The Family and Local History Handbook

incorporating **The Genealogical Services Directory**

9th Edition

In collaboration with

Edited & Compiled by
Robert Blatchford

Assistant Editor
Elizabeth Blatchford

Contents

7   *Feature Articles*

8	Getting Started in Genealogy	Robert Blatchford
14	County & Country Codes	
14	Census Returns	
15	Conservation and Preservation of your Family Archives	Doreen Hopwood
19	Bygone Days in a Lancashire Mill Town	Anne Harvey
25	19th Century Plagues of the Poor	Jean Cole
30	Civil Unrest in The Black Country 1766 – 1816	David Cox
35	The Black Country Society	Stan Hill
39	Faversham Gunpowder Factories	Arthur Percival
43	I'm not tracing my ancestors …… really!	Elsie Forster
45	Family Records Centre	David Annal
46	General Register Office - Certificate Services	Carol Quinn
53	Your Ancestors' Family Planning	Colin R Chapman
57	Death and the Victorians	Doreen Hopwood
63	A Wedding has been arranged	Doreen Berger
66	Rutland's Records - where to find them	Audrey Buxton
71	Finding South African Forebears -an introduction	Rosemary Dixon-Smith
76	Deceased Estates in South African Genealogy	Rosemary Dixon-Smith
80	The Clopton Oak	Gabriel Alington
83	West Dorset History and Genealogical Research Centre	Celia Martin
84	Windmills	Richie Green
88	The National Archives	John Wood
90	Blood's Thicker Than Water	Joan Dexter
97	Showing their Mettle … Industries of the West Midlands	Doreen Hopwood
102	Crime and Punishment in the 18th Century	Barry Redfern
105	People of the Parish	Anne Batchelor
109	Haigh Brewery	Glenys Shepherd
114	The Georgians at the Seaside	Prudence Bebb
117	Shovelling out the Poor: 19th Century Assisted Emigration	Simon Fowler
121	The Inspector calls...............	Richard Ratcliffe
124	London's Genealogy Village	Else Churchill
131	Understanding old trades and occupations	Doreen Hopwood
134	London Treacle, Syrup of Roses and Fish Kettles	Jill Groves
142	Pins for the People: the hatpin in England 1880 –1920	Dr Jane Batchelor
144	My Great Grand Aunt Maria	Jean Cole
147	How William Coleman lived: Probate Inventories	Stuart A. Raymond
149	Eavesdropping on the Dead Something to Write Home about	Joseph O'Neill
152	Captain of Industry: Gordon Armstrong	Martin Limon
154	No 2 Potash Cottages Pettistree	Ray Whitehand
157	Maria's murderer laid to rest – after 176 years	Paul Williams
160	A Hodge Podge of Duckenfields	Anne L Harvey
167	20th Century British State Registers of Merchant Mariners	Len Barnett
170	Registry of Shipping and Seamen	Neil Staples
176	The Little Drummer Boy	Glenys Shepherd
178	The History of Ferries - a research guide	Martin Limon
179	East Yorkshire Transport History: Wawne Ferry	Martin Limon
182	Hobby Bobbies	Fred Feather
186	Gas Workers - The National Gas Archive	Robert Blatchford
188	Ipswich Workhouses - The First in the County	Ray Whitehand
195	Britain's Hangmen	Paul Williams
199	Probate Records	
202	The National Library of Wales	Eirionedd Baskerville
204	J Llewellyn - An Aberystwyth Brigantine	W Troughton
208	Carmarthenshire Antiquarian Society	
211	The Public Record Office of Northern Ireland	Valerie Adams
214	Irish Censuses and Census Substitutes	David Webster
217	The Search for Scottish Sources	Rosemary Bigwood

220	General Register Office for Scotland	
221	Census Enumerators' Instructions	David Webster
225	An Irrestible Sense of Duty	Alastair Dinsmor
228	The Origin of Christianity in Scotland	David Webster
232	Scottish "Term Days"	David Webster

237 *Digital Genealogy*

238	A Basic Guide to Computers for Family History	Graham Hadfield
242	Easy Access to Records	David Tippey
246	Caveat Internet!	Robert Blatchford
247	Family History in the Media	Anthony Adolph
252	Electronic Indexes - Pain or Pleasure	David Tippey
255	The Archive CD Books Story	
258	Discovering family history with 1837online.com	John Coutts
263	www.oldbaileyonline.org	Barry Redfern
265	Trace Your British & Irish Family History using the Internet	Alan Stewart
270	DNA Heritage	Alastair Greenshields
274	If We Only Had Old Ireland Over Here	Joesph O'Neill
279	David Tippey's Top Research Websites	David Tippey
291	The Scotlands People Internet Service	Martin Tyson
292	Newsplan - Database of Local Newspaper Titles	Andrew Phillips
294	Heredis - a genealogy program	Robert Blatchford
295	Get Online! www.nationalarchives.gov.uk	John Wood
296	Irish Genealogy with Eneclann www.eneclann.ie	

297 *Military History*

298	What's new at the Imperial War Museum	Sarah Paterson
300	Tracing American Service Personnel	Sarah Paterson
303	Royal Air Force The Inter-War Years & Losses 1919 – 1939	David Barnes
309	Tracing Royal Naval Ancestry	Imperial War Museum
311	The Beckett Soldiers Index A – C	Brian Prescott
313	Waiting and Hoping	Joseph O'Neill
317	Belgian refugees in Britain during the First World War	Simon Fowler
321	A Red Cross VAD in Wartime	Jackie Evans
327	The Royal Navy - historical background for genealogists	Len Barnett
331	The Fleet Air Arm and Casualties 1939 – 1945	David Barnes
337	Touring the Western Front	Simon Fowler
342	Tracing Army Ancestry	Imperial War Museum

345 *The Genealogical Services Directory*

346	Family History & Genealogical Societies
357	Local and History Societies & Organisations
370	Family History Centres - The Church of Jesus Christ of The Latter Day Saints
372	Libraries
386	Cemeteries & Crematoria
393	Record Offices & Archives
408	Registrars of Births, Marriages & Deaths - England, Wales and Scotland
417	Registration Records in The Republic of Ireland
418	Museums
438	Military Museums
441	Police Records & Museums

443 *Index to Advertisers, Index & Miscellaneous Information*

443	Index to Advertisers
445	Index
447	Miscellaneous Information

Ever wondered how you got here?

Trace your family tree using our birth, marriage and death indexes for:

- England and Wales from 1837 to 2002

- British nationals overseas from 1761 to 1994 (including WW1, WW2 and consular records)

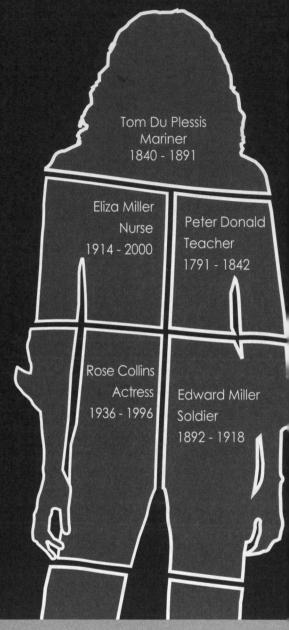

Tom Du Plessis
Mariner
1840 - 1891

Eliza Miller
Nurse
1914 - 2000

Peter Donald
Teacher
1791 - 1842

Rose Collins
Actress
1936 - 1996

Edward Miller
Soldier
1892 - 1918

www.1837online.com

Editorial

Welcome to the 9th Edition of the Handbook. By the time this edition appears the 8th edition will have completely sold out. The interest in family history research has certainly been stimulated by the BBC tv series '*Who Do You Think You Are?*' which followed various celebrities researching their ancestors.

The internet and other digital material is having an astounding effect on family history research. This is reflected by our new section - *Digital Genealogy*.

In our personal lives this year weddings, births and deaths. have all taken place and should be recorded for future generations. In February 2004 our own family saw the arrival of a new granddaughter, Libby, who is now crawling everywhere and trying to keep up with her two older brothers, William and Edward. Our son, Charles, and his wife, Rachel, are anticipating the arrival of their first child as this *Handbook* appears.

I again organised *The Great North Fair* in September 2004 and was ably asssted by Roger Kay. With over 2000 visitors and 105 exhibitors the success of the fair means it transcends a regional identity - it deserves the name national. We have therefore changed the fair's name to *The National Family History Fair*. The 2005 Fair will again be held at Gateshead International Stadium on Saturday 10th September 2005

Once again all design, layout and preparation is done in house on Apple Macintosh computers, a G4 Desktop and a G4 Power Book,using Quark Xpress 5, Adobe Photoshop CS and Adobe Acrobat CS. The *Handbook* is produced electronically and is transferred to paper only when it is printed.

I must acknowledge especially the help of my wife, Elizabeth for all her hard work and support. Her editorial contribution is now properly acknowledged with her name appearing on the title page. The family is thanked for their help, patience and forbearance.

Once again I am grateful to Nancy Redpath for her work in the final stages of preparation before the book goes to the printer.

Please support our advertisers as their contribution to the production of the *Handbook* is essential. I must emphasise this in relation to the 'sponsors' of somesections within the *Handbook - Stepping Stones Data CDs Ltd, ABM Publishing Ltd (publishers of Family Tree Magazine & Practical Family History magazine) and Family History monthly.*

If you do contact any of the advertisers please tell them that you saw their advertisement in *The Family and Local History Handbook*.

Suggestions from our readers are always welcome and where possible they are implemented in the next edition.We hope that you, our readers, enjoy this 9th edition as much as the previous ones.

Robert Blatchford

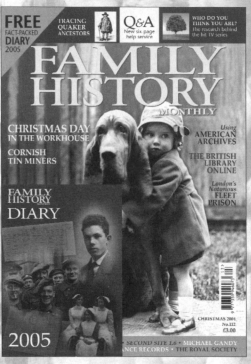

Feature Articles

In association with
FAMILY HISTORY
MONTHLY

"When I was a Girl" 7

Getting Started in Genealogy
Robert Blatchford

This article will have you up and running with your own research and if you have already started then the advice here will help you get the most from your hobby..........

There is no easy route to discovering your ancestors. It involves patience, luck and in some cases perseverance. Do not be put off. It is a great deal of fun. The more you discover the more you will want to know about your ancestors. There is some small cost to this fascinating hobby but the rewards will be great. Where your ancestors have moved around from area to area you will have a ready excuse to holiday in many places both at home and abroad - if some of your ancestors emigrated. There is nothing more satisfying than visiting a town, finding out about the historic events that took place some two hundred years previously and realising that an ancestor of yours

> **The Golden Rule**
> Whatever you do in your research the *golden rule* is to start with yourself and work backwards, generation by generation, ensuring that you have verified your sources. A mistake many people make is to take a name from the past and try to trace his or her ancestors or descendants believing they may be related. This rarely works and is definitely not recommended. In every family there are myths and legends most have some element of truth but as with many stories embellishment has probably occurred in the telling.

may have been a witness or perhaps even took part!

Preparation
You must be systematic and organised. You will collect a lot of information and data. This must be organised and filed for easy reference. In our busy lives it is not always possible to continually work on a hobby and there may be periods when your research has to take a back seat. This may a few days but could stretch into weeks and months. Revision is always useful and may provide new ideas for the future. It is also a record which verifies the value of your research.

What will I need?
A simple filing system using A4 binders with loose leaf pages and subject dividers, an index card file for each of the family names/members and events.

Somewhere to keep certificates and other documents. Avoid scraps of paper. Everything has its place. A note book is helpful for recording information as it is gathered for later transfer to your main file. It goes without saying that pens, pencils and the all important rubber are also needed.

How you organise the information is up to you. There are many printed recording aids available or you can create your own. Whatever system you use you must be methodical, identifying the source of the information and the date when it was found.

Do I need a computer?
The easy answer is that it is not a necessity. Many family historians prefer to keep paper records and hand drawn family trees charts. It is cheap and economic. If you would prefer to use a computerised system there are many programs available. However, remember that you do not need to wait until you have a computer or a suitable program to begin your work. If you do not have a computer but intend acquiring one make sure it is a system you want and not one a salesman wants to sell you. The computer is an efficient way of storing, copying, sharing and presenting information, and, along with the usual applications on a computer – word processor programs, email, access to the internet and the ability to scan, edit and print images – there are many programs specifically designed to help you draw up and publish your family tree and history. Genealogy computer programs are numerous; from shareware to proprietary ones with more features. Windows PC users have a choice between *Brother's Keeper* or the highly recommended *new* British program *Family Historian*. Users of Apple Mac computers can choose between shareware programs such as *Gene* or the highly recommended *Reunion 8*. Available from many software retailers such as S & N Genealogy – www.genealogysupplies.com or My History - www.my-history.co.uk *Heredis,* a new program is available to both Windows PC users and Apple Mac users - www.myheredis.com

Recording data and information
Whilst your record keeping may be methodical it should also be honest. There are always skeletons in the cupboard. Do not ignore them. They are part and parcel of the richness of your family history. You will find criminals, marital affairs and

illegitimacy - every family has them. They may not be recent but as your research progresses you will eventually find them.

Where should I start?

It is most important to assemble all the information

The GRO Index
Births, marriages and deaths are listed in separate indexes. Previously known as the St Catherine's Index its official title is now The General Register Office Index. These indexes can be seen at The Family Records Centre, 1 Myddelton Street, London EC1R 1UW. Microfilm copies of these indexes are held by some libraries, record offices, Family History Societies and Family History Centres of The Church of Latter Day Saints. It is also available on the internet at www.1837online.com
See the **Digital Genealoogy Section**

you can about your family from relatives. Gather together all the birth, marriage and death certificates of family members. Where certificates are not available the approximate dates of births, marriages and death should be obtained from family members. Copy certificates of these events can be obtained after consulting The General Register Office Indexes. Compulsory registration began in 1837 and births, marriages and deaths are listed in separate indexes. Birth certificate details give sufficient information to help find the marriage of parents, and the marriage certificate usually gives clues for the births of the marrying couple as well as the fathers of each. Microfilm copies of these indexes are held by many libraries, record offices and The Family Records Centre. These Indexes are searchable on the internet at www.1837online.com On this site you will find the entire indexes of Birth, Marriages and Deaths for England and Wales from 1837 to 2002 as well as overseas records - including WW1, WW2, Boer War, Marine and Consular indexes.

Once you have identified the entries in the indexes copy certificates of all registered births, marriages and deaths may obtained from The General Register Office or the Superintendent Registrar for the area where the registration was made. Certificates may also be ordered online by visiting www.gro.gov.uk/gro There is a fee to pay for copy certificates. A full list of Registrars for England, Wales and Scotland can be found in *The Family and Local History Handbook*.

Interviewing relatives

This sounds extremely formal but it is a source that is invaluable as you set out on your task. Talk to brothers and sisters, cousins, uncles, aunts, parents and grandparents. They will all have information some they will readily tell you but may be reluctant with revealing certain events. Speak to the eldest relatives. Don't make it sound like an interrogation. Ask them about events they have lived through, what they remember about their parents and grandparents. Gently coax the information. Make comprehensive notes. Tell them what you are doing and why. If they are happy use a tape recorder - a pocket memo is ideal. If you have a video camera use that to record discussions. Both of these will become very useful parts of your family history. Listen to the accounts several times to make sure you haven't missed anything. It may also prompt you to ask for more detail on certain events. Don't attempt to carry out the interview in one session. Several sessions are better and it will also help them to forget your recording system.

I was fortunate to find one of my mother's first cousins. George was 92 and in frail health. He told me a lot about my grandfather and my great grandfather, identifying him in some old photographs, his employment, his wife, his personality and about the other members of the family. But George was very reluctant to discuss a *family disagreement* that took place and never revealed anything about it before he died.

No matter how small the detail you learn about remember it is always worth noting. Once your

The National Archives
The Public Record Office is the national archive of England, Wales and the United Kingdom. In April 2003 the Public Record Office and the Historical Manuscripts Commission will combined to form the National Archives, based at Kew. The National Archives with over 100 miles of records houses one of the most definitive archive collections in the world representing the events and people of the past thousand years. The Public Record Office, Ruskin Avenue, Kew, Richmond, Surrey TW9 4DU Website: www.nationalarchives.gov.uk/

relative has passed on it will be too late. Your elderly relative may be happier jotting down his or her memories in a note book. This is what my wife has done with her own mother.

Surnames
Surnames are usually derived from one of four basic roots:

A Place - *Manchester, Dent, London, Durham*
An Occupation - *Taylor, Baker, Butcher, Smith*
From Patronymic (Relationship) - *Nelson* - son of Nell, *Robertson , Robson, McCarthy, Macpherson, Probert*
or a Nickname - *Redhead, Whitehead*.

The less common the surname, the easier searches can be, and some idea of the number of people bearing a certain surname and their distribution can be obtained by looking at local telephone directories.

Setting your sights
A fairly early decision needs to be made on where to concentrate your researches. You could aim to research your total ancestry. The implications for this are enormous. The data collected will soon overwhelm you. It is better to start with yourself, moving to your two parents and four grandparents then choosing a branch to follow. Most men research their surname whilst many women, if they are the last of the line to hold their father's surname, research his family. However at some point you may reach a *brickwall*. This is the time to pick up another branch of the family until a chance discovery lets you return to your first line of research. This has happened to me on several occasions.

Family History Classes
I always recommend that people join a family history class. Most areas in the country have short classes which give a good grounding in the essentials of family history research together with information written for magazines such as this one.

Should I join a Family History Society
The short answer is *yes*. I always recommend joining a family history society. In fact usually several unless you are positive that your family has lived for many generations in one place. Is there a family history society in your area? A full list of Family History Societies can be found in *The Family and Local History Handbook*.

The annual subscriptions are modest. Join the local family history society even if you do not research in their area. There are many benefits.
• The annual subscriptions are modest.
• Societies usually have books and information about your area
   • They will have Members' Interests lists of surnames being researched
• Many societies regularly publish a journal or newsletter
• They will have meetings with guest speakers,

Birth certificate details give sufficient information to help find the marriage of parents, and the marriage certificate usually gives clues for the births of the marrying couple as well as the fathers of each. Access is only to the quarterly indexes and no information is available except in the form of a certificate. There are separate indexes for the births, marriages and deaths of British Subjects returned by Consuls abroad (from 1809), in the Army (from 1761), and at sea (from 1837). Copy certificates for Births, Marriages, Deaths Certificates of all registered births, marriages and deaths since 1837 are obtainable by post from The General Register Office, Smedley Hydro, Southport, Merseyside PR8 2HH or the Superintendent Registrar for the area where the event was registered.

A birth certificate gives date and place where the event occurred, the child's forename(s), as well as the name and occupation of the father, the name and maiden surname of the mother with her usual residence if the birth took place elsewhere, and the name and address of the informant for the registration.

A **marriage certificate** gives the names and usually the ages of the marrying couple, their addresses and occupations, the names and occupations of their fathers, the date and place of marriage, and the names of the witnesses.

A **death certificate** records name(s), date, place, age, cause of death, occupation of the deceased, residence if different from âçthe place of death, and the name and address of the informant for registration. It does not show place of birth or parentage. After 1968 more details had to be recorded on the certificate.

FreeBMD project
FreeBMD stands for Free Births, Marriages, and Deaths.
The FreeBMD Project's objective is to provide free Internet access to the Civil Registration index information for England and Wales. The Civil Registration system for recording births, marriages, and deaths in England and Wales has been in place since 1837 and is one of the most significant single resources for genealogical research back to Victorian times. The FreeBMD project only contains index information for the period 1837-1902. The FreeBMD Database currently has over 88,000,000 records http://freebmd.rootsweb.com

covering items of interest and hints on how to do your own research
• Societies also often hold indexes of monumental inscriptions from churchyards and burial grounds as well as census and parish register indexes.

Research Etiquette

Once you have had your own research interests published with your society you may be contacted by other members researching the same name. They may have a great deal of information for you or they may have come across something they might consider useful to you. Please remember it is etiquette to express thanks as soon as possible even if the information is of no use. If you write to anyone seeking information then *always* as a courtesy include a stamped self addressed envelope. It is surprising how such a small gesture oils the wheels for further help.

Many people find interesting or famous people in their family history - such as murderers,

executioners, politicians, actors, or explorers - but a great many of us do not. Please tell the story about these *famous* ancestors to interested parties but refrain from *boring* everyone with the minutiae of your history and boasting about how far you have *got back*. Our individual family histories are really only interesting to our own families.

Should I use the Internet?

There is a great deal of very useful information available on the internet. If you have not already registered with an Internet Provider you will need to register and will pay telephone charges or a subscription fee. For more advice on using the intternet see the **Digital Genealoogy Section**

Where else can I look?

The list is endless. There are Indexes to search. These are usually published by Family History

Census Returns
A Census has been taken every 10 years since 1801 except in 1941 during the Second World War. The census returns for 1801, 1811, 1821, 1831 were not preserved.
However there are some areas where returns for these years have been found.
The first census that is useful to researchers is the one taken in 1841.
The Census returns were taken on:
1841 7th June 1841: 1851 30th March 1851:
1861 7th April 1861: 1871 2nd April 1871:
1881 3rd April 1881: 1891 5th April 1891:
1901 31st March 1901
These census returns can be consulted. They were subject to public closure for 100 years because of the sensitive personal information they contained.
The 1901 Census is now searchable on the internet, for payment, at http://www.census.pro.gov.uk/ There is a comprehensive name index search giving access to over 32 million individuals.

Scotland
Civil Registration for Births, Marriages and Deaths began in 1855 although the registration of baptisms and proclamation of marriages began in 1551. These records are held by the Registrar General at New Register House, Edinburgh EH1 3YT Microfiche copies of the register pages are then made available in the New Register House search rooms. By the end of 2003 the microfiche copies will have been replaced by digital images. To find out more see the GROS web site at http://www.gro-scotland.gov.uk. Pay-per-view search web site is http://www.scotlandspeople.gov.uk

societies, or individuals, and will include information about burials, servicemen, censuses, parish registers and monumental inscriptions as well as indexes for wills. You may like to know about the social history of the area. A family history society may have some but usually a great deal of our social history is uncovered and recorded by a Local History Society. There are records for occupations in all walks of life, Trade and Commercial Directories, electoral registers, newspapers, military service records, diaries and all the family memorabilia collected over the years.

You are about to embark upon a fascinating hobby that will show you your family's past both the pleasing and the not so pleasing. If may become an obsession but will be worthwhile record for you to leave to future generations.

Ireland
The General Register Office (Oifig An Ard-Chláraitheora), Joyce House, 8/11 Lombard Street, Dublin 2, Ireland is the main civil repository for records relating to Births, Deaths and Marriages in the Republic of Ireland. The records of marriages other than Roman Catholic marriages began in 1845 with the registration of Births, Deaths and Roman Catholic Marriages began in 1864. http://www.groireland.ie

The Proceedings of the Old Bailey London 1674 - 1834
This is a fully searchable database containing the accounts of over 100,000 criminal trials held at London's Central Criminal Court.
http://www.oldbaileyonline.org/

Trade, Street and Local Directories
These directories first appeared in the 17th century and are important sources for local and genealogical studies. They include lists of names, addresses and occupations of the inhabitants of the counties and towns they describe, and successive editions reflect the changes in the localities over a period of time. Many of these directories are now being reproduced for sale on CD. The University of Leicester has created a digital library of eighteenth, nineteenth and early twentieth century local and trade directories from England and Wales. High quality digital reproductions of a large selection of these comparatively rare books, previously only found in libraries and record offices, will be freely available online to anyone with an Internet connection. There is also a powerful search engine available so that names, occupations, addresses and other key words or phrases can be located to their exact places on pages within the text.
http://www.historicaldirectories.org

The International Genealogical Index (I.G.I.)
The Church of Jesus Christ of Latter Day Saints has produced the marvellous International Genealogical Index (known as the I.G.I.). The Index is unique source of information on family histories gathered world-wide. For many researchers it is the first location they check for leads in their quest for information on ancestors. It is an index to millions of records of births, deaths and marriages recorded in church records in many countries from medieval times prior to civil registration.

The I.G.I. is on the internet www.familysearch.org where it is also possible to search Ancestral File, Censuses - British 1881; United States 1880; Canada 1881, Pedigree Resource File, US Social security death Index, and the Vital Records Index

The National Family History Fair

Saturday 10th September 2005
10.00a.m. - 4.30.p.m.

Gateshead International Stadium
Neilson Road Gateshead NE10 0EF

Admission £3.00
Accompanied Children under 15 Free

Meet the national experts!

A must for family historians in 2005

Full list of exhibitors at:
www.nationalfamilyhistoryfair.com

2006 - **Saturday 9th September 2006**

County & Country Codes *(Pre 1974 counties)*

England	ENG
All Counties	ALL
Bedfordshire	BDF
Berkshire	BRK
Buckinghamshire	BKM
Cambridgeshire	CAM
Cheshire	CHS
Cornwall	CON
Cumberland	CUL
Derbyshire	DBY
Devonshire	DEV
Dorsetshire	DOR
Durham	DUR
Essex	ESS
Gloucestershire	GLS
Hampshire	HAM
Herefordshire	HEF
Hertfordshire	HRT
Huntingdonshire	HUN
Isle of Wight	IOW
Kent	KEN
Lancashire	LAN
Leicestershire	LEI
Lincolnshire	LIN
London (city)	LND
Middlesex	MDX
Norfolk	NFK
Northamptonshire	NTH
Northumberland	NBL
Nottinghamshire	NTT
Oxfordshire	OXF
Rutland	RUT
Shropshire	SAL
Somerset	SOM
Staffordshire	STS
Suffolk	SFK
Surrey	SRY
Sussex	SSX
Warwickshire	WAR
Westmorland	WES
Wiltshire	WIL
Worcestershire	WOR
Yorkshire	YKS
YKS E Riding	ERY
YKS N Riding	NRY
YKS W Riding	WRY

Wales	WLS
Anglesey	AGY
Brecknockshire	BRE
Caernarvonshire	CAE
Cardiganshire	CGN
Carmarthenshire	CMN
Denbighshire	DEN
Flintshire	FLN
Glamorgan	GLA
Merionethshire	MER
Monmouthshire	MON
Montgomershire	MGY
Pembrokeshire	PEM
Radnorshire	RAD

Scotland	SCT
Aberdeenshire	ABD
Angus	ANS
Argyllshire	ARL
Ayrshire	AYR
Banffshire	BAN
Berwickshire	BEW
Bute	BUT
Caithness-shire	CAI
Clackmannanshire	CLK
Dumfriesshire	DFS
Dunbartonshire	DNB
East Lothian	ELN
Fifeshire	FIF
Forfarshire	ANS
Inverness-shire	INV
Kincardineshire	KCD
Kinross-shire	KRS
Kirkcudbrightshire	KKD
Lanarkshire	LKS
Midlothian	MLN
Moray	MOR
Nairnshire	NAI
Orkney Isles	OKI
Peebles-shire	PEE
Perthshire	PER
Renfrewshire	RFW
Ross & Cromarty	ROC
Roxburghshire	ROX
Selkirkshire	SEL
Shetland Isles	SHI
Stirlingshire	STI
Sutherland	SUT
West Lothian	WLN
Wigtownshire	WIG

Ireland (Eire)	IRL
Antrim	ANT
Armagh	ARM
Carlow	CAR
Cavan	CAV
Clare	CLA
Cork	COR
Donegal	DON
Down	DOW
Dublin	DUB
Fermanagh	FER
Galway	GAL
Kerry	KER
Kildare	KID
Kilkenny	KIK
Leitrim	LET
Leix(Queens)	LEX
Limerick	LIM
Londonderry	LDY
Longford	LOG
Louth	LOU
Mayo	MAY
Meath	MEA
Monaghan	MOG
Offaly(Kings)	OFF
Roscommon	ROS
Sligo	SLI
Tipperary	TIP
Tyrone	TYR
Waterford	WAT
Westmeath	WES
Wexford	WEX
Wicklow	WIC

Channel Islands	CHI
Alderney	ALD
Guernsey	GSY
Jersey	JSY
Sark	SRK

Isle of Man	IOM

Australia	AUS
Capital Territory	CT
New South Wales	NS
Northern Territory	NT
Queensland	QL
South Australia	SA
Tasmania	TA
Victoria	VI
Western Australia	WA

Canada	CAN
Alberta	AB
British Columbia	BC
Manitoba	MB
New Brunswick	NB
Newfoundland	NF
North West Terr	NT
Nova Scotia	NS
Ontario	ON
Prince Edward Is	PE
Quebec	QC
Saskatchewan	SK
Yukon Territory	YT

Europe	
Austria	AUT
Belarus	BLR
Belgium	BEL
Croatia (Hrvatska)	HRV
Czech Republic	CZE
Denmark	DNK
Estonia	EST
Finland	FIN
France	FRA
Germany (1991)	DEU
Greece	GRC
Hungary	HUN
Italy	ITA
Latvia	LVA
Liechtenstein	LIE
Lithuania	LTU
Luxembourg	LUX
Netherlands	NLD
Norway	NOR
Poland	POL
Romania	ROU
Russian Federation	RUS
Slovakia	SVK
Slovinia	SVN
Spain (Espagne)	ESP
Sweden	SWE
Switzerland	CHE
Ukraine	UKR
United Kingdom	GBR
USSR	SUN
Yugoslavia	YUG

New Zealand	NZL
Papua New Guinea	PNG
South Africa	ZAF
United States	USA

These codes are used to avoid confusion in the use of abbreviations for countries and counties.
Those for the British Isles were created by Dr Colin Chapman.
A full list of International Codes can be found at **www.unicode.org/onlinedat/countries.html**
The codes are internationally recognised and should always be used.

Lochin Publishing, 19 Woodmancote, Dursley, Gloucestershire GL11 4AF

Census Returns

A Census has been taken every 10 years since 1801 except in 1941 during the Second World War. Most of the census returns for 1801, 1811, 1821, 1831 were not preserved. However there are some areas where returns for these years have been found - (see *Pre -1841 Censuses* by *Colin Chapman*) The first nationwide census returns useful to researchers are those for 1841.
The Census returns were taken on:

1841	7th June 1841	1851	30th March 1851	1861	7th April 1861
1871	2nd April 1871	1881	3rd April 1881	1891	5th April 1891
		1901	31st March 1901		

These census returns can be consulted. They were subject to public closure for 100 years because of the sensitive personal information they contained.

Archival Survival:
Conservation and Preservation of your Family Archives
Doreen Hopwood

The careful handling and storage of your family records is essential to ensure their survival for future generations. Here are some guidelines to help you to take the correct action to preserve them.

The main enemies of old documents and photographic items are:

You Over-handling them, or simply wrongly handling them, and how/where you store your family archive.

Light Direct sunlight and fluorescent lighting can cause serious damage.

Humidity This provides the ideal conditions for the growth of mould and mildew.

Chemicals These are present in many types of container which may be used for storage. It is worth investing in strong archival boxes and acid-free folders. Cigarette smoke and other pollutants are harmful too.

Pests Mice have been known to eat their way through parish registers – old papers make ideal nesting material and food. Gums and adhesive attract silverfish too, and a survey has identified over one hundred different varieties of insect which can endanger paper-based materials.

Documents, books and paper-based materials
Much primary source material, such as parish registers held by record offices and archives, has been microfilmed or digitised to minimise the handling of fragile originals. Family historians can follow some of the practices carried out by such repositories to prevent the deterioration of their own family's records.

If you are fortunate enough to possess a family bible, ensure that when you open it, it is supported (a cushion/pillow is sufficient for this purpose). Never lay an old book open flat on a surface, and try not to open it more than 90 degrees as the resulting structural stress may crack the spine and pull the binding apart. Turn the pages carefully and avoid touching the text or images of old books. No matter how clean your hands are, grease and other chemicals can easily be transferred onto documents, so it is worth investing in a pair of lint-free cotton gloves which will protect your archive from over-handling. Wherever possible, make a digital copy or scan, of the document, and use this for research purposes and showing to the family.

Any letters (or other paper documents), should be unfolded, and metal paper clips or staples carefully removed. Try to avoid clipping papers together, but if this has to be done, use brass fasteners or plastic-ended treasury tags, which will not rust and stain the items. Folded documents will eventually split along the fold, and tightly rolled maps will form ridges on the surface because the backing forces the map itself into a smaller space. If the maps are too large to be kept flat, they can be rolled around a tube (not placed in one) and protected with a calico cover.

Paper and parchment should not be kept together as the acidity of parchment can be harmful to paper. Wood pulp has been used in the manufacture of newspapers and paper for books for over a hundred years, and is not as durable as earlier paper. If a document needs to be repaired, it is imperative that adhesive tape or sellotape is not used. This degrades badly – firstly it turns yellow, then falls off and leaves a stain which cannot be removed. It is possible to purchase archival tape, but water-soluble glue and gummed paper (such as that on postage stamps) can be used if necessary, as their effects can generally be removed without damage to the documents. Don't be tempted to laminate your records.

Once you have sorted out your documents, they should be placed in protective sleeves made of acid-free material. Plastic sleeves and wallets must be avoided at all costs as the ink transfers from the document to the surface of the sleeve, thus destroying your archives.

The items should be stored in an archival box, made of acid-free material wherever possible. However, boxes lined with acid-free paper and containing a bag of silica gel can be used. Your collection needs to be stored at a fairly constant temperature with good ventilation and not exposed to direct sunlight or to fluorescent lighting. The latter will cause fading, brittleness and yellowing of paper, and high humidity is a recipe for mould growth. Don't be tempted to place your archives in the loft, cellar or garage – all of which may be dusty, damp and subject to fluctuations in temperature. Underneath the bed in a spare room, or inside a large cupboard/wardrobe are good storage places. If you find mould or mildew on any of your records do not try to move it whilst it's still damp. The items should be allowed to dry out in good ventilation, and then a soft brush can be used to clean the surface. As mould spores can be a hazard to health, a mask and gloves should be worn, and the cleaning done in a well-ventilated room – or outside in dry weather.

Photographs, Negatives and Transparencies
Handle with care is the most obvious piece of advice. Most photos have been passed around the family without any concern for their future. Every fingerprint is a potential threat to survival of the print, so hold it with the finger tips at the very corners of the paper. Better still, wearing lint-free cotton gloves will ensure minimal damage. These can be bought from specialist suppliers or good camera shops.

Don't be tempted to place each print in a plastic or polyester transparent slip because this will provide the perfect environment for mould and bacteria to grow. Whilst old shoe boxes (or even biscuit tins) are often used by people to store their loose photographs, it is worth purchasing archival boxes which have drop-down fronts, allowing easy access to the contents. Any particularly fragile print can be placed in a loose folder made of acid-free paper (similar to tissue paper).

Cataloguing your archive of photographs will enable you to find the one you are looking for easily, and without having to handle more prints than is necessary. Identifying each one can be done by writing on the reverse – as close to the edge as possible using a good quality drawing ink or an HB pencil. Never use a biro or felt-tip marker – the ink will bleed through onto the image. Some people suggest that each photo should be marked only by a reference number and the details entered into a notebook. Whilst this is an excellent method, there is always the danger that the notebook and print will become irrevocably separated, thus rendering both useless!

There have been numerous techniques used to produce photographs since William Henry Fox Talbot patented the calotype process in 1841, and each different type of photo requires its own method of conservation.

The calotype process was the first one to produce a negative from which multiple prints could be made – the birth of the present day system. Other processes, such as the daguerreotype and ambrotype were one-offs, thus making any surviving images unique. It is difficult to reproduce such images by means of conventional photography, but scanners can be used to produce a good copy. There are arguments both for and against taking such action, but it is probably less damaging to the original than placing it on display where it is open to environmental damage. However, don't be tempted to scan the image more than once. Set the scanner so that you get it right first time – you can then use an image editing package to clean up/enhance the scanned image as many times as you want without damaging the original, and print off as many copies as you want, or send the images electronically.

Ironically, photographs dating from before WW2 are often in better condition than ones produced more recently. Those printed on paper/card are especially vulnerable to mould, which develops through exposure to damp/humidity, so do value your recent photos as much as the older 'heirlooms'. Remember, today's pictures will become the archives of future family historians! Environmental conditions are important factors in the survival (or not!) of your photographs – humidity, light and temperature all can be detrimental. A relatively constant temperature is needed, so attics/lofts or garages are not ideal locations. As with other family archives, under a bed or in a wardrobe are good locations.

Self adhesive photo albums can cause untold damage – the ink will come off the print onto the transparent cover, whilst it is impossible to remove a photo once

By the 1970s, video recording techniques were starting to replace 8mm films for domestic use, but if you are fortunate to have any 8mm or its earlier counterparts or 9mm or 16mm, it can be copied onto DVD or video, and the original stored in aluminium reels. Other metals will gradually rust and cause the film to deteriorate.

There is an additional problem with video tapes – whether or not there will be machinery available in the future on which they can be played, so, even if our tapes are carefully preserved, we may not actually be able to view them. The answer lies with the transfer of video onto DVD, but there is still the debate about how long a life-span these may have. Similar problems arise with audio-tapes, but with these if you have a transcript of the interview (or at least the most important parts of it), all is not lost if the tape does not survive.

it has been placed in such an album for any length of time (as I found to my cost!). Any description/notes written on the reverse will be irretrievably lost.

If you have any 'carte-visites', the back of the photo contains information about the studio/photographer (and is often lavishly embellished), so remember to scan the reverse as well. It was popular to have photos in the form of postcards, so these may also contain information about the picture (and possibly show the postmark/address).

Chemical damage in the form of stains may appear from acid on mount board adhesive or from the deterioration of chemicals used in the developing process. There is little you can do about these yourself – professional advice should be sought, and, in the meantime, move the article a safe environment, and away from the rest of your collection.

If you find silverfish or other pests in your album, don't be tempted to spray insecticide around – whilst this will kill the pests, it will also destroy your collection. Most feed on starch, which was a common component of glues and rarely eat the photos themselves.

We have been entrusted with the care of our family's archives for future generations, so it is our responsibility to take what measures we can to ensure that they survive.

The National Preservation Office at the British Library has a website which includes advice on conservation, and can be found at www.bl.uk/services/preservation

In association with **FAMILY HISTORY MONTHLY**

Bygone Days in a Lancashire Mill Town
Anne Harvey

Nestling at the foot of what is rather grandly called the West Pennine Moors is the small town of Horwich which, although officially part of greater Manchester, used to be located in Lancashire (and most Lancastrians think it still should be!). High up on the old road from Bolton to Chorley there are some authentic stone cottages and shops, which constitute the old village, clustering around the parish church of Holy Trinity. With the Rivington Pike and the moors serving as a backdrop Horwich is now a pleasant and agreeable small town, much sought after by commuters from Bolton, Chorley and Wigan, all about 5 miles distant, and reflected in rising house prices.

It wasn't always so. The building of the Locomotive Works in the late 19th century by the Lancashire & Yorkshire Railway Co turned Horwich from a quiet backwater into an industrial town. The Railway Works, from which a blue sulphurous-smelling blue emission hung over the town, was the principal source of employment for the men of Horwich, bringing in migrants from all over Great Britain, including my ancestors. Traditionally, men worked at either the 'Works' or 'Dehavs', the local nickname for De Havilland Propellers Ltd. Along with two cotton mills, the Victoria and the Beehive, both producing terry towelling, these four industries formed the employment hub of Horwich from the late 19th century to the mid 20th century.

Not only tradition dictated that the women of Horwich went to work in either 'Vicky Mill' or 't'Beehive'. There was little career choice for women in the 1950s. University was for the academically minded, while office work attracted the clever few. The life of the mill girl, distinguishable by the cotton fluff in her hair and a permanent hole in her overall pocket where the weaver's scissors poke through, was for the also-rans. Yet these groups of girls and women who walked, arms linked and laughing, exuded an unmistakable air of confidence and bravado. It was not surprising that many a girl approaching the then-leaving school age of 15 aspired to join their ranks. I was one of those girls.

On my first day the shock of actually walking into a weaving shed was something no one had prepared me for. It was as if all the demons of hell had been released and the noise was like a physical blow to the stomach. With two other trainees I was assigned to an older woman, who taught us how to stop and start the looms, how to fix a loose thread or replace an empty shuttle. To begin with we found the task of rethreading a shuttle, a clumsy and painstaking process. Some older weavers sucked the thread through with their mouths, a process called 'kissing the shuttle' but we were told this wasn't advisable. As there was no chance of a normal conversation instructions were shouted into our ears. We quickly learned to lip-read, a skill that still comes in handy sometimes. Once I had mastered the basic tasks I progressed first to one loom, then two and finally to three.

Commencing at 7.30 am and finishing at 5.30 pm with a break at noon for dinner made for long and tiring days in the mill, 45 hours a week in total. One morning, in my early mill days, I fell asleep while sitting on the edge of the bed after my mother had called me. Typically my day would begin with me running down the hill and being packed with the rest of humanity into an over-crowded bus. Many of my fellow passengers worked at the Beehive Mill too and there would be a steady stream of mill workers wending their way either from the bus stop or local houses to the mill gates. In the gatekeeper's lodge we punched our cards into the clocking-on machine and made our way through the over-powering stench of the bleaching and dyeing rooms. The adjoining warp shed was a pleasant contrast, with the smell of oil coming from the stacked drums of spun cotton, called the warp, which was waiting to be lifted on to the looms. Next to it was the weaving shed, its high-ridged roof making it either piercingly cold in winter or uncomfortably hot in summer.

It could be dangerous too; if the leather holding the picking stick which batted the shuttles containing the weft backwards and forwards through the warp, broke, the shuttle had a tendency to fly out. Twelve inches of steel-tipped solid wood could cause considerable damage to both looms and any weaver who happened to be in the way. The belts that operated the central drive shaft broke occasionally too and snaked along the floor, catching many a passer-by a whip-like sting on the legs.

Reaching my silent looms, off would come my coat and, bundling it up with my bag, would be placed under a rarely used pullout stool. One by one my looms would be switched on and the day proper would begin. The threading of shuttles was a never-ending task, and filled shuttles rested against the wooden barrier that protected the weaver from the spiked roller as the towels were being woven. It was essential to keep a constant watch for loose ends of thread. If these were not 'drawn-in' with a reed hook they could break more threads to form a 'smash' and spoil the towel. Although the pay was good, we were paid on piecework and a ruined towel did not count. The loom had to be stopped when the roller was full so that the continuous towels could be 'taken off' the roller. This was the time when, with a quick glance around, many a towel was slipped into a bag. I never took one; I was always too scared I'd be caught. In the warehouse the towels were weighed and noted down against earnings.

Brew time was the first break of the day and first stop was always the toilet, not a place to linger for it was heavy with cigarette smoke, despite safety regulations. In the warp shed was a huge cistern, where weavers queued patiently glad to be able to chat, with their own mugs and a twist of greaseproof paper containing a teaspoon of tea and sugar.

The hooter went for our dinner break at 12 noon, when gradually the looms would fall silent; the giant pulleys and drive shafts slowed and stopped. As we made our way to the canteen across the mill yard, girls and women chattered, free from the restriction of deafening sound. While eating our dinner we were entertained by 'Workers Playtime' relayed over the loudspeakers. At the end of our dinner break the hooter that ruled our work lives warned us that it was time to make our way back to the weaving shed, to the rumble of the drive shafts and the swish of the belts as they started running once more. As the first loom clattered into operation, there were several catcalls of 'grabber'.

Life in the mill wasn't always serious or about

Anne (aged 18) and her friend on holiday at Blackpool during Wakes Week 1957

making money; there was lots of fun and laughter too. If one of the girls was getting married her looms would be decorated, usually with items useful in the new home, but often humorous and some downright suggestive. The tradition was, after work, to walk the prospective bride home, with 'L' plates and balloons attached to her coat and carrying a luridly decorated chamber pot.

At Christmas there was always a 'footing' with sherry and mince pies. The looms were adorned with

Cutlooker: "These ends are like tram lines."
Weaver: "Aye; Tram's a bit farther on."

balloons and tinsel and often, with a sprig of mistletoe, to catch the tacklers or warp-carriers unawares. Going home, mill workers would wend their way singing and slightly merry.

Another occasion looked forward to eagerly was the Wakes Weeks when, in common with other Lancashire cotton towns, the Works and the two mills closed down for the last two weeks in July. There was a mass exodus to the seaside, the obvious favourite being Blackpool. Those who could afford it stayed for a week in a boarding house; for those who couldn't there were special excursions from Horwich station and coach trips. Two of the most popular excursions were the Lake District and North Wales. For those two weeks Horwich itself would be a ghost town with most of the shops closed or only open for a short time in the morning.

In the 1950's there were still some old-fashioned shops in Horwich, including from a bygone era, a corn and feed merchant but which also sold dog biscuits and birdseed by the pound (everyone seemed to have a budgie in the 50s!) and always seemed to smell of mice. Buchanan's Ironmongers, with its aroma of firewood and paraffin, was a glory hole of pots and pans, tin pudding basins, nails and screws. Cases Confectioners very often had queues right round the block, so renowned were they for their meat or meat and potato pies.

Peacock Dyson's was a pharmacy of the old school with racks of wooden drawers marked with arrowroot, coltsfoot and sulphur and huge, shaped bottles filled with a nameless coloured fluid in the window. The steps to the Horwich Industrial Co-operative Society were worn down with the countless numbers of women collecting their 'divi' from the dark-panelled ledger-filled office. There used to be a saying 'If he fell off t'Co-op, he'd land in t'divi' to describe someone who always found a way out of trouble.

For the young people of Horwich, Ferretti's Ice Cream parlour (and there were two of them at opposite ends of the town) had areas where we could sit and consume a lip-smackingly good homemade ice cream in a glass with a tangy fruit sauce poured over it. Or there was Harry Stocker's Temperance Bar, where they served up hot Vimto in special white mugs. Decades of Horwich youth had carved their initials into the bare wooden tables and Harry Stocker's was one of the first to install a jukebox.

Apart from those places, there wasn't much for the young people of Horwich to do. We weren't allowed in pubs and we certainly never thought to try. There was a dance club in the Arcade, nicknamed the 'Fling' but that had a bit of a doubtful reputation, largely because at their Sunday club night, couples jived to the new rock 'n' roll. If we were 'courting', we usually met by pre-arrangement outside the cinema, watched the film (or we tried, depending on the determination of the boy), had a kiss and a cuddle in a doorway until the bus for home came. On Saturday nights, there was a dance in Rivington Hall Barn, for which Bolton Corporation laid on special buses. This was always a good way to meet someone new, with young people coming to the dances from the surrounding towns.

From the time when my mother was a girl and probably even before that, Sunday afternoons were reserved for a walk 'Up Rivi'. Although the village of Rivington gave the area its name, the whole was actually called Lever Park, after the first Lord Leverhulme, who built a large bungalow there as a country home and which was burnt down early in the 20th century. A walk 'Up Rivi' could constitute anything from the bungalow grounds; bluebell woods; a mock ruined castle; the Anglezarke reservoirs; a genuine tithe barn; and was not just for the youth of Horwich but also families. It is still popular on Sundays but more hazardous now as droves of motor bikers make Rivington Hall Barn their destination.

Dominating Lever Park stands the Rivington Pike, a small squat 18th century tower atop a hill. On Good Fridays, young and old alike would make the trek to the top, ostensibly to visit the fair round the base of the hill. The source of this pilgrimage is a mystery. Various theories suggest that it is because of its location on a hill in deference to Good Friday or that as it was to be used as a beacon during the threat of invasion, the annual trek was to commemorate Napoleon's defeat at Waterloo.

Fortunately, Horwich was blessed with three cinemas where, for a price most of us could afford, you could watch three different films a week, all at different cinemas. The 'Picture House' was the poshest, where the owner, Mr Rostron, walked up and down flashing his large torch on any miscreants. Alternatively, the 'Palace' had a tin roof so that when it rained it was impossible to hear the film. I was once sat on the toilet there when a mouse ran out between my legs

Rivington Pike from upper reaches of Horwich

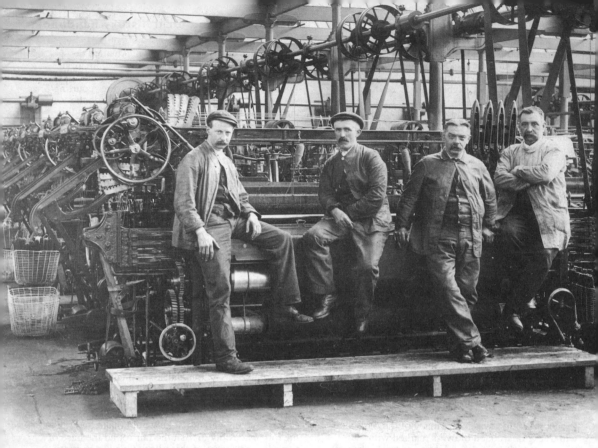

and disappeared under the gap of the door.

Some of the heart went out of Horwich with the scaling down of operations at the Locomotive Works in the late 1960s and its final closure in December 1983. Its vast acreage is now home to crumbling workshops and weeds, although great strides have been made to convert the site into an industrial estate. A victim of the jet age, Dehavilland Propellers has long since ceased production and the site now houses a minor subsidiary of British Aerospace. The Beehive Mill is home to light industrial units and although Victoria Mill is still in operation, it is no longer privately owned but part of a large national company.

But much has been gained too. A new retail park has been built, its heart the ship-like shape of the Reebok Stadium, home to Bolton Wanderers Football Club. Although the original railway station closed in 1960, a new station has been built adjacent to the Stadium. In the town centre itself some of the streets of closely packed terraced houses have been demolished to make way for more modern housing, but many remain the same and are now euphemistically called 'artisans' dwellings by enthusiastic estate agents. The air of Horwich is cleaner, the greenery more dominant, the views from the surrounding moors no longer obscured by mill and house chimneys spewing forth their noisome smoke.

From one hill in particular the view takes in the several reservoirs of Anzlezarke, descending into the distance. On a sunny day the sea at Blackpool can be seen glistening in the far distance. Often, if it is windy enough to blow any clouds away, there is a tantalising glimpse of Snowdonia while around another bend in the road, the fells of the Lake District beckon.

Although at the time I thought Horwich too parochial, it still has a special place in my heart. And although I hated worked in the mill, I'm glad now to have been a part of the last era of close participation by the weaver. For within only a few years full mechanisation and cheap imports had virtually destroyed the once giant cotton industry of Lancashire.

BIOGRAPHY NOTE:
Because of her early associations with the cotton industry, Anne has developed an interest in all textile industries. Now retired, she has written and published numerous genealogy and social history articles.

19th Century Plagues of the Poor
Jean Cole

Whilst searching the Longbridge Deverell (Wiltshire) Vestry meeting I came across this notice.

Notice read in Church on Sunday 2 September 1832
A meeting of the paymaster is requested in the Vestry at 12 o'clock on Friday next, the 7th day of September, to take into consideration the means best adopted under Divine Providence, to prevent the introduction, as well as to arrest the progress of Cholera in this parish. 7 September 1832, Committee appointed to enquire into the state of dwelling houses and gardens of the poor of this parish with a view to improve the ventilation of houses and to remove nuisances whereon an inspection thereof such regulations may be thought to be necessary.
Said Committee were requested to inspect the state of the poor generally and to report their opinion as to the formatting a Board of Health in this parish, on Friday, 14 September.

Committee, 14 September: reported found many instances of nuisances and want of ventilation in houses which required immediate attention and to continue inspection of other houses throughout the parish.

Official Board of Health appointed and contact to be made with the Board of Health in London.
The inspection continued until 2 October 1832 when Vestry decided a sum or sums of money to be invested for `proper carrying into effect the Board of Health's powers'. 16 December 1832.

This set me to thinking about how many preventable illnesses struck our vulnerable ancestors either causing long term debility and/or premature deaths. These, allied with poor ill-ventilated, damp dwellings and polluted water supplies, contributed to reoccurring illnesses and frailty with an inability to work and earn a regular wage.

Illnesses such as diarrhoea and ague (a type of

intermittent malaria) caused a progressive debility in health for even the strongest of men and women. Typhus (Asiatic Fever: Irish Fever) of which there was a countrywide epidemic in 1847, was caused through over-crowding, poor water and sanitation, body lice and was highly contagious. The symptoms were a purplish rash, an abnormally high temperature and prostration. Typhoid, which resembled typhus, also known as enteric fever, caused severe diarrhoea, weakness and rash.

Cholera or Asiatic cholera, as it was termed, had been known from earlier times. The first major epidemic occurred in Lower Bengal in 1817 and gradually spread outwards reaching Russia in 1830 and Germany in 1831, where many thousands of their respective populations died. In this country it reached Sunderland on 26 October 1831, Edinburgh on 6 February 1832 from where it spread into England and Wales causing great mortality. This was a disease, which was extremely swift and deadly and could kill a healthy person within 36 hours. Cholera symptoms were described in horrifying detail in this 1832 Report:

Vomiting or purging come on, the features become sharp and contracted, the eye sinks; the lips, face, neck, hands and feet and soon after the thighs, arms and whole surface assume a leaden blue, purple, black or deep brown tint; the pulse becomes small as a thread or else totally extinct. The skin is deadly cold, the tongue flabby and chilled like a piece of dead flesh. The patient speaks in a whisper. He struggles for breath. Sometimes there are rigid spasms of the legs, thighs and loins.

A Cholera remedy was issued by the Committee Room, Kingswood Hill, Bristol on 7th January 1834, but how efficacious it proved to be is not known!
Take in a tablespoonful of Brandy, as much powdered Rhubarb as will lie on a shilling.
Make a strong tea of camomile flowers, mallows, and mint, either dry or green, and take a tea-cup frequently.
Get two pieces of wood (if wood cannot be got, two pieces of tile will do)

Each six inches square, and one inch thick, place one of them against the bars of the fire grate, or in a heated oven, till quite hot, wrap it in flannel and lay it on the bowels. Heat one while the other is cooling.
It is strongly recommended that the above articles be procured in every family for immediate use, in case of attack of the bowels. Committee Room. Kingswood Hill, 7th January 1834.

Where parishes were obliged to deal with deaths from cholera it was reported burial grounds had become overfull. In Dudley, Staffordshire, the local Board of Health posted notices in September 1832 that churchyards there had become so full with people who had died from the cholera that no one who had died of it would be buried in the future in either of the parish burial grounds, and that all of those who had died of the disease for the foreseeable future were to be buried in the churchyard at nearby Netherton. In Devon, Exeter was another city to be badly affected by the dreaded cholera. During the middle of the 19th C Bristol enjoyed the unenviable distinction of being the third most unhealthy city in the country and in 1845 only Liverpool and Manchester had a higher general mortality rate. However, 20 years later, Bristol had become nearly the most healthy town in Great Britain!

Not far from Longbridge Deverell, over the border into Dorset, at Melbury Osmond, the cholera attacked, and Mr Selwood, the local physician, presented his bill to the parish authorities for the immense sum of £13. 9s 6d for just one year's attendance on the poor. A remedy used to combat the cholera in this parish was a mixture of white camphor and tobacco to fumigate infected buildings, but how effective this would have been is somewhat doubtful!

In 1831, the Government had forced local notables to serve on temporary boards of health in an endeavour to combat the cholera. Edwin Chadwick had been appointed by the Poor Law Commissioners to make an `Inquiry into the Sanitary Condition of the Labouring Population' and, in 1842, his report with its recommendations was published. The report's grim conclusions led to the Public Health Act of 1848 which set up local boards of health to deal with the problems of diet and disease, contaminated water and food. It was of interest to know that Chadwick also reported that where a person lived and what job they had was of vital importance in deciding how long they lived! The main cause of disease, he stated, was that the townspeople breathed in air, which had been poisoned by filth. His recommendation was that streets should be cleaned, drainage improved and houses to contain better ventilation which would let in more air and light and that sewerage systems and water supplies should be introduced.

By 1832 the threat of a cholera epidemic became imminent and suddenly the Government and parish vestries all over the country began to take hurried steps to try and deal with the situation. In Longbridge Deverell, the Vestry decided to investigate the condition of the dwellings of their poor parishioners which, obviously, according to the reports, were of the most inferior quality with little or no ventilation and spoil heaps outside their doors which could have caused not only cholera but other highly infectious and contagious diseases, some of which would eventually reach the higher echelons of Longbridge Deverell society. It was revealed disease was no respecter of persons, rich or poor! In this same year it had been estimated that 31,000 had died from cholera in England and Wales, and, by the second epidemic, 62,000 deaths over all were recorded. Further appearances of this dread disease occurred in 1853/4 and 1865/6 before subsiding. By 1 December 1866, it had been declared extinct in London, although other noxious diseases still held sway amongst the inhabitants of overcrowded houses and slums in towns and countryside alike.

An entry in Longbridge Deverell Vestry book for 16 December 1833 showed that £20 had been spent in removing earth from the foundations of the Church and the levelling of the churchyard – the sum to come from the rents of church lands. There is cause to

wonder whether the levelling of the churchyard had anything to do with the burial of cholera victims in the parish. However, it was not until July 1849, that cholera finally made its dread appearance in Crockerton, a neighbouring parish, as reported in a letter by George Vicary, MD to the Board of Guardians of Warminster Union.

A Report to the General Board of Health in 1852 concerning Longbridge Deverell and Crockerton, revealed the extent of the health and living conditions of their parishioners. William Lee, the Superintending Inspector, reported he had refrained from noting all the cases, because he would scarcely have had to omit a house in Crockerton! Lee wrote…

the people's face and hands appear bloodless, the lips almost white, and the countenance gloomy and depressed. There are probably 600 to 700 inhabitants in Crockerton, but I did not see one cheerful, smiling face – not even among the children. The population, with few exceptions, appears to be overwhelmed, pressed down, and utterly collapsed, with poverty and disease.

A brief extract from the Report illustrates the general conditions suffered by the parishioners:

At Daniel Payne's cottage, a back window opens on a large hole for slops and filth. The husband, wife, and 9 children, have had ague. Eli Tooze, living in the next house to Robert Ball, a strong young man who had also been badly affected by ague, stated:- We have had 5 children, but they are all dead. I have always lived in this parish. I had the ague first when I was 10 years of age: four years ago I was ill of it 25 weeks. I am ill now, and shall never be well again. My wife is unfit to do anything, she is so ill. She has not been well for some years, and has had the chill.

Unable to stand, this poor woman was sitting in a chair, endeavouring to wash a few clothes in some very dirty water. Both husband and wife looked more than half dead, Tears ran down both their faces while telling me their sorrowful tale They are on the parish.

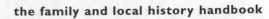

health. The case concerning Caroline Harris (WSRO B16/100/8) which came to the notice of the Hungerford Poor Law Union Guardians, related to the Public Health Act 1875.

29 January 1876. Charles Snell: I live at Hungerford and am an Inspector to Hungerford Union Rural Sanitary Authority. I, on 4 October, personally inspected a dwellinghouse, the property of defendant, situated at Lampiland in Ramsbury. I found the house utterly unfit for human habitation, exceedingly damp, very dilapidated, no water supply, no privy accommodation and the house is built of wattles and mud. It consists of one room only, there is no bedroom. The floor is of brick only, 14 " above the level of the water. Caroline Harris, defendant's sister, occupies the house...I reported the matter to the Sanitary Authority on 6 October. There was only one window in the house. The thatch is very imperfect. By the intervention of the Authority I served a notice at the house, calling attention of the defendant to the state of the premises, asking him either to shut them up or put them in proper authority so as to abate the nuisance. This notice I simply left on the premises. The house was then shut up...26 November 1876. The premises are still in the same state they were when I inspected them and are occupied by Caroline Harris. ... Defendant has given me to understand that he cannot do anything to the premises, that the premises are not worth it. Order made prohibiting the house as a human habitation. Defendant to pay the costs of this application.

Conclusion
After all this legislation concerning public health since the 19th century, many houses remained in a poor and insanitary condition for years. Well into the middle of the 20th century in my home town, there were still houses with dirt floor kitchens, one cold water tap, gaslight in one room only, and an outside dirt privy.

Reading
Gavin H. *Sanitary Ramblings* (1848, reprint 1967)
Large D and Round F. *Public Health in Mid-Victorian Bristol* (Bristol Local History Pamphlets)
Morgan KO. *History of Britain 1815-1851* (1985)
Rees *RA Britain 1815-1851* (1990)
Sharp RS. *Foul and Poisonous Air: Sanitation and Public Health in a Rural Community* (Local Historian article 1991)
Woods R & Woodward J *Urban Disease and Mortality in Nineteenth-Century England* (1984)
Poor Law Union Minute Books held in local record office collections and Ministry of Health correspondence in The National Archives.
Public Health Reports and Parliamentary enquiries should be available in some local record office collections and The National Archives.

It would have been interesting to discover just how much money and effort had been spent by the Longbridge Deverell Vestry in cleaning up these dwellings and whether they continued to improve the lot of the parish poor throughout the following decades.

The 1851 Report for Swindon bears comparison with other horrific reports from the rest of the country. Swindon Report - Dr HB Sealy, MD:
"...nearly every house in this town has a dead well and a privy close adjoining the well; and as the soil is very light, the water in many instances is not only much contaminated but rendered quite unfit for use. These dead wells generally are in a filthy state, and in some instances overflow into the houses. In 1848 I lived in a house in Victoria-street which although not altogether uncomfortable, had a very bad underground kitchen &c badly lighted, and a drain which emitted a most unhealthy smell. What was the consequence? For nearly two months, Mrs Sealy, myself and one of the servants were laid up with typhus fever of a most malignant type: and certainly for six months out of the twelve we lived there, we had illness of one kind or another in the family. Typhus is by no means an uncommon disease here...The poison, doubtless, must emanate from those abominable dead wells and open sewage holes which send out such a noxious and pestilential smell over the yards and houses in which they are situate.

It was well known in New Swindon, the home of the GWR workshops, that many housewives obtained their drinking water from the nearby canal with disastrous consequences and during 1853 in the new Railway Village, there was a severe outbreak of typhus fever. Analysis of parish burial registers can provide details of deaths from various epidemics. At the GWR church of St Mark's the burial registers of 1880 revealed 178 burials, of which 147 were for young children and babies. It was obvious from this figure that a virulent childhood disease outbreak had caused so many deaths.

In all counties later in the 19th century, the Poor Law Commissioners appointed officials to deal with public

In association with FAMILY HISTORY MONTHLY

Civil Unrest in The Black Country 1766 - 1816
David Cox

Pre-industrialised England is sometimes represented as a golden age of prosperity and plenty, with well-fed peasants happy with their lot in life, knowing their place in a benevolent and paternalistic society. Reality, as is so often the case, was somewhat different from the myth.

The 'Bread And Butter Riots' of 1766
In September 1766 the *Annual Register* (a yearly compendium of memorable events) remarked:

There having being many riots, and much mischief done, in different parts of England, in consequence of the rising of the poor; who have been driven to desperation and madness, by the exorbitant prices of all manner of provisions; we shall, without descending to minute particulars, or a strict regard as to the order of time, in which they happened, give a short abstract of these disturbances. [1]

It went on to describe over thirty popular uprisings throughout England, caused by a combination of factors concerned with the price and availability of staple foodstuffs *(see Figure 1)*. Such uprisings were not a new phenomenon in England, but they became increasingly common during the latter half of the eighteenth century due to the increasing cost of staple foods. The average price of wheat had remained relatively stable during the first half of the century, averaging 34s. 11d. per quarter-hundredweight for the period 1713-1764, but between 1765 and 1800 it rose to 55s. per quarter-hundredweight, reaching a peak of 128s. per quarter-hundredweight in 1800. [2]

The harvest of 1766 was a particularly poor one, and the number of popular uprisings rose dramatically – and 'something like sixty incidents were reported in the press in a dozen weeks'. [3] These uprisings were almost unfailingly described as 'riots', but this term is perhaps not apposite for all of the demonstrations witnessed throughout the Black Country in September 1766. The term 'riot' suggests an out-of-control mob, intent on pointless destruction, whereas contemporary sources such as the *Annual Register* or the *Gentleman's Magazine* often remark that although goods were seized by force, personal violence was not often employed. Self-control was often the guiding force of such demonstrations, rather than brute intimidation. E. P. Thompson, in his classic *The Making of the English Working Class*, quotes a contemporary report concerning an incident in 1766 at Honiton in Devon when 'lace-workers seized corn on the premises of the farmers, took it to market themselves, sold it, and returned the money and even the sacks back to the farmers'. [4] Similarly in the Black Country both the participants and many observers often regarded the uprisings as a justifiable method of righting a perceived wrong, rather than as mindless destructive rioting.

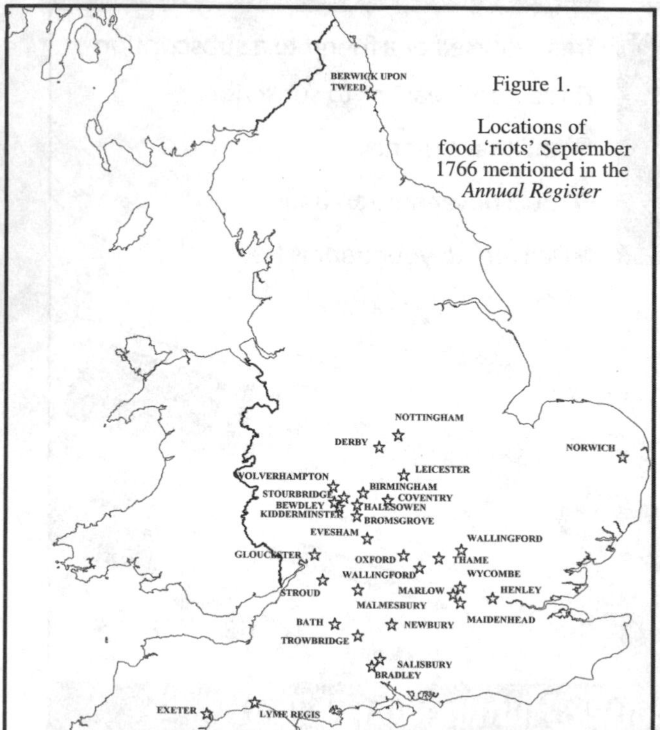

It is interesting to note that in many of these uprisings (commonly known as 'bread and butter riots'), the active participants were usually of the proto-urban working class, rather than agricultural workers or rural inhabitants. This seems to have been the case throughout the country, and the Black Country was no exception to this trend; in 1795, 1800 and 1810 the main body of 'rioters' was comprised of colliers. *Hue & Cry* (forerunner of *The Police Gazette*) stated on 16 June 1810 that:
Some disposition to riot, under the pretence of the high price of provisions shewed itself among the very lowest of the people of Birmingham and Wolverhampton, and the Colliers in the vicinity of Stourbridge a few days back; but [it] *was immediately suppressed by the prompt but humane interference of the Magistrates with other civil assistance, and the appearance of some Military parties.*

There was no doubt that occasionally the disturbances did take a violent and abusive turn; threatening letters such as the one reproduced below were sent to farmers and millers, often containing specific details of what could be expected if they were suspected of profiteering (spelling and punctuation is original):
Winter Nights is not past therefore your person shall not go home alive – or if you chance to escape the hand that guides this pen, a lighted Match will do eaqual execution. Your family I know not But the whole shall be inveloped in

Figure 1.

Locations of food 'riots' September 1766 mentioned in the *Annual Register*

BERWICK UPON TWEED

NOTTINGHAM
DERBY
NORWICH
LEICESTER
WOLVERHAMPTON
STOURBRIDGE
BIRMINGHAM
COVENTRY
BEWDLEY
HALESOWEN
KIDDERMINSTER
BROMSGROVE
EVESHAM
WALLINGFORD
GLOUCESTER
OXFORD
THAME
WALLINGFORD
WYCOMBE
STROUD
MARLOW
HENLEY
MALMESBURY
BATH
NEWBURY
MAIDENHEAD
TROWBRIDGE
SALISBURY
BRADLEY
EXETER
LYME REGIS
REDRUTH
ST. AUSTELL

Outline map reproduced from Ordnance Survey map data by permission of the Ordnance Survey

flames, your Carkase if any such should be found will be given to the Dogs if it Contains any Moisture for the Annimals to devour it[5]

A specific threat was received by Black Country magistrate and farmer, Thomas Biggs of Stourbridge, in September 1812 (spelling and punctuation is again original):

Mr Bigges,
Sir,
We right to let you know if you do not a medetley [immediately] *see that bread is made cheper you may and all your nebern* [neighbouring] *farmers expect all your houses rickes barns all fiered and bournd down to the ground. You are a gestes* [justice] *and see all your felley cretyrs* [fellow creatures] *starved to death. Pray see for som alterreshon in a mounth or you shall see what shall be the matter.* [6]

Local magistrates, aware of the tide of public opinion, often ensured that farmers and millers sold wheat and other staple foods at a reasonable rate during periods of shortage. The *Annual Register* informs its readers that 'at Kidderminster the populace obliged the farmers to sell their wheat at 5s a bushel', whilst at Stourbridge 'they lowered the price of butter, meat, and wheat'. Similarly, at Halesowen 'they rose, and forced the people to sell cheese at two-pence halfpenny, and flower *[sic]* for 5s. They destroyed two dressing-mills before they dispersed.'[7]

Despite the semi-official attempts by local magistrates to forestall such incidents by putting pressure on farmers and millers, the government of the day was not prepared to stand idly by and let matters worsen. Letters were sent to chief magistrates in each town where rioting had occurred, requiring the names of known offenders as evidence for special Commissions that were set up to prosecute the rioters. Repression could often be swift and final – eight rioters were reportedly shot dead on the road to Kidderminster during the uprising of 1766, and *The Times* stated in its edition of 5 May 1800 that thirty people were arrested during riots in Dudley, Stourbridge, Penn, Horton and Bilston.

However, the Government also took some positive steps to alleviate the problem. One of the main bones of contention between the rioters and the authorities was the export of grain to the Continent, which continued even in times of poor harvests. An Act to prohibit the export of corn, grain, meal, malt, flour, bread, biscuit and starch was passed on 26 September 1766, and another Act soon afterwards licensed the importation of duty-free grain from America and the Continent.

This had a beneficial short-term effect, but 'bread and butter' uprisings, together with other demonstrations about the high price of staple foods continued sporadically throughout the eighteenth and early nineteenth centuries. The Corn Laws and agitation for their repeal ensured that public unrest over staple food prices provided a continued threat to the social, political and economic *status quo* until the late 1840s.

The 'Colliers' March' of 1816
The period between 1815 and 1822 in particular was one of the most difficult and troubled in British

Sir Richard Birnie
Chief Magistrate
Bow Street
1821 - 1832

economic and social history – George Barnsby refers to it in his classic treatise *The Working Class Movement in the Black Country 1750-1867* as the 'Long Depression'.[8] The seemingly interminable wars with France had finally ended, and hundreds of thousands of soldiers and sailors had returned to their home country, thereby increasing the scarcity of both food and employment.

In 1816, although over sixteen million tons of coal were mined, over one half of the total public revenue was immediately swallowed up by payment of interest on the National Debt. Brian Murphy remarks in his *A History of the British Economy 1740-1970* that '1816 and 1817 were grim years for the iron-masters. More than one splendid fortune turned to dust'.[9] This obviously had a concomitant effect on those employed by the iron-masters, who provided a large proportion of employment within the Black Country. Once again, the scene was set for public unrest at both the price of staple foods and the scarcity of employment. However, the form of protest was gradually changing – George Barnsby stating that:

From 1815, permanent and highly sophisticated forms of organisation appeared whose members and leaders were working class people. The "mob" continued to play an important part in political and economic struggles, but response to injustice and repression was no longer entirely dependent on the vagaries of mob reaction.[10]

The reaction of the Bilston colliers and ironworkers seems partially to substantiate this view; although a "mob" was still involved in the immediate protests, the subsequent creation of relief funds for the downtrodden does seem to indicate a more sophisticated form of organization – however, these funds seem to have been largely the response of the concerned middle-class rather than the working-class.

As seen above, the late eighteenth and early nineteenth century had been a time of particular unrest and uncertainty with regard to food riots:

The industrial region of South Staffordshire was particularly likely to erupt in food riots. [There was] also a heavy concentration of occupations (such as that of collier) which had a reputation for collective direct action, in the form of riot, sabotage or other direct intimidation of employers and authorities, and the concentration of particular trades in certain parishes helped generalise the phenomenon.[11]

Increasingly intolerable distress faced by the colliers and ironworkers of the Black Country finally caused their despair to spill over in mid-1816, when groups of unemployed colliers decided to drag waggons containing Black Country coal to London and Liverpool in an effort to publicize their plight. Three waggons, each weighing in excess of two tons, were dragged by hand from the outskirts of Bilston to Oxford, a distance of over seventy miles. From there, the three groups split, with one heading to Maidenhead, another to St. Albans, and the third to Beaconsfield.

The Times of Friday 5 July 1816 contained the following account of what became known as the 'Colliers' March':

The colliers and labourers in the iron-works from Bilston, who have advanced towards London, have, it is said, at length been stopped by messengers from Government, advising them to wait at some distance from town until the result of their petitions shall be known. Government will doubtless give every possible attention to their petition; but it is utterly impossible that such wild projects should be attended with any beneficial result, which might not be much better obtained by remaining at home, and stating their grievances in writing to those who have it in their power to afford them relief. What good can possibly be obtained by losing many days labour, and incurring the expense of a long and tedious journey, it would puzzle the promoters of this ill-advised scheme to say. The waggon which was to proceed by the route of Oxford, has already reached the vicinity of Henley-upon-Thames; and another was reported yesterday to have reached the neighbourhood of St. Albans. In all that is stated about these unfortunate men, we do not learn that they have any wish to encourage riot or disorder. They foolishly entertain the opinion that the Prince Regent can order them employment, and they pride themselves upon being willing to work for an honest livelihood. Such is the curiosity excited to see these extraordinary petitioners, that many persons have actually left town in the expectation of meeting them.

This was the first of a series of reports that *The Times* carried on the 'Colliers' March'. On Saturday 6 July 1816, it published an 'eyewitness' account (reproduced below) of the progress of the waggon that had reached Maidenhead and which had attracted the attention of both the local magistracy and the Bow Street 'Runners'. The latter were experienced and professional police officers originally created by Henry Fielding the novelist, who was also Chief Magistrate at Bow Street in Westminster from 1748-1754. Fielding and his successors developed the 'Runners' into a small body of detectives who could

be employed throughout the country by the government (as in this case) or by private individuals or institutions.

Yesterday morning, Mr Birnie [Chief Magistrate] from Bow Street, accompanied by two officers, arrived at the Sun Inn here, and after consulting with Sir William Hearn, and other Magistrates of this place, swore in several extra constables; and as a matter of precaution, ordered a party of military to be under arms. [see Figure 2] This done, they sent forward the officers from Bow Street to meet the waggon that was approaching from Henley; it was met on Maidenhead Thicket, [...] and the crowd attending it, on being informed that they would not be permitted to proceed, instantly stopped, and conducted themselves with the greatest propriety. The waggon, which was 2 ton, 6cwt and 12lb, was drawn by forty-one men; and a leader or overseer rode on horseback and directed the whole. As soon as it was understood by the magistrates that the party wished to act in the way most agreeable to the lawful authorities, a negotiation was entered into, and the coals were permitted to be brought in here by four of the party and their leader, and were deposited with Wm. Pyne esq., who will distribute them among the poor of Maidenhead [...] The men refused to sell the coals, but gave them up as requested to Mr Pyne, and received a very handsome present instead. Mr Birnie, Sir William Hearn, Mr Pyne etc. went out and negotiated. The poor fellows were perfectly satisfied, but refused to go until the magistrates signed a paper that they had conducted themselves properly. At Henley, the day before yesterday, they behaved so well that the Mayor permitted them to go wherever they pleased in the town, and they had upwards of £40 given to them at that place. They left Bilston with three waggons in company, and parted at Oxford. One waggon was to be at Beaconsfield last night, and the other at St. Albans.

These accounts of the good behaviour of the protesters helped publicize their cause, and seemed to prick a few middle-class consciences. Letters from middle-class gentlemen from Coseley and Birmingham appeared in *The Times*, carrying accounts of the terrible suffering being endured by the colliers and ironworkers:

When I have told these poor creatures that the parish must find them food or labour, they have replied, 'Sir, they cannot do either', and some [...] have said, 'We would rather die, Sir, than be dependent on the parish'. Some, I believe, have really died of starvation.. An insufficiency of wholesome nourishment [...] produced diseases which terminated in dissolution [12]

Further letters of support and thanking those who had donated to the relief of the poor of the area were published on 29 and 31 July. On 5 August another letter was received:

The distress, Sir, is beyond everything that has been described [...]. I know, Sir, that other districts are in distress; but our sorrows are of an earlier date, and consequently of longer standing than those of any other county. Before the peace was concluded our staple manufacture – our iron-works – began to fail; and without help the pressure on our neighbourhood is insupportable.

Richard Smith, of Tibbington House near Birmingham, was the author of this letter. He, along with Reverend B. H. Draper of Coseley, helped co-ordinate the relief fund that had been created to help the distressed. Despite funds being received from such illustrious donors as Francis Freeling, Secretary

General of the Post Office, the distress continued unabated throughout the rest of the year. George Barnsby remarks that 'in Christmas week the Wolverhampton soup kitchen was issuing 4,200 quarts of soup weekly'.[13] In the following year the Reverend Doctor Luke Booker, JP and Vicar of Dudley, warned of seditious material issued by 'designing demagogues scattering their noxious notions over the prurient minds of an unwary people'.[14]

Although popular agitation in the Black Country area did diminish by the end of the decade, unrest in the area flared up again spasmodically throughout the second quarter of the nineteenth century, with the most serious unrest taking place in 1831, sparking real fears of a nation-wide revolution.[15]

With the benefit of hindsight, such popular agitation can be seen as the early stirrings of working-class demands for a fairer and more democratic society. That there was no widespread revolution in the late eighteenth or early nineteenth century is perhaps somewhat surprising; despite the popular image of working-class unrest, the majority of the population remained remarkably law-abiding and deferential to their unfortunate lot in society.

1. *Annual Register* vol. 9 (1766) p. 137
2. George Rud, *The Crowd in History* (London: Serif 1995), p. 39
3. ibid., p. 37
4. E. P. Thompson, *The Making of the English Working Class* (London: Penguin, 1991), p. 69
5. ibid., p. 68
6. *Hue & Cry* , 6 February 1813
7.. *Annual Register* vol 9 (17660 p 138
8. George Barnsby, *The Working Class Movement in the Black Country 1750 to 1867* (Wolverhampton: Integrated Publishing Services, 1977), p. 4
9. Brian Murphy, *A History of the British Economy 1740-1970* (London: Longman, 1973), p. 444
10. George Barnsby, *The Working Class Movement in the Black Country 1750 to 1867*, p. 4
11. Douglas Hay, 'Manufacturers and the Criminal Law in the Later Eighteenth Century: Crime and "Police" in South Staffordshire', *Past and Present Colloquium: Police and Policing* (1983)
12. *The Times*, 27 July 1816
13. George Barnsby, *The Working Class Movement in the Black Country 1750 to 1867*, p. 4
14. ibid., p. 6
15. These riots are covered in depth in a three-part article by J. Robert Williams in *The Blackcountryman* (vol. 7 nos. 3 & 4; vol. 8, no. 1, 1974/5)

David Cox is editor of The Blackcountryman the quarterly journal of The Black Country Society

www.blackcountrysociety.co.uk

**The Membership Secretary
25 Foxhills Park, Netherton
Dudley DY2 0AJ**

The Black Country consists of the area within the boundaries of the four West Midland metropolitan boroughs of Dudley, Walsall, Wolverhampton and Sandwell.

Founded in 1967, the aims of the Black Country Society, which has over 2,500 members worldwide, are to stimulate interest in the past, present and future of the Black Country and to encourage and facilitate the preservation of the Black Country's unique heritage.

The Society organises a yearly programme of varied activities including numerous walks and talks and also publishes a wide variety of books by Black Country writers and researchers on subjects ranging from humour to industrial archaeology.

The Blackcountryman, the Society's quarterly journal, is packed with articles about the Black Country and its hinterland, mainly written by Black Country people. Two national history publications have named The Blackcountryman as a leading magazine in the field of local history. Articles range from light-hearted contributions to in-depth research written by professional academics, and the journal also acts as a forum for members' queries and exchange of interests.

Help support the aims and objectives of the Society by becoming a member by writing to the address above and begin enjoying the many benefits of being a member of one of the best local societies in the country for as little as £10 per year!

Interested in the past, present and future of the Black Country?

Join the Black Country Society and enjoy the benefits of membership including excursions, walks, talks, book discounts and four copies (one each quarter) of *The Blackcountryman*, the Premier Magazine of the Black Country, delivered to your door each year.

The Red House Cone Wordsley, Stourbridge West Midlands

the best preserved glass cone in Britain and an example of the unique heritage of the Black Country

The Black Country Society

Stan Hill - Past President of The Black Country Society

The nineteenth-century nickname 'The Black Country' came to relate to an area of some 150 square miles north-west of Birmingham (but excluding that city), wherein lay a coal seam up to ten metres in depth known as 'The Thick'.

The discovery of outcrops of coal led to its extraction by simple opencast methods, just removing a few feet of top soil to expose it. Where the coal lay deeper, simple pits were dug until they became unsafe. The extractors would dig down to the seam and then sideways until it started to collapse; these simple pits were known as bell pits. They would then be abandoned and another one started a few yards away along the seam. On Cannock Chase (north of, but not in the Black Country), remainders of these can still be found. Over the next 200 years pits more familiar to us were developed. It was all done on an unco-ordinated scale.

The increase in the amount of coal produced in the seventeenth century coincided with Royal edicts forbidding the use of timber as a fuel because the demands of the emerging industries for their furnaces and kilns were decimating the forests and threatening the building of ships. For hundreds of years iron smelters had used wood in the form of charcoal as a fuel. This was very wasteful of timber for it took five tons of wood to produce one ton of charcoal. Britain's ancient forests and woodland were being destroyed, and her security was at risk.

Dud Dudley, a Royalist captain during the Civil War, and an illegitimate son of one of the lords of Dudley, had forges at Himley and on the River Stour. He claimed in a book called *Metallum Martis* that in about 1660 he had produced iron from iron ore using coal instead of charcoal. The discovery of the revolutionary process is however attributed to Abraham Darby, a Dudley-born man working at Coalbrookdale in 1709. This was really the start of the rolling snowball of the Industrial Revolution. The door was closing on wood as a fuel, whilst another opened with coal, which became available in increasing quantities just at the right time.

Water in the mines limited the depth to which pits could be sunk. Newcomen, a Cornishman working in the tin mines of Cornwall, developed a pumping engine. which was brought into use in the Black Country. One was installed at Tipton in 1712 and another in Bilston in 1713. These became widespread in the Black Country and coal production increased greatly. At the same time other minerals were found in abundance: iron ore, clay, and limestone, an essential item for the production of iron. All these materials were soon extensively mined or quarried throughout the area as the Industrial Revolution gathered pace.

In the south of the Black Country, around Brierley Hill and Stourbridge, were great reserves of fireclay, which proved an added incentive for glassmakers short of their traditional fuel of wood to come to the area in the 1600s. Fireclay was also important for the ironmakers as it was used to line their furnaces, and in the early nineteenth century for lining the fireboxes of thousands of railway locomotives.

Pre-1750 the Black Country was predominantly rural with much subsistence agricultural style life until the huge changes brought about by eighteenth-century Enclosure Acts. Small industries were craftsmen-

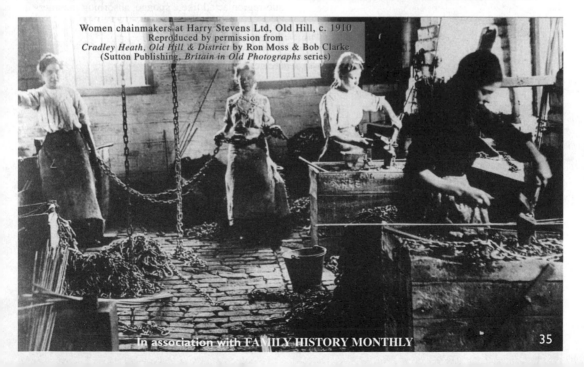

Women chainmakers at Harry Stevens Ltd, Old Hill, c. 1910
Reproduced by permission from
Cradley Heath, Old Hill & District by Ron Moss & Bob Clarke
(Sutton Publishing, *Britain in Old Photographs* series)

orientated and the original power sources were human, wind and water. The major subsequent developments which facilitated the growth of industry included the discovery of minerals, inventions of machines, steam engines, mechanised processes, expansion of the iron industry, building of canals and railways.

During the period of all these changes in the Black Country there was still a rural look about the landscape, particularly in areas where the coal near the surface had been exhausted and the despoiled land had reverted to nature. For example, even after the opening in 1927 of the Birmingham New Road (a more direct connection between Birmingham and Wolverhampton through the heart of the Black Country), traffic was still occasionally held up at Tividale while cattle crossed the road.

Over the 100 years of this transformation the population became close-knit through the hardships they experienced, families were large, infantile mortality was high, life expectancy was often low and there was a feeling of being different from others. Different customs developed, the language was peculiar to the coalfield (some experts say that it has Anglo-Saxon roots and was the language of Shakespeare), and despite all the influences of the modern media it remains strong.

Two transport developments within the space of fifty years greatly facilitated the expansion of the coal and iron industries in the Black Country. Canals used much iron in their mechanism and could also transport coal in great quantities. Railways used coal and iron in huge quantities, and both systems used and fed the demands of growing industry. From 1770 a great canal system grew over the Black Country and Birmingham, including the Staffordshire and Worcestershire Canal, which linked the Trent and the Severn. Railways were to follow some sixty years later.

The increasing industrial activity in the Black Country from the early eighteenth century onward led to an influx of country-folk from the surrounding counties. Housing settlements developed around pits and ironworks, or perhaps a small brickyard. Hovels were thrown up to accommodate newcomers and their families, and gradually industrial hamlets grew up without any planning over what was primarily a rural landscape.

Many of these industrial hamlets, after lasting for about a century, just withered away when the easily accessible coal had been exhausted. Other hamlets grew and joined with neighbouring settlements, perhaps to become an industrial village; some of them over the next 100 years became small industrial towns and developed specialisms e.g. Bilston (iron & steel), Wednesbury (iron & steel, heavy railway equipment, tubes), Willenhall (locks), Brierley Hill (iron & steel, maritime safety equipment), Cradley Heath (chains), Walsall (leather), Tipton (iron & steel), Wolverhampton (galvanized corrugated iron, locomotives). Throughout the Black Country, smaller industrial firms developed to produce all of the iron and steel products needed to feed the demands of the growing economy.

By 1860 the Black Country had reached the peak of industrial production. In 1860, within five miles of Dudley there were:
    441 collieries
    181 blast furnaces
    118 ironworks
    79 rolling mills
    1,500 puddling furnaces

One third of the region's men, some 40,000, were engaged in the heavy industries.

The uncontrolled, unplanned, unco-ordinated industrialisation continued. As industry expanded the sub-region acted like a sponge, absorbing incomers

'Landsale Wharf' at Haden Hill No. 1 Colliery
Reproduced by permission from
Cradley Heath, Old Hill & District by Ron Moss & Bob Clarke
(Sutton Publishing, *Britain in Old Photographs* series)

who were hastily accommodated in what were to become slums, there being no services such as water supply, sewage disposal, paved roads, street lighting or refuse collection.

Robert Southey, later to become Poet Laureate, travelled through the area in 1803. He wrote: *Everywhere the tower of some manufacturing was to be seen in the distance, vomiting up flames with smoke and blasting everything around with metallic vapours.*

One of the earliest, and certainly best known uses of the term the 'Black Country' was by Elihu Burritt, the American Consul based in Birmingham. He was a celebrated peace and anti-slavery campaigner appointed by Abraham Lincoln to assess the manufacturing capabilities of Birmingham and district in view of the lack of industry in the USA. He scoured the area and in 1868 published *Walks in the Black Country and its Green Borderland.*

Other early uses of the term Black Country include:

1851: In *Rides on Railways* by Samuel Sidney there is a complete chapter on the Black Country.
1860: Walter White's *All Around the Wrekin*, Chapter Two is entitled 'To the Black Country'.
1866: An article in *Punch* used the term to describe the area.

Some of these writers use the phrase 'known locally as the Black Country', so it is likely that the term was coined within the district itself in the 1830s-1840s.

Civil administration was totally inadequate to deal with the changing situation. The old Court Leets, Court Rolls and Parochial Church Councils continued, but certain old-established centres of population did manage to achieve some control over local affairs by obtaining Charters of Incorporation to become boroughs: Wolverhampton in 1848; Walsall in 1859; Dudley in 1865; West Bromwich in 1882. There followed Improvement Acts, Town Commissioners and Local Boards in Education and Health, all in an attempt to do something about the terrible effects of the Industrial Revolution.

A major step forward in civil administration came in 1888 with the creation of County Councils, which gradually absorbed the functions of the old established bodies and *ad-hoc* bodies. Counties were subdivided into districts in 1894. By this time, in the Black Country there were some twenty-three areas of joined-up small industrial townships which were granted their own local councils, urban district councils or rural district councils.

Since then there has been a succession of Local Government Acts of Parliament, the last one becoming operative in 1974 in which out of all of the local authorities in the Black Country, four Metropolitan Boroughs were created: Dudley, Wolverhampton, Sandwell, and Walsall.

Whatever the Black Country was (and there has been much uninformed speculation as to what it really was), it is now all incorporated in one or other of these four Boroughs. The new local authorities in some cases have added areas which used not to be considered part of the Black Country.

The four boroughs were later designated Black Country Metropolitan Boroughs and this was the first time that any lasting official recognition had been given to the 160-year-old nickname; although in 1987 the Government set up a body, the Black Country Development Corporation with huge sums of money available for dealing with the most polluted and neglected areas of the Black Country. The Corporation was able to clear such sites which it was not worthwhile for developers to do, and encourage the latter then to build houses and factory units. This was another use of the term 'The Black County' by officialdom.

The Black Country Society was founded in 1967 by enthusiasts who felt that the Black Country did not receive its fair share of recognition for its great contribution to the industrial development of Britain and the world. The stated aim was to foster interest in the past, present and future of the Black Country. Membership of the Society stands at around 2,500, whilst its renowned quarterly magazine, *The Blackcountryman* (of which will be published a celebratory 150th issue in March 2005), has so far included over 2,000 substantial articles on all aspects of the Black Country and reviews of over 600 books with Black Country references published since 1968.

For further information and membership details of the Society, see the Black Country Society advertisement in this *Handbook*.

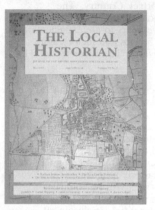

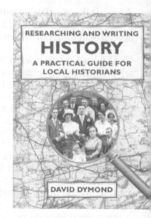

Faversham Gunpowder Factories – Staff and Operators
Arthur Percival

Factories places of beauty? Never, you'd probably respond. Yet you'd be wrong. Perhaps ironically, in view of their product, traditional gunpowder factories were invariably places of calm and charm, well-wooded and watered by rivers, streams and canals.

The woodland was managed to provide protection in the event of an accidental 'blow' (explosion). From the distance the Oare Works in Faversham, Kent, where over 200 people worked, could be mistaken for a game reserve. The biggest stand of alder in the UK is at the former Royal Gunpowder Factory at Waltham Abbey, Essex. It was grown because it made good charcoal, one of the key ingredients of gunpowder.

Before the advent of steam power, rivers and streams drove machinery. A conventional canal might serve for the delivery of raw materials, and despatch of the finished product. Within factories, as at Oare, there were often networks of narrow-gauge canals along which 'service-waiters' spent their working lives punting powder from process to process under the boughs of overhanging trees.

Think of gunpowder, and think of warfare. But this was not its only application. It is a key component, as it still is, of fireworks. Indeed over a thousand years ago it was an unknown Chinese pyrotechnician who invented it. It was used for sporting purposes. Most stone buildings would not exist without it - it made the job of quarrying so much easier. It made the Industrial Revolution possible, blasting routes for canals and railways.

Yet until quite recently it was the Cinderella of industrial history. For many applications it was succeeded by the new 'high' explosives, the first of which was invented in 1846; but not until the second half of the 20th century was any serious academic interest taken in it, nor any effort made to conserve the relics of its past.

In Kendal the late Paul Wilson pioneered study of the Cumbrian industry. The USA's first factory, started at Wilmington, Delaware, early in the 19th century by the Du Pont brothers from France, was restored by the Du Pont Foundation. The oldest surviving gunpowder mill in the world, on the former Home Works at Faversham, was rescued from the jaws of the bulldozer by the Faversham Society, and then restored and opened to the public.

Interest slowly gathered momentum. In the UK the main centres of the industry were in Cornwall, Cumbria, Essex, Kent, Scotland and Surrey; in Ireland at Ballincollig, Co Cork. Most of these have now been the subjects of detailed studies, many of them still in print. First the former Royal Gunpowder Factory at Ballincollig was restored for public access by Cork County Council and then its counterpart at Waltham Abbey in Essex. For English Heritage Wayne Cocroft undertook the first comprehensive UK-wide archaeological survey of the industry, published in 2000 as *Dangerous Energy*. As I write, the Oare Works at Faversham is being restored and will be open free of charge in 2005 as a countryside and industrial heritage park. A visit to this fascinating, beautiful site will not disappoint.

The Oare Works, the second of Faversham's three gunpowder factories, was started in the late 17th century by two Huguenot asylum-seekers, Peter Azire and James Tiphaine. Reputedly French powder was of better quality than English at the time, and they were encouraged to settle in the town by the 2nd Earl of Feversham (*sic*), himself a Huguenot refugee and the confidante (ironically) of the Catholic James II. Indeed in 1688 when James was imprisoned in Faversham it was the Earl who negotiated his release - but that is another story!

Huguenots were involved in the industry in Surrey as well as Faversham, and this prompted the question: Who exactly were they, and where in France had they come from? Ray Godfrey and I, both active Faversham Society members,

39

thought we ought to try to find out. But why, then, we asked, should we try to track down just Huguenots. Why not instead see if we could pinpoint as many as possible of those who worked in the local industry? And why not then publish the results for the benefit of local, social, family and economic historians? This was the origin of the *Faversham Gunpowder Industry Personnel Register 1573-1840*, which was recently published by the Society.

In style this is a little bit like Foster's *Alumni Oxonienses* and Venn's *Alumni Cantabrigieneses*. It names all those known to have worked in the three local factories, or who owned them or were otherwise involved, and records all that is at present known about them. Compiling it was no easy task. The only staff records which have survived are from the period, in the late 18th and early 19th centuries, when two of the factories were in Government ownership - and even these are far from complete. Other information therefore had to come from a wide range of sources, including printed books, genealogies, parish registers and title deeds.

The outcome was a 110-page book containing over 350 individual entries. Some are brief, one- or two-line entries, recording for example that Thomas Guttridge was a labourer extracting and refining saltpetre (another of the three main ingredients) in 1795 and 1796. Others, like that for Francis Grueber the elder (1657/8-1731), operator of both the Home and Oare Works, run to a whole page or more.

Grueber was another Huguenot asylum-seeker who had arrived in England in 1682. He had arrived in England from Lyon in 1682 with his parents and five siblings. His father, Daniel, had sought refuge with the specific intention of "making gunpowder after the French manner" and had acquired a lease of some Faversham mills in December 1684. He died in 1692, but Francis flourished in the industry. In 1692, when he was living in Seething Lane in the City of London, he was convicted of smuggling silk and trading with France in time of war, but neither he nor his business seems to have suffered as a result. By 1701 he was operating both the Home and the Oare Works, and supplying gunpowder to the Government's Board of Ordnance.

Gunpowder factories were places where a moment's carelessness could cost lives. In September 1703 Francis's son, also Francis, only 12 years old, was killed by flying débris from a 'blow' when he was "rowing across the river for his enjoyment." The tragedy was graphically described by Daniel Defoe, author of *Robinson Crusoe*.

Of Daniel Grueber's known descendants it seems most today live in India and Tasmania. In the summer of 2004 one of them, born in India but now living in England, played the leading part in a BBC Radio 4 *Meet the Descendants* programme. She came to Faversham and was able to see what remains of the two factories in which her forebears were involved, the spot where young Francis was killed, and the inscription over his grave in Faversham Parish Church.

It's not clear yet when the Faversham industry started, but the earliest local gunpowder-maker known to date is Thomas Gill, first recorded in 1573. There is a suspicion that he is identical with the person of the same name who - also in 1573 - was granted the lucrative office of keeping the lions, lionesses and leopards at the Tower of London. Improbable, you may say; but the job seems to have gone with being a gunpowder manufacturer, and may not have involved much personal contact with the animals. The Tower was then the nation's main arsenal, and gunpowder was also made there.

The *Faversham Gunpowder Personnel Register* makes clear that the town came to be regarded as a reservoir of gunpowder expertise. Staff were poached to start new factories elsewhere in the UK, in India and the USA. William Smith, who sailed for Bengal on the *Lord Anson* in 1760, took with him models of factory machinery so that he could build full-scale examples on arrival. In 1836 four brothers named Prickett were recruited from Faversham to rescue a factory near Enfield, Connecticut, which had failed to come up with decent-quality powder. The name of its site, perhaps appropriately, was Hazardville, but the derivation was not from the risks that the workers ran but from the owner, whose surname was Hazard.

In a few cases the *Register* records what workers looked like. Daniel Dane, a freeman of the Faversham Oyster Fishery Company (the oldest in the UK), was seaman serving on a powder vessel in 1791. He was 5' 3" tall, with a light brown complexion and dark brown hair. Thomas Dane, perhaps his brother, and another Oyster Fishery Company freeman, was skipper of the powder vessel *Wheatsheaf* in the same year. He was just as tall (or short), with a light complexion and red hair.

Because the gunpowder industry was a craft one, where experience, care and judgement counted, there were dynasties of employees. Son followed father, and sometimes grandson son. William Silver (1769-1848) worked till retirement at the Faversham factories - in 1789 at the cylinders, where charcoal was refined. Walter, his son, became foreman at the Thames-side magazine at Erith owned by the Low Wood Company, one of the Cumbrian factories. He was nearly killed in an explosion in 1864 but - nothing daunted - went on to be foreman of a magazine at East Tilbury, on the other side of the river.

By no means all staff retired. Some just went on

working. At the age of 78, after 43 years' service, Robert Wraight was still employed at the Faversham factories as a labourer. Later he became a warder (works policeman), and was still in post when he died in 1835 at the age of 89. He was evidently a saver rather than a spender. When he died he was worth £3,200, the equivalent of £300,000 today.

Faversham, now officially the hottest place in Britain, with a maximum of over 101° F recorded in August 2003, is said to be a healthy town, and in terms of longevity the gunpowder personnel records bear this out. In the 1770s two of the factories pioneered a BUPA-type private healthcare scheme. Workers who paid 6d (2 old pence) a week were guaranteed free medical treatment, as were members of their families. The only medical problem which persisted in the factories was that of what the records describe as 'ague'. In fact this was malaria, which was prevalent on the north-east Kent coastal fringe till the early 20th century, when spraying of watercourses finally wiped it out.

The *Faversham Gunpowder Personnel Register* excludes staff who started work in the factories after 1840. This is because with the 1841 Census employment information becomes available, and more specific records therefore begin. Another Faversham Society member, John Breeze, has been combing through these, and tracking down obituaries and reports (if this is not a terrible pun) of explosions. He and Ray Godfrey are working on a sequel *Register* which as well as covering the three gunpowder factories till their closure in 1934 will also list personnel working at the local high explosives factories which operated, ultimately on a huge scale, between 1874 and 1919.

The **Register** is on sale at the Faversham Society's Fleur de Lis Heritage Centre, 10-13 Preston Street, Faversham, Kent ME13 8NS, price £4.45 (£5.95 by post). The Centre stocks a wide range of books about the history of explosives manufacture, in Faversham and elsewhere. Request a list, or on the web for details go to www.faversham.org/history/explosivesbooks.asp. A free illustrated **Faversham Gunpowder Trail** is also available (please send second-class stamp if ordering by post).

Chart Gunpowder Mills, the oldest in the world, within a few minutes' walk of the town centre, are open free of charge on Saturdays, Sundays and Bank Holidays from 2 to 5 pm from Easter to the end of October The **Oare Gunpowder Works**, planned to be

UNCLE FUSBY GIVES ONE OF HIS DELIGHTFUL LECTURES, WITH A FEW SIMPLE CHEMICAL EXPERIMENTS, SUCH AS PHARAOH'S SERPENTS, THE MAGNESIUM WIRE, ETC. ALSO TO SHOW HOW GUNPOWDER CAN BE CONTAINED IN TWO INCOMBUSTIBLE POWDERS. STARTLING DÉNOÛMENT AND CHORUS OF DELIGHTED YOUNGSTERS, "OORAY!"

open in 2005, is about 2 km W of the town centre and reached on foot from the Market Place by walking along West Street, up Dark Hill and along Bysing Wood Road. By car take the A2, join the B2045 at the roundabout just west of the town, and after 1km take the first turning on the left. The entrance, 300m on, is on the right, and there is parking on site. Faversham, one of the UK's finest historic towns, with nearly 500 listed buildings, is easily accessible via the M2. Trains from London (Victoria) run half-hourly and take 69 minutes, and the station is five minutes' walk from the Market Place.

I'm not tracing my ancestors ...... really!
Elsie Forster

Four years ago, my older half-sister died and after some time had elapsed it occurred to me that I was the only one left with certain information about the family, and that it might be a good idea to write something down for the benefit of the younger members. I knew that Dad was from Cumrew, Cumberland, his father came from Lancashire and his mother from Cumberland; Mam was born in Gateshead and her father was Scottish but I wasn't sure about her mother who died before my mother was aged two. *(It turned out that she was half Scottish and half Northumbrian, born in North Shields, where I now live – surprise!).* My sister's mother also died young and I had a notion that she came from Spennymoor *(wrong! – she was actually born in the same village as my great-grandfather in Lancashire).* In this article I'll concentrate on Dad and his father's family, the Varleys.

Before I started writing anything down for others I jotted down what I knew, remembered, or half remembered and talked to other members of the family.

Dad was born on 14th October, 1893 in Cumrew and I remember him saying that his father nearly lost his life after registering his birth as a severe snowstorm blew up; grandfather was found half buried in a snowdrift. Grandfather was James Varley, a Church of England Schoolmaster from Lancashire who had attended the Church of England Teachers Training College in Chester. I remembered Dad saying that the Varleys came from Garstang and that James's father was a silk-weaver. *(How did James manage to get to college? – I still don't know).* I knew that James taught in Cumrew and, later, in Bewcastle.

To work: first I enquired about where I could obtain Dad's birth certificate then wrote to the Registry Office in Carlisle. Much to my surprise, they could not trace him although they do cover Cumrew. They informed me about the St. Catherine's Register; at the time the nearest copy was in Newcastle Central Library.

On searching the St. Catherine's Register I was surprised not to find Dad in the December 1893 quarter, but in the following one, and the area was given as Penrith. When I eventually received a copy of his birth certificate, the birth date was 14th October, but grandfather had registered the birth on 2nd January, 1894 at Kirkoswald. Dad was born in Cumrew Schoolhouse, Croglin, which was in a different registration district. *Although I had visited the area I had never spotted what looked like a parish school, and later discovered that the school was in an isolated situation between Cumrew and Croglin and that it no longer exists.*

Having discovered St. Catherine's Register I also searched for the births of Dad's brothers and sisters – I found all but one *(much later, with the help of the 1901 Census, I discovered that the 'missing' brother was born in Market Rasen, Lincs. about a year before Dad was born – I had no idea that the family had ever been there)*; I also found the eldest child of the family who just survived a few hours (and his name, John, was given to a later child whom I knew as my Uncle Jack).

So far so good – this research is a piece of cake! It would be interesting to find my grandparents' marriage – yes, they married at Lanercost Priory (part of which is used as the parish church) in 1890 – and the certificate gave the names and occupations of their fathers - so I now knew that my great grandfather was John Varley, silk dresser (not weaver as I had thought).

You're tracing your ancestors? - No, just checking one or two facts.

What next? – I may as well check on the births of the grandparents – *bingo!* – James born in Lancaster in 1860, parents John Varley, silk dresser and Eliza, maiden name Ashworth – *never heard of that name before – this is getting interesting!* Their marriage? John Varley, silk dresser, aged 26, (father Robert Varley, Joiner), and Eliza Ashworth, servant, aged 22 (father Richard Ashworth, Labourer) married in Lancaster in 1859.

English Street, Carlisle.

43

How about my great grandparents' births? *–registration only started in July 1837? – well that excludes John and possibly Eliza but let's see …. no luck unfortunately.*

In the meantime I had bought a computer, attended some classes to learn how to use it - and discovered the IGI and lots of people with family names who might belong to me – or might not! For example, the only John Varley I could find at around the right time was born near Scarborough – not impossible, I suppose, but how could I find out? – I might be able to get more from Census records? - the 1881 Census is in Newcastle Library?

Yes – there was John Varley, his wife Eliza and daughter Clara living in Ellel (just south of Lancaster) and John said he was born in Ellel, Eliza in Caton – and there was grandfather James Varley in residence in his college in Chester (I had found out after writing to the College that he left there in 1881).

This looking up the ancestors is interesting, isn't it? Perhaps, now that I've been doing it for a year, I should find out how to do it properly – and I attended some of the classes of Neil Richardson – great! – then joined the Northumberland and District Family History Society (NDFHS).

We later had family holidays in the different areas the family came from; in an apartment in Carlisle I left the slaves(!) to do the chores and entertain themselves while I spent each morning in the Records Office in the Castle where I got loads of information on the Cumbrian family which I won't go into here, but was also able to read the log-book of Cumrew School and the attendance book of the Park School, Bewcastle , both in my grandfather's handwriting, which were interesting in themselves and both of which gave more information in passing about the family. In the afternoons we explored the areas where the family lived – and the graveyards *(just the kind of holiday my lot always wanted!)*

We then visited Lancashire where we visited some of the places the family came from – the silk mill in Galgate (a listed building but now used for other purposes); the cottages nearby where the Varleys lived in 1881; Garstang; the various parish churches; not least, we enjoyed the countryside.

I also visited the Preston records office where I found John, Eliza and baby James in the 1861 Census, living in Lancaster. *Frustration though*, as I could not find Robert and family in any of the censuses in any of the areas I knew about (he died in Lancaster in 1870). Neither could I find the Christening of John in the Ellel parish register although he said in each Census that this was his place of birth. I did find the Christenings of Elizabeth and Thomas Varley *(the first I knew of them)*, with parents Robert Varley, joiner and his wife Margaret *(first time I'd got her name)* in 1839 and 1840, when they were living in Starbank then Dolphinholme. Time was limited and I left feeling that I hadn't learned much – *and why hadn't I looked at the parish records of Cockerham?* (Cockerham covered Ellel until its chapel of ease became a parish church in 1835).

Back home and I tried the IGI again – still no John, but I did find the marriage of Robert Varley and Margaret Standing in 1933 in Cockerham. (I had previously noted a marriage of Robert Varley and Alice Preston in 1824 in Garstang but could not be sure whether this was *my* Robert. I had looked in the parish records of St. Thomas, Garstang without finding them).

We returned to Lancashire this year, where we stayed on a farm in Ellel and I again visited the records office. In the Cockerham parish records there was the marriage of Robert and Margaret in 1933, but very little other information – and John wasn't Christened in Cockerham – *help!*

Visits around the area again included Dolphinholme this time and I acquired some very useful booklets in the parish church from which I learned that some of the area belonged to the parish of St. Helens, Garstang (which, just to complicate matters, is not in the town of Garstang at all but in Churchtown) and the rest to the parish of Cockerham, but that the Chapels of Ease at Ellel (before it became a parish in 1835) and Shireshead *(where???)* were sometimes used for Christenings and Burials because of the distance to the parish church. *I don't think anyone considered the difficulties for future family researchers!* Dolphinholme church was built by the local worsted wool mill owners in 1839 but did not become a parish church until much later. *Did Robert move to Dolphinholme to work on the church?*

Back to the records office – in St. Helens parish Robert Varley and Alice Preston, both 'of this parish' were married in 1824; in the Shireshead records *(obviously it's such a small place it's not been entered in the IGI)* Alice Varley, Robert's first wife, was buried in 1832, when they lived in Forton. I looked in the St. Helens Christenings and other areas in a couple of census records but found nothing – then my time was up.

Back home I requested the Preston Records Office to search the Shireshead Christenings for me, which they did for a small fee, and there were James, son of Robert and Alice Varley of Cleveley in 1831, then John *(hurrah!)*, son of Robert and Margaret

Varley of Ellel in 1833 and William, son of Robert and Margaret Varley of Ellel in 1835.

It's been a long hard road to get John's Christening. *Now about Robert, there are two alternatives ....(sounds of moaning as husband finally goes mad).*

This is only a small part of my search for my ancestors – and I feel as if I've only nibbled at the edges so far. The great thing is how helpful lots of people have been, whether in records offices, libraries, registry offices or fellow researchers who have often given freely of their time and to whom I am very grateful. Good luck with your own research!

The Family Records Centre

The Family Records Centre provides access to the following:

General Register Office

- Indexes of births, marriages and deaths in England and Wales from 1837
- Indexes of legal adoptions in England and Wales from 1927
- Indexes of some births, marriages and deaths of British nationals and British Armed Forces, which took place abroad, from the late 18th Century including both World Wars

Certificates can be purchased of any entry in the above. Please note that the certificates are not produced on the same day. If you need a certificate but cannot visit the Family Records Centre in person, you can place an order online at www.gro.gov.uk or by post, fax or telephone. Please ring 0845 603 7788 for further information and details of fees.

The National Archives

- Census returns for England and Wales (1841-1901)
- Wills and administrations from the PCC up to 1858
- Death Duty registers (1796-1858) and indexes (1796-1903)
- Records of nonconformist births, baptisms and burials (mainly pre-1837) and marriages (mainly pre-1754)
- Miscellaneous foreign returns of births, deaths and marriages from 1627 to 1964
- Access to online resources including DocumentsOnline (with free image downloads) and 1901 Census Online.

The Family Records Centre also offers the following services:

- Advice on family and local history research
- Family history reference area, including books, magazines and maps
- Family History Databases, including the International Genealogical Index (IGI) and the 1881 census index
- Free internet access
- Online indexes to Scottish registration and census records
- Bookshop, selling publications on family and local history
- Exhibitions, lectures and other events
- Self-service or staffed photocopying service on the first floor
- Regular users' consultations and quarterly newsletter
- Good facilities for customers with special needs
- Refreshment area with vending machines
- Baby changing room

Family Records Centre

1 Myddelton Street, London, EC1R 1UW
www.familyrecords.gov.uk
A service provided by The Public Record Office &
The Office for National Statistics (General Register Office)

Contact Details
Births, Marriages, Deaths, Adoptions and Overseas enquiries T: 0845 603 7788 F: 01704 550013
E: certificate.services@ons.gsi.gov.uk

Census and general enquiries T: 020 8392 5300
F: 020 8487 9214 E: frc@nationalarchives.gov.uk

Planning your visit
Opening hours
Monday 9:00 am – 5:00 pm: Tuesday 10:00 am – 7:00 pm:
Wednesday 9:00 am – 5:00 pm: Thursday 9:00 am – 7:00 pm: Friday 9:00 am – 5:00 pm: Saturday 9:30 am – 5:00 pm
The Centre is closed on Sundays and Public Holidays. Closure dates for Easter and Christmas are publicised in advance.
There is no need to book.

Group Visits
You are welcome to bring a group or coach party to the Family Records Centre (FRC) at any time during our normal opening hours. However, we would advise you to plan your visits to avoid our busiest times. On our busy days the lockers are often all in use so try to bring no more than you need for your research. Please let us know if you are planning to bring a large group to the FRC. Up to date information about coach parties planning to visit the FRC is available on our website.

How to get here
by rail
    Angel – Northern Line (City Branch)
    Farringdon – Circle, Metropolitan, Hammersmith & City Lines and Thameslink
    King's Cross – Victoria, Northern, Piccadilly, Circle, Metropolitan, Hammersmith & City Lines and National Rail services
by bus
    19, 38 and 341 along Rosebery Avenue
    63 along Farringdon Road
by car
    There is an NCP car park in Bowling Green Lane (off Farringdon Road) which is within easy walking distance of the Centre and limited Pay & Display parking in the surrounding streets. The FRC is located within the London Congestion Charging Zone (visit www.cclondon.com for details).

There is reserved parking for visitors with disabilities at the Centre, but spaces must be booked in advance. Please ring 020 7533 6436 before you visit.

General Register Office - Certificate Services

The General Register Office is part of the Office for National Statistics and is the central source of certified copies of register entries (certificates) in England and Wales. Since 1837 each entry made in a register of births, marriages or deaths in England and Wales has been copied to the centrally held national record maintained by General Register Office. Certificate Services is the name given to the arm of the General Register Office (GRO) that deals with applications for copies from this record of births, marriages and deaths and is based in Southport, Merseyside.

Many customers who apply to Certificate Services for a certificate do so for legal or administrative purposes such as applying for a passport or pension but increasingly a large proportion of applications are from family historians and professional genealogists. In 2002/2003 we received over 950,000 certificate applications. This is an increase of 42% over the past six years, and interest in family history accounts for most of that increase. GRO also has separate sections that deal with adoption certificates and certain overseas records.

Family Records Centre. Many of you will be familiar with the "public face" of Certificate Services, the Family Records Centre (FRC) at 1 Myddelton Street London EC1R 1UW. The FRC is run in partnership with The National Archives *formally The Public Record Office* and aims to provide a one-stop shop for family history research. The Family Record Centre provides access to:

Paper indexes of births, marriages and deaths registered in England and Wales from 1st July 1837.
Indexes of legal adoptions (England & Wales from 1927).
Indexes of births, marriages and deaths of some British citizen's abroad and those relating to British Armed Forces, posted overseas from the late 18th century. These include: Consular and High Commission returns since 1849; Marine births and deaths since 1837; aircraft births, deaths and missing persons from 1947; Army returns from 1881; Regimental registers 1761-1924; (these cover the UK, Ireland and abroad (including India) Army Chaplains returns 1796-1880; deaths in World Wars I and II and the Boer War; Ionic Islands and Indian State deaths.
A CD-ROM index of births which have taken place in Northern Ireland from 1922-1993.

How to go about finding a register entry
It is not possible for applicants to search through copies of the actual register entries themselves. However the indexes may be searched to identify the entry you seek. The indexes are arranged by year and then alphabetically by surname. Before 1983 the indexes are also split into the quarter of the year in which the event was registered e.g. events registered in January, February or March are indexed in the March quarter for the relevant year.

To apply for a certificate of the entry you can choose which method best suits you:
Application in person via the FRC
The Family Records Centre is open to the public at the following times: Monday, Wednesday, Thursday, Friday:9am-5pm Tuesday: 10am-7pm Saturday: 9.30am-5pm

Once you have searched the indexes and identified an entry you simply complete an application form, including the GRO Reference Number listed in the index and take it to the cashiers for payment. The fee for each certificate is £7.00.

Smedley Hydro
All applications made at the FRC are transported overnight to Certificate Services at Smedley Hydro, Southport, Merseyside. Many people have asked about the unusual name of the office where their certificates are produced. Smedley Hydro was build in early Victorian times and known as the Birkdale College for the education of young gentlemen. It then became a Hydropathic Hotel whose electro-chemical baths were extremely popular "in restoring the work-weary, the enfeebled and those of a naturally delicate organisation". With the outbreak of the Second World War the building was requisitioned by His Majesty's government for the purpose of National Registration and there are now 750 people working at the Southport Office with over 300 of them employed within Certificate Services.

Production Process
Once your application is received at Smedley Hydro the race then begins to have the applications sorted ready for the staff to retrieve the relevant microfilm, load the film onto a reader, find the entry, scan the image and produce the certificate ready for either posting out on the fourth working day or returning to the FRC for collection on the fourth working day. This is no mean feat when you consider that around ten thousand applications are received via the FRC every week.

Application direct to GRO Southport
If it is not convenient for you to go to central London and visit the FRC, you can apply directly to GRO Southport for your certificates. It would, of course, help us to have the index reference for the entry you want, so you may wish to look this up at one of the many centres around the country which hold copies of the national GRO index on microfiche. There are over 100 such locations including libraries, County Records Offices and Family History Centres within the UK and overseas. To find out the nearest one to you telephone Certificate Services on 0870 243 7788.

Alternatively you may wish to view the indexes on line. Recent changes to the conditions of sale of the GRO Indexes now mean that some organisations have made Index information available on the Internet.

Please note that it is not possible for members of the public to search the indexes at our Southport office itself. Personal callers are welcome to leave certificate applications between the hours of 9am – 5pm, Monday – Friday at GRO, Smedley Hydro, Trafalgar Rd, Birkdale, Southport.

Most applicants to GRO Southport prefer to apply by one of the following methods:

national STATISTICS

it cannot be found in that year. Due to the additional searches involved this service takes a little longer. Once the application is received the certificate is posted out within 15 working days. Should we be unable to find the entry, we will refund your fee minus a search fee of £4.50

By telephone:
Our call centre may be reached by dialling 0845 603 7788. You will hear a menu selection before being transferred to an operator who can take the details of the GRO reference number(s) you want and then arrange for your certificate(s) to be posted out to you within 5 working days. The fee for this service is £8.50, and payment can be made by Visa, Master or Switch. Please note we do not accept Electron or American Express Cards. The Call Centre is available 6 days a week (Monday – Friday 8am-8pm and Saturday 9am – 4pm) .

Our Call Centre deals with a variety of enquires relating to certificate services and each week a team of 25 staff deal with over four and a half thousand telephone calls.

By fax or post:
You may wish to fax your certificate application to 01704 550013. Alternatively you can post in your application enclosing a cheque or postal order payable to **ONS** to :
The General Register Office
PO Box 2, Southport, Merseyside PR8 2JD

On Line:
This is a secure website that can be used to place orders using the GRO Index reference number and for certificates in the twentieth century where the exact details are known. For further information visit our website at: www.statisitcs.gov.uk/registration

How to contact our office by email
As the e-revolution continues certificate services increasingly deal with a large number of enquiries from people who have visited our website. If you wish to contact us by email our address is certificate.services@ons.gov.uk

What if you do not know the GRO reference number of the entry you want?
If you do not wish to conduct you own search of the indexes we are happy to do this for you. For a fee of £11.50 we will undertake a search of the indexes for the year in which you tell us the event concerned occurred, and if necessary a year either side as well if

To assist us in the search you will need to provide as much information as possible about the person on the certificate you are trying to obtain. For a birth – full name, date of birth, place of birth and if known the parents names including the mothers maiden name. For a marriage, you will need to supply the names of both the bride and groom, date of marriage, place of marriage and if known, the fathers name for both bride and groom. For a death you will need to supply a full name, date of death, place of death and if a female their marital status. The occupation of the deceased is also helpful.

Smedley Hydro. Southport
Reproduced with the permission of Martin Perry, Southport Civic Society

Application to a local Register Office
If you know exactly where the birth, marriage or death that you are looking for took place you may also apply to the local Register Office covering that area. The Superintendent Registrar will be able to provide you with a certificate from his or her records. Please note that the GRO reference number does not refer to these local records, and will unfortunately be of no use to them in finding the entry for you. You will be asked to provide details similar to those listed in the paragraphs above so that they can locate the entry for you.

Other services provided by GRO:
Commemorative Certificates. Something that people may be unaware of is our Commemorative Certificate Section. For a cost of £40 they can provide a commemorative marriage certificate to mark silver, ruby, gold or diamond anniversaries. These certificates are colour printed on high quality paper and come mounted in frame within a presentation box, they do make an unusual and attractive gift. For further information call 0151 471 4256.

Certificate Services welcomes Feedback: We welcome feedback and customer input on the level and quality of service currently being provided. If you have any comments about our services please write to - Customer Service Unit Manager, PO Box 2, Southport, Merseyside, PR8 2JD or email certificate.services@ons.gov.uk

General Register Office Southport - a review of the year 2004
Carol Quinn Communications Manager - Certificate Services

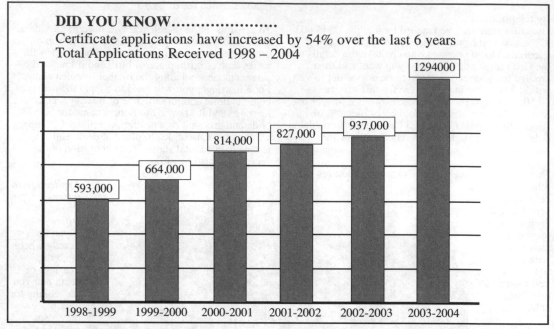

DID YOU KNOW........................
Certificate applications have increased by 54% over the last 6 years
Total Applications Received 1998 – 2004

1998-1999	593,000
1999-2000	664,000
2000-2001	814,000
2001-2002	827,000
2002-2003	937,000
2003-2004	1294000

The last year has seen a number of changes at GRO including the launch of the new look GRO website, the introduction of the new local rate telephone number for certificate ordering and general enquiries and the launch of certificate online ordering world wide.

New GRO Website – www.gro.gov.uk
On Wednesday 12 May 2004 the General Register Office's website was relaunched, setting high standards for usability and accessibility.

The site provides important information and advice on registration and related topics such as adoption, approved marriage premises and help for people wishing to find their individual records.

The structure and layout of the information has been reorganised around common activities rather than departments and each section (births, deaths, marriages, adoptions and stillbirths) offers links to relevant and useful topics, and ease of navigation helps users to easily switch between activities.

For more information and to have a look at the new, improved website, visit www.gro.gov.uk.

Certificate on line ordering
One of the more interesting features of the new website from a family historian's point of view is the introduction of an on-line certificate ordering service. Introduced initially in July 2003 for customers living within the UK the service was opened up to customers living overseas in July 2004.

Unfortunately only the actual ordering and payment is web based, the remainder of the process remains a manual operation in line with the legislation that supports the Registration Acts . Once received the order it is printed and passed to the certificate production area. A certificate is then produced, scrutinised for quality and despatched to the customer.

Since its launch in we have received over 505,000 applications via on-line ordering.

From 1 September 2004 the telephone number for certificate orders and enquiries is 0845 603 7788

Adoptions

Adoptions policy in England and Wales is governed by the Children's Branch at the Department for Education and Skills. The Registrar General administers the three national registration services, which have come into being since 1926 as part of his General Register Office functions.

When an adoption has been granted by a court in England or Wales, the court issues an order, which is the authority for an entry to be made in the Adopted Children Register. This is completed within six weeks and a free short certificate is sent to the adoptive parent(s).

A certificate of adoption is the equivalent of a normal birth certificate but in an adopted person's new name. It is a certified copy of an entry made in the Adopted Children Register and should be used by an adopted person in place of a birth certificate, which is a certified copy of the original birth entry.
Future replacement certificates can be easily purchased online at www.gro.gov.uk or by telephoning the General Register Office direct on 0845 603 7788. This number is available Monday to Friday 8am – 8pm and Saturday 9am – 4pm.

Information on access to Birth Details
If you were adopted through the courts of England or Wales and are 18 years or over, the law since 1976 has enabled you to find out more information relating to your birth details.

If you were adopted before 12 November 1975 and reside in England or Wales
You are required to attend an informal interview with an approved adoption worker. This can be someone at either your local Social Services, at the General Register Office in Southport or, under certain circumstances, at the agency that handled your adoption. You can also choose to see an adoption worker at another local authority but you will need to give a reason for your choice (for example, you may already work for your own local authority), otherwise they may not agree to see you.

If you were adopted on or after 12 November 1975

You have the choice whether you would like to see an approved adoption worker or have the information sent to you direct. You may find it helpful to see an adoption worker, as they may be able to offer practical advice and guidance as well as discussing any concerns or issues important to you.

If we are not able to help you, there are a number of other organisations you can contact to help you continue your search and these are listed on our website at www.gro.gov.uk

Adoption Contact Register
Created in 1991, the Adoption Contact Register is a database, which allows adopted adults and their birth relatives to register if they would welcome contact. To be eligible for registration applicants need to be 18 years or over.

The Register cannot help an adopted person to learn the whereabouts of a birth relative unless the relative has chosen to be entered on the Register.
The Contact Register is in two parts and there is a registration fee of £15 for Part 1 and £30 for Part 2.

Once the fee has been paid the details remain on the Register. However, if you change your mind about the registration of your name, a written request is required to have your name and address removed from the Register, and 28 days notice is required.

Part 1 of the Register is for any adopted adult to apply if they are hoping for contact to be made with a birth relative.

Part 2 of the Register is for any birth relative who can satisfy GRO of their relationship to the adopted person. When a Registration is entered on the database from either party, a search is made for matching details. If a link is made both parties will be notified, but only the adoptee will be provided with the current name and address. This is because the onus is on the adopted person to make initial contact. Some registrations remain on the database for many years and a link may not happen at all.

Overseas Adoption
Convention or overseas adoption may be registered by the Registrar General when the adoptive parents were habitually resident in England or Wales at the time the adoption was granted.

A convention adoption is one made under the Convention on the Protection of Children and the Co-operation in respect of Intercountry Adoption concluded at The Hague on 29 May 1993.

An overseas adoption is one made under the law of any of the countries on the designated list.

An application to register a foreign adoption may be made by:
- The adoptive parent (or in the case of an adoption by a married couple, one of the adoptive parents)

• Any other person who has parental responsibility for the adopted child within the meaning of Section 3 of the Children Act 1989
• The adopted person when aged 18 or over.

Future Changes
The Adoption and Children Act 2002, which the Government intends to implement in September 2005, will bring about many exciting changes in the world of adoption. Specifically with regard to the Registrar General's duties, the index to the Adopted Children Register will be available on computer, and will contain safeguards to protect illicit searching for the adoption of minors. The Contact Register will contain new features, such as specifying with whom contact

is wanted, and a desire for no contact. The biggest changes are in the field of Access to Birth Records. For new adoptions, access provisions will require adopted persons to approach agencies, rather than go direct to the Registrar General, who is not always best placed to assist them. For the first time, birth families will be legally entitled to seek details of their child given up for adoption by approaching new adoption support agencies, who will provide a tracing and intermediary service.

More information about these changes, and the consultation process prior to the new laws coming into effect are available on the DfES website at www.dfes.gov.uk

Overseas Records

The Overseas Section of the General Register Office holds records of births, marriages and deaths of British nationals and members of the British Armed Forces, where the event has taken place abroad and is registered with the British authorities concerned e.g. British Consuls, High Commissions, HM Forces, the Civil Aviation Authority and the Register of Shipping and Seamen. However, it should be noted that the majority of the registrations held are non-compulsory therefore it is possible that the record you are looking for may not be held at the General Register Office.

Furthermore you should be aware that there are certain countries where there is no provision for any form of British Consul or High Commission registration to be made, for example

Australia	Falkland Islands
Zimbabwe	New Zealand
Canada	South Africa

In which case you may have to apply to the relevant authority in the country concerned to try to obtain a locally issued certificate.

Although the records held at the General Register Office (GRO) do not cover every event which takes place involving a British national, we do hold the oldest records held by the GRO as we have the British Army 'Regimental Records' which date back to 1761. We also hold the death records of the men who fell during both World Wars as well as the Boer War.

The types of registrations held and relevant dates are as follows:
Regimental births/baptisms 1761-1924
Regimental marriages 1786-1924 (the regiment is needed for any search to be undertaken).
Ionian Islands births/baptisms, marriages and some burial records relating to the British civil and military population on the Islands of Corfu 1818-1864.
Marine births and deaths since 1837.
Consul births, marriages and deaths since 1849.
War Deaths:
• Boer War 1899-1902
• First World War 1914-1921
• Second World War 1939-1948
Entries held at GRO do not show place of burial or next of kin. Certificates only record Unit/Regiment, service number, name, age at death, country of birth, place

(normally theatre of war) and cause of death (normally 'killed in action' or 'died of wounds'.
Army births, marriages and deaths from 1880-1956.
High Commission births, marriages and deaths from date of Independence (e.g. India 1949).
Air births and deaths (events on British aircraft) since 1947.
Deposited Foreign marriage certificates since 1947.
Armed Forces births, marriages and deaths since 1957.
Hovercraft births and deaths (on British hovercraft) since 1972.
Offshore Installation deaths (on British gas and oilrigs) since 1972.

Although the indexes to overseas events are on view to the public at the Family Records Centre and are also available on microfiche the actual volumes holding the entries are housed at the General Register Office in Southport and any search made at the GRO carries a fee.

Certificates of Overseas events can be applied for in person at the Family Records Centre, or by post, fax or telephone to the General Register Office. Certificates can also be applied for online at www.gro.gov.uk Certificates are usually produced within 5 working days.
For further information visit us at www.gro.gov.uk .

KINSHIP

Family History Research
in
East and West Sussex
For details contact
Email: kinship2@hotmail.com
Sheila Haines & Leigh Lawson
23 Friar Road, Brighton
East Sussex BN1 6NG
 England

Your Ancestors' Family Planning
Colin R Chapman PhD FSG

When you search through censuses or civil registration records of the nineteenth century looking for your ancestors, or even work your way through parish registers of earlier centuries, you may find that families comprising father, mother and children were, potentially, considerably larger than those of today. I say "potentially" because in many cases, although copious children were born to a couple, and most of these were baptised or had their births registered, infant mortality in the past was very high - not insignificant numbers of the children died before reaching adolescence, some when only a few days old.

Looking more closely at baptism registers it will be noticed that the frequency with which some couples bring another child to the parish church for Holy Baptism is remarkably high, in some cases it seems to be almost an annual event. The mother is apparently spending all of her child-bearing years doing just that, and is rarely experiencing anything other than pregnancy or labour. But then, on careful scrutiny of the registers, you may find a break in the pattern of baptismal frequency, and no child of the couple you are studying appears in the records for two or three years. A common explanation is that the mother had suffered an accidental miscarriage, maybe more than one, or perhaps a still-birth with no subsequent baptism and possibly no recorded burial.

But have you considered that the parents were practising family planning or using some form of birth control or contraception? Such notions are not modern, indeed there is evidence of contraceptive techniques being used in Egypt in 1850 BC, and contraceptive advice was also offered by the Ancient Greeks, Romans and by Christian Fathers from the seventh century AD. Some of the techniques, such as women using vaginal pessaries of crocodile dung or acacia leaves and honey, or men smearing their penises with vinegar, appear strange today, but all of these have sound scientific explanations for their successes. Many of the spermicides and contraceptive creams used nowadays contain the same basic chemicals as did the ancient potions. There is also ample evidence that condoms, either of linen or sheep caeca (blind intestines), were in use from the sixteenth century or even earlier, but were employed to minimise the spread of venereal infections, rather than prevent conception. Even the female condom, often considered a twentieth century invention, is mentioned in Roman legends as a means of collecting the ejaculate of King Minos of Crete. His semen was thought to have contained serpents and scorpions and so deemed rather a nuisance for his partners.

Other suggestions to prevent conception, such as the woman spitting into the mouth of a frog or wearing a weasel's dried testicles as an amulet, were based on witchcraft or folklore and would have been effective only by coincidence or luck. Even sneezing immediately after coitus, advocated by Soranus in around AD 130, to dislodge the deposited semen, was seriously proscribed by the American, Dr Trall, in 1866. But, of course, the only guaranteed method of contraception, is sexual abstinence, promoted by some authorities, but deemed unrealistic by others. Attempts to enforce this included the fitting of chastity belts or performing male and female infibulation, the latter still practised today by some religious groups.

It is certain that some mothers passed on contraceptive advice, sound or otherwise, to their daughters, and sons may have picked up ideas from their peers, rather than from their fathers, but formal instruction from the medical profession emerged only slowly as understanding of human physiology, including reproduction, improved. Indeed, towards the end of the nineteenth century, as the knowledge of obstetrics and gynaecology developed, many doctors refused to offer any advice on contraception, particularly to the humbler members of society.

However, it was during eighteenth century Britain that interest in population numbers and family size was voiced in earnest [see *Pre-1841 Censuses and Population Listings in the British Isles* - Lochin Publishing]. Local censuses were conducted, population numbers were calculated from parish register entries and a whole range of surveys undertaken by the clergy and "philosophers", as many

Robert Dale Owen

mathematicians and scientists were termed at that time. Books and pamphlets were written on the topic, and politicians even introduced Bills into Parliament, advocating national censuses be held. Mary Woolstonecraft referred to breast feeding in 1792 as a means (lactation) of minimising pregnancy, but even if understood, the connection was not formally publicised until 1866. Nevertheless, you may notice from your family history research that "upper class" ladies, who put out their babies to wet nurses, produced children at a greater frequency than "working class" mothers who, not being able to afford this expedient, breast-fed their own children.

A major input to the debate came in 1798 when Rev Thomas Malthus claimed that the country's population was increasing far faster than its ability to feed the greater numbers of people. As a method of family size limitation, Malthus recommended couples postponed marriage until attaining their mid to late twenties. He pointed out that this measure would also reduce the burden on the Poor Rate, at that time a pressing economic problem for the whole country. Malthus was opposed to other methods of limiting family size, but his obsessive persistence on population numbers did, at least, result in regular national censuses being held from 1801.

Francis Place, a London tailor and advocate of "workers' rights", published some handbills in 1823 for the *Married of Both Sexes*. He suggested either the wife insert a vaginal sponge on a thread before coitus, or the husband employ a withdrawal technique (*coitus interruptus*, although he did not use this term). In 1825 the freethinker Richard Carlile, building on Place's suggestion, highly recommended a sponge moistened with water in his *Every Woman's Book*. But early nineteenth century Britain was not ready for such publications and Carlile's recommendations caused his opponents to describe him as "brutally bent on the destruction of all loyal, religious and moral feelings, in the lower and middle classes of this our great and happy land". Robert Dale Owen, another advocate of reform, who went to America to promote his ideas there, published a *Moral Physiology* in 1831 suggesting using a sponge, withdrawal or a condom. This work, which was reprinted in Britain, appears to have offered the first published account of condoms for only contraceptive purposes.

In 1832, also in America, Dr Charles Knowlton published *Fruits of Philosophy* in which he advocated using a syringe to douche the vagina after the male emission to dislodge the semen and destroy any that remained. He named a choice of chemicals but claimed that alum was the most convenient. Knowlton was not keen on the condom, believing it would not "come into general use", and he was totally opposed to abortion as among his patients he had seen too many cases of disastrous attempts at this by amateurs. Initially Knowlton's suggestions were passively accepted but then American medics accused him of "unnatural measures" and he suffered prosecutions, fines and a sentence of three months hard labour. He was the first birth control proponent in the world to be gaoled. Several others in England (and America) followed towards the end of the century as Victorian society decided that open discussion on such matters was unseemly, even obscene.

Abortion had been used quite commonly from ancient times to limit family size. Plato had recommended it for pregnant women over 40 or for younger women whose husbands were over 50. Aristotle had also advocated abortion as a method of family size limitation. Abortion was legal in England from 1307 until 1803 for a woman, up to her time of quickening. However, Ellenborough's Parliamentary Act made abortion at any time after conception illegal and punishable by being fined, imprisoned, whipped or transported for up to 14 years. After quickening the punishment was death as the crime, at that time, was regarded as murder. Nevertheless, abortifacients, such as Penny Royal, were openly sold in Britain well into the twentieth century, but disguised as pills to "keep ladies regular".

Whilst in Greek and Roman times, infanticide had been the main method used to limit family and community size, the practice never really went away. Responding to Malthus in 1801, William Godwin expressed the view that he would prefer "a child should perish in the first hour of its existence than that a man should spend 70 years of life in a state of misery and vice". Formalised infanticide, by gassing children of poor families during their first sleep was seriously proposed in England in 1838, though access to elaborate mausolea for the infant bodies was included in the proposals. It is well known that foundling hospitals passed on many of the babies in their care to old women known to be

Charles Bradlaugh

addicted to cheap gin who frequently added opium to this and gave to the infants to keep them occupied – but many children did not survive such cordials. Disraeli referred to this horror in his novel *Sybil*.

Knowlton's book was republished in England from 1833 but attracted little interest from the authorities. In 1854 Charles Drysdale, a British medical student and also a secularist, described four contraceptive methods: the "safe period" (though he gave incorrect data on when this occurred!), later termed the rhythm method, and the sponge, both meeting with his approval, and using withdrawal and condoms, both of which he thought inappropriate. The promotion of contraception was taken up by the Secularist Movement under the leadership of Charles Bradlaugh (later Member of Parliament for Northampton) who founded the Malthusian League in 1861. Malthus himself would have been horrified at this title as he disapproved of "unnatural" contraception. Fortunately some commentators called the members of this group Neo-Malthusians but the confusion remained in many people's minds and many authors today claim, incorrectly, that Malthus advocated contraceptive devices. Bradlaugh, however, became so busy attacking the Government and Churches on other fronts that his birth control interests took second place. Nevertheless, by 1876 Knowlton's book had sold over 40,000 copies and was republished by a Bristol bookseller who incorporated some illustrations. The result was regarded as obscene. As a test case, Bradlaugh with a fellow Secularist, Annie Besant, decided to raise the profile of birth control and republished Knowlton's book themselves in 1877. Amidst enormous publicity, which they encouraged, Bradlaugh and Besant were taken to court for a trial that lasted three months and initially found guilty, with the outcome that the publication sold another 120,000 copies, even though the Solicitor-General deemed it "a filthy, dirty, book".

A vaginal rubber diaphragm or synthetic rubber cap, designed as a physical barrier against sperm to cover the neck of the uterus, was invented in 1882 by Dr

Mensinga in Germany. This proved particularly popular in America where, before the discovery of vulcanisation, rubber condoms had suffered from the extreme temperature fluctuations of the North American climate. It was recommended that a doctor or trained person should make the correct "fitting" (take appropriate internal measurements) to be able to determine the correct size of diaphragm. A variation on this was the cervical cap, made of plastics or metal. These were designed to fit snugly over the neck of the womb but these too, had to be "fitted" by a physician. Although tricky to insert by the woman herself, it proved popular in Britain and Germany as it was often left in place from the end of one menstrual period to just before the start of the next.

Vaginal pessaries had been advocated in ancient times, as described above; but at the end of the nineteenth century another freethinker and secularist, W J Rendell in London, by trade a Chemist, designed a pessary of quinine and cacao-nut butter. His pessary proved popular long into the twentieth century. In 1887, Dr H A Allbutt of Leeds published a *Wife's Handbook* with a chapter on contraception. He described withdrawal, the safe period, douching, and using the sponge, condom, Mesinga's diaphragm or cap (and his own version of it) and Rendell's quinine pessaries. He included illustrated advertisements of "Malthusian Equipment". However, he caused enormous consternation within the medical profession, not for the illustrations, nor for the detail of the methods included, but for selling the booklet for 6d, and so placing it within the reach of the lower classes. For this Allbutt was struck off the Medical Register, although he was never prosecuted by the civil authorities.

The earliest birth control clinic in the world was opened in Amsterdam in 1882, soon headed by Dr Aletta Jacobs (the first woman to be qualified medically in The Netherlands), under the auspices of the Dutch Malthusian League founded in 1881. Dr Jacobs promoted the use of the recently developed Mensinga Diaphragm. Marie Stopes, with her second husband Henry Roe, opened the first clinic in England in March 1921 in Holloway and became the main champion of birth control in Britain. Stopes wrote many books and delivered lectures on the topic in the face of severe opposition from Church and State, until the Second World War. The first Family Planning Association on the American continent was established in 1917, resulting from the efforts of Margaret Sanger (who had first coined the term "birth control" in 1915), that in Australia in 1926, while the English Family Planning Association was set up in 1930.

It is not relevant here to describe other methods of family size limitation such as sterilisation, Intrauterine Devices (IUDs), Contraceptive or Morning-After Pills, or Hormonal techniques, for these were not generally available to our forebears. But the use of some form of contraception or birth control, as a means of family planning, could explain that "gap" in our ancestors' otherwise regular frequency of having children.

Obtainable from all Chemists Everywhere

2/6 PER BOX

7. J. Rendell, Ltd., will pay £1,000 to Charity if any person or persons an prove that each box of Pessaries contains one which is ineffective. There a false report spread by certain persons who endeavour to mislead the public to believing that every box contains a useless pessary, in some cases even pporting their statements by declaring it is made compulsory by law.

Our Solicitors are instructed to take proceedings against any person und to be circulating this false report.

VERY RENDELL PESSARY IS, AND ALWAYS HAS BEEN, ABSOLUTELY EFFICACIOUS.

Death and the Victorians
Doreen Hopwood

During the reign of Queen Victoria a whole industry evolved around death and its traditions. These included the building of cemeteries on a grand scale, elaborate funerals, large tombstones and a strict etiquette surrounding mourning.

At the beginning of the 19th century the established church was responsible for the baptism, marriage and burial of the population, but radical changes in legislation, which transferred the responsibility of recording births, marriages and death to the state, reflect the movement towards the secularisation and commercialisation of the rituals associated with death, burial and mourning.

When Queen Victorian came to the throne life expectancy varied greatly depending on where you lived and your place in society. Whilst the gentry could expect to reach the age of 45, an artisan or a tradesman might live to be 30, but for a labourer the average age at death was just 25. The high rates of infant mortality continued through Victoria's reign, and burial registers of churches and cemeteries bear witness to this. Between 1850 and 1901, the burial registers of Kingston upon Thames show that a fifth of all burials were for infants aged under one year.

However, by the 1830s, many of the church burial grounds, especially in the growing towns, were becoming full, thus robbing the dead of their dignity and endangering the health of the population who lived nearby. Cemetery companies were set up, funded by the sale of shares, and municipal cemeteries were established by the second half of the century. The overcrowded and insanitary church yards instigated Edwin Chadwick's 'Supplementary Report … into the Practice of Investment in Towns' in 1843, which included an account of funeral costs. These ranged from £100+ for the gentry to thirteen shillings for a pauper, with an average cost of £5 for an artisan. One social commentator suggested that '… the poor like funeral pomp because the rich like it – forgetting that during life, the condition of the dead was entirely different'.

The grand funerals of the aristocracy set the precedent which was initiated by the upper and middle classes. How much you spent on a funeral was an indication of your social standing, and, as early as 1843, Chadwick concluded in his report that over £4 million was '… annually thrown into the grave at the expense of the living'. Undertakers were accused of exploitation and greed at a time when people were most vulnerable. Many caricatures appeared in *Punch*, and undertakers (and their profession) were satirised by Dickens in many of his works. In 'Martin Chuzzlewit', the undertaker, Mr Mould, was described as '… a little elderly gentleman, bald and in a suit of black, with a notebook in his hand, a massive gold watch dangling from his fob, and a face in which a queer attempt at melancholy was at odds with a smirk of satisfaction'.

Chadwick's report acknowledged that whatever your place in society was '… the strongest and most widely diffused feeling among the population …' was to ensure a respectful interment for yourself and your family.

The stigma of a pauper's funeral, or being 'buried on the parish' was to be avoided at all costs, but the passing of Warburton's Anatomy Act in 1832 added a further fear for the poor. It was passed as a measure to curtail the actions of body-snatchers who stole cadavers and sold them to schools of anatomy. Under the Act, the unclaimed bodies of paupers who died in workhouses (or other institutions), could be passed to the anatomy schools for dissection. The growth of burial clubs and societies helped to lessen the fear, and Chadwick, some ten years later, suggested that between £6 million and £8 million were held in funeral or burial clubs. The average weekly

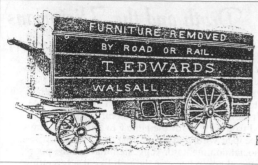

a flower bedecked bedroom or in a simple coffin in the kitchen.

Mourning Dress and Etiquette

The etiquette of mourning was governed by strict and complex rules. The restrictions imposed upon female mourners, especially widows, reinforced their inferior status in society, and the perception that a wife's whole identity (and sexuality) died along with her husband. The external signs of bereavement were evident in both the fashion and behaviour of the bereaved.

The most visible trappings of Victorian death were the wearing of mourning clothes. This served a threefold purpose; it identified the mourner, showed respect for the deceased and encouraged the sympathy of the community. It was believed that the wearing of dull black clothing made the living invisible to the dead, and is rooted in the fear of the dead returning. Mourning-departments appeared in large stores throughout the country, but the first to devote itself solely to mourning clothes was Jay's General

payment was a penny or 'tuppence' and, by the turn of the twentieth century, over four million people were members of one (or more) burial clubs.

The Funeral and the growth of commercialisation

The trend towards ostentatious funerals gathered momentum during the 1840s, and the practices copied the grand heraldic array of baronial funerals with all its attendant symbolism:

Two 'mutes' - men, dressed and paid to wear a gloomy expression, stood at each side of the door of the deceased's home, representative of the two porters at the castle. Each carried a black wand to represent their staves.

The man leading the procession wore a scarf, and represented the herald-at-arms. The esquire was symbolised by the man wearing a plume of black feathers on his head. The pall-bearers, with batons, were the companions-at-arms, and the men walking with wands represented the gentlemen ushers.

The Times, on 2 February 1875, commented 'It is within the last half century that prodigious funerals, awful hearses drawn by preternatural quadruplets, clouds of blacks plumes, solid and magnificent oak coffins … have spread downwards …'.

However, the elaborate funeral did not meet with wholehearted approval. The National Funeral and Mourning Association was formed in the 1850s to encourage simplicity and moderation. The Cremation Society of England was established in 1874, and the founder, Sir Henry Thompson, a leading surgeon, argued for cremation on sanitary and materialistic grounds, but it was dismissed as 'barbarous, heathen and unnatural' by the Bishop of Lincoln. The Cremation Act, passed in 1902, legalised the practice.

There was a strict set of regulations concerning the etiquette of the funeral, burial and mourning, and *Cassell's Household Guide* clearly set these out. The 1874 edition instructed that the blinds of the deceased's home should be drawn until the funeral had taken place, and that the door knockers should be hung with black crepe.

As most people died at home in the nineteenth century, the body would be laid out by a local woman in the working class areas, or by professionals in the homes of the upper and middle classes. The spouse of the deceased would then invite relatives and close friends to view the body, which may have been laid in

'Buying a Mourning Hat-Band',
Punch 1864

Customer. "A SLIGHT MOURNING HAT-BAND, IF YOU PLEASE."
Hatter. "WHAT RELATION, SIR?"
Customer. "WIFE'S UNCLE."
Hatter. "FAVOURITE UNCLE, SIR?"
Customer. "'UM—WELL, YES."
Hatter. "MAY I ASK, SIR, ARE YOU MENTIONED IN THE WILL?"
Customer. "NO SUCH LUCK."
Hatter (to his Assistant, briskly). "COUPLE O' INCHES, JOHN!"

Mourning Warehouse on Regent Street, London, in 1841.

A woman in deep mourning could not be mistaken for anything else, but the rules for men were more lax, as Henry Mayhew observed in 1865 '… a gentleman … attired for the gayest evening party would, apart from his jewellery, be equally presentable at the most sorrowful funeral'.

In Dickens' *Dombey and Son*, published in 1848, Mrs Pipchin's gown was of 'black bombazeen of such a lustreless deep, dead, sombre shade' that 'her presence was a quencher to any number of candles'. Crepe, a silk fabric which has a crimped appearance when heated, became synonymous with mourning clothes, and Courtaulds had a virtual monopoly on its manufacture, employing over 1,500 people by 1841.

Until a way was found for waterproofing crepe in 1897, problems arose both for the garment and its wearer. Remedies on how to remove rainwater marks on the cloth and 'black stains on the skin' appeared in journals. The antidote for the latter involved the use of a mixture of cream of tartar and oxalic acid – highly poisonous if swallowed or ingested.

Jet, a black hard coal-type material, had been popular for fashioning ornaments for sometime, and an industry grew near its main source at Whitby in Yorkshire. By 1850, several hundred workmen were fashioning jet into all forms of mourning jewellery, but 20 years later, cheaper imitations in the form of vulcanite,(an early type of plastic), were being produced on a large scale.

The period of mourning was long, and effectively cut a widow off from society, for she could not accept invitations or appear in public. For the year following the death of her husband, she had to wear full mourning dress, which could be replaced by plain black clothes twenty-one months after his death. This was followed by half-mourning for a further six months during which she could wear grey, lavender, violet or black, grey and white stripes.

A period of twelve months was required in respect of a child or parent, with a nine month period for grandparents, and six months for siblings. This was extended to include relations by marriage, and a second wife was expected to enter into 'complimentary' mourning when the parents of her husband's first wife died.

The After Life

Christian families took it for granted that they would be reunited in the next life, and this belief offered much-needed consolation for those left behind. In 1861, William Branks described heaven as '… a home with a great and happy loving family …', and tracts and pamphlets bearing titles such as 'Heaven and Home', 'Our children's rest', etc. were published in huge numbers by organizations such as The Religious Tract Society.

Most Victorian children would have witnessed the premature death of one of their siblings, and may have acted as pall bearers, dressed in white and carried the little white coffin (to denote innocence) in which their brother or sister lay. It was also common for Victorian children to be taken to view the corpse of any close family members – unless that person had died of an infectious disease. They grew up knowing that death was never far away, and much of the children's literature of the period included the death of a young child. It was agreed that raising the subject in this way taught Victorian children how to cope with the inevitable deaths among their family and friends. The deaths of children were often the subject of paintings such as Frank Holl's "Her Firstborn" and advances in print technology meant that copies could be found hanging on the walls of many working-class homes.

The concept of immortality shared not only with God, but with family members who had died before them was a source of solace. The (still legible) monument to the children of Samuel and Alice Brown in Aston Churchyard demonstrates the depth of their grief and consolation in knowing that their offspring had gone to a "better place":

Suffer little children to come unto me
In affectionate remembrance of Alice, daughter of Samuel
and Elizabeth Brown

REACTION.

Shortsighted Old Lady. "HI! OMLIBUS! HI!"

Hearse-Driver (unbending) "ALL RIGHT, MUM! MOST 'APPY, MUM! DI-RECTLY, MUM!"

She departed her life July 30th 1858 aged 6 years
The Spirit's fled life's latest sand is run
Father of mercies, let thy will be done
Not ours but thine, this fair this beauteous clay
Twas thine to give, and thine to take away
O May we meekly bow beneath the rod
And own thy chastening hand, O God
Also of Jessie Constance their daughter
who died December 29th 1864
aged 4 years
Ere sin could harm or sorrow fade
Death came with friendly care
The opening bud to Heaven convey'd
and bade it blossom there
Likewise of Arthur, their son,
who died January 1st 1865 aged 18 months

The epitaph to another young woman in the same burial ground describes her as "a tender wife, sister, friend".

The funeral and its practices had a therapeutic effect on those left behind. It gave them the opportunity to express their sorrow in a manner which made the grieving process easier to endure. The memory of deceased love ones was perpetuated through monuments, paintings, photographs, grave-visiting and mourning jewellery which often contain a lock of hair or image of the person. By the end of Victoria's reign, it was not unusual to have a photograph taken of the body, especially when an infant died. Their likenesses were posed so that the body looked as if he/she was simply asleep. The sending of mourning cards, printed on specially designed cards edged with black was another visible act of remembrance. These were often decorated with funerary symbols such as weeping willows and urns.

When Queen Victoria died, this was the last universal demonstration of mourning, and the ladies of the court, who had been forced to wear mourning dress since Prince Albert's death in 1861, had to endure it for yet another year.

CLEVELAND, NORTH YORKSHIRE and SOUTH DURHAM FAMILY HISTORY SOCIETY

Many indices and publications available by post for your research including 135 booklets on 1851 Census and over 270 lists of Monumental Inscriptions

1891 Census Microfiche nearing completion.

Send A5 SAE to the Secretary for full lists of publications and microfiche, or for details of membership.

Secretary:

Mr A Sampson
1 Oxgang Close
REDCAR
TS10 4ND

Tel/Fax: 01642 486615
Email: pjoiner@lineone.net

Web site: www.clevelandfhs.org.uk

Huddersfield & District Family History Society

Registered Charity No. 702199

The Huddersfield & District Family History Society caters for those researching and with interests in the Kirklees Metropolitan area which covers about 160 square miles. Within our boundaries lie the ancient parishes of Almondbury, Batley, Birstall, Dewsbury, Emley, Hartshead, Huddersfield, Kirkburton, Kirkheaton, Mirfield and Thornhill.

We have a research room and library at Meltham, which houses our transcriptions of the 1841 & 1851 census for our area, the 1881 census for England & Wales plus the 1992 edition of the IGI for the whole of Britain and the National Probate Calenders 1858 - 1943.

The Society has about 300 publications for sale of Parish Registers and the 1841 and 1851 censuses. We are also participating in the National Burial Index. Search Services on these and other databases are also available.

For further details please contact our
The Secretary - at
15 Market Place, Meltham, Huddersfield, West Yorkshire HD9 4NJ
or visit
our website at www.hdfhs.org.uk

A Wedding has been arranged
Doreen Berger

Family weddings should be occasions of joy and happiness, but when the families come from a totally different background, they may be looked upon with apprehension, with distaste or even with resignation. These were possibly some of the feelings felt by wedding guests on the dynastic marriages of the past.

Perhaps the most famous dynastic marriage in Jewish circles took place on Wednesday, March 20th, 1878, when a scion of the English nobility married a name well known in Anglo-Jewish dynastic circles. This wedding was of Miss Hannah de Rothschild, heiress to the magnificent estate at Mentmore, and granddaughter of Nathan Meyer Rothschild, founder of the English House of Rothschild. Her bridegroom was the Right Honourable Sir Archibald Philip Primrose, Bart., fifth Earl and Viscount of Rosebery, Viscount Invekeithing, Baron Rosebery of Rosebery, Baron Dalmeny and Primrose, owner of the beautiful house called Dalmeny.
Educated at Eton and Christ Church, Oxford, he was a supporter of the Liberal Party in the House of Lords.

Hannah was the only child of Mayer de Rothschild, fourth and youngest son of the originator of the English branch of the family, and his wife Juliana. He was amongst the principal landowners in Buckinghamshire and subscribed with great generosity to nearly every institution in the country. Known as a great country gentleman, he had horses that had won the Derby, Oakes Leger and the One Thousand Guineas, owned a valuable racing stud and was master of his own hounds. When he died in 1874, the funeral cortege included the private carriages of the Prince of Wales, his brother the Duke of Cambridge, the Russian Ambassador, Bavarian Minister and the Duke of Wellington. The funeral procession, extending a distance of about a quarter of a mile, caused great excitement along the route through which it passed. Along Piccadilly, where he had his town house, and Park Lane, the blinds of nearly all the residences were drawn. Special arrangements were made by the police authorities for facilitating the progress of the procession. It was rumoured that the fortune he had left would exceed three million pounds.

Juliana died at Nice, two years after the death of her husband, while on her yacht, the "Czarina". She was the eldest daughter of a well known philanthropic family, whose daughters married into the leading Anglo-Jewish families of the time. Mayer and Juliana were first cousins, Juliana's father, Isaac Cohen, being the brother of Mayer's mother, Hannah. Juliana is credited with the introduction of lip-reading among deaf-mutes. The Prince of Wales commented, soon after her death, at a festival in aid of the Association for the Oral instruction for the Deaf and Dumb, "I cannot forget one whom I know all interested in this institution will mourn deeply has been taken from us."

Hannah's birthday was always celebrated at Mentmore with entertainments for tenants and servants. We have descriptions in the Jewish newspapers of Hannah being presented at court, of meeting the Prince and Princess of Wales, together with the Czarewitch and Csarevana of Russia, at an evening party given by the Duke of Edinburgh, of endowing a Life Boat Station, of giving generously to charity.

Lord Rosebery had been introduced to the seventeen year old Miss Rothschild at Newmarket by Lady Disraeli. Rosebery was a great friend of the family and Hannah fell in love with him. Her mother was in favour of the match, but the family were nervous of public opinion. After her parents' death, Hannah found herself in possession of a considerable fortune, owner of the magnificent Mentmore, with its collection of art treasures, and alone.

After he was accepted by Hannah, Rosebery wrote to his sister: "I was engaged to Hannah yesterday. I love her so much that I can never be happy if you do not love her too."

The bridegroom's mother was not at all happy. Her house had stood alone against the inclusion of Jewish society among the aristocracy. "I myself do honestly, and from the bottom of my heart, disapprove of such marriages, and I could not say otherwise without acting against my conscientious convictions. For the present I would plead to be spared any agitating interviews on the score of my own health.", she wrote to her son.

Before ten o'clock in the morning of March 20, 1878, the civil ceremony was performed at the District Registrar's Office, Mount Street, Berkeley square. The bride wore a plain morning dress of cream silk brocade and a cream fur-lined cloak; her bonnet was trimmed with pearls, with a jewelled rose in the front. For ornament she wore a pearl necklace and diamond and ruby rings presented by Lord Rosebery. Hannah was accompanied by her uncle, John Samuel, who

63

was her legal guardian, and her grandmother, Mrs. Isaac Cohen. Lord Rosebery, who wore the blue dress-coat and light waistcoat of a bridegroom's attire, was accompanied by his friends, Lord Carrington, Lord Lascelles, and his brother, the Honourable Everard Primrose.

The second marriage ceremony was performed according to the ritual of the Church of England at half-past eleven at Christ Church, Down Street. Hannah was accompanied by her grandmother and her cousin, Baron Ferdinand de Rothschild. Wearing a princesse dress of pearl white satin, with trimmings and deep flounces of point d'Alencon, divided by orange-blossom fringes and a large veil, she was given away by a family friend, Benjamin Disraeli, the Earl of Beaconsfield. She wore no jewels except diamond and pearl earrings. Her bridesmaids were her cousins, the Misses Euphemia and Helen Lindsay, descendants of a previous Rothschild and English aristocratic alliance, the Honourable Mary Caroline Wyndham, niece of Lord Rosebery, and Emily Margaret Stanhope. The bridesmaids were attired in dresses in the style of the Louis XVI period, with long waistcoats richly embroidered in white silk and ruffles of white lace; white silk hats of the same period, trimmed with marabout feathers and embroidery, completed the ensemble. Each of the bridesmaids wore a gold pendant, with a monogram in rubies and diamonds, the gift of the bridegroom.

The ceremony was conducted by the Prebendary of St. Paul's and Rector of St. Botolph's, Bishopsgate. The Prince of Wales and the Duke of Cambridge signed the register.

After breakfast in Piccadilly, where the Prince of Wales proposed the health of the bride and bridegroom, they left for Petworth House, in Sussex, the seat of Lord Rosebery's brother-in-law, Lord Leconfield. Hannah's travelling dress was of sapphire blue velvet, with blue fox fur, with matching bonnets and muffs. Bridal gifts were of enormous value, conspicuous among them being the Rosebery family jewels.
A full description of the wedding and of Hannah's wardrobe can be read in The Illustrated London News.

The marriage was the subject of a dramatic editorial in the Jewish Chronicle. "A sad example has been set which, we pray God, may not be productive of dreadful consequences", the Jewish Chronicle, Anglo-Jewry's principal newspaper, wailed.

In the House of Convocation, the Rev. Prebendary Ainslie Henstridge obtained permission to read a petition, which included the following protest:

That two persons, one of them a Jewess, were married by civil contract before the Superintendent-Registrar of St. George's, Hanover Square. That on the same day these two persons, being married, presented themselves at Christ Church, Mayfair, for solemnising of their union with the marriage service of the Church of England. That a priest of this diocese did read the Church's service with them and according to that service, bless them. That this use of the service for

one who is an unbeliever in the Christian religion is a plain profanation of holiness, and a great scandal in the eyes of your petitioner and other Christians. That this ceremony was styled by the two persons "our well-beloved in Christ." That such licence might have been withheld at the discretion of the Bishop or his registrar.

Although Rosebery's famous remark is often quoted that "I am leaving tonight; Hannah and the rest of the heavy baggage will follow", it was well known that the marriage was a very successful one. From being a sheltered girl, spoiled by doting parents, Hannah became one of the most devoted and unselfish of wives. The Jewish public always held Hannah in great love and affection. Hannah, who was known to be devout, continued to practise her own religion.

Lord Rosebery's career, with Hannah's ardent support, went from strength to strength. He was appointed Under-Secretary for the Home Department after the 1880 General Election and became first commissioner of works and then Foreign Secretary. Mentmore became the centre of an influential social life.

When Hannah died unexpectedly in November, 1890, after contracting typhoid fever, Lord Rosebery was overcome with grief. She seemed to make a recovery, but had finally succumbed. He sank into a deep depression. Four years later he became the Premier of a Liberal Government until their defeat in the 1895 General Election, but resigned his leadership a year after that. Without Hannah, he had not the heart to continue.

So ended this remarkable love story.

The Roseberys had a family of two sons and two daughters. The eldest daughter, Sybil, married Sir Charles Grant, who served with distinction in the First World War. Peggy, the second daughter, married the Marquis of Crewe, who became Leader of the House of Lords. The eldest son, Harry Meyer (Dalmeny), the sixth Earl of Rosebery, served on General Allenby's staff in Palestine. Neil, the youngest, fell in 1917 in Palestine.

The contents of the magnificent Mentmore were sold in the nineteen seventies and raised over six million pounds. The house was then sold to the Maharishi Mahesh Yogi and for a while became the headquarters

Castle Howard
North Yorkshire

so, in 1884, this marriage took place.

And so we come to the present day.

The wedding of Simon Sebag-Montefiore, journalist and novelist, with Santa Palmer-Tompkinson, at the Liberal Synagogue, St. John's Wood, was the cause of much excitement and interest not only in the Jewish community, especially as Santa had undergone a religious conversion before the marriage. Simon is a descendant of a well known Anglo-Jewish family, who settled in this country at the end of the eighteenth century, and Santa Palmer-Tompkinson is a member of a family who have had a long friendship with the Prince of Wales. The presence of His Highness the Prince of Wales and Camilla Parker-Bowles at the ceremony added interest to the proceedings, especially as this was their first publicised appearance together.

Another young lady from a famous Jewish business dynasty has recently married into the ranks of the English aristocracy. Rebecca , the daughter of Jonathan Sieff and great- great- granddaughter of Michael Marks, founder of one of our most famous store groups, popularly known as "M. & S.", married Simon Howard, third son of the late Lord Howard of Henderskelle. This wedding took place at Castle Howard, the beautiful North Yorkshire country house. The Archbishop of York performed the blessing at the civil ceremony and the bride was given a diamond engagement ring once belonging to the bridegroom's grandmother.

Times change, and the marriages of people from very different backgrounds often take place with the blessing of their families and the acceptance of the social world from which they come.

Genealogical Reference Books by Doreen Berger
The Jewish Victorian: Genealogical Information from the Jewish Newspapers 1871-80 (600 pages)
The Jewish Victorian: Genealogical Information from the Jewish Newspapers 1861-70 (400 pages)
Containing all the births, marriages and deaths from the Jewish newspapers of the periods, with genealogies cross referenced, and so much more. Robert Boyd Publications, 260 Colwell drive, Witney, Oxfordshire OX8 7LW. Email: BOYDPUBS@aol.com

of the University of Natural Law. Nothing remains now in the mansion of the story of this unusual match.

Hannah was, in fact, following the example of her aunt, also called Hannah, who fell in love with Henry Fitzroy, a brother of Lord Southampton. After the death of her father, she, too, had married in a church. Four years earlier she had been sent hastily home from a stay with her uncle in Paris because a young Austrian aristocrat she met at a ball had wanted to marry her. The family were not ready for that. Her father had immediately ordered her home and added a clause to his will that his daughters would be disinherited if they married without the consent of the family. Now this Hannah again had made an unsuitable choice and there were terrible scenes. Fitzroy was told to go abroad for six months, but the two young people were determined. The marriage took place at St. George's, Hanover Square in 1839, with just her brother Nathaniel present and the bride wearing a simple morning dress. Her mother accompanied her only as far as the church in a simple coach. She received no wedding gifts, but only disapproving letters from the family. The young couple were happy, but the family considered any problems she later encountered as "divine retribution".

Another marriage which caused a sensation at the time was that of one of Hannah's many cousins. Charlotte Montefiore was the granddaughter of Henrietta Rothschild, Hannah's aunt. To the family's consternation, Charlotte became engaged to Lewis McIver, of the Indian Civil Service, who was not Jewish. Charlotte did not wish to marry in a church and Lewis did not wish to change his religion. Charlotte's brother, Claude, eventually found a Rabbi in Germany who was willing to marry a Jewish girl to a professing Christian in a religious ceremony. And

Rutland's Records - where to find them
Audrey Buxton

Rutland, squeezed between Lincolnshire, Nottinghamshire, Leicestershire and Northamptonshire, has always, it seems, been on the borders of everywhere. Not large enough - nor rich enough - to have a record office of her own, very few archives are to be found within her ancient borders. The few she had, painstakingly gathered by the late George Phillips, were pulped to help the 'War Effort' in World War II. Equally heinous, the Rutland Police records were allegedly partly burned in the yard of Melton Mowbray Police Station and the rest taken to a tip, during the mid 1980s.

Even more bewildering is the fact that having been passed around like a parcel so far as the Church of England is concerned, the parish registers have ended up in a different county from any of the dioceses who have had Rutland in their care, whilst original surviving Bishops Transcripts are in two other county record offices!

It is always difficult to write a definitive article about archives, and I have no doubt that when this one appears there will be a flurry of letters from readers who will be critical about some source I have not mentioned. However, this perforce is a brief guide only in which I shall mention the main documents and where they are to be found. If anyone knows of the whereabouts of other major holdings I will be pleased to hear from them.

The Leicestershire, Leicester & Rutland County Record Office holds the original deposited parish records and copies of Bishops Transcripts, some of which have been indexed by individuals; parish maps; an index of persons; all censuses, but only 1881 and 1851 (the latter indexed by the Leicestershire & Rutland Family History Society and also with information on public houses) by surname at the time of writing. The office (at Wigston), holds too the LRFHS-indexed Rutland marriages 1754-1837 and a partial Burials Index. There is an early International Genealogical Index for the whole country - some names do not appear in later editions - and some non-conformist registers of births/baptisms and burials on film. Leicester Marriage Licences are on card index and film, and it is worth searching these and other neighbouring counties as many Rutlanders crossed county borders to marry. Estate papers held at Wigston mention 21 Rutland villages. The Poor Law Index is worth a search, as are the surviving Quarter Sessions records.

Although they do not hold Rutland wills prior to 1858 except for the Lincoln Peculiars of Caldecott, Liddington and Ketton cum Tixover (Book I only; Book II wills are indexed here, but the wills are in Lincoln Archives), it is worth checking the Leicestershire index for testators dying there; these are indexed by place name 1495-1649. Likewise, try the 1801-37 Leicestershire Marriage Index and Marriage Licences, indexed from 1570. There is a large collection of local newspapers, but the Rutland & Stamford Mercury (of which more later) is held here only patchily from 1901 onwards. Do not forget Manorial rolls, school records, electoral rolls from 1973 (see below) and earlier Poll books, trade directories and the County Histories! If you are

Butter Cross
Oakham

coming from a distance it is worth booking a reader, and you will need identification, e.g. driving licence and a utilities bill if you intend to take out original archives.

Lincoln Archives.
Rutland was part of Lincoln Diocese (itself belonging to Northampton earlier still) before being transferred to Peterborough in 1541, but a few Rutland parishes remained 'peculiar' to Lincoln - see above. Empingham's Bishops Transcripts are held in Lincoln also, but there are huge gaps for the whole of the 18th century. Likewise there are some marriage licences pertaining to Rutland couples. Lincoln holds the electoral rolls for Rutland 1919-1974. Relevant Estate papers are to be found here, for example Ancaster, which is particularly rich in Rutland material and will be catalogued on A2A by early 2005. There are many maps in Lincoln Archives, a Persons Index with references to Rutland people, and a full, countrywide GRO index of births, marriages and deaths from 1837 to 1983. There is a considerable number of Lincoln Consistory Court Rutland wills, all indexed.

The Lincolnshire Family History Society, who seem to hold the record for publishing anything and everything, has indexed marriages by Deanery among other things; worth a search for cross-border weddings, as is their Poor Law index and Quarter Sessions. Census returns could be equally helpful: 1851, 1871, 1881, 1891 and 1901 are here, again indexed by the FHS by surname; the actual returns for 1841 and 1861 are in the Library nearby. Booking is essential for this record office, and not only do they ask for proof of identity; you need two passport-sized photographs. The researcher can also pre-book the photography studio. It is wise to pre-book for the Central Library; ask for the Local Studies section.

Northampton County Record Office
Northampton County Record Office holds all the remaining original Bishops Transcripts for Rutland after 1701, albeit with some missing. All years prior to 1701 were destroyed in a fire. It is interesting to compare these with Parish Register entries; sometimes they differ greatly. This record office holds all surviving Rutland Wills/Inventories and Marriage Bonds/Licences, all of which are indexed. The wills are available by surname and year, and are available either on film, or in books or the original where particular years have not been filmed.

The licences are on two separate card indexes, 1598-1684 and 1685-1771+. The former, in 12 boxes, includes many other snippets of information - e.g. marriages, burials, licences to teach, issue of tokens, descents and more. The later one, currently being added to by the Northamptonshire Family History Society, deals solely with the licences and bonds/bondholders. Information on both counties is intermingled, and one must take care, as villages with the same names occur in both and nearby counties, e.g. Pilton, Preston, Braunston. Spelling was at the mercy of the deanery scribe so 'Aston' - or even 'Ason' - may mean Ayston in Rutland, Easton-by-Stamford in Northamptonshire or Great Easton in Leicestershire. Usually 'Rut.' by the parish name provides solid identification, but not always. The original documents can be seen, and photographed by the researcher if a photocopy is not possible. Remember to look in the parish registers for villages close to Rutland's borders; and those of St. Martin's, Stamford Baron, is particularly important.

There are no Rutland non-conformist registers held here, but again, Estate papers for the Monckton, O'Brien and particularly Wingfield families hold a great deal of Rutland information. Poor Law documents are indexed by surname and a few are for Rutland families. Northampton CRO holds some Rutland Tithe maps and terriers, and the Boller-Blore marriage index, mostly compiled from Bishops Transcripts and somewhat fragile, which is searched on the enquirer's behalf by the Archivist on duty and may contain Rutlanders. This CRO does not take bookings but there is usually room on film and fiche readers. Following recent changes, there are Internet connections in reception and a large number of laptop stations are available. No proof of identity is required. Northampton's late night is Thursday, but no documents are produced after 4.30 pm. Do remember to bring your own food, as there is absolutely nowhere nearby to buy any.

Other records are to be found further afield. Huntingdon's record office has Estate papers which mention several Rutland villages, and some part-censuses.
Papers for the Manor of Essendine are held privately at Hatfield House, Hatfield, Hertfordshire and may be seen only by appointment.

Roman Catholicism was sparse in Rutland. Even today there is only the church in Oakham, and the private chapel at Exton Hall founded in 1868; very few events have been held here latterly, and records are not kept at the Hall. Before then worshippers had to cross borders following the closure of the only other Roman Catholic church at South Luffenham when its priest moved to Northamptonshire in 1803. Rutland lies in the Roman Catholic diocese of Nottingham. If your ancestors were Papists after 1850 try the Diocesan office, which is in Derby; if you are looking for records prior to that year, they should be in the Birmingham Diocesan Archives. In both cases you should write first and enclose an sae.

Non-conformism, in contrast, was well-represented in Rutland, although many chapels have closed and been sold off for housing, domestic garages and even a potato store. If you know which village your ancestors lived in, look for foundation stones for these; they may be named. There are no Rutland non-conformist monumental inscriptions at Wigston. (The Women's Institute did a national survey of gravestones which should be in the relevant record offices, but of course many stones were laid flat and covered over to save graveyard maintenance. The CRO at Wigston holds copies of their findings, but I believe coverage of non-conformist burials to be very poor in general, and did not form part of the W.I. survey.) Some registers are at Myddleton Place in London, and the Society of Genealogists have published a series of booklets covering the different denominations. Otherwise it is worth contacting the local chapel or meeting-house.

The Church of Jesus Christ of Latter-Day Saints, more familiarly known as the Mormons, had a branch in Empingham 1852-58 with 45 members on Roll. Six of them emigrated to Utah. Your local LDS Family History Centre will order films for you if you live a long way from the record offices holding Rutland material. If you are very lucky, they may have some Rutland film already in their collection. At the time of writing £2.70 covers short-term use, the film to be searched on their premises. All the libraries I have visited have been very friendly and the staff, all volunteers, more than helpful. No charge is made for using their history centres, but a donation towards more filming is gratefully received.

The library in Oakham and Oakham Museum both hold a surprising amount of local history and genealogy. The Rutland Record & Local History Society has published many articles and books including 'Tudor Rutland' and 'Rutland Hearth Tax 1665', plus 22 journals to date, some of which are still available for purchase in the Museum. The Society holds a large collection of books and is steadily adding to its library. Lottery money has meant the upgrading of facilities here for local history studies in a new purpose-built room. There are trades directories, and some material is available on film (all censuses), fiche (parish registers) and CD-Rom, including Rutland Tithe maps and an extensive collection of local photographs. Oakham Library also has a good Local History section with many books about Rutland and Rutlanders, and some material on film including censuses. Both venues hold a copy of the County History.

The library in Stamford holds on film the entire surviving run of the oldest British newspaper still in existence. The 'Stamford Mercury' (which has changed its name slightly several times over the years) is a goldmine, containing many local births, marriages and deaths; accounts of court cases, runaway servants, sales at auction, advertisements and scandals, as well as national and international news which sometimes provides quite an eye-opening opportunity to link family events to what was happening in the world. This library holds films of other local papers also, some long gone, some having been merged with others. Again, booking here is essential, as there is only one reader/printer. Make sure it is working before you set off! Census material for the eastern part of Rutland is held for 1851, 1861, 1871, 1881 and 1891 with the Lincolnshire Family History Society indexes and local parish records. Sadly, Stamford St. Martin's is not here as it is over the river in Northamptonshire; a great pity, as a surprising number of Rutlanders married there by Licence.

Leicester University has material, including the 1851 Religious Census. The first visit to their Library is free, and you will need identification. The Public Record Office at Kew has much more, including some early ale-house licences and pre-15th century coroners records, and many military and railway records.

For myself, I am working hard to complete a Rutland Marriage Index from all surviving parish records, of which 1650-1754 is now ready. In addition, I am indexing the Rutland marriage licences held in Northampton CRO mentioned above, of which there are many, and I may not live to finish since I am still working on letter 'C'!

To move to more modern times, the Roman Catholic records of St. Hugh, RAF Cottesmore are held at Aldershot; other denominations, and those of what was RAF North Luffenham are at RAF Andover. North Luffenham is now the home of the Royal Anglian Regiment.

Colin R. Chapman's 'Tracing Ancestors in Rutland' is a useful tool as are the detailed handbooks to be found in the various county record offices. I recommend the relevant CRO and Society web sites. All addresses are to be found in the relevant sections in the Handbook; Rutland Local History & Record Society can be accessed either through the County Museum in Oakham, or

I would like to acknowledge the help given me by archivists at the three main county record offices, chiefly Margaret Bonney and Sherry Nesbitt at Wigston (both of whom deserve gold medals), Crispin Powell at Northampton and Adrian Wilkinson at Lincoln Archives; and Robert Ovens, Chairman of the Rutland Local History Society, to give it its more manageable name.

Audrey Buxton is a member of theSociety of Genealogists and committee member of RLHS.

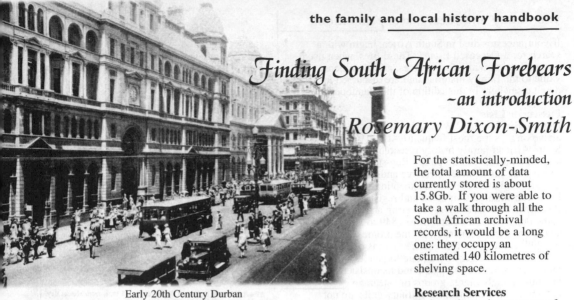

Finding South African Forebears
~an introduction
Rosemary Dixon-Smith

Early 20th Century Durban

For the statistically-minded, the total amount of data currently stored is about 15.8Gb. If you were able to take a walk through all the South African archival records, it would be a long one: they occupy an estimated 140 kilometres of shelving space.

The good news is that there has never been a more promising time than now to start researching your South African ancestry. Better still, much of your quest can be conducted from a distance. There are many opportunities open to the armchair family historian, particularly with the advantages of a computer and access to internet.

National Archives Index
Once as much information as possible has been obtained from sources within the family, first stop for anyone tracing South African connections is the NASA (National Archives of South Africa) web site **www.national.archives.gov.za/** Made available in 2001, with upwards of seven million records and additions at a rate of 250 000 a year, the resource is a mine of information and may well contain the precious nugget you require. User-friendly, the site offers comprehensive introductory pages which it is advisable to read carefully before taking the plunge, especially important being the explanation of information categories, acronyms used to identify the various archival repositories, source codes and tips for structuring search queries. Once you've mastered the simple navigation techniques, you'll return again and again. The online index, NAAIRS (National Automated Archival Information Retrieval System), should carry a government health warning – it's addictive. Be aware that it is an index, a tool enabling the identification and location of records. The original documents are in archival custody and are not accessible on-line.

Also included are two non-archival databases: that of the Bureau of Heraldry and Gravestone inscriptions recorded by the Genealogical Society of South Africa.

Be imaginative when searching the index: spellings of surnames may vary. The ancestor might even have used an alias, as emigrating to the colonies often provided an opportunity to wipe the slate clean.

NAAIRS has been likened to "the ears of the hippo", an analogy worth bearing in mind. Should you not find a reference to your ancestor on the index, don't despair; information is added on an on-going basis.

Research Services
To investigate the contents of any file identified on the index you'll need assistance. Archival staff are helpful and may do a limited number of simple retrievals, such as Death Notices. Alternatively, hire a local professional researcher to make transcripts or take digital photographs to be sent as e-mail attachments. The latter method works well, permitting a view of the actual document and eliminating transcription errors. Photocopying is not permitted in Deceased Estate files and access may also be denied to any documents in a fragile condition, preservation being the primary business of archivists. Contact details of free-lance researchers are available from the Archives Repository in each area and are also advertised on numerous web sites and in British and South African genealogical publications.

When contacting a local researcher, preferably by e-mail, it speeds things up if you've done your homework first and are able to provide full source references gleaned from the online index, copying and pasting these from the "Results Details" section. If you haven't been able to identify a relevant reference, try to supply the researcher of your choice with as much information as you can. You'll get short shrift with a question such as "My great grandfather fought in the Boer War; can you tell me more about him?"

Mailing Lists
Join one of the appropriate South African mailing lists and you could find a knowledgeable enthusiast willing to undertake voluntary look-ups. Phrase the request carefully and be specific about what you want, giving the exact file reference found, and inserting as a subject-heading the name you are researching, area and date parameters. "Can you help?" is unlikely to elicit a successful response, whereas "James Aloysius Higginbotham Cape 1823" will give you a fighting chance. Save time by visiting the list archives to see if anyone else is researching your topic. For instructions on subscribing to the mailing lists see Web Sites below.

Deceased Estates

If your ancestor died in South Africa, begin with a search for a Deceased Estate. These files, when used in conjunction with other sources, are of immense value to the family historian and are discussed in detail elsewhere in this edition of the Handbook.

Passenger Lists
Despite the fact that "What ship did my ancestor arrive on?" is the most frequently-asked question in South African family history research, passenger lists are not an ideal starting point. Registers which survive are far from all-inclusive and there are few indexes available. A notable exception is the European Immigration index and registers at Pietermaritzburg Archives, covering arrivals - and some departures - at Natal from 1849 to about 1911. There are gaps. Generally, as one progresses towards the 20th century the less chance there is of finding an individual passenger arrival, due to factors such as increased volume of shipping and inconsistent record-keeping. Usually, large groups of "steerage" passengers and members of military units are not identified separately. Some passenger lists appear in the Government Gazettes: check The National Archives UK catalogue for available copies. Tracing passengers from the British end requires knowledge of date and port of departure; BT 27 (at TNA Kew) contains outward lists from 1890 to 1960. There are no nominal indexes to these, many of the registers are fragile and searches take time. No British passenger lists before that period exist other than a few during the ten years between 1878 and 1888; the keeping of lists was discontinued in 1960.

If your ancestor went to South Africa as part of an organized immigration scheme, e.g. the 1820 settlers to the Cape, the Byrne settlers to Natal etc, he/she may be well-documented. Be warned, though, that published sources (of which there are many) for such groups often contain inaccuracies – one of my GADSDENS, listed as an 1820 settler, never actually left England.

Largely because of the time-intensive labour of transcription, online passenger lists are few and far-between. Some lists have been filmed by the LDS, so check their Family History Library Catalogue online or at Family History Centres and the Society of Genealogists, London. See Books below for a selection of published passenger lists.

Sources for South African immigration will be featured in greater detail in a forthcoming edition of the Handbook.

Civil registration
Compulsory registration of Births, Marriages and Deaths commenced in SA as follows:
Cape: Marriages 1700 Births and Deaths 1895
Natal: Marriages 1845 Births 1868 Deaths 1888
Transvaal: Marriages 1870 Births and Deaths 1901
Free State: Marriages 1848 Births and Deaths 1903

The registers are maintained by the Department of Home Affairs, Pretoria. There is no public access to indexes or registers. However, selected holdings have been transferred to Archives Repositories. Marriage and death registers older than 20 years may be

**Shipping Gazette
Natal Mercury June 9 1863**

consulted while in the case of births a 100 year closed period applies. Photocopying of the Archives of the Department of Home Affairs is not permitted.

Birth, Marriage and Death Certificates
Birth, Marriage and Death certificates are issued only by the Department of Home Affairs but full details of the individual and event are required to process an order.
Since these facts are usually what the family historian is seeking, you will perceive the anomaly. Obtaining a certificate of any kind may take up to six months. If a Death Notice is found you may not need a Death Certificate (see the companion article on Deceased Estates for the difference between the two documents) unless you are desperate to know cause of death, which is the only piece of information given on the Death Certificate that doesn't appear on the Death Notice. An Abridged Death Certificate often emerges among the papers in a Deceased Estate file and may obviate the necessity of ordering the Full Death Certificate. However, that's the one to request if you want the document **http://home-affairs.pwv.gov.za/**

Marriage certificates are no easier to obtain and aren't very informative, giving names of bride and groom and their marital status ("bachelor", "spinster" etc), no indication of age of either except for "of full age", and no parents' names (except where the bride is a minor and the consenting parent's signature appears). Sometimes witnesses' names may lead to identifying other family members though the relationship will not be stated on the certificate. It may not be essential to order a marriage certificate. Frequently, a copy is found in a later divorce file for the once-happy couple. Also see Church Registers below.

Church Registers

To embark on searches in South African church records, specifics as to date and place of event, and denomination the ancestors were likely to have chosen, are essential. Not all records are centralised. Among the older and larger denominations, the Dutch Reformed Church was the only official church in South Africa until 1778; its archives dating from 1665 are well-maintained (Dutch Reformed Church Archives, Cape Town). Note that English ancestors may have been baptised in the Dutch Reformed Church failing any other in the vicinity, just as Boer ancestors may be found in Anglican registers. The Church of the Province of South Africa (Anglican) came into being in 1806. Cullen Library at Witwatersrand University holds Anglican records. The Anglican Diocesan Archives in Pietermaritzburg has original Natal registers. Cory Library at Rhodes University, Grahamstown, has holdings of Presbyterian, Methodist and some Catholic records. Records of the Lutheran Evangelical Church up to 1890 are at Cape Archives.

There are a number of smaller denominations whose registers are still kept by the parish concerned, and thus may have been subjected to fire, flood and pest infestations – or, quoting instances in my own research experience, thrown into a river by thieves or kept in a belfry open to the weather.

A certificated copy of an entry in a church register, usually available at a minimal fee from the denomination concerned, can provide a substitute for an "official" marriage certificate.

The LDS have filmed South African church registers where allowed by the denominations concerned (Dutch Reformed and Anglican Churches are well-covered). Visit the Family History Centre in your area to order relevant films at minimal cost and do your own hands-on research.

Cemetery Registers

Municipal cemeteries keep burial registers, usually arranged according to year, and ideally giving the deceased's full name, date of burial and age at death, with block and plot number of the grave. Registers for cremations (20th century and onward) are kept at certain cemeteries. The Genealogical Society of South Africa (GSSA) has collected a large number of memorial inscriptions http://www.ggsa.info/

Census

It comes as a shock to family historians who regularly use this resource in Britain, that South African census records are not preserved. The only substitutes are selected electoral rolls, and these are found among Magisterial Archives, availability depending on area. Pre Union (1910) rolls occur in Government Gazettes. Some voters' rolls are available through the LDS.

Deeds Offices

Land registration began as early as 1685. The Surveyor-General's Office in the area concerned can provide the number of a farm, if its name and location are known. With that number, the Deeds Office should be able to offer a history of transactions pertaining to the property. Maps showing farm names may be among archival records: run a check on the online index. The Inventory which forms part of the Deceased Estate is a useful source for the legal description of a property. Mortgage Bonds often emerge on the index but aren't particularly helpful for family history purposes.

Newspapers

Any newspaper search is a time-consuming exercise, but may be worthwhile if a reasonable date parameter for an event is known (obituaries, reports of weddings, criminal trials etc). Some South African newspapers have been microfilmed, and some originals are preserved at local Archives Repositories and libraries. At the State Library Cape Town and other institutions, the Cape Town English Press Index covering part of the 1870s is available on microfiche. The Natal Society Library, Pietermaritzburg, has a large collection of original newspapers, as do other libraries. Selected South African newspapers are available at the British Library Newspaper Library, Colindale; online catalogue at http://prodigi.bl.uk/nlcat/

Museums

Museum collections provide a rich source of material on specific groups of people or local history background. The Albany Museum

---

O.P.-6.7139—1912-5—10.000-10   S.

ÚNIE VAN SUID-AFRIKA.   UNION OF SOUTH AFRICA.

B.M.D. 5.—Inkomste/Revenue 209.

GEBOORTESERTIFIKAAT.   BIRTH CERTIFICATE.

Uitgereik kragtens artikel 40 van Wet No. 17 van 1923.

Issued in terms of Section 40 of Act No. 17 of 1923.

Nº 930524

UITTREKSEL UIT die Geboorte-register ten opsigte van inskrywings-nommer

EXTRACT FROM the Births Register in respect of Entry Number

229 / 90

Distrik _____   District _Durban_

Voorname _Sydney_   _Bartle_   Christian Names.

Familienaam _GADSDEN ._   Surname.

Geslag _male_   Sex.

Ras van ouers   Race of Parents.

Geboortedatum _Third September 1880 ._   Date of Birth.

Geboorteplek _Durban ._   Place of Birth.

Gesertifiseer korrek/Certified Correct.

_E. _____

Registrateur/Distriksregistrateur.   Registrar/District Registrar.

Bedrag betaal.—Fee paid.

Datum _23 . 9 . 23 ._   Date.

2/6

Provinsie/ Distrik   _Durban ._   Provinsie/District.

DUPLIKAAT ORIGINEEL HUWELIKSREGISTER.
DUPLICATE ORIGINAL MARRIAGE REGISTER.

Since the ancestor didn't exist in a vacuum, but was subject to external forces beyond his control – military conflict, epidemics, economic and political changes, the influence of other human beings, even the weather – its essential to learn as much as possible about the backdrop against which his personal drama was enacted. Archival records provide exits and entrances and the names of the cast, but we need the context of a wider reality to illuminate the scene.

Grahamstown (1820 Settlers), Africana Museum Johannesburg, Kaffrarian Museum Kingwilliam's Town (German settlers) Huguenot Museum Franschhoek, Old Court House Durban and Campbell Collections Durban (Natal Settlers) are a small selection.   Contact details
for South African Museums can be found at
http://medial.mweb.co.za/mosa/find.asp

Military Records

It is impossible to do justice to this subject in limited space. Published sources are numerous. The National Archives UK holds Enrolment Forms and Nominal Rolls of South African Volunteer Units during the Anglo-Boer War (WO 126 and WO 127) as well as Medal Rolls (WO 100). At the end of this conflict, many British soldiers joined the South African Constabulary and personnel records are preserved in the National Archives of South Africa. Records post-1912 for all those who served in the South African Armed Forces including World War I and II, are kept by the South African Defence Force; information can be obtained from the Deputy Director, Documentation Centre (Personnel Archives) Private Bag X289 Pretoria 0001. The South African Military History Museum is an excellent resource; their online overview, "Researching Ancestors Who Were Servicemen", is recommended reading.
http://www.militarymuseum.co.za/

Placing the Ancestor in context

There's a greater likelihood of finding records about a South African ancestor if he became part of a public process such as litigation. If his business was liquidated, or his marriage ended in divorce or if he was involved in a criminal trial, a file giving the details will probably emerge. Ironically, the end of his life usually supplies more material than the preceding years. The upshot is that we may be left with a disproportionately dismal impression. His happiest moments - marriage, the births of children - do provide some leaven, but most of his ordinary daily routine remains invisible history.

Websites
http://whitlock.castlewebs.net/whitsend/tl.htm - A comprehensive Timeline: South African history at a glance
www.national.archives.gov.za/ - The portal to South African genealogy
http://home-affairs.pwv.gov.za/ - Dept of Home Affairs; downloadable forms
www.familysearch.org/ - LDS site; Family History Library Catalogue
http://www.ggsa.info/ - Genealogy Society of South Africa; includes details of a new virtual branch (eGSSA) founded in 2004
http://www.sun.ac.za/gisa/home.asp - Genealogical Institute of South Africa
www.genealogy.co.za - Links galore; selected passenger lists
http://home.global.co.za/~mercon/ - Overview and links; instructions on how to subscribe to SA mailing list
www.genealogyworld.net/ - Natal, Eastern Cape; beginners' tips; maritime pages, Natal passenger lists
www.1820Settlers.com - 1820 Settler community site
http://sa-passenger-list.za.net/ - Cape ships, Huguenots 1683-1756, Natal ships 1845-1858; only the tip of the iceberg
www.sagenealogy.co.za/DataArchive.htm - Selected Cape passenger lists
http://www.union-castle-line.com/ - History of this famous line, but no passenger lists
www.rhodes.ac.za/library/cory/ - Cory Library for Historical Research, Grahamstown
http://khozi2.nu.ac.za/kafricana.htm - Campbell Collections Durban; online photographs
www.ru.ac.za/affiliates/am/geneal.htm - Albany Museum, 1820 Settlers
http://home.global.co.za/~afrilib - Kimberley Africana Library, diamond mining, Anglo-Boer War
http://www.militarymuseum.co.za/ - South African National Museum of Military History
http://rapidttp.co.za/milhist/ - South African Military History Society
www.1879group.com - Researches Anglo-Zulu War, contacts descendants of participants; Living History section
http://www.rorkesdriftvc.com/ - Anglo-Zulu War;

active forum
http://media1.mweb.co.za/mosa/find.asp - South
African Museums' contact details
http://196.15.219.249/ - South African White Pages
www.geocities.com/Heartland/Valley/8140 - Huguenot
Society
www.jewishgen.org/SAfrica - Jewish South Africans
http://redcoat.future.easyspace.com/ - Officers who
died in Anglo-Boer War
www.sahra.org.za/f5.htm - Anglo-Boer War casualties
www.cwgc.org/ - Commonwealth War Graves
Commission

Books
Cameron & Spies ed., *An Illustrated History of South Africa*
(Jonathan Ball, Johannesburg 1986)
R T J Lombard, *Handbook for Genealogical Research in
South Africa* (HSRC Pretoria 1984); the bible of SA
ancestral research
Peter Philip, *British Residents at the Cape 1795-1819*
(David Philip, 1981), biographies of 4,800 early settlers
E Morse Jones, *Roll of the British Settlers in South Africa*
(A A Balkema, 1969) lists 1820 Settlers
Esme Bull, *Aided Immigration from Britain to South Africa
1857-1867* (Pretoria, HSRC, 1991); passenger lists and
12,000 names
G B Dickason, *Irish Settlers to the Cape: History of the
Clanwilliam 1820 Settlers from Cork Harbour* (Cape Town
1973)
G B Dickason, *Cornish Immigrants to South Africa: The
Cousin Jack's contribution to the development of mining and
commerce 1820 – 1920* (Cape Town 1978)
S. Spencer, *British Settlers in Natal* (University of Natal
Press); detailed biographies; 7 volumes (up to G)
Dr J Clark, Natal Settler Agent: *The Career of John
Moreland Agent for the Byrne emigration scheme of 1849-51*
(A A Balkema, 1972); detailed passenger lists and
descriptions of voyages
C G Botha, *The French Refugees at the Cape* (Cape Town,
1970)
C C de Villiers and C Pama, *Genealogies of old South
African families* (Cape Town, 1966)
D F du Toit Malherbe, *Family Register of the South African
Nation* (Tegniek, 1966)
S Watt, *Roll of Honour of Imperial Forces Anglo-Boer War
1899-190*2 (University of Natal Press Pietermaritzburg
2000)
J Wassermann & B Kearney ed., A Warrior's Gateway:
Durban and the Anglo-Boer War 1899-1902 (Protea Book
House Pretoria 2002)
Marischal Murray, Ships and South Africa, *A Maritime
Chronicle of the Cape with particular reference to Mail and
Passenger Liners from the Early Days of Steam down to the
Present* (Oxford University Press London 1933)

Addresses
**The National Archives and Records Service of South
Africa**
National Archives and Records Service of South Africa
Post: Private Bag X236, PRETORIA 0001 Address: 24
Hamilton Street, Arcadia, PRETORIA Tel: (012) 323 5300.
Fax: (012) 323 5287 E-mail: archives@dac.gov.za
Bureau of Heraldry, The State Herald, Post: Private Bag
X236, PRETORIA 0001 Address: 24 Hamilton Street,
Arcadia, PRETORIA
Tel: (012) 323 5300. Fax: (012) 323 5287 E-mail:
heraldry@dac.gov.za
Cape Town Archives Repository Post: Private Bag X9025,
CAPE TOWN 8000 Address: 72 Roeland Street, CAPE
TOWN Tel: (021) 462 4050. Fax: (021) 465 2960 E-mail:
Capearchives@mweb.co.za for General Correspondence
Caperm@mweb.co.za for Records Management
National Archives Repository Post: Private Bag X236,
PRETORIA 0001 Address: 24 Hamilton Street, Arcadia,
PRETORIA Tel: (012) 323 5300. Fax: (012) 323 5287 E-

mail: enquiries@dac.gov.za
National Film, Video and Sound Archives Post: Private
Bag X236, PRETORIA 0001l Address: 698 Church Street
East, Arcadia, PRETORIA Tel: (012) 343 9767. Fax: (012)
344 5143 E-mail: film01@hotmail.com

Provincial Archive Services
(Offices which are not part of National Archives and
Records Service of South Africa)
Eastern Cape Provincial Archives Post: Private Bag
X7486, KING WILLIAM'S TOWN, 5600 Address: Shop
no. 6, Public Works Building, Qasana Drive, BISHOTel:
(040) 609 4666/2/5/8 Fax: (040) 609 4664 E-Mail:
stofile@facmobp.ecape.gov.za
Port Elizabeth Archives Repository Post: Private Bag
X3932, North End, PORT ELIZABETH, 6056 Address: 1
De Villiers Street, PORT ELIZABETH Tel: (041) 484 6451.
Fax: (041) 484 6451
Umtata Archives Repository Post: Private Bag X5095,
UMTATA 5100 Address: corner of Owen Street and Nelson
Mandela Drive
Free State Provincial Archives Post: Private Bag X20504,
BLOEMFONTEIN 9300 Address: 29 Badenhorst Street,
BLOEMFONTEIN Tel: (051) 522 6762. Fax: (051) 522
6765 E-mail: fsarch@sac.fs.gov.za
KwaZulu-Natal Archives Post: Private Bag X75, ULUNDI
3838 Address: Block 4, Unit A, ULUNDI Tel: (035) 879
8500. Fax: (035) 879 8518 E-mail:
archives@uld.kzntl.gov.za
Durban Archives Repository Post: Private Bag X22,
GREYVILLE 4023 Address: Nashua House, 14 De
Mazenod Street, GREYVILLE Tel: (031) 309 5682. Fax:
(031) 309 5685 E-mail: dbnarchives@kznedu.kzntl.gov.za
Pietermaritzburg Archives Repository Post: Private Bag
X9012, PIETERMARITZBURG 3200 Address: 231
Pietermaritz Street, PIETERMARITZBURG Tel: (033) 342
4712. Fax: (033) 394 4353 E-mail:
pmbarchives@kznedu.kzntl.gov.za
Ulundi Archives Repository Post: Private Bag X75,
ULUNDI 3838 Address: Block 4, Unit A, ULUNDI Tel:
(035) 879 8500. Fax: (035) 879 8518 E-mail:
archives@uld.kzntl.gov.za
Limpopo Archives Service Post: Department of Sport, Arts
and Culture, Archives Service, Private Bag X9549,
POLOKWANE 0700 Address: 15 Grobler Road,
POLOKWANE Tel: (015) 299 7846 Fax: (015) 295 2043
Mpumalanga Provincial Archives Service:Postal Address:
P O Box 1243, NELSPRUIT, 1200 Tel: (013) 766 5062 Fax:
(013) 766 5594
Northern Cape Archives Services Post: Private Bag
X5004, KIMBERLEY 8300 Address: 6th Floor Dutoitspan
Building, Dutoitspan Road, KIMBERLEY Tel: (053) 831
1761. Fax: (053) 833 4353 E-mail: aluxton@ds.ncape.gov.za
North West Province Archives Service Post: Department
of Social Services, Arts, Culture and Sport, Private Bag X6,
MMABATHO, 2735 Address: Provident House, University
Drive, MMABATHO Tel: (018) 397 0244. Fax: (053) 833
4353 E-mail: lmokoena@nwpg.org.za

Deceased Estates in South African Genealogy
Rosemary Dixon-Smith

One of the accepted tenets of family history research is that we proceed from the "known" to the "unknown". The "known" event with which we begin our search is often the end of the ancestor's life: the inevitable, incontrovertible and usually recorded fact of Death. This is particularly true in the context of South African genealogy, where Deceased Estate documentation provides a valuable starting point for finding out more about our forebears.

If an ancestor died in South Africa, the chances of discovering more information are good – far better than if he was merely passing through on his way to another colony or making a temporary sojourn for some reason before returning to his place of origin. By using the Deceased Estate papers its possible to go back to his earlier history as well as forwards in quest of living descendants.

The first step is to identify a relevant Deceased Estate file for the ancestor by using the online SA National Archives index. **www.national.archives.gov.za/** (See accompanying article in this edition of The Handbook.) Some idea of the province in which the death took place would be helpful (though it is possible to search on all South Africa) plus a reasonable date parameter for the event. As always, if the name is a commonly-foundcommonly-found one this complicates matters: Algernon Rockafeller Entwhistle should be easily identified, whereas finding the "right" John Brown might take a little longer. Once a likely contender is pinpointedpinpointed, a local researcher will be needed to retrieve the original file and relay its contents, because the index is just that – a source locator; the documents themselves are not visible online.

Death Notice
Among the Estate documents, the Death Notice is the most significant for the family historian. It should give the following details: full name of deceased, birthplace, parents' names, the deceased's age at death (or date of birth), occupation, place of residence, marital status, place of last marriage, names of surviving and pre-deceased spouses, date and place of death, and names of major and minor children (if minor, with their dates of birth; if daughters, their appropriate married surnames may appear; if the deceased was unmarried, his siblings' names may be given). It There shouldis also give information as toregarding any assets in the estate, movable and immovable, whetherwhether these exceeded a certain value and

ifwhether the deceased left a will. The informant's signature appears on the document, with some indication as to whether they were present at the time and place of death.

The Death Notice is the key which unlocks many doors – but some remain firmly closed e.g. when the space on the form next to "Parents" gives that dreaded word "Deceased", or more starkly, "Dead", instead of the hoped-for names; or under "Birthplace", simply "England" instead of at least a County to provide as a starting point for the researcher. There's nothing much one can do about that except swallow one's disappointment and plod onwards. The fullness and accuracy of the information appearing on the Death Notice is in direct proportion to the knowledge of the Informant, usually but not always the next-of-kin. It may be that a son either never knew, or had forgotten, the names of his overseas grandparents, or where his parents were married. These Notices are completed under stress of bereavement and this may affect accuracy: a widow may not recall precisely where her husband was born. If the Informant was not a family member, details may be sketchy. However, additional information is often added after the completion of the Death Notice and this sometimes comes to light in documents filed later, one good reason for examining all the papers in any Deceased Eestate file.

There may also be cases of deliberate misinformation. Generally, though, the Death Notice should advance

DEATH NOTICE 1903

Country of origin England – in this case plus county

Age at death

Occupation

Date of death

Residence

No will

Deceased's name

Names of parents of deceased not always given

Marital status, name of spouse and whether mar Community of Property by Ante-Nuptial Contra

Date & place of last marriage

Minor children's full names & dates of birth given.

Property

Informant's (spouse's) signature

you several paces in your quest. Married names of the deceased's daughters may be the start of entirely new searches under those surnames and present opportunities for locating living relatives.

A Death Notice is not necessarily found for every person who died in South Africa, though theoretically there should be a Death Notice for anyone who died leaving inheritable assets in that country. Also, Death Notices didn't come into existence until 1834, so to find information for the period before that date other research avenues must be followed. Don't expect to find a Death Notice in an Insolvent Estate, incidentally – that's an entirely different kettle of fish from a Deceased Estate.

It's possible that a person who had lived in South Africa but died in England may have had both an English Death Certificate and a South African Death Notice, the reason being that though death occurred in UK the deceased owned property in South Africa. In an instance such as this, the country in whichwhere the estate was administered would depend on where the individual was resident at date of death. Delays and complications can ensue in these cases, and a South African Death Notice may not be filed for some months after death.

Finding two separate Death Notices in one Ddeceased Eestate file may indicate that the first form was filled in at the place of death e.g. during a military conflict (many examples during the Anglo-Boer War) and a later, a more detailed Notice followed. Or, the first Notice may have been issued in another area of SA , and a second Notice completed later.

The contents of the Death Notice vary slightly at different periods; more recent Notices include the SA Identity Number which first came into being in 1955/56. And Tthis ID Number can be important if you wish to acquire a South African Death Certificate.

Death Certificate
Not to be confused with the Death Notice, the Death Certificate is a much briefer document. The piece of information it offers which does not appear on the Death Notice is the cause of death, supplied by the doctor in attendance, with details as to duration of the final illness.

Ordering Certificates
The Department of Home Affairs is the only body which can issue certificates of any kind – birth, marriage or death. They have a web site at **http://home-affairs.pwv.gov.za** where application forms can be downloaded, or you can write to the Registration Office, Department of Home Affairs, Private Bag X114, Pretoria 001. There is a charge per certificate. If ordering a Death Certificate make sure you ask for a FULL certificate. If any certificate is required for Ancestral Visa purposes it's necessary to obtain a VAULT copy. Should you be delegating the task to a South African researcher, it is wise to mention the reason for wanting a certificate.

But pause before you embark on the frustrating and protracted course of certificate ordering. If a Death

Notice is located, it may not be worthwhile pursuing a Death Certificate, since the latter offers limited information. Sometimes a copy of a Death Certificate may turn up in an Eestate file and this provides cause of death – as mentioned above, the only fact not included on the Death Notice. There's a long waiting period, sometimes months, for the ordering process to grind through the Department's mill, and even if you have supplied all the particulars there's no guarantee that you'll eventually acquire a certificate.

Other Documents in the Estate File
Typically, there would also be a Will, Inventory, Final Liquidation and Distribution Accounts and correspondence. All of these are potential sources of information, so it's advisable not to stop the search at the Death Notice (or to allow your local researcher to do so). Surprising facts may emerge in the most unlikely pieces of paper.

Will
The Will is the next most significant document in an Eestate file. Many are in bland "standard" format and not particularly informative, though beneficiaries are named, of course, and specific bequests e.g. the medals of a military man, may be included. There may be unexpected revelations, or additions to the list of heirs: a favourite god-daughter, or an adopted or illegitimate child previously unknown to the family. Or even a mistress being rewarded "for services rendered". Don't make assumptions; check all the names: she might have been the housekeeper.

Family rifts may become apparent from the last wishes of the deceased: recently I found an angry clause from a father who stated in no uncertain terms that his daughter, who had "taken her mother's side" in her parents' divorce, would not benefit under his will. Forgiveness, alas, remains Divine.
A child not appearing as beneficiary in the Will isn't necessarily evidence of such a rift e.g. a father makes apology for non-inclusion of a son and says this shouldn't be taken as indication of disapproval or lack of appreciation for everything the son had done for the family business to date, but that this son was already well-established and other children were more in need.

Which leads on to the premise that it is essential to looksee beyond the stated facts: a list of children on a Death Notice of 1903 shows 5 sons and 3 daughters, only 2 of them Majors and "all residing with their mother", the surviving parent. The Minor children range in ages from 14 to 4 and obviously none of them were wage-earning. From the time of his father's death, the eldest Major son would be required to take on the role of breadwinner. The Death Notice reveals that the estate did not exceed a certain value and the deceased died intestate (no will), leaving no immovable property and not much in the way of movables either. Reading between the lines, a parlous situation for this family.

Instructions in the will as to choice of burial or cremation can be helpful when seeking the ancestor's last resting-place.

Inventory

One of the most intimate glimpses of our ancestor is offered in the Inventory, which lists his personal possessions: from the farm or house he owned to the porcelain basin and jug he used while shaving in the mornings. The full legal description of a piece of land as given under Immovable Assets can come in handy for searches in the Deeds Office. It's more difficult to quantify what is gained from details such as: "Machinery for Water Mill"; "Pair Cart Wheels, unmounted"; "Agricultural Implements old & worn out"; "Standing Wheat Crop 10 acres, can't be valued as it is liable to so many risks & enemies" - but such clues reveal the fabric of the ancestor's life and times and make all the difference when added to a basic family history narrative.

Tattersalls Bar,
HARRY PULHAM, "ECLIPSE."
...... Proprietor.

The Sporting House of Durban.

CORNER OF
WEST and GREY STREETS,
DURBAN,
15/11/11. 191

Liquidation & Distribution Account

This is essentially a balance sheet revealings details of all the assets including immovable property (land) or movable property (household furniture, jewellery etc), also listing claims which have been paid out of the estate such as advertisements in newspapers, funeral expenses etc. The "distribution" part refers to exactly how the amount left by the deceased was divided amongst the beneficiaries and is often useful for obtaining names of grandchildren who may not have been mentioned specifically at the time the will was made – again, this can take one forward to living descendants.

Correspondence

Typically grouped at the back of the file are various invoices e.g. from tradesmen claiming settlement from the estate. These are all worth looking at. The funeral parlour invoice merits special attention because frequently there is a note re the burial place, and sometimes even a plot number of the grave which can be a helpful short-cut. The undertaker's invoice may also tell us who paid for the obsequies and how much: the high cost of dying then, as now, becomes apparent. Some idea of the scale of the funeral can be obtained from references to "procession of 2 carriages and a special tram car for mourners". With the tradeplate of the undertaker emblazoned at the top, the invoice can provide an illustration for the family history – gloomy? Possibly, but interesting and decorative nevertheless.

Other less obvious invoices mention the minutiae of the ancestor's daily life, such as what medicines he bought from his local chemist (perhaps in an attempt to stave off the inevitable). A seemingly innocuous list of garments turned out to be my great great grandmother's mourning clothes, plus some for her daughters, ordered from the "Silk Mercer, Milliner & Straw Bonnet Manufacturer", so the family would be correctly attired for my great great grandfather's funeral in 1869.

Miscellaneous personal letters in the file may offer

examples of the handwriting of relatives of the deceased as well as throw light on arguments over division of property among the heirs – or who would pay for the tombstone.

Some letterheads are fine examples of the printer's art as well as giving intriguing snippets of information about a family business, its street as well as telegraphic address, who the directors were etc. The prize find in one file was an engraved letterhead bearing a picture of the building where the ancestor in question had lived, worked and died – an unimportant structure in itself and not likely to be found in any museum photo collection, but with a unique link to the deceased himself and a perfect illustration for a proposed book. It doesn't come much better than this in family history.

When a Deceased Estate file is not found

It should be emphasised that a Deceased Estate was not lodged for every person who died in South Africa. Reasons for not locating an Eestate file vary. There may have been insufficient assets, and hence literally no estate, although there are cases where the only asset was a negligible sum in a Post Office savings account and yet an estate was filed. If you find a Deceased Estate on the index, check the "Remarks" section at the bottom of the file reference: a number shown there may relate to the spouse's file. Where "No Trace" of a previously deceased's spouse's estate is mentioned, check the index for other provinces – the file may emerge elsewhere in the country.

Another reason for not finding a reference to a Ddeceased Eestate file on the online index is that it may be of too recent a date to have been handed over to archives and is still held by the Master of Supreme Court in the relevant area. There is a 25- year waiting period from the time that the estate is "wound up" before it is transferred to archives. These recent Eestate ffiles are grouped by year of death and if this is known the file can be viewed at the Master's Office – if you are at a distance, delegate the task to a local researcher who can take transcripts or digital photographs of the documents for you. The Cape Death Notice Index is a work in progress (by Western Cape Branch of the Genealogical Society of South Africa) making available online names and file numbers of estates held by the Master of Supreme Court in that area. This is not yet all-inclusive but worth checking at

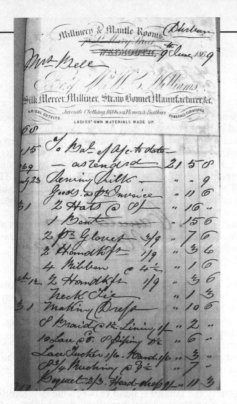

www.e-family.co.za/cdni/cdni_index.htm

Under the Cape system, the Death Notice and other estate papers are filed separately at archives, hence several references may appear on the online index in connection with one individual's estate. Speaking of Cape files, the significance of the code MOOC is a frequently-asked question. The initials refer to the Master's Office and Orphan Chamber. One of the legacies of the Dutch East India Company was the "Orphan Chamber": originally instituted to protect the inheritance of widows and orphans, it ceased to exist in 1833 and from then on Deceased Estate matters were handled by the Master of the Supreme Court.

While Deceased Estate files provide an excellent initial avenue to follow, the researcher cannot rely on them to the exclusion of the numerous other sources available for South African genealogy.
© Rosemary Dixon-Smith
dixonsmithbygad@eastcoast.co.za

The Clopton Oak
Gabriel Alington

England's history is full of oak trees. They have always been there, proud on the skyline, deepening the forests, standing apart majestically, sometimes famously.

The Celtic people worshipped their gods within groves of oaks. The first English navy was built of oak. King Charles hid inside a hollow oak. And it was under a certain Suffolk oak that, in 1615, John Winthrop asked Thomasine Clopton to marry him.

The tree stood in the grounds of the Clopton family manor, Castlings Hall at Groton near Boxford. It was a house John Winthrop must have known well for he lived only three miles away. The Winthrop estate, once glebe land, had been purchased from Henry VIII by John's grandfather, Adam Winthrop, in 1544. At that time the estate's principal house, Groton Hall, was already occupied under a long lease, so Adam Winthrop, having agreed a ninety-nine year lease to the rectory and glebe land, rebuilt and greatly enlarged the rectory, renaming it Groton Place. In time the Winthrops occupied both Groton Place and Groton Hall.

The history of Castlings Hall can be traced back to the 13th century when the lordship of the manor of Castelyns was Sir Gilbery de Chastelyn. The history of the estate goes back further still, possibly to the Iron Age. Long ridges to the north east of the manor as well as relics found in the soil, are indications of an early settlement there. Clearly evident in the same area is part of a 12th century castle moat, one of three built to defend local townships during King Stephen's turbulent reign.

It was in 1560 that Thomasine's grandfather, Sir William Clopton, acquired the ownership of Castlings from the Knyvet family and set about rebuilding the house; the result, a particularly fine Elizabethan manor. In front of the house Sir William planted a young oak tree.

The Cloptons had long been recognised as one of Suffolk's most presitigous familes. In the late 14th century, they built Kentwell Hall at Long Melford, a magnificent moated Tudor manor. A century later John Clopton provided Long Melford with a new church, for the medieval wool trade had brought prosperity to the little town; the population had multiplied; the old church was too small. John Clopton's church still stands on a rise at the edge of the town. Its long nave with a clerestory gives the whole building a rare sense of space and light. Altogether, with its wealth of carving and decoration, this glorious late-Perpendicular church is a place to wonder at. On the south side of the chancel a narrow passage leads to the Clopton chantry, a small private chapel where the figure of John's father, Sir William Clopton, lies on his tomb, and, set in the wall between the chapel and the main chancel, is the tomb of the John himself, who died in 1497, one of the great Clopton benefactors.

Indeed records show that the Clopton name had been held in high regard in East Anglia since the early Middle Ages, whereas the Winthrops had not risen to landowning status till the mid 16th century. It was, in fact, John's grandfather, Adam Winthrop, who, as a Lavenham clothier, had made the family fortune. He had enjoyed his wealth, establishing the family estate, developing his 'mansion house', as he called Groton Place, and embellishing it with fine carving and paintings. Like the Cloptons Adam Winthrop was a generous benefactor. Records show that in 1602 he bought land at nearby Boxford and gave it to the village for the building of a school.

John Winthrop and his four sisters would have grown up alongside the young Cloptons, meeting them on social occasions, riding out with them and, as the boys grew older, taking part in wild fowl shooting, perhaps around the ponds behind Castlings Hall. John, though extremely keen on the sport, was alledgedly a very poor shot. In his teens he went to Trinity College, Cambridge to read law.

Probably the strongest bond between the two families was their religion. They were Puritans, members of a nonconformist sect set up about 1564 with the aim of eliminating all traces of Roman Catholicism from their worship. Their services were absolutely plain, no hymns or anthems, simply Bible readings, quiet meditation and long sermons. Puritans believed in a moment of conversion, the moment of a soul's sudden emergence from darkness to divine enlightenment. In his autobiography, written late in life, John Winthrop describes experiencing his own conversion at the age of thirty.

Life was not easy for the Puritans. This was particularly true in the early 17th century when James I, who had succeeded the Protestant Elizabeth in 1603, had reinstated the faith of Rome. James was an ardent Catholic; he was also an ardent anti-Puritan.

Serious though this was, as John Winthrop rode to Castlings Hall to meet Thomasine on that day in 1615, he would have had other matters in mind. He needed a wife; he needed a mother for his four small children whose own mother had died six months before. John had first married at the age of 17 so that now, ten years later, he was still a comparatively young man. Thomasine, on the other hand, had probably resigned herself to spinsterhood. She was 32, nearly six years older than John. An offer of marriage from the Lord of Groton Place, albeit a widower with children, must have seemed like an answer to prayer.

And so on December 6th, 1615, at Castlings Hall, Thomasine became the second Mrs John Winthrop, stepmother to John, aged 9, Henry 7, Forth, 6 and Mary, aged about 3. John was devoted to Thomasine and, now, with children in her care , he was able to take on more legal work including a position on the

Suffolk Commission of Peace. Then a year to the day after their wedding, Thomasine gave birth to a daughter. The little girl lived only two days. On the following day Thomasine, weakened by the birth, collapsed with a fever which quickly grew worse. John, alarmed at her condition, is said to have broken down in tears while Thomasine struggled to comfort him. One by one her four married sisters, Mary, Margery, Elizabeth and Bridget, hurried to Castlings. It was clear they would not see her again. The next day at about five o'clock, while Mr Nicolson, the priest, prayed at her bedside, Thomasine died. On a bitterly cold December day she was buried with her child in the chancel of Groton church.

Once again John Winthrop faced widowhood. At first his grief at Thomasine's death and that of their child, seems to have completely overwhelmed him. But in time his deep religious faith - and by then he had experienced his moment of conversion - combined with his belief that '...the life which is most exercised with tryalls and temptations is the sweetest, and will prove the safeste', must have helped him face the future. He thought of taking holy orders but made no move to do so. There were, after all, the children to consider. What should he do? Doubtless John spent hours on his knees praying for guidance.

The answer to his prayer was a lady named Margaret Tyndal who, in April 1618, became the third Mrs Winthrop. Margaret proved a good wife for John. He became more outgoing, gave up considering holy orders and took on additional legal work. And, in a move which was to change the direction of his life, he joined in discussions with his Puritan neighbours on the grave situation facing them.

Since Charles I had succeeded his father in 1625, the plight of the Puritans had worsened. Charles was determined to get rid of them and he appointed two of his closest advisers, Sir Thomas Strafford and Bishop William Laud, to carry out a campaign against the sect. Puritans began to live in fear of their lives. It was the fact that they were being persecuted by the church, albeit Roman Catholic, that distressed them most. A number of their fellow Puritans had already emigrated to New England to find freedom to worship according to their faith. They had established a settlement on a plantation at Plymouth, Massachusetts. It was an idea that John Winthrop and his friends must have considered but one which, at that time, John was bound to reject, for in November 1628 he had the honour of being appointed to the Inner Temple.

Then in March 1629 came an event that stunned the country. The king announced the dissolution of parliament; in future he would govern the country himself. Among those summarily dismissed was the honourable member for Huntingdon, Oliver Cromwell.

Whether John Winthrop ever met Cromwell, who was eleven years younger, is not clear. Certainly they had much in common and Huntingdon is not so far from west Suffolk, even on horseback. It is also believed that at one time Cromwell was another who had thought of emigrating to the New World. It could be

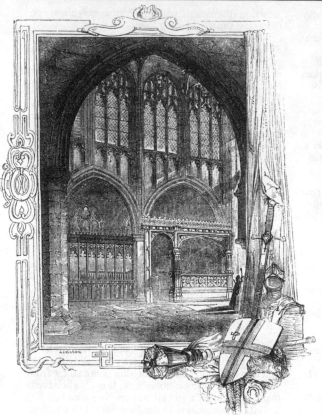

At one of the many services held on the Arbella during the voyage John Winthrop preached a memorable sermon. His words were heard again at the funeral of the late president, Ronald Reagan, on 11th June, 2004.

At last, after 66 days at sea, the ships reached New England. Crowding the deck rail to catch their first sight of this unfamiliar land, the emigrants must have been full of hope for their new life, but apprehension too. It was not going to be not easy. It was not. Indeed there were times when adapting to this strange environment was almost unbearably hard. But gradually life became easier. John Winthrop was a good governor and when his first term was up he was re-elected. As word reached England of the better conditions in the colony, more and more emigrants arrived. By 1633 the population had trebled to over 2,000.

Not everyone stayed; some, perhaps driven by homesickness, chose to go back. Walter Clopton was one who left after only one year and, though later he returned, again he did not stay long. The first permanent Clopton settler was, according to the records, William Clopton, Gentleman, who, in the early 1670's, came to Virginia, one of the other four colonies, and established his family at York County.

In 1643, when the four colonies were united into a confederation, John Winthrop was elected first as deputy governor and later as governor. He died on 26 March, 1649.

the two men discussed the idea. But while Cromwell, having decided against it, never reconsidered, John Winthrop did.

One reason was the death of his mother, Anne, who would have been too old to face a sea voyage and who he could not abandon. Another reason was the decision of the English proprietors of the Massachusetts plantation to convert it to a self-governing community. At a meeting in London John Winthrop and eleven other signatories agreed to set sail and, with their families, inhabit the plantation provided the government and patent of the plantation were legally and permanently transferred. One of the signatories was to be elected governor. The man chosen was John Winthrop.

For the next five months the families who had decided to go, doubtless after much angst and prayer, prepared for the voyage. There would be four ships; the departure date was set for 22 March, 1630.

On board the principal ship, the Arbella, was the Winthrop family, Walter Clopton, Thomasine's brother, and possibly other Cloptons too.

They embarked from Southampton and headed for the Isle of Wight. There they stayed waiting for a favourable wind. It is not hard to imagine their frustration and most probably mounting doubt. Had they made the right decision? Was this a sign from God? Then the wind changed and they sailed on.

Today descendants of the Winthrops and Cloptons take great pride in their history. A number pay regular visits to Groton calling in at their respective ancestral homes. On a recent visit members of the Winthrop family took part in a Remembrance service in Groton church. In recent years a Winthrop family fund has been set up through which regular and very generous donations are made to this small but special church.

Every six years a coach full of American Cloptons arrives to Castlings Hall. The house, which has never been unoccupied, has lost none of its original character and is still a perfect example of an early Elizabethan manor. With its many windows it is a house which looks alive; it has a lived-in air, a sense of the past, combined with the immediacy of today. As the present owners are a young couple with four small boys, that is no surprise. The Clopton visitors are warmly welcomed and entertained to tea. This now takes place in one of the two barns close to the house, which have recently been restored and are let for weddings, parties and other events to help finance the upkeep of the house and the gardens surrounding it. There, in the garden, standing apart, huge and stately, is a certain tree which the Cloptons unfailingly pay homage to. This must be the high spot of their trip to England for the tree is, of course, the Clopton oak.

It is the tree, you could say, that marks the spot where the story of the Cloptons and their Winthrop neighbours first began.

West Dorset History and Genealogical Research Centre
Celia Martin M.A.

The West Dorset History and Genealogical Society is based in Bridport in the county of Dorset a mile from the south coast. The town has been involved in the rope and net trade from before the first archival records relating to the industry in the early 13th century and the ancient craft has been passed down through generations. So Bridport has an interesting history of families and entrepreneurs and is a perfect place to set up a Research Centre. For those who come to visit us with members of the family not quite so interested in history there is the beach and some magnificent scenery to explore. This part of England was recently made a World Heritage Site with the title 'Jurassic Coast'.

Setting up the centre was made possible by serendipity, as with most good voluntary-run schemes, and we feel there must be many more people out there who could do the same with a bit of luck. We were all members of the Somerset & Dorset Family History Society when we put on an exhibition of the history of the rope and net trade of the Bridport area and were offered a place to store our display boards by a local factory. Two of us looked at the building and found we were being given a house that would make a perfect place to have a family history centre as it was right in the middle of Bridport. Then we were fortunate in getting the Society to back us and pay for the utilities. This was over three years ago and we have blossomed into a fully functioning centre with a group of over thirty dedicated volunteers all working hard on different projects. We open five days a week to the public and the task of building up our library is on-going.

Since June of 2004 we have run the centre independently, working with grant money and members' contributions to pay our way. We have a management committee of six volunteers who meet fortnightly to discuss the centre's progress; everything is run as democratically as possible! We are building up our book of clients and have had to become mercenary and charge for work we do for them. The Research Centre team consists of family historians, local historians, social historians as well as members who like to work on transcriptions or help with computer inputting; we have varied areas of expertise. People can either come into the centre to work or take work home. Many like to come in as we provide excellent coffee and biscuits in a kitchen where we can sit, chat and relax, and we also have a herb garden to sit in during the sunnier months. We are eager to hear from others who do the same as us. Record Offices and Museums may have more resources but not always the time to add the human helpful touch.

Our main project is the Dorset Migration Index and we have been compiling a database of names of people who left Dorset, mainly in the nineteenth century, to live elsewhere. We accept migrants who moved elsewhere in the United Kingdom as well as overseas. This was originally done with the help of members of the Somerset & Dorset Family History Society who sent in details of their ancestors after an article was published in the Society's magazine The Greenwood Tree. There are a number of questions on a form to fill in which can be sent out by post or by e-mail. When the forms come back, the migration team have a system of checking and collating the information before inputting the data. In case of electronic disasters we have a back-up duplicate system on old fashioned index cards - a case of belt and braces. New information on migrants is always welcome. We intend to put an indexed list of names on the Internet so that people can contact the centre for information on lost relatives, and we would like the work to be used for academic research. We know that the Cornish Migration Index was created ten years ago because they helped us start up our indexing system. We would like to hear if there are any more migration teams as it would be beneficial to everyone if we help each other and work towards the same goal. Of course, what we would really like to do is to set up is a Migration Centre for England down here in the South West. Scotland has a Migration Centre, as does Northern Ireland at Omagh, so why not England? There was much more movement within the country before the railways were built than we first realised, or are we in denial because so many of our ancestors became migrants who went abroad? We have found by looking at the censuses that over 100,000 people left Dorset in the 1800s. If you have a census for your part of the world that has some Dorset strays recorded please do send them to us.

We have also worked on transcribing censuses of our area, starting with the 1841. This work was incorporated into our second rope and net exhibition as so many people were involved in the industry at that time, and there were villagers working in mills and farmers growing hemp and flax in many of the surrounding rural parishes. Now we will put the research into use again with our Parish Packs project which we plan to work on for the next three years. This will include the work of local history societies as well as our own and we have been given a grant by Awards for All to set up the project which will eventually become self-financing.

This is a particularly fertile place in which to find your roots and we meet up regularly with other groups who are interested in history and heritage in the West Dorset area. The Bridport Museum has a Local History Centre and the Library has a Local Studies Collection in their Reference Section. So that visitors and residents don't go round in circles there is a Bridport Heritage leaflet that explains who has what and where, plus the times and places that the resources can be accessed. In our constitution our aim is to promote and support interest in social, family and local history and we enjoy doing exactly that.

West Dorset History & Genealogical Research Centre, 45, West Street, Bridport, Dorset DT6 3QW. Tel: 01308 458061 Email: wdhgrc@dorsetmigration.org.uk www.dorsetmigration.org.uk

Windmills
Richie Green

Imagine if you will the Hunter Gatherer running his fingers through the long grass realizing his outstretched hand was filling up with grains. Grasping them and putting them to his mouth he started to eat them, grinding them with his molars into an unpalatable paste and swallowing this barely acceptable food. This would have provided him with little nourishment since the grains would have been hard and very small but encouraged and curious, early man turned his attention to this strange food.

With the momentous inventions in farming from around 3500BC to 2000BC and the Scythes, Sickles, Hoes and Ploughs came ever increasing demands to grind the grain, the earliest ideas being based on pounding and then rubbing (pounder rubbers) the grain to produce rudimentary flour (meal). This led to improvements over thousands of years varying in output and efficiency but none the less steady progress from Mortars to the Saddlestone-Metates. The Saddle stone would feed a family of eight if used constantly throughout the day.

By this time, perhaps 1000BC, cultivation of the early barleys and rye led to a less nomadic lifestyle resulting in people putting down roots, creating small gatherings in the form of villages. Breadwheats appeared, einkhorn and emmer producing better quality flour and the almost magical yeast transformed the eating habits of most of the world of that period. Keeping up with farming became ever more difficult for the millers, the Egyptians leading the way because of their Alluvial ground, organisational skills and slaves. The grinding of grain became more businesslike, stones increased in size and more efficient types and styles meant that one man could produce more than enough food to feed his family, which led to bartering and trade. Slab and Push mills led to tabletop Lever mills eventually leading to the monumental Greek Hourglass mill.

The Hourglass mill used a true circular motion for the first time one stone placed upon another, the top stone revolving, grinding the grain between. From the Hourglass came the Delian (Possibly the other way around) the Quern and the Millstones used today.

There are some beautifully preserved Hourglass mills at Pompeii (albeit in horrendous circumstances). There are four in a row which were manned by slaves directly in front of the ovens for making the bread. It must have been horrible work in direct sunlight with the heat from the ovens too, although you appreciate the efficiency even today. The Romans fed their armies through the use of Hourglass and Querns being up to 12 times more effective

Cley Windmill, Norfolk

than Saddlestones and their bread was not too dissimilar to today's version although they often used to enhance their bread by the addition of Chalk. It made it whiter and a better texture. Woe betides the Miller who tries that today!

The Millstone, invented around 400BC, has changed little since, apart from being larger and more efficient but it's the driving force that has changed. Early on the stones were driven by Man, Horse (beasts of burden) and then the Watermill. The invention of the Watermill cannot be underestimated; it stands alongside the invention of the Hourglass as a huge step forward for the human race. George Long in his book The Mills of Man states: "The Water Mill was the Parent of Modern Industry". The earliest written reference to an English Watermill was in the Charter of Ethelberg of Kent dating from 762 with 5,624 Mills recorded in the Domesday book almost all of which were Watermills, but no Windmills.

At the height of milling in this country before Roller mills there were as many as 10.000 mills, as many as 4000 being Windmills. Today there are only 90 working Windmills in England with a possible further 140 ripe for preservation. The stones for all this milling effort came initially from local quarries but they were often of poor quality, left debris in the flour and wore away too quickly. Peak stones from the Derbyshire Peak district became popular especially for animal feeds but other materials were soon found. Cullin or Blue Lava stones from Cologne in Germany were one, but the best was the French Burr (Buhr) stones from the quarries around Paris (Ferte Sous Jouarre). Occasionally made from one piece of this freshwater Quartz but usually made up from a number of pieces shaped to fit together, cemented with plaster of Paris and held fast by the use of Iron bands around the circumference. These were imported at considerable expense (at one point the price of a new French Burr millstone was almost the same value as one of the smaller Post Mills).

The raising and lowering of the Runner Stone (Top stone) was critical. Called Tentering this was done by various levers and weights with manual adjustment the only option. Later automatic systems were used. A good flour relied upon the grain being ground not just with the correct gap between the stones but also required the right speed to keep the flour relatively cool, the dressing of the working faces of the stones to provide clean, sharp cutting and grinding edges and ventilation to prevent clogging and therefore ruination of the flour.

And so at last, might you say, to the English Windmill. There were many different types of windmills long before the invention of the English Windmill. These earlier types were very inefficient Persian, Italian and Chinese and were not improved in the same way as the English Windmill though I know not why. Indeed some of these are still in use today through necessity rather than design. The earliest written evidence of the English windmill was at Weedley near Skidby (Skidby is Yorkshire's only working windmill) in the parish of South Cave not far from Hull, dated probably around 1185 and costing 8 Shillings (40 pence) a year to rent. It would have been a Post mill so called because its whole structure

Holgate Windmill, York

was centred on a large Oak Post. English Oak selected from the best conditions properly seasoned can be enormously strong and hard, I myself had the occasion to come across such an Oak and attempted to hammer a 6 inch nail into it but to no avail, I only made a dent.

Sadly the initial designer of the Post mill is unknown. The purpose of the Post mill was to give shelter from the weather, storage and of course power to turn the stones. The first Post mills can be thought of as being a large wooden shed (Called a Buck) placed over an Oak trimmed to resemble a post with roots still intact and pivoting on it. Place your Sails on the front to provide the drive and there you have it if simply put. A long ladder from the ground to the Buck gave you access and a Tail Pole the ability to turn the Windmill into wind (by lifting up the ladder from the ground and physically hauling on the Tail Pole as at Wrawby Post mill in Lincolnshire). This was sometimes done by use of beasts of burden or geared and endless chains and eventually by Fantail.

Unfortunately the tree stumps would rot away and become unstable so the Millwrights raised the Post out of the ground and held it vertically by use of Quarterbars attached to Crosstrees laid on the ground (called an open Trestle). Essentially two beams of wood laid across each other on the floor and four pieces of wood fixed diagonally from the ends of the crosstrees to the Post in the middle. But this did not resolve the problem. The Crosstrees themselves would rot away too so the Millwrights raised the whole structure Buck, Sails, Stairs and Fantail on brick pillars from 3 to 12 feet high, an astonishing feat. Once raised in this way no weight would be carried by the post below the Quarterbars suspended by them in mid air, all the weight being taken through the Quarterbars and down through the pillars into the ground. The Millwrights were so confident of this design they did not even fasten the mill to the brick pillars, the mill just sat on them. The oldest working Post Mill in the country is Outwood (1665), Surrey and is Grade 1 listed.

There has been a recent disaster however (25th November 2003) with the newly renovated Chillenden Post mill being blown off the Pillars. It is hoped to rebuild it but the actual cause of the crash is not yet known. A brand new full sized Post mill is being built single-handedly at Pilson Green near South Walsham in Norfolk. It is of remarkable quality and is a tribute to the owner, designer and builder Millwright Richard Seago. It has a lovely aspect overlooking fields from a raised location. Ambitious and extraordinary.

The Dutch took the Post mill one step further in 1450 by taking a drive through the middle of the Post (called a Hollow Post mill) to a room below created by walling around the brick pillars called a Roundhouse. A good example of this is Wimbledon Common Windmill. This type of Mill never really caught on in England the English looking to revolve the Cap on a solid Tower. Nobody knows who invented the Tower Mill but Leonardo da Vinci sketched one in 1519. The tower mill provided more space and size for the Miller, better storage and safer

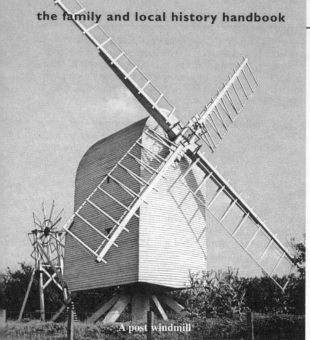

A post windmill

which turns the Cap through very low gearing on the Curb ring (an iron ring which sits on top of the Tower itself) so the sails face the wind. It was a wonderful invention but not taken up on the continent save for a few in Germany and Denmark. One wonders why.

Windmills had many champions often focusing on the sail design. Initially these were just canvas on a frame as at Burlesdon Windmill in Hampshire were improved by Captain Stephen Hoopers roller Reefing sails (just like roller blinds for windows) as fitted to Tollerton, Seaton Ross and Holgate Windmills to name a few in the past. The only working Windmill with this design is now Ballycopeland in Northern Ireland. It gave controllability if not reliability to the speed of the Sails., Andrew Meikle a Scottish Millwright invented the Spring sail, which opened and closed Shutters (just like Venetian blinds for windows) through the pressure on the spring. (The sail usually compartmented into eight bays, three shutters per bay). Finally William Cubit (later Sir), invented a progression of shuttered sails (Patent) by controlling the shutters through weights hanging on an endless chain counterbalancing the uneven pressure effect of the wind. The majority of working windmills today still use Patent sails. Numbers of sails on Windmills varies greatly from 2 to 8. There is an excellent 6 sailed at Heage in Derbyshire and the 8 sailed at Heckington in Lincolnshire is the only one of its type left working in England.

John Smeaton the well-known Engineer from Yorkshire and builder of Eddystone Lighthouse, turned his attention to Water and Wind power in 1759. His conclusions from various experiments had far reaching effects. He advised the weather (twist) of the sails to be 18 degrees at the centre and 7 degrees at the tip. He invented the five-sailed Windmill, which is the most efficient for catching the Wind. His introduction of Ironwork, the Ogee cap, and Sailbacks are just a few of his ideas turned into reality at Holgate Windmill York.

Putting the brakes on the sails was quite hazardous at times as the brake was attached to the Windshaft (Axle to the Sails) and enormous. Some Brakewheels were ten feet across and more. These Brakewheels were made from wood and around the wheel was a brake band also made of wood (sometimes metal), which created a lot friction when coming together. Many a Windmill has been burnt to the ground by the brakewheel catching fire during the Miller's desperate attempt to slow the sails in high winds. These are powerful machines and once out of control the end can come very quickly indeed.

And so we come to one particular Windmill close to my heart and home, Holgate Windmill in York. As Vice chair of the HWPS (Holgate Windmill Preservation Society) it is incumbent upon me to spread the word.

In 1770 George Waud - owner, builder and miller built a fine Lincolnshire style Windmill in Holdgate (Holgate). He must have been influenced by the esteemed Engineer and local lad John Smeaton born at Austhorpe Lodge in the Parish of Whitkirk (where he is buried) near Leeds. He incorporated a lot of his

working conditions. As they grew bigger and therefore higher they captured more wind and so generated more power. Sometimes this power was taken out of the Windmill as in the case of Colton Windmill near Leeds to an adjacent building to power other pairs of stones.

The first Tower mills were Smock (Frock) mills made almost entirely of wood usually 8, 10 or 12 sided, often with a brick base and sometimes with a square brick base as with Willesborough Smockmill in Kent. Frieston Smockmill in Lincolnshire was found to have had millstones as foundations under each of the Cants (corner posts) after it had burnt down. Tower mills superseded the Post mills throughout England although there are instances of Post mills surviving the Tower mills built to replace them. Tower mills were built from a variety of materials but usually Stone or Brick. Some were massive, High mill at South down Great Yarmouth in Norfolk had Sails 100 feet in diameter the usual size being 60 feet or thereabouts. The mill itself was 120 feet high and had a ground floor diameter of 40 feet. It has gone regretfully the way of many a mill, demolition. The largest Windmill in England is Moulton in Lincolnshire nearing completion after restoration 99 feet tall and 10 stories.

A tower mill has a rotating Cap, which carries the weight of the Sails, the Cap itself and the Fantail (the largest cap in England, 23 feet across is on Old Buckenham Windmill in Norfolk. It is big enough to party in and the views are stunning). The Fantail invented in 1745 by Edmund lee was an innovation to the English Miller with our contrary wind conditions as it always ensured that the sails faced into the wind. One of the greatest fears of any Miller is that of the sails being back winded (the wind blowing onto the backs of the sails. It usually ends in disaster or at least an expensive repair). The fantail is fitted diagonally opposed to the sails so whenever the wind blows on one side or the other it turns the Vanes

View from the top of Holgate Windmill, York
before the expansion of housing

new ideas into the Mill; five Sails, Sailbacks, Ironwork and Ogee shaped Cap as previously mentioned. This was heady stuff at the time, very progressive and forward looking.

Shortly after the Windmill's construction the Enclosure Act (1774) brought an end to the Manorial Rights and Holdgate was divided up amongst the residents and others. George was allotted 3 roods and 8 perches (0.35 hectares) of land on which stood the Mill. This is the Windmill which stands today on a "commanding eminence within a mile of the City of York" as an advertisement describes the site in 1855 when the Windmill was auctioned at, appropriately, The Windmill Inn, Blossom Street, York. Mr Waud his son and grandson ran the New Mill from the time it was built until 1851 when John Thackray took over and stayed for four years. Other Millers who followed (with the dates of their occupancy) were: Messrs. G. & J. Chapman (1855-1859); William Bean (1859-1867); Joseph Chapman and his son, Charles (1867-1902); Herbert Warters (1902-1924) and Thomas Mollett (1924-1933).

The mill today is denuded of sails and fantail, hemmed in on all sides by housing and sits forlornly on a roundabout.

I would like to pay tribute to the late David Lodge. His determination to preserve Holgate Windmill over many years has made the eventual restoration possible.

Unfortunately there is insufficient space to fully reflect all aspects of Windmills here. There are many omissions but If you wish to know more please contact the SPAB or buy their "Mills Open" 2004 book which has information on nearly 450 Mills of various types! Alternatively seek out Rex Wailes book "The English Windmill" or Stanley Freeses book "Windmills and Millwrighting". These are but two of many with many books dedicated to specific Counties.

"Imagine if you can, listening to the rhythmic rumble of apple wood teeth on to iron gears, to the sails shush by the windows, to the stones singing. Feeling the mill harassed by storms or seeing a glorious sunrise surprise the sails, smell the warm freshly ground flour and touch of ancient wood in your hand.

Windmills, like the old sailing ships are the living archives of English spirit and endeavour."

For further information about windmills contact:
SPAB Mills Section: 37 Spital Square London E1 6 DY.
Tel: 020 7456 0909 Fax: 020 7247 5296 Email: millsinfo@spab.org.uk
Holgate Windmill Preservation Society, York, England – HWPS : Brian Lambert, 2 Murray Street, York YO24 4JA Tel: 01904 799295 Email: lambert49@ntlworld.com Web site: www.holgatewindmill.org

Richie Green, the author, is one of Twins born to a nomadic lifestyle in 1952 in Hampshire. Graduated from the RAF after 22 years and happily married with two fine adult children and three miniature Dachshunds.

The National Archives
John Wood
Public Services Development Team

the national archives

The National Archives (commonly shortened to TNA) came into being in 2003 when the Public Record Office joined together with the Historical Manuscripts Commission. The National Archives, together with its sister organisation, The Family Records Centre is the prime resource for all interested in genealogy as well as local, national or international history. TNA attracts nearly 200000 visitors from around the world annually to its impressive facilities at Kew near Richmond in Surrey. TNA has one of the largest archival collections in the world, spanning 1000 years of British history from Domesday book onwards and all together has over 8.5 m documents available to all.

The TNA truly has something for everyone interested in family history. The gateway to the TNA is its website at www.nationalarchives.gov.uk (see separate section on online TNA) The website portal allows you to plan your visit in advance, search our online catalogue before your visit, order documents in advance, arrange for copies of documents to be made and also pre register for a reader' ticket. One of the popular features of the website is that it allows you to download an extensive range of research guides covering nearly 200 topics of interest to genealogists and historians. These replicate the guides available in the reading rooms at TNA.

A few good reasons
Why all those interested in family history should visit TNA...over 3 million records of soldiers up to the end World War 1, over a million merchant seamen's records, ships passenger lists, naturalisation records, railway staff records, over a million royal navy service records, RAF (RFC) WRAF, WRENS, Royal Marines, Tithe and Valuation plus over 2 million more maps, divorce, change of name, court records, transportation to the colonies, manorial documents register..........the list of sources available is endless.

Onsite Facilities
The modern Reception area is located within the main entrance to TNA. The ground floor houses:
An extensive modern bookshop
The free Museum featuring the treasures of TNA
Comprehensive restaurant facilities
Free cyber café
Free cloakroom and locker facilities

When you arrive
Admission to TNA is free and, other than for coach

parties and large groups, no advance booking is required. Researchers need to obtain a readers ticket at Reception to gain admission to the reading rooms. Registering to be a reader couldn't be easier, simply turn up during opening hours with proof of identity and register online. The whole process takes only a few minutes. Suitable means of identification for British visitors are a driving licence, passport, cheque card or credit card. If you have come from abroad then bring your national identity card, driving licence or your passport. If you are still at school or college, aged 14 or over, please bring a letter on headed notepaper, signed by your teacher or tutor, together with some evidence of your age (for example a birth certificate).

There are rules on what you can and cannot take into the reading rooms. For instance, coats and any bags have to be left in the free cloakroom and lockers, pencils only are to be used, and only a notebook, notepad or transparent wallet can be taken into the reading rooms (or you can use a portable pc in designated areas of the reading rooms). Full details can be found at www.nationalarchives.gov.uk/visit/whattobring.htm or our contact centre/ information line (see below) can help.

What you can do in the reading rooms
The newly refurbished first floor reading room facilities incorporate an information kiosk, specialist records advice desks and an extensive library and resource centre with browsery area. The main document reading room takes up a large part of the first floor, this is the point where documents that you order are delivered to your own reading room locker. It also has an excellent record copying centre so that you can make a permanent copy of that important family history document. You can also use your own digital camera to take photographs of some documents, subject to conditions.

The most popular records, including a large number of military service records have been made available in the self-service Microfilm Reading Room on the first floor where again there are extensive copying facilities.

Located on the 2nd floor is the Map and Large Document Reading Room On the 2nd floor. This is where documents too large to be produced elsewhere and where documents prior to 1688 are produced – not forgetting the millions of maps held at TNA.

Throughout the reading rooms are pc terminals where you can browse our catalogue as well as order documents and track your orders and staff are always on hand to give you expert knowledge as to how best pursue your research

Opening hours
We are open 6 days a week throughout the year except

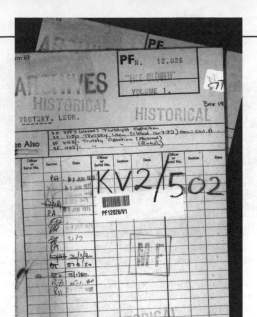

Secret Service file on Leon Trotsky
TNA KV2/502
©The National Archives

bank and public holiday weekends and the annual stocktaking week - usually in late November or early December. Up to date details of opening times and closure dates are on the website or can be checked with us direct via our contact centre/information line. It is always advisable to call us before visiting for the latest information on opening times, records availability, travel conditions and events.

Please allow plenty of time for your visit to find, order, read and copy your documents. The latest time you can place an order is 16:15 except on Tuesdays and Thursdays when it is 16:45. Please also note that on Saturdays document ordering is suspended between 12:00 and 13:30 and ends at 15:15.

Coach parties and groups
Coach parties are welcome to visit TNA. As space is limited for coaches all parties must be pre-booked. Bookings are taken up to 18 months in advance. All coach parties receive a dedicated orientation tour for newcomers in their party and are provided with an advance reader ticket registration service. To enquire about available dates and reserve your coach group booking telephone the coach party booking number or use the email facility listed below. NB: there is no access to the site for coaches that have not pre - booked.

Behind the scenes tours
TNA now offers visitors the chance to see 'behind the scenes' every Saturday that we are open. Our free behind the scenes tours provide a terrific opportunity to see the inner workings of Britain's most important archive and will give you a thorough introduction to the collection and workings of TNA. On the tours you can see and touch some of Britain's most significant historical documents, learn how government documents are selected for preservation and why some are not! As well as visiting our bomb proof, climate controlled storage facilities with over 100 miles of shelving. These immensely popular tours can only be booked in advance, you do so by calling the contact center/information line below, or via our website

Transport and Access
TNA is 200 yards level walk from Kew Gardens station, served by the District underground line and the Silverlink Metro rail service. Kew Bridge station is half a mile away. Local bus services run nearby. Road access to the motorway system is good. Free parking is available on site. There are easy access facilities for those with disabilities, including a lift to all floors.

Essential contacts and information
The National Archives, Kew, Richmond, Surrey TW9 4DU W: www.nationalarchives.gov.uk T: 020 8392 5200 F: 020 8392 5286 E: enquiry@nationalarchives.gov.uk Coach party bookings: 020 8392 5393 E: coaches@nationalarchives.gov.uk Events: 020 8392 5202 Publications or Bookshop enquiries: 020 8392 5271

Naval Ancestors?
©The National Archives

Blood's Thicker Than Water
~ The Search for a Family
Joan Dexter

Snape Castle, North Yorkshire.

Do you own a dog? Did your parents own a dog? Did your grandparents? Great-grandparents? Great-great-grandparents? Great-great-great-grandparents…? By now I suspect I can hear you muttering something along the lines of, "Stupid questions! How on earth can I know that far back in time?" Exactly! It isn't that they had or didn't have a dog, but that with each succeeding generation it becomes more difficult to *know*. Now for my punch-line: *I know* that my 10 x great-grandparents (that's right, 10 x, it's not a typing error), had a dog! How do I know? If you haven't already guessed, I'll let you into the secret: by researching my family history, of course!

In 1612, my paternal 10 x great-grandfather Francis Dinsdale was summoned before the manor court of Snape, his neighbour alleging that Francis' dog had killed her pig. The jury didn't believe her, perhaps realising that she may have brought the case in a fit of pique, they remembering that at the previous court, one of her relations had been accused of robbing Francis of the door to his calf pen. Was the case tit for tat?

Snape, in the parish of Well, is situated in what we now term North Yorkshire, but which not all that long ago was known as the North Riding, this being one of the three Ridings, from the old word meaning 'third'. It lies in the picturesque Vale of Mowbray, three miles west of the present A1 and three miles south of the market town of Bedale. The word 'Snape' means 'the mires or bog land', but the large lake or morass lying to the east of the village which my ancestors knew as 'The Mires' or 'Snape Water', was drained by means of ditches early in the 19th century and is now cultivated. Today, Snape is a pretty and well-kept village, centred upon a long and narrow village green which is split in two by the small stream known as Snape Beck. Another of my 10 x great-fathers, Thomas Crawe (say that aloud—don't you love the local dialect for Crow?) was fined at the Michaelmas manor court of 1613 because his wife had polluted the villagers' water supply. The actual wording is 'his wife washinge of Cloose within thee Yeads of the Towne becke', (washing of clothes within three yards of the Towne beck). The fine was 3s 4d which was quite steep, but she had ignored one of the jury's pains, and fines for breaching pains tended to be high.

Still commanding the western approach to the village stands Snape's main feature: Snape Castle, known in Francis' time as Snape Hall. A large and castellated building, formerly belonging to and occupied by the Latimers, a well-known, wealthy northern family, its greatest claim to fame lies in the fact that it was at one time the home of a future Queen of England. John Neville, third Lord Latimer, had married as his third wife, Katherine Parr, a distant cousin and also a Neville, and at the time of their marriage in 1533, a childless widow aged only 19. After Lord Latimer's death ten years later, even though her principal home was in London, Katherine must once in a while still have lived at Snape. At the time of the discovery of my family's connection with the village as tenants of these former owners of the castle, whilst part of the building was in ruins, a large part of the fabric was still inhabited. Although not open to the public, my parents, my husband and I were lucky enough to be shown around, even allowed out onto a part of the leaden roof to admire the graffiti of Tudor times, consisting of outlines of shoes scratched in the lead, with initials inside. Upstairs was a small room still known as 'Katherine's sewing room', complete with a beautiful stone Tudor fireplace. Local legend had it that King Henry VIII was a frequent visitor to Snape, and that from this window Katherine watched across the fields for his arrival to court her. No doubt the villagers watched, too, among them Francis' father Henry Dinsdale, my 11 x great-grandfather, a young man most likely in his middle teens. Our guide told us of the Castle's resident ghost, a young girl dressed in a blue Tudor-style dress, which had been seen by several witnesses including her daughter. She was at great pains to stress that it wasn't at all a frightening experience. Was she, I wondered, the spirit of Katherine Latimer, whose own days at Snape were perhaps amongst the happiest of her life?

Of course, I knew nothing of any of this on that day in 1960 when my late father and I made our first tentative move towards what was rapidly to become an all-consuming passion and take over our lives. We had never heard of Snape. But we *had* heard of the place Dinsdale, two of them in fact, on the banks of the River Tees. Surely the family's origins must lie there? We could see from a map that Low Dinsdale was in County Durham, whereas Over Dinsdale was across the river in Yorkshire. My father treated himself to an old second-hand book about the North Riding, published in 1859, and found that the two were connected by a cast iron bridge built on the stone piers of the wooden bridge erected twenty years earlier. Low Dinsdale appeared to be a parish in its own right, whereas Over Dinsdale, despite being in Yorkshire, appeared to be in the parish of Sockburn in County Durham. This was all a bit confusing, but we were greatly optimistic that we could sort it all out!

**The church of St John the Baptist
Low Dinsdale, County Durham**

Unlike today when tracing ancestors is such an up-and-coming hobby, with a plethora of books, magazines, courses, Family History Societies, television programmes and the Internet to get you started; in those far-off days there was very little. Eventually my father joined the Society of Genealogists which enabled him to borrow printed Parish Registers by post, but in the beginning we had nothing and nobody to rely upon except ourselves. There was no doubt in our minds, however, as to our initial step, and so one fine day that August my parents and I set off happily from our home in Nottinghamshire, northwards along what was in those days known as The Great North Road, on our first expedition to explore our roots, sublimely confident that if we combed the area we should somehow find a mine of information.

How naïve we were! We found Dinsdale church, but the interior was something of a disappointment, containing many monuments to the Surtees family with not a mention of a Dinsdale. Nevertheless, we took a photograph of the exterior of the church, and another of me posing on the railway platform beside the huge signboard bearing my name. We even hurried off to Newcastle-upon-Tyne to look at the Parish Registers for Sockburn and Dinsdale, only to find that from 1588–1812 the surname of Dinsdale wasn't mentioned once. Feeling not a little foolish to have drawn a blank, it began to dawn upon us that in our rush to chase our dream we had perhaps let our hearts rule our heads. Maybe a less emotional and more systematic and scholarly approach was needed? But it had been a pleasant family day's outing with the prospect of many more to come. All was not lost, for one thing was certain: this was only a minor set-back. *There would be a next time.*

Back home, we did what we should have done in the first place! With no known relatives bearing the name apart from his elderly widowed mother, who could tell him next to nothing, my father got out the motley

collection of 'treasures' inherited from his grandmother Lucy, who had died when he was 19 and who had had such an influence upon his boyhood. The old lady had outlived her husband and all their five children. I couldn't imagine anything worse. My father being her sole grandchild (daddy's father had died when daddy was seven), it was little wonder she had doted upon him and that various bits and bobs of her mementoes had found their way to him after her death. To this day I continue to be amazed at how she could safeguard these throughout her countless moves from one rented room to another. I have twenty different addresses for her in a period of eighteen years. Amongst the assortment Lucy had left was her mourning ring, a pitiful few photographs and a collection of Japanese odds and ends which my father knew was connected to his Uncle Herbert who had lived and worked in Japan. The biggest prize of them all was a scrap of paper measuring less than 4? x 7? inches, the top half being covered in her spidery, difficult to decipher hand. We eventually managed to make it out to be a list of the names, ages and dates of death of her loved ones, although it didn't strike us at the time that my grandfather Arthur's name was missing. It would be many years before we knew that the little boy George was known as 'our dear little Georgie' and not aged six but in his sixth year, that Lucy Winifred was Winifred Lucy, and that although Ethel was commemorated on the paper and on the headstone of the family grave, her ashes were interred at St. Albans. For the moment, none of that mattered. *We had the means to begin our search.*

From Lucy's scrap of paper, it was easy to calculate an approximate date of birth for her beloved husband Joseph, who was my great-grandfather. I was completely ignorant as to how to set about obtaining copies of birth, marriage and death certificates, yet somehow my father knew how to apply to the General Register Office at London's Somerset House. So off we sent, blithely confident in the knowledge that Joseph's death had been caused by a fall down the stairs during which he had broken his neck. After all, my father's mother had said so, hadn't she? When the replies arrived, we excitedly tore open the envelope and stared in horror and shock and disbelief. Surely there was some mistake? 'Suicide by Shooting Himself with a Revolver. Temporary Insanity.' That was our first lesson learned: you can't *always* believe family stories.

Joseph's birth certificate told us that he was born on 9 September 1842 at half past eight p.m., giving an address in north London, the son of Kay Dinsdale and Ann née Walker. Kay! My great-great-grandfather. What an unusual Christian name! His occupation was 'sadler' (sic). My father remembered Lucy's words to him had been, "The Dinsdales were saddlers, saddlers of repute, saddlers to royalty." Second lesson learned: you can *sometimes* believe family stories.

In anticipation that Joseph and Kay may have been members of the Worshipful Company of Saddlers, we wrote to the Clerk at their London address in Gutter Lane off Cheapside. Mr. Ralph Medley was so pleased to hear of our interests and couldn't have been more helpful. We realised that we were very lucky in that not only had both Joseph and Kay been members of the Company, but it looked on the face of it as if Mr. Medley's first reply might take us back another generation—to George, my great-great-great-grandfather. There was as yet no proof, but the inference was present. George had risen through the ranks of the Company to become Master in 1837.

Letters winged back and forth. Although most of the Company's records had been lost in that terrible night of 29/30 December 1940 when the Luftwaffe blasted much of the City of London and destroyed the old Saddlers' Hall, enough survived to begin to put flesh on the bones of a number of members of our family. Most intriguing of all was Mr. Medley's letter telling of an official report of some proceedings in the House of Lords which had fortuitously only just come to light. It appeared that in 1849 there had occurred a vacancy on the Court of the Saddlers' Company, the Court of Assistants being the governing body from which the Master and Wardens were elected. Kay Dinsdale was the senior qualified person for the post, but before election, the then Clerk asked him as a matter of routine, if he was or ever had been bankrupt, or if he could pay any debts he had in full. Kay replied that he was "as solvent as any member of the Court and could pay 20 shillings in the pound", (meaning he had no debts). Duly elected, he took his seat, attending two meetings. Two months later, he became bankrupt and paid 2s 8d (13.3p in current money) in the pound. The Saddlers' Company then dismissed him from the Court on the grounds that he must have given false answers to the questions put to him before nomination for election. Kay commenced proceedings, but it took eight years before the Court of Queen's Bench ruled, in 1860, that he was entitled to a writ of mandamus ordering the Company to reinstate him. Not surprisingly, the Company appealed, the Exchequer Chamber reversing the decision the following year. Not prepared to accept this judgment, Kay appealed in his turn, and eventually, fourteen years after the start of the Lawsuit, *Kay Dinsdale won his case in the House of Lords*. We were later to learn from an official at the Chamberlain's Court, Guildhall, that *"Kay Dinsdale is still very much remembered in the City. His lawsuit made history."*

The Worshipful Company of Saddlers must have been considerably out of pocket through the protracted litigation, but Christmas provided the ideal opportunity to bury the hatchet, with the result that the following summer we accepted the kind invitation to visit Saddlers' Hall. We received a warm welcome, Mr. Medley showing us round and permitting us to take a photograph of George Dinsdale's name on the list of Masters. (By that point, our research of London parish registers had divulged proof that he was indeed Kay's father.) It made us feel quite proud of the family connection as we basked in reflected glory.

By now, my mother's spring-cleaning had brought to light another document of immense importance, the will of the Uncle Herbert my father had never known: 'The last Will and Testament of Joseph Herbert Dinsdale of number 25 Nishi Kusabuka-cho, Shidzuoka, Japan, Bachelor', dated 10 April 1922. Herbert began by expressing the desire that his body be cremated and his ashes thrown into the sea. (We

Silouette of
George Dinsdale in 1828 aged 50
by Hervé of 172 Oxford Street, London.
George became Master of the Worshipful
Company of Saddlers in 1837

were in due course to learn the reason: that in countries prone to earthquakes, it isn't a pretty sight when the earth literally gives up its dead.) Although the name of one executor conveyed nothing, the unusual surname of the other matched that on one of the pile of postcards saved by Lucy. Of the legatees, one was clearly Japanese and one a Doctor with a foreign name, neither Japanese nor English. There was my father's mother, his grandmother and his aunt, but it was the others which drew our closest attention. Herbert had done us proud! He didn't just name names, but in most instances included relationships. Four were named as 'cousins' and three of these were Dinsdales. Manna from Heaven! There was 'my cousin Felix Amyas Dinsdale', 'my cousin Doris Muriel Dinsdale' and 'my cousin Geo. Kenneth Dinsdale'. What about 'my cousin Phillis Winifred de Courcy'? Could she be a married cousin? If these folk were Herbert's cousins, they were Arthur's cousins too. Taking this a stage further, they must be my father's first cousins once removed. *No relations?* Suddenly it seemed as if he did have Dinsdale relations, after all. Of course, there was a snag that we hardly dared think about. Forty years had elapsed. There had been a war in between. Would they still be alive? How were we to track them down? We resolved to work out how we could profit from our find.

Despite Dinsdale being a predominantly Yorkshire name, the addresses we had for Joseph, Kay and George were all in north London. Nottingham's main Post Office had telephone directories for the entire country, and from them we extracted the names and addresses of all the Dinsdales in the southern counties, precisely twenty-seven. Composing a letter asking if the names on our list meant anything to them, we posted them off to eagerly await results. About three quarters replied, most showing great interest and writing with details of their immediate

Marriage Register entry at St Gregory, Bedale of the flaxdresser George Dinsdale with Elizabeth Kay

Genealogists, eventually becoming a Fellow. He's now in his 97th year and we still correspond.) Mr. Rolfe knew, whereas we in our ignorance didn't, that in order to pursue a trade in the City of London, my 3 x great-grandfather George needed to become a Freeman of the City, and apart from paying the fee of 46s 8d, he had had to answer the question, "Who's your father?". His reply of *"George Dinsdale of Bedale, Yorkshire, flaxdresser",* took us back another generation, making that awkward cross-country jump to the North Riding of Yorkshire, to Lower Wensleydale.

The next major step was up to us, to find the whereabouts of Bedale's parish registers and trawl them for evidence of our more remote ancestors. It turned out to be a Herculean task. Ascertaining that no copies had been made, we finally discovered that the registers were still kept in Bedale church, locked away in the safe. But the safe key had been lost, the rector was ill in hospital and nothing could be done until he was well… Time dragged, although we put it to good use by corresponding with our new-found relatives and searching for our first family graves.

Easter 1962 heralded a day we would never forget. My parents, my then boy-friend (since husband) and myself were invited to the rectory for afternoon tea, my boy-friend being memorably referred to by the rector as "Miss Dinsdale's appendage!". Somehow or other, the safe was opened, and excitement knew no bounds when the registers as last revealed George the flaxdresser's marriage by licence on 26 December 1775 to Elizabeth *Kay.* On this, the first of a number of visits, we extracted about 50 Dinsdale entries of baptism, marriage and burial, making an attempt at home to link them together and finding about five separate families as well as 'odd bods' as my father termed them. Elizabeth had died leaving her parents to bring up her brood of children (one of many examples of blood being thicker than water, and thus my choice of title), whilst flaxdresser George disappeared from the scene. Had he gone elsewhere to search for work? We had solved one problem only to be confronted with another!

My father had the idea of laying a map on his desk and inserting a compass point upon the town of Bedale and drawing ever increasing circles. We would approach the incumbents of the parishes within the smallest circle first and seek their permission (easier said than done, we were to discover), to search their Parish Registers for George. So began a hunt through countless parish registers both within and without Wensleydale. The co-operation of the clergy wasn't always forthcoming. In fact, it was the attitude of those clergy which was to prove the biggest single help and the biggest single hindrance to us in achieving our objective. We crossed swords with

and not so-immediate family. We loved the letter which told of the two sayings from the head of Wensleydale: 'There are more Dinsdales in Hawes than fleas on a dog', and 'If you want to bury a Smith in Hawes, you have to dig up two Dinsdales to do it.' But it was letter number twenty-six which hit the jackpot! It had landed on the mat of a Mr. T. Dinsdale who lived in Berkshire. His full name turned out to be Mr. Timothy *Kay* Dinsdale, whose late father had been Felix Amyas. Tim was famous, having appeared on the BBC programme 'Panorama'—which we had missed, being so busy planning our assault upon the world of genealogy. An aeronautical engineer by profession, Tim had become interested in tales of the 'something' in Scotland's Loch Ness, and gone to see for himself. On the first of what was to be fifty-six private expeditions to the loch, he had actually seen the Loch Ness Monster and shot forty feet of film. Even now, 'The Dinsdale Film' as it became known, is still the most compelling evidence for the existence of Nessie.

Tim, his wife and four children lived near Reading, and eldest was Simon *Kay* Dinsdale. That Kay name was certainly proving useful though we still had no idea why it kept cropping up so frequently. Tim and Wendy extended an invitation to visit them for what proved to be a magical afternoon, with my father in his element having found his long-lost relations. Before we made our farewells, Tim gave us the telephone number of his Aunt Doris. Having married after the date of Herbert's will and so no longer bearing the name Dinsdale, she, of course, had not received one of our letters. We met Doris and her sister Phillis, were given the address of their brother in Canada, and embarked upon strong friendships which persist to this day with those who are still alive—and with the descendants of some of those who have passed on.

By now it was becoming increasingly clear that there was a limit as to how much more advancement we could make from home, when the records we needed to consult were only available in London. Soon after this we were given another lucky break with the name of a man who described himself as a semi-pro researcher, in reality an actor who was willing to help us when his television, film and theatrical work permitted. Left to our own devices, progress had been at snail's pace compared to what could be achieved with his aid. (Shortly afterwards, he became a fully fledged professional working for the Society of

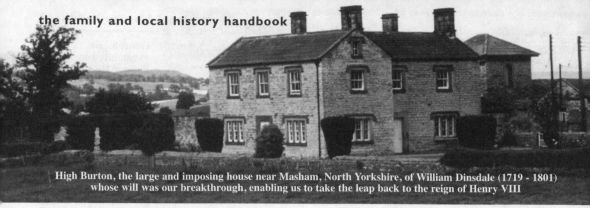

High Burton, the large and imposing house near Masham, North Yorkshire, of William Dinsdale (1719 - 1801) whose will was our breakthrough, enabling us to take the leap back to the reign of Henry VIII

many. It had never been our aim to alienate them, however hostile and rude some may have been. Yet others went out of their way to be friendly and helpful, even on occasions to the point of returning half the statutory fee if our search proved negative. In the mid 1970s we even began corresponding with one Yorkshire vicar surnamed Dinsdale who was chasing his forebears as keenly as we were. Memories ranged the whole gamut from a warming cuppa in a cosy study and a lift in a warm Riley to an outlying chapelry, to a freezing and draughty church—and worse—my husband and I once suffered the shock of being marooned without warning in a vestry whilst a funeral service was conducted in the body of the church!

By the beginning of 1964, much of the North Riding had been combed for the baptism and burial of George the flaxdresser. During the course of that year, we amassed a pile of probate documents, including one of a George Dinsdale at Leeds. A burial there only three weeks later under the name George *Tinsdale* looked on the face of it as if he could be our missing George Dinsdale. But how to prove it?

One parish adjacent to Bedale had been missed in our Parish Register search, Burneston's incumbent having slammed the vicarage door in our faces. The law entitled us to see his registers providing sufficient reason was given, and a polite letter to the Archdeacon of the Diocese might have done the trick, but this seemed a drastic move and one to which we never had recourse. We relied instead upon the more readily available Bishop's Transcripts, although it took a very long time to track them to earth, finally comparing them with the registers only after the death of Burneston's awkward incumbent. George the flaxdresser was notable by his absence but a scattering of other Dinsdales was present. How could we tell if these other folk were 'ours'?

With the emergence of another will that elusive proof did eventually fall into our laps. God bless Uncle William! Childless, yet well-to-do, his will was a dream, and all of a sudden the pile of wills, inventories and administrations, the gleanings from parish registers and the pedigrees we had tentatively made out, not only slotted together to make one proven whole, but joined forces with the later generations carefully garnered from London and Japan. Prior to Bedale, the family *had lived* in the parish of Burneston. All these years later, George's baptism still hasn't surfaced, but even without it the pedigree was water-tight back to 1690.

That didn't satisfy my father! He would turn back to his circles on the map. Were there at Leeds any probate documents for Dinsdale within the larger circle beyond Burneston? There were? At Snape… Henry 1586, Francis 1626, Robert 1667—and in our city library was a book listing wills proved in London at the time of the Protectorate, among them Henry of Snape 1655.

Snape's vicar turned out to be an enormously trusting and charitable soul, and our gratitude to him knew no bounds when he actually lent us his registers for a week. My father took them to the Nottingham archivist and together they looked at the earlier entries under ultra-violet light. *The generosity of the Revd. Mr. Lewin inked another four generations to the top of our family tree.*

To achieve his original aim of 'a Fifteen hundred and anything date' at the top of that tree had taken my father six years. Could he stop there? Of course not! He - and I - were well and truly 'hooked'. He had a fascinating collateral branch to begin to research, and after my father's death in 1984 I found another—and yet another. Having grown up with 'no relations' he would be amazed at the number of distant cousins on my Christmas list, some of them firm friends whilst others remain acquaintances. One newly-found fifth cousin wrote to me recently to say that he hadn't many relatives. My only reply could be, "Oh yes, you have, my address book's full of them!" I've found two more eighth cousins in recent months to add to the total. How? By visiting a cemetery in Worcester, and jamming polythene-wrapped notes down the sides of flower containers on what I knew to be family graves, notes giving the date of my visit, my name including maiden name, my address and phone number, and the information that I am a seventh cousin once removed of the man named on the headstone. Curiosity soon gets the better of whoever comes to tend their father's grave!

It is now over four decades since I began researching my paternal line through nearly five centuries, and the minutiae of wide-ranging detail uncovered never ceases to make me catch my breath. In such an article as this I can only give a brief snapshot. It ranges from the inventory of 1586 listing everything my smallholder Henry owned at his death, to the last letter written by my great-grandfather before he shot himself. I only wish I could have been a fly on the wall at ten o'clock on Saturday 3 July 1852 at my great-great-grandfather's summons to the Royal

The peacock quill harness for Her Majesty Queen Victoria

Mews in Pimlico to meet Her Majesty Queen Victoria and Prince Albert, but I do know what they said to one another as I have the documentation from the Public Record Office at Kew (now re-named The National Archives). I have been privileged to hold in my hands the harness Kay was making for his Queen. Now on display in the Mews, it is exquisite. Kay himself described it as "The most splendid ever seen", and who I am to argue with that? Even the gentleman at the Mews who was in charge of the harness at our visit in 1991 had great admiration for it, saying of the workmanship, "Look how many stitches there are to the inch." The leather was black patent and the metal pure silver. Peacocks' quills, for which I only recently found Kay's advertisement in 'The Times' newspaper, were originally white and have mellowed with the passage of the years into a creamy colour. The design of roses, thistles, leeks and shamrocks, together with the entwined cipher of V and R for Victoria Regina was Kay's own, but he had brought over three 'Austrian' workmen specially to do the embroidery. My only regret was that we hadn't been able to prove his granny Dinsdale's story of 'Saddlers to royalty' until after my father's death. It was some crumb of comfort that before she died, my mother at least had known that we had the proof, but such an eternal pity that the letter from the Royal Archives at Windsor Castle telling me the harness still existed and was on public view, had been dated the day after her funeral.

Truth really is stranger than fiction. I have the evidence so many times over. Would you expect a young girl of 22 to marry an elderly widower of 68, even if he did come from a wealthy, titled and armigerous family, and even if he was a Deputy Lieutenant of Berkshire and Oxfordshire? Would you expect to find the headline in a Canadian newspaper, 'Local Doctor Charged with Manslaughter'? (My collateral ancestor wasn't the doctor but the corpse.) Would you expect to find an ancestor marrying two women, one after the other, both bearing the same name? Would you expect to find ancestors in the Fleet Prison… the Queen's Prison… bankrupt not once but twice during a lifetime… in court charged with robbery… in court for non-payment of rent… in court for libel…? I have to say that *it's much more fun* when the ancestors were naughty! In that respect,

Snape's manor court rolls gave me a wealth of information as to minor misdemeanours and disputes within the community, very often the sole insight into the lives of females apart from the bare records of their names. My 10 x great-grandmother Frances (wife of Francis who owned the dog which didn't kill the pig), was accused in 1596 of breaking down the neighbours' 'sepes', which were their hedges or fences (sepes has both meanings so it isn't known which the clerk meant), and her husband was amerced 4d on her behalf. This is the kind of offence which poor people often committed, most usually in the winter-time, firewood being of such value for cooking and heating. The widowed Margaret, my 8 x great-grandmother, at regular October intervals from 1679 to 1682, was fined for the very ancient and common offence of not scouring her watercourse, presumably causing problems of flooding for her neighbours.

My hobby has transformed my life, taken me to some far-reaching destinations in time and place as well as some unusual places where the general public cannot go, and I've met some fascinating people along the way. I haven't finished yet, of course, and never will. That's the beauty of it. I never know what may lie around the corner ready to creep out of the woodwork and catch me unawares. Long may it continue.

Joan's book 'Blood's Thicker Than Water'—on the one hand a 300 page account of a family with its trials and tribulations throughout nearly five centuries, whilst on the other, an account of the search for these ancestors as well as present-day living relatives—is available from her:
Mrs J. Dexter, Maplebeck House, Maplebeck, Newark, Notts, NG22 0BS, price £12. 80 incl p&p

Showing their Mettle
... Industries of the West Midlands
Doreen Hopwood

extent of 8,000, buttons 150,000,000 … copper or bronze coins 6,000,000 … cut nails 500,000,000, gold and silver jewellery about £20,000 worth, wire and steel 4,500 miles long …"

The demand for labour brought migrants from both far and near. Initially many came from Staffordshire, Worcestershire and rural Warwickshire, but by the time that the 1851 census was taken, there were migrants from all over the world. Birmingham had never been a corporate or guild town, so there was no apprenticeship system to restrict the mobility of labour or prevent the establishment of new trades. In many other towns, local guilds operated to protect the market from usurpers and to subsidise the religious life of the town. An ordinance of Walsall, dated 1502, ordered that only men born or apprenticed in the town could practise their trade there. They were also obliged to pay an annual sum of 6s. 8d. to maintain the chapel of St Katherine and the light of St Anne in the parish church. It ends with the warning that "… if any man work contrary to this ordinance, the warden shall ask him to leave."

Birmingham could not have reached its eminent position without the ingenuity and flexibility of its workforce, and this is reflected in an old saying "Give a Birmingham man a guinea and a copper kettle and he'll make you a hundred pounds worth of jewellery!". Many of the patents taken out between 1750 and 1800 were by Birmingham inventors, and when Robert Rawlinson reported to the General Board of Health in 1849 he observed "There are about 520 distinctly classified manufacturers, traders or dealers and about 20 separate professions in Birmingham and each trade may certainly be divided into 5 branches which will give 2600 varieties of occupation".

Even a cursory glance through directories covering the West Midlands for the 1860s shows the sheer scope of goods being manufactured in the area. It was partly because of the number of diverse occupations that Birmingham's workers were deemed to have a reasonable standard of living. An enquiry in 1842 noted "… it rarely happens that all members of the same family work at the same trade so that if one trade is in a depressed state another may be in a thriving condition". Their nail-making contemporaries in the Black Country were not so fortunate, as a report of the same year stated "… the filthiness of the ground, the half-ragged, half-naked, unwashed persons at work and the smoke, ashes, water and clouds of dust are really dreadful".

Once described as "… not a place to promise much", Birmingham grew from a small village (hardly worth a mention in the Domesday Book) to become "the workshop of the world" by the mid-nineteenth century. Although it is well situated in the middle of England, it has no natural resources to speak of, is not located on any major river crossing, is a long distance from any port and is not an ancient religious or administrative centre. Birmingham made its mark through trade and manufacture. Its proximity to the Black Country, the source of many of the raw materials which Birmingham's workers transformed into finished goods meant that a lasting interdependence grew between the two areas.

In 1762, Matthew Boulton opened his Soho Manufactory on Handsworth Heath, on the outskirts of Birmingham, where he produced items known as "toys". These were not children's playthings, but trinkets and household goods made of metal, and included buckles, sword hilts, snuff boxes and inkstands. The scope and variety of such items made in Birmingham lead Edmund Burke to call it *"The Workshop of the World"* in 1777. Soho house was also the meeting place of the Lunar Society (so called because it convened on the Monday closest to the full moon so that members could travel safely on the moonlit lanes). It was made up of leading industrialists and intellectuals of the day including Josiah Wedgwood, Erasmus Darwin (grandfather of Charles) and Joseph Priestley. In 1774 Mathew Boulton formed a partnership with James Watt whose steam engine revolutionised the production of goods.

Writing in 1538, John Leland had observed the numbers of smiths and 'naylors', and in 1888 'The Guide to the Industrial Resources of The Midland Metropolis' stated that "… upwards of 20,000,000 pens are sent out every week … Guns are made to the

As the industrial revolution gathered pace, the towns and villages of the Black Country found themselves in a unique position, having all the necessary ingredients for the industrial age under and around them. Coal became a commodity in itself, rather than as charcoal to smelt iron, and steam replaced water power to fuel the huge boilers and furnaces. The transport revolution eased distribution and opened up new markets, whilst a combination of bad harvests and enclosures coincided with industrial opportunities, bringing country dwellers into the towns.

The first canal to be cut was from Birmingham through Smethwick, Oldbury and Tipton to Bilston and Wolverhampton, and the first loads were carried on 6th November 1769. It had an immediate effect on prices – within a week the cost of a ton of coal had nearly halved. By the beginning of the 18th century foundries, rolling mills, metal works and every kind of industry requiring heavy raw materials were established along the sides of the canal. 'Fly' boats competed with stagecoaches to transport passengers, and the building of the railway network not only provided better distribution of goods, but also employment as the manufacture of rolling stock became another industry in the area.

Although the majority of industries involved coal, limestone, glass or metal, each town and village had their own specialism. Generally speaking, the factory system was late in reaching the area, and many continued on a domestic basis until the late 19th century. This was partly because the tools and equipment needed were minimal, and some of the tasks could be performed by women and children. The fiercely independent nature of the workers was also part of the reason, as they did not want to be tied to a strict factory discipline. The observance of 'St Monday' (and sometimes Tuesday too!) was still commonplace, so the workers would remain absent from work on these days, and then cram a weeks labour into the remaining three days and nights. This could not be tolerated in the factories where the temporary loss of a key worker would hold up the whole production process. Instead, there was a form of contracting known as the 'butty' system, whereby a person would obtain a contract from a factory owner to produce a certain quantity of output for a fixed sum, to be paid on completion of the work.

He (or she) was known as a butty, overhand, charter-

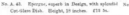

No. A. 43.   Epergne, superb in Design, with splendid   No. 44.   Flower Stand, rich in Design, with most beautiful
Cut-Glass Dish. Height, 18 inches. £12 5s.   Cut Glass. Height, 20 inches. £7.

master or piece-master, depending on the trade, and would then engage, supervise and pay the sub-workers he contracted There may have been as few as two or three in a chain shop, but could involve larger numbers in other trades.

Walsall has a long standing connection with saddlery, and, in 1540, John Leland noted that in "Waullesall, a little town in Staffordshire there be many lorimers and bytte makers … pittes of se cole and pyttes of lyme". Sketchley's 1767 directory of Walsall listed numerous branches of the saddle trade, including chapemakers, snuffermakers, spurriers and bridle cutters.

Wednesfield became a major centre for the manufacture of animal traps for export all over the world. These ranged from domestic vermin catchers to huge snares for the fur trade in Canada. Sidebottams' factory used an early form of assembly line to produce traps of all kinds, and these were packed at the side of the canal and sent by barge to the main ports.

Willenhall is famous for lock making – from tiny padlocks to those for prison gates, and, until it became mechanised, lock-makers spent long hours stooped over their workbenches, which caused disfiguration of the spine. This was so common in the town that it earned it the name of 'Umpshire'

Initially, chain-making was of the light variety, but, as the 19th century progressed, the demand for heavy chains, chain cables and anchors increased. Despite its distance from the coast, the Black Country became the national centre for the production of anchors and lighthouses. The cables for the world's largest ships were produced by Noah Hingley and Sons at

Casting a large roll

was between 210ºF and 220ºF, but that the workers were only exposed to this heat for 30 to 40 seconds, whereupon they immediately returned to a temperature of about 80ºF.

Birmingham saw its heyday of flint glass production in the 1840s when its glassmakers were producing beautifully cut items, such as scent bottles, table decorations and luxury goods. A twenty-feet high glass fountain was made as the centrepiece of the Great Exhibition by Oslers who became one of the country's finest crystal chandelier makers.

Nails and chain-making were two industries organised on the domestic system, and the hand-wrought nail trade was established in the area in the 16th century in several locations, whilst chain-making was a more localised trade. The baptism register of West Bromwich Parish Church for the period 1653 to 1659 has 212 entries, and of these 122 were children of nailers. In 1776, Arthur Young described the road for five or six miles through West Bromwich as "… one continued village of nailers". A few years later, it was estimated that there were between 35 and 45,000 nailers on the Staffordshire/Worcestershire border, and that half of Tipton's male population followed this trade. In order to survive competition from mechanisation in the cut-nail trade, nail making split into specialised branches in the 1830s, and continued as a home-based, family enterprise.

Many nail and chain makers had their own small forge attached to their homes. In an edition of *The Leisure Hour* in 1853, these were described as consisting of "… generally a small and dirty shanty about ten feet by twelve feet, ventilated only through the doorway and lighted by one or two unglazed apertures". Iron was usually supplied by the nailmaster, and the cost of materials was deducted from the price for paid for the completed nails when they were weighed in. Large nailmasters owned several warehouses across the region, and could have a thousand workers on his books. Some nailmasters also provided nailshops, which could be rented, or, on a smaller scale, a nailer could rent a standing from a fellow worker. The industry declined rapidly in the last part of the 19th century, with only 1,057 nailmakers listed in 1901 census – there had been 9,016 in 1861.

Where an industry declined, West Midlands manufacturers were quick to adapt or embrace a new challenge. As the demand for gun barrels declined after the Napoleonic Wars, the surplus were converted into gas tubes, and Wednesbury became the main

BIRMINGHAM MANUFACTORIES.

1. Messrs. Osler—Glass Works.
2. Messrs. D. F. Tayler & Co.—Pin and Wire Works.
3. Messrs. Elkington—Electro-plate Works.
4. Messrs. Perry & Co.—Steel Pen Works.

Netherton – including those for the *Titanic*. A team of twelve horses was needed to pull the flat wagon on which the anchor was loaded. Glass-making had long been established at Brierley Hill and Stourbridge, but the Spon Lane manufactory of Chance Brothers at Smethwick was the home of the Lighthouse Works, supplying all kinds of lantern for the coastal and shipping industry across the world. The huge sheets of plate glass for the Crystal Palace, for the Great Exhibition of 1851, were also produced by Chance Brothers, and much of the ironwork was manufactured in the region.

"The Report of the Sanitary Condition of the Labouring Population of Great Britain" was published in 1842, and its compilation had involved interviews with numerous employers and employees. At Chance Brothers, it was noted that at the place where the glass was removed from the furnace, the temperature

Birmingham Old Shipworks

centre of tube production earning the name of 'Tube Town'. Coach-iron manufacturers turned to making railway rolling stock as rail replaced horse power, and, as heavy industries and mining declined in the 20th century, lighter engineering has taken its place. In Birmingham, the demise of the buckle-making industry saw the emergence of button-making, which became one of the town's main industries until the late 19th century. Machinery was adapted to meet the demands of the trade, and, by 1850, buttons made of ivory, wood, glass, horn, pearl, and all kinds of metal were being produced.

When inspectors visited John Elliott's Button Manufactory on Regent Street in Birmingham on 6th January 1851, they noted "This is a well-ordered and conducted manufactory. The premises are large, spacious and generally airy. Some of the newer parts are fine rooms, particularly well-lighted and ventilated. The privies are quite separate. Very creditable attention is paid by Mr Elliott to the good conduct of his working people".

Demand for houses, as well as industrial buildings, continued to grow, and clay was just as prolific as coal and iron beneath the Black Country. High quality blue bricks were being produced at the rate of about 10,000 per week in the 1860s where much of the workforce was female. Brick-making was organised on the butty system where young girls (known a pages) would work for 10 to 12 hours a day for a shilling, carrying lumps of clay weighing about 25lbs.

Not all goods produced were industrial, Enamel work, japanned and papier maché ware were produced in large quantities, but one of the more unusual items was the Jews Harp. This was a primitive musical instrument made of brass or iron, which gave off a varying pitch when twanged against the teeth. At its zenith in the 1870s, John Barnsley's Netherton factory was producing nearly all of these instruments in the world, leading Horace Wapole to comment "Maryland was bought from the Indian with a quantity of vermillion and a parcel of Jews Harps".

Henry Clay took out a patent for papier maché in 1772, and, just eight years later, he was advertising articles such as tables, cabinets, coaches, chaises, sedans and snuff-boxes made of this material. Decoration was in the style of Japanese art, and became known as 'japanned ware'.

The growth in literacy rates in the early nineteenth century brought about a huge demand for pens, and the manufacture of steel pen nibs became an important Birmingham Trade. Several processes were required in their manufacture, and Birmingham's close association and history of metal-working helped to establish the pen trade as there was a ready supply of skilled workers and nimble-figured machine operators. The decline in the use of the 'dip-pen' saw the demise of the industry, but again, adaptability came to the fore and Birmingham's pen makers turned to the production of military materials.

The area which now makes up the West Midlands was known as the "Hardware District" in the mid-nineteenth century. This is hardly surprising, given the amount of metal being produced, refined and transformed into manufactured goods of all shapes and sizes. Gun-making had been important to Birmingham's economy since before the American War of Independence and in peacetime, production shifted to guns for sporting activities. Iron, brass and steel have always been used in the manufacture of heavy goods but also for ornate items such as door-knobs and letterbox covers for the home and church statues. Precious metals such as gold and silver were fashioned into intricate jewellery, and Birmingham still has a thriving Jewellery Quarter.

If your ancestor lived and worked the "Hardware District" he probably helped to manufacture one of the many items which earned it the name of *"Workshop of the World"*. More information about the Industrial Revolution and occupations of the area can be found at www.revolutionaryplayers.org.uk

LOCAL BLACK COUNTRY TRADES c1870

Town/Village	Trade and Industries
Bilston	Iron, coal, metal casting, japanned and hollow-ware, screw, chain, weighing machine, boiler, wire
Brierley Hill	Glass, coal, ironstone, clay, rolling mill, boiler, firebrick, agricultural tool
Cradley/Cradley Heath	Coal, fireclay, chain, nut and bolt
Darlaston	Gun lock, nut and bolt
Dudley	Iron, coal, stone quarrying, lime and coke burning, glass, fender and fire iron, tube, anchor, chain, brewing, brick, tile, wrought-nail, anvil, vice
Hales Owen	Wrought-nail, edge tool
Lye	Firebrick and retort, chains, anvil, vice
Netherton	Coal, iron, agricultural implements, nail, anchor, chain, brewing
Oldbury	Chemical, rolling stock, coal, iron
Rowley Regis	Coal, iron, nail, chain, brick making, quarrying, agricultural equipment, Jews harps
Sedgeley	Coal, iron, lime, nail, rivet, chain, fire-irons, lock, safe
Smethwick	Iron, glass, chemical, screw, nut and bolt
Stourbridge	Iron, flint and crown glass, fire brick, retort, edge tools
Tipton	Iron, coal, chain, wrought-nail, heavy engineering
Walsall	Coal, iron, clay, saddlers ironmongery, saddle, harness, whip, brush, key, lock, corn, glue, chemical, agricultural manure
Wednesbury	Iron, coal, tube-iron, gun lock
Wednesfield	Animal trap, key, lock, file, rasp, hinge
West Bromwich	Iron, coal, hollow-ware, spring, constructional engineering
Willenhall	Door lock, padlock, bolt, latch, currycomb varnish, brass and iron foundries
Wolverhampton	Coal, tinplate, japanned and papier mache ware, cut nail, iron tube, edge tool

Crime and Punishment in the 18ᵗʰ Century
Barry Redfern

We do not know how the quantity of crime in this country compares between our time and the 18ᵗʰ century. No comparable statistics were kept. But look at the records of that century, the newspapers, the broadsheets, the Hue and Cry, the warnings and pronouncements by justices and judges, and it is only too clear there was fear of crime. It was a period of history when the land was plagued with beggars and vagabonds. There were stark reminders of crime and punishment in every county and major town in the form of a gallows. This was a time when people believed that taking a piece of wood from a gibbet and rubbing it against a sore gum would ease the pain of toothache, and touching the hand of a newly hanged criminal to a diseased part of the body would bring about a cure. Travellers routinely carried firearms for protection and as they reached the crossroads outside the towns and villages they may pass the grave of a poor demented suicide buried in unhallowed ground with a wooden stake through his heart, as was the custom of the time. Conditions for prisoners were wretched and what we would see as harsh and cruel punishments were the norm.

Everyone in the community was required to band together under the leadership of the parish constable to deal with crimes. The constables should not be compared with the Peelers of the 19ᵗʰ century and the modern policeman. The official was an unpaid parish appointment, with no training for his task and had many other responsibilities apart from chasing criminals. Cities and large towns often paid for additional resources such as night watches or the Sergeants at Mace of Newcastle upon Tyne. (Examples from records in the north east of England are quoted here but apply equally around the country.) How did such a system work in practice to deal with a serious crime? In the autumn of 1791 an old woman named Margaret Crozier was found strangled in her house and country shop in a remote part of Northumberland. The building, a former bastle, had been burgled in the night and cleared of valuables. The parish constable called to this dreadful crime was John Brown, a local farmer not a trained investigator, but fortunately a man with much common sense and determination. Brown prepared for an inquest at which the coroner ordered Brown to arrange a meeting of the elders of the parish *'to decide what should be done to find the murderers'* .The parish

structure for communities played a much more active role in many matters than the present day. The meeting was held in the parish church at Elsdon and chaired by the curate. A reward for information and the other costs of the investigation had to be met by the parish. A small group of gypsies had come under suspicion and the elders decided to send out four teams each led by a parish constable to find them. The team led by John Brown actually arrested the gypsies many miles south towards the River Tyne several days after the murder. Everyone involved were missing from his or her work during this time and, of course, Brown was absent from his farm.

The justice of the peace now became involved. He was, often as not, the local squire. In the example explored here Brown took his prisoners to the country mansion of the local magistrate who had the power to commit the suspects to prison. In the cities and large towns there were courts where the prisoners could be taken. But the 18ᵗʰ century country justice of the peace worked from his home and he had an active investigation role in the matters brought to him. He examined witnesses found by the parish constable, took sworn statements from them and also interrogated the prisoners. Such tasks are now done by the police and presented to the magistrates for scrutiny before trial. Brown's prisoners were then committed to the Northumberland County Gaol at Morpeth.

The King's Gaols, as they were known, served a different purpose to a modern prison. Each shire county and county borough entitled to a sitting of the Assize court had a gaol which held prisoners awaiting trial at the local Assizes and in some cases the Quarter Sessions and also prisoners sentenced to hanged or transported. It was very unusual for a sentence to be passed of imprisonment in the gaols. Detention for a short period was much more likely to be ordered in a house of correction. The other major category in the prison population were debtor prisoners and some of them spent a very long time in custody. We are indebted to the work of John Howard who, through his inspections, revealed the poor state of the British prisons and many unfair practices.

The gaolers were paid a salary by the county authorities, but that income was supplemented by fees charged to prisoners on arrival and discharge, and money from the sale of liquor to prisoners. There was also the problem of 'garnish', money demanded from a new prisoner by those already there. Lack of cash led to seizure and sale of clothes or other effects from the new prisoner to provide money for liquor. The fees created great hardship and discomfort for destitute prisoners. Sexes were usually segregated but otherwise the prisoners, tried or untried, regardless of age were mixed together with inevitable consequences for young people.

The damp and cold buildings, poor quality food, cramped and unhygienic conditions all contributed to the awful smell that was characteristic of prisons of the time and to the spread of disease. It was the practice at the Newcastle courts to scatter sweet fragrant herbs to deal with the smell the prisoners brought into the buildings.

The Judges of Assize travelling around groups of courts in the provinces known as circuits dealt with the trials of all serious crime cases usually carrying the death penalty. There were more than 200 capital crimes on the statute book by the end of the 18th century. The justices sitting at Quarter Sessions handled the other problems. The punishment strategy for crimes in the 18th century appears to have had several basic elements, death, banishment, labour, pain and public humiliation. Death by hanging in public was the ultimate in pain and humiliation. However, such events attracted huge crowds, heavy drinking and disorder. Pickpockets were active around the gallows despite such crimes carrying the death penalty. Public executions were not the solemn measured punishment of an individual and a dramatic warning to the criminal community at large that the authorities wished them to be. The execution was a crude strangulation process. The prisoner, with his arms fastened, was put on a ladder leaning against the gallows and resting on the ground or a cart. The noose was adjusted on him then the executioner turned the prisoner off the ladder. The condemned man was left hanging usually about one hour. The bodies of murderers were often passed to the surgeons for public dissection, which in itself was another example of public humiliation.

Banishment, that is to say, transportation to America and the West Indies and later to Australia was a highly developed enterprise in the 18th century. Thousands of prisoners experienced extreme discomfort on long sea voyages only to be sold into slave labour for seven, fourteen years or life. Death on the gallows was the penalty for returning without permission.

Work and pain went hand in hand with sentences to the house of correction where prisoners were confined and put to hard manual labour to try to turn rogues, vagabonds and miscreants away from crime to an industrious life. Sentences at northeast courts usually ranged from 2 weeks to 3 months. Some hours in the pillory or public or private whipping were often added to a sentence to a spell in the house of correction

The 18th century authorities believed in public humiliation and pain as a deterrent to criminal behaviour and they had several means at their disposal. Each sitting of the Quarter Sessions at Newcastle upon Tyne was invariably followed by the public whipping of offenders through the streets stripped to the waist, male or female, and tied to the back of a cart. The justices set the distance and route to be taken through the town. That occasionally lethal apparatus, the pillory, was a public fixture in most towns. The offender was fixed in it upright with hands and head held fast. He had no way of protecting himself against things thrown at him and if a direct hit brought about a faint, then strangulation could easily follow. The stocks was a more parochial punishment for drunks, dishonest tradesmen and the like, where the offender had a sporting chance of protecting himself against flying objects. Humiliating exposure for a few hours was the main objective. However, similar offenders ordered to the ducking stool had no chance of avoiding the indignity of a thorough soaking. The branks was still in use in the 18th century for women spreading malicious gossip and false tales. This open helmet of metal straps had a sharpened metal strip that fitted into the woman's mouth to keep her tongue still. She was then led about the town with the added humiliation of a written notice fastened to her clothing proclaiming her misconduct. The metal strip in her mouth was liable to cause severe pain and injury during this extraordinary parade about the town. Examples survive in museums around the country including Morpeth and Newcastle upon Tyne.

Pain and humiliation by branding and disfigurement had been a feature of punishments in earlier times and survived into the 18th century as a link to benefit of clergy. For centuries this ancient practice permitted a literate person to claim membership of the clergy and the right not to be punished by lay courts, it was known as *"pleading his clergy"*. A person found guilty say of a capital crime could avoid death by reciting the first verse of Psalm 51. *"Have mercy upon me, O God, according to Thy great loving kindness; according unto the multitude of Thy tender mercies, blot out my transgressions."* To prevent a prisoner claiming benefit of clergy a second time he was branded with a letter 'F' at the base of his left thumb and then released. Newspaper reports of the time usually reported the result of such trials as A.N.Other "Burnt in the hand" without further comment. The authorities slowly adjusted this unfair system in new legislation and benefit of clergy was phased out in 1827.

Crime records often reveal fascinating details of domestic life so what records survive and where are they? Assize records are stored at the Public Record Office (PRO) at Kew, London. There are helpful guidance leaflets published by the PRO and can be seen on the PRO website. The records include such things as the circuit books recording the outcome of trials. Many bundles of original sworn depositions for the trials are available to seen at the PRO reading rooms. Personal details and relationships emerge in these statements by the witnesses. The PRO also holds records relating to the transportation of convicts; their leaflets and website guidance is the best starting point for that research. However Assize records for the 18th century tend to be incomplete.

Quarter Sessions records for the 18th century are usually found in the form of sturdy bound registers containing a hand written record of all the proceedings at the sessions, at least four times each year and sometime more often by adjournment. The Quarter Sessions did not simply deal with those offences not tried at the Assizes. The justices were responsible for a host of other matters relating to the good government of the counties such as roads and bridges, taxes for various purposes, appointments to official posts and so on. As a result these records are a superb source of names and, because of the nature of the record, can often be related to a place. Each volume of the northeast examples has an index of names and other things, which are crying out for transcription for family history purposes! These records are held in county record offices; researchers will usually find that Q.S. records have been transferred to microfilm and are easily accessed and copied in that way. The earliest court records may be found to be in Latin and there is also the problem of 17th/18th century scripts, but here and there some transcription work has been done to aid researchers. A handy guide to old scripts will be found very useful in exploring these records.

Probably the best starting point for exploring crime and punishment for local or family history is to look at the collections of 18th century newspapers held in the principal libraries around the country. The dates for the sittings of the Assize courts once or twice a year in the provinces and the Quarter Sessions, at least four times a year are predictable within a week or two. Reports of the results of trials yield information about dates of crimes and the original reports of those crimes can then be found in the same source. The Hue and Cry columns began to appear in the newspapers about 1772/1773 at the instigation of Sir John Fielding and contained names of victims and suspects and accounts of crimes around the country. Also in the libraries and record offices are collections of broadsheets or broadsides, specially printed accounts of executions, which often include family history data on the victim and the condemned person.

The other major source which should never be neglected is that extraordinary 20th century invention the Internet or the World Wide Web. Typing a name or a topic into one of the search engines can produce a breath-taking number of sites to explore; try 'transportation of convicts' for example. Relevant lists of one kind or another, executions for example, are available and new ones appear almost daily. The Public Record Office and most of the County Record Offices have their own websites and slowly more and more transcripts or images of interesting 18th century papers are appearing. On the Bodleian Library website it is possible to access images of the Gentlemen's Magazine for the early part of the 1700's together with an index search facility. The huge range of 18th century material available on a website about "The Proceedings of the Old Bailey" is discussed elsewhere in this publication.

What happened to the gypsies, two sisters and a man, who robbed and murdered the old woman in Northumberland? They were all hanged outside the West Gate in the town walls of Newcastle upon Tyne in 1792. The bodies of the women were given to the surgeons, but the body of the man was put on a gibbet south of Elsdon and a replica gibbet can still be seen there today. Another man condemned to death at the same Assizes for sheep stealing agreed to be the hangman and was reprieved for transportation to Australia. Hard times indeed!

Barry Redfern is a retired Chief Superintendent of the Northumbria Police and the author of "The Shadow of the Gallows, Crime and Punishment on Tyneside in the 18th Century", Tyne Bridge Publishing, Newcastle upon Tyne, October 2003, www.tynebridgepublishing.co.uk

People of the Parish
Anne Batchelor

Anne with a parish regsiter St Mary's, Chesham

I once met a lady who told me, with great excitement, that her nephew had researched her family tree. "He's got all the way back – to before the time of Jesus Christ!", she said. I smiled wanly, trying to look impressed and, taking her statement with an enormous pinch of salt, I said, "Oh, that's nice!"

Those of us engaged in the fascinating process of researching our families know how impossible that is. Nevertheless, there is great joy to be had in uncovering our family's story over a few hundred years. When I was taught history at school in the 1940's and 1950's it concerned only kings, queens, noblemen and politicians. As family historians we now know that real history is the story of the ordinary people – the blacksmith, the cordwainer, the strawplaiter, the village schoolmaster, and the good old 'ag.lab'. It is the records of their humble lives which tell the true history of our country.

The written records
I was fortunate to begin my family research almost twenty years ago when only a few eccentric people were to be found in county record offices, scrabbling about among heaps of dusty papers. In those days, I had the delight of being able to research from original documents. What a thrill there was in being able to handle an original parish register from 1538 or an indenture signed by "my Daniel" in 1586. To touch what they had touched – it gave me goose pimples.

Now, of course, due to the increased popularity of Family History, the originals have to be protected and can only be seen on film or under very strict regulations involving cotton gloves and plastic sheets. I do understand why, but I have to admit that some of the magic is lost.

Records of the parish, in whatever form we see them, give us a wonderful window into the past. Who can resist the old parish registers of Chesham (Bucks), full of stories such as the burial of Hugh Ovyot in July 1591, who was *'slayne by a faule out of a cherry tree'*, or in March 1596, *'Robt. Rederidge al Smith, sonne of the widoe franklin, wch Robt. dyed by cutting of his legg above the knee not lyving one*

hower after.' An agricultural accident, perhaps – or maybe an amputation which went wrong?

In North Church (Hertfordshire) in the year 1610 they buried *'Mother Clyfford, born in the time of King Henry Vll, being 105 years old and more.'* I love the vague *'and more'*. She must have been quite a lady! So much for those who say, "Of course, people didn't live long in those days."

I am reminded of Cornelius Vandun, who died in 1577 and who is buried in the beautiful church of St.Margaret, Westminster. His fine monument tells how he had been Yeoman of the Guard and Usher to King Henry, Edward, Queen Mary and Queen Elizabeth. He built twenty houses for poor widows at his own expense and died at the ripe old age of 94 – a good age even by modern reckoning.

I wonder what stories of despair lie behind the numerous suicides recorded in the Chesham registers? In February 1599, 'Jeremy Stanbridg – most fearfully by hanging him selfe ended this p(rese)nt lyfe.' Poor Isbell, the wife of Thomas Bowler of Botley, in July 1600, '…being greate with childe most fearfully by drowning her selfe in a ponde ended this present lyfe.'

The registers can also reveal 'strays' – that is genealogical missing persons, such as in a burial register for July 1589, 'Moris Lewys of Kynges Langeley in the Count. Of hart(ford), pedlar, being slayne in a fraye by an other pedlar comying togeather to this towne on the fayer even was buried.' Perhaps someone is searching the Kings Langley registers in a vain attempt to locate Moris's burial when, all the time, he lies snug in the churchyard at Chesham.

The same register reveals a small tragedy in my ancestors' lives, too. Mary, wife of my Peter Batchelor, carried her baby safely for many months, only to have him baptised and buried on the day of his birth, 24th June 1632. Even across all those years, discoveries like that touch me deeply.

Here, too, we see the baptism of illegitimate children recorded as 'Bridget and Elizabeth, the daughters of adultery', and 'Edward, sonne of an harlot.' Poor little souls! Then in 1635 there is the burial of '2 murdered infants'. I wonder what sad story lies behind that stark entry?

In parish records we see the tragic results of the Poor Law which condemned the destitute poor to return to their home parish. So often they never reached home. 'August, 1579 – buried Margarite, a poor strang travailling wonan.' Their children, too, often died on the journey. '4 Feb 1597 – Jonh up Robert, soone of a poore woman travailling by the high waye'. The Drayton Beauchamp register, about the same time, records the burial of 'a travilling great bellyd woman'. Poor soul, she was probably being pushed on from parish to parish in spite of her condition – or rather, because of it. Each parish would move her on quickly, before she could give birth and become a liability to their community. Sadly, she never managed to reach her home parish and was buried without anyone even knowing her name. Only in the burial registers do we find such touching entries.

However, you might be lucky enough to find a detailed marriage entry full of information about your family, such as – 'William makerith of the middle Temple in the Cittie of London gentl(eman) late s(er)vant to myles Sandys of latymersh in the Count. Of Buck. Esquyer, and Elyzabeth daughter of Frances marsh of Luton in the Count. Of Bedford gentl(eman).'

Baptisms tend to be recorded more simply, giving the child's name, both parents (if you are lucky) and perhaps father's occupation. However, the children's names can give great delight – who can resist Onesipherus Hands (who later married Dulcibella Meles), Love Lee (a lovely child?), Marfity Snipt (who later served in the scullery of the Earl of Dorset), Rowland Rubbish (violinist to Queen Elizabeth I – did she ever tell him, "Your music is rubbish, Rubbish!", Firebrace Cremer of Swanbourne, dear old Happy Nappy Stork of East Yorkshire - (was he perhaps Harry Napoleon ?), and, my favourites, the children of Thomas Holroyd, manager of the Gas Works at Castleford, West Yorks. In 1881, names Zerah, Zeuriah, Zelha, Ziha, Zillah, and Zibiah. I wonder why, in this forest of Zs, he named his second son 'Joe?' Some doubt about paternity, perhaps? – was Mrs Holroyd too friendly with the milkman?

I just can't resist collecting odd names. Mustn't forget poor Gertie Giggle who died in her teens, and eight year old Anastasia Galilee, a little rag-sorter in a Yorkshire mill. Such names make my Johns, Williams, Elizas, and Edwards seem very mundane.

Parish Officials
How we groan every time we have to fill in yet another form for officialdom. I remember whenever my late mother was assessed for Income Support I had a twenty-seven page document to complete for her. However, family history has changed my outlook on the recording of personal information. I now bless the penpushers of long ago who meticulously recorded the minute details of my ancestors' lives.

Foremost among these, of course, are the vicars and the parish clerks. Thanks to them we know about our family's 'hatches, matches, and despatches'. Studying parish records over many years we become familiar with individual clerics. One of my favourites is John James, vicar of Rickmansworth, Herts., in the early eighteenth century. He

decided that the country was going to the dogs and that the answer was to give the children of the poor a good Christian education. (Perhaps that is what is needed in today's society?) He explains, in 1711, when he draws up a subscription list for a charity school at Rickmansworth -

"Whereas the prophaness and debauchery are greatly owing to a gross ignorance of the Xian religion among the Poorer sort, and whereas nothing is more likely to promote the practise of Xianity and vertue than an early and pious education of youth, and whereas many poore people are desirous of haveing their children taught but are not able to afford a Xian and useful education, we whose names are underwritten do hereby agree to pay yearly at four quarterly payments the several sums of money over against our names respectively subscribe for the setting up of a charity school in the parish of Rickmansworth for teaching poor children to read and instructing them in the knowledge and practice of the Xn religion as professed and taught in the Church of England and for learning such other things as are suitable to their condition and capacity. May 21.1711." In a grovelling letter to two rich gentleman of London, Mr Jennings and Mr Cook, he explains that the school has "twenty boys and ten girls being taught all things necessary by a Mr and Mrs". The master and mistress were my 9xgreat grandparents, Edward and Rachel, whose signatures I have as they sign receipts for their salaries in 1711 - £3.10s per quarter for teaching the boys, and a measly £2 per quarter for teaching the girls!

Old Rev. John James pestered for money for his school – "for catechisms, books and ink", and when rich gentlemen sent him some, he thanked them profusely, and "dared to beg some more!" I imagine he was a caring and popular vicar. After all, in 1719 he authorised that "every public ringing day there should be allowed 15s and no more for drinks for the ringers". That was a great deal of beer money by 1719's standards. I reckon they got right merry, thanks to the vicar. I imagine that at the end of a long ringing day, their bells played a very garbled tune!

Other members of the parish played their part in the smooth running of their community. In 1672 Daniel Batchelor was guardian and churchwarden of the church at Hawbridge (Bucks). Earlier in 1662 he had reported to the Episcopal visitation team, "that the windows of the church – are much broken and the church in decay but prayeth tyme to be allowed him

THE OLD CHURCH AT LEE

for the amending thereof." Poor Daniel was threatened with excommunication, but was absolved less than a month later when he managed to get together enough money to pay the fee of the visitation. I'm sure present church treasurers will understand his problem!

Many hundreds of years ago, the parish fulfilled its Christian duty to care for the poor by appointing overseers whose job it was to collect the poor rate from well-to-do parishioners and redistribute it to the needy poor. For example, in the parish rate book for St. Margaret, Westminster, in 1604 Thomas Cardell, luterist and dancing master to Queen Elizabeth, paid a poor rate of "vs.quarterlie".

Bless the good old penpushers, - the overseers kept detailed records of payments to the poor - a mine of information to the family historian and a wonderful glimpse of life in parish. For example, St.Mary's, North Church (Herts), at the end of the eighteenth century records –
"April 19, 1795 - Paid for a hat forBatchelor's boy.
Paid for cloathes and shoes for   –do–
Jan, 1801 – Paid John Batchelor, his wife ill."

The parish paid for 'victuals' for those who couldn't afford food, for medical treatment and for the burial of the dead. It was the overseer's account books held at the Hertfordshire Record Office, that I read the brief, sad story of Mary Putnam –
"Paid for Mary Putnam's lying in – Paid for nurse and medicine for Mary Putnam's baby – Paid for a shroud for Mary Putnam's baby – "

These stark entries tell such a sad story. I feel for Mary across two hundred years. Was she a widow, a deserted wife or a "fallen girl?". Thank goodness the overseers were there to give her the help she needed.

The Parish at War
It never ceases to amaze me how much detail of ordinary lives was recorded and has survived to the present day. In a publication of the Buckinghamshire Record Society, I was able to find my 12xgreat grandfather Robert with his brothers William, Thomas, Andrew and Richard, paying a total of £38 tax for the war with the French in 1524! Thomas the Younger, my 11xgreat grandfather was also listed there, paying £5. These were considerable amounts of money almost five hundred years ago, but the people of the parish had to be prepared to pay

for the security of their country.

In 1636 Charles I raised a Ship Money Tax and the records of Buckinghamshire show how those who couldn't (or wouldn't) pay had their goods seized instead. "Harridge – Richard Scott distrayned 1 Brasse Potte, a brasse kettle and Warmeinge panne – 13s 4d" Poor Henry Meade, at Princes Risborough, pleaded that he had nothing worth seizing – "He rents 2 yarde lands and a halfe for which he is Asseste – iis. He complaynes of beinge a verrye poor man greatlye in debte haveinge no stocke but 4 poore horses and 3 Beasts for which 2 of them he owes for, upon his complaynte he hade Teares in his eyes beinge an olde man of 60 yeares of Age he did keepe himselfe in his House 7 years for debt." Poor soul! I wonder whether they made him pay up?

Militia Lists and Muster Rolls for individual parishes, available (if they have survived) at their County Record Office, give a picture of the size and make-up of the parish (males only, of course) and even, in the early ones, which were the bowmen and which the owners of bills and armour. All wonderful material for the family historian. As a child, I was a great fan of the stories of Robin Hood, so I was thrilled to find that my earliest Buckinghamshire ancestors were bowmen!

Printed records of the Parish
The people of the parish in more recent times are often revealed in magazines and newspapers. Who can resist the article in the Berkhamsted Deanery magazine telling of 'Mrs Batchelor, the crushed mother, mourning the death of her young son, cut off in the prime of life.' By playing Miss Marple I eventually identified the poor young man as Walter and found the full story of his accident in the local newspaper. He was bringing a prize fat bullock home from Hemel Hemstead show, walking alongside the cattlecart and leading the horses when he stumbled and fell, the wheel of the cart passing over his head. The Deanery magazine said that the people of the parish were doing their best to support the mother in her grief.

Newspapers often give wonderful detail of happier parish events. When Herbert Jukes married Winnie Cowing in Barnet in 1899, the local press described the weather, who supplied the flowers for the church, what hymns were sung and what was worn -"The bride looked charming in a Liberty costume of white crepe de chine (trimmed with silk embroidery, chiffon and lace) and a tulle veil with natural orange blossom." – who performed the ceremony (two ministers), who witnessed the register (SEVEN friends and relations) and even a complete list of their wedding presents! That included – "Mr and Mrs Clapham – Dresden afternoon tea service; Mrs Jukes – Family Bible and silver teaspoons; Mr W Ashby – a tea cosy; and Mr Russell – a hall gong". Reading this I almost felt I had been present.

When it comes to deaths, too, newspapers provide rich pickings for the family historian. Accidental deaths are often reported with

In Loving Memory

A tender Mother she has been,
And many troubles she has seen,
While she lived she did his best,
And now in Jesus she is blest.
Farewell dear children my life is past,
I lived and loved you to the last,
Since I am gone do not forsake,
But love each other for my sake

'Thy Will be Done.'

4, Duke Street, Featherstone.

In   Affectionate   Remembrance   of
Annie Harrap,
(Beloved wife of Ernest Harrap.)
Who Died Nov. 27th. 1917.
Aged 28 years.

Interred at Featherstone Cemetery Dec. 1st

details of the inquest, evidence given and the verdict reached. Through the Hemel Hemstead Gazette I know that William Batchelor of Boxmoor was "a bit queer in the head", when he fell in the canal in the middle of the night and drowned, in 1900.

I know that Augustus Frederick Manley, fearless climber of the Matterhorn and Eiger, had a foolish habit of thudding the stock of his gun on the ground as he waited for birds. Not a good idea when your gun has an unusually light trigger! He who had survived a fall down an ice crevass on a Swiss mountain accidentally shot himself through the chin, blowing his brains out.

The local newspaper reported details of the accident, given at the inquest, and lists all the local gentry who turned up for the funeral of this unfortunate young man. He is buried at the parish church in Weeford (Staffs) where I was able to pay my respects and leave a small bunch of roses to show he is not forgotten.

So – in both written and printed records, we can discover the people of the parish. They become, to us, not just "the parishioners" or "the poor". They have names. They were real people like us. They shared our experiences of anxiety, distress and joy. These are 'our' people and our research of their lives involves not just our head but also our heart.
God bless the people of the parish - past and present - and the long forgotten pen pushers who have recorded them for us.
Anne's three books are still available from 34 Bancroft Heights
Leeds LS14 1HP
A Batchelor's Delight £9.10 inc p & p
My Gallant Hussar £4.25 inc p&p

Haigh Brewery
Glenys Shepherd

A few years ago I was staying at a country guest house at Haigh (pronounced hay), in a rural part of Wigan. Whilst I was there, the manager lent me a document to copy. It was a collection of memories of Haigh Brewery, by a real character J.F.Moore, who had worked at the brewery all his life until 1931. It was a fascinating collection of stories of rural life in Haigh from the 1840's until 1931.

It is difficult to imagine that a five storey brewery stood at the top of Haigh Road next to the Balcarres Arms public house. This was one of the oldest breweries in the Wigan area. It was owned by John Summers. Summers had owned at least nine pubs in the Wigan area since the early 1800's and three of these were now owned privately by the Rawcliffe family. These were The Crispin Arms at Birkett Bank, The Bay Horse, and The Stanley at Whelley. The Crispin Arms and the Queens at Newton are the only ones still standing today. The Balcarres was originally a tied house but it did not pass to Greenhalls with the others and is now owned by Burtonwood.

Imagine you are standing under a canal bridge. You are now in a cellar about 60 yards long. Under the premises you would find six of these cellars plus one under Haigh School. This was just a walled area; the ceiling was the school floor so imagine the racket of the children's clogs on this floor.
The heart of the cellars was under the offices. Mr Parr was the cellar man.
This was the place where the barrels of beer came up in the lift to go on the wagons and a doorway in this also led to the Balcarres cellar. In addition to all this area, there was a tunnel under the main road to a massive cellar which went under Summers Row – I have taken part in football games under there! The stonework and flagged floors of these cellars were real works of art. This was all catered for in gullies, the whole network being connected to a well in the brew house which was about 40 feet deep. The drainage went from this well over the fields behind Culraven to septic tanks. I think you will find these at the right side of the path from Haigh Road to Toddington. Still on the subject of water; all over the premises you would find taps in pairs – one for the town's water and one for the Lodge. The Lodge water was for swilling down and finishing off which kept down expenses. Legend says that the windmill at Haigh was for pumping water, but for many years a

huge tank stood 30 feet high above the ground which must have been 15 feet square and 8 feet deep. This was kept filled with water from the Lodge which lay in the fields behind the brewery.

Take a walk down Bolton Road on the opposite side of the moor from the pub called The Mount Pleasant. At one time behind the old houses there was a malt kiln: you may still find the foundations of this building. Here the malt was spread out on the floors and sprayed with water. Underfloor heating caused the grain to grow and which was then killed off with extra heating. Why this took place I would not know. This building which was four floors high was demolished in 1912 From this date the barley must have been bought in ready malted.

Fifty years ago, what is now the entrance to Crawford Avenue was the gateway into Rawcliffe sidings. Here you would see five or six sets of tracks extending to where Aspull market now stands. On these tracks coal from Meadow Pit number 5 and Moor Pits was brought down the line to Alexander Pit where it would be shunted on the main lines. They were also used for the transportation of lime, manifolds, drainpipes and bricks from Accrington for house building. Beer sugar from Liverpool, hops from Kent, and malt from Lincoln also arrived for the brewery.

All this activity required plenty of horsepower. In its heyday, the company kept 45 workhorses and 4 ponies. The purchase of horses was undertaken by Mr Rawcliffe who used to go to Wales to the choose the ones he fancied. Before making his choice the horse had to go on the weighbridge and if it did not show over 18 hundredweight Mr Rawcliffe was not interested. When you consider the distances these horses had to cover you will realise why they had to be tip-top animals. They had to be able to travel from the brewery to Chequerbent station, The Punch Bowl at Atherton, The Brittania at Byrn, The Sportsman at Leigh, The George Inn at Pemberton, The Alison Arms at Chorley, and The Jolly Crofters in George Lane, at Horwich. Then there was always the climb back up to Haigh. By the time the brewery closed there were 84 pubs and 124 clubs. I suppose a dozen or so of these horses would be kept busy around the district as there was always coal to be brought from two Lancashire collieries; coke from Blackrod Gas Works and materials which were required for repairs to the various premises.

Many of the pubs had one, two or even three houses attached to them. Anyone here could obtain mortar made on the spot by a steam-driven water mill. All those beautiful signs along the roofs of pubs as you went along were made in their own joiner's shop at the brewery.

One regular task was carting grain down to the Malt Kiln and bringing it back to the brewery. Casks of black treacle came from Wigan on the wagons of J. Hall & Co. Also they had good horses, they were 'blown' (sic) when they arrived at Haigh. These horses were not the gentle giants they appeared to be. I have seen them going up Haigh Road like devils possessed with a piece of lead in the harness, and the driver and dray left behind. One fatal accident I remember was the death of Mr Bob Owens' grandfather – Bob Johnson. Returning home, he would call at the shop opposite Our Lady's Church in Haigh Road. When he left the shop to return to the horse, there was an almighty clap of thunder which caused the animal to rear up and it came down on top of him, killing him instantly.

Moving on, if you stand in front of Fred Wood's house you may find the remains of a long stretch of buildings along the side wall of Haigh House. This was the site of the blacksmith's shop, the plumbers, the coopers, and the engineering shop. About 1920, an extension was made opposite these buildings for the bottling department as well as a new joiner's shop and a power house. Electricity was made by a diesel engine – the flywheel was 10 feet in diameter and it drove a generator. At the rear of these buildings was a converted 12 stall stable occupied by long benches on which stood glass accumulators, which held the current when the engine was not running. In addition to providing the power for the brewery, it also supplied power to Culraven High House, Haigh School, and the church. Near here was the wash house and covered yard for storage of the barrels. A large cast iron tank of 3000 gallons was heated by a steam pipe, and always kept at boiling point. After having a good scrub, a bent pipe was inserted to clean the inside, and finally, a second pipe of town water was used for the final

swilling. A doorway led into the drying room with two long rooms of stillage which took about 60 barrels. Along the centre of this was an iron pipe intersected with a joint about 3 inches high. The bung holes of the newly washed barrels were placed over these joints and an air pump blew cold air inside to sweeten them. Even after this treatment, and before they went down to the cellars, a gas jet was put through the hole and a quick glance in the bung hole would show if it was perfectly clean. In hot weather, you could stand with your trouser legs over the pipes to get a little cooler.

On completion of the next brewing, hops, treacle, and water were added, a cover screwed on and the steam turned on. It was like a giant pressure cooker with a safety valve. Occasionally, froth would escape and as it came through the ventilators, it would float down Haigh Road like large lumps of candyfloss.

The Vat room resembled one of H.M. Prisons. Steel railings were erected to allow passageways around and between each vat, with yards and yards of flexible piping complete with brass unions which were detachable to allow for cleaning.

I must now mention Rebecca Seddon, who, with bare feet, and skirt pinned around her knees, emptied the mash tun as soon as it was possible to stand on the grains because of the heat when they were emptied onto the floor.
In the wall alongside, there were two chutes through which the grains were shovelled into carts below. A cart load cost 7 shillings and 6 pence. Rebbeca carried out this task for 41 years. Because of the heat of the grains, her feet turned outwards.
There seemed to be no end to the cleaning and polishing of the copper as this was most important. The fire men kept a supply of very fine dust on hand and this was used on a damp cloth much as you would use scouring powder. Climbing down to the copper by ladder and scouring every inch of it must have taken much effort and a job which was encouraged by two or three pints of beer.

Every brewing left a surplus of yeast, which was placed into a cheese press, and every Friday this was pressed tightly into barrels – on top was placed a layer of hop sacking and then the hoop was hammered over. Being of a volatile nature, this had to go by passenger train from Ladies Lane railway station at Hindley. On Saturday it was taken along with empty malt sacks which went to Lincoln. The yeast was then sent to manufacturing chemists at Welwyn Garden City. The carter taking the barrels to the station had to take sixpence to pass through the tollgate at Hindley.

Here I must mention an incident which took place relating to the tollgate.

Haigh School

A regular travelling fair was finishing its stay at Aspull Moor and moving on to Hindley. The fair would travel to Hindley via New Springs, Schofield Lane, and Ince. On arrival at the tollgate, the usual fee would be requested which would be a considerable fee for all the engines, trailers, caravans and carts. The cost of the toll upset the travelling 'fair' people who refused to pay it. There was a dreadful argument and the whole outfit drove at, and over the tollgate, which reduced it to a huge bundle of firewood. I gather that from that day to this, no one ever paid any toll again.

Another place where you were expected to pay was to pass through the farmyard and over the Wigan to Blackburn railway line crossing to get to The Boatmans Arms near Arley at Blackrod.

Many people were employed in the trade at the time. There was a Mr Hampson who toured the properties with his pony. He had in his employ 2 joiners, 2 bricklayers, 1 plumber, 1 slater, and 4 apprentices. A Mr Fred Wood was the mechanic, a Mr Fred Bamber was the electrician; Mr Bert Burnett and Mr Luke Duffy were boilermen. Mr George Fenton and his son were coopers and there were 10 general labourers. I suppose that before the use of motor wagons, there must have been around 100 employees. In addition to those named, there would be 24 carter, 2 blacksmiths and 1 harness mender. For the horses, a huge amount of hay was required and provender had to be mixed. On top of this, all the horses on the road had to take along a nose bag for their dinners.

Back to the buildings. Along the rear of the premises was a cart shed and close by the mortar mill the ashes were tipped. If anyone wanted a load of ashes you could go a help yourself. Behind all of this was another block of stables, sheds with haymaking machinery, pig sties, a dutch barn and 40 acres of

land. The land is now attached to Whittle Tag Farm. The high chimney was on the East Gate until 1920 when a large bottling store was built leaving the chimney in the centre of the building. Among the women who worked there were, Bella Berry, Martha Seddon, Alice Leach, Mary Ashcroft and Jenny Hamson. Their boss was Peggy Ashfield. About three times a year we would take all the bottles which belonged to other breweries and collect our own as well as 2000 empty wine and whisky bottles.

Mr J L Moore when writing down his memories described what it was like to work in Haigh Brewery more than 50 years ago.

When I went to work there, Mr Scotson was in charge of the wine and spirit stores. He lived in Summers Row and as the office only opened at 9.00am he came to work at 7.30am to attend to the wagons. I took over from him, leaving him free to take up an appointment at the offices. Every morning I would call at his house to collect the keys. Agnes Bradshaw would be waiting for me as she cleaned the offices. On a desk I would find 4 sets of invoices for the loads for the morning wagons. The beer then required was sent up by the cellarman. I would then give them the wine and spirits and cigarettes which I had prepared the day before. Every barrel had its number burned on at both ends. A landlord could saw a barrel in half and sell the two halves for use as washing tubs and he would get ten shillings for each half. As the barrel numbers were written on our statements, if a barrel failed to return to the brewery we could charge the landlord for its non-return. The actual number of barrels in use was 5,500 of 36 gallons, 3,500 of 18 gallons, 2,500 of 9 gallons and 1,000 'Tommy Thumpers'. When you consider that each pub and club could be holding from 3 to 12 barrels, there were always quite a number on the road. In summertime, pubs such as The Sportsman at Leigh, and The Yarrow Bridge at Chorley would each take 20 barrels as well as 30 dozen boxes. These made a load for a 5 or 6 ton Leyland Wagon and we had four of these. Standish bleach works also had four of these wagons taking cloth to Manchester every day. All the wagons had solid tyres and all the roads were paved. Driving these was none too comfortable. Great use had to be made of the gears as there were no power brakes then – all we had was a foot and hand brake on the rear wheels. Extra care had to be taken in wet weather as they could skid easily in the tram lines.

In addition to delivering the beer, the wagons also had other work. At least 40 of the licensed premises where we delivered had bowling greens attached and one or two always seemed to be in need of refurbishment. Drainpipes, ashes and sand would be needed. In order to kill two birds with one stone, we would load a wagon with spent hops at M.Molyneux of Newburgh and then continue to Southport. As the esplanade at Southport was often covered with 5 or 6 feet of sand blown from the beach in the wind, the Corporation welcomed anyone who took this away!

After I had been at work about 2 years, a new model Leyland became available which had pneumatic tyres. This was a great improvement and it was also more powerful. Unfortunately, the drivers found themselves in trouble with the police as the speed limit was

Culraven House

Haigh Hall

only 30 miles per hour. My own brother, Tom, was booked twice and fined £2.00 at Wigan and £5.00 at Bolton. Commenting on the differences in fines, it was stated that Bolton had its new Town Hall to pay for.

At this time Fred Wood was the owner of a 7 H.P. Harley Davidson motor cycle. One day he managed to get a tram wire standard firmly wedged between the sidecar and the bike. He was very badly injured and spent several weeks in Bolton Royal Infirmary. This meant that we were several weeks without a driver so Joseph Donnelly of Church Street would let me take the wagon and he would go as 'second' man. I was only 16 years of age and Jo and I got on very well but Arthur Scotson was none too happy with this arrangement. As the weeks went by it was evident that Fred Wood would not be able to resume wagon driving and handling barrels. As there was no other driver around a man came from Thwaites Brewery at Blackburn. I went back to the spirit store to get stocks built up for Christmas. At this time the directors were Henry Molyneux, Tom Winrow, Gerald Seddon, and Tom Moore. We had Mr Hughes and Mr Platt who were travellers. Mr Platt was, at a later date connected with Wigan Rugby Club at Central Park. In the offices Mr Jolley was the secretary to Mr Lawson, Mr Arthur Scotsman, Mr Ainscough, and Mr J. Anderton. Miss Miller and Miss Hartley were the general clerks.

Our travelling salesmen, Mr Hughes and Mr Platt were now supplied with a Morris Cowley car each. Two vans were bought for the wine shop. One shop was in Pall Mall at Chorley and the other in Lee Lane, Horwich. Once per week an order came in from them for wines and cigarettes. The bottled beer was delivered by wagon. On one occasion Tom Quigley from the Horwich shop spent the afternoon in the van running round the field at the rear of the brewery before taking it home. There were no driving schools in those days so the other drivers taught the new ones how to drive. We also bought a 30cwt Morris Commercial van for general use. Every vehicle was sent down to Fairs at Wigan to be painted and lettered in gold leaf, extolling the virtues of Sumners' Beer.

One perk of the job was that everyone who was working around the yard could, if they wished, place a pint bottle on the shelf between 10.00am and 3.00pm by the incline leading to Mr Parr's cellar and it would be filled ready to be collected when required. The men in the cellars could, if they wished, have a drink at any time. The back door of The Balcarres was inside the yard by the entrance gate. Every morning, Doris Southern, the daughter of the landlady used to take a tray of tea into the office staff. The women at the bottling store could brew their own drinks. However, I preferred to slip across the yard to the brew house and fill a glass of malt extract. This was a good drink on a cold morning. Even visitors who came to the yard on business could go down to the cellar for a drink from every brewing.

Another by-product of the industry was re-use of the hop sacks. The empty sacks were not returned as some were made into pinafores or 'brats' as they were called to protect men's clothing against the wet and dirty barrels. Another use for the empty sacks was for making peg rugs. There was quite a demand for them around the village at two shillings each.

In the spirit store were other items including a collection of pottery and glass ash-trays for the travellers to give out as well as beer mats and – the real piece de resistance – a few of the old cast iron spittoons, usually filled with sawdust!

A small building stood next to the Balcarres and from it could be accessed one of our stores. Inside you would notice 4 large casks of approximately 4 feet in diameter and 5 feet in height with copper hoops and taps, the latter being bolted in for safety. You could also see casks of French and Spanish ports, pale and brown sherry, brandy, gin and cheap Australian wines. After close discussions with the Customs and Excise Officer we were allowed to wait whilst he verified the cheque and banking details. Arriving back, the rum and whisky was pumped into casks and the remainder placed on the stillage. The spirits were 100% proof and we had to reduce them to 70%. A Mr Burston who lived at Riley House was our inspector and could come any time. On Sundays he was a preacher at the local Methodist church but he could put the fear of God into me any day of the week.

At the beginning of every November I would begin to prepare for Christmas, filling every available space. Filling the bottles required careful scrutiny to ensure the bottles were not cracked and a quick sniff to make sure they had not been used for paraffin. Sitting on a 3 legged stool I would put a dozen at a time into a specially made basket. The bottles were corked and labelled by hand. All that remained was to cover the tops with the right colour of sealing wax - blue for port and yellow or brown for the light or dark sherry.

The hotels were expected to buy from us but we had no authority over the clubs: the cigarettes we sold came from Manchester. I was quite intrigued by the wagons which brought them to us. . They were carrier wagons and the roof of the drivers cab overhung the engine a little bit which was to protect the driver as they had no windscreen. The most popular cigarettes were Woodbine, Robin, Star and Park Drive. A 250 pack of Woodbines was 5/11 pence and a 200 pack 4/11 pence. You may notice I make no mention of matches as they would be too dangerous to stock in a spirit store. Twist tobacco was in good demand - thin brown for chewing down the mines and black for smoking at home. Messrs Lawton, Gibson and Hampson were allowed a bottle of whisky and a siphon of soda each week, for their callers I suppose.

When I took over charge of the stores, I was given two very important instructions. Firstly I must never go out of sight of the door unless the keys were in my pocket. The second concerned a bottle of sherry, a wine glass and a napkin on a tray. The tray I placed on the hall stand every day of the week including Sunday when an extra bottle was left. Every evening a visitor had a key to the gate and the office. His usual time was 10.00.a.m. and the watchman's dog got used to him at that time, but on one occasion he arrived at 1.00.a.m. in the morning and was promptly bitten by the dog. This resulted in the loss of an arm and a few weeks later he died. The man was Mr

Peck who lived at Culraven House.

In those days my friend. John Anderton, who was a clerk and general run around for the offices), and myself, had a private sideline. Into every spirit cask that was emptied I would pour three gills of water, plug up the hole where the tap had been and then roll it away to the Dutch barn where the casks were stored. Every few days I would take a trip down there and give the cask a little "up and under". After a few weeks we drained the contents, our reward being a most palatable drink. This grogging was actually an offence by law.

From1.00.p.m. in the afternoon Mr Platt and Mr Hughes came in to make their reports and to cash in. This was an opportunity for me to deliver a few local orders using one of the cars - communion wine for the vicarage, orders for the Haighlands Moat House, Haigh Hall and Mr Maurice Stone at The Curfew. The cars had to be in the garage overnight and Mr Platt and Mr Hughes had to catch the bus into Wigan. There weren't many motor cars at this time. In Wigan in the 1920's most cars were ex- army and they must have been brought over from France at the end of the war. There were also Buicks, Chryselers and Lancias. Mr Gibson had a small Citroen car, but he never mastered the art of driving it. Mr Hampson had his pony and trap and he was very proud of it. He used to say he could beat any wagon home from the pub. I agree with him on that statement as the pony ran like the devil possessed.

One of our pubs was The Crawford Arms at Red Rock. The landlord was Mr Tarbuck. Entering the bar at that tine one was confronted by a big frying pan hanging on the wall. On this were painted the numerals and fingers of a clock. Below on a plaque was painted the following:-

Often on holiday weekends some customers would run short of beer and come with a pony and trap for supplies which the night watchman would supply. On one occasion, two young men came along in style with a motor cycle and sidecar but when placing the cask into the sidecar it slipped from their grasp which resulted in the bike and sidecar parting company. The watchman sent a message to John and me in the pub where we were playing billiards. We left the pub, got a wagon out of the garage and saw the two men safely back to Poolstock.

In the winter time the postmen would call on us so that they could thaw out in the boiler shop, but in the summer they went down to the cellar to quench their thirsts. Jim Bibby from near St.Elizabeths worked the Aspull round and Walter Conch, then living in a cottage at the rear of the Conservative Club with Molly Hook, delivered around Haigh and Red Rock.

Around Christmas time we were entertained to a grand party at The Running Horses and as a Christmas box we received a cash bonus. However, no one should get the idea that we worked for a free and easy establishment. We were a conscientious bunch as dedicated as any shareholder.

Out of the blue there was a rumour which became a reality when we were taken over. Two wagons came into the yard with 50 barrels of bitter beer from The Greenhall Whitley at St.Helens. From then on the clouds really gathered as more beer was brought in. My stock of cigarettes came to an end and the customers were left to make their own arrangements. The final blow came when the last brew was made and this was also the last visit by the farmers for their grain. All the orders were diverted to St.Helens and after a final check by Mr Purston the contents of the stores were taken away.

I was left with the cobwebs, to lock up and draw the boiler room fires. The premises to which we supplied electricity were then connected to the village supply and the engine was switched off. This gave us all the real churchyard feeling.1 think the only ones who went to St.Helens were Mr Lawton, Mr Jolley and the travellers. At the end of our one weeks notice we were given £10 for each years service. The hotels, stock and goodwill were sold for £250,000.

Thanks for asking me to jog my memory
J.F.Moore.Late of Haigh Road. Kitt Green, Wigan.

Some of the employees from 1840:
HAIGH BREWERY 1840
Crawford Arms at Red Rock and Balcarres Arms at Haigh.
Both of these built by Lord Crawford with ten year renewable leases.
The rent at close down was £1,200 per year.
Directors: -
Miss Dorothy Rawcliffe, Baroness
Mr Gerald Peck of Culraven House
Mr Molyneux of Newburgh
Mr Gerald Thwaites of Welwyn Garden City
Security – Mr Lawton
Brewer – Henry Gibson
Property Manager – Peter Hampson
Yard Foreman – John Wood.

The Georgians at the Seaside
Prudence Bebb

Bathers, Filey

The band played the national anthem as King George III stepped into the English Channel.

The Duke of Cumberland wrote: "...notre très cher père thinks sea bathing will comfort him in his old days." Fanny Burney said, "The king bathes and with great success, a machine follows the royal one into the sea, filled with fiddlers who play 'God save the king' as His Majesty takes the plunge." 'God save the king' was painted on bathing machines and children's hats were decorated with the same loyal prayer. The sea was good for you and the king could never have too much of it, leaving his bed and dressing before six in the morning when at Weymouth. Bathing was thought to do you more good in the early morning.

George III used an Admiralty barge to row him and his family out to a ship - well, not all his family for his wife suffered from seasickness. In fact, Queen Charlotte endured the holidays which the king enjoyed. Her daughters, Augusta and Elizabeth, took dips in the sea but the queen kept firmly on dry land and Princess Mary told the Prince of Wales that "Sophia and me do not intend to honour the sea with our charms this year." Dr Russell advocated seawater as a cure for various diseases. He bought a house in Brighthelmstone and some of his patients stayed there with him. His advice led to that little fishing town becoming the fashionable resort of Brighton despite the fearsome nature of his remedies. His belief that vipers, crabs' eyes and woodlice should be taken in a pill at night followed by a pint of seawater next morning might have deterred many of us but he was consulted by aristocrats and brought prosperity to Brighton.

King George's eldest son, who suffered from swellings on his neck, went to Brighton for the sea cure. He liked it so much that he bought a farmhouse there which, of course, ceased to be a farmhouse and was remodelled as a Greek villa.

Someone gave Prinny (as his friends called him) a present of Chinese wallpaper. Seldom has a gift caused the recipient to spend so much money because you couldn't paper a classical villa with oriental

designs. So the interior was radically changed. Dragons, fretwork, lotus flowers adorned it whilst pink wallpaper ornamented with blue birds and leaves met the guests' eyes. Thus the farmhouse underwent its second metamorphosis. The chinoiserie charm was not its last phase. Before the end of the Regency Prinny's architect, John Nash, was planning an Indian version and the prince's mother gave him £50,000 to help pay for it. Fifty thousand in those days! The Indian-style Pavilion now belongs to Brighton and gives delight to modern visitors. Where celebrities go, others follow; Brighton became fashionable. The Steine, where fishermen spread their nets to dry, was soon traversed by the sporting vehicles of the day, two-wheeled curricles drawn by pairs of well-matched horses. Near the narrow lanes, home to fishing families, elegant terraces of classical houses were built. Seaside holidays had come to stay.

People started to go for a dip - quite literally. When a lady wanted to benefit from contact with seawater, she hired a bathing machine which was not really a machine but a hut on wheels, pulled by a horse. This gave her privacy to change, not into a swimsuit because there weren't any; she donned a long flannel gown which would get heavy with seawater. She couldn't swim but when the driver turned the bathing machine round so the horse faced inland, a door at the back was opened and the bathing beauty stepped gingerly down the steps. Two paid 'dippers' stood either side of her, each holding one of her arms. Then they dunked her in the sea and she stood shivering in her clinging sodden gown. The most famous dipper in Brighton was Martha Gunn; most dippers were the wives of fishermen.

The south coast was too far for a Scottish peer to take his family. It would mean many changes of horses and several nights on the road but Scarborough was much nearer. Soon that shipbuilding town had rows of lodging-houses and those seeking healthful seawater also had the chance of drinking from a chalybeate spring. This was the spa at the bottom of the cliffs where poor widows were employed to lift beakers of water from the well for visitors.

A Georgian shop
Bridlington

certain way of having one's name in a list which included members of the nobility. Those lists may now be useful to family historians.

Most seaside places provided attractions to tempt money from the purses of the visitors. In 1814 Scarborough advertised the "Grandest Menagerie in Europe." Among the unfortunate animals in this travelling collection were "Two Majestic Bengal Tigers... A Noble Panther. A Beautiful Leopard and Leopardess" and some kangaroos. In those days when Australia was an unimaginable place, no one could expect to see its fauna in the wild. However, Mr Miles's collection of animals included two kangaroos with their offspring. The public was informed: "What renders these creatures particularly curious is that the Female lately brought forth her young ones, which come out of and retire into the Pouch at pleasure; and are allowed to be the first specimens of Nature, and not to be seen in any other collections..."

Those who preferred specimens of humankind could watch young men run races on the sand; the prize was usually money. In 1815 one race was abandoned before either party had a chance to win. One of the contestants lost his "drawers" which meant that his nether garment fell down and the lady spectators were quickly whisked out of the way in a variety of gigs and curricles.

There were no slot machines, no piers with ghost trains, no stalls selling iced lollies, not even fish and chip restaurants but people knew how to enjoy themselves.

Not that Scarborough was without its dippers. They were there on the sandy shore of the North Sea to dip the ladies in the briny, much to the delight of the men who stood on St Nicholas Cliff training their telescopes on the female bathers. It may have embarrassed the ladies and amused the gentlemen but it can't have been very exciting to watch sopping figures in shapeless flannel.

The men themselves actually went swimming. As no one had invented swimming trunks, they cleaved the water completely naked. This necessitated hiring a boat with an awning so they might undress without embarrassing the ladies and swim at a decent distance from the beach.

Theatre-goers were able to watch plays in most of the seaside resorts. The princesses went to the theatre in Weymouth. Travelling bands of actors performed; Bridlington s actors came from Lincolnshire and included some lovely young ladies which meant that there were plenty of young men in the audience. Perhaps Whitby's theatre would have benefitted from these thespians because George Young wrote in 1817: "Sometimes the house, which will seat about 500 is well filled: at other times the performers complain of want of encouragement..."

One of Whitby's other amenities was the Commercial Newsroom. This building, which is still in Haggersgate, was paid for by the public, who wanted somewhere to go for news and general information. Here one could meet friends and read the weekly newspapers. For avid readers most seaside resorts provided a library. You paid a subscription when you arrived and after that you could borrow books as you wanted. It didn't really matter if you hated reading, you would still pay because the newspaper recorded the names of persons staying at the seaside and they got the names from the subscription book. It was the

Assemblies were held weekly in most seaside resorts. Some places had an official Assembly Rooms; Scarborough had the Long Room which gave its name to Long Room Street (now St Nicholas Street). Many towns used the largest room in a local hostelry. In Brighton this was in the Old Ship Inn; at Whitby it was in the Angel Inn. An Assembly was an occasion for dancing, card games and light refreshments. Young people grew hot as they took part in country dances and had to be wary lest they slipped in candlegrease on the dance floor. Girls skipped up the line in a swirl of muslin whilst older ladies in silk and feathers sat alongside the wall, indulgently watching the pastel-coloured geometry on the floor. For these country dances formed sets in circles and parallel lines; the shapes changed like a kaleidoscope as the partners executed the steps of the dance whilst a group of fiddlers provided the music.

On the seashore people collected jet and amber, shells and fossils and when they returned home they put these trophies in glass-fronted cupboards for their friends to admire.

Young men cantered on the sand and sailed in the bay. Other men drilled on the clifftop, watched by admiring visitors, for these were the red-coated soldiers who prepared to meet and defeat Napoleon's troops if they should land on British soil.

The militia were quartered in a camp at Hilderthorpe, just south of Bridlington. The wives and children of the officers followed their men and stayed in

KEEP OF SCARBOROUGH,
Yorkshire

Respectability". Such folk may have been influenced by the Poetical Sketches of Scarborough, published in 1813, which declared:

> "Believe me, ma'am, a daily dip
> Will mollify the cheek and lip:
> If you're too fat 'twill make you thin;
> And if the bones invade the skin,
> 'Twill in a month their sharpness cover,
> And clothe them well with flesh all over,
> The sea"s the mill that people mean
> To make the old grow young again."

With such prognostications to entice the credulous, it is no wonder that shops at the seaside did an excellent trade during the Season.

Chemists provided for the hypochondriacs who drank seawater. Milliners and dressmakers designed and sewed for the ladies who wished to be seen walking by the sea or dancing in the assemblies. At Scarborough, the excellently named Mrs Peacock made bonnets and gowns.

Visitors to Brighton might receive an invitation to an evening's music in the overheated Pavilion. Such guests needed the latest high-waisted gowns and headdresses.

Visitors to Scarborough seem to have been particularly satisfied with the inns, especially those who were content with the "ordinary" which meant the basic meal of the day. In 1733 Edmund Withers wrote to a friend:

> "I am at one of the best inns in the town. We sit down at noon to a twelvepenny ordinary, when we have eight or ten dishes handsomely served up, of things best in season - Extraordinaries may amount to 4d. Then we have two or three hot dishes at supper... Daily charge of my horse 6d. Civil usage and as good accommodation for Lodging as I have at home..."

It was just as good in the Regency when guests at the Bell Inn ate splendid local prawns and had such a good breakfast that the Bell became famous for it.

Bridlington where they could enjoy the theatre and assemblies. They need not fear that Papa would be sent abroad because the militia existed to defend the homeland and were never sent out of the country.

In Scarborough troops were in barracks at the Castle. The militiamen were posted there for a short time where they were given training in the use of a musket. The other eleven months of the year they were at home doing their usual jobs. At the end of the training there was a review when the ladies came to admire the scarlet-jacketed men marching to the drumbeat and shouldering Brown Bess (the British musket). In July 1812 the militiamen paraded in a downpour but the newspaper recorded that they performed "nearly all" of the manoeures with precision. Afterwards the officers were given "a very handsome dinner, served up in the Town's Hall". Subsequently "the jolly god (sic) presided to a late hour..."

At Brighton the Sussex Militia, who were camped nearby, were not in a position to perform their manoeuvres with precision as they had imbibed at the local tavern previously and tottered around giggling helplessly, especially when a fierce gust blew the ladies' skirts upwards. The young colonel excused his men:

> "These poor fellows have just been paid their arrears, and it is so unusual for them to have a sixpence in their pockets that they know not how to keep it there."

There were plenty of ladies who felt as Jane Austen's Mrs Bennett, "A little sea-bathing would set me up for ever." So there was money to be made by people who lived beside the Channel or the German Ocean, as the North Sea was then called. Those who had spare rooms took in lodgers; in Scarborough they could earn £1.5s a week per lodger and charge an extra ten shillings for the bed. Gentlemen, who wanted a good investment, built houses which they could let to whole families who brought their own servants. These would be rented by "Persons of

Many inns provided a suitable room for public meetings. In Brighton they were held at the Old Ship. This inn also gave visitors a good address to head their letters when staying there because "the first families of the Nobility resorted thither". Sometimes they attended concerts there or played cards or danced. But the weary traveller, who had been jolted for miles, stopping at toll-gates, changing horses, feeling very squashed and hot, was just thankful to get into a four-poster bed in a room with a sea view. When the chintz curtains were drawn and the candle blown out, one could lie back on a downy mattress, soothed by the rhythmic sound of the retreating waves crunching the shingle.

Many of the seaside inns have survived and are now redeveloped as popular hotels. Some of the lodging houses are bed-and-breakfasts. The churches, where fisherfolk gave thanks alongside fashionable visitors, now house modern congregations. Surrounding all, the tides still come and go with eternal regularity while the seagulls screech and wheel.

Shovelling out the Poor:
Assisted Emigration in the 19th Century
Simon Fowler

During the nineteenth century between eight and ten million people departed the British Isles for the New World. That is roughly the total population of Britain in 1801. We think of the Irish fleeing the Famine in the 1840s, but they were only a small part of the flood which settled North America, Australasia, South Africa and South America.

Some emigrants went under their own steam, paying for their passage across the Atlantic and making their own way in their new home. Many more received assistance in some form. It may have been from 'landsmen' that is family or friends who had already settled in America or Australia, who sent money home for the voyage or made the promise of work. Alternatively emigrants may have received more formal grants from the authorities in Britain or from a charity or even a landowner, and this is the focus of this piece. Older readers may remember the 'ten pound Pom' scheme which enabled families to leave for Australia in the 1950s and 1960s, but similar programmes ran a century before.

Potential emigrants, assisted or not, had various reasons for going. The vast majority went either to join people they already knew or because they felt that the new lands offered new opportunities – even if this was just steady work and a decent wage, both less common in mid-Victorian England than might be imagined. Others went because they were forced to, such as convicts transported to Australia. Orphan and pauper children – known as home children - were also often sent abroad without really being consulted by charities. Lastly some went to settle religious communities. Thousands of Mormons, for example, left for Salt Lake City during the 1840s and 1850s. The types of emigrant and their motives are well summarized in a report in the Geelong Advertiser for May 1849. Their reporter describing emigrants at the Plymouth Emigration Depot said that: "Some were going out at the earnest wish of their friends who had previously emigrated and much improved their position; others were leaving England because work was scarce and poorly remunerated, and one stated that he left because in England 'masters were a deal too saucy and did not know how to treat working men'".

Although relatively few lists of assisted emigrants survive, we do know a reasonable amount about them. About half came from England and Wales, a third from Ireland and the remained from Scotland.

There was an emphasis on recruiting skilled agricultural labourers and their young families, such as shepherds and smiths, as there was a considerable demand for their skills in the colonies. However, there was already strong competition for people of this kind, and except in times of great economic depression there was normally enough work for the industrious and healthy in England. The governor of New South Wales received a petition in 1847 from 'certain land-holders, bankers, merchants, graziers… and others interested in welfare of colony" pointing out the "prevalent and increasing deficiency of labour and the urgent necessity for an immediate renewal of labour." In response the colonial government established a scheme which gave priority to the groups of workers for whom there was a ready demand — agricultural labourers, shepherds, farm servants, and country mechanics. They particularly were looking for families and young married childless couples. All adults had to be capable of labour and no support was to be offered to habitual paupers. However, there was great difficult to finding suitable candidates because there was a huge demand for labour in England as navvies to build the railways. The first ships to arrive in Sydney mainly consisted of Irish peasants who had fled the famine back home.

All too often the suitability and general physical health of the new arrivals left a lot to be desired. Newspaper articles and petitions to colonial governors all too often complain about the poor quality of the new arrivals. There were grumbles about the lack of morals (particularly among the female emigrants) and the lack of employable skills. And many arrivals were either disabled or diseased, which meant that they had to be supported by the authorities. In part at least, this was pure prejudice against the Irish and working class men and women in general, as well as a naïve belief in the stalwart quality of the English peasantry.

It is certainly true, however, that the poor law authorities took the opportunity to 'shovel out' their paupers as critics had it, particularly young women. In 1835, Lieutenant Low, the emigration agent at Liverpool complained to Whitehall that: "parish officers just getting rid of paupers without a just and proper regard to their comfort and accommodation during such a long voyage to Australia." But the authorities saw it as an opportunity to reduce the poor rates and, more positively, to give poor people the chance of a better life elsewhere.

It was said of the unemployed sent to Canada by the East London Emigrant Relief Committee in the early 1870s that 'their natal land would be better for their departure and their adopted country the worse'. It seemed as if their aim was to 'clear the neighbourhood of the most worthless and undeserving poor' and throw them on the charity of the Canadians.

In their defence migrants were largely victims of an imperfect economic system, which survived on a vast army of casual labourers who worked when there was a demand at harvest time or when there were orders in the factories, but were thrown aside when they were not required. By end of century, the quality of emigrants was generally better, as the result of improvements in public health and education in Britain, but the suspicion still remained that all the authorities in London wanted to do was to take the shirkers and ne'er-do-wells off the streets and send them to colonies.

Indeed the organisers of emigration schemes often argued that they were helping to remove surplus labour. The intention of the Petworth Emigration Society in Sussex, which sent hundreds of local agricultural labourers to Canada, was: "To remove from the minds of people of all classes that the notion of emigration is banishment and to cherish the idea that it is only a removal from a part of the British Empire, where there are more workmen than there is work to be performed to another, fertile, healthful and in every way delightful portion of the same Empire, where the contrary is the case."

Meanwhile protagonists for female emigration pointed to the surplus of women over men in the population —over 600,000 in 1861 — and the great shortage of marriageable women in the colonies. Others felt that emigration would help paupers and others migrants to restore their self-esteem and encourage self-help – that great nineteenth century panacea for all woes. By the end of the century Imperialists were increasingly arguing that there was a need to populate Greater Britain overseas, in order to boost trade and Imperial links across the Empire, and to boost these ties people should be encouraged to emigrate.

The assisted emigration study recently undertaken by the Family and Community History Research Society (FCAHRS) suggested that most people were pushed to apply by their circumstances, rather than attracted by the opportunities. The great distances involved and

the cost of travel meant emigration was generally for life. Emigrants had to be uprooted and compelled to adjust old habits and assumptions to new circumstances. If they found it hard in England to leave the land for the cities, it must have been doubly difficult for people offered the chance to go to the other side of the world. It is little wonder that perhaps a third of people changed their minds between applying and arriving on board ship at Liverpool or London – and why so many parties of emigrants were closely chaperoned to ensure members could not desert.

Assisted emigration schemes can roughly be divided into three although there was sometimes an overlap between them. Firstly there were formal ones organised by the state, either the Imperial government in London or colonial administrations – and most emigrants, particularly to Australia, went out this way. A number of charities also sent people, particularly children and young adults, to start new lives overseas. Canada was a favourite destination because it was relatively cheap destination. Lastly individual landowners informally dipped into their pockets to send deserving tenants to new lives in the colonies.

The British government in general was reluctant to pay for the passages of assisted emigrants, except in rare circumstances. One of which was the attempts to settle colonies with old soldiers who could defend the settlers in case they were attacked by the natives. Unfortunately this rarely worked, as most ex-servicemen had little experience of working the land. The best known of these schemes was in New Zealand, where European settlements around Auckland were defended by the Royal New Zealand Fencibles. The force consisted of 2500 discharged British soldiers and sailors of good character. They and their families came to Auckland between 1847 and 1852. The men served seven years, and were expected to do six days drill in spring and autumn.

But most eventually drifted to the city where they became labourers.

The most important government agency during the nineteenth century was the Colonial Land and Emigration Commission. Between 1842, when it was established, and 1878, when it was abolished, it sent out 340,000 settlers, as well as supervising the departure and passage of ordinary emigrants, and providing propaganda on the advantages of emigration. The Commission was funded by the profits from the sale of waste, or uncultivated, land in the colonies. Some 325,000 people were helped to go to New South Wales and Victoria at a cost of £5m, of which £4m came from land sales in the Australia. Its work declined in the 1860s as the colonies began to set up their own immigration procedures and agents in London. South Australia was the first in 1859, followed by New South Wales in 1861.

The peak of the Commission's work was in the late-1840s and early-1850s, at a time of serious economic depression. In 1848, thirty clerks were processing a thousand applications a week. Five years later an article in *Household Words* described 'the stream of fustian jackets, corduroy trousers and smock-frocks... the chattering excited parties of half-shaved mechanics, slatternly females and slip-shod children' thronging the 'much-sought office' of the Commissioners.

Until 1849 the Commission offered some free passages. Thereafter emigrants paid a deposit, which they promised to pay back from earnings in their new homes, although it was nearly impossible to enforce repayment. Emigrants were also expected to provide a set of clothes for the journey. For men this was two complete suits, six shirts, two pairs of shoes and six pairs of stockings. Women had to have two gowns, six shifts, two flannel petticoats, two pairs of shoes and six pairs of stockings. In addition each person had to supply four towels, 2lb soap and three sheets for their berth. Typically these expenses might amount to about £5 per person, a considerable sum for the period.

The other major government supported scheme took place in the decade before the First World War, when thousands of unemployed men and their families were sent to Canada and Australia by Unemployment Distress Committees which were set up in places where work was scarce. In early 1906 some 4500 unemployed men and their families were sent across the Atlantic to new lives in Canada, three quarters of whom came from London.

The Family and Community History Research Society project referred to above largely looked at emigrants who were helped by the poor law authorities. At the time of their establishment in 1834 poor law unions were given the power to pay for the emigration of suitable paupers. In practice this was a right which was rarely exercised, partly because it was discouraged by Whitehall. It was also difficult to find suitable candidates to help. Even so some 10,000 emigrants were helped by local poor law unions in the decade after 1836, thereafter numbers fell off considerably.

Many assisted passages were paid for by the colonial governments either through the Emigration Commissioners in London or from the 1860s by their own agents-general. A network of local agents was also recruited to spread the word and give lectures and magic lantern talks about the advantages of emigration.

In recruiting emigrants colonial governments faced a dilemma. They needed to attract labour, but the quality of emigrants was often poor which meant that they had to be provided for. Some 4200 girls from Irish workhouses, for example, were sent to New South Wales and Victoria between 1848 and 1850. Although care was taken to choose reputable girls, there were many complaints about receiving girls 'of the most abandoned character', their violent and disorderly conduct on voyage, gross and profane language. This was probably exaggerated. The Immigration Agent at Sydney reported in 1849 that he had found no fault with the girls except their ignorance of the duties of domestic service and inaptitude for learning them.

The colonies were increasingly keen to have a say on whom they received. Queensland, for example, objected to private emigration schemes and the arrival of assisted paupers because of fears about introduction of undesirable and unemployable people. Trade unions also objected to immigration at times of unemployment, when their members had difficulty in finding work let alone competing for places with people straight off the boat.

Charities were also important in running schemes, particularly during the last third of the nineteenth century when the British government lost interest in assisted emigration. Charitable bodies argued that they were offering slum-dwellers and other unfortunates a chance to start new lives in a decent

environment and where plenty of work was available. Unfortunately, although they sent chaperoned parties to the colonies, all too often there was the expectation that colonial governments and relief agencies would be able to deal with the migrants once they arrived. This was particularly true of the children, home children as they became known, who were sent out from the 1860s onwards. Often few preparations were made for their arrival in the colonies and there was little subsequent supervision, with the result that were often mistreated by foster parents and homes.

There were a large number of charities, many of whom only existed for a short period, perhaps to meet a short term crisis. Charities in the East End of London, for example, sent out 20,000 poor people to Canada in 1867 and 1868. A year later local charities migrated 1600 workers and their families to Canada when Woolwich Dockyard closed.

Charities were also used to send single young women overseas, for whom there was a constant demand. One of the most important was the Female Middle Class Emigration Society. In 1862, it despatched 99 teenagers to the infant colony of British Columbia as governesses, but most of the unfortunate girls were poor waifs and strays. It was not a happy experiment. One colonialist grumbled; "Half of them married soon after arrival or went into service, but a large proportion quickly went to the bad, and, from appearances had been there before… To speak gallantry, but truly many of these ladies were neither young nor beautiful."

A few emigrants had their passages paid for by local landlords. It was likely that the better sort of men and

their families might be supported in this way. Men whom it could be seen might prosper in the colonies and so would not become a burden on the poor rates in their home village. In most cases this was an informal arrangement. In Ham near Kingston in Surrey the local landowner Algernon Tollemarche paid for seven labourers and their families to go to New Zealand, where he had land. Occasionally it could be more organised. The third earl of Egremont paid for 1800 men and their families to go from the villages around his estates at Petworth in Sussex to Ontario in the mid-1830s.

Undoubtedly most migrants prospered in their new homes. Wages were generally higher for a start and there were plenty of opportunities for advancement. However, many families must have found it difficult to adapt to new conditions and learn new trades. And some, particularly the Irish, must have resented that they had to go at all.

For the Australian colonies, especially, it was the only real way to build up the population once transportation was phased out in the 1840s and 1850s. South Australia and, to a lesser degree, Western Australia was largely settled by assisted emigrants and their arrival also gave a powerful boost to the economies of New South Wales and Victoria. Canada too was a popular destination, but here there was always a considerable number of free emigrants so their influence was not so marked there. The dilemma for the colonies was that the quality of most emigrants did not match up to their expectations. There was always a shortage of intelligent hard-working men and women with the skills that the colonies needed. But these people could prosper at home or, perhaps, preferred to go to America where it was easier to make their fortune.

This migration seems to have gone largely unremarked in Britain. Between eight and ten million people left during the nineteenth century. Initially it was argued that this movement reduced the surplus population, who otherwise would have been a drain on the poor rates. Increasingly it was seen that helping people leave helped build up the Empire, who bought British goods and supplied raw material to British factories and dinner tables. But the greatest vindication, perhaps, came during the two world wars when tens of thousands of young colonials volunteered to help Britain in time of need.

The Inspector calls...............
Richard Ratcliffe F.S.G.

The children's version of education in an elementary school in the "Payment by Results " era is rarely recorded. Probably the most graphic account of an Annual Examination is to be found in Flora Thompson's autobiography "From Lark Rise to Candleford" published in 1929.

Flora, born Flora Timms in 1876 lived in the hamlet of Juniper in the North Oxfordshire parish of Cottisford. She attended the National School at Cottisford in the 1880s. In her book, Cottisford is called Fordlow , Juniper is renamed Lark Rise while the Mistress, Miss Susannah Holmyard becomes Miss Holmes and the Vicar of Cottisford [Fordlow], the Rev Charles Harrison is disguised as Rev Charles Ellison.

Flora describes life at Fordlow School in vivid detail. "At nine o'clock, the hamlet children set out on their mile and a half walk…soon after their seven o'clock breakfast, partly because they liked plenty of time to play on the road and partly because their mothers wanted them out of the way before house cleaning began.

Up the long straight road they straggled [an Enclosure Road?], in twos and threes and in gangs, their flat rush dinner baskets over their shoulders…In cold weather some of them carried two hot potatoes which had been in the oven or in the ashes, all night, to warm their hands on the way and to serve as a light lunch on their arrival. They were strong, lusty children let loose from control, and there was plenty of shouting, quarrelling and often fighting among them.

In more peaceful moments they would squat in the dust on the road and play marbles, or sit on a stone heap and play dibs with pebbles, or climb into the hedges after birds' eggs ..In spring they ate the young green from the hawthorn hedges which they called "bread and cheese"…. And in autumn there was an abundance of haws, blackberries, sloes and crab apples not so much because they were hungry as from habit and relish of wild food.

Although they started to school so early, the hamlet children took so much time on the way that the last quarter of a mile was always a race , and they would rush panting and dishevelled into school just as the bell stopped and the other children , spick and span, fresh from their mothers' hands would eye them sourly and murmur "That gipsy lot from Lark Rise[Juniper]."

Fordlow National School [Cottisford] was a grey one storied building…the one large classroom which served all purposes was well lighted with several windows … Beside and joined on to school was a tiny two roomed cottage for the schoolmistress. The school had a lobby with pegs for clothes, boys' and girls' earth closets and a back yard with fixed wash basins, although there was no water laid on.. the water supply was contained in a small bucket filled every morning by the old woman who cleaned the schoolroom, and every morning she would grumble because the children had been so extravagant that she had to fill it again.

The 19th century saw tremendous changes take place in the field of education. At the beginning of the century few of our ancestors received any kind of formal education. By the end of the century, elementary education had become compulsory for all children up to the age of 12 and was free.

Early in the 19th century two Church based societies had started to provide a limited form of elementary education using a method of teaching known as "the Monitorial System." The two societies were "The National Society" – a Church of England society – and "The British and Foreign Schoools Society" - linked to many Nonconformist Churches. By 1833, the two societies had opened over 3500 elementary schools which taught the basic skills of Reading, Writing and Arithmetic [the 3Rs].

In 1833, the recently elected Reform Parliament voted the first educational grants to the two societies to enable them to build more schools. In 1839, Parliament, set up an Education Committee of the Privy Council, increased the annual grant to the two societies and introduced inspection of schools to monitor standards of teaching and pupil achievement.

A year later the first Teacher Training College - at Battersea- was opened and by 1845 another 25 teacher training colleges had been opened.

As the Industrial Revolution of the 19th Century continued to gain momentum and with it a greater demand for workers with a good basic education, the Government set up a Commission of Enquiry in 1858 – the Newcastle Commission - to look into ways of improving educational standards. The Report of the Commission, published in 1861, recommended a system of education in elementary schools of "Payment by Results" by which the annual government grant would depend on the number of children who passed the annual examination in the 3Rs. A substantially enlarged Inspectorate of Schools would ensure that all schools were inspected. This system of education was introduced in 1862 and was to continue until 1902.

The keeping of School Log Books was made compulsory in 1862. In these books the results of the Annual Examinations were to be recorded as well as a summary of the Inspectors' Reports. The Log Books also record many of the day to day activities of schools and often show the considerable stresses under which the Headteachers operated as they prepared their pupils for the dreaded Annual Examination.

The average attendance was about 45 and even then to an outsider it would have appeared a quaint, old fashioned gathering; the girls in their ankle length frocks and long straight pinafores, with their hair strained back from their brows and secured on their crowns by a ribbon or black tape or a bootlace; the bigger boys in corduroys and hobnailed boots and the smaller ones in home made sailor suits or, until they were six or seven, in petticoats.

The school mistress in charge of Fordlow School at the beginning of the eighties had held that position for 15 years and seemed to her pupils as much a fixture as the school building, but for most of that time she had been engaged to the squire's head gardener. She was, at that time about 40, and was a small neat little body with a pale slightly pock marked face, snaky black curls hanging down to her shoulders.. she wore in school stiffly starched, holland aprons with bibs, one embroidered with red one week and one with blue the next and was seldom seen without a posy of flowers pinned on her breast..

[In the 1881 Census of Cottisford RG11/1508 F5 sch 13, Susannah Holmyard , a spinster of 35 and born in Marylebone, Middlesex, is the schoolmistress. In 1891 she is Susannah Tebby, wife of Henry Tebby, Gardener]

Reading, Writing and Arithmetic were the principal subjects, with a Scripture lesson every morning and needlework every afternoon for the girls. There was no assistant mistress, the Mistress taught all the classes simultaneously, assisted by two monitors - ex- scholars, aged about 12, who were paid a shilling a week each for their services.

Every morning at 10 o'clock the Rector arrived to take the older children for Scripture. He was a commanding figure, tall and stout with white hair, ruddy cheeks and an aristocratically beaked nose, and he was as far as possible removed by birth, education and worldly circumstances from his flock.

[In the 1881 Census of Cottisford RG11/1508 F5 sch 15, Rev Charles Harrison was a 66 year old Widower, born at Chester, living with his daughter Grace , a 29 year old Spinster born at Eton, Bucks, and 2 servants].

Flora refers to him as Mr Ellison. His lesson consisted of Bible Reading, turn and turn about the class, reciting from memory the names of the kings of Israel and repeating the catechism before the Rector delivered a little lecture on morals and behaviour.

Scripture over, ordinary lessons began - simple arithmetic extending only to the first four rules -

addition, subtraction, multiplication and division with money sums known as "bills of parcels" for the most advanced pupils. The writing lesson consisted of copying maxims in copperplate writing, " A fool and his money are soon parted," Waste not, want not," "Count ten before you speak." Once a week a composition in the form of a letter was set describing a recent event but was regarded chiefly as a spelling test.

For History readers were used containing stories about King Alfred, King Canute, the loss of the White Ship and Drake and Raleigh.

No Geography was taught but the walls of the classroom were hung with a series of maps: The World, Europe, North America, South America, England, Ireland and Scotland. The Royal Readers contained extracts from Ivanhoe, Fenimore Cooper's Prairie on Fire and Washington Irving's Capture of Wild Horses.

Flora describes the Annual Examination in great detail. The whole school year was centred around this event.

"Her Majesty's Inspector of Schools came once a year. There was no singing or quarrelling on the way to school that morning. The children, in clean pinafores and well blackened boots walked deep in thought , or with open spelling or table books in hand tried to make up in an hour for all their wasted yesterdays."

Although the date was known in advance, the time of his arrival was not stated, so some years he came in the morning and other years in the afternoon. He was an elderly clergyman and was accompanied by an Assistant Inspector, also a clergyman but younger.

The elder clergyman was a little man with an immense paunch and tiny grey eyes like gimlets…His voice was an exasperated roar and his criticism was a blend of outraged learning and sarcasm…he looked at the rows of children as if he hated them and at the mistress as if he despised her. The Assistant Inspector was by comparison almost human…Black eyes and very red lips shone through the bushiness of the whiskers which almost covered his face … The children in the lower classes, which he examined, were considered fortunate.

What kind of man the Inspector really was it is impossible to say. He may have been a great scholar, a good parish priest and a good friend to people of his own class. One thing is certain…he did not care for or understand children, at least National School children. In homely language he was the wrong man for the job. The very sound of his voice scattered the few wits of the less gifted, and those who could have done better were too terrified in his presence to be able to collect their thoughts to keep their hands from trembling.

The afternoon seemed endless. Classes came out to read; others classes bent over their sums or wrote letters to grandmothers describing imaginary summer holidays. Dictation always seemed to be full of hard spelling words. One year the great man caused extra confusion by adopting , to them, the new method of giving out the stops by name:

"Water fowl and other aquatic birds dwell on their banks semi-colon while on the surface of the placid water float the wide-spreading leaves of the Victoria regia comma and other lilies and water dash plants."

At last the ordeal was over. No one knew who had passed and who had not for a fortnight. When the papers arrived and the examination results were read out it was surprising to find that a number had passed. The standard must have been very low, for the children had never been taught some of the work set … and nervous dread prevented many from reaching their usual poor standard.

There was a great deal of jealousy and unkindness among the parents over the passes. The successful ones were spoken of as "favourites" and disliked. Disappointed mothers would say "Stands to reason that what he could do our Jimmy could do and better, too." " Examinations are all a lot of humbug, if you asks me." The parents of those who had passed were almost apologetic, "Tis all luck," they would say, apart from the parents of the boy who having passed the fourth standard could leave school and start work.

" Their ideal for themselves and their children was to keep to the level of the normal. To them outstanding ability was no better than outstanding stupidity."

M.K.Ashby in her biography "Joseph Ashby of Tysoe 1859-1919" describes the Annual Examination as related to her by her father.

"Two inspectors came once a year and carried out a dramatic examination. The schoolmaster came into school in his best suit; all the pupils and teachers would be listening till at ten o'clock a dog cart would be heard on the road even though it was eighty yards away. In would come two gentlemen with a deportment of high authority, with rich voices. Each would sit at a desk and children would be called in turn to one or other. The master hovered round calling children out as they were needed. The children could see him start with vexation as a good pupil stuck at a word in the reading book he had been using all year, or sat motionless with his sum in front of him. The master's anxiety was deep, for his earnings depended on the children's work. One year the atmosphere of anxiety so affected the lower standards that, one after another as they were brought to the Inspector, the boys howled and the girls whimpered. It took hours to get them through."

In her book, "The Victorian Country Child," Pamela Horn quotes from the School Log Book of Childrey Wesleyan School, Berkshire following the Annual Inspection of 1888.

"The discipline is good, and the scholars of the second and upper standards have made very fair progress in the obligatory subjects [i.e. the 3Rs]. The younger children

appear to have received insufficient attention."…

Average attendance – Boys 15.4; Girls 13.8 – 29.3 Total
Fixed Grant – 4s 6d; Merit Grant – 1s; Singing – 6d
Percentage – 5s 7d;   Total – 11s 7d
Needlework – 14s
Number presented and present at the examination – 24
Passes – Reading – 17; Writing – 16
       Arithmetic – 15 –Total – 48
Grant – 29 at 11s 7d =£16 15s 11d;
       Needlework - 14s;
Total Grant - £17 9s 11d

This would pay the Headteacher's salary for the next year. In a small school like Childrey, there would be only one teacher, the Headteacher, who would be assisted by a Monitor – usually a young girl aged 12 or 13 years of age who was paid between 1s 0d and 2s 0d a week by the Headteacher out of the annual grant. The Monitor would be taught the lessons for the day by the Headteacher before the pupils arrived at school. At Childrey it would seem the Monitor probably taught the younger children while the Headteacher concentrated on getting as many of the older children through the Annual Examination.

So if you find the word "Scholar" recorded against the names of your ancestors and their siblings in the 1871, 1881 and 1891 Censuses, spare a thought for the agonies that they and their teachers went through preparing for and taking part in the Annual Examinations in the 3Rs. And do check in the County Record Office if the School Log Books survive from 1862-1902 where you can read at first hand the Headteachers' weekly concerns about his pupils' ability to cope with the annual visit by Her Majesty's Inspectors of Schools.

Happy days!

Further Reading
Thompson, Flora; *Lark Rise* - Oxford University Press, 1939
Horn, Pamela; *The Victorian Country Child* – Alan Sutton 1985
Horn, Pamela, *The Victorian and Edwardian Schoolchild* - Alan Sutton 1980
Ashby, M.K., *Joseph Ashby of Tyso*e – Cambridge University Press 1961.

Visit the Society of Genealogists in London's Genealogy Village

Else Churchill Genealogy Officer

I'll wager you didn't know that genealogy can keep you fit in body as well as mind. Paris may have its Latin Quarter but apparently the Society of Genealogists can be found in what has now become London's Genealogy Village and it's no great distance from the Society to the other important family history archives centres that are our neighbours. With support from the *Archives Awareness* campaign and ITV's *Britain on the Move* campaign the major London Genealogical Libraries and Archives have produced the *Family History Map* that shows the ways to walk between key centres in the London Boroughs of Camden and Islington. The map is not just for Londoners: amazing local AND National resources can be found in this compact area – hence the "genealogical village." Along with information about the partners in the project there is information about accommodation provided during the vacations by London School of Economics Vacation Accommodation *www.lsevacations.co.uk* in Rosebery Hall, superbly located just moments from the Family Records Centre.

Whether you are starting your family history and need copies of certificates and census returns from the FRC to local information about London and its inhabitants or have ancestors who worked for the Post Office or served in India you'll find a tremendous amount of information within a very manageable walk from each other. And of course should your research lead you away from London before 1837 then the Society of Genealogists hold copies of registers and other sources of local genealogical material for approximately 10,000 parishes around the UK.

The following organisations are to be found in the village:

The British Library *www.bl.uk* 96 Euston Road London NW1 2DB
The principal resources used for family history are in the India Office Records, for ancestors in British India, and in the newspapers at the Newspaper Library in Colindale. Extensive collections include directories, oral history, pedigrees, maps and patents.

BT Archives *www.bt.com/archives* Third Floor Holborn Telephone Exchange 268-270 High Holborn London WC1V 7EE
BT Archives preserves the documentary heritage of BT and its predecessors. A major resource for family historians is the near-complete set of UK telephone directories dating from the first directory produced in 1880 to the present.

Camden Local Studies and Archives Centre
www.camden.gov.uk/localstudies Holborn Library 32-38 Theobalds Road London WC1X 8PA The Camden Local Studies and Archives Centre contains archives, printed material, illustrations and maps about the history of the area from the 17th century until the present day. Sources for family history research include ratebooks, electoral registers, local

directories, local newspapers, monumental inscriptions and Highgate Cemetery registers.

Family Records Centre (FRC)
www.familyrecords.gov.uk/frc 1 Myddelton Street London EC1R 1UW
The FRC holds indexes of births, marriages and deaths in England and Wales from1837, census returns for England and Wales (1841-1901), Prerogative Court of Canterbury (PCC) wills and administrations, and other records including death duty registers and non-conformist registers. We provide access to many online resources including the 1901 census, PCC wills, and other family history websites.

Islington Local History Centre
www.islington.gov.uk/libraries 245 St John Street London EC1V 4NB Family history sources include census returns for Islington & Finsbury (1841-1901), electoral registers (from 1870s onwards), parish registers for St. Mary Islington, ratebooks, maps, photographs and a range of archive and published material. Please book an appointment to visit.

London Metropolitan Archives (LMA)
www.cityoflondon.gov.uk/lma 40 Northampton Road London EC1R 0HB
LMA is the largest local authority record office in the UK, with 55km of records dating back nearly 900 years. LMA has records from the former county councils of London, Middlesex and Greater London. The main sources for family history include registers from over 800 parishes, poor law records and registers of electors; plus maps, plans, prints and photos.

Royal Mail Archive (Postal Heritage Trust)
www.royalmail.com/heritage Freeling House, Phoenix Place, London WC1X 0DL The Royal Mail Archive contains records for the history of The Post Office over four centuries. For family history research the main sources are the appointment books (1734-1774, 1831-1956) and establishment books (1742-1946). There are also records of pensions, postmasters/postmistresses, packet boat agents and captains and many other sources.

Society of Genealogists *www.sog.org.uk* 14 Charterhouse Buildings, London EC1M 7BA
The Society has the largest family history Library in the UK. It holds copies of family history sources, finding aids, indexes and unique research materials. The Library also has free Internet access to some major genealogical websites such as Ancestry.co.uk which indexes the 1891 and 1871 censuses and of course the SoG's own indexes and data on British origins. The Society is also proud to boast the largest collection of copies of parish registers in the UK, along with local histories, monumental inscriptions, thousands of directories and poll books and published sources materials covering the counties of the United Kingdom such as tax lists or indexes to wills. The

Society's unique collections of unpublished family histories and the remarkable wealth of miscellaneous manuscript research notes in the Document Collections are vital if anyone wishes to establish if any previous research has been undertaken into a family. The Society of Genealogists also holds thousands of rolled pedigrees amongst its archives. Also to be found in the Society's archive area in the lower library are the various manuscript and microfilmed special collections and finding aids that inlcude amongst many others the following:

Bernau index to miscellaneous chancery, exchequer and other 17th & 18th century sources
Teachers' Registration Council Registers 1902-48
Trinity House Petitions 1787-1854 (also some Apprentice Indentures 1788 & 1818-45 and miscellaneous Pensions and Petitions 1790-1889)
Great Card Index of miscellaneous sources (3 million entries)
Fawcett Index of Anglican Clergy and North Country families
Wagner Collection of notes on Huguenot families
Percy-Smith Collection of notes on British families in India
Colyier Fergusson Collection of notes on Jewish families.

When searching the special collections it is advisable to check the special collections card index which will tell if the surname name you are interested in can be found in any of the collections The Society will happily search its various catalogues and bibliographies (free of charge) to see if anything is held on a particular name. A quotation can then be

made for the costs of copying the relevant materials.

Enquiries should be made by: fax - (020) 7250 1800 e-mail library@sog.org.uk post - SoG, 14 Charterhouse Buildings, Goswell Road, London EC1M 7BA telephone 020 7702 5488 or 5489

For postal enquiries, please include a stamped self-addressed envelope or, if outside the UK, an addressed envelope and THREE International Reply Coupons.

Requests for catalogue enquiries and searches are dealt with in order of receipt. They are not acknowledged but the Society endeavours to answer within one month if possible. The Society is does not undertake professional genealogical research. Those unable to conduct their own research may wish to consider appointing a record agent or professional genealogist. The Society will not recommend any individual but several advertise in our own Genealogists' Magazine and other journals such as Family Tree Magazine. The Association of Genealogists and Researchers in Archives (AGRA) publishes a list of its members and can be found on-line at **www.agra.org.uk**

Personal searches can of course be made. Non-members are also welcome to use the Library as day searchers on payment of the appropriate fee (currently £3.30 per hour, £8.80 four hours or £13.20 a day). Photocopies or printouts can be made personally at a cost of 20p (A4) or 40p (A3) or by staff (in the case of fragile and or manuscript items in the lower library) at 30p (A4) or 50p (A3) per copy.

www.archiveawareness.com

---

1 The British Library

96 Euston Road London NW1 2DB
T +44 (0)870 444 1500
E reader-services-enquiries@bl.uk
   newspaper@bl.uk
W www.bl.uk

The principal resources used for family history are in the India Office Records, for ancestors in British India, and in the newspapers at the Newspaper Library in Colindale. Extensive collections (606km) include directories, oral history, pedigrees, maps and patents.

Check website for catalogues and opening hours of different reading rooms.

---

2 BT Archives

Third Floor Holborn Telephone Exchange
268–270 High Holborn London WC1V 7EE
T +44 (0)20 7440 4220
F +44 (0)20 7242 1967
E archives@bt.com
W www.bt.com/archives

BT Archives preserves the documentary heritage of BT and its predecessors. A major resource for family historians is the near-complete set of UK telephone directories dating from the first directory produced in 1880 to the present.

---

3 Camden Local Studies and Archives Centre

Holborn Library 32–38 Theobalds Road London WC1X 8PA
T +44 (0)20 7974 6342
F +44 (0)20 7974 6284
E localstudies@camden.gov.uk
W www.camden.gov.uk/localstudies

The Camden Local Studies and Archives Centre contains archives, printed material, illustrations and maps about the history of the area from the 17th century until the present day. Sources for family history research include ratebooks, electoral registers, local directories, local newspapers, monumental inscriptions and Highgate Cemetery registers.

---

4 Family Records Centre (FRC)

1 Myddelton Street London EC1R 1UW
T +44 (0)20 8392 5300
F +44 (0)20 8392 5307
E frc@nationalarchives.gov.uk
W www.familyrecords.gov.uk/frc

The FRC holds indexes of births, marriages and deaths in England and Wales from 1837, census returns for England and Wales (1841–1901), PCC wills and administrations, and other records including death duty registers and non-conformist registers. We provide access to many online resources including the 1901 census, PCC wills, and other family history websites.

---

5 Islington Local History Centre

245 St. John Street London EC1V 4NB
T +44 (0)20 7527 7988
E local.history@islington.gov.uk
W www.islington.gov.uk/libraries

Family history sources include census returns for Islington & Finsbury (1841–1901), electoral registers (from 1870s onwards), parish registers for St. Mary Islington, ratebooks, maps, photographs and a range of archive and published material. Please book an appointment to visit.

---

6 London Metropolitan Archives (LMA)

40 Northampton Road London EC1R 0HB
T +44 (0)20 7332 3820
F +44 (0)20 7833 9136
E ask.lma@corpoflondon.gov.uk
W www.cityoflondon.gov.uk/lma

LMA is the largest local authority record office in the UK, with 55km of records dating back nearly 900 years. LMA has records from the former county councils of London, Middlesex and Greater London. Main sources for family history include registers from over 800 parishes, poor law records and registers of electors; plus maps, plans, prints and photographs.

---

7 Royal Mail Archive (Postal Heritage Trust)

Freeling House, Phoenix Place, London WC1X 0DL
T +44 (0)20 7239 2570
F +44 (0)20 7239 2576
E heritage@royalmail.com
W www.royalmail.com/heritage

The Royal Mail Archive contains records for the history of The Post Office over four centuries. For family history research the main sources are the appointment books (1734–1774, 1831–1956) and establishment books (1742–1946). There are also records of pensions, postmasters/postmistresses, packet boat agents and captains and many other supporting sources.

---

8 Society of Genealogists

14 Charterhouse Buildings, London, EC1M 7BA
T +44 (0)20 7251 8799
F +44 (0)20 7250 1800
E library@sog.org.uk
W www.sog.org.uk

The Society has the largest family history library in the UK. It holds copies of family history sources, finding aids, indexes and unique research materials. The Library also has free Internet access to some major genealogical websites. The Society is also proud to boast the largest collection of copies of parish registers in the UK.

Get walking with ITV's Britain On The Move campaign.
www.britainonthemove.com

Camden & Islington
Family History Map

LSE

With so many centres for family history this close
in Camden and Islington, you can trace your
ancestors and get some exercise at the
same time!

The coloured routes will take you between
the centres. Average walking times are
shown.

This leaflet has been
produced by the partner archives
and LSE with financial support from
the British Library. ALM London
has given a grant as part of the
Archive Awareness Campaign.

LIBRARY BRITISH

ALM LONDON

---

1 **The British Library**
Oriental and India Office Reading Room
Open Mon 10.00am – 5.00pm
Tues–Sat 9.30am – 5.00pm
See www.bl.uk or call +44 (0)1870 444 1500 for
opening hours of other reading rooms.

2 **BT Archives**
Tues 10.00am – 4.00pm
Thurs 10.00am – 4.00pm
Please call to make an appointment.

3 **Camden Local Studies and Archives Centre**
Mon & Thurs 10.00am – 7.00pm
Tues & Fri 10.00am – 6.00pm
Sat 10.00am – 1.00pm, 2.00pm – 5.00pm

4 **Family Records Centre (FRC)**
Mon, Wed, Fri 9.00am – 5.00pm
Tues 10.00am – 7.00pm
Thurs 9.00am – 7.00pm
Sat 9.30am – 5.00pm

5 **Islington Local History Centre**
Mon & Thurs 9.30am – 1.00pm, 2.00pm – 8.00pm
Tues & alternate Saturdays 9.30am – 1.00pm,
2.00pm – 5.00pm
Fri 9.30am – 1.00pm

6 **London Metropolitan Archives (LMA)**
Mon, Weds, Fri 9.30am – 4.45pm
Tues & Thurs 9.30am – 7.30pm
Selected Saturdays 9.30am – 4.45pm – call +44(0)20 7332 3820 for dates.

7 **Royal Mail Archive
(Postal Heritage Trust)**
Mon–Fri 10.00am – 5.00pm
Thurs 10.00am – 7.00pm
Selected Saturdays 10.00am – 5.00pm –
call +44(0)20 7239 2570 for dates.

8 **Society of Genealogists**
Tues–Sat 10.00am – 6.00pm
Thurs 10.00am – 8.00pm
Saturday Library tours –
call +44(0)20 7251 8799 for details.

9 **LSE Vacation Accommodation**
If you are planning a visit to London to research family history, you can
make use of the excellent bed-and-breakfast rates at the London
School of Economics halls of residence. Open Easter,
Summer and Christmas, Rosebery Hall offers a welcoming
atmosphere and friendly service that is superbly located just
moments from the Family Records Centre. Facilities
include well-appointed comfortable bedrooms, a
cosy bar and a unique walled patio garden
where guests can enjoy a freshly cooked
full English breakfast, or a simple
afternoon tea.

For more information please
visit www.lsevacations.co.uk
or call 020 7955 7575

10 **The Court Service (Principal Registry
of the Family Division)**
Wills and divorce records for England and
Wales from 1858. Call +44(0)20 7947 6000
for opening times and information.

11 **Guildhall Library**
City of London parish
registers, maps,
directories and more.
Call +44 (0)20 7332 1868
for opening times and
information.

British Library Newspapers
Colindale Avenue
London NW9 5HE

Take the
Northern Line
to Colindale

Map labels:

KING'S CROSS, ST. PANCRAS, EUSTON, ANGEL, FARRINGDON, BARBICAN, ALDERSGATE, ST PAUL'S, CHANCERY LANE, HOLBORN, RUSSELL SQUARE

Euston Rd, Pancras Rd, Midland Rd, Judd Street, Woburn Place, Gray's Inn Road, Southampton Row, Guilford Street, Gulford Street, Bernard St, Brunswick Square, Grenville Street, Hunter Street, Lansdowne Terr, Lamb's Conduit St, Theobalds Road, High Holborn, Red Lion St, Drake St, Procter St, Holborn, Gray's Inn Gardens, Chancery Lane, Mount Pleasant, Phoenix Pl, Farringdon Rd, Clerkenwell Rd, Hatton Gdn, Holborn Viaduct, Shoe Lane, St Bride St, Newgate St, Cheapside, Le Grand, St Martin's, Gresham St, London Wall, Wood St, Aldermanbury, Beech St, Golden Lane, Barbican Centre, Carthusian St, Charterhouse St, Cowcross St, Chartarhouse St, St John Street, Percival St, Mdwin St, Skinner St, Emouth Mkt, Central St, Lever Street, City Road, Goswell Road, Old Street

St John St, Rosebery Ave, Myddelton St, Meredith St, Gloucester Way, Skinner St, Corporation Row, Rosoman St, Northampton Rd, Exmouth Mkt, Green Lane, Bowling Green Lane, Clerkenwell Close, Farringdon Rd

5 mins, 6 mins, 13 mins, 14 mins, 10 mins, 6 mins, 20 mins, 10 mins

WHERE CAN YOU

- Access over 100,000 items on local & family history?
- Use the largest collection of parish register & census index copies in Britain?
- Get immediate, valuable advice from experienced genealogists?
- Attend informative lectures presented by experts?
- Browse our great range of publications?
- Surf a growing range of online records?

YOU WILL GET ALL THESE AND MORE FROM

THE SOCIETY OF GENEALOGISTS
the one-stop resource for everyone in family & local history

Take advantage of our unique, refurbished **LIBRARY** with over 9,000 Parish Register copies and wide-ranging material on Civil Registration, Censuses, County Records, Poll Books, Heraldry & Family Histories - on microfilm, fiche and PC.

Visit our online sales ordering system at www.sog.org.uk for details of society **PUBLICATIONS** – over 150 titles containing valuable information on where to find source material. Titles include My Ancestor was a Merchant Seaman, My Ancestor was a Coalminer, National Index of Parish Registers (by county)

Join the Society – **MEMBERSHIP** gives you:

- FREE access to the library & borrowing rights
- A 10% discount on all Society publications, lectures & courses
- FREE copies of the highly respected Genealogists' Magazine
- FREE access to an increasing range of online records

all for **just £43 a year!***

For an **INFORMATION PACK**, simply email the Membership Team on:
membership@sog.org.uk   OR   Tel: 020 7553 3291

MAKE THE MOST OF YOUR RESEARCH WITH:
Society of Genealogists, 14 Charterhouse Buildings, Goswell Road, London EC1M 7BA
Tel: 020 7251 8799   Fax: 020 7250 1800   Web: www.sog.org.uk

* Initial Joining Fee £10.00

Registered Charity No. 233701. Company limited by guarantee. Registered No. 115703. Registered office, 14 Charterhouse Buildings, London, EC1M 7BA

Brick Making.

Understanding old trades and occupations
Doreen Hopwood

Pin Making.

For the majority of us today "going out to work" is a fact of life which we accept as the norm. However, until the early nineteenth century (and even later in some areas), this term was rarely heard. Our ancestors would have gone "out" to the fields or farmland of their employers, but for most, their place of residence and place of work was the same.

At the beginning of the eighteenth century, apart from London, there were only seven towns/cities with a population in excess of 100,000. These were Birmingham, Bristol, Liverpool, Manchester, Newcastle, Norwich and York, and, between them, they accounted for only 2% of the country's population. London accounted for a further 10%, leaving over 80% living in small villages, each with fewer than 300 inhabitants.

Domestic or cottage industries were prevalent, sometimes referred to as "proto-industrial", under which all the members of the family (or household) worked together as a unit in order to support themselves. They did not rely on cash, and often became self-provisioning by means of bartering or exchange of services. In pre-industrial society, seasonal farm work would generally be available to supplement the family's income, especially at harvest time. As time wore on, the home-based workers became more of a mini-industrial unit, selling their products on to "middlemen", (or "foggers" in the metal trades). Every member of the family was a potential contributor to the family income.

Daniel Defoe, writing of his tour through the country in 1724 noted that in Yorkshire "... the women and children ... always busy carding, spinning etc, so that

Butter Churning.

no hands being unemployed, all can gain their bread, even from the youngest to the ancient."

In areas such as the Black Country in the Midlands, home-based industries ran parallel with the growing numbers of factories and heavy-metal industries. Items such as chains and nails - both of which needed only a relatively small outlay in terms of equipment and space, continued to be made in small workshops, often attached to the family home well into the twentieth century.

The separation of home and work is a characteristic of industrialisation, when the household economy became reliant upon wages earned by individuals outside of the home. Until the mid-nineteenth century children and women joined their menfolk in the factories, mills and mines, but increasing legislation throughout the century restricted their employment and eventually the idea of the male-breadwinner working outside the home to support his wife and family became the accepted practice. This is often referred to as the asymmetrical family economy, but, in reality, many married women and daughters continued to work from home as dressmakers, milliners, laundresses or by taking in lodgers/boarders. However, this "employment" often remains absent from documents such as census returns, partly because the male head of the household did not want to appear unable to support his female dependents, and possibly to keep any additional earnings from the authorities.

We now freely speak of "multi-tasking", but this is by no means a new phenomenon. Many of our ancestors had more than one job, and would probably have skills which they could fall back on. My great-grandfather had learned his trade as a boot and shoemaker in Northamptonshire, but when he came to Manchester in 1861, he described himself as a soda water manufacturer and shoemaker. At another time he was a coffin-handle maker and a shoemaker simultaneously. In a 1869 advertisement, W Dawkes

Grinding Cutlery.

of Leamington Spa offered his services as "Builder, Plumber, Glazier, House Decorator and Undertaker" with "experienced workmen in all branches of the building trade".

The textile mills of Lancashire and the West Riding of Yorkshire were places where the factory operatives (or hands) first emerged, but even taking these into account, in 1831 the average number of employees per employer was a mere eight and a half persons. In 1851, the largest single occupational group in the country was the agricultural labourer. Many of these "ag-labs" became the urban builder's labourers working on the construction of houses, factories and civic buildings in the growing towns and replacing the early nineteenth century navigators (diggers of canals) to become the railway 'navvy'.

"Following in father's footsteps" may have become a popular music-hall song, but the majority of boys had little option, and it was usually accepted that they would follow their father's trade. Availability of work, which was limited where a town relied on only one major industry/employer, and a lack of skills and training opportunities further restricted any choice. In 1906 the local newsagent offered Thomas Jordan 5 shillings a week and training, but, as he would earn 6s 6d down the mines, his father was adamant that he took the latter job.

Most trades have their own district jargon and terminology, and mining is no exception. Thomas started working at a Durham coalmine in 1906 at the age of 13, and described a task which had hardly changed in 70 years "Dressed up as a little miner in a blue flannel shirt, short breeches and strong shoes … I descended the mine to earn my living. It was 9 p.m. and I may ascend that shaft at 8 a.m. if my relief came early. I was a 'trapper boy' pulling open and shutting the door to allow the 'putters' to come through … I must stay in position until relieved". Until factory legislation was effected, boys as young as seven worked as trappers. By the age of 12, he could 'progress' to become a 'putter', which involved the manual pushing (or putting) of trains of coal onto the cranes. They worked in gangs, led by a "headman" and assisted by 'half-marrows', 'foals' and 'helpers-up'.

It is easy to imagine that the working class formed a homogenous unit, but this has never been the case. In the Victorian period it was made up of a huge series of sub-classes which merged into each other, but with virtually nothing in common between the top and the bottom. Apart from the different strata across the

Japanner.

working class, each skilled occupation had its own hierarchy where every individual knew his place. Writing in 1837, W B Adams described the hierarchy among coachmakers. At the top were the bodymakers "… a species of aristocracy to which the workmen look up with feelings of respect, half of jealousy … carriage makers are entitled to a species of condescending familiarity … but working painters can at most be favoured with a nod".

The hierarchy within domestic service was even more rigid with little opportunity for social mobility beyond parlour maid or footman. Dickens reflected the "know your place" attitude in 'The Chimes', written in 1845:

"O let us love our occupations
Bless the Squire and his relations
Live upon our daily rations
And always know our proper stations"

The pessimistic view of the Industrial Revolution paints a grim picture of grimy, industrial towns (like Dicken's 'Coke Town' in Hard Times), and the destruction of craft skills and individuality. However, the process brought in new crafts too and made possible things that could not have been done by hand power alone. The 'electronic age' of the late twentieth century saw even more rapid changes in technology and the need to learn new skills. Ironically, twentieth century jobs, such as draughtsman and comptometer operator disappeared even more quickly than their nineteenth century predecessors in, for example, hand-loom weaving.

Occupations shown on census returns can confuse the modern family historian, and this is where it is important to look at our ancestors within their contemporary society. Many commonly used descriptions of the nineteenth century have a very different twenty-first century meaning. On the 1891 census, my grandmother's older sister (aged 18) was described as a "hooker", which is not to be confused with its present day interpretation. My great-grandfather was a boot and shoemaker, which used hooks and eyes as a means of fastening them.

The classification of the population by occupation has always been problematic for Registrar Generals, partly because the same occupation or trade could be called by a variety of names across the country. In some areas, a 'pigman' did work with animals, but in others, he was a dealer in crockery or a worker in an ironfoundry handling pig-iron. In 1891 the Registrar General complained about instances arising from "… the extremely inaccurate and inadequate manner in which uneducated, and often, indeed even educated persons, describe their calling". Initially, there were just three classification categories – "agriculture", "trade, manufacture or handicraft" and "other", but by the time the 1911 census was taken, a much more elaborate system had been drawn up.

People tended to aggrandise their work on census forms, such as the solicitor's clerk who became an attorney, or the bricklayer's labourer who said he was a bricklayer. There are numerous terms for the women who took in washing, ranging from laundress down to a lady who 'keeps a mangle'. You may find that an ancestor gave a very precise name for his work, and this can be most helpful, especially if it was connected with a localised trade, or one that no longer exists. Generally speaking, if your ancestor worked in a town associated with a particular industry (such as cotton in Manchester) you are likely to find out exactly what his daily worked involved. My ancestors regularly appeared as 'slubbers', 'tenters', 'strippers' and shuttlers', all inextricably linked to the cotton trade. You can be forgiven for thinking that a 'rogue spotter' was an early form of detective, but he inspected filled bottles at a bottling plant, and extracted any that were badly filled or damaged.

The dictates of fashion are also reflected in the types of occupations our ancestors may have undertaken. Before the discovery of aniline dyes, vast quantities of insects and vegetable matter were needed to produce the fashionable colours of the day, and huge quantities of leather and other animal skins were worked on by 'fullers', 'tanners' and 'hatters'. Many of these processes used highly dangerous substances, and the use of mercury in hat-making gives us the expression "mad as a hatter". When one fashion declined in favour, there was usually another to take its place. The demise of the buckle as a means of fastening clothes and shoes saw the rise of the button. The adaptability of workers was vital in order to remain employed, and patents were taken out in vast numbers during the nineteenth century to protect inventions or improvements to existing machines. W E Newton of London took out a patent for apparatus for "the manufacture of iced beverages" in 1869, and ice-cream vendors, known as "hokey-pokey men" were visible on the streets from the 1890s. The realisation of the danger of fires, together with the budding insurance industries brought about many patents, such as the forerunner of the fire extinguisher. Dick's patent portable self acting fire engine was patented in 1866. [see advert] The "Book

of Trades or Library of Useful Arts" was published in three volumes in 1806, and describes many now obsolete occupations such as 'currier', 'cork-cutter', 'wool-comber' and 'feather-worker'. The latter worked with ostrich, goose, heron, cock, swan and peacock feathers to fashion "… ornaments for the human head … for the beds on which we lie … for the pens with which we write". By the mid-nineteenth century, there was a huge demand for ostrich feathers for the newly created funeral industry. Undertakers often described themselves as 'Funeral and Feathermen'.

Sometimes a family headstone may provide a snippet about the deceased's occupation, as in the case of ironfounder Joseph Dowler, who died in 1787 and is buried at Aston Parish Church. His epitaph reads:

> *"My sledge and hammer lie reclined.*
> *My bellows too have lost their wind.*
> *My fires extinct, my forge decayed.*
> *And in the dust, my vice is laid.*
> *My coal is spent, my iron's gone.*
> *My nails are drove, my work is done".*

Inventories attached to wills up to the late eighteenth century provide a complete picture of both the home and the workshop of the deceased, and, from these, it is possible to get a glimpse of his daily work, and the equipment he used.

Directories for London were published from the seventeenth century, followed by provincial directories in the eighteenth century. These can be considered as a form of 'yellow pages' as they were (amongst other things) the advertising medium of their day. Those of the late eighteenth century reflect the fashions and luxuries of the time as well as the necessities of everyday life. Sketchley's Directory of Birmingham for 1784 includes peruke makers, sword cutlers and snuffer makers, and reflects the whole social and economic spectrum. In the days before health care was accessible, 'bleeders' (with leeches) and 'cuppers' were in demand, but I was stumped by the man described as a 'butter carer' on the 1901 census surname index. An examination of the census enumerator's book revealed that he was a 'button carver'! – a much more plausible explanation

Whatever your ancestors did for a living, finding out about their daily work can help us to understand about the society in which they lived.

Charcoal Burning.

London Treacle, Syrup of Roses and Fish Kettles
Food and cooking utensils in early modern probate inventories
Jill Groves

[This articles is based on two chapters (with additions) in
Piggins, Husslements and Desperate Debts by Jill Groves,
published by Northern Writers Advisory Services]

Sugar Trade.

Published Jan.1.1823 by Harris & Son, corner of St Pauls.

The Problems of food in Probate Inventories

Probate inventories are not a perfect source for diet.
In many ways they are very imperfect as a source
altogether as Margaret Spufford has pointed out. Fruit
like strawberries, rhubarb, raspberries, gooseberries,
apples, plums, cherries and pears, which must have
been grown in many gardens and orchards were
deemed by law not to belong to the executor(s) and so
should not be valued by the appraisers for the probate
inventories because they came 'mainly from the soil,
without the industry or manurance of man'. This takes
no account of the work of arborialists in the
seventeenth century. John Ryle of High Greaves,
Etchells, in Cheshire in his Memorandum Book of the
1680s mentions in passing that he had growing in his
orchard in the late seventeenth century apples, pears,
plums and cherries. A survey of Wythenshawe Hall
dated 1657 mentions 'many outlandish fruit trees' in
the courtyard orchards which may mean apricots,
peaches and quince trees. Richard Shireburne of
Stonyhurst, Lancashire listed in his account book of
1572 eight apple varieties and two pear varieties
which he had just planted.

Kitchen garden crops were not counted because 'roots
in garden, as carrots, parsnips, turnips [sic].., and
suchlike, shall not go to the executor, but to the heir',
since they could 'not be taken without digging and
breaking the soil'. Only goods, chatells and cattle
deemed to be administered by the executor had to be
listed in the inventory. The same might have also
applied to the roots in the field and to such vegetables
as onions, leeks and garlic.

Yet in Northenden in 1657 a schedule of all the three-
life-leased tenements showed that there were thirty-
six gardens, twenty-two orchards, six 'backsides' or
small backyards in which to grow vegetables and fruit
in a total of forty-three tenements.

However, apples, probably because they could be
stored as a crop in quantities, do appear in inventories
but not the apple trees. Tusser, the sixteenth century
farmer and poet, made it plain his wife specially
planted the soft fruit in her kitchen garden.
The gooseberry, raspberry and roses all three
With strawberries under them, trimly agreed

Raspberries, gooseberries and strawberries could not
be kept, except as conserves of some sort – however
jams, or their solid cousins the fruit cheeses, could be
cut into cubes and served at the end of a meal with
sweet wine. But that was in the wealthier households.

So it is to contemporary sources outside of
inventories that we must look for references to what
was grown in the kitchen garden or the orchard or to

utensils for gathering them or cooking them such as
apple pots, frying pans, spits and kneading troughs,
cheese presses, and fishing nets.

'Wee Find That William Browne and one Hart have
made a trespass in fishing in John Johnson pitts and
breakinge downe his hedge therefore they have lost
their amerciament either of them.' (Northenden Court
Leet Records)

Then there is the seasonal angle. An inventory taken
in April or May may have very little in the way of
food mentioned because all the seed corn should have
been planted and little or nothing would have been
harvested apart from the occasional vegetable from
the garden and the milk not yet fit to turn into cheese
or butter.

Food in the early modern period

The seventeenth and early eighteenth centuries were a
time of transition in English cuisine, in both gentry
houses and ordinary homes, from elaborate, spiced
meat dishes of the medieval period with their fruit
and vinegar sauces to what in some ways was a
plainer cuisine which used more sophisticated
cooking methods, but where the meat and vegetables
might be masked by nothing more than a butter sauce.
Puddings, in all their variety, sweet and savoury, were
the great feature of English cuisine from the late
seventeenth century onwards. Sugar was beginning to
supersede honey in the seventeenth century and
beekeeping was very much a declining occupation in
the eighteenth century.

Old fashioned flavourings for stews and meat
tenderisers, like crack verjuice or crab apple vinegar,
were still in favour in early seventeenth century
Stockport, and old-fashioned spices jostled still for
space on the shelves of local apothecaries alongside
newer food stuffs such as sugar candy, salad oils and
distilled waters. Medieval and early modern cooking
in the great houses used vinegar in meat stews and
people liked spicy sweet and sour dishes. William
Dickinson of Stockport, Cheshire, 1619, had crab
apples. Ursula Gerard of Stockport, the widow of
Rector Gerard, in 1624 had crab apple vinegar and
crab apples in her house. Henry Seele of Stockport,

Wheat Harvest.

yeoman, 1600, had crab apple vinegar or vargis in a barrel. Hale in Cheshire in the early seventeenth century had eight inventories mentioning apples and crab apples. This township also had the largest number of hives in the area in the early seventeenth century - forty-five altogether. Perhaps the bees were used to set the fruit on the trees.

Exotic spices such as East Indian ginger, candied ginger, oil of mace, molasses, syrups, London treacle, salad oil and distilled waters were on offer to customers of William Simkin of Stockport, apothecary, in 1623. John Bowland of Stockport, haberdasher, sold currants, spices and hops to his customers in 1638.

Edward Harpur of Stockport, Alderman, in 1650 had such spices as mustard seed, caraway seeds, fenugreek, aniseed, turmeric and 'long pepper' (chillies?) amongst his foodstuffs. Whether he sold them or just had them for consumption by himself and his family is not known. The accounts of his brother Francis in caring for Edward's four daughters after his death gives an insight into the extra food consumption habits of the Harpur family over and above what they could produce for themselves. Treacle was bought as a medicine to mix with wormseed. Sugar candy and white candy were used as much as medicines as sweetmeats. Francis Harpur bought from the local apothecary for the consumption of his nieces rose water, syrup of roses, mace, nutmeg, conserves (all of which could have made sweet-meats of the sort that graced the banqueting tables of aristocracy at the beginning of the seventeenth century). Prunes would have been dietary emetics for the nieces. Currants, sherry sack and a rack of veal were probably eaten by more members of the family than just the nieces. Some items of food were bought by Francis Harpur which Edward Harpur had the means to produce, such as milk and eggs. Vinegar and honey were produced locally but people would have bought them in.

Stockport people had access to the fashionable banqueting sweetmeats of the early seventeenth century. Frances Jodrell, spinster, 1631, a member of an esquire family, Jodrell of Yeardsley, Cheshire, had a one box of marmalade amongst her prize possessions. This was not the sort of marmalade bought today to spread on bread and toast, but a much thicker variety which could be cut into squares and served as a sweetmeat with sweet wines like petit fours at the end of a meal. Frances Jodrell had probably made the marmalade herself from bitter

Spanish oranges, boiling up the fruit first before adding it to the very hot sugar syrup and then pouring into an oiled wooden or tin box (this method achieves a set in a matter of minutes if not seconds). The modern equivalent is Portuguese quince paste.

Distilled waters, i.e. spirits or 'strong waters'/aquavitae ('water of life') distilled over fruits or herbs, were very popular amongst the aristocracy and gentry in the late sixteenth and early seventeenth centuries, accompanying the sweetmeats served in the banqueting course of a feast. Spirits, whether distilled at home or bought in, were also making an increased appearance in the late seventeenth century, but had not yet entirely lost their medicinal reputation. Distilled 'waters' appear in recipe books during the seventeenth and eighteenth centuries along with their medical uses. George Bolton and John Hollenpriest, both well-to-do yeomen of Hale, in 1614 and 1626 respectively enjoyed aquavitae, probably bought from an apothecary in the nearby town of Altrincham, Cheshire. George Bolton, a man of fashion in his own modest way, had wine glasses in which to serve his aquavitae. (George Bolton seems to have been an innkeeper with an upmarket establishment.)

Rosewater, a popular, non-alcoholic 'water' in Frampton Cotterell, Gloucestershire, was used to perfume food, clothes and people. It was the by-product of making oil of roses perfume (attar of roses). To make both oil and water needed access to the petals of at least an acre of rose bushes. Samuel Pill of Westerleigh, near Frampton Cotterell, gentleman, must have had such a rose garden to feed his rose still. The way of producing the oil of roses was only discovered by the Emperor of Persia in the early seventeenth century. It was then manufactured at Shiraz from 1612 onwards.

Thomas Poole of Frampton Cotterell, yeoman, 1679 had a still but probably he, or more likely his wife, only made alcoholic flower waters for medicine for the family. The same is probably true of Harry Symes of Frampton Cotterell, esquire, in 1687, and Jacob Hollister of Nibley, Westerleigh, yeoman in 1689, both of whom had stills. John Sorocold of Bowdon, Cheshire, a retired member of a cloth trade family from Manchester, had a limbeck or still in his house in 1649.

The brandy and port trade of the port of Bristol was growing, spirits were becoming cheaper to buy and so those who could not afford their own still could afford the occasional barrel of brandy. There were a number of people who enjoyed the occasional spirit and drank them from little dram dishes: John Smith of Westerleigh, feltmaker, 1690, Priscilla Brinkworth of Frampton Cotterell, widow, 1697, Margaret Smith of Nibley, Westerleigh, widow, 1698 and John Frape of Westerleigh, yeoman, 1697, had dram dishes but no mention of spirits in their possession. Two were widows, and Margaret Smith had a silver caudle cup, which may mean that the spirits supped from their dram dishes were more for medicinal purposes.

Maria Fields of Bricket Wood, Hertfordshire, in 1703 drank distilled spirits. In the parishes around Leicester only one inventory had an aquavitae bottle, John

North of Ratby, husbandman, in 1636.

Old-fashioned, comforting drinks such as possets and caudles were still popular in some eighteenth century homes in Clifton and Westbury, near Bristol. Richard Horwood of Westbury, slaughterman, 1717, had caudles cups to warm and nourish him after a day's work. In his case they were probably made of thin oatmeal gruel strengthened with beer and perhaps sweetened with a little honey.

William Cross of Shirehampton, Bristol, 1729, also liked caudles, but as these were served to him in a silver caudle cup it is likely that these were upmarket versions made with eggs, sugar and wine.

Frampton Cotterell people made cider in great quantities. Thomas Gyles of Winterbourne, husbandman, in 1618 had a great wooden wassail bowl and earthenware cups, which he probably used on *Twelfth Night* and other celebration days. It was probably beautifully carved and would be filled with hot, spiced cider, roasted apples and toasts. It could be that Thomas and his family went out the orchards with their neighbours and this great bowl to wassail the apple trees. This was a tradition reaching back to early medieval times.

'Apple tree, apple tree, I wassail thee!
To blow and to bear,
Hat vulls, cap vidls, dree-bushell-bag vulls!
And my pockets vull too!
Hi Hip Hip! Hooraw!'

Throughout the seventeenth century pies, cakes and other pastries were important in some areas and becoming more sophisticated and that meant that a greater variety of cakes, pies and tarts could be made. Most Whitby people had cast iron ranges. The ranges were a combination of fire grate, potracks, jacks, and chimney cranes for spits, pans, pots and hobs to take chafing dishes. It might be that side ovens were included. George Cockerill of Bagdale near Whitby, master mariner, 1725 ate tarts made in six tin tart pans and drank coffee and tea. Charles Lightfoot, Bailiff of Whitby Strand and innkeeper, 1744, served his customers pies and small cakes, and sliced eggs as well as wine in twenty-nine wine glasses. William Coulson of Whitby, shipbuilder, 1750, and his guests ate pies and cakes too. Frampton Cotterell people also made cakes and pies. Mary White of Frampton Cotterell, widow, 1795, baked pies in a tin pie pan. Samuel Codrington had pies and biscuits on his table baked in latten petty pans and a latten hoop for cakes. Elizabeth Hall of Westerleigh, widow, 1711, made pies in a pie pan. William Thomas of Says, Westerleigh, gentleman, 1717 had his pies baked in latten pie pans. Mary Trahern of Westerleigh, widow, 1729, baked hers on pie plates. However, the question is did they cook the pies and cakes in their own ovens. Hannah Trahern of Westerleigh, widow, 1709, had an oven, probably set into the thickness of the wall in the kitchen with an iron peel to take out the bread, pies and cakes she cooked there. Samuel Codrington almost certainly had at least one oven in his vast kitchen. So too did William Thomas of Says. But Widow White might have taken hers to the local baker. Nicholas Waterhouse, a non-confirmist

minister in Bowdon, Cheshire, in 1724 ate pies made on a 'pie iron' and little cakes made in petty tins by his wife Elizabeth, her daughters and the servants. Smethwick households (near Birmingham) baked and ate pasties, lunch pail food *par excellence* before the advent of the sandwich. Smethwick nailers were rather like Cornish miners in that they would be working all day long and might not have time to return to the house for a midday meal. Pasty tins or pans were found in four inventories.

There is some evidence that people, particularly those on higher status diets, ate salads and fruit. Salads were not unknown in early seventeenth century Frampton Cotterell. Thomas Baylie of Hambrook, Winterbourne, yeoman, 1640, had salad dishes and John Vidler of Stoke Gifford, husbandman, 1642, had a salad dish. Turnips appeared on the plate of John Weblie of Hambrook, Winterbourne, husbandman, 1639, about one hundred years before they began to be fashionable with agricultural improvers.

William Simkin of Stockport, apothecary, supplied salad oil to his customers in the 1620s. Richard Attwood of Hambrook, Winterbourne, yeoman, 1688, ate salad from his salad dishes but Elizabeth Rodman of Winterbourne, widow, 1676, ate fruit and vegetables, with her sauces, fricasses and roasts, so she may have had salads too.

James Ewer of Bricket Wood, husbandman, in 1694 had cherries to eat. Although cherry trees were probably quite common fruit trees in orchards throughout England, it is very unusual to find them in an inventory they were so perishable and their season relatively short.

Just as the cuisine of the country was changing in the seventeenth century, so too were the utensils on which the food was placed. From the late sixteenth century and into the second half of the seventeenth century if pottery was put on the table it was usually Ticknallware, pottery from Ticknall in Derbyshire which was sold throughout England. In areas close to ports Dutch blue and white Delftware (from Delft), itself an imitation of Chinese blue and white porcelain, was beginning to take the place of Ticknallware. In at least one case Ticknallware was replaced by real Chinese porcelain early in the seventeenth century. Henry Clarke of Stoke Gifford, vicar, 1620, had four 'porcelain' saucers in which to serve his condiments. Chinese porcelain had been imported into Bristol via Holland since 1609 and it is quite likely that this was true porcelain rather than earthenware imitations.

In 1761 Henry Wheatcroft of Frampton Cotterell, gentleman, had quite a collection of delft dishes, octagonal plates, platters and six delftware pots. By the 1760s these are likely to be Bristol manufactured delftware. One English firm had started making delftware in London in Limehouse in the 1740s, but moved to Bristol in about the 1750s. The remains of their small limehouse factory have recently been uncovered.

Knives and forks arrived in North-east Cheshire in the early eighteenth century and also in Whitby. Christopher Hill of Whitby, master mariner, 1718, had a set of nine knives and forks, so he, his family and guests could eat their meat and pudding without soiling their hands with gravy, an improvement in hygiene not yet come to many other households. Yet by the 1750s even Miles Sweeting of Whitby (1752) who was only worth £17 4s 3d, drank tea sweetened with sugar, and had knives and forks.

One of the most unusual cooking items found in the Frampton Cotterell inventories was a salamander which was owned by John Smith of Iron Acton, inn-holder, in 1728. A salamander was a flat disc of iron with a handle which was heated in the fire and used to brown pies and the tops of dishes like burnt cream, a very old English dish despite its modern French name of creme brulée.

All these changes in diet and in what food was served on and eaten with show that, as in furnishing of houses, there was growing sophistication and comfort. Things which had been the preserve of the aristocracy, Delftware, tea, coffee, sugar, knives and forks, were now bought and used by well-to-do yeomen and not so well-to-do husbandmen. However, one further change had yet to come. Sweet dishes were still alongside savoury at each course. Service à la Russe, with separate sweet and savoury courses, as we have it today arrived in the nineteenth century.

New Foods in the Eighteenth Century
Potatoes
Today the potato is so much a staple food it does seem very surprising that it was not widely grown or eaten in the eighteenth century outside of the North-west.

Potatoes - the smaller, round, South American variety, not the large, sweet potato of North America which arrived in aristocratic households via Spain in the late sixteenth century - arrived in Ireland some time between 1580 and 1600. They arrived in Lancashire before 1673 when they were being cultivated as a

garden crop at Swarthmoor Hall, Ulverston. Before the end of the 1680s they were known in North-east Cheshire. Samuel Peers of Sale, Cheshire, husbandman, in 1684 and Henry Chorlton of nearby Ashton-on-Mersey, in 1687, were growing potatoes to feed their families and possibly their livestock too. Edward Marsland of Sale, farmer, in 1757 was growing them on a commercial scale to supply the local markets.

J.H. Hodson says that potatoes were first adopted in the county for animal fodder and by the better-off farmers. However, by the 1730s potatoes were being grown in North-east Cheshire by husband men and poor craftsmen and probably not just for animal fodder.

Unfortunately for research into the subject, just as potato growing is taking off in Cheshire so the making of inventories to prove a will stops. But other sources such as the Manchester Court Leet Records and printed sources such as Aikins *A Description of the City from 30 to 40 miles Round Manchester* (1795) and the Reports for the Board of Agriculture appear towards the end of the eighteenth century.

Potato cultivation increased greatly in Cheshire between 1770 and 1790. Henry Holland noted in 1801 that a large number of varieties were being grown mainly around the market towns of Altrincham and Frodsham for the multiplying populations of Manchester and Liverpool. They would be sent to either town via the Bridgewater Canal. With the increasing price of grain, the potato had become the staple food in many parts of the North-west by the end of the eighteenth century.

Given that the population was nearly everywhere increasing during the mid to late eighteenth century, causing problems of adequate food supply to towns, why did the potato take so long to establish itself in many parts of the country? One reason may lie in the fact that most of Cheshire and Lancashire still practised a three or four field open field system, which allowed for a great deal of flexibility. In addition, most farm holdings in North-east Cheshire had small crofts of anything from a quarter of an acre to two acres in size close to the farmhouse, which were used for the growing of vegetables, hemp and flax. This is probably where potatoes were first grown and then transferred out into the fields.

One reason why potatoes were not grown for the markets until the end of the eighteenth is that landlords in the North-west imposed heavy fines on tenants who did so. The Tattons of Wythenshawe Hall, near Northenden, Cheshire, and their successors the Egerton-Tattons, lords of the manors of Northenden and Etchells imposed fines of £5 an acre on extra tillage over and above the normal third of the total acreage and stipulated in addition that no more potatoes be grown than could be consumed by a tenant and his family. In 1750 William Tatton told John Sumner, husbandman, that he could use no more than 20 roods for growing potatoes. In later leases the potato growing land was not stipulated but counted in with the rest of the tillage. One reason for the Tatton's (and other landlords') dislike of potatoes is that the

Hog Feeding.

crop took a lot out of the ground, and needed a lot of manure - making the ground too poor to grow other crops the following year, and the manure be better used elsewhere. However, from the 1720s onwards the Tattons had no control over potato growing on large parts of the two manors when they sold most of the customary three-life leases to their tenants.

Potatoes were getting to Manchester's markets, whether the landlords liked it or not. In October 1779 William Heywood of Altrincham was caught giving John Unsworth short weight of 3ozs on the 3lb of new potatoes the farmer sold to him. For this he was charged 2s 6d by the Manchester Court Leet.

Sugar or honey
Sugar was not a new food in the eighteenth century. The English gentry and aristocracy were making sweet-meats and even plates and cups out of it to grace their banquets and impress their friends. But at that time it was expensive and sales of it to those below the level of county aristocracy was mainly done through apothecaries, because sugar and things preserved or conserved in it or sweetened by it, such as rose-water and liqueurs, were considered to be medicinal. So in the 1620s William Simkin of Stockport, apothecary, sold syrups, conserves, London treacle, candied ginger and molasses to his customers and patients. London treacle cost 2s a pound, molasses 3d a pound at a time when the daily wage for a labourer was 1s. Treacle and 'wormseed' was a favourite cure for worms in children in the seventeenth century. Deborah Harpur of Stockport, daughter of Alderman Edward Harpur, was regularly dosed with this mixture in the 1650s.

Henry Best of Elmswell in Yorkshire made mead from his honey to which he added malt and hops to flavour and preserve.

In the eighteenth sugar became slightly cheaper and more available through grocers like Edward Dean of Northenden, who had 26lb of the stuff in his shop in 1742, John Lupton of Altrincham, chapman, who also sold sugar candy and treacle in 1701. However, although sugar was increasing replacing honey in cooking, from the evidence of inventories, even in gentry and wealthy households, its principal use was as a sweetener of the new drinks, tea and coffee. The principal sweetener and preserver in cooking for ordinary people probably continued to be honey. Fruits continued to be conserved in honey and honey was still used to sweeten feast day cakes, but the number of beehives declined.

Tea and Coffee
The first public sale of tea, (green leaf tea from China), in Britain took place in 1657. In the same year an advert for coffee appeared in the London *Publick Adviser*. ".....a very wholesome and Physical drink" that "doses the Orifice of the stomack, forticies the heat within, helpeth Digestion, quickeneth the Spirits, maketh the heart lightsom, is good against Eye-sores, Coughs, or Colds, Rhumes, Consumption Head-ach, Dropsie, Gout, Scurvy, King's Evil and many others".

Similar claims were also made for tea. Tea and coffee were taken to the British heart very quickly, despite their costliness. A pound of tea could make 300 cups. It could also be dried and sold for reuse.

From the early eighteenth century onwards the new, expensive drinks, tea, coffee and chocolate, appeared in Clifton, Westbury, Frampton Cotterell in Gloucestershire, Whitby, and Ashton-on-Mersey in Cheshire. William England of Shirehampton, butcher, 1730, took to the new drinking habits enthusiastically with five chocolate cups, five small tea dishes and one copper coffee pot. However, he was out-classed by Henry Wheatcroft of Clifton, gentleman, in 1761, thirty years later, who had a coffee mill, two tea boards, numerous cups and saucers for tea and coffee, plus five chocolate cups and two copper tea kettles.

In Whitby many people took to the expensive tea and coffee, to an extent not seen in other collections of inventories. (Was smuggling involved?) Some sailors, mariners and fishermen, people who spent very little time on shore and therefore needed little in the way of food or cooking utensils in their houses, had only teapots and china to drink it from. George Robinson of Whitby, mariner, 1756, had only tea which he drank from chinaware.

Samuel Codington of Frampton Cotterell, esquire, 1709, had a coffee pot and a coffee mill. Christopher Sturges of Frampton Cotterell, feltmaker, 1754, had a tea kettle.

The new drinks also arrived in Ashton-on-Mersey, Cheshire with the rector and his curate in the early eighteenth century. Thomas Ellison, the rector, had a copper teapot and a coffee pot in 1717. His curate, Samuel Bellis, in 1726, had a tea kettle, a teapot, a coffee pot and china in which to serve it and silver spoons with which to stir in the sugar.

The advent of tea and coffee at the time presented people in Britain with non-alcoholic drinks that were safe to drink (because the water to make them was boiled). Previously, because the water supply, even in the country, could not be guaranteed to be safe, only alcoholic drinks were considered to be safe (the water was heated to a high temperature in the brewing process and alcohol itself was a mild disinfectant). The weakest alcoholic drink was small beer (a weak beer) which was recommended for children and servants. The only non-alcoholic drink before the advent of tea and coffee was whey. It was available in rural areas, but only where it was not used to fatten the pigs. Tea was taxed heavily, but three-quarters of the annual tonnage of imports, 18 million pounds weight a year between 1770 and 1779, was said to be smuggled.

The evidence of the inventories in this study is that tea was far more popular than coffee. Possibly because coffee required a good deal of preparation, roasting and grinding the beans before long infusion, and because of its association with coffee houses, the reserve of men, it did not appeal to people as much as tea.

Tea, by contrast, was easy to prepare. It also introduced, to those who had the leisure and the wealth to indulge in it, an elaborate social ritual and a new meal, afternoon tea taken with friends and acquaintances. Heather Couttie described it in her glossary to Peter Pownall's diary:
'heated water was brought by the maid, and sometimes reheated by the hostess in a kettle over a spirit stove or 'Indian Furnace'', and the tea was made at the table. The teapot was of porcelain or silver, often with a stand and the tea was served in small handleless cups on saucers. If sweetmeats or tiny cakes were offered they were held in the fingers until eaten.'

Anne Hughes describes just such an occasion on 6 March 1796. "Yesterday we to the Lady Susan to drink tee. We did hay a verrie pleasant time, and did sat in my ladies little palour; me and Johns mother feeling verrie welcome there. The room was verne fine, with grand chaires and littel tables. I did see some dust in the chair legs. She did play some verrie pretty musick on her own spinette, which is bigger than mine, an a very sweet thing. Then we with her up to her bed-chamber to see her new furniture therein. Then to the tee drinking in her parlour, where her futman did wait up on us, as if we were the quality."

The Rise of Puddings
"They bake them in the oven, they boil them with the meat, they make them fifty several ways: BLESSED BE HE THAT INVENTED PUDDING, for it is a manna that hits the plates of all sorb of people ...[and they] are never weary of it." So wrote Monsieur Missons in the 1690s of the great English dish of the eighteenth century, facilitated by the invention of the pudding cloth. They could be plain batter puddings, baked under roast meat, light, moist egg custards or rich plum puddings. The commonest type, were the batter (soggy, egg custard type) or the Yorkshire (light, crisp) pudding which was baked or roasted under the meat in dripping pans.

Oysters.

By the early eighteenth century earthenware pudding basins, called 'pudding mugs', began to replace the pudding cloth. Puddings made in these and steamed over boiling water were lighter than those made in pudding cloths. The next development came with the advent of the cast-iron range when puddings could be poured into greased dishes and baked in the oven as pudding pies - the precursor of the souffle.

However, few appeared in eighteenth century North-east Cheshire beyond the Yorkshire pudding type roasted under the meat.

It is remarkable the range of sweet and savoury dishes that could be achieved with batter puddings: the sandwich fruit or vegetable saucer batters, which appear all along the Marches, and which Dorothy Hartley believed to be Welsh in origin, Tunbridge batter fritters, Nottingham batter and apple pudding (a sort of apple toad-in-the-hole) and Kentish fruit batters (like a clafoutis, a cross between an egg custard and a batter pudding) and, of course, toad-in-the-hole, a good dish when there were fresh sausages from a pig killing and the oven still very hot from bread baking.

Knives and forks
Knives and spoons had been commonly used to eat food since before the Middle Ages. Forks arrived in England in medieval times, but were only used by aristocrats for eating sticky sweetmeats. By the seventeenth century the use of forks was spreading to the rest of the meal. Tom Coryat is given the credit for introducing English society in 1607 to the use of the fork to help the knife cut the meat and then transfer it to the mouth without the food having been touched by human hand.

'the Italian cannot by any means indure to have his dish touched with fingers, seeing all men's fingers are not alike clean:'

As Ben Johnson pointed out in 1616, the use of forks saved the washing of meat juice-, oil- and sauce-stained napkins.

By the end of the seventeenth century forks had reached the gentry. In the 1720s matching sets of knives and forks reached the wealthy yeoman class in Bowdon and Hale, Cheshire. Nicholas Waterhouse, minister, of Bowdon, had a set of six forks and six knives in 1724. In 1729 George Ashley, yeoman, of Ollerbarrow Hall, Hale, had knives and forks. These sets of cutlery are often in silver and therefore expensive and represent status symbols. Peter Brears points out that forks were not adopted by the poor and the working class until the nineteenth century. Anne Hughes, at the end of the eighteenth century, still had to reprove her young serving girl, Sarah, for using her fingers not her fork. "Sarah bein' hungrie did ett a good dinner; pyking the mete off the bones with her teeth, for which I reproved her - but la, in 2 minuets she at it again."

Sarah came from a poor family and probably had not used a fork until she came to work for Anne Hughes.

Conclusions

Probate inventories can be used to study the diet of ordinary people, especially their deficiencies are corrected by information from other local documents. One hundred and sixty years is a short period in which to study changes in diet in this area of North-east Cheshire. Even so it is possible to see changes over time. There was growing materialism towards the end of the seventeenth century and in the first half of the eighteenth century. People were putting more of their money into comfortable furnishings for their houses and this extended to cooking utensils with the appearance of teapots and coffee pots and more sophisticated cooking equipment such as petty tins and pie tins indicating the use of ovens. More sophisticated ways of eating food such as knives, forks and spoons replaced fingers, hunting knives and spoons. Pewter replaced the wooden trenchers in many households for every day use by the end of the seventeenth and was replaced in its turn by the more decorative white metal (enamelled tin plate) and Ticknall ware.

There is a great deal more we could learn about the diet of ordinary people and the way they cooked food in the seventeenth and early eighteenth centuries. Some everyday recipes have survived into the twentieth century, such as Lancashire strong gingerbread, the making of cakes from a piece of bread-dough (West Country lardy cakes and Lancashire crushes), lobscouse (a sheep's head or beef and root vegetable stew, which, with variations, appear wherever the Vikings have been), Lancashire hot-pot (today served without the oysters under the potato crust), haverbread and mincemeat (now made almost without the meat). Some old recipes used by folk in the seventeenth and eighteenth centuries went over to America and returned to us in the twentieth century, for example, honey or sugar cured hams, waffles, alt pork and beans, and cooked cheese cakes.

Food historians have used the 'receipt books' of people like Lady Elinor Fettiplace, the writings of Gervaise Markham and the cookery books which were published from the mid-seventeenth century onwards, but these all originated with a well-to-do, even wealthy, and highly articulate section of English society who could afford sugar, sweet potatoes and servants to help them cook and clean the house. They do not give any idea of what the diet of ordinary people in the seventeenth and early eighteenth century was like. Probate inventories were not taken of the goods of the very poorest, but many better-off

labourers and poor husbandmen did have their goods and chattels inventoried, so these documents can be seen as able to give us information, though probably not 'chapter and verse', on what they ate and how they cooked it. Not until societies like the Manchester Statistical Society began surveying the food and drink consumed by poor families in Manchester slums from the 1850s onwards, do we have an idea of the diet of working people.

Food was an important part of the local everyday economy, perhaps more then than now because most of it was home-produced, home cured and home-made. More needs to be learnt about the history of diet and cooking to fully understand life in the seventeenth and eighteenth centuries.

Sources
Primary Sources
Manuscript
Cheshire Archives Probate Inventories of Hale, Northenden and Timperley, Cheshire
Stockport Local Studies Library
The Memorandum Book of John Ryle of Highgreaves, Etchells, 1649-1721, transcribed by Frank Mitchells, S/46E73.
John Rylands Library, University of Manchester Tatton Family Papers, 1657 Schedule Survey of Northenden dated 3rd March, 1656/57.
Archive Department, Central Reference Library, Manchester Etchells Court Baron Records, Midsummer 1662.

Printed
Mary Bodfish, editor, *Probate Inventories of Smethwick Residents 1647-1747*, Smethwick Local History Society, 1992.
All My Worldly Goods: An insight into family life from wills and inventories 1447-1742, Bricket Wood Society, 1991.
Heather Coutie, editor, *The Diary of Peter Pownall: A Bramhall farmer, 1785-1858*, Old Vicarage Publications, Congleton, Cheshire, 1989.
J.P. Earwaker, editor, *Manchester Court Leet Records, Vols I to VI*, 1888.
Henry Holland, *Report to the Board of Agriculture*, 1801.
Anne Hughes, *The Diary of a Farmer's Wife, 1796-97*, Penguin, London, 1984.
J.S. Moore, editor, *The Goods and Chattels of Our Forefathers: Frampton Cotterell and District Probate Inventories, 1539-1840*, Phillimore, Chichester, 1976.
J.S. Moore, editor, *Clifton and Westbury, Probate Inventories, 1609-1761*, University of Bristol, Department of Extra-Mural Studies, 1981.
Phillips, C.B., and Smith, J.H., editors, *Stockport Probate Records, 1590-1619*, Record Society of Lancashire and Cheshire, Vol.124, 1984-5.
Phillips, C.B., and Smith, J.H., editors, *Stockport Probate Records, 1620-1650*, Record Society of Lancashire and Cheshire, Vol.131, 1992.
Hilary Spurling, editor, *Elinor Fettiplace's Receipt Book*

Brewing.

Published Jan.ᵗ 1.1823 by Harris & Son corner of St Pauls.

Elizabethan Country House Cooking, Viking Salamander, London, 1986.
Noreen Vickers, editor, *A Yorkshire Town of the 18th Century: The Probate Inventories of Whitby, North Yorkshire, 1700-1800*, Brewin Books.
Wilshere, Jonathan, editor, *Ratby Probate Inventories 1532-1778*, paperback edition, Jonathan Wilshere publisher, Leicester, 1986.
Donald Woodward, editor, *Henry Best of Elmswell: The Farming and Memorandum Books of Henry Best of Elmswell l642*, Oxford University Press, 1984..

Secondary Sources
Jill Groves, *Piggins, Husslements and Desperate Debts: a social history of North-east Cheshire through wills and probate inventories, 1600-1760*, NWAS Publications, 1994.
Dorothy Hartley, *Food in England*, Macdonald and Jane's, paperback edition, London, 1971.
J.H. Hodson, *Cheshire, 1660-1780: Restoration to Industrial Revolution*, Cheshire Community Council, History of Cheshire Series, Vol. 9, Chester, 1975.
Elisabeth Luard, *European Peasant Cookery: The Rich Tradition*, Bantam Press, 1986.
Margaret Pannikar, 'An apple orchard in Tudor Lancashire',

Lancashire Local Historian, Vol.16, 2003.
Margaret Spufford, 'The limitations of the probate inventory', in *English Rural Society, 1500-1800: Essays in honour of Joan Thirsk* edited by John Chartres and David Hey, Cambridge University Press, 1990.
Reay Tannahill, *Food in History*, Penguin, 1988.
Jennifer Stead, *Food and Cooking in 18th Century Britain: History and Recipes*, English Heritage, 1985.
C. Anne Wilson, editor, *The Appetite and the Eye,* Food and Society Series, Edinburgh University Press, Edinburgh, 1991
C. Anne Wilson, editor, *Banqueting Stuffe,* Food and Society Series, Edinburgh University Press, Edinburgh, 1991
C. Anne Wilson, editor, *Liquid Nourishment: Potable Foods and Stimulating Drinks,* Food and Society Series, Edinburgh University Press, Edinburgh, 1991
C. Anne Wilson, editor, *Traditional Food East and West of the Pennines,* Food and Society Series, Edinburgh University Press, Edinburgh, 1991.
Rosemary Milward, *A Glossary of Household, Farming and Trade Terms from Probate inventories,* Derbyshire Record Society, Derby, 1986.

Pins for the People:
the hatpin in England 1880 -1920
Dr Jane Batchelor

If you go out today, will you put on a hat? Today hats in general are out of fashion, designer hats notwithstanding. It is no longer commonplace to wear hats in the street, except sunhats for summer and bobble hats for winter. Having said this, many people especially women still wear hats to weddings. Furthermore, to return to designer hats, when attending events which are part of the English social calendar eg Ascot and the Chelsea Flower Show everyone knows they can partake of a little English socialite glamour simply by wearing a hat in a place where it is good to be seen to be seen. Some of these hats are doubtless secured by hatpins. What is a hatpin? Quite simply, it is a pin that secures a woman's hat. If a hat especially a large hat is not pinned then it may fall off, or be carried away by the wind. For some older readers it is still a familiar object but for most younger people it may not be. This article examines briefly the hatpin in its heyday of 1880-1920, and aims to show how such small domestic objects should still have a place in the telling and retelling of local and family history.

Pins for the People: Mass production and the hatpin in the Victorian era
As Gladys Beattie Crozier observed in her article on the history of hats "Quaint Fashions in Headgear" which appeared in *The Lady's Realm magazine* in 1903 when interest in large decorative hats was at its height for centuries women have worn "elaborate" structures on their heads to make an impression on those around them. Of course those elaborate structures have always needed pinning up, so the hatpin was not new in this sense. However what was new as Eve Eckstein and June Firkins point out in their book *Hat Pins* (1992) was the availability of hatpins to the woman in the street. In the 1880s the fashion for ever larger hats coincided with the possibility to manufacture ever more hatpins. Sheffield factories for instance did not only produce steel for industry, but steel shafts for pins, and many of the workers making these pins were those cheapest to hire – women. It was possible to purchase a tablet (packet) of six – twelve glass topped steel pins for 6d-1s a packet (Eckstein, pages 11 and 24).As it was normal to use the pins and throw the packet away, pins which are still in their packets are now conversely much sought after as rare items. Not all manufacturers however saw hatpins as throwaway items. Charles Horner was a "prolific manufacturer" of hatpins, influenced by the Arts and Craft Movement which reacted against shoddy workmanship and sought to hark back to an ideal pre-machine age (O'Day, *Victorian Jewelry*, p.13); making use of the new machines Horner nevertheless produced "good quality" work made in a Celtic style emphasising an ancient tradition of craftsmanship and good designs, produced on his own premises to keep costs down (Eckstein, pp. 12-13).

I do like to be beside the seaside: holidays and hatpins
Hats were expanding; hatpins were ever larger and more decorative; the same combination of overblown optimism and technical expertise which allowed the mass production of hatpins in the nineteenth century was also reflected in the greatly improved transport system, especially the construction of the railways, which made travelling easier, cheaper and more convenient (O'Day, p. 8). Increasingly travel was something everyone could do, particularly when it was simply a matter of getting on a train and going to the seaside, the quintessentially English holiday. Whilst on holiday you could purchase a souvenir such as hatpin of Cornish serpentine or Whitby black jet (Eckstein, p.25). Hatpins were always useful, some becoming sentimental objects. You could buy the most basic steel and glass pin, but you could also buy hatpins with sequins, enamelled hatpins, pins of mother and pearl and pins in the shape of silver cupids. Or you could purchase a hatpin stand to keep your pins in made of for example silver, pottery, unglazed bisque or ceramic (Baker, *Hatpin and Hatpin Holders* p.101). The ceramic holders would often have a ceramic transfer of the shield of the local town to which they belonged. For instance Southend on Sea produced one with a boat, a churchman and an inscription "per mare per ecclesiam" linking the church to the sea.

The mourning hatpin: Whitby black jet
One of the most popular types of hatpins to be purchased at holiday or at home were hatpins made of black jet. Black was a practical colour for everyday wear, but also undoubtedly reflected the fashion for black mourning jewelry to remember deaths, especially the deaths of socially important people. As early as 1751 following the death of Prince Frederick ladies had carried black mourning fans (Llewellyn, *The Art of Death* pp. 94-95). But the fashion for wearing black mourning jewelry famously reached a height in the nineteenth century after the death of Prince Albert, the Prince Consort, after which Queen Victoria famously wore mourning for forty years. Moreover, before 1914 it was usual for all women to observe a two year period of mourning following the

lost of a relative (Baker,p.146). This enthusiasm for sombre jewelry was reflected in the flourishing of the jet industry at Whitby in Yorkshire, a popular seaside resort; as early as 1873 over 200 workshops were supplying Whitby jet to the home market, US and the empire (O'Day, p.37).

It is terrible to see the armoury of sharp pins that stick out of the sides of some women's hats – Mrs C E Humphrey: hatpins and women's suffrage
The late nineteenth century onwards had seen women becoming more active and joining in sports activities ranging from canoeing to cycling to driving, for those who could afford it: indeed manufacturers advertised special "wind defying" motoring pins for the newly liberated women (Nunn, *Fashion in Costume* p.133, Eckstein, p.25). As hatpins expanded, as horizons expanded, so did society's anxiety about where the pins might be stuck. In 1908 the Daily Mail reported that at the Clerkenwell Sessions suffragette prisoners were to appear in hats but without hatpins, just to be on the safe side (Eckstein, p.8). In December 1913 warnings were issued on London Underground not about what Al Qaeda might do, but about the hotly debated issue of the dangers of wearing hatpins. If a man lost his eye through a hatpin, would he get adequate compensation, especially if the woman was poor? ("That hatpin danger" letter to *London Times* March 31 1914 from "One for all", quoted by Baker, p.40). Having said this, on a practical level long pins probably did sometimes get in people's way, and by 1920 the "dagger" pins of the 1890s had shrunk to three inches (Baker p. 40, Eckstein p.10).

Buttons and pins: 1914 - 1918
Given the personal sentiment often attached to hatpins it is not surprising then that some people made their own hatpins personal to them, and one of the most striking examples of this is the way in which soldiers' buttons belonging to fathers, sons, brothers and husbands going to war were often turned into hatpins by removing the shank and attaching the button to the pin. It was also possible to have this done professionally. The button company Firmin took advantage by selling attachments for home use (Eckstein, p.20).

Finding out about hatpins today
It is increasingly difficult to find hatpins today, but there are various ways in which you can find out about them:
Elderly relatives – may have hatpins which they would be prepared to show you, but more crucially may be able to tell you more about when and where they or their relatives wore them.
•Museums – costume museums such as the Victoria and Albert in Museum where hats with pins may be on display. However it also worth investigating

military museums, where hatpins may be found among military memorabilia. Clearly a pin with a soldier's button is much more interesting if you know the person or family it belonged to.
Photographs – if you cannot find hatpins you may be able to find photographs. These can be of equal interest to the historian because they tell you the context in which pins were worn. It is also worth looking at old photographs in museums, archives, libraries and antique fairs.
Antique fairs, car boot sales, craft fairs, auctions - All places where pins can be rummaged for, but beware if the pin base is shiny or covered with glue, as this could be a new pin stuck on to an old base. Be aware that a hatpin head may be stuck on to an older longer pin to try and increase its value (Baker, p.97). If at an auction it makes sense to check out the catalogue so that you have a good idea of what you are buying before you take the plunge.
The Hat Pin Society of Great Britain has an interesting website, which tells more about the history of hatpins, articles on hatpins and hatpin collecting in general. It can be found at hatpinsociety.org.uk

To join the society you can email enquiries@hatpinsociety.org.uk or you can write to:
The Hat Pin Society of Great Britain, PO Box 110, Cheadle, Cheshire, SK8 1GG

In conclusion, hatpins may be "outdated" items but in their time they also represented a new industrial age and were part of a growing tourist industry; they were personal mementoes, objects of love and grief; they were innocuous items to be found on every woman's dressing table and possible weapons of destruction. In short, it is essential when writing about local and family history not to neglect the everyday items in our lives: it is often everyday items which are dearest to us, and which form the fabric of whom we were, are and may become.

Select Bibliography
Baker, Lilian *Hatpin and Hatpin Holders* (Kentucky, Collector Books, 1976)
Buck, Anne *Victorian Costume* (Ruth Bean Publishers, Carlton, Bedford, 1984)
Crozier, Gladys Beattie, "Quaint Fashions in Headgear" (*The Lady's Realm*, 1903, pp. 431-439.)
Eckstein, Eve and June Firkins *Hatpins* (Shire Album 282, Shire Publications Ltd, 1982)
Llewellyn, Nigel *The Art of Death: Visual Culture in the English Death Ritual* (Reaktion Books, London, 1991)
Nunn, Joan *Fashion in Costume 1200 –2000* (2nd edn, Herbert Press, London, 2000)
O'Day, Deirdre Victorian *Jewelry* (Charles Lett and Company, London, 1974)

My Great Grand Aunt Maria
Jean Cole

Sometime around 1964, my father and I decided to draw up a family tree from his memories and various family documents and mementoes. In 1977 when I first began to trace my family history, I looked at this sketchy family tree and set out to prove or disprove various theories. I discovered that although my father's memory had been quite good, he had managed to transfer some family members on to the wrong trees! One question posed by Dad that had intrigued me all those years was this – a family member had either become a Quaker or a Mormon. In the event, after much searching, I discovered that my great grand aunt, Maria Bidgood, the sister of my great grandfather, Abraham Bidgood, and the aunt of my grandmother, Annie Alice Elston Phillips, after many ventures into the aspects of various religious denominations, had eventually decided that the Church of Jesus Christ of Latter-day Saints was the true faith for her. Maria, it proved, had led a most interesting and intriguing life, so much so, that I decided to follow her life story through and discover all I could about her, her family and her life in Utah.

Maria, the fifth child of Abraham and Agnes (nee Gillard) Bidgood, was born in Halberton, Devon in 1832 and had been baptised into the Church of England on 11 March 1832 at the nearby parish of Willand. At 14 years of age, Maria left home to serve an apprenticeship with a milliner in Tiverton. On completion of her apprenticeship she moved to a responsible position as superintendent of a large millinery establishment in Bristol and from there to No 5 North Parade, Bath, with the Misses Beake and Headington, prestigious milliners to the gentry, where she remained for six years. She then moved to Leamington Spa to take charge of a millinery business but, after a while, now aged nearly 30, she decided the time had come for her to establish her own business in London. However, her health was not good and she was forced to move back home to Halberton. In 1861 she set up a millinery and dressmaking business at 115 Fore-street hill, Exeter. This was the period of time when millinery was at its most flamboyant and hats were a masterpiece of the milliner's art.

Although Maria had been raised in the Church of England she began to feel this Church no longer satisfied her religious needs. Deciding that baptism by total immersion was the right path, she joined the Baptist Church in Exeter where she worshipped and taught Sunday School. After a while she still felt something was missing and began to attend the Plymouth Brethren meetings. This turned out to be a fateful step, as this was where she was to meet her future husband, William Jarman, a widower, with a small son, Willie. It was not long before William Jarman was expelled from the Brethren as being an extortioner and a liar – a practice he seemingly continued nearly all the days of his life. The couple were married at Exeter Register Office in 1862 where William gave his age as 25 and Maria as 28 – a slight discrepancy on her part of two years or so! Their son Albert John was born two years later.

All was not well with their marriage, as William, it turned out, had a violent temper and was a gin drinker. He was declared a bankrupt and the couple lost everything they owned including all Maria had worked for. Fate had not been kind to the family as

Salt Lake City 1887

shortly after this Maria and her son, Albert, fell ill with the smallpox and, around the same time, little Willie Jarman died from a brain fever. To add to the family's woes, Jarman had been reported by their neighbours to the City authorities for smashing up the marital home, including the fact they thought he was insane. Hurriedly, the family left Exeter and moved to Chudleigh where their daughter, Maria, was born. William had a mental breakdown and was committed to an asylum, from where he managed to escape. Maria decided the time had come to take charge of her own life and moved back to Exeter where she worked diligently to reinstate her millinery and dressmaking business in order to make a living for herself and her children and life went on peacefully for a while. However, William was to reappear in her life and they were reconciled and moved back to Chudleigh. In 1865, they sent for a pamphlet entitled 'The True Faith' by Orson Pratt of the Mormon Church. They were so impressed by the promises of this Church that they decided this was the faith they had been seeking. By now, though, Maria had discovered that William had seduced her apprentice, Emily Richards. It seemed obvious that William had also decided that possibly a new beginning in a new country with a new faith could provide a new way of life for himself and his family. On 30 July 1866, the family with Emily Richards were baptised by Bishop McMaster of the LDS Church in the sea at Exmouth. Within four weeks they had sold their possessions and, with Emily, set off for Liverpool where they embarked on the 'City of Washington' on 22 August 1866 for the six week voyage to New York. On arrival In New York they passed through the official immigration depot at Castle Garden before leaving for Albany where they were to stay for the next two years working to earn the money for their final journey to Utah. In the event, however, there were no wagon trains westward from 1866 to 1868 because of the Indian Black Hawk wars that were ravaging the west. In Albany, it was not long before William was up to his old tricks once more, stealing money from his employers, Whitney and Myers Dry Good Store, drinking and generally being his old pompous and aggravating self.

In July 1868 at the end of the Black Hawk Wars, the family, with Emily, under the protection of Bishop McMaster, travelled by railroad to Fort Laramie, where they joined the John R Murdock Company travelling the Oregon trail by wagon to Salt Lake City. They were to be among the last of the pioneers, as by May 1869, the 'spike of gold' finally joined the railroad from east to west at Promontory Point. The 'Deseret News' of Tuesday, 26 August 1868 reported Murdock's mule train had arrived safely in 21 travelling days from Laramie, although there had been six deaths en route – four infants and two young children, but the immigrants were healthy and robust although they bore the marks of mountain travel.

William and Maria were re-married in the Mormon faith and at the same time, William took Emily Richards to wife. It was reported by William that relationships between the two women were strained! Jarman took to his old ways before long and whilst Maria was pregnant with her third child she applied for a divorce as William had threatened her with a

knife and a gun. The divorce was granted and she was given back her maiden surname of Bidgood. William was fined $25 dollars plus $5 dollars for contempt of court! Maria's third and last son, John, was born soon after. Maria was now obliged to earn her own living to keep herself and her three children. She took a position in the millinery department of the Auerbach Company store whilst her young daughter was obliged to help with the household chores as well as attending school. Maria worked, saved hard, and was able to sell her adobe house and purchase a city lot where she had a large new house built in 1870 and where it remained in the family until the death of Maria junior in 1953. It was here that Maria began her own millinery business setting her hats out on shining poles in the large bay window, according to her daughter's account of Maria's life. It was stated Paris fashions were not followed in America but that Philadelphia fashions took precedence. The Bidgood family showed in the 1870 and subsequent censuses as did William Jarman, carpenter, who showed only in 1870 as a married man with four in his household.

On 17 March 1881, Maria Bidgood married Robert Henry Ford, curator of the Salt Lake City Museum, according to the Salt Lake City directory. This was another unfortunate union, as neither party was happy in the marriage. Maria junior also disliked Ford immensely and moved away from home. William Jarman, in the meantime, had left Salt Lake City under a cloud and had gradually made his way back to New York, preaching against the Mormons along the way, eventually sailing for home and Exeter. In 1883, a scurrilous report about Maria, written by William, appeared in a Midland newspaper, including a statement that the Mormons had murdered his eldest child, Albert. Maria was obliged to refute this publicly stating that it was a pack of lies and that Albert was alive and well in Salt Lake. This same year, Robert Ford departed for England to perform his Mission for the Church. As he returned home, Maria sailed for England to visit her friends and relations and to pursue her genealogy. She recorded her travels in her journal adding she was sad to have to say goodbye to her sister and blind brother, Abraham as she boarded the train to begin her long journey back home to Salt Lake City, stating she knew she had found her true faith. By 1889, Maria obtained a divorce from Ford, as by this time he had 'taken to liquor' and had deserted her. In January 1890, Robert Ford died from a fall from the Temple building in Salt Lake City, then under construction. Some years after this, Maria was married to Mark Barnes and became known as Mrs Maria Bidgood Barnes. In 1919, Maria, now 87, rented out her home and went to live with her daughter and her husband, Samuel DeGrey. In 1922, the Church Relief Society celebrated her 90th birthday where it was reported…'it was an appropriate testimony to the respect and affection she had always retained in the community and her years of devoted service and sincerity in all things and under all circumstances'. Maria died in 1924.

But, what about William Jarman and his over-active imagination and whose own father had even declared him a 'son of Belial'? He had travelled across the States lecturing against the Mormons and, on his return to Britain, continued lecturing all over the country. He published several anti-Mormon tracts and a book with an immensely long title beginning `Hell upon Earth…' According to this book and various newspaper reports his notoriety in causing riots with the police being called out in Sheffield, Swansea and other places, gained him much publicity in his cause against Mormonism, In Sheffield in 1888, Jarman had instigated a confrontation with a Mormon Elder so that the police were called out to stop Jarman's armed supporters from causing injury to the Mormons.

However, around the age of 57, it seemed, William Jarman had begun to run out of steam and made a decision to settle down, setting up a business as a master confectioner and becoming an Exeter City councillor. Although he claimed to have been married several times, no evidence has been discovered to substantiate this. It was obvious he had made money out of his lecturing and publishing activities and was able to purchase a rather up-market house in Exeter.

William's son, Albert John Jarman, visited England on his Mission for the Church of Jesus Christ of Latter-day Saints and called upon his father who, true to his fashion, did his best to entice him away from the Mormon Church, without success. William Jarman died in 1917 at the age of 80 and, in his will, left everything he owned to Albert but nothing to his other two children from his marriage to Maria. Even to day, Jarman is still recorded in Mormon archives as a notorious apostate.

Conclusion: In this précis of my great grand aunt's life and times I have only been able to cover the finer points of Maria and William's story and have been obliged to omit much of my research into the lives of those who made the hazardous journey westwards towards their final goal. It was obvious that these were two strong-minded individuals who would have never lived amicably together – much like oil and water! Jarman lived in an age when it was considered that man was the superior being and a woman should know her place. From my point of view, research into two such lives and the times in which they lived proved to be an intriguing exercise. I was extremely fortunate to access the records of not only the Devon Record Office and West Country Studies Library in this country, but also those of the LDS Church Archives, the Daughters of the Pioneers Museum, the Family History Library and the Salt Lake City library. Nothing proved to be too much trouble for the staff of all these repositories who dealt with all my questions with efficiency and friendliness.

Bibliography
Church of Jesus Christ of Latter-day Saints chronology
Costume 1066-1966 J Peacock (1986)
Costumes of Everyday Life M Lister (Barrie and Jenkins)
`*Deseret News*' (British Library Newspaper Library, London)
Encyclopaedia of Dates (Penguin)
Expectations Westwards: the Mormons and the Emigration of British Converts in the 19th Century PAM Taylor (Oliver & Boyd)
History of the United States H Brogan (Longman)
If you travelled West in a Covered Wagon E Levine (Scholastic Inc)
`*Illustrated London News*' from 1848 onwards (Swindon Reference Library)
Life on Board an Emigrant Ship DH Pratt & PF Smart (Series 418. 1980)
Truth Will Prevail: The Rise of the Church of Jesus Christ of Latter-day Saints in the British Isles 1837-1987 ed. V Ben Bloxham, James R Moss, Larry C Porter (1987)

How William Coleman lived:
Probate Inventories and Living Conditions
Stuart A. Raymond

Can you imagine having to live without electricity? With no gas, and no taps with running water? With no carpets on the floor, and no soft chair to relax in? With no glass in the window, and no car to drive to work in? If you can, then you can imagine what it must have been like to live in England before 1800.

Our ancestors lives were conditioned by their three primary needs: food, shelter, and clothing. They were much more aware of these needs than we are: they had to be, as these commodities were not as easily procurable in their day as they are in ours. Their lives were much more precarious than ours, and where we tend to assume without thought that our basic needs will be met, they knew that it was quite possible that theirs would not. Famine stalked the towns and villages of England as recently as the nineteenth century; shelter was much more primitive than it is today, and sometimes poorer people could not afford to own more than the clothes they stood up in.

One of the best sources for studying the material conditions in which our ancestors lived are the inventories which are often found with wills and other probate records in the archives of the ecclesiastical courts. These inventories list the goods owned by them, and in so doing give us a picture of the conditions in which they lived. Sometimes they list goods room by room, so that it is possible to visualise the complete contents of each room. Thus the inventory of William Coleman of Writtle, mason, who died in 1635, includes goods in the hall, the buttery, the chamber over the hall, and in the chamber over the shop (the document is printed in F.W.Steer, ed. *Farm & cottage inventories of mid-Essex*. Phillimore, 1969). Unfortunately, it tells us nothing of any goods which may have been in the shop.

The hall was the principal room in Coleman's house. In some houses, it could be the only room. In this case, it was the only room with a hearth. This is demonstrated by the fact that it housed various items of equipment for use over the fire. It had a pair of

trammels - bars or hooks for suspending pots over the open fire. A pair of pot hooks are also mentioned, used for the same purpose. There was a gridiron, a framework of iron bars with short legs and a long handle, used for broiling food over the fire. The brass kettle that is also listed may have been used for boiling water on occasion; however, it was not a kettle in the modern sense. Rather, it was an open pot with semi-circular handles on both sides, which could be suspended over an open fire.

The hall also contained two pails, used for carrying water, or perhaps milk, three chairs, an old press cupboard, and an old powdering tub. The latter would have been used for salting meat. We do not know whether the tub actually contained meat at the date of death. If it did, it was probably bacon. Sides of bacon 'hung at the roof', i.e. hanging from the rafters, are frequently mentioned in inventories, although not in this one. The old press cupboard was probably used for storing clothes which were not in use; Coleman's 'wearing apparell', together with the money in his purse, were valued at ten shillings. His three chairs are the only items which would be found in the main living room of the modern home.

Also on the ground floor was the buttery. This was the cool room, used as a storeroom for food and drink away from the fire. Inventories frequently do not mention food and drink, and that is the case here; we do not know what perishables Coleman had in his buttery. We do know, however, what he would have placed on his table: eight pewter dishes, a salt cellar, five pewter spoons, a great wooden dish and other 'smale wooden dishes and other implements'. In the seventeenth century, pewter ware was fast replacing the older wooden dishes. Coleman, however, died a poor man, and probably could not afford to replace all his wooden dishes with pewter.

He did, however, own a 'joyned' table and six 'joyned' stools. These had been made by a carpenter, and were better than the rough furniture which many of his contemporaries owned. Probate inventories are full of 'table boards', that is, loose boards which could be placed on trestles (often described as 'horses') to form a table. Coleman's table stood in his 'chamber over the hall'. 'Chamber' was a word that could be used for any room, but often indicated an upstairs bedroom, or perhaps a parlour or other private room. In Coleman's case, it seems to have served a dual role; it housed a table, six joined stools, a chair and a cushion. Was this where his family ate their meals? But there was also a 'halfeheaded bedstedle', together with a small featherbed and feather bolster, and an old coverlet. The half headed bedstead was a bed with short corner posts, a head-board of medium height, and either no canopy, or one that only covered the head of the bed. The feather bed was not a bed in the modern sense, but rather a mattress stuffed with feathers, which lay on the bedstead; the bolster served as a pillow, the blanket and coverlet as coverings. The room also housed a pair of scales and weights, presumably used in Coleman's business as a mason.

The final room that can be described is Coleman's 'chamber over the shoppe'. This also housed a half-headed bedstead with what we would call its bedding; in this case, the latter included four 'towen' sheets, made from tow, the coarser fibres of flax or hemp. These presumably covered both beds. There was a 'little flockbedd', that is, a mattress stuffed with flock, perhaps used by a child or a servant. A table cloth was found in this room, presumably used for the table in the other chamber. If both half-headed bedsteads were double beds, that means there were beds for five people in this house. The probability is that they were all occupied at night. The question is, who by? Men like Coleman could not afford to have empty beds in their houses, and a count of the number of beds in probate inventories may give an indication of the number of people in each household.

This chamber also had four 'old huches' and two little boxes. A hutch was a small chest or box used for the storage of corn or meal; unfortunately there is no indication of what was in Coleman's hutches or boxes.

This inventory also notes that Coleman's working tools were worth five shillings, although it does not describe them. The total value of the items inventories was £6-11-08. This, by itself, suggests Coleman's poverty on the day he died. However, inventory totals are not necessarily a good guide to wealth; in this case, there are indications that death caught Coleman when he was going through a rough patch. His house had four rooms, with some relatively good furniture - the joined stools and tables, the two half-headed bedsteads. Pewter was not the mark of the poorest. A note at the foot of the inventory provides a possible explanation. It notes that he had a 'desperate debt' amounting to £11-00-00, due from John Luckyn of Little Waltham. Debts were 'desperate' when the assumption was made that they were non-recoverable.

Coleman's probate inventory is just one of the many thousands which have been printed, and I chose it as an example at random. It illustrates what could be found in the house of a working man in the seventeenth century. A similar inventory today would be far longer; the poorest person in the 21st century is likely to have more possessions than Coleman did. His house was bare by modern standards.

In one respect, however, Coleman was unusual. He had no livestock. It was normal even for tradesmen to have a pig or perhaps a cow. William Watkiss, blacksmith, of Dawley, Shropshire, for example, had three milking cows worth £5-10-00, and 'two yeare olds' worth £2-00-00, and a sheep worth four shillings. The total of his inventory was £16-07-06. The inventory is printed in Barrie Trinder & Jeff Cox, eds. *Yeomen & colliers in Telford*. Phillimore, 1980.

Coleman's probate inventory probably tells us more about him than any other document. However, it would probably be possible to discover much more information from other documents. His will, unfortunately, does not survive, or it might have given us useful information on his family and bequests. The parish register could, however, be consulted for his date of death, and for the baptisms, marriages and burials of his family. Deeds, leases, rentals, court rolls, etc., might be consulted to see if details of the tenancy of his house can be traced. Subsidy returns and parish records may reveal further information. If all these sources of information were to be compared with all the probate inventories for a particular parish, the history of that parish would be well on its way to being written.

Much work on probate records has been undertaken in the last few decades, but there is still a great deal that may be learnt from them. Numerous editions of probate records have been published, but there remain perhaps millions of documents which still lie in the archives unexamined. These records provide genealogists with much information on particular families, they enable local historians to reconstruct the culture of the people who wrote them, and they provide the basic data from which studies can be made of topics as diverse as housing, furniture, agriculture, and wealth. This examination of the inventory of William Coleman is intended to demonstrate some of their potentialities, in the hope of encouraging both genealogists and local historians to continue chipping away at this extremely rich source.

Stuart Raymond is a well known author of bibliographies and guide books for genealogists. He has recently returned to his earlier interest in local history, and published *Words from wills and other probate records* (F.F.H.S., 2004). This is a glossary of archaic words found in probate records, which will be of assistance to everyone wishing to use these documents. It is available from him at P.O.Box 35, Exeter, EX1 3YZ, price £9.50.

Eavesdropping on the Dead
Something to Write Home about
Joseph O'Neill

maintaining contact with home. As the barely literate Bridget Doorley wrote in one of her many letters from Bolton to her sister in Queensland 1887, "It taks me too days to writ a leter."

Letters are so valuable to the family historian because they were often written at seminal moments in people's lives – times of birth and death, after leaving home and in times of dire need. The world wars prompted a great surge of letters, often written by men and women who feared they might never again see loved ones. They knew that the letter they were writing might be their last chance to speak to mother or wife, lover or friend. It is impossible to read letters from this period without feeling the writers' heightened emotions and the intensity of their feelings as they confront the possibility of their own death.

We are not a generation of letter-writers. Telephones, faxes, e-mails and text-messaging mean instant communication. Once received, they disappear into the ether. Consequently, it is difficult for us to appreciate the importance of letters to our ancestors. They were the main means of communication before the mid- 20th century. The thrill of anticipation as the letterbox clattered and the mail fell to the mat is a thing of the past.

Yet for those far from home letters were a powerful focus in their lives, the joy of receiving them exceeded only by the catharsis of writing them. But it is only in recent centuries that letters became an option as a means of communication.

In medieval times hardly anyone other than priests and clerics were literate. It was only in the 16th and 17th centuries that the emerging professional class and tradesmen, whose work required it, acquired the ability to read and write. An analysis of marriage entries in parish registers suggests that in 1642 about 30% of men were able to write their name. It was during the early 19th century that there was a great surge in literacy.

By 1830 most children received some sort of education. By 1839, 66% of men and 50% of women signed the marriage register. By the end of the century these figures had risen to 95% and 94% respectively. But literacy wasn't the only obstacle to keeping in touch. The cheap and reliable postal system we have come to take for granted is of relatively recent vintage. Though Henry I appointed messengers to carry government letters as long ago as the 12th century, it was only with the appointment of Thomas Witherings as Chief Postmaster in the 17th century that the nucleus of the modern system emerged. Witherings established regular post roads, post houses with staff, and fixed charges. The modern postal system evolved on this foundation during the 19th century.

"I hope I never shall die until I see yea," wrote Michael Normile from New South Wales in 1886. "Believe me, my dear father, I feel myself at home when I am reading your valuable letters and newspapers. I read them over and over – but to my grief I expect I never will see home any more or the land that gave me birth. It's all I can say I wish yea and all the county you live in every good luck and prosperity."

One of the results of the growing interest in family history is the belated recognition of the importance of personal letters. Any fact about our ancestors, no matter how trivial, is fascinating simply because it tells us about someone who was our own flesh and blood. How much more enthralling to hold in your hands something their fingers once held, to touch something once warmed by their flesh? What could be better?

One thing is better. What wouldn't you give to hear your ancestor's voice? Wouldn't it be amazing to hear that distinctive cocktail of nuances, inflections, colloquialisms and rhythms that makes each person's speech unique? And how much better to hear him speaking about not only his everyday concerns but also about his deepest emotions, about home, love, his hopes and fears?

That is what personal letters allow us to do. More than any other source, they add flesh and blood to the ancestral bones.

Letters combine the deepest and most personal concerns of the writer with trivia. And it is often the detail that is most moving. ' Does the yard still flood during the winter?' asked Mary Brown in 1886, writing to her mother from Australia. John McCance, writing from Melbourne in 1856 asked his brother for detailed news of home. He added, " for all these things, be them ever so trifling, is precious to me."

The fact that many half literate emigrants regularly expended time and a great deal of effort on writing letters is itself a statement of their commitment to

Victorian developments speeded up internal mail, but contact with people in distant parts of the empire remained tortuous. As late as 1849 letters from Britain to New South Wales took up to five months. This time was gradually reduced during the second half of the century but even in 1914 the London to Sydney post took a month. But this too began to improve in 1911 with the introduction of the first air mail service. In 1919 this was extended to the London-Paris route and in 1937 the Empire Mail Scheme was introduced to carry first class mail throughout the Empire at a standard rate.

As the international postal system improved the volume of letters increased. These are the ones that are most useful to the family historian in helping to fill gaps in the family tree. Most valuable of all are those which are part of a network of communication between scattered relatives.

Recently a family historian chanced upon a 1911 letter from a great granduncle. The letter came from Butte, Montana and the writer, Denis Sullivan mentions the possibility of arranging for his brother Tim to join him in America. The researcher had no other information, apart from the address on the envelope. Armed with this he went to the American Family Immigration History Center website at www.ellisislandrecords.org In minutes he had discovered that Denis did in fact bring his brother to America in 1913. By accessing the ship's manifest he found not only a description of Tim, but the address to which he was travelling and that he had $40 when he arrived.

It is interesting how many emigrant letters jar against our 21st century expectations. We assume that emigrants left home to improve their material conditions and are enthusiastic about the life in their adopted country. Very often the opposite is the case. "Believe my word dear father," Michael Normile wrote in 1889, " you can't pick up money here as quick as the people at home thinks it."

Few writers actually encourage people at home to emigrate and a great number wrote seeking, not offering, financial help. As another emigrant wrote from Australian in the 1890s: " I suppose my uncle John will blame me for not sending for him. I am confident sure it is better for him to stop at home. There is a good many here that would wish to be back again."

Even if the message is no more than a few lines on a postcard, it helps the family historian locate his ancestors within their world more succinctly than even the best social history. William Fife, writing from Fermanagh, Ireland in 1870, summed up the plight of the rural poor: "There is many in this country and there is but one step between them and beggary."

Very often letters suggest relationships that are not otherwise easily determined. And explanations. The life of a maiden grand aunt is laid bare by a letter from a sweetheart who never returned from the trenches.

Letters invariably provide valuable references for events not recorded elsewhere. Nowhere is this better illustrated than in a collection I came across recently.

The Reynolds letters were written by William Reynolds of Manchester between 1866 and 1934 to his brother Laurence in Chicago. In October 1934 James Reynolds travelled from Chicago to Manchester to settle the estate of his late uncle, William Reynolds. As he sorted his uncle's belongings he found a metal box containing dozens of letters William had received from James's family. James took the letters back to Chicago where he discovered that his sister had kept the Manchester side of the correspondence. Together the letters covered the period 1866 to 1934. They gave a detailed account of how James's widowed mother and her six children had arrived in Manchester virtually destitute. They told how the family had established their own business and expanded it until William was one of the city's most successful entrepreneurs. The letters give a remarkable insight into one family's ascent through the echelons of Victorian society.

In October 1934 James Reynolds travelled from Chicago to Manchester to settle the estate of his late uncle, William Reynolds. As he sorted his uncle's belongings he found a metal box containing dozens of letters William had received from James's family. James took the letters back to Chicago where he discovered that his sister had kept the Manchester side of the correspondence. Together the letters covered the period 1866 to 1934. They gave a detailed account of how James's widowed mother and her six children had arrived in Manchester virtually destitute. They told how the family had established their own business and expanded it until William was one of the city's most successful entrepreneurs. The letters give a remarkable insight into one family's ascent through the echelons of Victorian society.

They are particularly fascinating because they tell us

about the life of a family eager to attain respectability and prosperity in a city renowned for the squalor of its living conditions. The Reynolds family lived near Little Ireland, a part of the city made famous by a host of social investigators, including Engels, who describes the wretchedness of the area in his *History of the Working Class in England*. It was also the subject of a street by street investigation by the Manchester and Salford Sanitary Association. Their report condemns its unhealthy back-to-back terraces, open drains, oozing sewers, overflowing privies and filthy piggeries.

Yet the Reynolds letters do not tell of hopeless paupers, oppressed by filth and ignorance. Instead we see an industrious and mutually supportive family dedicated to improving themselves. They are aware of the fine gradations of status within their community and move house whenever they see the opportunity for even the slightest improvement. They are a tea-total family, evangelical in their commitment to hard work and the value of education.

Their letters tell us that our image of the stereotypical slum dweller can hide a lot more than it reveals. They tell us how working class life in the big cities of the 19th century appeared to those who actually lived it. They are invaluable to any family historian whose ancestors shared that existence.

The difficulty with personal letters— other than those of the famous— is that they are among the most ephemeral of historical sources. They seldom retain their sentimental appeal after the death of the recipient and are usually thrown away as part of the ritual clear out. Where they do survive it is often as the result of oversight. Seldom filed away with business documents, they are more likely to turn up in attics, cellars and box rooms than in solicitors' collections.

Ireland's National Library spends half a million pounds every year extending its collection of heritage materials. A sizeable proportion of its acquisitions come from household attics, basements and box rooms. Among the most fascinating are letters, especially those written by people living abroad. They add depth and texture to the past and provide the personal dimension to social, economic and political history.

A large number of personal letters are found at flea-markets and bric-a-brac sales and they often turn up at house clearance sales and in the sort of antique shops that specialize in curiosities. Many turn up in the shops of antiquarian book dealers and I seldom attend a book fair without adding to my collection.

Postcards are more easily found. Most book fairs have at least a couple of dealers selling individual cards, most often sought for their pictures rather than the message on the other side. Collections of cards are still obtainable, though not as easily as formerly. In the early decades of the 20th century there was hardly a household without someone with a postcard scrapbook. Both cards and scrapbooks became very collectable during the 1940s.

Having found a collection of letters, either linked to my family or people who lived in similar circumstances, how do I follow them up?

One of the advantages of letters is that significant facets of their content is generally very accurate. Addresses, dates, the name of the sender and the recipient are likely to be correct. Surprisingly, letter writers seldom mention major historical events even when personally involved. They are far more likely to make reference to local events and very often they confine themselves to family affairs. All of these provide avenues for filling out the lives of our ancestors.

Any reference to local events should be followed up in the local press. When William Reynolds' business premises burnt down in July 1892, the *Manchester Chronicle* provided a detailed account of the fire. The same applies to births and deaths. Until about fifty years ago obituaries and the announcement of births received a great deal of coverage in local newspapers. Weddings were and remain the staple material of many local newspapers.

Details of crimes, accidents and disasters impinging on family life also warranted considerable coverage. Many areas of employment – particularly jobs like mining and agriculture, which tended to dominate the local economy — often have their own histories. Likewise with mention of interests and hobbies. Many golf clubs, for instance, have their own histories and most county records office have the papers of numerous clubs and societies.

Letters are particularly helpful in tracing emigrant ancestors. In the case of those who went to Australia knowledge of when they left and where they arrived makes it a great deal easier to locate them. This is exactly the sort of thing letters provide.

Even if you are not as fortunate as James Reynolds and never uncover a single letter linked to your 19th century ancestors, there are now so many collections available that you will surely find them by someone living in similar circumstances. Do not neglect it. Soon you will find yourself addicted and saying along with one Victorian writer, "I so look forward to your letters. They are my treasure and my joy."

Further Reading
The most engrossing collection of letters, with a splendid introduction and contextual information, is David Fiztpatrick's superb *Oceans of Consolation* – a must for family historians. It provides a wonderful insight into the outlook of the 19th century poor.
Lawrence W. McBride's edition of the *Reynolds Letters* tells us more than any social history about a poor family pulling themselves up from the slums.
Last Letters Home Ed Tamasin Day-Lewis, is a moving collection of last letters from men killed in the Second World War.
Olga Kenya's *800 Years of Women's Letters*, has something for everyone.
There are numerous superb web sites offering an extensive range of letters. The following are worth a visit:
<nttp:www.wendy.com/letterwriting/#collections> letters from Einstein to Yiddish speakers
<http:www.cyberpursuits.com/gen/gen-doc.asp> is a wonderful collection of American letters.

Captain of Industry:
Gordon Armstrong of Beverley (1885~1969)
Martin Limon

Less than fifty years ago the engineering firm of Armstrong Patents was a familiar sight in Beverley. With factories in Eastgate and Swinemoor Lane the company was a a major employer in the town. Once a household name in the manufacture of shock absorbers for the car industry, the company was founded by Gordon Armstrong.

It is often an indication of the past importance of a local person to a town when a building, road or street is named after them. Anyone arriving in Beverley today might be intrigued by the existence of an "Armstrong Way" or an "Armstrongs Social Club" since substantial evidence of the person they are named after has long since vanished.

Gordon Armstrong was not, in fact, a Beverlonian by birth: he was born in April 1885 at Border Rigg, Cumberland, of Anglo-Scottish parents. After serving an apprenticeship at an engineering firm in Gatesehead and attending classes at Gateshead Technical College he had a brief spell at sea as the fourth engineer on a ship working the North Atlantic route. The 22 year old Armstrong arrived in Beverley on January 1st 1907. He had decided to set up in business as a motor engineer having acquired knowledge of the new internal-combustion engine on the way. Armstrong rented a small engineering works, at Tiger Lane Beverley, for £8 a month and despite his lack of tools and equipment called his new business by the grand-sounding name of the *East Riding Garage and Engineering Works*. Although the motor trade was in its infancy Armstrong had chosen his career well for skilled motor engineers were in demand to repair and service the new and often temperamental horseless carriages. The business prospered and Armstrong was able to expand his Tiger Lane premises to incorporate three shops and twelve cottages (which he converted into a large showroom and workshop) and to hire two mechanics and three apprentices. Armstrong's skill as an engineer was shown when, in 1909, he designed and built his own car and drove it to York. A second model of the "Gordon" car was constructed and, in an era when building cars was still the job of a craftsman, contracts for building others (including orders from Australia and New Zealand) soon followed.

In 1910, three years after his arrival in Beverley, Armstrong was involved in another area of technological pioneering: that of aviation. The first powered flight, by the Wright Brothers, had only taken taken place seven years previously and flying was still both new and dangerous. Having witnessed aeroplanes in action at Doncaster, Armstrong decided to get his own and bought a Bleriot monoplane for £20. Having fitted a 25 horsepower petrol engine into the machine Armstrong approached the authorities for permission to use Beverley Westwood for a trial flight. On a Thursday evening, in the summer of

1910, Armstrong's plane was made ready for the flight witnessed, and hindered, by a large crowd that had assembled for the occasion. In the event no flight took place; in trying to start the engine Armstrong was injured when his left hand was struck by the propeller while there was a further mishap when, in trying to turn the machine, the back wheel buckled. Armstrong was forced to abandon his first attempt at flying complaining bitterly of the "thoughtlessness of the crowd" although he was later able, unhindered by people, to get the machine into the air for about one hundred yards.

When the First World War began Armstrong turned his garage business over to the production of munitions and such was the demand for his howitzer shells that in 1917 he bought an old cart and wagon works in Eastgate, Beverley, to expand production. There seems little doubt that Gordon Armstrong was both a skilled engineer and a workaholic but the long hours that he put into the business took a severe toll of his health. When the First World War ended in 1918 he suffered a nervous breakdown. Such was the nature of the man, however, that his agile mind was still at work during his convalescence when he turned his thoughts to the subject of car comfort. In 1919 Armstrong invented a simple but effective shock absorber and this became the basis for the future success of his business. Further development of his shock absorber and that of independent wheel suspension during the 1920s and 1930s led to orders from the Ford Motor Company and, in 1929, from William Morris. At a time of depression and high unemployment in the early 1930s Armstrong's factory was a major success story in Beverley's economy. By the outbreak of the Second World War in September 1939 Armstrong's works in Eastgate were producing 4,000 shock absorbers a day and employing 450 workers. In addition, the earlier roots of his business, motor vehicles, were not neglected. Armstrong was an agent for Austin, Rover, Morris and Standard cars and to add to his business in North Bar Street Beverley, Armstrong built a large 24 hour garage at the junction of Anlaby Road and Boothferry Road in Hull. This opened in 1932. The success of Armstrong's

THIS CAR CAN BE YOURS!

... accompanying photograph is a model ... Morris Eight Saloon Car, Series I., in ... with blue upholstery, which has been ... by Mr Gordon Armstrong, the well-... Beverley and Hull motor dealer, to ... he funds of the Beverley Carnival and ... ing Week in aid of the Hospital.

... car, which is an absolutely up-to-the-... production from the Morris works, ... nes all the valuable features of recent ... s with the latest innovations in the way ... curity, roominess, comfort, speed and

... does not differ in general design from a ... ar. It possesses a sound and excep-... ly efficient four-cylinder water-cooled ... e, with a totally enclosed three-speed ... romesh gear-box.

... cial features of the car are its generous ... sions, hydraulic shock absorbers, ... ulic brakes, and rear axle of three-... er floating type.

... a car, which will be supplied complete

with buffers front and rear, and electric traffic indicators, is valued at £128, and every person who fills in a coupon, selecting from 30 suggestions, the ten vegetables most suitable for hospital patients, stands an equal chance of winning this car for the outlay of a modest sixpence.

This Morris Eight is extremely economical to run, and its calls would not be beyond the poorest. The total road tax for the year is only £6, and the petrol consumption is just 45 miles to the gallon.

The car is capable of travelling at a speed of 60 miles an hour, and will seat four adults as comfortably as any bigger vehicle.

Coupons, which are priced at sixpence each, may be obtained from any of Messrs Gordon Armstrong's business establishments in Beverley or Hull, or from any member of the Carnival Committee. They should be filled in and returned as indicated on the coupon, where fuller particulars are also printed, as early as possible.

businesses meant changes in his lifestyle: by 1936 he had moved from a house in York Road, Beverley, to Longcroft Hall and was also able to indulge a passion for foreign travel and long sea voyages. Unfortunately during one of these to, South America, his wife Violet caught pneumonia and died on board the RMS Laconia at Rio de Janeiro (1937).

With the coming of the Second World War the Eastgate factory was once more turned over to the production of munitions. Between 1939 and 1945 over 1000 employees, both from Hull and Beverley, turned out a collection of products for the war effort ranging from tracer-shell casings for the Royal Navy to parts for Bofors guns. In many ways Armstrong was a progressive employer and a benefactor to Beverley and the war effort. He was one of the first employers in the country to introduce a five-day week for his workers and was active in providing money for the Beverley Cottage Hospital (1938). In the early stages of the war he was the first person in Britain to privately present an aircraft to the nation: a Hurricane fighter costing £8,500. Older Beverley residents may also remember the "Pale Moon Café": a mobile canteen which Gordon Armstrong established in Beverley's market place and which served free cups of tea and coffee, day and night, to anyone in uniform. In 1940 he offered his home, Longcroft Hall, to the Ministry of Health, free of charge, for use as a hospital.

After the war Gordon Armstrong left the running of the business to his younger son, William Armstrong. By the mid 1950s the workforce was 2,500 and there were soon factories in Beverley, Hull and York; these

were the boom years of the British car industry and Armstrong shock absorbers were much in demand. Gordon Armstrong retired to Weymouth in Dorset but remained the technical adviser to the firm. By 1968 Armstrong Patents had grown into a worldwide business with factories in Canada, Australia and South Africa. It is perhaps fortunate that Gordon Armstrong did not live to see the equally dramatic downturn of the business in the 1980s, which followed the catastrophic decline of British car industry. In 1981 the Eastgate Works closed with 300 redundancies while in 1989 the Armstrong business was sold to the American industrial giant Tenneco.

Gordon Armstrong died in Weymouth on July 30th 1969 aged eighty-four leaving, in his will, a considerable personal fortune of £98,423. His legacy for Beverley was also significant: as its foremost captain of industry, he made the town into a centre of component manufacture and brought both employment and prosperity to its people when both were sorely needed.

Biographies: suggestions

Every locality usually has examples of local streets, roads and buildings named after important local people. In many cases local historians will have produced books on the origins of street names and this could be a start for your own research on a person of local importance. Of course local celebrities may also have significance nationally and may be the subject of an entry in a standard reference work such as the *Dictionary of National Biography*.

Local historians looking for pictorial sources might also inquire at their local art gallery to discover portraits of their chosen research subject.
As with most local history topics local newspapers can be a good source of biographical material especially if your local studies library has indexed such entries. Obituaries in national/ local newspapers could also act as a stimulus to further research.

The site of Armstrong's Garage
Junction Tiger Lane and North Bar Within, Beverley

No 2 Potash Cottages Pettistree
~ A View From Inside and Out
Ray Whitehand

I was born at Potash Cottages, Pettistree in the February of 1948. I then spent the next twenty eight years building up a lifetime's memories, from childhood events, such as walking to school, or learning to ride a bicycle; or the daily routine of collecting drinking water from the village well, or the Saturday smells of mother's weekly cook; to recollections of the countryside, such as the sweet smell of harvest time to the distant sound of the east coast railway line. Yes Potash Cottages was Home, where Sunday roast would fill the air, and Christmas came around every year. However because of my lack of interest in things historical, I can confidently say that not in any of those 28 years did I give much consideration to the history of Potash cottages, or the lives of the people who had experienced the essence of life there before me, so it is I set out in my fifties to trace the story of Potash Cottages, Pettistree.

Pettistree is a rural parish, situated on the main London to Great Yarmouth trunk road, the A12, in the midst of Suffolk countryside. The village has always contained a diverse blend of properties from the manorial Pettistree House to the large number of modest labourers' cottages. While the former provided both employment and residence for a number of the inhabitants, it is to the latter most of the parishioners have found accommodation, for the bulk of its two hundred and fifty or so population have been either smallholders or agricultural labourers.

While now virtually all of these cottages have been modernised on the inside, much of the character of the old village can be still be felt by the conserved exteriors of these cottages, with their plastered walls of Suffolk pink, protected by the canopy of a reed or straw thatched roof. One of the best examples of this

is Coopers Cottages, situated only a few hundred yards from Potash Cottage. Situated in the oldest part of the village, along with its neighbouring community it remains as a testament to the old village life.

As for the origins of Potash Cottages, the date of its construction has been lost in the mists of time, though sources suggest it was built in the mid to latter part of the 18th centuries. A reference by the then owner of the property in 1936 claiming 150 years of land tax records, suggest a date c1786, which would tie in with the peak period for the industry of Potash manufacturing which occurred in the second half of the 18th century. The fact such an establishment existed on neighbouring lands suggest the dwelling may well have been built to house the workers at the factory. However the earliest identified recording of the dwelling is in the first Ordnance Survey map of 1839, with a second, more detailed description in the Tithe Map and Apportionment of Pettistree dated 1839 and 1842 respectively.

It is to the Tithe map and Apportionment we have to turn in order to get our first detailed look at both the property and its owners and occupiers. It shows the dwelling sited towards the rear of a wedge shaped plot, divided into three tenements, each with its own garden, with a fourth plot to the north of the building laid down as an orchard. Each tenement or plot wasgiven a unique number for identification purposes, a ploy emulated by this study in order to give continuity to the identification of the individual dwellings. The data of each plot is as follows: plot 160: area: 25 pole; usage orchard; plot 161: area 9 pole, usage: tenement & garden, occupier Henry Cooper; plot 162: area 7 pole, usage: tenement and garden, occupier Samuel Birt. Plot 163: area 15 pole, usage tenement and garden, occupier William Boon,

giving a total area of the whole plot of 1 rood 16 pole, or 0.35 acres. The details within the apportionment identifies Potash Cottages as being a part of the estate of Pettistree Lodge, with the owner named as Richard Brooks, with the ownership on his death in 1848 passing to his wife Mary. The inclusion of the acreage of each plot highlights the varied size of each tenement, information which while seemingly trivial, proved of considerable value in later identifying both the evolvement of the building and the occupiers of each dwelling.

By using the above information coupled with the detail of the 1841 census we can identify the make up of the families that were living in the dwelling in those early years of the reign of Queen Victoria. Census detail coupled with Poor Rent listings show us that Henry Cooper, his wife and family remained at Potash until c1860; Samuel Birt, his wife and their family moved from Potash to Ufford April 1844, to be replaced by Isaac Levett, while William Boon was the first of three generations of the Boon family to actually live at Potash Cottages, himself being the sole tenant of 163. After his death in 1880's the property was transformed from a triple dweller into a double one. The 1841 census shows there was a total of 6 adults and 11 children resident in the three tenements on 6 June 1841, being the date of the census.

We know from documents relating to a rebuild of the property in 1936, the original building was constructed of wattle and daub, set on a small brick wall no more than 2 feet high. The construction of such a wall involved inserting upright staves into horizontal crossbeams, which sat on the wall. These were then woven with 'withies' of hazel, willow or poplar. Onto this framework a coating of a mixture of clay, dung and horsehair would be daubed. This was then covered both inside and out with a coating of plaster. Finally the exterior would have been painted in Suffolk Pink, a colour originally achieved by a mixture of whitewash and cattle blood. Footings for the earlier building would have been minimal if any, while the original pitch of the roof demonstrates it was designed to be constructed with a thatched roof. This would have consisted of wheat straw, as opposed to the longer lasting, but more expensive Norfolk Reed. The three dwellings were each of brick flooring, while heating would have been an open fire. Water would have been from the skies, or drawn up from the Well situated in Stump Street, while sanitation was in the form of two outside 'dunnies'; existing plans illustrate a 'single seater' in plot 160 to the north of the property, while a doubleseater in 163 was provided for the purpose of both 162 and 163.

By using the combined data from census, rate books and tithe apportionment, it can be deduced the ownership of the property changed hands in 1874, when on the death of Mary Brooks, ownership passed to a Reverend Darling, possibly James G Darling, the Rector of neighbouring Eyke. This change of ownership proved to be a significant factor in the evolution of Potash, for farming was going through very lean times, meaning many of the farm cottages now fell into a state of disrepair. Thus it was as a direct result of the new owner not being reliant on the

land for his income, Potash Cottages underwent significant changes, seemingly between April 1883 and April 1884, the key renovation being the conversion of the property from a triple dweller into a double. This was achieved by incorporating the centre dwelling into the already larger one, making an even greater imbalance. This would seemingly have also been when the roof was converted from thatch to pan tiles. Many thatched cottages were converted in the second half of the 19th century. A drastic decline in the amount of suitable straw material had been brought about by the advent of the thrashing machines of the industrial revolution. While the substitution of tiles for thatch allowed for the pitch of the roof to be reduced, and for the raising of the ceilings in the bedrooms, we know this did not happen in the case of Potash, for while tiles had already replaced the thatch before 1936, the pitch of the roof was still severe at that time. Another pointer to this development is the appearance of a pond in the garden to the north of the properties, for while it was not marked on the map which accompanied a sales catalogue of 1874, when the property along with Pettistree Lodge was put up for Auction, it was definitely there by 1914, with the assumed reason for the excavation being to obtain clay for the building work. Data from the ten yearly census, coupled with that of surviving Rate books show a reasonably static number of tenants throughout the 19th century, with one family providing three generations of tenants. William Boon's son Robert and grandson Alfred both enjoyed periods of residence, with young Alf's appearance in the 1901 census, meaning there was a Boon living at Potash throughout the 19th century.

As the country moved into a new century, so Potash continued its passageway. To what effect the cottages suffered as a consequence of the first world war in unknown, though the fact by the mid 1930s, the property was noted as being unfit for human inhabitation does suggest a significant deterioration of the property over the post war years. It was in the 1930s, after Mr J. T. Lawn, had obtained Potash Cottage, possibly at the same time as he bought The Green Farm, that the property was next transformed. The survival of a detailed set of plans relating to this 'rebuild' with drawings of the property before and after renovation, have been instrumental in collaborating much of the history of this property. Examination of the 'before renovation' drawings shows the imbalance of the former property. With a single front door and two good-sized windows all well to the north end of 161/162 while a single diminutive window in the room, which is identified as the larder of 163, is all the morning sunlight its occupants receive. Equally a solitary dormer window in the bedroom of 162 is the only light supply from the front, to bedrooms with ceilings under 6 feet. As mentioned earlier the pitch of the roof contradicts its pan tile make up, showing that it was once constructed of thatch. . The existence of three stairwells, with the middle one now marked as disused, is testament to the original design of a triple dwelling, while the inclusion of the kitchen in the northern 'wing' of 161 demonstrates the extra space afforded to its tenant over the other two. Each room throughout the entire building benefits but a single window suggesting particularly gloomy living conditions especially during the winter months.

Turning to the proposed alterations it is clear how the construction of a new wing on the southern end of the property allowed for a balanced double-dweller of equal proportions to be designed with the new tenants each enjoying 3 bedrooms, a living room, kitchen and a scullery with the latter housing both a toilet and coal room. Outside the proposed planting of a new hedge and the digging of a ditch points to the extension of the garden at this time. A point, which is confirmed by comparing the acreage of the plot as shown in the Ordnance survey map of 1970, being 0.48 acres, compared to the tithe figure of 0.35. Gauging from the condition of the property in the 1950s virtually all of the proposals seem to have been undertaken, though possibly with one exception as by the time my parents moved into the dwelling both properties benefited from the erection of a lean-to building on the end of each wing. These were divided into two with the lavatory in the end nearest the back door, while the other end of these accommodated the coal shed. The inclusion of a copper turned this room in to the washroom.

As for the 20th century tenants of potash cottage. In 1948 there was only basic electricity inside the house with a single light socket and one round pin plug in each downstairs room, with just lighting upstairs. Heating was in the form of a cooking range in the kitchen, with an open fire in the front room to warm the centre of the house. Outside the property the two gardens, which were of roughly equal proportions were intensively cultivated and produced sufficient produce for the families. The next key construction at Potash was when mains water was introduced into the village. While East Suffolk County Council laid the actual mains pipe, it was the responsibility of each owner to fund their own linking pipe work. In the case of Potash it was agreed between landlord and tenant the former would fund the operation while the tenants would provide the labour, so tenants Frank Whitehand & Jack Smith dug out the trench to run from the house to mains pipe in the road, whereupon the Council came and laid the pipe work which provided Potash with its first running water. This finally ended the routine daily walk to the village well in stump street. Then in the summer of 1960 the builders moved into Potash again, this time it was to construct adjoining bathrooms and hallways for each property. The extension, which saw the demise of the wooden and tin shed which had been built in the 1950's to protect the rear of the house took the form of an infill to the rear of the two dwellings, and confined the Bungalow baths to the garden sheds, in case of emergency, though as far as the memory recalls they were never used again. While there were other cosmetic alterations, this was how I remember Potash Cottages as Home.

In order to identify the tenants of no 2 Potash in the 20th century we must turn to the Electoral registers of the parish, where we find a similar picture to that of the 19th. The family of Ablitts, which saw No 2 Potash into the new century, remained there for some 30 years until at least 1930. There was then a period of time, which saw a number of tenants come and go,

before my parents moved in in the Spring of 1947. They remained there until 1987, when they retired to Wickham Market. As for ownership in the 20th century, Reverend Darling was still the owner at the turn of the century, but the identity of other owners is unknown until the 1930's when Mr Lawn, a grocery retailer purchased the property. Following his transformation of the property he eventually sold it to Dickie Hayward during the Second World War, it then remaining in the Hayward family throughout the century.

So there we have the story of Potash Cottages, Pettistree, from its potential beginnings in the early part of the 19th century through to the end of the twentieth century, its various transformations, tenants and owners, with each and every one contributing to its History, proving that while it played such a big part in my early life, my part in its history was but a much smaller contribution.

About the author
In his early 50's Ray Whitehand turned his amateur experience in genealogy into a business. After a number of courses and several published articles in his first year, he has now produced census transcripts of East Suffolk parishes and a booklet about the history of a family cottage with guidance for others who want to research the history of their property. Ray has also undertaken considerable research into Suffolk Workhouses. If you need assistance with your Suffolk past, or research, Ray would be only too pleased to help. Contact Ray Whitehand, Local and Family History Research, 28 Lincoln Avenue, Saxmundham, Suffolk IP17 1BZ Email hrfw@supanet.com

MURDER *files*

Information available
on UK murders
Research undertaken

Maria's murderer laid to rest – after 176 years
Paul Williams
looks again at the Red Barn murder of 1827

As most genealogists will know, to trace your family history you need to work like a detective or sleuth leaving no stone unturned. You need to be a Sherlock Holmes with a large magnifying glass looking for minuscule details which often, annoyingly, completely changes all you have gleaned before. And just when you think you have it all, something else comes up and perhaps you find information on yet another lost relative.

In the 7th Edition of The Family and Local History Handbook I wrote an article called *'We've got a murderer in our family tree'*. One of the murder cases I wrote about in that article came about as a result of a lady from Middlesex writing to Murder Files enquiring about the murder of her great aunt, Maria Marten in 1828. Murder File records showed that Maria lived in the village of Polstead and after meeting a rich young farmer called William Corder in 1826 she became pregnant. At this time unmarried mothers were unacceptable to society so Corder promised to marry her. When the child died Maria's parents urged Corder to continue with the marriage.

In May 1827 Corder said he was taking Maria to Ipswich to marry her but said that the matter must be kept secret or she would no doubt be arrested for having bastard children. He told her to go to her parents' home and change into male clothing. In the meantime he took some of her clothing to the Red Barn, a red roofed building on his land. He later called for her and they both walked to his home where, he told her, was waiting a horse and carriage to take them both to Ipswich.

Two days later he returned, saying Maria was still in Ipswich as there were problems in getting a marriage licence. On 29th September Corder declared he was going to London to meet and marry Maria. Three weeks later he wrote to Maria's parents saying they were now married and living on the Isle of Wight. Her mother, however, had a dream that night that Maria had been murdered and buried in the Red Barn. So adamant was she that on the 19 April 1828 the barn was searched and Maria's body found.

By this time Corder had already married another girl in London. He was

Murder of Maria Marten

arrested and charged with Maria's murder. At his trial at Bury St Edmunds Assizes in August 1828 he pleaded Not Guilty and said that Maria had shot herself with one of his pistols that she had taken from his home. He did admit it was rather foolhardy in trying to conceal her body. The Jury were not convinced by this and listened to Corder's brother who said he had seen William leaving the barn with a pickaxe the day Maria disappeared. The Jury accordingly found Corder guilty of murder and he was hanged outside of Bury St Edmunds jail on Monday 11 August 1828 in front of a massive crowd. Strangely enough the murder was to be become the subject of several musicals for some years to follow.

That was the bare bones of the case – if you will excuse the expression. Beautiful young girl falls in love with rich young man who having made her pregnant does not want to remain with her so he murders her. And there was the added intrigue of the mother's dream. But what else can be gleaned about such murder cases? For example, remaining with the Maria Marten murder, what did Corder look like? How was he caught? What happened in Court? Was murder the only charge? Did he go to the gallows accepting his fate or have to be dragged struggling to the last minute? Local records, libraries and newspapers often hold a lot of additional information. If you are lucky and are prepared to sit for hours sifting through page after page, newspapers often provide the answers and more. Let's look at just a few of the added details found in the newspapers relating to this case.

The Times newspaper of 24 April 1828 tells of the pursuit of Corder to London:

" ....*the business (pursuit) was placed in the hands of Lea (the London police officer). With a loose clue afforded him by the country constable, he traced the prisoner first to Gray's Inn Terrace, and from thence through a number of intermediate places to his residence, in Ealing Lane, near Brentford, where he apprehended him"*.

We can also sometimes gain an insight into the officer's thinking. Having found Corder's residence, Lea then had to work out how to gain admittance.

" *A degree of stratagem was necessary to obtain an entrance, and he procured it by representing that he had a daughter whom he was anxious to place under the care of his wife. On going in, he found him (Corder) in the parlour with four ladies, at breakfast. He was in his dressing-gown* ...." .

Obviously the officer had done a bit of local questioning to find out what Corder and his wife did for a living.

The Times also refers to Corder's brother-in-law questioning his sister as to the length of time she had known Corder before she had married him.

"*She answered, only for three weeks, and that she first became acquainted with him through the medium of a matrimonial advertisement at a pastrycook's shop in Fleet Street, to which he had given a reference. She married him at the church of St Andrew, Holborn, in November last (1827), and was quite unaware of his being guilty of any offence"*.

Maria Marten's ghost shows where she is buried

So we now also have a place of marriage and a date which should on further research give us more information.

The Times, 1st May 1828, describes the scene where Maria's body was found:

" *The grave from which the poor victim has been taken is still open: the right layer of the barn had over it at least straw six inches deep, and a depth of the grave by our measurement, somewhat less than 18 inches; the picking up of a barn floor – solid as a public road – is no mean task for a common labourer; and it serves only to show the brute-like and insensible manner in which the monster proceeded to his work. If dug before the murder, it proclaims the deed to be of a most deliberate and premeditated nature; and if dug whilst the mangled remains were beside him, it exhibits the most remorseless and unpardon guilt"*.

The Times, 8th August 1828, gives detailed information of his Trial appearance and the indictments against Corder, The indictment contained 10 counts, the first being that of murder. So, as you can see, newspapers can provide a lot of background information and are certainly worth pursuing.

Even though this murder occurred way back in 1828, many articles about it have since been written and occasionally the odd new bit of information comes to light. Even this year another chapter was added to the Maria Marten murder.

In *The Times,* 18th August 2004 Michael Horsnell reported 'Red Barn murderer finally laid to rest' commenced:

"*The remains of the 19th-century killer William Corder have been cremated 176 years after his execution for the notorious 'red barn murder', as the result of a dogged campaign by a distant descendant .... Corder was publicly hanged and dissected on August 11, 1828, and, until last week, his skeleton was kept at the Royal College of Surgeons' Hunterian Museum in London, where it was taken in 1949.*

The crime gripped the public imagination and macabre relics, including an account of his trial in a book bound in his skin, remain as testimony to the fascination the murder has sustained ever since".

The cremation was the result of a 3 year campaign by Linda Nessworthy, a mental health nurse, from Great Yarmouth, who, whilst researching the family of her

Corder signs his confession in presence of the Prison Governor

Corder's Execution

grandmother, Laura Corder, who died aged 90 in 2000, came across the murder connection. Linda Nessworthy told Michael Horsnell:

"I told my grandmother what I was doing and she became very distressed. She told me I must not get involved because there was a murderer in the family. It was the first I had heard of it. I looked into it anyway and discovered that William Corder's great-grandfather was my grandmother's great-great grandfather from his second marriage"

Mrs Nessworthy believed Corder was not given a fair trial and was shocked by what happened to Corder's body after the execution.

"I understand that surgeons at the time would have wanted to dissect his body to study his anatomy but to open it up and put it on display for four hours was horrible and very undignified. I have been told that the research went so far that people in the market square were asked to taste his skin. It was such a disgrace. It was awful that his skeleton was then left in the local hospital foyer for decades."

The skeleton was displayed in the foyer until after the Second World War with the finger bones fused together so that the hand could be moved mechanically to point to a donation box.

Mrs Nessworthy wrote to the Royal College of Surgeons in 2001 asking for the skeleton to be returned to her. She had to prove first that she was a direct descendant before the society's heritage committee could agree and then the decision had to be ratified by the Culture Secretary. Mrs Nessworthy researched the case by examining court records, witness statements and trial reports. She consulted ballistics experts and was convinced Corder was telling the truth at his trial when he claimed that he shot his lover by accident as they scuffled. Mrs Nessworthy believes that the shot may have only injured her and Maria could have been finished off by another lover who stabbed her to death.

"I became very indignant and angry about the way Corder's death was handled and how he was treated" said Mrs Nesswworthy. "I felt it was only right to give him a Christian send-off that he was denied at the time. It has taken a long time to finally get his remains back but I was driven on by the injustice of it all. Hopefully this will close the final chapter of this episode in my family's history".

Mrs Nessworthy is now requesting the Moyse's Hall Museum, Bury St Edmunds to give up part of

Corder's scalp and a book about the murder, written by James Curtis, the *Times* journalist who covered the trial. It was this book that George Creed, a surgeon, had bound in leather made from the murderer's skin!

As well as finding out more information we now have two living enquirers related to victim and murderer. I wonder what Maria Marten and William Corder would think if both enquirers were to get together?

The message from this article? Newspapers and articles from books and magazines can be a valuable source of information. But always beware – some writers do unfortunately rather add in their own thoughts to embellish the case and in time everything gets distorted. I often get letters from enquirers telling me what they have learnt from relatives about a family murder. Sometimes it is completely wrong. Mind you, it can work the other way as well – dear old Uncle Harry may have murdered two or three people and not just one as they had been led to believe!

Family history can be frustrating, interesting, perhaps embarrassing but also fun. Perhaps I am slightly biased but I think it takes a lot to beat having a murderer or someone executed in the family tree.

Murder Files has information on thousands of British murders and the British Hangman. If you are looking for murder information either email Enquiry@murderfiles.com or write to Paul Williams, Dommett Hill Farm, Hare Lane, Buckland St Mary, Chard, Somerset, TA20 3JS. Have a look also at www.murderfiles.com

A Hodge Podge of Duckenfields
Anne L Harvey

The surname Duckenfield/Dukinfield is defined by the Oxford Dictionary of Surnames as an English habitation name from DUKINFIELD in Cheshire, probably from the Old English Dücena Field, a pasture of the ducks. There must be other definitions, equally valid.

It is an unusual surname which can be a blessing while searching ancient records because it stands out among all the others. Actually living with it, as I did for some 15 years, was another matter. The number of variations on a theme seemed to be endless especially when it came to putting in more consonants than necessary. DUCKINGFIELD was the most common, DUNKINFIELD was another.

To explain about my interest in the Duckenfield/Dukinfield name, it is necessary to introduce a personal note.

Harry Dukinfield was my first boyfriend when we were both growing up in the 1950s. Until then, I had not come across the surname before and I wasn't keen it. Despite my reservations, and with a good many years in between, Harry Dukinfield became my first husband. It wasn't until a few years later, when we were living in St Neots, Cambridgeshire, that I became more interested in the name.

A Registrar of Births, Marriages and Deaths, with whom my architect boss shared office premises, stopped me in the corridor one day. Since my married surname was most unusual, he wondered if I knew that W C Fields (1880-1946), the American comedian and actor, had changed his name to Fields from Dukinfield and that his father was an Englishman who'd emigrated to the United States sometime in the 19th century.

I didn't pursue this at the time as things were not working out well for Harry and I and we moved to Leeds in 1974, hopefully to make a new start. Unfortunately, that didn't work either and Harry and I eventually separated in 1978, finally divorcing in 1981. We did stay friends though and we often talked over the phone, especially about our two children.

In 1990 he and some friends were involved in a road accident and Harry was hospitalised for three weeks. On the day before he was due to be discharged, he collapsed and died from an embolism. I'd visited him in hospital and we'd chatted like the friends we still were. He was the same as he'd always been, unfailingly cheerful, with a dry sense of humour. Throughout his life, he was never malicious or deliberately unkind and everyone who came into contact with him liked him.

When my first Dukinfield grandson was born in 1992, it struck me that there was no one else around who could remember Harry's parents or other details of his earlier life. I started jotting down what I could remember and found that once I did that, other memories flooded in. It seemed a logical step to go further back, made easier by the fact that I'd been doing my own family history for some years.

I discovered that Harry's father, Ernest, had married Elsie Greatorex in 1928 in Oldham, Lancashire. Harry, their only child, was born in 1937, following which they moved to Horwich, near Bolton, Lancashire (where I met him). Ernest was born in 1898 in Mossley on the Yorkshire/Lancashire border. His parents, Henry Ashworth Dukinfield and Bessie Ann Jackson, were married a mere six weeks before his birth. I'd understood that Ernest had been orphaned quite young and been looked after by relatives, However, I discovered that although his mother had died in 1905, when Ernest was only seven, his father had died in 1922. The responsibility for caring for the young Ernest fell to his mother's elder sister, Harriet. He was brought up as one of her own, along with several cousins, to whom he remained close.

Somewhere between Henry Ashworth's birth in Saddleworth, Yorkshire in 1869, and his marriage in 1898, the spelling of the name changed from Duckenfield to Dukinfield. Henry himself was one of four brothers, all born in Saddleworth in the late1860s/early 1870s. His father was a Charles Duckenfield, born in Holmfirth, Yorkshire, in 1840.

Holmfirth Chapel about 1860

Holmfirth from Wooldale Cliff

Henry's middle name, Ashworth, was the maiden name of his mother Elizabeth. Charles and Elizabeth had been married in 1868 in Ashton-under-Lyne.

Charles Duckenfield was the eldest son of Joseph Duckenfield, born in Holmfirth in 1804, and baptised at Holmfirth Chapel in the parish of Kirkburton, near Huddersfield. Joseph and his wife Sarah Roebuck, whom he had married at Almondbury Parish Church in 1831, produced six children. Most of the family were textile workers, initially in wool, later in cotton. It may have been this change that caused them to move sometime between 1851 and 1861, first to Honley, near Huddersfield, then to Saddleworth, that large sprawling area straddling the Yorkshire/Lancashire border. During a four-year period in the early 1870s, first Joseph, then Sarah, then two daughters died. Joseph, who had initially been a fulling miller, a highly skilled job in the woollen industry, had been reduced to work as an outdoor labourer by the time of his death.

Joseph's father, John Duckenfield, was also a Holmfirth man, born in 1785. he had married a Sarah Heap in 1804, just a few months before Joseph, the eldest of six children, was born. Although the first three children were baptised at Holmfirth Chapel, the youngest three were born in Huddersfield and baptised at Queen Street Wesleyan Methodist Chapel. Both John and his wife Sarah were buried at Kirkheaton Church in Huddersfield.

John, in turn, was the son of a William Duckenfield and his wife, Ellen Mellor, of Snowgate Head, Holmfirth, the eldest of some ten children. William was also one of ten children of another John Duckenfield, born approximately 1722, and his wife Martha. Unfortunately, because of the cramped writing style of various parish clerks and curates, who tried to optimise space on costly parchment or vellum, it has not been possible to trace any further back.

The first Duckenfield in the Holmfirth area was an Edward Duckenfield, whose daughter Sarah was baptised in 1669 at Holmfirth Chapel (later Holy Trinity Church) . One has to wonder what brought Edward Duckenfield to the area. Was he perhaps some bye-blow of the landed gentry Dukinfield family of Dukinfield, Cheshire? It seems doubtful as there is a well-known published pedigree with all

issue apparently accounted for. There is, though, one small window of doubt. Robert Dokinfield of Dokinfield married Ellen Brereton, daughter of Sir William Brereton of Staffordshire in 1529. One of their sons, Edward, is unaccounted for and is thought to have died young as he was not mentioned in his father's will of 1547. Could he have perhaps survived as a disgraced son, to become the ancestor of the first Duckenfield in Holmfirth?

Or was the Edward Duckenfield of Holmfirth a victim of the divided loyalties of Royalists and Roundheads that possibly lingered in certain areas? The West Riding of Yorkshire was a major stronghold of Puritanism. The Dukinfields of Cheshire were fierce Puritans for another Robert Dukinfield was a well-known Colonel in the Army of Parliamentarians in the English Civil War of 1641-46. The Holmfirth Edward Duckenfield would have been born either during the Civil War or just after. There is an entry in the International Genealogical Index (IGI) of an Edward Dukinfield being baptised at the church of St Mary in Stockport, Cheshire, on 21 November 1646, his father also named Edward but it will be necessary to follow this up further.

The only mention of the Holmfirth Duckenfields in the Wakefield manorial records is an entry which states that Ralph Marsden surrendered two parcels of land in Holmfirth and Wooldale to the use of Edward Duckenfield and his wife Elizabeth and then to the heirs of their body, with remainder in default of such heirs to Roger Weedall of Meltham in the Court Rolls of 1677.

Published transcripts show that during the following 36 years, 12 or more children were born to Edward Duckenfield, a feat certainly possible for a man who would have been only in his fifties when his last child was baptised in January 1704/5. I thought at first that perhaps a son named Edward might have been the father of the later children. However, an Edward born in 1680 is thought to have died and a second Edward born in 1692 would not have been old enough to produce the later children. The solution lay in the fact that Edward the elder had two wives, Elizabeth who died in 1683 and Susannah, whom he married in 1685.

With such an unusual surname and one not local to the area (though more common in Sheffield) it seems

Interior of Holy Trinity Church (previously Holmfirth Chapel)

extremely likely that subsequent Duckenfields in the area were descended from the first Edward.

Between that first baptism and the mid 19th century, a period of some 200 years, there were Duckenfields in the Holmfirth area, seemingly at their most prolific in the late 18th/early 19th centuries. They married into local families, many of them with names familiar to the area such as Beaumont, Batty, Senior, Wimpenny, Addy, Haigh. Many, if not all, were involved in the domestic woollen industry which dominated the West Riding of Yorkshire. During that period, the Duckenfields experienced turbulent times, such as land enclosure, the introduction of mechanisation and the subsequent Luddite riots, the explosion of the Industrial Revolution, all of which combined to sound the death knell of the cottage woollen industry. By 1881, only a handful of Duckenfields were still in the area.

In the course of my research into the Duckenfields of Holmfirth, I have managed to piece together other family relationships and their connection, in many cases tenuous, to 'my' Duckenfields, as well as some intriguing facts.

A typical example was Ellis Winterbottom, a widower, who in October 1771 married Martha Duckenfield, a widow. Ellis Winterbottom had married his first wife Molly Taylor in July 1758 while Martha Rowbotham had married Thomas Duckenfield in October 1752. Between 1803 and 1804, Ellis Winterbottom, possibly a widower again, was receiving parish relief at the rate of 2s 6d a week which rose to 3s 6d , until 28 April 1804 after which payments ceased.

Family relationships previously only guessed at were confirmed in a will. John Duckenfield of Fulstone, who died in 1814, left legacies to his wife Sarah and siblings (including a brother William, one of 'my' Duckenfield direct ancestors) or their children, but with no mention of any children of his own. However, one haunting phrase says 'I give and bequeath unto Joseph Taylor otherwise Duckenfield, my natural son, the legacy of ten pounds.'

Holmfirth Chapel was originally licensed only for baptisms and burials so couples had to trek the nine or so miles to the parish church at Kirkburton to be married. This caused consternation among the chapel authorities who, in 1831, applied to Lord Brougham, the Lord Chancellor, to be allowed to carry out marriages in the chapel. The application stated that 'from the inconvenient distance the marriage parties have to travel, they are put to great expense in procuring refreshment and are often tempted to pass the bounds of sobriety so that the road from Holmfirth often presents, on the Lord's Day, scenes of shameful disorder.' (Many of the labouring classes were forced to marry on a Sunday as it was their only

day off.) Needless to say, the licence was granted! One of the first to marry at the newly licensed chapel was George Duckenfield, a shoemaker, who married Hannah Hardcastle on 25th December 1833. They had two children; a daughter Sarah, baptised 1839 (who later married Jonathan Woffenden in Huddersfield) and a son David, baptised 1835. Although David was baptised at Holmfirth Chapel, he seems to have transferred his allegiance to Lydgate English Presbyterian Chapel (later New Mill Unitarian Chapel) as he is mentioned several times in their records. His daughter Mary Hannah Duckenfield married George Frederick Charlesworth at Lydgate in December 1876. David himself died in 1901 and is buried at Lydgate together with his wife Hannah who died in 1906.

George's brother John was described in census records as a cordwainer, a shoemaker who worked on the softest finest leather on high quality shoes. Surprisingly, neither brother was mentioned in contemporary directories, though there were 14 shoemakers in the town at that time. In May 1834, John married Mary Hellawell at Kirkburton, with their son, Joseph, being born in 1835. In 1841, the family was at Underbank, Holmfirth, where they continued to live until at least 1912 when daughter Phoebe, born in 1843, died. She never married but had an illegitimate son, John William, to whom she left everything in her will.

Lydgate English Presbyterian Chapel (later New Mills Unitarian Chapel)

Her brother, Joseph, may have been apprenticed to a chemist in Leeds as he married Grace Craddock at Leeds Parish Church in 1860. By 1861, he was living back in Holmfirth and trading as a chemist and druggist. In 1871, he was trading in Armley Leeds, but in 1881, although living in South Milford, near Selby, he was listed in a directory as trading in Burmantofts, Leeds, quite a distance away. Perhaps he was able to travel there by train as the rail service was more effective then.

In the records, there were also many evidences of tragedies, death being an accepted part of life in those days. One James Duckenfield, baptised in 1789 lost three of his four children before adulthood, followed by his wife Elizabeth in 1819 aged only 30. The son who survived was William Duckenfield, baptised in 1812. Evidence suggests that he was the one who married Sarah Turner in July 1835. They went on to have three children, two of whom died in infancy, followed by William himself and then Sarah, all within two years.

The remaining child was John and census records have shown that his maternal grandfather, Jonathan Turner, brought him up. John, married a woman from Rotherham and was last heard of in 1891 in Staley(bridge) on the Cheshire side of the River Tame. Because of this, I believe he was a cousin of 'my' Duckenfields who were by then living in Mossley, only a few miles away.

As a postscript, one has to wonder why James Duckenfield of Cumberworth (an adjacent parish to Holmfirth), and Martha Holmes of Holmfirth had their banns called twice, first in October 1823 then again in April 1826. The couple were actually married in May 1824!

There is still much research to be done into the Duckenfields, not least to see if there is a connection between the Holmfirth Duckenfields and the Sheffield Duckenfields. This is particularly important because of the W C Fields connection. His father was a James Duckenfield born in Sheffield in 1840 who, after emigrating to the United States, served in a

Pennsylvania Regiment in the American Civil War. After all, Sheffield and Holmfirth are only some 25 miles or so apart and W C Fields bore a strong resemblance to my later father-in-law, Ernest Dukinfield.

Anne has been researching her own family history for some 20 years. She combines her interest in genealogy and local history with writing and has had numerous articles published.

YORKSHIRE
FAMILY HISTORY FAIR
KNAVESMIRE EXHIBITION CENTRE
YORK RACECOURSE

SATURDAY 25TH JUNE 2005
10.00.a.m. to 4.30.p.m.

Many Stalls including:
Society of Genealogists, Federation Publications
The Family & Local History Handbook
(The Genealogical Services Directory)
Family Tree Magazine, Local Archives,
Family History Societies from all over Great Britain
Maps, Postcards, Printouts,
New & Second-hand Microfiche Readers
Genealogy Computer Programs
Advice Table

248 Tables in 2003

FREE CAR PARKING
ADMISSION £3.00

Further Details from:
Mr A Sampson
1 Oxgang Close, Redcar TS10 4ND
Tel: 01642 486615

NOTE FOR YOUR DIARY:
YEAR 2006 - YORKSHIRE FAMILY HISTORY FAIR
SATURDAY 24TH JUNE 2006
YEAR 2007 - YORKSHIRE FAMILY HISTORY FAIR
SATURDAY 30TH JUNE 2007
YEAR 2008 - YORKSHIRE FAMILY HISTORY FAIR
SATURDAY 28TH JUNE 2008

FEDERATION OF FAMILY HISTORY SOCIETIES (PUBLICATIONS) LIMITED

Publishers and Suppliers of a wide range of books on Family History (and related subjects) to Family History Societies, individual Family Historians, Libraries, Record Offices and Booksellers, etc.

- *Well over 100 titles commissioned by the Federation of Family Historians and produced at attractive prices, plus a fine selection of titles from other publishers.*

- *A wide range of **'Basic Series'** and **'Introduction to'** books with detailed guidance on most aspects of family history research.*

- ***Gibson Guides** giving explicit advice on the precise extent and whereabouts of major record sources*

- ***Stuart Raymond's** extensive listings of published family history reference material at national and local level*

- ***Web Directories***

Titles available from your local Family History Society and by post from:-

**FFHS (Publications) Limited,
Units 15 and 16 Chesham Industrial Centre,
Oram Street, Bury, Lancashire, BL9 6EN**

Visit our 'On-line bookshop' and Catalogue at

www.familyhistorybooks.co.uk
Tel: 0161 797 3843 Fax: 0161 797 3846
Email enquiries to: sales@ffhs.co.uk

Research your Family History On-Line

We publish on-line records compiled by Family History Societies and others - quality data from experienced researchers with local knowledge, providing accurate details at fees that give real value for money.

Visit our 'pay per view' site at:
www.familyhistoryonline.net <http://www.familyhistoryonline.net/>

Ever wanted to chart your research?

Well now you can.

The Ancestral Arc
for

At The Chartists we've developed a range of template charts including arc, bow tie and circle formats, to allow you to present your research beautifully.

Our aim is to provide only the highest quality chart templates that your research deserves. We achieve this through a unique combination of traditional skills and the most up to date technology.

The Chartists

Display your research *Beautifully*

www.thechartists.co.uk

Twentieth Century British State Registers of Merchant Mariners
Len Barnett

There is a common perception that mercantile service was similar to that of the armed forces and therefore, that 'service sheets' should be available for genealogical study. But, in reality the 'Merchant Service' or 'Merchant Navy' as termed after the First World War was made up of many thousands of individual commercial entities: from the great passenger lines to one ship companies with shareholders spread through villages and rural communities. (Please see my article *The 19th and 20th British 'Merchant Navy' and its Links to State and Empire* in the seventh edition of *Family and Local History Handbook* for more background information.)

Of course, as of 1850 the Marine Department of the Board of Trade (and successor organisations) have overseen aspects of maritime mercantile activities. But, it should be stressed that unless circumstances demanded the opposite, generations of these civil servants took what is currently known as a 'light touch' in relation to their responsibilities.

With the above in mind, this short article is devoted primarily to the events leading to the formation of two registers that are highly important in tracing merchant mariners in the twentieth century. These are the Central Index Register operating between 1913 and 1941 (although only now effectively surviving from 1918-19 onwards) and the replacement Central Register of Seamen for 1941 to 1972: both available at the National Archives of the United Kingdom, Public Records Office, at Kew in Surrey. Hopefully, this will allow researchers to understand what is liable to be found within these and why.

Central Index Register
During the nineteenth century there had been a series of State efforts to keep registers showing the sea time of all Britons in British mercantile service. Apart from a register of seamen's tickets part way through, between 1835 and 1857 there were also registers of seamen: identified slightly inaccurately as series one to three. Essentially all these paper systems were designed as tools for the forced recruitment of merchant seamen for service on men-o-war in times of war. (Lower deck RN recruitment through the nineteenth century was complex and is greatly misunderstood. For more on this allied subject, see my other article *The Royal Navy - historical background and pointers for genealogists* in this publication.)

By the closing years of the nineteenth century there was support from different quarters within the shipping industry for a system of identification for merchant mariners in British service. Trades Unions and especially one representative, Havelock Wilson MP, wanted this in order to protect mariners' interests. An important element of this was in promoting a programme of certification for seamen in their arguments for introducing proper minimum manning levels on British merchantmen. The Shipping Federation (as the predominant voice of foreign-going shipowners) was also keen on such a register, but in order to be able to keep undesirables from signing onto their vessels.

Within Whitehall one recommendation of a departmental committee, that sat from 1899 to 1900 under Lord Dudley, brought about the introduction of books of continuous service and discharge for merchant mariners in October 1900 (*largely* but not completely replacing individual discharge certificates). To a degree, this made identification simpler, but neither unions nor shipowners were particularly satisfied. Said by advocates to enforce a section in the 1894 Merchant Shipping Act, a register of seamen was also costed by this committee, but not taken up. (A minor amending Act to the 1894 MSA three years later materially complicated the situation. Purporting to deal with undermanning on merchantmen, neither the Act nor the subsequent Board of Trade regulations arising from this were specific. So, this poorly drafted legislation was to be used continually as ammunition by advocates for the certification of seamen.)

THE HARBOUR
FOLKESTONE

Among recommendations that another internal committee of 1904 made, was one for a register of mariners. With the Tories falling from power the next year, the Liberal government acted on a number of these urgings in the Merchant Shipping Act 1906, but the mariners' register was not included. One result of this 1906 MSA was the setting up of the Merchant Shipping Advisory Committee. This was a sizeable body representing shipbuilders, shipowners and managers, along with mariners through various trades unions and professional associations (for officers). The question of a register of merchant mariners just would not go away and although support was not unanimous, the MSAC kept up pressure. Additionally, there had been a Colonial Shipping Conference held in London in 1907, whereby a resolution by Antipodean delegates called for a proper system of manning on British merchantmen.

There was unrelenting opposition from those at the highest levels of both the office of the Registrar General of Shipping and Seamen and also the Marine Department of the Board of Trade. Their arguments were multifarious and practised. In time the manning issue revolved around the word 'efficient'. The advocates maintained, therefore, that certification of seamen was required. The detractors regarded such a system as unnecessary, but also then fell back on an old standard and one used variously to cut the civil servants' workload. It was maintained that the nineteenth century registers had failed through deliberate abuse by mariners and an inability of the civil servants to identify the sailormen. (Funnily enough this apparent difficulty in identification was used again in the 1880s in justification of ceasing to log sea time for certificated seamen officers and engineers within their registers.) While undoubtedly not all nineteenth century mariners had complied properly, whether through illiteracy, fecklessness, malice or other reasons, apart from the sheer complexity of these hand-written paper systems, a *great* many of the errors can be traced directly to incompetence of civil servants. But, in the intervening time since the 1850s mandatory primary education had been introduced throughout Britain, so most mariners by the 1900s should at least have been partially literate. Even *if* the identification of mariners could be seen as being worthy, a prohibitively high setting up and operating cost could be mustered as a serious obstruction. This was a completely disingenuous argument. From the mid nineteenth century onwards the paper systems and personnel required by the merchant shipping legislation had been overwhelmingly paid for by the shipowners and mariners through fees. The only cost to the taxpayer had been for the permanent civil servants within the Board of Trade and only related to a very small percentage of the total. It is also interesting to note that the detractors' costing estimates were always high and the advocates' substantially lower.

There were two other positions taken by the civil servants. The first of these was that they were unable to introduce any such register because of the legislation then in force. The other, paradoxically, was that the crew lists lodged with the RGSS *already* constituted a 'register'. This latter point was argued for years, but had not been checked. However, with another departmental committee in 1909 and continuing pressure from the MSAC, when this matter finally *was* put before the government's most senior law officers in August 1911 they came down in favour of keeping a proper register. The reactionaries continued to fight paper rearguard actions and it was not until late 1913 that the Central Index Register (sometimes known as the 'Fourth Series') appeared.

Only a minimum of information was recorded in this. In relation to sea time (on CR2 cards) instead of *full* details of signing on and discharge that both unions and shipowners wanted, even when complete only ship's names (or more frequently their official numbers) along with dates of signing on are noted. In practical terms for modern research (especially since crew lists and official logs are spread half way across the world through decisions taken in the 1960s) this makes life unnecessarily difficult.

Towards the end of the First World War CR10 cards were introduced, creating a 'special index'. It would appear that this was due to an Order in Council issued on 2nd August 1918 (courtesy of the Defence of the Realm Act 1914). This instructed the Shipping Controller and Board of Trade to jointly ensure that all merchant mariners in British service carried certificates of identity and service. To comply with this legislation these government bodies were to provide for the 'registration' of those holding these certificates. Small 'passport' photographs are frequently, but not always attached.

This 'special index' was maintained until 1921. Complicating matters, additional to the normal CR1 and CR2 cards found in the system from 1921 onwards are some extra ones. Again often complete with photographs, these apparently are *only* of foreigners then serving on British merchantmen.

Anyway, post war there was much ill feeling towards foreigners of *all* nationalities, from Europeans through to those from the Empire: all who were seen as taking 'British' jobs. This erupted into violence and even killings, particularly in 1919 when there were numerous riots in mainland British ports. With this in mind, although the Aliens' Order did not come into force until 1925, there had been other measures through the continuance of emergency legislation imposed in the spring of 1919. So, these photographs *may* have been a way of keeping a theoretical if not particularly practical check on the identity of foreigners.

The Central Register of Seamen
Prior to the Second World War actually breaking out, conscription into the armed forces was introduced for males aged 20 to 23. This required all concerned to register with the Ministry of Labour. It was then not envisaged in official circles to take serving merchant mariners of this age group into the armed forces, assuming that they continued to sign onto merchantmen. Initially no further controls were seen as necessary, due to the make up of the merchant service. Excluding native labour, such as Lascars, that were not subject to conscription anyway, about 75 per cent of 'British' mariners were over 25. The normal casual way of employment was judged as containing a built in 'reserve' of mariners, and those who had been laid up due to the economic slumps of the 1930s were also thought would naturally return to the sea.

In time the Ministry of Shipping officials (that had taken over most of the responsibilities of the Marine Department of the Board of Trade) became concerned at an apparent inefficiency in shipping. The usual disciplinary problems of men not joining and deserting seemed to have increased; men were taking longer periods of leave between voyages; past mariners were not necessarily returning to the sea; others were leaving for better paid and less dangerous work ashore; and even those merchant mariners of conscription age having registered under the National Service Acts were able to slip ashore and remain there without getting called up (as the State machinery for enforcing this aspect failed). Even with *some* contraction due to the war and efforts such as retraining stewards as deck hands there were manning difficulties: such as a shortage of certificated engineers and second mates. Falling morale was also pondered on. One thing that these civil servants did not seemingly take into consideration though was the increased wastage of those killed, injured and sick by time at sea, as well as the escalating danger of actually serving.

With this as background, after the disasters of June 1940 control of civilian manpower generally became an important issue for maximising the war effort and the result was legislation giving the State the power of coercion. The first Essential Work Orders were made in March 1941. Initially, of more importance to merchant mariners (who were not subject to such an order until May 1942) was the Registration for Employment Order: also of March 1941.

Under the Employment Order all civilian males between 18 and 60 'who had served in merchant ships at any time since 1936 were required to register', where they could be 'compulsorily' directed to employment at sea. This was also used to allow a proportion of young men of military age into merchant service, rather than the merely to the armed forces.

The Merchant Navy Reserve Pool came about through the relevant 1942 Essential Work Order relating to the merchant service. This was a system of continuous employment, whereby officers and men who elected not to remain with vessels on reaching ports of final discharge would be sent to one of a number of pools, to await drafting to other vessels as required. (In time these were located throughout the world, with some temporarily run for specific operations, such as 'Overlord'.) Paid leave was also an entitlement and there were other schemes raising morale. With the details worked out by the National Maritime Board (an industry wide negotiating machinery set up in 1920), 'the pool' was run by the Shipping Federation (for and on behalf of the shipowners). With overall direction coming from the Ministry of War Transport (that had taken on the Ministry of Shipping's work in 1941) the office of the RGSS operated the Central Register of Seamen.

Post Second World War the British CRS was maintained. (It would appear from references on some entries that Colonial pools were run down within a year or so of peace in 1945.) Apart from the fact that MOWT officials were pleased with the improvements in record keeping over the old CIR there were other reasons. Perhaps ironically, by this time there was a perception that the CRS could actually be an aid to the shipping industry and hence, the moribund British economy. But, there was also another consideration - continued conscription. In the end the CRS outlived the military call up, lasting 1972.

Although there are indications within the very limited surviving sample of MOWT records in the public domain of much more paperwork, the Central Register of Seamen comprises two types of document. The more important are the docket books, made up of CRS10 forms and would seem to be almost complete. With a number of different series, these in effect, are 'service sheets' and often there is a substantial amount on mariners' sea time and associated information, including medal and pension entitlements. The other collection is made up of the 'pouches', officially known as CRS3s. Within these pouches can be a great variation of documents, including old CIR cards and can be well worth searching for. Unfortunately, a great many of these are missing. It is thought that the first 90,000 were destroyed relatively recently.

Also, not *all* wartime merchant mariners in British service were registered under the Employment Order: at least in the early stages of its operation. Those who were on very long haul voyages before this became law were not covered. As and when they returned to the UK, apparently they were then brought in. But, until this happened they continued to suffer the traditional pitfalls, such as having their pay stopped if their vessels were sunk.

Registry of Shipping and Seamen
Neil Staples – Records Officer

This is a guide to the library of seaman and ships records held at the Registry of Shipping and Seamen (RSS), P.O Box 420, Cardiff, CF24 5JW. T: 029 20 44 88 00, E: rss@mcga.gov.uk It also identifies records transferred to other locations. If you wish to obtain copies of any records held at RSS you should submit a written application to the Records Officer at the above address. The application should include as many details as you are able to provide together with the requisite fee. Further details on fees are shown against each category of record below

If you require information from records now held by other record offices you should contact them directly for details on how to make your application. Addresses and contact details for all organisations mentioned in this guide are given on the final pages. The information we give on these offices is accurate at the time of printing but we advise you to check with the organisation concerned before making personal applications.

1. MERCHANT NAVY SEAMAN'S SEA SERVICE RECORDS
2000 - 2004 Sea Service Records
This office is able to provide details of a merchant seaman's service for the above years. This information is **taken from the ships official logbooks and crew agreements** on which the seaman sailed. There is a charge of £11.00 per logbook to extract this information, the details of which are then included on a Certificate of Sea Service in respect of the seaman. Further charges are made for additional information and these are listed below.

1973 to 1999 Sea Service Records

This office is not able to supply information concerning the sea service details of individual Merchant Seamen from 1973 to 1999. After 1973 the Registrar General was not required by legislation to keep these records.

1941 to 1972 Fifth Register of Merchant Seaman's Service records are held at the National Archives in classification **BT 382. The Fifth Register of Seaman's Service 1941 to 1972.**

Records of individual Merchant Seamen's sea service details are held in alphabetical surname order. These details include the following information: Name of seaman, Date and place of birth, Discharge (Seaman's) book number, Rank, Details of the ships on which he served. These include:

Name of ship and official number, date of engagement (Joining ship), Date of discharge (Leaving ship), whether ship was a foreign going of home trade vessel, and records in some cases National Insurance contributions. Details shown in these records are similar to those contained in an individual seaman's discharge book.

1913 to 1940 Fourth Register of Merchant Seaman's service. These records are available at the National Archives and are held on Microfiche in the following classifications **BT 348: Register of Seamen, Central Index, Numerical Series (CR 2), BT 349: Register of Seamen, Central Index, Alphabetical Series (CR 1)** and **BT 350: Register of Seamen, Special Index, Alphabetical Series (CR 10).** These three classes were combined in one classification namely **BT 364 Register of Seaman, Combined Numerical Index** (CR1, CR 2 & CR 10) and were made up by extracting combinations of cards from the other three classes.

The original records for the above named classifications are now held at the following address: **Southampton Archives, Southampton City Council, South Block, Civic Centre, Southampton, S014 7LY.** This office is open Tuesdays to Fridays 9.30am to 4.30pm, with one late evening opening each month. There is no charge for a personal visit. Alternatively enquiries for information from the records may be made by post, E: or fax but there will be a charge for this.

1944 – 1945 SPECIAL OPERATIONS / D DAY RECORDS are held at the National Archives in their classification **BT 391 Merchant Seamen Special Operations Records** and details the sea service records of Merchant Seamen engaged in the liberation of Europe (6th June 1944 – 8th May 1945). They give the seaman's name, age, rank, rating/grade etc with details of the ships on which they served. The records are held in alphabetical order by seaman's name

These records are sometimes known as **COMNO** records, an abbreviation of **Combined Office Merchant Navy Operations.** The fifth register BT 381 (mentioned above) contain the annotation "See Comno pouches"; this leads to these pouches that contain the D Day/Comno service deliberately omitted from the seaman's service, for security reasons

MERCHANT SEAMEN WHO SERVED ON ROYAL NAVY SHIPS IN WW 2 1939 - 1946
These Merchant Seamen served on Royal Navy ships by special agreement with the Admiralty. The agreements were known as **T124X (Merchant ships)** and **T124T (Tugs)** agreements. This refers to the agreement form T124X

1835 to 1844 First Register of Merchant Seaman's service The registration of seamen was introduced by the Merchant Shipping Act 1835. These records are held at the National Archives under the following classifications: **BT 120: Register of Seamen Series 1.** (1835-1836).These records are arranged alphabetically. **BT 112: Register of Seamen: Series 11** (1835-1844). **BT 119 Alphabetical Index to Seamen**. This index provides the registration number of the seaman.

completed by the seaman.

Information is contained in pouches and includes personal details such as name, age, rank etc with details of the vessels on which the individual served. The pouches are presented in alphabetical order by the seaman's last name. These records are held at the National Archives in their classification BT 390.

1913 to 1940 Merchant Seaman's Pouches
These records are held at the National Archives in their classification **BT 372 Central Register of Seaman's Records ("Pouches")**. These are held in numerical order of the individual seaman's discharge book (Seaman's) number.

These pouches were a central repository for seaman's documents; these would comprise of the many documents that the sailor would have had to submit to the Registry of Shipping over the whole of his career and copies of those documents issued to him. These would comprise of Applications for Discharge Books (including photographs of the seaman), Sea Service records, records of certificates issued etc. The Pouches can sometimes include records cards extracted from the Forth Register of Seaman's Service.

* 1857 - 1918 for gaps between these records see section later on in leaflet concerning certificates of competency and service

1854 - 1856 Third Register of Merchant Seaman's service
This register of Merchant Seamen service was opened in 1854. This was arranged in alphabetical order and contained the following details of seaman: age, place of birth, details of voyage, including name of ship and port of departure. In 1856 it was considered that the obligation to maintain a register of seaman was satisfied by the crew list and the register was closed.

The records of this are held at the National Archives in the following classification **BT 116: Register of Seamen: Series 111.**

1845 - 1854 Second Register of Merchant Seaman's Service The Merchant Shipping Act 1844 stipulated that every British seaman should have a register ticket. The details given when applying for a ticket were: Name, Date and place of birth, Date and capacity of first going to sea, Capacity since: any Royal Navy ship served in, and capacity; Present employment at sea, home address.

These records are held at the National Archives under the following classifications: **BT 113: Registers of Seaman's Tickets**. (1845-1853), in Certificate number order. **BT 114: Alphabetical Index to registers of Seaman's Tickets. BT 115: Alphabetical Register of Masters Tickets**.

2. LOG BOOKS AND CREW AGREEMENTS
Logbooks are the records of a period of time in the life of a vessel; these usually are in existence for a one-year to eighteen-month period.

The logbook is divided up into two sections, the **tabular** section and the **narrative** section. The **tabular** section contains the information concerning "Notice of Freeboard" this is a record of all the ports the vessel docked at, and other information. This form is used for **tax purposes**. Births and deaths are also recorded in the tabular section along with other more routine information. The **narrative** section of the logbook contains written entries concerning various events that occur on each voyage: disciplinary matters, illness amongst the crew and accidents.

Fees for photocopies of logbooks
There is a charge of £11 to extract a logbook from our records and also additional photocopying charges. Please note blank pages with no information are not photocopied.

Crew Agreements
This document is a legal agreement between the crew of a vessel and the owners. It lists all the crew by name, includes their signatures and the last ship on which they sailed. When requesting a copy of a logbook the attached crew agreement would also be photocopied.

Log Books and Crew Agreements 2000 - 2002
These records are held at the Registry of Shipping and Seamen in their entirety. A certificate of sea service for individual seaman who sailed on ships from this period may be obtained from these records.
 (NB - No official logbooks and crew agreements have been retained between the years 1996 to 1999).

Log Books and Crew Agreements 1977 - 1995
A 10% sample of all log books for the above period 1977 to 1995 are held at the Public Record Office, in classification **BT 99: Agreements and Crew Lists, Series 11.**

Log Books and Crew Agreements 1951 to 1976
A 10% sample of all logbooks from the above period are held at the National Archives Office, in classification **BT 99 Agreements and Crew Lists, Series 11**. 80% of the records are now held at the **Maritime History Archive, Memorial University of Newfoundland, St. John's, Newfoundland, Canada, A1C 5S7**. The remaining 10% of these logbooks and crew agreements are kept at the **National Maritime Museum, Greenwich, London, SE10 9NF**. This last address keeps the years ending in "5", i.e. 1955, 1965, 1975.

Log Books and Crew Agreements 1947 to 1950
The Public Record Office holds all surviving logbooks and crew agreements for 1947 to 1950. These include both Merchant and Fishing vessels in their classification **BT 99 Agreements and Crew Lists, Series 11.**

Ships Logbooks and Crew Agreements 1939 to 1946
These records are held at the National Archives in their
classification **BT 381 WW 2 Logbooks and Crew
Agreements.** These are held in order of the ship's official
number; it is therefore advisable to find out the official
number of the ship in that you are interested before
researching these records. A Guide to Researching Logbooks
and Crew Agreements for the Period of World War 11 is also
available from this office.

The National Archives also holds index cards which record
all the official logbooks and crew agreements from WW 2
that are held in classification BT 381.This Index is held in
alphabetical order of ships name and can be used to obtain
the official number of the ship. These can be found in **BT
385 Index Cards for Ships Official Logbooks and Crew
Agreements.**
The cards contain some information on the ships and the
dates the log books where opened and then later concluded.

**WORLD WAR 2 MERCHANT SHIPPING
MOVEMENT CARDS** are held at the National Archives in
their classification **BT 389 World War 11, Merchant
Shipping Movements Cards.** Due to an Admiralty
instruction during WW 2 the Masters of Merchant vessels
were ordered not to record in the log books the ports at
which their ships called or details of their voyages in case
this information got into enemy hands. Instead, these details
were recorded on ships Movements Cards held and
maintained at the Registrar General of Shipping and
Seamen.

These cards are held in alphabetical order by ship's name.
They record the port at which the ship docked, intermediary
movements and the location of ships by latitude and
longitude if the ship sunk.

Allied Crew List 1939 - 1945
The following documents concerning allied vessels are held
at the National Archives, in alphabetical order of ship's
name: Return of British members of the crew of a foreign
Ship that has been requisitioned or chartered by, or on behalf
of H M Government and **Account of Changes** in the crew
of a foreign-going ship.

Agreement and list of the crew of a foreign-going ship.
Some Official Logbooks of these vessels are also held. The

records also include those records of the British crew of
allied vessels who were lost at sea. Please note that only in
rare cases were logbooks of any kind attached to these crew
lists. An additional record was also kept of the British
seamen who served on **Dutch** and **Norwegian** ships. These
are held in alphabetical ship order. These records are held in
their classification **BT 387. Allied Crew Lists from WW 2**.

Ships log books and Crew Lists 1861 to 1938
10% of logbooks and crew agreements for the above period
are held at the National Archives in classification **BT 99
Agreements and Crew Lists, Series 11.** 80% of the records
are held at the **Maritime History Archive, Canada**.

The remaining logbooks are held at the National Maritime
Museum, Greenwich. They hold the years where the last
digit ends in "5", from 1861 onwards: i.e. 1865, 1875, and
1885 etc.

Log books and crew agreements not included in the above
for the years 1861 to 1913 have been retained by some local
records office. If you wish to obtain a list of where these
records are held please write in to the Registry of Shipping
and this will be supplied. **Ships Log Books and Crew Lists
1835-1860**

From 1835 onwards the masters of foreign going British
ships over 80 tons were required to carry on board a written
agreement with every seaman employed. These
agreements contained the following: wage rate, The capacity
he served in, and the nature of the voyage.

These records are held at the National Archives under the
following classification: **BT 98. Agreement and Crew
Lists: Series 1.** Records prior to 1854 are arranged by the
port of registry numbers, later records are arranged in
official number order.

From 1852 onwards the official logbook of the vessel was
kept with the agreement and crew list.

Ships Log Books and Crew Lists 1747 - 1851
From 1747 onwards masters or owners of merchant ships
were obliged to keep muster rolls of each voyage. These
contained: names of the seamen employed on the ship, their
home address, when they joined ship and the last ship on
which they sailed. This system continued to be compiled
until 1851. These records are held at the National Archives
in **BT 98: Agreements and Crew
Lists: Series 1**.

Special Ships 1861 onwards
A selection was made of logbooks
and crew agreements from famous
ships, for example the SS Titanic and
Great Britain. These records are held
at the National Archives in category
**BT 100 Agreements and Crew
Lists Series 111**. A 10% sample of
similar records for fishing vessels of
less than 80 tons can be found at the
Public Record Office in category **BT
144 Agreements and Crew Lists
Series 1V** for the period 1884 -
1919. Later records of fishing vessel
are included in BT 99 (as above).

**World War 1 Log Books and Crew
Agreements**

**5 Agreements and Crew Lists.
Log Books containing entries of
Births and Deaths at Sea** were
segregated. These log books for the
years 1902 - 1938 are held at the
National Archives in classification
BT 165 Ship's Official Log Books.

Copyright
If you are planning to include a reproduction of a logbook or crew agreement or any part of these documents in a publication, you have to obtain written permission from this office to do so. You should acknowledge the Registry of Shipping and Seamen and include our full address. This should appear on the **same page** as the reproduced document.

3. DEATHS AT SEA: MERCHANT SEAMEN AND PASSENGERS The registers of deaths at sea are public documents and are open to inspection by the public. The various registers concerning deaths at sea contain the following information regarding Merchant Seamen and Passengers:

Name of person, Rank/Occupation, age/date of birth, address, date of death, place of death (This is often given in Lat. and Long.), cause of death: name, official number and port of registry of the ship.

Registers of Births and Deaths at Sea 1965 to present day These records are held at the Registry of Shipping and Seamen. A search may be made in these registers for the fee of £11.

Registers of Births, Marriages and Deaths at Sea Death Registers: 1891 to 1964 are held at the National Archives under category **BT 334: Registers and indexes of Births, Deaths and Marriages at Sea**. These records contain the death registers of those passengers and crew who died on the SS Titanic and SS Lusitania.

Registers of Births, Marriages and Deaths at Sea 1851 to 1890 From 1854 registers were compiled from ships official logbooks of births, marriages and deaths of passengers at sea. All these are recorded from 1854-1883, births and deaths only from 1883 -1887 and deaths only from 1888 onwards. These records are held at the National Archives in category **BT 158 Registers of Births, Marriages and Deaths of Passenger at Sea.**

Masters were also required from 1874 to report births and deaths of UK subjects and foreign subjects to the Registrar General of Shipping and Seamen. These records are held at the National Archives in category **BT 160: Registers of Births of British Nationals at Sea** and **BT 159: Registers of deaths at Sea of British Nationals.**

From 1851 onwards Masters of UK ships were required to surrender to the Board of Trade the wages and effects of any seaman who died during a voyage. These records included the following information concerning the seaman: name, date and place of joining the ship, date and cause of death, name, official number (after 1854) and port of ship: name of master, date and place of payment of wages, the amount of wages and date of receipt by Board of Trade.

These records are held at the National Archives in category **BT 153: Registers of Wages and Effects of Deceased Seamen (1852 to 1881).** To access these records you have to consult the following categories **BT 154: Indexes to Seamen's Names**
and Indexes to Ship's Names (1853 – 1889) These provide the relevant numbers of the pages in the register.

Monthly Lists of dead Seaman 1886 - 1889 were compiled giving name, age, rating, nationality and birthplace, home address and cause of death. Lists for 1886 - 1889 are at the National Archives in category **BT 156: Monthly Lists of Deaths of Seamen.** There are also nine manuscript registers of half yearly lists of deaths 1882-1888 classified by cause in category **BT 157 Registers of Seaman's Death Classified by Cause.**

Deaths at Sea - Returns of Death
When a death at sea occurs on an UK vessel the master is required to complete a Return of Death. This return includes the following information: name, official number and port of registry of ship, date and place of death, name, age, rank/occupation, address and cause of death of deceased.

The reverse of the form includes an extract of the ship's logbook that gives an account of the events that led to the death at sea. Please note however, that the log book extract is not always included. The return of death forms the basis of the death registration (See above).

The earliest surviving returns of death, date from1914 to 1919 are now held at the National Maritime Museum, Greenwich. No returns exist between 1920 - 1938, Returns from 1939 to 1946 & 1964 are also held at the National Maritime Museum. Returns from 1965 to the present day are held at the Registry of Shipping. Please note that there are also some gaps in these records.

Inquiries into Deaths at Sea, Papers and Reports
Inquiry reports concerning deaths at sea, conducted under the provisions of the Merchant Shipping Acts are held at the National Archives in classification: **BT 341 Inquiries into Deaths at Sea, Papers and Reports.** These documents contain statements, log book entries, medical reports and other relevant information regarding the particular death at sea. These cover the years 1939 to 1946 and the year 1964. The Returns of Death, which originally accompanied these papers, are now held at the National Maritime Museum (See above). These records are organised in year order and in alphabetical order of ship name. They correspond to the Registers of death held in BT 334.

Casualties and Deaths Lists (C & D)
When a vessel was lost at sea, the ship's official logbook would have been lost with the vessel. In these circumstances the owners of the vessel would submit a copy of the crew list to the Registrar General of Shipping and Seamen. These lists would be used for the registration of the deaths of the crewmembers.

Casualties and deaths lists (C & D) for the years 1920-1938 are held at the National Maritime Museum, Greenwich. **Casualties and deaths on fishing vessel's (List D)** for the years 1920-1938 have also been transferred to that office. These records are organised by the official number of the

ship. The official numbers of ships can be obtained from the extensive collection of Lloyds registers held at the National Maritime Museum. Many lists C & D are included in the 1939 - 1950 logbooks and crew agreements held at the Registry of Shipping.

Graves of Seamen/Memorials
The Registry of Shipping and Seamen holds no records of the last resting-place of seamen. Those who were lost or buried at sea and have no known grave are commemorated on the Tower Hill Memorial, London, and are also included in the Tower Hill Memorial Registers for both World Wars.

For information concerning the Tower Hill Memorial, you may wish to contact the following address: **The Commonwealth War Graves Commission, 2 Marlow Road, Maidenhead, Berkshire, SL6 7DX.**

Merchant seamen who are buried in various graves and war cemeteries around the world are included on index cards that have been transferred to the Commonwealth War Graves Commission. These cards also record those seamen included on the Halifax Memorial. There is also a small collection of cards held at the National Maritime Museum that date approx. 1939 to 1950 these include details of the deceased seaman and gives information regarding where the seaman is buried.

Rolls of Honour, Wars of 1914 - 1918 and 1939 - 1945 are held at The National Archives in their classification BT 339.

These include the Rolls of Honour of the Merchant Navy and Fishing Fleets, Ships list and Seaman list. The Albert Medal register, Nominal lists and Runnymede Memorial.

4. DAILY CASUALTY REGISTERS, WAR OF 1939 -

1945 comprise of 7 volumes of the daily casualties to Merchant Shipping between 8th June 1940 to 15th September 1945. These are held at the National Archives in their classification **BT 347**.

5. REGISTERS OF CERTIFICATES OF COMPETENCY AND SERVICE
Masters and Mates
From 1845 masters and mates of foreign going vessels took voluntary examinations of competency. These exams became compulsory in 1850, and from 1854 masters and mates of home trade vessels were also required to take these examinations.

The certificates were entered into registers arranged in numerical order and provide: name of seaman: place and date of birth, register ticket, if any, rank examined for, or served in, and date of issue of certificate.

Some additional information concerning the seamen may also be included in this record i.e. Deaths, injuries, previous ships etc.

Seamen judged by the examiners to have sufficient experience as a master or mate, and also men retiring from the Royal Navy were eligible, without formal examination, for certificates of service.

Those without sufficient service or wishing to progress in the ranks were granted certificates of competency on passing examinations.

These registers are arranged in 7 classes, which are held at the National Archives:
A. Certificates of Competency: Masters and Mates Foreign Trade. BT 122 (1845 - 1906). Held in Numerical order of certificate number.
B. Certificates of Service: Masters and Mates: Foreign Trade. BT 124. (1850 - 1888). Held in Numerical Order of Certificate number.
C. Certificates of Competency: Masters and Mates: Home Trade: BT 125. 1854 -1921. Held in Numerical order of Certificate number.
D. Registers of certificates of Competency: Masters and Mates of Steamships: Foreign Trade. BT 123. (1881 - 1921). Held in certificate number order.
E. Registers of Certificates of Service: Masters and Mates: Home Trade BT 126. (1855 - 1888). Held in certificate number order.
F. Alphabetical Register of Masters. BT 115. 1845 - 1854.
G. Certificates of Competency, Master and Mates. Colonial BT 128 1870 – 1921.
The means of reference to these series are the indexes to the registers **BT 127: Index to the Registers** that give the date and place of birth and the certificate number &

BT 352 Index to Certificate of Competency dates from 1910 to 1930. These cards are held in alphabetical order of seaman's name and list the certificates issued to the individual seaman with relevant number of the Certificate.

Application Forms for Certificates
All surviving Board of Trade Office copies of the above named certificates are held at the National Maritime Museum, these date from 1845 to 1927. These are arranged numerically by certificate number. The accompanying applications forms record the personal details of the candidate together with a list of vessels he served on with relevant dates of service.

Registers of Passes and Renewals of Master' and Mates'

Certificates 1917 to 1968
These are held at the National Archives in classification **BT 317**. These registers contain details of individual seamen passing certificate of competency examinations and also the replacement of lost certificates. These records are in numerical order of certificate number.

Registers of Changes of Masters 1893 to 1948
These records are held at the National Archives in their classification **BT 336**. The registers contain lists of those masters who were in command of vessels registered in the United Kingdom. The registers are arranged in numerical order by the official number of the individual ship. Each entry contains the name of the vessel: the port where the master joined the vessel with relevant date and also the name and seaman's number of the master.

Engineers
Examinations of competence were extended to engineers in 1862. The registers of certificates are held at the National Archives in the following classifications: **BT 139: Certificates of Competency: Engineers. (1863 – 1921)** and **BT 142: Certificates of Service: Engineers.** (1862 – 1921). The means of reference to these records are the indexes to registers in **BT 141: Certificates of Competency: Engineers.** This index is arranged alphabetically by surname, and gives date and place of birth and the certificate number **BT 143 Registers of Certificates of Competency and Service, Miscellaneous.** (1845 – 1849)

Fishing Boats
The Merchant Shipping (Fishing Boats) Act 1883 extended the examination system to the skippers and mates of fishing vessels. The registers of certificates are held at the National Archives in the following classifications **BT 129. Certificates of Competency: Skippers and Mates of Fishing Boats. (1880 – 1921)** and **BT 130: Certificates of Service: Skippers and Mates of Fishing Boats. (1883 – 1907)**

The means of reference to these records are **BT 138. Indexes to Registers of Competency and Service: Skippers and Mates of Fishing Boats.** These records are held in alphabetical order according to the seaman's surname.

5. MERCHANT SEAMEN PRISONER OF WAR
RECORDS 1939 to 1952 are held at the National Archives in classification **BT 373 Merchant Navy Prisoner of War Records.** The information is held in pouches and organised in alphabetical order by the name of ship from which the seamen were captured.

These records contain the names of those men captured from merchant ships and the names of the camps where they were held in captivity. These records also include additional information supplied by the Red Cross and also information regarding the deaths of POW's.

6. PRECEDENT BOOKS, ESTABLISHMENT PAPERS
etc This section can be regarded as a miscellaneous section contains a number of different types of records; these include policy files, precedent books and black books. These are books that deal with disciplinary conduct. These records are held at the National Archives in classification **BT 167.**

Marine Safety Agency (Now the Maritime and Coastguard Agency): **Business Plans.** These date from 1994 to 1998. These are held at the Public Record Office in classification **MT 173.**

7. APPRENTICES
These records are held at the National Archives the following classifications **Index of Apprentices BT 150 (1824 -1953), BT 151 Apprentices Indentures (1845 - 1962)** and **BT 152. Apprentices Indentures for Fishing (1895 to 1935)**

In accordance with the Merchant Seamen's act 1823 Masters of British merchant ships were required to carry a given number of indentured apprentices. In London they were registered with the Registrar General of Seamen, in other ports customs officers were required to submit quarterly list to the Registrar General.

These papers consist of indexes of all apprentices whose indentures were registered (BT 150), together with specimens taken at five-yearly intervals of the copy indentures (BT 151 and 152).

8. ROYAL NAVAL RESERVE (RNR): RATING RECORDS OF SERVICE 1908 - 1955
These are held at National Archives in their classification **BT 377.** This series contains microfiche copies of service record cards of Royal Naval Reserve rating, mainly covering men who served during the First World War. The filmed cards are arranged in service number order. Indexes to service numbers are included in the class.
The Royal Naval **Volunteer** Reserve (RNVR). This was a force of officer and ratings undertaking naval training in their spare time, but not professionally employed at sea like the RNR. During both world wars the RNVR was the principal means by which officers entered the Royal Navy for the period of the war only. In 1958 the RNVR was amalgamated with the RNR. Details of records related to the RNVR can be found in Public Record Office Handbook No 22 Naval Records for Genealogists.

Records of the **Merchant Navy Reserve Pool** WW2 are held at the National Maritime Museum.

9. PASSENGER LISTS 1878 - 1960
Passenger lists for the period before 1890 have not survived in England, with the exception of a few relating to vessels in the United Kingdom between 1878 and 1888. These, and the surviving lists for the period between 1890 and 1960, are held at the National Archives.

The classifications you would require at that address are as follow:
BT 26 Inwards Passenger Lists 1878 to 1960.
The information given in these lists include the age, occupation, address in the United Kingdom and the date of entering the country of passengers entering the United Kingdom by sea from ports outside Europe and the Mediterranean. They are arranged under the names of the ports of arrival.

The registers containing this information are held in classification **BT 32. Registers of Passenger Lists 1906 to 1951.** Prior to 1920 they are under the different ports, the names of ships and the month of arrival and departure: after 1920 the date of arrival or departure is recorded. Before 1908 the registers relate only to the ports of Southampton, Bristol and Weymouth.

BT 27 Outward Passenger Lists. 1890 to 1960
These give the names of all passengers leaving the UK where the ship's eventual destination was a port outside Europe and the Mediterranean Sea. Names of passengers who disembarked at European ports from these ships will be included in
these lists. They are arranged monthly by port of departure. For registers see **BT 32 (as above).**

There have been several resources published specifically aimed at helping family historians locate passenger lists outside the UK. Copies of these are now held at the following address: **The Guildhall Library, Aldermanbury, London, EC2P 2EJ.**

These include Filby, P.W.: **Passengers and immigration lists index (and annual supplements),** that cover North America. It can be found in the Reference Collection at R

325/2 and lists individuals by surname and shows where the passenger list can be found; **The Morton Allan Directory of European Steamship arrivals 1890 - 1930 at the ports of New York, Philadelphia, Boston & Baltimore,** Closed Access LB 286, is also useful. **British Immigration to Victoria - assisted immigrants 1839 - 1891** (microfiches 3), **Index of New South Wales Convict Indents** (microfiches 29) **Immigration Index to assisted immigrants arriving Sydney 1844 - 96,** Closed Access 387/5, and Hughes, 1A: **9 assorted list to Port Phillip, c 1839 - 51,** Closed Access 387/5, cover Australia.

Guildhall Library holds a number of shipping indexes that were compiled for the popular immigration ports in Australia and New Zealand. These include: **Shipping arrivals and departures, Victorian ports, 1798 - 1855** (2 vols.), **Shipping arrivals and departures, Sydney, 1788 - 1844** (3 vols.), **Shipping arrivals and departures, Tasmania, 1803 - 1843,** (2 vols.) and **Shipping to New Zealand 1839 - 1889** (known as the Comber Index), all Closed Access 387/2. Some other books held by the Library also provided potentially useful information, such as **Dictionary of Western Australians. 1829 - 1914,** Closed Access 325/941 and British settlers in Natal 1824 - 1857. Closed access 325/684.

10. MEDALS
The National Archives hold records of **World War 1 Medals** in their classification **BT 351: Index of First World War Mercantile Marine Medals.** These simply list the name of the seaman and the medals that they were issued to them. There are held in alphabetical order of the Seaman's name. A record of medals issued to Merchant Seamen for service in **World War 2** is also held at the Public Record Office in their classification **BT 395. Database of World War**

11 Medals issued to Merchant Seamen. These records mostly date from 1939 to 1950, however due to fact Merchant Navy medals are still issued in respect of service in WW 2 and other conflicts the record extents to 2002. The records are held in alphabetical order of seaman's name include the name of the seaman and the record the medals that were issued to him.

Recommended Reading:
Merchant Seamen: Registers of Service 1913 - 41 Public Record Office Leaflet Number DRI 90.
Records of the Merchant Shipping and Seamen. Public Records Office Readers' Guide No 20. PRO Publications.
A Guide to Researching Logbooks and Crew Agreements for the period of World War 11. MSF 5330 REV 5/02. (Can be obtained from this office).

1. The Registry of Shipping and Seamen P.O. Box 420 Cardiff CF24 5XR T: 029 20 44 88 00 F: 029 20 44 88 20 E: RSS@mcga.gov.uk W: :www.mcagency.gov.uk
2. The National Archives (formally The Public Record Office) Kew Richmond Surrey TW9 4DU T: 020 8876 3444 F: 020 8878 8905
E: enquiry@nationalarchives.gov.uk Website: www.nationalarchives.gov.uk
3. The National Maritime Museum, Greenwich London SE10 9NF T: 020 8858 4422 F: 020 8312 6632 Website: www.nmm.ac.uk.
4. The Archivist, Maritime History Archive Memorial University of Newfoundland St. John's Newfoundland A1C 5S7 T: 709 737 8428 F: 709 737 3123 Website: http://www.mun.ca/mha/ E: mha@mun.ca
5. The Guildhall Library Aldermanbury London EC2P 2EJ T: 020 7 332 1868/1870 F: 020 7 600 3384
6. The Southampton Archives Services Southampton City Council South Block Civic Centre Southampton S014 7LY T: 023 8083 2251 F: 023 8083 2156 E: city.archives@southampton.gov.uk

The Little Drummer Boy.
Glenys Shepherd

This is a continuation story from my family history which was published in the 7th edition of this Handbook, and described how I had begun to research my family history.

At that time the research was very much a matter of recording stories which had been handed down to me through family members; borrowing and copying photographs and making contact with newly discovered relations, as well as visiting the actual places where our ancestors had lived.

The next stage of my investigations was then to begin to investigate more formally by using sources of information such as birth, marriage and death certificates etc. In particular I was fascinated by the emerging story of my maternal grandfather, "The Little Drummer Boy."

George - aged 18 years

My great grandfather, George Dixon, was christened in 1850 in Chapel en le Frith in Derbyshire. His son, my grandfather was George Edward Shawcross Dixon and he was born in Denton in Manchester in 1870. He was the first son and second child of George and Sarah. Altogether there were 5 sons and 4 daughters. All the children were born in Scarborough except for George. He was born in Denton where his grandparents lived, possibly during a visit home with the firstborn child. The other children were born in Scarborough whilst great grandad George was a Professor of Music in York.

When grandad was 14 years old, he enlisted for a 12 year engagement in the second battalion of the Grenadier Guards. In the beginning he was a boy drummer but 3 years before his time was completed,

he became a full drummer. He enrolled on April 12th 1883 until 12th April 1895; he was a very small boy. He was 4 feet nine inches tall and weighed 5 stones and 12 pounds. His chest measurement was 27 inches. His religion was Wesleyan. At the time that he enlisted, his next of kin, his father, was back in Denton but during his period of service the address changed to 6, Deckhand, Bridge Street, Kirkaldy. This explained to me why I had a photograph of grandad's 4 brothers in a large grocery emporium in Edinburgh. Until then, I had not been able to work out the connection between Denton, York and Edinburgh.

Eliza Cant was my grandmother. She was born into a large family who lived in Great Gornard in Suffolk. She went to London to live and work in a large house in Sloane Square in Chelsea. Whilst she was there she met George and they fell in love. They were married at the Registry Office in Chelsea two years before his period of service finished.

Stories handed down have always to be questioned and verified if possible, but time and memories can distort the truth. I had always been led to believe that grandad was an officer of high rank. In fact he was a very talented musician who played the fife, the drums and the trumpet to a very high standard but through the years his rank had been exaggerated, probably said 'tongue in cheek'. In grandad's time, the little drummer boys were very much front line communicators because, of course, it was their drummed messages which kept everyone else informed of the action. George had a second class pass in Education which he obtained four months after enlisting. The Guards had a school which the soldiers could use. Children of the regiment could also attend but it was a very strict routine as they had to attend chapel and Sunday School as well as day school. They were not allowed to truant. George's brothers and sisters were listed as "scholars" in the census of 1881 from the age of only 3. George himself was listed as 'drummer', from the age of 11, so they had a good standard of education.

George's duties included general peacekeeping in London, Windsor and Dover. He was also in Dublin for almost 2 years. Generally the battalion had 6 months service in each place at home, but overseas the period of duty could be much longer. It was a very tough life. Many soldiers were recruited by special officers whose sole duty was to go round the major towns recruiting whoever they could persuade to join and by any means whatsoever, including getting them drunk, whatever their age. They were

Four of grandad's brothers in their shop in Edinburgh.
Waiting for George to visit

paid a bonus for everyone they recruited.

During grandad's period of enlistment, he spent 18 months in Bermuda. This puzzled me as I could not find any reason for him to be there. Apparently on July 7th 1881 the officer who was responsible for posting the men's duties in the mess hall had forgotten to do so and no one felt inclined to remind him. Early in the day it was realised that no one was getting up for duty. One officer managed to get a few men on duty and later in the day the battalion was assembled. Immediately, the offending officer resigned, but he and all the other officers were sentenced to varying periods of hard labour and dismissal from the service. Within 24 hours the remainder of the men were on a boat for Bermuda where they had to man what remained of a former penal colony. Most of the men treated it as a holiday but several died during the 18 month period.

George at The Grand Theatre, Bolton after leaving The Guards

Life was very hard for the privates such as grandad. A battalion was only allowed a certain number of married men and they received only a very small allowance. If the quota had been reached, they married secretly and did not receive an allowance. There were no married quarters so they rented rooms near to the barracks. Some wives followed their husbands around. Others carried on working or lived with their families. Sometimes the men were overseas for up to 9 years and when they returned they could not find their families. Many died overseas. Eliza married George 3 years before his period of enlistment finished. She was 18 at the time. Three months later he was posted to Dublin and she continued to work at 153, Sloane Street.

George was not happy during his period of service. He said his father had encouraged him to join as it would make a man of him. His punishment in Bermuda was not his only misdemeanour. He was frequently admonished for varying offences including losing his leggings; being late for duty; smoking in bed whilst a patient in hospital. And very improper conduct whilst on furlough. This last one was only two months before his completion of service. He left with a payment of £36.

By the time he left the guards, his father and brothers had moved to Kircaldy. Ellen Amelia, the eldest sister, was living in Denton with another sister and at least two of the sisters had married Denton businessmen. Grandad and grandmother moved first of all to Scunthorpe where he was an Orchestra Leader ; later to Bolton and finally to Wigan-They remained very much in love but he was not a very healthy person. He died at the age of 44 at 28,Taylors Lane, Spring View, Wigan, of pneumonia, tuberculosis and heart failure, on October 30th 1914. His funeral was a very grand affair, and a memorial keepsake was given to all who attended.

The memento included the following verse; -

Grieve not for me
My days are past,
Dearly you loved me to the last.
Grieve not for me
But comfort take,
And love each other
For my sake.

Grandfather's Funeral procession, Lower Ince, Wigan

The history of ferries ~ a research guide
Martin Limon B.A.(Hons)

Wawne Ferry in about 1900 with a Humber Keel sailing past. Close to the Wawne slipway stands the Windham Arms Public House

One hundred years ago river ferries were commonplace in Britain but in the twenty-first century they are comparatively rare. My own research on Wawne Ferry (East Yorkshire) came about because I lived close to where it once operated and since very little research on the ferry had ever been published I considered that it was a story worth telling.

For would-be researchers of the history of their own local ferries a good starting point is the Victoria County History (VCH). These volumes can be found in reference libraries/ local studies libraries and are useful not simply for the information they provide but also for their footnotes/ references. To pinpoint the volumes you will need go to www.englandpast.net on the internet. At the bottom of the webpage click on "county sites" for an indication of what VCH volumes have already been published in your own area. A trawl through the card index or online catalogue of your local studies library should also provide the titles/ authors of other secondary sources which may be helpful in your ferry research. To set your own local research into a national context the book *River Ferries by Nancy Martin* (Pub 1980) provides fascinating reading.

Remember that ferries are often intimately linked with the public houses on the riverbank where they operated from; ferry operators often supplemented their income by being publicans and farmers too! Check on local publications which cover the history of public houses in your area or surf the internet for these names through a good search engine like *Google*. The names of public houses can sometimes change and it can be helpful to look at and compare Ordnance Survey maps from the nineteenth and twentieth centuries to discover changes to a ferry service over time. These too can be found at Local Studies Libraries (or local authority *archives*) as are trade directories and census returns. The latter are usually available on microfilm. Don't be put off using

a microfilm reader because you think it's complicated; I have found that library staff are always willing to help in setting up the machine or adjusting it in use. The census took place every ten years and is a snapshot in time. A comparison between, say, the 1851 census and the 1861 census, can reveal a mass of fascinating details about the ferryman's household and of changes in the intervening period.

Examples of trade directories (eg. Genuki or Bulmers) can also be found on line. The microfilm reader may also be indispensable for a search through local newspapers of your area. Once you have done your groundwork through the VCH or other local history books you can fill in the details (for example, on the reasons for or the circumstances of a ferry's closure and attitudes of the time) by studying these press reports. The activities of local councils in resisting ferry closures are often covered too in newspapers of the time. Local newspapers can also provide stories of 'incidents' at river ferries. For example, while investigating late 19th century copies of the *Beverley Guardian* (for a topic totally unrelated to ferries) I came across the following:

Beverley Guardian: 10th June 1899
Trap Accident at Wawne Ferry
Horse drowned in River Hull

On Wednesday evening last a serious accident occurred at Wawne Ferry to a party of four gentlemen who were driving home to Sutton from Beverley. It appears that in descending the slope to the ferry, the horse was unable to hold properly in check the conveyance with the result that it missed its footing on the boat, swerved and fell headlong into the river. The horse dragged after it the trap and two of its occupants who were immersed in the deep water but who luckily escaped without receiving any further harm. The horse was however drowned before it could be rescued. One of the shafts of the trap was also broken. The horse was the property of Mr H. Webster, landlord of the Duke of York Inn, Sutton.

However, looking through newspapers can be a 'hit-and-miss' affair unless someone has produced an index of past copies.

The footnotes of the VCH and other secondary sources will also lead, hopefully, to the **Archives Service** of your local council. In some cases their *Archives Catalogue* may be available and searchable online which can considerably speed up your quest for relevant information on ferries. Since a ferry was considered, legally, to be part of the highway it can also be fruitful to examine the minutes of local authority highways committees.

Of course *archives* are not merely restricted to the ones held by local authorities. They are often held by university libraries or private institutions too. A useful tool for finding these is the *National Register of Archives* available on the internet. Given the close relationship between river ferries and public houses a useful source can be the *minute books of brewery companies*. Sometimes these can be found at the **Coors Visitor Centre** (formerly the Bass Museum) at Burton-upon-Trent. The address is :PO Box 220, Horninglow Street, Burton upon Trent, Staffordshire, DE14 1YQ. To avoid a fruitless visit you could also try emailing the Keeper of Documentation there at: Elizabeth.Press@Coorsbrewers.com

A major source of information about ferries in the 20th century is the *Report of the Committee on Ferries in Great Britain issued by the Minister of Transport (1948)*. If your own library does not have a copy (and it probably wont!) you can ask them to arrange an inter-library loan from a library which does. The late 1940s were a time of crisis for some ferries (though not all) and this Committee was set up to inquire into Britain's vehicle ferries. As well as their report you can also see the mass of evidence they based their recommendations on by visiting the National Archives in London. Members of the Ferries Committee went on a fact-finding mission to these river ferries as well as receiving correspondence and representations from breweries and other interested parties. Some examples of their investigations can be found at the National Archives (Kew) in Ministry of Transport files:

MT 41/51: Horning Ferry, Woodbastwick, Norfolk
(over the River Bure)
MT41/31: Loddon to Reedham Ferry, Norfolk
(over the River Yare)
MT41/49 Southrey Ferry, Lincolnshire
(over the River Witham)

The National Archives website is at:www.nationalarchives.gov.uk and their online catalogue is invaluable in discovering what is available. Finally, any study of a river ferry could incorporate the memories of those old enough to remember it in use (a diminishing group). An appeal in the *letters page* of your local newspaper or on your local radio station can often yield worthwhile results among the elderly who will happily reminisce about tales of a ferryboat in operation. A simple flyer (with a telephone contact number) posted through letterboxes can also produce significant results.

For over 800 years Wawne Ferry operated over the River Hull from Thearne on the east bank to Wawne on the west bank

East Yorkshire Transport History: Wawne Ferry
Martin Limon B.A.(Hons)

In an age before bridges, or when bridges were few in number, river ferries were a vital link in the road network of Yorkshire. It was the coming of the motor car which, more than any other factor, sounded the death knell of this ancient mode of transport. Of the many river ferries operating over the River Hull in East Yorkshire, Wawne Ferry was one of the more famous and long lasting. The ferry was a link in an ancient highway which led from the Roman town of Petuaria (modern-day Brough) to south-eastern Holderness. The ferry replaced a more ancient river crossing: a stone paved ford joining Thearne on the west bank of the River Hull with Wawne on the east bank. We know that the ferry was already in existence by the early 12th century for in 1136 William le Gros, an important local landowner, gave this "passage over the River Hull" to the Cistercian Abbey of Meaux which lay close by.

For the first four hundred years of its eight hundred year recorded history the ferry was owned by the

monks of Meaux Abbey. The abbey, during the Middle Ages, was a major wool-producer in East Yorkshire. The growth of the market town of Beverley and the rise of its wool manufacturing industry helps to explain the importance of Wawne Ferry which linked the Abbey's sheep farms with the spinners and weavers of Beverley. The ferry survived both the decline of Beverley's woolen industry in the later Middle Ages and the dissolution of the monasteries during 1536 - 1540 when ownership of Wawne Ferry was transferred, for about 90 years, to the crown. During the English Civil Wars of 1642 - 1646 the ferry was to thwart the attempts of the turncoat Governor of Hull, Sir John Hotham, to escape the clutches of his former Parliamentary friends. On June 29th 1643 Hotham fled from Hull and attempted to use Wawne Ferry to escape across the River Hull into Holderness. Arriving at the Thearne bank of the river Hotham found that the ferryboat had proceeded upriver. Forced to try and make his escape through the streets of Beverley he

Wawne Ferry in 1910. To the left of the Wawne slipway, in the punt, is the new ferryman, Donald Brewer . He holds the stour (or pole) which was used to propel the ferryboat across the River Hull. To the right of the slipway is the chain-operated pontoon ferry

was recognised and arrested by the Parliamentary commander there, Colonel Boynton.

In due course the ferry passed under the control of the lords of the manor of Wawne, the Windham family, who continued to own this important river crossing until 1911. For much of its history Wawne Ferry was a simple boat or punt which, because of the shallow nature of the River Hull at this point, would have been "poled" across the 45 feet of water which lay between the two banks of the river. This pole, called a **stour,** was about 8 feet long and generations of ferrymen learned how to judge the fickle tides and undercurrents of the River Hull to propel the boat across. However, there were occasional mishaps and an account book held in the East Riding Archive in Beverley records how in January 1780 the ferryboat sank. On January 26th 1780 the Windhams had to pay 12s 0d (about 60p in modern money) for "raising the ferryboat from the bottom of the river." A local boatbuilder called William Wiseman from Hull was asked to build a new ferryboat and was paid £60 for the work. The account book also records that when the new ferryboat was first launched in July 1780 the celebrations were marked with the spending of 8s 0d (40p) on ale!

Like many ferrymen of the 19th and 20th centuries those operating Wawne Ferry combined this work with inn-keeping and farming. On the eastern side of the river stood the ferryman's home: the Wawne Passage House, built around 1780, and a 33 acre farm which went with the tenancy. By the early nineteenth century the ferryman's home was also a public house and we have more evidence, in the form of local directories and census returns, on those living there. Dominant among the ferrymen in the later nineteenth and twentieth centuries were members of the Brewer family. By 1879 James Brewer, born in Little Weighton, was the ferryman and the 1881 census shows us that he had 12 children. His eldest daughter,

Transporting the horses and foxhounds of the Holderness Hunt c. 1930 on the pontoon ferry

Photograph of the 1930s. Hauling on the chain of the pontoon ferry is Donald Brewer. Being transported are Bob and Eliza Wray of Prospect Farm, Thearne, with a horse-drawn reaper.

move a tractor to the Wawne side, the regular use of the pontoon effectively ceased leaving only the punt to ferry foot passengers and cyclists during the years of the Second World War. The end of the ferry finally came in the summer of 1946 when the Windham Arms, its land and the ferry rights were sold to the Hull-based brewery firm of Moors and Robsons for £3,000. By the end of 1946 complaints were already being voiced about the closure of the ferry.

Alice, married John Wood of Wawne and Wood became the ferryman in 1895. At an early stage in his tenancy he was to show great courage when he prevented a suicide at the ferry crossing. In May 1895 Wood went into the river to rescue a middle-aged Hull woman called Emily Cousens who was trying to drown herself.

By about 1890 the ferryman at the Wawne crossing had two ferry craft at his disposal. Like many other river ferries in the country the small punt had been supplemented by a pontoon or floating bridge hauled manually across the river by chains fastened securely to both river-banks. The chain was pulled hand-over-hand sailor fashion in order to draw the pontoon from the Wawne slipway to the Thearne side. The pontoon ferry was large enough to transport animals (including the horses and foxhounds of the Holderness Hunt), farm machinery and cars and was particularly useful at high tide when operation of the punt was more difficult.

Continuing the family tradition James Brewer's son, Donald Brewer, took over as ferryman in 1909 and two years later he bought the ferry, the farm and the Windham Arms for £2,100 when all were sold at auction by the Windham family. Sales particulars from 1911 show that the takings from the ferry at that time were only £52 per year although combined with the profits from the public house and the farm they would have provided a reasonable income. Donald Brewer was to continue operating the ferry until almost the time it closed charging foot passengers 1d, cyclists 2d and the owners of small cars 6d for each crossing over the river. Passengers arriving at the Thearne side of the river had to ring a bell or shout "boat" to get his attention.

Although the rise of the motor vehicle at first provided increased opportunities for the ferry in the long term they were the cause of its downfall. With the rise of motorised road transport came pressure for road improvements and the building of more bridges. In July 1937 a new bridge over the River Hull was opened on the newly-constructed Sutton Road. Since this was only three miles south of Wawne Ferry any use of the pontoon for transporting vehicles declined rapidly. Although local agricultural contractors, like Mark Jackson of Thearne, occasionally used it to

The brewery appointed an elderly man called Walter Twidale as tenant of the Windham Arms and protestors were told that he believed that the ferryboat was no longer safe to use. Moors and Robsons insisted that the cost of repairs was not justified by the demand for the service. Despite a thorough investigation of the issues involved and pressure by the East Riding of Yorkshire County Council the ferry remained permanently closed after August 1946. The fate of Wawne Ferry was not unique in this respect.

The late 1940s were a time of crisis for river ferries and the government's concern was shown by a major investigation of ferries during 1947 - 1948 by the Ministry of Transport. This study showed that of thirteen pontoon and chain ferries of the type used at Wawne only five were still operating. The typical financial problems of Britain's smaller river ferries in the late 1940s are well illustrated by their investigations into the Stixwould Ferry in Lincolnshire. Here the ferry had been bought by Kesteven Council in 1937. However, such was the decline in ferry traffic that by 1945 they were in the unenviable position of paying someone £2 10s 0d (£2.50) a week to operate the ferry and allowing them to keep the ferry tolls of 7s 0d (35p) a week! In these circumstances it is not surprising that Moors and Robsons Ltd denied that they were responsible for maintaining a public ferry service at Wawne.

Martin Limon's book called " A Passage over the River Hull: the Story of Wawne Ferry" was published in 2003 and is available, price £4.50, from Browns Bookshop (Hull), the Beverley Bookshop or direct from him at 93 Thearne Lane, Thearne, Beverley, East Yorkshire, HU17 0SA.

Martin Limon was born in Hull and is a history graduate of Hull University and taught history in Hull secondary schools for 26 years.

Hobby Bobbies
Fred Feather

Early in my 1957 to 1998 police service I grew quite attached to those dedicated citizens who came, in uniform, to supplement us on a Friday evening. Some of my colleagues saw them as citizens performing civic duty; others as "*blacklegs*" that were "subverting a difficult job by doing it unpaid." Thus, whilst derided by some exponents of "Canteen culture" as "*Hobby Bobbies*," it soon became apparent to me that there were many among those members of the "Special Constabulary" who were officers with real police talent and who could offer skills that we could use to the public's advantage. I have had many well-respected friends who have served thus.

It was, however, some years before I realised that the history and formation of the "*specials*" long pre-dated that of the regular police (details of which I described in *Ancestors,* in an article in the February/March 2003 issue – "*Looking for a policeman*".) Given much of the task of producing a police museum from a basic four walls and a carpet, I was shortly afterwards asked the question "How many specials have been killed on duty in Essex?" and at first was delighted to answer "to the best of my knowledge – none." Soon after that I identified in this mournful category the Reverend J.B.Thomas of Hempstead, who was a "Special Corporal" when he fell from a bridge and died of his injuries during the Great War. It then became a pleasant and necessary project to learn more about the Special Constabulary and its varied appearances in the history of the policing of this country. I recalled that, of the four grandfathers of my wife and I, two had been special constables. My mother's father, a taxi driver, served during the Great War in the Metropolitan Police and my father-in-law's father, a gentlemen's outfitter, was in the Kent Constabulary. Of the latter's service, traces survived in a decorated truncheon, badges and a Special Constabulary Medal. As a matter of family pride I purchased a similar medal to represent my grandfather's service. At the police training school I was able to show the rest of the class the correct way to hold the, then, issue truncheon. "My mother taught me," I added.

Special constables regularly appear in histories of the Georgian and Victorian eras, at times of national disturbance. In 1819 they were used to help manage enormous meetings in Manchester during the Industrial Revolution, demonstrations which resulted in riots. Members of the public attending (who may

have been demonstrating) died and many more were injured. Following this the government passed an act confirming the magistrates' power to summon men to the role of Special Constable. Notable events of a similar nature were the "Peterloo" incident in Manchester in 1819, the "Cato Street Conspiracy" in London in 1820, and the Chartist incidents of 1848.

In 1831 the Special Constables Act allowed local authorities to recruit men to supplement the shortage of regular officers, when they were unable to keep law and order on their own. Also, Specials were given the full powers of regular police officers and the equipment needed for their protection whilst carrying out their duties. Three years later saw another enactment with an effect on the organisation of Special Constabulary. It contained two important factors, for it permitted them to act outside their parishes and townships and, more importantly, introduced the concept of the voluntary Special Constable.

One source quotes the number of specials enrolled in the panic before the events expected to culminate on Kennington Common in 1848 as 170,000. (*The Times* 1848). They were being sworn in, as many as 1000 daily, at each magistrate's court. Many were the workmen of major employers such as the Post Office, tanners, hatters, wool sorters, brewers and employees of the Archbishop at Lambeth. Because truncheons were in short supply they were warned to arm themselves with a "stout bludgeon." The majority of them would have been enrolled in London. The *Essex Standard* for April 1848 reported that Marylebone Magistrates Court in London had to postpone all of its normal business to accommodate and complete the swearing in of Special Constables. The numbers of attestations in this period alone were greater than the number of officers who serve in the whole of the

Times that, though he had not been in action that day, he would not put his body at risk again for the sort of fines levied on those who had attacked policemen. A citizen suggested a reward of an Easter meal of "Roast Beef" for all those citizens who had done their duty.

Specials and non-regular policemen

A general description of the use of the word "police" may be of assistance. Regular forces with paid officers date from 1829 in London, and between 1839 and 1856 in other cases, though Glasgow citizens and members of the River Thames Police in London claim earlier lineage. The grave of the founder of the latter organisation can be found at Church End, Paglesham, in Essex. There were police offices during the late 18th century and up to 1829 in London and other centres and the names of those serving there, sometimes described as policemen, can be found in newspaper reports and publications such as the *Newgate Calendar*. Some of these were "redbreasts" or Bow Street Runners and a contemporary report stated "A Horse Patrole of constables is to extend around the Metropolis in every direction at most 12 miles. Constables to have a brace of pistols and a sabre". (*Chelmsford Chronicle* 1805).

The origins of Special Constabulary were in an Act passed under King Charles II in 1673, which extended common law in order to summon any man to the role of temporary peace officer in times of unrest. Any citizen who refused to carry out this role could be heavily fined or even jailed. The legislation of 1673 had resulted in the formation of a body of men, nicknamed "*Charlies,*" from the name of their founder and ruling monarch. These static watchmen were still in their posts nation-wide until the 1840s and perhaps beyond. Their names are occasionally reported. In 1836 the Horse Patrols and the remaining Bow Street operatives were absorbed into the Metropolitan Police. Both that force and the Essex Police Museum hold lists of the Patrol Officers of that time. Parish Constables, High Constables and Chief Constables in the shires pre-dated the formation of the regular forces and sometimes acted in collusion with the regular police. Upon occasion they were in dispute over jurisdiction. In a crime of the 1850s, at Tollesbury in Essex, the suspect was "taken up by the constable" who was not a member of the Essex Constabulary, but who would no doubt be referred to as a constable in the 1851 census.

An attempt at large scale policing before most forces were formed.

The Specials Act of 1831 began a period of employment of temporary policemen, with emoluments and many, both mounted and on foot, were employed at the time of the "Swing riots." When Captain, later Admiral J.B.B.McHardy was made Chief Constable of Essex, his 1839 papers state "sworn in as a special Constable - to be Chief Constable of Essex." The Essex County Constabulary was not created until February 1840.

regular police of this country today.

The most famous personage to perform this civic duty in London was a soon to be Emperor of France, Louis-Napoleon Bonaparte, a recent sojourner in French prisons. He escaped to England and, in 1848, joined the Metropolitan Police, walking the beat in Kensington in that turbulent year. At least one of Louis-Napoleon's biographers suspected that he enrolled as a Special in order to impress on the French middle class that he was now on the side of law and order rather than espousing the revolutionary side of his Napoleonic inheritance. Many years later, during a subsequent State Visit to Queen Victoria, his aide presented various artefacts which commemorated this event to police officers serving at Buckingham Police. His duty armband was given to Chief Inspector Bocking of the Buckingham Palace Special Branch[1]. This was later left to his grandson, a Chief Inspector of Specials from the Essex Constabulary, and now resides in the collection of the Chelmsford and Essex Museum. It is about 6 inches long and 2 inches wide, made of rough white canvas, with brass fittings and with a thin crimson stripe close to the top and bottom edge. The word SPECIAL, in black, and the shape of a coat of arms, in black, are faded but just visible. Bonaparte, by then Emperor of the French, also had a staff or truncheon to give away and this survived by a parallel route, and is now in the West Country. It is similar to a tip-staff rather than the normal police truncheon designed for offence or defence[2].The owner had considered it as a possible exhibit for the proposed Metropolitan Police Museum, should this desirable project ever come to fruition. In the event the anticipated disorder of the Chartists came to nothing. A Special wrote to *The*

Between then and 1856 the regular paid officers took over the duties performed by their predecessors. The present 43 Home Office[3.] police services are the modern successors to over 200 smaller forces that have existed. It would be a natural assumption to seek the special constabulary service of a suspected ancestor within the administration of those bodies. This cannot be an exact science, for there have been many changes of geographical boundaries, of names, and of policing styles. From 1856 onward regular policing became "compulsory." I would suggest that a visit to a County Record Office or Local Studies Library would be useful, to see what forces existed at any given time. In my own county of Essex there were at least seven different such organisations which would have included specials in their line-up. Destruction policies of local authorities and police forces will have taken their toll on documentary evidence. Local newspapers will often have survived locally in microfilm and will carry many names of these officials.

That, in my opinion would be a sensible step. Documents may have survived, but they will not be uniform throughout the country. Perhaps you would be best served by my describing to you the sort of evidence which has survived in the museum I know best and hope that there are similar opportunities elsewhere. But then, I promise nothing.

Specials who can possibly be identified.
Before the Great War there were disturbances and threats of civil unrest in the south-west of our county and trainloads of specials were brought to the area of Grays and Tilbury. There was a mention of a threat by protesters to de-rail such a train. In our museum are a number of photographs of groups of specials in civilian clothing, but with uniform caps, truncheons and armbands, some of these photos are marked "Tilbury 1912." If the person being sought was in a reserved or vital occupation, which meant that they would not enter the armed forces during the Great War (perhaps even on the grounds of age), there are

other important documents. At the time of the armistice illuminated scrolls were placed in Magistrates Courts throughout the county, naming all the local specials. Some two dozen of these have survived the courts being redecorated and now are in the police museum at Chelmsford. The named officers have been incorporated into a computer programme held by the Curator, the sources include the four scrolls displayed on the wall of Grays Police Station, two at Halstead Magistrates Court and others in the local Maldon Museum. The same practice was not observed in the Borough of Southend on Sea, which had its own police, as did Colchester. The town of Romford, at one time the largest training establishment for the Essex Constabulary, has been in the Metropolitan Police District since 1965. The courts may have had such scrolls salted away somewhere, but the Epping Forest (Ex-Greater London Council boroughs), which only came into Essex Police District in the year 2000 were, during the Great War, in the Metropolitan Police District. I mention this to show the type of lateral thinking needed in order that the most effective enquiries can be carried out. Auxiliary women police officers appeared during the Great War, there were at least two in Romford, and these women often became regular officers during the 1920's. One organisation that performed police duty was the National Union of Women Workers. Other women served in London, Ireland and in towns with large factories employing women munitions workers.

During the World Wars regular police officers joined the army and navy in large numbers and often much of the day to day policing fell to the specials that remained. At the end of the Great War a medal was awarded for their service. It originally specified nine years service to qualify, or three years service during the Great War. Those with the latter war qualification received a bar to that effect. Over the following years the design of the obverse changed, but the ribbon remained the same, all types having the distinctive red, white and black ribbon. One group of specials, including Special Constable Edgar Nicholas at Great Wigborough, was also rewarded with silver watches for their part in the capture of the German naval crew of Zeppelin L33 in September 1916. There is also an apocryphal story that Arthur Morrison, the author of the famous book about the East End "A Child of the Jago" (Penguin 1896) was the first U.K. special constable to report sighting a Zeppelin raider, at Epping. Because soldiers of the Great War later sought service as specials in great numbers, the red, white and black ribbon can often be found after campaign stars and military medals on medal clusters. Essex is unique, I believe, in having a surviving register of all the county's recipients. For a description and pictures of the medals search on the Internet for "Special Constabulary Medals." Early in the War the use of army style titles such as Corporal was in fashion.

The period of the General Strike of 1926 was another occasion for the attestation of large numbers of specials and it came at the time of the proliferation of group photographs, many of which have survived, some with names, some without. Though the uniforms, if any, have a sameness about them,

buildings can help to identify the area. So can known local worthies such as the dashing special constabulary clergyman, photographed in gaiters and Homburg hat. On the subject of uniform, not all armbands had vertical stripes. The Colchester police used horizontal stripes. Bath stars and crowns, denoting ranks, were also sewn thereon. A few personnel records of special constabulary of these times have survived in various forms and card indexes.

Throughout World War Two Specials were again enrolled and used to replace regular officers serving in the armed forces. Badges which survive specify War Reserves and others identify the First Police Reserve. There were some women among them. Many wartime policemen were kept on as regular officers after the war and may have been entitled to the Defence Medal with a green orange and black ribbon. In my former home town of St. Albans the town was policed by the Special Constabulary on one Sunday each year, whilst the Hertfordshire Constabulary waited in reserve. Another word about ranks. Until quite recently specials used similar ranks to those held by regular officers; now a separate rank system operates.

Memorials
Coventry Cathedral is the place where the Memorial Book to the Special Constabulary of Great Britain and Northern Island is kept, originally maintained by a Special officer from the Merseyside area. It details the sacrifice of officers who died violently on duty and during wars. An entry was kindly accepted from me for the story of Henry Trigg, Parish Constable of Berden in Essex, who was murdered in 1814, to be included therein. Because of the keenness of the average Special officer it is likely that each modern

force will have someone who is knowledgeable on local service. A letter to a Police Headquarters, addressed to the Chief Constable or the Special Commandant may spark some response. Web-sites commemorate some sacrifices made on duty. Again, I repeat that this is not an exact science.

What is in a name.
The Special Constabulary is the only facet of U.K. police organisation that always identifies itself as "Constabulary." Those regular forces which date from before 1840 and town forces dating from 1836 usually use the title "Police." Counties are divided between those who use "Constabulary", and have done so since 1839, and those who have shortened the title to "Police" for other reasons. In 1974 the *Essex and Southend on Sea Joint Constabulary* was renamed as *Essex Police*. Thus around the Home Counties there serve Kent Constabulary, Hertfordshire Constabulary, Essex Police, Metropolitan Police, Surrey Police, the Thames Valley Police and others. They all have specials and all of them are known as Special Constabulary. I have consistently used the word "force" although it is a politically incorrect form and abhorred by exponents of "soft policing." The press and many otherwise correct officers, including Chief Constables on television, still use the old term. Many years ago the latter saw the absolute necessity of deploying the Special Constabulary as a part of front line policing and that is the situation at the present time. "Hobby Bobbies!" Never – rather an integral and essential part of modern policing.

Breaking news or epilogue.
As late as 20th March 2004 the following item came to light, it was entitled

"*Anecdote of the Emperor of the French*: It is well known (says a correspondent of the Preston Chronicle) that Prince Louis Napoleon acted as a special constable in London during the disturbances of April, 1848. At that time he occupied the very modest lodging in St. James, which he so proudly pointed out to his young wife, as they came up St. James Street on Monday. He was then, and still is, a member of the Army and Navy Club (otherwise the "Rag and Famish") and the members had many a merry laugh at him when he so gravely assured them "that he knew he should be Emperor before he died."

In those days the present ruler of millions of Frenchmen could not always muster enough money (1s-6d) to pay for a meal off the joint, but he was always certain of a welcome from the late Marquis of Londonderry, when in town, who gave the poor prince the "run" of Holderness House. The present historian cannot, however, tell where he dined when the Londonderry's were away - probably with "Duke Humphrey." Almost the first act of President Louis Napoleon was to send a magnificent piece of tapestry to the Army and Navy Club, who had just got into their splendid new club-house at the junction of St.James Square and Pall Mall "in remembrance of the many kindnesses he had received from the members and the pleasant hours he had passed among them." They were anxious to give him a banquet on the occasion of his visit to England, but his engagements would not permit him to accept their hospitality this time. At one of the first audiences given by the Emperor Louis Napoleon to Lord Cowley, the English Ambassador, in his library, he drew out of a desk the policeman's staff which he had carried when he went on his beat in Regent-street and said it had followed his fortune ever since."

Notes

1. The Special Branch – these officers have no direct connection with the Special Constabulary and this comment refers to detectives who then formed the executive arm of the security services.

2. The wording of a label on Napoleon's staff reads "This staff was used by Louis-Napoleon (afterwards Emperor of the French) as a special constable on the occasion of the great Demonstration in London 10 April 1848. It was given to me in November 187- *(date unreadable)*, by Ponsonby whose father walked next to Louis-Napoleon that day and received the staff from him." A Cambridge academic wrote in 1964 "The evidence that Louis-Napoleon did act as a special constable in April 1848 is of course overwhelming. But the only reference I can lay hands on at the moment to his staff, on that occasion, is Blanche Jerrold in his *"Life of Napoleon III"* - Volume 2 page 395 – ' On April 30 he was seen on his beat in Park Lane, armed with the staff of a special constable.' "

3. Home Office Police forces – these are the 43 police services of towns, counties and metropolitan areas that are under the aegis of the Home Office. There are also agencies of a similar appearance, like the Royal Parks Constabulary, the Transport Police, the London Transport Police and the Ministry of Defence Police. Space does not permit a description of those in this classification that may have employed specials, nor of the policing of Ireland, which could provide an article in its own right.

Acknowledgements - Thanks are offered to Dot Bedenham of the Chelmsford and Essex Museum, to Mr.D.Machin, to the Chelmsford Chronicle and to the Essex Police Museum.

Fred Feather is Chairman of the Essex Society for Family History and former Curator of the Essex Police Museum.

Gas Workers
The National Gas Archive

Some of the information in the article ***Finding out more about Gas Workers*** by *Simon Fowler* which appeared in the 8th edition has changed.

Until well into the 20th century the gas industry was characterised by the large number of undertakings which operated. Every town had its own gasworks, and large cities may have had several competing firms. In 1912, there were nearly 1,500 such firms throughout the British Isles, a quarter of whom were controlled by local authorities - the rest were privately owned companies. A few villages, like Debenham in Suffolk, Wedmore, Somerset and Rhayader, even had their own companies distributing gas to local people. The industry as a whole employed nearly a quarter of a million people.

It was an industry with strong family ties. It was not uncommon for three or four generations of the same family to work for one company. There are many sources of information, if you know where to look. Even if it is not possible to trace a particular person, you can often find something about the place in which they worked and the conditions they endured.

Gas Lighting, Carlton House 1823

Douglas Lacy, *The Rise of the Gas Industry in Great Britain* (Gas Council, 1949)
Maureen Dillon, *Artificial Sunshine: A Social History of Domestic Lighting* (National Trust, 2001)
Mary Mills, *Places and People in the Early East London Gas Industry*, available at £25 from M. Wright, 24 Hyde Road, London SE3 7LT.
Trevor I. Williams, *A History of the British Gas Industry* (Oxford University Press, 1981)
Hugh Barty-King, *New Flame: A History of Piped Gas, 1783-1984* (Graphmitre,1984)
The *Historic Gas Times* is a quarterly journal published by the Institute of Gas Engineers Panel for the History of the Industry. For details contact the Institute of Gas Engineers, 21 Portland Place, London W1B 1PY, *www.igasebg.com*.

Enquiries should be made in writing and an appointment has to be made before visiting the Archive.

Records of many gas companies, or undertakings, have been deposited with local record offices. Many Gas Light and Coke Company documents, for example, are held by the London Metropolitan Archives. The National Register of Archives, which is part of the National Archives, can tell you which records for individual companies survive and where they are stored. This information can be found on the web site *www.hmc.gov.uk* or by calling (020) 8392 5200.

Personnel records of individual workers are likely to be closed for 75 years or longer. There are other series of records that may provide additional information, including apprenticeship records, wage books and accident registers. Another useful source is company magazines and trade journals, which often mention individuals and include illustrations. The most important was the weekly *Gas Journal*, published from 1849. The oldest company magazine was the South Metropolitan Gas Company's *Co-partnership Journal*, first published in 1903.

Museums
There are several museums either devoted to the gas industry:
National Gas Museum, Aylestone Rd, Leicester LE2 7QH, tel. (0116) 250 3190, *www.gasmuseum.co.uk*. Claims to be the largest museum devoted to the gas industry in the world, but holds few archives.
Fakenham Museum of Gas and Local History, Hempton Rd, Fakenham NR21 9EP, tel. (01328) 855579, *www.fakenham.org. uk/gasmus1.htm* The Museum looks after the only surviving town gas production plant in Britain.
Biggar Gas Works, Biggar Museum Trust, Moat Park, Biggar ML12 6BT, tel. (01899) 221050 *http://www.redfern83.freeserve.co.uk/coal_gas_manufactur e/ia_003_biggar_gasworks.html*. The gasworks is the only remaining gas production plant in Scotland.
Societies
The North West Gas History Society produces an informative newsletter and organises meetings and visits. Despite the name, members are interested in the gas industry throughout England. The Society can be contacted via the treasurer Brian Bingham, 24 Greenhill, Timperley, Cheshire WA15 7BQ.

Terry Mitchell maintains the Gas Industry Genealogical Index, (GIGI) which includes some 250,000 names. He is willing to search it, for a small fee, as well as provide other help for people who had ancestors in the industry. His address is Old Barnshaw Cottage, Pepper St, Moberley, Cheshire WA16 6JH, or e-mail: tmm@tinyworld.co.uk.

Further Reading
There is no modern history about the gas industry and people who worked in it. There are however several books that may provide some background information:
Dean Chandler and A.

Normal Early Morning Load of Gas Appliances - Manchester 1932

Ipswich Workhouses ~ The First in the County

Ray Whitehand

St Mary Stoke Workhouse

Suffolk's first Workhouse was almost certainly in Ipswich. When Henry Tooley, 'the richest merchant in town' died in 1551, he left most of his fortune for the less fortunate of the borough. The Tooley Foundation was set up in 1552 to administer this request. In December 1568 the Burgesses of the Borough of Ipswich agreed to acquire premises to be used as a Municipal Poor House in order to complement the work of Tooley's Foundation. The former Priory of the Dominicans, Black Friars, was purchased in 1569, the purchase cost of which was met by the sale of some of Tooley's other properties in Ipswich, while the running costs were covered by a Poor Rate of between one and two pence per week per householder.

According to the Town Charter of 1572, Christ's Hospital, was intended to handle up to 40 inmates, who were grouped within two categories: 'Innocent victims of circumstances, namely the aged, orphaned, widowed, and sick', who were not only provided with clothing, and food, but were also given a weekly allowance for their efforts. In the early years they cooked their own meals, though it is unclear for how long this allowance continued. The second group being identified as the lazy drones of the Commonwealth, and the seminary of thieves, namely Vagrants and vagabonds begging without real necessity, were rounded up from the streets of Ipswich and its neighbouring parishes. The Governors

One of the purposes of the newly acquired Christ's Hospital, as it was now known was to provide work for those capable of but unable to find employment. The long and main halls together with the Refectory were set-aside as a workhouse for this very reason, while other parts of the Building took on the roles of House of Correction, Infirmary and Poor House.

parish contributions, private donations or bequests, though alternatively a Grant could be obtained under a 1576 Act of Parliament for such costs.

In the early 17th century, as a result of changes in the Law, together with the added pressures of an ever increasing population; a Workhouse was set up in each of Ipswich's fourteen parishes. This meant the demise of Christ's Hospital as a Borough Workhouse, though it maintained its role as a Charity School until the late 18th century. Some of these newly formed parish workhouses were the result of bequests of individual parishioners, while others were sought out by the parish officers as and when required. For this reason many were not ideal for the use they were required, often too small to provide even the basic requirement of a separation of the sexes. In 1698 Mary Wright made a bequest of five messuages in St Clement's to the trustees and churchwardens of the parish 'to be fitted up for the needy poor, partly as a workhouse for the children, who should be taught to read for one hour every day'. Isaac Blomfield left premises in St Peters in 1772, which were used as a workhouse for many years. In 1680 John Rednall gave a 'hay house and four small tenements, near the town ditches, together with their gardens', to the Churchwarden and Overseers of the poor of the parish of St Mary le Tower. This became the parish workhouse with some form of renovation work carried out in 1759 as this date was inscribed on the building. An entry in the Churchwardens book of St Margaret in 1822 acknowledges work done on workhouses at St Margaret's and St Mathews had 'remedied the most disgusting and promiscuous inter mixture in the sleeping rooms'. Now the aged and infirm as well as the women and young children were separated from the boys and able-bodied men during both the day and at night.

We can gauge a picture of the conditions and furnishings within these parish workhouses from surviving inventories, several of which survive for the Ipswich parishes. The Rates and Disbursements register of St Mary at the Elms lists the Goods and Chattels of the Workhouse on 19 May 1748 as follows (with spelling as in original):

In John Clarkes, room: one cupboard, one reel, one curtail rod, [other illegible items]
In Kitchen: one Dresser, one small square table, two old chairs
In Washroom one copper hinged with irons
In Han Samons chamber One large brass boiler, one brass frying pan, one small ion boiling pot, one iron fender, one pair of old bellows, one old brass skillet, one square table, one small cuboard, two old chairs, one old pail, one bedsted, one feather bed, one fether bolster, one pillow, one rug, one kabett, one old chest, one old washing basket, fire irons, one washing keele, two green curtains.

In the Chamber over John Clarkes room: one old bedstead, two old feather beds, one feather bolster, one old flock bolster, one matt, two wheels (at Sam Salmons one wheel more) one chest of drawers, four old chairs, one old table

In the old Chamber: two old bedsteds, a cradle

of the workhouse were instructed to search out beggars, drunkards, harlots, the idle and 'suche persons as shall be founde brekinge hedges, gates, pales, or other fences, or stelinge of wood.' In July 1573 a beadle (the forerunner of the modern police force) was employed for just this purpose. He was paid 2d. for every unruly person he brought in. In the first week he earned himself one shilling when he produced 6 'victims'. Within two months he had sent at least 95 culprits to the workhouse 'to be cured of their indolence'. Other inmates were sent or taken in by their parents or masters. Most of the work carried out by the inmates involved keeping the building clean and tidy. Thereafter other employment was found which would educate the children and reform the wayward in order to look after themselves and be of use to others. Provisions and a bed were provided as a reward for those who made the effort. It is not known whether the old building became dilapidated or whether as a consequence of general reorganization, but early in 1574, a new large workhouse was constructed on the same site, with a Dutchman now employed as Master of the House. Enough new tools and materials were bought to provide work for 40 people, which was mainly aimed at the linen and cloth trade, with jobs such as Carding, Spinning, & Weaving. Finances for purchasing of materials etc were often provided by

Ipswich Union Workhouse Christmas Party 1922

A picture of rather basic necessities. The number of beds suggesting a capacity of between seven and fourteen possible depending on sleeping arrangements, while the references to 'wheels' suggest spinning was a form of employment here,

The burden of the cost of the Workhouse, which fell on to the more fortunate of society, varied from parish to parish. Land tax figures for 1778 show that St Mathews had a yearly rate charge of 19 shillings while St Lawrence bore a bill of 12 shillings, a variation which may be explained by the location of St Lawrence in the more affluent part of the Borough, and hence not carrying the same Poor Relief burden as those parishioners of St Mathews. The Poor Rate in Ipswich in 1821 totalled more than £13,000, an enormous amount by the standards of the time. In 1822 a Committee set up to consider the running of workhouses and poor relief in general highlighted the fact that Ipswich was spending significantly more per head on its poor than other towns of a similar size. Rate payers of towns like Plymouth, Bristol and Lincoln, were receiving far less demands than their Ipswich counterparts, though there were mitigating factors such as the rural aspect, or indeed the quality level of the Poor relief in the borough which was deemed to be particularly good in this Suffolk town. The main recommendation of this committee suggested the parishes of the Borough unite and build one large workhouse capable of holding 500 inmates, who could be properly classified and usefully employed, with the Bosmere and Claydon union Workhouse at Barham given as a model, but nothing was done to implement the recommendations of the committee for some 12 years. The Committee, further concluded the Overseers of the Borough were a soft touch, with many able-bodied paupers far better

off than their employed compatriots. It was decreed any relief given to those who could not or would not work, should be confined to those actually resident in the workhouse. Relief payments were set at a basic level and had to be earned. Poorhouse meals were deliberately basic and repetitive. Bread, and cheese, meat, suet puddings, was washed down with beer. The rules also ordered that staff should have the same menu as the inmates, though in reality this was very open to abuse. It was estimated the cost to maintain each inmate was on average 3 shillings per week. With numbers in the workhouse rarely exceeding 250, this would equate to in the region of £1,600 per annum.

The 1835 Poor Law Act was a water shed for the whole system of Poor relief. It proved to be the demise of the small parish workhouse, with the new Union Workhouses for whole communities, run by a Board of Governors now the order of the day. The Ipswich Union was formed in 1836. One of its first significant moves was to streamline the housing of the Borough's current 176 paupers. The women and girls from the whole borough now became housed at St Margaret's, while the men and boys were sent to St Clements. St Mary le Tower became home for the aged and infirm paupers. The women and girls would spend days knitting sewing or mending garments such as stockings, socks and mittens, while the men's work including making rush mats, and the younger boys were taught the trade of shoe repairing. Remuneration was in the form of bed and provisions, no one got paid. This fact together with the poor living conditions provided the source of much trouble and rioting in the following months.

However, within three years a brand new workhouse costing £6000 was built in Great Whip Street, which

It was soon apparent, the new regime was proving an economical success. In 1834 the cost of Poor relief had amounted to over £15,000; by 1840 it had dropped to £13,000 and by 1850 £12,000, and this despite an ever-increasing population. However this was at a cost as life in the workhouse was now far more strict and disciplined. Relief which had varied from one to seven shillings, was now virtually standardised at 2 shillings a week, bearing in mind it had been 1s 8d in the 1760s, this equated to a 20 per cent rise in 90 years. No pets were allowed into the workhouse. The male / female ratio grew wider as while women and children continued to be admitted on grounds of destitution, health or age, fewer and fewer men of working age being accepted in the workhouse.

By 1870 the old building was starting to show signs of old age and decay. Murmurings were aplenty concerning replacing it with something more up to date. In 1872, partly in an attempt to ease the strain on the old building, the children from the Union house were resettled into the Children's Workhouse in St John's California, a suburb of Ipswich. While a significant number of them were from the Union House in Ipswich, more were brought in from the surrounding villages to help swell the numbers to something in the region of 230 inmates. Many said this was a retrograde step as it separated children further from society, indeed several of the children actually looked forward to being old enough to qualify for the adult building. The murmuring became

could accommodate 400 inmates. The Ipswich Union Workhouse was looked upon as a real chance for the town to both upgrade the conditions for the poor and lessen the burden on the ratepayers. It was designed by the London based Architect William Mason, who had also designed the Union Workhouse at Eye. The ground floor plans for the new building clearly shows how classification and segregation worked in the Union. Separate dining halls, day rooms, sleeping quarters, and toilets were allocated for each of the seven classified groups of paupers: infants, girls, boys, young men, and women, older men and women. Rooms for needlework, tailoring, shoe making and carpentry demonstrate the range of trades, which were carried out within the establishment.

As part of a cost cutting exercise the menu was totally reassessed. Meat rations in the workhouse were reduced by one third, with more bread and roots added to bulk up the meal. Beer was now banned. For a while the staff of the workhouse allowed fresh fruit and sweets to be brought in by visitors though when the Commissioners found out, this 'loop hole' was soon closed. A schoolmaster and mistress were brought into the Workhouse to teach the children to read and write. This was bitterly opposed by those outside as it was said this would give those in the workhouse an unfair advantage when they were released back into the real world where many did not get any education at all. The numbers of inmates were now on the increase, by 1838, there were 289 residents. This was such a concern, an advertising campaign was launched to encourage migration to the north of England or even America, where jobs were more plentiful.

of the Creed Register over a ten-year period suggests one in five inmates died in the workhouse.

Society was gradually moving away from the idea of the workhouse as the means of proving poor relief. The Old Age Pension was introduced in 1908, and the National Insurance in 1911. In order to keep up with the times the Union Commissioners decided to change the name of the workhouse to a less provocative one. Heathfields became the chosen name, reflecting its nearness to Rushmere Heath, while theoretically conjuring a more caring atmosphere. While there were still many a tale of hardship, neglect or cruelty, it was not all bad. Thomas Head whose father was the hairdresser in the workhouse in the 1920's recalled that while 'it was spartan with no luxuries, the homeless men and women forced to live there were treated with kindness and understanding of their plight'. The final demise of a workhouse in the Borough happened with the 1929 Act of Parliament, which abolished the Union and placed the responsibility for the poor of Ipswich on the shoulders of the newly formed Corporation's Public Health department. The building was converted into a 'home' for the elderly, until 1970 when it was rebuilt as the Borough and County's General Heath Road Hospital.

louder and louder, until in 1899 'a very expensive' new Workhouse was built at the north end of Woodbridge road. It was designed by architects Percy Adams and William Lister Newcombe, to have a capacity of up to 500 inmates. The new building was specifically planned for the comfort of the sick and elderly, but to deter the more able of society. A points system was implemented in an attempt to achieve this. Inmates categorised as Class One being those well behaved over 65, received additions to their diet in the form of half an ounce of tobacco a week or for the women the choice of 2 ounces of tea and half a pound sugar. Cake on the Sabbath and egg and butter on Friday gave added variety to their menu. Class two being those fairly well behaved over 65, received roughly half the proportions of the first class, while those deemed as Class three being every one else, received no additions at all.

The Creed register of the Union Workhouse of Ipswich serves to highlight how the comings and goings of the inmates varied at different times of the year. The register for 1901 –1910 show how one George Woodward, born 1878, and a resident of St Mathews and St Clements, was first admitted into the workhouse on 14 December 1907 at the age of 29. He was then discharged on 4 February 1908, but only to be readmitted on 14 February. However following his next discharge 9 April he remained out for most of the summer until 26th August. He then returned to the workhouse until the end of the year, apart from a brief two-week spell in early November. Further analysis

Sources:
Peter Bishop; *1500 years of Triumph and Disaster*; Unicorn Press 1995
Whites Directory Suffolk 1844
L. Redstone; *Ipswich through the Ages*; East Anglian Magazine Printers.
John Webb; *Poor Relief in Elizabethan Ipswich*; Suffolk Record Society 1966
Robert Malster; *A History of Ipswich*; Phillimore 2000
S.R.O. (I) FB1004/91/6 rates and disbursements of St Mary at the Elms
S.R.O. (I) FB101/69/2; rates and disbursements of St Peters
S.R.O. (I) C/1/9/4/3/18 land, window and retail tax Ipswich 1788
S.R.O. (I) DD1/44/1/1 *Creed Register Ipswich Union 1901-1911*

In his early 50's Ray Whitehand turned his amateur experience in genealogy into a business. After a number of courses and several published articles in his first year, he has now produced census transcripts of East Suffolk parishes and a booklet about the history of a family cottage with guidance for others who want to research the history of their property. Ray has also undertaken considerable research into Suffolk Workhouses. If you need assistance with your Suffolk past, or research, Ray would be only too pleased to help.

Contact Ray Whitehand, Local and Family History Research, 28 Lincoln Avenue, Saxmundham, Suffolk IP17 1BZ Email hrfw@supanet.com

The National Family History Fair

Saturday 10th September 2005
10.00a.m. - 4.30.p.m.

Gateshead International Stadium
Neilson Road Gateshead NE10 0EF

Admission £3.00
Accompanied Children under 15 Free

Meet the national experts!

A must for family historians in 2005

Full list of exhibitors at:
www.nationalfamilyhistoryfair.com

OFFICIAL SPONSORS
The National Family History Fair 2005

2006 - Saturday 9th September 2006

Have you missed a previous edition of The Family and Local History Handbook?

Whilst printed copies are no longer available we can provide copies in digital format as pdf files on CD

Volumes 1 - 3 Available on 1 CD £5.00

plus £1.00 p & p

 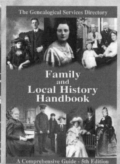 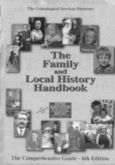 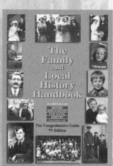 

Volumes 4 - 8 Available on CD £10.00 each volume post free

All 8 volumes (1 - 8) Available on CD £30.00 each post free

'This is quite literally *the* book to buy for family history research and if you only ever buy one genealogy book, it should be this one'
Your Family Tree Magazine May 2004

Full details at: www.genealogical.co.uk

To order please write to
Robert Blatchford Publishing Ltd
33 Nursery Road, Nether Poppleton, York YO26 6NN UK
All payments in £ sterling. Cheques payable to Robert Blatchford Publishing Ltd
Credit Card payments accepted for orders over £10.00
or email: sales@genealogical.co.uk

MURDER *files*

– Did one of them 'switch off any of your ancestors?

Britain's Hangmen

Paul Williams

discusses another aspect of *Murderfiles.com*

OK, hands up all those who have a murderer in their family tree. Judging by the number of enquiries *Murderfiles* receives, quite a few, but when you think about it, there aren't many days when one or more murders are not reported in the newspapers, so the chances are quite high.

Over the years I have found that, in many cases, our ancestors have not wanted to talk about the relative who cast a heavy cloud over the family name. They have hoped the matter would be forgotten about, brushed under the carpet. They have wanted to put to the back of the mind this relative who, in so doing this dastardly deed, probably caused huge family rifts with people taking sides; the parents, naturally loyally standing by their son or daughter. It is not uncommon for me to hear or read words like 'I remember my parents briefly mentioning that my Uncle had murdered someone but I could never find out the details'. The enquirer knows a murder took place and they know who the victim or murderer was, but what actually happened they don't know!

And that is where *Murderfiles* helps the many people who write or email saying 'What can you tell me about a family skeleton in the cupboard?' I must stress at this point that it is not the intention of *Murderfiles* to glorify the murderer or sanctify the victim. It regards murder as a part of our social history. It does not reinvestigate the case to try and prove that the accused really was innocent. It can, however, in many cases, let you know what happened: the accused, the victim, the circumstances, and/or the outcome.

Let's face it the words 'murdered' or 'hanged' in a family tree do add a bit of interest, especially when one can relate the circumstances. But how many can boast in their family trees to having a relative who was an Executioner? If your name is Pierrepoint, Binns, Calcraft, Incher, Marwood, Mitchell to name but a few, you might be related to one of our official hangmen but know nothing about it!

The Pierrepoints really made the task of Executioner a family affair. Henry Pierrepoint held the post from 1901 to 1910. His brother Thomas was also officiating from 1906 to 1946 and was succeeded by his son Albert who was executioner from 1932 to 1956.

During the nine years of Henry's term of office he executed 107 people. His customers included the hanging of 'baby farmer' Rhoda Wills in Cardiff in August 1907. Henry was eventually sacked from his job because he arrived at a Chelmsford execution in 1910 a little the worse for drink!

Thomas is credited with carrying out about 300 hangings and retired when in his mid seventies. He hanged Ethel Major in 1934 for the murder by strychnine poisoning of her husband Arthur. Unqualified 'nurse' Dorothea Waddingham who set up a 'Nursing Home for Aged and Chronic Cases' in Nottingham and looked after 80 year old Mrs Baguley and her 50 year old daughter Ada after they had handed over their savings in return for being looked after for the rest of their lives, also swung from Thomas's rope - she had poisoned them not long after they had signed their possessions away.

Albert Pierrepoint is probably the most well know of the Hangmen. He died in 1992 and will no doubt be remembered by many readers. During his 24 years service he executed in excess of 430 men and 17 women including 13 German war criminals. It was he who executed well know murderers such as Ruth Ellis, John Haigh, John Christie and Derek Bentley. Albert also kept a record of all his hangings showing the date of execution, name, age of person, his or her height, weight, length of drop and prison. A copy of this is with Murdefiles.

The last steps of a condemned man.

Ruth Ellis was hanged on 13 July 1955 in Holloway Prison amid a huge public outcry. She had shot dead her lover, racing driver David Blakely, outside the Magdalen Public House in Hampstead, North London. The bullet holes can still allegedly be seen in the wall to the left of the entrance. The case is described by some as a highly charged love affair and should have been regarded as a *crime passional*. In France Ruth would not have hanged; however in this country no such defence existed. At her Trial she was asked what she intended when she fired the revolver. She replied "I intended to kill him". Her own words in effect hanged her.   Pierrepoint wrote in his record after the hanging

    (date) 13 July 195
    (name) Ruth Ellis, (age) 28
    (height) 5' 2",
    (weight) 103 (lbs)
    (drop) 8'4",
    (Town) Holloway, (executioner) A
    (assisted by) Pickard.

Derek Bentley (19) was one of two youths who broke into a Croydon warehouse in November 1952. His accomplice Christopher Craig was 16. Craig had a revolver and Bentley had a knife. They had been seen entering the building. Police were called and on entering, PC Miles was shot dead by Craig. Prior to the shooting Bentley had just been detained and was technically in custody at the time of the murder. The case became famous because Craig, being under age, escaped hanging and served a long term of imprisonment. Bentley however, despite having already been arrested prior to the murder, was hanged. There was concern at the Trial that Bentley's remark to Craig just prior to the killing to 'Let him have it, Chris' was not an encouragement to Craig to shoot the officer but one of advice to hand the gun over to police. In 1998 however, following continued public outcries over the years, Bentley did receive a posthumous pardon.

One recent enquiry received at Murder Files was regarding Bartholomew Binns who was Hangman from 1883 to 1884. The enquirer had heard through the family of the ancestors 'occupation'. Records exist of whom he executed but nothing can be found of Binns's date and place of birth. Binns only held the position for a year but in that time he executed 11 people including 2 females. Complaints about the standard of his work led to his removal from the list. The Times reported on 12 March 1884 'The execution of Dutton (by Binns) at Liverpool in December last caused a painful sensation, not only on account of the bungling manner in which it was managed, but also on account of the shameless way in which the executioner misconducted himself before and after it'. The article went on 'The chaplain of the gaol affirmed that Binns smelt so strongly of liquor on the scaffold as to elicit from him a grave rebuke'.

If your name is Price you could be in for a double 'whammie' on your family tree; that is if you want to be associated with John Price, the holder of the Office of Common Hangman, from 1714 to 1715. Price distinguished himself by also being hanged for murder. He is described as being a 'coarse and brutal creature' and a 'compulsive liar'. We know his salary

Albert Pierrepoint The British Hangman

was small but payment was piece-work. He could claim the clothes of his 'clients' and fees were obtainable from the Company of the Barber Surgeons for the corpses he delivered for them to practise on. But he was unable to live within his means and women and drink soon put him into debt. In order to avoid his creditors he continually moved lodgings but was arrested in Holborn on his way back from an execution. His arrest was in respect of his owing 7s 6d. Managing to raise this amount on the spot he was released. The publicity of this however led to others finding him and his eventual incarceration in Marshalsea, the debtors' gaol in High Street, Southwark.

After being inside for three years he was eventually allowed out during the day provided he 'obeyed the rules' and returned at night. He picked up jobs as a labourer but, soon realising he would never be really released, he broke out of prison one night early in 1718. But drink again led to his downfall. On the night of Sunday 13 April Price was staggering through Upper Moorfields, near the Bunhill Fields burying ground when he chanced upon an elderly woman named Elizabeth White, a watchman's wife. White was at her stall of vegetables. Price flung her to the ground and attempted to rape her. When she screamed he hit her with a cudgel. Her screams were heard by two men and Price was taken into custody and placed in the watch-house in Old Street. Two watchmen then went in search of Mrs White who was found to have a broken leg, one eye almost knocked out, and bruises to her head and body. A surgeon and nurse were called but she died 4 days later. Price appeared at the Old Bailey on a charge of murder and being found guilty was sentenced to death. As was customary, a temporary gallows was erected at Bunhill Fields close to the scene of the crime. Vast crowds went to witness the execution. Price protested loudly of his innocence until just before he met his maker when he confessed to the crime whilst drunk. So Price held the distinction of being both executioner and executed. Jack Ketch, was another infamous hangman who served from 1663 to 1686. He was perhaps the most bloody, callous, brutal and incompetent of them all, so much so that his name became synonymous with hangmen long after his death. His incompetence comes within his first 12 months. Lord William Russell had been sentenced to death for his alleged complicity in the plot to assassinate Charles II. On 21 July 1683, at Lincoln's Inn Fields, it took Ketch three goes at severing Russell's head. Ketch claimed later that Lord Russell had moved as the axe fell.

A drawing of Jack Ketch.

As Hangman his duties also included whipping. After Titus Oates had been convicted of perjury he suffered appalling stoning whilst in the pillory. He was then dragged behind a horse and cart, being whipped unmercifully by Ketch. Two days later, unable to stand, he was tied to a sledge and flogged by Ketch all the way from Newgate to Tyburn. Accounts of the day report Oates receiving up to 3,000 lashes. So appalling was his punishment that even the crowd were baying for Ketch to stop.

Two months after this Ketch performed the worst act of his bloody career. James, the Duke of Monmouth had been captured at the Battle of Sedgemoor and his execution arranged at Tower Hill on 15 July 1685. Monmouth, relaxed and resigned to his fate, mounted the scaffold and seeing Ketch said 'Is this the man to do the business? Well, do your work well.' As was customary he then tipped Ketch six guineas to do a good job adding 'Do not serve me as you did my Lord Russell'. Monmouth laid his head upon the block but then raised himself up and feeling the edge of the axe with his thumb said 'I fear it is not sharp enough'. Ketch retorted that it was. Seconds later Ketch's first blow only cut the side of Monmouth's neck. The second blow went slightly deeper. The third missed all together. At this Ketch threw down his axe shouting 'I cannot do it!' With the crowd screaming threats of retaliation at Ketch, the sheriff ordered him to finish the job. Ketch picked up the axe and took a further three blows but still failed to sever the head. Monmouth died only after Ketch finished the job with a knife.

James Berry served as Hangman from 1884 to 1892. An ex Bradford policeman he had met William Marwood who had held office for the previous 10 years and observed his methods. On taking up the post he drew up a scale showing the distance of the drops depending on the condemned person's weight. These measurements were to be used by succeeding hangmen and refined over the years.

It was Berry who failed to hang John Lee in 1885. Lee had been convicted of murdering his elderly employer Ellen Keyse and was due to hang in Exeter Prison. When Berry pulled the lever to take Lee into the next world, the trap failed to open. Berry tried to force the trap open with his added weight but nothing happened so Lee was taken back to his cell. When the trap was tested again it worked. Lee was brought back for the sentence to be carried out. Berry pulled the lever but again nothing happened. Poor Lee was returned to his cell for a second time. When the trap was tested again it opened perfectly. There can be no doubt Lee was now thinking his chances of escaping the death sentence a third time were rather slim. He did however because when placed back on the trap it again for some reason jammed. By law, after three unsuccessful attempts, he could not be hanged. All the Prison Governor could do was return Lee to his cell and await instructions from the Home Secretary. His reprieve from the death sentence came within hours. Lee had dreamt the night prior to his planned execution that he would not hang. He said afterwards 'It was the Lord's hand which would not let the law take away my life ....'. He spent 22 years in prison and was released in 1907 whereupon he married, emigrated to America where he died in 1933.

Another of Berry's mishaps was the execution of Robert Goodale at Norwich Castle in 1885. With his table of drops Berry estimated that Goodale, who weighed 15 stone, should have a drop of 7ft 8inches. However, he decided that as Goodale was such a heavy man, his bones would be weak and decided to give him a drop of 5ft 9 inches only. The result was that, much to the horror of those witnessing the execution, Goodale was completely decapitated. After this, Berry adjusted his dropping distances. Basing his measurements on the striking force of bodies of various weights falling through different distances, he

Picture of executioner James Berry

Berry's visiting card

worked out that an average man required to strike the end of the rope with a force of 24 hundredweight, just over a ton.

Britain's last official hangman was Harry Allen. He had always been a lifelong supporter of capital punishment and when Albert Pierrepoint resigned, Allen and Steve Wade took over as joint Executioners. Allen had worked with Pierrepoint before; so too had Wade who had been assistant to both Tom and Albert Pierrepoint.

Executioner Harry Allen

Allen performed almost 100 executions and assisted at about another hundred. Travelling to an execution he always wore a bowler hat and suit, so , he said, passing himself off as a Solicitor if challenged by the gentlemen of the Press who always hovered around the doors of a Prison on such occasions. So slick was Allen at what he did that from the moment he entered the condemned cell to the time the trap door open was barely 11 seconds. He was always astonished at how calmly most met their death, no doubt because the prisoner had expected the end to come after a longer period! Amongst his 'clients' were three women. One of these, Gwynne Evans, he hanged at Strangeways Prison, Manchester. Her partner, Peter Allen, was executed the same time and day in Liverpool. They had both been convicted of murdering 53 year old John Alan West whilst carrying out a robbery. These were the last death penalties carried out in Britain. Allen commented some time after this that 'Since the rope was scrapped, discipline has gone right out of the window'. He died, aged 80, in August 1992.

There were many other official hangmen during the last few hundred years; far too many to mention in this article. The ones to hit the newspaper headlines were usually the murder victim or the accused. The one who completed the sentence of the law was not often referred to. In the usual two line article typical of newspapers such as the Times the day after the execution all that would be mentioned was that the accused had been executed at such and such prison.

The British Hangmen form just a small part of the information held by *Murderfiles*. *Murderfiles* is a private collection of information on murders that have occurred in Britain over the last 300 years. Information from this collection is available to enquirers, whether they be family historians or TV producers seeking murder details for a documentary. Details of cost involved are available on request.

Should you wish to know whether any information is stored on a particular case please do not hesitate to write or email giving as much information as possible. A stamped addressed envelope (if you are located in the UK) for your reply or an International Reply Coupon if enquiring from outside the UK, would be appreciated. Please write to '*Murderfiles*', Dommett Hill Farm, Hare Lane, Buckland St Mary, Chard, Somerset, TA20 3JS. Alternatively you can email on enquiry@murderfiles.com
Are there any 'skeletons' in your cupboard?

Paul Williams worked for the Metropolitan Police in London for 26 years during which time he not only spent several years in their Criminal Record Office but was for over 8 years responsible for their Force Museums. One of these Museums was the world famous Black Museum which holds crime exhibits from notorious criminal cases. Whilst there he lectured, with the Curator, to police officers, members of the Judiciary and eminent people including members of the British and foreign Royal families. Amongst the many interesting visitors he met were Albert Pierrepoint, the last British Hangman and Professor Sir Bernard Spilsby, the pathologist.

As well as running *Murder Files*, Paul Williams, who is a Winston Churchill Fellow, writes articles for books, magazines and CD-Roms. He provides storylines for TV documentaries and dramas and has been a narrator in front of the camera for a murder reconstruction.

Probate Records

Information from Probate records can provide vital pieces of the genealogical puzzle. Although often not as useful as records of births, marriages and deaths, which can evidence crucial links to previous generations, they can provide evidence of relatedness within generations, and often contain fascinating insights into the financial affairs of people in times past.

Probate is a process whereby some person or persons, usually the executor(s) of a Will if there was one, or one or more of the next-of-kin if there was no Will, are appointed in law to administer the estate of someone who has died. This is usually only necessary if the deceased person left fairly substantial assets, so don't expect to find any Probate record relating to the estate of a person who had little or no estate of their own. The Probate concept of 'estate' refers just to assets held in the sole name of the person who has died, and so Probate isn't necessary for the release of assets held jointly with another person. When an application for Probate is made, any Will that the deceased person left must be submitted to the Probate Registry. The Will, if judged to be valid, is thereafter kept on file, and it is normally possible for anyone to obtain a copy of it. There are exceptions, however, such as the Wills of members of the Royal family. The important point is that Wills are available from the Probate Registries only as a by-product of the Probate process: if Probate wasn't needed, then the Probate Registries have no record of the estate at all.

You should bear in mind that the Probate record, if any, will be dated some time after the date of death of the person concerned, so start searching from the year of death, or the year in which you think the person died. You should normally expect to find the Probate record within the first year or two after the date of

death, and, if you have not found it within three, you can usually assume that Probate wasn't necessary. However, in a very small number of cases, Probate is granted many years after the person in question died. Take a tip from the professionals: if you don't find a probate record within the first few years, the next most likely time to search is the year in which their heir(s) died. This is because unadministered estate is most likely to come to light at that time. How far you want to go with the search will probably depend on how crucial the person in question is to your research, but there is as yet no shortcut: you will have to search the index for each year separately.
Control of Probate record-keeping passed from the Church to the state in 1858, at which point the records were unified into one Calendar index. These indexes, which summarise all Probate grants for England and Wales during a given year, act as a table of contents for the vast store of records held by the Probate Registries. If the subject of your research died before 1858, it will be more difficult to trace their Will. However, if they were very wealthy or owned a lot of land, consult the indexes of the Prerogative Court of Canterbury (PCC) first, and then those of the lesser ecclesiastical courts of the region in which they lived. PCC records are held by the Family Records Centre in London (Tel: (020) 8392 5300), but records of the lesser ecclesiastical Probate courts are highly dispersed. Try the local authority archives, such as public libraries and County Record Offices of the appropriate region, and also any local historical research institutes. Major ecclesiastical centres are also likely to have their own archives.

The table below lists the Calendar indexes held by the various Probate Registries in England and Wales. You can usually call in to consult the indexes, but check with the Registry concerned first, especially if you intend to travel any distance. Probate grants for each year are listed alphabetically by surname. The crucial parts of the Probate record are the Grant type, which is usually 'Probate', 'Administration' or 'Administration with Will', the issuing Registry, and the grant issue date. They are normally written in sequence towards the end of the index entry, but the older books give the grant date first and highlight the issuing Registry in the text of the entry. The grant type can be inferred from the text, but note that the indexes prior to 1871 listed the 'Administration' grants in a separate part of the book from the 'Probate' and 'Administration with Will' grants, so be sure to search in both places for years prior to this. In addition, there may be a handwritten number next to entries for Wills proved in the Principal Probate Registry (London) between 1858 and 1930. This is the Folio number, which is used by the Probate Registries when obtaining copies of the Will. Always make a note of this if applicable.

If the grant type is 'Administration', this tells you that the person in question did not leave a valid Will. However, the Probate Registries can still supply a

Reading the Will

copy of the grant, which is the document naming the person appointed in law as the administrator of the estate. This can provide genealogical information, especially in older grants where the relationship of the applicant to the deceased was stated. It also gives the value of the estate, although in most cases this is stated as 'not exceeding' a certain figure rather than quoting an exact amount. In fact, the Probate record contains very little information about the estate at all, and no information about its composition. Don't expect to find inventories on file for records after 1858, although they sometimes form part of the Probate record prior to this.

In many cases you can save a lot of time and money by making the search yourself, but there is a postal service by which a search is made on your behalf for a period of four years. There is a fee of £5 for this, but this includes copies of the Will and/or grant if a record is found. It also gives you the benefit of the experience of Probate staff, for instance in knowing when to search and judging under which name the record is likely to be listed. If you want the Probate Registry to conduct a search for a period longer than the standard four years, there is an additional fee of £3 for each 4-year period after the first four. Thus, an 8-year search will cost £8, a 12-year search £11, and so on.

If you want to make a postal search, contact
The Postal Searches and Copies Department,
York Probate Sub-Registry, 1st Floor, Castle Chambers, Clifford Street, York YO1 9RG UK
Tel: +44 (1904) 666777   Fax: +44 (1904) 666776

Applications for searches must be made in writing, and give the full name, last known address and date of death of the person concerned. A search can normally be made using less detail, but if the date of death is not known, you must state the year from which you want the search to be made, or give some other evidence that might indicate when the person died. If you have information about any legal actions related to Probate or the disposition of assets, include that on your application. Many people find it convenient to order copies in this way even if they have already made a search of the Probate indexes and located a record relating to the subject of their research, but if this is the case, please include the grant type, issuing Registry and grant issue date on your application, as well as the Folio number if applicable (see above) as this can speed up the supply of copies considerably. The fee should be payable to "H.M.Paymaster General", and if it is paid from abroad, must be made by International Money Order or bank draft, payable through a United Kingdom bank and made out in £ sterling. If you are applying for a search as well, you can request a search of any length, and fees for this are outlined above.

The records referred to here relate only to estates in England and Wales.

The list shows what indexes the various Probate Registries hold. Most Registries will have had indexes dating back to 1858, but are not required to keep them for more than fifty years. Usually, the older indexes will have been donated to local authority archives. Contact your local public library or County/City Record Office to see what Probate records they have. If you know of any historical research institute in your area, find out if they have any Probate records. Please note that, since the York Probate Registry serves as a national centre for postal requests for searches and copies, it is not possible to inspect the Probate indexes in person there.

Probate Registries
& Sub-Registries

REGISTRY	RECORDS	TELEPHONE
Bangor Probate Sub-Registry	1946 to 1966 and 1973 to 1998	(01248) 362410
Council Offices, FFord, Bangor LL57 1DT		
Birmingham District Probate Registry	1948 to date	(0121) 681 3400
The Priory Courts, 33 Bull Street, Birmingham B4 6DU		
Bodmin Probate Sub-Registry	1858 to 1966 and 1973 to 1998	(01208) 72279
Market Street, Bodmin PL31 2JW		
Brighton District Probate Registry	1935 to date	(01273) 684071
William Street, Brighton BN2 2LG		
Bristol District Probate Registry	1901 to date	(0117) 927 3915
Ground Floor, The Crescent Centre, Temple Back, Bristol BS1 6EP		
Carmarthen Probate Sub-Registry	1973 to 1998	(01267) 236238
14 King Street, Carmarthen SA31 1BL		
Chester Probate Sub-Registry	1948 to 1966	(01244) 345082
5th Floor, Hamilton House, Hamilton Place, Chester CH1 2DA		
Exeter Probate Sub-Registry	1858 to 1966 and 1973 to 1998	(01392) 274515
Finance House, Barnfield Road, Exeter EX1 1QR		
Gloucester Probate Sub-Registry	1947 to 1966	(01452) 522585
2nd Floor, Combined Court Building, Kimbrose Way, Gloucester GL1 2DG		
Ipswich District Probate Registry	1936 to date	(01473) 253724
Level 3, Haven House, 17 Lower Brook Street, Ipswich IP4 1DN		
Leeds District Probate Registry	1949 to date	(0113) 243 1505
3rd Floor, Coronet House, Queen Street, Leeds LS1 2BA		
Leicester Probate Sub-Registry	1890 to 1966 and 1973 to date	(0116) 253 8558
5th Floor, Leicester House, Lee Circle, Leicester LE1 3RE		
Lincoln Probate Sub-Registry	1936 to 1966 and 1973 to 1998	(01522) 523648
Mill House, Brayford Side North, Lincoln LN1 1YW		
Liverpool District Probate Registry	1946 to date	(0151) 236 8264
Queen Elizabeth II Law Courts, Derby Square, Liverpool L2 1XA		
Manchester District Probate Registry	1947 to date	(0161) 834 4319
9th Floor, Astley House, 23 Quay Street, Manchester M3 4AT		
Middlesbrough Probate Sub-Registry	1973 to 1998	(01642) 340001
Teesside Combined Court Centre, Russell Street, Middlesbrough TS1 2AE		
Newcastle-upon-Tyne District Probate Registry	1929 to date	(0191) 261 8383
2nd Floor, Plummer House, Croft Street, Newcastle-upon-Tyne NE1 6NP		
Nottingham Probate Sub-Registry	1973 to 1998	(0115) 941 4288
Butt Dyke House, Park Row, Nottingham NG1 6GR		
Oxford District Probate Registry	1940 to date	(01865) 793050
Combined Court Building, St.Aldates, Oxford OX1 1LY		
Sheffield Probate Sub-Registry	1935 to 1966 and 1973 to 1998	(0114) 281 2596
PO Box 832, The Law Courts, 50 West Bar Sheffield S3 8YR		
Stoke-on-Trent Probate Sub-Registry	1973 to 1998	(01782) 854065
Combined Court Centre, Bethesda Street, Hanley, Stoke-on-Trent ST1 3BP		
Winchester District Probate Registry	1944 to date	(01962) 863771
4th Floor, Cromwell House, Andover Road, Winchester SO23 7EW		
Probate Registry of Wales	1951 to date	(029) 2037 6479
PO Box 474, 2 Park Street, Cardiff CF1 1ET		
Principal Probate Registry	1858 to date	(020) 7947 6939
First Avenue House, 42-49 High Holborn, London WC1		

The Service has undergone a process of computerisation, but as yet this covers only recently-issued grants, which will be of limited interest to genealogists. However, anyone who is interested in checking up on grants since 1996 can search the Probate Service database themselves. To date, workstations for public use have been installed at the Principal Probate Registry and Manchester District Probate Registry. The Postal Searches and Copies Department at York is also completing a long period of computerisation, which should see a much-improved service to family history researchers, with clearer and more comprehensive information and quicker supply of documents.

This information is based on details supplied by the Probate Service. The details are liable to change without notice. Always telephone the Registry before visiting, to check opening times and the availability of records. While every effort is made to ensure the accuracy of these details, the Probate Service cannot be held responsible for any consequence of errors.

Please check our website at www.courtservice.gov.uk before applying for searches or copy documents by post.

Llyfrgell Genedlaethol Cymru - The National Library of Wales
Eirionedd A. Baskerville

An interest in family history is part of the Welsh psyche. According to the Laws of Hywel Dda, it was necessary to know one's relatives to the ninth remove, and Giraldus Cambrensis on his crusading tour of Wales in 1188 noted that the humblest person was able to recite from memory his family tree, going back six or seven generations.

The National Library of Wales is the premier centre for family history research in Wales, holding as it does abundant records covering the whole of Wales. Amongst the printed sources are electoral lists, newspapers, journals and directories, while the non-print sources include plans, sale catalogues, Ordnance Survey maps, tithe maps and schedules together with manuscripts, archives and other original primary sources which are such a valuable resource from the point of view of genealogical research.

The Department has microform copies of the returns for the whole of Wales for each of the ten-yearly censuses 1841-1901, and microfiche copies of the index to the 1881 census for the English counties as well as those for Wales. In addition, some of the returns have been transcribed and indexed by enthusiastic individuals and societies who have kindly made them available to the Library's users.

Civil registration of births, marriages and deaths was introduced in England and Wales on 1 July 1837, and microfiche copies of the General Register Office's indexes of the registration records from 1837 to 1998 are available for searching free of charge at the National Library. The Library does not issue certificates, but a search of the indexes can be undertaken for a fee.

Before the introduction of civil registration, the 'rites of passage' were noted in parish registers, following the order of 5 September 1538 that a register of every baptism, marriage and burial in every parish should be kept. However, the earliest surviving registers for most Welsh parishes do not commence until after 1660, although starting dates vary greatly. Parish registers held at the National Library are available on microfilm to readers. The Library also holds transcript copies of some parish registers, which have been kindly donated by the compilers. In addition, the 1988 edition of the International Genealogical Index, while far from complete, can prove a useful starting point for tracing the parish in which a baptism or marriage was registered.

Although the ravages of weather and rodents, inept vicars and disrespectful parishioners have resulted in the disappearance of many original parish registers, the bishops transcripts (annual returns submitted by Anglican parish clergy to the bishops containing copies of all the entries recorded in their parish registers during the preceding twelve months), often come to the rescue of the family historian. Transcripts were ordered to be sent annually from 1597 onwards,

but there are no transcripts before 1661 in the records of the Church in Wales deposited in the Library. Even after this date there are many gaps in the returns, only a few transcripts before 1723 being extant for parishes in the diocese of Llandaff, and hardly any for the eighteenth century for parishes in the archdeaconries of Cardigan and St David's. The transcripts cease at dates varying from parish to parish during the middle of the nineteenth century, although there are a few examples from the early twentieth century from some parishes. Transcripts of marriage entries normally cease with the introduction of civil registration in 1837. The transcripts held by the Library are listed in schedules available in the South Reading Room. While the original transcripts for the dioceses of Bangor, St Asaph, St David's and Swansea and Brecon are still issued to readers, those for the diocese of Llandaff are now made available on fiche.

Marriage bonds and allegations are the next most important class of Anglican Church record of use to the genealogist. These documents were executed in order to obtain a licence to marry without having banns called publicly in Church on three Sundays before the solemnization of the marriage. Generally speaking, these records cover the eighteenth and nineteenth centuries and the first three decades of the twentieth century. The amount and nature of the information varies with the type of document, and are particularly valuable when the approximate date of a marriage is known but not its venue. The pre-1837 bonds and allegations in the Library have been indexed and may be searched on-line at http://www.llgc.org.uk:81/index.htm. Also available for the diocese of St David's are registers of marriage licences, mainly for the nineteenth century.

Another class of records of paramount interest to the genealogist is wills and administrations, and those which before the introduction of Civil Probate on 11 January 1858 were proved in the Welsh ecclesiastical courts, have been deposited in the Library. Roughly speaking, the covering dates of the surviving probate records of each of the consistory courts are: Bangor, 1635-1858; Brecon, 1543-1858; Chester (Welsh Wills), 1557-1858; Hawarden, 1554-1858; Llandaf, 1568-1857; St Asaph, 1565-1857; St David's, 1556-1858. These wills have also been indexed and may be searched either in volumes on the open shelves of the South Reading Room, or on a local database at the Library. It is hoped that they will be available for consultation on-line in the near future. For the period after 1858 the Library has custody of register copy wills from five registries, covering all but one (Montgomeryshire) of the Welsh counties, and a full set of the annual index of all wills and administrations granted in England and Wales (the Calendar of Grants), from 1858 to 1972.

Despite the fact that they are much less comprehensive than the records of the Anglican

Church in Wales, Nonconformist records are an important source of information for genealogists. Many registers of dissenting congregations were deposited with the Registrar-General after the Civil Registration Act of 1836, and the Library has microfilm copies of these. A few registers of that period which never found their way to London and some other later registers are now deposited at the Library. Other nonconformist records of genealogical value at the Library include manuscript lists of members and contribution books of individual chapels, printed annual reports, usually including lists of members and their contributions, which have been produced by many chapels since about 1880, and denominational periodicals, which often contain notices of births, marriages and deaths.

Records of the Court of Great Sessions of Wales, the most important legal and administrative body between the Act of Union and its abolition in 1830, may also prove useful for genealogical purposes. Occasionally challenge pedigrees were filed in connection with certain actions, and other documents of considerable value are depositions, which often state the age of the deponent, jury lists and coroners' inquests.

The Library has transferred its former holdings of Quarter Session Records to the appropriate County Record Offices, but some related materials are to be found among the archives of landed estates or solicitors' firms, for example a few sessional rolls and land tax records 1780-1839 from Cardiganshire, some land tax records (the most useful class of records for the genealogist) for Montgomeryshire and Breconshire, order books 1647-75 and rolls, 1643-99 for Denbighshire, and sessions records from Montgomeryshire.

Local government at a level between county and parish was practically non-existent before the formation of Poor Law Unions under the the the Poor Law Amendment Act 1834 Most Poor Law Union records are now deposited at the appropriate county record office, but there are some records at the Library, mainly from Montgomeryshire. Civil parish records are also mainly held by the appropriate county record office, although the Library holds vestry books and other parochial records for many parishes for which parish registers have been deposited.

The manorial records held by the Library are mainly to be found with the estate records and listed with them They are most comprehensive for Montgomeryshire (mainly the Powis Castle and Wynnstay estate records), with substantial holdings for Glamorgan and Monmouthshire also (mainly the Badminton, Bute and Tredegar estate records). It should be noted that in many parts of Wales the manorial system never really took root. In conjunction with HMC, the Library produced a manorial database for Wales which is available on (http://www2.hmc.gov.uk/Welsh_Manorial_Documents_Register.htm), and a volume entitled Welsh Manors and their Records by Helen Watt has also been published by the Library.

Most of the estate records and personal papers held by the Library are detailed in typescript schedules, many of which are now available on the Library's website. The estate records contain title deeds, rentals, account books, correspondence, etc. Rentals may prove particularly useful in indicating a death or change of residence when a name disappears from a series of rentals.

The Library also holds many manuscript pedigrees. These vary from descents of nobility, compiled in the later Middle Ages and copied time and again with additions by later genealogists, to charts which are the work of amateurs of modern times who have given copies of their compilations to the Library. For searchers particularly interested in the pedigrees of gentry families there are several important printed works available.

There is a general card index to most of the typescript schedules of the collections in the South Reading Room, and probably the most useful for the family historian are the sections devoted to wills, marriage settlements, inquisitions post mortem, and pedigrees. The index to the general collections of manuscripts (NLW MSS) may also be of use to genealogists. In addition, a basic inventory of the contents of the Library's Annual Report up to 1996 is available on-line.

For further information on sources for family history research at the National Library of Wales, it is worth consulting the Library's web site at: http://www.llgc.org.uk/ht/ht_s004.htm

J Llewellyn
An Aberystwyth Brigantine
W Troughton

J Llewellyn a 161 ton Aberystwyth built brigantine first came to my attention during research into Aberystwyth harbour and related shipping, in particular the barque *Hope*[1]. *Hope* had also been under the command of John Evans (1845-1923) of Aberystwyth. Further impetus for the article came about due to a chance contact with descendants of John Evans.

Although not an unusual vessel her story serves to touch on many aspects of maritime history. Most of the information contained here comes from crew agreements held at the National Library of Wales, shipping registers held at Ceredigion Archives and from local newspapers especially "The Cambrian News." Mrs Margot Heywood kindly supplied me with the illustrations used here.

J Llewellyn started life on the blocks in Jones & Williams shipyard in that part of Aberystwyth below South Road known as Y Geulan. She was launched on 4th September 1869 just after nine o'clock in the morning with a Mrs Llewellyn of Hay-on-Wye conducting the launching. The report in the following weeks Cambrian News reveals that she was to be captained by Captain Llewellyn and that she was to be engaged in the foreign trade. With regard to her ownership she was divided into the customary 64 shares. Of these 16 were held by Thomas Jones the Ropemaker, 13 by a Mary Davies and 35 by Capt Llewellyn himself, although he had to arrange a mortgage of £1458 7s 4d for 22 of these.

Following her launch it was necessary for the rigging to be fitted, sails made etc. This was not without incident and culminated in a tramping sailmaker being imprisoned for two months for theft of a ships clock valued at fifteen shillings as she lay at anchor in Aberystwyth.

J Llewellyn embarked on her maiden voyage from Aberystwyth in mid January 1870 bound for Newport, Monmouthshire presumably in ballast. As might be expected her crew for this voyage were mainly local and comprised the aforementioned Captain William Llewellyn aged 31, 23 year old mate James Griffiths, boatswain Edward Jones aged 30, three Able Bodied

(AB) seamen, namely Thomas Evans, David H Thomas, both aged 21 and Robert Pugh aged 19 who was listed as A B and ships carpenter. The only Ordinary Seaman (OS) was 18 year-old James Jones. The rank of ships boy fell to 12 year-old William Evans from Solva. With the addition of another AB Dutchman, Jan V Kalen, she sailed from Newport on 29th January. Of her crew seven were from Aberystwyth. The voyage took them to Cagliari, Barcelona (where they were forced to return in distress on March 31st), the Scilly Isles (where David H Thomas who had been mentioned three times in the ships log for unruly conduct was discharged by mutual consent) and finally to Antwerp where the crew were discharged.

Following a lay up in Antwerp she again sailed for the Mediterranean arriving in Genoa on 14th December 1871 before visiting Naples and Leghorn before returning to discharge her cargo in London in April. Her crew this time had a far more international flavour including three Norwegians. After this voyage her connection with Captain Llewellyn ceased.

Her long association with John Evans of Aberystwyth began following his purchase of 13 shares from William Llewellyn on 1st May 1871 with the help of a mortgage of £250 from Frederick Rowland Roberts of Aberystwyth.

William Llewellyn sold his remaining shares to Nelson Hewertson, tube merchant of Newport. Following the death of Hewertson in 1876 these shares were also purchased by John Evans. Eight of these were then sold on to John Evans' brother in law William Jones. Thomas Jones of Marine Terrace, Aberystwyth now became the registered managing owner until his death in 1880, following which this role fell to William Jones.

Her next two voyages with Thomas Jones at the managerial helm were both to the Caribbean. The first commenced from London on June 29th 1871 bound for Berbice (in present day Guyana) and back to London. The outward journey was achieved in a very respectable 34 days. The return journey took a more sedate 54 days. A contemporary guide-book said of Berbice "Mosquitoes abound here." One suspects that

Captain John Evans

the crew probably found this out for themselves quite quickly on arrival. The area was at this time wholly dominated by the sugar industry and it was this commodity that brought *J Llewellyn* to South America and later to other parts of the Caribbean. Her next voyage to this part of the world was to Grenada departing from London on 7th November 1871 and returning on 11th March 1872. The outward leg 43 days, the return leg 32 days. The delights of the Caribbean proved too much for one crew member, Canadian Jack Norton, who on the night of January 15th stowed his gear aboard the longboat and rowed ashore. His dash for liberty was short-lived as the next day he was arrested and jailed until the vessel sailed on 7th February. This act cost him a fine of his wages and probably the wrath of his fellow crew who would have had to load his share of the cargo whilst he languished in a prison cell.

For her next two voyages *J Llewellyn* headed south of the equator to present day South Africa. Her outward journey from London took 116 days. Both these voyages were to the relatively obscure Port Alfred situated between Port Elizabeth and East London. Amongst the crew members were mate John Jones from Borth, Jenkin Evans and John Isaac (both from Aberystwyth) who had sailed with Captain John Evans on *J Llewellyn's* previous voyages. Port Alfred was a popular destination for Aberystwyth vessels during the 1860's and 1870's. Amongst those who called there were *Ceredig, Hawendale, Maggie Phillips, Patriot, Retriever & Star of Wales*. This was despite being a notoriously difficult port to enter. The Cape Town Argus ventured the statement in 1870 that

"Within the last twelve months, of all the vessels that have entered or tried to enter the port, it is hardly an exaggeration to say that about one half came to grief."

The principal cause of the problems was a bar at the harbour mouth and the relatively narrow channel of the Kowie River once the bar had been negotiated. However the apprenticeship that most of these captains had along the rocky coastline of west Wales

evidently proved invaluable as none of these vessels ever came to grief there.

Port Alfred served the surrounding hinterland, in particular Grahamstown. An advertisement from the Grahamstown Journal of August 16th 1872 gives some clue as to the types of cargo carried in the hold of *J Llewellyn*. As well as listing a number of other vessels that have recently discharged cargoes on their behalf "Kennelly & Co, Grahamstown have on hand or are receiving Spirits, sherry, port, ale, soap, coffee, gunpowder, tea, milled flour, biscits, salmon, herrings, pickles, confectionery, barley, oatmeal, oysters, lobsters, potted meat, jam, Lea & Perrins sauce, macaroni, hams, raisins, salt, silks, cashmere, carpets, sewing machines"

The bar at the mouth of the Kowie proved the undoing of three members of the crew. To enable the vessel to cross the bar it was necessary to discharge part of the cargo into a lighter. During this process three crew members were spotted embezzling part of the cargo. This incurred a fine of £5 each. Not much by today's standards, but the equivalent of two months wages for two of the crewmen. Frustratingly it has not been possible to determine what cargo can have so tempted the crew and incurred such a hefty fine. Her return journey was accomplished in 68 days, the vessel arriving in London on 21st November 1872.

Her second journey to Port Alfred commenced from London on 3rd January 1873. This time her outward journey was completed in 116 days. After discharging her cargo, which, according to reports in the local papers, seems to have taken some weeks she loaded a part cargo in Natal. Returning to Port Alfred she departed on or after the 11th June (when an additional crew member was signed on) and arrived back in London on 24th August 1873.

After unloading her cargo and making good any damage sustained on her return voyage *J Llewellyn* sailed from London bound for St Lucia in the West Indies. Her outward voyage took 48 days, her return voyage back to London 53 days arriving on 11th February 1874. Her crew on this occasion included mate John Jones from Borth, Jenkin Evans, a 25 years old boatswain from Aberystwyth and James Evans, cook, aged 20, also from Aberystwyth. One of their crew mates was Augustus Antoine, a native of St Lucia who received wages of just £1 as when signing on he stated that he wished to be discharged at St Lucia. For the return leg another St Lucian 16 year old George Emile was recruited.

Two months later *J Llewellyn* departed from Cardiff for Cadiz, almost certainly carrying a cargo of coal. Here it can be surmised that she loaded with salt for Newfoundland. Arriving at St Johns after a 32 day crossing she spent some six weeks, presumably unloading her cargo and possibly loading a part cargo before moving along the coast to Greenspond where a stay of 17 days suggests more cargo being loaded. Her cargo from here was most likely copper ore. Greenspond is still associated with copper mining to this day. Her next ports of call were Alicante and Cadiz. As both visits were for ten days or so it is possible that the cargo was discharged at Alicante and a new cargo loaded at Cadiz. What is certain is that she departed from Cadiz in late October 1874 and arrived back in St Johns, Newfoundland on November 14th. She then sailed for Tilt Cove, Newfoundland where she loaded with a cargo of copper ore including 16 casks of No 1 Copper Ore and one cask of ore samples for Swansea, sailing on 14th December and arriving on 5th January 1875.

When she next sailed from Swansea on 11th February 1875 five of her seven crew were from Aberystwyth including John Isaac who had been a member of the crew on her voyage to Port Alfred in 1872. In comparison with previous convoluted voyages this was a straight forward voyage. Her destination was Saffi on the Atlantic coast of Morocco, a place that Captain John Evans was to become woefully familiar with at a later date. She sailed in ballast and loaded a cargo, possibly beans, sailing for Hull on 25th March where she arrived on 6th May 1875.

In the absence of definitive information her cargo when she sailed from Hull on 25th May can only be guessed as being fish. The destination of this cargo was Malaga. Her next port of call was Cadiz. After departure on 31st July 1875 a voyage of 37 days took her to Newfoundland. During her stay of 18 days she loaded a cargo of copper ore at Betts Cove before departing for Swansea and arriving on 26th October.

Unfortunately her crew agreements for 1876 are missing, consequently her movements are near impossible to track. Her next known port of call was sometime in July 1876 when she was surveyed in the Clyde. This was her half time survey as required by section 34 of Lloyds rules. The survey confirmed her A1 status. The fact that she was surveyed on the Clyde suggests that she may have been involved in importing sugar from the Caribbean during 1876. Glasgow at this time had several sugar refineries and in future years she was engaged in this trade. Her next known voyage commenced at Glasgow on 31st October 1877 and took her to Berbice, Barbados and St Lucia. Of the three ports her longest stay was at the latter port suggesting that it may have been here in the shadow of the Pitons that her return cargo of sugar was loaded for London. After arrival in London following a journey of 55 days once again her trail goes cold. This time she re-appears on 24th March 1879 in Hamburg where she signed on a multi-national crew which included a 25 year old mate from Borth, Richard Arter. Her first port of call was Lisbon, then onto Antigua where she loaded sugar for Greenock, arriving on 31st July after a journey of some 38 days.

During the next three years a similar trading pattern was followed with voyages to either French ports or the mediterranean alternating with voyages to load sugar in the Carribean. Two voyages were made to Berbice and both had their share of ill-luck. On 21st April 1881 cook and ordinary seaman Edward James of Aberystwyth was drowned at Berbice whilst attempting to step onto a lighter moored alongside the ship. Her return voyage the next year proved even more disastrous. Two of her crew, Thomas Rees of Aberystwyth and John Brooks from Bristol died of

fever in the Colonial Hospital within days of each other. Two other crew members John Keane from Liverpool and William Duff from Devonport were left behind at the same hospital. Captain John Evans chose not to take any chances and rapidly recruited three locals and a Dane and sailed for London the day after Thomas Rees died. The fate of the two seamen left behind is not known[2]. As though this was not enough after arrival in London a fire broke out whilst moored at the East [India?] Dock. The cargo was reported to contain oils and other inflammable materials and required two steam engines, one standpipe and a private hydrant to bring the blaze under control. The damage was listed as fore part of main hold and cargo severely damaged by fire; rest [of hold] and cargo by smoke, water and heat. The vessel was nearly filled with water.[3] Perhaps not suprisingly John Evans chose to end his connection with the Carribean.

The next destination was Newfoundland. Here *J Llewellyn* visited Halifax, St Johns and North Sydney before sailing back to Lisbon, onto Patras and eventually back to Bridgwater on 27th March 1883. Unfortunately no evidence has come to light regarding cargoes carried on this voyage. This was followed by a voyage from Cardiff to Messina and back to Hull between April and August 1883. It was on this voyage that a pierhead artist at Messina painted the incoming *J Llywelyn*, selling the result to John Evans. After her customary four weeks in port between voyages she crossed the Atlantic to St Johns, Newfoundland in 32 days before heading for the mediterranean. This time her first port of call was to Gibraltar to discharge Thomas Lloyd who had been injured when his leg became jammed between a cask and the stanchion to which he was attempting to secure it. He was to rejoin the vessel three weeks later at Malaga. Naturally he was not paid during his stay in hospital. Following the presumed discharge of her cargo a new destination revealed itself. This was Stettin, then in Germany, now in Poland. Here again it is surmised that she loaded with a cargo that was probably discharged during her five days stay at Dunkirk and subsequent return to Cardiff on 26th April 1884.

The final demise of *J Llewellyn* is probably best described by quoting verbatim the account that appeared in The Cambrian News of 25th December 1885. This in turn was probably based on the captain's depositions made to Lloyds Agent in Saffi.

Wrecks of Aberystwyth Ships
During the month of November two ships belonging to the port of Aberystwyth became total wrecks on the coast of Morocco, and the crews had narrow escapes from drowning. A terrific gale continued to to blow for several days and the sea became boisterous. The *Jane Llewellyn* [sic] went on shore on the 12th November and the *Solway* after holding on for five days longer parted her cables and drifted on to the rocks where she rolled over on her side to the imminent peril of the crew and rapidly went to pieces.

The *Jane Llewellyn* [sic] was a brigantine belonging to Aberystwyth and owned by Captain Evans, Mr

Edward Jones of Laura Place, Mrs Lloyd, St James Square and Mr William Jones, brother-in-law of the captain. Her master was Capt. Evans, Aberystwyth, the mate belonged to Aberdeen and of the crew only one man, William Thomas Jones, was from Aberystwyth. He was the son of the late Mr. Thomas Jones, carrier.

The vessel was loading beans at Saffi for Queenstown or Falmouth for orders and was anchored in the bay. About 3 o'clock on the afternoon of 12th November however she parted her cables and drifted on the sandy shore. The crew saved themselves by ropes and were subsequently enabled to get their clothes, but finally the ship was dashed to pieces by the breakers. The crew had been undergoing quarantine but the Saffi authorities held it to be insufficient and the men had to live for several days in a tent on the shore outside the walls of the town.

The *Solway* was wrecked on 17th November on the same coast. She was a brig built in Cumberland of about 340 tons and was owned by John Mathias, Bridge Street, Mr Thomas Hugh Jones, Captain Davies, Chalybeate Terrace and Mr Wm. Edwards, Cambrian Place. Her master was Captain Samuel Jones of 24 Mill Street, son-in-law of Mr Wm Edwards, who was accompanied by his wife and child, the latter being a little over 5 mths old. The mate was David Thomas of Vulcan Street, Mr Edward Jones boatswain, New Quay. Mr Wm. Jones the cook and amongst the crew were Arthur Jones, Grays Inn Lane, brother of the captain, a lad aged between 14 & 15. *Solway* was anchored in the bay like *J Llewellyn* and was also loading beans for Queenstown or Falmouth for orders, having been chartered by Mr Wm. Thomas, broker of Brunswick Street, Liverpool.

Between eight and nine o'clock on the evening of the 17th a terrific West South Westerly gale blew and *Solway* started to drag her anchors and drifted rapidly shorewards where Captain Evans had lit a fire to enable the crew to steer *Solway* onto the sandy beach, rather like that of the terrace. Solway drifted onto a reef under a bluff, rather like Craiglais. In a short time after her cables parted, she struck and after one or two rolls her cargo shifted and she listed. Captains wife and crew clung to the side of the ship whilst a rope was cast ashore and seized by Captain Evans and his mate. The rope was fastened and the crew began their passage over it, the baby tied to the breast of the boatswain. The captain left last and all then climbed up the cliffs before reaching shelter. The mate subsequently saw his muffler doing duty as a turban on the head of a moor, whilst another native was seen in one of the Captains Shirts. The British Consul entertained the crew and finally provided them with passages to London on the SS *Magadore*, the Shipwrecked Mariners Society paying to send them to their homes.

By the way of a postscript there is a tradition that the J Llewellyn was salvaged and refloated. There are no official records to support this. If it was the case it was likely that she was sold on to local owners.

1 See *The barque 'Hope' of Aberystwyth* in Ceredigion, journal of the Ceredigion Historical Society, XII vol 3 p85-101
2 To underline the nature of the climate of Berbice at this time the "West India Pocket Book, Book II", published in 1880 quotes the following statistics: in 1876 dysentry and diarhorea killed 1,160, consumption 576 and fever 915 persons. The population of Berbice in 1871 was 35,557
3 Cambrian News 23rd June 1882

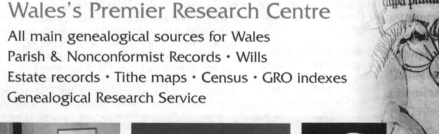

Carmarthenshire Antiquarian Society

Carmarthenshire Antiquarian Society wa founded on Friday 28 April 1905 (apparently at 7pm!) at a meeting attended by fewer than three dozen people, but by the first annual meeting a year later membership had grown to 125. The Society was founded at a time when there was little in the way of authoritative history of Carmarthenshire in published form. Indeed the primary research for such work was yet to be done. The Society was central in co-ordinating the collection and dissemination of all manner of historical and archaeological material. The first accommodation was in Walter Spurrell's printing office, but this was rapidly outgrown and moved in 1908 to 54 King Street where it remained until the move in 1920 to 5 Quay Street.

Through its well-attended field days members were able to see and hear about field monuments, and reports of these were published in The Welshman. So popular were these reports and notes that they were reprinted as our journal - the Transactions. Artefacts were also collected, and it was soon decided that the Society should have its own museum to hold these and the books and manuscripts that came flooding in from all corners of the County. From 1905 to the early 1920s the Society amassed so much material that its Museum in Quay Street, Carmarthen, became second only in size to the National Museum of Wales. However, it is clear that by the mid 1920s this by now priceless collection was ill housed in the Society's 'Rooms' in Quay Street. By 1929 things had come to a crisis point due to shortage of space and poor storage. Then dry rot set in. In December 1929 Sir Cyril Fox scathingly criticised the Society for continuing to gather material when its resources were inadequate. Fox hoped that the County Council would contribute.

The Society bought 5 Quay Street for £400 in 1931 from the executors of Mr D Howell Thomas, Starling Park, Carmarthen, having had the use of it rent-free since 1920. Four years later they bought No. 4, not only doubling the storage and display area of the

Museum but also reuniting two halves of a property built in 1670/71 and divided in the late nineteenth century. Cyril Fox wrote to the Society congratulating them on the purchase, adding that 'It is not a particularly good house, but it is something to be master in your own castle.' The Society now owned three properties in the town having bought 9 Bridge Street (complete with the castle sallyport circular tower) in 1907 for £90. Negotiations began with the County Council in the late 1930's for the transfer of the Museum into public ownership, instrumental in this was George Eyre Evans, one of the founding members, serving Secretary from the inception of the Society, and indefatigable collector and Curator of the Museum, but unfortunately he died in November 1939 before agreement was reached.

However, a year later in November 1940 the Society conveyed 4 and 5 Quay Street, 9 Bridge Street and all the objects, books and MSS for the sum of £800 to Carmarthenshire County Council. A brief (and wholly inadequate) catalogue included in the transfer gives some indication of the sheer vastness and range of the collections - Early Christian Memorials, objects of Folk Culture, glass and ceramics, much of it from Llanelli, quantities of love spoons, samplers, paintings, pictures and 60 cases of stuffed animals. The Society's collection of early Bibles was immense, including editions of 1611 and Y Beibl Cysegr Lan of 1620. Other printed works and incunabulae included editions of Camden, Speed and rare illustrated antiquarian tours of Egypt and the Middle East. Manuscript material included Carmarthen and Kidwelly borough records; police records; ecclesiastical records; poor law records; education records; maps; railway plans and a series of scrapbooks containing title deeds, cuttings, pictorial and antiquarian material. There was also a magnificent collection of journals accumulated through exchange agreements for the Transactions and also Alcwyn Evans' annotated set of Archaeological

Dolaucothy: Field Day 28 May, 1908.

Picton Frieze

Cambrensis.

The Society had provided much of the raw material and to some extent a synthesis for a better understanding of the development of the area from early times through to the modern era. The Transactions were continuously published and no doubt were invaluable to the authors of the Royal Commission Inventory (1917); and the County History, produced under the capable editorship of Sir John Lloyd in the 1930s. Field days continued to be popular and an important avenue for providing members with information about the County's antiquities, and landowners with information about the importance of sites on their land.

Under the County Council the Museum at best can be said to have remained stable. The Society maintained a presence on its management committee (a condition under the transfer agreement). However, the war years were a difficult period for the Society: it is clear that George Eyre Evans was sadly missed, and despite the stalwart efforts of the Officers, like E. G. Bowen, it was not possible to build up membership from the then very small base. It was a council member, J. F. (Fred) Jones, who became the curator in the 1950s and held the reins of both the Museum and Society through a decade that saw no material growth in membership.

A rebirth developed as a result of a number of factors that came together in the 1960s. An awakening interest in the past, especially in archaeology, coincided with local excavations lead by a young and enthusiastic Dr Barri Jones of Manchester University. His excavations in Carmarthen provided supporting evidence for his assertion that Carmarthen was not just a Roman Fort, but also a capital with its own walls distinct from the fort.

The Society's membership started to climb dramatically after a shake-up of the officers and the establishment of a new Council. Field days took on a new dimension, with much interest being shown in Roman sites. J. F. Jones had already discovered the important marching camp at Arosfa Garreg (which was not far from the already known overlapping camps at Y Pigwn). In addition, the survey work

proving the existence of Carmarthen's amphitheatre provided a further impetus for the archaeological work of the Society.

The Transactions had made way for the Carmarthenshire Antiquary from 1941 and by 1969 Barri Jones was able to publish interim results from his 1968 excavations. By 1970 more reports and the results of work at the Roman mines at Dolau Cothi appeared.

In the early 1970s local government reorganization was being planned and with the creation of Dyfed the new curator of the museum, John Little, along with the Society, lobbied for the removal of the Museum from Quay Street to the Old Palace at Abergwili (the latter had been vacated by the Bishop, leaving the Old Palace without a use).

In 1974 the Dyfed Archaeological Trust was set up making its headquarters in Carmarthen. The Trust brought in professionals who became involved in the Society's activities, helping cement the archaeological direction that had been the driving force for the growth in membership. One of the distinctive elements in the way the Society now developed was that its own members were carrying out field work and historical research, which often formed the subject matter for lectures and field days. This active work by our own members then formed (and still underpins) much of the subject matter of the Antiquary. Typical of such fieldwork and lectures was the pioneering work of the late M. C. S. (Mike) Evans on the early iron industry. His pre-Turnpike roads research produced one of the most successful series of lectures/field days and in turn became Antiquary articles that are warmly remembered by the membership. Excavations by the young Anthony Ward at Mynydd Llangyndeyrn and elsewhere, provided opportunities for members to become involved in excavations, and a project aimed at younger members included gravestone recording at St Ishmael's Church. It was the drive to provide ever better field days that sparked off the revisiting by members of the programme sub-committee of field monuments that had been left forgotten for decades. Attention was directed at the renewed interest in Industrial Archaeology, and members were surprised at how early Carmarthenshire's industrial history had developed. This provided a magnet for work in the south east of the county, with a spin-off of membership growth in the Llanelli area. The programme of field days thus became a forum for showing the results of fieldwork. The Antiquary, under the capable hands of the late Bill Morris, attained a well-deserved reputation with its exceedingly wide ranging subject matter, a mirror of the wide range of interests that the Society's members had.

Today the Programme of field days and lectures continues to keep abreast of new developments in archaeological and historical research in the County as well as West Wales in general, and the Antiquary continues to provide a forum for the publication of members' work as well as for academics and professionals. The publication of special volumes is central to the Society's aim to disseminate knowledge and educate a wide audience about Carmarthenshire's past.

At 100 years old the Society is far from 'antiquarian' and is very much an active one with regular attendances of over 70 at field days and lectures, drawn from a membership of over 400 spread across the UK and abroad.

The Public Record Office of Northern Ireland
Valerie Adams

The Public Record Office of Northern Ireland (PRONI) is the only dedicated archive repository in Northern Ireland, providing an integrated archival service for the whole country. It receives not only public records (those created by government departments, courts, local authorities and non-departmental public bodies) but also private records from a wide range of sources - individuals, families, businesses, charities, churches, societies, landed estates, etc. You might think that PRONI only holds archives relating only to the six counties of Northern Ireland but in fact there are archives relating to other parts of the island of Ireland and to numerous locations all over the world from Jamaica to India and from South Africa to China. This unique combination of private and public records and its extensive record holdings, amounting to over 35Km, makes PRONI the most important resource for anyone researching their family tree or their local area.

On PRONI's website you will find out how to make best use of the records. There is a 'Frequently Asked Questions' section, copies of all our information leaflets and details of our policies on preservation and copying. You will also find on the website the introductions to the major private archives and to the classes of records of the Ministry/Department of Education some of which will be of interest to the family historian if one of your ancestors was in the teaching profession. Also on the website will be news of new developments that are taking place.

Public Records
Because of the fire in the Public Record Office of Ireland in Dublin in 1922 many people are under the impression that there are no surviving public records before that date. In fact, there are many series of records that go back to the early 19th century and even into the 18th century in the case of the Grand Jury Presentment Books that will give the names of those who received money for the construction and repair of roads, bridges, gaols, etc. The most popular records for the family and local historian relating to the six counties of Northern Ireland are: the valuation records from the 1830s to the present; the tithe applotment books, 1823-37, giving details of landholders and the size of their holdings; copy wills from 1838 - c.1900 and all original wills from 1900 to 1998; registers and inspectors' observation books of c.1,600 national/public elementary/primary schools dating mainly from the 1870s; the grant-aid applications of the Commissioners of National Education which record the history and state of national schools from 1832 to 1889; the Ordnance Survey maps at various scales from 1831 to the present; the minutes, indoor and outdoor relief registers, etc of the Boards of Guardians who administered the workhouse system from 1838 to 1948; the records, including admission registers, of lunatic asylums, some dating back to the mid-19th

century (but these are subject to extended closure for 100 years); and the title deeds, leases and wills in the Irish Land Commission and the Land Purchase Commission archive some of which date back into the 18th century.

Guides to the tithe applotment books, the large scale town plans, education records and probate records are available in PRONI.

Private Archives
Because so many of the public records for the island of Ireland have not survived it is not surprising then that private archives have assumed a much greater importance for family and local history.

The most valuable are those of the great landed estates (many of which go back into the 17th and 18th centuries), of solicitors' firms which include copies of wills, leases and title deeds, of railway companies, and of churches. Equally important are family and personal papers and the working notes of antiquarians and genealogists who worked in the Public Record Office of Ireland prior to 1922 and who took copious notes from the records some of which date back to the17th century. Almost all the major estate archives are held in PRONI and you can find descriptions of many of them on the PRONI website. Among the more notable estate archives are: Downshire (Cos Down and Antrim); Antrim (Co Antrim); Abercorn (Co Tyrone); Belmore (Co Fermanagh); Gosford, Brownlow and Caledon (Co Armagh); and Drapers' Company (Co Londonderry). A comprehensive listing of all the estate records in PRONI will be found in the 'Guide to Landed Estates' available in PRONI or at the Local Studies Libraries of each Education and Library Board.

Church records are an invaluable source for the family historian, especially those that pre-date civil registration of births and deaths (births, deaths and all marriages from 1864 and Protestant marriages from 1845). Microfilm copies of almost all pre-1900 church records of the main denominations are available in the Self-Service Microfilm Room in PRONI. On the PRONI website you will find an index of reference numbers to many of these microfilmed church records but fuller details can be found in the 'Guide to Church Records', the most up to date version of which is available in PRONI.

Printed Sources
Street directories are often a neglected source of information for the family and local historian. PRONI holds a very comprehensive set of the Belfast and Ulster Street Directories from c.1840 to 1996 and of Thom's Directories from 1845 to 1958. Another useful source are the printed will calendars that give a brief summary of every will proved and of letters of administration taken out in the civil courts from 1858

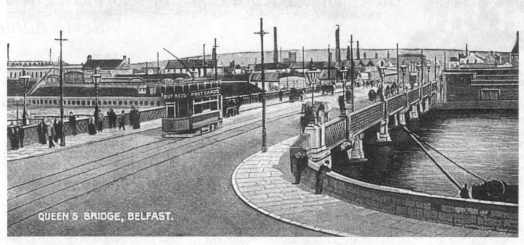

QUEEN'S BRIDGE, BELFAST.

to 1998; those from 1922 relate to Northern Ireland only.

Improvements to service
PRONI's commitment to raising standards of public services is reflected in the major re-furbishment and enlargement of the Public Search Room that took place in November and December 2003 - this included improved lighting and new furniture and additional computer terminals. PRONI can now provide modern, spacious and pleasant facilities for customers as well as an improved copying service. Regular consultation with users is vital to help identify where improvements are needed and to get feedback from users on improvements either implemented or planned. The PRONI Users Forum continues to provide the mechanism for doing so.

Forthcoming Developments
One of the largest projects (the 'eCATNI Project') that PRONI has ever embarked on and that is now well underway is the retrospective conversion of all our catalogues, right down to item level, which will eventually be accessible on the PRONI website. The project aims to create comprehensive, accurate and up-to-date electronic catalogues that can be accessed at the touch of a button. This will permit remote access to a rich archival heritage, opening up the opportunities for lifelong learning to a new and wider customer base and improving the efficiency and accessibility of PRONI's customer service. The first phase of the project will be available to the public by January 2005.

Self-Service Microfilm Room
In order to speed up access to the archives, the most popular sources on microfilm for the family and local historian are available in the specially equipped Self-Service Microfilm Room. There you can view microfilms of church records, the 1901 census for Northern Ireland, the copy will books, 1858-c.1900, the tithe applotment books, the civil birth indexes, 1864-1922, and the surviving fragments of the 1831-1851 census returns for some parishes in Cos Antrim, Fermanagh, Londonderry and Cavan.

Finding Aids
Besides our extensive catalogues which include virtual transcripts of important runs of estate correspondence, PRONI provides a range of finding aids: guides to different categories of records (eg women's history) and county guides; subject, place and personal name indexes (although the latter is by no means complete it is often a useful starting point if you do not know precisely where your ancestors came from); an extensive leaflet series on different types of records for family and local history and also leaflets on historical topics such as the Great Famine, the Act of Union and the Belfast Blitz.

New Acquisitions of interest to the family historian
Among the diverse range of archives either recently deposited or microfilmed and of most interest to the family historian are: additional records of Drumragh Parish Church, Co Tyrone, 1845 -1958 and of Bangor Parish Church, Co Down, 1845 - 1988, and marriage notice books for Templepatrick Presbytery, Co Antrim, 1869 -2002.

On-line records
PRONI's second large scale digitisation project was completed in September 2003, funded by the New Opportunities Fund - the indexing and scanning of the freeholders' records relating largely to the six counties of Northern Ireland from the mid 18th to early 19th centuries. These record the names and places of residence of those who were entitled to vote or who actually voted at elections. This new on-line resource of over 5,000 high quality images of the registers which is fully searchable and available on the PRONI website will provide speedier access to a unique resource for family and local history at a period when there is a scarcity of documentary sources. The current project that is now underway is to index and scan the wills for Northern Ireland from 1858 to c.1900.

External Relations
PRONI staff are available to give talks and lectures about PRONI and the sources we hold to outside

organisations, including family and local history societies. These can be delivered either on-site or off-site. Regular monthly series of talks on sources for tracing your family and local history are given in PRONI with occasional ones delivered elsewhere. These are open to everyone, especially if you have never been to PRONI before. PRONI's website will give details of forthcoming talks.

Facilities and Services

There is limited carparking within the PRONI site but space has been made available for those with a disability. Free off-street parking is available but you should park responsibly as residents do need to get in and out of their driveways.

Restaurant facilities are available on-site where you can purchase snacks, beverages and lunches that can be consumed in our new modernised and expanded restaurant area. It is possible to purchase a late evening meal on Thursdays when the Office is open until 8.45 but you must order this in advance at lunchtime.

IN PRONI you can access free of charge the websites of The National Archives, the National Archives of Scotland, the National Library of Scotland, the National Archives of Ireland and the National Library of Ireland. You can also now access the digital film archive of the Northern Ireland Film and Television Commission which contains 55 hours of film footage relating to Northern Ireland from 1897 to 2000.

Visiting PRONI and Opening Times

PRONI is open to the public without appointment and research is free for those pursuing personal and educational research. However, users will need to obtain a reader's ticket at Reception and will require proof of identity to gain admission and to use the computerised document ordering system. No advance booking is required. Group visits are very welcome but must be booked in advance.

Mon - Wed and Fri 9.00 – 16.45 Thurs - 10.00 – 20.45 (*please check in advance*) Last orders for documents -16.15 apart from Thursdays when it is 20.15 PRONI is closed annually for stocktaking during the last week in November and the first week in December and on public holidays (see the PRONI website for details as there are different public holidays in Northern Ireland). While there are detailed catalogues, guides and leaflets available, staff are always available at the Help Desk in the Public Search Room to give advice or help to researchers.

How to get there

If you are coming by car, there is easy access from the motorways and you should exit at Balmoral. While there is limited on-site carparking you can park in the vicinity of Balmoral Avenue. However, those with a disability will be accommodated on-site. If you are coming by bus, Nos 71 and 59 from the City Centre will take you to Balmoral Avenue and it is then is a short walk from the bus stop. Alternatively, Balmoral railway station on the Lisburn Road is only a short distance from PRONI.

Public Record Office of Northern Ireland
66 Balmoral Avenue, Belfast BT9 6NY T: 028 9025 5905 F: 028 9025 5999 E: proni@dcalni.gov.uk W: http://www.proni.gov.uk

Irish Censuses and Census Substitutes
David Webster

Introduction
To address the main subject of this article the history
of administrative jurisdictions in Ireland needs a brief
explanation. Up to 1922 records are centred in
Dublin. From 1922 Republic of Ireland records are in
Dublin while Northern Ireland records are in Belfast.
Belfast has some pre-1922 copies. Up to 1922 there
was the United Kingdom of Britain and Ireland. Since
then the country is correctly known as the United
Kingdom of Britain and Northern Ireland.

Be very careful about using the term "Ulster". In
historical terms there are 9 counties in Ulster, -
Donegal, Monaghan, Fermanagh, Tyrone, Antrim,
Down, Derry, Cavan, Armagh. (In genealogical terms
Belfast is also often regarded as a "county".) Cos.
Donegal, Monaghan & Cavan are in the Republic of
Ireland while the other 6 are in the United Kingdom
of Britain and Northern Ireland.

In the Republic of Ireland the main archives of
interest are GRO – General Register Office, which
holds BMDs up to 1922, and National Archives of
Ireland, which holds census and other records. In
Northern Ireland BMDs from 1922 onwards are held
by GRONI – General Register Office of Northern
Ireland, while PRONI – Public Record Office
Northern Ireland holds census and other records.

Irish Censuses
Full government censuses were taken of the whole
island in 1813, 1821, 1831, 1841, 1851, 1861, 1871,
1881, 1891, 1901, and 1911. The first five, for 1813,

1821, 1831, 1841, and 1851, were largely destroyed
in 1922, in the fire at the Public Record Office in
Dublin; surviving fragments are detailed under the
county source-lists. Those for 1861 and 1871 were
destroyed after use, and those for 1881 and 1891 were
completely destroyed during WWI, by order of the
government; as was a 1926 census of Northern
Ireland.

This means that the earliest surviving comprehensive
returns are for 1901 and 1911. Because of this, the
normal rule that census returns should not be
available to the public for 100 years has been
suspended in the Republic of Ireland, and the original
returns can be consulted in the National Archives; in
Northern Ireland the 1901 census is already available,
and the 1911 census will become available shortly,
with consideration being given to digitisation.

Full microfilm copies of the 1901 and 1911 censuses
are available at the LDS Family History Library in
Salt Lake City, and are also available through
LDS/GSU Family History Centres. Indexes,
published or database, are available for the 1901
returns of some counties. Copies of the 1901 returns
for the six counties now in Northern Ireland are
available at the Public Record Office of Northern
Ireland.

In 1901 and 1911 the Irish practice was different from
that in Scotland and England. In Scotland and
England the original household schedules, often
completed by the Head of the Household, were

destroyed soon after clerks had extracted the information required by government from the Enumeration Books, which had been created by the enumerators transcribing the individual household returns. In Ireland, the original household schedules survive!! So that, as long as the head of the household or someone else in the household, sometimes thought to have been a schoolchild, filled in the household schedule, you can look at the original handwriting of your ancestor.

The lack of censuses before 1901 had led to great interest in substitutes. A partial listing of these is as follows, -

Muster Rolls in the 17th century
Books of Survey and Distribution
Petty's 1655-67 Civil Survey of Ireland
Petty's 1659 Census
Hearth Money Rolls 1666
Subsidy Rolls 1662-66
Poll Tax Returns 1660
Tithe Applotment Books 1824-38
Occupiers of titheable land
Flax Growers' List
Freeholders' Records, various dates
Griffith's Valuation 1848-64 listing of every householder and occupier of land
The 1876 "Return of owners of land of one acre and upwards".
School records at PRONI

Possibly the most valuable of these to genealogists is "Griffiths" and the associated tithe applotment books.

Griffith's Valuation
Significant parts of what follows are taken from a post in a thread on the ScoltlandsPeople.gov.uk discussion group by Andy Keogh.

At the time of Griffith's (1848-1864) or to give it its proper name the Primary Valuation there was no Northern Ireland. The whole of the island was considered part of Britain, - the United Kingdom of Great Britain and Ireland (except by the indigenous Irish, mostly Catholics, who had lost their land and privileges when the English occupied the land by force).

Apart from a few entries from the 1851 census nothing survives of the original 6 useful censuses in Ireland (1821 and 1831 didn't give names). The earliest "Whole Country" (though 31 parishes out of 273 are missing) records are from the Tithe Applotment valuation between 1823 and 1838. The Tithe was an unpopular mandatory payment to the Church of Ireland, regardless of a person's religious affiliation. However some were exempt from the Tax and the valuation only lists Heads of household. *Griffith's Valuation (1848 -1864)* gives a complete list of occupiers of land, tenements and houses. But, again, only the immediate lease-holder (Head of Household) is named. Because of the severe lack of records in Ireland the usual "Burden of Proof" is often relaxed somewhat for Ireland.

In conducting genealogical research within Ireland it's essential to have a sound geographic knowledge down to townland

level, - the smallest recorded named subdivision of a parish, - similar to a Scottish fermtoun, milltoun, or similar, but never accorded the civil status in Scotland that was granted in Ireland, - I have an ongoing project to list place names in Scotland that end in "toun" or "ton", but it's proving to be a major task.

To set townland in context, a quick look at the hierarchy is helpful, -

Townland – smallest unit of land used in Ireland, 64,000+ in total
Civil parish – 2,500+, each containing 25 to 30 townlands
Diocese – religious jurisdiction of several faiths
County - From 1300s onwards, 36 counties
Barony – Portion of a county; 273 in total
Province – Originally 5, now 4
City, Town, Borough,Ward – separate administrative areas of varying size

It also helps to have an idea about the Land and Property Laws. For example: transfer of leased land could only occur upon the death of the immediate lease holder and, early in the 19th century, only the eldest surviving son was entitled to the land. However, if an eldest son (and only the eldest) married while his father was still living the father was allowed to give a portion of his leased land to that son, subject to the Landlord's approval.

How does this help? If you know your Paddy Murphy, born 1855, was from a particular townland and a Scottish record has thrown up a father's name, Tim Murphy, looking in Griffiths should yield a Tim Murphy (if he was married at the time of the valuation). If in the same townland you see a Ben Murphy that's perhaps the first indication of your Paddy's grandfather. That's where the Tithes come into play.

Being nearly a generation apart, the Tithes and Griffiths can work together. If you're fortunate, checking the Tithes for the same townland may show

a Ben Murphy and, in the same division of land, a Peter Murphy. This is called a "chain of occupancy", which can be a very accurate indication of paternal lineage, but only if the family didn't move around.

A real example is Andy Keogh's own ancestors, all from Northern Antrim for which there is, in addition, a fully extant Agricultural Census conducted in 1803. This survey was undertaken in preparation for a possible invasion by Napoleon. It included heads of households but additionally listed sons of military age as potential recruits, but not the various relationships.

From the death of Andy's great-grandmother in Scotland her parents are known to have been John Allan McQuilkin and Mary McCurdy and, given her age, born circa 1863. While the parents were probably married after the dates of *Griffith's Valuation*, it's fairly easy to guesstimate a rough period for her parents' births. It also help that it's known that she was from Rathlin Island.

Andy's aunt could remember stories about "Castle Quarter"; and it turns out to be the case that Castle Quarter is a "Clachan" a smaller, locally recognised, subdivision of a townland, usually occupied by family groups. Castle Quarter is in the Townland of Ballycarry on Rathlin.

In Griffith's Valuation for Ballycarry there are 9 families of relevance, -
  John WILKINSON, (cognate of McQUILKIN)
  Daniel M'ARTHUR
  John M'CURDY
  Donald M KINLEY
  Patrick M'CURDY
  Allen WILKINSON
  Donald M'CURDY
  John M'QUIG
  Patrick ANDERSON

Given a supposed date of marriage of Andy's John ALLAN as after Griffith's, even before other checks it would be fairly save to assume that the top John is Andy's John ALLAN's grandfather and Allan is the Father.

The Tithes records then come into play, -
The 1834 Tithe Applotment Book for Rathlin shows the following McQuilkins as the "Head of Household" by townland:
  Ballynagard - Alex McQUILKEN
  Mullindress - Daniel McQUILEN
  Ballycarry - Daniel McQUILKEN, Jn. McQUILKEN, and Allan McQUILKEN
  Coolnagrock - Michael McQUILKEN
  Craigmacagan - Alex McQUILKEN.

These records are generally set out terms of seniority, so that if there were three John SMITHs in the same townland the first would be John Sn., the second John Jr., and the third John B. (Beag), - father, son and grandson.

Given the date of birth of Andy's great-grandmother it's very unlikely that the John McQUILKIN in Ballycarry is her father but there is an Allan McQUILKIN so there is a highly probable chain of occupancy between the two valuations.

Back in 1803 there are the following McQUILKINs, this time spelled McQUILK, -
  ? McQUILK, Balleycarry
  Alexander McQUILK, Balleyconagan
  Alexander McQUILK, Cragmacagan
  Daniel McQUILK, Balleycarry
  Daniel McQUILK, Church Quarter
  Michael McQUILK, Balleycarry
  Neal McQUILK, Church Quarter

So in Ballycarry there are Daniel, Michael and an unknown McQuilkin with Daniel figuring between 1803 and the Tithes in 1832. Without even setting foot in Ireland this process results in a very possible lineage of Daniel to John to Allan to John Allan. In this particular case, the situation is greatly helped by extant monumental inscriptions (MIs) for Rathlin, which have been recorded, and which produce for this line, -

"Erected to the memory of John Wilkinson of Ballycarry who died 27th Jan 1863 aged 72 yrs" (after Griffiths and Tithe so this must be the John in Tithe and Griffiths)

"Also his father Dan'l who died 22nd January 1849 aged 85 yrs" (before Griffiths but after Tithe meaning he's the Daniel in 1803 and the Tithe)

Even though both died before statutory records started in Ireland (for everyone including Catholics) this is reasonable enough proof of Andy's lineage from his John ALLAN.

Andy also relates that he did, however, go to Ireland where I found that his John ALLAN (a blacksmith/farmer of Ballycarry) married in the Catholic Church on the Island in 1861. His father was Allan McQUILKIN (farmer of Ballycarry) who died 1877 aged 65. Allan's father was John of Ballycarry (Allan's wife was Susan ANDERSON, 10 years his senior she died 1869 aged 67).

All but two of John ALLAN and Mary McCURDY's children are in the statutory records but all were baptised on Rathlin Island.

This is an excellent example on the successful research in Ireland that is possible using Griffith's and associated sources, as well as other sources such as Memorial Inscriptions. Without knowing where the family came from and looking at the townlands and Land Laws this would have been impossible. Searching in Ireland is harder but very possible.

Griffith's on-line
The whole of Griffiths is now available on-line at http://www.irishorigins.com/ at a cost.
Access to Irish Origins exclusive Griffiths records costs:
  300 credits 7 days continuous access 8.50, US$9.75 or £6 GBP.
  600 credits 14 days continuous access 14.25, US$16.25 or £10 GBP.
  1 credit will enable you to retrieve one index record.
  20 credits will enable you to view an image of the original Griffith's Valuation.

The Search for Scottish Sources ~ Planning a Genealogical Journey

Rosemary Bigwood MA MLitt

The enthusiasm for tracing Scottish family history continues to grow and there are a wealth of opportunities for carrying out a great deal of research at home with the aid of internet sites and contacts or the facilities of a Family History Centre near you. If circumstances allow, however, a journey to Scotland will prove enormously rewarding, allowing the discovery of rich resources not available to you locally or which can only be found intside Scotland, to widen your research and your knowledge both of your ancestors and their background.

Planning a visit to Scotland in the quest of the ancestral past is not always an easy matter, especially if time is of the essence. A question frequently asked is "Should I go first to Edinburgh to the National Archives of Scotland and the General Register House or search in local record offices?" As with all travelling, some pre-journey preparations will be valuable. In the past it has often proved difficult to find out what source material is kept where and also to determine what records might be most fruitful to consult. Fortunately, work is now in hand to put most of the catalogues of the National Archives of Scotland and those of local and specialised archives on-line. This will be of great assistance in carrying out the planning of your research programme in Scotland.

One of the great interests in carrying out genealogical research is that you never know with certainty where it will lead in the end but in getting ready to embark on "on-site" work, it is important to make a list of your objectives – whether these are concerned with tracing back the family further, putting flesh on the bones by viewing the old family "stamping grounds" or trying to locate living relatives. Bring with you a summary of sources already searched so that you avoid duplication of work and a note of any index entries you have found relating to documents you may wish to view. Also, identify on a map the areas where the family are known to have lived in Scotland.

Where to start - Edinburgh

Many Scottish records which are concerned both with national and local administration are centralised in Edinburgh. Articles in the *Handbook* outline the rich resources of New Register House and the National Archives of Scotland. If you have work still to be done in extracting information from statutory registers of birth, death and marriage, in searching censuses or Old Parish Registers, then time spent in New Register House (also known as the General Register Office for Scotland) will be valuable. A day's ticket for access may seem expensive (currently £17) but, thanks to the self-service system which enables a

visitor to consult not only indexes but all the actual records, including copies of the statutory register pages and census returns (1841-1901) a great deal can be achieved within this time.

Having exhausted the resources of New Register House, it is time to assess what is now known about the family in which you are interested. What did these ancestors do - were they landlords or labourers? When did they live and where did they live? On this will depend the choice of records in which to carry out research "beyond" the parish registers.

Records are made by the contact of one person with another, with a group of people (perhaps at work or in the community) or with an authority such as a legal court or the church, for example. Thus a merchant or proprietor may have owned land, have left a testamentary disposition, had business and family dealings which are recorded in registers of deeds. He may have been involved in trade and have had a place in society, perhaps as a burgess in a burgh, member of the town council or acting as a JP – all of which matters may have resulted in the making of records. A tenant farmer is less likely to have owned land but could have left a testament, have had dealings with a landlord or initiated some legal proceedings. The labourer may be mentioned in poor law records, have appeared before a court for some misdemeanour, be listed in the local kirk session minutes or have had to serve in the militia if he lived at the time of the Napoleonic Wars – all contacts offering possible scope for research in specific classes of records, many of which can only be consulted in Scotland.

The second evaluation must be of the records themselves. How likely are they to throw light on a particular person and their circumstances? Are there indexes or finding aids and how long will it take to search them? Will the records be in Scots or Latin and will they be readable? Many documents, particularly those concerning the possession of land, were written in Latin until well on in the eighteenth

century. Handwriting changed around the beginning of the 1700's and there may be difficulties in reading the earlier, Old Scots hand. And lastly, where will these records be held?

The National Archives of Scotland
The National Archives of Scotland hold a vast and sometimes bewildering collection of material – much of it of vital interest to family historians. Some of this will be found on microfilm in Family History Centres but a great deal of it will not. Testaments, registers of deeds (both in the Books of Council and Session and in the sheriff and burgh courts), sasines, charters, retours, court records and a vast collection of church material, especially regarding the Established Church, are held there. There are muniments of many Scottish families, as well as records relating to national government – taxes and trade records. These sources are likely to be of prime importance in genealogical research. The new on-line catalogue of the NAS will provide some guidance as to the content of each class of records and be of assistance in selecting what may be relevant to your search. A preliminary study of published guides to records such as Cecil Sinclair's two books - *Tracing Your Scottish Ancestors in the Scottish Record Office* and *Tracing Scottish Local History in the Scottish Record Office* will meantime be of assistance in helping to identify source material which may be of value. *Tracing Scottish Ancestors* (Rosemary Bigwood) offers help in evaluating and selecting various classes of records, as well as indicating what may be found in the NAS and what is kept in local archives or to be found in libraries.

In the West Search Room in Charlotte Square, Edinburgh, the NAS has a very large collection of plans, mostly extracted from collections of family papers. These can shed considerable light on family history – illustrating land use, the whereabouts of old townships now vanished, buildings, plans of towns, providing information on field names and sometimes showing where named individuals lived.

The National Library of Scotland
This library, situated on George IV Bridge, Edinburgh, is a copyright library and has a huge collection of printed items. Their catalogue is on-line – www.nls.uk. They also have an extensive manuscript collection – including papers on families, estates, legal and financial matters. At present their detailed catalogue of manuscript material is not on-line and it is necessary to go to the library to search it.

A visit to the Map Library, which is part of the National Library of Scotland, (Causewayside Building, 33 Salisbury Place, Edinburgh) will almost certainly be of value in offering opportunities to look at their extensive collection of old printed maps of Scotland. They also have some manuscript ones. The maps include Scotland, Scottish counties, town plans, battles, railway and canal plans - to name only a few. The two volume work *The Early Maps of Scotland* published by the Royal Scottish Geographical Society is a useful guide to what is available.

Local Council Archives
In the past, the main administrative units in Scotland were the parish, the burgh and the sheriffdom or county. In 1975, as the result of the reorganisation of local government, burghs and counties were abolished and Scotland was divided into nine Regional Councils with a number of District Councils in the tier below. In 1996 there was yet another change when the present system of thirty-two local councils took over in charge of Scotland's local administration. These are listed below, with the administrative headquarters given in brackets after each:

Aberdeen City (Aberdeen) Inverclyde (Greenock) Aberdeenshire (Aberdeen) Midlothian (Dalkeith) Angus (Forfar) Moray (Elgin) Argyll & Bute (Lochgilphead) North Ayrshire (Irvine) City of Edinburgh (Edinburgh) North Lanarkshire (Motherwell) Clackmannanshire (Alloa) Orkney Islands (Kirkwall) Dumfries & Galloway (Dumfries) Perth & Kinross (Perth) Dundee City (Dundee) Renfrewshire (Paisley) East Ayrshire (Kilmarnock) Scottish Borders (Melrose) East Dumbartonshire (Glasgow) Shetlands Islands (Lerwick) East Lothian (Haddington) South Ayrshire (Ayr) East Renfrewshire (Glasgow) South Lanarkshire (Hamilton) Falkirk (Falkirk) Stirling (Stirling) Fife (Glenrothes) West Dumbartonshire (Dumbarton) Glasgow City (Glasgow) Western Isles (Stornoway) Highland (Inverness) West Lothian (Livingstone)

It is envisaged that each council will have an archivist but lack of funding and premises has in some cases made this difficult to implement immediately. Those currently in place are listed in the *Handbook* section on Record Offices and Archives.

Records of the Local Council Archives
It is first necessary to identify the local council which covers the district in which you are interested. Appendix 6 of *Tracing Scottish Ancestors* (Bigwood) gives a list of parishes and the local authority responsible for each.

CALLING OVER THE ROLL OF FAME.

Sergeant. "TUGAL M'TAVISH!"   *Tugal (hurrying up, too late for parade).* "HERE!"
Sergeant (indignant). "HERE! WHERE? YOU'LL ALWAYS CRY 'HERE!' WHEN YOU'RE ABSENT."

The holdings of the various local council archives vary widely. In Fife, for example, an archivist has only recently been appointed but a valuable body of material is being collected in the local council archive, including school board minutes, Commissioners of Supply books, parochial board minutes and various burgh and town council minutes. The largest collection of records for the area, however, is still held in the St. Andrews University archives – including deposits of records of a number of the Fife burghs – but other primary material is scattered in various centres, such as in the local history department of Dunfermline Library or in the Kirkcaldy Museum and Art Gallery. In other parts of Scotland, records are more centralised and one local council archive may hold most of the records of the royal burghs within their areas, as well as other local material relating to local administration, such as deeds, town council minutes, court records, lists of burgesses and parochial board minutes. Records of some kirk sessions (of both the Established Church and dissenting congregations), trade records, papers of associations of various kinds, collections of family papers, individuals and businesses, maps and plans may also be found in these archives.

Exploring Scottish History (2nd edition) edited by Michael Cox, is a directory of resource centres for Scottish local and national history and is an invaluable guide to what is held where. It includes a broad description of the holdings of each local archive. The book also notes the web-sites which can be useful, though the information provided on individual sites ranges from bare particulars of times of opening to quite detailed listings of holdings.

The Scottish Archive Network - SCAN - is currently working on giving on-line access (by 2003) to the "top level finding aids" of participating Scottish archives, providing a single searchable access point to their catalogues. Their web-site is: www.scan.org.uk. These finding aids will summarise the nature and content of each collection and show whether more detailed catalogues are available and in what form they can be consulted. The archives contributing to the network include all Scottish university archives, most local council and health board archives, and many specialist repositories. Details concerning surveys on private archives carried out by the National Register of Archives (Scotland) will also be incorporated. The web-site is *www.nas.gov.uk/reckeep/NRAS.asp*
When planning to visit a local council or specialised archive, it is wise to contact the archivist in advance. Not all archives (Stirling, for example) are open every day and in some there is limited space for researchers. The scope of material held, amount of help given, ease of access to records and premises themselves will, however, vary from place to place. Some provide facilities for photocopying, a user friendly cataloguing system and a café in the building. In others, archivists are struggling with inadequate storage space, understaffing and old premises. A great many of the archivists compensate for any such problems with their compendious knowledge of the district and its records and their willingness to help researchers.

University Archives
Many of the Scottish Universities have extensive holdings of primary material which may include papers of local families, estates and firms and large photographic collections, as well as records relating to the university itself and its students. For an outline description of university archives, consult *Exploring Scottish History* (Cox). A number of Scottish Universities are participating in the SCAN project and their entries will be cross-referenced to the descriptions of holdings on their individual web-sites. Another web-site dealing with the holdings of British universities is Archives Hub at www.archiveshub.ac.uk. Some of the university holdings include specialised collections. The University of Glasgow Business Records Centre is especially valuable in having a large collection of records of businesses of various kinds.

Specialist Archives and Museums
A number of organisations and professional bodies have archives – such as the Royal College of Physicians, Regimental Museums or the Royal Highland and Agricultural Society of Scotland - to mention just a few. As well as documentary evidence, artefacts, old agricultural machinery, presentations showing how people lived in the past displayed in local or specialised museums often add an extra dimension to family history. A wide range of both specialised archives and museums are mentioned in *Exploring Scottish History*.

Libraries
Local libraries often have very useful collections of regional books, town directories and copies of old newspapers, some of which may have been indexed. Small collections of primary material and photographic material may also be held there. The local knowledge of a librarian can be invaluable in pointing a researcher in the right direction. The telephone directory for the area will list both the local council library headquarters and also the branch libraries. For newspapers, *Directory of Scottish Newspapers* compiled by Joan P.S.Ferguson is invaluable in providing information about local newspapers, when they started publication and where runs of the paper are held in Scotland.

Family History Centres and Societies
Many family history centres and societies have premises which hold material of value to researchers – transcripts of monumental inscriptions, collections of published and unpublished genealogical works and reference books, as well as microfilm copies of parish registers, copies of the International Genealogical Index, and fiche indexes to census returns. Some of these centres make a small charge for non-members. Not all are open every day and it is well to check on this. Like the local libraries, these societies will provide opportunities for sharing local knowledge.

Rosemary Bigwood is a lecturer, researcher and genealogist, specialising in older Scottish records. Her handbook *Tracing Scottish Ancestors,* first published by Harper Collins in 1999, has been updated and republished in 2001. It provides detailed guidance on a wide range of sources, how to locate and use them. The book is available in the UK, America, Australia and New Zealand.

General Register Office for Scotland

Registration of births, deaths and marriages in Scotland

Registration of baptisms and proclamations of marriage was first enacted in Scotland by a Council of the Scottish clergy in 1551. The earliest recorded event - a baptism of 27 December 1553 - can be found in the register of baptisms and banns for Errol in Perthshire. Following the Reformation registration of births, deaths and marriages became the responsibility of the ministers and session clerks of the Church of Scotland. Standards of record-keeping varied greatly from parish to parish, however, and even from year to year. This together with evidence of the deterioration and loss of register volumes through neglect led to calls for the introduction of a compulsory and comprehensive civil registration system for Scotland. This came into being on 1 January 1855 with the establishment of the General Register Office for Scotland headed by the Registrar General and the setting up of 1027 registration districts. In 2004 registration districts numbered 231.

Records in the custody of the Registrar General

The main series of vital events records of interest to genealogists are held by the Registrar General at New Register House in Edinburgh. They are as follows:

Old Parish Registers (1553-1854): the 3500 surviving register volumes (the OPRs) compiled by the Church of Scotland session clerks were transferred to the custody of the Registrar General after 1855. They record the births and baptisms; proclamations of banns and marriages; and deaths and burials in some 900 Scottish parishes. They are far from complete, however, and most entries contain relatively little information. Microfilm copies of these records are available world-wide and there are computerised and microfiche indexes to baptisms and marriages. A project to index the death and burial entries got under way in 1997 and is still ongoing.

Register of neglected entries (1801-1854): this register was compiled by the Registrar General and consists of births, deaths and marriages proved to have occurred in Scotland between 1801 and 1854 but which had not been recorded in the OPRs. These entries are included in the all-Scotland computerised indexes.

Statutory registers of births, deaths and marriages (from 1855): these registers are compiled by district registrars. They are despatched by the district examiners to New Register House at the end of each calendar year. Microfiche and digital image copies of the register pages are then made available in the New Register House search rooms.

Adopted children register (from 1930): persons adopted under orders made by the Scottish courts. The earliest entry is for a birth in October 1909.

Register of divorces (from 1984): records the names of the parties, the date and place of marriage, the date and place of divorce and details of any order made by the court regarding financial provision or custody of children. Prior to May 1984 a divorce would be recorded in the RCE (formerly the Register of Corrected Entries, now the Register of Corrections Etc), and a cross-reference would be added to the marriage entry.

Births, deaths and marriages occurring outside Scotland (The Minor Records): these relate to persons who are or were usually resident in Scotland.
  Marine Register of Births and Deaths (from 1855)
  Air Register (from 1948)

GENERAL REGISTER OFFICE FOR SCOTLAND
New Register House
Edinburgh EH1 3YT
Scotland, UK
Tel: 0131 334 0380
Fax: 0131 314 4400

Email: records@gro-scotland.gov.uk

New Register House is at the east end of Edinburgh's Princes Street, directly opposite the Balmoral Hotel, a few minutes' walk from the main Waverley railway station, the bus station and the airport bus stop. There is no space for car parking or for baggage storage. If informed in advance we can make arrangements for customers with disabilities.

Opening hours:- 09:00 to 16:30 Mondays to Fridays (except some Scottish public holidays)
We have 100 places available for self-service searching. Booking is free but there is a statutory fee for access.
For further information please phone 0131 314 4433.
If you would like us to search in our records for a specific event and sell you an extract (an officially certified copy of an entry) please post or fax details to the above address. A 24-hour priority service is available.
To find out more about our records and services see our Web-site at
http://www.gro-scotland.gov.uk

Service Records (from 1881)
War Registers for the Boer War (1899-1902) and the two
World Wars
Consular returns (from 1914)
High Commissioners' returns (from 1964)
Foreign Marriages (from 1947)
Register of births, deaths and marriages in foreign
countries (1860-1965)

Census records (from 1841): these are the
enumerators' transcript books of the decennial census
of the population of Scotland. They record the name,
age, marital state, occupation and birthplace of every
member of a household present on census night.
Census records are closed for 100 years and only the
schedules for the 1841 to 1901 censuses are open to
the public.

To discover more details about the history of these
records please see GROS's publication "Jock
Tamson's Bairns: a history of the records of the
General Register Office for Scotland" by Cecil
Sinclair, ISBN 1 874451 591, 52 pages, cost GBP5.00
(USD8.00). See http://www.gro-scotland.gov.uk for
details of how to order.

Searching at New Register House
New Register House was opened in 1861 as a
purpose-built repository for Scotland's civil
registration records. Today it provides 100 search
places and is open to the public from 09:00 to 16:30,
Monday to Friday. Access to the indexes requires
payment of a statutory fee which also allows self-
service access to digital and microform copies of all
the open records. The fee can be for a day, part-day

(after 13:00 hours), a week, four weeks, a quarter or a
year. There are discount arrangements and a limited
number of seats can be booked in advance. There is
also provision for group evening visits.

Indexes to the statutory records (including overseas
events), OPR baptism and marriage entries, and the
1881, 1891 and 1901 census records are available on
computer, and most of these entries are now linked to
digital images created as part of the DIGROS
(Digitally Imaging the Genealogical Records of
Scotland's people) project. For records not yet in
digital form, there is self-service access to the
statutory register pages on microfiche and the OPR
and Census records on roll microfilm. It is also
possible to order official extracts of any entry.

Online Access to the New Register House Indexes
The all-Scotland computerised indexes and images
can also be accessed from local registration offices
which have links to the New Register House system.
Some local registration offices provide search room
facilities with access to microfiche copies of the
statutory registers for their area. The Family Records
Centre in London has also been provided with online
access (the "Scotlink"); while the indexes and images
to birth records over 100 years old, marriage records
over 75 years old and death records over 50 years old
have been made available for searching over the
Internet on the pay-per-view website
ScotlandsPeople. To find out more see the GROS
website at **http://www.gro-scotland.gov.uk**.
Pay-per-view search website is
http://www.scotlandspeople.gov.uk

Census Enumerators' Instructions.
David Webster

Introduction
Ever since I became seriously interested in genealogy
and family history what has particularly fascinated
me has been the benefit, I'd argue necessity, of
understanding records not just from the point of view
of superficial interpretation but also beyond that in
terms of understanding the "Why?" and the "How?"
in relation to various records. Quite often such an in-
depth understanding can lead to a different
perspective on the records in question, not least in
terms of a much better understanding of the possible
misunderstandings and errors on the part of the
informant or the enumerator or registrar.

This is why I'm the proud possessor (not owner, - it's
on long term loan) of a copy of the 1907 edition of
Bisset-Smith's thick book of instructions to Scottish
registrars, - "*Regulaioins for the Duties of Registrars
of Births, Deaths and Marriages.......*". For a busy
city district in the middle of Glasgow with well over
a 1,000 births and deaths in a year, not a reference
work that the registrar might have to refer to that
often, but imagine the position of the part-time
registrar in a remote, rural registration district with
perhaps only 15 births and deaths in the whole year.

The possession of such books, however, can have its
drawbacks. On my first trip to Salt Lake City a few
years ago, the American sitting next to me on the
flight from Glasgow probably still thinks back to that
lunatic they sat beside, as I broke out into
uncontrollable laughter on several occasions. One
such arose from Bissett-Smith's information on
illegitimacy.
Scottish law has always been and still is
fundamentally different from the system of law in
England. One aspect of this relates (perhaps more
correctly "related") to the treatment of illegitimacy. It
has always been the case in Scotland, with one
caveat, that the subsequent marriage of the parents
automatically legitimated any children born to the
couple before their marriage, and treated by the
registration system as illegitimate when registered.
The caveat is that that the parents must have been free
to marry at the time of the birth(s). If they were not
free to marry then the child is known in Scots law as
an "adulterine bastard". Now it's bad enough being a
bastard, but an adulterine bastard!!

Before we return to the main subject of this article, let

me appeal to readers for any information on example registration pages that were supplied to registrars. I've seen a few of these in LDS microfilms in Salt Lake City (LDS/GSU policy is always to film everything in a source), but didn't have enough time to carry out a systematic search for all the examples that there obviously were for births, deaths and marriages while I was there, and no-one in Scotland, even at the highest levels in GROS has been able to solve the problem for me in terms of the extant Scottish registers. From the few that I have seen, the intention was to provide registrars with an example of every single situation that they were ever likely to come across.

Censuses

Although censuses began in England, Wales and Scotland in 1801 the first four censuses recorded only the name of the head of the household, and the number of people in the household; and, in any case, all that survives apart from a few rare fragments is the statistical summaries, since the detailed returns were destroyed after the statistics had been calculated. Full government censuses were taken of the whole of Ireland in 1813, 1821, 1831, 1841, 1851, 1861, 1871, 1881, 1891, 1901, and 1911. The first five, for 1813, 1821, 1831, 1841, and 1851, were largely destroyed in 1922, in the fire at the Public Record Office in

Dublin; surviving fragments are detailed under the county source-lists. Those for 1861 and 1871 were destroyed after use, and those for 1881 and 1891 were completely destroyed during WWI, by order of the government; as was a 1926 census of Northern Ireland.

The Census Process

The schedule was left with the head of the household by the enumerator at some point in the few days leading up to census night, always a Sunday, filled in by the head and then collected some time after census night, normally the following day. Where necessary, the enumerator would assist with the completion of the schedule; this might not simply involve illiteracy, but unfamiliarity with such a form. It is believed, but I know of no proof, that many early census schedules were completed by children on the basis of instructions from their parents.

In Scotland the enumerator was most often the minister, the session clerk, the local headmaster, or the registrar himself, especially in the smaller, more remote rural parishes. In the larger, city parishes, others would have been required as well to act as enumerators.

In England, Wales and Scotland, the enumerator then transcribed the information from the individual

household schedules into the enumeration books with which we are familiar today.

After the necessary statistical information had been extracted by a team of clerks, the original household schedules were destroyed, except in Ireland for the 1901 and 1911 censuses, where the household schedules survive.

Obviously a very accurate process? Not always, as evidenced by a situation that Barney Tyrwhitt-Drake came across in two neighbouring enumeration districts in London (see his article in Computers in Genealogy a few years ago, - Vol.7, No.9, March/June 2002, p402) where confusion over the boundaries of two enumeration districts led to one street being covered by both enumerators. The resultant significant serious error, or should I write difference, rate is frighteningly high.

I've always hoped to come across a similar situation in a Scottish census, but the closest I've come to date is in a Glasgow enumeration district where it appears that the enumerator made a first draft of his transcription from the individual household schedules before making a fair copy after scoring out the draft, - perhaps he thought that he could be issued with

another enumeration book and was told by the registrar that he had to use the one with which he had been issued, - hence the scoring out of the draft transcription. Fortunately GSU/LDS standard practice is to photocopy everything in a source, regardless of whether or not it has, as in this case, subsequently been scored out. In the 16 or 17 pages that are duplicated there are only one or two significant differences, but quite a few smaller differences, such as the inclusion in the draft of a middle initial, but omission in the fair copy, and so on.

This brings me, finally!, to the aim of this article, in line with my belief in the value of understanding how records were made, which is to repeat the actual instructions given to the enumerators; in this case for the 1841 census. I've chosen this over the later censuses, for which the instructions are essentially the same but longer, as 1841 is interesting in terms of the different manner of recording the ages of adults, and the place of birth. Note also the instruction on how to delineate families within a household, and one household from another with the use of "/" and "//".

1841 Enumerator's Instructions

Respecting the manner in which Entries may be made in the Enumeration Schedule.

After "City or Borough of" write the name, if the District is in a City or Borough: if not, draw a line through those words, or through whichever of the two the District does not belong to. After "parish or Township of" write the name; if there is not Township in the Parish, draw a line through "Township:" if it is a Township, write the name of the Township and draw a line through "Parish". If it is Extra-parochial, draw a line through "parish or Township of," and write "Extra-Parochial" over those words, and after it the name.

In the column headed "Place," write the name of the house (if it has a name), or of the street or other part of the town, or of the village, hamlet, or extra-parochial place in which it stands, opposite to the mark denoting each house, or the first house in the street, etc, and write "do" opposite to every other in the same street, etc.

"Houses." Insert houses uninhabited or building in the manner shown in the Example, writing "1U" or "1B," as the case may be, in the proper column, opposite to the inhabited house to which each stands nearest. Every house which is unoccupied at the time of your visit and is believed not to have been slept in the night before, may be inserted as uninhabited. New houses, not yet inhabited, may be inserted as "Building." Where there is a row of such houses the total number may be inserted before the letter "B" instead of the separate insertion of each.

By "House" is meant Dwelling-House; and every building in which any person habitually sleeps must be considered a s dwelling-house; but buildings, such as churches or warehouses, or any others, which were never used or intended to be used as dwelling-houses, must not be inserted.

"Names of each Person who abode therein the preceding night." Insert, without distinction or omission, every

living person who abode or slept in each house. Leave no blank spaces between the names, but enter each immediately after the one preceding it, so that each page may contain 25. Set down one after the other those who have the same surname, beginning with the heads of the family, and put no others between them. As long as the surname is the same do not repeat it, but write "do." Where there are more Christian names than one, as in "John William," or "Maria Louisa," write down only the first.

When the person is a Peer or Peeress, the title may be written instead of the name. The words "Lord," "Lady," "Sir," "Rt Hon." "Hon," may be put before the names of those to whom they belong.

If no Christian name has been given to an infant write "n.k." for not known, as in the Example.

If, as may happen in a lodging-house or inn, a person who slept there the night before, has gone away early and the name is not known, write "n.k." where the name should have been.

At the end of the names of each family draw a line thus "/" as in the Example. At the end of the names of the inmates in each house draw a double line thus "//".

"Age and Sex." Write the age of each person opposite to the name in one of the two columns headed "Males" and "Females," according to the sex.

Write the age of every person under 15 years of age as it is stated to you. For persons aged 15 years and upwards, write the lowest of the term of 5 years within which the age is.
Thus - for Persons aged
15 years and under 20 write 15
20 years and under 25 write 20
25 years and under 30 write 25
30 years and under 35 write 30

35 years and under 40 write 35
40 years and under 45 write 40
45 years and under 50 write 45
50 years and under 55 write 50
55 years and under 60 write 55
60 years and under 65 write 60
65 years and under 70 write 65
70 years and under 75 write 70
and so on up to the greatest ages.

"Profession, Trade, Employment, or of Independent Means." Men, or widows, or single women, having no profession or calling, but living on their means, may be inserted as independent, which may be written shortly, thus "Ind."

The profession, etc, of wives, or of sons or daughters living with their husbands or parents, and assisting them, but not apprenticed or receiving wages, need not be set down.

All persons serving in Her Majesty's Land service as officers or privates in the Line, Cavalry, Engineers, or Artillery, may be entered as "Army," without any statement of their rank, adding "H.P." for Half-pay, and "P" for Pensioner.

All persons belonging to Her Majesty's Sea service, including Marines, may be entered as "Navy." Adding "H.P." for Half-Pay, and "P" for Pensioner.

All domestic servants may be entered as "M.S." for Male Servant, or "F.S." for Female Servant, without statement of their particular duties, as whether butler, groom, gardener, housekeeper, cook, etc, etc.

Insert all other professions, trades, or employments, as they are described by the parties, or by others on their

behalf, writing "J." for Journeyman, "Ap." for Apprentice, and "Sh" for Shopman, after a statement of the trade of those who are such. "Master" need not be inserted; everyone one will be so considered who is not entered as journeyman or apprentice.

Time may be saved by writing the following words, shortly thus, "M." for Manufacturer, "m." for Maker, as "shoem." For Shoemaker, "Cl." for Clerk, "Ag Lab." for Agricultural labourer, which may include all farming servants and labourers in husbandry. Use no other marks or abbreviations but those herein allowed.

Rank, or any such terms as "Esq." or "Gentleman" must not be entered in this column.

"Where born - Whether in the same County" Write opposite to each name except those of Irish, Scotch, or Foreigners,) "Y." or "N." for Yes or No, as they case may be.

Whether in Scotland, Ireland, or Foreign parts. Write in this column, "S." for those who were born in Scotland; "I." for those born in Ireland; and "F." for Foreigners. This latter mark is to be used only for those who are subjects of some Foreign State, and not for British subjects who happen to have been born abroad.

Enter the Totals at the bottom of each page as in the Example, and enter and add up all the Totals in the summary on the last page. This may be done at home, and must be written with ink.

The entries in the pages of the Enumeration Schedule (except the Totals) may be written with a pencil, which will be furnished for that purpose. All that is written in the 3 pages following them must be with ink.

An Irrestible Sense of Duty
Alastair Dinsmor

James Straiton
1946

For thirty years, James Straiton had been a policeman. Born in Stirling in 1884, he worked on the railways before joining the Lanarkshire Constabulary on 4 May 1903.
He was posted to Tollcross just beyond the Glasgow city boundary and when Glasgow annexed the area in 1912, Constable Straiton was absorbed into the Eastern Division of the City of Glasgow Police. In 1923 he was appointed to the Criminal Investigation Department and reached the rank of Detective Sergeant in 1925, having been commended by the Chief Constable on ten occasions. He retired from the police in 1934 at the age of fifty.

After his retiral, James worked as an investigator for a furniture company, but his period of retiral had been particularly poignant as one of his sons had been killed in Libya during the Second World War. He was pleased when his other son followed in his footsteps into the police. James lived with his wife in a semi-detached house at 528 Edinburgh Road, Carntyne, on the East Side of Glasgow and was well known and respected in the area. He had not been in good health with heart trouble during the month of February 1946.

At about 8.30pm on the evening of Tuesday 26 March 1946, the couple who lived just two houses away from the Straitons, Mr. and Mrs. Deaken, got off a 'bus on Edinburgh Road, just opposite their house at No. 524. As they crossed the road, James Deaken asked his wife Annie if she had left the light on in their house when they left earlier that evening. When she said that she had not left the light on, they realised that someone had been in their house during their absence. Mr. Deaken told his wife to go to No. 528 and ask Mr. Straiton to help them, knowing that he had been a policeman.

When Mrs. Deaken came to his door and explained their suspicions, James Straiton did not hesitate. He knew what he had to do and did not flinch, despite his deteriorating health. His wife was at the cinema and he was alone in his house at the time. He fetched his old police baton and went immediately to help his neighbour.

In the meantime, James Deaken had tried his key in his front door lock, but it would not open, confirming his earlier suspicions that the house had been broken into. At that point, Straiton arrived to assist him and Mr. Deaken suggested that he would climb in one of the rear windows and open the door from the inside, while Straiton covered the front.

James Deaken entered by the rear window, switched on the downstairs light and opened the front door. He heard a noise upstairs and on looking up, saw two men at the top of the stairs. Instantly, the men ran down the stairs towards the front door and to his horror Deaken saw that one of the men was carrying two pistols, one in each hand.

As they reached the door, Mr. Deaken tried to block the door, but the armed intruder fired a pistol at him, narrowly missing him. As Deaken and Straiton moved towards the man who had fired, the other burglar ran past. There was a violent struggle and the armed intruder was struck on the forehead by the police baton wielded by Straiton. The blow knocked the intruder to his knees, but as he did so, he fired one of the pistols and the bullet struck the retired detective in the stomach. Both intruders then ran off, leaving Straiton lying, dying, in the garden, but not before firing another shot at Annie Deaken who was by the garden gate. She was uninjured.

It was not until after ten o'clock that same evening

524 Edinburgh Road

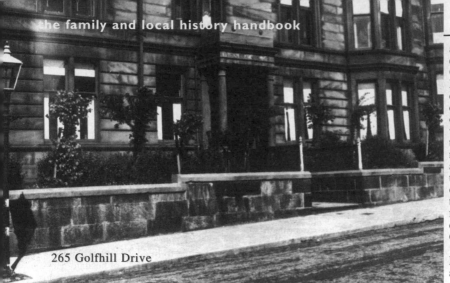

265 Golfhill Drive

a lack of forensic evidence, the Modus Operandi index of the Identification Bureau could be searched for criminals between the ages of twenty and twenty-five who had previously used the method of climbing a rone-pipe before breaking an upper window during their crimes. Fingerprints of those so identified could then be compared to a fingerprint left at the scene of the housebreaking in Golfhill Drive.

It seemed a daunting task and, as it was a Sunday, only a skeleton staff was on duty. A total of 450 criminals were selected from the index and the painstaking comparison of their fingerprints began what they thought would be an endless task. After just ten minutes had elapsed, Detective Constable Douglas Hamilton paused, then checked and re-checked a fingerprint card with the Golfhill Drive print…they were identical! The information was passed to Detective Chief Superintendent Ewing.

The thumbprint belonged to John Caldwell, a twenty-year-old absentee soldier, who lived in Fielden Street, Bridgeton, Glasgow. He was arrested at 2 o'clock on the morning of 1 April 1946, by Detective Lieutenant Robert Colquhoun, head of the Eastern Division C.I.D., together with Detective Lieutenant Dow and Detective Inspector McCartney.

that Mrs. Straiton returned from the cinema and saw a large crowd outside her house. She broke down in disbelief when told of her husband's murder, as she had been worried about his heart condition.

Chief Superintendent William Ewing, the head of Glasgow's C.I.D., was on the scene without delay and his men interviewed the witnesses, obtaining detailed descriptions of the two intruders who had brutally murdered the former policeman. Circulation of the men's descriptions also included Glasgow's hospitals as it was felt that the young man struck by the police baton might seek medical attention.

A search of the garden revealed that the burglars had entered the house by climbing a rone pipe and one of them had removed his shoes to allow him to climb. The shoes, three spent .45 cartridge cases from a semi-automatic pistol and other articles were taken away for forensic examination.

Despite the activity of scores of detectives working night and day on the case, five days went by without any positive evidence, which might lead to the identity of the murderer.

During their enquiries, the detectives had become aware of distinctive similarities in three housebreakings that had occurred in the East-end of the City where the rone pipe method of entry had been used and, crucially, a pistol had been involved. They were:

1. 18 March 1946 - 2 Whitehill Street - Jewelry stolen and pistol fired at lock of lock fast interior door;
2. 25 March 1946 - 265 Golfhill Drive - Jewelry stolen and pistol pointed at the householder who returned to find intruder in her house;
3. 26 March 1946 – 524 Edinburgh Road – Small household items stolen and pistol used to murder James Straiton, to evade arrest.

Detective Superintendent Gilbert McIlwrick, Head of the Identification Bureau suggested another method, which could be employed to increase the possibility of identifying the culprit. He suggested that as there was

Det Supt Gilbert McIlwrick

Following Caldwell's arrest, the detectives also arrested a youth of 15 years who was charged with acting along with Caldwell in the housebreakings and subsequent murder of Mr. Straiton. Both young men were taken to the Eastern Police Office in Tobago Street, Glasgow, where, later that morning, they appeared separately at the Eastern Police Court and were remanded in custody. Caldwell's father James, aged 57, also appeared at the Court on charges relating to receiving large quantities of clothing and jewelry from the housebreakings.

The trial of John Caldwell at Glasgow High Court took place in June 1946, and the public galleries were filled with spectators every day. The 15 year old youth who had been charged with Caldwell had previously been found to be mentally ill and committed to Lennox Castle Certified Institution, Lennoxtown, Stirlingshire. Caldwell stood alone to face the capital charges, which he denied.

The fingerprint evidence coupled with the ballistic evidence were the key to the case and fingerprint, forensic and ballistic experts were on hand to give the crucial evidence for the prosecution. The eminent Professor John Glaister, Regius Professor of Forensic Medicine at Glasgow University, had examined James

Det Lieutenant
Robert Colquhoun

Straiton's body. He found that he had died from massive haemorrhaging due to the fatal bullet, fired at a distance of between three to eight inches (7.5 - 20cm), penetrating his jacket and the waistband of his trousers.

Dr. Scott of Barlinnie Prison in his evidence, stated that he had observed Caldwell extensively and concluded that there was no evidence of insanity, but he was not 'normal'. He said that he was more likely to be rash in his actions than a normal person was and not likely to have feelings of remorse for the consequences. He was also, in an emotional sense, below the normal standard and that there was insanity in his family. Mr. Gordon Thomson, K.C., the defence counsel, seized on this evidence and drew a conclusion from Dr. Scott that the blow to the head by Straiton's baton could have produced a reaction from Caldwell different to a normal person. This ignored the obvious fact that Caldwell had fired the pistol at Mr. Deaken before he was struck on the head by Straiton, thereby indicating his intention to kill to escape if necessary, an observation which was clear for all to see.

In his concluding presentation to the fifteen jurors, Mr. Douglas Johnston, Advocate-Depute, appearing for the prosecution, said that "seldom in this court, where there have been many similar trials, could there have been such an overwhelming body of evidence against an accused person". In conclusion, he told them to "steel their hearts and do their duty as citizens of Glasgow and return a verdict that the accused is guilty".

The defence counsel, Mr. Thomson, in his concluding presentation asked the jury to consider the medical evidence that had been placed before them and accept that Caldwell was acting under 'dimished responsibility' when he committed the crimes.

The Jury was not long in their deliberations and returned a majority verdict of 'Guilty' to all charges, although they did add a recommendation for mercy. Notwithstanding the recommendation of the Jury, the trial judge produced the dreaded black cap and placed it briefly over his judicial wig while he passed the sentence of death on John Caldwell. A subsequent appeal for mercy was dismissed by the Criminal Appeal Court in Edinburgh on 23 July 1946.

At two minutes past eight on Saturday, 10 August 1946, John Caldwell was executed at Barlinnie Prison. When the Notice of Execution was posted to the prison door by the Deputy Governor, Mr. A. E. Edwards, only seven men and one woman turned up to read the notice, then walk quickly away.

Caldwell's Shoes found behind
524 Edinburgh Road

As is the case with executions, evidence of the execution was given before Sheriff Berry at Glasgow Sheriff Court by Bailie Scott Adamson, who said that Caldwell had declined to say anything before the sentence was carried out. Dr. Scott, who had given evidence as to the medical condition of Caldwell at his trial, also gave evidence of his examination of the body before it was buried in the grounds of the prison.

Throughout the investigation and subsequent trial, one thing that stood out above all the forensic and ballistic evidence given was the courage and sense of duty that James Straiton had displayed on the fateful night. Here was a man in his early sixties, in questionable health, who had 'done his bit' over a period of thirty years in the police being asked to 'stand up and be counted' one more time to assist a neighbour. He could have shrunk back from the challenge and 'hid behind his pension', but he was not that kind of man and had not been that kind of policeman. It was the policeman's sense of duty that James Straiton found irresistible and he paid for it with his life.

This story, and other interesting material can be seen at the new Glasgow Police Museum, 68 St. Andrew's Square, Glasgow. The Museum is open 7 days (Monday to Saturday 10am - 4.30pm : Sundays 12noon – 4.30pm). Admission is free.

You can also read more of the people, the stories and the history of Glasgow Police by visiting:
The Glasgow Police Heritage Society website :
www.policemuseum.org.uk

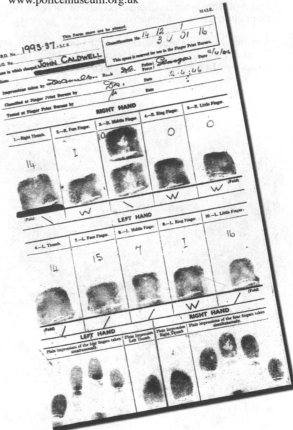

Caldwell's Fingerprints signed by DC Hamilton

The Origin of Christianity in Scotland and The Catholic Church
David Webster

Introduction

Only recently I realised that some North American researchers lack even an elementary, never mind a proper understanding, of the history of the church in Scotland. In one particular example there was the belief that Scotland was still a purely Catholic country, and in yet another, Antipodean example, that the many Presbyterian secession churches were no more than closely associated "branches" of the Established Church of Scotland, instead of the correct situation, - completely separate and independent Presbyterian churches, although liturgically close or very close to the Established Church of Scotland in terms of the wide range of Christian beliefs across different churches.

A proper appreciation of the situation is very likely to assist the researcher in terms of understanding better the possibility of extant records, their likely content and location. Given the important part that the church played in everyday life, such an understanding will also allow researchers to understand better the daily life of their ancestors.

This short article deals with the origin of Christianity in Scotland, and Catholic Church records. It does not deal with Presbyterian Church records, or those of other churches, e.g. Methodist.

Anyone wanting a much more detailed treatment of Scottish Catholic records is referred to the 3 excellent books by Michael Gandy, - see end of this article for details.

History

The Celtic history of Scotland is full of fable, and was a battlefield of Romanists and Protestants, Episcopalians and Presbyterians, who have claimed it for their respective systems of doctrine and church-politics, never mind the sectarian issues of the Culdean controversy.

In 325 AD, Christianity was proclaimed the official religion of the Roman Empire by Emperor Constantine the Great.

Christianity then came to Scotland in the late 4th century when St Ninian established the monastery known as Candida Casa at Whithorn in Wigtownshire in 397.

If a Scotsman, St Patrick, was responsible for establishing the Christian Church once and for all in Ireland, it was an Irishman who returned the favour for Scotland. St Columba was born in Donegal in 521 and was ordained at the age of 30. He continued where St Patrick had left off in Ireland, and founded several religious establishments in his home country. In 563, he sailed east with 12 disciples and settled on the island of Iona, where he built a church and monastery.

By now, Ninian's early Christian influence in what would later become Scotland had all but disappeared and it was Columba who took it upon himself to re-establish Christianity here.

His missionary work took him eventually to Inverness, the Pictish capital of King Brude, where, after winning a miracle working contest with the local pagan priests, Columba convinced Brude that his was the true religion. Brude duly converted to Christianity, and his Pictish subjects dutifully followed suit.

Better known to posterity by his nickname of Mungo ("dear friend"),

Kentigern is the patron saint of Glasgow and laid the foundations for the great cathedral that stands there today. St Mungo brought Christianity to this area in the latter part of the 6th century.

It's important to understand that Christianity came to Scotland from Ireland and from Southern Europe, possibly through links that had existed for centuries with the Iberian Peninsula, and beyond that, North Africa. As a result the usages of the Celtic Church differed in significant details from those of Rome, introduced in the south of Britain by St. Augustine. Conflict between the two was settled in favour of Roman usage at the Synod of Whitby in 663, but Scottish Christianity only slowly adopted the Roman forms over the next few centuries.

In a paper delivered to an ecclesiastical society entitled "Church life in the time of St. Blane" by J. Hutchison Cockburn, a former Minister of Dunblane Cathedral, Scotland, the author observes: "The Celtic Church in Ireland and in Scotland owed its origin not to Rome, but to Egypt and the East; its customs, traditions, methods, government came from Egypt through Athanasius of Alexandria, Hilary, Martin of Tours, Ninian, and through that religious channel, more than a little independent of Rome. The religious ideas of Egypt came to Scotland and Ireland and were absorbed easily into the tribal life of these countries. There is no doubt that the Celtic Church owed its ritual, its architecture, its worship and its law to Syria, Egypt and Palestine, and that its allegiance to Rome was slight." Anyone wanting to research this further should have a look at material on the Culdees, and the Chaldean churches that still are very active in the Middle East.

One consequence of this is that the Church in Scotland was monastic rather than diocesan in the beginning.

The impact of monasticism on Scotland was profound and long lasting. The arrival of the monks brought a whole new conception of society to its pagan tribes - ideas of a Christian community, education and the responsibilities of leadership and government that still under-pin Scottish society today. Along with Scotland's warrior kings, they shaped the very idea of the Scottish nation.

A genealogically significant consequence of this is the parish structure, which was adopted as the initial basis for the system of registration districts used for statutory registration and censuses in the1800s.

Originally, the parishes were based on the land ownership of monasteries, abbeys, friaries, etc., and were more often than not far from contiguous. In other words, areas of land owned by one monastery could be some distance away in the middle of land owned by another. Over the succeeding centuries, especially from 1855 onwards, this situation involving detached parts of parishes was rationalised, but there is still one county that is not contiguous as a result, - Dunbartonshire.

Another consequence was the commissary courts, - the pre-Reformation church courts, which survived the Reformation in terms of being the continuing method of administering testaments (wills) up until the first couple of decades of the 19th century when the Sheriff Courts took over. The borders of the areas covered by the commissary courts bear little or no relation to the administrative county structure introduced at that time. This is now of less relevance to researchers due to the introduction of the on-line index and digitised images of over 520,000 Scottish testaments up to 1900 available at scottishdocuments.com. In other words, there is less need to understand the areas covered by the commissary courts.

In effect, around the end of the first millennium, the Scottish church had come fully under the influence of Rome, so that it would be correct only then to call the church in Scotland Catholic.

Over the next few centuries, this lead to the same excesses becoming prevalent as in the rest of Europe, which eventually led to the Reformation.

That there are some records of genealogical significance for this period in the archives of the Vatican, there is no doubt, but little is known about their content.

As for the heads of monasteries and their inmates, there is little evidence to suggest that there was widespread corruption and sinful behaviour within the monastic system or, for that matter, the friaries. Where criticism was certainly justified was in the case of the nunneries, which were universally condemned for their illiteracy and scandalous conduct. For much of the 1540s there are instances of sporadic heretical activities (in the eyes of the Catholic church) in places like Dundee, Perth and their hinterland. The culmination of these was the murder at St Andrews in May 1546 of David Beaton, Archbishop of St

Andrews, at least partly in revenge for the execution of the Protestant George Wishart earlier in the year. Even the accession of Edward VI (1537-53) to the English throne, followed by the introduction of the Protestant faith into England, had little effect on Scotland despite the English strategy of infiltrating translations of the Bible during both the "Rough Wooing" and thereafter.

In fact, Protestantism, apart from certain radical enclaves in Angus, Ayrshire, Fife and the Lothians remained a predominantly underground affair still lacking the catalyst that could make it become a serious threat to the established Church. Where it existed in the 1550s, as the visitations of John Knox (c. 1512-72) in these years confirm, it was no longer Lutheran but Calvinist doctrines that it was supporting.

Finally, in 1560 the Scottish Parliament rejected papal authority, followed by the formation of the Scottish Reformed "Kirk" in 1561. That this date should be regarded as that of the Scottish Reformation is a moot point, but the Scottish Reformed "Kirk" can be regarded as a daughter church of the Reformed Church of Geneva.

John Knox (1514 – 1572) should be considered as important a figure and influential outside Scotland in the Reformation in Europe as Martin Luther (1483 – 1546), Ulrich Zwingli (1484 – 1531), and John Calvin (1509 – 1564).

Up until the early 1800s with the changes in the law with respect to Catholicism, and the large influx of Catholic Irish from famine-struck Ireland, it can be said that Calvinism was practically the only religion in Scotland from the Reformation onwards.

Attempts by Charles I and Charles II to control the Kirk (to use the Scots term) met with protest, including the signing of the National Covenant at

Greyfriars Church in Edinburgh in 1638.

The Modern Catholic Church in Scotland.
After several centuries of repression, officially or otherwise, the Catholic church was able to start operating again in public in the early 1800s, from which time the earliest modern records exist (see Michael Gandy: *Catholic Missions and Registers 1700 – 1880: Vol 6 – Scotland;* published by the author).)
The current diocesan system was set up in 1878. The senior dioceses carried on the work of the former vicariates and regions, inheriting their records. The current parish system did not come into force until after WWI.
While it may be possible to research ancestors in the records of individual parishes and the various diocesan archives (rules for access differ widely between different parishes and diocesan archives), the following is some information on the Scottish Catholic Archives. For much more detailed information, readers are referred to the three Michael Gandy books listed at the end of this article.

The Scottish Catholic Archives
Introduction
The Scottish Catholic Archives is responsible for maintaining the diverse manuscript collections relating to the Catholic Church in Scotland. The main body of the collection dates from before 1878, when the Hierarchy was restored in Scotland, but added to this are the records of the Dioceses of Argyll and the Isles; Dunkeld; St Andrews and Edinburgh; Galloway and Motherwell. The records of the Scots Colleges at home: Blairs, Scalan, Aquhorties; and abroad: Paris, Douai, Madrid and Rome are also a part of their holdings.
The Scottish Catholic Archives does not have sufficient resources to offer a family history research service, however every attempt will be made to answer specific enquires about material in the collections.

Parish Registers at SCA
The Scottish Catholic Archives holds minimal parish registers for certain parts of Scotland. These registers are un-indexed. Researchers are welcome to visit the Archive and conduct their own research. Limited searches can be made of the registers held at Columba House, but requests must be very specific. There is a fee for searches conducted by staff.

The National Archives of Scotland has photocopied all pre-1855 Roman Catholic parish registers and they are to be found in the RH21 series of records. These registers are un-indexed and you must either visit yourself or engage a private researcher to conduct research.

Roman Catholic parish registers are not available on microfilm to purchase nor are they obtainable through LDS Family History Centres.
The Scottish Catholic Archives hold the following types of parish registers:
Baptismal registers will normally provide the child's name, names of parents and sponsors, date of birth, date of baptisms, and the name of the priest administering the Sacrament. They do not provide the

address of the family at the time of the baptism nor do they provide information on place of origin. If a marriage later took place elsewhere, there may the record of the enquiry from that other parish's priest seeking confirmation of details.

Marriage registers will normally provide the names of the bride and groom, the names of the witness(es), and the name of the officiating priest. They will not provide an address at the time of the marriage, nor do they normally provide information about date or place of birth.

Death Registers are not common. Normally they will only give the name and date of death.
Other listings occur for:
Conditional baptisms, conversions and reconciliations
Confirmations
Communicants: Easter duties or first communion
Obituaries
Status animarum (state of souls)
Bona mors (confraternity of a happy death)
School registers
Monumental inscriptions

Post-1855 Parish Registers, i.e. registers with a starting date later than 1855 are normally kept in the parishes. Please note that for searches after 1855, the exact date of birth and marriage should be provided if you make direct contact with the parish priest.
In *Catholic Missions and Registers 1700 – 1880: Vol. 6 – Scotland;* Michael Gandy fully documents the mission and parish records known to exist.

SCA Catalogues
The Scottish Catholic Archives has begun a program of retro-conversion of the manuscript catalogues, which will produce ISAD(G) compliant catalogues and full ISAD(G) identity statements at appropriate levels. The Scottish Catholic Archives is participating in SCAN (Scottish Archives Network), and top level finding aids will be available for searching there in the future.

B/	Bishops	1729-1996
BC/	Blairs Charters	1366-1841
BL/	Blairs Letters	1627-1887
CA/	Colleges Abroad	1544-1964
CB/	Blairs College	1764-1988
CC/	Canon Clapperton	18th cent-20th cent
CG/	Gillis College	1924-1988
CS/	Colleges in Scotland	1722-1899
DA/	Diocese of Argyll & the Isles	1493-1996
DD/	Diocese of Dunkeld	1559-1996
DE/	Diocese of St Andrews & Edinburgh 1846-1998	
DG/	Diocese of Galloway	1847-1995
DM/	Diocese of Motherwell	1837-1987
ED/	Eastern District Vicariate	1713-1986
FA/	Fort Augustus Abbey	1597-1998
FL/	Families and Lands	1406-1851
GC/	Gifted Compilations: Research work by Individuals	
GD/	Gifts and Deposits	
GP/	Photocopies and Transcripts of Original Documents	
HC/	House Collections	
IM/	Individual Mission Stations	1738-1895
JB/	Archbishop James Beaton's Paper 12th -19th cent	
JO/	St John Ogilvie	1615-1673
KA/	Keeper: William James Anderson 1822-1972	

KB/	Keeper: David McRoberts	1926-1983
KC/	Keeper: Rev Mark Dilworth	1882-1995
KJ/	King James VII and II	1633-1701
LIT/	Liturgy	18th -20th cent
LS/	Lectures and Sermons	1675-1890
MC/	St Margaret's Convent, Edinburgh 1809-1984	
MM/	Miscellaneous Manuscripts	13th-19th cent
OL/	Oban Letters [Highland]: Western District Vicariate	1764-1901
P/	Persons	1520-1988
PL/	Preshome Letters: Northern District Vicariate	1641-1933
PP/	Photographs and Plans	
RE/	Religious Education	1799-1985
SK/	Schottenkloester (Scots abbeys in Germany) 1177-late 19th cent	
SM/	Scottish Mission	1560-1959
SmP/	Small Printed Material	
SS/	Synods	1881-1961
TM/	Thomson-McPherson: History of the Scottish Mission [1560-1853]	

Access to SCA
Access is available to those engaged in bona fide research. Academics, research students and undergraduates are welcome as are local and family historians.
Identification is required on a first visit to complete a Reader's Application. A letter of recommendation is not essential, however, it might be necessary to obtain a letter of consent to consult certain material.

It is advisable to contact the Archivist before planning a visit to ensure the material required for study is free from any restrictions.

SCA Location
The Scottish Catholic Archives is located in the historic New Town of Edinburgh. Columba House is located at the west end of Drummond Gardens, on the corner of Drummond Place and Great King Street.
Address: Scottish Catholic Archives, Columba House, 16 Drummond Place, Edinburgh EH3 6PL
Telephone: 0131 556 3661 *Email:* sca@catholic-heritage.net
Web site *www.catholic-heritage.net -*
Opening Hours: Monday to Friday 10 am - 4 pm by appointment

Useful Books
All by Michael Gandy and published by the author, 3 Church Crescent, Whetstone, London N20 0JR.
Catholic Family History: A Bibliography for Scotland. A 47 page (A5) booklet with as comprehensive a listing that I've ever seen of sources for Scottish Catholic family history; worth every penny of the £4.50 that it cost me a few years ago.
Catholic Parishes in England, Wales and Scotland: An Atlas. A 32 page (A5) booklet covering all of England, Wales and Scotland. Although only 7 pages relate to Scotland, an essential source for understanding the province, diocesan, and parish structure.
Catholic Missions and Registers 1700 – 1880: Vol. 6 – Scotland. An essential companion to the bibliography; 50 A5 pages, 40 of which are a detailed parish by parish listing of the extant records, plus a 5 page index.

Scottish "Term Days", Festivals, Dating & the Gregorian Calendar
David Webster

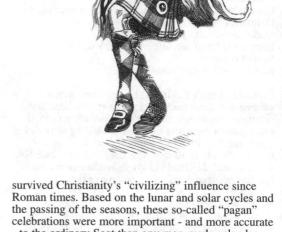

Scottish Term Days

In England, Ireland and Wales the concept of "quarter days" is well known, these being the four days dividing the legal year, - Lady Day – 25th March, Midsummer – 24th June, Michaelmas – 29th September, and Christmas – 25th December.

In Scotland the same principle of dividing the legal year into 4 parts is followed with the Scottish equivalent of the English quarter days being "term days". Term days were when rent and interest on loans were due, when ministers' stipends were due for payment, when servants in town and country were hired and paid, and when contracts and leases often began or ended.

The term days in Scotland were and are Candlemas, Whitsun, Lammas, and Martinmas.
- **Candlemas**, on 2nd February, was originally the date of the feast of the Purification of the Virgin Mary. In pre-Reformation times this was celebrated by candlelit processions.
- **Whitsun** was originally the feast of Pentecost, around which a great many christenings seemed to occur and therefore became associated with the colour white. In Scotland the legal term day was fixed as 26th May Old Style, and then 15th May New Style (see below), irrespective of the day of the week that Whitsun fell on.
- **Lammas** was traditionally a harvest festival on 1st August, at which the first fruits of the harvest were offered. The name derives from the Anglo-Saxon for "loaf-mass" or "bread-feast".
- **Martinmas** was on 11th November. It was originally the feast of Saint Martin of Tours, a 4th century bishop and hermit.

In 1886 the term dates for the removal and hiring of servants in towns were changed to 28th May and 28th November.

Dating

Up to 1600 the year ended in Scotland on 24th March, with the "New Year" beginning on 25th March (the Feast of Annunciation in the Catholic Calendar) but termed the start of Spring by the Presbyterian Church of Scotland. In other words, the year, say 1555/56, ran from 25th March 1555 to 24th March 1556!

While this may come as a surprise to those who associate Scottish New Years with the Hogmanay festival held on January 1, historically the Scots had always celebrated the New Year four days after the Vernal Equinox, on March 21, also known as the beginning of Spring, or Alban Eiler. Anglicized as "Lady Day", the traditional Scottish New Year was just one of many ancient Druid religious practises that survived Christianity's "civilizing" influence since Roman times. Based on the lunar and solar cycles and the passing of the seasons, these so-called "pagan" celebrations were more important - and more accurate - to the ordinary Scot than any man-made calendar could ever claim to be.

That changed in 1600, with that year being the first when New Year's Day was the 1st January.

> ...his Majestie with the advise of the Lordis of his Secreit Counsall statutis and ordanis that in all tyme cuming the first day of the yeir sal begin yeirlie upoun the first day of Januare....
>
> **Register of the Privy Council, 17 December, 1599**

Whether or not this was in conjunction with the change from the Julian Calendar to the Gregorian Calendar is a matter of debate among experts. In many other countries in Europe the Julian/Gregorian change was accompanied by the adjustment of the beginning of the year to 1st January.

Julian and Gregorian Calendars

Classical astronomers calculated that the solar year (i.e. the time taken for the earth to orbit the sun) was 365 days. The Julian calendar (introduced in 45 BC) was based on this calculation, and had a standard year of 365 days, with every fourth year (a 'leap year') having an extra day to take account of the day. The Julian calendar was used throughout Europe until 1582, and in some countries for several years or even centuries further. This method of fixing the date is known as 'Old Style'. In medieval Europe, including Scotland, the beginning of the year was usually 25 March, so that the day after 24 March 1490 was 25 March 1491. Medieval scholars discovered that the year of 365 days was a slight over-estimate, and by the sixteenth century a discrepancy of about 10 days had accumulated between the calendar year and the solar year.

Pope Gregory XIII corrected the error by cutting 10 days from the calendar in 1582 (so that 15 October 1582 followed 4 October 1582), and reformed the calendar to make only the last year of centuries divisible by 400 a leap year, i.e. 2000 was a leap year, but 1900 and 1800 were not. This calendar became known as the 'Gregorian Calendar', and dates calculated by the Gregorian Calendar are often described as "New Style", previous Julian dates being "Old Style", - you may see the date given in the format, for example", "10th Sep 1752 Old Style/22nd Sept New Style".

In addition he decreed that the year should begin on 1st January. However, Pope Gregory's reformation of the calendar was not accepted by most protestant states until the eighteenth century (and the twentieth century in Russia, the Balkans and Greece). The Russian Orthodox Church still calculates the dates of its festivals by the Julian Calendar.

Scotland adopted the change to the start of the year in 1599 (31 December 1599 was followed by 1 January 1600). In the rest of the British Isles the start of the year change did not take place until 1 January 1752, under Chesterfield's Act (24 Geo. II, c.23), which also removed the days (eleven by this time) required to bring the British Isles into the Gregorian New Style (2 September 1752 was followed by 14 September 1752).

Some correspondents in the seventeenth and eighteenth centuries would mark two dates on a letter, e.g. '11/21 March 1651', to take account of the different calendars operating in different parts of Europe. Where it becomes complicated in terms of Scotland is when the Julian/Gregorian change took place, - 1st January 1600, 2nd September 1752, or some date in between, - pick your expert and take your choice !!

What probably happened was that Scotland did change to the Gregorian Calendar in 1600 but then ran a dual calendar system depending on whether or not the matter involved an internal Scottish situation or correspondence, or trading with Catholic Europe, or those confusing people south of the Border in England, a situation not made easier by the Union of Crowns in 1603, - James VI of Scotland becoming also James I of England and moving his court and the centre of power in Scottish terms from Edinburgh to London; and the Union of Parliaments in 1707, when the hitherto, separate Scottish parliament ceased to exist, with the Westminster parliament assuming powers over Scotland – it was supposed to be a "Union" of parliaments, but that's another story! (The Scottish parliament was restored a few years ago, albeit with limited powers).

The tax year in the UK starts on the 6th April! Why ? Because the government year used to start on 25th March, which changed by +11 days in 1752, - by this time the adjustment required was 11 days, - thus becoming 6th April.

And if you think that's complicated, then pity the poor Swedes, - Sweden decided to make a gradual change from the Julian to the Gregorian calendar, presumable thereby hoping to avoid the major civil disturbance, including riots, that there had been in some countries over the "loss" of 10 or 11 days from peoples' lives. By dropping every leap year from 1700 through 1740 the eleven superfluous days would be omitted and from 1 Mar 1740 they would be in synchronisation with the Gregorian calendar. (But in the meantime they would be in sync with nobody!) So 1700 (which should have been a leap year in the Julian calendar) was not a leap year in Sweden. However, by mistake, 1704 and 1708 became leap years. This left Sweden out of synchronisation with both the Julian and the Gregorian world, so they decided to go back to the Julian calendar. In order to do this, they inserted an additional extra day in 1712, making that year a

double leap year! So in 1712, February had 30 days in Sweden. Later, in 1753, Sweden changed to the Gregorian calendar by dropping 11 days like everyone else.

Scottish Festivals

Travel around Scotland and you will come across in most places the remnants of a rich history of "high" days and holidays, and fairs and festivals, holy and otherwise. What remains today, however, is often little appreciated or understood as being the puny modern-day remnant of a year full of such events, national and local, across the whole country.

For centuries there was a calendar of festivals, many based on seasonal events, very often following the course of the Sun. Many of these festivals, such as Beltane, Halloe'en or Samhain were ancient in origin, - Celtic. There were fire festivals, many of which survive, but whose origin is now little understood, to mark the power of the sun to enrich and renew the crops, and to mourn its disappearance.

Yule covered the period including Christmas and New Year and continued up until the date of the old New Year, - January 6th – Twelfth Night, - which was Scandinavian in origin.

Scots absorbed folklore from many cultures, including Celtic, Scandinavian, Roman, and other European countries. Generally, in the West of Scotland, the Celtic influence is strongest, while Norse influence is greatest in the Northeast and especially Orkney and Shetland.

Feriae in Latin means holidays, and applied to festivals held on the feast days of saints. In the 6th century A.D. Pope Gregory sent St Augustine to Britain as a missionary with the instruction to adapt existing, more ancient customs to Christianity. Up to the Reformation these were strictly religious occasions, but thereafter the religious aspect dropped away, although the habit of there being a holiday remained, often with a fair being held, as a place for the buying and selling of goods and animals. Such fairs originally took place in church property but later expanded to the nearby streets and parks. The post-reformation church attempted to force people to abandon the celebration of such saints' days, but the customs were very deeply entrenched, so that most continued.

Other festivals had grown out of the formalities surrounding confirming the extent of a town or village by means of an annual inspection of the boundary. Particularly in the Borders, these survive as Riding of the Marches.

The great majority of festivals

and fairs have disappeared, with quite often only one major particular tradition surviving in any particular town although there is an increasing interest in reviving fairs and festivals as people become more interested in the history of their area. Quite often certain traditions surrounded a festival or a fair, and some of these survive but their origin is now little understood.

Spring and summer festivals involved seeds, greenery, and flowers, while those held later in the year in autumn were most often a celebration of the harvest and sufficient grain, vegetables, meat and dairy products to see people through the winter at least until spring crops and the next main harvest. The main winter festivals most often involved fire, i.e. light, in one way or another, as a reminder, originally the hope, that the disappearing sun would return.

Very many customs that survive to the present day and that have become attached to particular times of the year derive from ancient festivals. These include first footing, guising, the hiding of trinkets, dancing around fires, and bringing greenery indoors to ensure good fortune.

From ancient times it appears that Scotland adopted the particular Norwegian custom of beginning a festival day at sunset on the previous day, and ending it at sunset on the day of the festival.

Back in the late 1700s Sir John Sinclair decided that it would be a good idea to record Scottish society by commissioning an article from the minister of every Established Church of Scotland parish on their parish. It took a few years and many reminders to the dilatory, but this resulted in a quite amazing picture of Scottish society of the time in 1796, - known as the First Statistical Account, - "First", as the New or Second Statistical Account followed the First in 1841. (There has since been a more modern Third Statistical Account

published in 1950.)

While the entries for a very few parishes are short and relatively uninteresting, the great majority of the entries in the many volumes of the First Statistical Account are much longer and quite detailed, and include extensive information on the habits and customs of the locality, including locally celebrated festivals, as well as the manner in which national festivals were particularly celebrated in the parish. Sheila Livingstone's *Scottish Festivals* , Birlinn Edinburgh 1997, ISBN 1 874744 785, and her companion volume, *Scottish Customs*, are well worth their price for anyone looking for further, more detailed information.

The Family and Local History Handbook
Digital Genealogy Section
in association with

A Basic Guide to Computers for Family History.

Graham Hadfield

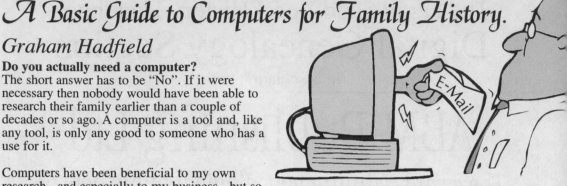

Do you actually need a computer?

The short answer has to be "No". If it were necessary then nobody would have been able to research their family earlier than a couple of decades or so ago. A computer is a tool and, like any tool, is only any good to someone who has a use for it.

Computers have been beneficial to my own research - and especially to my business - but so have conventional mail and interacting with fellow researchers (through membership of a number of family history societies for instance).

What sort of computer?

We've all seen the adverts on TV and in the press for the latest and fastest machines but do we really need all that power? It's always tempting to buy the latest specification, thinking that anything less isn't good enough. It's worth remembering, though, that the world of computers moves so fast that the top specifications of today could well be the budget models of 6 months or a year hence.

At a family history fair in the Autumn of 2001 I met a gentleman who told me that there were two computers in his household. His wife used a fairly new PC but he used an Amstrad word processor, complete with dot matrix printer, which he had purchased around 20 years previously. He found it simple to use and it still did all he demanded of it. That gentleman had absolutely the right attitude. As I wrote previously, computers are tools, and, just like the hammer that feels right in the hand, for each of us the one we are comfortable with is the one we will use.

Of course, that gentleman's requirements were not all that "sophisticated". He had no requirement for colour printing, or for processing of graphics, audio or video files. It is the latter file types (audio and video especially) which demand the higher specifications because they need so much computing power to manipulate them. If, however, your requirements mainly revolve around a family history database program plus a word processor and reasonably simple photo editing then you probably do not need "cutting edge" hardware. I purchased the computer which I currently use in November 2002. It has a 1.7 GHz processor, 40 GB hard disk and 128 MB of RAM. The PC magazines at the time were reviewing machines with 2.8 GHz processor, 80 GB hard disk and 512 MB of

RAM. All I have added to my machine since I bought it are an extra 128 MB of RAM (comparatively cheap and the more memory the better) plus (recently) a second, 120 GB, hard disk (and that simply because of the amount of space taken up by all the books and maps we are scanning).

One thing to bear in mind, if you are buying a computer for family history use, is that the "IBM" PC format is more popular than Mac and, on PC, the Microsoft Windows operating systems are more popular than Linux. The result is that software packages for PC tend to be numerous and more readily available than for Mac or Linux. Having said that, there is a Mac version of Microsoft Office. In fact, you don't even need to pay for an office suite - OpenOffice is a free package which, is compatible with MS Office, and has versions for Windows, Mac and Linux. It's a similar story with specialised genealogy software. For instance, the Generations Family Tree PC package has its "roots" in Reunion, which is still available for the Mac, and the Heredis package is available in versions for both platforms. A Google search for Linux "genealogy software" produced over 7,500 results, including LifeLines which has versions for Windows, Mac and Linux. So, the message is that there is plenty to choose from for the platform which you prefer to work with.

What peripherals are needed?

First and foremost is probably a printer - what goes in will probably need to come out at some time. The choice is basically between laser (if black and white text is all that is required) and inkjet if colour printing (including photographs) is what you want. Many PCs are sold in a "bundle" together with a printer (and, possibly, a scanner and/or digital camera) which can offer value for money. One thing to watch with any printer is the cost of the ink/toner cartridges. There are, of course, compatible cartridges on the market. Very good results can be obtained

with many of them but using compatibles can invalidate the warranty. Some inkjets will read the storage cards used by digital cameras and produce prints without the need for a computer at all. Most printers for home use handle up to A4/Letter size paper but there are a number of A3 printers available now and a few which will print larger formats (though most of these are aimed at commercial usage).

Digital cameras are useful for taking photos both of your modern day relatives and of places where your family lived. The quality has increased dramatically over the last couple of years whilst prices have dropped equally dramatically. Another use for digital cameras is in taking photos of old documents and photographs, though you have to watch out for the effects of parallax. Features to look for are the resolution (expressed as a number of megapixels) and the optical and digital zoom capabilities.

A much better piece of kit for copying old documents and photographs is a flatbed scanner. The range of these on sale is as wide as the ranges of computers and printers. Some take their power from the cable used to attach them to the PC whilst others require a separate power supply. As with printers, most models handle up to A4 size paper though larger ones are available. Scanners are also rated by the resolution (e.g. 4800 x 9600 dpi (dots per inch) though this may be partially "interpolated", i.e. software generated rather than being part of the initial scan, and colour depth (e.g. 48 bit). Some scanners come with an adapter for scanning of film transparencies.

What software is needed?
Sometimes PCs come with big software bundles covering everything from games to garden design. If the software is of use to you then fine - but if you will never use it then its value to the package you are buying has to be questioned. Many PCs will come with "office" packages (e.g. Microsoftt Office, Microsoft Works or Lotus Smartsuite) which contain word processing, spreadsheet and, possibly, database and desktop publishing (DTP) programs. On a all Macs Appleworks is the standard office program. The simplest of these is probably enough for most family historians and a word processor program is probably sufficient if a DTP program is not included - I produced a 60 page illustrated book of my family history research in 1995 using the Ami Pro word processor which was first released in 1988.

Being a family historian you will probably want a specialised family history database program to store your research results and produce reports. There are a number of programs on the market ranging from those which are free to download from the Internet (or sometimes available on the CDs mounted on magazine covers) to programs which cost £50 or more. Some programs are available from high street stores but the largest ranges are stocked by specialist suppliers. In some cases, programs come together with a number of data CDs. As with the software bundles supplied with some PCs the value of these will depend on your area of research. If, for instance, none of your ancestors left the UK then a United States census database will be worthless. On the other hand, if you are looking for a long lost cousin who emigrated, the same database might just contain the answer you are looking for. Like the price range, the reporting capabilities of the different programs varies considerably, as does the "user interface" - the screen that you use to input and update your data. As with the computer itself, the software is a tool and the one to buy is the one which suits you best.

Another type of program which you may require is a photo editor. Most scanners come with programs bundled with them. Many of these are quite sufficient for the needs of most home users but different programs have different capabilities. The two most sophisticated packages for home use are Jasc Paint Shop Pro and the cheaper versions of Adobe Photoshop (e.g. Elements). Photo processing software can also often be found on the cover CDs of magazines devoted to PCs or digital photography - it usually won't be the latest version but provides a reasonably cheap way of trying out a number of options.

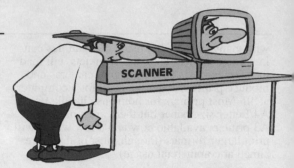

Storing files in a logical structure

Some programs and operating systems have a habit of assuming that they know best where the files created using them should be stored. This is usually within the program's own folder or within a folder such as "My Documents" or "My Pictures". That may be fine if you only use one program or are happy to have all your files together. It's much easier to keep track of your different files if you create your own simple hierarchical structure. An example, of a possible structure if shown by Figure 1. Here we have a folder called "Family History Files". Within that folder there are individual folders for all the different surnames being researched (e.g. "Hadfield", "Platt", "Robinson"). Within the folder for each name are standard folders such as "Census", "Civil Registration", "Correspondence" and so on.

Backup regimes

The frequency with which you back up your files and the medium you choose is up to you. The Golden Rule is **do it**. One of our PCs went wrong last year, so wrong that it had to be replaced by a new one (luckily it was still under warranty). It was inconvenient, having to spend time setting up a new machine, but it was not a disaster as all the data files from that PC were backed up on a CD and could simply be reloaded once the new machine was ready for use. Whilst we were in the shop

collecting the replacement, the salesman told us of a young lady who had visited the shop in similar circumstances the previous week. She had used her PC to store all her "A" level course work - which was all lost when the PC went wrong, merely because she had not taken regular backup copies.

In a home situation a simple regime can probably be implemented, all data files being copied to a CD each week (this is easier if a logical structure for data files has been set up as described above). Off-site backup is often easier to achieve than might be supposed - just take the CDs to work and put them in your locker or desk, or make an arrangement with a friend to look after each other's copies. It is still possible to use floppy disks for backup but many files these days are too large for them. Other options are CD-Rs (re-writable CDs) or zip disks - you pays your money and you makes your choice, but always remember the Golden Rule, **do it**.

We sometimes read of the limited life of floppy disks, CDs and other media. Some of these are scare stories but it would be a very unlucky person taking regular backups to find that all copies had failed. One thing to watch out for, though, is that you always have facilities available to read whatever medium you have used for your backup files. When I bought my first IBM PC I found that I could not transfer the files from an earlier, Amstrad, computer because that machine used a proprietary type of floppy disk. I've not made that mistake again. We have facilities to read 5.25" and 3.5" floppy disks, and 100 MB zip disks plus CDs and DVDs of all current formats.

Using the Internet (and avoiding viruses and spam)

The number of family historians connected to the Internet has grown tremendously over the last few years. Once again, though, the Internet is only a tool. Basically, it is simply another way of getting in touch with people and of accessing information - but remember that much of the information is transcribed and/or interpreted by its maintainers and, as such, needs to be treated in just the same way as similar information in paper form - i.e. check back to the source. A broadband connection is preferable because of

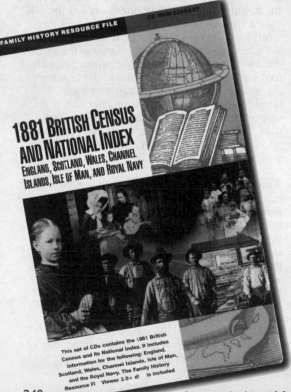

FAMILY HISTORY RESOURCE FILE

CD ROM LIBRARY

1881 BRITISH CENSUS AND NATIONAL INDEX

ENGLAND, SCOTLAND, WALES, CHANNEL ISLANDS, ISLE OF MAN, AND ROYAL NAVY

This set of CDs contains the 1881 British Census and its National Index. It includes information for the following: England, Scotland, Wales, Channel Islands, Isle of Man, and the Royal Navy. The Family History Resource Fi   Viewer 2.0+ d   is included

the faster speed but the type of connection you use will depend on availability in your area and what you can afford. An Internet browser program will probably be built into the operating system but there are alternatives on the market if you prefer something different.

One problem of the Internet is that of viruses. It is important to maintain up to date anti-virus software. There are many programs on the market, some of which are free for home users. It is a must, though, to keep the "virus signatures" up to date. Most programs can be set to do this automatically or to tell you when it needs doing. Another weapon against viruses and invasions by similar rogue programs is to implement a firewall. Users of broadband connections can buy hardware firewalls which sit between the modem and the PC. The alternative (or you can, of course, use both) is a software firewall. Your PC operating system might include a basic firewall but I find it preferable to use a separate package. As with anti-virus programs, some software is free for home users.

You will also need an e-mail program. As with the browser, there will probably be one built into the operating system but there are alternatives available. It is e-mail that brings with it the second problem of the Internet, that of "spam", the electronic version of junk mail. Some e-mail programs are able to be upgraded with plug-ins which reject spam and others have built-in filtering tools which enable you to direct "good" and "bad" messages to appropriate folders.

Data CDs

Data on CD (and now DVD as well) has started to replace microfiche and microfilm in a big way in the last few years. With the advent of more modern scanners and faster CD writers, CDs are easier and cheaper to produce than microfiche and easier to use - not least

because they can be run on the computer you use for other things, rather than having to buy a microfiche/film reader. Some CDs contain scanned images of the pages of books and maps whilst others contain transcripts or indexes created by their publishers. The same caveats as ever apply to transcripts and indexes - and, of course, to scans from a book which is itself a transcript. The main advantage of the CD medium is that it makes rare and expensive items available for a much larger number of people to use at home than would otherwise be possible. Perhaps the most important records available on CD are census records, both images and transcripts. Figure 2 shows examples of these from various suppliers.

Many family history societies and commercial companies have produced transcripts of parish registers and memorial inscriptions. Other types of data in scanned form are Directories, Maps, Histories and Topographical Guides. Even if these publications do not mention your ancestor they are valuable in that they give you the background to the areas and times that they lived in. Once again, there are various suppliers of such publications - Figure 3 shows a few from our own range.

Graham Hadfield spent over 30 years in IT before forming JiGraH Resources with wife, Jill, in September 2001. The company provides computer services for family and local historians including printing of large family trees, photo restoration, data rescue and a growing range of old books and maps on CD.

Easy Access to Records - the cost and benefits of the revolution
David Tippey

The internet is starting to revolutionise the way we can carry out research, as more resources are becoming available online. Companies are now fighting to get a share in what they believe will become a lucrative new market, but not all researchers are totally happy about it, believing that these records should be provided for free.

The first website to seriously upset people was the 1901 census online, whose launch brought many mutterings about having to pay to use the census as access had always been free. After all they belonged to the nation, the argument went, so we should be able to use them at no cost - they are charging us to use 'our records.' This argument continues to rumble on in the background and there is also talk about companies making vast profits from publishing data and images of primary sources on CD or online There is little truth in this, as a massive outlay in both time and capital has to be made just to provide the service before any income is generated, so profits are in the future, not the present.

Of course it is true that the the census records were free to access, but that statement needs to be examined a little closer. Unless you lived within 5 minute's walk of the Family Record Centre or the National Archives, free was only a relative term. For most users there has always been a considerable cost implication in using such records, both in terms of time, travel and possibly even food and accommodation. You needed to be in London to access the records for the full country, local record offices and libraries only held local records.

The 1901 records were still provided at no charge, as they always had been. In the traditional filmed format you can use the 1901 census for 'free', with full sets at the Family Records Centre and county sets at record offices around the country. With county record offices and libraries having only local coverage and not the full country, your travel costs might not be too great if your research is local to where you live. However if you live in a rural area or need to research outside your local area, the cost implications of access can be prohibitive and you can then start to see what a bargain the online services are.

The online access to the 1901 census was an additional service made available because of the advances in technology since the previous census releases. Wider computer ownership and access to the internet made the idea viable, but commercial assistance was necessary to turn that idea into a reality. It was a tremendous achievement, despite the initial problems caused by underestimating the demand and the several month's wait whilst the system was restructured, but it wasn't just the delays that brought criticism.

The trouble was researchers had been spoiled by the earlier release of the 1881 census index, an amazing accomplishment in providing cheap, accessible mass data before anything similar was available to the public. Before uttering facile comments about commercial companies making vast profits, the complainants should consider the vast amounts of time and other hidden costs that went into carrying out that single pioneer project. The work was performed by hundreds of volunteers and took years, plus the non profit making resources of the LDS Church to publish the final result. This project led the way for volunteer projects and others will eventually provide excellent free resources for family historians. One such is the FreeBMD project, also still to be completed, but already with enough data to save many people from having to pay for a commercial BMD index site. These are mammoth projects, undertaken by willing volunteers who have effectively funded the work out of their own pockets. However large the projects and their number, added together they don't even scratch the surface of the vast pile of records that researchers are regularly using, never mind the more obscure sources. The FreeBMD project has taken years of work but pales into insignificance against the mammoth task of making the 1841-2001 census available. If this were to be attempted by

© Apple Computer

volunteers, it will be our grandchildren who reap the benefits not us. However commercial sites giving access to all that information should be completed in the next few years, but we will have to be prepared to pay for the information.

The government can't be expected to provide computer access to records. In a country which fails to fully resource much more important aspects of life such as education, hospitals and transport, why should family and local historians expect their hobby to be funded by the other tax payers? As a nation we undertake to preserve the records and make them freely available via the Family Record Centre, the National Archives or County Record offices. That hasn't changed, but technology has now made it possible to do much more. However although it is now possible, there is no funding for such gigantic digitisation and indexing projects which have no real benefit to the community. It would be akin to the government nationalising all the golf clubs in the country and giving us all free membership and a bag of clubs, we wouldn't be very pleased with the use of our taxes, especially if we played rugby, tennis or just watched TV!

So in an ideal fully funded world, all the records in our archives would be digitised, fully indexed and freely available online? This utopian dream is less likely than the development of a flying pig by genetic engineering! Only commercial organisations can even begin to make that dream a reality. The costs in staff and equipment to create digital images of just one census year are great, but this is a relatively mechanised process. The real expense comes in the indexing which is required to make these images more accessible than they were before. These costs all have to be met to get the project up and running and then recouped before companies make any profit from the work.

Companies such as Ancestry in the USA and S&N in the UK have committed large amounts of money to large scale publishing projects covering many data sets, with no guarantee that they will ever fully recoup the costs. It is a large commercial risk which is looking at long term profits, not a quick gain. Other commercial projects offering just a single database such as the National Archives/QuinetiQ partnership and 1837Online, who seized the opportunity to publish a database they had already created for their own use, are taking much less risk and are more likely to be profitable in the short term. If they are successful some of the profits go back into improving and extending their services, as can be seen at 1837Online who have re-indexed the data as well as adding some new resources.

There are benefits both to the company and the family historian in this relationship.

Whichever way you look at it, only commercial companies are going to bring us the records and indexes we would like online and they are going to want a return on their investment. The good news is that there is competition in the data market, with each company offering slightly different products in terms of levels of accuracy, ease of use, service and payment options. This means researchers have choice of whose Census records or BMD indexes and images they pay for, so we should get the service we want.

Aside from the sheer convenience, the real advantage of paying to view records is that you know exactly what they are costing you. Of course you can see those records for 'free' at the local Record Office, when it is open, which rules out many people still working for a living. However few of us will have actually worked out the real cost of finding a record at the archives and obtaining a copy. The archive's records are unlikely to be fully indexed and your transport, photocopies and other hidden costs are likely to add up to considerably more than using an online service. Having spent several all day sessions at a record office 40 miles from where I live, trawling the filmed GRO indexes for a particular death, I found it in an hour using a commercial BMD index service which had full name indexing. I considered that and a few other events that I checked at the same time were well worth the £5 pounds on my credit card, especially as the bus to my nearest library costs £4 each way!

Online records are fast to use and can be accessed anytime you have a few minutes to spare. The last record copies I obtained at a record office cost 35p each for an A4 and even self copied items are around 20p. They also had to be ordered and sent to me, arriving about a week later. Online I would have found the records much faster, and at a time convenient to me, so even if they do cost 75p per copy the price is quite reasonable.

On balance the benefits are considerable, I can achieve more in the limited research time I have available and I know exactly what my hobby is costing, as other than my internet cost which is a few pence per hour, there are no hidden costs for the likes of transport and food - Long Live the Data Revolution!

Caveat Internet!

Robert Blatchford

The Internet has made family history research material even more accessible but there are pitfalls for the unwary! Caveat Internet – Let the Internet user beware!

Brancaster Castle, Norfolk!

Family history research has been transformed by the Internet and the growth in online resources has been quite phenomenal. Before the internet information between family researchers was shared by 'snail mail' and in the early days of the internet by bulletin boards. Today there are millions of websites containing billions of family history information. Many websites have been established by government archives offices, libraries and other organizations with archive material but by far the largest number of websites contain information from individuals.

The problem for researchers arises when we rely too heavily upon third party information which invariably contains inaccurate or wrong information, or has been incorrectly transcribed. As I travel about the country attending Family History Fairs I am quite often told that a person has 'done' their family tree and that they 'got it all off the internet'. If this is symptomatic of a lot of research today then there may be many families relying upon false information.

Unless you verify the source of your information it is always advisable to check and confirm it with the original or a photocopy/film of that material.

I can understand the logic of using the internet because it is much easier these days for a researcher to access information from his or her computer rather than visiting the local library, record office or archive which may be some distance from their home. The basic elements of your family tree will be easily traced. The caveat is to ensure that it is accurate.

Family historians have always been faced with false genealogies, incorrect information, and sometimes complete fabrications of a family history. A news report in The Times newspaper in April 2001 said that American tourists had fallen for an ancestral castle spoof sending a steady stream of transatlantic visitors in search of their ancestral home - a non existent Castle at Brancaster in Norfolk.

They based their connection with Brancaster on a book in the Library of Congress, published in 1906, "*The History and Genealogy of the Rix Family of America*". Guy S. Rix wrote "an accurate and scholarly work, of how the Rix family emigrated from England in the 17th century" but included a letter apparently written in 1894 telling of the family's glorious past in a Norfolk castle with "12ft thick walls, which had been visited by Henry VIII". He presumably inserted the letter in the belief "that more namesakes would buy his book if they thought they were descended from English castle-owning nobility." This is just one of many written examples.

With the growth in the use of computers, CD-Roms, and the Internet there is even more scope for inaccuracy. Errors in transcription abound amongst the many web sites and the fact that if it is there 'it must be gospel' will lead many people to include the information provided in their histories. Always remember when dealing with any information from original documents and particularly modern transcriptions they can all be subject to human error. Eric Budgen of The Somerset and Dorset Family History Society advises everyone 'to adopt a critical attitude – never take anything for granted! And always check back to the original, where possible.'

It is essential that our descendants are able to rely upon the accuracy of our researches because if we go wrong in those endeavours the result is really not worth the paper it is written on. By following this advice you could create a family history which will become an heirloom.

Family History in the Media - a personal view
Anthony Adolph

Roots and Honeycombs

As long as family history has been a popular pastime, it has exercised a fascination for the media. Back in 1977, Alex Hailey's *Roots* held the nation glued to the TV as his quest for his pre-slavery origins in Africa unfolded. Four years later, Gordon Honeycombe took his viewers on a quest for his Honeycombe ancestry, explaining, step-by-step, how he went about tracing his family tree.

Both series, in very different ways, inspired viewers not just to watch and enjoy, but also to emulate. People left their sofas in droves and went out (for yes, in the days before the Internet, they needed to go out) to trace their own roots.

Talking to people who have been in the profession from that period, I have confirmed again and again that those two programmes between them had a significant an impact on the growth of family history's popularity. A further series, *Family Trees*, broadcast in 1982, cashed in on this, focussing the 'message' at children and (inadvertently) launching the career of Aneka Rice. A surprising number of the very same people who have been in the profession since that era were involved in the show. Catholic Family History Society chairman Michael Gandy, for example, contributed the material for an episode in which his two young daughters Isabel and Rachel discovered family links with Thomas Hardy and the Battle of Culloden.

A paucity of programmes

And then, something odd happened. Whilst the family history movement went from strength to strength, its relationship with TV, which had seemed set to flourish, came to nothing. Of course, the subject didn't absolutely vanish from our screens, but nothing of such significance as *Roots* or Honeycombe was commissioned again for a long time. There isn't a single reason for that, but I believe it was due, mainly, to TV having becoming at once more sophisticated and also less cerebral. The great era of David Attenborough at BBC2, which saw such intellectual masterpieces as *Life on Earth* and *Civilisation*, was edging towards to the dawn of the era of makeover show. Commissioning editors wanted snappy, slick shows to wow their audiences, and were repeatedly drawn to but then repelled from a subject which, they feared, would require too much mental effort from their viewers.

Towards the end of the 1990's, I and many other professional genealogists started to receive requests from an increasing number of production companies eager to overcome these issues and plug such an obvious gap in the TV market. The key to success, it seemed, was not so much content, as format. Broadcasting heavyweight Joan Bakewell made a concerted effort to break the stalemate, whilst comedian-turned-producer Jimmy Mulville launched his own bid to find the elusive formula that would convince the broadcasters that genealogy really was sexy enough to be allowed back onto our screens. It was like a love affair, in which two parties yearn for each other, yet whenever one plucks up the courage to woo the other, the courted party shies away.

BBC2 temporarily side-stepped the issue by commissioning a series on, of all things, old documents, which must have got through the system because its presenter, Bethany Hughes (amongst her many other qualities), was extremely young, attractive and enthusiastic. Yet they still couldn't convince themselves that any of the pure family history proposals flooding across their desks would achieve the viewing figures they knew they had to achieve.

Melanie Sykes and Anthony Adolph
outside the Island Record Office in Spanish Town, Jamaica

The growth of Internet genealogy did a huge amount to convince broadcasters that public interest in family history was very substantial. When the Mormon's website - www.familysearch.org- went online for the first time in May 1999 and was crashed by the vast amount of hits it received, broadcasters realised they had to act. So, just like London busses, two commissions came along at once. Within two heady weeks in early summer that year, BBC2 and Channel 4, quite unaware of what the other one was doing, commissioned TV genealogy programmes. I know that for a fact because, quite by coincidence, I was the genealogist both successful production companies had selected to participate in their shows.

I know I wasn't the only genealogist keen to be involved, but of the enthusiastic ones I think I was the youngest (I was 31 and still had most of my own hair), and I'd clocked up a modest collection of TV and radio interviews, including a very memorable (for me, I mean) 'phone-in on the Dennis and Muffin Show on South African radio (Dennis interviewed me: Muffin, being a poodle, barked).

Blood ties and Extraordinary Ancestors

For an exciting weekend, I thought I would be able to do both series simultaneously, until it was quietly explained that such a thing was out of the question. A colleague, Steve Thomas, very ably took on the BBC2 series, *Blood Ties*, produced by RDF and presented by Martha Carney. With a short deadline and restricted budget, he came up with some fantastic stories, of which the best had to be the story of the Ind family of brewers, a white, English family of whom one had gone to Rhodesia and fathered a black line of the family. Having traced two descendants, one white English, one black Zimbabweian, Steve introduced them in an Ind pub and rapidly found the family similarities which underpinned their apparently very different racial and ethnic origins. Colour difference, he discovered as the two long-lost cousins made friends on-screen, really was only skin deep.

Channel 4 chose a proposal from a then virtually unknown production company called Freeform TV, run by Ann Lavelle and Antoine Palmer, now best known for producing *a Place in the Sun*. They had started off trying to make a holiday show with a difference, and realised that ancestry could be an excellent reason for people to visit unusual places, in Britain and abroad. Patrick Younge, head of Channel 4's Multiracial Department, loved the idea for a different reason- like the Ind story, this could be a fantastic vehicle for showing how diverse and interconnected modern British families really were.

If anyone ever asks you to be in a TV show, agree unconditionally. Participating takes a lot of time and effort- it can feel as if it's taking over your whole life- but the fun, the buzz, the excitement of making a programme, never mind actually watching it afterwards, is extraordinary. From a fairly calm desk job as a professional genealogist, I found myself frenetically pursuing lines of ancestry in Britain; Ireland; America; Jamaica; Latvia, all with the seemingly impossible mandate of 'find us some extraordinary ancestors, preferably by this time next week'.

There's quite a mixture of opinion on researching family history for TV programmes. Traditional research is thorough, eclectic and reasonably slow. When you trace your own family tree, you spend time researching great granny's links with the local gentry, and also her career on the stage, and if she moonlighted as a button maker you explore that as well. When you're working on a short time-scale with a tiny research budget handed down from the TV executives far, far above and you know you've *got* to get a good story, you take a different

approach. You don't sacrifice accuracy- believe me, when you're putting together a story which hundreds of thousands of people are going to watch and scrutinise, you make jolly sure you get it right. But you do have to be ruthless about focussing on a single, strong story-line rather than butterflying between different 'fascinating' elements of a family tree.

Many people- most people- are terribly keen to help, and thank goodness for that. Without a legion of wonderful record agents; librarians; archivists; record office staff; museum curators and members of the public bending over backwards to help, TV genealogy wouldn't exist. Occasionally, though, you do encounter a few individuals who seem to take a pride in *not* helping. 'You want the answer now, but how long has it taken you to get in touch?' asked one clever-dick archivist in London. Actually, we'd thought of contacting him three days earlier, but a day's filming and two other days' hectic trying to sort out other stories for the same series meant that, without being super-human, I couldn't have rung earlier. I think the problem is that some people think TV programmes are made by well-paid celebrities with huge budgets and all the time in the world. Well, the truth is somewhat different: the more people are prepared to help, the better the resulting programmes will be, and I can't see how that will make anybody lose out.

For *Extraordinary Ancestors*, Ann and Antoine actually gave me six weeks, working from information provided by a host of eager would-be participants found through a series of announcements on local radio stations. 'Nine to five' suddenly became 'seven to eleven' and I lost the plot of my favourite soap opera altogether- yet, remarkably, the stories emerged.

I remember getting off the phone to a very crackly-sounding man in America and 'phoning Ann with the breathless news- Martin Morris, a mixed-race P.E. instructor from Oldham, had a line of ancestry going back through the Trench family of Trenchtown, Jamaica, to Irish landed gentry, and beyond. 'He's related to the Queen!' I exclaimed. 'Wow!' came Ann's response, followed by a cheer in the background from Antoine. I didn't understand exactly why then, but I do now- up to that point, success had been uncertain. Now, we had an extraordinary story: *Extraordinary Ancestors* would live up to its name.
The excitement of the research process, though, was nothing to filming. I'd never done more on TV than sit and answer questions before. Now, I was expected to remember lines, walk about, gesticulate- all the sort of stuff which sounds really easy until you actually have to do it on camera. But to guide me through these minefields was a wonderful presenter- and the real reason why I'd chosen Channel 4 over BBC2- Melanie Sykes. As an ex-girlfriend of one of the twins from Bros and a close friend of the likes of Ulrika Johnson and

Paul Gascoigne, I assumed she'd be aloof and snooty, but she wasn't at all. 'Come and 'elp me learn me lines', she said in her smiley, Mancunian drawl, and we soon became firm friends.

The filming took us to the Jewish cemetery in Cheetham Hill, Manchester; down a coal mine in Wakefield (I went down: Mel stayed on the surface with the claustrophobic participant) and a replica 18th century sailingship in St Catherine's Dock, London (which you'll have seen if you watched *Hornblower*). But best of all, we flew to the suppurating heart of Trenchtown, where Martin kicked a football around with the local boys, and specially hired members of the local mob protected us from being shot or stabbed by the suburb's older residents. Later, I had a moment of genealogical epiphany when I showed Martin the grave of his great-grandmother- the black servant whose relationship with her white master had created the link to the Trenches- in a yard behind a bar on Jamaica's north coast. At that moment, as the pathos of the location sunk in and Martin's tears began to flow, Mel and I also realised that this long-dead ancestor of his had been a real person, whose real bones lay in the damp earth beneath our feet- and we started crying too!

The pilot was a huge success. Patrick and Channel 4 in general were delighted, and commissioned a series, which was broadcast in October 2000. The format was a series of roadshows, held in Bristol, Cardiff and Edinburgh- the latter bang in the middle of the petrol strike, when the country almost came to a standstill. We were worried people wouldn't be able to make it, but many told us they had saved their last litres of petrol specially to be there.

As before, we had advertised for participants and I'd pre-traced their stories. Mel had other commitments at the time, so we had Shilpa Mehta as a presenter, with the task of scurrying all over the planet at break-neck speed, from India to the Forest of Dean and Paris to Vladivostok; Trinidad to South Wales, bringing a series of astonished participants into direct contact with their ancestors' old haunts. My on-screen role was to reveal stories from nearer-at-hand: a Victorian great-great uncle who was the much-publicised Giant Welsh Baby; a proven line of descent back to a Viking; a Trinidadian whose French colonial ancestors were connected to Chopin. My wonderful director, Lizzie Becker, gave me props to help tell the stories, of which the most bizarre was a Gloucester Old Spot piglet (clue to an ancestral Gloucestershire faming family), which was about two feet long, very sharp toothed and very, very cross about being made to sit on a table under bright lights. I will never forget the visceral edge to its squeals, and the pure fear I felt when it turned its curly-tailed bottom to face my lovely new, cream-coloured suit.

I have dwelt on *Extraordinary Ancestors* because

of the impact it made on me both personally and professionally- it taught me a lot about TV presenting and also made me a much better, more focussed genealogist- and also because it brought a very great number of new people into family history, especially (as Patrick Younge had hoped), from families with mixed-race backgrounds.

The cost of what was effectively a three-ring media circus, however, had been enormous, and nobody seemed to have the energy to embark on a second series. *Blood Ties*, meanwhile, underwent a complete format-revamp and became *The People Detective,* changing from a magazine-style to focussed half-hour story-lines and presented by panama-hatted Daru Rooke. It included the astonishingly good story of a missionary's descendant being taken back to a Pacific island to receive a friendly apology from the descendants of the natives who had *eaten* her ancestor. After a single series, though, *Blood Ties*, rolled over on its back and died.

Back to square one
The next couple of years were decidedly disappointing. Media interest continued unabated, of course, and every time a new website was launched and/or crashed, the press and TV were clamouring for exciting stories and interviews. My most exciting one was an appearance on Ruby Wax's daytime show, Ruby. 'We want someone who'll stand up to her', the producer explained in advance'. Ruby's interest, though, seemed less in

family history as in catching her guests out. But I came forewarned and fore-armed. 'What does Wax mean?', asked fellow-guest, Michelle Collins (who had played the schemeing Cindy Beale in *EastEnders*, yet turned out in real life to be considerably nicer than our hostess). 'It means a wax-seller', said I, who had looked it up the day before in a German surname dictionary. 'You're wrong, Mister!' exploded La Wax: 'Originally it wasn't Wax- it was German, spelled 'W-A-C-H-S!' Luckily, I'd known that when I looked it up. 'Yes, I know', I said. '*Wachs* was the German for wax'.

Other magazine and chat-shows picked up on the popularity of family trees too. *Working Lunch* gave it a 10 minute slot, in which I gave the presenter as much of a family tree as I'd been able to rush together in a week. John Titford did the same for Richard and Judy- though Judy obviously hadn't been bitten by the genealogy bug and only managed with some effort to mouth the words 'that's quite interesting' when poor John postulated that the Finnegans had come from Ireland.

Publicity shot for *Extraordinary Ancestors* - Shilpa Mehta and Anthony A

Motherland

We had to wait until spring 2003 for the Next Big Thing. Although it was only one programme, BBC2's *Motherland* really changed the face of family history and, again, it was focussed on mixed-race ancestry. Most descendants of slaves simply cannot trace their ancestry: records of their ancestors speak of them as commodities, and don't provide sufficient information to construct a family tree or pinpoint where in Africa a slave originated. Even Alex Hailey needed to take a leap of faith to bring *Roots* to its successful conclusion- but now a new technology had emerged. D.N.A. can't trace a family tree, but it can pinpoint a place of origin for the direct male and direct female line.

Motherland took three black British people with slave ancestry on journeys to discover their African roots. The results were moving, surprising and relentlessly fascinating. A mixed-race woman who was proud of her white, plantation ancestry came to terms with the brutality of slavery and her own black origins; a black Englishwoman was reunited with the tribe from which, according to the DNA, her ancestor was abducted, but soon realised that her new-found relatives might be expecting financial as well as emotional ties with her. Finally, a mixed-race man was appalled to find that his male-line ancestry was not African, but German (through, no doubt, a German plantation owner), whilst his female-line lead him back not to innocent Africans, but to black slave-traders. Such was the impact of *Motherland* that a group still exists for all those who applied to be on the show but could not be included, whilst versions of the show are set to be made all around the world.

A helping hand from the psychics

While Motherland was reverberating through the airwaves, I had been invited to co-present another big, and many thought batty, project- *Antiques Ghostshow*. Format, as I have said, is the major factor which either attracts or repels commissioning editors. Craig and Hillary Goldman of production company IPM had already achieved success in televising psychic readings, and realised that, if psychics really could talk to the dead, it would be quite interesting to have a genealogist around to verify that the deceased individuals really had existed. To keep the TV watchdogs happy, the show's resident psychic Derek Acorah didn't communicate directly with the dead, but did so instead by the process of psychometry, whereby he claimed to pick up residual energies of the long-departed left behind in objects they had owned-objects now owned by their living descendants. Having heard of cases where psychics apparently had helped genealogists, I was delighted to join in. Myself, Derek, and the show's antiques expert, Chris Gower, gelled immediately, and spent most of the time off-camera (and some of the time on-camera) roaring with laughter and thoroughly enjoying ourselves. Chris regaled us with tales of his earlier TV career, including a part in *To the Manor Born*, and Derek's dinner conversations glittered with tales of celebrities for whom he had performed readings- Cher used to ring him regularly- and many more famous names whom he had encountered in the 'world of spirit'.

In the course of the pilot and eight-part series which followed, I saw Derek at work a great deal. The pressure and pace of work was so intense that cheating was out of the question, and when I investigated the family histories of the heirloom owners I was astonished how many times things Derek had said turned out to be accurate. Derek, of course, was a convinced believer- he was, he said, a reincarnation of an Etheopian boy who had lived 2,000 years ago. On a couple of occasions I got uncomfortably close to ancestors myself. When Derek seemed almost possessed by the spirit of a Zulu War Victoria Cross hero, I asked if he could provide his rank and number. The man- part Derek, part soldier, I suppose- snapped to attention and barked out both details so suddenly that I almost dropped my pen. Later that year, I had a psychic reading myself, on Colin Fry's show *6th Sense*, and received what seemed to be some accurate advise and admonitions from my late grandfather. Yet, whilst I suspect no dishonesty, I still can't, personally, bring myself to believe that the spirits really are out there. But I now know that many people are truly convinced.

Antiques Ghostshow raised many eyebrows in the genealogical world when it was broadcast on Living TV in summer 2003, and again at New Year 2004, and also on satellite stations in Canada, New Zealand and Australia. But the effect of the show, as far as I was concerned, was to bring family history to a vast new audience who had never engaged with the subject before. I know from the e-mails I still receive about it that there are many people who have started tracing their ancestry because they were inspired to do so by the show.

The History Channel picked up on family history too- about time, you'd think, given their name- and launched their Family History Project. Guided by Nick Barrat, formerly researcher of *House Detectives*, they collected and broadcasted short films about people's family stories. Discovery Channel dipped its toe into the water as well, commissioning *Mongrel Nation*, in which comedian Eddie Izzard fronted a three-part show investigating the many foreign roots of the British people. The show could have taken a genealogical element but instead chose a more culturally-based approach, (tea-drinking was introduced from India via Portugese Queen Catherine in the 17th century, for example).

Radio catches up
But where Eddie missed a trick, Radio 4 cashed in with *Meet the Descendants*. Producer Colin Davies was absolutely fascinated by the idea of white British people having non-British, even non-European roots, and commissioned me to find and research some good examples. In the first series, which was broadcast in spring and summer 2003, we had some marvellous finds, including a white woman from Ramsgate with a black sailor ancestor from Sierra Leone and a very 'normal', middle-class couple from Guildford whose ancestor, Sake Dean Mohamed, opened the first Indian restaurant in Britain in 1809.

Jim Walvin, a professor of history at York University and an authority on black British history- a wonderful, warm, humorous man who is great fun to work with- presented the shows, and I developed my role as enthusiast revealer of the genealogical facts. We were delighted when we made it to *Pick of the Week*, and even more when a second series was commissioned for summer 2004. Again, the stories worked like dreams- including a white female descendant of an India Prince (and, incidentally, of the prophet Mohamed) and a Wiltshire smallholder descended from the child of a Capetown slave and an Irish nobleman. My most nerve-wracking moment was when, having spent

four months trying to track down a living descendant of Munnoo, an India servant boy brought here in the early 19th century, I finally spoke to one. How would he react? Would he agree to participate, or was he a racist? The relief when he said, 'I think I've heard he was my ancestor' was enormous.

Radio 4's radio waves get everywhere. Friends doing the washing up or driving down motorways said they'd heard it- many of them people who'd never deliberately tune in to a genealogy programme- and I was contacted by many more people who had been inspired to tell me their family stories, or wanted me to take them on as private clients to start solving their family mysteries. I'm convinced that all these genealogy programmes, and the many other short features and slots on the subject which have been broadcast over the years and which I haven't mentioned here, have helped increase the number of people engaging in the subject.

The future
And the more people who get involved, the more the Internet is used for family history, and the more genealogy websites appear and become so inundated with hits that they crash, which in turn sends new waves of interest through the press and back into the media, who then start commissioning new programmes. The dark days of the 1990's, when the subject all but vanished from the airwaves, seems well and truly in the past now, especially in these times of proliferating channels. As I write this in summer 2004, I am looking forward to BBC2's new series focussing on celebrity genealogies, which will start in the autumn (I did some work on Jeremy Clarkson's story): I've just finished a pilot with Leopard Films for Discovery Channel, called *Ancestor Hunters*, in which we investigated a Sussex family's links with the great highwayman Dick Turpin, and all sorts of new ideas for yet more shows are in the air.

I'd like to think that the elements of these programmes which emphasise the interconnections between black and white; rich and poor; famous and obscure, help, in their own small way, to make Britain a better place. Surely, knowing that 'pure' white people are almost all partly descended from black immigrants in the past, and that most black people, especially of Caribbean ancestry, have a dose of white blood, takes much of the appeal out of racism. Recently, I asked a black genealogist, Patrick Vernon, if he agreed with that. He said no- such broadcasting preaches to the converted, and the racists will always have counter-arguments. Be that as it may, I can't help but feel- or perhaps it is just a hope- that these programmes are not mere entertainment, but serve in some way to help make Britain a better place.

And, besides, they are entertaining, educational, and great fun- what more could anyone want?

Electronic Indexes ~ Pain or Pleasure
David Tippey

Most of the time they work but when you don't get the result you are looking for, it is very easy to sit at your computer and complain that the indexing is poor. Accurate indexing of even a single data set, takes a considerable amount of time and labour, with the original data often containing inaccuracies which are added to by human errors when transcribing. Coping with indexing a small project is a very different matter to producing indexes for every year of the census, 1841-1901, for the whole country, so should we expect better indexes than we have at present?

Dumb machines
The index is important because computers are basically stupid and can often only find exact matches to a search. If you don't ask the right question, they can't find the information. This situation is improved on some databases by the ability to use "wild card", synonym or "fuzzy" searching techniques to improve the chances of a partial match to your query. Indexes are never going to be 100% accurate, as even with extensive checking, errors will get through. Even the benchmark 1881 census project wasn't immune, as despite the fact that the transcriptions had been done and carefully checked by Family History Societies with local knowledge, by the time the 1881 census was published, new errors had been introduced.

The money aspect
Indexes produced commercially have to balance the need for accuracy with the requirement to complete the index within a manageable time scale and budget. This may mean that we don't always get the quality of index we would like, however the situation is still considerably better than it would have been, when no index was available at all. At least you should find the answers to the bulk of your queries speedily.

Get results
The trick with using all electronic indexes is to use the "less is more" rule. Start all searches using the minimum of information and only put in additional facts if you need to trim down the results. If you fill in too many boxes in your query at the outset, you are more likely to get no results because generally, everything you enter has to match the entry exactly for it to be found. The chances of you achieving this on multiple search fields is small.

OCR indexing
Indexing of printed material can be automated to some degree, but optical character recognition programs are far from perfect. Handwritten records need to be manually transcribed, as there is no computer program that can convert the handwritten documents to editable text. The indexing of the Ancestry parish records, which was produced by OCR indexing of scanned, printed transcripts, is rather poor and exhibits the typical errors introduced by OCR programs. Their census indexing however was performed abroad and is somewhat better. Many of the PDF reproductions of old books and trade directories are "fully searchable," but this is done by using an OCR program and hiding the results behind the scan of the actual page. The OCR version can't be checked when it is automatically produced by Adobe Acrobat, so it retains all the usual OCR mistakes that anyone who has tried the process will be familiar with. So the electronic search for a word may work, but may not, leaving you to go back to the old fashioned methods and actually use the index or read the book.

Manual transcription and indexing
This is an expensive operation to perform, no matter how you do it, and various use has been made of cheaper labour, such as prison inmates or countries such as India or China with much lower wages. Without adequate checking of the results this could be a recipe for disaster. S&N originally started a volunteer project to provide indexes to their census CD images but are now using an Indian company to speed up the provision of indexes to all census years. To ensure as high a quality index as possible, a very important requirement a far as their MD is concerned, they created software tools for the transcribers to use to check personal and place names and set up a large department at their headquarters whose main purpose is to check the incoming indexes. Their indexing company are paid a bonus for achieving higher accuracy and are achieving 98+% accuracy, which is far better than some indexes appear to provide.

1901 census
When the 1901 census was released, which had used a combination of prison and foreign indexers, it received a lot of criticism. Stephen Miller of LeedsIndexers said *"We checked the first person in every Enumeration District for the whole of Yorkshire (in the 1901 census) and found approximately 10% errors."* Well 90% isn't bad for a first attempt, but surely better checking of the work would have raised this to a more acceptable level?

But was it 90%? Before QuinetiQ altered the 1901 website to prevent their use, Jeanne Bunting and John Hanson had been using data mining utilities to compare the 1901 online Index to the enumerators book images from the S&N 1901 census CDs. They found *"...in the Enumeration District of Rotherhithe (about 300 people) there were 1,000 errors in First name, Surname, Place of Birth and Occupation."* This seems rather extreme, however all but 2% of these have been accepted by the National Archives for correction. Was that just an isolated occurrence or an indication that this might be the case elsewhere?

Without the correct infrastructure to evaluate the accuracy of indexes and transcripts as they are made, commercially produced indexes can fail to provide the level of accuracy expected by the users. The 1901 index has slowly improved and corrections have been made, but in the main it's only after someone using it has identified and reported the errors!

BMD indexes

The 1837online Birth, Marriage and Death indexes were originally only indexed by the first three letters of the surname, which wasn't good if you had a popular surname. They have now been re-indexed and like their rival BMDindex, are now indexed using the full name and forename or initials, making searches faster and downloads fewer. Of course the level of accuracy on a project like this should be very high, as it only required the first and last name on each page to be indexed. However this indexing of images still doesn't tell you if a name actually appears on the page in question, only that it fits into the range of names to be found there. Only a full transcript of the GRO indexes such as FreeBMD volunteer project will do that.

GRO records from 1984 to date were already computerised by the GRO and so are fully searchable on both 1837online and BMDindex, although the latter also allows you to map the distribution of surnames from the post 1984 data and to instantly look up details of spouses.

Is it an index? Is it a transcript?

Indexes and transcripts are not the same thing, a transcript is an exact copy of the original entry, mistakes and all, so it doesn't make a particularly good index. An index would normally standardise or group together spellings of place names for instance, so that they can be more easily found. In census entries the reported place where born is frequently miss spelled and if any of the first letters are incorrect, you have no chance of finding them when you use the place name as a search term. This is why the "less is more" rule should be applied to your searches.

The National Archive's 1901 Census Index use the transcript and as transcripts aim to reproduce even the obvious errors, such as spelling or the reversal of forename and surname, they don't make the best indexes. However as well as the original errors, many new ones were introduced when the census was indexed, and this combination can make it extremely difficult to find

people, even if you know a considerable amount about them already. Had an index been created from the transcript with standardised spellings, and obvious mistakes such as name reversals corrected, then in combination you would have a better chance of finding the entries you want.

Although QuinetiQ have now edited some of the original errors, the current "index" is still neither an accurate transcript or a true index. Shortcomings in the search and problems associated with the quality and implementation of this transcription/index itself can make it extremely difficult to positively identify an individual unless you already know the very details you are trying to find. Some individuals known to have been around in 1901 still refuse to surface, did they all manage to evade the enumerator?

When technology fails

Unfortunately it is all too easy to become reliant upon the electronic indexing, what started as a luxury is becoming an essential to some. In fact new researchers seem rather disgruntled when records can't be searched using a keyboard, whilst those who have been at it longer, appreciate the time saving it usually brings. However it can also be frustrating when your computer search fails to come up with the goods, but at least we can go back to the old fashioned, if rather slower, methods of research. Even viewing the images page by page and slowly widening the search is easier when you can use CDs or online resources instead of going to the record office and winding microfilm readers all day.

Just because your computer can't find it, doesn't mean that the information is not there, it's probably slightly deformed and buried in the index! However when the index works, which is most of the time, and the information you are seeking just pops up without all the hard slog, technology is truly wonderful.

The Archive CD Books Story

The Archive CD Books Project began four years ago, since when it has produced more than 1,500 CDs containing scanned images of old and rare books, church records, maps, 19th century censuses, and more, of interest to genealogists and historians. Probably the largest collection of family history resources available!

The project's founder, Rod Neep has a great interest in family history. In March 2000 Rod saw a message on the Nottinghamshire genealogy internet discussion group. "Can anyone tell me how to obtain a copy of the Nottingham Date Book", to which a reply had been posted: "We have been trying for about fifteen years to borrow the book from the Nottinghamshire Archives, to put it on microfiche, but unfortunately we have always been told that it is impossible for the book to be removed from the county record office. It is so rare, and there are only a handful of known copies". Rod knew of the book's usefulness to family historians and had referred to it regularly during research trips to Nottingham. There had been two copies at the record office, one had been stolen, and the remaining copy was in very poor condition. Rod had an idea. "If we could persuade the Nottinghamshire Archives to loan the book for a few days, it could be scanned, reproduced on CD and made accessible to anyone. The proceeds from the sale of CDs could pay for the conservation and rebinding of the book, and CD copies could be given to Nottinghamshire Archives, local museums and libraries." Rod phoned the principal archivist and put forwards his idea, and was surprised by the response. "Excellent. When would you like to collect it?"

The model for the Archive CD Books Project was established and exists to make reproductions of old books, documents and maps available on CD to genealogists and historians, and help libraries, museums and record offices by providing funds for the renovation of old books in their collection, and to donate books to their collections for conservation for future generations. CD copies would then be available for genealogists and historians at a reasonable price. It is a "user supported" project, and intended to be a non profit organisation. Rod Neep says "It gives me a lot of pleasure to make these old and rare books available to historians and those interested in researching their family history."

For the first six months, Rod laboured with a normal flatbed scanner and a single CD maker, but it soon became clear that a more professional system was required, and so he purchased his first specialist book camera, a Bookeye scanner. It was so much faster with the book being scanned in its normal open relaxed position causing no damage to the book. A small CD making machine was purchased from the USA which with the camera was a large personal investment for Rod. With the increase of the number of books being scanned, and the growth of the project, more people were needed to handle the scanning, mastering, CD making, order processing and mailing, and Rod gradually increased the team, employing more people. The work force was all drawn from the local job centre, providing work for unemployed local people. "But I was eager to stand by those original principles. Despite increasing overheads, it was important to continue paying for books to be renovated, and to give away rare and valuable books, purchased from book dealers, to record offices, museums and libraries. And it was

important to keep CD costs down so that they could be affordable." Archive CD books has continued to grow, there are now five book cameras, a film scanner, several CD making machines, and fifteen members in the team at the Gloucestershire base.

The Archive CD Books Project is very much supported by its "customers". In fact, most of them don't consider themselves to be customers, but "supporters". In addition to the web site and on-line catalogue on the net, (www.archivecdbooks.org), there is an active discussion forum, The CD Books mailing list, where people throw around ideas for the development of the project, suggestions for improvements, book sources, etc. In addition, the supporters of the project are keen to help others on the internet family history mailing lists with information from their CDs. It's not like a business, it's more like a club, and Rod Neep is very visible and approachable at its head. Rod's mailbox is full of emails each day with queries, suggestions and thanks.

"I'd like to thank Rod and all the fine folk who are working on this project. I believe it is one of the most significant projects going on today in genealogy. I have really enjoyed the 1844 Pigot's Directory – Gloucestershire and Herefordshire. It not only confirmed some residence and address information for me but it has added much to my understanding of the times in which my ancestors lived."

The Archive CD Books Project doesn't just scan the "juicy" books to put onto CD. There are some pretty obscure and esoteric ones too, some of which would never cover their costs. Last year, for example, Rod was visiting a book dealer in Sheffield, and was rummaging through an old chest of drawers in a cellar, when he discovered a whole pile of manorial documents relating to the village of Burnham Thorpe in Norfolk. There were over sixty of them, which the dealer was selling at £10 each. Rod immediately bought them all, scanned them and made them available on CD, and then drove over to Norwich to give the documents to the Norfolk County Record Office. "I think we may have sold four CDs", Rod says, "But that isn't the point. Those old unique documents are now where they belong. It's still a success story for the project".

Rod Neep
Founder of Archive CD Books

Not all church records are stored at the county record offices. Some are still at the churches. Archive CD Books was approached by a church in Cumbria who still held their own registers of baptisms, marriages and burials, in old vellum books dating back into the 1600s. They wanted them to be digitised. After all, these were unique and extremely important records, and copies *needed* to be made. So the registers were scanned, at no cost to the church, and made available on CD. Now anyone can have easy access to them. When Rod later visited the Cumbria Record Office at Barrow in Furness, and gave them copies of the CDs, the archivist was somewhat surprised! They had been trying to get the church to deposit the books with the record office for safe-keeping. But the story doesn't end there. The Barrow in Furness Record Office had some other rare books which the other branches didn't have, and so those were loaned to Archive CD Books for scanning. All four of the Cumbria Record Offices now have copies for their visitors to use, and they are also accessible to anyone on CD, anywhere in the world. The Barrow Record Office also had a request. They had been trying to obtain a copy of the last Kelly's Directory of Lancashire, published in 1924, but not only were such books very expensive, but just about impossible to find. Rod Neep offered to help. Amazingly, one was spotted at a book auction just a few weeks later. It cost Archive CD Books £450.00 to purchase. The huge book was scanned and made available on CD, and the original book was donated to the Barrow in

✂ -

Name	
Address	
Post Code	

☐ I enclose a cheque for £1.50 made payable to **"Archive CD Books"**

Furness Record Office, together with copies of the CDs.

Another of Archive CD Books' success stories is with The National Archives in London. The Family Records Centre at Myddleton Street had a huge collection of county directories dating back to the early 1800s. They were in very heavy daily use by members of the public, and they were being destroyed by over use. Bindings were loose, fragile pages were torn. They were in a very sad state. This was an ideal project for Archive CD Books. Over a year the books went to Gloucestershire for scanning. The resulting CDs were given to the Public Record Office and visitors can now browse the books on The National Archives computers. The original books have been removed from the open shelves for conservation. The cost of the project was paid with the sale of the CDs from the Archive CD Books web site.

Many family history societies also use Archive CD Books for their own CD publications. Many societies publish the CDs themselves whilst some are on a royalty basis, with Archive CD Books doing the marketing. The family historian that gains by having access to numerous old and rare resources. In the past these rare books and records could normally only be viewed at local libraries, museums and record offices. Now they are available for anyone to browse on their own computer.

Last year, Archive CD Books embarked on a new project - digitising the censuses of England and Wales. Films of the censuses are purchased from The National Archives, scanned using a film scanner, and then transferred onto CDs for each county's registration districts. Despite some of the censuses being made available on the internet, many people prefer to have a copy for browsing on their own computer. It's so much easier and faster. Archive CD Books have developed special scanning and image enhancement techniques to make even the notoriously faded and difficult-to read 1841 census pages legible.

The Archive CD Books Project is now developing in other countries too. Partner projects have already been set up in Australia, Canada, the USA and the Netherlands, all working to the same model, and working with books and documents from their own country. It won't be long before we see Archive CD Books in New Zealand, South Africa and Ireland too. Each country's project concentrates on producing its own CDs, but all CDs from other partner projects are available locally in each country.

For more details of the Archive CD Books project, visit **www.archivecdbooks.org**

DON'T MISS OUT - ON YOUR CHANCE TO GET A **FREE** (£1.50 P&P) **ARCHIVE CD BOOKS** CD WORTH £34.95! SEE COUPON FOR DETAILS.

Discovering family history with 1837online.com
John Coutts

Birth, marriage and death records are the building blocks of genealogical research. But until last year, the only way you could see the complete indexes of these events was to go to a library or record office. Now, though, anybody with internet access can search the indexes for British nationals overseas (including WW1, WW2 and Consular indexes) as well as the complete index for England and Wales from 1837 to the present day by visiting www.1837online.com.

Using 1837online.com is like having the real indexes in front of you. Once you've logged on, you can search, print and save authentic images of index pages. Searching is free – viewing a page costs a maximum of ten pence – and the system works equally well on PCs and Macs. The site has a link to the General Register Office (GRO), so users can order birth, marriage and death certificates online too.

Registration of births, marriages and deaths in England and Wales was introduced in 1837, the year Queen Victoria came to the throne. Despite some minor changes, the civil registration system remains in operation to this day. These records have always been an invaluable resource for family historians. But using the indexes in their traditional form was a time-consuming business.

"Birth, marriage and death records are the one record set that you always need to come back to if you are researching your family tree," says Colin Miller, managing director of 1837online.com. "The concept was to allow family historians to access the core data set online."

1837online.com is an offshoot of Title Research, a company that provides specialist genealogy services to the legal community. Title Research has been in the business for nearly 40 years and it's the only company of its sort endorsed by the Law Society. To streamline operations, the decision was taken to computerise the entire index. It was an enormous task: the database includes some 2.5 million individual index pages spanning nearly 150 years.

The screen-based system was originally designed for professional use only. But it soon became clear that it would be a valuable public resource – and 1837online.com was born. The system, which contains high-resolution scans of the entire index and features a sophisticated cataloguing system, was fine-tuned for more than a year and tested by the genealogical community for six months before its public launch.

1837online.com is unique in that it has the only complete version of the England and Wales

indexes on the web as well as now hosting the additional British nationals' overseas indexes. All the data is offered in its original form.

"I think if you were to speak to anyone – whether they would class themselves as a professional genealogist or even a very enthusiastic hobbyist – they would probably join me in saying where you can, do look at the primary source" says 1837online's Colin Miller. "Anything that has been transcribed, whether professionally or otherwise, does have potential faults in it. That can mean the difference between a positive and negative result. We have to be 100% sure. Of course, we know the original GRO indexes are flawed to some degree but they're still the most useful source out there."

By accessing images of the original indexes, users of 1837online.com can rely on their own judgement when interpreting the data. As a testament to its reliability, professional researchers – including those serving the legal community – use 1837online.com to help them get the right results. Even the General Register Office uses 1837online.com as part of its record-keeping tool kit.

The website relaunched in April 2004 with a range of enhancements. The revamp improves the look and feel of the site and includes comprehensive new guidance pages for researchers, as well as a site tour. And as part of the ongoing enhancement process, the home page now includes links to news and events so users can keep up to date with the latest genealogical issues.

1837online.com prides itself on maintaining a personal connection with its users. As part of their training, staff at 1837online.com have to prepare their own family tree. So when users call the helpline, they can be certain of getting the best possible advice. "It's really important for us to be able to talk to our customers and to allow them to contact us as easily and as quickly as possible," says Mr. Miller. "Whist we are there for technical support, we have become an unofficial genealogical helpline. But it's something we love doing and we're quite happy to answer questions. In that sense, it's a real passion."

SURNAME of Person	NAME (if any) or SEX of CHILD	SUP. REGISTRAR'S DISTRICT	Vol.	Page
Findall	Sarah	Lincoln	xiv	527
Findall	Sarah	Soulcoates	xxii	171
Findall	William Higginbotham	Rochdale	xxii	664
Findel	Ellen	St Geo. East	1c	163
Findell	Christiana	Eccles	xxii	517
Findle	Martin	Durham	xxiv	74
Findle	Robert	Sunderland	xxii	374
Findlay	George	Rotherho'	xv	340
Findly	Rachael	Downham	xii	69
Findly	Male	Biggleswade	vi	68
Findly	Male	Biggleswade	vi	61
Findly	Elizabeth	Downham	xii	80
Findly	George	Belper	xiv	272

Getting started

To register, simply go to **www.1837online.com** and click the **new visitor** link. The whole process – including downloading free DjVu software to view the indexes – normally takes between five and ten minutes.

Searching the indexes

The indexes on the website fall into three distinct groups. From 1837 to 1983 and for the overseas records they are stored as image files that are opened and navigated using DjVu software. Indexes from 1984 to date are stored in database format.

Births, marriages and deaths from 1837 – 1983

When searching for ancestors in the 1837 – 1983 indexes, users can search on the full surname as well as the full first name too. Searches can be for a maximum of 10 years and if, for example, you have searched for a James Smith born between July and December 1867, the search results will be displayed as follows:

Jul-Aug-Sep 1867 SMITH, George William - SMITH, John VIEW Oct-Nov-Dec 1867 SMITH, Hannah - SMITH, John Fallows VIEW

Users should note that these are the first and last names on these particular pages. You can see other names on these pages, such as James, that fall alphabetically between George William and John, or Hannah and John, once you have clicked on 'VIEW to look at the actual image'.

Births, marriages and deaths of British nationals overseas from 1761 – 1994

The overseas indexes can be searched by full surname only, not by first name. However searches do not have to be limited to a 10 year time frame. The search results for overseas records will be displayed as follows:
GRO Marine Birth Indices 1837 – 1862
RENNER to STEIN VIEW
These are again the first and last names on these particular pages if you have searched on 'Smith' for example.

Births, marriages and deaths from 1984 – 2002

Relatives can be found in the 1984 – 2002 indexes by searching under any combination of event, month, year, forename(s), middle initial(s), surname, district(s), mother's maiden name (for birth indexes), birth date (for death indexes) and spouse's surname (for the marriage indices).

The search results will tell users exactly how many records match the criteria entered and how many units will be used to view the results. It will also prompt customers to redefine their search if many results are listed.

Please note that the search results for all the indexes show the page or pages which may contain the index entry relating to the person users are looking for. There is no guarantee that a person of that name will be on each page in the search results.

What do indices and certificates tell you?

Indexes contain basic data about individuals. Certificates paint a more detailed picture. You can order birth, marriage and death certificates from the General Register Office via 1837online.com.

Births

Birth index entries from 1837 and the June quarter 1911 contain the following information: surname, two full forenames, subsequent initials, registration district and reference number. From the September quarter 1911 to present, the index contains: surname, one forename, subsequent initials, mother's maiden surname, registration district and reference number. Recent records contain two forenames.

SURNAME of Parent	NAME (if any) or SEX of CHILD	SUP. REGISTRAR'S DISTRICT	Vol.	Page
		172		
Couchman	Hannah	Dartford	V	100
Couchman	John William	Faversham	V	172
Couchman	Mary Elizabeth	St Saviour's	IV	472
Coucill	Deni	Bolton	XXI	153
Coucl	Eliza	Witham	XII	301
Couerdale	Matthew Sandem	Stockton	XXIV	183
Coughlan	Anne	Merthyr Tydfil	XXVI	364
Coughlan	Joanna Coughlan	Bristol	XI	152
Coughlan	Julia	Birmingham	XVI	303

A **birth certificate** gives the date and place of the birth, the child's forename(s), the name and occupation of the father, the name and maiden surname of the mother. It also includes her usual place of residence if the birth took place elsewhere, and the name and address of the informant for the registration. A birth certificate provides sufficient information to help find the marriage of parents.

For the overseas records, the birth certificates will vary greatly depending on the country reporting the birth.

Marriages

Marriage index entries from 1837 to the December quarter 1911 contain: the surname of the person married, first two forenames, subsequent initials, registration district and reference number. From the March quarter 1912 to the September quarter 1962, if the woman was previously married, the index shows both maiden and married names. From the March quarter 1912, the index includes the surname of the spouse.

A **marriage certificate** gives the names and usually the ages of the marrying couple, their addresses and occupations, the names and occupations of their fathers, the date and place of the marriage and the names of the witnesses. A marriage certificate usually gives clues for the births of the marrying couple as well as the fathers of each. Because a marriage certificate contains so much detail, it's potentially one of the most useful civil registration records there is.

For the overseas records, the marriage certificates will vary greatly depending on the country reporting the birth.

Names of persons married.	District.		Vol.	Page.
Verrell, Lily A.	Kidd	Wandsworth	1 d	1176
Verrier, Annie	Cruse	Pontypridd	11 a	995
Verrill, Edward	Colbourne	Steyning	2 b	649
Verrimat, Lucien M.	Foulcher or Smith	St.Giles	1 b	852
Verrin, Mary C.	Sleeman	Liskeard	5 c	96
Verrinder, Bertha L.	Jensen	Croydon	2. a	752
— Margaret A.	Smith	Croydon	2 a	751
Verrion, Arthur T.	Kippen	Thanet	2 a	2117
— Dorothy M.	Millington	Brighton	2 b	501
Verry, Nelson G.	Rees	Cardiff	11 a	498

Deaths

Death index entries from 1837 to the June quarter 1911 record surname, two full forenames, subsequent initials, registration district and reference number. Age at death is included in the index from the March quarter 1866. From the June quarter 1969, the exact date of birth – rather than the age – is given. From the September quarter 1911 only one forename and subsequent initials are provided. Recent indexes record two forenames and subsequent initials.

Name	Date of Birth	REFERENCE	
		District	Vol	Page
JONES			
Thomas George	20 Mr 1886	Lichfield	9b 563
Thomas Henry	22 Oc 1905	St.Asaph	8a2711
Thomas Humphreys	25 Se 1888	Bangor	8a 334
Thomas Ifor	20 No 1893	Caerleon	8c 364
Thomas Inman	29 De 1896	St.Asaph	8a2483
Thomas John	11 No 1895	Conway	8a 572

A **death certificate** includes the name, date, place, age, cause of death, occupation, place of residence if different from the place of death and the name and address of the informant of the registration. Death certificates do not record the place of birth or parentage.

For the overseas records, the birth certificates will vary greatly depending on the country reporting the birth.

Anybody can order certificates - you don't have to be a relative. The service is now available to visitors based in the UK or overseas. You need a credit/debit card and index details for the person and event concerned. Simply click on **order certificates** on the right-hand side of the blue tool bar and follow the link to the GRO's online order centre. Certificates cost £7 each and are dispatched on the fourth working day of order. Priority dispatch costs £23. (The delivery time may be between 5 and 10 days for overseas certificates.)

Using DjVu

Civil registration indexes have been produced in a number of different forms over the last century and a half. Early indexes were written by hand; later indexes were typeset or typed. DjVu image software is designed to help you make the most of these original records.

You can move pages up and down using the mouse – simply press the left-hand button and slide the mouse backwards and forwards, or use the inner scroll bar on the right-hand side of the screen.

To zoom in or out, simply choose a magnification factor from the drop-down list in the centre of the toolbar, or use the + or - buttons next to it. You can also rotate pages.

You can select an area to zoom in on by clicking on the magnifying-glass icon and then selecting the area of text you want to scrutinise by holding down the left mouse button, dragging open a box and simply releasing the mouse button. To undo any action, simply click the green 'back' arrow on the right-hand side of the toolbar. To print the whole page, simply click on the 'print' icon, select 'fit to page' then hit 'OK'.

DjVu lets you save page images so you can view them offline. To save an image, click on the floppy disc icon on the extreme left of the toolbar.

DjVu tips

Printing pages: original records sometimes contain handwritten insertions called interlineations – these are entries added after the index is compiled, and could mean the name you're looking for is at the bottom of the page where you're not expecting to find it. If you print the page first, there's less risk of missing something.

Saving your work: DjVu allows you to allocate your own file names to saved images. To make recording your results easier, it's worth developing your own file-naming convention at an early stage.

Identify your records: because the handwritten pre-1860 index pages do not have titles, it's worth writing page location details at the top of your print out.

Troubleshooting: if you encounter any difficulties using DjVu, follow the link at the top of the index

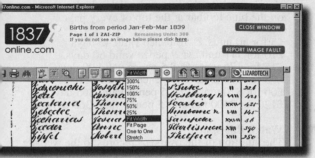

page you're viewing. If you're anywhere else in the 1837online.com website, simply click **help** at the top of the page in the centre, or **faqs** on the far right-hand side. DjVu is fully supported for Windows 98 or later, Mac OS X, Mac OS 9 and Unix. If you can't fix the problem yourself, contact 1837online.com on **0870 777 1837** or via **info@1837online.com**.

Working with Civil Registration data

1837online.com provides comprehensive guidance on tracing your family tree using civil registration records, so before you start searching the records it's worth looking at the **getting started** and **resources & guidance** pages first. Here are a few things to bear in mind before you start using indexes and certificates.

Births: a child does not have to have a name to be registered. If a child is not named at registration, only a gender reference is recorded. Where parents were not married, the child should be registered under the surname of the mother; where paternity was acknowledged, the birth may also be registered under the surname of the father. It's also worth bearing in mind that when registration began, parents had three weeks in which to register a birth - and after three months, they couldn't register it at all.

Marriages: for every one marriage there are two index entries. Previous marriages were sometimes concealed from partners and bigamy was not uncommon – declarations of marital status found on certificates may not always be reliable. And even in the nineteenth century, not every couple that lived together was necessarily married.

Deaths: a death is registered in the district or country in which it occurs – this is not necessarily the same area the person lived in.

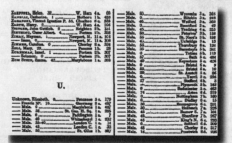

Calendar quarters: indexes for England and Wales from 1837 to 1983 were compiled by calendar quarter. Each quarter index is described by the name of the last month included in it, so an index for January, February and March would be described as the March index.

Compulsory registration: registration only became compulsory in 1875. It's believed that between six and 10% of births before 1875 were not recorded. Registration is not compulsory for British nationals overseas however.

Registration lag: there's often a considerable gap between an event taking place and registration. Marriage details in particular may take a long time to reach the central register because the information is collated from a large number of churches and other religious establishments. Modern index data has to be 'cleaned' before it becomes available to the public – so anything that has happened in the last 18 months is unlikely to be immediately available.

Age errors: people sometimes modify their ages – for example, the age stated on a marriage certificate might not be correct. Whilst age slippage is not uncommon, it's rare for anybody to alter the day and month of their birth. Ages on death certificates are also potentially unreliable. When searching for an expected birth entry, be prepared to check before and after the expected year.

Variant spellings and interpreting old indexes: name spellings change through time. Sometimes families make a deliberate decision to alter a name spelling; occasionally the registration process generates spelling errors. Equally, it's quite easy for researchers to make interpretation errors when viewing some of the early handwritten index entries.

Name indexing: names are arranged alphabetically from A to Z. The convention for indexing **Mac** and **Mc** surnames has changed over time - before the June quarter 1969, they were indexed separately but they are interfiled for the period to December 1983 under MAC. **Double-barrelled** surnames may be wrongly indexed if the hyphen is ignored. Births and deaths of **'unknowns'** may be registered at the end of surnames beginning with the letter Z.

Registration errors: the indexes contain about two billion name references, all of which were originally transcribed from either the district records to create the national indexes, or military, consular or high commission records to create the overseas records. Inevitably, there will be a small number of errors.

How much does it cost?

1837online.com pricing plans start from £5. You can order units online via a secure connection using a credit or debit card, or through BT click&buy, the secure online account which can be settled using direct debit or your BT phone bill. You can purchase units from any page on the site –

simply click on the **buy units** link which appears on the blue toolbar at the top of every page.

£5 for 50 units @ 10 pence valid 45 days
£10 for 111 units @ 9 pence valid 60 days
£15 for 176 units @ 8.5 pence valid 90 days
£25 for 313 units @ 8 pence valid 120 days
£60 for 810 units @ 7.5 pence valid 365 days
£120 for 2400 units @ 5 pence valid 365 days

Watch this space!

The addition of the overseas records to the website shows the commitment of 1837online.com to continue to improve and grow as an invaluable resource to the genealogical community. You can expect to see a number of exciting changes to the site over the coming year and 1837online.com will e-mail their registered users with any new developments.

www.oldbaileyonline.org
Barry Redfern

There are some remarkable archive collections becoming available on the internet, but amongst the leaders is a site that will attract everyone interested in family and local history. Type www.oldbaileyonline.org into a web search engine, press 'Go' and you will enter the records of 18th century criminal trials at the most famous court in the world, the Old Bailey, London. This web site called *"The Proceedings of the Old Bailey"*, is the product of work led by Professor Tim Hitchcock of the University of Hertfordshire and Professor Robert Shoemaker, Sheffield University and supported by the New Opportunities Fund and Enrich UK.

As the Home Page appears take an immediate sample of what this site is all about. Click on the option *"On this day"* which will open an account of an interesting trial on an 18th century date corresponding to the day you happen to visit the site. There will be the name of the prisoner, the charge (or indictment as it is known) transcripts of the evidence, the result of the trial and the sentence.

What is on view here is the painstaking transcription of old publications, under a variety of titles, describing trials at the Old Bailey. Alongside the transcripts appears a small (enlargeable) image of the original printed page. When the project is complete the site will reproduce all the surviving accounts of trials at the Old Bailey from 1674 to 1834. The 'Publishing History' section of the site reports the views of a Frenchman in 1726 who said that the proceedings *"are one of the most diverting things a man can read in London."* That remains so today but the proceedings can now be read throughout the world.

A prodigious amount of work has been done on these old records and the stories open up many aspects of 18th century life such as work, use of leisure, family relationships, domestic life, how people travelled and of course the main business of the range of crimes, punishments and how society

went about dealing with them. This large body of text lends itself to studies of various kinds. The designers of the site have taken care to help schools and colleges. Terms, court procedures, punishments etc., are carefully explained. There is an evocative description of the journey from Newgate Prison to the gallows at Tyburn..

Browsing this user-friendly site could not be simpler. The search facility permits comprehensive exploration of the site in many ways, including names, occupations, places, crimes, punishments, statistics and so on. There are thousands of names of victims, witnesses, officials and prisoners to check and, as will be seen below, the names are usually related to places. Whilst London is the base or host for the trials, the net spreads wide to catch hundreds of place names around the country and elsewhere. A search on Newcastle upon Tyne, for example, produces many references including Mary Brown cleared of picking pockets in 1755, a charge involving a watch containing a paper with the name James Smoak, a watchmaker of that town. A search on Plymouth at the other end of England reveals, as the 1st of 71 hits, Bridget Potter alias Hamlet alias Ward. Potter was convicted of bigamously marrying Edward Ward whilst legally married to James Hamlet. She claimed that Hamlet had another wife in Plymouth. She could not prove that fact and Hamlet denied it. So, married there or not, it appears there was connection between Plymouth and James Hamlet. When it came to sentence Potter pleaded benefit of clergy. She was *"burnt in the hand"* that is to say branded with a letter F at the base of her left thumb to prevent pleading her clergy a second time, and was released.

The reports of evidence by witnesses are often written in the first person. This style serves to draw the reader into the drama of the court-room, rather like reading a play, and beyond that into the homes, taverns, theatres, workshops and the bustling life on the streets of 18th century London. No better example can be found than the shocking and heart-breaking account of the death in 1767 of young Mary Clifford, a fourteen years old servant girl. Mary was starved and systematically beaten by her mistress Elizabeth Brownrigg. The girl was often beaten whilst stripped naked with her hands tied to a hook specially fixed to a beam for the purpose. She was imprisoned and fastened in a cellar with a collar and chain around her neck and this continued until Clifford died after eighteen months of the savage treatment. Brownrigg was hanged for murder on Monday 14th September 1767 and her body was delivered to the Surgeon's Hall to be anatomised. Her husband James and son John tried with her were cleared.

Here to conclude is a short case study, an example of how brief information from one source can be linked to greater detail on the Old Bailey web site. A researcher may pick up in the Gentleman's Magazine for June 1732 (page 823) a tale of tragedy told in a few short lines:

Tuesday 13th June 1732. *John Waller* was kill'd by the Mob, as he stood on the Pillory at the *Seven Dials*.
Wednesday 14th June 1732. The Coroner's Inquest having sat on the Body of *Waller*, gave their Verdict *Wilful Murder by Persons Unknown*.

Limited information surely, but if the researcher's interest is in the family name Waller or in the history of crime and punishment then there is a wealth of information to be found in the 'Proceedings of the Old Bailey.' Entering the name 'John Waller' into the web site search engine brings up, amongst other things, "John Waller, Perverting Justice, 25th May 1732." The trial summary reveals that John Waller passing himself off as John Trevor falsely accused John Edlin and Uriah Davis of being footpads who robbed him on the highway at a place called Colney in Hertfordshire. Waller's motive was to seek a reward. The magistrate was uneasy about the accusation thinking he had seen Waller somewhere before that day, however, after having enquiries made and receiving assurances he committed Edlin and Davis to prison.

When the time came for the trial at Hertfordshire Assizes Waller and his witnesses failed to appear at court to give evidence and the charge against Edlin and Davis was dismissed. A deeper enquiry into Waller alias Trevor revealed that he had made similar false allegations against two other men at Cambridge. Evidence of his lies and bad character came through just in time to save the two men from execution at Cambridge.

The place of making the original accusation against Edlin and Davis brought Waller under the jurisdiction of the Old Bailey. On the 25th May 1732 Waller was found guilty of perverting the course of justice and given an unusual combination of punishments. He was to stand in the pillory at the Seven Dials (a famous London landmark near

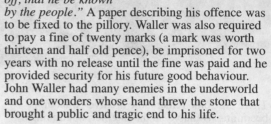

Covent Garden) in St. Giles in the Fields and in the pillory against Hick's Hall (Peter Street) for one hour at each place and again at the same places for one hour each at a different time *"with his Hat off, that he be known by the people."* A paper describing his offence was to be fixed to the pillory. Waller was also required to pay a fine of twenty marks (a mark was worth thirteen and half old pence), be imprisoned for two years with no release until the fine was paid and he provided security for his future good behaviour. John Waller had many enemies in the underworld and one wonders whose hand threw the stone that brought a public and tragic end to his life.

So much can be learned from this resource now available through modern technology. Researchers interested in the name Waller have new districts to check. The transcripts of evidence against Waller make it possible to say he had connections to central London, Colney Herts., Cambridge, Thetford and Bury St. Edmunds. Within this one story there were sixty-nine other surnames mentioned in the trial and session punishment summaries for the case including uncommon names such as Giggle, Noden, Scrivener, D'Angre and Ketcher.

The historian will pick up on many things in covering this ground. One reassuring thing is the sense of reservation and caution that comes from the way the magistrate dealt with Waller's initial complaint. The justice felt uneasy and did not take it at face value. There were also points of detail; the judges at the Hertfordshire Assizes in 1732 sat on the last day until three or four o'clock in the morning to clear the calendar, as it was called, of cases in time for them to move on to the next assize in the circuit. The combination of punishments for Waller was unusual in that it included a sentence of imprisonment. The locations are established for two of the many pillories in London and the death of this man is yet further proof of how dangerous an hour or two in the pillory could be.

This is a web site that should carry a time-consumer warning! Searching a name or topic draws you in, getting out requires a firm resolve not to read one fascinating story after another and another and another …………..

Barry Redfern is a retired Chief Superintendent of the Northumbria Police and the author of T*he Shadow of the Gallows, Crime and Punishment on Tyneside in the 18th Century* - Tyne Bridge Publishing, Newcastle upon Tyne - October 2003 - *www.tynebridgepublishing.co.uk*

Trace Your British and Irish Family History Using the Internet
Alan Stewart

As recently as 2002, it would have been a gross overstatement to have suggested that you *could* trace your ancestors in Britain and Ireland using the Internet. Now, however, you can carry out a great deal of Scottish research online. Scotland's civil registration, censuses for 1881-1901 and wills are already accessible via the Internet, with the 1841-1871 censuses and the Old Parish Registers set to join them in 2005.

Fewer English and Welsh primary records are online, although the situation is constantly improving. The 1871-1901 censuses, many wills and the indexes to the civil registration are now online, with more records being digitised or transcribed every year.

Griffith's land valuation (which act as a census-substitute, because all the 19th century censuses were destroyed) is the only all-Ireland primary source available online so far. An index of surviving Irish wills is also available online. This has been compiled from transcripts, copies, etc as most of the originals were destroyed by fire in 1922.

A. General Britain and Ireland
1. Commonwealth War Graves Commission
www.cwgc.org
At this website, you can search free of charge for information on the 1.7 million Canadian, Australian, New Zealand, South African, Indian and UK servicemen and -women (and some civilians) who were killed in the First and Second World Wars.

2. Documents Online
www.documentsonline.nationalarchives.gov.uk
One million wills proved at the Prerogative Court of Canterbury (covering the south of England and most of Wales) between 1384 and 1858 are indexed on this site. This index is searchable free

of charge, as are indexes of First World War campaign medals and medals issued to merchant seamen after the Second World War. You do have to pay £3.50 to view an image, however.

3. FreeCEN *freecen.rootsweb.com*
Volunteers are transcribing and indexing the 1841-1891 censuses for England, Scotland and Wales, and these are being made available on this website free of charge. Only a few counties have been completed so far, including Cornwall for 1841 and 1891 and Bute and East Lothian for 1841.

4. GENUKI *www.genuki.org.uk*
This free "virtual reference library" about the UK and Ireland contains all sorts of useful information for family historians. The information is organised at national, county and parish level, and covers topics such as monumental inscriptions, photographs, descriptions of the countryside, its history, maps, and population figures.

5. LDS FamilySearch *www.familysearch.org*
The Church of Jesus Christ of Latter-day Saints (the 'Mormons') have made the International Genealogical Index (IGI) of parish register (and some civil registration) entries available on this website free of charge. You can also search the 1881 census there for England, Wales, the Isle of Man, and the Channel Islands (but not Scotland).

6. National Archives Catalogue
www.catalogue.nationalarchives.gov.uk
This is a free online index to documents held by the UK National Archives. If you're looking for soldier ancestors, you'll find entries in the index if you search with a name and series code "WO 97" or "WO 121". These record series contain information on privates and non-commissioned officers (but not commissioned officers) in the British Army who left and received a pension between 1760 and 1913.

B. England and Wales
1. 1837online.com *www.1837online.com*
Before FreeBMD *(see below)* made its images of the birth, marriage and death indexes available free of charge, 1837online had put similar images (covering the period 1837-1983) on to its website on a pay-per-view basis. Each page costs one unit to view, with units costing between £5 for 55 units (which are valid for 45 days) and £120 for 2,640 units (valid for 365 days). Records from 1984 onwards are held in a fully-computerised database. The site also contains indexes of consular, high commission, and armed forces births, marriages and deaths.

2. 1901 Census
www.1901census.nationalarchives.gov.uk
The UK National Archives has made the 1901 census (for England and Wales) available at this site, with a full index that can be searched free of charge. It costs 75p to view the image of a page from the census, or 50p for a transcription of one person's details, and a further 50p for a transcription of the rest of the household. For £5, you can buy a 48-hour credit card session, although £5, £10, and £50 vouchers are valid for six months from the date of first use.

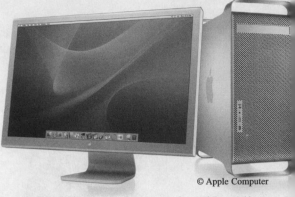
© Apple Computer

3. Ancestry.co.uk *www.ancestry.co.uk*
This is the UK website for the American family history company Ancestry.com. The most useful of the many databases accessible through an annual subscription of £59.95 (or £24.95 quarterly) are the English and Welsh censuses for 1871-1901. Ancestry also holds the Pallot marriage index 1780-1837, covering mainly London and Middlesex.

4. BMD Index.co.uk *www.bmdindex.co.uk*
This is another site providing access to the English and Welsh birth, marriage and death indexes, this time on a subscription basis. The site holds a fully-computerised index of births from 1900 to 1983, as well as for births, marriages and deaths from 1984 onwards. A three-month subscription will cost you £5, or you can pay £14.95 for a year.

5. British Origins *www.britishorigins.com*
Formerly a pay-per-view site known as English Origins, this website is now subscription-based and provides access to a number of databases. Some of these contain data provided by the Society of Genealogists, the UK's oldest genealogical society. The databases include Boyd's Marriage Index, which contains over six million entries for marriages in England and Wales that took place between 1538 and 1840. A 72-hour trial will cost you £5.95, almost as much as the cost of a month's subscription (£7.95). The charge for three months is £12.50 and for a year £22.50.

6. Cornwall On-line Parish Clerks *west-penwith.org.uk/opc.htm*
Volunteers are collecting, collating and transcribing parish registers, census records, monumental inscriptions, and local histories for each Cornish parish, and making them available online free of charge. This site contains links to six other counties with similar on-line parish clerk schemes.

7. FamilyHistoryOnline
www.familyhistoryonline.net
The Federation of Family History Societies has set up this pay-per-view website. Instead of having to buy several little booklets and microfiches, you can view online various indexes compiled by family history societies. These include baptisms, marriages, burials, monumental inscriptions and census returns for the majority of English counties and some Welsh ones. Payments from £5 to £50 can be made online, with individual items costing between 2p and 9p each.

8. FreeBMD *freebmd.rootsweb.com*
There aren't yet complete online indexes to the civil registration of births, marriages and deaths that took place in England and Wales from 1st July 1837 onwards. You'll find the next best thing at this website, where a band of volunteers is well on the way to creating indexes up to 1910. The organisers expect the database to be complete by 2007. You can also view free of charge the images of the original paper indexes used by FreeBMD's volunteers.

9. The Genealogist *thegenealogist.sandn.net*
Over two dozen English census name indexes have been put on to this subscription site by S&N Genealogy, publishers of the British Data Archive census CDs, which are not indexed. The charge for access to the index for one census (e.g. Durham 1891) is £5 for 90 days or £14.95 for a year.

10. General Register Office *www.gro.gov.uk*
Wherever you live in the world, you can place an online order for English and Welsh birth, marriage and death certificates at this official website. The certificates, which cost £7 each, will then be delivered to you by post.

11. The National Archivist
www.nationalarchivist.com
You can view the images of a variety of records at this pay-per-view site. These include army lists, births, marriages and deaths at sea (1854-90), death duty registers (1796-1903), and passport applications (1851-62 and 1874-1903). Searching the indexes is free of charge. There is a charge of 1-4 credits for viewing a record, where 35 credits (valid for 45 days) will cost you £7, and 360 credits (valid for 75 days) £50.

12. UKBMD *www.ukbmd.org.uk*
Around 15 local indexes of births, marriages and deaths in England and Wales can be reached through this site. These are free of charge, apart from the index for Derbyshire County Council, which is available on FamilyHistoryOnline *(see above)*. The indexes have been put online by local registry offices, the first to do so having been that

of Cheshire County Council in 2000. You can order a certificate from a local office for £7.

C. Scotland

1. Scotland's People *www.scotlandspeople.gov.uk*
At this official pay-per-view website, you can view and download images of the Scottish civil registration births (1855-1904), marriages (1855-1929) and deaths (1855-1954). In addition, the records of the 1881-1901 censuses are available online. All of these records are indexed, as are the Old Parish Register baptisms and marriages (1553-1854). The 1841-1871 census records and images of the baptisms and marriages are expected to follow in 2005, with burials coming later. Thirty 'page credits', valid for 48 hours, will cost you £6, with unused credits added to your next session. One credit buys a page of up to 25 names from one of the indexes, while the image of one of the records costs five credits.

2. Scottish Documents
www.scottishdocuments.com
You can find 520,000 Scottish wills and inventories (1500-1901) at this site. Searching the index is free of charge, but downloading the image of a will or inventory costs £5.

3. Scottish Strays Marriage Index
www.m&lfhs.org.uk
An index of marriages that took place outside Scotland, where at least one spouse was born in Scotland, has been compiled by the Anglo-Scottish Family History Society (ASFHS). You can search the index free of charge at the website of the Manchester & Lancashire FHS, which is the parent of the ASFHS.

4. The Statistical Accounts of Scotland
edina.ac.uk/statacc
This site provides free access to digitised copies of these descriptions of life in the 938 parishes of Scotland in the 1790s and 1830s/40s. The fascinating accounts were compiled by the local Church of Scotland ministers, and give a great deal of information about the parishes, but mention few people by name.

D. Ireland

1. Irish Ancestors *scripts.ireland.com/ancestor*
Irish genealogist John Grenham runs this website together with *The Irish Times*. You can use the site to search for a surname in Griffith's Valuation, and also for a second surname in the same parish. The site also contains placename and ancestor search facilities. The latter lists resources you can use to search for records of your ancestor, with more information available through a pay-per-view payment of US$8 or a subscription payment of $60 for 30 credits.

2. Irish Genealogy *www.irishgenealogy.ie*
At this website, you can search free of charge in the computer index of records held by some of the Irish Genealogical Project's 33 county-based family history research centres. In addition, you can order and pay online for research to be carried out at one of the centres, and download a free booklet entitled *Tracing Your Ancestors in Ireland*.

3. Irish Origins *www.irishorigins.com*
You can view Griffith's Valuation at this pay-per-view site, as well as Irish wills (1484-1858). The wills consist of a mixture of original documents, copies, transcripts, abstracts and extracts. A 72-hour trial of the site costs £3.95, while subscriptions cost £7.95 for a month, £12.50 for three months, and £22.50 for a year.

4. Leitrim-Roscommon Genealogy Website
www.leitrim-roscommon.com
This site contains various databases created by volunteers and accessible free of charge. The databases include the 1901 census, complete for the counties of Leitrim and Roscommon, and partial for Mayo, Wexford and Sligo. Other databases provide details of the townlands (subdivisions of a parish) for Leitrim and Roscommon, and also for the whole of Ireland.

5. Otherdays *www.otherdays.com*
This subscription-based website includes fully-indexed images of Griffith's Valuation, as well as Dublin wills and marriage licences (1270-1857), and a census of County Antrim taken in 1803. There are also over 120 further databases of Irish records, including county and occupational directories, indexes of births, marriages and deaths for certain counties, and burial indexes for some graveyards. Charges range from US$8 for 72 hours to $44 for a year's subscription.

6. Ulster Historical Foundation
www.ancestryireland.co.uk
Member of the Foundation's Ulster Genealogical Historical Guild (which has an annual subscription charge of £20) can carry out online searches of the Foundation's indexes. These cover over half a million records including lists of householders and flax growers. Another 2.5 million records have been digitised and are expected to become available online in the future.

Miscellaneous websites
Several other websites (with free access) contain information useful to family historians:

Access to Archives (A2A) *www.a2a.org.uk* (the catalogue of over 350 English archives)
British History Online *www.british-history.ac.uk* (includes parts of several *Victoria County Histories* of a number of English counties)
Cobh Genealogical Project *www.cork.anglican.org* (computerising all Church of Ireland (Anglican) registers for County Cork)
Cyndi's List *www.cyndislist.com* (over 240,000 links to family history sites worldwide)
Dumfries and Galloway Historical Indexes

www.dumgal.gov.uk/services/depts/comres/library/archives.asp (includes a local index to the 1851 census, as well as kirk session minutes)

Family History in India
members.ozemail.com.au/~clday (all about the British in India)

Federation of Family History Societies
www.ffhs.org.uk (with links to nearly 90 family history societies in England, eight in Wales, three in Ireland, and many around the world)

Friends of Dundee City Archives
www.fdca.org.uk (includes databases of burials and Methodist baptisms)

Genealogical Society of Ireland
www.gensocireland.org (contains interesting comments on the computerisation of the civil registration in the Irish Republic)

Gloucestershire Genealogical Database
www.gloucestershire.gov.uk/genealogy/genealogy.dll (includes an index of wills, non-conformist church records, and gaol registers)

Historical Directories
www.historicaldirectories.org (local and trade directories for England and Wales)

Irish Ancestral Research Association *tiara.ie* (contains links to many Irish family history and cultural websites)

JCR-UK All UK Database
www2.jewishgen.org/databases/UK (combined database of Jewish records)

London Signatures
www.cityoflondon.gov.uk/corporation/wills (wills proved in the Archdeaconry Court of Middlesex. £4 to download a will)

Moving Here *www.movinghere.org.uk* (information on Irish, Jewish, South Asian and West Indian immigration to Britain)

Police, 'Black Sheep' and Other Indexes
www.lightage.demon.co.uk (various useful indexes)

Proceedings of the Old Bailey
www.oldbaileyonline.org (records of around 100,000 trials at the Central Criminal Court in London)

Scottish Association of Family History Societies
www.safhs.org.uk (with links to 20 family history societies in Scotland, and many others worldwide)

Welsh Family History Archive
home.clara.net/wfha/wales (all about Welsh family history)

Workhouses *www.workhouses.org.uk* (all about the workhouses of the British Isles)

Future Digitisation and Other Projects
The UK Government is in the process of consulting on changes to the existing civil registration system for England and Wales. The changes are expected to come into law by the end of 2005, with electronic registration of new births, marriages and deaths beginning in 2006. The Government plans to digitise the existing registers from 1993-2005, but whether earlier registers are also digitised will depend on funding being available!

FreeREG *(freereg.rootsweb.com)* is a sister project of FreeBMD and FreeCEN, and aims to index all parish and non-conformist registers in the UK, starting with those in England and Wales. The index is still being built and not yet open for searching. As the IGI already indexes most parish records, this project may be rather "re-inventing the wheel".

Ancestry.co.uk has a non-exclusive agreement with the Office of National Statistics to digitise and index the remaining censuses (1841-1861) for England and Wales, and will be doing so over the coming years.

In Scotland, a project is under way to digitise the records of the kirk sessions (church courts dealing with the moral transgressions of their congregations), which will probably take another five years to complete. In addition, 19th century poor relief registers are being digitised, with those for the historic counties of Caithness, Ross & Cromarty, and Wigtownshire being tackled first. The National Archives of Scotland's collection of sasines (land records dating back to 1599), and taxation records may also be digitised later.

Also in Scotland, the Court of the Lord Lyon King of Arms *(www.lyon-court.com)*, which is the government agency in charge of registering Scottish coats of arms, is digitising its "Lyon Register". This records all coats of arms authorised since 1672, and contains genealogical information on well-to-do Scottish families.

The register is expected to be online by 2007, and will form part of the forthcoming Scottish Family History Research Service, which should be fully operational by 2006. This will provide an integrated online service with access to the resources available at present through the *Scotland's People* and *Scottish Documents* websites.

Despite an all-Ireland initiative to transcribe parish registers and make them available electronically, these records are not finding their way online. Unfortunately, the Government of the Irish Republic seems more interested in promoting tourism to Ireland than making records available to family historians worldwide.

New civil registrations in the Republic of Ireland are being carried out electronically, and existing civil records are being digitised. Unfortunately, these will not be initially accessible via the Internet either. We can but hope that the Irish Government will see the benefit of putting all these transcribed and digitised records on to the Internet, as has happened in Scotland.

Alan Stewart is the author of Gathering the Clans: Tracing Scottish Ancestry on the Internet *(Phillimore, 2004). (www.phillimore.co.uk)*

DNA Heritage
Alastair Greenshields

It's an unusual request to make! Usually when you write to your genealogical contacts you are after a GEDCOM file or a copy of a will or possibly some family photos. This time you've sent them a few cotton bud-like swabs and asked them to rub them on the inside of their mouths. This time you want their DNA.

This isn't such an odd request. Your father gave you 'the family nose', your hair is wavy like your mother's and you have her sense of humour. This isn't surprising as between them they also gave you a combined mixture of DNA, their genetic code.

So genetically, you are a blend of your parents. And your parents a blend of their parents. As is every living human. It's a scenario that has caused philosophers to ask if we are just placed on earth to safely look after our DNA to pass on the next generation. But how does this tie in with asking your relatives and genealogical friends to give up their own? The answer lies in a tiny part of the DNA called the Y-chromosome.

When a baby is conceived, it's up to genes within the body that tell the baby which sex to grow into. The Y-chromosome has a genetic switch that when

Cumbria, but that's as much as you can find out. Or maybe you've been in contact with a gentleman living in the US with a slightly different surname to your own but you suspect that he's actually is related to your line. Any evidence of a paper trail was lost as his ancestors made the trip across the Atlantic. Both are perfect scenarios of where DNA testing comes into its own.

By testing certain males within the different lines, we can look at the results, compare and conclude if the theories are correct. And the cost per test? Good, high-resolution tests start at about $138. It is entirely sexist in that only males can participate, but female relatives usually contribute to the test fund. If you compare this with the cost of a genealogical field trip to a records centre visit, it's not too expensive. And it can be a powerful genealogical tool when the records no longer exist.

Just what are we actually looking for and comparing? Essentially a series of numbers. This series of numbers is called a 'haplotype' and may look like this: (Fig 1)

*As you can see, the haplotypes for the two cousins are identical as would be expected. This is how we

Your results, called a 'haplotype', will look similar to this. This is used to compare with putative cousins.

	DYS19	DYS385a	DYS385b	DYS388	DYS389i	DYS389ii	DYS390	DYS391	DYS392 etc.
Haplotype	14	12	17	12	13	29	24	11	13

turned on, starts a cascade of events within the body that "It's a boy" are the first words it will hear.

But this Y-chromosome is special in that the baby didn't receive it from both parents like the rest of the DNA. Only males possess Y-chromosomes and so the baby must have received his copy from his father. And in turn the father received his copy from the grandfather. This has gone on for thousands of generations and the new baby boy is just the bottom in a long genetic lineage.

Conveniently for genealogists, the passing on of the Y-chromosome usually follows the same path of the surname. So if you pick a great-grandfather in your family tree, all of his direct male descendants will have the same (or very nearly the same) Y-chromosome. If we're able to read and compare these Y-chromosomes we can prove that they are related. Conversely, we can compare other people with the same or similar sounding surnames and see if we can tie them into your own genetic line.

Imagine the usefulness that this could have for your own research. There is a group of you who share the same surname and can all trace your origins to

match people up. This also answers another question about DNA testing; "Will it identify me as an individual?". The answer is no. You'll share your haplotype with many, many people and it's only by limiting comparisons with people who share the same surnames that we make sense of the results (by effectively only comparing against a much smaller group of people). Y-chromosome testing is very different from a forensic DNA profile in this regard.

If we focus on one single genetic 'marker' in the above haplotype, say DYS390, the number 24 pertains to how many times a part of the Y-chromosome is repeated at that particular location. Using DYS390 as an example, the genetic letters of TCTA are repeated several times (in this case 24). What is important to note is that this is the same number of repeats as the father and his grandfather. This is proved by the fact that the cousin also shares the same number of repeats at that marker.

When we take a step back, we've managed to prove that these cousins are related and have also worked out the haplotype for the grandfather. If we then test more distantly related cousins, we can confirm that this new cousin really is related and also

270

deduce the haplotype for a much older ancestor.

Now you can begin to see just how powerful 'genetic genealogy' can be. If we go further and test people who we believe may also be related e.g. the surnames are the same, we can also test this theory too. In fact, this is precisely what is being carried out already by hundreds of Surname Project and thousands of people around the world; and most Projects have members from all around the world (mostly from North America, Europe and Oceania).

Many people receive their results and 'bank' them into the Ybase public-access database at www.ybase.org. Because the results won't identify someone as an individual and because the results are not medically informative, it is a great way to help your genetic cousins to find you. People enter their genealogical information along with their Y-chromosome data. It's possible to search by haplotype and surname. Ybase also contains the Ybase Forums (at www.ybase.org/forum) which is designed to help people with the same or similar surname connect up and discuss their possible genetic links.

You may be asking how, if the DNA stays the same over time, do I and my next door neighbour differ? Good question. In fact when the DNA is copied within the body, small mistakes are occasionally made. This means that where a father may have 24 repeats at DYS390, his son may only have 23. These differences are called 'mutations' but aren't as bad as they may sound. This doesn't harm the son at all (the Y-chromosome tests are not medically informative) and he carries that slightly different Y-chromosome with no adverse effects.

These mutations are actually fairly rare; and happen approximately once every 500 generations. This is a hugely long period of time and it doesn't sound like it would makes us very different from our neighbour. But if we consider that this has been going on for millions of years and if we look at enough genetic markers, on average, we are very

different from our neighbours. Luckily for genealogy, the number of genetic markers now available and the timescales that we are able to compare people within fits well with the relatively few centuries that surnames have been around.

A common desire is to try and find a link between yourself and a distant cousin who share their most recent common ancestor, say back in the 17th century. This theory can be tested - if we test the right people. If for example, you just compare yourself and that distant cousin of yours, and the results don't match, then you come up with the conclusion that you aren't genetically related. This will be true but will probably not tell the whole story.

In every generation, there is a small chance that a 'non-paternity' event has occurred. This may be adoption or illegitimacy, essentially any situation where the genetic line differs from that of the surname. This happens at about 2-5% every generation and varies with socio-economic groups. But what it does mean for genealogists is that if you go far enough back, the genetic line has a fairly good chance of being broken. So testing just two people may not give the right picture.

Here is a good testing scenario. Have yourself and a close-ish cousin tested. A 2nd cousin is a good choice. This should be a match. You've just determined the haplotype for your great-grandfather. Then test a slightly more distant cousin. If this result matches (or is very close), you will have determined the haplotype for a more distant ancestor. By this method, you will provide a clearer picture of your genealogy and differences to the norm will show up quite clearly. Test enough selected cousins and you can effectively 'walk' back up your own genetic line and can then connect to and provide this information to countless cousins who also share the same genetic lineage. And once you've got a clear picture of your lineage, you can confidently compare with others who share your surname to see if they are also related – and this works for variant spellings too.

About 4 and a half years ago, the first genetic services for genealogy were offered to the public. The technology was straight out of the research labs and although the scientific techniques used had been around for many years, the analysis of the Y-chromosome was a brand new application. As such, the people being tested were pioneers in a sense although the results they received were only low-resolution tests. These were using 10 or 12 marker tests. The conclusions formed from the tests weren't as accurate as they can be (i.e. the conclusions of if someone was related or not weren't always correct) and as technology has improved, this has been borne out.

If we take this to the extreme, and only compare people using one single marker, you might share it with as many as half a billion people around the world. Clearly you are not related to this many people within the timeframes that most genealogists are looking at. As we increase the number of markers, the number of matches reduces dramatically. So generally, the more markers you compare against, the better.

When we compare two people, how many non-matches do we need for them to be unrelated? This depends on the number of markers used. Whilst some people do have themselves tested on just 10 or 12 markers (which we can't recommend – more on this later), the majority of people have themselves tested on at least 20 markers. If we take 23 as an example, at this number of markers, a 23/23 match is an exact match, a 22/23 match is where one of the markers doesn't match and a 21/23 match is where two of the markers do not match.

means that you may get an answer back that you are related when in fact you aren't. And vice-versa.

As an example of this, a survey, http://blairgenealogy.com/dna/markers.html carried out on the results that surname group studies had published on the web who had both 12 and 25 markers tested showed that if only 12 markers were used to compare with, in at least 21% of the time, the wrong conclusions were formed. Only when they compared using extra markers was the correct picture shown. This 21% figure should be as near to 0% as possible.

Many people stay at the 12 marker level and don't purchase extra markers thus more than 1 in 5 people will have come to the wrong conclusions regarding their relationship with another person. This is an unacceptable situation and results in people wrongly adjusting their family trees based on the results. Back in the Elizabethan period, birth and marriage records were often forged by professional historians and researchers to make it appear as though there were connections to the aristocracy. If low-resolution tests are relied upon, a similar situation occurs, only with DNA testing providing the 'proof'. Yet to get valid results is surely the reason why people have themselves tested in the first place.

The key is, don't stick at the lower level of testing – like everything else in life, you do get what you pay for. However, valid results can be gained with 20+ marker tests and will cost only marginally more. You will also save time and money if you purchase enough markers straight off.

These cousins share surnames but aren't haplotype matches, yet are close enough to be considered related.

Cousin 1	14, 11, 14, 12, 13, 29, 24, 11, 13, 13, 12, 15, 13, 11, 13, 12, 12, 11, 14, 24, 19, 30, 11
Cousin 2	15, 11, 14, 12, 13, 29, 24, 11, 13, 13, 12, 15, 13, 11, 13, 12, 12, 11, 14, 25, 19, 30, 11

Clearly, where a 23/23 match exists, this is an identical result and provides very good support that the two people are related. But because the mutations are random and can happen at any time, we may also include the 22/23 and 21/23 matches as also related, but usually more distantly. This is with the caveat that any comparisons must be made within the same surname spelling (or similar)

Any more than a difference of two at this number of markers and we can say that the two people are not related. The testing companies will provide help people compare their results.

Whilst it is possible to purchase up to 43 markers in a single test, some companies will still sell 10 or 12 marker tests. The main reason people purchase these are because they can be low-cost, but caution must be taken as the wrong conclusions are often formed at this low-resolution level of testing. This

So why do people purchase more markers than 20, if 20 are enough? There are three main reasons:
i) you might have a popular surname, in which case it's advisable to test at about the 30-marker level (to reduce the possibility of a random, incorrect match)
ii) you may want to show finer branching and structure within your surname group which is often possible by comparing more markers.
ii) you may want to compare with markers tested by other companies.

Whilst all of the above points are important, the last point needs further explanation. There are in total about 49 genetic markers in use by test companies. It's possible to purchase as many as 43 markers in a single test although a total of 49 markers can be purchased if you order from more than one company. However, in the recent past, the test companies have not always used the same markers

These men share their surnames, a common ancestry and...

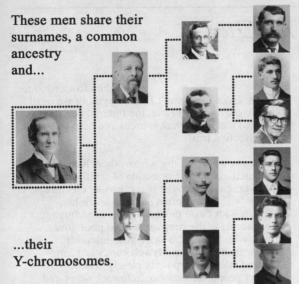

...their Y-chromosomes.

By analysing their DNA, you can connect them where the paper records might not be so strong.

You can also test other cousins to climb further up the family tree...

...and can compare other men with the same surname to see if they are related too.

What is also interesting is that some haplogroups aren't seen outside Africa, which supports the theory that modern humans originated in Africa - mostly likely East Africa. These humans can then be seen to travel around the globe, which the genetic evidence from the Y-chromosome also supports.

Most companies will perform this correlation for you and although they are usually fairly spot on, be aware that all haplogroup predictions may contain error. It should also be made clear that it is not possible to pin the origin/path of the Y-chromosome to a narrow region or country and only a wide region can be given.

As an example Haplogroup R1b is very common within Western Europe. This haplogroup has its origin's within Iberia at the end of the last ice age (10-12,000 years ago). As the huge ice sheet that covered much of Europe retreated, the peoples held up within this Iberian region essentially followed the food. This would have carried these people with the R1b pattern from Spain and Portugal across France and eventually to the UK and Ireland. It is still observed in these regions today has spread a little into Central Europe and is almost non-existent in Eastern Europe. We do however see the same patterns appear all over South America and shows the dramatic influx of Y-chromosomes into this region over the last 500 years.

Within Ybase (www.ybase.org), there is an excellent correlation between user reported haplogroups and what their patterns suggest so it can be a very good guide as to the European haplogroups.

which has meant that it wasn't always easy to compare with people tested elsewhere.

This problem of marker incompatibility has been resolved with newer, more universal tests and it's now even possible to have a choice over the markers you want to buy, meaning that if you wished to compare with others tested elsewhere, you can. This has also opened the market up rather than restrict cousins to testing with the same lab. And with a more open market comes a reduction in price.

So if you have genealogical questions that you'd like answered, try genetic genealogy!

There is also another use for Y-chromosome testing. 'Deep' ancestry is of interest to people as they try and get as much information from their results as possible. The results you'd receive is called a haplotype. From this haplotype it is possible (for the majority of the time) to predict a haplogroup from your haplotype results.

A haplogroup is a broad grouping to which many males belong to. If you consider a tree structure, the origin of the human Y-chromosome can be considered the trunk. Every so often, a chromosome will change slightly where in this case, a single letter of the DNA code changes. Again with this type of mutation, the altered chromosome is passed on unchanged to any sons. By doing do, the tree effectively splits into a thick branch with this mutation as a marker of the newer branch. After many more generations (and usually several thousand years later) the chromosome will mutate again. Eventually, we can see a tree-like structure for the Y-chromosome. These branches are our haplogroups. You can see a diagram of this at http://www.le.ac.uk/genetics/maj4/JoblingTS.03.NRG.Review.pdf

If We Only Had Old Ireland Over Here
Joesph O'Neill

There's a sentimental Irish song that tells of an emigrant wishing that someone would bring Galway Bay and other parts of Ireland to him. His wish is echoed by family historians frustrated that information about their Irish ancestors is beyond their reach. The Internet is not able to transport the Mountains of Mourne but it can give us access to many records once available only in Ireland.

One of the exciting things about the Internet is that it is in a constant state of flux. New sites are appearing all the time, every day more data is accessible on-line.

What's more, the Internet is ideal for those activities central to genealogy: consulting records and making contact with those who share our interests. It revolutionises the speed with which we can do this. As the number of on-line genealogists increases so does the ease with which we can search data and share information.

Recent research suggests that about 60% of UK genealogists are currently on-line and the number is steadily increasing, and while books, microfilm and other media remain important, the Internet is the publishing medium of choice of all major genealogical data projects and most small ones.

These advantages are highlighted when we need to access data from outside Britain. Even if we can't find everything we need without leaving the house, the Internet can tell us where to locate relevant sources and help us to plan effective trips.

'There is no need to dig where others have already excavated', is a basic principle of family history. The average genealogist is a generous creature usually willing and often eager to share his research with those ploughing the same furrow. The Internet is the simplest way to pool your efforts with those who share your interests. Rootsweb at <**www.rootsweb.com**> is a long-standing site. Its purpose is clearly stated: "to connect people so they can help each other and share genealogical research." In addition it has its own search engine and many large and searchable databases. Genealogy Mall, <**www.genealogy-mall.com**>, Irish Origins discussion group, <**groups.yahoo.com/group/irish-origins**>, Origins.net mailing list, <**www.origins.net/maillist.html**> and the Index to RootsWeb's 23,404 genealogy mailing lists at <**lists.rootsweb.com**> all serve a similar purpose. The gateway site to genealogy in the United Kingdom and Ireland is Genuki at <**www.genuki.org.uk**>. Organised and searchable geographically, you can see immediately what information is available on your chosen area. A

OUR FRIEND, BRIGGS, RECEIVES A PRESSING INVITATION TO COME OVER AGAIN TO IRELAND DURING THE HUNTING SEASON, AND HAVE A WEEK WITH THE GALWAY BLAZERS!
[Mr. B. says he should like it extremely, as he has never ridden in a Stone Wall country.

great strength of the site is its search engine. Not only does it trawl all connected sites but it also combs the site of the Public Record Office at Kew. The British Isles page is at <www.genuki.org.uk/big> and the Irish page at <www.genuki.org.uk/big/irl>.

Cyndi's List sets out to be all things to all genealogists and largely succeeds. It consists of links to genealogy web sites arranged in five main categories –a main list, topical, alphabetical, no frills and text only. Once you are familiar with this site you will find yourself returning to it again and again. You'll find it at <www.cyndislist.com>.

Peter Christian, author of *The Genealogist's Internet*, the best general guide, is the leading authority in his field. His splendid site 'Finding Genealogy on the Internet' at <www.spub.co.uk/fgi/> is clear and concise and includes genealogy gateway sites from a British perspective.

A particularly good search engine is 'Irish Origins' at **www.irishorigins.com**. Part of the subscription service 'Origin Search', it is a free service. It has a number of sophisticated name-matching features and a facility, which allows you to search by category of document.

Another guiding principle is to check compiled or secondary records before looking at original or primary records. Eventually, you will verify information from compiled records by reference to original records. But the advantage of consulting sources in the correct order is that it can save you a great deal of time and unnecessary work. You may well discover that the research you are planning has already been done.

Genealogists or historians create compiled or secondary records possibly years after the events to which they refer. They are often compiled from original records, such as registers of births, marriages and deaths or from other compiled records. They are always easier to search than the original sources and are thus a boon to the genealogist.

Irish surnames are still associated with specific areas of the country. This is one reason why maps are essential secondary sources for the family historian. The University of Wisconsin - Madison has several historical maps of Ireland including a Poor Law map at <history.wisc.edu/archdeacon/famine/>. The National Library of Ireland's large collection of maps is listed at **www.nli.ie/co_maps.htm**

In the early stages of research, when searching for family and local histories, newspaper files containing obituaries and relevant news items, you will want to contact local libraries, historical, family history and genealogical societies — which are also sources of invaluable shortcuts. The following are invaluable at this stage: British Isles Genealogy at <www.bigenealogy.com>, Research

UK at <www.research-uk.com>, British Isles Gen Web at <www.britishislesgenweb.org>, the UK and Ireland Genealogical Information Service (GENUKI) at <www.genuki.org.uk> and Family History Resources in Public Libraries in Britain and Ireland at <www.familia.org.uk>.

Begin your search for family histories and surname background at Surname Web on <www.surnameweb.com> and Surname Search at <www.surnamesearch.com>.

You will certainly contact kindred spirits sharing your particular interests through The Society of Genealogists at <www.sog.org.uk>, The Federation of Family History Societies at <www.ffhs.org.uk> or the North of Ireland Family History Society, <www.nifhs.org>. Family Tree, <www.familytree.com> and Genealogy Links, <www.genealogylinks.net> provide further means of tapping into those who mining the same seam.

The most famous compiled sources is the International Genealogical Index. It consists of millions of names combed from birth, christening, marriage and other records. It is available at the Family History Library, FamilySearch™ Centre and at many Family History Centres. You can find out about it on <www.familysearch.org>.

Before you plunge into your search for the primary sources remember that most Church of Ireland parish registers, and census records, were destroyed when the Irish national archives were burnt in 1922. You can find details of what survives on the Fianna site at www.rootsweb.com/~fianna/guide/census.html. The good news, however, is that there are some substitute records and that many Catholic parish registers survive, though few from the pre-1800 period.

Full civil registration began in Ireland on 1 January 1864, though registration of Protestant marriages dates from 1 April 1845. The Registrar General in Dublin holds records for the whole of Ireland up to 31 December 1921 and for the Republic thereafter at **www.groireland.ie**. The equivalent records for Northern Ireland are the responsibility of the General Register Office (Northern Ireland) at **www.groni.gov.uk/index.htm**. You will find information on records of births, marriages and deaths at the National Archives of Ireland site at www.nationalarchives.ie/birthsmarrdeaths.html .

There are a number of sites with census data for individual counties. Data from the 1901 census is available on-line at www.leitrim-roscommon.com/1901census/ However, the only all-Ireland material currently on-line is at FamilySearch <www.familysearch.org> where you may access the IGI which contains the births for the first five years of registration, 1864-1868.

Because of the gaps in Irish census material, the

'census substitutes' are vital. The best guide to these is on the Fianna site at **www.rootsweb.com/~fianna/guide/cen2.html** The Primary Valuation of Ireland (Griffith's Valution) is the key "census substitute" for mid-19th century Ireland. The first systematic valuation of all property holdings in Ireland, many genealogists regard Griffith's as an indispensable resource. The PRONI has a guide to the use of the Valuation at **www.proni.gov.uk/research/family/griffith.htm** and you can access it on the Otherdays subscription site at www.otherdays.com where you can correlate entries with Ordnance Survey maps. Searching records for the period before national registers means relying mainly on parish registers. The Society of Genealogists – at <www.sog.org.uk> — has copies of many Irish registers. Family history and parish register societies have indexed many more, but there is very little of this material actually on-line. What there is can be found on three sites.

RootsWeb has user-submitted databases which are listed at <**userdb.rootsweb.com/regional.html**>. You can access some parish register material through the Irish Ancestor site at <**scripts.ireland.com/ancstors/browse/links/coun ties/**>. There is also a section covering church records on the Genuki site at **www.genuki.org.uk/big/irl/**.

If you can't access many church records online, you can certainly locate them. IrelandGenWeb at **www.irelandgenweb.com** and NorthernIrelandGenWeb at **www.rootsweb.com/~nirwgw/** have county pages with information on the parishes whose registers have been filmed by the LDS. Details of PRONI's Church of Ireland and Presbyterian records on microfilm are available at **www.proni.gov.uk/records/USING/using.htm** For the Nonconformist churches, consul Fianna's guide to 'Baptist, Methodist, Presbyterian and Quaker Records in Ireland' at **www.rootsweb.com/~fianna/country/churches.ht ml**.

Cemetery records may enable you to locate names and dates not found anywhere else. The clustering of headstones and their epitaphs can also help establish relationships. Many family history societies are recording tombstone and monumental inscriptions, thousand of which have been deposited with the Society of Genealogists. You can find the details at <**www.sog.org.uk**>. Unfortunately graves and monuments, like those they commemorate, are subject to the ravages of time. You are unlikely to find many from the 17th century. Most are from the 19th and 20th centuries. One of the most comprehensive sites is Cemeteries of Ireland at **http://www.interment.net/ireland/**, which provides links to cemetery sites throughout the thirty-two counties. Others well worthy a visit Ireland Cemetery Preservation - SavingGraves.co.uk, Churches & Cemeteries -

Shamrock Cottage and Cemetery Inscriptions - A Little Bit of Ireland.

Of course, many of our Irish forebears did not find their final resting-place in Ireland. This is because of the unique significance of emigration in Ireland's history and its effect on almost every family. Sooner or later you will be consulting emigration records.

When tracing an ancestor who emigrated from the British Isles, it is often easiest to search the records of their country of destination. New arrivals overseas were more likely to have been recorded than those leaving the British Isles. Many Irish emigrants, especially during the 19th century, were convicts, transported to British colonies and penal settlements as an alternative to imprisonment. The experience of these unfortunates is generally well documented.

Your starting point should be the National Archives' leaflet, 'Emigration', which is the definitive on-line guide at <**catalogue.pro.gov.uk/Leaflets/ri2272.htm**>. You will find excellent leaflets on convict transportation to North America and the West Indies at < **catalogue.pro.gov.uk/Leaflets/ri2234.htm**> and to Australia at <**catalogue.pro.gov.uk/Leaflets/ri2235.htm**>

Passenger lists are key records when searching for emigrant ancestors. There are several sites with information about surviving lists or data transcribed from them. Cyndi's List 'Ships and Passenger Lists' page at **www.cyndislist.com/ships.htm/** has links to numerous lists and lists of ship arrivals.

Another splendid site is that of the Immigrant Ships Transcribers Guild at <**istg.rootsweb.com**>. It allows you to search over 5,000 passenger lists by date, port of departure, port of arrival, and captain's name. The Guild's Compass site at <**istg.rootsweb.com/newcompass/pcindex.html**> provides links to an enormous number of on-line passenger list sites. Of particular interest to those working on Irish ancestry is the ScotlandsClans site at www.scotlandsclans.com/irshiplists.htm which provides links to many relevant sites.

Passenger lists for emigrants from Ireland to the United States and Canada, arranged in date order, are available at **http://freespace.virgin.net/alan.tupman/sites/iris h.htm**. A superb site is the American Family Immigration History Centre website at <**www.ellisislandrecords.org**>. Its facilities allow you to search by passenger name and even view the original ship's manifest and the ship. There are also many good mailing lists for immigrant ships. The most extensive is TheShips List at **www.theshipslists.com**.

you still can't locate that elusive ancestor?

A good starting point for your review is the information you were working from when you searched Griffith's Valuation. Try to verify the dates you were using. Check the place name. Did the area have a different name at the relevant time? And what about the form of the surname for which you are searching? Is it possible the spelling has changed?

If this fails to produce a breakthrough, you should try a different index resource for the Valuation. Each index is unique in that there are slight variations between them all. And, of course, they all contain mistakes due to human error when the index was compiled.

Apart from sites specialising in specific areas of family history, there are many general sites, which offer a range of information and search aids. These are constantly developing as more material becomes available online.

UK and Ireland Genealogical Information Service (GENUKI) at <**www.genuki.org.uk**> is an excellent reference sources. Though surname sites have a specific focus they are also a good means of contacting those working in your area. Among the most useful for Irish family historian are Surname Web at <**www.surnameweb.com**> and Surname Search at<**www.surnamesearch.com**>. The North of Ireland Family History Society at <**www.nifhs.org**>, the Irish Origins discussion group at <**groups.yahoo.com/group/irish-origins**> and the Index to RootsWeb's, with links to over 23,000 genealogy mailing lists at <**lists.rootsweb.com**> should provide links with all the contacts you require.
The most convenient way to survey the material in the Irish county heritage centres is through http://www.irish-roots.net/Cork.htm. There are many online lists, including the religious census of 1776 which you can access at **http://www.interment.net/ireland/**. Irish Genealogy Links at **http://www.genealogylinks.net/uk/ireland/** also organises its material according to county. Genealogy Resources on the Internet at **http://www.personal.umich.edu/~cgaunt/irish.html** is an excellent site very well organised and clearly set out in a logical manner.
And what if, after patiently trawling these sites,

One option is the Householders Index, available on film through the Family History Centres. There is a guide among the Research Helps for Ireland at **www.familysearch.org**.
Ultimately, you may have to accept that the information you seek is not there. Some people were not recorded. Most of these people were town dwellers living in rented accommodation. They owned no land and so escaped the compilers' attention.

But this does not mean that you have to give up, only that you should try another approach. There are other many other online resources, including a number of versions of the Valuation, some for counties and some targeting particular areas. Try these. Turn to other records of the period and examine the later valuation books for the place you have searched.

The Internet is not a panacea. It cannot transport Cork City to Adelaide or make Killarnay's lakes flow into Botany Bay. But in many instances it brings into our homes records which were once half a world away. It's something we shouldn't be blasé about. It's as wonderful as Shandon Bells ringing out in Sydney Harbour.

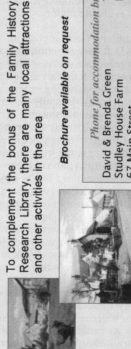

David Tippey's Top Research Websites

The number of websites making available actual research material and useful indexes, rather than help and advice has blossomed over the last couple of years. We now have a number of useful sites, some free, others with various payment models:

Some sites offer a free index and then sell single copies of documents at a fixed price each.

Others have a free index, plus a minimum subscription charge giving a fixed number of credits to be redeemed against data downloads over a fixed period.

A third method has access to both index and data using a fixed period subscription and download credits.

Finally there is the flat rate subscription where a fixed fee is paid for a period of access no matter what the usage.

They all have some pros and cons and most users will have their own preference, but all offer quite good value when you take into consideration the convenient access, relatively cheap price for copies (you can save them to disk rather than print them) and lack of hidden costs. If you don't have much money to spare, make sure you plan your research and optimise the use of your access by having a list of alternative, but less pressing, facts to check at the same time.

The free sites tend to be created by volunteers, non commercial organisations such as the LDS Church or a combination of the two. You might expect that to mean less impressive and less useful sites, but the likes of FreeBMD, Ellis Island and Family Search with its 1881 census, IGI and Vital Records databases certainly dispel that thought. There are also a myriad of smaller websites hosting useful data and resources. They are far too numerous, and most too small and specialised to mention here, but many researchers will find a small site somewhere on the web that holds a nugget of information that they will cherish.

This list pulls together the best of the websites that will prove most useful to researchers wanting to access English, Welsh or Scottish material from their home computer.

© Apple Computer

Research Sites to pay for-

1901 Census
www.1901census.nationalarchives.gov.uk

Despite the criticism it received in the past, the 1901 census is an extremely useful resource which has proved a boon for researchers. Searching the index is free and you then pay 50p for a transcript of an individual's details and a further 50p for the rest of the household. However it is generally preferable to view the original census book image so that you can verify the transcription yourself. This costs 75p per page. The minimum payment is £5 worth of credits, which last just 24 hours, making prepayment vouchers a more attractive option as they have a much longer life

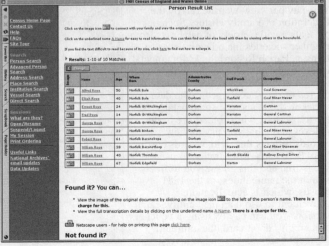

Documents Online

www.documentsonline.nationalarchives.gov.uk

The complete collection of over 1 million Prerogative Court of Canterbury wills has been indexed and can be searched. Except for the Commonwealth period, most of the entries are for the south of England, as those for much of the North were proved at York. In addition, details of the entitlement to World War 1 campaign medals and World War 2 Merchant Seaman's medals are now being digitised and put online. There is no fixed subscription, with the use of the indexes being free. Single copies of the wills or medal details can be instantly purchased online in PDF format at £3.50 per document.

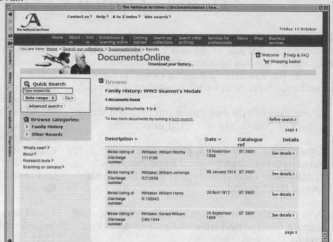

Scotlands People

www.scotlandspeople.gov.uk

This site holds an extensive set of records from the General Register Office of Scotland, covering Census; Birth, Marriage and Death registrations, and Parish Registers. A good feature of this site is that registered users, even with no credits, can see their previously viewed images again and also to save their searches. You do need to be in credit to actually search the indexes or view new images though and this costs a minimum of £6 for 30 credits lasting 48 hours.

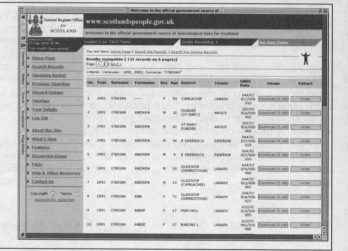

Family History Online

www.familyhistoryonline.net

This pay per view website run by the Federation of Family History Societies presents a wide variety of databases from member societies including indexes to Census, Parish Records and Monumental Inscriptions, as well as holding the latest version of the National Burial Index. The degree of detail contained in the data varies with the society, some databases are transcripts, whilst others are basic indexes and what you pay to view records reflects this, with records costing from 3-9p each. Registration to use the site is free and this allows you to freely search the name index, or the 1881 census, which is actually more convenient to use than the FamilySearch version. You can pay by using a voucher or a credit / debit card, the minimum payment being £5 which has a very generous 6 months of life

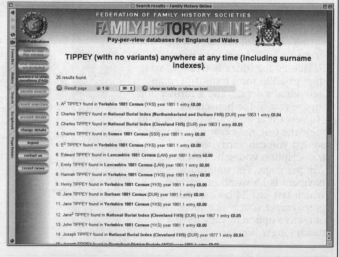

1837 Online *www.1837online.com*
The first website to place all the General
Register Office's Civil Registration indexes
online. The indexes to Births, Marriages and
Death registrations are split into two sections.
From 1984 onwards the records are fully
searchable by name and the individual record
can be viewed. From 1837 -1983 the records are
in the form of images of the original index book
pages. These are arranged in four quarter year
batches for each event and are indexed by
surname and forename or initial, Because the
pages are indexed by name range, there is the
possibility that the name searched for doesn't
actually appear on that page. Recently, various
indexes to overseas events have been added to
extend the range of the service. The minimum
payment is £5 for 55 units (one page download
costs 1 unit) which last 45 days, larger volumes
of units are cheaper and last for longer periods.

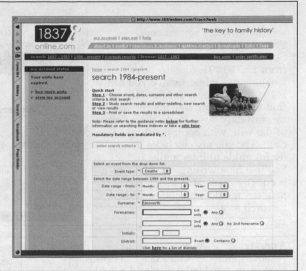

National Archivist
www.nationalarchivist.com
With a free search, after your initial
registration, this is a pay per view
site which includes a collection of
more unusual databases to extend
the range of resources available to
genealogists, These include Army
Lists; Passport Applications, Bank
of England Death Duty Registers
and a range of Indian Colonial
material. There are also some free
to view items, which mainly consist
of ancillary information pages
about the main data sets. The
minimum subscription costs £7 and
provides 35 Credits with a life of
45 days

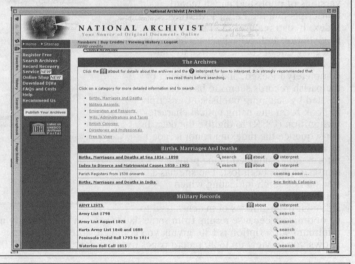

The Origins Network *www.origins.net*
The Origins website consists of three main
sections: British Origins containing an
eclectic collection of indexes from the
SOG plus a gazetteer and some 1871
census material; Irish Origins which
contains databases from Eneclann,
previously only available on CD, plus
uniquely, the maps which accompany the
Griffith's Valuation; Origin Search Pro, a
search engine which only returns
genealogy related web pages. Scots
Origins is still represented but reduced to
little more than a research service and a
free Scottish IGI search (not available
elsewhere online) since the data was move
to the new ScotlandsPeople website. A
minimum of 72 hours access to all Origins
services costs £7.50 (£34.50 annually), or
£5.95 for 72 hour access to British Origins
and Origins Search Pro only.

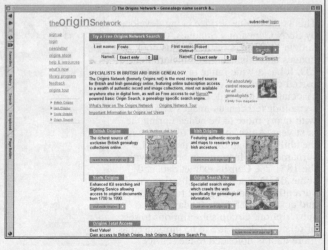

Scottish Documents

www.scottishdocuments.com

Providing an online database to Scottish wills and testaments dating from 1500-1901, like the NA's Documents Online service you can search the database for free. If you find what you are looking for you can instantly download a digital copy of the will, with copies costing £5 each. The site also includes a very useful guide to interpreting old Scottish handwriting, most of which is equally applicable to any old handwritten documents, and other research tools.

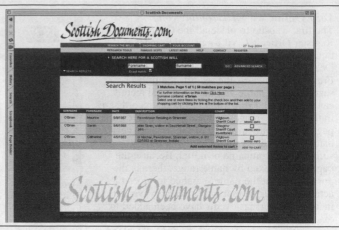

Ancestry   *www.ancestry.co.uk*

A subscription site with a range of census page images and indexes, plus digitised versions of published parish record transcripts and the Pallot's Marriage Index. It also features the FreeBMD Civil Registration Indexes which are hosted by Ancestry but of course are free to view. Not all the document images are completely indexed, and the indexing of the parish records seems to have been created by scanning published transcripts in book form and using optical character recognition (OCR) to digitise the data. In consequence the indexing is not as good as it might be and some of the additional information contained in the printed transcripts has been lost. The site has a free name search indicating which databases hold matching records, although the estimates of matches tend to be optimistic, because results from some databases don't necessarily match your full search criteria. The minimum subscription is £30, giving you complete access for a quarter, and a trial pay per view option allows you to view up to 20 record pages over a 7 day period for £7.00

The Genealogist

www.thegenealogist.co.uk

This is the online service being developed by S&N Genealogy Supplies, the well known publishers of the Census book images and other research material on CD. It has a wide range of complete and partial census indexes available, and the associated BMD index. It already has some indexed census images available, with many more to be added during the next year. A useful feature of the site is the ability to map the distribution of surnames. this feature can be used with the 1851 2% Census extract data and some BMD index data. Subscriptions are currently per database, not for the full site and cost from £5 for a 90 day access subscription. Group subscriptions to sets of related indexes are to be introduced as more data is uploaded to the service

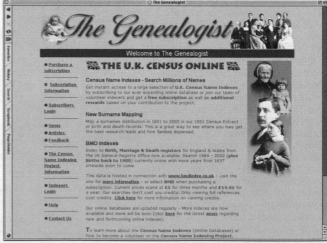

BMDindex *www.bmdindex.co.uk*

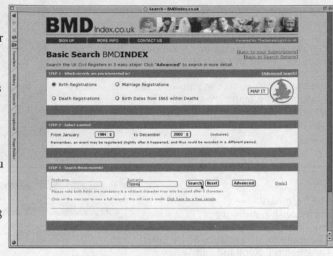

The BMDindex has fully searchable GRO indexes from 1984 to date and for the period 1900-1983 the images are indexed by the full surname and forename, making it easy to find the entry you want. The subscription prices cost from £5 for a 90 day access subscription, you receive credits which allow you to view the full records but using the name search is free and doesn't deduct any credits from your account. Credits are deducted when you download and view a page image, but as the indexing accurately takes you to the correct page the credits go a long way as you will probably only use 4 - 8 to search a full year. For post 1983 records the free index contains all the available information except the Volume and Page references needed to obtain a certificate. These newer records also have an automatic spouse look up for marriages and all post 1983 events can be mapped by surname to show the distribution of the events around the country.

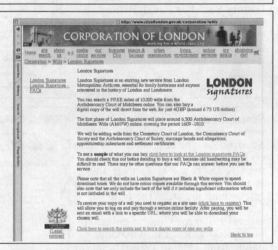

London Signatures
www.cityoflondon.gov.uk/Corporation/wills
This is another will website, this time from the London Metropolitan Archives. Again the model is similar to Documents Online and you are allowed to search a free index to the wills proved in the Archdeaconry Court of Middlesex. If you find what you want you can purchase a digital copy of the will for £4. Wills from other courts, as well as other document types are planned to be added.

Free sites for both Data and Research

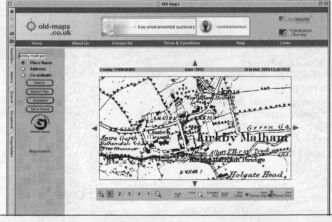

Old Maps *www.old-maps.co.uk*
This excellent resource gives you free access to the first edition 6 inch series Ordnance Survey mapping. These date from the middle of the 19th Century and include lots of small places that have now been swallowed up by larger towns and cities. The maps cover most areas of England, Scotland and Wales and can be freely downloaded and printed.

Get a Map

www.ordnancesurvey.co.uk/oswebsite/getamap
This service from the Ordnance Survey allows you to download and print small sections of the current mapping for all of Great Britain including Northern Ireland. It is useful for finding addresses, archives and churches and to compare with the 19th century mapping. The maps are available in various scales up to 1:25,000 and you will also find a comprehensive online gazetteer on the OS website.

1881 Census

www.familysearch.org :
www.familyhistoryonline.com
The transcription of the 1881 census for England, Scotland and Wales is freely available on the LDS Church's FamilySearch website, but not many people know that England and Wales is also on the Federation of Family History Society's FamilyHistory Online website. It is still free to use and the query system is different from the LDS version, which I think makes it easier to use.

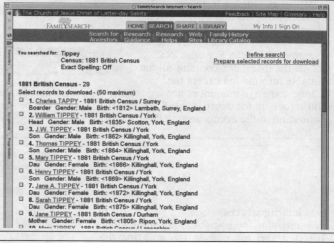

Scottish maps

www.nls.uk/collections/maps
Scotland has the best online collection of maps of any area in the UK and if you enjoy maps this is a site to visit even if you aren't researching the area. The National Library of Scotland has provided around 1,300 map images covering nearly 400 years of map making, dating from 1560 to 1928. These are not the horrible, small, pixilated images you often find on the web, but first class reproductions.

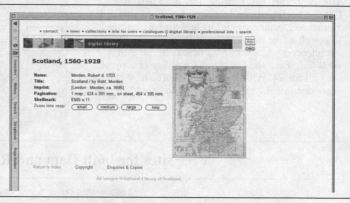

The Old Bailey

www.oldbaileyonline.org
This fully searchable account of proceedings at the country's most famous court, will when complete. hold details of over 100,000 criminal trials which were held there between 1674 and 1834

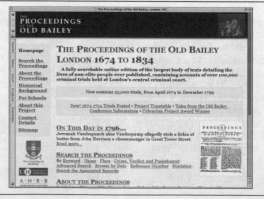

freeBMD
www.freebmd.org.uk
If you want to find references to Births, Marriages and Deaths and obtain the information required to order copies of civil registration certificates, then try this site first, before you sign up for one of the paid for services. It is a volunteer transcription project, with one of the best search engines you will find on any database and although not complete, the coverage from 1837 to 1900 is very good.

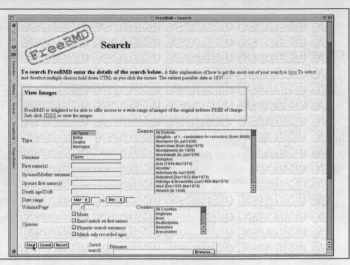

Ellis Island *www.ellisisland.org*
If you suspect anyone may have travelled to America between 1892 and 1924 this site is a must, allowing you to search the passenger lists and to view images of the original records for all the vessels arriving during this period. Most entries into The United States and some bound for Canada arrived via New York. So whether your ancestors emigrated, went on a short business trip or were members of the crew, they could appear on the arrivals paperwork for Ellis Island. The site also has details of the ships, usually accompanied by pictures too.

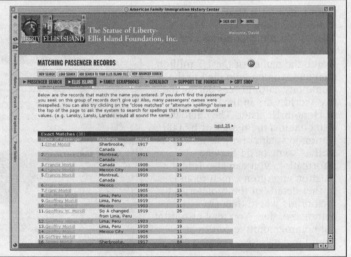

Immigrant Ships Transcribers Guild
www.immigrantships.net

This is useful site where you can find a wide range of passenger list transcriptions covering ships travelling to all destinations, not just the USA. It is a volunteer project and the coverage of dates and places is very variable, but it is well worth looking at just in case you find those ancestors who fell off your tree.

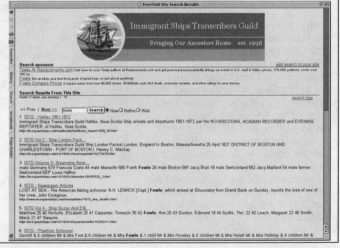

GENUKI *www.genuki.org.uk*

This site is a mine of information and resources covering all aspects of research in the United Kingdom and Ireland. Whenever you start to use a new resource or look at a new area of the country, it will give you quick access to a host of useful pages. The site is organised in levels from country to county, and down to parish, and is packed with useful research information, addresses and even some, but not a lot, of actual data too

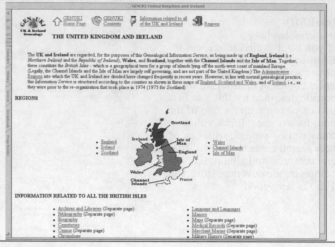

Commonwealth War Graves Commission
www.cwgc.org

The 20th century conflicts caused many family losses and you can search the names of the 1.7 million men and women who died in the Commonwealth Forces during the two world wars in the CWGC Debt of Honour Register. The database also contains the names of 67,000 Commonwealth civilians killed. As well as some basic Service information, you can also find the location and often a picture and further details of the cemeteries or memorials where they are commemorated. You may also print out commemorative certificates from the database.

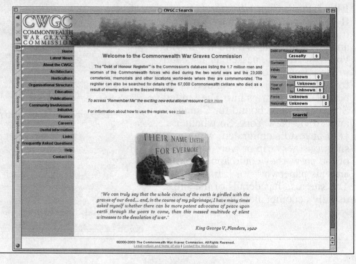

Trade Directories
www.historicaldirectories.org

This is a Leicester University project which aims to make a range of online Trade Directories available for every County. They intend to provide at least one example from each of the following decades: 1850s, 1890s and 1910s for every county, but some already have greater coverage than this. It is a digital library of directory images, fully searchable by location, decade or keyword. The site is a bit slow, but if you are lucky enough to have broadband this won't be a problem.

FamilySearch *www.familysearch.org*
The excellent website created by the Church of Jesus Christ of Latter-day Saints (LDS) has a series of useful databases which can be search individually or together. Transcripts for the 1881 Canadian and 1880 American census are available as well those for the England, Scotland and Wales. The International Genealogical Index (IGI) contains many transcribed sets of Parish Records, although there are some poor quality early LDS Church member submissions. The Vital Records Index contains the more recent extractions of church and chapel records and Ancestral File contains deposited genealogies from various researchers, which are generally less useful and should not be taken at face value.

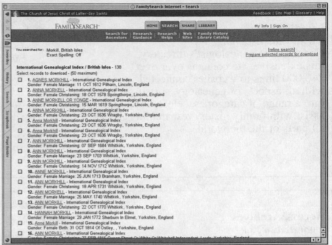

Manorial Documents Register
www.mdr.nationalarchives.gov.uk/mdr
Now part of the National Archives website, this site contains a computerised catalogue identifying the location of Manorial documents for many parts of the country. At present you can search for documents from Hampshire, Isle of Wight, Norfolk, Surrey, Middlesex and the three Ridings of Yorkshire; and all of Wales. They are searchable by manor or probably more useful for most people, by parish.

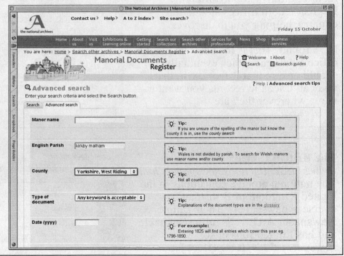

Charles Booth Online Archive
http://booth.lse.ac.uk
Definitely a site for those with London ancestors, it details Charles Booth's survey into life and labour in London. The site includes the Poverty Maps of London and digitised notebooks detailing his walks with the police around the different areas of the city.

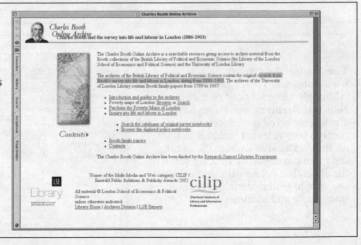

Cyndis List

www.cyndislist.com
The ultimate genealogist's directory, this extensive site contains over over 240,000 links to websites connected with all aspects of genealogy, sorted into a range of categories, selected to assist with family history research in all parts of the the world.

Access2Archives

www.a2a.org.uk
Using this ever growing catalogue, you can search details of over 7 million record holdings at 360 different English record offices around the country, helping you to discover information you may never otherwise have found. This is the ultimate record office catalogue which eventually should ensure that if they exist, that you can trace the records you want to view, wherever they are

The British Library

www.bl.uk/collections/newspapers.html
The national archive collections in the United Kingdom of British and overseas newspapers. Their Online Newspaper Archive is fully searchable and has limited runs of some newspaper titles, It is perfect for finding period background information, even if you can't find specific family references.

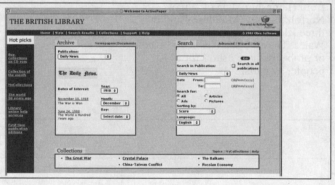

The National Archives

www.nationalarchives.gov.uk
Although some sections of the National Archives web pages have already received a mention, there is plenty more relevant material to find on their extensive website. Searching the main catalogue or viewing some of the specialist online exhibitions, you are sure to find material that is both interesting and useful.

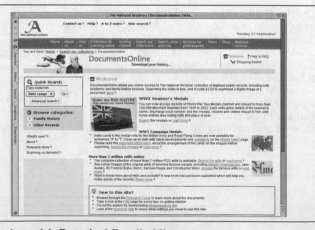

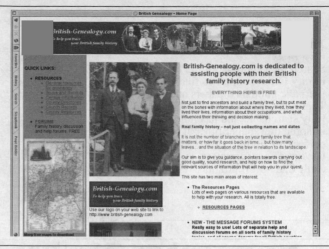

British-Genealogy
www.british-genealogy.com
The very informative and usable website set up by Archive CD Books to assist people to research and build their family trees. It contains information on all the main sources used by family historians, is well written and easily understandable and uses lots of examples taken from relevant documents.

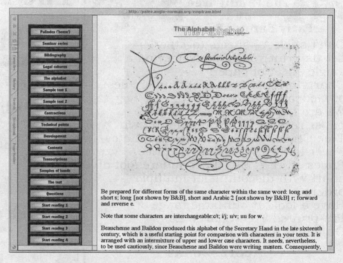

Paleography
http://paleo.anglo-norman.org
Developed by Prof. Dave Postles of Leicester University, this is probably the best old handwriting site and will help you learn or brush up the transcription skills necessary for working with old documents, whether they are medieval or from the 17th and 18th centuries, you will find excellent example and guidance.

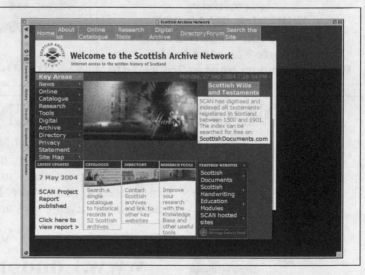

Scottish Archive Network
www.scan.org.uk
This is the Scottish version of A2A and similarly aims to provide a single searchable catalogue of the record holdings in Scotland. Like A2A it is a 'work in progress' but already has representative catalogues from 52 Scottish archives.

The British Library
www.bl.uk
Search the catalogue of the largest library in the country to find books, journals, published papers and more. Their Online Newspaper Archive is fully searchable and has limited runs of some newspaper titles, It is perfect for finding period background information, even if you can't find specific family references.

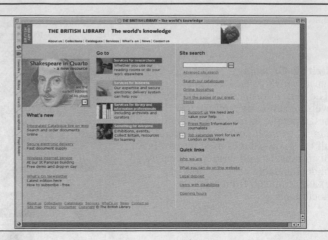

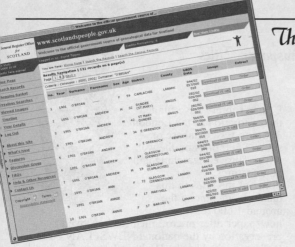

The Scotlands People Internet Service
Martin Tyson
General Register Office for Scotland

Since September 2002, *ScotlandsPeople* has been giving access to indexes and digitised images of GROS's historical records on the Internet. It is a fully searchable pay-per-view website provided in partnership with Scotland On Line, a well-known Internet provider with a particular interest in Scottish heritage (and replaces the successful *Scots Origins* website).

ScotlandsPeople.gov.uk gives access to a uniquely comprehensive range of Scottish genealogical data. This includes:

• Indexed digital images of the statutory registers of births for Scotland, 1855-1904
• Indexed digital images of the statutory registers of marriages for Scotland, 1855-1929
• Indexed digital images of the statutory registers of deaths for Scotland, 1855-1954
• Indexed digital images of the 1891 and 1901 census returns for Scotland
• Indexes to the 1881 census returns for Scotland
• Indexes to the Old Parochial Registers of baptisms and proclamations/marriages for Scotland, 1553-1854

In addition, digital images of the Old Parochial Registers of baptisms, proclamations of banns/marriages and deaths, and of the 1841-1881 census returns will become available on scotlandspeople.gov.uk during 2005/6.

The various cut-off dates detailed above have been applied to the statutory registers to avoid raising concerns about browsing on the Internet among records relating to living people. An additional year of index data and images will be added at the beginning of each year, so 1905 birth data, 1930 marriage data, and 1955 death data will be available from January 2006.

Features
The site includes a number of free features, including a free surname search where the customer can see how many entries there are under their name on the indexes, a regularly updated feature on Famous Scots, giving access to data on the site regarding well-known figures in Scottish history, a place-name search, and news items.

Registration
Customers need to register the first time they access the database. Once registered, customers only need to use their customer name and password when they return to the site. It uses customer registration forms and order forms so that customers can request particular products, but does not handle credit- or debit-card details. This information is entered once customers have been directed to the Streamline secure payment gateway of the Royal Bank of Scotland Group, a major UK bank. Credit card or debit-card information, including account number, is not held by Scotland On Line or GROS at any time.

It costs £6, payable by credit card, to access the index database. This gives 30 'page credits' and allows access for a period of 48 hours (starting from the time a credit card payment is authorised), however many times the customer logs on and off in that time. Further credits can be purchased. Customers can access any of the previous records they have downloaded, outside the 48-hour registration period. The site also offers a timeline feature to help customers keep track of the records they have found. Customers can also order hard copies from any of the previously viewed records without having to pay the £6 again.

Searching
Searching is straightforward, with soundex and wild card search options available. The customer can search across all the records on the database, or narrow their search by type of record, time period or geographical area. Each time a search is done, the number of records found is displayed; each record refers to a specific event, ie a particular birth/baptism, marriage or death. When the customer decides to download these records to their PC, they are displayed in pages each containing a maximum of 25 records. Each page they choose to download costs 1 credit. The index page will indicate if a digital image of each record is available - if so, it can be accessed at the click of a mouse. To view a digital image costs 5 credits.

If a customer wishes to order an extract of any register entry found in the index, they can do this on-line, again making a credit card payment. The system automatically transfers the request to the General Register Office for Scotland to fulfil the order and mail the extract. A fixed fee of £10 is payable per extract.

You can access the records of ScotlandsPeople at http://www.scotlandspeople.gov.uk

Newsplan ~ Database of Local Newspaper Titles
Andrew Phillips

NEWSPLAN is the co-operative newspaper programme involving UK libraries and archives, the British Library, the National Libraries of Scotland, Wales & Ireland and newspaper publishers.

It is one of the success stories of British librarianship and information provision. Since the 1980s NEWSPLAN has been recording, preserving and microfilming local newspapers, both historic and recent, in the ten library and archive regions of the UK (and in Ireland) and in the national library collections. Previously unrecorded holdings of newspapers have been identified. All kinds of newspaper information have been conserved and made accessible to users and students by NEWSPLAN. The study of family and local history particularly benefits since surveys show that between 50% and 60% of local newspaper readers in libraries are researching these. Now, increasing digitisation of newspaper texts – accompanied by sophisticated searching and automatic indexing - will unlock ever more stories and snippets to engage, delight and perplex readers.

The London & South East region is among the most complex in extent and variety of its newspapers and, indeed, in public library reorganisation down the years. During the 1990s the former LASER agency produced the NEWSPLAN original database for the region. Now the new Laser Foundation together with the

British Library have funded the restoration of the London & South East database of some 2,500 titles on the web, with improved searching and new features.

Some of the titles in this database are among the around 1,600 local newspaper titles microfilmed for improved preservation by the national NEWSPLAN 2000 Project, backed by the Heritage Lottery Fund and by UK regional newspaper publishers.

Click on *www.newsplan.co.uk* to search for local newspaper titles in London & the South East (via the Search Newspapers page) and open doors to find, in the New York Times motto, "All the news that's fit to print" – and, doubtless, some that isn't.

Why are local newspapers so important? They are key sources for anyone studying family history or the local and social history of communities. They provide information for students and readers of all ages whether they are doing school projects or writing university theses, drawing up family trees or researching pictures and illustrations.

What can you read there? Family history and genealogy in the births, marriages and deaths notices and some obituaries. Accident, crime, court and coroners' inquest reports. Local histories of schools, churches, houses and events. Political, council and official matters. Reports of sports, games and local shows. Notes and notices of local business, shops, industry and finance. And, of course, photographs, engravings and masses of advertisements.

What might you find there? Newspapers give all kinds of contemporary accounts of historic events. Though the national news tends to make the main headlines remember that, especially before the railways came, local newspapers reported much national and international news. Remember, too, that local newspaper reporters were right on the spot to witness the terror of Jack the Ripper in London's East End in the 1880s, the tragedy of the Hungerford massacre in 1987, the 'little ships' bringing an army safe home from the Dunkirk beaches in 1940 – to take only three historical examples from London & South East newspapers – and countless other events.

What may the search and the chase bring? See how subjects return with different coverage: Bosnia was reported in 1909 as well as 1992. See attitude changes over time to murder, civil rights,

cricketer WG Grace in Bexley in 1915. Yet another traced a rogue shipping agent in 1870s Littlehampton, while one reader regarded his getting a first class degree to be due in part to reading about immigration appeals in his London local newspaper.

The web-site's Links page provides a gateway into other regional (and national) newspaper databases and related web-sites. Not all UK regions' local newspaper title lists are currently accessible via the internet, but several are. In any case, you will find some information here about newspaper collections in all the UK and Ireland NEWSPLAN regions: namely, London & South East, the North West, the South West, the North East, Yorkshire & Humberside, East Midlands, West Midlands, Scotland, Wales, Northern Ireland and the Republic of Ireland.

divorce and so many other issues – for example, Battersea Dogs' Home was vilified when first set up while Queen Victoria's death practically extinguished all other international and local news at the time. One local newspaper reader, in a previous London & South East survey, found lists of Sussex prisoners of war in French prisons during the Napoleonic wars. Another discovered one of the last local matches played by the great

So, buy another ticket into history via the newspaper booking hall of www.newsplan.co.uk and see again Speaker 'Tip' O'Neill's truism that 'all politics is local' while at the same time glimpsing the lives of so many who were of their communities and who, as the poet Geoffrey Grigson quoted from his local church memorial, "…were all christened in this church and were lovers of this parish".

Heredis - a genealogy program
Robert Blatchford

There are many family history programs in the market place. Invariably the program has either been written for a Windows PC or an Apple Macintosh computer. The transfer of data between all programs is by the GEDCom standard. This enables everyone to share their data with others. It is therefore a refreshing change to find a program which has versions for both a Windows PC and a Macintosh and is also GEDCOM compatible.

Heredis is a truly cross platform genealogy program. The writers have really made data entry and viewing easy for the researcher.

Heredis 7.2 for Windows
Standard Edition for Windows is the free version of this genealogy program. It is a full featured, easy to use powerful genealogy program. It offers numerous innovative and purpose-built functions without any limits to data entry! Apart from charting and good reports, you can create a multimedia CD ROM of your genealogy file (which can then be read by any computer). In addition there is the ability to arrange data for internet publishing, a descendant family wheel and a unique global 3D tree feature. The Standard Edition for Windows is available as a free download from http://www.myheredis.com/

The Premium Edition for Windows has many more features gives you absolutely everything! Everything you may possibly need for handling your genealogy. The Premium Edition for Windows is available for purchase as a download. This version has many more features which can be viewed by visiting http://www.myheredis.com/ You may place your order via the secure server of Digibuy and you may pay by credit card. You may also order the Heredis Program by phone or fax. The cost is $29.99

When the order has been processed, Digibuy sends an email with the Registration Code and details of the site page from where the program may be downloaded.

Heredis X (Version 10.1.2) for Macintosh
With over 80 000 users in Europe this genealogy program has gone from strength to strength since its creation in 1994. Heredis Mac X is a powerful, complete and reliable tool which even the novice genealogist will know how to handle. Its interface is fully adapted for managing genealogical data and integrates perfectly into the Mac OS X environment. Each item of data will find its natural place in the limitless database: civil status, all the events of life, with witnesses, sources and images, addresses, notes and commentaries, personal references, acts to be researched. The program also controls and helps you with the entry of your data : validity of dates, coherence of data, evolution of family names and of place names over the centuries, personalized data entry shortcuts, permanent control of duplicates.

The writers of the program have paid a lot of attention to producing one of the best presented family history programs.
Linda Steward reviewing the program in MacWorld Magazine said: 'Heredis has everything I have hoped for! With its easy navigation and data entry, powerful search capabilities, database merging and – best of all – the ability to display and access all functions on one screen, it makes data management and the creation of family trees a breeze. Original documents of all kinds may be scanned and stored ready for integration with sound and video recordings – and photographs can be displayed on screen as well as in printed trees of numerous kinds, including a rather terrifying 3D version which places you at the centre of your own family universe. The most complex of family relationships can be handled with sensitivity and respect for privacy.'

Similar praise was expressed by Mike Ratcliff in MacFormat magazine (September 2004): 'Heredis is an excellent tool for the genealogist. Packed with features and extremely good value for money.'
Both MacFormat and Macworld magazines gave the program an excellent rating.
Full details at http://www.softlineuk.com/
The program costs £45.00. Resellers can be found via the Softline website.

One or two features of Heredis will require some learning and there is cheaper shareware. the pros outweigh the cons. However, having used the program for a short time I can certainly recommend it.

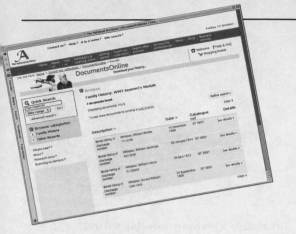

Get Online!
www.nationalarchives.gov.uk
John Wood
Public Services Development Team

The National Archives award winning new website at www.nationalarchives.gov.uk tells you all you need to know about The National Archives and hosts millions of online records.

Starting research online
Our 'getting started' section points you in the right direction and gives you starting points for our most popular topics including family, local and military history. From there you can download for free copies of the hundreds of research guides available.

Search our collections
The search our collections section gives you options to search numerous databases for free including 'The Catalogue'. The Catalogue has an advanced search facility and online help that allows you to search over 9 million record descriptions and order in advance before your visit to The National Archives.

Documents online
The DocumentsOnline section of our website allows you to freely search the indexes, access and download The National Archives ever growing collection of digitised record images. Included on DocumentsOnline are thousands of WW2 Merchant Seamen's medals, millions of WW1 Campaign Medals and over 1 million PCC Wills.

Searching is free, there is online help and images cost £3.50 to download. DocumentsOnline at www.documentsonline.nationalarchives.gov.uk/ is growing rapidly – you will need to frequently check the website to keep up to date with the latest projects.

1901 Census
www.1901census.nationalarchives.gov.uk/ id the official genealogy site of the English and Welsh census information for 1901. The free search facility allows you to search over 32 million people and 6 million properties. Discover your ancestors as well as find out who lived at a particular address.

Plus
You can use The National Archives website portal - www.nationalarchives.gov.uk to
Keep up with the latest news and record releases
Subscribe to a free monthly newsletter jam packed with research information
Buy books and gifts from The National Archives shop, delivered to your door
Book tickets for the free behind the scenes tour and events at Kew
Learn online aimed at helping children with their own research whether for homework or just for fun
Browse 1000 years of history online - see famous images and transcripts of documents such as The Domesday Book or Jack the Ripper's letters
Use The National Archives online image library

Essential contacts and information
The National Archives, Kew, Richmond, Surrey, TW9 4DU
Website: www.nationalarchives.gov.uk
Tel: 020 8392 5200
Email: enquiry@nationalarchives.gov.uk
Publications or bookshop: 020 8392 5271

Do these shelves contain your family history?
©The National Archives

Irish Genealogy with Eneclann
www.eneclann.ie

A Stroll through Dublin Max Matthews ISBN 0 9537557 8 9 This CD brings the streets, buildings and people of Dublin City alive containing over 2,000 high quality photographs, details on over 500 buildings throughout the city, as well as over 500 biographies of famous Dubliners, histories of over 300 streets, and general histories of the city, and historic maps. Released to celebrate the anniversary of Joyce's *Ulysses* there is commentary on how the city would have looked at the time with photographs from the *Ulysses* trail. Details are also included of all the major flashpoints during the 1916 rebellion, and the War of Independence in the city. (PC and Macintosh).

Irish Records Index Vol.1 Index of Irish Wills 1484-1858 ISBN 0 9537557 0 3 A comprehensive index to the Testamentary Records in the National Archives of Ireland and includes records in all the card catalogues as well as the Inland Revenue Will Registers and Administration Registers 1828-1839. Contains over 70,000 individual records and 100,000 names and surnames (and variants). PC and Macintosh (VirtualPC) computers.

Irish Records Index Vol.2 The William Smith O'Brien Petition ISBN 0 9537557 2 X This petition was signed by over 80,000 people from every part of Ireland, Liverpool, Manchester, and other parts of England, between 1848 and 1849. It is a unique historical and genealogical source from the period of the Famine. Following the failure of the 1848 rising, O'Brien was sentenced to death, and this petition was collected to gain clemency for the rebel leader. As a consequence his sentence was commuted and O'Brien was transported to Australia for life. Contains over 80,000 names, addresses and occupations (PC and Macintosh).

Irish Records Index Vol.3 The 1851 Dublin City Census ISBN 0 9537557 3 8 The destruction of the 19th century Irish Census returns is probably the greatest loss that genealogy in Ireland has suffered. Prior to the destruction of the 1851 census, Dr. D.A. Chart of the Public Record Office compiled a comprehensive list of the names and addresses of heads of households for Dublin City. Contains over 60,000 names and addresses (and some occupations) in the city of Dublin and scanned images of the original 1847 Ordnance Survey Town Plans. PC and Macintosh (VirtualPC) computers.

Irish Memorial Inscriptions Vol.1 Memorials of the Dead *Counties Galway & Mayo (Western Seaboard)* ISBN 0 9537557 4 6 This CD provides comprehensive coverage of the western half of counties Galway and Mayo and includes full transcripts of the surviving memorials found in the 128 graveyards in that part of Ireland. There are also detailed maps of the area covered, over 3,000 memorials up to 1901. Memorials were often erected by American relatives, and their details are included. PC and Macintosh (VirtualPC) computers.

Grenham's Irish Surnames ISBN 0 9537557 6 2 Ireland was one of the first European countries to adopt hereditary surnames. Nine centuries of change and with immigration, colonisation and linguistic upheaval, have produced an extraordinary legacy: This CD provides an unparalleled resource for anyone interested in his or her Irish surname. It includes details of 26,756 Irish surnames and 104,058 surname variants. PC and Macintosh (VirtualPC) computers.

Counties in Time ISBN 0-9540750-0-5 A sample of the records held in the National Archives of Ireland which exist for the 32 counties of Ireland covering the period from the late sixteenth century to the mid-twentieth century. Contains almost 1000 documents, including sixteenth century Chancery Pleadings, seventeenth century Books of Survey and Distribution, eighteenth century Proclamations, nineteenth century Famine papers, and twentieth century records of the first Dáil. The included documents range from proclamations against Catholics holding arms during the penal days to family returns for the 1901 and 1911 Censuses, from the records of seventeenth century land redistribution to police reports on 1930s IRA activity, and from mid-nineteenth century crime reports to 1867 photographs of Fenian suspects. (PC and Macintosh).

The 1831 Tithe Defaulters ISBN 0 9537557 7 0 The records on this CD are of the people involved in the infamous Tithe War 1831-38. All occupants of land were required to pay an annual tithe (or religious tax) of 10% of the agricultural produce generated by that holding. This money was demanded from all landholders, irrespective of their religion, and was paid directly to the official state church, the Anglican (Episcopalian) Church of Ireland. However, in 1831 many people refused to pay this tithe, and so started the Tithe War, which was fiercest in the southeast. The names that appear on this CD are of those people recorded by the Church of Ireland clergy who refused to pay their tithe. The CD contains all personal details from the original files, as well as copious information about the parishes that the people resided in. The people most affected by the Tithe War are precisely those most affected by emigration and the famine in the next generation. It includes details of nearly 30,000 individual defaulters as well as the addresses, occupations and other details about the defaulters appearing on the original record. A list of the parishes covered can be viewed at www.eneclann.ie PC and Macintosh (VirtualPC) computers.

What's new at the Imperial War Museum

Sarah Paterson - *Department of Printed Books*

The main news this year is that you can now look through the Imperial War Museum catalogues at your leisure in the comfort of your own home. Last year we reported that the catalogues for the Department of Documents, the Film Archive and the Sound Archive were now available online. From April 2004, these were joined by the databases of the other collecting departments within the Museum (Art, Exhibits and Firearms, Photographs and the Department of Printed Books). 160,000 records can be found on this, with at least 85,000 of these coming from the library. The website address is: www.iwmcollections.org.uk

Collections Online enables you to search the catalogues yourselves. You can make arrangements to see anything on this (although in all cases you will need an appointment to do so). Appointments to visit the Reading Room (where you can view collections from the Departments of Documents and Printed Books) need to be made at least 24 hours in advance of your visit. Most of the items held in the other departments are unique to the Museum, but because the library contains printed and published materials many of these are not. You can use the Department of Printed Books catalogue to see what is available on a given subject. It should be stressed that for various reasons, not everything appears on these computerised catalogues. If you don't see what you are looking for, please contact us for more advice.

Many of the books we have will be available through the inter-library loan scheme (although we do not loan our own materials because they need to be available for use in our Reading Room at all times). They can also be viewed in our Reading Room (well worth a visit in itself, as this used to be the former chapel for the Bethlem Mental Hospital). One of our great strengths is having a specialist library under one roof – you can view rolls of honour from all over the country (and abroad), regimental, squadron and ship histories,

trench newspapers, as well as recipe books and leaflets to prepare for your Victory street parties in 2005.

Our updated family history notes leaflets for tracing those who served in the Army and Royal Navy have been reproduced here. It is very difficult to ensure these are totally up to date because as soon as a new edition has been produced, there will inevitably be a change of telephone number, or a new website address, organisations cease to exist while new ones open, records move, and we are kept constantly on our toes...

Those new to family history research concerning the armed forces in the twentieth century may find our Tracing your family history series helpful. These sell for £5.50 each, and we have titles covering the Army, Merchant Navy and Royal Air Force. The Royal Navy book has recently been republished as a second edition.

These can be purchased though the Museum's website, where a copy of the Museum's publications catalogue, can be downloaded at www.iwm.org.uk Other recent publications that might be of interest include a paperback facsimile of the 1919 **Report on shell-shock** produced by the War Office (which features a useful current bibliography and an historical essay). The price is

IMPERIAL WAR MUSEUM

£13.99 and the ISBN is 1-901-62366-1. A book of great interest (and an excellent gift) for any former crew member of HMS Belfast or their family is **In trust for the nation: HMS Belfast, 1939-1972** by John Wingate. Originally published in 1972, this is a facsimile reprint that has been brought up to date and includes a bibliography. It sells for £12.99 and the ISBN is 1-901623-72-6.

If you wish to make an appointment to visit our Reading Room, or have a question you would like to ask (bearing in mind that we cannot embark on detailed research for you), please contact us in one of the following ways:
Telephone (enquiries): (020) 7416 5342
Post: Imperial War Museum, Department of Printed Books, Lambeth Road, London SE1 6HZ
Email: books@iwm.org.uk Website: www.iwm.org.uk

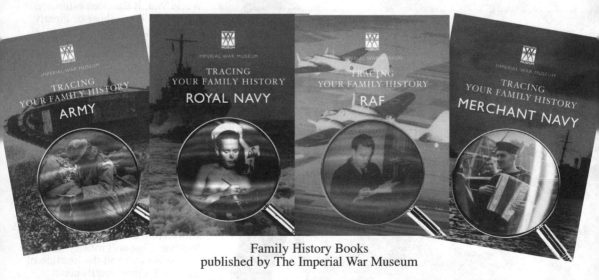

Family History Books
published by The Imperial War Museum

Tracing American Service Personnel

Sarah Paterson *Department of Printed Books Imperial War Museum*

This information provides guidance on tracing American service personnel and advice about sources for useful background information on their activities. The term serviceman is used throughout, although the information does apply equally to servicewomen. The Imperial War Museum does not hold any official personal service records or documentation, although this sheet provides addresses for finding these in the USA. The Department of Printed Books has a very good library relating to all aspects of American history since 1914. Visitors are welcome to visit our Reading Room by prior appointment between 10 am and 5 pm, Monday to Saturday, subject to weekend closures for Bank Holidays.

All other departments within the Collections Division – Art, Documents, Exhibits and Firearms, Film and Video Archive, Photograph Archive and the Sound Archive – are open to the public by prior appointment.

Service records
All post 1917 service records of military personnel (Army, Navy, United States Marine Corps, United States Air Force and Coast Guard) who no longer have any service obligation are held at the **National Personnel Records Center, Military**

Personnel Records, 9700 Page Avenue, St Louis, MO 63132-5100, USA. There is a very helpful website at http://www.archives.gov/facilities/mo/st_louis/mili tary_personnel_records.html that provides full details of what is held and how to apply.

In July 1973 a fire destroyed many of the records, although information about personnel can often be put together from various other sources. Roughly 80% of records for Army discharges between November 1912 and January 1960 were lost, as were about 75% of records for Air Force discharges between 25 September 1947 and 1 January 1964 (although records for the early part of the alphabet up to Hubbard are still largely intact). The United States Air Force only became a separate service in 1947. Before and during the Second World War airmen served either in the Army or the Navy.

If you are trying to trace your father, you may find it helpful to consult some of the books listed below, or have a look at the website at http://freespace.virgin.net/j.munro/trace.htm before proceeding further.

Casualty records

The American Battle Monuments Commission is the equivalent of the British Commonwealth War Graves Commission, but differs from it in that the United States did allow repatriation of bodies, and those who died overseas could be returned to America to be buried at home. For the Second World War, it has been estimated that only 39% of those originally buried now lie in one of the fourteen ABMC Cemeteries abroad. The website at http://www.abmc.gov contains a World War I Honor Roll, World War II Honor Roll and a Korean War Honor Roll listing those buried overseas or named on one of the memorials to the missing (if a serviceman's body was never recovered).

If you are searching for someone who died in action or overseas, he should have an Individual Deceased Personnel File. The information contained in these does vary, but will usually include at least his unit and the location of his burial. Often details about

where and when he died together with reports about the action in which he died will be included. If his body was never recovered, this file will include the results of research to find out what had happened to him, sometimes including testimonies by his comrades. For those who were repatriated there will usually be information about identification and reburial. Records covering the Second World War, Korea and Vietnam are held, and the information does take some months to be released. Application must be made by post, and the address to write to is: **Freedom of Information Act (FOIA) Office, Total Army Personnel Command, Attention: TAPC-PAO (FOIA), 200 Stovell Street, Alexandria, VA 22332-0404, USA**. Both Army and Air Force records can be obtained from this address. Equivalent information for the Marine Corps is held at: **Headquarters, United States Marine Corps, Manpower and Reserve Affairs (MRC), 3280 Russell Road, Quantico, VA 22134-5103, USA**. Similar information for Naval personnel is probably held by: **Officer in Charge, Naval Medical and Dental Affairs, Mortuary Affairs Branch, PO Box 886999, Great Lakes, IL 60099-6999, USA.**

If repatriated servicemen were not buried in a local cemetery they may now rest in one of the 120 Veterans Affairs National Cemeteries. These were established during the American Civil War, and anyone who has had military service is eligible to be buried in one (consequently, they include veterans who may have died in recent years). The genealogical information held is extremely limited, but this is still an avenue to be pursued. The address to contact is: **United States Department of Veterans Affairs, National Cemetery Administration (402B), Burial Location Request, 810 Vermont Avenue, NW, Washington, DC 20420, USA**. The website is at http://www.cem.va.gov/

There are also other types of cemeteries in which veterans may be buried including State Veterans

Cemeteries and the two maintained by the Department of the Army (of which Arlington National Cemetery is one). Although there are plans to have a searchable database for those buried in National Cemeteries, this will not be available in the near future because of the verification of records that needs to be applied. In the meantime, some non-comprehensive databases of different types of veterans cemetery can be found at http://www.interment.net/us/nat/veterans.htm

Further information
Other institutions that might prove helpful include:
United States Center of Military History
103 3rd Avenue, Fort Lesley J. McNair DC 20319-5058 USA W: http://www.army.mil/cmh-pg/
United States Air Force Historical Research Agency, 600 Chenault Circle, Maxwell Air Force Base, AL 36112-6424 USA
W: http://www.au.af.mil/au/afhra
Air Force History Support Office
AFHSO/HOR, Reference and Analysis Division, B-3 Brookley Avenue, Box 94 Bolling Air Force Base, DC 20032-5000 USA
W: http://www.airforcehistory.hq.af.mil/
Naval Historical Center
Department of the Navy, 805 Kidder Breese SE, Washington Navy Yard Washington DC 20374-5060 USA W: http://www.history.navy.mil/
Marine Corps Historical Center
1254 Charles Morris Street SE Washington Navy Yard DC 20374-5040 USA   W: http://hqinet001.hqmc.usmc.mil/HD/Home_Page.htm

Further Reading
All these titles (mainly relating specifically to finding GI fathers) can be consulted by appointment at the Imperial War Museum Dome Reading Room, but many of them may be available through other libraries via the inter-library loan scheme. The Department of Printed Books has also produced some booklists on American Forces in the United Kingdom, British War Brides and the American 8th Air Force. Some of these can be found on our website at www.iwm.org.uk or they can be requested from the Department of Printed Books. We also have a good

collection of official histories, regimental, squadron and ship histories, personal experiences, rolls of honour and journals.

Those living in the East Anglia area may also wish to visit the **Second Air Division Memorial Library, The Forum, Millennium Plain**, **Norwich, Norfolk NR2 1AW (Website: http://www.2ndair.org.uk**), as this should have an excellent collection of books relating to the Americans in Britain in the Second World War (concentrating on aviation).

How to locate anyone who is or has been in the military: Armed Forces locator guide Richard S. Johnson & Debra Johnson Knox.- 8th ed. Military Information Enterprises, 1999. ISBN: 1-8776-3950-8
Bye bye baby: the story of the children the GIs left behind / Pamela Winfield. Bloomsbury, 1992 ISBN 0-7475-1123-3
Somewhere out there: an Englishwoman's search for her G.I. father / Norma Jean Clarke-McCloud. - Enfield: Maka Books ISBN 0-9533749-0-4
Melancholy baby: the unplanned consequences of the G.I.s' arrival in Europe for World War II / Pamela Winfield. - Westport, Connecticut: Bergin and Garvey, 2000.ISBN 0-89789-639-4
"GI Baby" in **After the battle** issue 64 (pages 45-49)

Those searching for GI fathers may wish to contact the following addresses:
TRACE, Membership Secretary: Norma Jean Clarke-McCloud, Heron's Flight, 1H Bycullah Road, Enfield, Middlesex EN2 8EE Website: http://freespace.virgin.net/j.munro/trace.htm

WAR BABES, c/o Shirley McGlade, 15 Plough Avenue, South Woodgate, Birmingham B32 3TQ

The Internet
The proliferation of websites relating to veterans organisations and different conflicts have revolutionised the possibilities of searching for people or people who may have known the serviceman you are seeking. Most sites have links that will progress the possibilities of research further. Many servicemen will have socialised with friends, and it is always worth contacting websites relating to war brides to see whether those who went to America may have recollections of people or events in their home towns. Two sites that are useful starting points are http://uk-pages.net/Guestbook/warbrides.html and http://geocities.com/Heartland/Meadows/9710/WarBrides.html

A very good starting point, that has many varied links, and good suggestions for contacting veterans associations is: http://members.aol.com/dadswar

Finally, anyone especially interested in American aviation may wish to visit the American Air Museum at **Imperial War Museum Duxford, Cambridgeshire CB2 4QR**. More information can be found on the website http://www.iwm.org.uk/duxford/aam.htm The only **American Battle Monuments Commission Cemetery** in Britain (containing 3,811 graves and commemorating 5,125 missing) is at Madingley, near Cambridge www.usabmc.com/ca.htm.

© Department of Printed Books, Imperial War Museum, Lambeth Road, London SE1 6HZ T: (+44) 020 7416 5342 F: (+44) 020 7416 5246 Email: books@iwm.org.uk

The Imperial War Museum does not hold any service records, official documentation or comprehensive listings of Prisoners of War, but it does have extensive material that will be helpful for providing information and understanding about their experience. This article should be read in conjunction with the relevant Imperial War Museum leaflet for the individual's branch of service – Army, Royal Air Force, Royal Navy or Merchant Marine.

The Department of Printed Books welcomes visitors by appointment (Monday to Saturday, from 10am to 5pm). Other reference departments in the Museum – Art, Documents, Exhibits and Firearms, Film and Video Archive, Photograph Archive, and the Sound Archive – may also be able to assist. Advance appointments are required.

Royal Air Force
The Inter-War Years and Losses 1919 - 1939
David Barnes

Between the end of the First World War in November 1918, and the beginning of the Second World War in September 1939 the Royal Air Force carried out a wide variety of duties at home and abroad.

At home the Royal Air Force was involved in Defensive duties, on which there were four primary roles;

The protect our country

To preserve the trade routes upon which we defend for food and raw materials

To defend British territories overseas from attack

To co-operate with the defence of our allies

To maintain high standards set during the First World War there were a number of specialist schools set up for training.

The Central Flying School at Upavon, Wiltshire, ensured that a high standard of flying was upheld by flying instructors, and exhibitions of these skills were demonstrated to the public at flying displays, such as the annual displays held at Hendon. Originally called the Royal Air Force Tournament, the first display was held at Hendon on 3 July 1920.

The R.A.F. Cadet College was opened at Cranwell, Lincolnshire on 5 February 1920 to 'create an Air Force spirit' and to train new officers for the new service.

The R.A.F. Staff College was opened at Andover, Hampshire on 4 April 1922 and is devoted to the higher professional education of permanent R.A.F. Officers. The course was 1 year duration and trained officers in detailed air planning for tasks / operations they may be required to carry out.

No.1 School of Technical Training was set up at Halton, near Aylesbury, Buckinghamshire and was used for training apprentices in the R.A.F. trades of Fitter Grade ll and Fitter (Armourer), both courses were of three years duration. There was also the Electrical and Wireless School at Cranwell, Lincolnshire which trained Officers, Airmen, Aircraft Apprentices, and Boys as Signal Officers, Wireless Operators, Wireless Operator Mechanics

or Instrument Repairers. Courses were of various lengths from 12 months to three years.

Abroad, the Royal Air Force was involved in a number of 'local' wars in various parts of, the world, including

North and South Russia 1918-1920
British Somaliland 1919-21
Northern Iraq and Kurdistan 1919
India 1919 - 1939
Mesopotamia 1919 - 1939
Palestine and Jordan 1918 –1948
Aden 1917 - 1939
Chanak Crisis, Turkey 1922-23
China / Shanghai 1927
Afghanistan 1928
Aden 1927 – 1928
Iraq 1928 -1935
Abyssinian Crisis 1935-1936,
Egypt, Cyprus, Sudan,
Algeria 1937.

The first time, after the First World War, that the Royal Air Force played the primary part in a Military Policing Operation was Z Unit, in Somaliland in 1920, when in three weeks it caused the defeat of the 'Mad Mullah', who had defied the British Administration for 25 years. Strenuous work was also undertaken on the North-West Frontier of India. The Royal Air Force performed the first major evacuation by air, flying some 586 people out of Kabul, Afghanistan in December 1928.

Bristol Bulldog II - 17 Squadron 1930
K 1085 - Delivered 30 January 1930.
Flew into ground in fog, Arundel Park, Sussex 30 September 1930,
K1081 - Delivered 30 January 1930.
Collided with J9590 during practice attack on bombers and abandoned, Wardington, near Banbury, Oxfordshire 6 May 1931

ROYAL AIR FORCE	ROYAL NAVY	ARMY
Marshal of the Air	Admiral of the Fleet	Field Marshal
Air Chief-Marshal	Admiral	General
Air Marshal	Vice-Admiral	Lieutenant-General
Air Vice-Marshal	Rear-Admiral	Major-General
Air Commodore	Commodore	Brigadier-General
Group Captain	Captain	Colonel
Wing Commander	Commander	Lieutenant-Colonel
Squadron Leader	Lieutenant-Commander	Major
Flight Lieutenant	Lieutenant	Captain
Flying Officer (Observer Officer)	Sub-Lieutenant	Lieutenant
Pilot Officer	Midshipman	Second Lieutenant

Flying boats, which had the ability to fly from harbours, rivers and lakes, operated by the Royal Air Force, made it possible to police the remote colonies of the British Empire.

It was not just aircraft that the Royal Air Force operated, it had a number of Armoured Car Units, these operated in places such as; Aden, Iraq, Palestine and Trans-Jordan. Amongst the duties undertaken by these units were touring outlying posts, guarding the overland mail route through Iraq, surveying desert areas as well as co-operating with aircraft in isolated areas to disperse rebel tribesmen etc in peace-keeping duties.

Members of the Royal Air Force were encouraged in activities which would lead to improved performance in the air and participated in record attempts and contests such as ;
the Supermarine S.6B, winner of the Schneider Trophy, holder of the World air speed record of 407.5 mph in 1931
Fairey Long Range Monoplane, world distance record of 5,309 miles from Cranwell, Lincolnshire to Walvis Bay, South Africa 6-8 February 1933
Worlds Height Record of 53,937 feet in Bristol 138a aircraft in 1937
Vickers Wellesley, world distance record of 7,162 miles from Ismailia, Egypt to Darwin, Australia in 1938

Some of the long distance flights and record inter-city flights undertaken by the Royal Air Force 1918-1938 pioneered air routes for civil airlines abroad. Often regarded officially as 'Training Flights', the purpose of these flights was for communication between outposts and cities of the British Empire. It was also an opportunity to carry out aerial photography to assist in accurate mapping of uncharted jungles and deserts in the 1920's and 1930's.
These flights, often using three or more aircraft, with the associated support required for fuel, spares etc,

were also used to test the mobility of Royal Air Force units and to test the capabilities of both aircraft and crew.

It should be remembered that in the 1920's there were a number of well publicised aerial record flights undertaken by both male and female civilian pilots in solo aircraft.

This was the 'Golden Age' of flying. The Department of Civil Aviation was created in February 1919 by the Air Ministry to apply Air Navigation Regulations etc. Work was also undertaken in aircraft design with the help of a number of different aircraft manufacturers and experiments at the Aircraft Experimental Establishment at Martlesham Heath.

At the signing of the Armistice in November 1918, the strength of the Royal Air Force was 27,333 Officers (of which more than one half were trained pilots) and 263,837 other ranks. General J E B Seely stated on 8 June 1920 that "in 1918 we were incomparably the best equipped of all nations in the air".

Shortly after November 1918, with the end of hostilities the demobilisation of this vast force commenced. In the course of the six months between July and December 1919 the personnel of the Royal Air Force was reduced (in round figures) from 10,500 officers, to 4,000 officers, and from 62,500 men to 31,500.

Practice attack carried out on Handley Page Heyford bomber by Hawker Demon two-seater biplane fighter in the mid-1930's

The following shows the changes in strength of the Royal Air Force, based on statistics of the Authorised R.A.F. Strength paid for by Parliament. The tables do not include men serving in India, as these were paid separately by the Government of India

Year	Officers	Other Ranks	Total
1920	3059	22984	26043
1921	2932	25607	28539
1922	3085	26295	29380
1923	3217	27105	30322
1924	3360	28600	31960
1925	3627	30190	33817
1926	3547	28025	31572
1927	3436	25545	28981
1928	3430	25318	28748
1929	3338	25300	28638
1930	3339	24858	28197
1931	3238	25432	28670
1932	3238	25886	29124
1933	3195	25662	28857
1934	3191	25949	29140
1935	3298	26550	29848
1936	4290	40590	44880
1937	5314	56953	62267
1938	7011	67512	74523
1939			140882

Strength on the Outbreak of War September 1939
RAF: 118,000 WAAF: 2,000   Total: 20,000
Peak Strength Mid-1944
RAF: 1,012,000 WAAF: 174,000
                              Total   1,186,000
Total strength May 1945   1,079,835

In 1923 the Government had decided that a Home Defence force of 52 Squadrons was necessary for our security and that such a force should be completed by 1928. (By 1933 only 42 Squadrons had been formed!). On 14 March 1924, Sir Samuel Hoare, the Secretary of State for Air, informed the House of Commons that "today we have 371 first-line aircraft as compared with 3,300 in November 1918!"

Although a number of expansion plans had been put forward during the late 1920's, there was a lack of political motivation to provide adequate funding for the Royal Air Force, leaving it short of aircraft and equipment and without likelihood of improvement.

However in the early 1930's with a number of Political crises in Europe, and the threat of Hitler's Germany, the Government took stock of the situation and finally began to appreciate the under-funding; for example most of the aircraft were biplanes such as the Hart, Hind, Fury and Gladiator, which were generally of lower performance than contemporary monoplanes.

In February 1934 the Royal Air Force had only 850 first-line aircraft (at home and overseas) compared

An announcement in Air Ministry Weekly Orders in July 1919 stated that some 2,500 temporary officers were required for the Royal Air Force for a basic period of three years. Although this was aimed at Pilots who had served in the Aerial Services in the First World War, it was the beginning of the Short Service Commission scheme, which was extended to civilian candidates at the end of 1920.

The first post-war permanent commissions to be granted in the Royal Air Force were gazetted on 1 August 1919. The list comprised six Major-Generals, seventeen Colonels, seventy-nine Lieutenant-Colonels, 179 Majors, 294 Captains and 493 Lieutenants, making a total of 1,064 Officers. The distinctive rank titles for R.A.F. officers came into force during August 1919. The selection of these 'new' rank titles was, according to the Official Order, "to preserve and emphasise the principle of the independence and integrity of the Royal Air Force as a separate service among the fighting services of the Crown". The new titles and their equivalents are set out below.

Plans for a permanent air force were presented to Parliament in December 1919 in a Memorandum prepared by Sir Hugh Trenchard.

with France's 1,650. In the House of Commons on 8 March 1934, Stanley Baldwin announced "This Government will see to it that in air strength and in air power this country shall no longer be in a position inferior to any country within striking distance of our shores." Re-arming began in 1935-36, expanding the size of the Royal Air Force and using this country's well-established engineering industry to produce all-metal, low wing aircraft, such as the Blenheim, Battle, Hurricane and Spitfire. By September 1939 the Royal Air Force had some 2,000 first-line aircraft with a further 2,200 in reserve. Also a great building construction programme was started in 1936 with a number of large aerodromes being built, mainly in the eastern half of Great Britain, which were capable of accommodating two or three units and new Flying Training Schools were formed.

The Reserve of Air Force Officers, formed in Spring 1933, was divided into three sections; Class A consisted of flying personnel, Class B were Technical or Professional Specialists and Class C were civilians employed by the service, all of whom had had R.A.F. Training. All these men were liable for recall and would be obliged to return for refresher flying training each year.

The formation of the Royal Air Force Volunteer Reserve on 30 July 1936 went some way towards creating the necessary pool of pilots and observers. These reservists were to train as weekend flyers with some thirteen civil flying clubs at airfields close to major towns. However the Flying Training Schools were becoming congested and as the prospect of war drew closer, the Empire Air Training Scheme was inaugurated in Autumn 1939 and schools in Canada, Australia and New Zealand were opened up.

The Losses

Set against all the work that the Royal Air Force carried out there was a dark side - the losses. It was inevitable that there would be casualties to both men and machines during small wars and local uprising. There were those that were killed in training and flying accidents as well as those who died from disease in some far corner of the British Empire and those whose died from natural causes. Who were they and how do we find them?

In William Spencer's book 'Air Force Records for Family Historians' it stated that specific casualty records for the inter-war years (1919-1938) are not easily located. If a death occurred in a specific unit, it suggests that you try to consult that unit''s records in the National Archives.

It is fortunate that during this period (1919-1938) there is a section in the monthly Air Force List, which lists the names of Royal Air Force Officers who had died since the previous listing. From July 1919 to September 1939 some 3,434 Officer's names are recorded as being Killed or Died whilst

Statistics gathered by the R.A.F Medical Branch are as follows

YEAR	Strength	Home	Abroad	Total Deaths
1920	25,932	21,454	4,478	115
1921	28,322	21,936	6,386	134
1922	28,926	21,074	7,852	124
1923	29,771	20,239	9,532	116
1924	31,622	22,559	9,063	143
1925	33,028	23,838	9,027	138
1926	32985	23,958	9,190	153
1927	30,123	21,254	8,158	126
1928	30,470	21,981	7,677	137
1929	31,159	22,300	8,033	105
1930	32,000	22,701	8,451	135
1931	32,448	23,050	8,552	143
1932	31,877	22,528	8,452	115
1933	30,826	21,874	8,994	115
1934	30,624	21,424	9,200	94
1935	35,098	25,242	9,856	167
1936	47,834	35,823	12,011	181
1937	59,232	48,697	10,535	243
1938	75,895	64,031	11,864	347
1939	140,882	123,430	17,432	950

1920-1939		Total Deaths		3781

The 1939 figure does include Second World War Deaths from September to December 1939 - approximately some 630 deaths

 * Note the difference in strength figures to list earlier in this article is due to figures being compiled at different times in the year.

Taking the Commonwealth War Graves Statistics
For 12 November 1918 to 30 June 1919   1,543
Taking RAF Medical Branch Statistics
For 1 July 1919 - 31 August 1939
3,434
Approx total for Inter War Casualties
4,977
Of these over 1,500 were deaths in flying accidents

serving in the Royal Air Force. However, some of the names in the 1918/1919 Lists are officers who had been posted missing during the First World War. These were then listed as 'Presumed to have been killed on the date they had been posted Missing' as no further trace of them had been found by the Imperial War Graves Commission or the R.A.F. Search Teams that went to France and Flanders after the end of the war.

The Commonwealth War Graves Commission's records for Royal Air Casualties from 12 November 1918 to 31 August 1921 includes some 2,261 names of both Officers and Other Ranks.

A number of R.A.F. deaths in India can be found on the internet, graves at Peshawar and Quetta are listed on www.angelfire.com/mp/memorials/RAFmen1.htm

Names on the Peshawar Memorial are at www.angelfire.com/mp/memorials/rafpesh.htm

And those at Quetta earthquake memorial can be found at www.angelfire.com/mp/memorials/rafmemsx.htm

SEE THE WORLD WITH THE Royal Air Force

Apply: **INSPECTOR OF RECRUITING.**
4 HENRIETTA St. COVENT GARDEN. LONDON, W.C. 2.
Or any R.A.F Unit or Depôt.

If you are interested in finding out about an aircraft crash near where you live, then it may be best to start your research locally. Visiting local libraries, archives and newspapers, or even just asking around and talking to people who have lived in the area for a while may be a useful starting point. The National Archives holds some useful information concerning crashes and accidents. For example it has Squadron and Unit Operations Records Books.

The Royal Air Force Museum holds copies of aircraft accident reports, mainly dating from 1929 onwards. In order to trace a specific accident it is essential to know the date (within a month) and type of aircraft involved.

The RAF Museum also holds copies of Aircraft Movement Cards, which record details such as units to which an aircraft was allocated, repairs and accidents. These are arranged by aircraft type, and then by serial number.

For further information, please contact Department of Research and Information Services

Royal Air Force Museum, Graham Park Way, Hendon, London NW9 5LL

Amongst one of the heaviest losses of life to R.A.F. Personnel during this period was on 31 May 1935 when 53 men of No.3 India Wing lost their lives in an earthquake at Quetta, Baluchistan, India.

A tablet was erected with a list of names of those who died, along with names of two children of airmen. Details of this memorial can be found on

http://www.angelfire.com/mp/memorials/rafmemsx.htm

Another useful source of post war deaths are the Rolls of Honour held at R.A.F. Church, St Clement Danes, London. These books record the first name(s) and surname along with month and year of death, and are useful for cross referencing the officers names from the Air Force List and getting an idea of the number of 'other ranks' who were killed or died. The St Clement Danes Roll of Honour for the period between July 1919 and September 1939 contains 1,708 names.

There are detailed reports of some crashes involving Military Aircraft from 1919 in the Ministry of Aviation Accident Investigation Branch records held in AVIA 5, in the National Archives. However only a sample of these records have been retained. They are arranged chronologically by aircraft type and serial number. Very often the crew does not get mentioned at all as these reports.

Currently there is no central source where data is held listing inter-war R.A.F. Burials. This period is outside of the general remit of the Commonwealth War Graves Commission, who are responsible for the maintenance of headstones relating to servicemen who died during the First World War between 4 August 1914 - 31 August 1921 and the Second World War deaths between 3 September 1939 - 31 December 1947.

The R.A.F.'s Central Casualty Section does ensure that post-World War Two headstones of personnel who died in service are maintained. The Section arranges for all the R.A.F. headstones to be checked annually, usually by the nearest R.A.F. unit, and if any fall into disrepair, can arrange replacements. Whist they have a database of post 1947 graves, they will not release this information

The RAF Roll of Honour Project is currently compiling information based upon the entries in the Air Force Lists, the limited data held by the Commonwealth War Graves Commission and St Clement Danes Roll of Honour concerning Royal Air Force inter-war (1919 - 1939) deaths.

The RAF Roll of Honour Project would welcome any information, especially concerning where these casualties are buried.

Please contact R.A.F. Roll of Honour Project c/o 148 Parkinson Street, Burnley, Lancashire BB11 3LL

It is planned that the details recorded on the index will be able to be searched by Surname, by Squadron, Aircraft type, Aircraft serial number etc, once all the details are collated. Quite clearly this is a mammoth task and help and assistance in gathering information is always welcome. In particular, locations of graves and inscriptions concerning Royal Air Force deaths 1919-1939 would be very useful, as would loan of old copies of 'Flight' or 'The Aeroplane' magazines for the period 1919 -1938 since these can often record deaths.

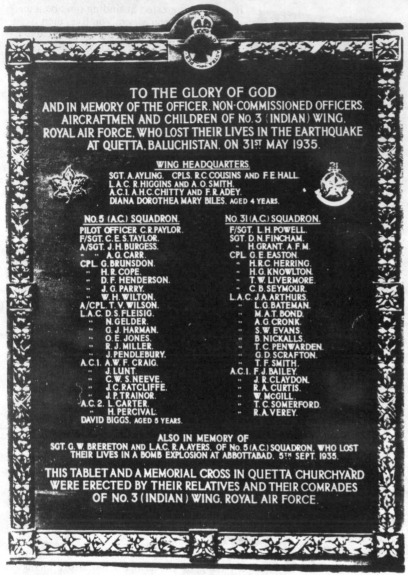

TO THE GLORY OF GOD
AND IN MEMORY OF THE OFFICER, NON-COMMISSIONED OFFICERS, AIRCRAFTMEN AND CHILDREN OF No. 3 (INDIAN) WING, ROYAL AIR FORCE, WHO LOST THEIR LIVES IN THE EARTHQUAKE AT QUETTA, BALUCHISTAN, ON 31ST MAY 1935.

WING HEADQUARTERS.
SGT. A. AYLING. CPLS. R.C. COUSINS AND F.E. HALL.
L.A.C. R. HIGGINS AND A. O. SMITH.
A.C.I. A.H.C. CHITTY AND F.R. ADEY.
DIANA DOROTHEA MARY BILES, AGED 4 YEARS.

NO. 5 (A.C.) SQUADRON.
PILOT OFFICER C.R. PAYLOR.
F/SGT. C.E.S. TAYLOR.
A/SGT. J.H. BURGESS.
     " A.G. CARR.
CPL. G. BRUNSDON.
  " H.R. COPE.
  " D.F. HENDERSON.
  " J.G. PARRY.
  " W.H. WILTON.
A/CPL. T.V. WILSON.
L.A.C. D.S. FLEISIG.
  " N. GELDER.
  " G.J. HARMAN.
  " O.E. JONES.
  " R.J. MILLER.
  " J. PENDLEBURY.
A.C.I. A.W.F. CRAIG.
  " J. LUNT.
  " C.W.S. NEEVE.
  " J.C. RATCLIFFE.
  " J.P. TRAINOR.
A.C. 2. L. CARTER.
  " H. PERCIVAL.
DAVID BIGGS, AGED 5 YEARS.

NO. 31 (A.C.) SQUADRON.
F/SGT. L.H. POWELL.
SGT. D.N. FINCHAM.
  " H. GRANT. A.F.M.
CPL. G.E. EASTON.
  " H.R.C. HERRING.
  " H.G. KNOWLTON.
  " T.W. LIVERMORE.
  " C.B. SEYMOUR.
L.A.C. J.A. ARTHURS.
  " L.G. BATEMAN.
  " M.A.T. BOND.
  " A.G. CRONK.
  " S.W. EVANS.
  " B. NICKALLS.
  " T.C. PENWARDEN.
  " G.D. SCRAFTON.
  " T.F. SMITH.
A.C.I. F.J. BAILEY.
  " J.R. CLAYDON.
  " R.A. CURTIS.
  " W. MCGILL.
  " T.C. SOMERFORD.
  " R.A. VEREY.

ALSO IN MEMORY OF
SGT. G.W. BRERETON AND L.A.C. R.A. AYERS, OF No. 5 (A.C.) SQUADRON, WHO LOST THEIR LIVES IN A BOMB EXPLOSION AT ABBOTTABAD, 5TH SEPT. 1935.

THIS TABLET AND A MEMORIAL CROSS IN QUETTA CHURCHYARD WERE ERECTED BY THEIR RELATIVES AND THEIR COMRADES OF No. 3 (INDIAN) WING, ROYAL AIR FORCE.

to the public, due to the Data Protection Act. R.A.F.'s Central Casualty Section does not maintain, or hold a register of any inter-war burials.

The policy for service personnel who died between the First and Second World Wars, in the period 1 September 1921 to 2 September 1939, was that the Unit concerned or the family of the deceased were responsible for the headstones and grave site. There is no record of the location of these grave sites, apart from what may be held on an individual's service record or information that may be held in Units' records, which may in the National Archives.

Maintenance of headstones relating to ex-Service men who die in retirement is a private responsibility of the family.

Further Reading:
RAF Operations 1918 - 1938 Chaz Bowyer. Published William Kimber & Co Ltd, London 1988
The Paladins John James. Macdonald & Co Ltd, London 1999. (Paperback edition - Futura Publications 1991)
The Source Book of the Royal Air Force Ken Delve. Airlife Publishing Ltd, Shrewsbury 1994

Tracing Royal Naval Ancestry
Family History notes from the Imperial War Museum

The Museum does not hold any personal service records or official documentation, but can help the enquirer as long as some basic facts are known. The Department of Printed Books welcomes visitors by appointment and is able to provide useful reading material and advice for finding out more about those who served. Other reference departments in the Museum – Art, Documents, Exhibits and Firearms, Film and Photograph Archives, and the Sound Archive – may also be able to assist.

Where to find Royal Navy Service Records
The Imperial War Museum only covers the period from the First World War onwards. Most of the relevant records relating to naval genealogical research are either still held by **Ministry of Defence** agencies or the **National Archives** (formerly the **Public Record Office**). Genealogical enquiries to the various Ministry of Defence agencies must be made in writing, but do not receive priority as their principal concern is to respond to official enquiries concerning welfare, pensions and other legal matters. The basic search fee, if levied, is currently £25.

Personnel records available to the public are now held by the **National Archives, Ruskin Avenue, Kew, Richmond, Surrey TW9 4DU (Tel: 020 8392 5200 Website: www.nationalarchives.gov.uk)**. Please note that The National Archives (TNA) does not undertake research on behalf of the public; it is necessary to either visit in person or employ a professional researcher, details of which are available direct from Readers' Services at the National Archives. For anyone intending to do their own research TNA has produced invaluable guides to their holdings; of particular importance are *Tracing your Ancestors in the Public Record Office*, 6th revised edition edited by Amanda Bevan (Richmond, Surrey: PRO, 2002), *Naval Records for Genealogists* by N.A.M. Rodger (Richmond, Surrey: PRO, 1998) and *Tracing your Naval Ancestors* by Bruno Pappalardo (Richmond, Surrey: PRO, 2003).

Pre-First World War service records, and ratings' personnel files and officers' records dating to 1923, are now held at TNA. For service records dating from 1924 to 1939 please write to the **Ministry of Defence, Directorate of Personnel Support (Navy), (Hayes), Bourne Avenue, Hayes, Middlesex UB3 1RF** (subsequently referred to as DPS Hayes).

For records of officers and ratings who saw service from 1939 (including 'Hostilities Only' service in the Second World War and Korea), write to the **Directorate of Naval Pay and Pensions, NPP(Acs)1E Centurion Building, Grange Road, Gosport, Hampshire PO13 9XA** (subsequently referred to as DNPP Gosport).
Service records for officers of the **Royal Naval Reserve** (RNR) and **Royal Naval Volunteer Reserve** (RNVR) for the First World War have now been transferred to TNA. Officers' records for the Second World War and Korea are held at DPS Hayes, thereafter at DNPP Gosport. Records of RNR ratings for the First World War are also at TNA, and Second World War records have recently been transferred there; later records are held at DNPP Gosport. Records of RNVR ratings for the First World War are at TNA, Second World War records are still held at DPS Hayes, while post-1945 records are held at DNPP Gosport.

First World War **Royal Naval Division** records of service are now at TNA.

Records of **Royal Marines** officers and men in service up to 1924 are at TNA. Subsequent records are still held by the **Royal Marines Drafting and Record Office, Centurion Building, Grange Road, Gosport, Hampshire PO13 9XA**.

Records of those who served in the **Royal Naval Air Service** can be found at TNA. **Fleet Air Arm** records are held at DNPP Gosport.

The NA holds the records for the **Women's Royal Naval Service**, 1917-1919. Records of WRNS who entered service before 1955 are at DPS Hayes, thereafter at DNPP Gosport.

Pre-1929 **Queen Alexandra's Royal Naval Nursing Service** records are held at TNA. Records of those

© Robert Blatchford

The Battle of Jutland 1916

who entered service up to 1956 are at DPS Hayes, with subsequent records at DNPP Gosport.

The careers of naval officers can be traced through the *Navy List*, a regular official publication. (No such listing exists for other ranks.) These contain seniority lists of all officers, cross referred to individual ships. A full set is held by TNA but the Department of Printed Books (DPB) holds a near complete run from 1914 to date.

Casualty Records

Casualty records are available for consultation at TNA. In addition, the **Commonwealth War Graves Commission, 2 Marlow Road, Maidenhead, Berkshire SL6 7DX (Tel: 01628 507200 Website: www.cwgc.org)** holds details of the burial place or commemoration site for all those who died in service during the period 1914-1921 and 1939-1947. A search fee may be levied but their website provides free access to the *Debt of Honour* database. Details of naval personnel who were buried at sea are contained in memorial registers produced by the Commission. The DPB holds a complete set of memorial and cemetery registers, together with various operational and unit histories, some of which may make reference to casualties, and many published rolls of honour.

Details of service personnel buried in 'non-World War' graves are available from the **Ministry of Defence, NP-Sec2(b), Room 222 Victory Building, HM Naval Base, Portsmouth, Hampshire PO1 3LS**.

Medal Records

Records of campaign and gallantry awards and available citations, for the period up to 1921, are lodged with TNA. For awards after that date write to the **Directorate of Naval Pay and Pensions, NPP(Acs)1F Centurion Building, Grange Road, Gosport, Hampshire PO13 9XA**. The NA holds a full set of the *London Gazette*, another good source of reference for awards and citations, complete with indexes. The *London Gazette* is also available on line at www.gazettes-online.co.uk. However, please note that during the Second World War, publication of all citations for gallantry awards was suspended. For possible information on these 'unpublished' citations write to the **Ministry of Defence, Honours and Awards, Room 115 Victory Building, HM Naval Base, Portsmouth, Hampshire PO1 3LS.**

The Department of Printed Books holds published sources only, but recommends in particular the volume *Seedie's Roll of Naval Honour and Awards, 1939-1959* compiled by B.C. Dickson (Tisbury, Wiltshire: Ripley Registers, 1989).

Other Sources

The **Royal Naval Association** produces a monthly magazine *Navy News* **(Tel: 02392 826040 Website: www.navynews.co.uk)** which carries a column for contacting and tracing ex-servicemen. Details of other publications and other associations, which offer a similar service, are available from the DPB. Researchers will also find operational accounts, unit and ship histories held by the Department, invaluable for background detail. Official documentation such as operational records, unit diaries and ships' logs are now with *The National Archives*.

Once the recommended archives have been approached, researchers are welcome to forward their findings to the DPB for advice on other relevant works and addresses. The Printed Books Reading Room is open to the public, by prior appointment, from Monday to Saturday between 10.00am and 5.00pm.

Other museums that might be able to offer further assistance are listed below:
Royal Naval Museum, HM Naval Base (PP66), Portsmouth, Hampshire PO1 3NH
Tel: 02392 727562
Website: www.royalnavalmuseum.org
Fleet Air Arm Museum, Box D6, RNAS Yeovilton, near Ilchester, Somerset BA22 8HT Tel: 01935 840565
Website: www.fleetairarm.com
Royal Marines Museum, Southsea, Hampshire PO4 9PX Tel: 02392 819385
Website: www.royalmarinesmuseum.co.uk
Royal Navy Submarine Museum, Haslar Jetty Road, Gosport, Hampshire PO12 2AS
Tel: 02392 529217 Website: www.rnsubmus.co.uk
National Maritime Museum, Romney Road, Greenwich, London SE10 9NF Tel: 020 8858 4422
Website: www.nmm.ac.uk

More detailed information can be found in our publication *Tracing your Family History: Royal Navy* – this can be purchased from the Imperial War Museum for £5.50.
Department of Printed Books, Imperial War Museum, Lambeth Road, London SE1 6HZ Tel: (+44) 020 7416 5342 Fax: (+44) 020 7416 5246
Website: www.iwm.org.uk
Email: books@iwm.org.uk

Naval Review
at Spithead
1914

2/59th (2nd NOTTINGHAMSHIRE) REGT.
1813

SERGEANT LIGHT COY.   OFFICER BATTALION COY.   PRIVATE GRENADIER COY.

The Beckett Soldiers Index A–C
Brian Prescott

James Deuchar Beckett is a much respected family historian well known for his contribution to the interest. He has, for almost forty years, been very active in the north of England. His knowledge of the subject is immense and his memory prodigious for names that other members are interested in.

For the period before B.M.D. Registration began in 1837 military records are a valuable, worthwhile source of information about our ancestors. The difficulty was, and still is, that to access a soldier's papers you need to know the regiment in which he last served. This is because the man's papers are kept, in the case of the WO97 series of 'soldiers' documents', in 6,383 boxes. It would, I think, take the best part of a lifetime to search those boxes methodically until 'your man' was found by chance. Jim Beckett realised this about twenty years ago and determined to solve the problem by compiling a 'soldiers index' to aid his fellow family historians. Such an index would not only solve a knotty problem but save the fortune on travel, meals and accommodation required for frequent visits to Kew.

Since 1984, Jim has compiled an extensive index of soldiers, comprising more than 300,000 names with service between 1793 and 1854. These are arranged in alphabetical order with surname, forename, regiment and some useful biographical detail to help you find 'your man'. The basic information, in the form of full name and birthplace, was originally extracted from the source WO120, the Chelsea Hospital Regimental Registers at the National Archives at Kew, London. However, it became evident that many men were not recorded in conventional Army pension sources; therefore, it was decided to supplement the index from wherever reference to soldiers could be found.

Thousands more soldiers were added from Parish Registers and innumerable 1841 Census Returns. The detail may consist of birth date and place; place and date of baptism; date and place of marriage with the name of the bride; if the man received the Military General Service Medal, the Army of India Medal or the Long Service and Good Conduct Medal; if he was at Waterloo; if he was wounded or, if he was in the 59th Regiment of Foot, whether he was involved in the fateful *Sea Horse* disaster in 1816.

The Beckett Index was greatly expanded by appending the extensive transcripts of the late Ian Rowbotham, medal collector, who had transcribed thousands of Napoleonic War veterans, from Muster and Medal Rolls, as well as pensioners from source WO116. The latter source was especially interesting, consisting of men discharged fit before 1830 but later granted pensions on hardship grounds, often many years after 1854.

The compiler was fortunate in acquiring indexes from military historians who had particular interests in Wales, Herefordshire, Leicestershire, Nottinghamshire, Suffolk, Sussex and abroad. In recent times more than 20,000 army deserters, for the period 1828-1841, have been included, although some did later re-enlist, complete their service and were pensioned. A great number of the men recorded in WO97 are duplicated in WO120, but duplication has been kept down to a minimum by excluding two sections and by running a comparison check to eliminate *exact* duplicates.

The Beckett Index also contains thousands of men who were induced to forfeit a pension and reside overseas. No birthplace is given but often there is a place and date of death. Leon Metzner, for the Anglo-German Society, has recorded pensioners of the King's German Legion. Again no birthplace is noted, but most seem to originate from the States of Hanover or Saxony and many men of European origin served in the 60th Foot (King's Royal Rifle Corps).

At the National Archives there are several pensioner sources. None seem to be complete without the others. Prior to 1823 many men were discharged through Kilmainham Hospital, Dublin. Registers in source WO118 and 119 would seem to concern men who completed their service in Ireland. Over 42% of the Army of this period was born in Ireland, very useful for the Ireland searcher where very little of the 19th century Census survives.

Recent years have seen great progress with the indexing of soldiers' records, particularly sources WO97 and WO121, covering the period 1770-1854. This was organised by the 'Friends of the P.R.O.' team and must be one of the greatest indexes ever produced and it is available at the National Archives. Although it contains about 250,000 names we must be aware of its limitations. Some authorities assert that about two-thirds of the men from the Peninsular period were not pensioned and so do not appear on the WO97 index. This was due to a number of factors including death in service or late claims for pension. The pension was not paid automatically, at that time, it had to be applied for. Unfortunately, many men took years to apply (some Waterloo veterans as late as the 1870s) and others died in poverty and ignorance – never having known of their entitlement to a pension.

Hence the decision to publish the Beckett Soldiers Index. As with many military indexes, commissioned officers are excluded, presuming that they are adequately represented in Hart's Annual Army Lists from 1840, official Army Lists and others. It will be some time before the entire index can be published. Meanwhile, the next volume D–G is being prepared by Jade Publishing while Jim is beavering away completing H–K and so the work will continue until the monster Index is finished with about 300,000 names to aid the family historian.

Foster's *Military General Service Medal* volume is worthy of study as is the more accurate and complete later work of the same title by A.L.T. 'Tony' Mullen, who generously gave permission to quote from his book. The recipients of the M.G.S. Medal did noble service during the Napoleonic War from 1795-1814 and must have lived until 1848, when the medal was belatedly awarded to survivors of that prolonged and bloody conflict. It is presumed that most of the veterans not on the Medal Roll died before 1849. There were those who survived but did not claim the medal and so are not recorded. Similarly, recipients of the Army of India Medal had to be alive in 1851, almost 60 years after the first campaigns in India that the award sought to acknowledge. Ian McInnes, author of many fine military reference books of particular interest to medal collectors kindly gave permission to extract from his two main works *The Army Long Service and Good Conduct Medal 1830–1848* and *The Annuity Meritorious Service Medal 1847–1953* and its subsequent *First Supplement*.

Another important indexing project, processing at present, is the combined Muster Rolls of 1806, P.R.O. source WO25/909, which comprises virtually a list of the entire British Army in that year. This task has been undertaken by Barbara Chambers and she has printed books and microfiches of some regiments. So far about 40 regiments have been indexed. She has also produced an Index of the Army of Reserve by county and, typically, three or four counties are listed in each booklet. From these lists one should proceed to Description Books or Casualty Rolls. The Muster Rolls include many men not in pension sources; thousands were later killed in Egypt, at Maida (Italy), at Martinique and Guadeloupe, in the Peninsular campaigns, died at, or as a result of malaria caught at, Walcheren. There were others who died in America during the war of 1812-1814 and at the great battle of Waterloo.

For a variety of reasons many men seem to have escaped the net of pensioner lists. Muster Rolls include a large number of soldiers not in pensioner sources. Deserter Lists and Barrack Census Returns appear to have some men not on Muster Rolls. Cross-referencing seems to be the order of the day when searching for your early military forebear.

In the compiling of the Beckett Soldiers Index over a period of twenty years Jim has received much valuable assistance from many people, who made a very real and vital contribution to this work. In the main, these unnamed helpers are the many willing members of the Manchester and Lancashire Family History Society, who either collected names for inclusion, or who helped with computer input. Jade Publishing has been involved with Jim's project for eleven years. It has been a mammoth task. Happily, it is now available with the recent release of the first volume of *The Beckett Soldiers Index A–C* available from Jade Publishing Limited, 5, Leefields Close, Uppermill, Oldham, Lancashire, OL3 6LA at only £9.95 or from many Family History Societies. Postage and packing is £2.35. Trade terms for Societies on request: telephone 01457–870944.

References:
WO97 index at the National Archives on the Internet at http//catalogue.pro.gov.uk/.
WO120 Chelsea Hospital Regimental Registers,
WO116 and WO117 are the Admission Books for out-pensioners with disabilities or who had qualified under the terms of long service,
WO121 Soldiers' Documents,
WO17 and WO73 Army Monthly Returns give regiments at particular places,
Muster Rolls WO25/871-1121 for 24 June, 1806 – the last complete Muster Roll for the British Army before the Peninsular War,
Pension Returns WO22 for 1842-1862 are arranged by pension district and give many men of the Napoleonic period who changed status by arrival, departure or death,
Especially recommended is the excellent *My Ancestor was in the British Army – How can I find out more about him?* by Michael J. and Christopher T. Watts which lists fully the Army Records held at the National Archives. It was published in 1992 and is being updated for republishing.
British Pensioners Abroad by Norman K. Crowder, Genealogical Publishing Co. Inc., 1001, North Calvert Street, Baltimore, MD21202, USA (Published 1995)
Barbara Chambers has printed books and microfiches of some regiments and copies can be bought by writing to her at 39, Chatterton, Letchworth Garden City, Hertfordshire, SG6 2JY, or from her web site http://members.aol.com/BJCham2909/homepage.html, or by email at BJCham2809@aol.com.
Finally, a series of books of interest to medal collectors has been published by Jade Publishing Limited, who will supply direct. See address details above. The books contain many details of interest to family historians. They are: *The Army Long Service and Good Conduct Medal 1830–1848*, which details about 2,900 men; *The Annuity Meritorious Service Medal 1847–1953* and its subsequent *First Supplement*.; which list about 6,000 men with much biographical information; *Sudden Death, Sudden Glory* the story of the 59th Foot from 1793–1830 with biographical details and casualty returns of the officers and men who served in the Peninsular 1808-1809 and 1812-1814, at Walcheren 1809, at Java 1811, at Waterloo in 1815, Bhurtpoor 1825-26; *The Yeomen of the Guard including the Body of Yeoman Warders of H.M. Tower of London, members of the Sovereign's Body Guard (Extraordinary) 1823–1903* contains much biographical information on 477 men who served during that period and there are almost 200 illustrations of the men and their medals.

Brian Prescott, Managing Director of Jade Publishing Limited is President of The Northern Branch of the Orders and Medals Research Society and a member of The Manchester and Lancashire Family History Society

Waiting and Hoping
Joseph O'Neill

British and French
Prisoners of War 1915

Every prisoner of war's story is a unique tale of personal heroism. Yet there is one aspect of the experience common to all.

Not one of them had anticipated capture. They had all imagined being wounded or killed – but the possibility of spending years in captivity only occurred to them when it became a reality. For over 500,000 Allied troops in the Second World War it was the defining experience of their lives.

The Japanese captured 140,000 Allied troops. The suffering of PoWs in the Far East is well documented. In the final months of the war the Japanese government decided to murder the survivors. Only the Allied victory saved those who had survived years of brutality. Amazingly, prior to the war, Japanese generals seem to have made no provision for prisoners. When the first American troops fell into their hands on Wake Island, Japanese officers argued whether or not to shoot them all. Every prisoner's life hung on his captors' whim. Anthony Hewitt, a British officer serving in Hong Kong, was appalled at the Japanese attitude to him and his men. He told his men they had fought bravely and could surrender with honour. It soon became clear that this idea was anathema to the Japanese who were expressly forbidden to surrender under any circumstances.

Hewitt and the rest of the Middlesex Regiment spent their first days of captivity in an abandoned barracks at Sham Shui Po. With no sanitation, few of the huts had roofs and they slept on concrete. Their food was a small portion of rice twice a day and the guards routinely beat anyone guilty of imagined discourtesy. They beat Hewitt, as they did other officers, with sheathed bayonet blades. When he fell they kicked him to his feet. This was typical of the treatment of most POWs. For Hewitt it was a foretaste of his experience of captivity.

Unsurprisingly, he formed an unfavourable opinion of his captors. "There was absolutely no link between normal, civilised behaviour and the way these Japanese troops were behaving. No reason at all why they had to behave in this awful, cruel and sadistic manner." The treatment of POWs, from all Allied armies, who were forced to build the Burma – Siam railway was as cruel as any war atrocity. But as the war progressed and its tide turned against Japan, conditions became even worse. Increasing numbers of POWs experienced the horrors of the 'hellships', used to ship them to the Japanese home islands for slave labour. Conditions were so brutal that many never saw Japan. Others were bombed or torpedoed by the Allies because these ships were always unmarked. The fate of those transported in the Rakuyo Maru and the Kashidoki Maru in September 1944 pushed them to the limits of human endurance and rank among the most harrowing of all war stories. The Japanese transports, both unmarked, carried 2,300 POWs. American U-boats, lying in wait, sank the ships and other members of the convoy. Most of the prisoners were killed outright but a thousand managed to make it into the waters of the South China Sea, where they scrambled for oil barrels and flotsam. Japanese lifeboats picked up a few. The rest spent four days in the water before American vessels arrived and rescued one hundred survivors. The rest were left for a further two days during which the forty feet waves of a typhoon hurled them across the sea. Some survived even this and were able to struggle aboard the American submarines that came to their rescue – six days after they went into the water.

Almost as grim are the accounts of prisoners made to work on Japanese building projects. After capturing Borneo the Japanese set their captives to work building an airport at Sandakan. Conditions there displayed the full gambit of Japanese barbarity.

British Prisoners of War
near Berlin 1915

The camp commanders ordered prisoners to sign a written pledge not to escape. Thereafter, the guards shot all escapers. For lesser offences there was the cage. Placed in the middle of the compound in the blistering sun, guards locked the prisoner in a wooden cage three feet square. Once a day they released the prisoner and beat him senseless. Some men endured forty days of this. Others went insane. Their screams tormented their comrades.

As work on the airport fell behind schedule, the beatings increased in frequency and brutality. Those who witnessed this testify that the Japanese officers were equally brutal in the treatment of their subordinates, frequently subjecting their own men to merciless and sustained assaults. This in turn increased the brutality of the guards' treatment of the prisoners.

As a further punishment they reduced the rations of the emaciated prisoners and forced even the sick to work. When an Allied invasion was imminent the authorities evacuated the camp, forcing the inmates to march 120 miles to Api. Many marched barefoot. The guards shot those who fell behind. Of the 700 British and 1,800 Australian prisoners , six survived.

Twenty-seven per cent of Allied POWs captured by the Japanese died in captivity, as to 4% of those held by the Germans and Italians. Even this gruesome statistic pales beside the figure for Soviet prisoners captured by the Germans, more than half of whom – 3.3 million – perished.

Like their comrades in the East, many British POWs captured in Europe, fell into captivity early in the war. The German blitzkrieg of May 1940 knocked France out of the war and delivered thousands of British troops into the hands of the Axis. Soon after this Rommel's advance in North Africa swelled the number of captives thronging the camps. More daunting than the constant hunger and boredom was the uncertainty that was part of every prisoner's lot.

Each man had to find his own way of adapting to captivity. Memoirs show a whole range of initial reactions. Some suffered a desolating sense of loneliness, cut off from home and family for an indeterminate time. Others reacted with a pervasive irritability fuelled by a sense of injustice. A small minority channelled their frustration into an obsession with escaping. These were the ones who spent every waking moment scheming and planning how to outwit their captors.

Young men plucked from the exhilaration of battle, found the enforced inactivity of captivity intolerable. Churchill, himself a prisoner during the Boer War, summed up this frustration. " You are in the power of your enemy. You owe your life to his humanity and your daily bread to his compassion."

The Geneva Convention sought to ensure that prisoners received humane treatment. Their food, clothing and shelter was to be as good as that of their captives' soldiers and they had the right to communicate with their family. Though the brutality of the Germans on the Eastern front exceeded even the Japanese, they did generally adhere to the Convention in their treatment of British, French and American troops captured in Africa and the West. This is because most Allied POWs were held in camps run by the Wehrmacht and the Lutwaffe. It was only escapees who ran the risk of falling into the hands of the Gestapo, who had no regard for the Geneva Convention.

The procedure for captives was uniform. First they were taken to a transit camp for interrogation. It was only when they reached the camp where they were to be held that the reality of the situation struck them. A cocktail of shame, anger and relief kept them in emotional turmoil but the nature of their day-to-day experience was determined by their guards and especially the camp commandant. He set the tone for their captivity.

Most commandants were retired army officers, recalled for the duration. The guards had usually seen active service before being wounded or reaching retirement. Few were convinced Nazis and generally behaved with decency. The problem was that as the war progressed they increasingly came under pressure from Punishment Companies, who demanded they adhere rigidly to the ethos of the regime and treat prisoners with appropriate severity.

For many prisoners, captivity was a release. They

recall their sense of gratitude at surviving and escaping the fear of death that was the constant companion of the soldier on active service.

Lord Haig, the son of Douglas Haig, the British commander on the Western Front in the Great War, remembers feeling relieved that he no longer had to live up to his father's reputation.

Ken Rees, shot down over Germany, was concerned about his wife and family. Would they learn that he was not dead?

Initially there were comrades' suspicions to deal with. Every prisoner was a potential German 'stooge'. Until someone vouched for you or you won the trust of your fellows they treated you warily. Once you had won their trust you were united with your comrades in common experiences and shared preoccupations. First among these was hunger. The nagging throb of an empty stomach was ever present. Rations were meagre, the same as those for a non-working civilian.

The Red Cross parcels, which started to arrive in the spring of 1941, became the focus of prisoners' longing. They not only supplemented a dull and inadequate diet – they boosted morale to an extent almost impossible to appreciate. More than anything else it was food which determined prisoners' morale. During the final months of the war hunger made them dull and inactive, too depressed to do anything but lie on their bunks. Boredom tortured most prisoners for most of the time. It was at times like this that 'goon bating' became an attractive way of venting their frustrations on the guards.

The Germans too realised ennui led to restlessness. So they encouraged harmless pastimes, helping inmates to build up libraries, to further their education and take part in sports. Many an accommodating commandant made available to aspiring thespians theatrical costumes from Berlin. One insightful prisoner, divided his fellow inmates into five categories: the students, the administrators, the creators, sleepers and the escapers. Despite the myths and the products of the Ealing Studios, the latter were always a small minority.

The majority preferred to come to terms with captivity. Lord Haig, for instance, admitted that he never considered the possibility of breaking out. Some prisoners resented the habitual escaper as he created trouble for his fellow inmates.

Yet prisoners made thousands of breakout bids. Some were meticulously planned over many months. Others were impulsive actions, sparked by a careless guard leaving a rubbish lorry unattended or a door unlocked. Either way, luck was essential.

The first problem was to get out of the camp. Camps such as Stallag Luft III were purpose built, designed to frustrate escapers. Seismographs peppered the earth around the huts and anti-escape specialists – 'ferrets' – were always active.

Once outside the camp an escaper's problems were just beginning. To make the coveted 'home run' he had to cross many miles of enemy territory, find food and shelter and evade road blocks and posses, often without an adequate map. In addition, he had two additional burdens: recapture was more than a personal blow – it would deflate all those who had helped with planning, forged documents and clothing. Further, once he left the confines of the camp, he lost his status as a combatant and was subject to German civil law, an area increasingly dominated by the Gestapo.

Stallag Luft III in Lower Silesia, was the Luftwaffe's most famous camp. By the end of the war it housed over 10,000 officers who in the summer of 1942 made forty escape attempts. Only one succeeded but it was to prove the most significant breakout of the war, later immortalised as the 'Great Escape'. The plan involved two hundred men escaping through a tunnel. In fact seventy-six succeeded. When Hitler heard the news he flew into a rage, called a national alert and summoned Himmler, the head of police and the most feared man in the Reich. He ordered that every airmen be shot when recaptured.

The German military were unhappy with this and pointed out that such action could invite reprisals against German POWs. Hitler later relented, for fear of reprisals against German POWs. He would not have them all shot. Instead, Himmler was to pick fifty to face the firing squad. Of those involved, only three reached home. One of the recaptured, Jimmy James was despatched to Sachsenhausen concentration camp. On arrival an inmate told him the only way out was up the chimney. Yet James managed to tunnel out. Sleeping by day and travelling across fields by night, he reached Germany's Baltic border. With freedom in sight, two vigilant members of the Volkssturm (Home Guard) recaptured him and returned him to Sachsenhausen. He was prepared for the worst, especially when he learnt that the Gestapo had blamed the camp commandant for his escape and shot him.

Amazingly, James survived. Confined in solitary, he expected every day to be his last. After five months his guards pulled him from his cell and threw him into the back of a lorry. He had hardly got his bearings before he arrived at Flossenburg concentration camp. The commandant there was not

British Prisoners of War
World War II

RAF British Prisoner of War
Italian Prisoner of War Camp
World War II

Jimmy James, *Moonlight Night*, (Sentinel, 1993) and Walter Morrison, *Flak and Ferrets* (Sentinel,1995).

There are few records in TNA relating to POWs in the Second World War. Bombs destroyed some, others shredded as part of government policy. Most of those that survived were passed on to the International Committee of the Red Cross for safekeeping. The National Archive leaflet, *Prisoners of War, British 1939-53, Military Information Leaflet 27,* provides a complete guide to all the relevant documents held by the National Archive. It also appears on http://catalogue.pro.gov.uk/leaflets/ri2020.htm and includes the most comprehensive listings of British and Commonwealth POWs held in Germany, German-occupied territory and Italy. It also includes a register of captives of the Japanese and all merchant navy captives.

A further section details the National Archive's holdings of Red Cross reports on POW camps and on war crimes relating to prisoners.

The Centre for Internees Rights on http://www.expows.com/ has a large section on prisoners of the Japanese during the Second World War.

http://www.aim25.ac.uk/ deals with war crimes and contains many cases relating to POWs during the Second World War.

The International Committee of the Red Cross has compiled records of POWs from all nations involved in the Second World War. Researchers cannot consult them but the Red Cross will supply information in response to written requests and payment of a fee.

prepared to take any risks – he immediately ordered that James and the other POWs be shot. It was an SS guard who pointed out that this was illegal and by so doing saved James' life. James survived both Flossenburg and later Dachau before the Americans liberated him.

Others, the 'prominente', feared they would not see liberation and that in one last act of vengeance Himmler would slaughter them. These men were relations of prominent members of the British establishment. The Nazis regarded prisoners such as George Lascelles, son of the Earl of Harewood and Giles Romilly, Churchill's nephew, as possible bargaining counters. In the last days of the war the authorities shipped them out of Colditz to an unknown destination.

Fortunately the chaos that swamped the Reich in the final weeks of the war derailed the Nazi plans and the Americans liberated the 'prominente'. But even then their ordeal was not over. The immediate post-war years were a time of slow and often painful readjustment. Many suffered from a profound anticlimax. Some, like Dawyck Haig, were indelibly marked by their experiences, their personalities fundamentally changed. Others missed the camaraderie. They suffered from a profound loneliness. They realised that captivity was for them a defining experience.

SOURCES
Many Prisoners of War have written accounts of their wartime experiences. None is without interest but the following are among the best: Michael Alexander, *A Privileged Nightmare* (Pan, 1956), Dawyck Haig, My Father's Son, (Pen & Sword Books, 2000),

German Prisoners of War
Flanders 1914

Belgian refugees in Britain during the First World War
Simon Fowler

Refugees at Tirlemont Belgium 1914

It is a truism to say that Britain drifted into World War I over a hot bank holiday weekend. And although there were detailed plans to send a military force to France, almost no thought had been given to directing the civilian population.

The end of August 1914 saw the arrival of the first Belgian refugees fleeing the invading German forces. Nothing like this had ever occurred in Britain before. Some refugees had escaped across the Channel from other continental conflicts, particularly during the Napoleonic wars, but they were small in numbers and generally wealthy. But now and until the beginning of November 1914 nearly 200,000 destitute men women and children from the upper, middle and working classes arrived in the ports up and down the East Coast.

The first arrivals were chiefly people with enough money to pay their way at least for a few days. Later arrivals, the destitute as *The Times History of the War* somewhat unkindly called them started arriving in London in early September at the rate of 500 a day. The fall of Antwerp rapidly increased those numbers. At Folkestone, 11,000 arrived in one day. Numbers accelerated after the fall of Ostend, with 26,000 arriving at Folkestone, among them wounded Belgian soldiers. During November, 45,000 refuges came to Britain. Thereafter the numbers decreased as it became increasingly difficult to cross the English Channel.

By June 1915, it is estimated 265,000 refugees had made their way to the fate of their families and property, which is why it is impossible to say exactly how many refugees there were. A census was taken of the 211,000 refugees in June 1915, in order to determine who was suitable for military service or work in the war economy. It found that there were 65,000 men over 16; 80,000 women over 16, and 66,000 children.

Inevitably a few people were hostile to their arrival, but they were small in number. Winston Churchill,

for instance, grumbled 'They ought to stay there and eat up continental food and occupy German policy attention. This was no time for charity.'

Within a matter of days of the arrival of the first refugees a network of relief charities sprang up — some 2000 in all, most of whom were very small and only cared for one or two Belgian families, usually in houses donated by local well-wishers. In larger towns committees tended to be set up under the chairmanship of the mayor, which gave them official authority of sorts. In Croydon, such a committee was formed in late August 1914. It consisted of councillors and members of local charities. They provided housing and clothing for the 900 refugees who arrived during the early months of the war. They also arranged schooling for children and employment for their parents, and opened a workshop where a dozen men were employed making furniture and a smaller number of women made clothes which was sent to Le Havre for use by Belgian refugees in France.

Refugees were spread fairly evenly through the country, although there were concentrations in London and seaside resorts where there was plenty of spare accommodation out of season. Blackpool for example housed 8000 Belgians.

The government stepped in on 9th September and appointed the Local Government Board to co-ordinate the work of local charities. The Board however preferred to work through the War Refugees Committee, which had itself been set up a few days earlier. They had immediately issued an appeal for hospitality, money, clothes, food and volunteers. On the first day the Committee received a thousand letters each offering accommodation for the refugees, within two weeks offers of hospitality for 100,000 people had been received from all social classes. One working man wrote to the War Refugee Committee: 'I have five [children] of my own, but I'd like to keep a Belgian.'

Fleeing Belgian Refugees 1914

For much of the war the upper classes received a sympathetic hearing, and were protected from the reality of the situation with considerable resources were dedicated to their support. In the autumn of 1914 aristocratic ladies fought to look after the richer refugees. Lady Lyttleton campaigned to have hostels for better class men saying 'they are very nice people some of them – I mean men one could have to stay with one.' A Hostel for First Class Belgians in Chelsea was specifically set up to house 'best class' Belgians unlikely to be able to work in London.

The WRC also attempted to organise relief efforts and co-ordinate activities, not always successfully. Its headquarters in the Aldwych soon became the centre of a great deal of activity for refugees from being a receiving centre to a clothing store. It ran centres at Olympia and Alexandra Palace in London which housed refugees and provided employment in workshops. By the end of the war it employed 140 staff.

Despite a general welcome in the early months of the war, most refugees soon found themselves in the position of unwanted pets grown too big. The Hostel for Best-Class Belgians closed in late 1916 'as we found Belgians in the house were very difficult.' Indeed, by 1916, publicity was likely to be negative concentrating on those Belgians who were unwilling to contribute to the war effort. A year later many supporters would have agreed with Mr H.G. Smith of Oundle who wrote to Canon Elwes in Peterborough: "I am enclosing a cheque for £1 for the Belgian Relief Committee. I am afraid this has to be the last contribution… we do not like to ask for money for the Belgians here as we feel that they ought by now to be entirely self-sufficient."

Elsewhere when the charitable donations ran out, they found the welcome was not as warm as it had once been. The British public, as is so often the case, found other causes more immediately important to support. There were also grumbles that the refugees were content to live off others rather than fend for themselves. This was not a new sentiment as there had been constant complaints about the supposedly large number of scroungers and shirkers among pre-war charity recipients.

To an extent the problem resolved itself because of the increasing demand for labour, particularly in the munitions factories. By the middle of 1916 most adult Belgians could find work if they so choose and there was constant pressure upon them to do so.

It was much more difficult to handle the upper class refugees, most of whom were unaccustomed to manual labour. They fought to retain their pre-war social status with a passionate determination. Members of the professions for example wanted to continue as advocates or teachers and nothing else. This increasingly caused antagonism in a society engaged in total war, where social divisions were becoming blurred.

By and large there was little attempt to integrate the refugees into the host population. In part this was due to the language barrier. Few British people spoke French, let alone Flemish, and relatively few Belgians had any English or in many cases even French. The diarist Rev Andrew Clark noted on 24th September 1914 that one of his parishioners Mrs Scott: "has great difficulty in conversation with her refugees. She speaks French and German. They only speak Flemish."

In addition their British hosts expected the Belgians to be much like themselves with a tinge of continental exoticism – and to adapt the traditional subservient position of the 'deserving poor'. Instead the Belgians came from a very different culture, and many of the refugees were equally unwilling to adjust to their new circumstances. By 1916 and 1917 this was no longer forthcoming.

The result was often friction and disillusionment. Miss G.M. West, a vicar's daughter in the West Country, noted in her diary as early as November 1914, that: "Most people agree that they are fat, lazy, greedy amiable and inclined to take all the benefits heaped upon them as a matter of course."

The greatest complaint was that Belgian young men were reluctant to enlist in their army, while the other refugees were unwilling to pull their weight in the war effort. Similar pressure was placed on their British counterparts. In the Spring of 1916, Baron Hymans, the Belgian minister to London, reported to the Belgian government in exile in Le Havre that Londoners, fed up with seeing refugees out of uniform, were shouting; "Bloody Belgians" even at those too young to bear arms. He himself was once upbraided, which he took as a compliment because of his age. However he thought that Belgians must contribute more to the war effort and to be seen to be doing so.

The two communities – host and guest – largely preferred to keep themselves to themselves, perhaps the various petty resentments ensured that this would be the case. The division is best shown in the North

Belgian Refugees reach London

gendarmerie and a shot was fired. In the end, sense prevailed and gradually conditions improved. Eventually a small town of 6,000 people was established. The community was kept separate and enclosed by iron fencing. They had prefabricated homes (with inside toilets), a school, a church, a hospital and a village store.

Undoubtedly many Belgians were very grateful for the care they and their families received, even if they occasionally fell foul of the unwritten expectations of the English class system. The annual report of the Putney and Roehampton Fund in 1915: 'It is frequently asked 'Do you find the Belgians grateful?' The experience has been that they are most grateful.' Of course it was in the interest of the Fund to stress the supplicant nature of the applicants. And in October 1917 a tree was planted in Queen's Park in Glasgow by the city's refugee community: 'In remembrance of the hospitality and kindness extended

East. A special housing estate, named Elisabethville after the Belgian Queen, was built for refugee workers at the munitions factory in Birtley south of Newcastle. It was run according to Belgian law and protected by Belgian gendarmes. Flemish and Walloon were spoken and the currency used was Belgian. At first the accommodation was inadequate, the pay was less than it ought to have been, and there was resentment because at work they were required to wear full military uniform. This led to a riot in December 1916 when 2,000 men marched on the

to them during their sojourn.'

After the Armistice the refugees went home to their now devastated country. Very few elected to remain in Britain. Indeed there is almost nothing left today to show that this country played host to 160,000 men, women and children. The name and its original purpose of the settlement at Birtley was almost forgotten. For most people Agatha Christie's Hercule Poirot, the retired Belgian police detective, is the only reminder.

Most refugees returned within a few weeks of the Armistice. Their reception on their return Belgium was mixed. Undoubtedly there was some resentment that they missed out the privations endured by that country at the hands of the Germans. The Rev Andrew Clark noted in May 1919 that he had been told: "the little children cannot speak French and the older children had got into English ways which are not approved of by the Belgians." The appalling conditions they found at home made a few people nostalgic for their lives in England. The historian of Croydon's war effort noted that the council had received many a letter from former refugees expressing the wish that they 'might be in Croydon again'.

Finding out more

Although the Belgian refugees have been all but forgotten it is still possible to find out about individuals and their reception locally. The most important genealogical resource is the individual history cards, which were recreated by the War Refugees Committee. These are at the National Archives at Kew in series MH 8 and record personal details of the refugees and where they were looked after in Britain. The series also has the remaining papers of the Committee itself including minutes and correspondence. Other correspondence can be found in HO 45 and RG 20.

Locally the best bet are newspapers which will record the reception of refugees locally in 1914 as well as the establishment of local care committees and related fundraising activities, although as the war progressed Belgians are less likely to appear unless they fell foul of the law in some way. A few records of the charities which were formed to care for the refugees may be found at local archives. Probably more useful are local authority minute books which will indicate how refugee children were educated and the provision of work for their parents.

Sometimes you may find graves for refugees and the occasional memorial. There is a large monument, for example, in the City Road Cemetery in Sheffield. In the early 1920s the Belgian government seems to have presented memorials to local councils in thanks which may have been erected in the town hall.

A few local historians have written about the Belgian refugees (I know of studies in Birtley, Swindon and Sheffield), but there is no general book on them and their experiences. If you have memories or know where graves or memorials can be found I'd be interested to hear from you. My personal email is sfowler@sfowler.force9.co.uk.

The Western Front Association

Registered Charity 298365 was founded to further interest in the period 1914-1918.
Its main aim is to perpetuate the memory, courage and comradeship, of those, on all sides, who served their countries. It does not seek to glorify war, is non-political, and welcomes members of all ages.

Benefits of membership include:-
National and local meetings, where members can hear high quality lectures and meet like minded people.

Publications
Stand To! (an authoritative journal of the period) and *The Bulletin* (our in house magazine)
are sent to all members 3 times annually.

Members services
including trench maps, a full range of commodities, and advice and help relating
to historical and genealogical research.

For details of membership, please apply to

THE WESTERN FRONT ASSOCIATION
PO BOX 1914 KIDDERMINSTER WORCS. DY10 2WZ

http://www.westernfrontassociation.com

A Red Cross VAD in Wartime
Jackie Evans

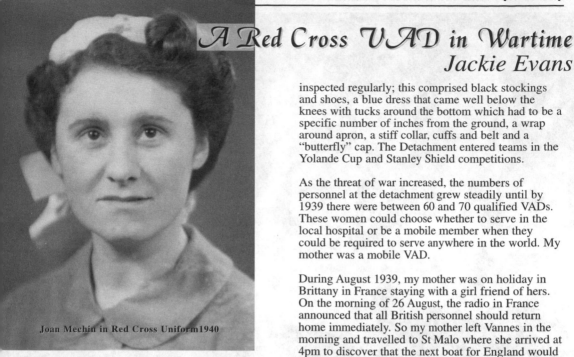

Joan Mechin in Red Cross Uniform 1940

My mother, Joan Alexander Evans nee Mechin, was the niece of Frederick Matthias Alexander who bequeathed to the world the Alexander Technique. In 1933, when Joan's father, George Mechin, died, Alexander offered his sister, Amy and her two daughters, Marjory and Joan accommodation at a cottage on his estate at Penhill in Sidcup in Kent. In January 1934, Amy and her girls moved to the house of another brother, a widower whose son was the same age as Joan, in High View Road, Sidcup.

In 1935, there was a small Red Cross Detachment (Kent 62) in Sidcup that Joan joined in November as a probationer and a year later she was accepted as a qualified Voluntary Aid Detachment (VAD). Discipline within the detachment was strict and members took their obligations very seriously. Their duties involved one Sunday a month working on the wards of the local cottage hospital, frequent attendance at the 1st Aid Post on the busy A 20 road and weekly meetings of the detachment. There was an Annual Inspection at which appearance was obligatory or one year's service was discounted. Their uniforms were inspected regularly; this comprised black stockings and shoes, a blue dress that came well below the knees with tucks around the bottom which had to be a specific number of inches from the ground, a wrap around apron, a stiff collar, cuffs and belt and a "butterfly" cap. The Detachment entered teams in the Yolande Cup and Stanley Shield competitions.

As the threat of war increased, the numbers of personnel at the detachment grew steadily until by 1939 there were between 60 and 70 qualified VADs. These women could choose whether to serve in the local hospital or be a mobile member when they could be required to serve anywhere in the world. My mother was a mobile VAD.

During August 1939, my mother was on holiday in Brittany in France staying with a girl friend of hers. On the morning of 26 August, the radio in France announced that all British personnel should return home immediately. So my mother left Vannes in the morning and travelled to St Malo where she arrived at 4pm to discover that the next boat for England would not sail until the following morning. She joined the queue and spent the night sleeping in the open on the quay, a very cold experience! The ship sailed at 10am and she was able to get home to Sidcup that night. As a result of her night at St Malo, she contracted a very bad infection and spent the next 2 weeks in bed. This meant that when her call up papers for the Army came through she was unfit to travel. War was declared on 3 September and on 23 September she began duty, on 8-hour shifts, 7 days a week, at the mobile unit in Sidcup. A couple of weeks later her Commandant informed her that she was to join the Navy and on 18 October she reported to the Naval Hospital at Chatham. This was to change her life.

NAVAL HOSPITAL, CHATHAM.

Kent 62 Red Cross Terretorial Camp 1937

When she left Sidcup she was a young 23 year old who had spent only short periods of time away from the family. Now she was on her own in the big wide world going to a place where she knew nobody. Her friend, Ivor Evans, that she would later marry drove her to the station and saw her on to the train. He returned to duty as a TA Officer at RAF Biggin Hill.

My mother arrived at Chatham hospital and was taken to the VAD mess where she found that she was sharing a room with two other girls. She met the Sister in charge of the VADs and Matron. Later Sister took her on a tour of the hospital and told her that the next day she would be working on one of the surgical wards. The hospital at Chatham was based on a central corridor alleged to be a quarter of a mile long with wards opposite each other and at right angles to the corridor.

It is hard to imagine what the poor Matron and the Sisters thought of the arrival of these VADs. They were trained in First Aid and Home Nursing, they had undertaken courses on hygiene and sanitation as well as Gas Warfare and they could all plan gas proof 1st Aid posts. For the previous two years my mother had attended an annual tented TA camp and manned a tented hospital but not all the VADs had done this. She remembers to her shame the day she brought in an unconscious casualty by ambulance who proved to be drunk. The incident was soon forgotten when the angry MO insisted on her helping with the stomach pump. Part of my mother's training included two weeks on the wards at Shorncliffe Military Hospital, an extremely useful experience for those VADs who were shortly to be sent for duty in a service hospital on the out break of war. Some VADs had not experienced this in fact some of them had never

worked in their lives and a number had been debutantes. This limited training fell a long way short of the standard that Matron and the Sisters were used to from their staff. Keen, enthusiastic and energetic the VADs certainly were but the nursing skills required in a war situation were seriously lacking. At Chatham there were about 28 VADs and on the 44 bedded wards there were 3 on each of the 2 day shifts and 2 on the night shift, the only staff. A Sister looked after 3 wards at night. It must be remembered that in addition to nursing duties the VADs were responsible for cleaning the wards.

It was perhaps fortunate for all concerned that for the first few months there were relatively few casualties and so the VADs could be trained. They worked a 7 day week with half day off which meant that because my mother lived relatively close to Chatham she could often go home. The patients on her minor surgical ward comprised men suffering from boils, carbuncles, septic hands and other slight ailments. They were only in hospital a short time but there were a certain number of treatments to be undertaken and dressings to be changed. These were carried out by the sister so that the VADs could watch and learn. The wards had to be tidied, lockers cleaned and all the beds had to be in a straight line. Inspections took place regularly and as was normal practice in all the services, not only then but for many years after the war, the inspecting officer wore white gloves. They climbed on chairs and ran their gloved hands over the top of the curtain rail, underneath the bed and along all the ledges. Woe betide the person who was responsible for a speck of dust on the inspecting officer's white glove. The cry would go up that many of us remember so well, "this is filthy and has not been dusted for weeks". Certainly, life in any service

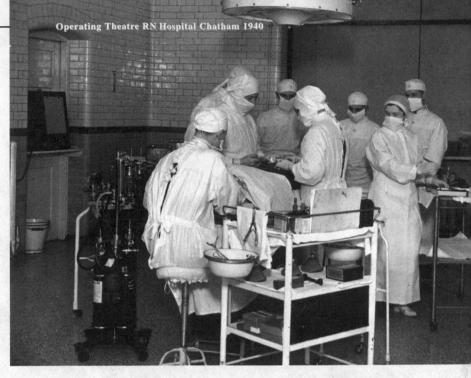

Operating Theatre RN Hospital Chatham 1940

taught people how to clean and the importance of hygiene; most of us have never forgotten this vital aspect so essential for healthy living.

After about a fortnight on the minor surgical ward, my mother was transferred onto a medical ward on 8 November. There she looked after men with pneumonia, bronchitis and other medical conditions. There were, of course, no anti-biotics in those days. On 19 December, she started her time on night duty; this was a 12 hour shift for 31 continuous nights and of course included Christmas. She had the advantage of knowing the patients; this was a great help on such a long and arduous duty but Christmas involved day time activities as well as her night shift. This proved to be a very taxing time. It is interesting that during all the time she was nursing she never once had to shave anyone. The up patients always undertook this task; those men who were sufficiently fit helped around the wards as much as possible and always supported the VADs when Sister or Matron criticised them. On night duty, by 8am all the ward of 44 men had to be washed and ready for inspection. Frequently my mother started washing the men at 4am so that they would all be ready in time; none of them ever complained or even commented about this rather early start! She remembers the joy and evil amusement of the men who were intent on disrupting the weekly gas drill. Dressed in cap and apron, the nurses donned their gas masks and tin hats for half an hour and continued with their duties. If they laughed, which the men tried to achieve, then the gas mask steamed up and it was impossible to see.

My mother had a few days leave after her night duty before, on 2 February, she returned to day duty on the same medical ward. Life moved steadily along with the VADs learning all the time. They gained in confidence and with the exception of one elderly VAD they were young and very adaptable. At Chatham they were treated as officers and so there were many parties and dances with the medical officers. They went to the cinema regularly or as often as their 10s a week would allow and walked considerable distances around the area. As spring approached they played tennis on the courts just outside their mess. Life was really quite enjoyable but little did they realise what was about to happen.

Early in May, my mother's friend, Ivor Evans went with his Royal Artillery regiment to France. They were tasked to go to Arras to support the troops there but events overtook them. On 10 May, the German forces advanced into Belgium and Holland and the next day Chamberlain resigned and Winston Churchill became Prime Minister of a coalition government. By 15 May the Dutch capitulated and on 17 May the Germans entered Brussels and Belgium capitulated formally on 27 May. The position of the British troops on the continent was dire and on 24 May the first 1000 of them were evacuated from Boulogne but within a few hours the Germans had entered the port. Operation *Dynamo,* the evacuation from Dunkirk began two days later. This operation continued until midnight on 2 June when General Alexander and Captain Tennant toured the harbour area and inspected the beaches and were content that there was nobody left. They went back to the pier and embarked for Britain; the total evacuated was 338,226 personnel in 7 days. This included Ivor Evans who came back with his men, after their retreat from near Arras, on the *Lady of Man* which was the last civilian ship to leave the beachhead. Five days later the King of Norway embarked for England and his troops ceased hostilities; the evacuation of the British troops at Narvik was completed a day later on 8 June.

Life at Chatham changed radically. The wounded were loaded on to trains at Dover and the red labels, life expectancy 24 hours, were detrained at Chatham, the orange labels went to London and the yellow and green labels went further north. The 44 bed wards filled quickly, mattresses were placed between the beds and the stretchers were put up and down the long corridor. The medical officers went round inspecting the injured, ordering the evacuation of the less seriously ill patients already in the hospital and filling the empty beds from the stretchers in the corridors. The nurses had to cut the men out of their

323

Ward F2 - RN Hospital Chatham 1940

uniforms and remove the dressings that had been administered at the field hospitals and dressing stations in France. To say that things were hectic is an understatement. My mother's diary for this period contains nothing, she was obviously too busy and when she came off duty too tired and emotionally exhausted to consider writing anything down. On 2 June, she was transferred to the Burns Unit. To this day she cannot cope with the smell of Laburnum because as they walked on duty they passed the wonderful avenue of Laburnum trees. To her the smell of those trees is always mingled with smell of burned flesh. It brings back the sight of burned faces covered with gentian violet making a black mask that stared from so many beds. Sister started at one end of the ward irrigating eyes only to start all over again when she had finished one round. Hands resting on white sheets, almost immovable, leaving pools of disgusting puss beneath them when the hands were moved; legs encased in bags of saline; feeding tiny flecks of boiled egg to patients almost unable to open their lips were unforgettable memories especially the courage and bravery of those so heavily afflicted. These totally weary men were so pleased to be home.

After 6 days on the Burns Unit, my mother moved to A1, a surgical ward. It was here that she experienced something that she would never forget. She had just come on duty when she was called to a bed by a man with a cage over his leg who asked her "please move my leg it pains me so much". Trying to show no emotion when the removed covers revealed no leg at all, she rustled the sheets and could hardly bear his gratitude when he said "oh nursie, that feels so much better."

The news from the war got progressively worse; France capitulated on 21 June and by now the Germans had just over one and a half million French prisoners of war in addition to a considerable number of British ones. Meanwhile, the evacuation, entitled Operation *Ariel*, from the ports of Northern France continued and, between 16 and 24 June, 163,225 British, Canadian and Polish servicemen were brought to England by the Royal Navy and the Merchant Navy. Britain and the Empire stood alone against Germany and an invasion of Britain was expected to start at any time. First the Germans had to gain control of the skies and so on 15 July began the Battle of Britain. The battle raged over southern England particularly Kent where of course Chatham is situated. During August the Germans launched intensive day operations against coastal radar stations and fighter airfields in the London area. Then, on 7 September, the day light assault on London itself began. Attacks on the docks, though serious in themselves, brought vital relief to the fighter airfields which had been under great pressure. The climax of the battle was reached on 15 September when over 1000 sorties were flown against the capital. At one time during that day the RAF had all their aircraft in the air, there were no reserves and no more pilots; these men flew sortie after sortie. Winston Churchill described this "as one of the decisive battles of the war".

My mother remembers that hot summer as if it were yesterday; the bombing of Chatham; the sky lighted up by the burning of London; leaning out of the train window one Saturday between Dartford and Sidcup watching the silver fish enemy aircraft flying up the Thames; returning from the cinema in Chatham while a raid was in progress and hearing the guns booming

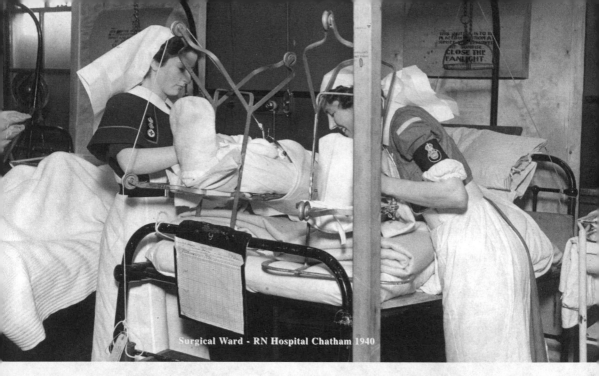

Surgical Ward - RN Hospital Chatham 1940

out from the ships in the harbour and a group of VADs my mother included kneeling on the ground with their heads buried and their tin hats firmly covering their bottoms. It was an incredibly difficult time for everyone but the people my mother felt most sorry for were the foreign casualties particularly those who could hardly speak English. During the Battle of Britain, there were 147 Polish and 101 Czech pilots and many were killed or wounded. Some of the wounded were brought to Chatham. These young, frightened men so far from friends, home and everything that was familiar to them needed special care and comfort. It was during night duty that it was so important to help the patients. For 12 hours, the two nurses on the ward were literally run off their feet but my mother learnt that time expands to cover the work that needs to be done and that if one is really busy then the impossible can be achieved. It was perhaps fortunate for her that before this particular period of night duty which lasted all of August, she had been given two weeks leave some of which she spent in Penzance.

The punishing schedule for the nurses continued for the rest of the year and the war went relentlessly on. The London Blitz as it became known went on throughout the autumn and winter causing unbelievable destruction and a high loss of life. On 29 December the Germans launched a massive raid against London; Guildhall and eight Wren churches were destroyed or severely damaged and St Paul's Cathedral engulfed in flames was saved on the specific orders of Churchill and the amazing vigilance and bravery of the fire fighters who had to contend with an ebbing tide. As 1940 became 1941, the war news became worse and worse. My mother continued to nurse at Chatham and became engaged to Ivor Evans on 29 June 1941. On her birthday, on 10 August, she was posted to a blood transfusion unit. The unit went to Plymouth, Slough, Exeter and

Pwllheli and then on 22 September, the unit was moved to Leeds. Here my mother and the rest of the VADs lived in an establishment that had previously been a home for "fallen women". During the next 15 months, they bled every town and village in Yorkshire and my mother will always remember the kindness, generosity and hospitality of the Yorkshire people. On 22 May 1942, my mother married Ivor Evans; she was dressed in blue the only appropriate dress available at the time and they had a chocolate wedding cake. The baker and all the neighbours had selflessly given their coupons for the occasion. The Guard of Honour was provided by VADs. In January 1943, my mother was posted to the Naval hospital at Haslar and then in February was moved to Golden Square, just behind Piccadilly Circus, where she was in charge of a WREN hostel. This hostel was for girls who were going overseas. They stayed there a few days while my mother checked that they were not pregnant, did not have bugs in their hair and had had all their inoculations. One girl arrived at the hostel with diphtheria, my mother looked down her throat and when she saw that the membrane had already formed, she was horrified. She rang the doctor who told her to give the girl a particular injection. She did so and the girl passed out during the injection but my mother decided to give her the full dose anyway. The girl recovered and my mother did not catch diphtheria. My mother became pregnant and left Golden Square on 22 June 1943 to await my birth. During May, she had nursed patients with German Measles but, fortunately, did not catch the disease so I survived without any damage.

After the war, my mother continued to work for the Red Cross on a voluntary basis. She took a mobile shop around our local TB hospital and later formed a Red Cross Members group which she ran for many years. In 1964, she was appointed President of the Red Cross in the newly formed London borough of

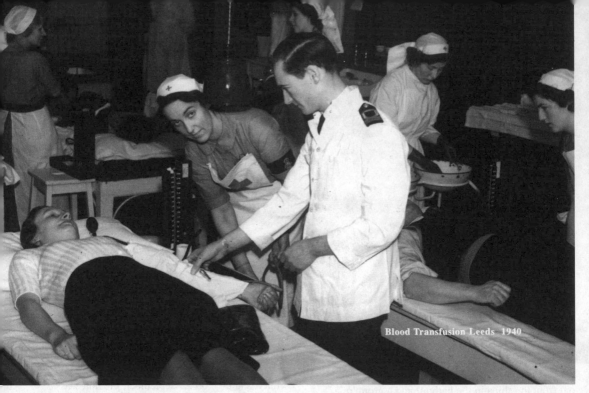

Blood Transfusion Leeds 1940

Bexley and was instrumental in starting 3 different clubs for the disabled in various parts of the borough. Two of them still operate today. She negotiated for a Red Cross charity shop to open in Sidcup and, in 1972, she was appointed Chairman of South East London; a very busy job that required long hours and much hard work from which she retired in 1981. She was awarded the Badge of Honour for distinguished service, made a Life Member of the Society and, later, a Vice President of the London Branch. Throughout the post war period until a couple of years ago, my mother undertook a vast amount of welfare work. As a youngster, I shall never forget visiting a First World War veteran and his wife. The lady was lying on a couch and the rest of the sitting room was furnished with orange boxes. My mother told me to put the food we had brought into a kitchen cupboard and I could not believe it when I opened the doors of the cupboards that there was absolutely nothing in them!

My mother says to this day that her time nursing with the Navy changed her forever. She learnt about suffering, sorrow, joy and total exhaustion coupled with satisfaction. But overriding everything she learnt about the importance of comradeship and teamwork. She made friendships during her time in the Navy that have lasted a lifetime- a shared experience that can never be repeated.

Most of the information for this article was extracted from my mother's diaries. For clarification of factual information about the 2nd World War, Martin Gilbert, *Second World War* (London: Phoenix Giant, (1989) 1996) was used.

Jackie Evans is the author of *Frederick Matthias Alexander, A Family History*. The book gives a detailed account of the Alexander family, transportation to Australia, life in the early days of Tasmania and the development of the Alexander Technique. The publishers are Phillimore & Co. Ltd of Chichester on www.phillimore.co.uk or in Australia the book is available at Einstein's Moon Bookshop, 336 Clarendon Street, South Melbourne, Victoria 3205, Australia.

The Royal Navy
~ historical background and pointers for genealogists
Len Barnett

doctrine first formulated, a code of discipline came into use as of 1653 that became the Articles of War within a decade. After the Restoration in 1660 there was far reaching naval reform, largely but not completely through the efforts of a Navy Board official named Samuel Pepys. It is from this post Restoration era that the earliest useful body of records can be drawn and it is important to state that by this time both administrative and executive affairs were effectively conducted through the one office of the Navy Board. (*Some* aspects of administration, such as victualling and medical issues, were dealt with variously by other boards, mostly set up as of the latter part of the seventeenth century.)

Arguably, one of Pepys' greatest achievements was in introducing a system of professional examinations for those applying for lieutenancies as of 1677. Apparently a revolutionary idea at the time, this went a long way to forging an officer corps recognisable in modern terms.

'Typical Pusser' is a term that has been used within the Royal Navy for a long time. It has rather a fluid meaning though. To some it engenders a warmth for all the colourful if slightly idiosyncratic ways of the service. For others, often the more cynical, these two words instead encapsulate all the inequities, operational chaos and administrative muddles that they get caught up in.

I, therefore, begin this article with a suggestion that genealogists tracing their naval forebears *might* like to keep this phrase in mind. It obviously depends on researchers' own temperaments and experiences as to which of the two definitions is closer to their own mindsets.

With a dearth of realistically usable personnel records prior to the seventeenth century, an outline of naval organisation in Britain is not necessary here. Nevertheless, amazingly some earlier administrative documents from the sixteenth century survive. Saliently, unless otherwise stated, all records referred to in this article are to be found at the Public Records Office, Kew, Surrey as part of the United Kingdom's National Archives.

Ironically for the 'Royal' Navy it was during the Puritan Commonwealth (1649-59) that the State's warships first began to act effectively as a disciplined force. After serious defeats inflicted by the Dutch, something of the character of the New Model Army was instilled afloat. Not only was a tactical battle fleet

Through the eighteenth century to the nineteenth the monarch's navy not only grew in size, but also in complexity. The relationship between the various boards altered, with the Admiralty (as an executive in its own right) gradually gaining the ascendancy. And, for the first time, in 1748, commissioned officers (and midshipmen) became instantly recognisable, with the introduction of uniforms for them. (The only others then wearing uniforms in naval service were Royal Marines, or 'lobster-backs' as they were known and even then, generally not at sea.)

By the mid eighteenth century, apart from sea officers with monarch's commissions there were also others holding warrants from the boards already briefly alluded to. These were specialists - sailing masters (navigators), gunners, carpenters, boatswains, surgeons and pursers. With the *possible* exception of masters, they were all essential in running men-o-war. In the sense of the time they were also sea officers, with their own professional career paths and often highly respected in their own rights. All but one class were also required to pass examinations. (Pursers were different and in a strange position, partly responsible to the Navy Board, but also in business on their own account.)

Below the sea officers were 'inferior' or petty officers. Confusingly, some of these also held warrants, such as armourers, sailmakers, masters-at-arms, cooks, surgeons' mates, chaplains and schoolmasters. In the final decade of the century caulkers, ropemakers and coopers, who had been purely dockyard workers up until then joined them at sea. Another group of petty officers were rated onboard (but with recourse to higher authority) and included 'young gentlemen', midshipmen, masters' mates and gunners' mates. (Midshipmen were then seen as senior petty officers, not necessarily young, or even on their way to commissions.)

The 'people' formed the bulk of ships' companies. There was yet another class of petty officers, who were rated onboard locally by ships' commanders. Some of these rates were as quartermasters, boatswains' mates, armourers' mates, pursers' stewards and captains' clerks. The rest were 'private' men and again there were gradations in rating.

There was also another way of splitting up companies: those that kept watches and those that did not. This cut across all onboard. Those that were not seamen and hence, watchkeepers were rather unfairly called 'idlers'.

War always having been an *extremely* expensive pursuit and warships being particularly costly to build and operate, accounting has been a very important facet of British naval record keeping for centuries. These bodies of records, while often highly complex are the basis for modern genealogical study. Incidentally, even captains', lieutenants' and masters' logs were kept partially at least in relation to proving accounts submitted, before payment.

Genealogically commissioned officers up to 1815 are best served, with much academic work previously conducted on their careers. Through published lists, it is not even necessary to go to *any* original documents to find when and where individuals served: at least on gaining their lieutenancies. Passing certificates, as introduced by Pepys, can then be consulted for earlier service and these stretch back to the 1690s. Anyway, for researchers wanting more detail there are numerous types of records by and devoted to those holding commissions. One favourite is in lieutenants' logs (over 5,000 of which are held at the National Maritime Museum, Greenwich). Although in the apparent name of particular officers, what is not generally realised is that very often not only are the entries in captains' and lieutenants' logs absolutely identical, when directly compared so too is the *handwriting*. Taken from deck logs, it is far from clear who actually routinely wrote up these documents.

Warrant Officers have received much less scholarship. Nevertheless, as well as certificates of service (that were used for a variety of uses from applying for employment and promotion to pensions), there are a number of classes of original documents specifically relating to them that are greatly useful, if sometimes difficult to use. Disposition lists are one possibility (also for commissioned officers), although these are far from complete, time consuming in use and frequently the wanted dates of discharge and new appointments are missing.

Representatives of the people pose *infinitely* more problems, but if one has a ship and a year, it can be possible to trace careers through ships' musters and especially pay books: as well as gaining other snippets such as places and years of birth. (Please note these personal details are not shown for those with warrants or commissions in musters and pay books.) Such salient information can *sometimes* be gleaned through certificates of service, but the lower

the rate the less chance that there will have been such a certificate raised. Unfortunately, without an initial way into the musters and pay books it is not possible to locate individuals. There are also further complications due to the nature of recruitment of the lower deck. Technically at least, boys and men signed on per voyage. More often than not this equated as per war and men could also be transferred from ship to ship, at least sometimes. But, once discharged they could then sign on elsewhere: on other men-o-war, merchantmen of all types including Indiamen, or even privateers. As ships of the Royal Navy not infrequently had to resort to impressment in times of war, men taken from merchantmen might already have served the monarch: willingly or otherwise. Unless showing up in the records as, for instance, a returned prisoner of war, normally it cannot be determined whether one bout of service had been the only one.

Even before the long era of peace post 1815 there were social changes in the Royal Navy. In 1808 masters, surgeons, pursers and chaplains became 'Warrant Officers of Wardroom Rank'. Later, in 1843, all but chaplains were commissioned (with masters becoming navigating lieutenants and pursers becoming paymasters). This elevation also followed in 1859 for 'sky pilots', as chaplains were *already* known. Early in the Victorian era a new junior commissioned rank appeared. Initially designated as mate, twenty years later this was renamed sub-lieutenant. Also, with changed training regimes, especially as of the 1850s, the *rank* of midshipman became that of officers under training (with naval cadet below midshipman).

On the other hand, other classes of warrant officer did not fare so well. Although retaining their titles, both boatswains and carpenters lost status as technology evolved into iron and steel: progressively into the nineteenth century. Gunners did marginally better, with some getting into the gunroom at least as commissioned gunners *much* later in the century. The 'inferior officers' holding warrants of old also

evolved. Schoolmasters were elevated first to 'Warrant Officers of Wardroom Rank' in 1836, with an intermediate step in 1842 as 'Naval Instructors' and finally they were commissioned in 1861. Others, such as armourers, masters-at-arms, sailmakers, ropemakers and caulkers remained in petty officer rates. By the early 1860s they had been joined by other technical rates such as shipwrights and plumbers. All of the above were required to pass examinations before gaining their rates.

Recruitment for the lower deck was massively overhauled in a truncated way throughout the nineteenth century. The writing was already very much on the wall. Apart from the social unrest and political agitation of the lower orders post 1815 already by the 1830s industrial technology was making an imprint with steam-powered paddlers and even some screw-driven warships. On the subject of manpower, in 1835 there were two apparently separate experiments begun. One related to a series of attempts to monitor all British mariners in *merchant* service, with the view to forcing selected men onto men-o-war when required. Essentially these failed and the last register was wound up in 1857. But, more importantly there was also a limited scheme of engagements of continuous service introduced for boys and seamen *joining* the RN. This became the norm for entry to the seamen branch in 1853 and nine years later made mandatory. From then onwards this was opened to some in other branches, on the recommendation of commanding officers. Additionally, uniforms for the lower deck were first adopted in 1857 and rank structures became formalised: especially in the 1860s. There had always been 'superior' able rates and recognising this, a leading rate was introduced below petty officer. Two classes of petty officer also appeared over and above chief petty officers' rates. Warrant officers became departmental heads of the lower deck.

Some of the older rates evolved. When continuous service was being made mandatory for seamen joining as of 1862, this was not allowed for ships' stewards and their assistants. Unlike seamen, they were required to be able to read, write and count and were obviously employed as clerks. By the late 1870s stewards had generally become 'plate layers' and were still not offered this long term security, while new writers' rates existed: *some* on continuous service.

In these same decades other new rates appeared, such as signalmen and they too were accorded engagements of CS. But, in 1879's *Queen's Regulations* there was still a long list of those on non-continuous service. Apart from 'domestics' (a wide variety of cooks, stewards and servants) there were also butchers, bakers, barbers, tailors, shoemakers, musicians and native labour among this group. By the 1893 regulations this tally had become more limited, but had by no means ended.

Organisationally, in 1832 the Admiralty subsumed all the other boards. An opportunity to sensibly overhaul old procedures, *by and large* this does not appear to have happened.

One might also think that new arms of service starting from scratch might have been developed along more modern lines - such as that of the engineering branch. For those in positions of responsibility, engineers were first warranted as of 1837 and commissioned ten years later. For stokers, at the other end of the equation, for a considerable period continuous service was seen as a reward rather than a right.

Although service sheets came into use, variously and apparently haphazardly (for both officers and men) throughout the nineteenth century, many of the old ways of administration continued. In one way at least, this can be helpful to genealogists. The traditional certificates of service remained in use until almost the end of the century. Although these are not service histories as such, they can be extremely useful when service sheets are not available. Of course, far from all requested these, so they only give a tantalising glimpse of what might have been had the RN adopted some disciplined form of service sheets earlier. (Incidentally, long before there had also been *limited* 'service sheets' produced for commissioned officers in Pepys' time, but unfortunately for genealogists, were not then continued permanently.)

In relation to record keeping nineteenth century service sheets can sometimes be disappointing, particularly for commissioned officers. Surgeons are a case in point. Service histories for these officers are *very* deficient indeed, but at least until the early 1870s their pay records yield their full time in great detail. So, other sources, such as the *Navy List* need to be consulted. But, for others and especially executive officers, between their service sheets and the confidential reports kept by the First Lord's Office, it is often possible to see how individuals were judged by their superiors.

The RN's personnel records of the twentieth century follow all the basic patterns of the late nineteenth and so do not warrant further explanation: at least until after the First World War. But, these more recent documents are generally still held by the Ministry of Defence and need to be directly applied for by closely related descendants. Intriguingly, non-continuous service on the lower deck, for a dwindling number of rates, including domestics and native labour, continued *well* into the twentieth century.

One type of records not yet referred to relate to pensions. This is an extremely involved subject all on its own. Surprisingly, as early as the seventeenth century already there were various pension schemes for those on British men-o-war: State funded, or contributory. Far from all encompassing, through the eighteenth century many of these were expanded, but much remained chaotic. From 1832 onwards reorganisations and centralisation made these far more efficient.

Another subject deliberately not tackled is that of medal rolls. Apart from honours awarded to senior officers for services rendered, during the seventeenth and eighteenth centuries there were only occasional private medallions struck. Although not until 1847, a naval general service medal (with 230 different clasps) for the Revolutionary and Napoleonic Wars (1793-1815) was issued. This was the first of many, with many other awards instituted for other reasons. All these require space in their own rights.
© Len Barnett 2004

H.M. GUNBOAT "MEDINA" CONVEYING THE MARINES TO THE DOCKYARD   H.M.S. "ORONTES" LEAVING PORTSMOUTH

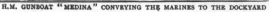

THE CRISIS IN EGYPT—WAR PREPARATIONS AT PORTSMOUTH 1882

The Fleet Air Arm and Casualties 1939 - 1945
David Barnes

HMS Ark Royal

would play an important role in any future air defence and a programme of expansion was put together.

The Fleet Air Arm was formed in April 1924 when the Admiralty was given a certain degree of control over the Royal Air Force units embarked on Aircraft Carriers and other surface ships. A maximum quota (70%) of naval officers were permitted to hold commissions in that part of the Royal Air Force known as the 'Fleet Air Arm'. Units embarked on carriers and ships came under the operational and disciplinary control of the Navy whilst at sea, but they reverted to Air Force control when they came 'ashore' and were accommodated at R.A.F. Stations.

The origins of British Naval Aviation go back to 1911, when the owner of the aerodrome at Eastchurch, on the Isle of Sheppey, made an offer to the Admiralty, to have four naval officers taught to fly at his own expense. There were around 200 volunteers to take up the offer, but the four selected were;

Lieutenant Charles Rumney Samson, Royal Navy
Lieutenant Reginald Gregory, Royal Navy
Lieutenant Arthur Murray Longmore, Royal Navy
Captain Eugene Louis Gerrard, Royal Marine Light Infantry

They all qualified for their Royal Aeronautical Society's Aviators Certificates in April and May 1911. In April 1912 the Royal Flying Corps was formed, this had two branches, a Naval Wing and a Military Wing, along with the Central Flying School. The Naval Wing was responsible for nine Royal Naval Air Stations and five airships. At first the Admiralty used the title 'Royal Flying Corps - Naval Wing', but in July 1914 the title 'Royal Naval Air Service' was officially adopted.

Since the first duty of the British Fleet was to protect the British Isles, the Royal Naval Air Service assumed responsibility for our Air Defences from September 1914 to February 1916.

The Royal Naval Air Service carried out anti-submarine and anti-zeppelin patrols as well as operating in France and the Eastern Mediterranean. On 1st April 1918 the Royal Flying Corps and the Royal Naval Air Service were merged to form the Royal Air Force.

After the end of the First World War, a programme of demobilising personnel was implemented, along with enrolments in the much smaller, Royal Air Force. Permanent commissions for officers were granted from August 1919. In December 1919 R.A.F. units working with the Royal Navy were placed under a new command called "Coastal Area." In 1922 it was decided that the Royal Air Force

This system of 'dual control' persisted with a few minor adjustments until the summer of 1937, then the Government announced its decision to transfer the administrative control, of all aircraft borne in ships of the Royal Navy, to the Admiralty. The Air Ministry was still responsible for research, development and supply of aircraft and equipment.

In 1938 the Admiralty was authorised by Parliament to implement a 300% increase in Fleet Air Arm personnel. There was consequently a considerable increase in the numbers of Naval personnel engaged in air duties in the Fleet Air Arm, as they replaced Royal Air Force personnel who were attached to the Fleet Air Arm, and to meet the pre-war expansion programme of the Fleet Air Arm. The Admiralty also drew up plans for short service commissions in the Royal Navy (Air Branch) and for the training of rating pilots. The Air Ministry still remained responsible for the training of pilots for the Fleet Air Arm, until they reach the stage when specialisation in Naval Duties begins, at which point the Admiralty assumes responsibility.

Personnel

Under the original agreement between the Admiralty and the Air Ministry 70% of the flying personnel of the Fleet Air Arm was made up of officers of the Royal Navy and Royal Marines. Officers who volunteered for service with the Fleet Air Arm were attached to the Royal Air Force and were granted Air Force rank during their period of attachment, irrespective of their rank in the Royal Navy or Royal Marines. When qualified as pilots, officers were eligible for promotion in R.A.F. rank, whilst in the zones of their naval or marine seniority. If they passed out of the zones of their naval or marine seniority before promotion, these officers automatically reverted to naval duties.

The minimum period of attachment to the Fleet Air

Royal Navy Officers' rank titles and their equivalents:		
ROYAL NAVY (inc Fleet Air Arm)	**ARMY**	**ROYAL AIR FORCE**
Admiral of the Fleet	Field Marshal	Marshal of the Air
Admiral	General	Air Chief-Marshal
Vice-Admiral	Lieutenant-General	Air Marshal
Rear-Admiral	Major-General	Air Vice-Marshal
Commodore	Brigadier-General	Air Commodore
Captain	Colonel	Group Captain
Commander	Lieutenant-Colonel	Wing Commander
Lieutenant -Commander	Major	Squadron Leader
Lieutenant	Captain	Flight Lieutenant
Sub-Lieutenant	Lieutenant	Flying Officer (Observer Officer)
Midshipman	Second Lieutenant	Pilot Officer

The training schedule for officers of the Royal Navy (Air Branch) would be as follows;
• Three months' preliminary naval training at Devonport
• Ten months flying training at a R.A.F. or civil flying school
• Six months specialised training in air duties peculiar to the Fleet Air Arm. These included; training in naval types of aircraft; torpedo work; advance navigation and wireless courses; deck-landing and catapult take-off training. This period was divided between naval training bases at; Ford, Sussex, Gosport, Hampshire and Lee-on-Solent, Hampshire. Following this officers usually embarked on a short training course in the training carrier, H.M.S. *'Furious'*
• Officer would then be appointed to a carrier or catapult unit at home or abroad.

Arm was for four years, but a large proportion of the officers continued to serve the whole of their Lieutenant or Lieutenant-Commander's time in the Fleet Air Arm. All officers, during their period of attachment to the R.A.F., returned to naval service or marine duties for two consecutive years after they had completed roughly five years' flying duties.

Officers if the Royal Navy (Air Branch) were required to serve with the Royal Navy for air duties for seven years. The first two years were spent in training. Both primary naval training and flying training from both ships and from shore stations. Subsequent years would, generally, be spent in ships of the Fleet, including service abroad, on foreign stations.

After seven years on the Active List, officers were transferred to an Emergency List for a period of eight years, during which they were required to keep themselves in flying practice, arranged at an aerodrome (not necessarily naval) as near as possible to the officer's home, and completing at least twelve hour's flying practice per year. In addition, they were to undergo periodic training in H.M. ships or naval establishments, either a fortnight annually or a month biennially.

Fairy Swordfish

After completion of their eight years' Emergency List service, officers were transferred to the Retired List of the Royal Navy, and were no longer required to keep themselves in flying training or to carry out further training. However they would be liable for recall to the service in the event of war or an emergency. After completing seven years service on the Active List, officers could volunteer to be retained on the Active List for a further period of eight years, this offer could be accepted at the Admiralty's discretion, and these officers were usually promoted to Lieutenant-Commander. A few officers, selected from those who completed fifteen years service on the Active List, could be allowed to remain for a further period, with a view to them qualifying for retired pay. Officers qualified for retired pay on attaining the age of forty, or completing twenty year's service.

There was an agreement between the Admiralty and the Air Ministry that a limited number of Royal Air Force officers could be transferred to the Air Branch. These officers were already qualified pilots, fit for full flying duties, but they did not need to have any previous Fleet Air Arm experience.

Naval ratings of the seaman, signal and telegraphist branches were eligible to serve as pilots. The first entry of twenty ratings, with the grades of able-seaman and leading seaman, started training on 1 May 1938. Initial shore training lasted one year, followed by eight weeks training at sea on a training aircraft carrier. On qualification they were known as: "rating pilots", corresponding with sergeant pilots in the Royal Air Force and were promoted to the rank of Petty Officer. The normal period of service of ratings pilots was to be seven years, after which they could opt to continue on full flying duties for a further three years, or pass into the flying reserve, or cease flying and return to normal naval duties.

Observers in the Fleet Air Arm have always been either naval officers or ratings unattached to the Royal Air Force.

In 1935 the non-substantive rating of telegraphist-air-gunner was replaced by a non-substantive rating of air gunner, this was open to seamen, signal and telegraphist branches, and a new, higher, non-substantive rating of Observer's mate, open to selected air-gunners, was created. Observer's mates perform air duties similar to those of the earlier rating of telegraphist-air-gunner, but were required to reach a higher standard of efficiency and training to enable them to carry out duties previously carried out by officer observers.

Ratings in the Air-Gunner Branch who qualify and were recommended for Observer's mate, were taken by roster, for courses at the Signal School, Gunnery School and School for Naval Co-operation at Ford, Sussex. These courses were similar to those undertaken by Observers (officers) An air section was also created in the Royal Naval Volunteer Reserve.

World War Two
The splendid achievements of the Fleet Air Arm during the Second World War are often forgotten about. Certainly at the time it was not realised how successful the torpedo-carrying would be. The torpedo was one of the surprised of the war and enabled the Fleet Air Arm to become a deadly force. This was certainly demonstrated in the Battles of Matapan and Taranto when a number of ships of the Italian Fleet were sunk or badly damaged by aircraft of the Fleet Air Arm.

The Fleet Air Arm was also responsible for reconnaissance. Reconnaissance spotter aircraft enabled the Navy, notably in the Mediterranean to find enemy ships and engage them, thus limiting the effectiveness of the enemy's naval forces. In the first action involving Naval Aircraft, it was a Fleet Air Arm Fairey Seafox that first spotted the *Admiral Graf Spee* in December 1939 and enabled the British Cruisers *Ajax, Achilles* and *Exeter* to engage her and force the Germans to scuttle her.

In the Norwegian Campaign between April and June 1940, the Gloster Gladiators operated without air superiority from frozen lakes. Further aircraft, Swordfish and Skua's were taken to Norway by the

Aircraft Carriers, H.M.S. Furious, H.M.S. Glorious and H.M.S. Ark Royal. In appalling conditions they attacked shipping and shore targets as well as supporting the Army during it's landings. The Skua dive bombers suceeded in sinking the German Cruiser *Konigsberg* in Bergen harbour. The aircrew losses during this campaign were severe, the Fleet Air Arm lost one third of its total strength.

Swordfish Biplanes from H.M.S. Illustrious and H.M.S. Eagle launched a daring raid on the night of 11 November 1940 on Taranto. Flying in two waves, the aircraft attacked targets with their torpedoes in the Max Grande. Three Italian battleships were crippled, a cruiser and two destroyers and an oil depot damaged and a seaplane base destroyed. Of the twenty one British Aircraft that took part in the raid, two were shot down

During the hunt for the *Bismark* 22-27 May 1941, fifteen Swordfish aircraft flew from H.M.S. Ark Royal in a full Atlantic gale, to make a twilight torpedo attack on her, succeeding in crippling the German battleship.

Sea Hurricanes proved successful in the raids on the ports of Petsamo and Kirkenes, north of the Arctic Circle, in July 1941. Further raids on hostile coastlines were carried out by carrier-borne fighter aircraft throughout the war, in places such as Madagascar, North Africa, Salerno, the South of France, and later in the Pacific.

With the increasing U-boat threat, in September 1941 the Fleet Air Arm started convoy protection duty and a number of small escort carriers, were brought into service.

Fleet Air Arm Strengths		
Date	Squadrons	Aircraft
September 1939	15	176
September 1940	26	247
September 1941	33	327
September 1942	55	461
September 1943	61	688
September 1944	74	1194
April 1945	66	1326
September 1945	67	945

Fairy Swordfish

HMS Glorious

In mid 1944 the emphasis of the sea war had swung towards the Far East. Flying largely American-built aircraft the Fleet Air Arm attacked the oil refineries at Pelambang, which supplied the Japanese forces with over half their oil supplies. With four Fleet Carriers operating in the Indian Ocean, The Fleet Air Arm could put some 250 modern aircraft into the air. In March 1945 the British Pacific Fleet, consisting of two battleships and four aircraft carriers, joined the U.S. Pacific Fleet. In July 1945 the combined forces targeted the Japanese mainland. In one period of eight days the British Pacific Fleet alone destroyed 450 Japanese aircraft on the ground and sank 350,000 tons of shipping.

Starting the war as a fairly small unit, the strength of the Fleet Air Arm was continually increased, new Squadrons were formed and more and more aircraft taken on strength.

Victoria Cross Awards
Lieut-Comander Eugene Kingsmill Esmonde
Led six Swordfish from 825 Squadron, in attack on German battleship *Prinz Eugen* in the English Channel 12 February 1942
The following details are given in the London Gazette of 3rd March, 1942 : The King has been graciously pleased to approve the grant of the Victoria Cross, for valour and resolution in action against the enemy, to Lieut-Commander Eugene Esmonde, DSO, R.N. On 12th February, 1942, Lieut-Commander Esmonde was in command of a squadron of six Swordfish ordered to attack the German battle-cruisers Scharnhorst and Gneisenau and the cruiser Prinz Eugene, which were entering the Straits of Dover strongly escorted by some thirty surface craft. After ten minutes' flight his squadron was attacked by a strong force of enemy fighters. Touch was lost with his fighter escort and all his aircraft were damaged. Nevertheless, cool and resolute, challenging hopeless odds, he flew on towards the target through the deadly fire of the battle-cruisers and their escorts. The port wing of his aircraft was shattered, but still he led his squadron on, only to be quickly shot down. His high courage and splendid resolution will live in the traditions of the Royal Navy and remain for many generations a fine and stirring memory

Lieutenant Robert Hampton Gray, RCNVR
Leading Corsair's from H.M.S. Formidible's 1841 and 1842 Squadrrons in strike against Japanese shipping in Onagawa Wan 9 August 1945
The citation in the London Gazette of 16th January, 1946, gives the following particulars: For great valour in leading an attack on a Japanese destroyer in Onagawa Wan on 9th August, 1945. In the face of fire from shore batteries and a heavy concentration of fire from some five warships, Lieutenant Gray pressed home his attack, flying very low in order to ensure success. Although he was hit and his aircraft was in flames, he obtained at least one direct hit, sinking the destroyer. Lieutenant Gray constantly showed a brilliant fighting spirit and most inspiring leadership.

Memorials
Fleet Air Arm Lee-on-Solent Memorial, Hampshire is located on the main sea front, near the former principal base of the Fleet Air Arm. It was chosen as the site for the Memorial to the men of the Fleet Air Arm who died during the Second World War and who have no known grave. The Memorial consists of a rectangular column of

Aircraft Carrier Losses
H.M.S. Ark Royal
Torpedoed in Mediterranean near Gibraltar by U-81 on 13 November 1941. Sank whilst under tow 14 November 1941 Built by Cammel Laird 1938. 60 aircraft (Official complement 72 aircraft)
H.M.S. Avenger
Torpedoed and sunk west of Gibraltar by U-155 on 15 November 1942
Ex mercantile ship – Rio Hudson. USN Lease/Lend 1941 20 Aircraft
H.M.S. Courageous
Torpedoed and sunk west of Ireland by U-29 on 17 September 1939 Built by Armstrong, Whitworth and Co. Newcastle 1916 as light battle cruiser. Converted to Aircraft Carrier at H.M. Dockyard, Devonport 1924-1928. 48 aircraft
H.M.S. Dasher
Lost in petrol explosion, south of Cumbraes. Firth of Clyde 27 March 1943
Ex mercantile ship – Rio de Janero. USN Lease/Lend 1942 20 Aircraft
H.M.S. Eagle
Torpedoed and sunk in Mediterranean, north of Algiers by U-73 on 11 August 1942, whilst escorting a large Malta-bound convoy Laid down by Armstrong, Whitworth and Co. Newcastle as Chilean battleship1913, hull taken over in 1917 Converted to Aircraft Carrier by H.M. Dockyard, Portsmouth 1923. 21 aircraft
H.M.S. Glorious
Sunk in action, by gunfire from German Battlecruisers *Scharnhorst* and *Gneisenau* west of Narvick 8 June 1940 Built by Harland and Wolff, Belfast 1916 as a light battlecruiser. Converted to Aircraft Carrier by H.M. Dockyards, Rosyth and Devonport 1924-1930. 48 aircraft
H.M.S. Hermes
Sunk by Japanese aircraft, south of Ceylon 9 April 1942 Built by Armstrong, Whitworth and Co. Newcastle and H.M. Dockyard, Devonport 1923.
12 aircraft (Official complement 15 aircraft)

Convoys were vital to the war effort, examples were across the Atlantic, to Russia and to the Mediterranean. Perhaps one of the more familiar ones were the convoys to Malta, the most famous being Operation Pedestal in August 1942 when, during a four-day running battle, 72 naval fighters faced the onslaught of some 600 available enemy aircraft. Thirteen Aircraft were lost, H.M.S. Eagle. Two cruisers and a destroyer were sunk and H.M.S. Indomitable was badly damaged.

Portland stone bearing the inscription: *THESE OFFICERS AND MEN OF THE FLEET AIR ARM DIED IN THE SERVICE OF THEIR COUNTRY AND HAVE NO GRAVE BUT THE SEA. 1939-1945.* Almost 2,000 names are carved on the panels.

The Commonwealth War Graves Commission Memorial Registers listed all these names, and these can be searched in the CWGC 'Debt of Honour' website. www.cwgc.org.uk . Whilst the CWGC 'Debt of Honour' lists all Naval Deaths, it does not specifically identify all Fleet Air Arm casualties. Those few that are listed as Fleet Air Arm, their Squadron or unit is not listed.

With the valuable assistance from the Commonwealth War Graves Commission; Fleet Air Arm Memorial Church, St Bartholomews, Yeovilton; Captain R F Shercliff, R.N.; David J Barnes and Don L Kindell, a complete listing of casualties for the Fleet Air Arm 1939 - 1947. This listing has been produced based upon Admiralty Records which were cross-referenced and checked against the Commonwealth War Graves Files, and logged in Excel spreadsheet format. The spreadsheet can be searched by any of the following categories; Surname, Crew Names; Service Number; Date of death; Squadrons; Ships; Aircraft Type ; Aircraft Serial Number; Where Buried / Commemorated.

This Excel spreadsheet is available on Data-CD for £25 post free from **David J Barnes 148 Parkinson Street, Burnley, Lancashire, BB11 3LL** and is also available via the E-bay auction site.

The Fleet Air Arm Museum

Further information regarding the Fleet Air Arm can be obtained from the Fleet Air Arm Museum Records and Research Centre, which assists hundreds of enquirers each year, providing assistance to genealogists and historians, from all parts of the globe.
The Museum Collection holds a wide range of documents from official and private sources, related to the British Naval Aviation. They cover areas such as aircraft,

Types of Naval Aircraft
The following is a list of principal types of aircraft used by the Fleet Air Arm. A number of other types were also used in smaller numbers for communication, transport and training duties etc

Name	Type	In Service
Blackburn Roc	Fighter	1940 1943
Blackburn Skua	Fighter / Dive Bomber	Late 1938 – August 1941
Fairey Albacore	Torpedo Bomber	March 1940 – December 1943
Fairey Barracuda	Torpedo Bomber	January 1943 - 1945
Fairey Fulmar	Fighter	June 1940 – March 1945
Fairey Firefly	Fighter	May 1943 - 1945
Fairey Seafox	Reconnaissance Seaplane	1938 - 1942
Fairey Swordfish	Torpedo Bomber	July 1936 – July 1945
Gloster Sea Gladiator	Fighter	1933 - 1940
Grumman Martlet / Wildcat	Fighter	September 1940 - 1945
Grumman Hellcat	Fighter	July 1943 - August 1943
Grumman Avenger	Torpedo Bomber	April 1943 - 1945
Hawker Sea Hurricane	Fighter	July 1941 –1945
Supermarine Seafire	Fighter	June 1942 - 1945
Supermariine Sea Otter	Reconnaissance Amphibian	1944 - 1945
Vickers-Armstrong Walrus	Reconnaissance Amphibian	1935 - 1944
Voight Corsair	Fighter Bomber	June 1943 - 1945

Blackburn Skua

Battle Honours
Thirty Battle Honours were awarded to Naval Air Squadrons, these show the extent of the actions and areas that the Fleet Air Arm operated in.

Aegean 1943-44	English Channel 1939-45	Norway 1940-45
Artic 1941-45	Japan 1945	Okinawa 1945
Atlantic 1939-45	Libya 1940-42	Palembang 1945
Biscay 1940-45	Malaya 1942-45	River Plate 1939
Bismark 1941	Malta Convoys 1942-45	Sabang 1944
Burma 1944-45	Matapan 141	Salerno 1943
Calabria 1940	Mediterranean 1940-45	Sicily 1943
Crete 1941	Normandy 1944	South of France 1944
Diego Suarez 1943	North Africa 1942-43	Spartivento 1940
Dunkirk 1940	North Sea 1939-45	Taranto 1940

Grumman Martlet/Wildcat

ships, equipment, air stations, operations and personnel. Amongst the most regularly consulted are the Squadron Line Books and Record Books, Air Publications and aircraft accident records. The Centre also holds the enlistment papers for First World War Royal Navy ratings and some Royal Marines.
The very large photograph collection covers all areas within the Museum's remit. It includes material from both official and private sources.

Research Services and Facilities Enquirers may conduct their research either in person or by post. Please contact the Centre in advance to discuss your area of research and to book an appointment. Please be aware that a research fee will be levied.

Records & Research Centre Fleet Air Arm Museum, Box D6, RNAS Yeovilton, Near Ilchester, Somerset BA22 8HT Tel: +44 (0) 1935 840565 Fax: +44 (0) 1935 842630 E-mail: research@fleetairarm.com

The Fleet Air Arm Memorial Church
The Royal Navy has enjoyed a close friendship with the parish church of St. Bartholomew, which began in 1940 with the commissioning of RNAS Yeovilton (HMS Heron). During 1940-42 fifteen victims of air accidents were buried in the churchyard before the opening of the Naval Cemetery on its southern boundary in 1942. In 1988, much of the church structure having become unsafe, it was made redundant.

It was then that the often-discussed idea of using St. Bartholomew's as the Anglican Church for RNAS Yeovilton was put into action. The Royal Navy seized the opportunity and bought the 'job-lot' for £1. This triggered a series of national and international appeals to restore the church to its former glory under the guardianship of the newly formed Trustees.

An Order in Council signed by the Prince of Wales and Queen Elizabeth the Queen Mother formally sealed this process. 'St. Bart's', as it has come to be affectionately known, passed from the local Diocese of Bath and Wells to assume the mantle of the Fleet Air Arm Memorial Chapel.

RNAS Yeovilton has five Chaplains. There is the Church of England Chaplain, The Roman Catholic Chaplain, The Church of Scotland and Free Church of Scotland, The Sea Harrier Force Chaplain and The Commando Helicopter Force Chaplain. There is also a Verger, a Custodian for the Church and a Chaplaincy Runner.

Fleet Air Arm Memorial Church. St Bartholomew's Church, RNAS Yeovilton, near Ilchester, Somerset BA22 8HT The Fleet Air Arm Memorial Church (and Naval Cemetery) is open to the Public Daily from 1400 - 1600 (Fridays 1300 - 1500) and for family Eucharist (Sundays at 1030). The Church has a Roll of Honour, which can be seen by the public between 1400 - 1600 hours daily.

In 2003 the Prince of Wales unveiled a new memorial dedicated to the 6,000 men and women who have lost their lives on active Service with the Fleet Air Arm of the Royal Navy. The memorial features a bronze winged figure of Daedalus, and bears the inscription: *"To the everlasting memory of all the men and women from the United Kingdom, the British Commonwealth and the many Allied Nations who have given their lives whilst serving in the Royal Naval Air Service and the Fleet Air Arm"*

Further Reading
Fleet Air Arm. Prepared for the Admiralty by the Ministry of Information. H.M.S.O. London 1943
Fleet Air Arm at War Ray Sturtivant. Published Ian Allan Ltd, Shepperton, Surrey 1982
The Fleet Air Arm Handbook 1939-1945 David Wragg Sutton Publishing 2001
Flying Marines Major A E Marsh. R.M. (Retired). Privately Published April 1980
The Hamlyn Concise Guide to British Aircraft of World War II David Mondey. Hamlyn Publishing Group 1982, Republished by Chancellor Press 1994

Touring the Western Front
Simon Fowler

Almost as soon as the armistice was signed tourists began to visit the shattered villages and the battlefields of the Western Front. Between the wars the British Legion organised pilgrimages for the families of those who had fallen and so that old comrades could visit the places they had spent their youth. The old sites of France and Flanders remain extremely popular destinations particularly with British visitors. Indeed if you have any interest in the First World War you should try to visit the sites of the great battles and the memorials they left behind. On the whole there isn't much to see on the ground, as the scars of war have all but healed, however the cemeteries and the great memorials are very moving. There are also several excellent museums. You won't regret a visit.

Numerous tour operators run regular trips to the battlefields (including those at Gallipoli and outside Europe). Tours are geared either for first time visitors or perhaps examine particular battles or other aspects of the war. Included in the fare is the accommodation, meals, coach travel and the services of an expert guide. Provided they have advanced notice, most are only too happy to detour to a particular cemetery so that you can visit an individual grave. A three-day introductory trip to France and Flanders costs in the region of £420 per person. Three of the most reputable operators are:

Holts Tours, HiTours House, Crossoak Lane, Salford, Tel: 01293-455300 www.battletours.co.uk
Flanders Tours, PO Box 240, Ellington, Huntington PE28 0YE, Tel: 01480-890966, www.flanderstours.co.uk
Tours with Experts, Red Lion Building, 9 Liverpool Road North, Maghull L31 2HB, Tel :0151- 520 1290 www.tours-with-experts.com
Western Front Battlefield Tours, Kenilworth, Gannock Road, Deganwy, Conwy LL31 9HJ www.battlefield-toursonline.co.uk

However, it is perfectly possible to tour the Western Front under your own steam. You can easily travel by car from central London to the market place at Ypres in five hours (back in 1916 it took at least eighteen), so a day trip to the salient is possible. Indeed I've done it. Roads in the area are excellent and there are motorway links both to Flanders and to the Somme from Calais. Unfortunately it is not a journey you can so easily do by public transport, although Ypres and Poperinghe are on a railway branch line from Kortrijk (Courtrai), and Amiens and Arras are served by French railways. There's also a bus service in Flanders run by the regional carrier De Lijn, whose Flemish language website (www.delijn.be) has comprehensive if confusing timetables. The French are less well organised.
Many of the towns, particularly in Belgium, offer a range of hotels and restaurants, Ypres in particular is

pretty geared up to catering to battlefield visitors, although I prefer to stay in Poperinghe (stay at the Gasthof de Kring, eat at the Café de la Paix, drink at the Hotel Palace). The choice is rather less good in France – too many tour groups end up staying at featureless hotels on the bleak outskirts of Lille, but there are small hotels in Albert, Arras and Amiens. There are also a number of B&Bs and camping sites.

There are a number of guidebooks covering the battlefields in varying degrees of detail. One that covers the whole area is Rose E. Coombs, *Before Endeavours Fade: A Guide to the Battlefields of the First World War* (After the Battle, 1994). Another comprehensive guide is Tonie and Valmai Holt, *Major & Mrs Holt's Battlefield Guide to World War One Battles* (3rd edition, Pen and Sword, 2003). Pen and Sword also publish a series of more detailed guides in their excellent 'Battlefield Europe' series. Richard Holmes, *War Walks* (BBC, 1997) is a guide to six battlefields of northern France and Belgium, including Mons and Le Cateau, the Somme, and Arras. A website, run by the military historian and tour guide leader Paul Reed, offering useful advice to people wishing to visit the battlefields can be found at: The Old Front Line web site: http://battlefields1418.50megs.com/

In association with the Commonwealth War Graves Commission, Michelin has produced two modern road maps of the areas showing war cemeteries in northern France and Belgium. The maps in Michelin's 1:200,000 series (Nos 51 and 52) are overprinted with the exact location of each cemetery and memorial and are indexed. They cost £4 each and can be obtained from the Commission and museums and bookshops in the area.

Whether you go with a tour or just by yourself remember to be careful when you tour the battlefields. Every year farmers plough up thousands of unexploded shells, bullets and barbed wire, which can often be seen in piles by the side of the road waiting to be taken away by the French and Belgian armies. For good reason this is known as the 'harvest of death' and even after ninety years remains extremely dangerous. However, tempting it might be, please do not pick up any of these items. A friend of mine was hospitalised for months with mustard gas poisoning after touching a shell for a few seconds.

The most important sites, which you should probably include in any visit to the battlefields, are:

The Somme

Museums

Historial de la Grand Guerre, Chateau de Peronne, F-80201 Peronne, tel. (0033) 322 831418, www. historial.org The superb Historial is the major museum for the area with extensive displays and exhibitions (in English as well as French) on all aspects of the First World War. Admission is 7 for adults, and 3.50 for children.

Musée Somme, The Ramparts, F-80203 Albert, tel (0033) 322 75537, www.somme-1916.org. A museum based in the tunnels under the old town walls. Admission 4 adults, 2.50 children.

Musée des Abris - Somme 1916, Rue Anicet Godin , F80300 Albert, tel (0033) 322 751617, www.cr-picardie.fr/uk/page.cfm?pageref=culture~patrimoine~musees ~abris. The Musée is based in a Second World War underground shelter in the centre of the town with numerous displays about the Battle of the Somme and its aftermath. Admission 4 adults, 2.50 children

Musée des Abris - Somme 1916
Rue Anicet Godin , F80300 Albert France

Battlefield remnants

Beaumont Hamel Memorial Park (Beaumont Hamel) is dedicated to the memory of men of the Newfoundland Regiment who fought and died here on 1st July 1916. In less than thirty minutes, 710 of the 776 men who had left the trenches had been killed, wounded or reported missing: probably the greatest loss of any unit on the day. The site still contains the trenches, shell holes and twisted remains of 'Danger Tree', which were left after the Armistice, although after 85 years they are little more than hollows in the ground. The site is dominated by a giant caribou: the emblem of the Newfoundland Regiment.

...chnagar Crater (**La Boiselle**) is the only surviving site
...the 17 mines which were exploded under the German
...es at the time of the British advance in July 1916.

Monuments

The Thiepval Anglo-French Memorial dominates much of the local skyline. It commemorates the 73,000 British men who fell on the Somme between July 1915 and March 1918, and who have no known grave. Sir Edward Lutyens designed the 141 feet tall monument, which was unveiled in 1932. A new visitors centre and interpretation area opened in July 2004.

Monuments

Delville Wood, which South African battalions attempted to take in late July 1916. It was the site of some of the bloodiest fighting of the war. It now houses the moving South African National War Memorial.

Ulster Tower, near Thiepval, commemorates the men of the Ulster Division who died on 1st July. The memorial is a replica of Helen's Tower, a well-known Northern Ireland landmark. It is now dedicated to improving relationships between the two communities in the province. For more information contact the Somme Heritage Centre, Whitespots County Park, 233 Bangor Rd, Newtownards BT23 7PH, or visit *www.irishsoldier.org*.

Serre Road Cemeteries, near Auchonvilliers. These three cemeteries contain the bodies of nearly 20,000 men who died during the battle. French, German and British graves are found here. There are numerous other cemeteries nearby which testify to the great losses during the battle.

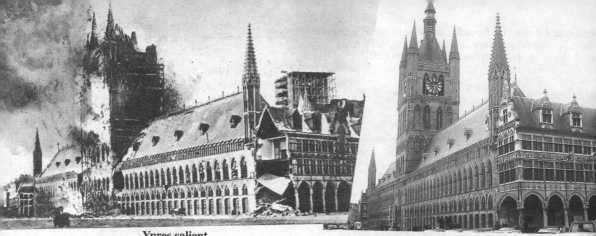

Ypres salient

There is a useful (if frustratingly incomplete) web site which contains much information about battlefield tourism around Ypres: www.greatwar.be

Museums

In Flanders Fields, Lakenhalle, Grote Markt 34, B-8000 Ypres, tel: (0032) 57 228584. www.inflandersfields.be, admission 7.50 (adults), 3.50 (children).An award winning museum in the restored Lace Hall looking at the experience of soldiers in the Salient and the civilians whose lives were dramatically altered by the war.

Passchendaele Memorial Museum 1917, Zonnebeke Chateau, c/o Tourist Information Centre, Ieperstraat 5, B-8980 Zonnebeke, Belgium tel (0032 51 77 04 41), www.passchendaele.be. Admission 5. A new museum in the grounds of the local chateau with 'a classical tradition style of presentation' concentrating on the five battles of Ypres and chance to visit a British dugout with communication and dressing posts. Open daily 25 April – 15 November (2pm-6pm)

Battlefield remnants

Talbot House (Poperinghe). Strictly not a battlefield, but a building that housed a unique social club for officers and other ranks run by the Revd Tubby Clayton during the war (and which led to the Toc H movement). The premises have been sensitively restored to how they looked during the war. The history of the House and Clayton himself is told in Paul Chapman, *A Haven in Hell* (Pen and Sword, 2000)

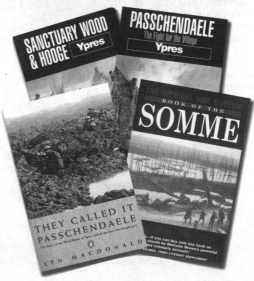

Sanctuary Wood, Menen Road (south east of Ypres). One of the strangest places to visit on the whole of the Western Front: part locals' bar, part museum and, frankly, part freak show. Most people come to visit the now almost entirely eroded remains of the trenches in the wood behind the museum. There is a good range of artefacts which have been dug up locally on display. Many of the museum exhibits, however, are not for the squeamish. There is an admission charge.

Monuments
Tyne Cot Cemetery (near Zonnebeke).
The largest British war cemetery with 12,000 graves (including 1350 Australian, 1000 Canadian and 500 New Zealander).

Menin Gate (Ypres).
A few metres from the Grote Markt, is the memorial to the British and Empire men who lost their lives in the salient and have no known grave. Nearly 55,000 soldiers who died between October 1914 and 15 August 1917 are commemorated here. The 35,000 men who died subsequently are commemorated at Tyne Cot Cemetery. Designed by Sir Reginald Blomfield, it was unveiled in July 1927 by Field Marshal Lord Plumer. If you are in Ypres overnight you should attend the ceremony that takes place at 8pm each evening, where buglers from the local fire brigade play the Last Post. Even the hordes of English teenage school parties are momentarily silenced by this simple ritual.

Langemarck German Cemetery (Langemarck)
is the only German cemetery on the salient houses 44,292 bodies in mass graves. The sombre black tombstones and the general arrangement provide a chilling reminder that the enemy too suffered enormous losses during the war.

Elsewhere
Vimy Ridge (between Arras and Lens) is the principle Canadian monument on the Western Front and commemorates a successful Allied assault on German lines. As well as the very impressive memorial which dominates the local skyline (and look out for the miniature beavers!), there are preserved trenches, a tunnel system and a visitor's centre.

Family history notes from the Imperial War Museum – Tracing Army Ancestry

The purpose of this article is to provide guidance on tracing Army personnel. More detailed information can be found in the Imperial War Museum publication *Tracing your family history: Army* which can be purchased from the museum. The Museum does not hold any personal service records or official documentation, but can help the enquirer as long as some basic facts are known. The Department of Printed Books welcomes visitors by appointment and is able to provide useful reading material and advice for finding out more about those who served. Other reference departments in the Museum - Art, Documents, Exhibits and Firearms, Film and Photograph Archives, and the Sound Archive - may also be able to assist.

Department of Printed Books, Imperial War Museum, Lambeth Road, London SE1 6HZ
T: (+44) 020 7416 5342 F: (+44) 020 7416 5246
W: www.iwm.org.uk E: books@iwm.org.uk

Where to find army service records
The most important piece of information is the unit that an individual served with (it is a sad fact that those who died during the World Wars will be easier to trace than those who survived, and this information is readily obtainable from the **Commonwealth War Graves Commission**). The personal service record should be the starting point, but not all of these records for the First World War survived Second World War bombing. Records are located according to an individual's date of discharge.

The Imperial War Museum only covers the period from the First World War onwards. Military history from 1485 to date is covered by the **National Army Museum, Royal Hospital Road, Chelsea, London SW3 4HT (Tel: 020 7730 0717; Website: www.national-army-museum.ac.uk)**. Pre-1914 service records are held at **The National Archives, Ruskin Avenue, Kew, Richmond, Surrey TW9 4DU (Tel: 020 8392 5200; Website: www.nationalarchives.gov.uk)**. The National Archives (TNA), formerly Public Record Office, also holds all surviving First World War service records for officers who left the Army before 1922. Surviving First World War service records for other ranks who ceased service before 1920 are now held at the TNA where they can be consulted on microfilm (unfortunately large numbers of these were destroyed by bombing in the Second World War). The publication *Army Service Records of the First World War* by William Spencer is essential reading for those interested in First World War records, and *Army Records for Family Historians* by Simon Fowler and William Spencer will also prove helpful.

The records of any First World War soldier who saw service after these cut-off dates or who rejoined the Army are held by the Ministry of Defence. These can

be applied for by post from **Army Personnel Centre, Historical Disclosures, Mailpoint 400, Kentigern House, 65 Brown Street, Glasgow G2 8EX**. Initial contact with the Army Personnel Centre (APC) can be made by telephone (0141 224 3030) or e-mail – please include your postal address (apc_historical_disclosures@dial.pipex.com). Records will be released to proven next of kin for a £25 fee, but there may be a lengthy wait for this service.

The Brigade of Guards form an exception to this as records for other ranks (officers' records are held by TNA/APC) are held by the **Regimental Headquarters Grenadier / Coldstream / Scots / Irish / Welsh Guards, Wellington Barracks, Birdcage Walk, London SW1E 6HQ**. Household Cavalry records are held at TNA but are also accessible on microfiche at the **Household Cavalry Museum, Combermere Barracks, Windsor, Berkshire SL4 3DN (Website: www.householdcavalry.co.uk)**.

The careers of Army officers can be traced using the regular official publication *The Army List*, and the Department of Printed Books holds an almost complete set of these from 1914 to date.

Casualty Records
The **Commonwealth War Graves Commission, 2 Marlow Road, Maidenhead, Berkshire SL6 7DX (Tel: 01628 507200)** has details of all service personnel who died between the dates 4 August 1914-31 August 1921 and 3 September 1939-31 December 1947. The Commonwealth War Graves Commission (CWGC) may charge a fee for postal enquiries, but the website containing their computerised database, *Debt of Honour* can be consulted at **www.cwgc.org**.

Details about the burial places of soldiers who died outside the dates covered by the CWGC are held by the **Ministry of Defence, PS4 (A) (Cas/Comp), Building 43, Trenchard Lines, Upavon, Pewsey, Wiltshire SN9 6BE**. They also have some details relating to soldiers' wives or children who may have died outside the UK.

Sources held by the Department of Printed Books (DPB) include a complete set of the CWGC's memorial and cemetery registers and the 80 volume *Soldiers died in the Great War, 1914-19*. This was originally published in 1921 by HMSO but was republished by J B Hayward in 1989. It is also now available on a CD-ROM produced by Naval and Military Press. *Officers died in the Great War, 1914-19* is less detailed and has probably been superseded by *Officers who died in the service of British, Indian and East African Regiments and Corps, 1914-1919* by S D and D B Jarvis (Reading: Roberts Medals, 1993).

A CD-ROM for Army personnel who died in the Second World War has also been produced by Naval and Military Press, and can be consulted in our Reading Room. Rolls of honour for other later conflicts are also held, and in addition the DPB has a large collection of published rolls of honour for localities, schools, institutions, etc. Regimental histories and journals often contain rolls of honour.

The soldiers' own home area should not be forgotten when researching an individual's service - there may be local war memorial records, a local account of war service may have been published, and contemporary local newspapers can prove very helpful. It is also possible that school, church or workplace records may still exist.

Medal Records
Campaign medals are those given to soldiers who are eligible for them because they were in a particular theatre of war within given dates. The First World War Medal Roll which provides a listing of all those who qualified for the 1914 Star, 1914/15 Star, British War Medal, Victory Medal, Territorial Force War Medal and/or the Silver War Badge is held at TNA. If a First World War record was destroyed some basic information about a soldier's service may be found in this.

Gallantry medals are those medals awarded for an especially heroic deed or action. Records for these are held at TNA, but may not be very detailed. Notifications and citations (if published, which was not the case for awards such as the Military Medal and Mentions in Despatches) appeared in the official journal *London Gazette*. A complete set of this, and the all important indexes, is held at TNA. **The London Gazette Online Archive** at www.gazettes-online.co.uk provides access to First and Second World War entries. The DPB has some published listings of medal awards for decorations such as the Victoria Cross and Distinguished Conduct Medal. Usually you will need to go either to the official unit war diary (held at TNA) or to a published unit history to see whether you can find out more about the action for which the decoration was awarded.

Regimental histories
The DPB has an excellent collection of regimental histories. For those unable to visit our Reading Room (open 10am-5pm, Monday to Saturday), *A bibliography of regimental histories of the British Army* compiled by Arthur S White (London: London Stamp Exchange, 1988) provides details of published histories that may be available through your local library's inter-library loan scheme. Regimental journals and forces newspapers should not be overlooked.

A useful title for locating regimental museums (although these are unlikely to hold information about individuals) is *A guide to military museums: and other places of military interest* by Terence and Shirley Wise (Knighton, Powys: Terence Wise, 2001).

We can also advise on the addresses of Old Comrades Associations. The internet has made it easier to establish contact with people who may have served in the Forces, or who may be conducting research similar to your own. The British Legion website at **www.britishlegion.org.uk** is a good place to start. An excellent site for First World War Orders of Battle and Army information is **www.1914-1918.net**. Other websites of interest include The Western Front Association at **www.westernfront.co.uk** and Land Forces of Britain, the Empire and Commonwealth at **www.regiments.org**.

The Genealogical Services Directory

In association with

STEPPING STONES
Data CDs Ltd

Family History Societies

British Association for Local History PO Box 6549, Somersal Herbert, Ashbourne, Derbyshire, DE6 5WH Tel: 01283 585947 Fax: 01722 413242 E: mail@balh.co.uk (Enquiries) W: www.balh.co.uk

East Anglian Group of Family History Societies 42 Crowhill, Godmanchester, Huntington, Cambrideshire, PE29 2NR E: secretary@huntsfhs.org.uk W: www.huntsfhs.org.uk

Federation of Family History Societies, PO Box 2425, Coventry, CV5 6YX Tel: 070 41 492032 Fax: 070 41 492032 E: info@ffhs.org.uk W: www.ffhs.org.uk

Institute of Heraldic and Genealogical Studies 79 - 82 Northgate, Canterbury, Kent, CT1 1BA T: 01227 462618 Fax: 01227 765617 E: ihgs@ihgs.ac.uk W: www.ihgs.ac.uk

The North East Group of Family History Societies 11 Collins Street, Great Horton, Bradford, West Yorkshire, BD7 4HF, Group for Societies in North East of England. No individual members.

North West Group of FHS Family History Fairs see Lancashire

Society of Genealogists - Library, 14 Charterhouse Buildings, Goswell Road, London, EC1M 7BA T: 020-7251-8799 T: 020-7250-0291 Fax: 020-7250-1800 E: library@sog.org.uk - Sales at sales@sog.org.uk W: www.sog.org.uk

South West Group of Family History Societies see Somerset

Yorkshire Consortium of Family History Societies London Group see Yorkshire

England
Avon
Bristol & Avon FHS see Bristol
Sodbury Vale Family History Group see Bristol

Bedfordshire
Bedfordshire FHS P0 Box 214, Bedford, Bedfordshire, MK42 9RX E: bfhs@bfhs.org.uk W: www.bfhs.org.uk

Berkshire
Berkshire FHS Research Centre, Yeomanry House, 131 Castle Hill, Reading, Berkshire, RG1 7TJ T: 0118 966 3585 E: secretary@berksfhs.org.uk W: www.berksfhs.org.uk

Birmingham
Birmingham & Midland Society for Genealogy and Heraldry 2 Castle Croft, Oldbury, West Midlands, B68 9BQ T: 0121 429 9712 E: birmingham@terrymorter.fsnet.co.uk W: www.bmsgh.org

Bristol
Bristol & Avon FHS 60 Pound Road, Kingswood, Bristol, BS15 4QY T: 0117 967 7288 E: secretary@bafhs.org.uk W: www.bafhs.org.uk

Sodbury Vale Family History Group 36 Westcourt Drive, Oldland Common, Bristol, BS30 9RU T: 0117 932 4133 E: sladekf@supanet.com

Buckinghamshire
Buckinghamshire FHS PO Box 403, Aylesbury, Buckinghamshire, HP21 7GU E: secretary@bucksfhs.org.uk W: www.bucksfhs.org.uk

Buckinghamshire Genealogical Society Varneys, Rudds Lane, Haddenham, Buckinghamshire, HP17 8JP T: 01844 291631 E: eve@varneys.demon.co.uk W: http://met.open.ac.uk/group/kaq/bgs.htm

Cambridgeshire
Cambridgeshire FHS 45 Wachard Road, Cambridge CB3 0HZ E: secretary@cfhs.org.uk W: www.cfhs.org.uk

Cambridge University H & G S, c/o Crossfield House, Dale Road, Stanton, Bury St Edmunds, Suffolk, IP31 2DY T: 01359 251050 Fax: 01359 251050 E: president@one-name.org W: www.cam.ac.uk/societies/cuhags/

Fenland FHS Rose Hall, Walpole Bank, Walpole St Andrew, Wisbech PE14 7JD W: www.cambridgeshirehistory.com/Societies/ffhs Covers Fenland areas of Cambridgeshire, Lincolnshire and Norfolk

Huntingdonshire FHS 42 Crowhill, Godmanchester, Huntingdon, Cambridgeshire, PE29 2NR T: 01480 390476 E: secretary@huntsfhs.org.uk W: www.huntsfhs.org.uk

Peterborough & District FHS 33 Farleigh Fields, Orton Wistow, Peterborough, Cambridgeshire, PE2 6YB T: 01733 235956

Cheshire
Family History Society of Cheshire, 10 Dunns Lane, Ashton, Chester, Cheshire, CH3 8BU T: 01829 759089 E: info@fhsc.org.uk W: www.fhsc.org.uk

North Cheshire FHS 2 Denham Drive, Bramhall, Stockport, Cheshire, SK7 2AT T: 0161-439-9270 E: roger@demercado.demon.co.uk W: www.genuki.org.uk/big/eng/CHS/NorthChesFHS

South Cheshire FHS incorporating S E Cheshire Local Studies Group PO Box 1990, Crewe, CW2 6FF W: www.scfhs.org.uk

Cleveland
Cleveland FHS 1 Oxgang Close, Redcar, Cleveland, TS10 4ND T: 01642 486615 F: 01642 486615 W: www.clevelandfhs.org.uk

Cornwall
Cornwall FHS 5 Victoria Square, Truro, Cornwall, TR1 2RS T: 01872-264044 E: secretary@cornwallfhs.com W: www.cornwallfhs.com

Cornish Forefathers Society Credvill, Quakers Road, Perranwell, Truro, Cornwall, TR3 7PJ T: 0777 992 9361 (Mobile) E: forefathers@ukonline.co.uk W: www.cornish-forefathers.com

Fal Worldwide Family History Group 57 Huntersfield, South Tehidy, Camborne, Cornwall, TR14 0HW T: 01209-711557 E: cfdell@clara.net W: http://beehive.thisiscornwall.co.uk/falwwfhg

Cumbria/Cumberland
Cumbria FHS Ulpha, 32 Granada Road, Denton, Manchester, M34 2LJ W: www.genuki.org.uk/big/eng/CUL/cumbFHS/membership.html The Society caters for those with interests in the old counties of Cumberland & Westmorland and those parts of Lancashire known as 'Lonsdale North of the Sands' Founded to help Cumbrians and those with Cumbrian Ancestors carry out their family history research in the area covered by the modern county of Cumbria

Furness FHS 64 Cowlarns Road, Hawcoat, Barrow-in-Furness, Cumbria, LA14 4HJ T: 01229-830942 E: julia.fairbairn@virgin.net W: www.members.aol.com/furnessfhs/fpw.htm

Derbyshire
Buxton & District U3A - Family History Group, Yarrow, 8 Carlisle Grove, Buxton SK17 6XP T: 01298 70959 E: iw.taylor@ic24.net

Chesterfield & District FHS 16 Mill Crescent, Wingerworth, Chesterfield, Derbyshire, S42 6NN T: 01246 231900 E: cadfhs@aol.com

Derbyshire FHS Bridge Chapel House, St Mary's Bridge, Sowter Road, Derby, Derbyshire, DE1 3AT T: 01332 608101 W: www.dfhs.org.uk

Derbyshire Ancestral Research Group 86 High St, Loscoe, Heanor, Derbyshire, DE75 7LF T: 01773-604916

Devon
Devon FHS PO Box 9, Exeter, Devon, EX2 6YP T: 01392 275917 E: members@devonfhs.org.uk W: www.deveonfhs.org.uk

Thorverton & District History Society Ferndale, Thorverton, Exeter, Devon, EX5 5NG T: 01392 860932

Dorset
Dorset FHS Unit 40 Mannings Heath Works, 18 Mannings Heath Road, Parkstone, Poole, Dorset, BH12 4NJ T: 01202 736261 E: contact@dorsetfhs.freeserve.co.uk W: www.dfhs.freeserve.co.uk/index.html

Somerset & Dorset FHS see Somerset

West Dorset Research Centre, 45 West Street, Bridport DT6 3QW T: 01308 458061 E: wdhgrc@dorsetmigration.org.uk W: www.dorsetmigration.org.uk Dorset Migration Index

Durham
Cleveland FHS see Cleveland

Elvet Local & Family History Groups, 37 Hallgarth Street, Durham, County Durham, DH1 3AT T: 0191-386-4098 Fax: 0191-386-4098 E: Turnstone-Ventures@durham-city.freeserve.co.uk

Newton Aycliffe FHS 4 Barnard Close, Woodham Village, Newton Aycliffe, County Durham, DL5 4SP T: 01325 315959 E: jtb2@totalise.com

Northumberland & Durham FHS see Northumberland

Essex
Essex Society for Family History, Research Centre, Essex Record Office, Wharf Road, Chelmsford, Essex CM2 6YT T: 01245 244670 E: secretary@esfh.org.uk W: www.esfh.org.uk

Waltham Forest FHS 49 Sky Peals Road, Woodford Green, Essex, IG8 9NE

Gloucestershire
Gloucestershire FHS 37 Barrington Drive, Hucclecote, Gloucester GL3 3BT T: 01452 524344 (RESOURCE CENTRE) T: 01452 535608 F: 01452 615143 E: alexwood@blueyonder.co.uk W: www.gfhs.org.uk

Campden & District Family History Group 9 Wolds End, Chipping Campden, Gloucestershire, GL55 6JW T: 01386 840561 E: familyhistory@judithellis.org.uk

Bristol & Avon FHS see Bristol
Gloucestershire - South
Sodbury Vale Family History Group see Bristol

Hampshire
Hampshire Genealogical Soc 198A Havant Rd, Drayton, Portsmouth PO6 2EH E: society@hgs-online.org.uk W: www.hgs-online.org.uk

Herefordshire
Herefordshire FHS 6 Birch Meadow, Gosmore Road, Clehonger, Hereford, Herefordshire, HR2 9RH T: 01981-250974 E: prosser_brian@hotmail.com W: www.roortsweb.com/~ukhfhs

Hertfordshire
Hertfordshire FHS 26 Vale Close, Harpenden, Hertfordshire, AL5 3LX E: secretary@hertsfhs.org.uk W: www.hertsfhs.org.uk
Royston & District FHS Baltana, London Road, Barkway, Royston, Hertfordshire, SG8 8EY T: 01763 848228 E: keith-curtis@lineone.net
Welwyn & District Local History Society 40 Hawbush Rise, Welwyn, Hertfordshire, AL6 9PP T: 01438 716415 E: p.jiggens-keen@virgin.net W: www.welwynhistory.org
Letchworth & District Family History Group 84 Kings Hedges, Hitchin, Hertfordshire, SG5 2QE
Codicote Local History Society 34 Harkness Way, Hitchin, Hertfordshire, SG4 0QL T: 01462 622953

Isle of Wight
Isle of Wight FHS 9 Forest Dell, Winford, Sandown PO36 0LG W: www.isle-of-wight-fhs.co.uk
Roots Family & Parish History - Disbanded 2003

Kent
Folkestone & District FHS 81 Wear Bay Road, Folkestone, Kent, CT19 6PR E: alisonfhs@aslan consultancy.freeserve.co.uk W: www.folkfhs.org.uk
Kent FHS Bullockstone Farm, Bullockstone Road, Herne Bay, CT6 7NL W: www.kfhs.org.uk
North West Kent FHS 58 Clarendon Gardens, Dartford, Kent, DA2 6EZ E: secretary@nwkfhs.org.uk W: www.nwkfhs.org.uk Covers ancient parishes of Deptford, Greenwich Woolwich
Tunbridge Wells FHS The Old Cottage, Langton Road, Langton Green, Tunbridge Wells, Kent, TN3 0BA E: s.oxenbury@virgin.net W: www.tunwells fhs.co.uk
Woolwich & District FHS 54 Parkhill Road, Bexley, Kent, DA5 1HY E: FrEdnafhs@aol.com

Lancashire
Accrington Uncovered, 15 Christ Church Street, Accrington, Lancashire, BB5 2LZ T: 01254 398579 E: jhunt@christchurch92.freeserve.co.uk W: www.accringtonuncovered.com
Bolton & District FHS 205 Crompton Way, Bolton, Lancashire, BL2 2RU T: 01204 525472 E: bolton@mlfhs.demon.co.uk W: www.mlfhs.demon.co.uk A branch of Manchester and Lancashire FHS
Lancaster Family History Group 116 Bowerham Road, Lancaster LA1 4HL
Liverpool & S W Lancashire FHS 11 Bushbys Lane, Formby, Liverpool, L37 2DX W: www.liverpool genealogy.org.uk Society consists of eight groups: Liverpool, St Helens, Southport, Skelmersdale & Upholland, Warrington, Leigh, Widnes & special interest group Anglo Irish
Manchester and Lancashire FHS Clayton House, 59 Piccadilly, Manchester, M1 2AQ T: 0161 236 9750 Fax: 0161 237 3512 E: office@mlfhs.org.uk W: www.mlfhs.org.uk
North Meols FHS 6 Millars Pace, Marshside, Southport PR9 9FU E: nadine@xplorasia.freeserve.co.uk W: www.users.zetnet.co.uk/nmfh
North West Group of FHS Family History Fairs, North West Group of Family History Societies, 4 Lawrence Avenue, Simonstone, Burnley, Lancashire, BB12 7HX T: 01282 771999 E: ed@gull66.freeserve.co.uk
Oldham & District FHS Clayton House, 59 Piccadilly, Manchester, M1 2QA T: 0161 236 9750 Fax: 0161 237 3512 E: office@mlfhs.org.uk W: www.mlfhs.org.uk
Ormskirk & District FHS c/o Ormskirk College, Hants Lane, Ormskirk, Lancashire, L39 1PX T: 01695 578604 E: odfhs@skelmersdale.ac.uk W: www.odfhs.freeserve.co.uk
Wigan FHS 678 Warrington Road, Goose Green, Wigan WN3 6XN W: www.ffhs.org.uk/members/wigan.htm

Leicestershire
Leicestershire & Rutland FHS 11 Spring Lane, Wymondham, Leicester, Leicestershire, LE14 2AY T: 01572 787331 E: secretary@lrfhs.org.uk W: www.lrfhs.org.uk CC accepted

Lincolnshire
Lincolnshire FHS 10 Windsor Avenue, Holbeach, Spalding, Lincolnshire, PE12 7AN E: chairman@lincolnshirefhs.org.uk W: www.lincolnshirefhs.org.uk
Isle of Axholme FHS Alwinton, 51 Mill Road, Crowle, Isle of Axholme, North Lincolnshire, DN17 4LW T: 01724 710578 E: secretary@axholme fhs.org.uk W: www.axholme fhs.org.uk www.linktop.demon.co.uk/axholme/

Liverpool
Liverpool & S W Lancashire FHS see Lancashire

London
East of London FHS 23 Louvaine Avenue, Wickford SS12 0DP E: ean23@btopenworld.com W: www.eolfhs.org.uk
London, Westminster and Middlesex FHS 57 Belvedere Way, Kenton, Harrow HA3 9XQ T: (020) 8204 5470 E: william.pyemont@virgin.net W: wwww.lnmfhs.dircon.co.uk
Society of Genealogists Library see National

Manchester
Manchester and Lancashire FHS see Lancashire

Merseyside
Liverpool & S W Lancashire FHSty see Lancashire

Middlesex
Hillingdon FHS 20 Moreland Drive, Gerrards Cross, Buckinghamshire, SL9 8BB T: 01753 885602 E: gillmay@dial.pipex.com W: www.hfhs.co.uk
London & North Middlesex FHS incorporating Westminster & Central Middlesex **FHS** see London
West Middlesex FHS 32 The Avenue, Bedford Park, Chiswick, London W4 1HT E: secretary@west-middlesex-fhs.org.uk W: www.west-middlesex-fhs.org.uk

Norfolk
Norfolk FHS Headquarters, Library & Registered Office, Kirby Hall, 70 St Giles Street, Norwich, Norfolk, NR2 1LS T: 01603 763718 T: E: nfhs@paston.co.uk W: www.norfolkfhs.org.uk
Mid - Norfolk FHS 47 Greengate, Swanton Morley, Dereham NR20 4LX E: keasdown@aol.com W: http://www.uea.ac.uk/~s300/genuki/NFK/organisations/midnfh

Northamptonshire
Northamptonshire FHS 22 Godwin Walk, Ryehill Estate, Northampton NN5 7RW E: angela.malin@btinternet.com W: http://www.fugazi.demon.co.uk

Northumberland
Northumberland & Durham FHS 2nd Floor, Bolbec Hall, Westgate Road, Newcastle on Tyne, Tyne and Wear, NE1 1SE T: 0191 261 2159 W: www.ndfhs.org.uk Secretary Mrs Frances Norman, 23 Monkton Avenue, Simonside South Shields, Tyne & Wear, NE34 9RX.

Nottinghamshire
Nottinghamshire FHS 26 Acorn Bank, West Bridgford, Nottingham NG2 7SH W: http://www..nottsfhs.org.uk
Mansfield & District FHS 15 Cranmer Grove, Mansfield, Nottinghamshire, NG19 7JR E: betty@flintham.freeserve.co.uk

Oxfordshire
Oxfordshire FHS 19 Mavor Close, Woodstock, Oxford, Oxfordshire, OX20 1YL T: 01993 812258 E: secretary@ofhs.org.uk W: www.ofhs.org.uk

Rutland
Leicestershire & Rutland FHS see Leicestershire

Shropshire
Shropshire FHS Redhillside, Ludlow Road, Church Stretton, Shropshire, SY6 6AD T: 01694 722949 E: secretary@sfhs.org.uk W: www.sfhs.org.uk
Cleobury Mortimer Historical Society The Old Schoolhouse, Neen Savage, Cleobury Mortimer, Kidderminster, Shropshire, DY14 8JU T: 01299 270319 E: paddy@treves.freeserve.co.uk

Somerset
Somerset & Dorset FHS PO Box 4502, Sherborne, Dorset, DH9 6YL T: 01935 389611 Fax: 01935 389611 E: society@sdfhs.org W: www.sdfhs.org
Weston Super Mare FHS 32 Marconi Close, Weston Super Mare, Somerset, BS23 3HH T: 01934 627053 E: kes.jack@virgin.co.uk
South West Group of Family History Societies, 32 Marconi Close, Weston Super Mare, Somerset, BS23 3HH T: 01934 627053
Sodbury Vale Family History Group see Bristol

Staffordshire
Ancestral Rescue Club, 19 Mansfield Close, Tamworth, Staffordshire, B79 7YE T: 01827 65322 E: ancestral@rescue.fsnet.co.uk W: www.rootsweb.com/~engarc/index.html
Audley & District FHS 20 Hillside Avenue, Endon, Stoke on Trent ST9 9HH E: hamhist@audley.net
Birmingham & Midland Society for Genealogy and Heraldry see Birmingham
Burntwood Family History Group The Annexe, Green Lane Farm, Green Lane, Burntwood, Staffordshire, WS7 9HB E: gassor@ukonline.co.uk W: www.geocities.com/bfhg1986

Suffolk
Felixstowe FHS Drenagh, 7 Victoria Road, Felixstowe, Suffolk, IP11 7PT T: 01394 275631 Fax: 01394 275631 E: W: www.btinternet.com/~woodsbj/tths
Suffolk FHS Egg Hall Cottage, 14 Birch Street, Nayland, Colchester CO6 4JA T: 01206 263116 W: http://www.genuki.org.uk/big/eng/SFK/Sfhs/Sfhs.htm

Surrey - East
East Surrey FHS 119 Keevil Drive, London SW19 6TF E: secretary@eastsurreyfhs.org.uk W: www.eastsurreyfhs.org.uk
Surrey - West
West Surrey FHS Deer Dell, Botany Hill, Sands, Farnham, Surrey, GU10 1LZ T: 01252 783485 E: secretary@wsfhs.org W: www.wsfhs.org

Sussex
Sussex Family History Group 40 Tanbridge Park, Horsham, RH12 1SZ E: secretary@sfhg.org.uk W: www.sfhg.org.uk Latest publications include Brighton Census Index 1851 Horsham Census index 1841 & 1851. Aim of the Group is to promote study of family history and preservatioin, transcription & publication of relevant documents & records.
Sussex - East
Eastbourne & District (Family Roots) FHS 8 Park Lane, Eastbourne BN21 2UT E: sarahlslaughter@madasafish.com W: www.eastbournefhs.org.uk
Hastings & Rother FHS 73 Harley Shute Road, St Leonards on Sea, East Sussex, TN38 8BY T: 01424 436605 W: www.hrfhs.org.uk

Tyne and Wear
Northumberland & Durham FHS see Northumberland

Waltham Forest - Waltham Forest FHS see Essex

Warwickshire
Birmingham & Midland Society for Genealogy and Heraldry see Birmingham
Coventry FHS PO Box 2746, Coventry, Warwickshire, CV5 7YD T: (024) 7646 4256 E: enquiries@covfhs.org W: www.covfhs.org
Nuneaton & North Warwickshire FHS PO Box 2282, Nuneaton CV11 6ZT W: www.nnwfhs.org.uk
Rugby Family History Group Springfields, Rocherberie Way, Rugby, Warwickshire, CV22 6EG T: 01788 813957 E: j.chard@ntlworld.com W: www.rugbyfhg.co.uk
Warwickshire FHS 44 Abbotts Land, Coundon, Coventry, Warwickshire, CV1 4AZ E: n.wetton.@virgin.net W: www.wfhs.org.uk

Westmorland - Cumbria FHS see Cumbria

West Midlands
Birmingham & Midland Society for Genealogy and Heraldry see Birmingham
Sandwell FHS, 9 Leacroft Grove, Hill Top, West Bromwich, West Midlands, B71 2QP T: 0121 556 0731 E: a.hale@talk21.com

Wiltshire
Wiltshire FHS 10 Castle Lane, Devizes, Wiltshire, SN10 1HJ T: 01225 762648 E: society@wiltshirefhs.co.uk W: www.wiltshirefhs.co.uk
Worcestershire
Birmingham & Midland Society for Genealogy and Heraldry
Malvern Family History Group D'Haute Rive, 37 Tennyson Drive, St James' Park, Malvern, Worcestershire, WR14 2TQ T: 01684 561872 W: www.mfhg.org.uk
Yorkshire
Yorkshire Archaeological Society Family History Section, Claremont, 23 Clarendon Road, Leeds, LS2 9NZ W: www.users.globalnet.co.uk/~gdl/yasfhs.htm
Yorkshire Consortium of Family History Societies - London Group 121 Layhams Road, West Wickham BR4 9HE
Yorkshire - City of York
City of York & District FHS 140 Shipton Road, York, Yorkshire, YO30 5RU E: yorkfamilyhistory@btopenworld.com W: www.yorkfamilyhistory.org.ukResearch Room at The Study Centre, Community House, 10 Priory street, York YO1 6EZ T: 01904 652363
Yorkshire – East
Boothferry Family & Local History Group 17 Airmyn Avenue, Goole, Yorkshire, DN14 6PF E: howardrj@madasafish.com
City of York & District FHS see Yorkshire
East Yorkshire FHS 12 Carlton Drive, Aldbrough HU11 4SF E: secretary@eyfhs.org.uk W: www.eyfhs.org.uk Research Facilities at Room 21, Hull Business Centre, Guildhall Road, Hull, HU1 1BH (Tel: 01482 222262)
Yorkshire – North
City of York & District FHS see above
Cleveland FHS see Cleveland

Ripon Historical Society & Ripon, Harrogate & District Family History Group 16 Swinburne Close, Harrogate, North Yorkshire, HG1 3LX W: http://web.onetel.net.uk/~gdlawson/rh1.htm
Upper Dales Family History Group Croft House, Newbiggin in Bishopdale, Nr Leyburn, North Yorkshire, DL8 3TD T: 01969 663738 E: glenys@bishopdale.demon.co.uk W: www.bishopdale.demon.co.uk
Yorkshire – South
Barnsley FHS 58A High Street, Royston, Barnsley, South Yorkshire, S71 4RN E: secretary@barnsleyfhs.org.uk W: www.barnsleyfhs.co.uk
Doncaster & District FHS 'Marton House', 125 The Grove, Wheatley Hills, Doncaster, South Yorkshire, DN2 5SN T: 01302 367257 E: marton house@blueyonder.co.uk W: www.doncasterfhs.freeserve.co.uk
Grenoside & District LHG, 4 Stepping Lane, Grenoside, Sheffield S35 8RA T: 0114 257 1929 T: 0114 245 6959 E: info@grenosidelocalhistory.co.uk W: www.grenosidelocalhistory.co.uk Local and FHS
Sheffield & District FHS 5 Old Houses, Piccadilly Road, Chesterfield, Derbyshire, S41 0EH E: secretary@sheffieldfhs.org.uk W: www.sheffieldfhs.org.uk
Rotherham FHS 7 St Stephen's Road, Rotherham, South Yorkshire, S65 1PJ W: www.rotherhamfhs.f9.co.uk
Yorkshire – West
Bradford FHS 5 Leaventhorpe Avenue, Fairweathergreen, Bradford BD8 0ED W: http://www.genuki.org.uk/big/eng/YKS/bfhs/
Boothferry Family & Local History Group see Yorkshire - East
Calderdale FHS incorporating Halifax & District, 61 Gleanings Avenue, Norton Tower, Halifax, West Yorkshire, HX2 0NU T: 01422 360756 W: www.users.globalnet.co.uk/~cfhs/
Huddersfield & District FHS 15 Huddersfield Road, Neltham, Huddersfield, West Yorkshire, HD9 4NJ T: 01484 852420 E: secretary@hdfhs.org.uk W: www.hdfhs.org.uk
Keighley & District FHS 2 The Hallows, Shann Park, Keighley, West Yorkshire, BD20 6HY T: 01535 672144
Morley & District Family History Group 1 New Lane, East Ardsley, Wakefield WF3 2DP, W: www.morleyfhg.co.uk
Pontefract & District FHS 14 Sandringham Close, Carleton Rise, Pontefract WF8 4RF E: r.thrall@btopenworld.com W: http://freespace.virgin.net/richard.lockwood www.pontefract-fhs.co.uk
Wharfedale Family History Group 1 West View Court, Yeadon, Leeds, West Yorkshire, LS19 7HX T: 0113 258 5597 T: 0113 250 7249 E: wfhg@yorksgen.org.uk W: www.wfhg.org.uk http://web.onetel.net.uk/~gdlawson/wfhg1.htm
Wakefield & District FHS 32 Blenheim Road, Wakefield, West Yorkshire, WF1 3JZ T: 01924 373310 T: 01924 250882 (Membership Secretary) E: secretary@wdfhs.co.uk W: www.wdfhs.co.uk

Isle of Man
Isle of Man FHS Pear Tree Cottage, Llhergy Cripperty, Union Mills, Isle of Man, IM4 4NF T: 01624 622188 T: 01624 862088 W: www.isle-of-man.com/interests/genealogy/fhs

Channel Islands
Guernsey
Family History Section of La Société Guernesiaise, PO Box 314, Candie, St Peter Port, Guernsey, GY1 3TG
Jersey
Channel Islands FHS P0 Box 507, St Helier, Jersey, JE4 5TN E: cifhs@localdial.com W: www.user.itl.net/~glen/AbouttheChannelIslandsFHS.html

Wales
London Branch of the Welsh Family History Societies, 27 Princes Avenue, Carshalton Beeches, Surrey, SM5 4NZ E: regandpaddy@btinternet.com
Breconshire - see Powys FHS
Cardiganshire
Cardiganshire FHS Adran Casliadau, National library of Wales, Aberystwyth, Ceredigion, SY25 3BU W: www.cardiganshirefhs.org.uk www.cgnfhs.org.uk
Carmarthenshire
Dyfed FHS 12 Elder Grove, Llangunnor SA31 2LG T: 01267 232637 E: secretary@dyfedfhs.org.uk W: www.dyfed.org.uk
Ceredigion - see Dyfed FHS
Clwyd
Clwyd FHS The Laurels, Dolydd Road, Cefn Mawr, Wrexham, LL14 3NH T: 01978 822218 E: secretary@clwydfhs.org.uk W: www.clwydfhs.org.uk Covers the pre 1974 counties of Denbighshire and Flintshire
Denbighshire - see Clwyd FHS
Flintshire - see Clwyd FHS
Glamorgan
Glamorgan FHS 22 Parc y Bryn, Creigiau, Cardiff, Glamorgan, CF15 9SE E: secretary@glamfhs.org W: www.glamfhs.org, Glamorgan FHS covers the Old County of Glamorgan. Monthly meetings at all six branches.

Extensive search facilities available to members. Quarterly journals

Gwent
Gwent FHS 11 Rosser Street, Wainfelin, Pontypool, Gwent, NP4
6EA E: secretary@gwentfhs.info W: www.gwentfhs.info

Gwynedd
Gwynedd FHS 36 Y Wern, Y Felinheli, Gwynedd, LL56 4TX T:
01248 670267 E: Gwynedd.Roots@tesco.net W:
www.gwynedd.fsbusiness.co.uk

Monmouthshire - see Gwent FHS

Montgomeryshire
Montgomeryshire Genealogical Society Cambrian House, Brimmon
Lane, Newtown, Powys, SY16 1BY T: 01686 624753 W:
home.freeuk.net/montgensoc

Pembrokeshire - see Dyfed FHS

Powys
Powys FHS Waterloo Cottage, The Vineyards, Llandeilo Graban,
Builth Wells, Powys, LD2 3SJ E: rspearson@breathemail.com W:
www.rootsweb.com/~wlspfhs/faq/, Credit card facilities via secure
server at GENfair for membership, services and publications

Radnorshire - see Powys FHS

Scotland

Scottish Genealogy Society 15 Victoria Terrace, Edinburgh, EH1
2JL T: 0131-220-3677 T: 0131-220-3677 E:
info@scotsgenealogy.com W: www.scotsgenealogy.com

Aberdeen
Aberdeen & North East Scotland FHS 158 - 164 King Street,
Aberdeen, AB24 5BD T: 01224 646323 T: 01224 639096 E:
enquiries@anefhs.org.uk W: www.anesfhs.org.uk

Angus
Tay Valley FHS & Family History Research Centre see Dundee

Argyll - see Glasgow & West of Scotland FHS

Ayrshire
Alloway & Southern Ayrshire FHS c/o Alloway Public Library,
Doonholm Road, Alloway, Ayr, Ayrshire, KA7 4QQ E:
asafhs@mtcharlesayr.fsnet.co.uk

East Ayrshire FHS c/o Dick Institute, Elmbank Avenue,
Kilmarnock, East Ayrshire, KA1 3BU E:
enquiries@eastayrshirefhs.org.uk W: www.eastayrshirefhs.org.uk

Glasgow & West of Scotland FHS see Glasgow

Largs & North Ayrshire FHS Bogriggs Cottage, Carlung, West
Kilbride, Ayrshire, KA23 9PS T: 01294 823690 W:
www.freeyellow.com/members7/lnafhs/index.html

Troon @ Ayrshire FHS c/o M.E.R.C., Troon Public Library, South
Beach, Troon, Ayrshire, KA10 6EF E: info@troonayrshirefhs.org.uk
W: www.troonayrshirefhs.org.uk

**South West Scotland Local/Family History Maybole Historical
Society** 15F Campbell Court, Ayr, Ayrshire, KA8 0SE T: 07776
445033 E: maybole@scotsfamilies.co.uk W: www.maybole.org

Berwickshire / Borders
Borders FHS 2 Fellowhills, Ladykirk, TD15 1XN T: 01289 382060
E: hloughAukonIine.co.uk
Family History Room at Old Gala House, Galashiels.

Bute - see Glasgow

Caithness
Caithness FHS Mill Cottage, Corsback, Dunnet, Caithness, KW1
48XQ E: a.e.lewis@btinternet.com W: www.caithnessfhs.org.uk

Central Scotland
Central Scotland FHS 11 Springbank Gardens, Dunblane,
Perthshire, FK15 9JX T: 01786 823937 E: margaret.turner@tesco.net
W: www.csfhs.org.uk

Dumfries
Dumfries & Galloway FHS Family History Research Centre, 9
Glasgow Street, Dumfries DG2 9AF T: 01387-248093 E:
shop@dgfhs.org.uk W: www.dgfhs.org.uk

Dunbartonshire - see Glasgow

Dundee
Tay Valley FHS & Family History Research Centre Family
History Research Centre, 179–181 Princes Street, Dundee, DD4 6DQ
T: 01382-461845 T: 01382 455532 E: tvfhs@tayvalleyfhs.org.uk W:
www.tayvalleyfhs.org.uk

Edinburgh
Lothians FHS c/o Lasswade High School Centre, Eskdale Drive,
Bonnyrigg, Midlothian, EH19 2LA T: 0131 660 1933 T: 0131 663
6634 E: lothiansfhs@hotmail.com W: www.lothiansfhs.org.uk
Scottish Genealogy Society 15 Victoria Terrace, Edinburgh, EH1
2JL T: 0131-220-3677 T: 0131-220-3677 E:
info@scotsgenealogy.com W: www.scotsgenealogy.com

Fife
Fife FHS Glenmoriston, Durie Street, Leven, Fife, KY8 4HF T:
01333 425321 E: fife@ffhoc.freeserve.co.uk W:
www.fifefhs.pwp.bluyonder.co.uk
Tay Valley FHS & Family History Research Centre see Dundee

Glasgow
Glasgow & West of Scotland FHS Unit 5, 22 Mansfield Street,
Partick, Glasgow, G11 5QP T: 0141-339-8303 W:

www.gwsfhs.org.uk

Highland/Invernesshire
Highland FHS c/o Reference Room, Inverness Public Library,
Farraline Park, Inverness, IV1 1NH
**Kinross-shire - Tay Valley FHS & Family History Research
Centre** see Dundee

Lanarkshire
Lanarkshire FHS Local History Lab, Motherwell Heritage Centre,
1 High Road, Motherwell, Lanarkshire, ML1 3HU

Lothian
Lothians FHS see Edinburgh
Midlothian see Edinburgh
North East Scotland - see Aberdeen

Orkney
Orkney FHS Community Room, The Strynd, Kirkwall, Orkney,
KW15 1HG T: 01856 761582 (Home) E: olaf.mooney@virgin.net W:
www.orkneyfhs.co.uk

Peebleshire - see Borders FHS
Perthshire - see Tay Valley FHS
Refrewshire - Glasgow & West of Scotland FHS
Renfrewshire FHS c/o Museum and Art Galleries, High Street,
Paisley, Renfrewshire, PA1 2BA W: www.renfrewshire.org.uk
Roxburghshire - see Borders FHS
Selkirkshire - see Borders FHS

Shetland
Shetland FHS 6 Hillhead, Lerwick, Shetland, ZE1 0EJ E:
secretary@shetland-fhs.org.uk W: www.shetland-fhs.org.uk
Stirlingshire - see Central Scotland and Glasgow

Northern Ireland

Irish Heritage Association A.204 Portview, 310 Newtownards
Road, Belfast, BT4 1HE T: (028) 90455325
North of Ireland FHS c/o Graduate School of Education, 69
University Street, Belfast, BT7 1HL E: R.Sibbett@tesco.net W:
www.nifhs.org
Ulster Historical Foundation Balmoral Buildings, 12 College
Square East, Belfast, BT1 6DD T: (028) 9033 2288, 028 9023 9885
E: enquiry@uhf.org.uk W: www.uhf.org.uk
www.ancestryireland.com

Ireland

Council of Irish Genealogical Organisations, 186 Ashcroft,
Raheny, Dublin 5
Ballinteer FHS, 29 The View, Woodpark, Ballinteer, Dundrum,
Dublin, 16 T: 01-298-8082, Mobile: 086 8120463 E:
ryanct@eircom.net Annual publication - 'Gateway to the Past'
Membership 12.00
Cork Genealogical Society c/o 4 Evergreen Villas, Evergreen Road,
Cork City, Co Cork T: 086 8198359 E: micaconl@eircon.ie W:
http://homepage.eircon.net/~adcolemen
Flannery Clan / Clann Fhlannabhra, 81 Woodford Drive,
Clondakin, Dublin, 22 E: oflannery@eircom.net W:
www.flanneryclan.ie
Genealogical Society of Ireland, 11 Desmond Avenue, Dun
Laoghaire, Co Dublin T: 353 1 284 2711 E: GenSocIreland@iol.ie
W: www.gensocireland.org
Irish Ancestry Group Clayton House, 59 Piccadilly, Manchester,
M1 2AQ T: 0161-236-9750 T: 0161-237-3512 E:
office@mlfhs.org.uk W: www.mlfhs.org.uk A specialist group of
Manchester and Lancashire FHS
Irish FHS P0 Box 36, Naas, Co Kildare E: ifhs@eircom.net W:
http://homepage.eircom.net/~ifhs/
Wicklow County Genealogical Society 1 Summerhill, Wicklow
Town, Co Wicklow
Irish Genealogical Research Society 18 Stratford Avenue, Rainham,
Gillingham, Kent, ME8 0EP E: info@igrsoc.org W: www.igrsoc.org,
Raheny Heritage Society 68 Raheny Park, Raheny, Dublin 5,
Dublin T: 01 831 4729 E: jussher@softhome.net
Wexford FHS 24 Parklands, Wexford, Co Wexford T: 053-42273 E:
murphyh@tinet.ie

Specialist Family History Societies

Ambleside Oral History Group 1 High Busk, Ambleside, Cumbria,
LA22 0AW T: 01539 431070 E: history@amblesideonline.co.uk W:
www.aoghistory.f9.co.uk
Anglo-French FHS 31 Collingwood Walk, Andover, Hampshire,
SP10 IPU W: www.anglo-french-fhs.org
Anglo-German FHS 5 Oldbury Grove, Beaconsfield,
Buckinghamshire HP9 2AJ T: 01494 676812 E:
gwendolinedavis@aol.com W: www.agfhs.org.uk www.art-
science.com/agfhs
Anglo-Italian FHS 3 Calais Street, London, SE5 9LP T: 020 7274
7809 E: membership@anglo-italianfhs.org.uk W: www.anglo-
italianfhs.org.uk
Anglo-Scottish FHS Clayton House, 59 Piccadilly, Manchester, M1
2AQ T: 0161 236 9750 T: 0161 237 3512 E: mlfhs.demon.co.uk A
specialist group of Manchester and Lancashire FHS

Anglo-Zulu War Historical Society Woodbury House, Woodchurch Road, Tenterden, Kent TN30 7AE T: 01580-764189 F: 01580-766648 W: www.web-marketing.co.uk/anglozuluwar

Association of Denominational Historical Societies and Cognate Libraries 44 Seymour Road, Wandsworth, London SW18 5JA T: 020 8874 7727

Australian Society of the Lace Makers of Calais Inc, PO Box 946, Batemans Bay, New South Wales, 2536 T: 0244 718168 T: 0244 723421 E: carolynb@acr.net.au

British Ancestors in India Society 2 South Farm Avenue, Harthill, Sheffield, South Yorkshire, S26 7WY T: +44 (0) 1909 774416 T: +44 (0) 1909 774416 E: editorial@indiaman.com W: www.indiaman.com

British Association for Cemeteries in S.Asia, 76 1/2 Chartfield Avenue, London, SW15 6HQ T: (020) 8788-6953 W: www.bacsa.org.uk Records Cemeteries. Published over 40 surveys of cemeteries in Pakistan, India, Bangladesh, Burma, Malaysia, Indonesia, Thailand and Japan

Catholic FHS 45 Gates Green Road, West Wickham, Kent, BR4 9DE W: www.catholic-history.org.uk Regular meetings in London, Birmingham, Derwentside & South Lancashire

Cawdor Heritage Group Family & Local History Room, Nairn Museum, Viewfield Drive, Nairn, Nairnshire, IV12 4EE T: 01667 456791 T: 01667 455399 E: manager@nairnmuseum.freeserve.co.uk W: www.nairnmuseum.co.uk Information available on Nairnshire, census returns and Old Parish Registers

Chapels Heritage Society - CAPEL, 2 Sandy Way, Wood Lane, Hawarden, Flintshire, CH5 3JJ T: 01244 531255

Descendants of Convicts Group PO Box 12224, A'Beckett Street, Melbourne 3000, Victoria

Every Generation, Unit 4-5 First Floor West, Universal House, 88-94 Wentworth Street, London E1 7SA T:, 020 7247 5565 E: info@everygeneration.co.uk W: www.everygeneration.co.uk

Families in British India Society 51 Taylor's Ride, Leighton Buzzard, Bedfordshire LU7 3JN E: lawrie.butler@talk21.com

Genealogical Society of Utah (UK) 185 Penns Lane, Sutton Coldfield, West Midlands B76 1JU T: 0121 384 2028

Heraldry Society PO Box 32, Maidenhead, Berkshire, SL6 3FD T: 0118-932-0210 T: 0118 932 0210 E: heraldry-society@cwcom.net

Historical Medical Equipment Society 8 Albion Mews, Apsley, Hertfordshire, HP3 9QZ E: hmes@antiageing.freeserve.co.uk

Holgate Windmill Preservation Society 2 Murray Street, York YO24 4JA T: 01904 799295 E: lambert49@ntlworld.com W: www.holgatewindmill.org

Hugenot & Walloon Research Association, Malmaison, Church St, Great Bedwyn, Wiltshire, SN8 3PE

International Police Association - British Section - Genealogy Group Thornholm, Church Lane, South Muskham, Newark, Nottinghamshire, NG23 6EQ T: 01636 676997 E: ipagenuk@thornholm.freeserve.co.uk

International Society for British Genealogy & Family History, PO Box 3115, Salt Lake City, Utah, 84110-3115 T: 801 272 2178 W: www.homestart.com/isbgfh/

Irish Ancestry Group Clayton House, 59 Piccadilly, Manchester, M1 2AQ T: 0161-236-9750 T: 0161 237 3512 E: office@mlfhs.org.uk W: www.mlfhs.org.uk A specialist group of Manchester and Lancashire FHS

Irish Genealogical Research Society 18 Stratford Avenue, Rainham, Gillingham, Kent, ME8 0EP E: info@igrsoc.org W: www.igrsoc.org, The Society has a library of over four thousand books and two and a half thousand manuscripts

Jewish Genealogical Society of Great Britain, 48 Worcester Crescent, Woodford Green, Essex, IG8 0LU T: 020 8504 8013 E: pnking@onetel.net.uk W: www.jgsgb.org.uk

Lancashire Parish Register Society 135 Sandy Lane, Orford, Warrington, Lancashire, WA2 9JB E: tom_obrien@bigfoot.com W: www.genuki.org.uk/big/eng/LAN/lprs

Lighthouse Society of Great Britain, Gravesend Cottage, Gravesend, Torpoint, Cornwall, PL11 2LX E: k.trethewey@btinternet.com W: www.lsgb.co.uk Holds databases of lighthouses and their keepers. SAE required for enquiries

London & North Western Railway Society - Staff History Group 34 Falmouth Close, Nuneaton, Warwickshire, CV11 6GB T: 024 76 381090 T: 024 76 373577 E: nuneazon2000@aol.com W: www.progsol.co.uk/lnwr

North East England Family History Club, 5 Tree Court, Doxford Park, Sunderland, Tyne and Wear, SR3 2HR T: 0191-522-8344

Quaker FHS 1 Ormond Crescent, Hampton, Middlesex, TW12 2TJ E: info@qfhs.co.uk W: www.qfhs.co.uk

Police History Society 37 Greenhill Road, Timperley, Altrincham, Cheshire WA15 7BG T: 0161-980-2188 E: alanhayhurst@greenhillroad.fsnet.co.uk W: www.policehistorysociety.co.uk Whilst the Society is not primarily interested in family history and having no personal records of its own is unable to answer enquiries re individual officers. However members may contact each other

Railway Ancestors FHS Lundy, 31 Tennyson Road, Eastleigh, Hampshire, SO50 9FS T: (023) 8049 7465 T: (023) 8090 0923 Fax: (023) 8049 7465 E: jim@railwayancestors.org.uk W:

www.railwayancestors.org.uk

Rolls Royce FHS 25 Gisburn Road, Barnoldswick, Colne, Lancashire, BB18 5HB T: 01282 815778 E: ken@ranson.org.uk

Romany & Traveller FHS 6 St James Walk, South Chailey, East Sussex, BN8 4BU W: http://website.lineone.net/~rtfhs

Scottish Association of Family History Societies, c/o 9 Glasgow Street, Dumfries, Dumfrieshire, DG2 9AF W: www.safhs.org.uk

Shap Local History Society The Hermitage, Shap, Penrith, Cumbria, CA10 3LY T: 01931 716671 E: liz@kbhshap.freeserve.co.uk

Society for Name Studies in Britain & Ireland, 22 Peel Park Avenue, Clitheroe, Lancashire, BB7 1ET T: 01200-423771 T: 01200-423771

Society of Brushmakers Descendants FHS 13 Ashworth Place, Church Langley, Essex, CM17 9PU T: 01279-629392 E: s.b.d@lineone.net W: www.brushmakers.com

Tennyson Society Central Library, Free School Lane, Lincoln, Lincolnshire, LN2 1EZ T: 01522-552862 T: 01522-552858 E: linnet@lincolnshire.gov.uk W: www.tennysonsociety.org.uk

The Clans of Ireland Ltd, 2 Westbourne Terrace, Quinsboro Road, Bray, County Wicklow, Ireland T: 01365-322353 E: theclansofireland@ireland.com

Victorian Military Society PO Box 5837, Newbury, Berkshire, RG14 7FJ T: 01635 48628 E: vmsdan@msn.com W: www.vms.org.uk The leading Society covering military history of all nations and races from 1837 to 1914

One Name Societies

Guild of One Name Studies, 14 Charterhouse Buildings, Goswell Road, London, EC1M 7BA T: 01293-411136 E: guild@one-name.org W: www.one-name.org

Alabaster Society No 1 Manor Farm Cottages, Bradenham, Thetford, Norfolk, IP25 7QE T: 01362-821243 E: Laraine_Hake@compuserve.com W: www.alabaster.org.uk

Alderson FHS 13 Spring Grove, Harrogate, North Yorkshire, HG1 2HS

Alderton Family 16 Woodfield Drive, Gidea Park, Romford, Essex RM2 5DH

Allsop Family Group 86 High Street, Loscoe, Heanor, Derbyshire, DE75 7LF

Andy Punshon, 173 Derwent Road, Thatcham, Berkshire, RG79 3UP T: 01635 867448 E: apunshon@vodaphone-corporate.co.uk Researching the Punshon name in NE England and worldwide.

Armstrong Clan Association, Thyme, 7 Riverside Park, Hollows, Canonbie, Dumfriesshire, DG14 0UY T: 013873 71876 E: ted.armclan@aol.com W: www.armstrongclan.info

Badham One Name Society Woodlands Grange, Highwood, Uttoxeter, ST14 8JX E: gamebill@hotmail.com W: www.badham.co.uk

Beresford Family Society 2 Malatia, 78 St Augustines Avenue, South Croydon, Surrey, CR2 6JH T: (020) 8686 3749 T: (020) 8681 3740 E: beresford@atlas.co.uk W: www.beresfordfamilysociety.org.uk

Birkbecks of Westmoreland and Others One Name Study, 330 Dereham Road, Norwich, Norfolk, NR2 4DL E: Seosimhin@btopenworld.com W: www.jgeoghegan.org.uk

Blanchard FHS 10 Stainers, Bishop Stortford, Hertfordshire, CM23 4GL W: www.blanshard.org

Bliss FHS Old Well Cottage, Washdyke Lane, Fulbeck, Lincolnshire, NG32 3LB T: 01400 279050 E: bliss@one-name.org W: www.members.aol.com/keithbliss/fhs/main.htm

Braund Society 12 Ranelagh Road, Lake, Sandown, Isle of Wight PO36 8NX E: braundsociety@fewiow.freeserve.co.uk

Brooking FHS 48 Regent Close, Edgbaston, Birmingham, West Midlands, B5 7PL T: 0121 249 1226 E: marylogan@blueyonder.co.uk W: www.brookingsociety.org.uk

Bunting Society 'Firgrove', Horseshoe Lane, Ash Vale, Surrey, GU12 5LL T: 01252-325644E: firgrove@compuserve.com W: http://freespace.virgin.net/teebee.axmeister/BuntingSociety.htm

Caraher FHS 142 Rexford Street, Sistersville, VA 26175

Cave FHS 45 Wisbech Road, Thorney, Peterborough, Cambridgeshire, PE6 0SA T: 01733 270881 E: hugh-cave@cave-fhs.org.uk W: www.cave-fhs.org.uk

Clan Davidson Assoc Aisling, 67 Shore Road, Kircubbin, Newtownards, Co Down, BT22 2RP T: 028 427-38402 E: clan.davidson@virgin.net

Clan Gregor Society Administrative Office, 2 Braehead, Alloa, Clackmannanshire, FK10 2EW T: 01259 212076 T: 01259 720274 E: clangregor@sol.co.uk W: www.clangregor.com/macgregor

Cobbing FHS 89a Petherton Road, London, N5 2QT T: (020) 7226-2657, Covers Cobbing, Cobbin and other variations

Cory Society 3 Bourne Close, Thames Ditton, London, KT7 0EA W: www.corysociety.org.uk

Courtenay Society Powderham Castle, Kenton, Exeter, Devon, EX6 8JQ T: 01626-891554 T: 01626 891367 Fax: 01626 890729 E: courtenay@courtsoc.demon.co.uk W: www.courtenaysociety.org

Dalton Genealogical Society 11 Jordan Close, Leavesden, Watford, Hertfordshire, WD25 7AF T: 01923 661139 E: pam-

lynam@lineone.net W:
http://members.aol.com/daltongene/index.html

East Family History Soc 45 Windsor Road, Ealing, London W5 3UP

Entwistle FH Association, 58 Earnsdale Road, Darwin, Lancashire, BB3 1HS W: www.entwistlefamily.org.uk

Family History Soc of Martin PO Box 9, Rosanna, Victoria, 3084

Family History Society of Martin (UK), 63 Higher Coombe Drive, Teignmouth, Devon, TQ14 9NL

Geoghegan/McGeoghegan One Name Study, 330 Dereham Road, Norwich, Norfolk, NR2 4DL E: josi@geoghegan18.fsnet.co.uk W: www.jgeoghegan.org.uk

Hamley, Hambly & Hamlyn F H Soc (International), 59 Eylewood Road, West Norwood, London, SE27 9LZ T: (020) 8670-0683 E: hamley@one-name.org W: www.hhh-fhs.com

Hards Family Society Venusmead, 36 Venus Street, Congresbury, Bristol, BS49 5EZ T: 01934 834780 T: 01934 834780 E: rogerhards-venusmead@breathemail.net W: www.hards.freewire.org.uk

Holdich FHS 19 Park Crescent, Elstree, Hertfordshire, WD6 3PT T: (020) 8953 7195 E: apogee.dtaylor@btopenworld.com

Holt Ancestry 26a Avondale Road, Bath, Somerset BA1 3EG E: victoria-holt@holtancestry.co.uk W: www.holtancestry.co.uk

Hotham/Owst One Name Study 65 Northolme Road, Hessle, Hull East Yorkshire HU13 9JB E: jbresearch870@hotmail.com

International Haskell Family Society 36 Hedley Davis Court, Cherry Orchard Lane, Salisbury, Wiltshire, SP2 7UE T: 01722 332873 T: 01722 410004 E: suzyflip@hotmail.com

International Relf Society Chatsworth House , Sutton Road, Somerton, Somerset, TA11 6QL T: 01458-274015 E: chris.relf@bucklebury.demon.co.uk

Kay Family Association UK 47 Moorway, Poulton le Flyde, Lancashire, FY6 6EX T: 01253 886171

Krans-Buckland Family Association, P0 Box 1025, North Highlands, California, 95660-1025 T: (916) 332 4359 E: jkbfa@worldnet.att.net

Leather FHS 134 Holbeck, Great Hollands, Bracknell, Berkshire, RG12 8XG T: 01344 425092 E: s.leather@ic.ac.uk

Lin(d)field One Name Group Southview, Maplehurst, Horsham, West Sussex, RH13 6QY T: 01403 864389 E: lindfield@one-name.org W: www.lindfield.force9.co.uk/long

Mackman FHS Chawton Cottage, 22a Long Ridge Lane, Nether Poppleton, York, North Yorkshire, YO26 6LX T: +44 (0)1904 781752 E: mackman@one-name.org

Mayhew Ancestory Research, 28 Windmill Road, West Croydon, Surrey, CR0 2XN

Morbey Family History Group 23 Cowper Crescent, Bengeo, Hertford, Hertfordshire, SG14 3DZ

Morgan Society of England & Wales, 11 Arden Drive, Dorridge, Solihull, West Midlands, B93 8LP T: 01564 774020 T: 01564 774020 E: morgansociety@tesco.net W: http://freepages.genealogy.rootsweb.com/~morgansociety http://homepages.tesco.net/n.morganpublications/morganpu.htm

Moxon Family Research Trust, 1 Pine Tree Close, Cowes, Isle of wight, PO31 8DX T: 01983 296921 E: john.moxon@virgin.net W: www.moxon.org.uk

Offley Family Society 39 Windmill Fields, Old Harlow, Hertfordshire CM17 0LQ T: 01438-820006 E: jrrichards@onetel.net.uk W: www.offleysociety.co.uk/

Orton FHS 25a Longwood Avenue, Bingley, West Yorkshire, BD16 2RX E: derek@beckd.freeserve.co.uk W: www.redflag.co.uk/ortonfhs.htm

Palgrave Society Crossfield House, Dale Road, Stanton, Bury St Edmunds IP31 2DY T: 01359 251050 E: DerekPalgrave@btinternet.com W: www.ffhs.org.uk/members/palgrave.htm,

The Patterson Heritage Museum 2 - 6 Station Approach, Birchington on Sea, Kent CT7 9RD T: 01843 841649 E: pattersonheritage@tesco.net W: www.pattersonheritage.co.uk Please address all mail to 4 Station Approach, Birchington on Sea Kent CT7 9RD. No fees Donations welcome

Penty Family Name Society Kymbelin, 30 Lych Way, Horsell Village, Surrey, GU21 4QG T: 01483 764904 E: pentytree@aol.com, W:

Percy-Piercy FHS 32 Ravensdale Avenue, North Finchley, London, N12 9HT T: 020 8446 0592 E: brian.piercy@which.net

Rix Family Alliance, 4 Acklam Close, Hedon, Hull, HU12 8NA W: www.rix-alliance.co.uk

Rose Family Society - disbanded 1st March 2002

Serman, Surman FHS 24 Monks Walk, Bridge Street, Evesham WR11 4SL T: 01386 49967 T: 01386 49967 E: design@johnsermon.demon.co.uk W: www.johnsermon.demon.co.uk,

Silverthorne Family Association, 1 Cambridge Close, Swindon, Wiltshire, SN3 1JQ T: 01793 537103

Society of Cornishes, 1 Maple Close, Tavistock, Devon, PL19 9LL T: 01822 614613 T: 01822 614613 E: cornish@one-name.org W: www.societyofcornishes.org

Sole Society 49 Kennel Ride, North Ascot, Berkshire, SL5 7NJ T: 01344 883700 E: info@sole.org.uk W: www.solesociety.freeserve.co.uk Interest in family names Sole, Saul, Sewell and Solly including spelling variations

Spencer Family, 1303 Azalea Lane, Dekalb, Illinois, 60115

Stendall & Variants One Name Study, PO Box 6417, Sutton in Ashfield, Nottinghamshire, NG17 3LE T: 01623 406870 W: www.genealogy-links.co.uk

Stockdill FHS 6 First Avenue, Garston, Watford, WD2 6PZ T: 01923-675292 E: roystock@compuserve.com W: http://ourworld.compuserve.com/homepages/roystock

Swinnerton Society 30 Coleridge Walk, London, NW11 6AT T: (020) 8458-3443 E: roger.swynnerton@whichnet

Talbot Research Organisation, 142 Albemarle Ave, Elson, Gosport PO12 4HY T: 023 92589785 E: mjh.talbot@tinyworld.co.uk W: www.kiamara.demon.co.uk/index.html

The Goddard Association of Europe, 2 Lowergate Road, Huncoat, Accrington, Lancashire, BB5 6LN T: 01254-235135 E: johnc.goddard@virgin.net W: www.goddard-association.co.uk

The Metcalfe Society 57 Westbourne Avenue, Hull, East Yorkshire, HU5 3HW T: 01482 342516 E: enquiries@metcalfe.org.uk W: www.metcalfe.org.uk

The Stockton Society The Leas, 28 North Road, Builth Wells, Powys, LD2 3BU T: 01982 551667 E: cestrienne@aol.com

Toseland Clan Society 40 Moresdale Lane, Seacroft, Leeds, West Yorkshire, LS14 5SY T: 0113 225 9954

Tyrrell FHS 16 The Crescent, Solihull, West Midlands, B91 7PE W: www.tyrrellfhs.org.uk

Watkins FHS PO Box 1698, Douglas, Georgia, 31534-1698 T: 912 383 0839 E: watkinsfhs@alltel.net buzzwatk@aol.com W: www.iinet.net.au/~davwat/wfhs/

Witheridge FHS 16 Haven Close, Dunster, Minehead, Somerset, TA24 6RW

AUSTRALIA

Australasian Federation of Family History Organisations (AFFHO) PO Box 3012, Weston Creek ACT 2611

The Heraldry & Genealogy Society of Canberra Inc GPO Box 585, Canberra ACT 2601 T: 02 6282 9356 (library) E: hagsoc@hagsoc.org.au W: www.hagsoc.org.au

Australian Institute of Genealogical Studies PO Box 359, Blackburn, Victoria 3130 E: info@aigs.org.au W: www.aigs.org.au

Society of Australian Genealogists Richmond Villa, 120 Kent Street, Observatory Hill, Sydney 2000 T: 61-02-92473953 Fax: 61-02-92414872 E: socgenes@ozemail.com.au

NEW SOUTH WALES

1788-1820 Pioneer Association PO Box 57, Croydon, New South Wales, 2132 T: (02)-9797-8107

Australian Society of the Lace Makers of Calais Inc PO Box 946, Batemans Bay, New South Wales, 2536 T: 0244-718168, 0244-723421 E: carolynb@acr.net.au

Bega Valley Genealogical Society Inc PO Box 19, Pambula, New South Wales, 2549

Berrima District Historical & FHS Inc PO Box 851, Bowral, New South Wales, 2576

Blayney Shire Local & FHS Group Inc c/o The Library, 48 Adelaide Street, Blayney, New South Wales, 2799 E: blayney.library@cww.octec.org.au

Blue Mountains FHS PO Box 97, Springwood, NSW, NSW 2777 Fax: 02-4751-2746

Botany Bay FHS Inc PO Box 1006, Sutherland, New South Wales 1499 W: mypage.southernx.com.au/~bbfhs

Broken Hill Family History Group PO Box 779, 75 Pell Street, Broken Hill, New South Wales, 2880 T: 08-80-881321

Burwood Drummoyne & District Family History Group c/o Burwood Central Library, 4 Marmaduke Street, Burwood2134

Cape Banks FHS PO Box 67, Maroubra, New South Wales, NSW 2035 E: hazelb@compassnet.com.au W: www.ozemail.com.au/mhazelb/capebank

Capital Territory Historical & Genealogical Society of Canberra GPO Box 585, Canberra, ACT 2601

Casino & District Family History Group Inc PO Box 586, Casino, New South Wales, 2470 E: hughsie@nor.com W: www.rootsweb/~nswcdfhg

Central Coast FHG Inc PO Box 4090 East Gosford NSW 2250 WWW: centralcoastfhs.org.au

Coffs Harbour District FHS Inc PO Box 2057, Coffs Harbour, New South Wales, 2450

Cowra FHG Inc PO Box 495, Cowra, New South Wales, 2794

Deniliquin Family History Group Inc PO Box 144, Multi Arts Hall, Cressy Street, Deniliquin, New South Wales, 2710 T: (03)-5881-3980 Fax: (03)-5881-1270

Dubbo & District FHS Inc PO Box 868 Dubbo NSW 2830

F H S of Singleton Inc PO Box 422, Singleton NSW 2330

Fellowship of First Fleeters First Fleet House, 105 Cathedral Street, Woolloomooloo, New South Wales, 2000 T: (02)-9360-3988

Forbes Family History Group Inc PO Box 574, Forbes, New South Wales, 2871 T: 0411-095311-(mobile)

Goulburn District FHS Inc PO Box 611, Goulburn, New South Wales, 2580

Griffith Genealogical & Historical Society Inc PO Box 270, Griffith, New South Wales, 2680

Gwydir FHS PO Box EM61, East Moree 2400 T: (02)-67549235
Hastings Valley Family History Group Inc
PO Box 1359, Port Macquarie, New South Wales, 2444
Hawkesbury FHG
C/o Hawkesbury City Council Library, Dight Street, Windsor, 2756
Hill End Family History Group Sarnia, Hill End 2850
Hornsbury Kuring-Gai FHS Inc PO Box 680, Hornsby, 2077
Illawarra FHG PO Box 1652 South Coast Mail Centre, Wollongong 2521
Inverell District FHG Inc PO Box 367, Inverells, 2360
Leeton FHS PO Box 475, Centre Point, Pine Avenue, Leeton 2705
T: 02-6955-7199, 02-6953-2301
Lithgow & District FHS PO Box 516, Lithgow, NSW, 2790
Little Forest FH Research Group PO Box 87, 192 Little Forest Rd,
Milton, 2538 T: 02-4455-4780 E: cathyd@shoalhaven.net.au
W: www.shoalhaven.net.au/~cathyd/groups.html
Liverpool & District FHS PO Box 830, Liverpool NSW 2170
Maitland FH Circle Inc PO Box 247, Maitland, New South Wales
2320WWW: www.rootsweb.com/~ausmfhc
Manning Wallamba FHS c/o Greater Taree City Library, Pulteney
Street, Taree, New South Wales, 2430
Milton Ulladulla Genealogical Society Inc PO Box 619, Ulladulla,
New South Wales, 2539 T: 02-4455-4206
Nepean FHS PO Box 81, Emu Plains 2750 T: (02)-47-353-798 E:
istack@penrithcity.nsw.gov.au W:
www.penrithcity.nsw.gov.au/nfhs/nfhshome.htm
New South Wales Association of Family History Societies
PO Box 48, Waratah, New South Wales, 2298
Newcastle FHS PO Box 189, Adamstown, New South Wales, 2289
Orange FHS PO Box 930, Orange, New South Wales, 2800
Port Stephens-Tilligerry & Districts FHS PO Box 32, Tanilba Bay,
New South Wales, 2319
Richmond River Historical Society Inc PO Box 467, 165
Molesworth Street, Lismore2480 T: 02-6621-9993
Richmond-Tweed FHS PO Box 817, Ballina 2478 E:
warmer@nor.com.au
Ryde District Historical Society Inc 770 Victoria Road, Ryde 2112
T: (02)-9807-7137
Scone & Upper Hunter Historical Society Inc PO Box 339,
Kingdon Street, Upper Hunter, Scone 2337 T: 02-654-51218
Shoalhaven FHS Inc PO Box 591, Nowra NSW 2541 T: 02-
44221253 E: wvost@shoal.net.au
Snowy Mountains Family History Group PO Box 153, Cooma,
New South Wales, 2630
Wagga Wagga & District FHS Inc PO Box 307, Wagga Wagga,
New South Wales, 2650
Wingham FHGPO Box 72, Wingham, New South Wales, 2429
Young & District FHG Inc PO Box 586, Young 2594
NORTHERN TERRITORY
Genealogical Society of the Northern Territory PO Box 37212,
Winnellie, Northern Territory, 0821 T: 08-898-17363
QUEENSLAND
Queensland FHS
PO Box 171, Indooroonilly, Brisbane, Oueensland, 4O68
Beaudesert Branch Genealogical Soc of Queensland Inc
PO Box 664, Beaudesert, Queensland, 4285
Bundaberg Genealocical Association Inc
PO Box 103, Bundaberg, Queensland, 4670
Burdekin Contact Group Family Hist Assn of N Qld Inc
PO Box 393, Home Hill, Queensland, 4806
Caboolture FH Research Group Inc
PO Box 837, Caboolture, Queensland, 4510
Cairns & District FHS Inc
PO Box 5069, Cairns, Queensland, 4870 T: 07-40537113
Central Queensland Family History Asociation
PO Box 8423, Woolloongabba Queensland 4102
Charters Towers & Dalrymple F H Association Inc
PO Box 783, 54 Towers Street, Charters Towers, Queensland, 4820
T: 07-4787-2124
Cooroy Noosa Genealogical & Historical Research Group Inc PO
Box 792, Cooroy, Queensland 4563 E: info@genealogy-noosa.org.au
W: www.genealogy-noosa.org.au
Dalby FHS IncPO Box 962, Dalby, Queensland, 4405
Darling Downs FHS
PO Box 2229, Toowoomba, Queensland, 4350
Genealogical Society of Queensland Inc
PO Box 8423, Woolloongabba, Queensland, 4102
Gladstone Branch G.S.Q.
PO Box 1778, Gladstone, Queensland, 4680
Gold Coast & Albert Genealogical Society
PO Box 2763, Southport, Queensland, 4215
Gold Coast Family History Research Group
PO Box 1126, Southport, Gold Coast, Queensland, 4215
Goondiwindi & District FHS
PO Box 190, Goondiwindi, Queensland, 4390 T: 0746712156
Fax: 0746713019 E: pez@bigpond.com
Gympie Ancestral Research Society Inc
PO Box 767, Gympie, Queensland, 4570
Ipswich Genealogical Society Inc.PO Box 323, 1st Floor, Ipswich

Campus Tafe, cnr. Limestone & Ellenborough Streets, Ipswich,
Queensland, 4305 T: (07)-3201-8770
Kingaroy Family History Centre
PO Box 629, James Street, Kingaroy, Queensland, 4610
Mackay Branch Genealogical Society of Queensland Inc
PO Box 882, Mackay, Queensland, 4740 T: (07)-49426266
Maryborough District FHS
PO Box 408, Maryborough, Queensland, 4650
Mount Isa FHS IncPO Box 1832, Mount Isa, Queensland, 4825 E:
krp8@+opend.com.au
North Brisbane Branch - Genealogical Soc of Queensland Inc
PO Box 353, Chermside South, Queensland, 4032
Queensland FHS Inc
PO Box 171, Indooroophilly, Queensland, 4068
Rockhampton Genealogical Society of Queensland Inc
PO Box 992, Rockhampton, Queensland, 4700
Roma & District Local & FHS
PO Box 877, Roma, Queensland, 4455
South Burnett Genealogical & FHS
PO Box 598, Kingaroy, Queensland, 4610
Southern Suburbs Branch - G.S.Q. Inc
PO Box 844, Mount Gravatt, Queensland, 4122
Sunshine Coast Historical & Genealogical Resource Centre Inc
PO Box 1051, Nambour, Queensland, 4560
Toowoomba Family History Centre c/o South Town Post Office,
South Street, Toowoomba, Queensland, 4350 T: 0746-355895
Townsville - Fam Hist Assoc of North Queensland Inc
PO Box 6120, Townsville M.C., Queensland, 4810
Whitsunday Branch - Genealogical Soc of Queensland Inc
PO Box 15, Prosperpine, Queensland, 4800
SOUTH AUSTRALIA
Fleirieu Peninsula FHG Inc Oarlunga Library, PO Box 411,
Noarlunga Centre South Australia 5168 E:
fleurpengroup@yahoo.co.uk W: www.rootsweb.com/~safpfhg
South Australian Genealogical & Heraldic Society GPO Box 592,
Adelaide 5001, South Australia T: (08)-8272-4222 W:
www.saghs.org.au
South East FHG Inc PO Box 758, Millicent, South Australia, 5280
Southern Eyre Peninsula FHG
26 Cranston Street, Port Lincoln 5606
Whyalla FHG
PO Box 2190, Whyalla Norrie, South Australia, 5608
Yorke Peninsula Family History Group - 1st Branch SAGHS
PO Box 260, Kadina, South Australia, 5554
TASMANIA
Tasmanian FHS (Launceston Branch) PO Box 1290, Launceston,
Tasmania 7250 Email; secretary@tasfhs.org W: www.tasfhs.org
Tasmanian FHS Inc PO Box 191, Launceston, Tasmania 7250 W:
www.tasfhs.org
VICTORIA
Ararat Genealogical Society inc PO Box 361, Ararat, Victoria, 3377
Australian Institute of Genealogical Studies PO Box 339,
Blackburn, Victoria, 3130 E: aigs@alphalink.com.all W:
www.alphalink.com.au/~aigs/index.htm
Benalla & District Family History Group Inc PO Box 268, St
Andrews Church Hall, Church Street, Benalla, Victoria, 3672 T:
(03)-57-644258
Bendigo Regional Genealogical Society Inc
PO Box 1049, Bendigo, Victoria, 3552
Cobram Genealogical Group PO Box 75, Cobram, Victoria, 3643
East Gippsland Family History Group Inc
PO Box 1104, Bairnsdale, Victoria, 3875
Echuca/Moama Family History Group Inc
PO Box 707, Echuca, Victoria, 3564
Emerald Genealogy Group
62 Monbulk Road, Emerald, Victoria, 3782
Euroa Genealogical Group 43 Anderson Street, Euroa, Victoria, 3666
First Fleet Fellowship Victoria Inc Cnr Phayer & Barnet Streets,
South Melbourne, Victoria, 3205
Geelong Family History Group Inc PO Box 1187, Geelong, 3220
E: flw@deakin.edu.au W:
www.home.vicnet.net.au/wgfamhist/index.htm
Genealogical Society of Victoria Ancestor House, 179 Queen
Street, Melbourne 3000, Victoria T: +61-03-9670-7033 E:
gsv@gsv.org.au W: www.gsv.org.au The second biggest Society in
Australia and the first to put their library catalogue on line. The
Society covers the whole of Australia and has resources for other
areas of the world
Hamilton Family & Local History Group PO Box 816, Hamilton,
Victoria, 3300 T: 61-3-55-724933 Fax: 61-3-55-724933 E:
ham19.@mail.vicnet.net.au W: www.freenet.com.au/hamilton
Italian Historical Society 185 Faraday Street, Carlton3053
Kerang & District Family History Group
PO Box 325, Kerang, Victoria, 3579
Mid Gippsland FHS Inc PO Box 767, Morwell, Victoria, 3840
Mildura & District Genealogical Society Inc
PO Box 2895, Mildura, Victoria, 3502
Mornington Peninsula FHS 16 Tavisstock Road, Frankston South,

Victoria 3199 T: 61 3 9783 8773 E: marjoryknight@bigpond.com W: http://mpfhs.org
Narre Warren & District FHG PO Box 149, Narre Warren, Victoria, 3805 W: www.ozemail.com.au/~narre/fam-hist.html
Nathalia Genealogical Group Inc
R.M.B. 1003, Picola, Victoria, 3639
Port Genealogical Society of Victoria Inc
PO Box 1070, Warrambool, Victoria, 3280 E: joyceaustin@start.co.au
Sale & District FH Group Inc PO Box 773, Sale, Victoria, 3850
Stawell Biarri Group for Genealogy Inc
PO Box 417, Stawell, Victoria, 3380
Swam Hill Genealogical & Historical Society Inc
PO Box 1232, Swan Hill, Victoria, 3585
Toora & District FHG Inc PO Box 41, Toora, Victoria, 3962
Wangaratta Gen Soc Inc PO Box 683, Wangaratta, Victoria, 3676
West Gippsland Genealogical Society Inc PO Box 225, Old Shire Hall, Queen Street, Warragul, Victoria, 3820 T: 03-56252743 E: watts@dcsi.net.au W: www.vicnet.net.au/~wggs/
Wimmera Assoc for Genealogy PO Box 880, Horsham Victoria, 3402
Wodonga FHS Inc PO Box 289, Wodonga, Victoria, 3689
Yarram Genealogical Group Inc
PO Box 42, 161 Commercial Road, Yarram, Victoria, 3971
WESTERN AUSTRALIA
Australasian Federation of FH Orgs Inc 6/48 May Street, Bayswater, WA 6053 W: www.affho.org
Geraldton FHS PO Box 2502, Geralton 6531, Western Australia W: www.com.au/gol/genealogy/gfhs/gfhsmain.htm
Goldfields Branch West Australian Genealogical Society Inc
PO Box 1462, Kalgoorlie, Western Australia, 6430
Melville Family History Centre PO Box 108 (Rear of Church of Jesus Christ Latter Day Saints), 308 Preston Point Road, Attadale, Melville, Western Australia, 6156
Western Australia Genealogical Society Inc 6/48 May St Bayswater, WA 6053 T: 08-9271-4311 F: 08-9271-4311 E: wags@cleo.murdoch.edu.au W: www.cleo.murdoch.edu.au/~wags

NEW ZEALAND
Bishopdale Branch NZ Society of Genealogists Inc.
c/o 19a Resolution Place, Christchurch, 8005 T: 03 351 0625
Cromwell Family History Group
3 Porcell Court, Cromwell, 9191
Fairlie Genealogy Group c/o 38 Gray Street, Fairlie, 8771
General Research Institute of New Zealand
PO Box 12531, Thorndon, Wellington, 6038
Hawkes Bay Branch NZ Society of Genealogists Inc.
P O Box 7375, Taradale, Hawkes Bay
Kapiti Branch NZ Society of Genealogists Inc.
P O Box 6, Paraparaumu, Kapiti Coast, 6450
Mercury Bay Branch NZ Society of Genealogists Inc.
31 Catherine Crescent, Whitianga, 2856 T: 0 7 866 2355
Morrinsville Branch NZ Society of Genealogists Inc.
1 David St., Morrinsville, 2251
N.Z. Fencible Society
P O Box 8415, Symonds Street, Auckland, 1003
New Zealand FHS
P O Box13,301, Armagh, Christchurch T: 03 352 4506 E: ranz@xtra.co.nz
New Zealand FHS Inc
PO Box 13301, Armagh, Christchurch E: ranz@extra.co.nz
New Zealand Society of Genealogists Inc
PO Box 8795, Symonds Street, AUCKLAND, 1035 T: 09-525—0625 Fax: 09-525-0620
Northern Wairoa Branch NZ Society of Genealogists Inc.
60 Gordon Street, Dargaville, 300
NZ Society of Genealogists Inc. - Alexandra Branch
21 Gregg Street, Alexandra, 9181
Palmerston North Genealogy Group
P O Box 1992, Palmerston North, 5301
Panmure Branch NZ Society of Genealogists Inc.
29 Mirrabooka Ave, Howick, Auckland, 1705
Papakura Branch NZ Society of Genealogists Inc.
P O Box 993, Papakura, Auckland
Polish Genealogical Society of New Zealand
Box 88, Urenui, Taranaki T: 06 754 4551 E: pgs.newzealand@clear.net.nz
Rotorua Branch NZ Society of Genealogists Inc.
17 Sophia Street, Rotorua, 3201 T: 0 7 347 9122
Scottish Interest Group NZ Society of Genealogists Inc.
P O Box 8164, Symonds Street, Auckland, 1003
South Canterbury Branch NZ Society of Genealogists Inc.
9 Burnett Street, Timaru, 8601
Tairua Branch NZ Society of Genealogists Inc.
c/o 10 Pepe Road, Tairua, 2853
Te Awamutu Branch NZ Society of Genealogists Inc.
Hairini, RD1, Te Awamutu, 2400
Te Puke Branch NZ Society of Genealogists Inc.
20 Valley Road, Te Puke, 3071

Waimate Branch NZ Society of Genealogists Inc.
4 Saul Shrives Place, Waimate, 8791
Wairarapa Branch NZ Society of Genealogists Inc.
34 Rugby Street, Masterton, 5901
Whakatane Branch NZ Society of Genealogists Inc.
P O Box 203, Whakatane, 3080
Whangamata Genealogy Group
116 Hetherington Road, Whangamata, 3062
Whangarei Branch NZ Society of Genealogists Inc.
P O Box 758, Whangarei, 115 T: 09 434 6508

SOUTH AFRICA
Genealogical Institute of South Africa 115 Banheok Road, Stellenbosch, Western Cape, South Africa T: 021-887-5070 E: GISA@RENET.SUN.AC.ZA
Genealogical Society of South Africa
Suite 143, Postnet X2600, Houghton, 2041, South Africa
Human Sciences Research Council Genealogy Information, HSRC Library & Information Service, Private Bag X41, Pretoria 0001, South Africa T: (012)-302-2636 Fax: (012)-302-2933 E: ig@legii.hsrc.ac.za
West Rand FHS
The Secretary, PO Box 760, Florida 1710, South Africa

ZIMBABWE
Heraldry & Genealogy Society of Zimbabwe
Harare Branch, 8 Renfrew Road, Eastlea, Harare, Zimbabwe

NORTH AMERICA
CANADA
ALBERTA
Alberta Family Histories Society
PO Box 30270, Station B, Calgary, Alberta, T2M 4P1
Alberta Genealogical Society (Edmonton Branch)
Room 116, Prince of Wales Armouries, 10440-108 Avenue, Edmonton, Alberta, T5H 3Z9 T: (403)-424-4429
Fax: (403)-423-8980 E: agsedm@compusmart.ab.ca W: www.compusmart.ab.ca/abgensoc/branches.html
Alberta Genealogical Society Drayton Valley Branch
PO Box 6358, Drayton Valley, Alberta, T7A 1R8 T: 403-542-2787 E: c_or_c@telusplanet.net
Alberta Genealogical Society Fort McMurray Branch
PO Box 6253, Fort McMurray, Alberta, T9H 4W1
Alberta Gene Soc Grande Prairie & District Branch
PO Box 1257, Grande Prairie, Alberta, T8V 4Z1
Alberta Gen Society Medicine Hat & District Branch
PO Box 971, Medicine Hat, Alberta, T1A 7G8
Alberta Gen Society Red Deer & District Branch
PO Box 922, Red Deer, Alberta, T4N 5H3 E: evwes@telusplanet.net
Brooks & District Branch Alberta Genealogical Society
PO Box 1538, Brooks, Alberta, T1R 1C4
Ukrainian Genealogical & Historical Society of Canada
R.R.2, Cochrane, Alberta, T0L 0W0 T: (403)-932-6811
BRITISH COLUMBIA
British Columbia Genealogical Society
PO Box 88054, Lansdowne Mall, Richmond V6X 3T6
Campbell River Genealogy Club
PO Box 884, Campbell River, British Columbia, V9W 6Y4 E: rcase@connected.bc.ca W: www.connected.bc.ca/~genealogy/
Comox Valley Family History Research Group
c/o Courtenay & District Museum & Archives, 360 Cliffe Street, Courtenay, British Columbia, V9N 2H9
Kamloops Genealogical Society
Box 1162, Kamloops, British Columbia, V2C 6H3
Kelowna & District Genealogical Society
PO Box 501, Station A, Kelowna, British Columbia, V1Y 7P1 T: 1-250-763-7159 E: doug.ablett@bc.sympatico.ca
Nanaimo FHS PO Box 1027, Nanaimo, British Columbia, V9R 5Z2
Port Alberni Genealogy Club
Site 322, Comp. 6, R.R.3, Port Alberni V9Y 7L7
Powell River Gen Club PO Box 446, Powell River BC V8A 5C2
Prince George Genealogical Society
PO Box 1056, Prince George, British Columbia, V2L 4V2
Revelstoke Genealogy Group
PO Box 2613, Revelstoke, British Columbia, V0E 2S0
Shuswap Lake Genealogical Society
R.R.1, Site 4, Com 4, Sorrento, British Columbia, V0E 2W0
South Okanagan Genealogical Society
c/o Museum, 785 Main Street, Penticton V2A 5E3
Vernon & District FHS PO Box 1447, Vernon V1T 6N7
Victoria Gen Soc PO Box 45031, Mayfair Place, Victoria V8Z 7G9
MANITOBA
Canadian Federation of Gen & Family History Societies
227 Parkville Bay, Winnipeg, Manitoba, R2M 2J6 W: www.geocities.com/athens/troy/2274/index.html
East European Genealogical Society

PO Box 2536, Winnipeg, Manitoba, R3C 4A7
La Societe Historique de Saint Boniface
220 Ave de la Cathedral, Saint Boniface, Manitoba, R2H 0H7
Manitoba Genealogical Society
Unit A, 1045 St James Street, Winnipeg, Manitoba, R3H 1BI
South West Branch of Manitoba Genealogical Society
53 Almond Crescent, Brandon, Manitoba, R7B 1A2 T: 204-728-2857
E: mla@access.tkm.mb.ca
Winnipeg Branch of Manitoba Genealogical Society
PO Box 1244, Winnipeg, Manitoba, R3C 2Y4
NEW BRUNSWICK
Centre d'Etudes Acadiennes
Universite de Moncton, Moncton, New Brunswick, E1A 3E9
New Brunswick Genealogical Society
PO Box 3235, Station B, Fredericton E3A 5G9
NEWFOUNDLAND & LABRADOR
Newfoundland & Labrador Genealogical Society
Colonial Building, Military Road, St John's A1C 2C9
NOVA SCOTIA
Archelaus Smith Historical Society
PO Box 291, Clarks Harbour, Nova Scotia, B0W 1P0 E:
timkins@atcon.com
Cape Breton Genealogical Society
PO Box 53, Sydney, Nova Scotia, B1P 6G9
Genealogical Association of Nova Scotia
PO Box 641, Station Central, Halifax, Nova Scotia, B3J 2T3
Queens County Historical Society
PO Box 1078, Liverpool, Nova Scotia, B0T 1K0
Shelburne County Genealogical Society
PO Box 248 Town Hall, 168 Water St, Shelburne B0T 1W0
ONTARIO
British Isles FHS of Greater Ottowa
Box 38026, Ottawa, Ontario, K2C 1N0
Bruce & Grey Branch - Ontario Genealogical Society
PO Box 66, Owen Sound, Ontario, N4K 5P1
Bruce County Genealogical Society
PO Box 1083, Port Elgin, Ontario, N0H 2C0
Elgin County Branch Ontario Genealogical Society
PO Box 20060, St Thomas, Ontario, N5P 4H4
Essex County Branch Ontario Genealogical Society
PO Box 2, Station A, Windsor, Ontario, N9A 6J5
Haliburton Highlands Genealogy Group Box 834, Minden, Ontario
K0M2K0 T: (705) 286-3154 E: hhggroup@hotmail.com
Halton-Peel Branch Ontario Genealogical Society PO Box 70030,
2441 Lakeshore Road West, Oakville, Ontario, L6L 6M9 E:
jwatt@ica.net W: www.hhpl.on.c9/sigs/ogshp/ogshp.htm
Hamilton Branch Ontario Genealogical Society
PO Box 904, LCD 1, Hamilton, Ontario, L8N 3P6
Huron County Branch Ontario Genealogical Society
PO Box 469, Goderich, Ontario, N7A 4C7
Jewish Genealogical Society of Canada
PO Box 446, Station A, Willowdale, Ontario, M2N 5T1 E:
henry_wellisch@tvo.org
Kawartha Branch Ontario Genealogical Society
PO Box 861, Peterborough, Ontario, K9J 7AZ
Kent County Branch Ontario Genealogical Society
PO Box 964, Chatham, Ontario, N7M 5L3
Kingston Branch Ontario Genealogical Society
PO Box 1394, Kingston, Ontario, K7L 5C6
Lambton County Branch Ontario Genealogical Society
PO Box 2857, Sarnia, Ontario, N7T 7W1
Lanark County Genealogical Society
PO Box 512, Perth, Ontario, K7H 3K4 E: gjbyron@magma.ca W:
www.globalgenealogy.com/LCGs
Marilyn Adams Genealogical Research Centre
PO Box 35, Ameliasburgh, Ontario, K0K 1A0 T: 613-967-6291
Niagara Peninsula Branch Ontario Genealogical Society
PO Box 2224, St Catharines, Ontario, L2R 7R8
Nipissing District Branch Ontario Genealogical Society
PO Box 93, North Bay, Ontario, P1B 8G8
Norfolk County Branch Ontario Genealogical Society
PO Box 145, Delhi, Ontario, N4B 2W9 E:
oxford.net/~mihaley/ogsnb/main.htm
Nor-West Genealogy & History Society
PO Box 35, Vermilion Bay, Ontario, P0V 2V0 T: 807-227-5293
Norwich & District Historical Society
c/o Archives, R.R. #3, Norwich, Ontario, N0J 1P0 T: (519)-863-3638
Ontario Genealogical Society
Suite 102, 40 Orchard View Boulevard, Toronto, Ontario, M4R 1B9
W: www.ogs.on.ca
Ontario Genealogical Society (Toronto Branch)
Box 513, Station Z, Toronto, Ontario, M4P 2GP
Ottawa Branch Ontario Genealogical Society
PO Box 8346, Ottawa, Ontario, K1G 3H8
Perth County Branch Ontario Genealogical Society
PO Box 9, Stratford, Ontario, N5A 6S8 T: 519-273-0399
Simcoe County Branch Ontario Genealogical Society
PO Box 892, Barrie, Ontario, L4M 4Y6

Sioux Lookout Genealogical Club
PO Box 1561, Sioux Lookout, Ontario, P8T 1C3
Societe Franco-Ontarienne DHistoire et de Genealogie
C.P.720, Succursale B, Ottawa, Ontario, K1P 5P8
Stormont Dundas & Glengarry Genealogical Society
PO Box 1522, Cornwall, Ontario, K6H 5V5
Sudbury District Branch Ontario Genealogical Society
c/o Sudbury Public Library, 74 MacKenzie Street, Sudbury, Ontario,
P3C 4X8 T: (705)-674-9991 E: fredie@isys.ca
Thunder Bay District Branch Ontario Genealogical Soc
PO Box 10373, Thunder Bay, Ontario, P7B 6T8
Upper Ottawa Genealogical Group
PO Box 972, Pembroke, Ontario, K8A 7M5
Waterdown East Flamborough Heritage Society
PO Box 1044, Waterdown, Ontario, L0R 2H0 T: 905-689-4074
Waterloo-Wellington Branch Ontario Genealogical Soc 153
Frederick Street, Ste 102, Kitchener, Ontario, N2H 2M2 E:
lestrome@library.uwaterloo.ca
WWW: www.dos.iwaterloo.ca/~marj/genealogy/ww.html
West Elgin Genealogical & Historical Society
22552 Talbot Line, R.R.#3, Rodney, Ontario, N0L 2C0
Whitby - Oshawa Branch Ontario Genealogical Society
PO Box 174, Whitby, Ontario, L1N 5S1
QUEBEC
Brome County Historical Society
PO Box 690, 130 Lakeside, Knowlton, Quebec, J0E 1V0 T:
450-243-6782
Federation Quebecoise des Societies de Genealogie
C.P. 9454, Sainte Foy, Quebec, G1V 4B8
Les Patriotes Inc
105 Prince, Sorel, Quebec, J3P 4J9
Missisquoi Historical Society
PO Box 186, Stanbridge East, Quebec, J0J 2H0 T: (450)-248-3153 E:
sochm@globetrotter.com
Quebec FHS
PO Box 1026, Postal Station, Pointe Claire, Quebec, H9S 4H9
Societ de Genealogie de la Maurice et des Bois Francs
C.P. 901, Trois Rivieres, Quebec, G9A 5K2
**Societe de Conservation du Patrimoine de St Fracois de la Riviere
du Sud** C P 306, 534 Boul St Francois Ouest, St Francois, Quebec,
G0R 3A0
Societe de Genealogie de Drummondville
545 des Ecoles, Drummondville, Quebec, J2B 8P3
Societe de Genealogie de Quebec
C.P. 9066, Sainte Foy, Quebec, G1V 4A8
Societe de Genealogie des Laurentides C.P. 131, 185 Rue Du
Palais, St Jerome, Quebec, J7Z 5T7 T: (450)-438-8158
W: www.societe-genalogie-laurentides.gc.ca
Societe de Genealogie et d'Histoire de Chetford Mines
671 boul. Smith Sud, Thetford Mines, Quebec, G6G 1N1
Societe d'Histoire d'Amos
222 1ere Avenue Est, Amos, Quebec, J9T 1H3
Societe d'Histoire et d'Archeologie des Monts
C.P. 1192, 675 Chemin du Roy, Sainte Anne des Monts, Quebec, G0E 2G0
Societe d'Histoire et de Genealogie de Matane
145 Soucy, Matane, Quebec, G4W 2E1
Societe d'Histoire et de Genealogie de Riviere du Loup
300 rue St Pierre, Riviere du Loup, Quebec, G5R 3V3 T:
(418)-867-4245 E: shgrd@icrdl.net W:
www.icrdl.net/shgrdl/index.html
Societe d'Histoire et de Genealogie de Verdun
198 chemin de lAnce, Vaudreuil, Quebec, J7V 8P3
Societe d'histoire et de genealogie du Centre-du-Quebec
34-A, rue Laurier est, Victoriaville, Quebec, G6P 6P7
E: geneatique@netscape.net W: www.genealogie.qc.ca
Societe d'Histoire et de Genealogie Maria Chapdeleine
1024 Place des Copains, C.P. 201, Dolbeau, Quebec, G8L 3N5
Societe d'Histoire et Genealogie de Salaberry de Valley Field
75 rue St Jean Baptiste, Valleyfield, Quebec, J6T 1Z6
Societe Genealogie d'Argenteuil
378 Principale, Lachute, Quebec, J8H 1Y2
Societe Genealogique Canadienne-Francaise
Case Postale 335, Place d Armes, Montreal, Quebec, H2Y 2H1
Societie de Genealogie de L'Outaouaid Inc
C.P. 2025, Succ. B , Hull, Quebec, J8X 3Z2
SASKATCHEWAN
Saskatchewan Genealogical Society 1870 Lorne Street, Regina,
Saskatchewan S4P 3E1
Battleford's Branch S askatchewan Genealogical Society
8925 Gregory Drive, North Battleford, Saskatchewan, S9A 2W6
Central Butte Branch Saskatchewan Genealogical Society
P.O. Box 224, Central Butte, Saskatchewan, S0H 0T0
Grasslands Branch Saskatchewan Genealogical Society
P.O. Box 272, Mankota, Saskatchewan, S0H 2W0 T: 306-264-5149
Grenfell Branch Saskatchewan Genealogical Society
P.O. Box 61, Grenfell, Saskatchewan, S0G 2B0 T: (306)-697-3176

Moose Jaw Branch Saskatchewan Genealogical Society
1037 Henry Street, Moose Jaw, Saskatchewan, S6H 3H3
Pangman Branch Saskatchewan Genealogical Society
P.O. Box 23, Pangman, Saskatchewan, S0C 2C0
Radville Branch Saskatchewan Genealogical Society
P.O. Box 27, Radville, Saskatchewan, S0C 2G0
Regina Branch Saskatchewan Genealogical Society
95 Hammond Road, Regina, Saskatchewan, S4R 3C8
Saskatchewan Genealogical Society
1870 Lorne Street, Regina, Saskatchewan, S4P 3E1
South East Branch Saskatchewan Genealogical Society
P.O. Box 460, Carnduff, Saskatchewan, S0C 0S0
West Central Branch Saskatchewan Genealogical Society
P.O. Box 1147, Eston, Saskatchewan, S0L 1A0
Yorkton Branch Saskatchewan Genealogical Society
28 Dalewood Crescent, Yorkton, Saskatchewan, S3N 2P7
YUKON
Dawson City Museum & Historical Society
P.O. Box 303, Dawson City, Yukon, Y0B 1G0 T: 867-993-5291
Fax: 867-993-5839 E: dcmuseum@yknet.yk.ca

FAMILY HISTORY SOCIETIES - EUROPE
AUSTRIA
Heraldisch-Genealogische Gesellschaft 'Adler'
Universitatsstrasse 6, Wien, A-1096, Austria
BELGIUM
Cercle de Genealogie Juive de Belgique
74 Avenue Stalingrad, Bruxelles, B-1000, Belgium T: 32 0 2 512 19
63 Fax: 32 0 513 48 59 E: mjb<d.dratwa@mjb-jmb.org>
Federation des Associations de Famille
Bruyeres Marion 10, Biez, B-1390, Belgium
Federation Genealogique et Heraldique de Belgique
Avenue Parmentier 117, Bruxelles, B-1150, Belgium
Office Genealogique et Heraldique de Belgique
Avenue C Thielemans 93, Brussels, B-1150, Belgium
CROATIA
Croatian Genealogical Society
2527 San Carlos Ave, San Carlos, CA, 94070, USA
CZECHOSLOVAKIA
Czechoslovak Genealogical Society International
PO Box 16225, St Paul, MN, 55116-0225, USA
DENMARK
Danish Soc. for Local History
Colbjornsensvej 8, Naerum, DK-2850, Denmark
Sammenslutningen af Slaegtshistoriske Foreninger
Klostermarker 13, Aalborg, DK-9000, Denmark E:
ulla@silkeborg.bib.dk
Society for Danish Genealogy & Biography
Grysgardsvej 2, Copenhagen NV, DK-2400, Denmark W:
www.genealogi.dk
ESTONIA
Estonia Genealogical Society
Sopruse puiestec 214-88, Tallin, EE-0034, Estland
FINLAND
Genealogiska Samfundet i Finland
Fredsgatan 15 B, Helsingfors, SF-00170, Finland
Helsingfors Slaktforskare R.F.
Dragonvagen 10, Helsingfors, FIN-00330, Finland
FRANCE
Amicale des Familles d'alliance Canadiennne-Francaise
BP10, Les Ormes, 86220, France
Amities Genealogiques Bordelaises 2 rue Paul Bert, Bordeaux,
Aquitaine, 33000, France T: 05 5644 8199 Fax: 05 5644 8199
Assoc. Genealogique et Historique des Yvelines Nord
Hotel de Ville, Meulan, 78250, France
Association Catalane de Genealogie
BP 1024, Perpignan Cedex, Languedoc Rousillon, 66101, France
Association de la Bourgeoisie Ancienne Francaise
74 Avenue Kleber, Paris, 75116, France
Association Genealogique de la Charente
Archives Departementales, 24 avenue Gambetta, Angouleme, Poitou
Charentes, 16000, France
Association Genealogique de l'Anjou
75 rue Bressigny, Angers, Pays de la Loire, 49100, France
Association Genealogique de l'Oise
BP 626, Compiegne Cedex, Picardie, 60206, France
Association Genealogique des Bouches-du-Rhone
BP 22, Marseilles Cedex, Provence Alpes Cote d'Azur, 1,
Association Genealogique des Hautes Alpes
Archives Departementales, route de Rambaud, Gap, Provence Alpes
Cote d'Azur, 5000, France
Association Genealogique du Pas de Calais
BP 471, Arras Cedex, Nord-Pas de Calais, 62028
Association Genealogique du Pays de Bray
BP 62, Serqueux, Normandie, 76440 Fax: 02 3509 8756
Association Genealogique du Var
BP 1022, Toulon Cedex, Provence Alpes Cote d'Azur, 83051

Association Genealogique Flandre-Hainaut
BP493, Valenciennes Cedex, Nord-Pas de Calais, 59321
Association Recherches Genealogiques Historique d'Auvergne
Maison des Consuls, Place Poly, Clermont Ferrand, Auvergne, 63100
Bibliotheque Genealogique
3 Rue de Turbigo, Paris, 75001, France T: 01 4233 5821
Brive-Genealogie Maison des Associations, 11 place J M Dauaier,
Brive, Limousin, 19100, France
Centre de Recherches Genealogiques Flandre-Artois
BP 76, Bailleul, Nord-Pas de Calais, 59270, France
Centre d'Entraide Genealogique de France 3 Rue de Turbigo,
Paris, 75001, France T: 33 4041 9909 Fax: 33 4041 9963 E:
cegf@usa.net W: www.mygale.org/04cabrigol/cegf/
Centre Departemental d'Histoire des Familles 5 place Saint Leger,
Guebwiller, Alsace, 68500, France E: cdhf@telmat-net.fr W:
web.telemat-net-fr~cdhf
Centre Entraide Genealogique Franche Comte
35 rue du Polygone, Besancon, Franche Comte, 25000
Centre Genealogique de la Marne
BP 20, Chalons-en-Champagne, Champagne Ardennes, 51005
Centre Genealogique de Savoie
BP1727, Chambery Cedex, Rhone Alpes, 73017, France
Centre Genealogique de Touraine
BP 5951, Tours Cedex, Centre, 37059, France
Centre Genealogique des Cotes d'Armor3bis rue Bel Orient, Saint
Brieuc, Bretagne, 22000, France Fax: 02 9662 8900
Centre Genealogique des Landes
Societe de Borda, 27 rue de Cazarde, Dax, Aquitaine, 40100
Centre Genealogique des Pyrenees Atlantique
BP 1115, Pau Cedex, Aquitaine, 64011, France
Centre Genealogique du Perche 9 rue Ville Close, Bellame,
Normandie, 61130, France T: 02 3383 3789
Centre Genealogique du Sud Ouest Hotel des Societes Savantes, 1
Place Bardineau, Bordeaux, Aquitaine, 33000, France
Centre Genealogique et Heraldique des Ardennes
Hotel de Ville, Charleville Mezieres, Champagne Ardennes, 8000
Centre Genealogique Protestant
54 rue des Saints-Peres, Paris, 75007, France
Cercle de Genealogie du Calvados Archives Departementales, 61
route de Lion-sur-Mer, Caen, Normandie, 14000, France
Cercle de Genealogie et d'Heraldique de Seine et Marne
BP 113, Melun Cedex, 77002, France
Cercle de Genealogie Juive (Jewish)
14 rue St Lazare, Paris, 75009, France T: 01 4023 0490 Fax: 01
4023 0490 E: cgjgeniefr@aol.com
Cercle d'Etudes Genealogiques et Heraldique d'Ile-de-France
46 Route de Croissy, Le Vesinet, 78110, France
Cercle d'Histoire et Genealogique du Perigord
2 rue Roletrou, Perigueux, Aquitaine, 24000, France
Cercle Genealogique Bull
rue Jean Jaures, BP 53, Les-Clayes-sous-Bois, 78340,
Cercle Genealogique d'Alsace
Archives du Bas-Rhin, 5 rue Fischart, Strasbourg, Alsace, 67000
Cercle Genealogique d'Aunis et Saintonge c/o Mr Provost, 10 ave
de Metz, La Rochelle, Poitou Charentes, 17000, France
Cercle Genealogique de la Manche
BP 410, Cherbourg Cedex, Normandie, 50104, France
Cercle Genealogique de la Meurthe et Moselle
4 rue Emile Gentil, Briey, Lorraine, 54150, France
Cercle Genealogique de la Region de Belfort
c/o F Werlen, 4 ave Charles de Gaulle, Valdoie, Franche Comte, 90300
Cercle Genealogique de l'Eure Archives Departementales, 2 rue de
Verdun, Evreux Cedex, Normandie, 27025, France
Cercle Genealogique de Saintonge
8 rue Mauny, Saintes, Poitou Charentes, 17100, France
Cercle Genealogique de Vaucluse
Ecole Sixte Isnard, 31 ter Avenue de la Trillade, Avignon, Provence
Alpes Cote d'Azur, 84000, France
Cercle Genealogique des Deux-Sevres
26 rue de la Blauderie, Niort, Poitou Charentes, 79000, **Cercle
Genealogique des P.T.T.** BP33, Paris Cedex 15, 75721, France
Cercle Genealogique d'Ille-et-Vilaine
6 rue Frederic Mistral, Rennes, Bretagne, 35200 T: 02 9953 6363
**Cercle Genealogique du C.E. de la Caisse d'Epargne Ile de
France-Paris** 19 rue du Louvre, Paris, 75001, France
Cercle Genealogique du Finistere Salle Municipale, rue du
Commandant Tissot, Brest, Bretagne, 29000 Fax: 02 9843 0176 E:
cgf@eurobretagne.fr W: www.karolus.org/membres/cgf.htm
Cercle Genealogique du Haut-Berry place Martin Luther King,
Bourges, Centre, 18000 F: 02 4821 0483 E: cgh-b@wanadoo.fr
Cercle Genealogique du Languedoc 18 rue de la Tannerie,
Toulouse, Languedoc Rousillon, 31400, France T: 05 6226 1530
Cercle Genealogique du Loir-et-Cher
11 rue du Bourg Neuf, Blois, Centre, 41000 T: 02 5456 0711
Cercle Genealogique d'Yvetot et du Pays de Caux
Pavillion des Fetes, Yvetot, Normandie, 76190, France
Cercle Genealogique et Historique du Lot et Garonne
13 rue Etienne Marcel, Villeneuve sur Lot, Aquitaine, 47340

Cercle Genealogique Poitevin
22bis rue Arsene Orillard, Poitiiers, Poitou Charentes, 86000
Cercle Genealogique Rouen Seine-Maritime
Archives Departementales, Cours Clemenceau, Normandie, 76101
Cercle Genealogique Saone-et-Loire
115 rue des Cordiers, Macon, Bourgogne, 71000, France
Cercle Genealogique Vendeen Bat.H, 307bis, Cite de la Vigne aux
Roses, La Roche-sur-Yon, Pays de la Loire, 85000, France
Cercle Genealogique Versailles et Yvelines Archives
Departementales, 1 avenue de Paris, Versailles, 78000, France T: 01
3952 7239 Fax: 01 3952 7239
Cercle Genelogique du Rouergue Archives Departementales, 25 av
Victor Hugo, Rodez, Midi-Pyrenees, 12000, France
Club Genealogique Air France CE Air France Roissy Exploitation,
BP 10201, Roissy CDG Cedex, 95703, France Fax: 01 4864 3220
Club Genealogique Group IBM France CE IBM St Jean de
Braye-Ste Marie, 50-56 ave Pierre Curie, St Jean de Braye Cedex,
45807, France
Confederation Internationale de Genealogie et d'Heraldique
Maison de la Genealogie, 3 rue Turbigo, Paris, F - 75001
Etudes Genealogiques Drome-Ardeche
14 rue de la Manutention, Valence, Rhone Alpes, 26000
Federation Francaise de Genealogie 3 Rue de Turbigo, Paris,
75001, France T: 01 4013 0088 F: 01 4013 0089 W:
www.karolus.org
France-Louisuane/Franco-Americanie Commission Retrouvailles,
Centre CommercialeGatie, 80 avenue du Maine, Paris 75014 Fax: 01
4047 8321 W: www.noconnet.com:80/forms/cajunews.htm
Genealogie Algerie Maroc Tunisie Maison Marechal Alphonse, Juin
28 Av. de Tubingen, Aix en Provence, 13090, France
Genealogie Entraide Recherche en Cote d'Or
97 rue d'Estienne d'Orves, Clarmart, Bourgogne, 92140
Genealogie et Histoire de la Caraibe Pavillion 23, 12 avenue
Charles de Gaulle, Le Pecq, Overseas, 78230, France E:
ghcaraibe@aol.com W: //members.aol.com/ghcaraibe
Groupement Genealogique de la Region dy Nord
BP 62, Wambrechies, Nord-Pas de Calais, 59118, France
Groupement Genealogique du Havre et de Seine Maritime
BP 80, Le Havre Cedex, Normandie, 76050 T: 02 3522 7633
Institut Francophone de Genealogie et d'Histoire 5 rue de
l'Aimable Nanette, le Gabut, La Rochelle, Overseas, 17000 T: 05
4641 9032 Fax: 05 4641 9032
Institut Genealogique de Bourgogne 237 rue Vendome, BP 7076,
Lyon, Bourgogne, 69301
Loiret Genealogique BP 9, Orleans Cedex, Centre, 45016, France
Salon Genealogique de Vichy et du Centr48 Boulevard de Sichon,
Vichy, Auvergne, 3200, France W: www.genea.com
Section Genealogique de l'Assoc. Artistique-Banque de France
2 rue Chabanais, Paris, 75002, France
Societe Genealogique du Bas-Berr Maison des Associations, 30
Espace Mendez France, Chateauroux, Centre, 36000, France
Societe Genealogique du Lyonnais
7 rue Major Martin, Lyon, Rhone Alpes, 69001, France
GERMANY
Arbeirkreis fur Familienforschung e.V Muhlentorturm,
Muhlentortplatz 2, Lubeck, Schleswig-Holstein, D - 23552, Germany
Bayerischer Landesverein fur Familienkunde Ludwigstrasse 14/1,
Munchen, Bayern, D - 80539 E: blf@rusch.m.shuttle.de W:
www.genealogy.com/gene/reg/BAY/BLF-d.html
Deutsche Zentalstelle fur Genealogie
Schongaver str. 1, Leipzig, D - 04329, Germany
Dusseldorfer Verein fur Familienkunde e.V Krummenweger
Strasse 26, Ratingen, Nordrhein Westfalen, D - 40885, Germany
Herold - Verein fur Genealogie Heraldik und Reiwandte
Wissen-Scahaften Archiv Str. 12-14, Berlin, D -14195, Germany
Niedersachsischer Gesellschaft fur Familienkunde e.V Stadtarchiv,
Am Bokemahle 14 - 16, Hannover, Niedersachsen, D - 30171
Oldenburgische Gesellschaft fur Familienkunde
Lerigauweg 14, Oldenurg, Niedersachsen, D - 26131, Germany
Verein fur Familien-U. Wappenkunde in Wurttemberg und
Baden Postfach 105441, Stuttgart, Baden-Wuerttemberg, D - 70047,
Germany
Westdeutsche Gesellschaft fur Familienkunde e.V Sitz Koln Unter
Gottes Gnaden 34, Koln-Widdersdorf, Nordrhein Westfalen, D -
50859, Germany T: 49 221 50 48 88
Zentralstelle fur Personnen und Familiengeschichte
Birkenweg 13, Friedrichsdorf, D - 61381, Germany
GREECE
Heraldic-Genealogical Society of Greece
56 3rd Septemvriou Str., Athens, GR - 10433, Greece
HUNGARY
Historical Society of Hungary University of Eoetveos Lorand, Pesti
Barnabas utca 1, Budapest, H - 1052, Hungary T: 267 0966
ICELAND
The Genealogical Society
P O Box 829, Reykjavick, 121, Iceland Fax: 354 1 679840

ITALY
Ancetres Italien 3 Rue de Turbigo, Paris, 75001, France T: 01 4664
2722 W: //members.aol.com/geneaita/
NETHERLANDS
Centraal Bureau voor Genealogie P O Box 11755, The Hague, NL -
2502 AT T: 070 315 0500 F: 070 347 8394 W: www.cbg.nl
Koninklijk Nederlandsch Genootschap voor Geslacht-en
Wapen-KundeP O Box 85630, Den Haag, 2508 CH, Netherlands
Nederlandse Genealogische Vereniging Postbus 976, Amsterdam,
NL - 1000 AZ, Netherlands E: info@ngu.nl W: www.ngu.nl
Stichting 'Genealogisch Centrum Zeeland'
Wijnaardstraat, Goes, 4416DA T: 0113 232 895
The Caledonian Society
Zuiderweg 50, Noordwolde, NL 8391 KH T: 0561 431580
NORWAY
Norsk Slektshistorik Forening Sentrum Postboks 59, Oslo, N -
0101, Norway T: 2242 2204 Fax: 2242 2204
POLAND
Polish Genealogical Society of America
984 N. Milwaukee Ave, Chicago, IL, 60622, USA
Polish Genealogical Society of New Zealand Box 88, Urenui,
Taranaki, New Zealand T: 06 754 4551 E:
pgs.newzealand@clear.net.nz
SLOVAKIA
Slovak GHS At Matica Slovenska
Novomeskeho, 32, 036 52 Martin, Slovakia
SPAIN
Asociacion de Diplomados en Genealogia y Nobilaria
Alcala 20, 2 Piso, Madrid, 28014 T: 34 522 3822 Fax: 34 532 6674
Asociacion de Hidalgos a Fuerto de Espana
Aniceto Marinas 114, Madrid, 28008, Spain
Cercle Genealogic del Valles
Roca 29, 5 2, Sabadell, Barcelona, 8208, Spain
Circulo de Estudios Genealogicos Familiares
Prado 21, Ateneo de Madrid, Madrid, 28014, Spain
Instituto Aragones de Investigaciones Historiograficas
Madre Sacramento 33, 1', Zaragoza, 50004, Spain
Instituto de Estudios Heraldicos y Genealogicos de Extremadura
Lucio Cornelio Balbo 6, Caceres, 1004, Spain
Real Academia Matritense de Heraldica y Genealogia
Quintana 28, Madrid, 28008, Spain
Sociedad Toledana de Estudios Heraldicos y Genealogicos
Apartado de Correos No. 373, Toledo, Spain
Societat Catalana de Genealogia Heraldica Sigillografia
Vexillologia P O Box 2830, Barcelona, 8080, Spain
Societat Valenciana de Genealogia Heraldica Sigillografia
Vexillologia Les Tendes 22, Oliva, 46780, Spain

SWEDEN
Sveriges Slaktforskarforbund Box 30222, Stockholm, 104 25,
Sweden T: 08 695 0890 Fax: 08 695 0824 E:
genealog@genealogi.se
SWITZERLAND
Genealogical & Heraldry Association of Zurich
Dammbodenstrasse 1, Volketswil, CH-8604, Switzerland
Swiss Genealogical Society Eggstr 46, Oberengstringen, CH 8102,
Switzerland W: www.eye.ch/swissgen/SGFF.html
Swiss Society for Jewish Genealogy
P O Box 876, Zurich, CH-8021, Switzerland
Zentralstelle fur Genealogie Vogelaustrasse 34, CH-8953,
Switzerland Fax: 44 1 742 20 84 E: aicher@eyekon.ch

Local and History Societies & Organisations

The 1805 Club (Royal Navy History) 81 Pepys Road, Wimbledon, London SW20 8NW

The Airfield Research Group 33A Earls Street, Thetford, Norfolk, IP24 2DB T: 01842 765399, E: ray.towler@btinternet.com W: http://members.aol.com/peritrack/argindex.htm

Ancient Monuments Society St Anne's Vestry Hall, 2 Church Entry, London EC4V 5HB T: 0207 236 3934 F: 0207 329 3677 E: ancientmonuments@vol21.com

Anglo-Zulu War Historical Society Woodbury House, Woodchurch Road, Tenterden, TN30 7AE T: 01580-764189W: www.web-marketing.co.uk/anglozuluwar

Association of Local History Tutors 47 Ramsbury Drive, Earley, Reading, RG6 7RT T: 0118 926 4729 E: ray.dils@lineone.net

Battlefields Trust, 33 High Green, Brooke, Norwich, NR15 1HR T: 01508 558145 F: 01508 558145 E: BattlefieldTrust@aol.com W: www.battlefieldstrust.com

Black and Asian Studies Association, 28 Russell Square, London, WC1B 5DS T: (020) 7862 8844 E: marikas@sas.ac.uk

Brewery History Society, Manor Side East, Mill Lane, Byfleet, West Byfleet, KT14 7RS E: jsechiari@rmcbp.co.uk W: www.breweryhistory.com

British Association for Local History, PO Box 6549, Somersal Herbert, Ashbourne, DE6 5WH T: 01283 585947 F: 01722 413242 E: mail@balh.co.uk W: www.balh.co.uk

British Association of Paper Historians, 47 Ellesmere Road, Chiswick, London, W4 3EA E: baph@baph.freeserve.co.uk W: www.baph.freeserve.co.uk Occupational/Genealogical Index Contact: Jean Stirk, Shode House, Ightham Kent TN15 9H

British Brick Society, 9 Bailey Close, High Wycombe, HP13 6QA T: 01494-520299 E: michael@mhammett.freeserve.co.uk W: www.britishbricksoc.free-online.co.uk www.tengula.freeserve.co.uk/acbmg/bt.htm,

British Records Association, 40 Northampton Road, London, EC1R 0HB T: (020) 7833 0428 F: (020) 7833 0416 E: britrecassoc@hotmail.com W: www.hmc.gov.uk/bra

British Records Society Stone Barn Farm, Sutherland Road, Longsdon, ST9 9QD T: 01782 385446 E: carolyn@cs.keele.ac.uk britishrecordsociety@hotmail.com W: www.britishrecordsociety.org.uk Will indexes, Hearth Tax, Probate Inventories

British Society for Sports History, Dept of Sports & Science, John Moore's University, Byrom Street, Liverpool, L3 3AF

Chapels Heritage Society - CAPEL, 2 Sandy Way, Wood Lane, Hawarden, CH5 3JJ T: 01244 531255

Chapels Society, 25 Park Chase, Wembley, HA9 8EQ T: 020 8903 2198 E: agworth296@hotmail.com

Coble and Keelboat Society, 19 Selwyn Avenue, Whitley Bay, NE25 9DH T: 0191 251 4412

Conference of Regional and Local Historians, The School of Humanities, Languages & Social Sciences, University of Wolverhampton, Dudley Campus, Castle View, Dudley, DY1 3HR T: 01902 321056 E: M.D.Wanklyn@wiv.ac.uk

Congregational History Circle, 160 Green Lane, Morden, SM4 6SR

Costume Society, St Paul's House, 8 Warwick Road, London, EC4P 4BN W: www.costumesociety.org.uk

Current Archaeology, 9 Nassington Road, London, NW3 2TX T: (020) 7435-7517 F: (020) 7916-2405 E: editor@archaeology.co.uk W: http://www.archaeology.co.uk CC accepted

Assoc of Denominational Historical Societies & Cognate Libraries 44 Seymour Road, Wandsworth, London SW18 5JA T: 020 8874 7727

Ecclesiastical History Society, 6 Gallows Hill, Saffron Walden, CB11 4DA

English Place Name Society, c/o School of English Studies, University of Nottingham, Nottingham, NG7 2RD T: 0115 951 5919 F: 0115 951 5924 E: janet.rudkin@nottingham.ac.uk W: www.nottingham.ac.uk/english/

Family & Community Historical Society Woburn Lane, Aspley Suise, Milton Keynes, MK17 8JR W: www.fachrs.com

Family & Community Historical Society, 73 Derby Road, Cromford, Matlock, DE4 3RP W: www.fachrs.com

Friends Historical Society, c/o The Library, Friends House, 173-177 Euston Road, London, NW1 2BJ

Friends of War Memorials, 4 Lower Belgrave Street, London, SW1W 0LA T: (020) 7259-0403 F: (020) 7259-0296 E: fowm@eidosnet.co.uk W: http://www.war-memorials.com

Furniture History Society c/o The Furniture and Woodwork Collection, Victoria and Albert Museum, Kensington, London, SW7 2RL T: 01444 413845 F: 01444 413845 E: furniturehistorysociety@hotmail.com

Garden History Society, 70 Cowcross Street, London, EC1M 6EJ T: (020) 7608 2409 F: (020) 7490 2974 E: enquiries@gardenhistorysociety.org W: www.gardenhistorysociety.org

Glasgow Hebrew Burial Society, 222 Fenwick Rd, Griffnock, Glasgow, G46 6UE T: 0141 577 8226

Historical Association (Local History), 59A Kennington Park Road, London, SE11 4JH T: (020) 7735-3901 F: (020) 7582 4989 E: enquiry@history.org.uk W: http://www..history.org.uk

Historical Medical Equipment Society, 8 Albion Mews, Apsley, HP3 9QZ E: hmes@antiageing.freeserve.co.uk

Holgate Windmill Preservation Society 2 Murray Street, York YO24 4JA T: 01904 799295 E: lambert49@ntlworld.com W: www.holgatewindmill.org

Hugenot Society of Great Britain & Ireland, Hugenot Library University College, Gower Street, London, WC1E 6BT T: 020 7679 5199 E: s.massil@ucl.ac.uk W: (Library) www.ucl.ac.uk/ucl-info/divisions/library/huguenot.htm (Society) www.hugenotsociety.org.uk

Labour Heritage, 18 Ridge Road, Mitcham, CR4 2EY T: 020 8640 1814 F: 020 8640 1814,

Association of Local History Tutors, 47 Ramsbury Drive, Earley, Reading, RG6 7RT T: 0118 926 4729

Local Population Studies Society, School of Biological Sciences (Dr S Scott), University of Liverpool, Derby Building, Liverpool, L69 3GS

Mercia Cinema Society, 5 Arcadia Avenue, Chester le Street, DH3 3UH

Military Historical Society, Court Hill Farm, Potterne, Devizes, SN10 5PN T: 01980 615689 Daytime T: 01380 723371 Evenings F: 01980 618746

Oral History Society, British Library National Sound Archive, 96 Euston Road, London, NW1 2DB T: (020) 7412-7405 T: (020) 7412-7440 F: (020) 7412-7441 E: rob.perks@bl.uk W: www.oralhistory.org.uk

Police History Society 37 Greenhill Road, Timperley, Altrincham, Cheshire WA15 7BG T: 0161-980-2188 E: alanhayhurst@greenhillroad.fsnet.co.uk W: www.policehistorysociety.co.uk

Postal History Society, 60 Tachbrook Street, London, SW1V 2NA T: (020) 7821-6399 E: home@claireangier.co.uk

Pub History Society, 13 Grovewood, Sandycombe Road, Kew, Richmond, TW9 3NF T: (020) 8296-8794 E: sfowler@sfowler.force9.co.uk W: www.uk-history.co.uk/phs.htm

Railway & Canal Historical Society 16 Priory Court, Berkhamsted, Hertfordshire HP4 2DP, E: rjtatberk@aol.com

Richard III Society - Norfolk Group, 20 Rowington Road, Norwich, NR1 3RR

Royal Geographical Society (with IBG), 1 Kensington Gore, London, SW7 2AR T: 020 7291 3001 F: 020 7591 3001 W: www.rgs.org

Royal Photographic Society Historical Group 7A Cotswold Road, Belmont, Sutton, SM2 5NG T: (020) 8643 2743

Royal Society, 6 - 9 Carlton House Terrace, London, SW1Y 5AG T: 020 7451 2606 E: library@royalsoc.ac.uk W: www.royalsoc.ac.uk

Royal Society of Chemistry Library & Information Centre, Burlington House, Piccadilly, London, W1J 0BA T: (020) 7437 8656 F: (020) 7287 9798 E: library@rsc.org W: www.rsc.org

Society for the Protection of Ancient Buildings - Mills Section 37 Spital Square, London, E1 6DY T: 020 7456 0909 F: 020 7247 5296 E: millsinfo@spab.org.uk W: www.spab.org.uk

Society for Landscape Studies, School of Continuing Studies, Birmingham University, Edbaston, Birmingham, B15 2TT

Society for Nautical Research, Stowell House, New Pond Hill, Cross in Hand, Heathfield TN21 0LX

Society of Antiquaries, Burlington House, Piccadilly, London, W1J 0BE T: (020) 7479 7080 E: admin@sal.org.uk W: www.sal.org.uk

Society of Jewellery Historians, Department of Scientific Research, The British Museum, Great Russell Street, London, WC1B 3DG E: jewelleryhistorians@yahoo.com

Society for the Protection of Ancient Buildings - Mills Section 37 Spital Square, London E1 6DY T: 020 7456 0909 F: 020 7247 5296 E: millsinfo@spab.org.uk W: www.spab.org.uk

Strict Baptist Historical Society, 38 Frenchs Avenue, Dunstable, LU6 1BH T: 01582 602242 E: kdix@sbhs.freeserve.co.uk W: www.strictbaptisthistory.org.uk

The Tool and Trades History Society Church Farm, 48 Calne Road, Lyneham, Chippenham, Wiltshire SN15 4PN E: taths@aol.com W: www.taths.org.uk

Thoresby Society, 23 Clarendon Road, Leeds, LS2 9NZ T: 0113 245 7910 W: www.thoresby.org.uk

Unitarian Historical Society, 6 Ventnor Terr, Edinburgh, EH9 2BL

United Kingdom Reminiscence Network, Age Exchange Reminiscence Centre, 11 Blackheath Village, London, SE3 9LA T: 020 83189 9105 E: age-exchange@lewisham.gov.uk

United Reformed Church History Society, Westminster College, Madingley Road, Cambridge, CB3 0AA T: 01223-741300 (NOT Wednesdays), Information on ministers of constituent churches not members

University of London Extra -Mural Society For Genealogy And History of The Family, 136 Lennard Road, Beckenham, BR3 1QT
Vernacular Architecture Group, Ashley, Willows Green, Chelmsford, CM3 1QD T: 01245 361408 W: www.vag.org.uk
Veterinary History Society, 608 Warwick Road, Solihull, B91 1AA
Victorian Military Society, PO Box 5837, Newbury, RG14 7FJ T: 01635 48628 E: vmsdan@msn.com W: www.vms.org.uk
Victorian Revival, Sugar Hill Farm, Knayton, Thirsk, YO7 4BP T: 01845 537827 F: 01845 537827 E: pamelagoult@hotmail.com
Victorian Society, 1 Priory Gardens, Bedford Park, London, W4 1TT T: (020) 8994 1019 F: (020) 8747 5899 E: admin@victorian-society.org.uk W: http://www.victorian-society.org.uk CC accepted
Voluntary Action History Society, National Centre for Volunteering, Regent's Wharf, 8 All Saints Street, London, N1 9RL T: (020) 7520 8900 F: (020) 7520 8910 E: instvolres.aol.com W: www.ivr.org.uk/vahs.htm
War Research Society, 27 Courtway Avenue, Birmingham, B14 4PP T: 0121 430 5348 F: 0121 436 7401 E: battletour@aol.com W: www.battlefieldtours.co.uk
Wesley Historical Society, 34 Spiceland Road, Northfield, Birmingham, B31 1NJ E: edgraham@tesco.net W: www.wesleyhistoricalsociety.org.uk
The Waterways Trust, The National Waterways Museum, Llanthony Warehouse, Gloucester Docks, Gloucester, GL1 2EH T: 01452 318053 F: 01452 318066 E: info@nwm.demon.co.uk W: www.nwm.org.uk
The West of England Costume Society, 4 Church Lane, Long Aston, Nr. Bristol, BS41 9LU T: 01275-543564 F: 01275-543564

Bedfordshire
Ampthill History Forum 10 Mendham Way, Clophill, Bedford, MK45 4AL E: forum@ampthillhistory.co.uk W: www.ampthillhistory.co.uk
Ampthill & District Archaeological and Local History 14 Glebe Avenue, Flitwick, Bedford, MK45 1HS T: 01525 712778 E: petwood@waitrose.com W: www.museums.bedfordshire.gov.uk/localgroups/ampthill2/html
Ampthill & District Preservation Society, Seventh House, 43 Park Hill, Ampthill, MK45 2LP
Ampthill History Forum, 10 Mendham Way, Clophill, Bedford, MK45 4AL E: forum@ampthillhistory.co.uk W: www.ampthillhistory.co.uk
Bedfordshire Local History Association 29 George Street, Maulden, Bedford, MK45 2DF T: 01525 633029
Bedfordshire Archaeological and Local History Society 7 Lely Close, Bedford, MK41 7LS T: 01234 365095 W: www.museums.bedfordshire.gov.uk/localgroups
Bedfordshire Historical Record Society, 48 St Augustine's Road, Bedford, MK40 2ND T: 01234 309548 E: rsmart@ntlworld.com W: www.bedfordshirehrs.org.uk
Biggleswade History Soc 6 Pine Close, Biggleswade, SG18 QEF
Caddington Local History Group, 98 Mancroft Road, Caddington, Nr. Luton, LU11 4EN W: www.caddhist.moonfruit.com
Carlton & Chellington Historical Society, 3 High Street, Carlton, MK43 7JX
Dunstable & District Local History Society, 7 Castle Close, Totternhoe, Dunstable, LU6 1QJ T: 01525 221963
Dunstable Historic and Heritage Studies, 184 West Street, Dunstable, LU6 1 NX T: 01582 609018
Harlington Heritage Trust, 2 Shepherds Close, Harlington, Near Dunstable, LU5 6NR
Knoll History Projext, 32 Ashburnham Road, Ampthill, MK45 2RH
Leighton-Linslade Heritage Display Society, 25 Rothschild Road, Linslade, Leighton Buzzard, LU7 7SY T:
Luton & District Historical Society 22 Homerton Road, Luton, LU3 2UL T: 01582 584367
Social History of Learning Disability Research Group, School of Health & Social Welfare, Open University, Milton Keynes, MK7 6AA
Toddington Historical Society, 21 Elm Grove, Toddington, Dunstable, LU5 6BJ W: www.museums.bedfordshire.gov.uk/local/toddington.htm
Wrestlingworth History Society 18 Braggs Lane, Church Lane, Wrestlingworth, SG19 2ER

Berkshire
Berkshire Industrial Archaeological Group 20 Auclum Close, Burghfield Common, Reading, RG7 DY
Berkshire Archaeology Research Group Wayfield, 20 Rances Lane, Wokingham, RG40 2LH T: 0118 978 2161 W: www.berkshire-archaeology.info
Berkshire Local History Association, 18 Foster Road, Abingdson, OX14 1YN E: secretary@blha.org.uk W: www.blha.org.uk
Berkshire Record Society Berkshire Record Office, 9 Coley Avenue, Reading, RG1 6AF T: 0118-901-5130 F: 0118-901-5131 E: peter.durrant@reading.gov.uk
Bracknell & District Historical Society 16 Harcourt Road, Bracknell, RG12 7JD T: 01344 640341

Brimpton Parish Research Association Shortacre, Brimpton Common, Reading, RG7 4RY T: 0118 981 3649
Chiltern Heraldry Group, Magpie Cottage, Pondwood Lane, Shottesbrooke, SL6 3SS T: 0118 934 3698
Cox Green Local History Group 29 Bissley Drive, Maidenhead, SL6 3UX T: 01628 823890
Datchet Village Society 86 London Road, Datchet, SL3 9LQ T: 01753 542438 E: janet@datchet.com W: www.datchet.com
Eton Wick History Group 47 Colenorton Crescent, Eton Wick, Windsor, SL4 6WW T: 01753 861674
Finchampstead History & Heritage Group 134 Kiln Ride, California, Wokingham, RG40 3PB T: 0118 973 3005
Friends of Reading Museums, 15 Benyon Court, Bath Road, Reading, RG1 6HR T: 0118 958 0642
Friends of Wantage Vale & Downland Museum 19 Church Street, Wantage, OX12 8BL T: 01235 771447
Goring & Streatley Local History Society 45 Springhill Road, Goring On Thames, Reading, RG8 OBY T: 01491 872625
Hare Hatch & Kiln Green Local History Group Shinglebury, Tag Lane, Hare Hatch, Twyford, RG10 9ST T: 0118 940 2157 E: richard.lloyd@wargrave.net
Hedgerley Historical Society, Broad Oaks, Parish Lane, Farnham Common, Slough, SL2 3JW T: 01753 645682 E: brendakenw@tiscali.co.uk
Heraldry Society, PO Box 32, Maidenhead, SL6 3FD T: 0118-932-0210 F: 0118 932 0210 E: heraldry-society@cwcom.net
History of Reading Society 5 Wilmington Close, Woodley, Reading, RG5 4LR T: 0118 961 8559 E: peterrussell7@hotmail.com
Hungerford Historical Association 23 Fairview Road, Hungerford, RG170PB T: 01488 682932 E: mandm.martin@talk21.com W: www.hungerfordhistorical.org.uk
Maidenhead Archaeological & Historical Society 70 Lambourne Drive, Maidenhead, SL6 3HG T: 01628 672196
Middle Thames Archaeological & Historical Society 1 Saffron Close, Datchet, Slough, SL3 9DU T: 01753 543636
Mortimer Local History Group 19 Victoria Road, Mortimer, RG7 3SH T: 0118 933 2819
Newbury & District Field Club, 4 Coombe Cottages, Coombe Road, Crompton, Newbury, RG20 6RG T: 01635 579076
Project Purley 4 Allison Gardens, Purley on Thames, RG8 8DF T: 0118 942 2485
Sandhurst Historical Society, Beech Tree Cottage, Hancombe Road, Little Sandhurst, GU47 8NP T: 01344 777476 W: www.sandhurst-town.com/societies
Shinfield & District Local History Societies Long Meadow, Part Lane, Swallowfield, RG7 1TB
Swallowfield Local History Society Kimberley, Swallowfield, Reading, RG7 1QX T: 0118 988 3650
Thatcham Historical Society 72 Northfield Road, Thatcham, RG18 3ES T: 01635 864820 W: www.thatchamhistoricalsociety.org.uk
Twyford & Ruscombe Local History Society 26 Highfield Court, Waltham Road, Twyford, RG10 0AA T: 0118 934 0109
Wargrave Local History Society 6 East View Close, Wargrave, RG10 8BJ T: 0118 940 3121 E: peter.delaney@talk21.com history@wargrave.net W: www.wargrave.net/history
Windsor Local History Publications Group 256 Dedworth Road, Windsor, SL4 4JR T: 01753 864835 E: windlesora@hotmail.com
Wokingham History Group 39 Howard Road, Wokingham, RG40 2BX T: 0118 978 8519

Birmingham
Alvechurch Historical Society, Bearhill House, Alvechurch, Birmingham, B48 7JX T: 0121 445 2222
Birmingham & District Local History Association, 112 Brandwood Road, Kings Heath, Birmingham, B14 6BX T: 0121-444-7470
Small Heath Local History Society, 381 St Benedicts Rd, Small Heath, Birmingham B10 9ND

Bristol
Alveston Local History Society, 6 Hazel Gardens, Alveston, BS35 3RD T: 01454 43881 E: jc1932@alveston51.fsnet.co.uk
Avon Local History Association, 4 Dalkeith Avenue, Kingswood, Bristol, BS15 1HH T: 0117 967 1362
Bristol & Avon Archaeological Society 3 Priory Avenue, Westbury on Trym, Bristol, BS9 4DA T: 0117 9620161 (evenings) W: http://www-digitalbristol.org/members/baas/
Bristol Records Society, Regional History Centre, Faculty of Humanities, University of the West of England, St Maththias Campus, Oldbury Court Road, Fishponds, Bristol, BS16 2JP T: 0117 344 4395 W: http://humanities.uwe.ac.uk/brs/index.htm
Congresbury History Group Venusmead, 36 Venus Street, Congresbury, Bristol, BS49 5EZ T: 01934 834780 F: 01934 834780 E: rogerhards-venusmead@breathemail.net
Downend Local History Society, 141 Overndale Road, Downend, Bristol, B516 2RN
Whitchurch Local History Society, 62 Nailsea Park, Nailsea, Bristol, B519 1BB

Yatton Local History Society, 27 Henley Park, Yatton, Bristol, BS49 4JH T: 01934 832575

Buckinghamshire

Buckinghamshire Archaeological Society County Museum, Church Street, Aylesbury, HP20 2QP T: 01269 678114

Buckinghamshire Record Society Centre for Buckinghamshire Studies, County Hall, Aylesbury, HP20 1UU T: 01296 383013 F: 01296-382771 E: archives@buckscc.gov.uk W: www.buckscc.gov.uk/archives/publications/brs.stm

Chesham Bois One-Place Study, 70 Chestnut Lane, Amersham, HP6 6EH T: 01494 726103 E: cdjmills@hotmail.com

Chesham Society, 54 Church Street, Chesham, HP5 IHY

Chess Valley Archealogical & Historical Society, 16 Chapmans Crescent, Chesham, NP5 2QU T: 01494 772914

Lashbrook One-Place Study, 70 Chestnut Lane, Amersham, HP6 6EH T: 01494 726103 E: cdjmills@hotmail.com Covers Bradford, Talaton, Thornbury in Devon and Shiplake, Oxfordshire see also Lashbrook One-Name Study (Under Family History Societies)

Pitstone and Ivinghoe Museum Society, Vicarage Road, Pitstone, Leighton Buzzard, LU7 9EY T: 01296 668123 W: http://website.lineone.net/~pitstonemus Pitstone Green Museum and Ford End Watermill

Princes Risborough Area Heritage Society Martin's Close, 11 Wycombe Road, Princes Risborough, HP27 0EE T: 01844 343004 F: 01844 273142 E: sandymac@risboro35.freeserve.co.uk

Cambridgeshire

Cambridge Antiquarian Society, PO Box 376, 96 Mill Lane, Impington, Cambridge , CB4 9HS T: 01223 502974 E: liz-allan@hotmail.com

Cambridge Group for History of Population and Social History, Sir William Hardy Building, Downing Place, Cambridge, CB2 3EN T: 01223 333181 F: 01223 333183 W: http://www-hpss.geog.cam.ac.uk

Cambridgeshire Archaeology , Castle Court, Shire Hall, Cambridge, CB3 0AP T: 01223 717312 F: 01223 362425 E: quentin.carroll@cambridgeshire.gov.uk W: http://edweb.camcnty.gov.uk/archaeology www.archaeology.freewire.co.uk

Cambridgeshire Local History Society 1A Archers Close, Swaffham Bulbeck, Cambridge, CB5 0NG

Cambridgeshire Records Society County Record Office, Shire Hall, Cambridge, CB3 0AP W: www.cambridgeshirehistory.com/societies/crs/index.html

Hemingfords Local History Society, Royal Oak Corner, Hemingford Abbots, Huntingdon, PE28 9AE T: 01480 463430 E: hemlocs@hotmail.com

Houghton & Wyton Local History Society, Church View, Chapel Lane, Houghton, Huntingdon, PE28 2AY T: 01480 469376 E: gerry.feake@one-name.org

Huntingdonshire Local History Society, 2 Croftfield Road, Godmanchester, PE29 2ED T: 01480 411202

Saffron Walden Historical Society, 9 High Street, Saffron Walden, CB10 1AT T:

Sawston Village History Society, 21 Westmoor Avenue, Sawston, Cambridge, CB2 4BU T: 01223 833475

Upwood & Raveley History Group, The Old Post Office, 71-73 High Street, Upwood, Huntingdon, PE17 1QE

Cheshire

Altrincham History Society, 10 Willoughby Close, Sale, M33 6PJ T: 0161 962 7658

Ashton & Sale History Society, Tralawney House, 78 School Road, Sale, M33 7XB T: 0161 9692795

Bowdon History Society, 5 Pinewood, Bowdon, Altrincham, WA14 3JQ T: 0161 928 8975

Cheshire Heraldry Society, 24 Malvern Close, Congleton, CW12 4PD

Cheshire Local History Association Cheshire Record Office, Duke Street, Chester, CH1 1RL T: 01224 602559 F: 01244 603812 E: chairman@cheshirehistory.org.uk W: www.cheshirehistory.org.uk

Chester Archaeological Society Grosvenor Museum, 27 Grosvenor Street, Chester, CH1 2DD T: 01244 402028 F: 01244 347522 E: p.carrington@chesterccc.gov.uk W: http://www.chesterarchaeolsoc.org.uk

Christleton Local History Group, 25 Croft Close, Rowton, CH3 7QQ T: 01244 332410

Society of Cirplanologists, 26 Roe Cross Green, Mottram, Hyde, SK14 6LP T: 01457 763485

Congleton History Society 48 Harvey Road, Congleton, CWI2 2DH T: 01260 278757 E: awill0909@aol.com

Department of History - University College Chester, Department of History, University College Chester, Cheveney Road, Chester, CH1 4BJ T: 01244 375444 F: 01244 314095 E: history@chester.ac.uk W: www.chester.ac.uk/history

Disley Local History Society 5 Hilton Road, Disley, SK12 2JU T: 01663 763346 F: 01663 764910 E: chgris.makepeace@talk21.com

Historic Society of Lancashire & Cheshire East Wing Flat, Arley Hall, Northwich, CW9 6NA T: 01565 777231 F: 01565 777465

Lancashire & Cheshire Antiquarian Society 59 Malmesbury Road, Cheadle Hulme, SK8 7QL T: 0161 439 7202 E: morris.garratt@lineone.net W: www.lancashirehistory.co.uk www.cheshirehistory.org.uk

Lawton History Group, 17 Brattswood drive, Church Lawton, Stoke on Trent, ST7 3EF T: 01270 873427 E: arthur@aburton83.freeserve.co.uk

Macclesfield Historical Society 42 Tytherington Drive, Macclesfield, SK10 2HJ T: 01625 420250, SAE for all enquiries

Northwich & District Heritage Society, 13 Woodlands Road, Hartford, Northwich, CW8 1NS, Several publications available for Mid Cheshire area

Poynton Local History Society, 6 Easby Close, Poynton, SK12 1YG

South Cheshire FHS incorporating S E Cheshire Local Studies Group, PO Box 1990, Crewe, CW2 6FF W: www.scfhs.org.uk

Stockport Historical Society 59 Malmesbury Road, Cheadle Hulme, Stockport, SK8 7QL T: 0161 439 7202

Weaverham History Society, Ashdown, Sandy Lane, Weaverham, Northwich, CW8 3PX T: 01606 852252 E: jg-davies@lineone.net

Wilmslow Historical Society, 4 Campden Way, Handforth, Wilmslow, SK9 3JA T: 01625 529381

Cleveland

Cleveland & Teesside Local History Society 150 Oxford Road, Linthorpe, Middlesbrough, TS5 5EL, Membership Secretary: 43 Petrel Crescenet, Norton, Stockton on Tees TS20 1SN

Cornwall

Bodmin Local History Group 1 Lanhydrock View, Bodmin, PL31 1BG

Cornwall Association of Local Historians, St Clement's Cottage, Coldrinnick Bac, Duloe, Liskeard, PL14 4QF T: 01503 220947 E: anne@coldrinnick.freeserve.co.uk

Cornwall FHS , 5 Victoria Square, Truro, TR1 2RS T: 01872-264044 E: secretary@cornwallfhs.com W: http://www.cornwallfhs.com Secretary/Administrator Mrs Frances Armstrong

Lighthouse Society of Great Britain, Gravesend Cottage, Gravesend, Torpoint, PL11 2LX E: k.trethewey@btinternet.com W: http://www.lsgb.co.uk Holds databases of lighthouses and their keepers.

Royal Institution of Cornwall, Courtney Library & Cornish History Research Centre, Royal Cornwall Museum, River Street, Truro, TR1 2SJ T: 01872 272205 E: RIC@royal-cornwall-museum.freeserve.co.uk W: www.cornwall-online.co.uk/ric

Cumbria

Ambleside Oral History Group, 1 High Busk, Ambleside, LA22 0AW T: 01539 431070 E: history@amblesideonline.co.uk W: www.aoghistory.f9.co.uk

Appleby Archaeology Group, Pear Tree Cottage, Kirkland Road, Skirwith, Penrith, CA10 1RL T: 01768 388318 E: martin@fellside-eden.freeserve.co.uk

Appleby In Westmorland Record Society, Kingstone House, Battlebarrow, Appleby-In-Westmorland, CA16 6XT T: 017683 52282 E: barry.mckay@britishlibrary.net

Caldbeck & District Local History Society, Whelpo House, Caldbeck, Wigton, CA7 8HQ T: 01697 478270

Cartmel Peninsula Local History Society, Fairfield, Cartmel, Grange Over Sands, LA11 6PY T: 015395 36503

Centre for North West Regional Studies, Fylde College, Lancaster University, Lancaster, LA1 4YF T: 01524 593770 E: christine.wilkinson@lancaster.ac.uk W: www.lancs.ac.uk/users/cnwrs

Crosby Ravensworth Local History Society, Brookside, Crosby Ravensworth, Penrith, CA10 3JP T: 01931 715324 E: david@riskd.freeserve.co.uk

Cumberland and Westmorland Antiquarian & Archaeological Society County Offices, Kendal, LA9 4RQ T: 01539 773431 F: 01539 773539 E: info@cwaas.org.uk W: www.cwaas.org.uk

Cumbria Amenity Trust Mining History Society, The Rise, Alston, CA9 3DB T: 01434 381903 W: www.catmhs.co.uk

Cumbria Industrial History Society, Coomara, Carleton, Carlisle, CA4 0BU T: 01228 537379 F: 01228 596986 E: gbrooksvet@tiscali.co.uk W: www.cumbria-industries.org.uk

Cumbria Local History Federation Oakwood, The Stripes, Cumwhinton, Carlisle, CA4 0AP

Cumbrian Railways Association, Whin Rigg, 33 St Andrews Drive, Perton, Wolverhampton, WV6 7YL T: 01902 745472 W: www.cumbrian-rail.org

Dalton Local History Society, 15 Kirkstone Crescent, Barrow in Furness, LA14 4ND T: 01229 823558 E: davidhsd@aol.co.

Dudden Valley Local History Group Seathwaite Lodge, Dudden Valley, Broughton in Furness, LA20 6ED

Friends of Cumbria Archives, The Barn, Parsonby, Aspatria, Wigton, CA7 2DE T: 01697 320053 E: john@johnmary.freeserve.co.uk W: www.focasonline.org.uk

Friends of The Helena Thompson Museum, 24 Calva Brow, Workington, CA14 1DD T: 01900 603312

Holme & District Local History Society, The Croft, Tanpits Lane, Burton, Carnforth, LA6 1HZ T: 01524 782121

Keswick Historical Society, Windrush, Rogersfield, Keswick, CA12 4BN T: 01768 772771

Lorton and Derwent Fells Local History Society, Clouds Hill, Lorton, Cockermouth, CA13 9TX T: 01900 85259 E: michael@lorton.freeserve.co.uk

Matterdale Historical and Archaeological Society, The Knotts, Matterdale, Penrith, CA11 0LD T: 01768 482358

North Pennines Heritage Trust, Nenthead Mines Heritage Centre, Nenthead, Alston, CA9 3PD T: 01434 382037 F: 01434 382294 E: administration.office@virgin.net W: www.npht.com

Sedbergh & District History Society, c/o 72 Main Street, Sedbergh, LA10 5AD T: 015396 20504 E: history@sedbergh.org.uk

Shap Local History Society, The Hermitage, Shap, Penrith, CA10 3LY T: 01931 716671 E: liz@kbhshap.freeserve.co.uk

Solway History Society, 9 Longthwaite Crescent, Wigton, CA7 9JN T: 01697 344257 E: s.l.thornhill@talk21.com

Staveley and District History Society, Heather Cottage, Staveley, Kendal, LA8 9JE T: 01539 821194 E: Jpatdball@aol.com

Upper Eden History Society, Copthorne, Brough Sowerby, Kirkby Stephen, CA17 4EG T: 01768 341007 E: gowling@kencomp.net

Whitehaven Local History Society, Cumbria Record Office & local Studies Library, Scotch Street, Whitehaven, CA28 7BJ T: 01946 852920 F: 01946 852919 E: anne.dick@cumbriacc.gov.uk

The 68th (or Durham) Regiment of Light Infantry Display Team, 40 The Rowans, Orgill, Egremont, CA22 2HW T: 01946 820110 E: PhilMackie@aol.com W: www.68dli.com

Derbyshire

Allestree Local Studies Group, 30 Kingsley Road, Allestree, Derby, DE22 2JH

Arkwright Society, Cromford Mill, Mill Lane, Cromford, DE4 3RQ T: 01629 823256 F: 01629 823256 E: info@cromfordmill.co.uk W: www.cromfordmill.co.uk CC accepted not American Express

Chesterfield & District Local History Society Melbourne House, 130 Station Road, Bimington, Chesterfield, S43 1LU T: 01246 620276

Derbyshire Archaeological Society, 2 The Watermeadows, Swarkestone, Derby, DE73 1JA T: 01332 704148 E: barbarafoster@talk21.com W: www.DerbyshireAS.org.uk

Derbyshire Local History Societies Network Derbyshire Record Office, Libraries & Heritage Dept, County Hall, Matlock, DE4 3AG T: 01629-580000-ext-3520-1 F: 01629-57611 E: recordoffice@derbyshire.gov.uk W: www.derbyshire.gov.uk

Derbyshire Record Society 57 New Road, Wingerworth, Chesterfield, S42 6UJ T: 01246 231024 E: neapen@aol.com W: www.merton.dircon.co.uk/drshome.htm

Holymoorside and District History Society, 12 Brook Close, Holymoorside, Chesterfield, S42 7HB T: 01246 566799 W: www.holymoorsidehistsoc.org.uk

Ilkeston & District Local History Society 16 Rigley Avenue, Ilkeston, DE7 5LW

New Mills Local History Society, High Point, Cote Lane, Hayfield, High Peak, SK23 T: 01663-742814

Old Dronfield Soc 2 Gosforth Close, Dronfield, S18 INT

Nottinghamshire Industrial Archaeology Society, 18 Queens Avenue, Ilkeston, DE7 4DL T: 0115 932 2228

Pentrich Historical Society, c/o The Village Hall, Main Road, Pentrich, DE5 3RE E: mail@pentrich.org.uk W: www.pentrich.org

Devon

Chagford Local History Society, Footaway, Westcott, Chagford, Newton Abbott, TQ13 8JF T: 01647 433698 E: cjbaker@jetdash.freeserve.co.uk

Dulverton and District Civic Society, 39 Jury Road, Dulverton, TA22 9EJ,

Holbeton Yealmpton Brixton Society 32 Cherry Tree Dr, Brixton, Plymouth, PL8 2DD W: http://beehive.thisisplymouth.co.uk/hyb

Moretonhampstead History Society, School House, Moreton, Hampstead, TQ13 8NX

Newton Tracey & District Local History Society, Home Park, Lovacott , Newton Tracey, Barnstaple, EX31 3PY T: 01271 858451

Tavistock & District Local History Society, 18 Heather Close, Tavistock, PL19 9QS T: 01822 615211 E: linagelliott@aol.com

The Devon & Cornwall Record Society 7 The Close, Exeter, EX1 1EZ T: 01392 274727 W: www.cs.ncl.ac.uk/genuki/DEV/DCRS

The Devon History Society, c/o 112 Topsham Road, Exeter, EX2 4RW T: 01803 613336 T: 01392 256686 F: 01392 256689

The Old Plymouth Society 625 Budshead Road, Whitleigh, Plymouth, PL5 4DW

Thorverton & District History Society, Ferndale, Thorverton, Exeter, EX5 5NG T: 01392 860932

Wembury Amenity Society, 5 Cross Park Road, Wembury, Plymouth, PL9 OEU

Yelverton & District Local History Society, 4 The Coach House, Grenofen, Tavistock, PL19 9ES T: W: www.floyds.org.uk/ylhs

Dorset

Bournemouth Local Studies Group 6 Sunningdale, Fairway Drive, Christchurch, BH23 1JY T: 01202 485903 E: mbhall@onetel.net.uk

Bridport History Society 22 Fox Close, Bradpole, Bridport, DT6 3JF T: 01308 456876 E: celia@cgulls.fsnet.co.uk

Dorchester Association For Research into Local History, 7 Stokehouse Street, Poundbury, Dorchester, DT1 3GP

Dorset Natural History & Archaeological Society Dorset County Museum, High West Street, Dorchester, DT1 1XA T: 01305 262735 F: 01305 257180

Dorset Record Society Dorset County Museum, High West Street, Dorchester, DT1 1XA T: 01305-262735

Verwood Historical Society, 74 Lake Road, Verwood, BH31 6BX T: 01202 824175 E: trevorgilbert@hotmail.com W: www.geocities.com/verwood_historical

William Barnes Society, Pippins, 58 Mellstock Avenue, Dorchester, DT1 2BQ T: 01305 265358, William Barnes is primarily (but not exclusively) a Dorest Dialect Poet

Dorset - West

Bridport History Society, 22 Fox Close, Bradpole, Bridport, DT6 3JF T: 01308 456876 E: celia@cgulls.fsnet.co.uk

Durham

Elvet Local & Family History Groups, 37 Hallgarth Street, Durham, DH1 3AT T: 0191-386-4098 F: 0191-386-4098 E: Turnstone-Ventures@durham-city.freeserve.co.uk

Architectural & Archaeological Society of Durham & Northumberland, Broom Cottage, 29 Foundry Fielkds, Crook, DL15 9SY T: 01388 762620 E: belindaburke@aol.com

Durham County Local History Society 21 St Mary's Close, Tudoe Village, Spennymoor, DL16 6LR T: 01388 816209 E: johnbanham@tiscali.co.uk W: www.durhamweb.org.uk/dclhs

Durham Victoria County History Trust, Redesdale, The Oval, North Crescent, Durham, DH1 4NE T: 0191 384 8305 W: www.durhampast.net

Lanchester Local History Society, 11 St Margaret's Drive, Tanfield Village, Stanley, DH9 9QW T: 01207-236634 E: jstl@supanet.com

Monkwearmouth Local History Group, 75 Escallond Drive, Dalton Heights, Seaham, SR7 8JZ

North-East England History Institute (NEEHI), Department of History University of Durham, 43 North Bailey, Durham, DH1 3EX T: 0191-374-2004 F: 0191-374-4754 E: m.a.mcallister@durham.ac.uk W: http://www.durham.ac.uk/neehi.history/homepage.htm

St John Ambulance History Group, 3 The Bower, Meadowside, Jarrow, NE32 4RS T: 0191 537 4252

Teesdale Heritage Group, Wesley Terrace, Middleton in Teesdale, Barnard Castle, DL12 0Q T: 01833 641104

The Derwentdale Local History Society, 36 Roger Street, Blackhill, Consett, DH8 5SX

Tow Law History Society, 27 Attleee Estate, Tow Law, DL13 4LG T: 01388-730056 E: RonaldStorey@btinternet.co.uk W: www.historysociety.org.uk

Wheatley Hill History Club, Broadmeadows, Durham Road, Wheatley Hill, DH6 3LJ T: 01429 820813, Mobile 0781 112387 E: wheathistory@onet.co.uk W: http://mypages.comcast.net/dcock104433/HISTORY/index.htm

The 68th (or Durham) Regiment of Light Infantry Display Team see Cumbria

Essex

Barking & District Historical Society, 449 Ripple Road, Barking, IG11 9RB T: 020 8594 7381 E: barkinghistorical@hotmail.com Covers the London Borough of Barking and Dagenham

Barking & District Historical Society, 16 North Road, Chadwell Heath, Romford, RM6 6XU E: barkinghistorical@hotmail.com Postal and Email enquiries only

Billericay Archaeological and Historical Society, 24 Belgrave Road, Billericay, CM12 1TX T: 01277 658989

Brentwood & District Historical Society 51 Hartswood Road, Brentwood, CM14 5AG T: 01277 221637

Burnham & District Local History & Archaeological Society The Museum, The Quay, Burnham on Crouch, CM0 8AS

Colchester Archaeological Group, 172 Lexden Road, Colchester, CO3 4BZ T: 01206 575081 W: www.camulos.com//cag/cag.htm

Dunmow & District Historical and Literary Society, 18 The Poplars, Great Dunmow, CM6 2JA T: 01371 872496

Essex Archaeological & Historical Congress, 56 Armond Road, Witham, CM8 2HA T: 01376 516315 F: 01376 516315 E: essexahc@aol.com

Essex Historic Buildings Group, 12 Westfield Avenue, Chelmsford, CM1 1SF T: 01245 256102 F: 01371 830416 E: cakemp@hotmail.com

Essex Society for Archaeology & History 2 Landview Gardens, Ongar, CM5 9EQ T: 1277363106 E: family@leachies.freeserve.co.uk W: www.leachies.freeserve.co.uk

Friends of Historic Essex, 11 Milligans Chase, Galleywood, Chelmsford, CM2 8QD T: 01245 436043 F: 01245 257365 E: geraldine.willden2@essexcc.gov.uk

Friends of The Hospital Chapel - Ilford, 174 Aldborough Road South, Seven Kings, Ilford, IG3 8HF T: (020) 8590 9972 F: (020) 8590 0366

Halstead & District Local History Society, Magnolia, 3 Monklands Court, Halstead, CO9 1AB

(HEARS) Herts & Essex Architectural Research Society , 4 Nelmes Way, Hornchurch, RM11 2QZ T: 01708 473646 E: kpolrm11@aol.com

High Country History Group, Repentance Cottage, Drapers Corner, Greensted, Ongar, CM5 9LS T: 01277 364305 E: rob.brooks@virgin.net Covers the rural area of S W Ongar being the parishes of Greensted, Stanford Rivers, Stapleford Tawney and Theydon Mount

Ingatestone and Fryerning Historical and Archaeological Society 36 Pine Close, Ingatestone, CM4 9EG T: 01277 354001

Loughton & District Historical Society, 6 High Gables, Loughton, IG10 4EZ T: (020) 8508 4974

Maldon Society 15 Regency Court, Heybridge, Maldon, CM9 4EJ

Saffron Walden Historical Society 9 High Street, Saffron Walden, CB10 1AT

Nazeing History Workshop 16 Shooters Dr, Nazeing, EN9 2QD T: 01992 893264 E: d_pracy@hotmail.com W: www.eppingforectmuseum.co.uk/socvieties/php/NazeingHistoryWorkshop

Romford & District Historical Society 67 Gelsthorpe Road, Collier Row, Romford, RM5 2LX T: 01708 728203 E: caroline@wiggins67.freeserve.co.uk

The Colne Smack Preservation Society, 76 New Street, Brightlingsea, CO7 0DD T: 01206 304768 W: www.colne-smack-preservation.rest.org.uk

Thurrock Heritage Forum, c/o Thurrock Museum, Orsett Road, Grays, RM17 5DX T: 01375 673828 E: enquiries@thurrockheritageforum.co.uk W: www.thurrockheritageforum.co.uk

Thurrock Local History Society, 13 Rosedale Road, Little Thurrock, Grays, RM17 6AD T: 01375 377746 E: tcvs.tc@gtnet.gov.uk

Waltham Abbey Historical Society, 28 Hanover Court, Quaker Lane, Waltham Abbey, EN9 1HR T: 01992 716830

Walthamstow Historical Society, 24 Nesta Road, Woodford Green, IG8 9RG T: (020) 8504 4156 F: (020) 8523 2399

Wanstead Historical Soc 28 Howard Road, Ilford, IG1 2EX

Witham History Group, 35 The Avenue, Witham, CM8 2DN T: 01376 512566

Woodford Historical Society, 2 Glen Rise, Woodford Green, IG8 0AW

Gloucestershire

Bristol and Gloucestershire Archaeological Society 22 Beaumont Road, Gloucester, GL2 0EJ T: 01452 302610, david_j._h.smith@virgin.net W: http://www.bgas.org.uk, Calandar of Apprentice Registers of City of Gloucester 1595-1700

Campden & District Historical & Archaeological Society (CADWAS), The Old Police station, High Street, Chipping Campden, GL55 6HB T: 01386 848840 E: enquiries@chippingcampdenhistory.org.uk W: www.chippingcampdenhistory.org.uk

Charlton Kings Local History Society, 28 Chase Avenue, Charlton Kings, Cheltenham, GL52 6YU T: 01242 520492

Cheltenham Local History Society, 1 Turkdean Road, Cheltenham, GL51 6AP

Cirencester Archaeological and Historical Society 8 Tower Street, Cirencester, GL7 1EF T: 01285 651516 F: 01285 651516 E: dviner@waitrose.com

Forest of Dean Local History Society Patch Cottage, Oldcroft Green, Lydney, GL15 4NL T: 01594 563165 E: akear@patchcottage.freeserve.co.uk W: www.forestofdeanhistory.co.uk

Frenchay Tuckett Society and Local History Museum, 247 Frenchay Park Road, Frenchay, BS16 1LG T: 0117 956 9324 E: raybulmer@compuserve.com W: www.frenchay.org/museum.html

Friends of Gloucestershire Archives, 17 Estcourt Road, Gloucester, GL13LU T: 01452 528930 E: patricia.bath@talk21.com

Gloucestershire County Local History Committee, Gloucestershire RCC, Community House, 15 College Green, Gloucester, GL1 1LZ T: 01452 528491, Fax:, 01452-528493 E: glosrcc@grcc.org.uk

Lechlade History Society, The Gables, High Street, Lechlade, GL7 3AD T: 01367 252457 E: Gillkeithnewson.aol.com Archivist: Mrs Maureen Baxter Tel; 01367 252437

Leckhampton Local History Society 202 Leckhampton Road, Leckhampton, Cheltenham, GL53 OHG W: www.geocities.com/llhsgl53

Moreton-In-Marsh & District Local History Society, Chapel Place, Longborough, Moreton-In-Marsh, GL56 OQR T: 01451 830531 W: www.moretonhistory.co.uk

Newent Local History Society, Arron, Ross Road, Newent, GL18 1BE T: 01531 821398

Painswick Local History Society, Canton House, New Street, Painswick, GL6 6XH T: 01452 812419

Stroud Civic Society, Blakeford House, Broad Street, Kings Stanley, Stonehouse, GL10 3PN T: 01453 822498

Stroud Local History Society, Stonehatch, Oakridge Lynch, Stroud, GL6 7NR T: 01285 760460 E: john@loosleyj.freeserve.co.uk

Swindon Village Society, 3 Swindon Hall, Swindon Village, Cheltenham, GL51 9QR T: 01242 521723

Tewkesbury Historical Society 20 Moulder Road, Tewkesbury, GL20 8ED T: 01684 297871

Hampshire

Aldershot Historical and Archaeological Society, 10 Brockenhurst Road, Aldershot, GU11 3HH T: 01252 26589

Andover History and Archaeology Society, 140 Weyhill Road, Andover, SP1O 3BG T: 01264 324926 E: johnl.barrell@virgin.net

Basingstoke Archaeological and Historical Society, 57 Belvedere Gardens, Chineham, Basingstoke, RG21 T: 01256 356012

Bishops Waltham Museum Trust, 8 Folly Field, Bishop's Waltham, Southampton, S032 1EB T: 01489 894970

Bitterne Local History Society Heritage Centre, 225 Peartree Avenue, Bitterne, Southampton T: 023 8049 0948 W: www.bitterne.net

Botley & Curdridge Local History, 3 Mayfair Court, Botley, SO30 2GT

Fareham Local History Group Wood End Lodge, Wood End, Wickham, Fareham, PO17 6JZ W: www.cix.co.uk/~catisfield/farehist.htm

Fleet & Crookham Local History Group 33 Knoll Road, Fleet, GU51 4PT W: www.hants.gov.uk/fclhg

Fordingbridge Historical Society, 26 Lyster Road,, Manor Park, Fordingbridge, SP6 IQY T: 01425 655417

Hampshire Archives Trust 3 Scott-Paine Drive, Hythe, S045 6JY

Hampshire Field Club and Archaeological Society, 8 Lynch Hill Park, Whitchurch, RG28 7NF T: 01256 893241 E: jhamdeveson@compuserve.com W: www.fieldclub.hants.org.uk/

Hampshire Field Club & Archaeological Society (Local History Sect) c/o Hampshire Record Office, Sussex St, Winchester, SO23 8TH

Havant Museum, Havant Museum, 56 East Street, Havant, P09 1BS T: 023 9245 1155 F: 023 9249 8707 E: musmop@hants.gov.uk W: www.hants.gov.uk/museums Also Friends of Havant Museum - Local History Section Local Studies Collection open Tuesday to Saturday

Lymington & District Historical Society Larks Lees, Coxhill Boldre, Near Lymington, 5041 8PS T: 01590 623933 E: birchsj@clara.co.uk

Lyndhurst Historical Society - disbanded May 2003, Books and Documents handed into the New Forest Museum

Milford-on-Sea Historical Record Society, New House, New Road, Keyhaven, Lymington, S041 0TN

North East Hampshire Historical and Archaeological Society, 36 High View Road, Farnborough, GU14 7PT T: 01252-543023, E: nehhas@netscape.net W: www.hants.org.uk/nehhas

Parish Register Transcription Society, 50 Silvester Road, Waterlooville, PO8 5TL T: E: mail@prtsoc.org.uk W: www.prtsoc.org.uk

Porchester Society Mount Cottage, Nelson Lane, Portchester, PO17 6AW

Somborne & District Society, Forge House, Winchester Road, Kings Somborne, Stockbridge, SO20 6NY T: 01794 388742 E: w.hartley@ntlworld.com W: www.communigate.co.uk/hants/somsoc

South of England Costume Society , Bramley Cottage, 9 Vicarage Hill, Hartley Witney, Hook, RG27 8EH E: j.sanders@lineone.net

Southampton Local History Forum Special Collections Library, Civic Centre, Southampton, England T: 023 8083 2462 F: 023 8022 6305 E: local.studies@southampton.gov.uk

Southern Counties Costume Society, 173 Abbotstone, Alresford, SO24 9TE T:

Stubbington & Hillhead History Society, 34 Anker Lane, Stubbington, Fareham, PO14 3HE T: 01329 664554

Tadley and District History Soicty (TADS) PO Box 7642, Tadley, RG26 3AF T: 0118 981 4006W: www.tadhistorey.com

History of Thursley Society, 50 Wyke Lane, Ash, Aldershot, GU12 6EA E: norman.ratcliffe@ntlworld.com W: http://home.clara.net/old.norm/Thursley

West End Local History Society, 20 Orchards Way, West End, Southampton, S030 3FJ T: 023 8057 5244 E: westendlhs@aol.com W: www.telbin.demon.co.uk/westendlhs, Museum at Old Fire Station, High Street, West End

Herefordshire

Eardisland Oral History Group, Eardisland, Leominster E: info@eardislandhistory.co.uk W: www.eardislandhistory.co.uk

Ewyas Harold & District WEA, c/o Hillside, Ewyas Harold, Hereford, HR2 0HA T: 01981 240529

Kington History Society, Kington Library, 64 Bridge Street, Kington, HR5 3BD T: 01544 230427 E: vee.harrison@virgin.net

Leominster Historical Society Fircroft, Hereford Road, Leominster, HR6 8JU T: 01568 612874

Weobley & District Local History Society and Museum Weobley Museum, Back Lane, Weobley, HR4 8SG T: 01544 340292

Hertfordshire

1st or Grenadier Foot Guards 1803 -1823 - Napoleonic Wars, 39 Chatterton, Letchworth, SG6 2JY T: 01462-670918 E: BJCham2809@aol.com W: http://members.aol.com/BJCham2809/homepage.html

Abbots Langley Local History Society, 19 High street, Abbots Langley, WD5 0AA E: allhs@btinternet.com W: http://www.allhs.btinternet.co.uk

Abbots Langley Local History Society, 159 Cottonmill Lane, St Albans, AL1 2EX

Baptist Historical Society, 60 Strathmore Avenue, Hitchin, SG5 1ST T: 01462-431816 T: 01462-442548 E: slcopson@dial.pipex.com W: www.baptisthistory.org.uk

Barnet & District Local History Society 31 Wood Street, Barnet, EN4 9PA

Black Sheep Research (Machine Breakers, Rioters & Protesters), 4 Quills, Letchworth Garden City, SG6 2RJ T: 01462-483706 E: J_M_Chambers@compuserve.com

Braughing Local History Society, Pantiles, Braughing Friars, Ware, SG11 2NS

Codicote Local History Society, 34 Harkness Way, Hitchin, SG4 0QL T: 01462 622953

East Herts Archaeological Society, 1 Marsh Lane, Stanstead Abbots, Ware, SG12 8HH T: 01920 870664

The Harpenden & District Local History Society The History Centre, 19 Arden Grove, Harpenden, AL5 4SJ T: 01582 713539

Hertford Museum (Hertfordshire Regiment), 18 Bull Plain, Hertford, SG14 1DT T: 01992 552100 F: 01992 534797 E: enquiries@hertfordmuseum.org W: www.hertfordmuseum.org

Hertford & Ware Local History Society, 10 Hawthorn Close, Hertford, SG14 2DT

Hertfordshire Archaeological Trust, The Seed Warehouse, Maidenhead Yard, The Wash, Hertford, SG14 1PX T: 01992 558 170 F: 01992 553359 E: herts.archtrust@virgin.net W: www.hertfordshire-archaeological-trust.co.uk

Hertfordshire Association for Local History c/o 64 Marshals Drive, St Albans, AL1 4RF T: 01727 856250 E: ClareEllis@compuserve.com

Hertfordshire Record Society 119 Winton Drive, Croxley Green, Rickmansworth, WD3 3QS T: 01923-248581 E: info@hrsociety.org.uk W: www.hrsociety.org.uk

Hitchin Historical Society, c/o Hitchin Museum, Paynes Park, Hitchin, SG5 2EQ

Kings Langley Local History & Museum Society Kings Langley Library, The Nap, Kings Langley, WD4 8ET T: 01923 263205 E: frankdavies4@hotmail.com alan@penwardens.freeserve.co.uk W: www.kingslangley.org.uk

London Colney Local History Society, 51A St Annes Road, London Colney St. Albans, AL2 1PD

North Mymms Local History Society 89 Peplins Way, Brookmans Park, Hatfield, AL9 7UT T: 01707 655970 W: www.brookmans.com

Rickmansworth Historical Society 20 West Way, Rickmansworth, WD3 7EN T: 01923 774998 E: geoff@gmsaul.freeserve.co.uk, Search service for Rickmansworth (old Parish area) - militia lists, census, baptisms, marriage & burials, from 1700 app to 1st World War; Watford Observer quotes to 100 years ago

Royston & District Local History Society, 8 Chilcourt, Royston, SG8 9DD T: 01763 242677 E: david.allard@ntlworld.com W: www.royston.clara.net/localhistory

South West Hertfordshire Archaeological and Historical Society 29 Horseshoe Lane, Garston, Watford, WD25 0LN T: 01923 672482

St. Albans & Herts Architectural & Archaeological Society 24 Rose Walk, St Albans, AL4 9AF T: 01727 853204

The Harpenden & District Local History Society, The History Centre, 19 Arden Grove, Harpenden, AL5 4SJ T: 01582 713539

Welwyn Archaeological Society, The Old Rectory, 23 Mill Lane, Welwyn, AL6 9EU T: 01438 715300 F: 01438 715300 E: tony.rook@virgin.net

Welwyn & District Local History Society, 40 Hawbush Rise, Welwyn, AL6 9PP T: 01438 716415 E: p.jiggens-keen@virgin.net W: www.welwynhistory.org

Hull

Yorkshire Quaker Heritage Project Brynmore Jones Library, University of Hull, Hull, HU6 7RX

Isle of Wight

Isle of Wight Natural History & Archaeological Society, Salisbury Gardens, Dudley Road, Ventnor, PO38 1EJ T: 01983 855385

Newchurch Parish Register Society 1 Mount Pleasant, Newport Road, Sandown, PO36 OLS

Roots Family & Parish History - Disbanded 2003,

St. Helens History Society, c/o The Castle, Duver Road, St Helens, Ryde, PO33 1XY T: 01983 872164

Kent

Appledore Local History Society, 72 The Street, Appledore, Ashford, TN26 2AE T: 01233 758500 F: 01233 758500 E: trothfw@aol.com

Ashford Archaeological and Historical Society, Gablehook Farm, Bethersden, Ashford, TN26 3BQ T: 01233 820679,

Aylesford Society, 30 The Avenue, Greenacres, Aylesford, Maidstone, ME20 7LE

Bearsted & District Local History Society, 17 Mount Lane, Bearsted, Maidstone, ME14 4DD

Bexley Civic Society, 58 Palmeira Road, Bexleyheath, DA7 4UX

Bexley Historical Society, 36 Cowper Close, Welling, DAI6 2JT

Biddenden Local History Society, Willow Cottage, Smarden Road, Biddenden, Ashford, TN27 8JT

Brenchley & Matfield Local History Society, Ashendene, Tong Road, Brenchley, Tonbridge, TN12 7HT T: 01892 723476

Bridge & District History Soc, La Dacha, Patrixbourne Road, Bridge, Canterbury, CT4 5BL

Broadstairs Soc, 30 King Edward Avenue, Broadstairs, CT10 lPH T: 01843 603928 E: mike@termites.fsnet.co.uk

Bromley Borough Local History Soc, 62 Harvest Bank Road, West Wickham, BR4 9DJ T: 020 8462 5002

Canterbury Archaeology Soc, Dane Court, Adisham, Canterbury, CT3 3LA E: jeancrane@tiscali.co.uk

Charing & District Local History Soc, Old School House, Charing, Ashford, TN27 0LS

Chatham Historical Soc, 69 Ballens Road, Walderslade, Chatham, ME5 8NX T: 01634 865176

Council for Kentish Archaeology, 3 Westholme, Orpington, BR6 0AN E: information@the-cka.fsnet.co.uk W: www.the-cka.fsnet.co.uk

Cranbrook & District History Soc, 61 Wheatfield Way, Cranbrook, TN17 3NE

Crayford Manor House Historical and Archaeological Soc, 17 Swanton Road, Erith, DA8 1LP T: 01322 433480

Dartford History & Antiquarian Soc, 14 Devonshire Avenue, Dartford, DA1 3DW T: F: 01732 824741

Deal & Walmer Local History Soc, 7 Northcote Road, Deal, CT14 7BZ T:

Detling Society., 19 Hockers Lane, Detling, Maidstone, ME14 3JL T: 01622 737940 F: 01622 737408 E: johnowne@springfield19.freeserve.co.uk

Dover History Soc, 2 Courtland Drive, Kearsney, Dover, CT16 3BX T: 01304 824764

East Peckham Historical Soc, 13 Fell Mead, East Peckham, Tonbridge, TNI2 5EG

Edenbridge & District History Soc, 17 Grange Close, Edenbridge, TN8 5LT

Erith & Belvedere Local History Soc, 67 Merewood Road, Barnehurst, DA7 6PF

Farningham & Eynsford Local History Soc, Lavender Hill, Beesfield Lane, Farningham, Dartford, DA4 ODA

Faversham Society 10-13 Preston St, Faversham, ME13 8NS T: 01795 534542 F: 01795 533261 E: faversham@btinternet.com W: http://www.faversham.org CC accepted.

Fawkham & District Historical Soc, The Old Rectory, Valley Road, Fawkham, Longfield, DA3 8LX

Folkestone & District Local History Soc, 7 Shorncliffe Crescent, Folkestone

Friends of Lydd 106 Littlestone Rd New Romney TN28 8NH

Frittenden History Soc, Bobbyns, The Street, Frittenden, Cranbrook, TN17 2DG T: 01580 852459 F: 01580 852459

Gillingham & Rainham Local History Soc, 23 Sunningdale Road, Rainham, Gillingham, ME8 9EQ

Goudhurst & Kilndown Local History Soc, 2 Weavers Cottages, Church Road, Goudhurst, TN17 1BL

Gravesend Historical Soc, 58 Vicarage Lane, Chalk, Gravesend, DA12 4TE T: 01474 363998 W: www.ghs.org.uk Encompassess Northfleet and surrounding Parishes in 'The Gravesham Borough Council Area'

Great Chart Soc, Swan Lodge, The Street, Great Chart, Ashford, TN23 3AH

Hadlow History Soc, Spring House, Tonbridge Road, Hadlow, Tonbridge, TN11 0DZ T: 01732 850214 E: billanne@hadlow12.freeserve.co.uk

Halling Local History Soc, 58 Ladywood Road, Cuxton, Rochester, ME2 1EP T: 01634 716139

Hawkhurst Local History Soc, 17 Oakfield, Hawkhurst, Cranbrook, TN18 4JR T: 01580 752376 E: vcw@lessereagles.freeserve.co.uk

Headcorn Local History Soc, Cecil Way, 2 Forge Lane, Headcorn, TN27 9QQ T: 01622 890253 W: www.headcorn.org.uk

Herne Bay Historical Records Soc, c/o Herne Bay Museum, 12 William St, Herne Bay, CT6 5EJ

Higham Village History Group, Forge House, 84 Forge Lane, Higham, Rochester, ME3 7AH

Horton Kirby & South Darenth Local History Soc, Appledore, Rays Hill, Horton Kirby, Dartford, DA4 9DB T: 01322 862056

Hythe Civic Soc, 25 Napier Gardens, Hythe, CT2l 6DD
Isle of Thanet Historical Soc, 58 Epple Bay Avenue, Birchington on Sea
Kemsing Historical & Art Soc, 26 Dippers Close, Kemsing, Sevenoaks, TN15 6QD T: 01732 761774
Kent Archaeological Rescue Unit, Roman Painted House, New Street, Dover, CTl7 9AJ T: 01304 203279 T: 020 8462 4737 F: 020 8462 4737 W: www.the-cka.fsnet.co.uk
The Kent Archaeological Society Three Elms, Woodlands Lane, Shorne, Gravesend, DA12 3HH T: 01474 822280 E: secretary@kentarchaeology.org.uk W: www.kentarchaeology.org.uk
Kent History Federation 14 Valliers Wood Rd, Sidcup, DA15 8BG
Kent Mills Group, Windmill Cottage, Mill Lane, Willesborough, TN27 0QG
Kent Postal History Group, 27 Denbeigh Drive, Tonbridge, TN10 3PW
Lamberhurst L H S, 1 Tanyard Cotts, The Broadway, Lamberhurst, Tunbridge Wells, TN3 8DD
Lamorbey & Sidcup Local History Soc, 14 Valliers Wood Road, Sidcup, DA15 8BG
Legion of Frontiersmen of Commonwealth, 4 Edwards Road, Belvedere, DA17 5AL
Leigh and District History Soc, Elizabeths Cottage, The Green, Leigh, Tonbridge, TN11 8QW T: 01732 832459
Lewisham Local History Soc, 2 Bennett Park, Blackheath Village, London, SE3 9RB E: tom@trshepherd.fsnet.co.uk
Loose Area History Soc, 16 Bedgebury Cl, Maidstone, ME14 5QY
Lyminge Historical Soc, Ash Grove, Canterbury Road, Etchinghill, Folkestone, CTl8 8DF
Maidstone Area Archaeological Group, 40 Bell Meadow, Maidstone, Kent ME15 9ND
Maidstone Historical Society 37 Bower Mount Road, Maidstone, ME16 8AX T: 01622 676472
Margate Civic Soc, 19 Lonsdale Avenue, Cliftonville, Margate, CT9 3BT
Meopham Historical Soc, Tamar, Wrotham Road, Meopham, DA13 0EX
Orpington History Soc, 42 Crossway, Petts Wood, Orpington, BR5 1PE
Otford & District History Soc, Thyme Bank, Coombe Road, Otford, Sevenoaks, TNl4 5RJ
Otham Soc, Tudor Cottage, Stoneacre Lawn, Otham, Maidstone, ME15 8RT
Paddock Wood History Soc, 19 The Greenways, Paddock Wood, Tonbridge, TNl2 6LS
Plaxtol Local History Group, Tebolds, High Street, Plaxtol, Sevenoaks, TN15 0QJ
Rainham Historical Soc, 52 Northumberland Avenue, Rainham, Gillingham, ME8 7JY
Ramsgate Soc, Mayfold, Park Road, Ramsgate, CT11 7QH
Ringwould History Soc, Back Street, Ringwould, Deal, CT14 8HL T: 01304 361030 T: 01304 380083 E: julie.m.rayner@talk21.com jeanwinn@beeb.net W: www.ringwould-village.org.uk
Romney Marsh Research Trust, 11 Caledon Terrace, Canterbury, CT1 3JS T: 01227 472490 E: s.m.sweetinburgh@kent.ac.uk W: www.kent.ac.uk/mts/rmrt/
Rye Local History Group, 107 Military Road, Rye, TN31 7NZ
Sandgate Soc, The Old Fire Station, 51 High Street, Sandgate, CT20 3AH
Sandwich Local History Soc, Clover Rise, 14 Stone Cross Lees, Sandwich, CT13 OBZ T: 01304 613476 E: frankandrews@FreeNet.co.uk
Sevenoaks Historical Soc, 122 Kippington Road, Sevenoaks, TN13 2LN E: wilkospin@beeb.net
Sheppey Local History Soc, 34 St Helens Road, Sheerness
Shoreham & District Historical Soc, The Coach House, Darenth Hulme, Shoreham, TNl4 7TU
Shorne Local History Group, 2 Calderwood, Gravesend, DAl2 4Q11
Sittingbourne Soc, 4 Stanhope Avenue, Sittingbourne, ME10 4TU T: 01795 473807 F: 01795 473807 E: mandbmoore@tinyonline.co.uk
Smarden Local History Soc, 7 Beult Meadow, Cage Lane, Smarden, TN27 8PZ T: 01233 770 856 F: 01233 770 856 E: franlester@fish.co.uk
Snodland Historical Soc, 214 Malling Road, Snodland, ME6 SEQ E: aa0060962@blueyonder.co.uk W: www.snodlandhistory.org.uk
St Margaret's Bay History Soc, Rock Mount, Salisbury Road, St Margarets Bay, Dover, CT15 6DL T: 01304 852236
Staplehurst Soc, Willow Cottage, Chapel Lane, Staplehurst, TN12 0AN T: 01580 891059 E: awcebd@mistral.co.uk
Tenterden & District Local History Soc, Little Brooms, Ox Lane, St Michaels, Tenterden, TN30 6NQ
Teston History Soc, Broad Halfpenny, Malling Road, Teston, Maidstone, ME18 SAN
Thanet Retired Teachers Association , 85 Percy Avenue, Kingsgate, Broadstairs, CT10 3LD
The Marden Soc, 6 Bramley Court, Marden, Tonbridge, TN12 9QN T: 01622 831904 W: www.marden.org.uk

Three Suttons Soc, Henikers, Henikers Lane, Sutton Valence, ME17 3EE T:
Tonbridge History Society 8 Woodview Crescent, Hildenborough, Tonbridge, TN11 9HD T: 01732 838698 E: s.broomfield@dial.pipex.com
Wateringbury Local History Soc, Vine House , 234 Tonbridge Road, Wateringbury, ME18 5NY
Weald History Group, Brook Farm, Long Barn Road, Weald, Sevenoaks
Wealden Buildings Study Group, 64 Pilgrims Way, East Otford, Sevenoaks, TN14 5QW
Whitstable History Soc, 83 Kingsdown Park, Tankerton, Whitstable
Wingham Local History Soc, 67 High Street, Wingham, Canterbury, CT3 1AA
Woodchurch Local History Soc, Woodesden, 24 Front Road, Woodclnurch, Ashford, TN26 3QE
Wrotham Historical Soc, Hillside House, Wrotham, TN15 7JH
Wye Historical Soc, I Upper Bridge Street, Wye, Ashford, TN2 5 SAW

Lancashire

Aspull and Haigh Historical Soc, 1 Tanpit Cottages, Winstanley, Wigan, WN3 6JY T: 01942 222769
Blackburn Civic Soc, 20 Tower Road, Blackburn, BB2 5LE T: 01254 201399
Burnley Historical Society 66 Langdale Road, Blackburn, BB2 5DW T: 01254 201162
Centre for North West Regional Studies, Fylde College, Lancaster University, Lancaster, LA1 4YF T: 01524 593770 F: 01524 594725 E: christine.wilkinson@lancaster.ac.uk W: www.lancs.ac.uk/users/cnwrs
Chadderton Historical Soc, 18 Moreton Street, Chadderton, 0L9 OLP T: 0161 652 3930 E: enid@chadderton-hs.freeuk.com W: http://www.chadderton-hs.freeuk.com
Ewecross History Soc, Gruskholme, Bentham, Lancaster, LA2 7AX T: 015242 61420
Fleetwood & District Historical Society 54 The Esplanade, Fleetwood, FY7 6QE
Friends of Smithills Hall Museum, Smithills Hall, Smithills Deane Road, Bolton, BL1 7NP
Garstang Historical & Archaelogical Soc, 7 Rivermead Drive, Garstang, PR3 1JJ T: 01995 604913 E: marian.fish@btinternet.com
Holme & District Local History Soc, The Croft, Tanpits Lane, Burton, Carnforth, LA6 1HZ T: 01524 782121
Hyndburn Local History Soc, 20 Royds Avenue, Accrington, BB5 2LE T: 01254 235511
Lancashire & Cheshire Antiquarian Society 59 Malmesbury Road, Cheadle Hulme, SK8 7QL T: 0161 439 7202 E: morris.garratt@lineone.net W: www.lancashirehistory.co.uk www.cheshirehistory.org.uk
Lancashire Family History and Heraldry Society 21 Baytree Road, Clayton le Woods, PR6 7JW W: www.lfhhs.org.uk
Lancashire Local History Federation, 25 Trinity Court, Cleminson Street, Salford, M3 6DX E: secretary@lancashirehistory.co.uk W: www.lancashirehistory.co.uk
Lancashire Parish Register Soc, 135 Sandy Lane, Orford, Warrington, WA2 9JB E: tom_obrien@bigfoot.com W: http://www.genuki.org.uk/big/eng/LAN/lprs
Lancaster Military Heritage Group, 19 Middleton Road, Overton, Morecombe, LA3 1HB
Leyland Historical Soc, 172 Stanifield Lane, Farington, Leyland, Preston, PR5 2QT
Littleborough Historical and Archaeological Soc, 8 Springfield Avenue, Littleborough, LA15 9JR T: 01706 377685
Mourholme Local History Soc, The Croft, Croftlands, Warton, Carnforth, LA5 9PY T: 01524 734110 E: nt.stobbs@virgin.net
Nelson Local History Soc, 5 Langholme Street, Nelson, BB9 0RW T: 01282 699475
North West Sound Archive, Old Steward's Office, Clitheroe Castle, Clitheroe, BB7 1AZ T: 01200-427897 E: nwsa@ed.lancscc.gov.uk W: www.lancashire.gov.uk/education/lifelong/recordindex
Saddleworth Historical Soc, 7 Slackcote, Delph, Oldham, OL3 5TW T: 01457 874530
Society for Name Studies in Britain & Ireland, 22 Peel Park Avenue, Clitheroe, BB7 1ET T: 01200-423771 F: 01200-423771
Urmston District Local History Soc, 78 Mount Drive, Urmston, Manchester, M41 9QA

Leicestershire

Desford & District Local History Group, Lindridge House, Lindridge Lane, Desford, LE9 9FD T: 01455 824514 E: jshepherd@freeuk.com
East Leake & District Local History Soc, 8 West Leake Road, East Leake, Loughborough, LE12 6LJ T: 01509 852390
Glenfield and Western Archaeological and Historical Group, 50 Chadwell Road, Leicester, LE3 6LF T: 1162873220
Great Bowden Historical Society 14 Langdon Road, Market Harborough, LE16 7EZ

Leicestershire Archaeological & Historical Society The Guildhall, Leicester, LE1 5FQ T: 0116 270 3031: E: alan@dovedale2.demon.co.uk W: www.le.ac.uk/archaeology/lahs/lahs.html
Sutton Bonington Local History Soc, 6 Charnwood Fields, Sutton Bonington, Loughborough, LE12 5NP T: 01509 673107
Vaughan Archaeological and Historical Soc, c/o Vaughan College, St Nicholas Circle, Leicester, LE1 4LB

Lincolnshire
Lincoln Record Society Cathedral Library, The Cathedral, Lincoln, LN2 1PZ T: 01522 544544 E: librarian@lincolncathedral.com W: www.lincolncathedral.com
Long Bennington Local History Soc, Kirton House, Kirton Lane, Long Bennington, Newark, NG23 5DX T: 01400 281726
Society for Lincolnshire History & Archaeology, Jews' Court, Steep Hill, Lincoln, LN2 1LS T: 01522-521337 F: 01522 521337 E: slha@lincolnshirepast.org.uk W: www.lincolnshirepast.org.uk
Tennyson Soc, Central Library, Free School Lane, Lincoln, LN2 1EZ T: 01522-552862 E: linnet@lincolnshire.gov.uk W: www.tennysonsociety.org.uk

London
Acton History Group 30 Highlands Avenue, London, W3 6EU T: (020) 8992 8698
Birkbeck College, Birkbeck College, Malet Street, London, WC1E 7HU T: (020) 7631 6633 F: (020) 7631 6688 E: info@bbk.ac.uk W: www.bbl.ac.uk
Brentford & Chiswick Local History Society 25 Hartington Road, London, W4 3TL
Brixton Society 82 Mayall Road, Brixton, SE24 0PJ T: (020) 7207 0347 F: (020) 7207 0347 E: apiperbrix@aol.com W: www.brixtonsociety.org.uk
Centre for Metropolitan History, Institute of Historical Research, Senate House, Malet Street, London, WC1E 7HU T: (020) 7862 8790 F: (020) 7862 8793 E: olwen.myhill@sas.ac.uk W: www.history.ac.uk/cmh/cmh.main.html
Croydon Local Studies Forum, c/o Local Studies Library, Catherine Street, Croydon, CR9 1ET T:
Croydon Local Studies Forum, Flat 2, 30 Howard Road, South Norwood, London, SE25 5BY T: (020) 8654-6454
East London History Soc, 42 Campbell Road, Bow, London, E3 4DT T: 020 8980 5672 E: elhs@mernicks.com W: www.eastlondon.org.uk
Fulham And Hammersmith Historical Soceity, Flat 12, 43 Peterborough Road, Fulham, London, SW6 3BT T: (020) 7731 0363 E: mail@fhhs.org.uk W: www.fhhs.org.uk
Fulham & Hammersmith History Soc, 85 Rannoch Road, Hammersmith, London, W6 9SX
The Garden History Society 70 Cowcross Street, London, EC1M 6EJ T: (020) 7608 2409 F: (020) 7490 2974 E: enquiries@gardenhistorysociety.org W: www.gardenhistorysociety.org
Hendon & District Archaeological Society 13 Reynolds Close, London, NW11 7EA T: (020) 8458 1352 F: (020) 8731 9882 E: denis@netmatters.co.uk W: www.hadas.org.uk
Hornsey Historical Society The Old Schoolhouse, 136 Tottenham Lane, London, N8 7EL T: (020) 8348 8429 W: www.hornseyhistorical.org.uk
London & Middlesex Archaeological Society Placements Office, University of North London, 62-66 Highbury Grove, London, N5 2AD
London Record Society c/o Institute of Historical Research, Senate House, Malet Street, London, WC1E 7HU T: (020) 7862-8798 F: (020) 7862 8793 E: heathercreaton@sas.ac.uk W: http://www.ihrininfo.ac.uk/cmh
Mill Hill Historical Society 41 Victoria Road, Mill Hill, London, NW7 4SA T: (020) 8959 7126
Newham History Soc, 52 Eastbourne Road, East Ham, London, E6 6AT T: (020) 8471 1171 W: www.pewsey.net/newhamhistory.htm
Paddington Waterways and Maida Vale Society (Local History), 19a Randolph Road, Maida Vale, London, W9 1AN T: 020 7289 0950
Royal Arsenal Woolwich Historical Soc, Main Guard House, Royal Arsenal Woolwich, Woolwich, London, SE18 6ST E: royalarsenal@talk21.com W: http://members.lycos.co.uk/RoyalArsenal
Royal Society of Chemistry Library & Information Centre Burlington House, Piccadilly, London, W1J 0BA T: (020) 7440 3376 F: (020) 7287 9798 E: library@rsc.org W: www.rsc.org, Records and information on the history of chemistry and obituary notices on RSC members
The Peckham Soc, 6 Everthorpe Road, Peckham, London, SE15 4DA T: (020) 8693 9412
The Vauxhall Soc 20 Albert Square, London, SW8 1BS
Walthamstow Historical Soc, 24 Nesta Road, Woodford Green, IG8 9RG T: (020) 8504 4156 F: (020) 8523 2399

Wandsworth Historical Society 31 Hill Court, Putney Hill, London, SW15 6BB, Covers the areas of Balham, Southfields, Tooting, Wandsworth, Roehampton, Earlsfield, Putney, Battersea
Willesden Local History Society (London Borough of Brent), 9 Benningfield Gardens, Berkhamstead, HP4 2GW T: 01442 878477, Covers the parishes of Cricklewood, Willesden, Kilburn, Park Royal, Harlesden, Neasden, Park Royal & Kensal Rise
Victorian Soc, 1 Priory Gardens, Bedford Park, London, W4 1TT T: (020) 8994 1019 F: (020) 8747 5899 E: admin@victorian-society.org.uk W: http://www.victorian-society.org.uk CC accepted

Manchester
Denton Local History Society 94 Edward Street, Denton, Manchester, M34 3BR
Stretford Local History Society 26 Sandy Lane, Stretford, Manchester, M32 9DA T: 0161 283 9434 E: mjdawson@cwcom.net W: www.stretfordlhs.cwc.net

Merseyside
Birkdale & Ainsdale Historical Research Soc, 20 Blundell Drive, Birkdale, Southport, PR8 4RG W: www.harrop.co.uk/bandahrs
Friends of Williamson's Tunnels, 15-17 Chatham Place, Edge Hill, Liverpool, L7 3HD T: 0151 475 9833 F: 0151 475 9833 E: info@williamsontunnels.com W: www.williamsontunnels.com To ensure the preservation of the mysterious 19th century labyrinth under Liverpool and to further understanding of the life and times of its creator Joseph Williamson (1769 - 1840)
Historic Society of Lancashire & Cheshire see Cheshire
The Guild of Merseyside Historians and Tourist Guides 49 Parkhill Road, Prenton, Birkenhead, L42 9JD T: 0151 608 3769
Liverpool Historical Society 46 Stanley Avenue, Rainford, WA11 8HU E: liverpoolhistsoc@merseymail.com W: www.liverpoolhistorysociety.merseyside.org
Maghull and Lydiate Local History Soc, 15 Brendale Avenue, Maghull, Liverpool, L31 7AX
Merseyside Archaeological Soc, 20 Osborne Road, Formby, Liverpool, L37 6AR T: 01704 871802
Society of Cirplanologists, 26 Roe Cross Green, Mottram, Hyde, SK14 6LP T: 01457 7634857

Middlesex
Borough of Twickenham Local History Soc, 258 Hanworth Road, Hounslow, TW3 3TY E: pbarnfield@post.com
British Deaf History Soc, 288 Bedfont Lane, Feltham, TW14 9NU E: bdhs@iconic.demon.co.uk
Edmonton Hundred Historical Society Local History Unit, Southgate Town Hall, Green Lanes, London, N13 4XD T: (020) 8379 2724, Covers Tottenham, Wood Green, Palmers Green, Winchmore Hill, and Southgate (All London Postal Districts besides Enfield and Muken Hadley)
Hoouslow Chronicle, 142 Guildford Avenue, Feltham, TW13 4E
Hounslow & District History Soc, 16 Orchard Avenue, Heston, TW5 0DU T: (020) 8570 4264
Middlesex Heraldry Soc, 4 Croftwell, Harpeden, AL5 1JG T: 01582 766372
Northwood & Eastcote Local History Soc, 3 Elbridge Close, Ruislip, HA4 7XA T: 01895 637134 W: www.rnelhs.flyer.co.uk
Pinner Local History Society 8 The Dell, Pinner, HA5 3EW T: (020) 8866 1918 E: mwg@pinnerlhs.freeserve.co.uk W: www.pinnerlhs.freeserve.co.uk/index.html
Ruislip Northwood & Eastcote Local History Society 3 Elmbridge Close, Ruislip, HA4 7XA T: 01895 637134 E: www.rnelhs.flyer.co.uk
Sunbury and Shepperton Local History Society 30 Lindsay Drive, Shepperton, TW17 88JU T: 01932 226776 E: H.L.Brooking@eggconnect.net W: http://users.eggconnect.net/h.l.brooking/sslhs

Norfolk
Blakeney Area Historical Society 2 Wiveton Road, Blakeney, NR25 7NJ T: 01263 741063
Federation of Norfolk Historical & Archaeological Organisations 14 Beck Lane, Horsham St Faith, Norwich, NR10 3LD
Feltwell (Historical and Archaeological) Soc, 16 High Street, Feltwell, Thetford, IP26 4AF T: 01842 828448 E: peterfeltwell@tinyworld.co.uk The Museum is at The Beck, Feltwell Open Tuesday & Saturday April to September 2.00.p.m. to 4.00.p.m.
Holt History Group 6 Kelling Close, Holt, NR23 6RU
Narborough Local History Society 101 Westfields, Narborough, Kings Lynn, PE32 ISY W: www.narboroughaerodrome.org.uk, Narborough Aerodrome 1915-1919 ongoing research - Narborough Airfield Research group. Over 1000 names of Officers Men & Women who served at Narborough. 15 Military graves
Norfolk and Norwich Archaeological Soc, 30 Brettingham Avenue, Cringleford, Norwich, NR4 6XG T: 01603 455913
Norfolk Archaeological and Historical Research Group 50 Cotman Road, Norwich, NR1 4AH T: 01603 435470

Norfolk Heraldry Soc, 26c Shotesham Road, Poringland, Norwich, NR14 7LG T: 01508 493832 F: 01508 493832 W: www.norfolkheraldry.co.uk
Norfolk Record Society 17 Christchurch Road, Norwich, NR2 2AE

Northamptonshire
Bozeat Historical and Archaeological Soc, 44 Mile Street, Bozeat, NN9 7NB T: 01933 663647
Brackley & District History Society 32 Church Lane, Evenley, Brackley, NN13 5SG T: 01280 703508
Higham Chichele Soc, 3 Bramley Close, Rushden, NN10 6RL
Houghtons & Brafield History, 5 Lodge Road, Little Houghton, NN7 IAE
Irchester Parish Historical Soc, 80 Northampton Road, Wellingborough, NN8 3HT T: 01933 274880 F: 01933 274888 W: www.irchester.org www.iphs.org.uk
Northamptonshire Association for Local History 6 Bakers Lane, Norton, Daventry, NN11 5EL T: 01327 312850 E: enquiries@northants-history.org.uk W: www.northants-history.org.uk
Northamptonshire Record Society Wootton Park Hall, Northampton, NN4 8BQ T: 01604 762297
Oundle Historical Soc, 13 Lime Avenue, Oundle, Peterborough, PE8 4PT
Rushden & District History Soc, 25 Byron Crescent, Rushden, NN10 6BL E: rdhs.rushden@virgin.net W: www.rdhs.org.uk
Weedon Bec History Soc, 35 Oak Street, Weedon, Northampton, NN7 4RR
West Haddon Local History Group, Bramley House, 12 Guilsborough Road, West Haddon, NN6 7AD T:

Northumberland
Felton & Swarland L H Soc, 23 Benlaw Grove, Felton, Morpeth, NE65 9NG T: 01670 787476 E: petercook@felton111.freeserve.co.uk
Hexham Local History Society Dilstone, Burswell Villas, Hexham, NE46 3LD T: 01434 603216
Morpeth Antiquarian Soc, 9 Eden Grove, Morpeth, NE61 2EN T: 01670 514792 E: hudson.c@virgin.net W: www.morpethnet.co.uk
Morpeth Nothumbrian Gathering, Westgate House, Dogger Bank, Morpeth, NE61 1RF
Friends of War Memorials Bilsdale, Ulgham, Morpeth, NE61 3AR T: 01670 790465 E: gjb@bilsdale.frecserve.co.uk
Northumbrian Language Society Westgate House, Dogger Bank, Morpeth, NE61 1RE T: 01670 513308 E: kim@northumbriana.org.uk W: www.northumbriana.org.uk
Prudhoe & District Local History Soc, Prudhoe Community Enterprise Office, 82 Front Street, Prudhoe, NE42 5PU
Stannington Local History Society Glencar House, 1 Moor Lane, Stannington, Morpeth, NE61 6EA
The Ponteland Local History Soc, Woodlands, Prestwick Village, Ponteland, NE20 9TX T: 01661 824017 E: jmichaeltaylor@talk21.com W: www.ponthistsoc.freeuk.com

Nottinghamshire
Epperstone History Soc, Sunny Mead, Main Street, Epperstone, NG14 6AG
Basford & District Local History Soc, 44 Cherry Tree Close, Bucinsley, Nottingham, NG16 5BA T: 0115 927 2370
Beeston & District Local History Soc, 16 Cumberland Avenue, Beeston, NG9 4DH T: 0115 922 3008
Bingham & District Local History Soc, 56 Nottingham Road, Bingham, NG13 8AT T: 01949 875866
Bleasby Local History Soc, 5 Sycamore Lane, Bleasby, NG14 7GJ T: 01636 830094
Bulwell Historical Soc, 19 Woodland Avenue, Bulwell, Nottingham, NG6 9BY T: 0115 927 9519
Burton Joyce and Bulcote Local History Soc, 9 Carnarvon Drive, Burton Joyce, Nottingham, NG14 5ER T: 0115 931 3669
Caunton Local History Soc, Beech House, Caunton, Newark, NG23 6AF T: 01636 636564
Chinemarelian Soc, 3 Main Street, Kimberley, NG16 2NL T: 0115 945 9306, covers Kimberley
Cotgrave Local History Soc, 81 Owthorpe Road, Cotgrave, NG T: 0115 989 2115
East Midlands Historian School of Continuing Education, Nottingham University, University Park, Nottingham, NG7 2RD T: 0115 951 4398 F: 0115 846 6477 E: susan.clayton@nottingham.ac.uk
Eastwood Historical Soc, 18 Park Crescent, Eastwood , NG16 3DU T: 01773 712080
Edwalton Local History Soc, 85 Tollerton Lane, Tollerton, Nottingham, NG12 4FS T: 0115 937 2391 F: 0115 986 1215 E: elviahugh@yahoo.co.uk
Edwinstowe Historical Soc, 12 Church Street, Edwinstowe, NG21 9QA T: 01623 824455
Farndon & District Local History Soc, 22 Brockton Avenue, Farndon, Newark, NG24 4TH T: 01636 610070
Flintham Soc, Flintham Museum, Inholms Road, Flintham, NG23 5LF T: 0163.6 525111 E: flintham.museum@lineone.net W: www.flintham-museum.org.uk

Gotham & District Local History Society 108A Leake Road, Gotham, NG11 0JN T: 0115 983 0494 F: 0115 983 0494
Hucknall Heritage Soc, 68 Papplewick Lane, Hucknall, Nottingham, NG15 8EF E: marion.williamson@ntlworld.com
Keyworth & District Local History Soc, Innisfree, Thelda Avenue, Keyworth, Nottingham, NG12 5HU T: 0115 937908 F: 0115 9372908 E: info@keyworth-history.org.uk W: www.keyworth-history.org.uk
Lambley Historical Soc, 11 Steeles Way, Lambley, Nottingham, NG4 4QN T: 0115 931 2588
Lenton Local History Soc, 53 Arnesby Road, Lenton Gardens, Nottingham, NG7 2EA T: 0115 970 3891
Long Bennington Local History Soc, Kirton House, Kirton Lane, Long Bennington, Newark, NG23 5DX T: 01400 281726
Newark Archaeological & Local History Soc, 13 Main Street, Sutton on Trent, Newark, NG23 6PF T: 01636 821781 (Evenings) E: jill.campbell@ic24.net
North Muskham History Group, Roseacre, Village Lane, North Muskham, NG23 6ES T: 01636 705566
Nottingham Civic Soc, 57 Woodhedge Drive, Nottingham, NG3 6LW T: 0115 958 8247 F: 0115 958 8247 E: membership@nottinghamcivicsoc.org.uk
Nottingham Historical and Archaeological Soc, 9 Churchill Drive, Stapleford, Nottingham, NG9 8PE T: 0115 939 7140
Nottinghamshire Industrial Archaeology Soc, 18 Queens Avenue, Ilkeston, DE7 4DL T: 0115 932 2228
Nottinghamshire Local History Association, 128 Sandhill Street, Worksop, S80 1SY T: 01909 488878, Mobile: 07773887803 E: drossellis@aol.com
Nuthall & District Local History Soc, 14 Temple Drive, Nuthall, Nottingham, NG16 1BE T: 0115 927 1118 E: tony.horton@ntlworld.com
Old Mansfield Soc, 7 Barn Close, Mansfield, NG18 3JX T: 01623 654815 E: dcrut@yahoo.com W: www.old-mansfield.org.uk
Old Mansfield Woodhouse Soc, Burrwells, Newboundmill Lane, Pleasley, Mansfield, NG19 7QA T: 01623 810396
Old Warsop Soc, 1 Bracken Close, Market Warsop, NG20 0QQ
Pentagon Soc, Dellary, Mill Road, Elston, Newark, NG23 5NR T: 01636 525278, covers Elston, Shelton, Sibthorpe, East Stoke & Syerston CC accepted
Pleasley History Group, 8 Cambria Road, Pleasley, Mansfield, NG19 7RL T: 01623 810201
Radford Memories Project, 25 Manston Mews, Alfreton Road, Radford, Nottingham, NG7 3QY T: 0115 970 1256
Retford & District Historical & Archaeological Soc, Cambridge House, 36 Alma Road, Retford, DN22 6LW T: 7790212360 E: joan@granto.demon.co.uk
Ruddington Local History Soc, St Peter's Rooms, Church Street, Ruddington, Nottingham, NG11 6HA T: 0115 914 6645
Sherwood Archaeological Soc, 32 Mapperley Hall Drive, Nottingham, NG3 5EY T: 0115 960 3032 E: pjneale@aol.com
Shireoaks Local History Group, 22 Shireoaks Row, Shireoaks, Worksop, S81 8LP
Sneinton Environmental Soc, 248 Greenwood Road, Nottingham, NG3 7FY T: 0115 987 5035
Southwell & District Local History Soc, Fern Cottage, 70 Kirklington Road, Southwell, NG25 0AX T: 01636 812220
Stapleford & District Local History Soc, 25 Westerlands, Stapleford, Nottingham, NG9 7JE T: 0115 939 2573
Sutton Heritage Soc, 8 Sheepbridge Lane, Mansfield, NG18 5EA T: 01623 451179 E: lildawes@yahoo.co.uk
Sutton on Trent Local History Soc, 14 Grassthorpe Road, Sutton on Trent, Newark, NG23 6QD T: 01636 821228
Thoroton Society of Nottinghamshire, 59 Briar Gate, Long Eaton, Nottingham, NG10 4BQ T: 0115-972-6590 E: thoroton@keithgoodman.com W: www.thorotonsociety.org.uk
Tuxford Heritage Soc, 140 Lincoln Road, Tuxford, Newark, NG22 0HS
West Bridgford & District Local History Soc, 30 Repton Road, West Bridgford, NG2 7EJ T: 0115 923 3901
Whitwell Local History Group, 34 Shepherds Avenue, Worksop, S81 0JB E: wlhg@freeuk.com jandpwalker34@aol.com W: www.wlhg.freeuk.com
Wilford History Soc, 10 St Austell Drive, Wilford, Nottingham, NG11 7BP T: 0115 981 7061
Woodborough Local History Group, The Woodpatch, 19 Sunningdale Drive, Woodborough, NG14 6EQ T: 0115 965 3103 W: www.woodborough-heritage.org.uk
Worksop Archaeological & Local History Soc, 42 Dunstan Crescent, Worksop, S80 1AF T: 01909 477575

Oxfordshire
Abingdon Area Archaeological and Historical Soc, 4 Sutton Close, Abingdon, OX14 1ER T: 01235 529720 E: rainslie@hotmail.com W: www.aaahs.org.uk
Banbury Historical Society c/o Banbury Museum, Spiceball Park Road, Banbury, OX16 2PQ T: 01295 672626

Blewbury Local History Group, Spring Cottage, Church Road, Blewbury, Didcot, OX11 9PY T: 01235 850427 E: aud@spcott.fsnet.co.uk

Bloxham Village History Group, 1 Hyde Grove, Bloxham, Banbury, OX15 4HZ T: 01295 720037

Chadlington Local History Soc, 5 Webbs Close, Chadlington, Chipping Nortro, OX7 3RA T: 01608 676116 E: kagewinter@aol.com

Charlbury Soc, 7 Park Street, Charlbury, OX7 3PS T: 01608 810390 E: charles.tyzack@btinternet.com

Chinnor Historical & Archealogical Soc, 4 Beech Road, Thame, OX9 2AL T: 01844 216538 E: kendmason@macunlimited.net

Chipping Norton History Soc, 9 Toy Lane, Chipping Norton, OX7 5FH T: 01608 642754

Cumnor and District History Soc, 4 Kenilworth Road, Cumnor, Nr Oxford, OX2 9QP T: 01865 862965 F: 01865 862965

Dorchester Historical Soc, 20 Watling Lane, Dorchester on Thames, Wallingford, OX10 7GJ T: 01865 340422 E: david.lucas1@which.net

Enstone Local History Circle, The Sheiling, Sibford Ferris, Banbury, OX15 5RG

Eynsham History Group, 11 Newland Street, Eynsham, OX29 4LB T: 01865 883141

Faringdon Archaeological & Historical Society 1 Orchard Hill, Faringdon, SN7 7EH T: 01367 240885 E: fdahs@bigfoot.com W: www.faringdon.org/hysoc

Finstock Local History Soc, 81 High Street, Finstock, OX7 3DA T: 01993 868965 E: jon@joncarpenter.co.uk

Hanney History Group, Willow Tree House, The Green, East Hanney, Wantage, OX12 0HQ T: 01238 68375 E: creason@EastHanney.demon.co.uk

Henley on Thames Archaeological and Historical Group, 52 Elizabeth Road, Henley on Thames, RG9 1RA T: 01491 578 530

Hook Norton Local History Group, Littlenook, Chapel Street, Hook Norton, OX15 5JT T: 01608 730355 E: sheila@littlenook.ndo.co.uk

Iffley Local History Soc, 4 Abberbury Avenue, Oxford, OX4 4EU T: 01865 779257

Kidlington and District Historical Soc, 18 Oak Drive, Kidlington, OX5 2HL T: 01865 373517 W: www.communigate.co.uk/oxford

Launton Historical Soc, Salamanca, Launton, OX26 5DQ T: 01869 253281 E: p_tucker@tesco.net

Longworth Local History Soc, 7 Norwood Avenue, Southmoor, Abingdon, OX13 5AD T: 01865 820522 F: 01865 820522 E: keene@thematictrails.u-net.com W: www.kbsonline.org.uk http://freepages.history.rootsweb.com/~lhs1, Covers villages of Hinton Waldrist and Kingston Bagpuize with Southmoor

Marcham Soc, Prior's Corner, 2 Priory Lane, Marcham, Abingdon, OX13 6NY T: 01865 391439 E: e.dunford@btinternet.com

Over Norton History Group, Fountain Cottage, The Green, Over Norton, OX7 5PT T: 01608 641057

Oxfordshire Architectural and Historical Soc, 53 Radley Road, Abingdon, Oxford, OX14 3PN T: 01235 525960 E: tony@oahs.org.uk W: www.oahs.org.uk

Oxfordshire Local History Association 12 Meadow View, Witney, OX28 6TY T: 01993 778345

Oxfordshire Record Society Bodleian Library, Oxford, OX1 3BG T: 01865 277164 E: srt@bodley.ox.ac.uk

Shrivenham Local History Soc, Ridgeway, Kings Lane, Loncot, Faringdon, SN7 7SS T: 01793 783083

Thame Historical Soc, 12 Park Terrace, Thame, OX9 3HZ T: 01844 212336 E: Csear58229@aol.com W: www.thamehistory.net

The Bartons History Group, 18 North Street, Middle Barton, OX7 7BJ T: 01869 347013 E: edbury@midbar18.freeserve,co.uk

Volunteer Corps of Frontiersmen, Archangels' Rest, 26 Dark Lane, Witney, OX8 5LE

Wallingford Historical and Archaeological Society Wallingford Museum, Flint House, 52a High Street, Wallingford, OX1O 0DB T: 01491 835065

Whitchurch: The Ancient Parish of Whitchurch Historical Soc, Ashdown, Duchess Close, Whitchurch on Thames, RG8 7EN

Witney & District Historical & Archaeological Soc, 16 Church Green, Witney, OX28 4AW T: 01993 703289 F: 01993 703281

Wolvercote Local History Soc, 18 Dovehouse Close, Upper Wolvercote, OX2 8BG

Wootton, Dry Sandford & District History Soc, 46 Church Lane, Dry Sandford, Abingdon, OX13 6JP T: 01865 390441

Wychwoods Local History Society Littlecott, Honeydale Farm, Shipton Under Wychwood, Chipping Norton, OX7 6BJ T: 01993 831023, Enquiry letters should be accompanied by an SAE or 2 IRCs if from abroad

Yarnton with Begbroke Hist Soc, 6 Quarry End, Begbroke OX5 1SF

Rutland

Rutland Local History & Record Society c/o Rutland County Museum, Catmos Street, Oakham, LE15 6HW T: 01572 758440 F: 01572 757576 E: rutlandhistory@rutnet.co.uk W: www.rutnet.co.uk/rlhrs

Shropshire

Cleobury Mortimer Historical Soc, The Old Schoolhouse, Neen Savage, Cleobury Mortimer, Kidderminster, DY14 8JU T: 01299 270319 E: paddy@treves.freeserve.co.uk

Council for British Archaeology - West Midlands, c/o Rowley's House Museum, Barker Street, Shrewsbury, SY1 1QH T: 01743 361196 F: 01743 358411 E: mikestokes@shrewsbury-atcham.gov.uk W: www.shrewsburymuseums.com www.darwincountry.org

Field Studies Council, Head office, Preston Montford, Montford Bridge, Shrewsbury, SY4 1HW T: 01743 852100 F: 01743 852101 E: fsc.headoffice@ukonline.co.uk W: www.field-studies-council.org

Shropshire Archaeological and Historical Society Lower Wallop Farm, Westbury, Shrewsbury, SY5 9RT T: 01743 891215 F: 01743 891805 E: walloparch@farming.co.uk W: www.shropshirearchaeology.com

Whitchurch History and Archaeology Group, Smallthythe, 26 Rosemary Lane, Whitchurch, SY13 1EG T: 01948 662120

Somerset

Axbridge Archaeological and Local History Soc, King John's Hunting Lodge, The Square, Axbridge, BS26 2AR T: 01934 732012

Bathford Soc, 36 Bathford Hill, Bathford, BA1 7SL

Bruton Museum Soc, The Dovecote Building, High Street, Bruton T: 01749 812851 W: www.southsomersetmuseum.org.uk

Castle Cary & District Museum & Preservation Soc, Woodville House, Woodcock Street, Castle Cary, BA7 7BJ T: 01963 351122 T: 01963 350680 (Museum) Curator: Mrs P M Schiffer, Rosemary Cottage, Bailey Hill, Castle Cary BA7 7AD

Chard History Group, 17 Kinforde, Chard, TA20 1DT T: 01460 62722 E: carterw@globalnet.co.uk W: www.users.globalnet.co.uk/~carterw

Freshford & District Local History Soc, Quince Tree House, Pipehouse Lane, Freshford, Bath, BA2 7UH T: 01225 722339

Oakhill & Ashwick Local History Society Bramley Farm, Bath Road, Oakhill, BA3 5AF T: 01749 840 241 F: 01749 841195

Notes and Queries for Somerset and Dorset Marston House, Marston Bigot, Frome, BA11 5DU

Somerset Archaeological & Natural History Society Taunton Castle, Taunton, TA1 4AD T: 01823 272429 F: 01823 272429 E: secretary@sanhs.freeserve.co.uk

Somerset Record Society Somerset Studies Library, Paul Street, Taunton, TA1 3XZ T: 01823-340300 F: 01823-340301

South East Somerset Archaeological and Historical Soc, Silverlands, Combe Hill, Templecombe, BA8 OLL T: 01963 371307 F: 01963 371307

South Petherton Local History Group Cobbetts Droveway, South Petherton, TAI3 5DA T: 01460 240252

Somerset - North

Nailsea & District Local History Society PO Box 1089, Nailsea, BS48 2YP

Staffordshire

Berkswich History Society 1 Greenfield Road, Stafford, ST17 OPU T: 01785 662401

Birmingham Canal Navigation Soc, 37 Chestnut Close, Handsacre, Rugeley, WS15 4TH

Landor Soc, 38 Fortescue Ln, Rugeley, WS15 2AE T: 01889 582709

Lawton History Group, 17 Brattswood drive, Church Lawton, Stoke on Trent, ST7 3EF T: 01270 873427 E: arthur@aburton83.freeserve.co.uk

Mid-Trent Historical Association 36 Heritage Court, Lichfield, WS14 9ST T: 01543 301097

North Staffordshire Historians' Guild, 14 Berne Avenue, Newcastle under Lyme, ST5 2QJ

Ridware History Soc, 8 Waters Edge, Handsacre, Nr. Rugeley, WS15 7HP T: 01543 307456 E: davidandmonty@carefree.net

Stafford Historical & Civic Society 86 Bodmin Avenue, Weeping Cross, Stafford, ST17 OEQ T: 01785 612194 E: esj@supanet.com

Staffordshire Archaeological and Historical Society 6 Lawson Close, Aldridge, Walsall, WS9 0RX T: 01922 452230 E: sahs@britishlibrary.net W: www.sahs.uk.net

Suffolk

Framlingham & District Local History & Preservation Society 28 Pembroke Road, Framlingham, IP13 9HA T: 01728 723214

Lowestoft Archaeological and Local History Society 1 Cranfield Close, Pakefield, Lowestoft, NR33 7EL T: 01502 586143

Suffolk Institute of Archaeology and History Roots, Church Lane, Playford, Ipswich, IP6 9DS T: 01473-624556 E: brianseward@btinternet.com W: www.suffolkarch.org.uk

Suffolk Local History Council Suffolk Community Resource Centre, 2 Wharfedale Road, Ipswich, IP1 4JP E: admin@suffolklocalhistorycouncil.org.uk W: www.suffolklocalhistorycouncil.org.uk

Surrey

Addlestone History Society 53 Liberty Lane, Addlestone, Weybridge, KT15 1NQ

Beddington Carshalton & Wallington History Society 7 Mortlake Close, Beddington, Croydon, CR0 4JW T: (020) 8726 0255

Bourne Society 54 Whyteleafe Road, Caterham, CR3 5EF T: 01883 349287 E: robert@friday-house.freeserve.co.uk W: www.bournesociety.org.uk Covers the districts of Caterham, Chaldon, Chelsham, Chipstead, Coulsdon, Farleigh, Godstone, Kenley, Old Coulsdon, Parley, Sanderstead, Whyteleafe, Warlingham and Woldingham.

Carshalton Soc 43 Denmark Road, Carshalton, SM5 2JE

Centre for Local History Studies, Faculty of Human Sciences, Kingston University, Penrhyn Road, Kingston, KT1 2EE T: (020) 8547 7359 E: localhistory@kingston.ac.uk W: http://localhistory.kingston.ac.uk

Croydon Natural History & Scientific Society Ltd 96a Brighton Road, South Croydon, CR2 6AD T: (020) 8688 4539 W: http://www.grieg51.freeserve.co.uk/cnhss

Domestic Buildings Research Group (Surrey), The Ridings, Lynx Hill, East Horsley, KT24 5AX T: 01483 283917

Dorking Local History Group Dorking & District Museum, The Old Foundry, 62a West St, Dorking, RH4 1BS T: 01306 876591

Esher District Local History Soc, 45 Telegraph Lane, Claygate, KT10 0DT

Farnham and District Museum Soc, Tanyard House, 13a Bridge Square, Farnham, GU9 7QR

Friends of Public Record Office, The Public Record Office, Ruskin Avenue, Kew, Richmond, TW9 4DU T: (020) 8876 3444 ext 2226 E: friends-pro@pro.gov.uk W: www.pro.gov.uk/yourpro/friends.htm

Guildford Archaeology and Local History Group, 6 St Omer Road, Guildford, GU1 2DB T: 01483 532201 E: H.E.Davies@surrey.ac.uk

Hayward Memorial Local History Centre, The Guest House, Vicarage Road, Lingfield, RH7 6HA T: 01342 832058 F: 01342 832517

Leatherhead and District Local History Society Leatherhead Museum, 64 Church Street, Leatherhead, KT22 8DP T: 01372 386348, cc accepted

Nonsuch Antiquarian Soc, 17 Seymour Avenue, Ewell, KT17 2RP T: (020) 8393 0531 W: www.nonsuchas.org.uk

Puttenham & Wanborough History Soc, Brown Eaves, 116 The Street, Puttenham, Guildford, GU3 1AU

Richmond Local History Society 9 Bridge Road, St Margarets, Twickenham, TWI IRE

Send and Ripley History Society St Georges Farm House, Ripley, GU23 6AF T: 01483 222107 F: 01483 211832 E: slatford@johnone.freeserve.co.uk

Shere Gomshall & Peaslake Local History Society Twiga Lodge, Wonham Way, Gomshall, Guildford, GU5 9NZ T: 01483 202112 E: twiga@gomshall.freeserve.co.uk W: www.gomshall.freeserve.co.uk/sglshhp.htm

Surrey Archaeological Soc, Castle Arch, Guildford, GU1 3SX T: 01483 532454 E: surreyarch@compuserve.com W: www.ourworld.compuserve.com/homepages/surreyarch

Surrey Local History Council Guildford Institute, University of Surrey, Ward Street, Guildford, GU1 4LH

Surrey Record Society c/o Surrey History Centre, 130 Goldsworth Road, Woking, GU21 1ND T: 01483 594603, This is a publishing society only. No research can be undertaken by the honorary officers.

Walton On The Hill District Local History Soc, 5 Russell Close, Walton On The Hill, Tadworth, KT2O 7QH T: 01737 812013

Walton & Weybridge Local History Society 67 York Gardens, Walton on Thames, KT12 3EN

Westcott Local History Group, 6 Heath Rise, Westcott, Dorking, RH4 3NN T: 01306 882624 E: info@westcotthistory.org.uk W: www.westcotthistory.org.uk

Sussex

Danehill Parish Historical Soc, Butchers Barn, Freshfield Lane, Danehill, RH17 7HQ T: 01825 790292

Eastbourne Local History Soc, 12 Steeple Grange, 5 Mill Road, Eastbourne, BN21 2LY

Lewes Archaeological Group, Rosemary Cottage, High Street, Barcombe, near Lewes, BN8 5DM T: 01273 400878

Sussex Local History Forum, Anne of Cleves House, 52 Southover, High Street, Lewes, BN7 1JA

Sussex - East

Blackboys & District Historical Society 18 Maple Leaf Cottages, School Lane, Blackboys, Uckfield, TN22 5LJ E: baturner.18maple@btinternet.com

Brighton & Hove Archealogical Soc, 115 Braeside Avenue, Patcham, Brighton, BN1 8SQ T:

Eastbourne Natural History and Archaeological Soc, 11 Brown Jack Avenue, Polegate, BN26 5HN T: 01323 486014

Family & Community Historical Research Soc, 56 South Way, Lewes, BN7 1LY T: 01273 471897

Friends of East Sussex Record Office, The Maltings, Castle Precincts, Lewes, BN7 1YT T: 01273-482349 F: 01273-482341 W:

www.esrole.fsnet.co.uk

Maresfield Historical Soc, Hockridge House, London Road, Maresfield, TN22 2EH T: 01825 765386

Mid Sussex Local History Group, Saddlers, Stud Farm Stables, Gainsborough Lane, Polegate, BN26 5HQ T: 01323 482215

Peacehaven & Telscombe Historical Soc, 2 The Compts, Peacehaven, BN1O 75Q T: 01273 588874 F: 01273 589881 E: paths@openlink.org W: www.history-peacehaven-telscombe.org.uk

Rye Local History Group, 107 Military Road, Rye, TN31 7NZ

Sussex Archaeological Society & Sussex Past Barbican House, 169 High Street, Lewes, BN7 1YE T: 01273 405738 F: 01273 486990 E: library@sussexpast.co.uk W: sussexpast.co.uk

Sussex History Forum Barbican House, 169 High Street, Lewes, BN7 1YE T: 01273-405736 F: 01273-486990 E: research@sussexpast.co.uk W: www.sussexpast.co.uk

Uckfield & District Preservation Soc, 89 Lashbrooks Road, Uckfield, TN22 2AZ

Warbleton & District History Group Hillside Cottage, North Road, Bodle Street Green, Hailsham, BN27 4RG T: 01323 832339 E: junegeoff.hillside@tiscali.co.uk

Sussex - West

Beeding & Bramber Local History Soc, 19 Roman Road, Steyning, BN44 3FN T: 01903 814083

Billingshurst Local History Society 2 Cleve Way, Billingshurst, RH14 9RW T: 01403 782472 E: jane.lecluse@atkinsglobal.com

Bolney Local History Soc, Leacroft, The Street, Bolney, Haywards, RH17 5PG T: 01444 881550 E: constable@lespres.freeserve.co.uk

Chichester LH Soc, 38 Ferndale Rd, Chichester, PO19 6QS

Horsham Museum Soc, Horsham Museum, 9 The Causeway, Horsham, RH12 1HE T: 01403 254959 E: museum@horsham.gov.uk

Midland Railway Soc, 4 Canal Road, Yapton, BN18 0HA T: 01243-553401 E: BeeFitch@aol.com W: www.derby.org/midland

The RH7 History Group, Bidbury House, Hollow Lane, East Grinstead, RH19 3PS

Steyning Soc, 30 St Cuthmans Road, Steyning, BN44 3RN

Sussex Record Society West Sussex Record Office, County Hall, Chichester, PO19 1RN T: 01243 753600 F: 01243-533959 E: peter.wilkinson@westsussex.gov.uk

The Angmering Soc, 45 Greenwood Drive, Angmering, BNI6 4JW T: 01903-775811 E: editor@angmeringsociety.org.uk W: www.angmeringsociety.org.uk

West Sussex Archives Soc, c/o West Sussex Record Office, West Sussex CountyCouncil County Hall, Chichester, PO19 IRN T: 01243 753600 F: 01243 533959 E: records.office@westsussex.gov.uk W: www.westsussex.gov.uk/cs/ro/rohome.htm

Wivelsfield Historical Soc, Wychwood, Theobalds Road, Wivelsfield, Haywards Heath, RH15 0Sx T: 01444 236491

Tyne and Wear

Association of Northumberland Local History Societies c/o The Black Gate, Castle Garth, Newcastle upon Tyne, NE1 1RQ T: 0191 257 3254

Cullercoats Local History Soc 33 St Georges Road, Cullercoats, North Shields, NE30 3JZ T: 0191 252 7042

North East Labour History Soc, Department of Historical & Critical Studies, University of Northumbria, Newcastle upon Tyne, NE1 8ST T: 0191-227-3193 F: 0191-227-4630 E: joan.hugman@unn.ac.uk

North Eastern Police History Soc, Brinkburn Cottage, 28 Brinkburn Street, High Barnes, Sunderland, SR4 7RG T: 0191-565-7215 E: harry.wynne@virgin.net W: http://nepolicehistory.homestead.com

Southwick History and Preservation Soc, 8 St Georges Terrace, Roker, Sunderland, SR6 9LX T: 0191 567 2438 T: 07833 787 481 E: pamela.tate@freedomnames.co.uk W: www.rootsweb.com/~engshps/index.htm

Sunderland Antiquarian Society 22 Ferndale Avenue, East Boldon, NE36 0TN T: 0191 536 1692

Society of Antiquaries of Newcastle upon Tyne, The Black Gate, Castle Garth, Newcastle upon Tyne, NE1 1RQ T: 0191 261 5390 E: admin@newcastle-antiquaries.org.uk W: www.newcastle-antiquaries.org.uk

Southwick History and Preservation Society 8 St Georges Terrace, Roker, Sunderland, SR6 9LX T: 0191 567 2438 E: pamela.tate@freedomnames.co.uk W: www.southwickhistory.org.uk

South Hylton Local History Society 6 North View, South Hylton, Sunderland, SR4 0LH T: 0191 534 4251 E: south.hylton@ntlworld.com W: www.shlhs.com

St John Ambulance History Group, 3 The Bower, Meadowside, Jarrow, NE32 4RS T: 0191 537 4252

Warwickshire

Kineton and District Local History Group The Glebe House, Lighthorne Road, Kineton, CV35 0JL T: 01926 690298 F: 01926 690298 E: p.holdsworth@virgin.net,

Warwickshire Local History Society 9 Willes Terrace, Leamington Spa, CV31 1DL T: 01926 429671

Watford
Watford and District Industrial History Soc, 79 Kingswood Road, Garston, Watford, WD25 0EF T: 01923 673253

West Midlands
Aldridge Local History Soc 45 Erdington Road, Walsall, WS9 8UU,
Barr & Aston Local History, 17 Booths Farm Road, Great Barr, Birmingham, 642 2NJ
Birmingham & District Local History Association 112 Brandwood Road, Kings Heath, Birmingham, B14 6BX T: 0121-444-7470
Birmingham Heritage Forum 95 Church Hill Rd, Solihull, B91 3JH
Birmingham War Research Soc, 43 Norfolk Place, Kings Norton, Birmingham, B30 3LB T: 0121 459 9008 F: 0121 459 9008
Black Country Local History Consortium, Canal St, Tipton Rd, Dudley, DY1 4SQ T: 0121 522 9643 F: 0121 557 4242 E: info@bclm.co.uk W: www.bclm.co.uk
Black Country Society PO Box 71, Kingswinford, DY6 9YN E: mick@mickandlinpearson.co.uk W: www.blackcountrysociety.co.uk
Local History Consortium, The Black Country Living Museum, Tipton Road, Dudley, DY1 4SQ T: 0121 557 9643
Local Studies Group of CILIP - Formerly the Library Assoc, 25 Bromford Gardens, Edgbaston, Birmingham, B15 3XD T: 0121 454 0935 F: 0121 454 7330 E: prthomaspdt@aol.com
Quinton Local History Soc, 15 Worlds End Avenue, Quinton, Birmingham, B32 1JF T: 0121-422-1792 F: 0121 422 1792 E: qlhs@bjtaylor.fsnet.co.uk W: www.qlhs.org.uk
Romsley & Hunnington History Soc, Port Erin, Green Lane, Chapmans Hill, Romsley, Halesowen, B62 0HB T: 01562 710295 E: ejhumphreys@mail.com
Small Heath Local History Society 381 St Benedicts Road, Small Heath, Birmingham, B10 9ND
Smethwick Local History Society 47 Talbot Road, Smethwick, Warley, B66 4DX W: www.smethwicklocalhistory.co.uk

Wiltshire
Amesbury Society 34 Countess Road, Amesbury, SP4 7AS T: 01980 623123
Ashbury Local History Society Claremont , Asbury, Swindon, SN6 8LN E: marionlt@waitrose.com
Atworth History Group, 48D Post Office Lane, Atworth, Melksham, SN12 8JX T: 01225 702351 E: joan.cocozza@btinternet.com
Chiseldon Local History Group, 3 Norris Close, Chiseldon, SN4 0LW T: 01793 740432 E: DavidBailey22@aol.com
Devizes Local History Group 9 Hartfield, Devizes, SN10 5JH T: 01380 727369
Highworth Historical Soc, 6 Copper Beeches, Highworth, Swindon, SN6 7BJ T: 01793 763863
Marshfield & District Local History Soc, Weir Cottage, Weir Lane, Marshfield, Chippenham, SN14 8NB T: 01225 891229
Melksham & District Historical Assoc, 13 Sandridge Road, Melksham, SN12 7BE T: 01225 703644
Mere Historical Soc, Bristow House, Castle Street, Mere, BA12 6JF T: 01747 860643
Mid Thorngate Soc, Yewcroft, Stoney Batter, West Tytherley, Salisbury, SP5 ILD T:
Pewsey Vale Local History Soc, 10 Holly Tree Walk, Pewsey, SN9 5DE T: 01672 562417 F: 01972 563924 E: westerberg@onetel.co.uk
Purton Historical Soc, 1 Church Street, Purton, SN5 4DS T: 01793 770331
Redlynch & District Local History Soc, Hawkstone, Church Hill, Redlynch, Salisbury, SP5 2PL E: pat.mill@btinternet.com
Salisbury Civic Soc, 4 Chestnut Close, Laverstock, Salisbury, SP1 1SL
Salisbury Local History Group 67 St Edmunds Church Street, Salisbury, SP1 1EF T: 01722 338346
Swindon Society 4 Lakeside, Swindon, SN3 1QE T: 01793-521910
South Wiltshire Industrial Archaeology Society 2 Byways Close, Salisbury, SP1 2QS T: 01722 323732 E: jackson.douglas@btinternet.com W: www.southwilts.co.uk/site/south-wiltshire-industrial-archaeology-society
Swindon Soc, 4 Lakeside, Swindon, SN3 1QE T: 01793-521910
The Hatcher Soc, 11 Turner Close, Harnham, Salisbury, SP2 8NX
The Historical Association (West Wiltshire Branch), 24 Meadowfield, Bradford on Avon, BA15 1PL T: 01225 862722
Tisbury Local History Soc, Suzay House, Court Street, Tisbury, SP3 6NF
Trowbridge Civic Soc, 43 Victoria Road, Trowbridge, BA14 7LD
Warminster History Society 13 The Downlands, Warminster, BA12 0BD T: 01985 216022 F: 01985 846332
Wilton Historical Society 3 Wiley Terrace, North Street, Wilton, SP2 0HN T: 01722 742856,
Wiltshire Archaeological and Natural History Soc, Wiltshire Heritage Library, 41 Long Street, Devizes, SN10 1NS T: 01380 727369 E: wanhs@wiltshireheritage.org.uk W: www.wiltshireheritage.org.uk
Wiltshire Buildings Record, Libraries HQ, Bythesea Rd, Trowbridge, BA14 8BS T: 01225 713740 E:

dorothytreasure@wiltshire.gov.uk W: www.wiltshire.gov.uk
Wiltshire Local History Forum Tanglewood, Laverstock Park, Salisbury, SP1 1QJ T: 01722 328922 F: 01722 501907 E: sarumjeh@aol.com
Wiltshire Record Society County Record Office, County Libraries HQ, Trowbridge, BA14 8BS T: 01225 713136 F: 01225 713515
Wootton Bassett Historical Soc, 20 The Broadway, Rodbourne Cheney, Swindon, SN25 3BT, Small local history Society with no genealogical information.
Wroughton History Group, 32 Kerrs Way, Wroughton, SN4 9EH T: 01793 635838

Worcestershire
Alcester & District Local History Society Applecross, Worcester Road, Inkberrow, Worcester, WR7 4ET E: cjjohnson@care4free.net
Bewdley Historical Research 8 Ironside Close, Bewdley, DY12 2HX T: 01299 403582 E: angela.ironside@clara.co.uk
Dodderhill Parish History Project - Discovering Wychbol's Past, 9 Laurelwood Close, Droitwich Spa, WR9 7SF
Droitwich History and Archaeology Soc, 45 Moreland Road, Droitwich Spa, WR9 8RN T: 01905-773420
Feckenham Forest History Soc, Lower Grinsty Farmhouse, Callow Hill, Redditch, B97 5PJ T: 01527-542063
Feckenham Parish, Worcestershire One Place Study, 33c Castle Street, Astwood Park, Worcester, B96 6DP E: benwright3@hotmail.com
Kidderminster District Archaeological and Historical Soc, 178 Birmingham Road, Kidderminster, DYIO 2SJ T: 01562 823530 W: www.communigate.co.uk/worcs/kidderminsterhistorysoc/index.phtml
Kidderminster & District Local History Soc, 39 Cardinal Drive, Kidderminster, DY104RZ E: kidderhist.soc@virgin.net W: www.communigate.co.uk/worcs/kidderminsterhistorysoc/index.phtml
Kidderminster Field Club, 7 Holmwood Avenue, Kidderminster, DYL 1 6DA
Open University History Society 111 Coleshill Drive, Chapel End, Nuneaton, CV10 0PG T: (024) 76397668, The Open University History Society is a natioanlly based Society with a widely scattered membership. To keep in touch with members a quarterly magazine Open History written mainly by members themselves
Pershore Heritage & History Soc, 6 Abbey Croft, Pershore, WR10 1JQ T: 01386 552482 E: kenmar.abcroft@virgin.net,
Suckley Local History Soc Knowle Cottage, Suckley, WR6 5DJ T: 01886 884357 E: sea.bird@virgin.net
Wolverley & Cookley Historical Soc, 18/20 Caunsall Road, Cookley, Kidderminster, DYL 1 5YB or:The Elms, Drakelow Lane, Wolverley, Kidderminster, DY11 5RU T: 01562 850215, History of parishes of Wolverley & Cookley
Worcestershire Archaeological Service, Woodbury Hall, University College of Worcester, Henwick Grove, Worcester, WR2 6AJ T: 01905 855455 F: 01905 29054 E: archaeology@worcestershire.gov.uk W: http://www.worcestershire.gov.uk/archaeology
Worcestershire Archaeological Soc, The , 26 Albert Park Road, Malvern, WR14 1HN T: 01684 565190
Worcestershire Industrial Archealogy & Local History Society 99 Feckenham Road, Headless Cross, Redditch, B97 5AM
Worcestershire Local History Forum 45 Moreland Road, Droitwich, WR9 8RN T: 01905-773420
Wythall History Soc, 64 Meadow Road, Wythall, Birmingham, B47 6EQ E: val@wythallhistory.co.uk W: www.wythallhistory.co.uk

Yorkshire
York Georgian Soc, King's Manor, York, YO1 7EW
Yorkshire Architectural & York Archaeological Soc, c/o Cromwell House, 13 Ogleforth, York, YO1 7FG W: www.homepages.tesco.net/~hugh.murray/yayas/,
Yorkshire Philosophical Soc, The Lodge, Museum Gardens, Museum Street, York, YO1 7DR T: 01904 656713 F: 01904 656713 E: yps@yorkphil.fsnet.co.uk W: www.yorec.org.uk
Yorkshire Quaker Heritage Project Brynmore Jones Library, University of Hull, Hull, HU6 7RX
Yorkshire Vernacular Buildings Study Group, 18 Sycamore Terrace, Bootham, York, YO30 7DN T: 01904 652387 E: dave.crook@suleacy.freeserve.co.uk W: www.yvbsg.org.uk
Yorkshire - City of York
York Archaeological Trust, 13 Ogleforth, York, YO1 7FG T: 01904 663000 E: enquiries@yorkarchaeology.co.uk W: www.yorkarchaeology.co.uk
Yorkshire - East
East Riding Archaeological Soc, 455 Chanterland Avenue, Hull, HU5 4AY T: 01482 445232
East Yorkshire Local History Society 13 Oaktree Drive, Molescroft, Beverley, HU17 7BB
Yorkshire - North
Forest of Galtres Soc, c/o Crawford House, Long Street, Easingwold, York, YO61 3JB T: 01347 821685
Holgate Windmill Preservation Society 2 Murray Street, York, YO24 4JA T: 01904 799295 E: lambert49@ntlworld.com W: www.holgatewindmill.org

Northallerton and District Local History Society 17 Thistle Close, Romanby Park, Northallerton, DL7 8FF T: 01609 771878

Poppleton History Soc, Russett House, The Green, Upper Poppleton, York, YO26 6DR T: 01904 798868 F: 01904 613330 E: susan.major@virgin.net W: www.poppleton.net/historysoc

Scarborough Archaeological and Historical Society 10 Westbourne Park, Scarborough, YO12 4AT T: 01723 354237, F: E: archaeology@scarborough.co.uk W: www.scarborough-heritage.org

Snape Local History Group, Lammas Cottage, Snape, Bedale, DL8 2TW T: 01677 470727 W: www.communigate.co.uk/ne/slhg/index.phtml

Stokesley Local History Study Group, Cropton Lodge, Belbrough Lane, Hutton Rudby, Yarm TS15 0HY Tel: 01642 700306 E: christinemiller46@hotmail.com W: http://pride.webspace.co.uk/stokesley.htm

Upper Dales Family History Group Croft House, Newbiggin in Bishopdale, Nr Leyburn, DL8 3TD T: 01969 663738 E: glenys@bishopdale.demon.co.uk W: www.bishopdale.demon.co.uk

Upper Wharfedale Field Society (Local History Section), Brookfield, Hebden Hall Park, Grassington, Skipton, BD23 5DX T: 01756-752012

Wensleydale Railway Assoc, WRA Membership Administration, PO Box 65, Northallerton, DL7 8YZ T: 01969 625182 (Railway Shop, Leyburn) W: www.wensleydalerailway.com

Yorkshire Dialect Soc, 51 Stepney Avenue, Scarborough, YO12 5BW

Yorkshire - South

Barnscan - The Barnsdale Local History Group, 23 Rushymoor Lane, Askern, Doncaster, DN6 0NH T: 01302 700083 E: barnscan@btinternet.com W: www.barnscan.btinternet.co.uk

Bentley with Arksey Heritage Soc, 45 Finkle Street, Bentley, Doncaster, DN5 0RP T:

Chapeltown & High Green Archives, The Grange, 4 Kirkstead Abbey Mews, Thorpe Hesley, Rotherham, S61 2UZ T: 0114 245 1235 E: bellamyted@aol.com W: www.chgarchives.com

Doncaster Archaeological Society a Group of the Yorkshire Archaeological Soc, The Poplars, Long Plantation, Edenthorpe, Doncaster, DN3 2NL T: 01302 882840 E: d.j.croft@talk21.com

Friends of Barnsley Archives and Local Studies, 30 Southgate, Barnsley, S752QL E: hazel@snowie48.freeserve.co.uk

Grenoside & District Local History Group 4 Stepping Lane, Grenoside, Sheffield, S35 8RA T: 0114 257 1929 E: info@grenosidelocalhistory.co.uk W: www.grenosidelocalhistory.co.uk

Wombwell Heritage Group, 9 Queens Gardens, Wombwell, Barnsley, S73 0EE T: 01226 210648

The Yorkshire Buildings Preservation Trust, c/o Elmhirst & Maxton Solicitors, 17-19 Regent Street, Barnsley, S70 2HP

The Yorkshire Heraldry Society 2 Woodhall Park Grove, Pudsey, Leeds, LS28 7HB

Yorkshire - West

Beeston Local History Soc, 30 Sunnyview Ave, Leeds, LS11 8QY T: 0113 271 7095 Beeston, Leeds not to be confused with Beeston, Nottinghamshire

East Leeds Historical Soc, 10 Thornfield Drive, Cross Gates, Leeds, LS15 7LS, Also East Leeds Heritage Centre

Halifax Antiquarian Soc, 66 Grubb Lane, Gomersal, Cleckheaton, BD19 4BU T: 01274 865418

Kippax & District History Society 8 Hall Park Croft, Kippax, Leeds, LS25 7QF T: 0113 286 4785 E: mdlbrumwell@tinyworld.co.uk W: www.kippaxhistoricalsoc.leedsnet.org

Lowertown Old Burial Ground Trust, 16 South Close, Guisley, Leeds, LS20 8TD, Reg Charity 1003823 Lowertown Old Burial Ground is at Oxenhope, Keighley. The Trust has transcribed the Memorial Inscriptions and hold some family trees.

Northern Society of Costume and Textiles, 43 Gledhow Lane, Leeds, LS8 1RT

Olicana Historical Soc, 54 Kings Road, Ilkley, LS29 9AT T: 01943 609206

Ossett & District Historical Soc, 29 Prospect Road, Ossett T: 01924 279449

Shipley Local History Soc, 68 Wycliffe Gardens, Shipley, BD18 3NH E: ian@slhs.abelgratis.co.uk

Wetherby & District Historical Society 73 Aire Road, Wetherby, LS22 7UE T: 01937 584875

Yorkshire Archaeological Society - Local History Study Section, Claremont, 23 Clarendon Road, Leeds, LS2 9NZ T: 0113-245-7910 F: 0113-244-1979

Wales

Pentyrch & District Local History Soc, 34 Castell Coch View, Tongwynlais, Cardiff, CF15 7LA

Carmarthenshire

Carmarthenshire Antiquarian Society 24 Hoel Beca, Carmarthen, SA31 3LS E: arfon.rees@btinternet.com W: www.carmantiqs.org.uk, **Llanelli Historical Society** Gwynfryn, Mountain Road, Trimsaran, Kidwelly, SA17 4EU T: 01554 810677

Gwendraeth Valley Hist Soc, 19 Grugos Avenue, Pontyberem, Llanelli, SA14 5AF

Ceredigion

Ceredigion Antiquarian Soc, Archives Department, Ceredigion County Council, Aberystwyth, SY23 T: 01970 633697 E: info@ceredigion.gov.uk

Friends of The Clwyd Archives, Bryn Gwyn, 2 Rhodea Anwyl, Rhuddlan, LL18 2SQ T: 01745 591676 F: 01745 591676 E: coppack@timyworld.co.uk

Conwy

Abergele Field Club and Historical Soc, Rhyd y Felin, 47 Bryn Twr, Abergele, LL22 8DD T: 01745 832497

Llandudno & District Historical Soc, Springfield, 97 Queen's Road, Llandudno, LL30 1TY T: 01492 876337,

Denbighshire

Flintshire Historical Society 69 Pen y Maes Avenue, Rhyl, LL18 4ED T: 01745 332220

Ruthin Local History Group, 27 Tan y Bryn, Llanbedr D.C., Ruthin, LL15 1AQ T: 01824 702632 F: 01824 702632 E: gwynnemorris@btinternet.com

Flintshire

Chapels Heritage Society - CAPEL, 2 Sandy Way, Wood Lane, Hawarden, CH5 3JJ T: 01244 531255

Llantrisant & District Local History Soc, Cerrig Llwyd, Lisvane Road, Lisvane, Cardiff, CF14 0SG T: 029 2075 6173 E: BDavies203@aol.com

Gwent

Abertillery & District Museum, 5 Harcourt Terrace, Glandwr Street, Abertillery, NP3 ITS

Abertillery & District Museum Soc, The Metropole, Market Street, Abertillery, NP13 1AH T: 01495 211140

Gwent Local History Council, 8 Pentonville, Newport, NP9 5XH T: 01633 213229 F: 01633 221812 E: byron.grubb@gavowales.org.uk

Newport Local History Soc, 72 Risca Road, Newport, NP20 4JA

Pontypool Local History Soc, 24 Longhouse Grove, Henllys, Cwmbran, NP44 6HQ T: 01633 865662,

Gwynedd

The Anglesey Antiquarian Society & Field Club 1 Fronheulog, Sling, Tregarth, Bangor, LL57 4RD T: 01248 600083 W: www.hanesmon.btinternet.co.uk

Caernarvonshire Historical Soc, Gwynedd Archives, County offices, Caernarfon, LL555 1SH T: 01286 679088 E: caernarvonshirehistoricalsociety@btinternet.com W: www.caernarvonshirehistoricalsociety.btinternet.co.uk

Cymdeithas Hanes a Chofnodion Sir Feirionnydd Meirioneth Historicial and Record Soc, Archifdy Meirion Cae Penarlag, Dolgellau, LL40 2YB T: 01341 424444 F: 01341 424505,

Cymdeithas Hanes Beddgelert - Beddgelert History Soc, Creua, Llanfrothen, Penrhyndeudraeth, LL48 6SH T: 1766770534

Federation of History Societies in Caernarvonshire, 19 Lon Dinas, Cricieth, LL52 0EH T: 01766 522238,

Glamorgan

Glamorgan History Soc, 7 Gifford Close, Two Locks, NP44 7NX T: 01633 489725 (Evenings Only) E: rosemary_hewlett@yahoo.co.uk

Kenfig Soc, 6 Locks Lane, Porthcawl, CF36 3HY T: 01656 782351 E: terry.robbins@virgin.net W: www.kenfigsociety.supanet.com

Glamorgan - Mid

Merthyr Tydfil Historical Soc, Ronamar, Ashlea Drive, Twynyrodyn, Merthyr Tydfil, CF47 0NY T: 01685 385871,

Pembrokeshire

The Pembrokeshire Historical Society Dolau Dwrbach, Fishguard, SA65 9RN T: 01348 873316 E: mike.eastham@btinternet.com

Powys

Radnorshire Soc, Pool House, Discoed, Presteigne, LD8 2NW E: sadie@cole.kc3ltd.co.uk

Wrexham

Denbighshire Historical Society 1 Green Park, Erddig, Wrexham, LL13 7YE, Covers the old county of Denbighshire as defined by the 1536 Act of Union.,

Scotland,

Scottish Local History Forum, 45 High Street, Linlithgow, EH54 6EW T: 01506 844649 F: 0131 260 6610 E: chantal.hamill@dial.pipex.com

Scottish Records Assoc, National Archives of Scotland, H M General Register House, Edinburgh, EH1 3YY T: 0141 287 2914 F: 0141 226 8452

Society of Antiquaries of Scotland Royal Museum of Scotland, Chambers Street, Edinburgh, EH1 1JF T: 0131 247 4115 F: 0131 247 4163 E: r.lancaster@nms.ac.uk W: www.socantscot.org

Ayrshire

Ayrshire Federation of Historical Societies, 11 Chalmers Road, Ayr, KA7 2RQ

South West Scotland Local/Family History Maybole Historical Society 18A Shawfarm Place, Prestwick, KA9 1JQ T: 07776 445033 E: maybole@scotsfamilies.co.uk W: www.maybole.org

Ayrshire - East
Stewarton Library, Cunningham Institute, Stewarton, KA3 5AB T: 01560 484385
Dundee
Abertay Historical Society 90 Dundee Road, Broughty Ferry, Dundee, DD5 1DW T: 01382 731607 E: abertay@dmcsoft.com W: www.dcmsoft.com/abertay
Friends of Dundee City Archives 21 City Square, Dundee, DD1 3BY T: 01382 434494 E: richard.cullen@dundeecity.gov.uk W: http://www.dundeecity.gov.uk/archives
Falkirk
Falkirk Local History Soc, 11 Neilson Street, Falkirk, FK1 5AQ
Glasgow
Glasgow Hebrew Burial Society 222 Fenwick Road, Griffnock, Glasgow, G46 6UE T: 0141 577 8226
Midlothian
Monklands Heritage Soc, 141 Cromarty Road, Cairnhill, Airdrie, ML6 9RZ T: 01236 764192,
Perthshire
Dunning Parish Historical Society The Old Schoolhouse, Newtown of Pitcairns, Dunning, Perth, PH2 0SL T: 01764 684448 E: postman@dunning.uk.net W: www.dunning.uk.net
Renfrewshire
Bridge of Weir History Society 41 Houston Road, Bridge Of Weir, PA11 3QR, No archive material available and no family history research undertaken
Renfrewshire Local History Forum 15 Victoria Crescent, Clarkston, Glasgow, G76 8BP T: 0141 644 2522 W:, www.rlhf.info
Stirlingshire
Drymen Library The Square, Drymen, G63 0BL T: 01360 660751 E: drymenlibrary@stirling.gov.uk
West Lothian
Linlithgow Union Canal Soc, Manse Road Basin, Linlithgow, EH49 6AJ T: 01506-671215 E: info@lucs.org.uk W: www.lucs.org.uk
Northern Ireland,
Federation for Ulster Local Studies, 18 May Street, Belfast, BT1

4NL T: (028) 90235254 F: (028) 9043 4086 E: fulsltd@aol.com W: www.ulsterlocalhistory.org
Co Tyrone
Centre for Migration Studies, Ulster American Folk Park, Mellon Road, Castletown, Omagh, BT78 5QY T: 028 82 256315, 028 82 242241 E: uafp@iol.ie W: www.qub.ac.uk/cms/ www.folkpark.com
County Londonderry
Roe Valley Historical Soc, 36 Drumachose Park, Limavady, BT49 0NZ
Presbyterian Historical Society of Ireland, Church House, Fisherwick Place, Belfast, BT1 6DW T: (028) 9032 2284

Isle of Man
Isle of Man Natural History & Antiquarian Soc, Ballacrye Stream Cottage, Ballaugh, IM7 5EB T: 01624-897306
Isle of Man Natural History & Local History Soc, Stream Cottage, Ballacrye, Ballaugh, IM7 5EB

Channel Islands
Societe Jersiaise, 7 Pier Road, St Helier, Jersey, 01534 730538 T: 01534 888262 E: societe@societe-jersiaise.org

Republic of Ireland
Federation of Local History Societies - Ireland, Rothe House, Kilkenny
Presbyterian Historical Society of Ireland, Church House, Fisherwick Place, Belfast, BT1 6DW T: (028) 9032 2284
Dublin
Raheny Heritage Soc, 68 Raheny Park, Raheny, Dublin 5 T: 01 831 4729 E: jussher@softhome.net
County Mayo
Mayo North Family Heritage Centre, Enniscoe, Castlehill, Ballina T: 00 44 096 31809 F: 00 44 096 31885 E: normayo@iol.ie W: www.mayo-ireland.ie/motm.htm,
South Mayo Family Research Centre, Main Street, Ballinrobe T: 353 92 41214 E: soumayo@iol.ie W: http:/mayo.irish-roots.net/

Family History Centres ~ *The Church of Jesus Christ of The Latter Day Saints*

Church of Jesus Christ of Latter Day Saints - North America Distribution Centre 1999 West 1700 South, Salt Lake City, Utah, 84104 United States of America
Church of Jesus Christ of Latter Day Saints - UK Distribution Centre 399 Garretts Green Lane, Birmingham, West Midlands, B33 0HU Tel: 0870-010-2051
Bedfordshire
St Albans Family History Centre London Road/Cutenhoe Road, Luton LU1 3NQ Tel: 01582-482234
Berkshire
Reading Family History Centre 280 The Meadway, Tilehurst, Reading RG3 4PF Tel: 0118-941 0211
Bristol
Bristol Family History Centre 721 Wells Road, Whitchurch, Bristol BS14 9HU Tel: 01275-838326
Cambridgeshire
Cambridgeshire Family History Centre 670 Cherry Hinton Road, Cambridge CB1 4DR Tel: 01223-247010
Peterborough Family History Centre Cottesmore Close off Atherstone Av, Netherton Estate
Peterborough PE3 9TP Tel: 01733-263374
Cleveland
Billingham Family History Centre The Linkway, Billingham TS23 3HG T: 01642-563162
Cornwall
Helston Family History Centre Clodgey Lane, Helston T: 01326-564503
Cumbria
Carlisle Family History Centre Langrigg Road, Morton Park, Carlisle CA2 5HT T: 01228-26767
Devon
Exeter Family History Centre Wonford Road Exeter T: 01392 250723
Plymouth Family History Centre Mannamead Road Plymouth PL3 5QJ T: 01752-668666
Dorset
Chickerell Family History Centre 396 Chickerell Road Chickerell Weymouth DT4 9TP T: 01305 787240
Poole Family History Centre 8 Mount Road Parkstone Poole BH14 0QW T: 01202-730646
Essex
Romford Family History Centre 64 Butts Green Road Hornchurch RM11 2JJ T: 01708-620727
Gloucestershire
Cheltenham Family History Centre Thirlestaine Road Cheltenham GL53 7AS T: 01242-523433
Forest of Dean Family History Centre Wynol's Hill Queensway

Coleford T: 01594-542480
Yate Family History Centre Wellington Road Yate BS37 5UY T: 01454-323004
Hampshire
Portsmouth Family History Centre 82 Kingston Crescent Portsmouth PO2 8AQ T: (023) 92696243
Isle of Wight
Newport Family History Centre Chestnut Close Shide Road Newport PO30 1YE T: 01983-529643
Kent
Maidstone Family History Centre 76b London Road Maidstone ME16 0DR T: 01622-757811
Lancashire
Ashton Family History Centre Patterdale Road Ashton-under-Lyne OL7 T: 0161-330-1270
Blackpool Family History Centre Warren Drive Cleveleys Blackpool FY5 3TG T: 01253-858218
Chorley Family History Centre Preston Temple Chorley PR6 7EQ T: 01257 226147
Lancaster Family History Centre Ovangle Road Lancaster LA1 5HZ T: 01254-33571
Manchester Family History Centre Altrincham Road Wythenshawe Road Manchester M22 4BJ T: 0161-902-9279
Rawtenstall Family History Centre Haslingden Rawtenstall Rossendale BB4 6PU T: 01706 213460
Leicestershire
Leicestershire Family History Centre Wakerley Road Leicester LE5 4WD T: 0116-233-5544
Lincolnshire
Lincoln Family History Centre Skellingthorpe Road Lincoln LN6 0PB T: 01522-680117 Email: dann.family@diamond.co.uk
Lincolnshire - North East
Grimsby Family History Centre Linwood Avenue (NO LETTER BOX) Scartho Grimsby DN33 2NL T: 01472-828876
London
Hyde Park Family History Centre 64 - 68 Exhibition Road South Kensington London SW7 2PA T: (020) 789-8561
Wandsworth Family History Centre 149 Nightingale Lane Balham London SW12 T: (020) 8673-6741
Merseyside
Liverpool Family History Centre 4 Mill Bank Liverpool L13 0BW T: 0151-228-0433 Fax: 0151-252-0164
Middlesex
Staines Family History Centre 41 Kingston Road Staines TW14 0ND T: 01784-462627
Norfolk
Kings Lynn Family History Centre Reffley Lane Kings Lynn PE30

3EQ T: 01553-67000
Norwich Family History Centre 19 Greenways Eaton Norwich NR4 6PA T: 01603-452440
Northamptonshire
Northampton Family History Centre 137 Harlestone Road Duston Northampton NN5 6AA T: 01604-587630
Nottinghamshire
Mansfield Family History Centre Southridge Drive Mansfield NG18 4RJ T: 01623-26729
Nottingham Family History Centre Stanhome Square, West Bridgford, Nottingham NG2 7GF T: 0115 914 4255
Shropshire
Telford Family History Centre 72 Glebe Street Wellington
Somerset
Yeovil Family History Centre Forest Hill Yeovil BA20 2PH T: 01935 426817
South Yorkshire
Sheffield Family History Centre Wheel Lane Grenoside Sheffield S30 3RL T: 0114-245-3124
Staffordshire
Lichfield Family History Centre Purcell Avenue Lichfield WS14 9XA T: 01543-414843
Newcastle under Lyme Family History Centre PO Box 457 Newcastle under Lyme ST5 0TD T: 01782-620653 Fax: 01782-630178
Suffolk
Ipswich Family History Centre 42 Sidegate Lane West Ipswich IP4 3DB T: 01473-723182
Lowestoft Family History Centre 165 Yarmouth Road Lowestoft T: 01502-573851
Tyne and Wear
Sunderland Family History Centre Linden Road off Queen Alexandra Road Sunderland SR2 9BT T: 0191-528-5787
West Midlands
Coventry Family History Centre Riverside Close Whitley Coventry T: (024) 76301420
Harborne Family History Centre 38 Lordswood Road Harborne Birmingham B17 9QS T: 0121-427-9291
Sutton Coldfield Family History Centre 185 Penns Lane Sutton Coldfield Birmingham B76 1JU T: 0121-386-1690
Wednesfield Family History Centre Linthouse Lane Wednesfield Wolverhampton T: 01902-724097
Sussex – East
Crawley Family History Centre Old Horsham Road Crawley RH11 8PD T: 01293-516151
Sussex – West
Worthing Family History Centre Goring Street Worthing BN12 5AR
Wirral
Birkenhead Family History Centre Reservoir Road off Prenton Lane Prenton Birkenhead CH42 8LJ T: 0151 608 0157
Worcestershire
Redditch Family History Centre 321 Evesham Road Crabbs Cross Redditch B97 5JA T: 01527-550657
Yorkshire
Yorkshire - East
Hull Family History Centre 725 Holderness Road Kingston upon Hull HU4 7RT T: 01482-701439
Yorkshire – North
Scarborough Family History Centre Stepney Drive/Whitby Road Scarborough
Yorkshire – West
Huddersfield Family History Centre 12 Halifax Road Birchencliffe Huddersfield HD3 3BS T: 01484-454573
Leeds Family History Centre Vesper Road Leeds LS5 3QT T: 0113-258-5297
York
York Family History Centre West Bank Acomb York T: 01904-785128
Wales
Denbighshire
Rhyl Family History Centre Rhuddlan Road Rhyl
Glamorgan
Merthyr Tydfil Family History Centre Swansea Road Merthyr Tydfil CF 48 1NR T: 01685-722455
Glamorgan
Swansea Family History Centre Cockett Road Swansea SA2 0FH T: 01792-419520
South Glamorgan
Cardiff Family History Centre Heol y Deri Rhiwbina Cardiff CF4 6UH T: (029) 20620205
Isle of Man
Douglas Family History Centre Woodbourne Road Douglas IM2 3AP T: 01624-675834
Jersey
St Helier Family History Centre La Rue de la Vallee St Mary JE3 3DL T: 01534-82171
Scotland

Ayrshire
Kilmarnock Family History Centre Wahtriggs Road Kilmarnock KA1 3QY T: 01563-26560
Dumfrieshire
Dumfries Family History Centre 36 Edinburgh Road Albanybank Dumfries DG1 1JQ T: 01387-254865
Edinburgh
Edinburgh Family History Centre 30a Colinton Road Edinburgh EH4 3SN T: 0130-337-3049
Fife
Kirkcaldy Family History Centre Winifred Crescent Forth Park Kirkcaldy KY2 5SX T: 01592-640041
Glasgow
Glasgow Family History Centre 35 Julian Avenue Glasgow G12 0RB T: 0141-357-1024
Grampian
Aberdeen Family History Centre North Anderson Drive Aberdeen AB2 6DD T: 01224-692206
Highlands
Inverness Family History Centre 13 Ness Walk Inverness IV3 5SQ T: 01463-231220
Johnstone
Paisley Family History Centre Campbell Street Paisley PA5 8LD T: 01505-20886
Shetland
Lerwick Family History Centre Baila Croft Lerwick ZE1 0EY T: 01595-695732 Fax: 01950-431469
Tayside
Dundee Family History Centre 22 - 26 Bingham Terrace Dundee DD4 7HH T: 01382-451247
Northern Ireland
Belfast
Belfast Family History Centre 401 Holywood Road Belfast BT4 2GU T: (028) 90768250
Londonderry
Londonderry Family History Centre Racecourse Road Belmont Estate Londonderry T: Sun-only-(028) 71350179
Ireland
Co Dublin
Dublin Family History Centre The Willows Finglas Dublin 11 T: -4625962

Libraries

National

Angus Library Regent's Park College, Pusey Street, Oxford, OX1 2LB T: 01865 288142 F: 01865 288121

Birmingham University Information Services - Special Collections, Main Library, University of Birmingham, Edgbaston, Birmingham, B15 2TT T: 0121 414 5838 F: 0121 471 4691 E: special-collections@bham.ac.uk W: www.is.bham.ac.uk

Bristol University Library - Special Collections, Tyndall Avenue, Bristol, BS8 1TJ T: 0117 928 8014 F: 0117 925 5334 E: library@bris.ac.uk W: www.bris.ac.uk/depts/library

British Genealogical Survey Library, Kingsley Dunham Centre, Keyworth, Nottingham, NG12 5GG T: 0115 939 3205 F: 0115 936 3200 E: info@bgs.ac.uk W: www.bgs.ac.uk

British Library, British Library Building, 96 Euston Road, London, NW1 2DB T: (020) 7412 7676 Bookings E:Reader/admissions@bl.uk W: www.portico.bl.uk

British Library - Early Printed Collections, 96 Euston Road, London, NW1 2DB T: (020) 7412 7673 F: (020) 7412-7577 E: rare-books@bl.uk W: http://www.bl.uk

Cambridge University Library - Department of Manuscripts & University Archives see Cambridgeshire

House of Commons Library, House of Commons, 1 Derby Gate, London, SW1A 2DG T: (020) 7219-5545 F: (020) 7219-3921

Institute of Heraldic and Genealogical Studies seeKent

Jewish Studies Library, University College, Gower Street, London, WC1E 6BT T: (020) 7387 7050

National Gallery Library and Archive, Trafalgar Square, London, WC2N 5DN T: 020 7747 2542 F: 020 7753 8179 E: iad@ng-london.org.uk W: www.nationalgallery.org.uk

National Maritime Museum, Romney Road, Greenwich, London, SE10 9NF T: (020) 8858-4422 F: (020) 8312-6632 W: http://www.nmm.ac.uk

National Maritime Museum - Caird Library, Park Row, Greenwich, London, SE10 9NF T: (020) 8312 6673 F: (020) 8312-6632 E: ABuchanan@nmm.ac.uk W: http://www.nmm.ac.uk

Nuffield College Library, Oxford, OX1 1NF T: 01865 278550 F: 01865 278621 E: library-archives@nuf.ox.ac.uk W: www.nuff.ox.ac.uk/library/archives-information.asp

Rhodes House Library, Bodleian Library, South Parks Road, Oxford, OX1 3RG T: 01865 270909 F: 01865 270912

Robinson Library seeTyne & Wear

Royal Armouries, H.M Tower Of London, Tower Hill, London, EC3N 4AB T: (020) 7480 6358 ext 30 F: (020) 7481 2922 E: Bridgett.Clifford@armouries.org.uk W: www.armouries.org.uk

Royal Commonwealth Society Library, West Road, Cambridge, CB3 9DR T: 01223 333198 F: 01223 333160 E: tab@ula.cam.ac.uk W: www.lib.cam.ac.uk/MSS/

Royal Society of Chemistry Library & Information Centre, Burlington House, Piccadilly, London, W1J 0BA T: (020) 7437 8656 F: (020) 7287 9798 E: library@rsc.org W: www.rsc.org

Society of Antiquaries of London, Burlington House, Piccadilly, London, W1J 0BE T: 020 7479 7084 F: 020 7287 6967 E: library@sal.org.uk W: www.sal.org.uk

Society of Friends (Quakers) - Library (Ireland) see Ireland

Society of Genealogists - Library, 14 Charterhouse Buildings, Goswell Road, London, EC1M 7BA T: 020-7251-8799 T: 020-7250-0291 E: library@sog.org.uk -sales@sog.org.uk W: www.sog.org.uk

Sussex University Library, Manuscript Collections, Falmer, Brighton, BN1 9QL T: 01273 606755 F: 01273 678441

The Kenneth Ritchie Wimbledon Library, The All England Lawn Tennis & Croquet Club, Church Road, Wimbledon, London, SW19 5AE T: (020) 8946 6131 F: (020) 8944 6497 W: www.wimbledon.org, Contains the world's finest collection of books and periodicals relating to lawn tennis

The Library & Museum of Freemasonry, Freemasons' Hall, 60 Great Queen Street, London, WC2B 5AZ T: (020) 7395 9257 W: www.grandlodge-england.org

The National Coal Mining Museum for England, Caphouse Colliery, New Road, Overton, Wakefield, WF4 4RH T: 01924 848806 F: 01924 840694 E: info@ncm.org.uk W: www.ncm.org.uk

Trinity College Library, Cambridge University, Trinity College, Cambridge, CB1 1TQ T: 01223 338488 F: 01223 338532 E: trin-lib@lists.cam.ac.uk W: http://rabbit.trin.cam.ac.uk

United Reformed Church History Society, Westminster College, Madingley Road, Cambridge, CB3 0AA T: 01223-741300 (NOT Wednesdays) Information on ministers of constituent churches not members

University of Wales Swansea Library seeGlamorgan-West

Victoria & Albert Museum - National Art Library, Cromwell Road, South Kensington, London, SW7 2RL T: (020) 7938 8315 F: (020) 7938 8461 W: www.nal.vam.ac.uk

Victoria & Albert Museum - National Art Library - Archive of Art & Design, Blythe House, 23 Blythe Road, London, W14 0QF T: (020) 7603 1514 F: (020) 7602 0980 E: archive@vam.ac.uk W: www.nal.vam.ac.uk

Specialist Records & Indexes

Berkshire Medical Heritage Centre, Level 4, Main Entrance, Royal Berkshire Hospital, London Road, Reading, RG1 5AN T: 0118 987 7298 W: www.bmhc.org

British Library Newspaper Library, Colindale Avenue, London, NW9 5HE T: 020-7412-7353 F: 020-7412-7379 E: newspaper@bl.uk W: www.bl.uk/collections/newspaper/ The National archive collections of British and Overseas newspapers as well as major collections of popular magazines. Open Mon to Sat 10am to 4.45pm. Readers must be over 18yrs of age and provide proof of identity bearing their signature.

British Library of Political and Economic Science, London School of Economics, 10 Portugal Street, London, WC2A 2HD T: 020 7955 7223 F: 020 7955 7454 E: info@lse.ac.uk W: www.lse.ac.uk

British Library Oriental and India Office Collections, 96 Euston Road, London, NW1 2DB T: (020) 7412-7873 F: (020) 7412-7641 E: oioc-enquiries@bl.uk W: www.bl.uk/collections/oriental

Catholic Central Library, Lancing Street, London, NW1 1ND T: (020) 7383-4333 F: (020) 7388-6675 E: librarian@catholic-library.demon.co.uk W: www.catholic-library.demon.co.uk

Department of Manuscripts and Special Collections, Hallward Library, Nottingham University, University Park, Nottingham, NG7 2RD T: 0115 951 4565 F: 0115 951 4558 E: mss-library@nottingham.ac.uk W: www.mss.library.nottingham.ac.uk

Dr Williams's Library, 14 Gordon Square, London, WC1H 0AR T: (020) 7387-3727 The collections of the library are primarily concerned with the history and theology of religious dissent or nonconformity, principally Unitarians and Congreationalists. The libary has few registers.The General Registers of Protestant Dissenters (so called Dr Williams's Library Registers) were surrendered to the Registrar General and are now at The Public Record Office (RG4/4666-4673)

Huguenot Library, University College, Gower Street, London, WC1E 6BT T: (020) 7679 7094 E: s.massilk@ucl.ac.uk W: www.ucl.ac.uk/ucl-info/divisions/library/hugenot.htm

John Rylands University Library see Manchester

Lambeth Palace Library Lambeth Palace Road, London SE1 7JU T: (020) 7898 1400 F: (020) 7928-7932 W: www.lambethpalacelibrary.org

Library of the Religious Society of Friends (Quakers), Friends House, 173 - 177 Euston Rd, London, NW1 2BJ T: 0207 663 1135 T: 0207 663 1001 E: library@quaker.org.uk W: www.quaker.org.uk/library Limited opening hours. Letter of introduction required. Please send SAE for details or enclose IRCs

Library of the Royal College of Surgeons of England, 35-43 Lincoln's Inn Fields, London, WC2A 3PN T: (020) 7869 6520 F: (020) 7405 4438 E: library@rseng.ac.uk W: www.rseng.ac.uk Research enquiries are not undertaken. Appointments required.

Lifelong Learning Service, Theodore Road, Port Talbot, SA13 1SP T: 01639-898581 F: 01639-899914 E: lls@neath-porttalbot.gov.uk W: www.neath-porttalbot.gov.uk

Liverpool University Special Collections & Archives, see Liverpool

Methodist Archives and Research Centre, John Rylands University Library, 150 Deansgate, Manchester, M3 3EH T: 0161 834 5343 F: 0161 834 5574

Methodist Evangelical Library 78a Chiltern Street, London, W1M 2HB

Museum of the Order of St John St John's Gate, St John's Lane, Clerkenwell, London EC1M 4DA T: (020) 7253-6644 F: (020) 7336 0587 W: www.sja.org.uk/history

Library of Primitive Methodism, Englesea Brook Chapel and Museum, Englesea Brook, Crewe, Cheshire, CW2 5QW E: engleseabrook-methodist-museum@supanet.com W: www.engleseabrook-museum.org

Museum of the Order of St John, St John's Gate, St John's Lane, Clerkenwell, London, EC1M 4DA T: (020) 7253-6644 F: (020) 7336 0587 W: www.sja.org.uk/history

National Gallery Library and Archive Trafalgar Square, London, WC2N 5DN T: 020 7747 2542Fax: 020 7753 8179 E: iad@ng-london.org.uk W: www.nationalgallery.org.uk

National Maritime Museum - Caird Library, Park Row, Greenwich, London, SE10 9NF T: (020) 8312 6673 F: (020) 8312-6632 E: ABuchanan@nmm.ac.uk W: http://www.nmm.ac.uk

River & Rowing Museum, Rowing & River Museum, Mill Meadows, Henley on Thames, RG9 1BF T: 01491 415625 F: 01491 415601 E: museum@rrm.co.uk W: www..rrm.co.uk Thames linked families especially lock keepers , boat builders

Royal Institute of British Architects' Library, Manuscripts & archives Collection, 66 portland Place, London, W1N 4AD T: 020 7307 3615 F: 020 7631 1802

Royal Society of Chemistry Library & Information Centre Burlington House, Piccadilly, London W1J 0BA T: (020) 7440 3376 F: (020) 7287 9798 E: library@rsc.org W: www.rsc.org Records and information on the history of chemistry and obituary notices on RSC members

School of Oriental and African Studies library, Thornhaugh Street, Russell Square, London, WC1H 0XG T: 020 7323 6112 F: 020 7636 2834, E: lib@soas.ac.uk W: www.soas.ac.uk/library/
Society of Antiquaries of London Burlington House, Piccadilly, London, W1J 0BE T: 020 7479 7084Fax: 020 7287 6967 E: library@sal.org.uk W: www.sal.org.uk
Society of Genealogists - Library see National
South Wales Miners' Library - University of Wales, Swansea, Hendrefoelan House, Gower Road, Swansea, SA2 7NB T: 01792-518603 F: 01792-518694 E: miners@swansea.ac.uk W: www.swan.ac.uk/lis/swml
The Science Museum Library, Imperial College Road, South Kensington, London, SW7 5NH T: 020 7938 8234 T: 020 7938 8218 F: 020 7938 9714
The Women's Library, Old Castle Street, London, E1 7NT T: (020) 7320-1189 F: (020) 7320-1188Email: fawcett@lgu.ac.uk W: W: http://www.lgu.ac.uk./fawcett
Thomas Plume Library see Essex
Trades Union Congress Library Collections - University of North London, 236 - 250 Holloway Road, London, N7 6PP F: 0171 753 3191Email: tuclib@unl.ac.uk W: www.unl.ac.uk/library/tuc
United Reformed Church History Society see National
Wellcome Library for the History and Understanding of Medicine : Contemporary Medical Archives Centre : Wellcome Library for the History of Medicine - Department of Western Manuscripts, 183 Euston Road, London, NW1 2BE T: (020) 7611-8582 F: (020) 7611 8369 E: library@wellcome.ac.uk W: www.wellcome.ac.uk/library Library catalogue is available through the internet: telnet://wihm.ucl.ac.uk

England
Bedfordshire
Bedford Central Library Harpur Street, Bedford, Bedfordshire, MK40 1PG T: 01234-350931Fax: 01234-342163 E: stephensonB@bedfordshire.gov.uk W: www.bedfordshire.gov.uk
Biggleswade Library Chestnut Avenue, Biggleswade, Bedfordshire, SG18 0LL T: 01767 312324
Dunstable Library Vernon Place, Dunstable, Bedfordshire, LU5 4HA T: 01582 608441 , 1901 census
Leighton Buzzard Library Lake Street, Leighton Buzzard, Bedfordshire, LU7 1RX T: 01525 371788 , 1901 census
Local Studies Library Luton Central Library St George's Square, Luton, Bedfordshire, LU1 2NG T: 01582-547420 T: 01582-547421, E: local.studies@luton.gov.uk W: www.luton.gov.uk
Berkshire
Ascot Heath Library Fernbank Road, North Ascot, Berkshire, SL5 8LA T: 01344 884030Fax: 01344 885472
Berkshire Medical Heritage Centre Level 4, Main Entrance, Royal Berkshire Hospital, London Road, Reading, Berkshire, RG1 5AN T: 0118 987 7298 W: www.bmhc.org
Binfield Library Benetfeld Road, Binfield, Berkshire, RG42 4HD T: 01344 306663Fax: 01344 486467
Bracknell Library - Local Studies Town Square, Bracknell, Berkshire, RG12 1BH T: 01344 352515Fax: 01344 411392
Crowthorne Library Lower Broadmoor Road, Crowthorne, Berkshire, RG45 7LA T: 01344 776431Fax: 01344 776431
Eton College, College Library Windsor, Berkshire, SL4 6DB T: 01753 671269 E: archivist@etoncollege.org.uk W: www.etoncollege.com Open by appointment 9.30.a.m. to 1.00.p.m. and 2.00.p.m. to 5.00.p.m. Monday to Friday
Newbury Reference Library Newbury Central Library The Wharf, Newbury, Berkshire, RG14 5AU T: 01635 519900Fax: 01635 519906 E: newburylib@westberks.gov.uk W: www.westberks.gov.uk
Reading Local Studies Library 3rd Floor, Central Library Abbey Square, Reading, Berkshire, RG1 3BQ T: 0118 901 5965Fax: 0118 901 5954 E: info@readinglibraries.org.uk W: www.readinglibraries.org.uk
Reading University Library Whiteknights PO Box 223, Reading, RG6 6AE T: 0118-931-8776 W: www.reading.ac.uk/
Royal Borough of Windsor & Maidenhead Local Studies Collections Maidenhead Library St Ives Road, Maidenhead, Berkshire, SL6 1QU T: 01628 796978Fax: 01628 796971 E: maidenhead.ref@rbwm.gov.uk W: www.rbwm.gov.uk
Sandhurst Library The Broadway, Sandhurst, Berkshire, GU47 9BL T: 01252 870161Fax: 01252 878285
Slough Local Studies Library Top Floor, Slough Library High Street, Slough, Berkshire, SL1 1EA T: 01753 787511E: librarytop@sloughlibrary.org.uk W: www.sloughlibrary.org.uk
Whitegrove Library 5 County Lane, Warfield, Berkshire, RG42 3JP T: 01344 424211Fax: 01344 861233
Wokingham Library Local Studies The Library Denmark Street, Wokingham, Berkshire, RG40 2BT T: 0118 978 1368Fax: 0118 989 1214 E: libraries@wokingham.gov.uk W: www.wokingham.gov.uk/libraries
Birkenhead
Wirral Central Library Borough Road, Birkenhead, CH41 2XB T: 0151 652 6106 T: 0151 652 6107/8, F: 0151 653 7320 E: birkenhead.library@merseymail.com,

Birmingham
Birmingham Central Library - The Genealogist, Local Studies & History Service Floor 6, Central Library Chamberlain Square, Birmingham, West Midlands, B3 3HQ T: 0121 303 4549Fax: 0121 464 0993 E: local.studies.library@birmingham.gov.uk W: www.birmingham.gov.uk, 1901 census
Bolton
Central Library Civic Centre Le Mans Crescent, Bolton, BL1 1SE T: 01204-333185 ,
Bournemouth
Bournemouth Library see Hampshire
Bracknell Forest Borough
Ascot Heath Library see Berkshire
Binfield Library see Berkshire
Bracknell Library - Local Studies see Berkshire
Crowthorne Library see Berkshire
Sandhurst Library see Berkshire
Whitegrove Library see Berkshire
Brighton & Hove
Brighton & Hove Council Library Service see Sussex - East
Brighton Local Studies Library see Sussex - East
Bristol
Bristol Central Library Reference Section, College Green, Bristol, BS1 5TL T: 0117 903 7202
Buckinghamshire
County Reference Library Walton Street, Aylesbury, Buckinghamshire, HP20 1UU T: 01296-382250Fax: 01296-382405
High Wycombe Reference Library Queen Victoria Road, High Wycombe, Buckinghamshire, HP11 1BD T: 01494-510241 E: lib-hiwref@buckscc.gov.uk W: www.buckscc.gov.uk
Milton Keynes Reference Library 555 Silbury Boulevard, Milton Keynes, Buckinghamshire, MK9 3HL T: 01908 254160 E: mklocal@milton-keynes.gov.uk W: www.mkheritage.co.uk/mkl
Cambridgeshire
The Cambridge Library Lion Yard Cambridge, Cambridgeshire, CB2 3QD
Cambridge University Library - Department of Manuscripts & University Archives West Road, Cambridge, Cambridgeshire, CB3 9DR T: 01223 333000 ext 33143 (Manuscripts) T: 01223 333000 ext 33148 (University Archives), F: 01223 333160 E: mss@ula.cam.ac.uk W: www.lib.cam.ac.uk/MSS/
Homerton College Library The New Library Hills Road, Cambridge, Cambridgeshire, CB2 2PH
Norris Library and Museum The Broadway, St Ives, Cambridgeshire, PE27 5BX T: 01480 497317, E: bob@norrismuseum.fsnet.co.uk,
Peterborough Local Studies Collection Central Library, Broadway, Peterborough PE1 1RX T: 01733 742700 F: 01733 555277 E: libraries@peterborough.gov.uk W: www.peterborough.gov.uk
Cheshire
Alderley Edge Library Heys Lane, Alderley Edge, Cheshire, SK9 7JT T: 01625 584487Fax: 01625 584487, W: www.cheshire.gov.uk
Alsager Library Sandbach Road North, Alsager, Cheshire, ST7 2QH T: 01270 873552Fax: 01270 883093 E: alsager.infopoint@cheshire.gov.uk W: www.cheshire.gov.uk
Barnton Library Townfield Lane, Barnton, Cheshire, CW8 4LJ T: 01606 77343Fax: 01606 77343, W: www.cheshire.gov.uk
Bishops' High School Library Vaughans Lane, Chester, Cheshire, CH3 5XF T: 01244 313806Fax: 01244 320992, W: www.cheshire.gov.uk
Blacon Library Western Avenue, Blacon, Chester, Cheshire, CH1 5XF T: 01244 390628Fax: 01244 390628, W: www.cheshire.gov.uk
Bollington Library Palmerston Street, Bollington, Cheshire, SK10 5JX T: 01625 573058Fax: 01625 573058, W: www.cheshire.gov.uk
Chester Library Northgate Street, Chester, Cheshire, CH1 2EF T: 01244-312935Fax: 01244-315534 E: chester.infopoint@cheshire.gov.uk W: www.cheshire.gov.uk
Congleton Library Market Square, Congleton, Cheshire, CW12 1ET T: 01260 271141Fax: 01260 298774 E: congleton.infopoint@cheshire.gov.uk W: www.cheshire.gov.uk
Crewe Library Prince Albert Street, Crewe, Cheshire, CW1 2DH T: 01270 211123Fax: 01270 256952 E: crewe.infopoint@cheshire.gov.uk W: www.cheshire.gov.uk
Disley Library Off Buxton Old Road, Disley, Cheshire, SK12 2BB T: 01663 765635Fax: 01663 765635, W: www.cheshire.gov.uk
Ellesmere Port Library Civic Way, Ellesmere Port, South Wirral, Cheshire, L65 0BG T: 0151-355-8101Fax: 0151-355-6849 E: eport.infopoint@cheshire.gov.uk W: www.cheshire.gov.uk
Frodsham Library Rock Chapel, Main Street, Frodsham, Cheshire, WA6 7AN T: 01928 732775Fax: 01928 734214
Great Boughton Library Green Lane, Vicars Cross, Chester, Cheshire, CH3 5LB T: 01244 320709Fax: 01244 320709, W: www.cheshire.gov.uk
Halton Lea Library Halton Lea, Runcorn, Cheshire, WA7 2PF T: 01928-715351Fax: 01928-790221, W: www.cheshire.gov.uk
Handforth Library The Green, Wilmslow Road, Handforth, Cheshire, SK9 3ES T: 01625 528062Fax: 01625 524390, W: www.cheshire.gov.uk

Helsby Library Lower Robin Hood Lane, Helsby, Cheshire, WA5 0BW T: 01928 724659 W: www.cheshire.gov.uk

Holmes Chapel Library London Road, Holmes Chapel, Cheshire, CW4 7AP T: 01477 535126Fax: 01477 544193 E: homeschapel.infopoint@cheshire.gov.uk W: www.cheshire.gov.uk

Hoole Library 91 Hoole Road, Chester, Cheshire, England T: 01244 347401Fax: 01244 347401, W: www.cheshire.gov.uk

Hope Farm Library Bridge Meadow, Great Sutton, Cheshire, CH66 2LE T: 0151 355 8923 W: www.cheshire.gov.uk

Hurdsfield Library 7 Hurdsfield Green, Macclesfield, Cheshire, SK10 2RJ T: 01625 423788Fax: 01625 423788, W: www.cheshire.gov.uk

Knutsford Library Brook Street, Knutsford WA16 8BP T: 01565 632909 E: knutsford.infopoint@cheshire.gov.uk

Lache Library Lache Park Avenue, Chester, Cheshire, CH4 8HR T: 01244 683385 T: 01244 683385 W: www.cheshire.gov.uk

Little Sutton Library Chester Road, Little Sutton, Cheshire, CH66 1QQ T: 0151 339 3373Fax: 0151 339 3373, W: www.cheshire.gov.uk

Macclesfield Library 2 Jordongate, Macclesfield, Cheshire, SK10 1EE T: 01625-422512Fax: 01625-612818 E: macclesfield.infopoint@cheshire.gov.uk W: www.cheshire.gov.uk

Macclesfield Silk Museums Paradise Mill, Park Lane, Macclesfield, Cheshire, SK11 6TJ T: 01625 612045 E: silkmuseum@tiscali.co.uk W: www.silk-macclesfield.org

Malpas Library Bishop Herber High School, Malpas, Cheshire, SY14 8JD T: 01948 860571Fax: 01948 860962, W: www.cheshire.gov.uk

Middlewich Library Lewin Street, Middlewich, Cheshire, CW10 9AS T: 01606 832801Fax: 01606 833336, W: www.cheshire.gov.uk

Nantwich Library Beam Street, Nantwich, Cheshire, CW5 5LY T: 1270624867, F: 01270 610271 E: nantwich.infopoint@cheshire.gov.uk W: www.cheshire.gov.uk

Northwich Library Witton Street, Northwich, Cheshire, CW9 5DR T: 01606 44221Fax: 01606 48396 E: northwich.infopoint@cheshire.gov.uk W: www.cheshire.gov.uk

Poynton Library Park Lane, Poynton, Cheshire, SK12 1RB T: 01625 876257Fax: 01625 858027 E: poynton.infopoint@cheshire.gov.uk W: www.cheshire.gov.uk

Prestbury Library The Reading Room, Prestbury, Cheshire, SK10 4AD T: 01625 827501 W: www.cheshire.gov.uk

John Rylands University Library see Manchester

Sandbach Library The Common, Sandbach, Cheshire, CW11 1FJ T: 01270 762309Fax: 01270 759656 E: sandbach.infopoint@cheshire.gov.uk W: www.cheshire.gov.uk

Sandiway Library Mere Lane, Cuddington, Northwich, Cheshire, CW8 2NS T: 01606 888065Fax: 01606 883743, W: www.cheshire.gov.uk

Stockport Local Heritage Library Central Library Wellington Road South, Stockport, Cheshire, SK1 3RS T: 0161-474-4530Fax: 0161-474-7750 E: localheritage.library@stockport.gov.uk W: www.stockport.gov.uk

Tameside Local Studies Library Stalybridge Library Trinity Street, Stalybridge, Cheshire, SK15 2BN T: 0161-338-2708 E: localstudies.library@mail.tameside.gov.uk W: www.tameside.gov.uk

Tarporley Library High School, Eaton Road, Tarporley, Cheshire, CW6 0BJ T: 01829 732558 W: www.cheshire.gov.uk

Upton Library Wealstone Lane, Upton by Chester, Cheshire, CH2 1HB T: 01244 380053, F: 01244 377197, W: www.cheshire.gov.uk

Warrington Library & Local Studies Centre Museum Street, Warrington, Cheshire, WA1 1JB T: 01925 442890 F: 01925 411395 E: library@warrington.gov.uk W: www.warrington.gov.uk

Weaverham Library Russett Road, Weaverham, Northwich, Cheshire, CW8 3HY T: 01606 853359, F: 01606 853359, W: www.cheshire.gov.uk

Weston Library Heyes Hall, Weston, Macclesfield, Cheshire, SK11 8RL T: 01625 614008, F: 01625 614008, W: www.cheshire.gov.uk

Wharton Library Willow Square, Wharton, Winsford, Cheshire, CW7 3HP T: 01606 593883, F: 01606 593883, W: www.cheshire.gov.uk

Wilmslow Library South Drive, Wilmslow, Cheshire, SK9 1NW T: 01625 528977, F: 01625 548401 E: wilmslow.infopoint@cheshire.gov.uk W: www.cheshire.gov.uk

Winsford Library High Street, Winsford, Cheshire, CW7 2AS T: 01606 552065, F: 01606 861563 E: winsford.infopoint@cheshire.gov.uk W: www.cheshire.gov.uk

Cleveland

Hartlepool Central Library 124 York Road, Hartlepool, Cleveland, TS26 9DE T: 01429 263778 , 1901 census

Middlesbrough Libraries & Local Studies Centre Central Library Victoria Square, Middlesbrough, Cleveland, TS1 2AY T: 01642 729001 E: reference_library@middlesbrough.gov.uk W: www.middlesbrough.gov.uk

Stockton Reference Library Church Road, Stockton on Tees, Cleveland, TS18 1TU T: 01642-393994, F: 01642-393929 E: reference.library@stockton.bc.gov.uk W: www.stockton.bc.gov.uk

Cornwall

The Cornwall Centre , Alma Place, Redruth, Cornwall, TR15 2AT T: 01209-216760, F: 01209-210283 E: cornishstudies@library.cornwall.gov.uk W: www.cornwall.gov.uk Cornwall Libraries main library of local studies material. Printed and published items about Cornwall incl books, pamphlets, journals, newspapers, maps, photographs etc. 1901 census

Royal Institution of Cornwall, Courtney Library & Cornish History Research Centre Royal Cornwall Museum, River Street, Truro, Cornwall, TR1 2SJ T: 01872 272205, F: 01872 240514 E: RIC@royal-cornwall-museum.freeserve.co.uk W: www.cornwall-online.co.uk/ric

County Durham

Darlington Local Studies Centre The Library Crown Street, Darlington, County Durham, DL1 1ND T: 01325-349630, F: 01325-381556 E: crown.street.library@darlington.gov.uk W: www.darlington.gov.uk 1901 census

Durham City Reference & Local Studies Library Durham Clayport Library Millennium Place, Durham, County Durham, DH1 1WA T: 0191-386-4003 E: durhamcityref.lib@durham.gov.uk W: www.durham.gov.uk

Durham Cultural Services, Library and Museums Department, County Hall, Durham, County Durham, DH1 5TY T: 0191 384 3777, F: 0191 384 1336 E: culture@durham.gov.uk W: www.durham.gov.uk

Durham University Library Archives and Special Collections, Palace Green Section, Palace Green, Durham, DH1 3RN T: 0191-374-3032, E: pg.library@durham.ac.uk W: www.durham.ac.uk

Cumbria

Carlisle Library 11 Globe Lane, Carlisle, Cumbria, CA3 8NX T: 01228-607310 E: carlisle.library@cumbriacc.gov.uk W: www.cumbriacc.gov.uk

Cumbria Record Office and Local Studies Library (Whitehaven) Scotch Street, Whitehaven, Cumbria, CA28 7BJ T: 01946-852920, F: 01946-852919 E: whitehaven.record.office@cumbriacc.gov.uk W: www.cumbria.gov.uk/archives

Cumbria Record Office & Local Studies Library 140 Duke St, Barrow in Furness, Cumbria, LA14 1XW T: 01229-894363, F: 01229-894371 E: barrow.record.office@cumbriacc.gov.uk W: www.cumbria.gov.uk/archives

Kendal Library Stricklandgate, Kendal, Cumbria, LA9 4PY T: 01539-773520, F: 01539-773530 E: kendal.library@cumbriacc.gov.uk W: www.cumbriacc.gov.uk

Penrith Library St Andrews Churchyard, Penrith, Cumbria, CA11 7YA T: 01768-242100, F: 01768-242101 E: penrith.library@dial.pipexcom W: www.cumbria.gov.uk

Workington Library Vulcans Lane, Workington, Cumbria, CA14 2ND T: 01900-325170, F: 01900-325181 E: workington.library@cumbriacc.gov.uk W: www.cumbriacc.gov.uk

Derbyshire

Chesterfield Local Studies Department Chesterfield Library New Beetwell Street, Chesterfield, Derbyshire, S40 1QN T: 01246-209792, F: 01246-209304 E: chesterfield.library@derbyshire.gov.uk 1901 census - North Derbyshire only on microfilm

Derby Local Studies Library 25b Irongate, Derby, Derbyshire, DE1 3GL T: 01332 255393, E: localstudies.library@derby.gov.uk W: www.derby.gov.uk/libraries/about/local_studies.htm, 1901 census

Matlock Local Studies Library County Hall, Smedley Street, Matlock, Derbyshire, DE4 3AG T: 01629-585579 E: ruth.gordon@derbyshire.gov.uk W: www.derbyshire.gov.uk/librar/locstu.htm

Devon

Exeter University Library Stocker Road, Exeter, Devon, EX4 4PT T: 01392 263870, F: 01392 263871 E: library@exeter.ac.uk W: www.library.exeter.ac.uk

Plymouth Local Studies Library Central Library Drake Circus, Plymouth PL4 8AL T: 01752 305909 E: localstudies@plymouth.gov.uk W: www.plymouth.gov.uk

Torquay Library Lymington Road, Torquay, Devon, TQ1 3DT T: 01803 208305

West Country Studies Library Exeter Central Library Castle Street, Exeter, Devon, EX4 3PQ T: 01392 384216 E: dlaw@devon-cc.gov.uk http://www.devon-cc.gov.uk/library/locstudy

Devon & Exeter Institution Library 7 The Close, Exeter, Devonshire, EX1 1EZ T: 01392 251017, F: 01392-263871 E: m.midgley@exeter.ac.uk W: www.ex.ac.uk/library/devonex.html

Dorset

Dorchester Reference Library Colliton Park, Dorchester, Dorset, DT1 1XJ T: 01305-224448, F: 01305-266120

Dorset County Museum High West Street, Dorchester, Dorset, DT1 1XA T: 01305 262735, F: 01305 257180 E: dorsetcountymuseum@dor-mus.demon.co.uk W: www.dorsetcc.gov.uk

Poole Central Reference Library Dolphin Centre , Poole, Dorset, BH15 1QE T: 01202 262424 E: centrallibrary@poole.gov.uk W: www.poole.gov.uk

Weymouth Library The Local Studies Library, Great George Street, Weymouth DT4 8NN T: 01305 762410 E: weymouthlibrary@dorsetcc.gov.uk W: www.dorsetcc.gov.uk

East Yorkshire

Bridlington Local Studies Library Bridlington Library King Street, Bridlington, East Yorkshire, YO15 2DF T: 01262 672917, F: 01262 670208 E: bridlingtonref.library@eastriding.gov.uk W: www.eastriding.gov.uk 1841 to 1901 Censuses for bridlington area

East Riding Heritage Library & Museum Sewerby Hall, Church Lane, Sewerby, Bridlington, East Yorkshire, YO15 1EA T: 01262-677874 T: 01262-674265, E: museum@pop3.poptel.org.uk W: www.bridlington.net/sew

Goole Local Studies Library Goole Library Carlisle Street, Goole, East Yorkshire, DN14 5DS T: 01405-762187, F: 01405-768329 E: goolref.library@eastriding.gov.uk W: www.eastriding.gov.uk

Essex

Central Reference Library - London Borough of Havering Reference Library St Edward's Way, Romford, Essex, RM1 3AR T: 01708 432393 T: 01708 432394Fax: 01708 432391 E: romfordlib2@rmplc.co.uk

Chelmsford Library PO Box 882, Market Road, Chelmsford, Essex, CM1 1LH T: 01245 492758, F: 01245 492536 E: answers.direct@essexcc.gov.uk W: www.essexcc.gov.uk 1901 census

Clacton Library Station Road, Clacton on Sea, Essex, CO15 1SF T: 01255 421207

Colchester Central Library Trinity Square, Colchester, Essex, CO1 1JB T: 01206-245917 E: jane.stanway@essexcc.gov.uk W: www.essexcc.co.uk

Harlow Library The High, Harlow, Essex, CM20 1HA T: 01279 413772

Ilford Local Studies and Archives Central Library Clements Road, Ilford, Essex, IG1 1EA T: 020 8708 2417

London Borough of Barking & Dagenham Local Studies Library Valence House Museum, Beacontree Avenue, Dagenham, Essex, RM8 3HT T: 020 8270 6896E: localstudies@bardaglea.org.uk W: www.barking-dagenham.gov.uk

Loughton Library Traps Hill, Loughton, Essex, IG10 1HD T: 020 8502 0181

Redbridge Library Central Library Clements Road, Ilford, Essex, IG1 1EA T: (020) 8708-2417 E: Local.Studies@redbridge.gov.uk W: www.redbridge.gov.uk

Saffron Walden Library 2 King Street, Saffron Walden, Essex, CB10 1ES T: 01799 523178

Southend Library Central Library Victoria Avenue, Southend on Sea, Essex, SS2 6EX T: 01702-612621, F: 01792-612652 and 01702 469241 E: library@southend.gov.uk W: www.southend.gov.uk/libraries/, Minicom 01702 600579

Thomas Plume Library Market Hill, Maldon, Essex, CM9 4PZ T: , No facilities for incoming telephone or fax messages

Valence House Museum, Valence House Museum, Becontree Avenue, Dagenham, Essex, RM8 3HT T: 020 8270 6866, F: 020 82706868, W: www.barking-dagenham.gov.uk Heritage service includes a local history museum, and archive section. A list of resources is available upon request. Archives of the Essex Parishes of Barking and Dagenham and the London Boroughs of the same names

Gloucestershire

Cheltenham Local Studies Centre Cheltenham Library Clarence Street, Cheltenham, Gloucestershire, GL50 3JT T: 01242-532678, F: 01242 532673

Gloucester Library, Arts & Museums County Library Quayside, Shire Hall, Gloucester, Gloucestershire, GL1 1HY T: 01452-425037, F: 01452-425042 E: clams@gloscc.gov.uk http://www.gloscc.gov.uk

Gloucestershire County Library Brunswick Road, Gloucester, GL1 1HT T: 01452-426979, F: 01452-521468 E: clams@gloscc.gov.uk W: www.gloscc.gov.uk The Gloucester Collection at Gloucester Library is the largest local studies library in the County. Other libraries specialising in their particular areas are Cheltenham, Cinderford, Cirencester, Stow on the Wold, Stroud and Tewkesbury

Yate Library 44 West Walk, Yate, S Gloucestershire, BS37 4AX T: 01454 865661 E: yate_library@southglos.gov.uk W: www.southglos.co.uk

Gloucestershire – South

Thornbury Library St Mary Street, Thornbury, South Gloucestershire, BS35 2AA T: 01454-865655 E: thornbury.library@southglos.gov.uk W: www.southglos.gov.uk

Hammersmith

Hammersmith Central Library Shepherds Bush Road, London, W6 7AT T: 020 8753 3816, F: 020 8753 3815, W: www.lbhf.gov.uk

Hampshire

Aldershot Library 109 High Street, Aldershot, Hampshire, GU11 1DQ T: 01252 322456 ,

Andover Library Chantry Centre , Andover, Hampshire, SP10 1LT T: 01264 352807 E: clceand@hants.gov.uk W: www.hants.gov.uk

Basingstoke Library North Division Headquarters, 19 - 20 Westminster House, Potters Walk, Basingstoke, Hampshire, RG21 7LS T: 01256-473901, F: 01256-470666, W: www.hants.gov.uk

Bournemouth Library 22 The Triangle, Bournemouth, Hampshire, BH2 5RQ T: 01202 454817Fax: 01202 454830

Eastleigh Library The Swan Centre , Eastleigh, Hampshire, SO50 5SF T: 01703 612513 E: clweeas@hants.gov.uk W: www.hants.gov.uk

Fareham Library South Division Headquarters, Osborn Road, Fareham, Hampshire, PO16 7EN T: 01329-282715, F: 01329-221551 E: clsoref@hants.gov.uk W: www.hants.gov.uk

Farnborough Library Pinehurst, Farnborough, Hampshire, GU14 7JZ T: 01252 513838 E: clnoref@hants.gov.uk W: www.brit-a-r.demon.co.uk

Fleet Library 236 Fleet Road, Fleet, Hampshire, GU13 8BX T: 01252 614213 E: clnofle@hants.gov.uk W: www.hants.gov.uk

Gosport Library High Street, Gosport, Hampshire, PO12 1BT T: (023) 9252 3431 E: clsos@hants.gov.uk W: www.hants.gov.uk

Hampshire County Library West Division Headquarters, The Old School, Cannon Street, Lymington, Hampshire, SO41 9BR T: 01590-675767 E: clwedhq@hants.gov.uk W: www.hants.gov.uk

Hampshire Local Studies Library Winchester Library Jewry Street, Winchester, Hampshire, SO23 8RX T: 01962 841408 E: clceloc@hants.gov.uk W: www.hants.gov.uk/library

Lymington Library Cannon Street, Lymington, Hampshire, SO41 9BR T: 01590 673050 E: clwelym@hants.gov.uk W: www.hants.gov.uk

Portsmouth City Libraries Central Library Guildhall Square, Portsmouth, Hampshire, PO1 2DX T: (023) 9281 9311 X232 (Bookings) T: (023) 9281 9311 X234 (Enquiries)Fax: (023) 9283 9855 E: reference.library@portsmouthcc.gov.uk W: www.portsmouthcc.gov.uk

Royal Marines Museum, Eastney, Southsea, Hampshire, PO4 9PX T: (023) 9281 9385-Exts-224 Fax: (023) 9283 8420 E: matthewlittle@royalmarinesmuseum.co.uk W: www.royalmarinesmuseum.co.uk No charges for research other than material costs. Donations welcome. Visits by appointment Mon to Fri 10am to 4.30pm

Royal Naval Museum, H M Naval Base (PP66), Portsmouth, Hampshire, PO1 3NH T: (023) 9272 3795 (023) 9272 3942, W: www.royalnavalmuseum.org

Southampton City Libraries - Special Collections Southampton Reference Library Civic Centre , Southampton, Hampshire, SO14 7LW T: 023 8083 2205E: local.studies@southampton.gov.uk W: www.southampton.gov.uk Special collections include information on Southampton and Hampshire, genealogy and maritime topics

Southampton University Library Highfield, Southampton, Hampshire, SO17 1BJ T: 023 8059 3724 T: 023 8059 2721

Waterlooville Library The Precinct Waterlooville, Hampshire, PO7 7DT T: (023) 9225 4626 E: clsowvl@hants.gov.uk W: www.hants.gov.uk

Winchester Reference Library 81 North Walls, Winchester, Hampshire, SO23 8BY T: 01962-846059 E: clceref@hants.gov.uk W: www.hants.gov.uk

Herefordshire

Bromyard Library 34 Church Street, Bromyard, Herefordshire, HR7 4DP T: 01885 482657 , No Genealogical information held

Colwall Library Humphrey Walwyn Library Colwall, Malvern, Herefordshire, WR13 6QT T: 01684 540642 ,

Hereford Cathedral Archives & Library 5 College Cloisters, Cathedral Close, Hereford HR1 2NG T: 01432 374225 E: library@herefordcathedral.co.uk W: www.herefordcathedral.co.uk

Hereford Library Broad Street, Hereford, Herefordshire, HR4 9AU T: 01432-272456 E: herefordlibrary@herefordshire.gov.uk W: www.libraries.herefordshire.gov.uk The main local studies collection for the county of Herefordshire

Ledbury Library The Homend Ledbury, Herefordshire, HR8 1BT T: 01531 632133

Leominster Library 8 Buttercross, Leominster, Herefordshire, HR6 8BN T: 01568-612384

Ross Library Cantilupe Road, Ross on Wye, Herefordshire, HR9 7AN T: 01989 567937

Hertfordshire

Bushey Museum, Art Gallery and Local Studies Centre Rudolph Road, Bushey, Hertfordshire, WD23 3HW T: 020 8420 4057 E: busmt@bushey.org.uk W: www.busheymuseum.org

Hertfordshire Archives and Local Studies County Hall, Pegs Lane, Hertford, Hertfordshire, SG13 8EJ T: 01438 737333 E: herts.direct@hertscc.gov.uk http://hertsdirect.org/hals

Welwyn Garden City Central Library Local Studies, Campus West, Welwyn Garden City, Hertfordshire, AL8 6AJ T: 01438 737333

Hull

Brynmor Jones Library - University of Hull Cottingham Road, Hull, HU6 7RX T: 01482 465265 E: archives@acs.hull.ac.uk W: www.hull.ac.uk/lib W: www.hull.ac.uk/lib/archives

Hull Central Library Family and Local History Unit Central Library Albion Street, Kingston upon Hull, HU1 3TF T: 01482 616828 01482 616827 E: gareth@ukorigins.co.uk W: www.hullcc.gov.uk/genealogy/famhist.php, Free membership. Meets second Tuesday of every month 1901 census

Hull College - Local History Unit James Reckitt Library, Holderness Road, Hull HU9 1EA T: 01482 331551 E: historyunit@netscape.net W: www.historyofhull.co.uk

Hull Local Studies Library Central Library Albion Street, Kingston upon Hull, HU1 3TF T: 01482 210077
E: local.studies@hullcc.gov.uk W: www.hullcc.gov.uk/genealogy/
Isle of Wight
Isle of Wight County Library Lord Louis Library Orchard Street, Newport, Isle of Wight, PO30 1LL T: 01983-823800 01983-825972 E: reflib@postmaster.co.uk W: www.iwight.com/thelibrary
Kent
Ashford Library Church Road, Asford, Kent, TN23 1QX T: 01233 620649 W: www.kent.gov.uk 1901 census
Broadstairs Library The Broadway, Broadstairs, Kent, CT10 2BS T: 01843-862994 W: www.kent.gov.uk
Canterbury Cathedral Library The Precincts, Canterbury, Kent, CT1 2EH T: 01227-865287 01227-865222 E: catlib@ukc.ac.uk W: www.canterbury-cathedral.org
Canterbury Library & Local Studies Collection 18 High Street, Canterbury, Kent, CT1 2JF T: 01227-463608 01227-768338, W: www.kent.gov.uk 1901 census
Dartford Central Library - Reference Department Market Street, Dartford, Kent, DA1 1EU T: 01322-221133 01322-278271, W: www.kent.gov.uk
Deal Library Broad Street, Deal, Kent, CT14 6ER T: 01304 374726 W: www.kent.gov.uk 1901 census
Dover Library Maison Dieu House, Biggin Street, Dover, Kent, CT16 1DW T: 01304 204241 01304 225914, W: www.kent.gov.uk 1901 census
Faversham Library Newton Road, Faversham, Kent, ME13 8DY T: 01759-532448 01795-591229, W: www.kent.gov.uk 1901 census
Folkestone Library & Local Heritage Studies 2 Grace Hill, Folkestone, Kent, CT20 1HD T: 01303-256710 01303-256710 E: janet.adamson@kent.gov.uk W: www.kent.gov.uk
Gillingham Library High Street, Gillingham, Kent, ME7 1BG T: 01634-281066 01634-855814 E: Gillingham.Library@medway.gov.uk W: www.medway.gov.uk
Gravesend Library Windmill Street, Gravesend, Kent, DA12 1BE T: 01474 352758 01474-320284, W: www.kent.gov.uk 1901 census
Greenhill Library Greenhill Road, Herne Bay, Kent, CT6 7PN T: 01227 374288 W: www.kent.gov.uk
Herne Bay Library 124 High Street, Herne Bay, Kent, CT6 5JY T: 01227-374896 01227-741582, W: www.kent.gov.uk
Institute of Heraldic and Genealogical Studies, 79 - 82 Northgate, Canterbury, Kent, CT1 1BA T: 01227 462618 01227 765617 E: ihgs@ihgs.ac.uk W: www.ihgs.ac.uk
London Borough of Bromley Local Studies Library Central Library High Street, Bromley, Kent, BR1 1EX T: 020 8460 9955 020 8313 9975 E: localstudies.library@bromley.gov.uk W: www.bromley.gov.uk 1901 census
Maidstone Reference Library St Faith's Street, Maidstone, Kent, ME14 1LH T: 01622 701943 W: www.kent.gov.uk 1901 census
Margate Library Local History Collection, Cecil Square, Margate, Kent, CT9 1RE T: 01843-223626 01843-293015, W: www.kent,gov.uk
Ramsgate Library and Museum, Guildford Lawn, Ramsgate, Kent, CT11 9QY T: 01843-593532 01843-852692, W: www.kent.gov.uk
Ramsgate Library Local Strudies Collection & Thanet Branch Archives Ramsgate Library Guildford Lawn, Ramsgate, Kent, CT11 9AY T: 01843-593532 W: www.kent.gov.uk Archives at this library moved to East Kent Archives CentreEnterprise Zone, Honeywood Road, Whitfield, Dover, Kent CT16 3EH. A Local Studies Collection will remain
Sevenoaks Library Buckhurst Lane, Sevenoaks, Kent, TN13 1LQ T: 01732-453118 01732-742682, W: www.kent.gov.uk 1901 census
Sheerness Library Russell Street, Sheerness, Kent, ME12 1PL T: 01795-662618 01795-583035, W: www.kent.gov.uk 1901 census
Sittingbourne Library Central Avenue, Sittingbourne, Kent, ME10 4AH T: 01795-476545 01795-428376, W: www.kent.gov.uk 1901 census
Sturry Library Chafy Crescent, Sturry, Canterbury, Kent, CT2 0BA T: 01227 711479 01227 710768, W: www.kent.gov.uk
Tonbridge Library Avenbury Avenue, Tonbridge, Kent, TN9 1TG T: 01732 352754 W: www.kent.gov.uk 1901 census
Tunbridge Wells Library Mount Pleasant, Tunbridge Wells, Kent, TN1 1NS T: 01892-522352 01892-514657, W: www.kent.gov.uk 1901 census
University of Kent at Canterbury Library Canterbury, Kent, CT2 7NU T: 01227 764000 01227 823984
Whitstable Library 31-33 Oxford Street, Whitstable, Kent, CT5 1DB T: 01227-273309 01227-771812
Lancashire
Bacup Library St James's Square, Bacup, Lancashire, OL13 9AH T: 01706 873324 , 1901 census
Barnoldswick Library Fernlea Avenue, Barnoldswick, Lancashire, BB18 5DW T: 01282-812147 1901 census
Blackburn Central Library Town Hall Street, Blackburn, BB2 1AG T: 01254 587920 E: reference.library@blackburn.gov.uk W: www.blackburn.gov.uk/library

Burnley Central & Local Studies Library Grimshaw St, Burnley BB11 2BD T: 01282-437115 E: burnley.reference@lcl.lancscc.gov.uk W: www.lancscc.gov.uk 1901 census
Bury Central Library - References and Information Services Bury Central Library Manchester Road, Bury, Lancashire, BL9 0DG T: 0161-253-5871 E: information@bury.gov.uk Bury.lib@bury.gov.uk W: www.bury.gov.uk/culture.htm
Chethams Library Long Millgate, Manchester, M3 1SB T: 0161 834 7961 0161 839 5797 E: librarian@chethams.org.uk W: www.chethams.org.uk
Chorley Central Library Union Street, Chorley, Lancashire, PR7 1EB T: 01257 277222
Clitheroe Library Church Street, Clitheroe, Lancashire, BB7 2DG T: 01200 428788
Colne Library Market Street, Colne, Lancashire, BB8 0AP T: 01282-871155 01282 865227 E: colne.reference@lcl.lancscc.gov.uk
Haslingden Library Higher Deardengate, Haslingden, Rossendale, Lancashire, BB4 5QL T: 01706 215690
Heywood Local Studies Library Heywood Library Church Street, Heywood, Lancashire, OL10 1LL T: 01706 360947 01706 368683
Hyndburn Central Library St James Street, Accrington BB5 1NQ T: 01254-872385 E: accrington.localstudies@lcl.lancscc.gov.uk W: www.lancscc.gov.uk
John Rylands University Library see Manchester
Lancashire Record Office Bow Lane, Preston PR1 2RE T: 01772 263039 01772 263050 E: record.office@ed.lancscc.gov.uk W: www.lancashire.gov.uk/education/lifelong/recordindex.shtm The Lancashire Local Studies Collection is now housed here 1901 census
Leigh Library Turnpike Centre Civic Centre, Leigh WN7 1EB T: 01942-404559 01942 404567 E: heritage@wiganmbc.gov.uk W: www.wiganmbc.gov.uk 1901 census
Leyland Library Lancastergate, Leyland PR25 2EX T: 01772 432804 01772 456549 E: leyland.library@lcl.lancscc.gov.uk W: www.lancashire.gov.uk/libraries
Morecambe Library Central Drive, Morecambe, Lancashire, LA4 5DL T: 01524 402110 , 1901 census - Lancaster District
Nelson Library Market Square, Nelson, Lancashire, BB9 7PU T: 01282 692511 01282 449584 E: nelson.reference@lcl.lancscc.gov.uk W: www.lancashire.gov.uk/libraries/
Oldham Local Studies and Archives 84 Union Street, Oldham, Lancashire, OL1 1DN T: 0161-911-4654 E: archives@oldham.gov.uk localstudies@oldham.gov.uk W: www.oldham.gov.uk/archives W: www.oldham.gov.uk/local_studies
Ormskirk Library Burscough Street, Ormskirk, Lancashire, L39 2EN T: 01695 573448
Prestwich Library Longfield Centre , Prestwich, Lancashire, M25 1AY T: 0161 253 7214 T: 0161 253 7218, 0161 253 5372 E: Prestwich.lib@bury.gov.uk W: www.bury.gov.uk
Radcliffe Library Stand Lane, Radcliffe, Lancashire, M26 9WR T: 0161 253 7160 0161 253 7165 E: Radcliffe.lib@bury.gov.uk W: www.bury.gov.uk
Ramsbottom Library Carr Street, Ramsbottom, Lancashire, BL0 9AE T: 01706 822481 01706 824638 F: Ramsbottom.lib@bury.gov.uk W: www.bury.gov.uk
Rawtenstall Library Haslingden Rd, Rawtenstall, Rossendale, BB4 6QU T: 01706 227911 E: rawtenstall.reference@lcl.lancscc.gov.uk W: www.lancashire.gov.uk/libraries
Rochdale Local Studies Library Touchstones, The Esplanade, Rochdale, Lancashire, OL16 1AQ T: 01706 864915 01706 864944 E: localstudies@rochdale.gov.uk W: www.rochdale.gov.uk
Salford Local History Library Peel Park, Salford, Lancashire, M5 4WU T: 0161 736 2649 E: salford.museums@salford/gov.uk W: www.salford.gov.uk
Salford Museum & Art Gallery, Peel Park, Salford, Lancashire, M5 4WU T: 0161 736 2649 E: Email: info@lifetimes.org.uk W: www.lifetimes.org.uk
Skelmersdale Central Library Southway, Skelmersdale, Lancashire, WN8 6NL T: 01695 720312 , 1901 census
St Anne's Library 254 Clifton Drive, St Anne's on Sea, Lancashire, FY8 1NR T: 01253 643900 , 1901 census
The Harris Reference Library Market Square, Preston, Lancashire, PR1 2PP T: 01772 404010 01772 555527 E: harris@airtime.co.uk 1901 census
Tameside Local Studies Library Stalybridge Library Trinity Street, Stalybridge, Cheshire, SK15 2BN T: 0161-338-2708 T: 0161-338-3831 and 0161 303 7937Fax: 0161-303-8289 E: localstudies.library@mail.tameside.gov.uk W: www.tameside.gov.uk 1901 census
Working Class Movement Library Jubilee House, 51 The Crescent, Salford, Lancashire, M5 4WX T: 0161 736 3601 0161-737 4115 E: enquiries2wcml.org.uk W: www.wcml.org.uk
Leeds
Brotherton Library see Yorkshire- West
Leicestershire
Hinckley Library Local Studies Collection Hinckley Library Lancaster Road, Hinckley, Leicestershire, LE10 0AT T: 01455-635106 01455-251385 E: hinckleylibrary@leics.gov.uk W: www.leics.gov.uk

Leicester Reference and Information Library Bishop Street, Leicester, Leicestershire, LE1 6AA T: 0116 299 5401 , 1901 census
Leicestershire Libraries & Information Service 929 - 931 Loughborough Road, Rothley, Leicestershire, LE7 7NH T: 0116 267 8023 0116 267 8039 E: skettle@leics.gov.uk W: www.leicestershire.gov.uk/libraries
Loughborough Library Local Studies Collection Granby Street, Loughborough LE11 3DZ T: 01509-238466 E: Jslater@leices.gov.uk W: www.leices.gov.uk/libraries
Market Harborough Library and Local Studies Collection Pen Lloyd Library Adam and Eve Street, Market Harborough, Leicestershire, LE16 7LT T: 01858-821272 01858-821265
Melton Mowbray Library Wilton Road, Melton Mowbray, Leicestershire, LE13 0UJ T: 01664 560161 01664 410199, W: www.leics.gov.uk
Southfields Library Reader Development Services, Saffron Lane, Leicester, Leicestershire, LE2 6QS
Lincolnshire
Boston Library County Hall Boston PE21 6LX T: 01205 357760
Gainsborough Library Cobden Street, Gainsborough DN21 2NG T: 01427 614780 E: gainsborough.library@lincolnshire.gov.uk
Grantham Library Issac Newton Centre , Grantham, Lincolnshire, NG1 9LD T: 01476 591411 01476 592458
Lincoln Cathedral Library Lincoln Cathedral Library The Cathedral, Lincoln LN2 1PZ England T: 01522-544544E: librarian@lincolncathedral.com W: www.lincolncathedral.com
Lincolnshire County Library Local Studies Section, Lincoln Central Library Free School Lane, Lincoln, Lincolnshire, LN1 1EZ T: 01522-510800 E: lincoln.library@lincolnshire.gov.uk W: www.lincolnshire.gov.uk/library/services/family.htm
Stamford Library High Street, Stamford, Lincolnshire, PE9 2BB T: 01780 763442 01780 482518
Lincolnshire - North
Scunthorpe Central Library Carlton Street, Scunthorpe DN15 6TX T: 01724-860161 E: scunthorpe.ref@central-library.demon.co.uk W: www.nothlincs.gov.uk/library
Lincolnshire - North East
Grimsby Central Library Reference Department Central Library Town Hall Square, Great Grimsby DN31 1HG T: 01472-323635 E: jennie.mooney@nelincs.gov.uk W: www.nelincs.gov.uk
Liverpool
Liverpool Record Office & Local History Dept Central Library William Brown Street, Liverpool, L3 8EW T: 0151 233 5817 E: recoffice.central.library@liverpool.gov.uk W: www.liverpool.gov.uk
Liverpool University Special Collections & Archives University of Liverpool Library PO Box 123, Liverpool, L69 3DA T: 0151-794-2696 W: www.sca.lib.liv.ac.uk/collections/index.html The University holds the records of a number of charities, especially those which looked after children or encouraged emigration
London
Bancroft Library 277 Bancroft Road, London, E1 4DQ T: 020 8980 4366 , 1901 census
London Borough of Barking & Dagenham Local Studies Library see Essex
Bishopsgate Institute, Reference Librarian, 230 Bishopsgate, London, EC2M 4QH T: (020) 7392 9270 (020) 7392 9275 E: library@bishopsgate.org.uk W: www.bishopsgate.org.uk
Brent Community History Library & Archive 152 Olive Road, London, NW2 6UY T: (020) 8937 3541 (020) 8450 5211 E: archive@brent.gov.uk W: www.brent.gov.uk 1901 census
British Film Institute - Library & Film Archive 21 Stephen Street, London, W1T 1LN T: 020 7957 4824 W: www.bfi.org.uk
British Library see National
British Library - Early Printed Collections see National
British Library Newspaper Library see National
British Library of Political and Economic Science see National
British Library Oriental and India Office Collections see National
Catholic Central Library Lancing Street, London, NW1 1ND T: (020) 7383-4333 (020) 7388-6675 E: librarian@catholic-library.demon.co.uk W: www.catholic-library.demon.co.uk
Chelsea Public Library Old Town Hall, King's Road, London, SW3 5EZ T: (020) 7352-6056 T: (020) 7361-4158, (020) 7351 1294 Local Studies Collection on Royal Borough of Kensington & Chelsea south of Fulham Road
Dr Williams's Library see Special
Ealing Local History Centre Central Library 103 Broadway Centre Ealing, London, W5 5JY T: (020) 8567-3656-ext-37, (020) 8840-2351 E: localhistory@hotmail.com W: www.ealing.gov.uk/libraries
Fawcett Library London Guildhall University, Old Castle Street, London, E1 7NT T: (020) 7320-1189 (020) 7320-1188 E: fawcett@lgu.ac.uk W: http://www.lgu.ac.uk./fawcett
The Library & Museum of Freemasonry see National
Guildhall Library, Manuscripts Section Aldermanbury, London, EC2P 2EJ T: (020) 7332-1863 (020) 7600-3384 E: manuscripts.guildhall@corpoflondon.gov.uk
http://ihr.sas.ac.uk/ihr/gh/ Records: City of London parish records, probate records, City Livery companies, business records, Diocese of London, St Pauls Cathedral, etc. Prior booking unnecessary except

some records on 24 hrs call/restricted
Hammersmith Central Library Shepherds Bush Road, London, W6 7AT T: 020 8753 3816, F: 020 8753 3815, W: www.lbhf.gov.uk
Hounslow Library (Local Studies & Archives) Centrespace, Treaty Centre High Street, Hounslow, London, TW3 1ES T: 0845 456 2800 0845 456 2880, W: www.cip.com
House of Commons Library see National
Huguenot Library University College, Gower Street, London, WC1E 6BT T: (020) 7679 7094 E: s.massilk@ucl.ac.uk W: www.ucl.ac.uk/ucl-info/divisions/library/hugenot.htm
Imperial College Archives London University, Room 455 Sherfield Building, Imperial College, London, SW7 2AZ T: 020 7594 8850 020 7584 3763 E: archivist@ic.ac.uk W: www.lib.ic.ac.uk
James Clavell Library Royal Arsenal (West), Warren Lane, Woolwich, London, SE18 6ST T: 020 8312 7125 E: library@firepower.org.uk W: www.firepower.org.uk
Jewish Museum, The Sternberg Centre for Judaism, 80 East End Road, Finchley, London, N3 2SY T: 020 8349 1143 020 8343 2162 E: enquiries@jewishmuseum.org.uk W: www.jewishmuseum.org.uk
Jewish Studies Library see National
The Kenneth Ritchie Wimbledon Library see National
Lambeth Palace Library see Special
Library of the Religious Society of Friends (Quakers) see Special
Lewisham Local Studies & Archives, Lewisham Library 199 - 201 Lewisham High Street, Lewisham, London, SE13 6LG T: (020) 8297-0682 (020) 8297-1169 E: local.studies@lewisham.gov.uk W: www.lewisham.gov.uk Covering the Parishes of Lewisham, Lee & St Paul's, Deptford. Appointments advisable. 1901 census
Linnean Society of London Burlington House, Piccadilly, London, W1J 0BF T: 020 7437 4479 T: 020 7434 4470, 020 7287 9364 E: gina@linnean.org W: www.linnean.org
Local Studies Collection for Chiswick & Brentford Chiswick Public Library Dukes Avenue, Chiswick, London, W4 2AB T: (020) 8994-5295 (020) 8995-0016 and (020) 8742 7411, Restricted opening hours for local history room: please telephone before visiting
London Borough of Barnet, Archives & Local Studies Department Hendon Library The Burroughs, Hendon, London, NW4 3BQ T: (020) 8359-2876, (020) 8359-2885 E: hendon.library@barnet.gov.uk W: www.barnet.gov.uk
London Borough of Bromley Local Studies Library see Kent
Hertfordshire Archives and Local Studies, see Hertfordshire
London Borough of Camden Local Studies & Archive Centre Holborn Library 32 - 38 Theobalds Road, London, WC1X 8PA T: 020 7974 6342 020 7974 6284 E: localstudies@camden.gov.uk W: www.camden.gov.uk
L Borough of Croydon Library & Archives Service see Surrey
London Borough of Enfield Libraries, Southgate Town Hall, Green Lanes, Palmers Green, London, N13 4XD T: (020) 8379-2724
London Borough of Greenwich Heritage Centre Museum and Library Building 41 Royal Arsenal, Woolwich, London, SE18 6SP T: (020) 8858 4631 (020) 8293 4721 E: local.history@greenwich.gov.uk W: www.greenwich.gov.uk
Central Ref Library - London Borough of Havering see Essex
London Borough of Islington Finsbury Library 245 St John Street, London, EC1V 4NB T: (020) 7527 7994 (020) 7527 8821, W: www.islington.gov.uk/htm
London Borough of Islington History Centre Finsbury Library 245 St John Street, London, EC1V 4NB T: (020) 7527 7988 E: local.history@islington.gov.uk W: www.islington.gov.uk , Collection covers the LB of Islington. Material relating to (1) the former Metropolitan Borough of Islington; (2) the present London Borough of Islington and (3) the civil parish of St Mary, Islington (to 1900). The north and south part of the present London Borough of Islington - the former Metropolitan Borough of Finsbury and its predecesors, the former civil parishes of Clerkenwell and St Lukes, Finsbury. 1901 census. The Local History Service operates through an appointment system. Users must make an appointment, preferably by telephone. A postal enquiry service (SAE required) is available. A charge is made for extended research.
London Borough of Lambeth Archives Department Minet Library 52 Knatchbull Road, Lambeth, London, SE5 9QY T: (020) 7926 6076 (020) 7936 6080 E: lambetharchives@lambeth.gov.uk W: www.lambeth.gov.uk
London Borough of Newham Archives & Local Studies Library Stratford Library 3 The Grove, London, E15 1EL T: (020) 8430 6881 W: www.newham.gov.uk
London Borough of Waltham Forest Local Studies Library Vestry House Museum, Vestry Road, Walthamstow, London, E17 9NH T: (020) 8509 1917 E: Vestry.House@al.lbwf.gov.uk W: www.lbwf.gov.uk/vestry/vestry.htm
London Borough of Wandsworth Local Studies Local Studies Service, Battersea Library 265 Lavender Hill, London, SW11 1JB T: (020) 8871 7753 E: wandsworthmuseum@wandsworth.gov.uk W: www.wandsworth.gov.uk
Library of the Royal College of Surgeons of England see Special
London Hillingdon Borough Libraries, Central Library High Street, Uxbridge, Middlesex, UB8 1HD T: 01895 250702 01895 811164 E: clib@hillingdon.gov.uk W: www. hillingdon.gov.uk

London Metropolitan Archives, 40 Northampton Road, London, EC1R 0HB T: 020 7332 3820 T: Mini com 020 7278 8703, 020 7833 9136 E: ask.lma@ms.corpoflondon.gov.uk W: www.cityoflondon.gov.uk

London University - Institute of Advanced Studies Charles Clore House, 17 Russell Square, London, WC1B 5DR T: (020) 7637 1731 (020) 7637 8224 E: ials.lib@sas.ac.uk W: http://ials.sas.ac.uk

Manuscripts Room, Library Services, University College, Gower Street, London, WC1E 6BT T: (020) 7387 7050 E: mssrb@ucl.ac.uk W: www.ucl.ac.uk/library/special-coll/

Minet Library 52 Knatchbull Road, Lambeth, London, SE5 9QY T: (020) 7926 6076 E: lambetharchives@lambeth.gov.uk W: www.lambeth.gov.uk

Museum in Docklands Library & Archives Library & Archive, No 1 Warehouse, West India Quay, Hertsmere Road, London, E14 4AL T: (020) 7001 9825 (Librarian), (020) 7001 9801 E: bobaspinall@museumindocklands.org.uk W: www.museumindocklands.org.uk

Museum of London 150 London Wall, London, EC2Y 5HN T: 020 7814 5588 020 7600 1058 E: info@museumoflondon.org.uk W: http://museumoflondon.org.uk

Museum of the Order of St John St John's Gate, St John's Lane, Clerkenwell, London, EC1M 4DA T: (020) 7253-6644 (020) 7336 0587, W: www.sja.org.uk/history

National Gallery Library and Archive see National

National Maritime Museum - Caird Library see National

Royal Armouries see National

Royal Borough of Kensington and Chelsea Libraries & Arts Service Central Library Phillimore Walk, Kensington, London, W8 7RX T: (020) 7361-3036 T: (020) 7361 3007, E: information.services@rbkc.gov.uk W: www.rbkc.gov.uk

Royal Botanic Gardens, Library & Archives, Kew, Richmond, Surrey, TW9 3AE T: 020 8332 5414

Royal Society of Chemistry Library & Info Centre see Special

School of Oriental and African Studies Library see Special

Society of Antiquaries of London see Special

Society of Genealogists - Library see National

Southwark Local Studies Library 211 Borough High Street, Southwark, London, SE1 1JA T: 0207-403-3507 0207-403-8633 E: local.studies.library@southwark.gov.uk W: www.southwark.gov.uk

Tower Hamlets Local History Library & Archives Bancroft Library 277 Bancroft Road, London, E1 4DQ T: (020) 8980 4366 Ext 129, (020) 8983 4510 E: localhistory@towerhamlets.gov.uk W: www.towerhamlets.gov.uk

Trades Union Congress Library Collections - University of North London see Special

Twickenham Library Twickenham Library Garfield Road, Twickenham, Middlesex, TW1 3JS T: (020) 8891-7271 (020) 8891-5934 E: twicklib@richmond.gov.uk W: www.richmond.gov.uk The Twickenham collection moved to Richmond Local Studies Library

United Reformed Church History Society see National

University of London (Library - Senate House) Palaeography Room, Senate House, Malet Street, London, WC1E 7HU T: (020) 7862 8475 020 7862 8480 E: library@hull.ac.uk W: www.ull.ac.uk

Victoria & Albert Museum - National Art Library see National

Victoria & Albert Museum - National Art Library - Archive of Art and Design see National

Wellcome Library - Contemporary Medical Archives Centre :
Wellcome Library for the History of Medicine - Department of Western Manuscripts : The Wellcome Trust : Wellcome Library for the History and Understanding of Medicine see Special

Westminster Abbey Library & Muniment Room Westminster Abbey, London, SW1P 3PA T: (020) 7222-5152-Ext-4830, (020) 7226-4827 E: library@westminster-abbey.org W: www.westminster-abbey.org

Westminster University Archives Information Systems & Library Services, 4-12 Little Titchfield Street, London, W1W 7UW T: 020 7911 5000 ext 2524, 020 7911 5894 E: archive@westminster.ac.uk W: www.wmin.ac.uk The archive is organisationally within the Library but is a separate entity. The University of Westminster Libraries do not have special collections relating to family and local histrory but the archive may be of interest to researchers

The Women's Library see Special

Luton BC

Local Studies Library Luton Central Library St George's Square, Luton, Bedfordshire, LU1 2NG T: 01582-547420 T: 01582-547421, F: 01582-547450 E: local.studies@luton.gov.uk W: www.luton.gov.uk 1901 census

Manchester

JJohn Rylands University Library Special Collections Division, 150 Deansgate, Manchester M3 3EH T: 0161-834-5343 F: 0161-834-5343 E: spcoll72@fs1.li.man.ac.uk W: http://rylibweb.man.ac.uk Holdings include family muniment collections especially relating to Cheshire and major Non Conformist Archives Few genealogical records held except for family muniment collections, especially for Cheshire and Methodist Circuit plans, records, ministers

Manchester Archives & Local Studies Central Library St Peter's Square, Manchester, M2 5PD T: 0161-234-1979E: lsu@libraries.manchester.gov.uk W: www.manchester.gov.uk/libraries/index.htm

Methodist Archives and Research Centre John Rylands University Library 150 Deansgate, Manchester, M3 3EH T: 0161 834 5343 0161 834 5574

Medway

Medway Archives and Local Studies Centre , Civic Centre Strood, Rochester, Kent, ME2 4AU T: 01634-332714 01634-297060 E: archives@medway.gov.uk local.studies@medway.gov.uk W: www.medway.gov.uk 1901 census

Merseyside

Crosby Library (South Sefton Local History Unit), Crosby Road North, Waterloo, Liverpool, Merseyside, L22 0LQ T: 0151 257 6401 0151 934 5770 E: local-history.south@leisure.sefton.gov.uk W: www.sefton.gov.uk The Local History Units serve Sefton Borough Council area. The South Sefton Unit covers Bootle, Crosby, Maghull and other communities south of the River Alt. The North Sefton Unit covers Southport, Formby.

Huyton Central Library Huyton Library Civic Way, Huyton, Knowsley, Merseyside, L36 9GD T: 0151-443-3738 0151 443 3739 E: eileen.hume.dlcs@knowsley.gov.uk W: www.knowsley.gov.uk/leisure/libraries/huyton/index.html

Liverpool University Special Collections & Archives see Liverpool,

Southport Library (North Sefton Local History Unit), Lord Street, Southport, Merseyside, PR8 1DJ T: 0151 934 2119 0151 934 2115 E: local-history.north@leisure.sefton.gov.uk The Local History Units serve Sefton Borough Council area. The North Sefton Unit covers Southport, Formby. The South Sefton Unit covers Bootle, Crosby, Maghull and other communities south of the River Alt

St Helen's Local History & Archives Library Central Library, Gamble Institute, Victoria Square, St Helens, Merseyside, WA10 1DY T: 01744-456952 01744 20836 No research undertaken 1901 census

Middlesbrough

Middlesbrough Libraries & Local Studies Centre see Cleveland

Middlesex

London Borough of Harrow Local History Collection Civic Centre Library, PO Box 4, Station Road, Harrow, Middlesex, HA1 2UU T: 0208 424 1055 T: 0208 424 1056, 0181-424-1971 E: civiccentre.library@harrow.gov.uk W: www.harrow.gov.uk 1901 census

Hertfordshire Archives and Local Studies see Hertfordshire

Milton Keynes

Milton Keynes Reference Library see Buckinghamshire

Newcastle upon Tyne

Robinson Library see Tyne & Wear

Norfolk

Family History Shop & Library The Family History Shop, 51 Horns Lane, Norwich, Norfolk, NR1 1ER T: 01603 621152 E: jenlibrary@aol.com W: www.jenlibrary.u-net.com

Great Yarmouth Central Library Tolhouse Street, Great Yarmouth, Norfolk, NR30 2SH T: 01493-844551 T: 01493-842279, 01493-857628 E: yarmouth.lib@norfolk.gov.uk W: www.library.norfolk.gov.uk 1901 census

Heritage Centre, Norfolk and Norwich Millennium Library Millennium Plain, Norwich, Norfolk, NR1 T: 01603 774740 01603-215258 E: norfolk.studies.lib@norfolk.gov.uk W: www.norfolk.gov.uk 1901 census

Kings Lynn Library London Road, King's Lynn, Norfolk, PE30 5EZ T: 01553-772568 T: 01553 761393, 01553-769832 E: kings.lynn.lib@norfolk.gov.uk W: www.norfolk.gov.uk 1901 census

Thetford Public Library Raymond Street, Thetford, Norfolk, IP24 2EA T: 01842-752048 01842-750125 E: thetford.lib@norfolk.gov.uk W: www.culture.norfolk.gov.uk 1901 census

Northumberland

Alnwick Library Green Batt, Alnwick, Northumberland, NE66 1TU T: 01665-602689 01665 604740, W: www.northumberland.gov.uk

Berwick upon Tweed Library Church Street, Berwick upon Tweed, Northumberland, TD15 1EE T: 01289-307320 01289-308299, W: www.northumberland.gov.uk

Blyth Library Bridge Street, Blyth, Northumberland, NE24 2DJ T: 01670-361352 W: www.northumberland.gov.uk

Border History Museum and Library Moothall, Hallgate, Hexham, Northumberland, NE46 3NH T: 01434-652349 01434-652425 E: museum@tynedale.gov.uk W: www.tynedale.gov.uk

Hexham Library Queens Hall, Beaumont Street, Hexham, Northumberland, NE46 3LS T: 01434 652474 01434-606043 E: cheane@northumberland.gov.uk W: www.northumberland.gov.uk

Nottinghamshire

Arnold Library Front Street, Arnold, Nottinghamshire, NG5 7EE T: 0115-920-2247 0115-967-3378, W: www.nottscc.gov.uk

Beeston Library Foster Avenue, Beeston, Nottinghamshire, NG9 1AE T: 0115-925-5168 0115-922-0841, W: www.nottscc.gov.uk

Eastwood Library Wellington Place, Eastwood, Nottinghamshire, NG16 3GB T: 01773-712209 W: www.nottscc.gov.uk

Mansfield Library Four Seasons Centre Westgate, Mansfield, Nottinghamshire, NG18 1NH T: 01623-627591 01623-629276 E: mansfield.library@nottscc.gov.uk W: www.nottscc.gov.uk

Newark Library Beaumont Gardens, Newark, Nottinghamshire, NG24 1UW T: 01636-703966 01636-610045, W: www.nottscc.gov.uk

Nottingham Central Library : Local Studies Centre Angel Row, Nottingham, Nottinghamshire, NG1 6HP T: 0115 915 2873 0115 915 2850 E: local-studies.library@nottinghamcity.gov.uk W: www.nottinghamcity.gov.uk/libraries

Retford Library Denman Library Churchgate, Retford, Nottinghamshire, DN22 6PE T: 01777-708724 01777-710020, W: www.nottscc.gov.uk

Southwell Minster Library Minster Office, Trebeck Hall, Bishop's Drive, Southwell NG25 0JP T: 01636-812649 E: mail@southwellminster.org.uk W: www.southwellminster.org.uk

Sutton in Ashfield Library Devonshire Mall, Sutton in Ashfield, Nottinghamshire, NG17 1BP T: 01623-556296 01623-551962, W: www.nottscc.gov.uk

University of Nottingham, Hallward Library University Park, Nottingham, NG7 2RD T: 0115-951-4514 0115-951-4558, W: www.nottingham.ac.uk/library/

Department of Manuscripts and Special Collections see Special

West Bridgford Library Bridgford Road, West Bridgford, Nottinghamshire, NG2 6AT T: 0115-981-6506 0115-981-3199, W: www.nottscc.gov.uk

Oxfordshire

Abingdon Library The Charter, Abingdon, Oxfordshire, OX14 3LY T: 01235-520374 01235 532643 E: abingdon_library@yahoo.com W: www.oxfordshire.gov.uk

Angus Library Regent's Park College, Pusey Street, Oxford, Oxfordshire, OX1 2LB T: 01865 288142 01865 288121

Banbury Library Marlborough Road, Banbury, Oxfordshire, OX16 8DF T: 01295-262282 01295-264331

Centre for Oxfordshire Studies Central Library Westgate, Oxford, Oxfordshire, OX1 1DJ T: 01865-815749 01865-810187 E: cos@oxfordshire.gov.uk W: www.oxfordshire.gov.uk

Henley Library Ravenscroft Road, Henley on Thames, Oxfordshire, RG9 2DH T: 01491-575278 01491-576187

Middle East Centre St Anthony's College, Pusey Street, Oxford, Oxfordshire, OX2 6JF T: 01865 284706 01865 311475

Nuffield College Library see National

Pusey House Library Pusey House, 61 St Giles, Oxford, Oxfordshire, OX1 1LZ T: 01865 278415 01865 278416 E: pusey.house@ic24.net,

River & Rowing Museum see National

Rhodes House Library see National

The Bodleian Library Broad Street, Oxford, Oxfordshire, OX1 3BG T: 01865 277000 01865 277182, W: www.bodley.ox.ac.uk The Bodleian is the largest of the libraries operated by Oxford University and includes the Old Library, the New Library and the Radcliffe Camera. In addition to the Central Bodleian, the library has 7 dependant libraries: The Indian Institute Library, The Bodleian Law Library, Rhodes House Library, the Radcliffe Science Library, The Bodleian Japanese Library, the Oriental Institute Library and the Philosophy Library

Wantage Library Stirlings Road, Wantage, Oxfordshire, OX12 7BB T: 01235 762291 01235 7700951

Witney Library Welch Way, Witney, Oxfordshire, OX8 7HH T: 01993-703659 01993-775993

Peterborough

Peterborough Local Studies Collection see Cambridgeshire

Redcar & Cleveland BC

Redcar Reference Library Coatham Road, Redcar, Cleveland, TS10 1RP T: 01642 489292 E: reference_library@redcar-cleveland.gov.uk

Rutland

Oakham Library Catmos Street, Oakham, Rutland, LE15 6HW T: 01572 722918 , 1901 census

Shropshire

Wrekin Local Studies Forum Madeley Library Russell Square, Telford, Shropshire, TF7 5BB T: 01952 586575 01952 587105 E: wlst@library.madeley W: www.madeley.org.uk

Slough BC

Slough Local Studies Library see Berkshikre

Somerset

Bath Central Library 19 The Podium, Northgate Street, Bath, Somerset, BA1 5AN T: 01225 787400 1225787426 E: Bath_Library@bathnes.gov.uk W: www.bathnes.gov.uk 1901 census. GRO Index 1837 - 1950

Bristol University Library - Special Collections Tyndall Avenue, Bristol, BS8 1TJ T: 0117 928 8014 0117 925 5334 E: library@bris.ac.uk W: www.bris.ac.uk/depts/library

Nailsea Library Somerset Square, Nailsea, Somerset, BS19 2EX T: 01275-854583 01275-858373

Reference Library Binford Place, Bridgewater, Somerset, TA6 3LF T: 01278-450082 01278-451027 E: pcstoyle@somerset.gov.uk W: www.somerset.gov.uk

Reference Library Justice Lane, Frome, Somerset, BA11 1BA T: 01373-462215 01373-472003

Somerset Studies Library Paul Street, Taunton, Somerset, TA1 3XZ T: 01823-340300 01823-340301 E: somstud@somerset.gov.uk W: www.somerset.gov.uk/libraries

Weston Library The Boulevard, Weston Super Mare, Somerset, BS23 1PL T: 01934-636638 01934-413046 E: weston.library@n-somerset.gov.uk W: www.n-somerset.gov.uk 1901 census

Yeovil Library King George Street, Yeovil, Somerset, BA20 1PY T: 01935-421910 01935-431847 E: ransell@somerset.gov.uk W: www.somerset.gov.uk

Southampton

Southampton City Libraries - Special Collections see Hampshire

Staffordshire

Barton Library Dunstall Road, Barton under Needwood, Staffordshire, DE13 8AX T: 01283-713753 W: www.staffordshire.gov.uk

Biddulph Library Tunstall Road, Biddulph, Stoke on Trent, Staffordshire, ST8 6HH T: 01782-512103 W: www.staffordshire.gov.uk

Brewood Library Newport Street, Brewood, Staffordshire, ST19 9DT T: 01902-850087 W: www.staffordshire.gov.uk

Burton Library Burton Library Riverside, High Street, Burton on Trent, Staffordshire, DE14 1AH T: 01283-239556 01283-239571 E: burton.library@staffordshire.gov.uk W: www.staffordshire.gov.uk

Cannock Library Manor Avenue, Cannock WS11 1AA T: 01543-502019 01543-278509 E: cannock.library@staffordshire.gov.uk W: www.staffordshire.gov.uk

Cheslyn Hay Library , Cheslyn Hay, Walsall, Staffordshire, WS56 7AE T: 01922-413956 W: www.staffordshire.gov.uk

Codsall Library Histons Hill, Codsall, Staffordshire, WV8 1AA T: 01902-842764 W: www.staffordshire.gov.uk

Great Wyrley Library John's Lane, Great Wyrley, Walsall, WS6 6BY T: 01922-414632 W: www.staffordshire.gov.uk

Keele University Library , Keele, ST5 5BG T: 01782 583237 E: library@keele.ac.uk W: www.keele.ac.uk/library

Kinver Library Vicarage Drive, Kinver, Stourbridge, Staffordshire, DY7 6HJ T: 01384-872348 W: www.staffordshire.gov.uk

Leek Library Nicholson Institute, Stockwell Street, Leek, Staffordshire, ST13 6DW T: 01538-483210 01538-483216 E: leek.library@staffordshire.gov.uk W: www.staffordshire.gov.uk

Lichfield Library (Local Studies Section) Lichfield Library The Friary, Lichfield WS13 6QG T: 01543 510720 01543 510716

Newcastle Library Ironmarket, Newcastle under Lyme, ST5 1AT T: 01782-297310 E: newcastle.library@staffordshire.gov.uk W: www.staffordshire.gov.uk

Penkridge Library Bellbrock, Penkridge ST19 9DL T: 01785-712916 W: www.staffordshire.gov.uk

Perton Library Severn Drive, Perton WV6 7QU T: 01902-755794 01902-756123 E: perton.library@staffordshire.gov.uk W: www.staffordshire.gov.uk

Rugeley Library Anson Street, Rugeley, Staffordshire, WS16 2BB T: 01889-583237 W: www.staffordshire.gov.uk

Staffordshire & Stoke on Trent Archive Service -Stoke on Trent City Archives Hanley Library Bethesda Street, Hanley, Stoke on Trent, Staffordshire, ST1 3RS T: 01782-238420 01782-238499 E: stoke.archives@stoke.gov.uk W: www.staffordshire.gov.uk/archives

Tamworth Library Corporation Street, Tamworth, Staffordshire, B79 7DN T: 01827-475645 01827-475658 E: tamworth.library@staffordshire.gov.uk W: www.staffordshire.gov.uk/locgov/county/cars/tamlib.htm

Uttoxeter Library High Street, Uttoxeter, Staffordshire, ST14 7JQ T: 01889-256371 01889-256374, W: www.staffordshire.gov.uk

William Salt Library Eastgate Street, Stafford, Staffordshire, ST16 2LZ T: 01785-278372 01785-278414 E: william.salt.library@staffordshire.gov.uk W: www.staffordshire.gov.uk/archives/salt.htm

Wombourne Library Windmill Bank, Wombourne, Staffordshire, WV5 9JD T: 01902-892032 W: www.staffordshire.gov.uk

Stockport MBC

Local Heritage Library see Cheshire

Suffolk

Chantry Library Chantry Library Hawthorne Drive, Ipswich, Suffolk, IP2 0QY T: 01473 686117

Surrey

Bourne Hall Library Bourne Hall, Spring Street, Ewell, Epsom, Surrey, KT17 1UF T: 020 8394 0372 020 8873 1603, W: www.surrey.gov.uk

Caterham Valley Library Caterham Valley Library Stafford Road, Caterham, Surrey, CR3 6JG T: 01883 343580 01883 330872, W: www.surrey.gov.uk

Cranleigh Library and Local History Centre High Street, Cranleigh, Surrey, GU6 8AE T: 01483 272413 01483 271327, W: www.surrey.gov.uk

London Borough of Croydon Library & Archives Service Central Library Katharine Street, Croydon, CR9 1ET T: (020) 8760-5400-ext-1112 E: localstudies@croydononline.org W: www.croydon.gov.uk/

London Borough of Lambeth Archives Department see Lambeth

Epsom and Ewell Local History Centre Bourne Hall, Spring Street, Ewell, Epsom, Surrey, KT17 1UF T: 020 8394 0372 020 8873 1603, W: www.surrey.gov.uk

Horley Library Horley Library Victoria Road, Horley, Surrey, RH6 7AG T: 01293 784141 01293 820084, W: www.surrey.gov.uk

Lingfield Library The Guest House, Vicarage Road, Lingfield, Surrey, RH7 6HA T: 01342 832058 01342 832517, W: www.surrey.gov.uk

London Borough of Merton Local Studies Centre Merton Civic Centre London Road, Morden, Surrey, SM4 5DX T: (020) 8545-3239 (020) 8545-4037 E: local.studies@merton.gov.uk W: www.merton.gov.uk/libraries

Minet Library see London

London Borough of Richmond upon Thames Local Studies Library Old Town Hall, Whittaker Avenue, Richmond upon Thames, Surrey, TW9 1TP T: (020) 8332 6820 (020) 8940 6899 E: localstudies@richmond.gov.uk W: www.richmond.gov.uk

Redhill Library Warwick Quadrant, Redhill, Surrey, RH1 1NN T: 01737 763332 01737 778020, W: www.surrey.gov.uk

Southwark Local Studies Library see London

Surrey History Centre and Archives Surrey History Centre 130 Goldsworth Road, Woking, Surrey, GU21 1ND T: 01483-594594 01483-594595 E: shs@surreycc.gov.uk W: www.surrey.gov.uk

Sutton Central Library St Nicholas Way, Sutton, Surrey, SM1 1EA T: (020) 8770 4745 (020) 8770 4777 E: sutton.information@sutton.gov.uk W: www.sutton.gov.uk

Surrey Heath Museum Knoll Road, Camberley GU15 3HD T: 01276 707284 E: museum@surreyheath.gov.uk W: www.surreyheath.gov.uk/leisure

Sussex

Sussex University Library Manuscript Collections, Falmer, Brighton, Sussex, BN1 9QL T: 01273 606755 01273 678441

Sussex – West

Worthing Reference Library Worthing Library Richmond Road, Worthing, West Sussex, BN11 1HD T: 01903-212060 01903-821902 E: worthing.reference.library@westsussex.gov.uk W: www.westsussex.gov.uk Largest library in West Sussex and specialist centre for family history sources.

Sussex-East

Brighton & Hove Council Library Service Bibliographic Services, 44 St Annes Crescent, Lewes, East Sussex, BN17 1SQ T: 01273-481813

Brighton Local Studies Library 155 Church Street, Brighton, East Sussex, BN1 1 UD T: 01273 296971, F: 01273 296962 E: brightonlibrary@pavilion.co.uk 1901 census

Hove Reference Library 182 - 186 Church Road, Hove, East Sussex, BN3 2EG T: 01273-296942 01273-296947 E: hovelibrary@brighton-hove.gov.uk W: www.brighton-hove.gov.uk

Tameside

Tameside Local Studies Library see Cheshire

Tyne and Wear

City Library & Arts Centre , 28 - 30 Fawcett Street, Sunderland, Tyne and Wear, BR1 1RE T: 0191-514235 0191-514-8444

North Shields Local Studies Centre Central Library Northumberland Square, North Shields, NE3O 1QU T: 0191-200-5424 0191 200 6118 E: eric.hollerton@northtyneside.gov.uk W: www.northtyneside.gov.uk/libraries.html

South Tyneside Central Library Prince George Str, South Shields NE33 2PE T: 0191-427-1818-Ext-7860, E: reference.library@s-tyneside-mbc.gov.uk W: www.s-tyneside-mbc.gov.uk

Central Library Northumberland Square, North Shields, NE3O 1QU T: 0191-200-5424 E: local.studies@northtyneside.gov.uk W: www.northtyneside.gov.uk/libraries/index.htm

Gateshead Central Library & Local Studies Department Prince Consort Road, Gateshead, Tyne & Wear, NE8 4LN T: 0191 477 3478 E: a.lang@libarts.gatesheadmbc.gov.uk http://ris.niaa.org.ukw W: www.gateshead.gov.uk/ls

Newcastle Local Studies Centre City Library Princess Square, Newcastle upon Tyne, NE99 1DX T: 0191 277 4116 E: local.studies@newcastle.gov.uk W: www.newcastle.gov.uk

Robinson Library University of Newcastle upon Tyne, Newcastle Upon Tyne, Tyne & wear, NE2 4HQ T: 0191 222 7671 0191 222 6235 E: library@ncl.ac.uk W: www.ncl.ac.uk/library/

Warwickshire

Atherstone Library Long Street, Atherstone, Warwickshire, CV9 1AX T: 01827 712395 T: 01827 712034 & 01827 718373 - for requests, 01827 720285 E: atherstonelibrary@warwickshire.gov.uk W: www.warwickshire.gov.uk

Bedworth Library 18 High Street, Bedworth, Nuneaton, Warwickshire, CV12 8NF T: 024 7631 2267 024 7664 0429 E: bedworthlibrary@warwickshire.gov.uk W: www.warwickshire.gov.uk

Kenilworth Library Smalley Place, Kenilworth, Warwickshire, CV8 1QG T: 01926 852595 T: 01926 850708, 01926 864503 E: kenilworthlibrary@warwickshire.gov.uk W: www.warwickshire.gov.uk

Modern Records Centre University of Warwick Library Coventry, Warwickshire, CV4 7AL T: (024) 76524219 (024) 7652 4211 E: archives@warwick.ac.uk W: www.modernrecords.warwick.ac.uk

Nuneaton Library Church Street, Nuneaton, Warwickshire, CV11 4DR T: 024 7638 4027 T: 024 7634 7006, 024 7635 0125 (Megastream 6739) E: nuneatonlibrary@warwickshire.gov.uk W: www.warwickshire.gov.uk

Rugby Library Little ElborowStreet, Rugby, Warwickshire, CV21 3BZ T: 01788 533250 01788 533252 & Public Fax 01788 533267 E: rugbylibrary@warwickshire.gov.uk W: www.warwickshire.gov.uk

Shakespeare Birthplace Trust - Library Shakespeare Centre Library Henley Street, Stratford upon Avon, Warwickshire, CV37 6QW T: 01789-204016 T: 01789-201813, 01789-296083 E: library@shakespeare.org.uk W: www.shakespeare.org.uk 1901 census

Stratford on Avon Library 12 Henley Street, Stratford on Avon, Warwickshire, CV37 6PZ T: 01789 292209 T: 01789 296904 & 01926 476760 (Megastream), 01789 268554 & 01926 476774 (Megastream) E: stratfordlibrary@warwickshire.gov.uk W: www.warwickshire.gov.uk

Sutton Coldfield Library & Local Studies Centre 43 Lower Parade, Sutton Coldfield, Warwickshire, B72 1XX T: 0121-354-2274 T: 0121 464 0164, 0121 464 0173 E: sutton.coldfield.reference.lib@birmingham.gov.uk W: www.birmingham.gov.uk

Warwick Library - Warwickshire Local Collection (County Collection) Warwick Library Barrack Street, Warwick, Warwickshire, CV34 4TH T: 01926 412189 T: 01926 412488, 01926 412784 E: warwicklibrary@warwickshire.gov.uk W: www.warwickshire.gov.uk

Warwickshire County Library Leamington Library Royal Pump Rooms, The Parade, Leamington Spa, Warwickshire, CV32 4AA T: 01926 742721 T: 01926 742722 & 01926 742720(Renewals), 01926 742749 (Staff) & 01926 742743 (Public Fax) E: leamingtonlibrary@warwickshire.gov.uk W: www.warwickshire.gov.uk

West Midlands

Birmingham University Information Services - Special Collections see National

Dudley Archives & Local History Service, Mount Pleasant Street, Coseley, Dudley, West Midlands, WV14 9JR T: 01384-812770 E: archives.pls@mbc.dudley.gov.uk W: www.dudley.gov.uk

Coventry Local Studies Library Central Library Smithford Way, Coventry, West Midlands, CV1 1FY T: 012476 832336 02476 832440 E: covinfo@discover.co.uk W: www.coventry.gov.uk/accent.htm

MLA West Midlands: the Regional Council for Museums, Libraries and Archives see Worcestershire

Sandwell Community History & Archives Service Smethwick Library High Street, Smethwick, West Midlands, B66 1AB T: 0121 558 2561, 0121 555 6064

Sandwell Community Libraries Town Hall, High Street, West Bromwich, West Midlands, B70 8DX T: 0121-569-4909 0121-569-4907 E: dm025@viscount.org.uk

Solihull Heritage and Local Studies Service Solihull Central Library Homer Road, Solihull, West Midlands, B91 3RG T: 0121-704-6977 0121-704-6212 E: info@solihull.gov.uk W: www.solihull.gov.uk/wwwlib/#local

Walsall Local History Centre , Essex St, Walsall, West Midlands, WS2 7AS T: 01922-721305 E: localhistorycentre@walsall.gov.uk W: www.walsall.gov.uk/culturalservices/library/welcome.htm

Wolverhampton Archives & Local Studies 42 - 50 Snow Hill, Wolverhampton, West Midlands, WV2 4AG T: 01902 552480 01902 552481 E: wolverhamptonarchives@dial.pipes.com W: www.wolverhampton.gov.uk/archives

Wigan MBC

Abram Library Vicarage Road, Abram, Wigan, Lancashire, WN2 5QX T: 1942866350

Ashton Library Wigan Road, Ashton in Makerfield, Wigan, Lancashire, WN2 9BH T: 01942 727119 ,

Aspull Library Oakfield Crescent, Aspull, Wigan, Lancashire, WN2 1XJ T: 01942 831303 ,

Atherton Library York Street, Atherton, Manchester, Lancashire, M46 9JH T: 01942 404817 T: 01942 4044816

Beech Hill Library Buckley St West, Beech Hill, Wigan, WN6 7PQ

Golborne Library Tanners Lane, Golborne, Warrington, WA3 3AW T: 01942 777800 ,

Hindley Library Market Street, Hindley, Wigan, WN2 3AN T: 01942 255287 ,

Ince Library Smithy Green, Ince, Wigan, WN2 2AT T: 01942 255287 ,

Leigh Library Turnpike Centre Civic Square, Leigh, WN7 1EB T: 01942 404557 01942 404567

Marsh Green Library Harrow Road, Marsh Green, Wigan, WN5 0QL T: 01942 760041

Orrell Library Orrell Post, Orrell, Wigan, WN5 8LY T: 01942 705060 ,

Shevington Library Gathurst Lane, Shevington, Wigan, WN6 8HA T: 01257 252618

Standish Library Cross Street, Standish, Wigan, WN6 0HQ T: 01257 400496

Tyldesley Library Stanley Street, Tyldesley, Manchester, M29 8AII T: 01942 882504

Wigan Library College Avenue, Wigan, WN1 1NN T: 01942 827619 01942 827640
Wigan Metropolitan Borough Council - Leisure Services Department Information Unit, Station Road, Wigan WN1 1WA
Wiltshire
Salisbury Reference and Local Studies Library Market Place, Salisbury, Wiltshire, SP1 1BL T: 01722 411098 01722 413214, W: www.wiltshire.co.uk
Swindon Borough Library Reference Library Regent Circus, Swindon, Wiltshire, SN1 1QG T: 01793 463240 01793 541319 E: reference.library@swindon.gov.uk W: www.swindon.gov.uk 1901 census
Swindon Local Studies Library Swindon Central Library Regent Circus, Swindon, Wiltshire, SN11QG T: 01793 463240 01793 541319 E: swindonref@swindon.gov.uk W: www.swindon.gov.uk
Wiltshire Archaeological & Natural History Society Wiltshire Heritage Library 41 Long St, Devizes SN10 1NS T: 01380 727369 E: wanhs@wiltshireheritage.org.uk W: www.wiltshireheritage.org.uk
Wiltshire Buildings Record Libraries and Heritage HQ, Bythesea Road, Trowbridge, Wiltshire, BA14 8BS T: 01225 713740 E: dorothytreasure@wiltshire.gov.uk W: www.wiltshire.gov.uk
Wiltshire Heritage Museum Library Wiltshire Archaeological & Natural History Society, 41 Long Street, Devizes, Wiltshire, SN10 1NS T: 01380 727369 01380 722150 E: wanhs@wiltshireheritage.org.uk W: www.wiltshireheritage.org.uk
Wiltshire Studies Library Trowbridge Reference Library Bythesea Road, Trowbridge, Wiltshire, BA14 8BS T: 01225-713732 T: 01225 713727, 01225-713715 E: libraryenquiries@wiltshire.gov.uk W: www.wiltshire.gov.uk
Worcestershire
Bewdley Museum Research Library Load Street, Bewdley, Worcestershire, DY12 2AE T: 01229-403573 E: museum@online.rednet.co.uk angela@bewdleyhistory.evesham.net W: www.bewdleymuseum.tripod.com
Bromsgrove Library Stratford Road, Bromsgrove, Worcestershire, B60 1AP T: 01527-575855 01527-575855, W: www.worcestershire.gov.uk
Evesham Library Oat Street, Evesham, Worcestershire, WR11 4PJ T: 01386-442291 01386-765855 E: eveshamlib@worcestershire.gov.uk W: www.worcestershire.gov.uk
Kidderminster Library Market Street, Kidderminster, Worcestershire, DY10 1AD T: 01562-824500 01562-827303 E: kidderminster@worcestershire.gov.uk W: www.worcestershire.gov.uk
Malvern Library Graham Road, Malvern, Worcestershire, WR14 2HU T: 01684-561223 01684-892999, W: www.worcestershire.gov.uk
MLA West Midlands: the Regional Council for Museums, Libraries and Archives 2nd Floor, Grosvenor House, 14 Bennetts Hill, Worcestershire, B2 5RS T: 01527 872258 01527 576960
Redditch Library 15 Market Place, Redditch, B98 8AR T: 01527-63291 01527 68571 E: redditchlibrary@worcestershire.gov.uk W: www.worcestershire.gov.uk
Worcester Library Foregate Street, Worcester, Worcestershire, WR1 1DT T: 01905 765312 01905 726664 E: worcesterlib@worcestershire.gov.uk W: www.worcestershire.gov.uk/libraries
Worcesterhire Library & History Centre History Centre Trinity Street, Worcester, Worcestershire, WR1 2PW T: 01905 765922 01905 765925 E: wlhc@worcestershire.gov.uk W: www.worcestershire.gov.uk/records
Yorkshire
York Minster Library York Minster Library & Archives, Dean's Park, York, YO1 2JQ T: 01904-625308 Library T: 01904-611118 Archives, 01904-611119 E: library@yorkminster.org archives@yorkminster.org W: www.yorkminster.org
Yorkshire Family History - Biographical Database York Minster Library & Archives, Dean's Park, York YO1 7JQ T: 01904-625308 Library T: 01904-611118 Archives F: 01904-611119 E: library@yorkminster.org archives@yorkminster.org W: www.yorkminster.org
Yorkshire - City of York
City of York Libraries - Local History & Reference Collection Central Library Library Square, Museum Street, York, YO1 7DS T: 01904-655631 01904-611025 E: reference.library@york.gov.uk W: www.york.gov.uk
Yorkshire – North
Catterick Garrison Library Gough Road, Catterick Garrison, North Yorkshire, DL9 3EL T: 01748 833543 W: www.northyorks.gov.uk or **Harrogate Reference Library** Victoria Avenue, Harrogate, North Yorkshire, HG1 1EG T: 01423-502744 01423-523158, W: www.northyorks.gov.uk 1901 census
Malton Library St Michael's Street, Malton, North Yorkshire, YO17 7LJ T: 01653 692714 W: www.northyorks.gov.uk 1901 census
North Yorkshire County Libraries 21 Grammar School Lane, Northallerton, DL6 1DF T: 01609-776271 01609-780793 E: elizabeth.melrose@northyorks.gov.uk W: www.northyorks.gov.uk

Northallerton Reference Library 1 Thirsk Road, Northallerton, DL6 1PT T: 01609-776202 E: northallerton.libraryhq@northyorks.gov.uk W: www.northyorks.gov.uk 1901 census
Pickering Reference Library The Ropery, Pickering, YO18 8DY T: 01751-472185 W: www.northyorks.gov.uk
Richmond Library Queen's Road, Richmond DL10 4AE T: 01748 823120 W: www.northyorks.gov.uk 1901 census
Ripon Library The Arcade, Ripon HG4 1AG T: 01765 792926 W: www.northyorks.gov.uk 1901 census
Scarborough Reference Library Vernon Road, ScarboroughYO11 2NN T: 01723-364285 E: scarborough.library@northyorks.gov.uk W: www.northyorks.gov.uk 1901 census
Selby Reference Library 52 Micklegate, Selby YO8 4EQ T: 01757-702020 01757 705396, W: www.northyorks.gov.uk 1901 census
Skipton Reference Library High Street, Skipton BD23 1JX T: 01756-794726 01756-798056, W: www.northyorks.gov.uk
Whitby Library Windsor Terrace, Whitby, North Yorkshire, YO21 1ET T: 01947-602554 01947 820288 1901 census
Yorkshire – East
Beverley Local Studies Library Beverley Library Champney Road, Beverley, East Riding of Yorkshire, HU17 9BG T: 01482 392755, F: 01482 881861 E: beverleyref@eastriding.gov.uk W: www.eastriding.gov.uk 1841 to 1901 East Riding Census
Hull Central Library Family and Local History Unit see Hull
Yorkshire – South
Barnsley Archives and Local Studies Department Central Library Shambles Street, Barnsley, South Yorkshire, S70 2JF T: 01226-773950 T: 01226-773938 E: Archives@barnsley.gov.uk librarian@barnsley.gov.uk W: www.barnsley.gov.uk
Doncaster Libraries - Local Studies Section Central Library Waterdale, Doncaster, South Yorkshire, DN1 3JE T: 01302-734307 01302 369749 E: reference.library@doncaster.gov.uk W: www.doncaster.gov.uk
Rotherham Archives & Local Studies Central Library Walker Place, Rotherham, South Yorkshire, S65 1JH T: 01709-823616 E: archives@rotherham.gov.uk W: www.rotherham.gov.uk
Sheffield Central Library Surrey Street, Sheffield, South Yorkshire, S1 1XZ T: 0114 273 4711 0114 273 5009 E: sheffield.libraries@dial.pipex.com,
Sheffield University Library Special Collections & Library Archives, Western Bank, Sheffield, South Yorkshire, S10 2TN T: 0114 222 7230 0114 222 7290
Yorkshire – West
Batley Library Market Place, Batley, West Yorkshire, WF17 5DA T: 01924 326021 01924 326308 E: batley.library@kirklees.gov.uk W: www.kirklees.gov.uk
Bradford Local Studies Reference Library Central Library Prince's Way, Bradford, West Yorkshire, BD1 1NN T: 01274 433661 01274 753660 E: local.studies@bradford.gov.uk W: www.bradford.gov.uk 1901 census.
British Library , Boston Spa, Wetherby, West Yorkshire, LS23 7BY
British Library Acquisitions Unit - Monograph Ordering The British Library Boston Spa, Wetherby, West Yorkshire, LS23 7BQ T: 01937-546212
Calderdale Central Library Northgate House, Northgate, Halifax, West Yorkshire, HX11 1UN T: 1422392631 01422-349458, W: www.calderdale.gov.uk
Cleckheaton Library Whitcliffe Road, Cleckheaton, West Yorkshire, BD19 3DX T: 01274 335170
Dewsbury Library Dewsbury Retail Park, Railway Street, Dewsbury, West Yorkshire, WF12 8EQ T: 01924 325080 , 1901 census
Huddersfield Local History Library Library & Art Gallery, Princess Alexandra Walk, Huddersfield HD1 2SU T: 01484-221965 E: ref-library@geo2.poptel.org.uk W: www.kirkleesmc.gov.uk
Keighley Reference Library North Street, Keighley BD21 3SX T: 01535-618215 E: keighleylibrary@bradford.gov.uk W: www.bradford.gov.uk
Leeds Local Studies Library Leeds Central Library Calverley Street, Leeds, West Yorkshire, LS1 3AB T: 0113 247 8290 E: local.studies@leeds.gov.uk W: www.leeds.gov.uk/library/services/
Mirfield Library East Thorpe Lodge, Mirfield, West Yorkshire, WF14 8AN T: 01924 326470 1901 census
The National Coal Mining Museum for England see National
Olicana Historical Society 54 Kings Road, Ilkley, West Yorkshire, LS29 9AT T: 01943 609206
Pontefract Library & Local Studies Centre Pontefract Library Shoemarket, Pontefract, West Yorkshire, WF8 1BD T: 01977-727692
Wakefield Metropolitan District Libraries & Information Services Castleford Library & Local Studies Dept, Carlton Street, Castleford, West Yorkshire, WF10 1BB T: 01977-722085
Wakefield Library Headquarters - Local Studies Department Balne Lane, Wakefield, West Yorkshire, WF2 0DQ T: 01924-302224 01924-302245 E: wakehist@hotmail.com W: www.wakefield.gov.uk 1901 census

Yorkshire Archaeological Society Claremont, 23 Clarendon Rd, Leeds, West Yorkshire, LS2 9NZ T: 0113-245-6342 T: 0113 245 7910, 0113-244-1979 E: j.heron@sheffield.ac.uk (Society business) yas@wyjs.org.uk (Library and Archives) W: www.yas.org.uk
Brotherton Library Department of Special Collections, Leeds University, Leeds LS2 9JT T: 0113 233 55188 E: special-collections@library.leeds.ac.uk W: http://leeds.ac.uk/library/spcoll/

WALES
National Library of Wales Penglais, Aberystwyth, Ceredigion, SY23 3BU T: 01970 632800 T: 01970 632902 Marketing, 01970 615709 E: holi@llgc.org.uk W: www.llgc.org.uk
South Wales Miners' Library - University of Wales, Swansea Hendrefoelan House, Gower Road, Swansea, SA2 7NB T: 01792-518603 01792-518694 E: miners@swansea.ac.uk W: www.swan.ac.uk/lis/swml
University of Wales Swansea Library see Glamorgan - West
Blaenau Gwent
Ebbw Vale Library Ebbw Vale Library 21 Bethcar Street, Ebbw Vale, Gwent, NP23 6HH T: 01495-303069 01495-350547
Tredegar Library The Circle Tredegar, Gwent, NP2 3PS T: 01495-722687
Caerphilly
Bargoed Library The Square, Bargoed, Caerphilly, CF81 8QQ T: 01443-875548 01443-836057 E: 9e465@dial.pipex.com
Caerphilly Library HQ, Unit 7 Woodfieldside Business Park, Penmaen Road, Pontllanfraith, Blackwood, Caerphilly, NP12 2DG T: 01495 235584 01495 235567 E: cael.libs@dial.pipex.com,
Cardiff
Cardiff Central Library (Local Studies Department) St Davids Link, Frederick Street, Cardiff, CF1 4DT T: (029) 2038 2116 (029) 2087 1599 E: p.sawyer@cardlib.gov.uk W: www.cardiff.gov.uk
Carmarthenshire
Carmarthen Library St Peters Street, Carmarthen, Carmarthenshire, SA31 1LN T: 01267-224822
Llanelli Public Library Vaughan Street, Lanelli, Carmarthenshire, SA15 3AS T: 01554-773538 01554 750125
Ceredigion
Aberystwyth Reference Library Corporation Street, Aberystwyth, Ceredigion, SY23 2BU T: 01970-617464 01970 625059 E: llyfrgell.library@ceredigion.gov.uk W: www.ceredigion.gov.uk/libraries
Flintshire
Flintshire Reference Library Headquarters County Hall Mold, Flintshire, CH7 6NW T: 01352 704411 01352 753662 E: libraries@flintshire.gov.uk W: www.flintshire.gov.uk
Glamorgan
Bridgend Library & Information Service Coed Parc, Park Street, Bridgend, Glamorgan, CF31 4BA T: 01656-767451 01656-645719 E: blis@bridgendlib.gov.uk W: www.bridgendlib.gov.uk
Dowlais Library Church Street, Dowlais, Merthyr Tydfil, Glamorgan, CF48 3HS T: 01985-723051
Merthyr Tydfil Central Library (Local Studies Department) Merthyr Library High Street, Merthyr Tydfil, Glamorgan, CF47 8AF T: 01685-723057 01685-722146 E: library@merthyr.gov.uk W: www.merthyr.gov.uk Specialises in the Borough of Merthyr Tydfil - all census returns 1841 - 1891 arranged by surname for the Borough
Glamorgan - Vale of
Barry Library King Square, Holton Road, Barry, Glamorgan, CF63 4RW T: 01446-735722 01446 734427
Glamorgan – West
Neath Central Library (Local Studies Department) 29 Victoria Gardens, Neath, Glamorgan, SA11 3BA T: 01639-620139 W: www.neath-porttalbot.gov.uk
Port Talbot Library 1st Floor Aberafan Shopping Centre Port Talbot, Glamorgan, SA13 1PB T: 01639-763490 W: www.neath-porttalbot.gov.uk
University of Wales Swansea Library Library & Information Centre Singleton Park, Swansea, SA2 8PP T: 01792 295021 01792 295851
Swansea Reference Library Alexandra Road, Swansea, SA1 5DX T: 01792-516753 01792 516759 E: central.library@swansea.gov.uk W: www.swansea.gov.uk
West Glamorgan Archive Service - Port Talbot Access Point Port Talbot Library 1st Floor, Aberavon Shopping Centre Port Talbot, SA13 1PB T: 01639 763430 W: www.swansea.gov.uk/archives
Rhondda Cynon Taff
Aberdare Library Green Street, Aberdare, Rhondda Cynon Taff, CF44 7AG T: 01685 880053 01685 881181 E: alun.r.prescott@rhondda-cynon-taff.gov.uk W: www.rhondda-cynon-taff.gov.uk/libraries/aberdare.htm
Pontypridd Library Library Road, Pontypridd, Rhondda Cynon Taff, CF37 2DY T: 01443-486850 01443 493258 E: hywel.w.matthews@rhondda-cynon-taff.gov.uk W: www.rhondda-cynon-taff.gov.uk/libraries/pontypri.htm
Treorchy Library Station Road, Treorchy, Glamorgan, CF42 6NN T: 01443-773204 01443-777407

Gwent
Abertillery Library Station Hill, Abertillery, Gwent, NP13 1TE T: 01495-212332
Gwynedd
Canolfan Llyfrgell Dolgellau Library FforddBala Dolgellau, Gwynedd, LL40 2YF T: 01341-422771 01341-423560, W: www.gwynedd.gov.uk
Llyfrgell Caernarfon, Lon Pafiliwn Caernafon, Gwynedd, LL55 1AS T: 01286-679465 E: library@gwynedd.gov.uk W: www.gwynedd.gov.uk
Merthyr Tydfil
Merthyr Tydfil Central Library (Local Studies Department) see Glamorgan
Treharris Library Perrott Street, Treharris, Merthyr Tydfil, CF46 5ET T: 01443-410517 01443 410517
Monmoputhshire
Chepstow Library & Information Centre Manor Way, Chepstow, Monmoputhshire, NP16 5HZ T: 01291-635730 E: chepstowlibrary@monmouthshire.gov.uk W: www.monmouthshire.gov.uk/leisure/libraries
Neath Port Talbot
Lifelong Learning Service Theodore Road, Port Talbot, SA13 1SP T: 01639-898581 E: lls@neath-porttalbot.gov.uk W: www.neath-porttalbot.gov.uk
Newport
Newport Library & Information Service Central Library John Frost Square, Newport NP20 1PA T: 01633-211376 E: reference.library@newport.gov.uk W: www.earl.org.uk/partners/newport/index.html
Pembrokeshire
Pembrokeshire Libraries, The County Library Dew Street, Haverfordwest, Pembrokeshire, SA61 1SU T: 01437 775248 E: sandra.matthews@pembrokeshire.gov.uk W: www.pembrokeshire.gov.uk
Powys
Brecon Area Library Ship Street, Brecon, Powys, LD3 9AE T: 01874-623346 E: breclib@mail.powys.gov.uk W: www.powys.gov.uk
Llandrindod Wells Library Cefnllys Lane, Llandrindod Wells, Powys, LD1 5LD T: 01597-826870 llandod.library@powys.gov.uk W: www.powys.gov.uk 1901 census
Newtown Area Library Park Lane, Newtown, Powys, SY16 1EJ T: 01686-626934 01686 624935 E: nlibrary@powys.gov.uk W: www.powys.gov.uk 1901 census
Wrexham CBC
Wrexham Library and Arts Centre , Rhosddu Road, Wrexham, LL11 1AU T: 01978-292622 01978-292611 E: joy.thomas@wrexham.gov.uk W: www.wrexham.gov.uk

SCOTLAND
National
Edinburgh University Library, Special Collections Department George Square, Edinburgh, EH8 9LJ T: 0131 650 3412 0131 650 6863 E: special.collections@ed.ac.uk W: www.lib.ed.ac.uk
Edinburgh University New College Library Mound Place, Edinburgh, EH1 2UL T: 0131 650 8957 0131 650 6579 E: New.College.Library@ed.ac.uk W: www.lib.ed.ac.uk
Glasgow University Library & Special Collections Department Hillhead Street, Glasgow, G12 8QE T: 0141 330 6767 0141 330 3793 E: library@lib.gla.ac.uk W: www.gla.ac.uk/library
National Library of Scotland George IV Bridge, Edinburgh, EH1 1EW T: 0131-226-4531 0131 622 4803 E: enquiries@nls.uk W: www.nls.uk
National Monuments Record of Scotland Royal Commission on the Ancient & Historical Monuments of Scotland, John Sinclair House, 16 Bernard terrace, Edinburgh, EH8 9NX T: 0131 662 1456 0131 662 1477 or 0131 662 1499 E: nmrs@rcahms.gov.uk W: www.rcahms.gov.uk
National Museums of Scotland Library Royal Museum, Chambers Street, Edinburgh, EH1 1JF T: 0131 247 4137 0131 247 4311 E: library@nms.ac.uk W: www.nms.ac.uk Holds large collection of family histories, esp Scottish
National War Museum of Scotland Library The Castle, Museum Square, Edinburgh, EH1 1 2NG T: 0131 225 7534 Ext 2O4 T: 0131 225 3848 E: library@nms.ac.uk W: www.nms.ac.uk/library
Royal Botanic Garden, The Library 20a Inverleith Row, Edinburgh, EH3 5LR T: 0131 552 7171 0131 248 2901
Scottish Genealogy Society, 15 Victoria Terrace, Edinburgh, EH1 2JL T: 0131-220-3677 0131-220-3677 E: info@scotsgenealogy.com W: www.scotsgenealogy.com
St Andrews University Library - Special Collections Department North Street, St Andrews, Fife, KY16 9TR T: 01334 462339 E: speccoll@st-and.ac.uk W: http://specialcollections.st-and.ac.uk
Strathclyde University Archives McCance Building, 16 Richmond Street, Glasgow, G1 1XQ T: 0141 548 2397 0141 552 0775
Aberdeen
Aberdeen Central Library - Reference & Local Studies Rosemount Viaduct, Aberdeen, AB25 1GW T: 01224-652511E: refloc@arts-rec.aberdeen.net.uk W: www.aberdeencity.gov.uk

University of Aberdeen DISS: Heritage Division Special Collections & Archives Kings College, Aberdeen, AB24 3SW T: 01224-272598 F: 01224-273891 E: speclib@abdn.ac.uk W: www.abdn.ac.uk/diss/heritage

Aberdeenshire Library & Information Service The Meadows Industrial Estate, Meldrum Meg Way, Oldmeldrum, AB51 0GN T: 01651-872707 T: 01651-871219/871220 F: 01651-872142 E: ALIS@aberdeenshire.gov.uk W: www.aberdeenshire.gov.uk

Angus

Angus Archives, Montrose Library 214 High Street, Montrose, DD10 8PH T: 01674-671415 E: angus.archives@angus.govuk W: www.angus.gov.uk/history/history.htm

Angus District, Montrose Library 214 High Street, Montrose, MO10 8PH T: 01674-673256

Dundee University Archives Tower Building, University of Dundee, Dundee, DD1 4HN T: 01382-344095 F: 01382 345523 E: archives@dundee.ac.uk W: www.dundee.ac.uk/archives/

Tay Valley FHS & Research Centre see Dundee,

Argyll

Argyll & Bute Council Library Service - Local Studies Highland Avenue, Sandbank, Dunoon, PA23 8PB T: 01369 703214 F: 01369 705797 E: eleanor.harris@argyll-bute.gov.uk W: www.argyll-bute.gov.uk Census 1841-1901 and OPR.

Argyll & Bute Library Service Library Headquarters, Highland Avenue, Sandbank, Dunoon, PA23 8PB T: 01369-703214 F: 1369705797 E: andyewan@abc-libraries.demon.co.uk W: www.argyll-bute.gov.uk

Campbeltown Library and Museum Hall St, Campbeltown, PA28 6BU T: 01586 552366 F: 01586 552938 E: mary.vanhelmond@argyll-bute.gov.uk W: www.argyle-bute.gov.uk/content/leisure/museums

Ayrshire

East Ayrshire Council District History Centre & Museum Baird Institute, 3 Lugar Street, Cumnock, KA18 1AD T: 01290-421701 F: 01290-421701 E: Baird.institute@east-ayrshire.gov.uk W: www.east-ayrshire.gov.uk

East Ayrshire Libraries Dick Institute, Elmbank Avenue, Kilmarnock, KA1 3BU T: 01563 554310 T: 01290 421701 F: 01563 554311 E: baird.institute@east-ayrshire.gov.uk W: www.east-ayrshire.gov.uk

North Ayrshire Libraries Library Headquarters, 39 - 41 Princes Street, Ardrossan, KA22 8BT T: 01294-469137 F: 01924-604236 E: reference@naclibhq.prestel.co.uk W: www.north-ayrshire.gov.uk

South Ayrshire Library Carnegie Library 12 Main Street, Ayr, KA8 8ED T: 01292-286385 F: 01292-611593 E: carnegie@south-ayrshire.gov.uk W: www.south-ayrshire.gov.uk

Ayrshire – East

East Ayrshire Libraries – Cumnock 25-27 Ayr Road, Cumnock, KA18 1EB T: 01290-422804, W: www.east-ayrshire.gov.uk

Auchinleck Library Well Road, Auchinleck, KA18 2LA T: 01290 422829, W: www.east-ayrshire.gov.uk

Bellfield Library 79 Whatriggs Road, Kilmarnock, KA1 3RB T: 01563 534266 E: libraries@east-ayrshire.gov.uk W: www.east-ayrshire.gov.uk

Bellsbank Library Primary School, Craiglea Crescent, Bellsbank, KA6 7UA T: 01292 551057 E: libraries@east-ayrshire.gov.uk W: www.east-ayrshire.gov.uk

Catrine Library A M Brown Institute, Catrine, KA5 6RT T: 01290 551717 E: libraries@east-ayrshire.gov.uk W: www.east-ayrshire.gov.uk

Crosshouse Library 11-13 Gatehead Road, Crosshouse, KA2 0HN T: 01563 573640 E: libraries@east-ayrshire.gov.uk W: www.east-ayrshire.gov.uk

Dalmellington Library Townhead, Dalmellington, KA6 7QZ T: 01292 550159 E: libraries@east-ayrshire.gov.uk W: www.east-ayrshire.gov.uk

Dalrymple Library Barbieston Road, Dalrymple, KA6 6DZ E: libraries@east-ayrshire.gov.uk W: www.east-ayrshire.gov.uk

Darvel Library Town Hall, West Main Street, Darvel, KA17 0AQ T: 01560 322754 E: libraries@east-ayrshire.gov.uk W: www.east-ayrshire.gov.uk

Drongan Library Mill O'Shield Road, Drongan, KA6 7AY T: 01292 591718 E: libraries@east-ayrshire.gov.uk W: www.east-ayrshire.gov.uk

Galston Library Henrietta Street, Galston, KA4 8HQ T: 01563 821994 E: libraries@east-ayrshire.gov.uk W: www.east-ayrshire.gov.uk

Hurlford Library Blair Road, Hurlford, KA1 5BN T: 01563 539899 E: libraries@east-ayrshire.gov.uk W: www.east-ayrshire.gov.uk

Kilmaurs Library Irvine Road, Kilmaurs, KA3 2RJ T: E: libraries@east-ayrshire.gov.uk W: www.east-ayrshire.gov.uk

Mauchline Library 2 The Cross, Mauchline, T: 01290 550824 E: libraries@east-ayrshire.gov.uk W: www.east-ayrshire.gov.uk

Muirkirk Library Burns Avenue, Muirkirk, KA18 3RH T: 01290 661505 E: libraries@east-ayrshire.gov.uk W: www.east-ayrshire.gov.uk

Netherthird Library Ryderston Drive, Netherthird, KA18 3AR T: 01290 423806 E: libraries@east-ayrshire.gov.uk W: www.east-ayrshire.gov.uk

New Cumnock Library Community Centre, The Castle, New Cumnock, KA18 4AH T: 01290 338710 E: libraries@east-ayrshire.gov.uk W: www.east-ayrshire.gov.uk

Newmilns Library Craigview Road, Newmilns, KA16 9DQ T: 01560 322890 E: libraries@east-ayrshire.gov.uk W: www.east-ayrshire.gov.uk

Ochiltree Library Main Street, Ochiltree, KA18 2PE T: 01290 700425 E: libraries@east-ayrshire.gov.uk W: www.east-ayrshire.gov.uk

Patna Library Doonside Avenue, Patna, KA6 7LX T: 01292 531538 E: libraries@east-ayrshire.gov.uk W: www.east-ayrshire.gov.uk

Clackmannanshire

Clackmannanshire Archives, Alloa Library 26/28 Drysdale Street, Alloa, FK10 1JL T: 01259-722262 F: 01259-219469 E: libraries@clacks.gov.uk W: www.clacksweb.org.uk/dyna/archives

Clackmannanshire Libraries, Alloa Library 26/28 Drysdale Street, Alloa, FK10 1JL T: 01259-722262 F: 01259-219469 E: clack.lib@mail.easynet.co.uk

Dumfriesshire

Ewart Library Ewart Library Catherine Street, Dumfries, DG1 1JB T: 01387 260285 T: 01387-252070 F: 01387-260294 E: ruth_airley@dumgal.gov.uk libsxi@dumgal.gov.uk W: www.dumgal.gov.uk Fee paid research service availble

Dumbartonshire

Dumbarton Public Library Strathleven Place, Dumbarton, G82 1BD T: 01389-733273 F: 01389-738324 E: wdlibs@hotmail.com W: www.wdcweb.info

Dundee, Dundee Central Library The Wellgate, Dundee, DD1 1DB T: 01382-434377 E: local.studies@dundeecity.gov.uk W: www.dundeecity.gov.uk/dcchtml/nrd/loc_stud.htm

Tay Valley FHS & Family History Research Centre Family History Research Centre, 179–181 Princes Street, Dundee, DD4 6DQ T: 01382-461845 F: 01382 455532 E: tvfhs@tayvalleyfhs.org.uk W: www.tayvalleyfhs.org.uk

East Dunbarton

Bishopbriggs Library 170 Kirkintilloch Road, Bishopbriggs, G64 2LX T: 0141 772 4513 F: 0141 762 5363 W: www.eastdunbarton.gov.uk

Craighead Library , Milton of Campsie, G66 8Dl T: 01360 311925, W: www.eastdunbarton.gov.uk

Lennoxtown Library Main Street, Lennoxtown, G66 7HA T: 01360 311436 F: 01360 311436,

Lenzie Library 13 - 15 Alexandra Avenue, Lenzie, G66 5BG T: 0141 776 3021, W: www.eastdunbarton.gov.uk

Milgarvie Library Allander Road, Milngarvie, G62 8PN T: 0141 956 2776 F: 0141 956 2776 W: www.eastdunbarton.gov.uk

Westerton Library 82 Maxwell Avenue, Bearsden, G61 1NZ T: 0141 943 0780 F: 0141 943 0780,

East Dunbartonshire Local Record Offices and Reference Libraries William Patrick Library 2 West High Street, Kirkintilloch, G66 1AD T: 0141-776-8090 F: 0141-776-0408 E: libraries@eastdunbarton.gov.uk W: www.eastdunbarton.gov.uk

East Renfrewshire,

Giffnock Library Station Road, Giffnock, Glasgow, G46 6JF T: 0141-577-4976 F: 0141-577-4978 E: devinem@eastrenfrewshire.co.uk W: www.eastrenfrewshire.co.uk

Edinburgh

Edinburgh Central Library Edinburgh Room, George IV Bridge, Edinburgh, EH1 1EG T: 0131-242 8030 F: 0131-242 8009 E: eclis@edinburgh.gov.uk W: www.edinburgh.gov.uk

Scottish Genealogy Society - Library see Scotland National

Falkirk

Falkirk Library Hope Street, Falkirk, FK1 5AU T: 01324 503605 F: 01324 503606 E: falkirk-library@falkirk-library.demon.co.uk W: www.falkirk.gov.uk Holds Local Studies Collection

Falkirk Museum History Research Centre Callendar House, Callendar Park, Falkirk, FK1 1YR T: 01324 503778 F: 01324 503771 E: ereid@falkirkmuseums.demon.co.uk callandarhouse@falkirkmuseums.demon.co.uk W: www.falkirkmuseums.demon.co.uk Records held: Local Authority, business, personal and estate records, local organmisations, trade unions, over 28,000 photographs Falkirk District

Fife

Dunfermline Library - Local History Department Abbot Street, Dunfermline, KY12 7NL T: 01383-312994 F: 01383-312608 E: info@dunfermline.fifelib.net W: www.fife.gov.uk

Fife Council Central Area Libraries Central Library War Memorial Grounds, Kirkcaldy, KY1 1YG T: 01592-412878 F: 01592-412750 E: info@kirkcaldy.fifelib.net W: www.fife.gov.uk

Tay Valley FHS & Research Centre see Dundee

St Andrews Library Church Square, St Andrews, KY16 9NN T: 01334-412685 F: 01334 413029 E: info@standres.fiflib.net W: www.fife.gov.uk

St Andrews University Library North Street, St Andrews, KY16 9TR T: 01334-462281 F: 01334-462282 W: www.library.st-and.ac.uk

St Andrews University Library - Special Collections Department
see Scotland National
Glasgow
Brookwood Library 166 Drymen Road, Bearsden, Glasgow, G61
3RJ T: 0141-942 6811 F: 0141 943 1119 W:
www.eastdunbarton.gov.uk
Glasgow City Libraries & Archives Mitchell Library North Street,
Glasgow, G3 7DN T: 0141 287 2937 F: 0141 287 2912 E:
history_and_glasgow @gcl.glasgow.gov.uk W:
www.glasgow.gov.uk/html/council/cindex.htm
Glasgow University Library & Special Collections Department
Hillhead Street, Glasgow, G12 8QE T: 0141 330 6767 F: 0141 330
3793 E: library@lib.gla.ac.uk W: www.gla.ac.uk/library
Social Sciences Department - History & Glasgow Room The
Mitchell Library North Street, Glasgow, G3 7DN T: 0141-227-2935
T: 0141-227-2937 & 0141-227-2938 F: 0141-227-2935 E: history-
and-glasgow@cls.glasgow.gov.uk W: www.libarch.glasgow
Highland
North Highland Archive Wick Library Sinclair Terrace, Wick, KW1
5AB T: 01955 606432 F: 01955 603000
Isle of Barra
Castlebay Community Library Community School, Castlebay,
HS95XD T: 01871-810471 F: 01871-810650
Isle of Benbecula
Community Library Sgoil Lionacleit, Liniclate, HS7 5PJ T: 01870-
602211 F: 01870-602817
Isle of Lewis
Stornoway Library 19 Cromwell Street, Stornoway, HS1 2DA T:
01851 708631 F: 01851 708676/708677 E: dfowler@cne-siar.gov.uk
Kinross-shire
Perth & Kinross Libraries, A K Bell Library 2 - 8 York Place,
Perth, PH2 8EP T: 01738-477062 F: 01738-477010 E:
jaduncan@pkc.gov.uk W: www.pkc.gov.uk
Tay Valley FHS & Family History Research Centre see Dundee
Kirkcudbrightshire
Ewart Library Ewart Library Catherine Street, Dumfries, DG1 1JB
T: 01387 260285 T: 01387-252070 E: libsxi@dumgal.gov.uk W:
www.dumgal.gov.uk
Lanarkshire
Airdrie Library Wellwynd, Airdrie, ML6 0AG T: 01236-763221 T:
01236-760937 F: 01236-766027 W: www.northlan.gov.uk
Cumbernauld Central Library 8 Allander Walk, Cumbernauld, G67
1EE T: 01236-735964 F: 01236-458350 W: www.northlan.org.uk
Leadhills Miners' Library 15 Main Street, Leadhills, ML12 6XP T:
01659-74326 E: anne@leadshilllibrary.co.uk W:
www.lowtherhills.fsnet.co.uk
Midlothian
Midlothian Archives and Local Studies Centre 2 Clerk Street,
Loanhead, EH20 9DR T: 0131 271 3976 F: 0131 440 4635 E:
local.studies@midlothian.gov.uk W: www.midlothian.gov.uk
Midlothian Libraries Local History Centre Midlothian Council
Libraries Headquarters, 2 Clerk Street, Loanhead, EH20 9DR T:
0131-440-2210 F: 0131-440-4635 E:
local.studies@midlothian.gov.uk W:
www.earl.org.uk.partners/midlothian/index.html
Morayshire
Buckie Library Clunu Place, Buckie, AB56 1HB T: 01542-832121
F: 01542-835237 E: buckie.lib@techleis.moray.gov.uk W:
www.moray.gov.uk
Forres Library Forres House, High Street, Forres, IV36 0BJ T:
01309-672834 F: 01309-675084 W: www.moray.gov.uk
Keith Library Union Street, Keith, AB55 5DP T: 01542-882223 F:
01542-882177 E: keithlibrary@techleis.moray.gov.uk W:
www.moray.gov.uk
Moray Local Heritage Centre Grant Lodge, Cooper Park, Elgin,
IV30 1HS T: 01343 562644 E: graeme.wilson@techleis.moray.gov.uk
W: www.morray.org/heritage/roots.html
North Lanarkshire
Kilsyth Library Burngreen, Kilsyth, G65 0HT T: 01236-823147 F:
01236-823147 W: www.northlan.org.uk
Motherwell Heritage Centre High Road, Motherwell, ML1 3HU T:
01698-251000 F: 01698-253433 E: heritage@mhc158.freeserve.co.uk
W: www.northlan.org.uk
Shotts Library Benhar Road, Shotts, ML7 5EN T: 01501-821556,
W: www.northlan.org.uk
Orkney
Orkney Library The Orkney Library Laing Street, Kirkwall, KWI5
1NW T: 01856-873166 F: 01856-875260 E:
karen.walker@orkney.gov.uk W: www.orkney.gov.uk
Perthshire
Perth & Kinross Libraries, A K Bell Library 2 - 8 York Place,
Perth, PH2 8EP T: 01738-477062 F: 01738-477010 E:
jaduncan@pkc.gov.uk W: www.pkc.gov.uk
Tay Valley FHS & Research Centre see Dundee
Renfrewshire
Renfrewshire Council Library & Museum Services Central
Library & Museum Complex, High Street, Paisley, PA1 2BB T: 0141-
889-2350 F: 0141-887-6468 E:

local_studies.library@renfrewshire.gov.uk W:
www.renfrewshire.gov.uk
Watt Library 9 Union Street, Greenock, PA16 8JH T: 01475 715628
F: 01475 712339 E: library.watt@inverclyde.gov.uk W:
www.inverclyde-libraries.info
Scottish Borders
Scottish Borders Archive & Local History Centre Library
Headquarters, St Mary's Mill, Selkirk, TD7 5EW T: 01750 20842 T:
01750 724903 F: 01750 22875 E: archives@scotborders.gov.uk W:
www.scotborders.gov.uk/libraries
Shetland
Shetland Library Lower Hillhead, Lerwick, ZE1 0EL T: 01595-
693868 F: 01595-694430 E: info@shetland-library.gov.uk W:
www.shetland-library.gov.uk
Stirling
Bridge of Allan Library Fountain Road, Bridge of Allan, FK9 4AT
T: 01786 833680 F: 01786 833680 W: www.stirling.gov.uk
Dunblane Library High Street, Dunbland, FK15 0ER T: 01786
823125 F: 01786 823125 E: dunblanelibrary@stirling.gov.uk W:
www.stirling.gov.uk
St Ninians Library Mayfield Centre, St Ninians, FK7 0DB T: 01786
472069 E: stninlibrary@stirling.gov.uk W: www.stirling.gov.uk
Stirling Central Library Central Library Corn Exchange Road,
Stirling, FK8 2HX T: 01786 432106 F: 01786 473094 E:
centrallibrary@stirling.gov.uk W: www.stirling.gov.uk
West Lothian
West Lothian Council Libraries Connolly House, Hopefield Road,
Blackburn, EH47 7HZ T: 01506-776331 F: 01506-776345 E:
localhistory@westlothian.org.uk W: www.wlonline.org
Wigtownshire
Ewart Library see Dumfries

NORTHERN IRELAND
Belfast
Belfast Central Library Irish & Local Studies Dept, Royal Avenue,
Belfast, BT1 1EA T: (028) 9024 3233 (028) 9033 2819 E:
info@libraries.belfast-elb.gov.uk W: www.belb.org.uk
Belfast Linen Hall Library 17 Donegall Square North, Belfast, BT1
5GD T: (028) 90321707
County Antrim
Local Studies Service, Area Library HQ, Demesne Avenue,
Ballymena, Co Antrim, BT43 7BG T: (028) 25 664121 (028) 256
46680 E: yvonne_hirst@hotmail.com W: www.neelb.org.uk
North Eastern Library Board & Local Studies Area Reference
Library Demesne Avenue, Ballymena, Antrim, BT43 7BG T: (028) 25
6641212 (028) 256 46680 E: yvonne_hirt@hotmail.com W:
www.neelb.org.uk
County Fermanagh
Enniskillen Library Halls Lane, Enniskillen, Co Fermanagh, BT1
3HP T: (028) 66322886 01365-324685 E:
librarian@eknlib.demon.co.uk
County Londonderry
Central and Reference Library 35 Foyle Street, Londonderry, Co
Londonderry, BT24 6AL T: (028) 71272300 01504-269084 E:
trishaw@online.rednet.co.uk
Irish Room, Coleraine County Hall, Castlerock Road, Ballymena,
County Londonderry, BT1 3HP T: (028) 705 1026 (028) 705 1247,
W: www.neelb.org.uk
County Tyrone
Centre for Migration Studies, Ulster American Folk Park, Mellon
Road, Castletown, Omagh, Co Tyrone, BT78 5QY T: 028 82 256315
028 82 242241 E: uafp@iol.ie W: www.qub.ac.uk/cms/
Omagh Library 1 Spillars Place, Omagh, Co Tyrone, BT78 1HL T:
(028) 82244821 01662-246772 E: librarian@omahlib.demon.co.uk
County Down
South Eastern Library Board & Local Studies Library HQ,
Windmill Hill, Ballynahinch, County Down, BT24 8DH T: (028)
9756 6400 (028) 9756 5072 E: ref@bhinchlibhq.demon.co.uk
South Antrim
South Eastern Library Board & Local Studies Library HQ,
Windmill Hill, Ballynahinch, County Down, BT24 8DH T: (028)
9756 6400 (028) 9756 5072 E: ref@bhinchlibhq.demon.co.uk

IRELAND
National Library of Ireland, Kildare Street, Dublin, 2 T: 661-8811
676-6690 E: coflaherty@nli.ie,
Society of Friends (Quakers) - Historical Library Swanbrook
House, Bloomfield Avenue, Dublin, 4 T: (01) 668-7157 , By 2001
will have completed computerisation of card index
Dublin
Dublin Public Libraries, Gilbert Library - Dublin & Irish
Collections, 138 - 142 Pearse Street, Dublin, 2 T: 353 1 674 4800 353
1 674 4879 E: dublinpubliclibraries@dublincity.ie W:
www.dublincity.ie
County Clare
Clare County Library The Manse, Harmony Row, Ennis, Co Clare
T: 065-6821616 065-6842462 E: clarelib@iol.ie W:
www.iol.ie/~clarelib

County Cork
Cork City Library Grand Parade, Cork, Co Cork T: 021-277110 021-275684 E: cork.city.library@indigo.ie W: www.corkcity.ie/
Mallow Heritage Centre , 27/28 Bank Place, Mallow, Co Cork T: 022-50302 W: www.corkcoco.com/
County Dublin
Dun Laoghaire Library Lower George's Street, Dun Laoghaire, Co Dublin T: 2801147 2846141 E: eprout@dlrcoco.ie W: www.dlrcoco.ie/library/lhistory.htm
County Kerry
Kerry County Library Genealogical Centre Cathedral Walk, Killarney, Co Kerry T: 353-0-64-359946
County Kildare
Kildare County Library , Newbridge, Co Kildare T: 045-431109 045-432490 W: www.kildare.ie/countycouncil/
Kildare Hertiage & Genealogy Kildare County Library Newbridge, Co Kildare T: 045 433602 045-432490 E: capinfo@iol.ie W: www.kildare.ie
County Mayo
Central Library , Castlebar, Co Mayo T: 094-24444 094-24774 E: cbarlib@iol.ie W: www.mayococo.ie
County Sligo
Sligo County Library Westward Town Centre Bridge Street, Sligo, Co Sligo T: 00-353-71-47190 00-353-71-46798 E: sligolib@iol.ie W: www.sligococo.ie/
County Tipperary
Tipperary County Library Local Studies Department Castle Avenue, Thurles, Co Tipperary T: 0504-21555 0504-23442 E: studies@tipplibs.iol.ie W: www.iol.ie/~TIPPLIBS
County Waterford
Waterford County Library Central Library Davitt's Quay, Dungarvan, Co Waterford T: 058 41231 058 54877 W: www.waterfordcoco.ie/
County Wexford
Enniscorthy Branch Library Lymington Road, Enniscorthy, Co Wexford T: 054-36055 W: www.wexford.ie/
New Ross Branch Library Barrack Lane, New Ross, Co Wexford T: 051-21877 W: www.wexford.ie/
Wexford Branch Library Teach Shionoid, Abbey Street, Wexford, Co Wexford T: 053-42211 053-21097 W: www.wexford.ie/
County Donegal
Donegal Local Studies Centre Central Library & Arts Centre Oliver Plunkett Road, Letterkenny, County Donegal T: 00353 74 24950 00353 74 24950 E: dgcolib@iol.ie W: www.donegal.ie/library
County Dublin
Ballyfermot Public Library Ballyfermot, Dublin, 10 T: W: www.dublincity.ie
County Limerick
Limerick City Library The Granary, Michael Street, Limerick, County Limerick T: 061-314668 061 411506 E: doyledolores@hotmail.com W: www.limerickcoco.ie/

Australia
ACT
National Library of Australia Canberra, 2600 T: 02 6262 1111 WWW: http://www.nla.gov.au
New South Wales
Mitchell Library Macquarie Street Sydney, 2000 T: 02 9230 1693 Fax: 02 9235 1687 E: slinfo@slsw.gov.au
State Library of New South Wales Macquarie Street Sydney, 2000 T: 02 9230 1414 F: 02 9223 3369 E: slinfo@slsw.gov.au
Queensland
State Library of Queensland PO Box 3488, Cnr Peel and Stanley Streets, South Brisbane, Brisbane, 4101 T: 07 3840 7775 Fax: 07 3840 7840 E: genie@slq.qld.gov.au
WWW: http://www.slq.qld.gov.au/subgenie/htm
South Australia
South Australia State Library PO Box 419 Adelaide, 5001 T: (08) 8207 7235 F: (08) 8207 7247 E: famhist@slsa.sa.gov.au W: http://www.slsa.sa.gov.au/library/collres/famhist/
Victoria
State Library of Victoria 328 Swanston Street Walk Melbourne, 3000 T: 03 9669 9080 E: granth@newvenus.slv.vic.gov.au W: http://www.slv.vic.gov.au/slv/genealogy/index
Western Australia
State Library Alexander Library, Perth Cultural Centre Perth, 6000 T: 09 427 3111 F: 09 427 3256

New Zealand
Auckland Research Centre Auckland City Libraries PO Box 4138, 44 46 Lorne Street Auckland T: 64 9 377 0209 F: 64 9 307 7741 E: heritage@auckland library.govt.nz
National Library of New Zealand PO Box 1467 Thorndon, Wellington T: (0064)4 474 3030 F: (0064)4 474 3063 WWW: http://www.natlib.govt.nz
Alexander Turnbull Library PO Box 12 349 , Wellington, 6038 T: 04 474 3050 F: 04 474 3063

Canterbury Public Library PO Box 1466 , Christchurch T: 03 379 6914 F: 03 365 1751
Dunedin Public Libraries PO Box 5542, Moray Place Dunedin T: 03 474 3651 F: 03 474 3660 E: library@dcc.govt.nz
Fielding Public Library PO Box 264 , Fielding, 5600 T: 06 323 5373
Hamilton Public Library PO Box 933, Garden Place Hamilton, 2015 T: 07 838 6827 F: 07 838 6858
Hocken Library PO Box 56 , Dunedin T: 03 479 8873 Fax: 03 479 5078
Porirua Public Library PO Box 50218 , Porirua, 6215 T: 04 237 1541 F: 04 237 7320
Takapuna Public Library Private Bag 93508 , Takapuna, 1309 Tel: 09 486 8466 F: 09 486 8519
Wanganui District Library Private Bag 3005, Alexander Building, Queens Park, Wanganui, 5001 T: 06 345 8195 F: 06 345 5516 E: wap@wdl.govt.nz

South Africa
South African Library PO Box 496 , Cape Town, 8000 T: 021 246320 F: 021 244848

Canada
Alberta
Calgary Public Library 616 MacLeod Tr SE Calgary, T2G 2M2 T: 260 2785
Glenbow Library & Archives 130 9th Avenue SE Calgary, T2G 0P3 T: 403 268 4197 F: 403 232 6569
British Columbia
British Columbia Archives 865 Yates Street Victoria, V8V 1X4 T: 604 387 1952 F: 604 387 2072 E: rfrogner@maynard.bcars.gs.gov.bc.ca
Cloverdale Library 5642 176a Street Surrey, V3S 4G9 T: 604 576 1384 E: GenealogyResearch@city.surrey.bc.ca
WWW: http://www.city.surrey.bc.ca/spl/
New Brunswick
Harriet Irving Library PO Box 7500 Fredericton, E3B 5H5 T: 506 453 4748 **Loyalist Collection & Reference Library** PO Box 7500 Fredericton, E3B 5H5 T: 506 453 4749
Newfoundland
Newfoundland Provincial Resource Library Arts and Cultural Centre, Allandale Road St Johns, A1B 3A3 T: 709 737 3955 E: genealog@publib.nf.ca W: http://www.publib.nf.ca
Ontario
National Library 395 Wellington Street Ottawa, K1A 0N4 Tel: 613 995 9481 E:reference@nlc bnc.ca W: http://www.nlc bnc.ca
Toronto Reference Library 789 Yonge Street Toronto, M4W 2G8 T: 416 393 7155 **James Gibson Reference Library** 500 Glenridge Avenue St Catherines, L2S 3A1 Tel: 905 688 5550 F: 905 988 5490
Public Library PO Box 2700, Station LCD 1 Hamilton, L8N 4E4 Tel: 546 3408 E: speccol@hpl.hamilton.on.ca
Public Library 85 Queen Street North Kitchener, N2H 2H1 Tel: 519 743 0271 F: 519 570 1360
Public Library 305 Queens Avenue London, N6B 3L7 Tel: 519 661 4600 F: 519 663 5396
Public Library 301 Burnhamthorpe Road West Mississauga, L5B 3Y3 T: 905 615 3500 E: library.info@city.mississauga.on.ca WWW: http://www.city.mississauga.on.ca/Library
Toronto Public Library North York (Central Library) Canadiana Department, 5120 Yonge Street North York, M2N 5N9 Tel: 416 395 5623 W: http://www.tpl.tor.on.ca
Public Library 74 Mackenzie Street Sudbury, P3C 4X8 Tel: 01673 1155 F: 01673 9603

St Catharines Public Library 54 Church Street St Catharines, L2R 7K2 T: 905 688 6103 F: 905 688 2811 E: scpublib@stcatharines.library.on.ca W: http://www.stcatharines.library.on.ca
Quebec
Bibliotheque De Montreal 1210, Rue Sherbrooke East Street , Montreal, H2L 1L9 T: 514 872 1616 F: 514 872 4654 Email: daniel_olivier@ville.montreal.qc.ca WWW: http://www.ville.montreal.qc.ca/biblio/pageacc.htm
Saskatchewan
Public Library PO Box 2311 Regina, S4P 3Z5 T: 306 777 6011 Fax: 306 352 5550 E: kaitken@rpl.sk.ca
Public Library 311 23rd Street East Saskatoon, S7K 0J6 T: 306 975 7555 F: 306 975 7542

Cemeteries & Crematoria

This list is not exhaustive and we would be pleased to receive details of other cemeteries & crematoria to add to our future lists.

England

Avon

Bristol General Cemetery Co, East Lodge, Bath Rd, Arnos Vale, Bristol, BS4 3EW T: 0117 971 3294

Canford Crematorium & Cemetery, Canford Lane, Westbury On Trym, Bristol, BS9 3PQ T: 0117 903 8280 Fax: 0117 903 8287 Administration Office for: Canford Crematorium, Canford Cemetery, Shirehampton Cemetery, Henbury Cemetery, Avonview Cemetery, Brislington Cemetery, Ridgeway Park Cemetery

Cemetery of Holy Souls, Bath Rd, Bristol, BS4 3EW T: 0117 977 2386

Haycombe Crematorium & Cemetery, Whiteway Rd, Bath, BA2 2RQ T: 01225 423682

South Bristol Crematorium & Cemetery, Bridgwater Rd, Bristol, BS13 7AS T: 0117 963 4141

Westerleigh Crematorium, Westerleigh Rd, Westerleigh, Bristol, BS37 8QP T: 0117 937 4619

Weston Super Mare Crematorium, Ebdon Rd, Worle, Weston-Super-Mare, BS22 9NY T: 01934 511717

Bedfordshire

Norse Rd Crematorium 104 Norse Rd, Bedford, MK41 0RL Tel: 01234 353701

Church Burial Ground, 26 Crawley Green Rd, Luton, LU2 0QX T: 01582 722874 T: 01582 721867 W: www.stmarysluton.org Correspondence to; St Mary's Church, Church Street, Luton LU1 3JF

Dunstable Cemetery, West St, Dunstable, LU6 1PB T: 01582 662772

Kempston Cemetery, Cemetery Lodge, 2 Green End Rd, Kempston, Bedford, MK43 8RJ T: 01234 851823

Luton Crematorium, The Vale, Butterfield Green Road, Stopsley, Luton, LU2 8DD T: 01582 723700 T: 01582 723730

Luton General Cemetery, Rothesay Rd, Luton, LU1 1QX T: 01582 727480

Berkshire

Easthampstead Park Cemetry & Crematorium, Nine Mile Ride, Wokingham, RG40 3DW T: 01344 420314

Henley Road Cemetery & Reading Crematorium, All Hallows Road, Henley Road, Caversham, Reading, RG4 5LP Tel: 0118 947 2433

Larges Lane Cemetery, Larges Lane, Bracknell, RG12 9AL Tel: 01344 450665

Newbury Cemetery, Shaw Hill, Shaw Fields, Shaw, Newbury, RG14 2EQ T: 01635 40096

Slough Cemetery & Crematorium, Stoke Rd, Slough, SL2 5AX T: 01753 523127 (Cemetery) Fax: 01753 520702 (Crematorium) E: sloughcrem@hotmail.com W: www.slough.gov.uk

Bristol

South Bristol Crematorium and Cemetery, Bridgwater Road, Bedminster Down, Bristol, BS13 7AS T: 0117 903 833 Fax: 0117 903 8337 Administration Office for South Bristol Crematorium, South Bristol Cemetery, Greenbank Cemetery

Buckinghamshire

Crownhill Crematorium, Dansteed Way, Crownhill, Milton Keynes, T: 01908 568112

Chilterns Crematorium, Whielden Lane, Winchmore Hill, Amersham, HP7 0ND T: 01494 724263

Cambridgeshire

American Military Cemetery, Madingley Rd, Coton, Cambridge, CB3 7PH T: 01954 210350 Fax: 01954 211130 E: Cambridge.Cemetery@ambc-er.org W: http://www.ambc.gov

Cambridge City Crematorium, Huntingdon Rd, Girton, Cambridge, CB3 0JJ T: 01954 780681

City of Ely Council, Ely Cemetery, Beech Lane, Ely, CB7 4QZ T: 01353 669659

Marholm Crematorium, Mowbray Rd, Peterborough, PE6 7JE T: 01733 262639

Cheshire

Altrincham Cemetery, Hale Rd, Altrincham, WA14 2EW T: 0161 980 4441

Altrincham Crematorium, White House Lane, Dunham Massey, Altrincham, WA14 5RH T: 0161 928 7771

Chester Cemetries & Crematorium, Blacon Avenue, Blacon, Chester, CH1 5BB T: 01244 372428

Dukinfield Crematorium, Hall Green Rd, Dukinfield, SK16 4EP T: 0161 330 1901

Macclesfield Cemetery, Cemetery Lodge, 87 Prestbury Rd, Macclesfield, SK10 3BU T: 01625 422330

Middlewich Cemetery, 12 Chester Rd, Middlewich, CW10 9ET T: 01606 737101

Overleigh Rd Cemetery, The Lodge, Overleigh Rd, Chester, CH4 7HW T: 01244 682529

Walton Lea Crematorium, Chester Rd, Higher Walton, Warrington, WA4 6TB T: 01925 267731

Widnes Cemetery & Crematorium, Birchfield Rd, Widnes, WA8 9EE T: 0151 471 7332

Cleveland

Teesside Crematorium, Acklam Rd, Middlesbrough, TS5 7HE T: 01642 817725 Fax: 01642 852424 E: peter_gitsham@middlesbrough.gov.uk W: www.middlesbrough.gov.uk Also contact address for: Acklam Cemetery, Acklam Road, Middlesbrough; Linthorpe Cemetery, Burlam Road; Thorntree Cemetery, Cargo Fleet Lane; Thorntree RC Cemetery, Cargo Fleet Lane; North Ormesby Cemetery; St josephs Cemetery, Ormesby Road, Middlesbrough

Cornwall

Glynn Valley Crematorium, Turfdown Rd, Fletchers Bridge, Bodmin, PL30 4AU T: 01208 73858

Penmount Crematorium, Penmount, Truro, TR4 9AA T: 01872 272871 Fax: 01872 223634 E: mail@penmount-crematorium.org.uk W: www.penmount-crematorium.org.uk

County Durham

Birtley Cemetery & Crematorium, Windsor Rd, Birtley, Chester Le Street, DH3 1PQ T: 0191 4102381

Chester Le Street Cemetery, Chester Le Street District Council Civic Centre, Newcastle Rd, Chester Le Street, DH3 3UT T: 0191 3872117

Horden Parish Council, Horden Cemetery Lodge, Thorpe Rd, Horden, Peterlee, SR8 4TP T: 0191 5863870

Mountsett Crematorium, Ewehurst Rd, Dipton, Stanley, DH9 0HN T: 01207 570255

Murton Parish Council, Cemetery Lodge, Church Lane, Murton, Seaham, SR7 9RD T: 0191 5263973

Newton Aycliffe Cemetery, Stephenson Way, Newton Aycliffe, DL5 7DF T: 01325 312861

Princess Road Cemetery, Princess Rd, Seaham, SR7 7TD T: 0191 5812943

Trimdon Foundry Parish Council, Cemetary Lodge, Thornley Rd, Trimdon Station, TS29 6NX T: 01429 880592

Trimdon Parish Council, Cemetery Lodge, Northside, Trimdon Grange, Trimdon Station, TS29 6HN T: 01429 880538

Wear Valley District Council, Cemetery Lodge, South Church Rd, Bishop Auckland, DL14 7NA T: 01388 603396

Cumbria

Carlisle Cemetery, Richardson St, Carlisle, CA2 6AL T: 01228 625310 Fax: 01228 625313 E: junec@carlisle-city.gov.uk

Penrith Cemetery, Beacon Edge, Penrith, CA11 7RZ T: 01768 862152

Wigton Burial Joint Committee, Cemetery House, Station Hill, Wigton, CA7 9BN T: 016973 42442

Derbyshire

Bretby Crematorium, Geary Lane, Bretby, Burton-On-Trent, DE15 0QE T: 01283 221505 Fax: 01283 224846 E: bretby.crematorium@eaststaffsbc.gov.uk WWW: www.eaststaffsbc.gov.uk CC accepted

Castle Donington Parish Council, Cemetery House, The Barroon, Castle Donington, Derby, DE74 2PF T: 01332 810202

Chesterfield & District Joint Crematorium, Chesterfield Rd, Brimington, Chesterfield, S43 1AU T: 01246 345888 Fax: 01246 345889

Clay Cross Cemetery, Cemetery Rd, Danesmoor, Chesterfield, S45 9RL T: 01246 863225

Dronfield Cemetery, Cemetery Lodge, 42 Cemetery Rd, Dronfield, S18 1XY T: 01246 412373

Glossop Cemetery, Arundel House, Cemetery Rd, Glossop, SK13 7QG T: 01457 852269

Markeaton Crematorium, Markeaton Lane, Derby, DE22 4NH T: 01332 341012 Fax: 01332 331273

Melbourne Cemetery, Pack Horse Rd, Melbourne, Derby, DE73 1BZ T: 01332 863369

Shirebrook Town Council, Common Lane, Shirebrook, Mansfield, NG20 8PA T: 01623 742509

Devon

Drake Memorial Park Ltd The, Haye Rd, Plympton, Plymouth, PL7 1UQ T: 01752 337937

Exeter & Devon Crematorium, Topsham Rd, Exeter, EX2 6EU T: 01392 496333

Littleham Church Yard, Littleham Village, Littleham, Exmouth, EX8 2RQ T: 01395 225579

Mole Valley Green Burial Ground, Woodhouse Farm, Queens Nympton, South Molton, EX36 4JH T: 01769 574512 Fax: 01769 574512 E: woodhouse.org.farm@farming.co.uk

North Devon Crematorium, Old Torrington Rd, Barnstaple, EX31 3NW T: 01271 345431

Ford Park Cemetery Trust, Ford Park Rd, Plymouth, PL4 6NT T: 01752 665442 Fax: 01752 601177 E: trustees@ford-park-cemetery.org W: www.ford-park-cemetery.org

Tavistock Cemetery, Cemetery Office, Plymouth Rd, Tavistock, PL19 8BY T: 01822 612799 Fax: 01822 618300 E: tavistocktc@aol.com W: www.tavistock.gov.uk

Torquay Crematorium & Cemetery, Hele Rd, Torquay, TQ2 7QG T: 01803 327768

Dorset, Dorchester Cemetery Office, 31a Weymouth Avenue, Dorchester, DT1 2EN T: 01305 263900

Parkstone Cemetery, 134 Pottery Rd, Parkstone, Poole, BH14 8RD T: 01202 741104

Poole Cemetery, Dorchester Rd, Oakdale, Poole, BH15 3RZ T: 01202 741106

Poole Crematorium, Gravel Hill, Poole, BH17 9BQ T: 01202 602582

Sherborne Cemetery, Lenthay Rd, Sherborne, DT9 6AA T: 01935 812909

Weymouth Crematorium, Quibo Lane, Weymouth, DT4 0RR T: 01305 786984

Essex

Basildon & District Crematorium, Church Rd, Bowers Gifford, Basildon, SS13 2HG T: 01268 584411

Chadwell Heath Cemetery, Whalebone Lane, North Chadwell Heath, Romford, RM6 5QX T: 0181 590 3280

Chelmsford Crematorium, Writtle Rd, Chelmsford, CM1 3BL T: 01245 256946

Chigwell Cemetery, Frog Hall LaneChapman, Manor Rd, Chigwell, IG7 4JX T: 020 8501 4275 E: chigwell@tesco.net

Colchester Cemetery & Crematorium, Mersea Rd, Colchester, CO2 8RU T: 01206 282950

Eastbrookend Cemetery, Dagenham Rd, Dagenham, RM10 7DR T: 01708 447451

Federation of Synagogues Burial Society, 416 Upminster Rd North, Rainham, RM13 9SB T: 01708 552825

Great Burstead Cemetery, Church St, Great Burstead, Billericay, CM11 2TR T: 01277 654334

Parndon Wood Crematorium and Cemetery, Parndon Wood Rd, Harlow, CM19 4SF T: 01279 446199 T: 01279 423800, E: chris.brown@harlow.gov.uk

Pitsea Cemetery, Church Rd, Pitsea, Basildon, SS13 2EZ T: 01268 552132

Romford Cemetery, Crow Lane, Romford, RM7 0EP T: 01708 740791

Sewardstone Road Cemetery, Sewardstone Rd, Waltham Abbey, EN9 1NX T: 01992 712525

South Essex Crematorium, Ockendon Rd, Corbets Tey, Upminster, RM14 2UY T: 01708 222188

Sutton Road Cemetery, The Lodge, Sutton Rd, Southend-On-Sea, SS2 5PX T: 01702 603907 Fax: 01702 603906 CC accepted

Weeley Crematorium, Colchester Rd, Weeley, Clacton-On-Sea, CO16 9JP T: 01255 831108 Fax: 01255 831440 Also covers and is contact address for: Clacton Cemetery; Kirby Cross Cemetery; Dovercourt Cemetery; Walton on the Naze Cemetery

Wickford Cemetery, Park Drive, Wickford, SS12 9DH T: 01268 733335

Gloucestershire

Cheltenham Cemetery & Crematorium, Bouncers Lane, Cheltenham, GL52 5JT T: 01242 244245 Fax: 01242 263123 E: cemetery@cheltenham.gov.uk WWW: www.cheltenham.gov.uk

Coney Hill Crematorium, Coney Hill Rd, Gloucester, GL4 4PA T: 01452 523902

Forest of Dean Crematorium, Yew Tree Brake, Speech House Rd, Cinderford, GL14 3HU T: 01594 826624

Mile End Cemetery, Mile End, Coleford, GL16 7DB T: 01594 832848

Hampshire

Aldershot Crematorium, 48 Guildford Rd, Aldershot, GU12 4BP T: 01252 321653

Anns Hill Rd Cemetery, Anns Hill Rd, Gosport, PO12 3JX T: 023 9258 0181 Fax: 023 9251 3191 W: www.gosport.gov.uk

Basingstoke Crematorium, Manor Farm, Stockbridge Rd, North Waltham, Basingstoke, RG25 2BA T: 01256 398784

Magdalen Hill Cemetery, Magdalen Hill, Arlesesford Rd, Winchester, SO21 1HE T: 01962 854135

Portchester Crematorium, Upper Cornaway Lane, Portchester, Fareham, PO16 8NE T: 01329 822533

Portsmouth Cemeteries Office, Milton Rd, Southsea, PO4 8 T: 023 9273 2559

Southampton City Council, 6 Bugle St, Southampton, SO14 2AJ T: 01703 228609

Warblington Cemetery, Church Lane, Warblington, Havant, PO9 2TU

Worting Rd Cemetery, 105 Worting Rd, Basingstoke, RG21 8YZ T: 01256 321737

Herefordshire

Hereford Cemetery & Crematorium, Bereavement Services office, Westfaling Street, Hereford, HR4 0JE T: 01432 383200

Hertfordshire

Vicarage Road Cemetery, Vicarage Road, Watford, WD18 0EJ T: 01923 672157 Fax: 01923 672157

Almonds Lane Cemetery, Almonds Lane, Stevenage, SG1 3RR T: 01438 350902

Bushey Jewish Cemetery, Little Bushey Lane, Bushey, Watford, WD2 3TP T: 0181 950 6299 One of the burial grounds maintained by the United Synagogue

Chorleywood Road Cemetery, Chorleywood Rd, Rickmansworth, WD3 4EH T: 01923 772646

Dacorum Borough Council, Woodwells Cemetery, Buncefield Lane, Hemel Hempstead, HP2 7HY T: 01442 252856

Harwood Park Crematorium Ltd, Watton Rd, Stevenage, SG2 8XT T: 01438 815555

Hatfield Road Cemetery, Hatfield Rd, St. Albans, AL1 4LU T: 01727 819362 Fax: 01727 819362 E: stalbans@cemeteries.freeserve.co.uk St Albans City & District Council administers three Cemeteries from Hatfield Road. The other two are situated London Road, St Albans and Westfield Road, Harpenden

North Watford Cemetery, North Western Avenue, Watford, WD25 0AW T: 01923 672157 Fax: 01923 672157

Tring Cemetery, Aylesbury Rd, Aylesbury, Tring, HP23 4DH T: 01442 822248

Vicarage Road Cemetery, Vicarage Rd, Watford, WD1 8EJ T: 01923 225147

Watton Rd Cemetery, Watton Rd, Ware, SG12 0AX T: 01920 463261

West Herts Crematorium, High Elms Lane, Watford, WD25 0JS T: 01923 673285 Fax: 01923 681318 E: postmaster@weshertscrem.org W: www.weshertscrem.org CC accepted

Western Synagogue Cemetery, Cheshunt Cemetery, Bulls Cross Ride, Waltham Cross, EN7 5HT T: 01992 717820

Weston Road Cemetery, Weston Rd, Stevenage, SG1 4DE T: 01438 367109

Woodcock Hill Cemetery, Lodge, Woodcock Hill, Harefield Rd, Rickmansworth, WD3 1PT T: 01923 775188

Isle Of Wight

Shanklin Cemetery, 1 Cemetery Rd, Lake Sandown, Sandown, PO36 9NN T: 01983 403743

Kent

Barham Crematorium, Canterbury Rd, Barham, Canterbury, CT4 6QU T: 01227 831351 Fax: 01227 830258

Beckenham Crematorium & Cemetery, Elmers End Rd, Beckenham, BR3 4TD T: 0208650 0322

Chartham Cemetery Lodge, Ashford Rd, Chartham, Canterbury, CT4 7NY T: 01227 738211 T: 01227 738211 Minicom, Fax: 01227 738211 All burial records computerised

Gravesham Borough Council, Old Rd West, Gravesend, DA11 0LS T: 01474 337491

Hawkinge Cemetery & Crematorium, Aerodrome Rd, Hawkinge, Folkestone, CT18 7AG T: 01303 892215

Kent & Sussex Crematorium, Benhall Mill Rd., Tunbridge Wells, TN2 5JH T: 01892 523894

Kent County Crematorium plc, Newcourt Wood, Charing, Ashford, TN27 0EB T: 01233 712443 Fax: 01233 713501

The Cremation Society, 2nd Floor Brecon House, 16/16a Albion Place, Maidstone, ME14 5DZ T: 01622 688292/3 Fax: 01622 686698 E: cremsoc@aol.com W: www.cremation.org.uk

Medway Crematorium, Robin Hood Lane, Blue Bell Hill, Chatham, ME5 9QU T: 01634 861639 Fax: 01634 671206 E: paul.edwards@medway.gov.uk CC accepted

Northfleet Cemetery, Springhead Rd, Northfleet, Gravesend, DA11 8HW T: 01474 533260

Snodland Cemetery, Cemetery Cottage, Cemetery Rd, Snodland, ME6 5DN T: 01634 240764

Thanet Crematorium, Manston Rd, Margate, CT9 4LY T: 01843 224492 Fax: 01843 292218 Also covers: Margate Cemetery, Kent; Ramsgate and St Lawrence Cemeteries

Vinters Park Crematorium, Bearstead Rd, Weavering, Maidstone, ME14 5LG T: 01622 738172 Fax: 01622 630560 CC accepted

Lancashire

Accrington Cemetery & Crematorium, Burnley Rd, Accrington, BB5 6HA T: 01254 232933 Fax: 01254 232933

Atherton Cemetery, Leigh Road, Atherton

Audenshaw Cemetery, Cemetery Rd, Audenshaw, Manchester, M34 5AH T: 0161 336 2675

Blackley Cemetery & Crematorium, Victoria Avenue, Manchester, M9 8 T: 0161 740 5359

Burnley Cemetery, Rossendale Rd, Burnley, BB11 5DD T: 01282 435411 Fax: 01282 458904 W: www.burnley.gov.uk

Carleton Crematorium, Stocks Lane, Carleton, Poulton-Le-Fylde, FY6 7QS T: 01253 882541

Central & North Manchester Synagogue Jewish Cemetery, Rainsough Brow, Prestwich, Manchester, M25 9XW T: 0161 773 2641**Central & North Manchester Synagogue Jewish Cemetery,** Rochdale Rd, Manchester, M9 6FQ T: 0161 740 2317

Chadderton Cemetery, Cemetery Lodge, Middleton Rd, Chadderton, Oldham, OL9 0JZ T: 0161 624 2301

Gidlow Cemetery, Gidlow Lane, Standish, Wigan, WN6 8RT T: 01257 424127

Greenacres Cemetery, Greenacres Rd, Oldham, OL4 3HT T: 0161 624 2294

Hindley Cemetery, Castle Hill Road Road, Ince, Wigan, WN3

Hollinwood Cemetery (incorporating Oldham Crematorium), Central Cemeteries Office, Roman Rd, Hollinwood, Oldham, OL8 3LU T: 0161 681 1312 Fax: 0161 683 5233 E: oper.cemeteries@oldham.gov.uk W: www.oldham.gov.uk The Central Cemeteries Office covers seven cemeteries and one crematorium: Hollinwood, Greenacres, Crompton, Royton, Lees, Chadderton and Failswoprth Cemeteries and Oldham Crematorium
Howe Bridge Crematorium, Crematorium Management Ltd, Lovers Lane, Atherton, Manchester, M46 0PZ T: 01942 870811
Howebridge Cemetery, Lovers Lane, Atherton
Ince in Makerfield Cemetery, Warrington Road, Lower Ince, Wigan
Leigh Cemetery, Manchester Rd, Leigh, WN7 2 T: 01942 671560 Fax: 01942 828877 W: www.wiganbc.gov.uk
Lower Ince Cemetery and Crematorium, Cemetery Road, Lower Ince, Wigan, WN3 4NH T: 01942 866455 Fax: 01942 828855 E: t.bassett@wiganmbc.gov.uk
Lytham Park Cemetery & Cremarotium, Regent Avenue, Lytham St. Annes, FY8 4AB T: 01253 735429 Fax: 01253 731903
Manchester Crematorium Ltd, Barlow Moor Rd, Manchester, M21 7GZ T: 0161 881 5269
Middleton New Cemetery, Boarshaw Rd, Middleton, Manchester, M24 6 T: 0161 655 3765
New Manchester Woodland Cemetery, City Rd, Ellenbrook, Worsley, Manchester, M28 1BD T: 0161 790 1300
Overdale Crematorium, Overdale Drive, Chorley New Rd, Heaton, Bolton, BL1 5BU T: 01204 840214
Padiham Public Cemetery, St. Johns Rd, Padiham, Burnley, BB12 7BN T: 01282 778139
Preston Cemetery, New Hall Lane, Preston, PR1 4SY T: 01772 794585 Fax: 01772 703857 E: m.birch@preston.gov.uk W: www.preston.gov.uk All burial records are available on microfilm at the Lancashire Record Office, Bow Lane, Preston as well as at the Cemetery Office
Preston Crematorium, Longridge Rd, Ribbleton, Preston, PR2 6RL T: 01772 792391 Fax: 01772 703857 E: m.birch@preston.gov.uk W: www.preston.gov.uk All records relating to Preston Crematorium are held at Preston Cemetery office, New Hall Lane, Preston PR1 4SY T: 01772 794585
Rochdale Cemetery, Bury Rd, Rochdale, OL11 4DG T: 01706 645219
Southern Cemetery, Barlow Moor Rd, Manchester, M21 7GL T: 0161 881 2208
St. Mary's Catholic Cemetery, Manchester Rd, Wardley, Manchester, M28 2UJ T: 0161 794 2194 E: cemeteries@salforddiocese.org
St Joseph's Cemetery, Moston Lane, Manchester, M40 9QL T: 0161 681 1582 E: cemeteries@salforddiocese.org
Tyldesley Cemetery, Hough Lane, Tyldesley
United Synagogue Burial Ground, Worsley Hill Farm, Phillips Park Rd, Whitefield, Manchester, M45 7ED T: 0161 766 2065
Wigan Council Cemeteries and Crematorium Section, 1 - 3 Worsley Terrace, Standishgate, Wigan, WN1 1XW T: 01942 828993 T: 01942 828994, Fax: 01942 828877 E: t.boussele@wiganmbc.gov.uk
Whitworth Cemetery, Edward St, Whitworth, Rochdale, OL16 2EJ T: 01706 217777
Westwood Cemetery, Westwood Lane, Lower Ince, Wigan,
Leicestershire
Cemetery Lodge, Thorpe Rd, Melton Mowbray, LE13 1SH T: 01664 562223
Loughborough Crematorium, Leicester Rd, Loughborough, LE11 2AF T: 01743 353046
Saffron Hill Cemetery, Stonesby Avenue, Leicester, LE2 6TY T: 0116 222 1049
Lincolnshire
Boston Crematorium, Cemeteries and Crematorium Office, Marian Rd, Boston, PE21 9HA T: 01205 364612 Fax: 01205 364612 E: martin.potts@boston.gov.ukW: www.boston.gov.uk Administers Boston Cemetery (1855), Fosdyke Cemetery (1952) and Boston Crematorium (1966)
Bourne Town Cemetery, South Rd, Bourne, PE10 9JB Tel: 01778 422796
Grantham Cemetery & Crematorium, Harrowby Rd, Grantham, NG31 9DT T: 01476 563083 T: 01476 590905 Fax: 01476 576228
Horncastle Cemetery, Boston Rd, Horncastle, LN9 6NF Tel: 01507 527118
Stamford Cemetery, Wichendom, Little Casterton Rd, Stamford, PE9 1BB T: 01780 762316
Tyler Landscapes, Newport Cemetery, Manor Rd, Newport, Lincoln, LN4 1RT T: 01522 525195
Lincolnshire - North East
Cleethorpes Cemetery, Beacon Avenue, Cleethorpes, DN35 8EQ T: 01472 324869 Fax: 01472 324870
North East Lincolnshire Council Crematorium & Cemeteries Department, Weelsby Avenue, Grimsby, DN32 0BA T: 01472 324869 Fax: 01472 324870

Lincolnshire - North
Woodlands Crematorium, Brumby Wood Lane, Scunthorpe, DN17 1SP T: 01724 280289 Fax: 01724 871235 E: crematorium@northlincs.gov.uk W: www.northlincs.gov.uk/environmentalhealth/cemetery.htm Central Office for holding documents for: Barton Upon Humber Cemetery, Brumby Cemetery, Crosby Cemetery, Brigg Cemetery, Scawby Cemetery, Winterton Cemetery and Woodlands Cemetery
London
Abney Park Cemetery, The South Lodgfe, Stoke Newington High St, Stoke Newington, London, N16 0LH T: 020 7275 7557 Fax: 020 7275 7557 E: abney-park@ges2.poptel.org.uk W: www.abney-park.org.uk
Brockley Ladywell Hithergreen & Grove Park Cemeteries, Verdant Lane, Catford, London SE6 1TP T: 0181 697 2555
Brompton Cemetery, Fulham Rd, London, SW10 9UG T: 0171 352 1201
Cemetery Management Ltd, The City of Westminster Office, 38 Uxbridge Rd, London, W7 3PP T: 0181 567 0913
Charlton Cemetery, Cemetery Lane, London, SE7 8DZ T: 0181 854 0235
Chingford Mount Cemetery London Borough of Waltham Forest, Old Church Rd, London, E4 6ST T: 020 8524 5030
City of London Cemetery & Crematorium, Aldersbrook Rd, London, E12 5DQ T: 0181 530 2151
Coroners Court, 8 Ladywell Rd, Lewisham, London, SE13 7UW T: 0208690 5138
East London Cemetery Co.Ltd, Grange Rd, London, E13 0HB Tel: 020 7476 5109 Fax: 020 7476 8338 E: enquiries@eastlondoncemetery.co.uk W: www.eastlondoncemetery.co.uk
Edmonton Cemetery, Church St, Edmonton, London, N9 9HP T: 0208360 2157
Eltham Cemetery & Crematorium, Crown Woods Way, Eltham, London, SE9 2RF T: 0181 850 2921 (Cemetery) Fax: 0181 850 7046 (Crematorium)
Gap Road Cemetery, Gap Rd, London, SW19 8JF T: 0208879 0701
Golders Green Crematorium, 62 Hoop Lane, London, NW11 7NL T: 0208455 2374
Greenwich Cemetery, Well Hall Rd, London SE9 6TZ T: 0181 856 8666
London Borough of Hackney Mortuary, Lower Clapton Rd, London, E5 8EQ T: 0181 985 2808
Hendon Cemetery & Crematorium, Holders Hill Rd, London, NW7 1NB T: 0181 346 0657
Highgate Cemetery, Swains Lane, London, N6 6PJ T: 0181 340 1834
Honor Oak Crematorium, Brenchley Gardens, London, SE23 3RB T: 020 7639 3121 Fax: 020 7732 3557 E: terry.connor@southwark.gov.uk
Islington Cemetery & Crematorium, High Rd, East Finchley, London, N2 9AG T: 0208883 1230
Kensal Green Cemetery, Harrow Road, London, W10 4RA T: 020 8969 0152 Fax: 020 8960 9744
L B S Cemeteries, Brenchley Gardens, London, SE23 3RD T: 020 7639 3121 Fax: 020 7732 3557 E: terry.connor@southwark.gov.uk
Lambeth Cemetery and Crematorium, Cemetery Lodge, Blackshaw Rd, Tooting, London, SW17 0BY T: 0181 672 1390
Lewisham Crematorium, Verdant Lane, London, SE6 1TP T: 0208698 4955
Liberal Jewish Cemetery, The Lodge, Pound Lane, London, NW10 2HG T: 0181 459 1635
Manor Park Cemetery Co.Ltd, Sebert Rd, Forest Gate, London, E7 0NP T: 020 8534 1486 Fax: 020 8519 1348 E: supt@manorpark15.fsbusiness.co.uk W: www.mpark.co.uk CC accepted Grave of John Cornwell VC
New Southgate Cemetery & Crematorium Ltd, 98 Brunswick Park Rd, London, N11 1JJ T: 0181 361 1713
Newham, London Borough of, High St South, London, E6 6ET T: 0181 472 9111
Plumstead Cemetery, Wickham Lane, London, SE2 0NS T: 0181 854 0785
Putney Vale Cemetery & Crematorium, Kingston Rd, London, SW15 3SB T: 0181 788 2113
South London Crematorium & Streatham Park Cemetery, Rowan Rd, London, SW16 5JG T: 0181 764 2255
St. Marylebone Crematorium, East End Rd, Finchley, London, N2 0RZ T: 0208343 2233
St. Pancras Cemetery (London Borough Of Camden), High Rd, East Finchley, London, N2 9AG T: 0181 883 1231
St. Patrick's Catholic Cemetery, Langthorne Rd, London, E11 4HL T: 0181 539 2451
St.Mary's Catholic Cemetery, Harrow Rd, London, NW10 5NU T: 0181 969 1145
Tottenham Park Cemetery, Montagu Rd, Edmonton, N18 2NF T: 0181 807 1617
United Synagogue, Beaconsfield Rd, Willesden, London, NW10 2JE T: 0208459 0394
West End Chesed V'Ameth Burial Society, 3 Rowan Rd, London, SW16 5JF T: 0181 764 1566

West Ham Cemetery, Cemetery Rd, London, E7 9DG T: 0208534 1566

West London Synagogue, Hoop Lane, London, NW11 7NJ T: 0208455 2569

West Norwood Cemetery & Crematorium, Norwood Rd, London, SE27 9AJ T: 0207926 7900

Woodgrange Park Cemetery, Romford Rd, London, E7 8AF T: 0181 472 3433

Woolwich Cemetery, Kings Highway, London, SE18 2BJ T: 0181 854 0740

Merseyside

Anfield Crematorium, Priory Rd, Anfield, Liverpool, L4 2SL T: 0151 263 3267

Southport Cemeteries & Crematoria, Southport Rd, Scarisbrick, Southport, PR8 5JQ T: 01704 533443

St. Helens Cemetery & Crematorium, Rainford Rd, Windle, St. Helens, WA10 6DF T: 01744 677406 Fax: 01744 677411

Thornton Garden Of Rest, Lydiate Lane, Thornton, Liverpool, L23 1TP T: 0151 924 5143

Middlesex

Adath Yisroel Synagogue & Burial Society, Carterhatch Lane, Enfield, EN1 4BG T: 0181 363 3384

Breakspear Crematorium, Breakspear Rd, Ruislip, HA4 7SJ T: 01895 632843 Fax: 01895 624209

Enfield Crematorium, Great Cambridge Rd, Enfield, EN1 4DS T: 0181 363 8324

Heston & Isleworth Borough Cemetry, 190 Powder Mill Lane, Twickenham, TW2 6EJ T: 0181 894 3830

South West Middlesex Crematorium, Hounslow Rd, Hanworth, Feltham, TW13 5JH T: 0208894 9001

Spelthorne Borough Council, Green Way, Sunbury-On-Thames, TW16 6NW T: 01932 780244

Norfolk

Colney Wood Memorial Park, Colney Hall, Watton Rd, Norwich, NR4 7TY T: 01603 811556

Mintlyn Crematorium, Lynn Rd, Bawsey, King's Lynn, PE32 1HB T: 01553 630533 Fax: 01553 630998 E: colin.houseman@west-norfolk.gov.uk W: www.west-norfolk.gov.uk

Norwich & Norfolk Crematoria - St. Faiths & Earlham, 75 Manor Rd, Horsham St. Faith, Norwich, NR10 3LF T: 01603 898264

Sprowston Cemetery, Church Lane, Sprowston, Norwich, NR7 8AU T: 01603 425354

North Tyneside - North Tyneside Metropolitan Borough Council

Earsdon Cemetery, Earsdon, Whitley Bay, NE25 9LR T: 0191 200 5861 0191 200 5860

Longbenton Cemetery, Longbenton, Newcastle Upon Tyne, NE12 8EY T: 0191 2661261

Whitley Bay Cemetery, Blyth Rd, Whitley Bay, NE26 4NH T: 0191 200 5861 Fax: 0191 200 5860

Northamptonshire

Counties Crematorium, Towcester Rd, Milton Malsor, Northampton, NN4 9RN T: 01604 858280

Dallington Cemetery, Harlstone Rd, Dallington, Northampton, NN5 7 T: 01604 751589

Northumberland

Alnwick Cemetary, Cemetery Lodge Office, South Rd, Alnwick, NE66 2PH T: 01665 602598 T: 01665 579272, Fax: 01665 579272 W: www.alnwicktown.com

Blyth Cemetery, Links Rd, Blyth, NE24 3PJ T: 01670 369623

Cowpen Cemetery, Cowpen Rd, Blyth, NE24 5SZ T: 01670 352107

Embleton Joint Burial Committee, Spitalford, Embleton, Alnwick, NE66 3DW T: 01665 576632

Haltwhistle & District Joint Burial Committee, Cemetery Lodge Haltwhistle, NE49 0LF T: 01434 320266 Fax: 01434 320266

Rothbury Cemetery, Cemetery Lodge, Whitton Rd Rothbury, Morpeth, NE65 7RX T: 01669 620451

Nottinghamshire

Bramcote Crematorium, Coventry Lane, Beeston, Nottingham, NG9 3GJ T: 0115 922 1837

Mansfield & District Crematorium, Derby Rd, Mansfield, NG18 5BJ T: 01623 621811

Northern Cemetery, Hempshill Lane, Bulwell, Nottingham, NG6 8PF T: 0115 915 3245 Fax: 0115 915 3246 E: alec.thomson@nottinghamcity.gov.uk W: www.nottinghamcity.gov.uk/bereavement Also covers: ~Basford Cemetery Npottingham Road, General Cemetery Waverley Street, Canning Circus and Church (Rock) Cemetery, Mansfield Road

Southern Cemetery & Crematoria, Wilford Hill, West Bridgford, Nottingham, NG2 7FE T: 0115 915 2340

Tithe Green Woodland Burial Ground, Salterford Lane, Calverton, Nottingham, NG14 6NZ T: 01623 882210

Oxfordshire

Oxford Crematorium Ltd, Bayswater Rd, Headington, Oxford, OX3 9RZ T: 01865 351255

Shropshire

Bridgnorth Cemetery, Mill St, Bridgnorth, WV15 5NG T: 01746 762386

Emstrey Crematorium, London Rd, Shrewsbury, SY2 6PS T: 01743 359883

Hadley Cemetery, 85 Hadley Park Rd, Hadley, Telford, TF1 4PY T: 01952 223418

Longden Road Cemetery, Longden Rd, Shrewsbury, SY3 7HS T: 01743 353046

Market Drayton Burial Committee, Cemetery Lodge, Cemetery Rd, Market Drayton, TF9 3BD T: 01630 652833

Oswestry Cemetery, Cemetery Lodge, Victoria Rd, Oswestry, SY11 2HU T: 01691 652013 Fax: 01691 652013 E: graham.lee2@btinternet.com

Whitchurch Joint Cemetery Board, The Cemetery Lodge, Mile Bank Rd, Whitchurch, SY13 4JY T: 01948 665477

Somerset

Burnham Area Burial Board, The Old Courthouse, Jaycroft Rd, Burnham-on-Sea, TA8 1LE T: 01278 795111

Chard Town Council, Holyrood Lace Mill, Hollyrood Street, Chard, TA20 12YA T: 01460 260370 Fax: 01460 260372

Minehead Cemetery, Porlock Rd, Woodcombe, Minehead, TA24 8RY T: 01643 705243

Sedgemoor District Council, The Cemetery, Quantock Rd, Bridgwater, TA6 7EJ T: 01278 423993

Taunton Deane Cemeteries & Crematorium, Wellington New Rd, Taunton, TA1 5NE T: 01823 284811 Fax: 01823 323152 W: www.tauntondeane.gov.uk/TDBCsites/crem

Wells Burial Joint Committee, 127 Portway, Wells, BA5 1LY T: 01749 672049

Yeovil Cemetery, Preston Rd, Yeovil, BA21 3AG T: 01935 423742

Yeovil Crematorium, Bunford Lane, Yeovil, BA20 2EJ T: 01935 476718

Staffordshire

Bretby Crematorium, Geary Lane, Bretby, Burton-On-Trent, DE15 0QE T: 01283 221505 Fax: 01283 224846 E: bretby.crematorium@eaststaffsbc.gov.uk WWW: www.eaststaffsbc.gov.uk CC accepted

Cannock Cemetery, Cemetery Lodge, 160 Pye Green Rd, Cannock, WS11 2SJ T: 01543 503176

Carmountside Cemetery and Crematorium Leek Rd, Milton, Stoke-On-Trent, ST2 7AB T: 01782 235050 Fax: 01782 235050 E: karendeaville@civic2.stoke.gov.uk

Leek Cemetery, Condlyffe Rd, Leek, ST13 5PP T: 01538 382616

Newcastle Cemetery, Lymewood Grove, Newcastle, ST5 2EH T: 01782 616379 Fax: 01782 630498 E: jeanette.hollins@newcastle-staffs.gov.uk

Newcastle Crematorium, Chatterley Close, Bradwell, Newcastle, ST5 8LE T: 01782 635498 Fax: 01782 710859

Stafford Crematorium, Tixall Rd, Stafford, ST18 0XZ T: 01785 242594

Stapenhill Cemetery, 38 Stapenhill Rd, Burton-On-Trent, DE15 9AE T: 01283 508572 Fax: 01283 566586 E: cemetery@eaststaffsbc.gov.uk W: www.eaststaffsbc.gov.uk

Stilecop Cemetary, Stilecop Rd, Rugeley, WS15 1ND T: 01889 577739

Uttoxeter Town Council, Cemetery Lodge, Stafford Rd, Uttoxeter ST14 8DS T: 01889 563374

Suffolk

Brinkley Woodland Cemetery, 147 All Saints Rd, Newmarket, CB8 8HH T: 01638 600693

Bury St. Edmunds Cemetery, 91 Kings Rd, Bury St. Edmunds, IP33 3DT T: 01284 754447

Hadleigh Town Council, Friars Rd, Hadleigh, Ipswich, IP7 6DF T: 01473 822034

Haverhill Cemetery, Withersfield Rd, Haverhill, CB9 9HF T: 01440 703810

Ipswich Cemetery & Crematorium, Cemetery Lane, Ipswich, IP4 2TQ T: 01473 433580 Fax: 01473 433588 E: carol.egerton@ipswich.gov.uk

Leiston Cemetery, Waterloo Avenue, Leiston, IP16 4EH T: 01728 831043

West Suffolk Crematorium, Risby, Bury St. Edmunds, IP28 6RR T: 01284 755118 Fax: 01284 755135

Surrey

American Cemetery, Cemetery Pales, Brookwood, Woking, GU24 0BL T: 01483 473237

Bandon Hill Cemetery Joint Committee, Plough Lane, Wallington, SM6 8JQ T: 0181 647 1024

Brookwood Cemetery, Cemetery Pales, Brookwood, Woking, GU24 0BL T: 01483 472222

Confederation of Burial Authorities, The Gate House, Kew Meadow Path, Richmond, TW9 4EN T: 0181 392 9487

Guildford Crematorium & Cemetaries, Broadwater, New Pond Rd, Goldaming GU7 3DB T: 01483 444711

Kingston Cemetary & Crematorium, Bonner Hill Rd, Kingston Upon Thames, KT1 3EZ T: 020 8546 4462 Fax: 020 8546 4463

London Road Cemetery, Figs Marsh, London Rd, Mitcham, CR4 3 T: 020048 4115

Merton & Sutton Joint Cemetery, Garth Rd, Morden, SM4 4LL T: (020) 8337 4420 Fax: (020) 8337 4420

Mortlake Crematorium Board, Kew Meadow Path, Town Mead Rd, Richmond, TW9 4EN T: 0181 876 8056
Mount Cemetery, Weyside Rd, Guildford, GU1 1HZ T: 01483 561927
North East Surrey Crematorium Board, Lower Morden Lane, Morden, SM4 4NU T: 020 8337 4835 Fax: 020 8337 8745 E: nescb.crematorium@talk21.com W: www.nes-crematorium.org.uk Opened May 1958
Randalls Park Crematorium, Randalls Rd, Leatherhead, KT22 0AG T: 01372 373813
Redstone Cemetery, Philanthropic Rd, Redhill, RH1 4DN T: 01737 761592
Dorking Cemetery, Reigate Rd, Dorking, RH4 1QF T: 01306 879299 Fax: 01306 876821 E: carole.brough@mole-valley.gov.uk W: www.mole-valley.gov.uk Victorian Cemetery concecrated in 1855 (listed Grade II in 1999)
Richmond Cemeteries, London Borough of Richmond upon Thames, Sheen Rd, Richmond, TW10 5BJ T: 020 8876 4511 Fax: 020 8878 8118 E: cemeteries@richmond.gov.uk
Surbiton Cemetery, Lower Marsh Lane, Kingston Upon Thames, KT1 3BN T: 0208546 4463
Sutton & Cuddington Cemeteries, Alcorn Close, off Oldfields Road, Sutton, SM3 9PX T: 020 8644 9437 Fax: 020 8644 1373
The Godalming Joint Burial Committee, New Cemetery Lodge, Ockford Ridge, Godalming, GU7 2NP T: 01483 421559
Woking Crematorium, Hermitage Rd, Woking, GU21 8TJ T: 01483 472197 Oldest crematorium in the UK. Search fee payable
Sussex - East
Afterthoughts Grave Care, 16 Derwent Rd, Eastbourne BN20 7PH T: 01323 730029
Brighton Borough Mortuary, Lewes Rd, Brighton, BN2 3QB T: 01273 602345
Downs Crematorium, Bear Rd, Brighton, BN2 3PL T: 01273 601601
Eastbourne Cemeteries & Crematorium, Hide Hollow, Langney, Eastbourne, BN23 8AE T: 01323 766536 (Cemetery) Fax: 01323 761093 (Crematorium)
Woodvale Crematorium, Lewes Rd, Brighton, BN2 3QB T: 01273 604020
Sussex - West
Chichester Crematorium, Westhampnett Rd, Chichester, PO19 4UH T: 01243 787755
Midhurst Burial Authority, Cemetery Lodge, Carron Lane, Midhurst, GU29 9LF T: 01730 812758
Surrey & Sussex Crematorium, Balcombe Rd, Crawley, RH10 3NQ T: 01293 888930
Worthing Crematorium & Cemeteries, Horsham Rd, Findon, Worthing, BN14 0RG T: 01903 872678 Fax: 01903 872051 E: crematorium@worthing.gov.uk
Tyne And Wear
Byker & Heaton Cemetery, 18 Benton Rd, Heaton, Newcastle Upon Tyne, NE7 7DS T: 0191 2662017
Gateshead East Cemetery, Cemetery Rd, Gateshead, NE8 4HJ T: 0191 4771819
Heworth Cemetery, Sunderland Rd, Felling, Gateshead, NE10 0NT T: 0191 4697851
Preston Cemetery & Tynemouth Crematorium, Walton Avenue, North Shields, NE29 9NJ T: 0191 2005861
Saltwell Crematorium, Saltwell Road South, Gateshead, NE8 4TQ T: 0191 4910553
St. Andrews Cemetery, Lodges 1-2, Great North Rd, Jesmond, Newcastle Upon Tyne, NE2 3BU T: 0191 2810953
St. Johns & Elswick Cemetery, Elswick Rd, Newcastle Upon Tyne, NE4 8DL T: 0191 2734127
St. Nicholas Cemetery, Wingrove Avenue Back, Newcastle Upon Tyne, NE4 9AP T: 0191 2735112
Union Hall Cemetery, Union Hall Rd, Newcastle Upon Tyne, NE15 7JS T: 0191 2674398
West Road Cemetery, West Rd, Newcastle Upon Tyne, NE5 2JL T: 0191 2744737
Warwickshire
Mid-Warwickshire Crematorium & Cemeteries, Oakley Wood, Bishops Tachbrook, Leamington Spa, CV33 9QP T: 01926 651418
Nuneaton Cemetery, Oaston Rd, Nuneaton, CV11 6JZ T: 024 7637 6357 Fax: 024 7637 6485
Stratford-on-Avon Cemetery, Evesham Rd, Stratford-Upon-Avon, CV37 9AA T: 01789 292676
West Midlands
Robin Hood Cemetery and Crematorium, Sheetsbrook Road, Shirley, Solihull, B90 3NL T: 0121 744 1121 Fax: 0121 733 8674
Widney Manor Cemetery, Widney Manor Road, Bentley Heath, Solihull, B93 3LX
Birmingham Crematorium 1973, 389 Walsall Rd, Perry Barr, Birmingham, B42 2LR T: 0121 356 9476
Birmingham Hebrew Congregation Cemetery, The Ridgeway, Erdington, Birmingham, B23 7TD T: 0121 356 4615
Brandwood End Cemetery, Woodthorpe Rd, Kings Heath, Birmingham, B14 6EQ T: 0121 444 1328

Coventry Bereavement Services, The Cemeteries & Crematorium Office, Cannon Hill Rd, Canley, Coventry, CV4 7DF T: 01203 418055
Handsworth Cemetery, Oxhill Rd, Birmingham, B21 8JT T: 0121 554 0096
Lodge Hill Cemetery & Cremetorium, Weoley Park Rd, Birmingham, B29 5AA T: 0121 472 1575
Quinton Cemetery, Halesowen Rd, Halesowen, B62 9AF T: 0121 422 2023
Stourbridge Cemetry & Crematorium, South Rd, Stourbridge, DY8 3RQ T: 01384 813985
Streetly Cemetery & Crematorium, Walsall Metropolitan Borough Council - Bereavement Services Division, Little Hardwick Road, Aldridge, Walsall, WS9 0SG T: 0121 353 7228 Fax: 0121 353 6557 E: billingss@walsall.gov.uk Also administers: Bentley Cemetery (opened 1900), Wolverhampton Road West, Willenhall; Bloxwich Cemetery, Field Road, Bloxwich, Walsall (opened 1875), James Bridge Cemetery (opened 1857), Cemetery Road, Darlaston, Walsall; North Walsall Cemetery (opened 1996), Saddleworth Road, Bloxwixh, Ryecroft Cemetery (opened 1894), Coalpool Lane, Walsall; Steetley Cemetery & Crematorium (opened 1938/1984); Willenhall Lawn Cemetery (opened 1966); Wood Street Cemetery (opened prior to 1857), Willenhall
Sutton Coldfield Cemetery, Rectory Rd, Sutton Coldfield, B75 7RP T: 0121 378 0224
Sutton Coldfield Cremetorium, Tamworth Rd, Four Oaks, Sutton Coldfield, B75 6LG T: 0121 308 3812
West Bromwich Crematorium, Forge Lane, West Bromwich, B71 3SX T: 0121 588 2160
Willenhall Lawn Cemetery, Bentley Lane, Willenhall, WV12 4AE T: 01902 368621
Witton Cemetery, Moor Lane Witton, Birmingham, B6 7AE T: 0121 356 4363 Fax: 0121 331 1283 E: wittoncem@birmingham.gov.uk
Woodlands Cemetery and Crematorium, Birmingham Rd, Coleshill, Birmingham, B46 2ET T: 01675 464835
Wiltshire
Box Cemetery, Bath Road, Box, Corsham, SN13 8AA T: 01225 742476
The Cemetery Chippenham, London Road, Chippenham, SN15 3RD T: 01249 652728
Devizes & Roundway Joint Burial Committee, Cemetry Lodge, Rotherstone, Devizes, SN10 2DE T: 01380 722821
Salisbury Crematorium, Barrington Road, Salisbury, SP1 3JB T: 01722 333632
Swindon Crematorium Kingsdown, Swindon, SN25 6SG T: 01793 822259 Holds records for Radnor Street and Whitworth Road Cemeteries, Swindon
West Wiltshire Crematorium, Devizes Road, Semington, Trowbridge, BA14 7QH T: 01380 871101
Wirral
Landican Cemetery, Arrowe Park Rd, Birkenhead, CH49 5LW T: 0151 677 2361
Worcestershire
Pershore Cemetery, Defford Rd, Pershore, WR10 3BX T: 01386 552043
Redith Crematorium & Abbey Cemetery, Bordesley Lane, Redditch, B97 6RR T: 01527 62174
Westall Park Woodland Burial, Holberrow Green, Redditch, B96 6JY T: 01386 792806
Worcester Crematorium, Astwood Rd, Tintern Avenue, Worcester, WR3 8HA T: 01905 22633
Yorkshire - East
East Riding Crematorium Ltd, Octon Cross Rd, Langtoft, Driffield, YO25 3BL T: 01377 267604
East Riding of Yorkshire Council, Cemetery Lodge, Sewerby Rd, Bridlington, YO16 7DS T: 01262 672138
Goole Cemetery, Hook Rd, Goole, DN14 5LU T: 01405 762725
Yorkshire - North
Fulford New Cemetery, Cemetery Lodge, Fordlands Rd, Fulford, York, YO19 4QG T: 01904 633151
Mowthorpe Garden of Rest, Southwood Farm, Terrington, York, YO60 6QB T: 01653 648459 Fax: 01653 648225 E: robert@robertgoodwill.co.uk
Stonefall Cemetery & Cremetoria, Wetherby Rd, Harrogate, HG3 1DE T: 01423 883523
Waltonwrays Cemetery, The Gatehouse, Carlton Rd, Skipton, BD23 3BT T: 01756 793168
York Cemetery, Gate House, Cemetery Rd, York, YO10 5AF T: 01904 610578
Yorkshire - South
Barnsley Crematorium & Cemetery, Doncaster Rd, Ardsley, Barnsley, S71 5EH T: 01226 206053
City Road Cemetery, City Rd, Sheffield, S2 1GD T: 0114 239 6068
Ecclesfield Cemetery, Priory Lane, Ecclesfield, Sheffield, S35 9XZ T: 0114 239 6068 Fax: 0114 239 3757
Eckington Cemetery, Sheffield Rd, Eckington, Sheffield, S21 9FP T: 01246 432197
Grenoside Crematorium, 5 Skew Hill Lane, Grenoside, Sheffield, S35 8RZ T: 0114 245 3999
Handsworth Cemetery, 51 Orgreave Lane, Handsworth, Sheffield, S13 9NE T: 0114 254 0832

Hatfield Cemetery, Cemetery Rd, Hatfield, Doncaster, DN7 6LX T: 01302 840242

Mexborough Cemetery, Cemetery Rd, Mexborough, S64 9PN T: 01709 585184

Rose Hill Crematorium, Cantley Lane, Doncaster, DN4 6NE T: 01302 535191

Rotherham Cemeteries & Crematorium, Ridgeway East, Herringthorpe, Rotherham, S65 3NN T: 01709 850344

Sheffield Cemeteries, City Rd, Sheffield, S2 1GD T: 0114 253 0614

Stainforth Town Council, Cemetery Office, Church Rd, Stainforth, Doncaster, DN7 5AA T: 01302 845158

Yorkshire - West

Brighouse Cemetery, Cemetery Lodge, 132 Lightcliffe Rd, Brighouse, HD6 2HY T: 01484 715183

Cottingly Hall, Elland Rd, Leeds, LS11 0 T: 0113 271 6101

Dewsbury Moor Crematorium, Heckmondwike Rd, Dewsbury, WF13 3PL T: 01924 325180

Exley Lane Cemetery, Exley Lane, Elland, HX5 0SW T: 01422 372449

Killingbeck Cemetery, York Rd, Killingbeck, Leeds, LS14 6AB T: 0113 264 5247

Lawnswood Cemetery & Crematorium, Otley Rd, Adel, Leeds, LS16 6AH T: 0113 267 3188

Leeds Jewish Workers Co-Op Society, 717 Whitehall Rd, New Farnley, Leeds, LS12 6JL T: 0113 285 2521

Moorthorpe Cemetery, Barnsley Rd, Moorthorpe, Pontefract, WF9 2BP T: 01977 642433

Nab Wood Crematorium, Bingley Rd, Shipley, BD18 4BG T: 01274 584109 Fax: 01274 530419

Oakworth Crematorium, Wide Lane, Oakworth, Keighley, BD22 0RJ T: 01535 603162

Park Wood Crematorium, Park Rd, Elland, HX5 9HZ T: 01422 372293

Pontefract Crematorium, Wakefield Rd, Pontefract, WF8 4HA T: 01977 723455

Rawdon Crematorium, Leeds Rd, Rawdon, Leeds, LS19 6JP T: 0113 250 2904

Scholemoor Cemetery & Crematorium, Necropolis Rd, Bradford, BD7 2PS T: 01274 571313

Sowerby Bridge Cemetery, Sowerby New Rd, Sowerby Bridge, HX6 1LQ T: 01422 831193

United Hebrew Congregation Leeds, Jewish Cemetery, Gelderd Rd, Leeds, LS7 4BU T: 0113 263 8684

Wakefield Cemetery, Standbridge Lane, Crigglestone, Wakefield, WF4 3JA T: 01924 303380

Wetherby Cemetery, Sexton House, Hallfield Lane, Wetherby, LS22 6JQ T: 01937 582451

Wales

Bridgend

Coychurch Crematorium Coychurch, Bridgend, CF35 6AB T: 01656 656605 Fax: 01656 668108

Clwyd

Golden Memorial Care, 5 Golden Grove, Rhyl, LL18 2RR T: 0800 9178281

Mold Town Cemetery, Cemetery Lodge, Alexandra Rd, Mold, CH7 1HJ T: 01352 753820

Wrexham Cemeteries & Crematorium Pentre Bychan, Wrexham, LL14 4EP T: 01978 840068

Wrexham Cemetery Lodge, Ruabon Rd, Wrexham, LL13 7NY T: 01978 263159

Conwy County

Colwyn Bay Crematorium, Bron y Nant, Dinerth Rd, Colwyn Bay, LL28 4YN T: 01492 544677

Dyfed

Aberystwyth Crematorium, Clarach Rd, Aberystwyth, SY23 3DG T: 01970 626942

Carmarthen Cemetery, Elim Rd, Carmarthen, SA31 1TX T: 01267 234134

Llanelli District Cemetery, Swansea Rd, Llanelli, SA15 3EX T: 01554 773710

Milford Haven Cemetery, The Cemetery Milford Haven, SA73 2RP T: 01646 693324

Gwent

Christchurch Cemetry Christchurch, Newport, NP18 1JJ T: 01633 277566

Ebbw Vale Cemetery, Waun-y-Pound Rd, Ebbw Vale, NP23 6LE T: 01495 302187

Gwent Crematorium, Treherbert Rd, Croesyceiliog, Cwmbran, NP44 2BZ T: 01633 482784 Opened 1960. Records mainly on computer. No search fees payable

Gwynedd, Bangor Crematorium, Llandygai Rd, Bangor, LL57 4HP T: 01248 370500

Mid Glamorgan

Cemetery Section, Monks St, Aberdare, CF44 7PA T: 01685 885345

Ferndale Cemetery, Cemetery Lodge, Highfield, Ferndale, CF43 4TD T: 01443 730321

Llwydcoed Crematorium Llwydcoed, Aberdare, CF44 0DJ T: 01685 874115 Fax: 01685 874115 E: enquiries@crematorium.org.uk W: www.crematorium.org.uk

Maesteg Cemetery, Cemetery Rd, Maesteg, CF34 0DN T: 01656 735485

Penrhys Cemetery, Cemetery Lodge, Penrhys Rd, Tylorstown, Ferndale, CF43 3PN T: 01443 730465

Trane Cemetery, Gilfach Rd, Tonyrefail, Porth, CF39 8HL T: 01443 670280 T: 01443 673991, Fax: 01443 676916

Treorchy Cemetery, The Lodge, Cemetery Rd, Treorchy, CF42 6TB T: 01443 772336

Ynysybwl Cemetery, Heol Y Plwyf, Ynysybwl, Pontypridd, CF37 3HU T: 01443 790159

South Glamorgan

Cardiff Crematorium and Thornhill Cemetery, Bereavement Services, Thornhill Road, Cardiff, CF14 9UA T: 029 2062 3294 Fax: 029 20692904 W: www.cardiff.gov.uk Opened 1953 Administered from: Bereavement Services, Thornhill Road, Llanishen, Cardiff CF14 9UA Tel 029 2062 3294 Fax 029 2069 2904 Also administers: Pantmawr Cemetery, Radyr Cemetery, Llanishen Cemetery, Llandaff Cemetery, Cathay Cemetery, Western Cemetery, Thornhill Cemetery and Cardiff (Thornhill) Crematorium

Cathays Cemetery, Fairoak Rd, Cathays, Cardiff, CF24 4PY T: 029 2062 3294 W: www.cardiff.gov.uk Opened 1859

Administered from: Bereavement Services, Thornhill Road, Llanishen, Cardiff CF14 9UA Tel 029 2062 3294 Fax 029 2069 2904

Western Cemetery, Cowbridge Road West, Ely, Cardiff, CF5 5TF T: 029 2059 3231 W: www.cardiff.gop.uk Opened 1936 - Administered from: Bereavement Services, Thornhill Road, Llanishen, Cardiff CF14 9UA Tel 029 2062 3294 Fax 029 2069 2904

West Glamorgan, Goytre Cemetery, Neath Port Talbot CBC, Abrafan House, Port Talbot, SA13 1PJ T: 01639 763415

Margam Crematorium, Longland Lane, Margam, Port Talbot, SA13 2PP T: 01639 883570

Oystermouth Cemetery, Newton Road, Oystermouth, Swansea, SA3 4GW T: 07980 721 559 First internment in 1883

Wrexham

Coedpoeth Cemetery, The Lodge, Cemetery Rd, Coedpoeth, LL11 3SP T: 01978 755617

Scotland

Aberdeenshire

Springbank Cemetery, Countesswells Rd, Springbank, Aberdeen, AB15 7YH T: 01224 317323

St. Peter's Cemetery, King St, Aberdeen, AB24 3BX T: 01224 638490

Trinity Cemetery, Erroll St, Aberdeen, AB24 5PP T: 01224 633747

Aberdeen Cemeteries, St Nicholas House, Broad Street, Aberdeen, AB10 1BX T: 01224 523 155

Aberdeenshire (except Aberdeen City) Cemeteries (North), 1 Church Street, Macduff, AB44 1UR T: 01261 813387

Angus

Barnhill Cemetery, 27 Strathmore St, Broughty Ferry, Dundee, DD5 2NY T: 01382 477139

Dundee Crematorium Ltd, Crematorium, Macalpine Rd, Dundee, DD3 8 T: 01382 825601

Park Grove Crematorium, Douglasmuir, Friocheim, Arbroath, DD11 4UN T: 01241 828959

Dundee City Cemeteries, Tayside House Dundee, DD1 3RA T: 01382 434 000 E: parks.burials@dundeecity.gov.uk

Angus (except Dundee City) Cemeteries, County Buildings, Market Street, Forfar, DD8 3WA T: 01307 461 460 Fax: 01307 466 220

Argyll

Argyll & Bute Council Cemeteries, Amenity Services, Kilmory, Lochgilphead, PA31 8RT T: 01546 604 360 Fax: 01546 604 208 E: alison.mcilroy@argyll-bute.gov.uk W: www.argyll-bute.gov.uk/couninfo/dev.htm

Ayrshire

Ardrossan Cemetery, Sorbie Rd, Ardrossan, KA22 8AQ T: 01294 463133

Dreghorn Cemetery, Station Rd, Dreghorn, Irvine, KA11 4AJ T: 01294 211101

Hawkhill Cemetery, Kilwinning Rd, Saltcoats, Stevenston, KA20 3DE T: 01294 465241

Holmsford Bridge Crematorium, Dreghorn, Irvine, KA11 4EF T: 01294 214720

Kilwinning Cemetery, Bridgend, Kilwinning, KA13 7LY T: 01294 552102

Largs Cemetery, Greenock Rd, Largs, KA30 8NG T: 01475 673149

Maybole Cemetery, Crosshill Rd, Maybole, KA19 7BN T: 01655 884852 Fax: 01655 889621 E: maybole.registrars@south-ayrshire.gov.uk Also contact for Crosshill, Dunure, Kirkmichael, Kirkoswald and Straiton Cemeteries

Newmilns Cemetery, Dalwhatswood Rd Newmilns, KA16 9LT T: 01560 320191

Prestwick Cemetery, Shaw Rd, Prestwick, KA9 2LP T: 01292 477759

Stewarton Cemetery, Dalry Rd, Stewarton, Kilmarnock, KA3 3DY
T: 01560 482888
West Kilbride Cemetery, Hunterston Rd, West Kilbride, KA23 9EX
T: 01294 822818
North Ayrshire Cemeteries, 43 Ardrossan Road, Saltcoats, KA21
5BS T: 01294 605 436 Fax: 01294 606 416 E:
CemeteriesOffice@north-ayrshire.gov.uk Administers: Irvine Area
Dreghorn Cemetery, Station Road, Dreghorn; Knadgerhill Cemetery,
Knaderhill, Irvine; Kilwinning Cemetery, Glasgow Road, Kilwinning;
Shewalton Cemetery, Ayr Road, Irvine; Old P
South Ayrshire Cemeteries, Masonhill Crematorium, By Ayr, KA6
6EN T: 01292 266 051 Fax: 01292 610 096
Banffshire
Moray Crematorium, Clochan, Buckie, AB56 5HQ T:
01542 850488
Berwickshire
Scottish Borders Council Cemeteries, Council Offices, 8 Newtown
Street, Duns, TD11 3DT T: 01361 882 600
Bute
Arran and Cumbrae Cemeteries, 43 Ardrossan Road, Saltcoats,
KA21 5BS T: 01294 605 436 Fax: 01294 606 416 E:
CemeteriesOffice@north-ayrshire.gov.uk
Caithness
Caithness Cemeteries, Wick, Caithness, KW1 4AB T: 01955 607
737 Fax: 01955 606 376
Clackmannanshire
Alva Cemetery, The Glebe, Alva, FK12 5HR T: 01259 760354
Sunnyside Cemetery, Sunnyside Rd, Alloa, FK10 2AP T:
01259 723575
Tillicoultry Cemetery, Dollar Rd, Tillicoultry, FK13 6PF T:
01259 750216
Dumfrieshire
Dumfrieshire Cemeteries, Kirkbank, English Street, Dumfries, DG1
2HS T: 01387 260042 Fax: 01387 260188
Annan & Eskdale Cemeteries, Dumfries and Galloway Council,
Dryfe Road, Lockerbie, DG11 2AP T: 01576 205 000
Dumbartonshire
Cardross Crematorium, Main Rd, Cardross, Dumbarton, G82 5HD
T: 01389 841313
Dumbarton Cemetery, Stirling Rd, Dumbarton, G82 2PF
Tel: 01389 762033
Vale Of Leven Cemetery, Overton Rd, Alexandria G83 0LJ
Tel: 01389 752266
West Dumbartonshire Crematorium, North Dalnottar, Clydebank,
G81 4SL T: 01389 874318
West Dumbartonshire Crematorium, Richmond Street, Clydebank,
G81 1RF T: 01389 738709 Fax: 01389 738690 E:
helen.murray@westdunbarton.gov.uk
East Dumbartonshire Cemeteries, Broomhill Industrial Estate,
Kilsyth Road, Kirkintilloch, G66 1TF T: 0141 574 5549 Fax: 0141
574 5555 E: Alan-Copeland@EastDunbarton.gov.uk
West Dumbartonshire Cemeteries, Roseberry Place, Clydebank,
G81 1TG T: 01389 738 709 Fax: 01389 733 493
Dumbartonshire - East Cadder Cemetery, Kirkintilloch Road,
Bishopbriggs, Glasgow, G64 2QG T: 0141 772 1977 Fax: 0141 775 0696
Edinburgh
Edinburgh Crematorium Ltd, 3 Walker St, Edinburgh, Midlothian,
EH3 7JY T: 0131 225 7227
Fife
Dunfermline Cemetery, Halbeath Rd, Dunfermline, KY12 7RA T:
01383 724899
Dunfermline Crematorium, Masterton Rd, Dunfermline,
KY11 8QR T: 01383 724653
Kirkcaldy Crematorium, Rosemount Avenue, Dunnikier, Kirkcaldy,
KY1 3PL T: 01592 260277 Fax: 01592 203438
Central Fife Cemeteries, Rosemount Avenue, Dunnikier, Kirkcaldy,
KY1 3PL T: 01592 260 277 Fax: 01592 203 438
East Fife Cemeteries, St Catherine Street, Cupar, KY15 4TA T:
01334 412 818 Fax: 01334 412 896
East Fife Cemeteries, Masterton Road, Dunfermline, KY11 8QR T:
01383 724 653 Fax: 01383 738 636
Inverness-Shire
Inverness Crematorium, Kilvean Rd, Kilvean, Inverness, IV3 8JN
T: 01463 717849 Fax: 01463 717850
Invernesssshire Cemeteries, Fulton House, Gordon Square, Fort
William, PH33 6XY T: 01397 707 008 Fax: 01397 707 009 Service
restructuring in late 2002 transferred responsibility for all burial grounds in
Lochaber area will be transferred to Highland Council, TEC Services, Carrs
Corner, Fort William, PH33 6TQ
Badenoch & Strathspey Cemeteries, Ruthven Road, Kingussie,
PH21 1EJ T: 01540 664 500 Fax: 01540 661 004
Inverness Cemeteries, Administration Office, Kilvean Cemetery,
Kilvean Road, Inverness, IV3 8JN T: 01463 717849 Fax: 01463
717850 E: derek.allan@highland.gov.uk and
fiona.morrison@highland.gov.uk W: www.highland.gov.uk
Highland Council Cemeteries, T.E.C. Services, Broom Place,
Portree, Isle of Skye, IV51 9HF T: 01478 612717 Fax: 01478 612255

Isle Of Cumbrae, Millport Cemetery, Golf Rd, Millport,
KA28 0HB T: 01475 530442
Kirkcudbright
Kirkcudbright Cemeteries, Daar Road, Kirkcubright, DG6 4JG
Tel: 01557 330 291
Lanarkshire
Airbles Cemetery, Airbles Rd, Motherwell, ML1 3AW T:
01698 263986
Bedlay Cemetery, Bedlay Walk, Moodiesburn, Glasgow, G69 0QG
T: 01236 872446
Bothwellpark Cemetery, New Edinburgh Rd, Bellshill, ML4 3HH
T: 01698 748146
Cambusnethan Cemetery, Kirk Road, Wishaw, ML2 8NP T:
01698 384481
St. Patrick's Cemetery, Kings Drive, New Stevenson, Motherwell,
ML1 4HY T: 01698 732938
Glasgow
Campsie Cemetery, High Church of Scotland, Main Street,
Lennoxtown, Glasgow, G66 7DA T: 01360 311127
Cardonald Cemetery, 547 Mosspark Boulevard, Glasgow, G52 1SB
T: 0141 882 1059
Daldowie Crematorium, Daldowie Estate, Uddingston, Glasgow,
G71 7RU T: 0141 771 1004
Glasgow Crematorium, Western Necropolis, Tresta Rd, Glasgow,
G23 5AA T: 0141 946 2895
Glebe Cemetery, Vicars Rd, Stonehouse, Larkhall, ML9 3EB T:
01698 793674
Glenduffhill Cemetery, 278 Hallhill Rd, Glasgow, G33 4RU T:
0141 771 2446
Kilsyth Parish Cemetery, Howe Rd, Kirklands, Glasgow, G65 0LA
T: 01236 822144
Larkhall Cemetery, The Cemetery Lodge, Duke St, Larkhall,
ML9 2AL T: 01698 883049
Old Aisle Cemetery, Old Aisle Rd, Kirkintilloch, Glasgow,
G66 3HH T: 0141 776 2330
St. Conval's Cemetery, Glasgow Rd, Barrhead, Glasgow, G78 1TH
T: 0141 881 1058
St. Peters Cemetery 1900 London Rd, Glasgow, G32 8RD T: 0141 778 1183
The Necropolis 50 Cathedral Square, Glasgow, G4 0UZ T: 0141 552 3145
Glasgow Cemeteries, 20 Trongate, Glasgow, G1 5ES T: 0141 287
3961 Fax: 0141 287 3960 inc crematoria Linn and Daldowie
North Lanarkshire Cemeteries
Old Edinburgh Road, Bellshill, ML4 3JS T: 01698 506 301 Fax:
01698 506 309
Lanarkshire - South
South Lanarkshire Cemeteries, Atholl House East Kilbride, G74
1LU T: 01355 806 980 Fax: 01355 806 983
Midlothian
Dean Cemetery, Dean Path, Edinburgh, EH4 3AT T: 0131 332 1496
Seafield Cemetery & Crematorium, Seafield Rd, Edinburgh,
EH6 7LQ T: 0131 554 3496
Warriston Crematorium, 36 Warriston Rd, Edinburgh, EH7 4HW
T: 0131 552 3020
Midlothian Council Cemeteries, Dundas Buildings, 62A Polton
Street, Bonnybrigg, EH22 3YD T: 0131 561 5280 Fax: 0131 654
2797 E: nancy.newton@midlothian.gov.uk
City of Edinburgh Council Cemeteries, Howdenhall Road,
Edinburgh, EH16 6TX T: 0131 664 4314 Fax: 0131 664 2031 Five
private cemeteries in Edinburgh - council does not have access to their records
Lothian - West
West Lothian Cemeteries, County Buildings, High Street,
Linlithgow, EH49 7EZ T: 01506 775 300 Fax: 01506 775 412
Moray
Morayshire Cemeteries, Cooper Park, Elgin, IV30 1HS T: 01343
544 475 Fax: 01343 549 050 E: graeme.wilson@moray.gov.uk W:
www.moray.org/heritage/roots.html
Perthshire
Perth Crematorium, Crieff Rd, Perth, PH1 2PE T: 01738 625068
Fax: 01738 445977 E: dpmartin@pkc.gov.uk
Renfrewshire
Hawkhead Cemetery, 133 Hawkhead Rd, Paisley, PA2 7BE T: 0141
889 3472
Paisley Cemetery Co.Ltd, 46 Broomlands St, Paisley, PA1 2NP T:
0141 889 2260
Renfrewshire Cemeteries, Tweedie Halls, Ardlamont Square,
Linwood, PA3 3DE T: 01505 322 135 Fax: 01505 322135
Cemeteries Division - Renfrewshire Council, Environmental
Services Department, Cotton Street, South Building, Paisley, PA1
1BR T: 0141 840 3504 Fax: 0141 842 1179
Renfrew Cemeteries, 3 Longcroft Drive, Renfrew, PA4 8NF T: 0141
848 1450 Fax: 0141 886 2807
**East Renfrewshire - including Neilston, Newton Mearns and
Eaglesham Cemeteries,** Rhuallan House, 1 Montgomery Drive,
Giffnock, G46 6PY T: 0141 577 3913 Fax: 0141 577 3919 E:
sandra.donnelly@eastrenfrewshire.gov.uk
Roxburghshire
Roxburghshire Environmental Health - Burials, High Street,
Hawick, TD9 9EF T: 01450 375 991

Scottish Borders
Scottish Borders Council - Burials, Paton Street, Galashiels, TD1
3AS T: 01896 662739 Fax: 01896 750329
Scottish Borders Council Burial Grounds Department, Council
Offices, Rosetta Road, Peebles, EH45 8HG T: 01721 726306 Fax:
01721 726304 E: p.allan@scot.borders.gov.uk
Shetland
Shetland Burial Ground Management Grantfield Lerwick, ZE1
0NT T: 01595 744 871 E: jim.grant@sic.shetland.gov.uk W:
www.users.zetnet.co.uk/eats-operations
Stirlingshire
Larbert Cemetery, 25 Muirhead Rd, Larbert, FK5 4HZ T:
01324 557867
Stirlingshire Cemeteries, Viewforth, Stirling, FK8 2ET T: 01786
442 559 Fax: 01786 442 558 E: mcbrier@stirling.gov.uk
WWW: www.stirling.gov.uk
Falkirk Cemeteries and Crematorium, Dorrator Road, Camelon,
Falkirk, FK2 7YJ T: 01324 503 654 Fax: 01324 503 651 E:
billbauchope@falkirk.gov.uk
Wigtown
Wigtown Cemeteries, Dunbae House, Church Street, Stranraer, DG9
7JG T: 01776 888 405

Northern Ireland
County Antrim
Ballymena Cemetery, Cushendall Rd, Ballymena, BT43 6QE T:
01266 656026
Ballymoney Cemetery, 44 Knock Rd, Ballymoney, BT53 6LX T:
012656 66364
Blaris New Cemetery, 25 Blaris Rd, Lisburn, BT27 5RA T:
01846 607143
Carnmoney Cemetery, 10 Prince Charles Way, Newtownabbey,
BT36 7LG T: 01232 832428
City Cemetery, 511 Falls Rd, Belfast, BT12 6DE T: 028 90323112
Greenland Cemetery, Upper Cairncastle Rd, Larne, BT40 2EG T:
01574 272543
Milltown Cemetery Office, 546 Falls Rd, Belfast, BT12 6EQ T:
01232 613972
County Armagh, Kernan Cemetery, Kernan Hill Rd, Portadown,
Craigavon, BT63 5YB T: 028 38339059
Lurgan Cemetery, 57 Tandragee Rd, Lurgan, Craigavon, BT66 8TL
T: 028 38342853
County Down

City of Belfast Crematorium, 129 Ballgowan Road, Crossacreevy,
Belfast, BT5 7TZ T: 028 9044 8342 Fax: 028 9044 8579 E:
crematorium@belfastcity.gov.uk
WWW: www.belfastcrematorium.co.uk
Ballyvestry Cemetery, 6 Edgewater Millisle, Newtownards, BT23 5
T: 01247 882657
Banbridge Public Cemetery, Newry Rd, Banbridge, BT32 3NB T:
018206 62623
Bangor Cemetery, 62 Newtownards Rd, Bangor, BT20 4DN T:
028 91271909
Clandeboye Cemetery, 300 Old Belfast Rd, Bangor, BT19 1RH T:
028 91853246
Comber Cemetery, 31 Newtownards Rd, Comber, Newtownards,
BT23 5AZ T: 01247 872529
Down District Council, Struell Cemetery, Old Course Rd,
Downpatrick, BT30 8AQ T: 01396 613086
Down District Council - Lough Inch Cemetery, Lough Inch
Cemetery, Riverside Rd, Ballynahinch, BT24 8JB T: 01238 562987
Kirkistown Cemetery, Main Rd, Portavogie, Newtownards,
BT22 1EL T: 012477 71773
Movilla Cemetery, Movilla Rd, Newtownards, BT23 8EY T:
01247 812276
Redburn Cemetery, Old Holywood Rd, Holywood, BT18 9QH T:
01232 425547
Roselawn Cemetery, 127 Ballygowan Rd, Crossnacreevy, Belfast,
BT5 7TZ T: 01232 448288
Whitechurch Cemetery, 19 Dunover Rd, Newtownards, BT22 2LE
T: 012477 58659
County Londonderry
Altnagelvin Cemetery, Church Brae, Altnagelvin, Londonderry,
BT47 3QG T: 01504 343351
City Cemetery, Lone Moor Rd, Londonderry, BT48 9LA T: 02871
362615 F: 02871 362085
County Tyrone
Greenhill Cemetery, Mountjoy Rd, Omagh, BT79 7BL T: 028 8224
4918
Westland Road Cemetery, Westland Rd, Cookstown, BT80 8BX T:
016487 66087
France
**Russian Cemetery, Cimetiere Russe de Sainte Genevierve des
Bois (Russian Cemetery),** 8 Rue Léo Lagrange, 91700, Sainte
Genevierve des Bois

Record Offices & Archives

NATIONAL
The National Archives Public Records Office Ruskin Avenue Kew
Richmond Surrey TW9 4DU T: (020) 8392 5271 F: (020) 8392 5266
W: www.nas.gov.uk/
BBC Written Archives Centre see Berkshire
The Boat Museum & David Owen Waterways Archive South Pier
Road Ellesmere Port Cheshire CH65 4FW T: 0151-355-5017 F:
0151-355-4079 E: boatmuseum@easynet.co.uk Records relating to
the management, maintenance and operation of inland waterways in
England, Scotland and Wales. Substantial Waterways library. Date
range: late 17th century to 20th century. Information held on some
boatmen and boatwomen.
**Birmingham University Information Services - Special
Collections** see West Midlands
Black Cultural Archives 378 Coldharbour Lane London SW9 8LF
T: (020) 7738 4591 F: (020) 7738 7168 E: info@99mbh.org.uk W:
www.99mbh.org.uk
Bristol University Library - Special Collections see Somerset
British Airways Archives Trident House - Block E S583 London
heathrow airport Hounslow Middlesex TW6 2JA
British Library Newspaper Library Colindale Avenue London
NW9 5HE T: 020-7412-7353 F: 020-7412-7379 E: newspaper@bl.uk
W: www.bl.uk/collections/newspaper/
British Library of Political and Economic Science London School
of Economics 10 Portugal Street London WC2A 2HD T: 020 7955
7223 F: 020 7955 7454 E: info@lse.ac.uk W: www.lse.ac.uk
British Film Institute - Library & Film Archive 21 Stephen Street
London W1T 1LN T: 020 7957 4824 W: www.bfi.org.uk
British Waterways Archives and The Waterways Trust Llanthony
Warehouse Gloucester Docks Gloucester Gloucestershire GL1 2EJ T:
01452 318041 F: 01452 318076 E:
roy.jamieson@britishwaterways.co.uk W:
www.britishwaterways.org.uk Records relating to the management,
maintenance and operation of inland waterways in England, Scotland
and Wales for which British Waterways is the statutory undertaker.
Date range: late 17th to 20th Centuries. NB The archive is NOT part
of the National Waterways Museum. Opening Hours Mon-Fri 1000 to
1700 by prior appointment only.
**Cambridge University Library - Department of Manuscripts &
University Archives** see Cambridgeshire

College of Arms Queen Victoria Street London EC4V 4BT T: (020)
7248-2762 F: (020) 7248-6448 E: enquiries@college-of-arms.gov.uk
W: www.college-of-arms.gov.uk The College of Arms maintains the
official registers of arms for England and Wales
Commonwealth War Graves Commission 2 Marlow Road
Maidenhead Berkshire SL6 7DX T: 01628-634221 F: 01628-771208
E: General Enquiries: General.enq@cwgc.org Casualty & Cemetery
Enquiries: casualty.enq@cwgc.org W: www.cwgc.org
Department of Manuscripts and Special Collections Hallward
Library Nottingham University University Park Nottingham NG7
2RD T: 0115 951 4565 F: 0115 951 4558 E: mss-
library@nottingham.ac.uk W: www.mss.library.nottingham.ac.uk
Family Records Centre 1 Myddelton Street London EC1R 1UW T:
(020) 8392-5300 F: (020) 8392-5307 E: info@familyrecords.gov.uk
W: www.familyrecords.gov.uk
Postal Heritage Trust Freeling House, Phoenix Place, London
WC1X 0DL T: (020) 7239 2570 T: (020) 7239 2561 F: (020) 7239
2576 E: heritage@royalmail.com W: www.royalmail.com/heritage
House of Lords Record Office - The Parliamentary Archives
House of Lords London SW1A 0PW T: (020) 7219-3074 F: (020)
7219-2570 E: hlro@parliament.uk W: www.parliament.uk Holdings
include protestation returns of 1642 and evidence of witnesses on
private bills
Huguenot Library University College Gower Street London WC1E
6BT T: (020) 7679 7094 E: s.massilk@ucl.ac.uk W:
www.ucl.ac.uk/ucl-info/divisions/library/hugcnot.htm
Imperial War Museum - Department of Documents Department of
Documents Lambeth Road London SE1 6HZ T: (020) 7416-
5221/2/3/6 F: (020) 7416-5374 E: docs@iwm.org.uk W:
www.iwm.org.uk
Imperial War Museum Film and Video Archive Lambeth Road
London SE1 6HZ T: 020 7416 5291 E: W:
www.iwm.org.uk/collections/film.htm
Institute of Heraldic and Genealogical Studies see Kent
Liverpool University Special Collections & Archives University of
Liverpool Library PO Box 123 Liverpool L69 3DA T: 0151-794-
2696 F: 0151-794-2081 W:
www.sca.lib.liv.ac.uk/collections/index.html The University holds the
records of a number of charities, especially those which looked after
children or encouraged emigration

Labour History Archive and Study Centre People's History Museum 103 Princess Street Manchester M1 6DD T: 0161 228 7212 F: 0161 237 5965 E: archives@nmlhweb.org W: http://rylibweb.man.ac.uk

Lloyds Register of Shipping Information Services 71 Fenchurch Street London EC3M 4BS T: (020) 7423 2531 F: (020) 7423 2039 W: www.lr.org Personal callers only. Reserarch cannot be undertaken

Ministry of Defence - Fleet Air Arm Records Service CS(R)2, Bourne Avenue, Hayes UB3 1RF F: 0181 573 9078 E: lhearn.defencerecords.hayes@gtnet.gov.uk

Ministry of Defence - Army Records Centre CS(R)2b, Bourne Ave, Hayes UB3 1RF E: lhearn.defencerecords.hayes@gtnet.gov.uk

Museum of the Order of St John, St John's Gate, St John's Lane, Clerkenwell, London EC1M 4DA T: (020) 7253-6644 F: (020) 7336 0587 W: www.sja.org.uk/history

National Gallery Library and Archive Trafalgar Square London WC2N 5DN T: 020 7747 2542 F: 020 7753 8179 E: iad@ng-london.org.uk W: www.nationalgallery.org.uk

The National Gas Archive Unit 1 Europa Court, Europa Boulevard, Warrington WA5 7TN T: 01925 425740 F: 01925 425748 E: enquiries@gasarchive.org W: www.gasarchive.org

National Monuments Record Enquiry and Research Services 55 Blandford Street London W1H 3AF T: 020 7208 8200 F: 020 7224 5333 W: www.english-heritage.org.uk/knowledge/nmr

National Museum of Photography, Film and Television Bradford West Yorkshire BD1 1NQ T: 01274-202030 F: 01274 -723155 W: www.nmpft.org.uk

National Portrait Gallery Heinz Archive & library 2 St. Martins Place London WC2H 0HE T: (020) 7306 0055 F: (020) 7306 0056 W: www.npg.org.uk

National Railway Museum Leeman Road York YO26 4XJ T: 01904 621261 F: 01904 611112 E: nrm@nmsi.ac.uk W: www.nrm.org.uk Does not hold Railway Company staff records generally at PRO and NAS. Does hold a good run of railway staff magazines which often contain information about named staff members especially if they were senior or killed/missing in action in both World Wars.

North West Sound Archive Old Steward's Office Clitheroe Castle Clitheroe Lancashire BB7 1AZ T: 01200-427897 F: 01200-427897 E: nwsa@ed.lancscc.gov.uk W: www.lancashire.gov.uk/education/lifelong/recordindex

Probate Service Probate Sub Registry, 1st Floor, Castle Chambers, Clifford Street York YO1 9RG T: 01904 666777 W: www.courtservice.gov.uk Designated Office for dealing with postal enquiries concerning probate records for the whole of England and Wales

Registry of Shipping PO Box 420, Cardiff CF24 5JW T: 029 2044 8800 Agency is concentrating on active seafarers and most of its historical records will transfer to the National Archives

Royal Air Force Museum Grahame Park Way, Hendon, London NW9 5LL T: (020) 8200 1763 F: (020) 8200 1751 E: groupbusiness@refmuseum.org.uk W: www.rafmuseum.org.uk

The Royal College of Physicians 11 St Andrews Place London NW1 4LE T: (020) 7935 1174 ext 312 F: (020) 7486 3729 E: info@rcplondon.ac.uk W: www.rcplondon.ac.uk Holds records relating to administration and members from 1518 to date

Royal College of Obstetricians & Gynaecologists College Archives 27 Sussex Place Regents Park London NW1 4RG T: 020 7772 6277 F: 020 7723 0575 E: archives@rcog.org.uk W: www.rcog.org.uk

Royal Commission on Historical Manuscripts Quality House Quality Court Chancery Lane London WC2A 1HP T: (020) 7242-1198 F: (020) 7831-3550 E: nra@hmc.gov.uk W: www.hmc.gov.uk Maintains the National Register of Archives and the Manorial Documents Register

Royal Society 6 - 9 Carlton House Terrace London SW1Y 5AG T: 020 7451 2606 F: 020 7930 2170 E: library@royalsoc.ac.uk W: www.royalsoc.ac.uk

Royal Marines Historical Records & Medals Centurion Building, Grange Road, Gosport PO13 9XA

John Rylands University Library Special Collections Division 150 Deansgate Manchester M3 3EH T: 0161-834-5343 F: 0161-834-5343 E: spcoll72@fs1.li.man.ac.uk W: http://rylibweb.man.ac.uk Holdings include family muniment collections especially relating to Cheshire and major Non Conformist Archives Few genealogical records held except for family muniment collections, especially for Cheshire and Methodist Circuit plans, records, ministers

School of Oriental and African Studies library Thornhaugh Street Russell Square London WC1H 0XG T: 020 7323 6112 F: 020 7636 2834 E: lib@soas.ac.uk W: www.soas.ac.uk/library/

Shakespeare Birthplace Trust - Records Office Henley Street Stratford Upon Avon Warwickshire CV37 6QW T: 01789 201816 T: 01789 204016 F: 01789 296083 E: records@sharespeare.org.uk W: www.shakespeare.org.uk 1901 census

Society of Antiquaries of London Burlington House Piccadilly London W1J 0BE T: 020 7479 7084 F: 020 7287 6967 E: library@sal.org.uk W: www.sal.org.uk

Society of Genealogists - Library 14 Charterhouse Buildings Goswell Road London EC1M 7BA T: 020-7251-8799 T: 020-7250-0291 F: 020-7250-1800 E: library@sog.org.uk - Sales at sales@sog.org.uk W: www.sog.org.uk

Tate Archive Collection Tate Britain Millbank London SW1P 4RG T: 020 7887 8831 F: 020 7887 8637 Tate Gallery, Millbank, London SW1P 4RG :Tate Modern, Bankside, London SE1 9TG

Tennyson Research Centre Central Library Free School Lane Lincoln Lincolnshire LN2 1EZ T: 01522-552862 F: 01522-552858 E: sue.gates@lincolnshire.gov.uk W: www.lincolnshire.gov.uk The collection concentrates on Alfred Lord Tennyson and his immediate family. Do not hold detailed genealogical information nor details of any other generations of the Tennysons

TRAP - Tracking Railway Archives Project Al Mafrak George Hill Road Broadstairs Kent CT10 3JT E: d.kelso@btinternet.com

Victoria & Albert Museum - National Art Library - Archive of Art and Design Blythe House 23 Blythe Road London W14 0QF T: (020) 7603 1514 F: (020) 7602 0980 E: archive@vam.ac.uk W: www.nal.vam.ac.uk

Wellcome Library for the History & Understanding of Medicine 183 Euston Road London NW1 2BE T: (020) 7611-8582 E: library@wellcome.ac.uk W: www.wellcome.ac.uk/library W: http://library.wellcome.ac.uk

Specialist Records
Brewing
Bass Museum Horninglow Street Burton on Trent Staffordshire DE14 1YQ T: 0845 6000598 F: 01283 513509 W: www.bass-museum.com

Guinness Archive Park Royal Brewery London NW10 7RR

Southern Courage Archives Southern Accounting Centre PO Box 85 Counterslip Bristol BS99 7BT

Whitbread Archives - Permanently Closed The Brewery Chiswell Street London EC1Y 4SD

The Archives of Worshipful Company of Brewers Brewers' Hall Aldermanbury Square London EC2V 7HR T: (020) 7606 1301

Young's & Co's Brewery Archives Ram Brewery High Street Wandsworth London SW18 4JD

Church Records
Church of England Record Centre 15 Galleywall Road South Bermondsey London SE16 3PB T: 020 7898 1030 F: 020 7898 1031 W: www.church-of-england.org

Church of Ireland Archives Representative Church Body Library Braemor Park Churchtown Dublin 14 Co Dublin T: 01-492-3979 F: 01-492-4770 E: library@ireland.anglican.org W: www.ireland.anglican.org/

Lambeth Palace Library Lambeth Palace Road London SE1 7JU T: (020) 7898 1400 F: (020) 7928-7932 W: www.lambethpalacelibrary.org

Presbyterian Historical Society of Ireland Church House Fisherwick Place Belfast BT1 6DW T: (028) 9032 2284

Scottish Catholic Archives Columba House 16 Drummond Place Edinburgh EH3 6PL T: 0131-5563661 W: www.scottishcatholicarchives.org Minimal parish registers are held - all have been copied and are available at The National archives of Scotland

Methodist
Archives of the Independent Methodist Churches Independent Methodist Resource Centre, Fleet Street, Pemberton, Wigan WN5 0DS T: 01942 223526 F: 01942 227768 E: archives@imcgb.org.uk W: www.imcgb.org.uk Visits by appointment. Monday to Friday

Evangelical Library 78a Chiltern Street London W1M 2HB

Methodist Archives and Research Centre John Rylands University Library 150 Deansgate Manchester M3 3EH T: 0161 834 5343 F: 0161 834 5574

Jewish
Aberdeen Synagogue 74 Dee Street Aberdeen AB11 6DS T: 01224 582135

Dundee Synagogue St Mary Place Dundee DD1 5RB

Edinburgh Synagogue 4 Salisbury Road Edinburgh EH16 5AB

Glasgow Jewish Representative Council 222 Fenwick Road Giffnock Glasgow G46 6UE T: 0141 577 8200 F: 0141 577 8202 E: jrepcouncil@aol.com W: www.j-scot.org/glasgow

Scottish Jewish Archives Centre Garnethill Synagogue 129 Hill Street Garnethill Glasgow G3 6UB T: 0141 332 4911 F: 0141 332 4911 E: archives@sjac.fsbusiness.co.uk W: www.sjac.org.uk

Quakers
Library of the Religious Society of Friends (Quakers) Friends House 173 - 177 Euston Rd London NW1 2BJ T: 0207 663 1135 T: 0207 663 1001 E: library@quaker.org.uk W: www.quaker.org.uk/library Limited opening hours. Letter of introduction required. Please send SAE for details or enclose IRCs

United Reformed Church History Society Westminster College Madingley Road Cambridge CB3 0AA T: 01223-741300 (NOT Weds) Information on ministers of constituent churches not members

Gypsy
The Gypsy Collections University of Liverpool PO Box 229 Liverpool L69 3DA T: 0151 794 2696 F: 0151 794 2081 W: www.sca.lib.liv.ac.uk/collections/index.html The University holds the records of a number of charities, especially those which looked after children or encouraged emigration

The Robert Dawson Romany Collection Rural History Centre, University of Reading Whiteknights PO Box 229 Reading RG6 6AG T: 0118-931-8664 F: 0118-975-1264 E: j.s.creasey@reading.ac.uk W: www.ruralhistory.org/index.html Appointments required
The Romany Collections Brotherton Library Leeds University Leeds West Yorkshire LS2 9JT T: 0113 233 55188 F: 0113 233 5561 E: special-collections@library.leeds.ac.uk W: http://leeds.ac.uk/library/spcoll/

Masonic
The United Grand Lodge of England Freemasons' Hall 60 Great Queen Street London WC2B 5AZ T: (020) 7831 9811 W: www.grandlodge.org
Canonbury Masonic Research Centre Canonbury Tower London N1 2NQ W: www.canonbury.ac.uk
Grand Lodge of Ireland Freemasons' Hall 17 Molesworth Street Dublin 2 T: 00 353 01 6760 1337
Grand Lodge of Scotland Freemasons' Hall 96 George Street Edinburgh EH2 3DH T: 0131 225 5304
The Library & Museum of Freemasonry Freemasons' Hall 60 Great Queen Street London WC2B 5AZ T: (020) 7395 9257 W: www.grandlodge-england.org

Military Records
Ministry of Defence - Fleet Air Arm Records Service CS(R)2, Bourne Avenue, Hayes, Middlesex UB3 1RF F: 0181 573 9078 E:lhearn.defencerecords.hayes@gtnet.gov.uk
Ministry of Defence - Army Records Centre CS(R)2b, Bourne Avenue, Hayes Middlesex UB3 1RF F: 0181 573 9078 E: lhearn.defencerecords.hayes@gtnet.gov.uk
Ministry of Defence - Royal Naval Personnel Records Centre CS(RM)2, Navy Search, Bourne Avenue, Hayes, Middlesex UB3 1RF F: 0181 573 9078**Royal Marines Historical Records and Medals** Centurion Building, Grange Road, Gosport, Hampshire PO13 9XA

Police
Metropolitan Police Archives Room 517, Wellington House 67-73 Buckingham Gate London SW1E 6BE T: 020 7230 7186 E: margarter.bird@met.police.uk The Metropolitan Police do not hold any records. All records that have survived are in the National Archives. Do not hold records for City of London Police or other police forces or constabularies. The Archives have some finding aids. SAE for information
Thames Valley Police Museum Sulhamstead Nr Reading Berkshire RG7 4DX T: 0118 932 5748 F: 0118 932 5751 E: ken.wells@thamesvalley.police.uk W: www.thamesvalley.police.uk Thames Valley Police formed April 1968 from Berkshire, Oxfordshire, Oxford City and Reading Borough constabularies. Only records of officers are those who served in Reading Borough and Oxfordshire. Appointments only with Curator

England
Bath & North East Somerset Record Office Guildhall, High Street, Bath BA1 5AW T: 01225-477421 F: 01225-477439 E: archives@bathnes.gov.uk
Bedfordshire
Bedfordshire & Luton Archives & Record Service County Hall Cauldwell Street Bedford MK42 9AP T: 01234-228833 T: 01234-228777 F: 01234-228854 E: archive@csd.bedfordshire.gov.uk W: www.bedfordshire.gov.uk 1901 census
Berkshire
BBC Written Archives Centre Caversham Park Reading Berkshire RG4 8TZ T: 0118 948 6281 F: 0118 946 1145 E: wac.enquiries@bbc.co.uk W: www.bbc.co.uk/thenandnow Access by appointment only. Brief enquiries can be answered by post or telephone
Berkshire Medical Heritage Centre Level 4, Main Entrance Royal Berkshire Hospital London Road Reading Berkshire RG1 5AN T: 0118 987 7298 W: www.bmhc.org
Berkshire Record Office 9 Coley Avenue, Reading RG1 6AF T: 0118-901-5132 F: 0118-901-5131 E: arch@reading.gov.uk W: www.reading.gov.uk/berkshirerecordoffice 1901 census
Eton College College Library Windsor Berkshire SL4 6DB T: 01753 671269 E: archivist@etoncollege.org.uk W: www.etoncollege.com Open by appointment Monday to Friday
Museum of English Rural Life, Rural History Centre University of Reading Whiteknights PO Box 229 Reading RG6 6AG T: 0118-931-8664 F: 0118-975-1264 E: j.s.creasey@reading.ac.uk W: www.ruralhistory.org/index.html Appointments required
The Museum of Berkshire Aviation Trust Mohawk Way, Bader Way Woodley Reading RG5 4UE T: 0118 944 8089 E: museumofberkshireaviation@fly.to W: http://fly.to/museumofberkshireaviation
West Berkshire Heritage Service - Newbury The Wharf Newbury Berkshire RG14 5AS T: 01635 30511 F: 01635 38535 E: heritage@westberks.gov.uk W: www.westberks.gov.uk/tourism
Bristol
Bristol Record Office B Bond Warehouse Smeaton Road Bristol BS1 6XN T: 0117-922-4224 F: 0117-922-4236 E: bro@bristol-city.gov.uk W: www.bristol-city.gov.uk/recordoffice 1901 census

British Empire & Commonwealth Museum Clock Tower Yard Temple Meads Bristol BS1 6QH T: 0117 925 4980 F: 0117 925 4983 E: staff@empiremuseum.co.uk W: www.empiremuseum.co.uk
Buckinghamshire
Buckinghamshire Record Office County Offices Walton Street Aylesbury Buckinghamshire HP20 1UU T: 01296 383013 F: 01296-382274 E: archives@buckscc.gov.uk W: www.buckscc.gov.uk/leisure/libraries/archives
Cambridgeshire
Cambridge University Library - Department of Manuscripts & University Archives West Road Cambridge Cambridgeshire CB3 9DR T: 01223 333000 ext 33143 (Manuscripts) T: 01223 333000 ext 33148 (University Archives) F: 01223 333160 E: mss@ula.cam.ac.uk W: www.lib.cam.ac.uk/MSS/
Cambridgeshire Archive Service (Huntingdon) County Record Office Huntingdon Grammar School Walk Huntingdon Cambridgeshire PE29 3LF T: 01480-375842 F: 01480 375842 E: county.records.hunts@cambridgeshire.gov.uk W: www.cambridgeshire.gov.uk 1901 census
Cambridgeshire Archives Service County Record Office Shire Hall Castle Hill Cambridge Cambridgeshire CB3 0AP T: 01223 717281 F: 01223 717201 E: County.Records.Cambridge@cambridgeshire.gov.uk W: www.cambridgeshire.gov.uk/ 1901 census
Centre for Regional Studies Anglia Polytechnic University East Road Cambridge Cambridgeshire CB1 1PT T: 01223-363271 ext 2030 F: 01223-352973 E: t.kirby@anglia.ac.uk W: www.anglia.ac.uk APU also offers a degree course (BA Combined Honours) in family and Community History
Peterborough Local Studies Collection Central Library Broadway Peterborough PE1 1RX T: 01733 742700 F: 01733 555277 E: libraries@peterborough.gov.uk W: www.peterborough.gov.uk The telephone number may change in 2002 1901 census
Cheshire
Cheshire & Chester Archives & Local Studies Duke Street Chester Cheshire CH1 1RL T: 01244-602574 F: 01244-603812 E: recordoffice@cheshire.gov.uk W: www.cheshire.gov.uk/recoff/home.htm In April 2000 management of all original archives was transferred to Cheshire & Chester Archives & Local Studies, Duke Street, Chester. All archives must be consulted there. Secondary sources such as Chester Census, Cemetery Registers, Parish Records etc are also available at Chester History & Heritage, St Michael's Church 1901 census
Cheshire Military Museum The Castle Chester Cheshire CH1 2DN T: 01244 327617 Cheshire Yeomanry elements of 3rd Carabiniers and 5th Royal Inniskilling Dragoon Guards)
Chester History & Heritage St Michaels Church Bridge Street Row Chester Cheshire CH1 1NW T: 01244 402110 E: s.oswald.gov.uk W: www.chestercc.gov.uk/chestercc/htmls/heritage.htm
Macclesfield Silk Museums Paradise Mill Park Lane Macclesfield Cheshire SK11 6TJ T: 01625 612045 F: 01625 612048 E: silkmuseum@tiscali.co.uk W: www.silk-macclesfield.org Reference library and archive. Museums cover the history of silk in macclesfield use the centre of the industry. Demonstartions of hand weaving, exhibitions and models. cc accepted
Stockport Archive Service Central Library Wellington Road South Stockport Cheshire SK1 3RS T: 0161-474-4530 F: 0161-474-7750 E: localheritage.library@stockport.gov.uk W: www.stockport.gov.uk
Tameside Local Studies Library Stalybridge Library Trinity Street Stalybridge Cheshire SK15 2BN T: 0161-338-2708 T: 0161-338-3831 and 0161 303 7937 F: 0161-303-8289 E: localstudies.library@mail.tameside.gov.uk W: www.tameside.gov.uk 1901 census
The Boat Museum & David Owen Waterways Archive see National
Warrington Library & Local Studies Centre Museum Street Warrington Cheshire WA1 1JB T: 01925 442890 F: 01925 411395 E: library@warrington.gov.uk W: www.warrington.gov.uk
Cleveland
Tees Archaeology - The Archaeological Service for Teeside Sir William Gray Clarence Road Hartlepool TS24 8BT T: 01429 523455 F: 01429 523477 E: tees-archaeology@hartlepool.gov.uk W: www.hartlepool.gov.uk
Teesside Archives Exchange House 6 Marton Road Middlesbrough Cleveland TS1 1DB T: 01642-248321 F: 01642 248391 E: teesside_archives@middlesbrough.gov.uk W: www.middlesbrough.gov.uk 1901 census
Cornwall
Cable & Wireless Archive & Museum of Submarine Telegraphy Eastern House, Porthcurno Penzance Cornwall TR19 6JX T: 01736 810478 T: 01736 810811 F: 01736 810640 E: info@tunnels.demon.co.uk W: www.porthcurno.org.uk Housed in one of Porthcurno's former telegraph ststion buildings, and adjacent to the Museum of Submarine Telegraphy, the archive is a unique resource for learning about: the history of Porthcurno; cable communications linking Cornwall with the rest of the world; the company, and the people who have worked for it over the years.
Cornish-American Connection Murdoch House Cross Street Redruth Cornwall TR15 2BU T: 01209 216333 E: m.s.tangye@exeter.ac.uk W: www.ex.ac.uk/~cnfrench/ics/welcome.htm

Cornwall Record Office County Hall Truro Cornwall TRI 3AY T: 01872-323127 F: 01872-270340 E: cro@cornwall.gov.uk W: www.cornwall.gov.uk

Royal Institution of Cornwall, Courtney Library & Cornish History Research Centre Royal Cornwall Museum River Street Truro Cornwall TR1 2SJ T: 01872 272205 F: 01872 240514 E: RIC@royal-cornwall-museum.freeserve.co.uk W: www.cornwall-online.co.uk/ric

The Cornwall Centre Alma Place Redruth Cornwall TR15 2AT T: 01209-216760 F: 01209-210283 E: cornishstudies@library.cornwall.gov.uk W: www.cornwall.gov.uk Cornwall Libraries main library of local studies material. Printed and published items about Cornwall incl books, pamphlets, journals, newspapers, maps, photographs etc. 1901 census

Cumbria

Centre for North West Regional Studies Fylde College Lancaster University Lancaster Lancashire LA1 4YF T: 01524 593770 F: 01524 594725 E: christine.wilkinson@lancaster.ac.uk W: www.lancs.ac.uk/users/cnwrs cc accepted Oral History Archives; Elizabeth Roberts Archive: Penny Summerfield Archive

Cumbria Archive Service Cumbria Record Office The Castle Carlisle Cumbria CA3 8UR T: 01228-607285 T: 01228-607284 F: 01228-607270 E: carlisle.record.office@cumbriacc.gov.uk W: www.cumbriacc.gov.uk/archives 1901 census

Cumbria Record Office County Offices Stricklandgate Kendal Cumbria LA9 4RQ T: 01539 773540 F: 01539 773538 E: kendal.record.office@cumbriacc.gov.uk W: www.cumbria.gov.uk/archives 1901 census

Cumbria Record Office and Local Studies Library (Whitehaven) Scotch Street Whitehaven Cumbria CA28 7BJ T: 01946-852920 F: 01946-852919 E: whitehaven.record.office@cumbriacc.gov.uk W: www.cumbria.gov.uk/archives

Cumbria Record Office & Local Studies Library 140 Duke St Barrow in Furness Cumbria LA14 1XW T: 01229-894363 F: 01229-894371 E: barrow.record.office@cumbriacc.gov.uk W: www.cumbria.gov.uk/archives

Ulverston Heritage Centre Lower Brook St Ulverston Cumbria LA12 7EE T: 01229 580820 F: 01229 580820 E: heritage@tower-house.demon.co.uk W: www.rootsweb.com/~ukuhc/

Derbyshire

Derby Local Studies Library 25b Irongate Derby Derbyshire DE1 3GL T: 01332 255393 E: localstudies.library@derby.gov.uk W: www.derby.gov.uk/libraries/about/local_studies.htm 1901 census

Derby Museum & Art Gallery The Strand Derby Derbyshire DE1 1BS T: 01332-716659 F: 01332-716670 W: www.derby.gov.uk/museums No archive material as such, but some local genealogical information available and numerous indices on local trades, etc eg clock makers, gunmakers, etc

Derbyshire Record Office County Hall Matlock Derbyshire DE4 3AG T: 01629-580000-ext-35207 F: 01629-57611 The Record Office for Derbyshire - City and County and the Diocese of Derby. The Record Office is located New Street, Matlock, Derbyshire DE4 3AG. The address at County Hall is for correspondence only. Fee paid family history search service available. 1901 census

Erewash Museum The Museum High Street Ilkeston Derbyshire DE7 5JA T: 0115 907 1141 F: 0115 907 1121 E: museum@erewash.gov.uk W: www.erewash.gov.uk

Devon

Beaford Photograph Archive Barnstaple Devon EX32 7EJ T: 01271 288611

Bill Douglas Centre for the History of Cinema and Popular Culture University of Exeter Queen's Building Queen's Drive Exeter Devon EX4 4QH T: 01392 264321 W: www.ex.ac.uk/bill.douglas

Devon Record Office Castle Street Exeter Devon EX4 3PU T: 01392 384253 F: 01392 384256 E: devrec@devon.gov.uk W: www.devon.gov.uk/dro/homepage.html

North Devon Record Office Tuly Street Barnstaple Devon EX31 1EL T: 01271 388607 T: 01271 388608 E: ndevrec@devon.gov.uk W: www.devon.gov.uk/dro/homepage Open: Mon, Tues, Thurs & Fri 9.30 to 5pm;Wed 9.30 to 1pm; 2 Sats per month 9.30 to 4pm. Admission charges £2 per day

Plymouth & West Devon Record Office Unit 3 Clare Place Coxside Plymouth Devon PL4 0JW T: 01752-305940 E: pwdro@plymouth.gov.uk W: www.plymouth.gov.uk/star/archives.htm

South West Film and Television Archive Melville Building Royal William Yard Stonehouse Plymouth Devon PL1 3RP T: 01752 202650 W: www.tswfta.co.uk

The Devonshire and Dorset Regiment (Archives) RHQ, Devonshire and Dorset Regiment, Wyvern Barracks Barrack Road Exeter Devon EX2 6AR T: 01392 492436 F: 01392 492469

Dorset

Dorset Archives Service 9 Bridport Road Dorchester Dorset DT1 1RP T: 01305-250550 F: 01305-257184 E: dcc_archives@dorset-cc.gov.uk W: www.dorset-cc.gov.uk/archives Research service

available. Search fee The service covers the areas served by Dorset County, Bournemouth Borough and the Borough of Poole. 1901 census

Poole Central Reference Library Dolphin Centre Poole Dorset BH15 1QE T: 01202 262424 F: 01202 262442 E: centrallibrary@poole.gov.uk W: www.poole.gov.uk The local studies collection was relocated to The Waterfront Museum, Poole Some records moved to Dorset Record Office. Retains only general local history and national family history indexes.

Waterfront Musuem and Local Studies Centre 4 High St Poole Dorset BH15 1BW T: 01202 683138 T: 01202 262600 F: 01202 660896 E: museums@poole.gov.uk mldavidw@poole.gov.uk W: www.poole.gov.uk 1901 census

Dorset – West

Bridport Museum Trust - Local History Centre The Coach House Grundy Lane Bridport Dorset DT6 3RJ T: 01308 458703 F: 01308 458704 E: sh-bridportmus@btconnect.com Wide range of resources. The service is free. Open Tues - Thurs 10.a.m. to 1.p.m. and 2.p.m. to 4.p.m. year round

Durham

Darlington Local Studies Centre The Library Crown Street Darlington County Durham DL1 1ND T: 01325-349630 F: 01325-381556 E: crown.street.library@darlington.gov.uk W: www.darlington.gov.uk 1901 census

Durham County Record Office County Hall Durham County Durham DH1 5UL T: 0191-383-3474 T: 0191-383-3253 F: 0191-383-4500 E: record.office@durham.gov.uk W: www.durham.gov.uk/recordoffice 1901 census

Durham University Library Archives and Special Collections Palace Green Section, Palace Green, Durham DH1 3RN T: 0191 334 2932 F: 0191 334 2942 E: pg.library@durham.ac.uk W: www.dw.ac.uk/library/asc

Essex

Central Reference Library - London Borough of Havering Reference Library St Edward's Way Romford Essex RM1 3AR T: 01708 432393 T: 01708 432394 F: 01708 432391 E: romfordlib2@rmplc.co.uk

Chelmsford Library PO Box 882 Market Road Chelmsford Essex CM1 1LH T: 01245 492758 F: 01245 492536 E: answers.direct@essexcc.gov.uk W: www.essexcc.gov.uk 1901 census

Essex Record Office Wharf Road Chelmsford Essex CM2 6YT T: 01245 244644 F: 01245 244655 E: ero.enquiry@essexcc.gov.uk (General Enquiries) ero.search@essexcc.gov.uk (Search Service) W: www.essexcc.gov.uk/ero 1901 census

Essex Record Office, Colchester & NE Essex Branch Stanwell House Stanwell Street Colchester Essex CO2 7DL T: 01206-572099 F: 01206-574541 W: www.essexcc.gov.uk/ero

Essex Record Office, Southend Branch Central Library Victoria Avenue Southend on Sea Essex SS2 6EX T: 01702-464278 F: 01702-464253 W: www.essexcc.gov.uk/ero 1901 census

London Borough of Barking & Dagenham Local Studies Library Valence House Museum Beacontree Avenue Dagenham Essex RM8 3HT T: 020 8270 6896 F: 020 8270 6897 E: localstudies@bardaglea.org.uk W: www.barking-dagenham.gov.uk

Redbridge Library Central Library Clements Road Ilford Essex IG1 1EA T: (020) 8708-2417 F: (020) 8553 3299 E: Local.Studies@redbridge.gov.uk W: www.redbridge.gov.uk

Valence House Museum Valence House Museum Becontree Avenue Dagenham Essex RM8 3HT T: 020 8270 6866 F: 020 82706868 W: www.barking-dagenham.gov.uk Heritage service includes a local history museum, and archive section. A list of resources is available upon request. Archives of the Essex Parishes of Barking and Dagenham and the London Boroughs of the same names

Gloucestershire

Gloucestershire Record Office Clarence Row Alvin Street Gloucester GL1 3DW T: 01452-425295 F: 01452-426378 E: records@gloscc.gov.uk W: www.gloscc.gov.uk Daily admission charge £2 (£1.50 for over 60's.) I/d required 1901 census

Hampshire

Hampshire Local Studies Library Winchester Library Jewry Street Winchester Hampshire SO23 8RX T: 01962 841408 F: 01962 841489 E: clceloc@hants.gov.uk W: www.hants.gov.uk/library 1901 census

Hampshire Record Office Sussex St Winchester Hampshire SO23 8TH T: 01962-846154 F: 01962-878681 E: enquiries.archives@hants.gov.uk W: www.hants.gov.uk/record-office

Portsmouth City Libraries Central Library Guildhall Square Portsmouth Hampshire PO1 2DX T: (023) 9281 9311 X232 (Bookings) T: (023) 9281 9311 X234 (Enquiries) F: (023) 9283 9855 E: reference.library@portsmouthcc.gov.uk W: www.portsmouthcc.gov.uk 1901 census

Portsmouth City Museum and Record Office Museum Road Portsmouth Hampshire PO1 2LJ T: (023) 92827261 F: (023) 92875276 E: Email: portmus@compuserve.com 1901 census

Portsmouth Roman Catholic Diocesan Archives St Edmund House Edinburgh Road Portsmouth Hampshire PO1 3QA T: 023 9282 5430 E: archive@portsmouth-dio.org.uk These are private archives and arrangements to visit have to be agreed beforehand.

Royal Marines Museum Eastney, Southsea PO4 9PX T: (023) 9281 9385 Exts 224 E: matthewlittle@royalmarinesmuseum.co.uk W: www.royalmarinesmuseum.co.uk No charges for research other than material costs. Donations welcome. Visits by appointment Mon to Fri

Southampton Archive Service Civic Centre Southampton Hants SO14 7LY T: (023) 80832251 T: (023) 8022 3855 x 2251 F: (023) 80832156 E: city.archives@southampton.gov.uk W: www.southampton.gov.uk

Southampton City Libraries - Special Collections Southampton Reference Library Civic Centre Southampton Hampshire SO14 7LW T: 023 8083 2205 F: 023 8033 6305 E: local.studies@southampton.gov.uk W: www.southampton.gov.uk Special collections include information on Southampton and Hampshire, genealogy and maritime topics. 1901 census

Wessex Film and Sound Archive Hampshire Record Office Sussex Street Winchester Hampshire SO23 8TH T: 01962 847742 W: www.hants.gov.uk/record-office/film.html

Herefordshire

Hereford Cathedral Archives & Library 5 College Cloisters Cathedral Close Hereford Herefordshire HR1 2NG T: 01432 374225 F: 01432 374220 E: library@herefordcathedral.co.uk W: www.herefordcathedral.co.uk

Herefordshire Record Office The Old Barracks Harold Street Hereford Herefordshire HR1 2QX T: 01432 260750 F: 01432 260066 E: shubbard@herefordshire.gov.uk W: www.herefordshire.gov.uk 1901 census

Hertfordshire

Ashwell Education Services 59 High Street Ashwell Baldock Hertfordshire SG7 5NP T: 01462 742385 F: 01462 743024 E: aes@ashwell-education-services.co.uk W: www.ashwell-education-services.co.uk Research into the History and family histories of ashwell and its people

Bushey Museum, Art Gallery and Local Studies Centre Rudolph Road Bushey Hertfordshire WD23 3HW T: 020 8420 4057 F: 020 8420 4923 E: busmt@bushey.org.uk W: www.busheymuseum.org 1901 census for Bushey and aldenham

Hertfordshire Archives and Local Studies County Hall Pegs Lane Hertford Hertfordshire SG13 8EJ T: 01438 737333 F: 01923 471333 E: herts.direct@hertscc.gov.uk W: http://hertsdirect.org/hals

Hull

Brynmor Jones Library - University of Hull Cottingham Road Hull HU6 7RX T: 01482 465265 F: 01482 466205 E: archives@acs.hull.ac.uk W: www.hull.ac.uk/lib W: www.hull.ac.uk/lib/archives

Hull City Archives 79 Lowgate Kingston upon Hull HU1 1HN T: 01482-615102 T: 01482-615110 F: 01482-613051 E: city.archives@hcc.gov.uk W: www.hullcc.gov.uk

Local History Unit Hull College Park Street Centre Hull HU2 8RR T: 01482-598952 F: 01482 598989 E: historyunit@netscape.net W: www.historyofhull.co.uk

Isle of Wight

Isle of Wight Record Office 26 Hillside Newport Isle of Wight PO30 2EB T: 01983-823820/1 F: 01983 823820 E: record.office@iow.gov.uk W: www.iwight.com/library/default.asp 1901 census

Kent

Bexley Local Studies and Archive Centre Central Library Bourne Townley Road Bexleyheath Kent DA6 7HJ T: (020) 8301 1545 F: (020) 8303 7872 E: archives@bexleycouncil.freeserve.co.uk W: www.bexley.gov.uk As well as being a designated local authority record office the Local Studies Centre is Diocesan Record Office for all the (C of E) Parishes within the Borough ie Rochester & Southwark Dioceses 1901 census

Canterbury Cathedral Archives The Precincts Canterbury Kent CT1 2EH T: 01227 865330 F: 1227865222 E: archives@canterbury-cathedral.org W: www.canterbury-cathedral.org

Canterbury Library & Local Studies Collection 18 High Street Canterbury Kent CT1 2JF T: 01227-463608 F: 01227-768338 W: www.kent.gov.uk 1901 census

Centre for Kentish Studies / Kent County Archives Service Sessions House County Hall Maidstone Kent ME141XQ T: 01622-694363 F: 01622 694379 E: archives@kent.gov.uk W: www.kent.gov.uk/e&l/artslib/ARCHIVES/archiveshome.htm 1901 census

East Kent Archives Centre Enterprise Zone Honeywood Road Whitfield Dover Kent CT16 3EH T: 01304 829306 F: 01304 820783 E: eastkentarchives@kent.gov.uk W: www.kent.gov.uk 1901 census

Institute of Heraldic and Genealogical Studies 79 - 82 Northgate Canterbury Kent CT1 1BA T: 01227 462618 F: 01227 765617 E: ihgs@ihgs.ac.uk W: www.ihgs.ac.uk

London Borough of Bromley Local Studies Library Central Library High Street Bromley Kent BR1 1EX T: 020 8460 9955 F: 020 8313 9975 E: localstudies.library@bromley.gov.uk W: www.bromley.gov.uk 1901 census

Margate Library Local History Collection Cecil Square Margate Kent CT9 1RE T: 01843-223626 F: 01843-293015 W: www.kent.gov.uk

The Patterson Heritage Museum 2 - 6 Station Approach, Birchington on Sea, CT7 9RD T: 01843 841649 E: pattersonheritage@tesco.net W: www.pattersonheritage.co.uk, Please address all mail to 4 Station Approach, Birchington on Sea Kent CT7 9RD. No fees Donations welcome

Ramsgate Library Local Strudies Collection & Thanet Branch Archives Ramsgate Library Guildford Lawn Ramsgate Kent CT11 9AY T: 01843-593532 W: www.kent.gov.uk Archives at this library moved to East Kent Archives CentreEnterprise Zone, Honeywood Road, Whitfield, Dover, Kent CT16 3EH. A Local Studies Collection will remain

Sevenoaks Archives Office Central Library Buckhurst Lane Sevenoaks Kent TN13 1LQ T: 01732-453118 T: 01732-452384 F: 01732-742682

Lancashire

Blackburn Cathedral & Archives Cathedral Close Blackburn Lancashire BB1 5AA T: 01254 51491 F: 01254 689666 E: cathedral@blackburn.anglican.org W: www.blackburn.anglican.org

Blackburn Central Library Town Hall Street Blackburn Lancashire BB2 1AG T: 01254 587920 F: 01254 690539 E: reference.library@blackburn.gov.uk W: www.blackburn.gov.uk/library 1901 census

Bolton Archive & Local Studies Service Central Library, Civic Centre Le Mans Crescent Bolton Lancashire BL1 1SE T: 01204-332185 F: 01204 332225 E: archives.library@bolton.gov.uk W: www.bolton.gov.uk 1901 census

Bury Archive Service 1st Floor, Derby Hall Annexe Edwin Street off Crompton Street Bury Greater Manchester BL9 0AS T: 0161-797-6697 F: 0161 797 6697 Telephone before faxing E: archives@bury.gov.uk W: www.bury.gov.uk/culture.htm May be moving to new premises in 2002 check before visiting

Lancashire Record Office Bow Lane Preston Lancashire PR1 2RE T: 01772 533039 E: record.office@ed.lancscc.gov.uk W: www.archives.lancashire.gov.uk Lancashire Local Studies Collection is now housed here

North West Sound Archive Old Steward's Office Clitheroe Castle Clitheroe Lancashire BB7 1AZ T: 01200-427897 F: 01200-427897 E: nwsa@ed.lancscc.gov.uk W: www.lancashire.gov.uk/education/lifelong/recordindex

Oldham Local Studies and Archives 84 Union Street Oldham Lancashire OL1 1DN T: 0161-911-4654 F: 0161-911-4654 E: archives@oldham.gov.uk localstudies@oldham.gov.uk W: www.oldham.gov.uk/archives W: www.oldham.gov.uk/local_studies 1901 census

Rochdale Local Studies Library Touchstones The Esplanade Rochdale Lancashire OL16 1AQ T: 01706 864915 F: 01706 864944 E: localstudies@rochdale.gov.uk W: www.rochdale.gov.uk 1901 census. GRO Index 1837 - 1999

Salford City Archives Salford Archives Centre 658/662 Liverpool Rd Irlam Manchester M44 5AD T: 0161 775-5643

Salford Local History Library Peel Park Salford Lancashire M5 4WU T: 0161 736 2649 F: 01161 745 9490 E: salford.museums@salford/gov.uk W: www.salford.gov.uk

The Documentary Photography Archive - Manchester c/o 7 Towncroft Lane Bolton Lancashire BL1 5EW T: 0161 832 5284 T: 01204-840439 (Home) F: 01204-840439

Traceline PO Box 106 Southport Lancashire PR8 2HH T: 0151 471 4811 F: 01704-563354 E: traceline@ons.gov.uk W: www.ons.gov.uk To be put in touch with lost relatives and acquaintances. The ONS must be satisfied that contact would be in the best interests of the person being sought. Traceline uses the NHS Central Register. NHSCR does not officially operate under the name Traceline and adheres to other strict criteria

Trafford Local Studies Centre Public Library Tatton Road Sale M33 1YH T: 0161-912-3013 F: 0161-912-3019 E: traffordlocalstudies@hotmail.com The collection covers the former Lancashire and Cheshire towns of Stretford, Old Trafford, Urmston, Daveyhulme, Flixton, Altincham, Bowdon, Hale, Dunham Massey, Sale, Ashton-o-Mersey, Carrington, Partington, Warburton, etc. 1901 census

Wigan Heritage Service Town Hall Leigh Wigan Greater Manchester WN7 2DY T: 01942-404430 F: 01942-404425 E: heritage@wiganmbc.gov.uk W: www.wiganmbc.gov.uk Open by appointment: Mon, Tues, Thurs & Fri

Wigan Heritage Service Museum History Shop Library Street Wigan Greater Manchester WN1 1NU T: 01942 828020 F: 01942 827645 E: heritage@wiganmbc.gov.uk W: www.wiganmbc.gov.uk

Leicestershire
East Midlands Oral History archive Centre for Urban History University of Leicester Leicester Leicestershire LE1 7RH T: 0116 252 5065 E: emoha@le.ac.uk W: www.le.ac.uk/emoha
Melton Mowbray Library Wilton Road Melton Mowbray Leicestershire LE13 0UJ T: 01664 560161 F: 01664 410199 W: www.leics.gov.uk
Record Office for Leicestershire, Leicester and Rutland Long Street Wigston Magna Leicestershire LE18 2AH T: 0116-257-1080 F: 0116-257-1120 E: recordoffice@leics.gov.uk W: www.leics.gov.uk
Lincolnshire
Lincolnshire Archives St Rumbold Street Lincoln Lincolnshire LN2 5AB T: 01522-526204 F: 01522-530047 E: archive@lincolnshire.gov.uk W: www.lincolnshire.gov.uk/archives 1901 census
Lincolnshire County Library Local Studies Section Lincoln Central Library Free School Lane Lincoln Lincolnshire LN1 1EZ T: 01522-510800 F: 01522-575011 E: lincoln.library@lincolnshire.gov.uk W: www.lincolnshire.gov.uk/library/services/family.htm 1901 census
North East Lincolnshire Archives Town Hall, Town Hall Square, Grimsby DN31 1HX T: 01472-323585 F: 01472-323582 E: john.wilson@nelincs.gov.uk W: www.nelincs.gov.uk
Liverpool
Liverpool Record Office & Local History Department Central Library William Brown Street Liverpool L3 8EW T: 0151 233 5817 F: 0151-233 5886 E: recoffice.central.library@liverpool.gov.uk W: www.liverpool.gov.uk

London
Alexander Fleming Laboratory Museum / St Mary's NHS Trust Archives St Mary's Hospital Praed Street Paddington London W2 1NY T: (020) 7886 6528 F: (020) 7886 6739 E: kevin.brown@st-marys.nhs.uk W: www.st-marys.nhs.uk
Bank of England Archive Archive Section HO-SV The Bank of England Threadneedle Street London EC2R 8AH T: (020) 7601-5096 F: (020) 7601-4356 E: archive@bankofengland.co.uk W: www.bankofengland.co.uk
Bethlem Royal Hospital Archives and Museum Monks Orchard Road Beckenham Kent BR3 3BX T: (020) 8776 4307 T: (020) 8776 4053 F: (020) 8776 4045 E: museum@bethlem.freeserve.co.uk The archives of the Bethlem and Maudsley NHS Trust (the Bethlem Royal Hospital and the Maudsley Hospital). Records relating to individual patients are closed for 100 years. The museum does not contain material relating to genealogy or family history
Black Cultural Archives see National
Brent Community History Library & Archive 152 Olive Road London NW2 6UY T: (020) 8937 3541 F: (020) 8450 5211 E: archive@brent.gov.uk W: www.brent.gov.uk 1901 census
British Library Oriental and India Collections 197 Blackfriars Rd London SE1 8NG T: (020) 7412-7873 F: (020) 7412-7641 E: oioc-enquiries@bl.uk W: www.bl.uk/collections/oriental
British Library Western Manuscripts Collections 96 Euston Road London NW1 2DB T: (020) 7412-7513 F: (020) 7412-7745 E: mss@bl.uk W: www.bl.uk/ Note: can only respond to enquiries related to their own collections
British Red Cross Museum and Archives 44 Moorfields, London EC2Y 9ALT: 0870 170 7000 F: (020) 7562 2000 E: enquiry@redcross.org.uk W: www.redcross.org.uk/museum&archives Open by appointment 10am to 4pm Monday to Friday.
Centre for Metropolitan History Institute of Historical Research Senate House Malet Street London WC1E 7HU T: (020) 7862 8790 F: (020) 7862 8793 E: olwen.myhill@sas.ac.uk W: www.history.ac.uk/cmh/cmh.main.html
Chelsea Public Library Old Town Hall King's Road London SW3 5EZ T: (020) 7352-6056 T: (020) 7361-4158 F: (020) 7351 1294 Local Studies Collection on Royal Borough of Kensington & Chelsea south of Fulham Road
City of Westminster Archives Centre 10 St Ann's Street London SW1P 2DE T: (020) 7641-5180 F: (020) 7641-5179 W: www.westminster.gov.uk Holds records for whole area covered by City of Westminster incl former Metropolitan Boroughs of Paddington and St Maryleborne. 1901 census
Corporation of London Records Office PO Box 270 Guildhall London EC2P 2EJ T: (020) 7332-1251 F: (020) 7710-8682 E: clro@corpoflondon.gov.uk W: www.cityoflondon.gov.uk/archives/clro
Deed Poll Records Section Room E 15 Royal Courts of Justice Strand London WC2A 2LL T: (020) 7947 6528 F: (020) 7947 6807
Documents Register Quality House Quality Court Chancery Lane London WC2A 1HP T: (020) 7242-1198 F: (020) 7831-3550 E: nra@hmc.gov.uk W: www.hmc.gov.uk
Dr Williams's Library 14 Gordon Square London WC1H 0AR T: (020) 7387-3727 E: enquiries@dwlib.co.uk
Ealing Local History Centre Central Library 103 Broadway Centre Ealing London W5 5JY T: (020) 8567-3656-ext-37 F: (020) 8840-2351 E: localhistory@hotmail.com W: www.ealing.gov.uk/libraries
Family Records Centre see National

Grenadier Guards Record Office Wellington Barracks Birdcage Walk London London SW1E 6HQ E: rhqgrengds@yahoo.co.uk Access is by appointment made in advance. Search fee of £25.00 per search
Guildhall Library, Manuscripts Sect Aldermanbury London EC2P 2EJ T: (020) 7332-1863 E: manuscripts.guildhall@corpoflondon.gov.uk W: http://ihr.sas.ac.uk/ihr/gh/ Records: City of London parish records, probate records, City Livery companies, business records, Diocese of London, St Pauls Cathedral, etc. Prior booking unnecessary except some records on 24 hrs call/restricted
Hackney Archives Department 43 De Beauvoir Road London Borough of Hackney London N1 5SQ T: (020) 7241-2886 F: (020) 7241-6688 E: archives@hackney.gov.uk W: www.hackney.gov.uk/history/index.html Covers Hackney, Shoreditch & Stoke Newington
Heritage Royal Mail see National
Hillingdon Local Studies & Archives Central Library High Street Uxbridge London Middlesex UB8 1HD T: 01895 250702 F: 01895 811164 E: ccotton@hillingdon.gov.uk W: www.hillingdon.gov.uk/goto/libraries 1901 census
Hounslow Library (Local Studies & Archives) Centrespace, Treaty Centre High Street Hounslow London TW3 1ES T: 0845 456 2800 F: 0845 456 2880 W: www.cip.com 1901 census
Imperial College Archives London University Room 455 Sherfield Building Imperial College London SW7 2AZ T: 020 7594 8850 F: 020 7584 3763 E: archivist@ic.ac.uk W: www.lib.ic.ac.uk
Institute of Historical Research University of London Senate House Malet Street London WC1E 7HU T: (020) 7862 8740 F: 020 7436 2145 E: ihr@sas.ac.uk http://ihr.sas.ac.uk
King's College London Archives Kins College Strand London WC2R 2LS T: 020 7848 2015 E: archives@kcl.ac.uk W: www.kcl.ac.uk/depsta/iss/archives/top.htm includes Student records, staff records and hospital records for Kings College Hospital
L B of Hammersmith & Fulham Archives & Local History Centre The Lilla Huset 191 Talgarth Road London W6 8BJ T: 0208-741-5159 F: 0208-741-4882 W: www.lbhf.gov.uk 1901 census
Lewisham Local Studies & Archives Lewisham Library 199 - 201 Lewisham High Street Lewisham London SE13 6LG T: (020) 8297-0682 F: (020) 8297-1169 E: local.studies@lewisham.gov.uk W: www.lewisham.gov.uk Covering the Parishes of Lewisham, Lee & St Paul's, Deptford. Appointments advisable. 1901 census
Library of the Royal College of Surgeons of England 35-43 Lincoln's Inn Fields London WC2A 3PN T: (020) 7869 6520 F: (020) 7405 4438 E: library@rseng.ac.uk W: www.rseng.ac.uk Research enquiries are not undertaken. Appointments required.
Liddell Hart Centre for Military Archives King's College London Strand London WC2R 2LS T: 020 7848 2015 T: 020 7848 2187 F: 020 7848 2760 E: archives@kcl.ac.uk W: www.kcl.ac.uk/lhcma/top.htm
Linnean Society of London Burlington House Piccadilly London W1J 0BF T: 020 7437 4479 T: 020 7434 4470 F: 020 7287 9364 E: gina@linnean.org W: www.linnean.org
Local Studies Collection for Chiswick & Brentford Chiswick Public Library Dukes Avenue Chiswick London W4 2AB T: (020) 8994-5295 F: (020) 8995-0016 and (020) 8742 7411 Restricted opening hours for local history room: please telephone before visiting
London Borough of Barnet, Archives & Local Studies Department Hendon Library The Burroughs Hendon London NW4 3BQ T: (020) 8359-2876 F: (020) 8359-2885 E: hendon.library@barnet.gov.uk W: www.barnet.gov.uk
London Borough of Camden Local Studies & Archive Centre Holborn Library 32 - 38 Theobalds Road London WC1X 8PA T: 020 7974 6342 F: 020 7974 6284 E: localstudies@camden.gov.uk W: www.camden.gov.uk
LBorough of Croydon Library and Archives Service see Surrey
London Borough of Enfield Archives & Local History Unit Southgate Town Hall Green Lanes Palmers Green London N13 4XD T: (020) 8379-2724 F: (020) 8379 2761 The collections specifically relate to Edmonton and Enfield (both formerly in Middlesex)
London Borough of Greenwich Heritage Centre Museum and Library Building 41 Royal Arsenal Woolwich London SE18 6SP T: (020) 8858 4631 E: local.history@greenwich.gov.uk W: www.greenwich.gov.uk
London Borough of Haringey Archives Service Bruce Castle Museum Lordship Lane Tottenham London N17 8NU T: (020) 8808-8772 F: (020) 8808-4118 E: museum.services@haringey.gov.uk W: www.haringey.gov.uk
London Borough of Islington History Centre Finsbury library 245 St John Street London EC1V 4NB T: (020) 7527 7988 E: local.history@islington.gov.uk W: www.islington.gov.uk Collection covers the LB of Islington.
Material relating to (1) the former Metropolitan Borough of Islington; (2) the present London Borough of Islington and (3) the civil parish of St Mary, Islington (to 1900). The north and south part of the present London Borough of Islington - the former Metropolitan Borough of Finsbury and its predecessors, the former civil parishes of Clerkenwell and St Lukes, Finsbury. 1901 census. The Local History Service operates through an appointment system. Users must make an appointment, preferably by telephone. A postal enquiry service (SAE required) is available. A charge is made for extended research.

London Borough of Lambeth Archives Department Minet Library 52 Knatchbull Road Lambeth London SE5 9QY T: (020) 7926 6076 F: (020) 7936 6080 E: lambetharchives@lambeth.gov.uk W: www.lambeth.gov.uk

London Borough of Newham Archives & Local Studies Library Stratford Library 3 The Grove London E15 1EL T: (020) 8430 6881 W: www.newham.gov.uk

London Borough of Wandsworth Local Studies Local Studies Service Battersea Library 265 Lavender Hill London SW11 1JB T: (020) 8871 7753 F: (020) 7978-4376 E: wandsworthmuseum@wandsworth.gov.uk W: www.wandsworth.gov.uk Open Tues & Wed 10am to 88pm, Fri 10am to 5pm, Sat 9am to 1pm - Research service offerred - £7.00 per half hour (the minimum fee) apointment advised to ensure archives, hard copy newspapers (if not microfilmed) and other items are available

London Metropolitan Archives 40 Northampton Road London EC1R 0HB T: 020 7332 3820 T: Mini com 020 7278 8703 F: 020 7833 9136 E: ask.lma@ms.corpoflondon.gov.uk W: www.cityoflondon.gov.uk

London University - Institute of Advanced Studies Charles Clore House 17 Russell Square London WC1B 5DR T: (020) 7637 1731 F: (020) 7637 8224 E: ials.lib@sas.ac.uk W: http://ials.sas.ac.uk

London University - Institute of Education 20 Bedford Way London WC1H 0AL T: 020 7612 6063 F: 020 7612 6093 E: lib@ioe.ac.uk W: www.ioe.ac.uk/library/

Manorial Documents Register Quality House Quality Court Chancery Lane London WC2A 1HP T: (020) 7242-1198 F: (020) 7831-3550 E: nra@hmc.gov.uk W: www.hmc.gov.uk

Manuscripts Room Library Services University College Gower Street London WC1E 6BT T: (020) 7387 7050 F: 020 7380 7727 E: mssr@ucl.ac.uk W: www.ucl.ac.uk/library/special-coll/

Museum of London Library 150 London Wall London EC2Y 5HN T: 020 7814 5588 E: info@museumoflondon.org.uk W: http://museumoflondon.org.uk

Museum of the Order of St John St John's Gate St John's Lane Clerkenwell London EC1M 4DA T: (020) 7253-6644 F: (020) 7336 0587 W: www.sja.org.uk/history

Museum of the Royal Pharmaceutical Society Museum of the Royal Pharmaceutical Society 1 Lambeth High Street London SE1 7JN T: (020) 7572 2210 F: (020) 7572 2499 E: museum@rpsgb.org.uk W: www.rpsgb.org.uk CC accepted. Records of pharmacists from 1841 Research fee charged £20 per person or premises researched to Non members of the Society, £10 per person or premises researched for members(Genealogical Enquiries) Enquirers may visit and undertake research themselves by appointment only at a cost of £10.00 per day

National Army Museum Royal Hospital Road London London SW3 4HT T: (020) 7730-0717 F: (020) 7823-6573 E: info@national-army-museum.ac.uk W: www.national-army-museum.ac.uk incorporating Middlesex Regiment Museum & Buffs regiment Museum

National Army Museum Department of Archives (Photographs, Film & Sound) Royal Hospital Road London SW3 4HT T: (020) 7730-0717 F: (020) 7823-6573 E: info@national-army-museum.ac.uk W: www.national-army-museum.ac.uk

National Register of Archives Quality House Quality Court Chancery Lane London WC2A 1HP T: (020) 7242 1198 F: (020) 7831 3550 E: nra@hmc.gov.uk W: www.hmc.gov.uk The National Register of Archives (NRA) is maintained by the Historical Manuscripts Commission (HMC) as a central collecting point for information concerning the location of manuscript sources for British History, outside the Public RecordsHMS's Archives in Focus website (W: www.hmc.gov.uk/focus) provides an introduction to archives in the UK including guides to local and family history

Probate Principal Registry of the Family Division First Avenue House 42 - 49 High Holborn London WC1V 6NP T: (020) 7947 6939 F: (020) 7947 6946 W: www.courtservice.gov.uk Postal Searches: York Probate Sub Registry, Duncombe Place, York YO1 7EA

Royal Air Force Museum Grahame Park Way Hendon London NW9 5LL T: (020) 8205-2266 F: (020) 8200 1751 E: groupbusiness@refmuseum.org.uk W: www.rafmuseum.org.uk

Royal Borough of Kensington and Chelsea Libraries & Arts Service Central Library Phillimore Walk Kensington London W8 7RX T: (020) 7361-3036 T: (020) 7361 3007 E: information.services@rbkc.gov.uk W: www.rbkc.gov.uk

Royal Botanic Gardens Library & Archives Kew Richmond Surrey TW9 3AE T: 020 8332 5414 T: 020 8332 5417 F: 020 8332 5430 CC Accepted

Royal London Hospital Archives and Museum Royal London Hospital Newark Whitechapel London E1 1BB T: (020) 7377-7608 F: (020) 7377 7413 E: r.j.evans@mds.qmw.ac.uk W: www.bartsandthelondon.org.uk

Southwark Local Studies Library 211 Borough High Street Southwark London SE1 1JA T: 0207-403-3507 F: 0207-403-8633 E: local.studies.library@southwark.gov.uk W: www.southwark.gov.uk

St Bartholomew's Hospital Archives & Museum Archives and Museum West Smithfield London EC1A 7BE T: (020) 7601-8152 F: (020) 7606 4790 E: marion.rea@bartsandthelondon.nhs.uk W: www.brlcf.org.uk Visitors to use the archive by appointment only - Mon to Fri 9.30am to 5pm

The Galton Institute 19 Northfields Prospect London SW18 1PE

Tower Hamlets Local History Library & Archives Bancroft Library 277 Bancroft Road London El 4DQ T: (020) 8980 4366 Ext 129 F: (020) 8983 4510 E: localhistory@towerhamlets.gov.uk W: www.towerhamlets.gov.uk

Twickenham Library Twickenham Library Garfield Road Twickenham Middlesex TW1 3JS T: (020) 8891-7271 F: (020) 8891-5934 E: twicklib@richmond.gov.uk W: www.richmond.gov.uk The Twickenham collection moved to Richmond Local Studies Library

University of London (Library - Senate House) Palaeography Room Senate House Malet Street London WC1E 7HU T: (020) 7862 8475 F: 020 7862 8480 E: library@ull.ac.uk W: www.ull.ac.uk

Waltham Forest Archives Vestry House Museum Vestry Road Walthamstow London E17 9NH T: (020) 8509 1917 E: vestry.house@al.lbwf.gov.uk W: www.lbwf.gov.uk/vestry/vestry.htm Visits by prior appointment only 1901 census

Westminster Abbey Library & Muniment Room Westminster Abbey London SW1P 3PA T: (020) 7222-5152-Ext-4830 F: (020) 7226-4827 E: library@westminster-abbey.org W: www.westminster-abbey.org

Westminster Diocesan Archives 16a Abingdon Road Kensington London W8 6AF T: (020) 7938-3580 This is the private archive of the Catholic Archbishop of Westminster and is not open to the public. Pre 1837 baptismal records have been transcribed and copies are with the Society of Genealogists. No registers earlier than 18th century. Appointments and enquiries through the Catholic FHS

Westminster University Archives Information Systems & Library Services 4-12 Little Titchfield Street London W1W 7UW T: 020 7911 5000 ext 2524 F: 020 7911 5894 E: archive@westminster.ac.uk W: www.wmin.ac.uk
The archive is organisationally within the Library but is a separate entity. The University of Westminster Libraries do not have special collections relating to family and local histrory but the archive may be of interest to researchers

Manchester

Greater Manchester County Record Office 56 Marshall St New Cross Manchester Greater Manchester M4 5FU T: 0161-832-5284 F: 0161-839-3808 E: archives@gmcro.co.uk W: www.gmcro.co.uk

Manchester Archives & Local Studies Manchester Central Library St Peter's Square Manchester M2 5PD T: 0161-234-1979 F: 0161-234-1927 E: lsu@libraries.manchester.gov.uk W: www.manchester.gov.uk/libraries/index.htm 1901 census

Methodist Archives and Research Centre see Methodist

North West Film Archive Manchester Metropolitan University Minshull House 47-49 Chorlton Street Manchester M1 3EU T: 0161 247 3097 W: www.nwfa.mmu.ac.uk

Medway

Medway Archives and Local Studies Centre Civic Centre Strood Rochester Kent ME2 4AU T: 01634-332714 F: 01634-297060 E: archives@medway.gov.uk local.studies@medway.gov.uk W: www.medway.gov.uk 1901 census

Merseyside

Crosby Library (South Sefton Local History Unit) Crosby Road North Waterloo Liverpool Merseyside L22 0LQ T: 0151 257 6401 F: 0151 934 5770 E: local-history.south@leisure.sefton.gov.uk W: www.sefton.gov.uk The Local History Units serve Sefton Borough Council area. The South Sefton Unit covers Bootle, Crosby, Maghull and other communities south of the River Alt. The North Sefton Unit covers Southport, Formby.

Huyton Central Library Huyton Library Civic Way Huyton Knowsley Merseyside L36 9GD T: 0151-443-3738 F: 0151 443 3739 E: eileen.hume.dlcs@knowsley.gov.uk W: www.knowsley.gov.uk/leisure/libraries/huyton/index.html 1901 census

Merseyside Maritime Museum Maritime Archives and Library Albert Dock Liverpool Merseyside L3 4AQ T: 0151-478-4418 T: 0151 478 4424 F: 0151-478-4590 E: archives@nmgmarchives.demon.co.uk W: www.nmgm.org.uk

Southport Library (North Sefton Local History Unit) Lord Street Southport Merseyside PR8 1DJ T: 0151 934 2119 F: 0151 934 2115 E: local-history.north@leisure.sefton.gov.uk The Local History Units serve Sefton Borough Council area. The North Sefton Unit covers Southport, Formby. The South Sefton Unit covers Bootle, Crosby, Maghull and other communities south of the River Alt

St Helen's Local History & Archives Library Central Library, Gamble Institute Victoria Square St Helens Merseyside WA10 1DY T: 01744-456952 F: 01744 20836 No research undertaken 1901 census

Wirral Archives Service Wirral Museum, Birkenhead Town Hall Hamilton Street Birkenhead Merseyside CH41 5BR T: 0151-666 3903 F: 0151-666 3965 E: archives@wirral-libraries.net W: www.wirral-libraries.net/archives Open: Thursday & friday 10.00.a.m. to 5.00.p.m. Saturday: 10.00.a.m. to 1.00.p.m.

Middlesex

British Deaf History Society 288 Bedfont Lane Feltham Middlesex TW14 9NU E: bdhs@iconic.demon.co.uk

London Borough of Harrow Local History Collection Civic Centre Library, PO Box 4 Station Road Harrow Middlesex HA1 2UU T: 0208 424 1055 T: 0208 424 1056 F: 0208 424 1971 E: civiccentre.library@harrow.gov.uk W: www.harrow.gov.uk 1901 census

Norfolk
East Anglian Film Archive University of East Anglia Norwich Norfolk NR4 7TJ T: 01603 592664 W: www.uea.ac.uk/eafa
Kings Lynn Borough Archives The Old Gaol House Saturday Market Place Kings Lynn Norfolk PE30 5DQ T: 01553-774297 T: 01603 761349 F: 01603 761885 E: norfrec.nro@norfolk.gov.uk W: http://archives.norfolk.gov.uk
Norfolk Record Office Gildengate House Anglia Square Upper Green Lane Norwich Norfolk NR3 1AX T: 01603-761349 F: 01603-761885 E: norfrec.nro@norfolk.gov.uk W: www.norfolk.gov.uk

Northamptonshire
Northamptonshire Central Library Abington Street Northampton Northamptonshire NN1 2BA T: 01604-462040 F: 01604-462055 E: ns-centlib@northamptonshire.gov.uk W: www.northamptonshire.gov.uk Northamptonshire Studies Room collection includes census returns 1841 to 1891, name indexes to 1851 & 1881 census, Parish Registers on microfiche, I.G.I., trade and street directories, poll books, electoral registers for Northampton Borough, biographical indexes and newscuttings. GRO index 1837 - 1983 Free internet access to many family history websites
Northamptonshire Record Office Wootton Hall Park Northampton Northamptonshire NN4 8BQ T: 01604-762129 F: 01604 767562 E: archivist@nro.northamptonshire.gov.uk W: www.nro.northamptonshire.gov.uk also holds Peterborough Diocesan Record Office

Northumberland
Berwick upon Tweed Record Office Council Offices Wallace Green Berwick-Upon-Tweed Northumberland TD15 1ED T: 01289 301865 T: 01289-330044-Ext-265 01289-330540 E: lb@berwick-upon-tweed.gov.uk W: www.swinhope.demon.co.uk/genuki/NBL/Northumberland RO/Berwick.html GRO indexes 1837-1940: Pre 1855 OPR Christening & Marriage inedxes for all Scottish counties Office open Wed & Thurs 9.30am to 1pm and 2pm to 5pm. Research service - £8 per half hour. 1901 census
Friends of Northumberland Archives 19 Rodsley Court Rothbury Northumberland NE65 7UY
Northumberland Archive Service Morpeth Records Centre The Kylins Loansdean Morpeth Northumberland NE6l 2EQ T: 01670-504084 F: 01670-514815 E: archives@northumberland.gov.uk W: www.swinnhopc.myby.co.uk/nro 1901 census

Nottinghamshire
Media Archive for Central England Institute of Film Studies University of Nottingham Nottingham Nottinghamshire NG7 2RD T: 0115 846 6448 W: www.nottingham.ac.uk/film/mace
Nottingham Catholic Diocese Nottingham Diocesan Archives Willson House Derby Road Nottingham Nottinghamshire NG1 5AW T: 0115 953 9803 F: 0115 953 9808 E: archives@nottinghamdiocese.org.uk W: www.nottinghamdiocese.org.uk
Nottingham Central Library : Local Studies Centre Angel Row Nottingham Nottinghamshire NG1 6HP T: 0115 915 2873 F: 0115 915 2850 E: local-studies.library@nottinghamcity.gov.uk W: www.nottinghamcity.gov.uk/libraries
Nottinghamshire Archives Castle Meadow Road Nottingham Nottinghamshire NG2 1AG T: 0115-950-4524 Admin T: 0115 958 1634 Enquiries F: 0115-941-3997 E: archives@nottscc.gov.uk W: www.nottscc.gov.uk/libraries/archives/index.htm 1901 census
Southwell Minster Library Minster Office, Trebeck Hall Bishop's Drive Southwell Nottinghamshire NG25 0JP T: 01636-812649 F: 01636 815904 E: mail@southwellminster.org.uk W: www.southwellminster.org.uk

Oxfordshire
Oxfordshire Archives St Luke's Church Temple Road Cowley Oxford Oxfordshire OX4 2EX T: 01865 398200 F: 01865 398201 E: archives@oxfordshire.gov.uk W: www.oxfordshire.gov.uk 1901 census

Peterborough
Peterborough Local Studies Collection Central Library Broadway Peterborough PE1 1RX T: 01733 742700 F: 01733 555277 E: libraries@peterborough.gov.uk W: www.peterborough.gov.uk The telephone number may change in 2002 1901 census

Rutland
Record Office for Leicestershire, Leicester and Rutland Long Street Wigston Magna Leicestershire LE18 2AH T: 0116-257-1080 F: 0116-257-1120 E: recordoffice@leics.gov.uk W: www.leics.gov.uk

Shropshire
Ironbridge Gorge Museum, Library & Archives The Wharfage Ironbridge Telford TF8 7AW T: 01952 432141 F: 01952 432237 E: library@ironbridge.org.uk W: www.ironbridge.org.uk
Shropshire Archives Castle Gates Shrewsbury Shropshire SY1 2AQ T: 01743 255350 F: 01743 255355 E: research@shropshire-cc.gov.uk W: www.shropshire-cc.gov.uk/research.nsf 1901 census
Wrekin Local Studies Forum Madeley Library Russell Square Telford Shropshire TF7 5BB T: 01952 586575 F: 01952 587105 E: wlst@library.madeley.uk W: www.madeley.org.uk

Somerset
Bath & North East Somerset Record Office Guildhall, High Street, Bath BA1 5AW T: 01225-477421 F: 01225-477439 E: archives@bathnes.gov.uk
Bristol University Library - Special Collections Tyndall Avenue Bristol BS8 1TJ T: 0117 928 8014 F: 0117 925 5334 E: library@bris.ac.uk W: www.bris.ac.uk/depts/library
Somerset Archive & Record Service Somerset Record Office Obridge Road Taunton Somerset TA2 7PU T: 01823-337600 Appointments T: 01823 278805 Enquiries F: 01823-325402 E: archives@somerset.gov.uk W: www.somerset.gov.uk 1901 census

Staffordshire
Burton Archives Burton Library Riverside High Street Burton on Trent Staffordshire DE14 1AH T: 01283-239556 F: 01283-239571 E: burton.library@staffordshire.gov.uk W: www.staffordshire.gov.uk
Coal Miners Records Cannock Record Centre Old Mid-Cannock (Closed) Colliery Site Rumer Hill Road Cannock Staffordshire WS11 3EX T: 01543-570666 F: 01543-578168 Employment and training records held for ex mineworkers post 1917
Keele University Special Collections & Archives Keele Staffordshire ST5 5BG T: 01782 583237 F: 01782 711553 E: h.burton@keele.ac.uk W: www.keele.ac.uk/depts/li/specarc
Lichfield Record Office Lichfield Library The Friary Lichfield Staffordshire WS13 6QG T: 01543 510720 F: 01543-510715 E: lichfield.record.office@staffordshire.gov.uk W: www.staffordshire.gov.uk/archives/ Advance booking required. Lichfield Records Research Service. Covers all the holdings of the office, including Lichfield Diocesan records such as wills including, bishop's transcripts and marriage bonds for Staffordshire, Derbyshire, north east Warickshire and North Shropshire
Staffordshire Record Office Eastgate Street Stafford Staffordshire ST16 2LZ T: 01785 278373 (Bookings) T: 01785 278379 (Enquiries) F: 01785 278384 E: staffordshire.record.office@staffordshire.co.uk W: www.staffordshire.gov.uk/archives For research into all Staffordshire records including parish and nonconformist registers, census and electoral registers contact:Staffordshire Record Office, Eastgate Street, Stafford ST16 2LZ Lichfield Records Research Service For research into all Lichfield Diocesan records including will, bishop's transcripts and marriage bonds for Staffordshire, Derbyshire, north east Warickshire and North Shropshire 1901 census
Staffordshire & Stoke on Trent Archive Service -Stoke on Trent City Archives Hanley Library Bethesda Street Hanley Stoke on Trent Staffordshire ST1 3RS T: 01782-238420 F: 01782-238499 E: stoke.archives@stoke.gov.uk W: www.staffordshire.gov.uk/archives 1901 census
Tamworth Library Corporation Street Tamworth Staffordshire B79 7DN T: 01827-475645 F: 01827-475658 E: tamworth.library@staffordshire.gov.uk W: www.staffordshire.gov.uk/locgov/county/cars/tamlib.htm IGI (Derby, Leics, Notts, Shrops, Staffs, Warks, Worcs). Parish registers for Tamworth. Census for Tamworth and District, 1841 - 91. Street directories for Staffs and Warks.
William Salt Library Eastgate Street Stafford Staffordshire ST16 2LZ T: 01785-278372 F: 01785-278414 E: william.salt.library@staffordshire.gov.uk W: www.staffordshire.gov.uk/archives/salt.htm

Suffolk
Suffolk Record Office - Bury St Edmunds Branch 77 Raingate Street Bury St Edmunds Suffolk IP33 2AR T: 01284-352352 F: 01284-352355 E: bury.ro@libher.suffolkcc.gov.uk W: www.suffolkcc.gov.uk/sro/ 1901 census
Suffolk Record Office Ipswich Branch Gatacre Road Ipswich Suffolk IP1 2LQ T: 01473 584541 F: 01473 584533 E: ipswich.ro@libher.suffolkcc.gov.uk W: www.suffolkcc.gov.uk/sro/ 1901 census
Suffolk Record Office Lowestoft Branch Central Library Clapham Road Lowestoft Suffolk NR32 1DR T: 01502-405357 F: 01502-405350 E: lowestoft.ro@libher.suffolkcc.gov.uk W: www.suffolkcc.gov.uk/sro/ 1901 census
Suffolk Regiment Archives Suffolk Record Office 77 Raingate Street Bury St Edmunds Suffolk IP33 2AR T: 01284-352352 F: 01284-352355 E: bury.ro@libher.suffolkcc.gov.uk W: www.suffolkcc.gov.uk/sro/

Surrey
Cranleigh Library and Local History Centre High Street Cranleigh Surrey GU6 8AE T: 01483 272413 F: 01483 271327 W: www.surrey.gov.uk

Domestic Buildings Research Group (Surrey) The Ridings Lynx Hill East Horsley Surrey KT24 5AX T: 01483 283917
Epsom and Ewell Local History Centre Bourne Hall Spring Street Ewell Epsom Surrey KT17 1UF T: 020 8394 0372 F: 020 8873 1603 W: www.surrey.gov.uk
Horley Local History Centre Horley Library Victoria Road Horley Surrey RH6 7AG T: 01293 784141 F: 01293 820084 W: www.surrey.gov.uk
Kingston Museum & Heritage Service North Kingston Centre Richmond Road Kingston upon Thames Surrey KT2 5PE T: (020) 8547-6738 F: (020) 8547-6747 E: local.history@rbk.kingston.gov.uk W: www.kingston.gov.uk/museum/ Research service available £7.50 per half hour - max 3 hours
London Borough of Lambeth Archives Department see London
London Borough of Wandsworth Local Studies see London
London Borough of Merton Local Studies Centre Merton Civic Centre London Road Morden Surrey SM4 5DX T: (020) 8545-3239 F: (020) 8545-4037 E: local.studies@merton.gov.uk W: www.merton.gov.uk/libraries Open: Mon to Fri 9.30 to 7.00: Weds 9.30 to 1.00: Sats 9.30 to 5.00
London Borough of Croydon Library and Archives Service Central Library Katharine Street Croydon CR9 1ET T: (020) 8760-5400-ext-1112 F: (020) 8253-1012 E: localstudies@croydononline.org W: www.croydon.gov.uk/
London Borough of Sutton Archives Central Library St Nicholas Way Sutton Surrey SM1 1EA T: (020) 8770-4747 F: (020) 8770-4777 E: local.studies@sutton.gov.uk W: www.sutton.gov.uk
North Tandridge Local History Centre Caterham Valley Library Stafford Road Caterham Surrey CR3 6JG T: 01883 343580 F: 01883 330872 W: www.surrey.gov.uk
Redhill Centre for Local and Family History Redhill Library Warwick Quadrant Redhill Surrey RH1 1NN T: 01737 763332 F: 01737 778020 W: www.surrey.gov.uk
Surrey History Centre and Archives Surrey History Centre 130 Goldsworth Road Woking Surrey GU21 1ND T: 01483-594594 F: 01483-594595 E: shs@surreycc.gov.uk W: www.surrey.gov.uk
Southwark Local Studies Library see London
Surrey History Centre and Archives Surrey History Centre, 130 Goldsworth Road, Woking GU21 1ND T: 01483-594594 F: 01483-594595 E: shs@surreycc.gov.uk W: www.surrey.gov.uk 1901 census
East Sussex Record Office see Sussex - East
South East Film and Video Archive University of Brighton Grand Parade Brighton Sussex BN2 2JY T: 01273 643213 W: www.bton.ac.uk/sefva

Sussex
Sussex - East
Brighton History Centre Brighton Museum and Art Gallery Royal Pavilion Gardens Brighton East Sussex BN1 1EE T: 01273 296972(Bookings) F: 01273 296962 E: localhistory@brighton-hove.gov.uk W: www.citylibraries.info/localhistory
East Sussex Record Office The Maltings, Castle Precincts, Lewes BN7 1YT T: 01273-482349 E: archives@eastsussexcc.gov.uk W: www.eastsussexcc.gov.uk/archives/main.htm
Sussex - West
West Sussex Record Office County Hall Chichester West Sussex PO19 1RN T: 01243-753600 F: 01243-533959 E: records.office@westsussex.gov.uk W: www.westsussex.gov.uk/ro/
Worthing Reference Library Worthing Library Richmond Road Worthing West Sussex BN11 1HD T: 01903-212060 F: 01903-821902 E: worthing.reference.library@westsussex.gov.uk W: www.westsussex.gov.uk Largest library in West Sussex and specialist centre for family history sources.

Tyne and Wear
Local Studies Centre Central Library Northumberland Square North Shields NE3O 1QU T: 0191-200-5424 F: 0191 200 6118 E: eric.hollerton@northtyneside.gov.uk W: www.northtyneside.gov.uk/libraries.html
South Tyneside Central Library Prince George Street South Shields Tyne and Wear NE33 2PE T: 0191-427-1818-Ext-7860 F: 0191-455-8085 E: reference.library@s-tyneside-mbc.gov.uk W: www.s-tyneside-mbc.gov.uk 1901 census
Gateshead Central Library & Local Studies Department Prince Consort Road Gateshead Tyne & Wear NE8 4LN T: 0191 477 3478 F: 0191 477 7454 E: a.lang@libarts.gatesheadmbc.gov.uk W: http://ris.niaa.org.uk W: www.gateshead.gov.uk/ls 1901 census
Newcastle Local Studies Centre City Library Princess Square Newcastle upon Tyne NE99 1DX T: 0191 277 4116 F: 0191 277 4118 E: local.studies@newcastle.gov.uk W: www.newcastle.gov.uk 1901 census
Northumberland County Record Office Melton Park North Gosforth Newcastle upon Tyne NE3 5QX T: 0191-236-2680 F: 0191-217-0905 E: archives@northumberland.gov.uk W: www.swinnhopc.myby.co.uk/nro 1901 census
Tyne & Wear Archives Service Blandford House Blandford Square Newcastle upon Tyne Tyne and Wear NE1 4JA T: 0191-232-6789 F: 0191-230-2614 E: twas@dial.pipex.com W:

www.thenortheast.com/archives/ 1901 census

Warwickshire
Coventry City Archives Mandela House Bayley Lane Coventry West Midlands CV1 5RG T: (024) 7683 2418 F: (024) 7683 2421 E: coventryarchives@discover.co.uk W: www.theherbest.co.uk
Modern Records Centre University of Warwick Library Coventry Warwickshire CV4 7AL T: (024) 76524219 F: (024) 7652 4211 E: archives@warwick.ac.uk W: www.modernrecords.warwick.ac.uk

Rugby School Archives Temple Reading Room Rugby School Barby Road Rugby Warwickshire CV22 5DW T: 01788 556227 F: 01788 556228 E: dhrm@rugby-school.warwks.sch.uk W: www.rugby-school.warwks.sch.uk
Sutton Coldfield Library & Local Studies Centre 43 Lower Parade Sutton Coldfield Warwickshire B72 1XX T: 0121-354-2274 T: 0121 464 0164 F: 0121 464 0173 E: sutton.coldfield.reference.lib@birmingham.gov.uk W: www.birmingham.gov.uk
Warwick County Record Office Priory Park Cape Road Warwick Warwickshire CV34 4JS T: 01926 738959 F: 1926738969 E: recordoffice@warwickshire.gov.uk W: www.warwickshire.gov.uk

West Midlands
Birmingham City Archives Floor 7, Central Library Chamberlain Square Birmingham West Midlands B3 3HQ T: 0121-303-4217 F: 0121-464 1176 E: archives@birmingham.gov.uk W: www.birmingham.gov.uk/libraries/archives/home.htm 1901 census
Birmingham Roman Catholic Archdiocesan Archives Cathedral House St Chad's Queensway Birmingham West Midlands B4 6EU T: 0121-236-2251 F: 0121 233 9299 E: archives@rc-birmingham.org W: www.rc-birmingham.org
Birmingham University Information Services - Special Collections Main Library University of Birmingham Edgbaston Birmingham West Midlands B15 2TT T: 0121 414 5838 F: 0121 471 4691 E: special-collections@bham.ac.uk W: www.is.bham.ac.uk
Dudley Archives & Local History Service Mount Pleasant Street Coseley Dudley West Midlands WV14 9JR T: 01384-812770 F: 01384-812770 E: archives.pls@mbc.dudley.gov.uk W: www.dudley.gov.uk Family History Research Service (fee paying) available 1901 census
Sandwell Community History & Archives Service Smethwick Library High Street Smethwick West Midlands B66 1AB T: 0121 558 2561 F: 0121 555 6064
Solihull Heritage and Local Studies service Solihull Central Library Homer Road Solihull West Midlands B91 3RG T: 0121-704-6977 F: 0121-704-6212 E: info@solihull.gov.uk W: www.solihull.gov.uk/wwwlib/#local
Walsall Local History Centre Essex Street Walsall West Midlands WS2 7AS T: 01922-721305 F: 01922-634594 E: localhistorycentre@walsall.gov.uk W: www.walsall.gov.uk/culturalservices/library/welcome.htm
Wolverhampton Archives & Local Studies 42 - 50 Snow Hill Wolverhampton West Midlands WV2 4AG T: 01902 552480 F: 01902 552481 E: wolverhamptonarchives@dial.pipes.com W: www.wolverhampton.gov.uk/archives 1901 census

Wiltshire
Images of England Project National Monuments Records Centre Kemble Drive Swindon Wiltshire SN2 2GZ T: 01793 414779 W: www.imagesofengland.org.uk
Salisbury Reference and Local Studies Library Market Place Salisbury Wiltshire SP1 1BL T: 01722 411098 F: 01722 413214 W: www.wiltshire.gov.uk
Wiltshire and Swindon Record Office Libraries HQ Bythesea Road Trowbridge Wiltshire BA14 8BS T: 01225 713709 F: 01225-713515 E: wrso@wiltshire.gov.uk W: www.wiltshire.gov.uk 1901 census
Wiltshire Buildings Record Libraries and Heritage HQ Bythesea Road Trowbridge Wiltshire BA14 8BS T: 01225 713740 E: dorothytreasure@wiltshire.gov.uk W: www.wiltshire.gov.uk
Wiltshire Studies Library Trowbridge Reference Library Bythesea Road Trowbridge Wiltshire BA14 8BS T: 01225-713732 T: 01225 713727 F: 01225-713715 E: libraryenquiries@wiltshire.gov.uk W: www.wiltshire.gov.uk

Worcestershire
MLA West Midlands: the Regional Council for Museums, Libraries and archives 2nd Floor, Grosvenor House 14 Bennetts Hill Worcestershire B2 5RS T: 01527 872258 F: 01527 576960
St Helens Record Office - Worcestershire St Helens Record Office Fish Street Worcester Worcestershire WR1 2HN T: 01905-765922 F: 01905-765925 E: recordoffice@worcestershire.gov.uk W: www.worcestershire.gov.uk/records
Worcesterhire Library & History Centre History Centre Trinity Street Worcester Worcestershire WR1 2PW T: 01905 765922 F: 01905 765925 E: wlhc@worcestershire.gov.uk W:

www.worcestershire.gov.uk/records
Worcestershire Regimental Archives RHQ The Worcestershire & Sherwood Foresters Regiment Norton Barracks Worcester Worcestershire WR5 2PA T: 01905-354359 01905-353871 E: rhq_wfr@lineone.net W: www.wfrmuseum.org.uk Records of the Regiment and predecessors from1694, some bibliographical details

Yorkshire
Borthwick Institute of Historical Research University of York, Heslington, York YO10 5DD T: 01904 321166 - archives T: 01904 321160 - Publication sales W: www.york.ac.uk/inst/bihr T: www.york.ac.uk/borthwick Appointment necessary to use Archives. Research Service Available
Yorkshire Family History - Biographical Database York Minster Library & Archives Dean's Park York Yorkshire YO1 7JQ T: 01904-625308 Library T: 01904-611118 Archives F: 01904-611119 E: library@yorkminster.org archives@yorkminster.org W: www.yorkminster.org
Yorkshire - City of York
City of York Libraries - Local History & Reference Collection York Central Library Library Square Museum Street York YO1 7DS T: 01904-655631 F: 01904-611025 E: reference.library@york.gov.uk W: www.york.gov.uk
York City Archives Exhibition Square Bootham York YO1 7EW T: 01904-551878/9 F: 01904-551877 E: archives@york.gov.uk W: www.york.gov.uk
Yorkshire - East
East Yorkshire Archives Service County Hall Champney Road Beverley East Yorkshire HU17 9BA T: 01482 392790 F: 01482 392791 E: archives.service@eastriding.gov.uk W: www.eastriding.gov.uk/learning Correspondence to County Hall, Champney Road, Beverley, HU17 9BA . Reading Room at The Chapel, Lord Roberts Road, Beverley HU17 9BQ T: 01482 392790 F: 01482 392791 Appointments necessary
Hull Central Library Family and Local History Unit Central Library Albion Street Kingston upon Hull HU1 3TF T: 01482 616828 F: 01482 616827 E: gareth@ukorigins.co.uk W: www.hullcc.gov.uk/genealogy/famhist.php Free membership. Meets second Tuesday of every month 1901 census
Yorkshire - North
Catterick Garrison Library Gough Road Catterick Garrison North Yorkshire DL9 3EL T: 01748 833543 W: www.northyorks.gov.uk Extensive collection of over 1350 military history books available for reference or loan. Open Mon 10.am to 12, 1pm to 5.30pm; Wed 10am to 12, 1pm to 5pm; Fri 10am to 12 noon.
North Yorkshire County Record Office County Hall Northallerton North Yorkshire DL7 8AF T: 01609-777585 W: www.northyorks.gov.uk
Ripon Local Studies Centre, 42 Market Place, Ripon HG4 1BZ T: 01765 692200 F: 01765 692200 E: riponlsrc@supanet.com W: www.riponlsrc.supanet.com
Royal Dragoon Guards Military Museum (4th/7th Royal Dragoon Guards & 5th Royal Inniskilling Dragoon Guards) 3A Tower Street York North Yorkshire YO1 9SB T: 01904-662790 T: 01904 662310 F: 01904 662310 E: rdgmuseum@onetel.net.uk W: www.rdg.co.uk co located with Prince of Wales' Own Regiment of Yorkshire Military Museum (West & East Yorkshire Regiments)
Whitby Pictorial Archives Trust Whitby Archives & Heritage Centre, 17/18 Grape Lane, Whitby YO22 4BA T: 01947-600170 F: 01947 821833 E: info@whitbyarchives.freeserve.co.uk W: www.whitbyarchives.freeserve.co.uk
Yorkshire Film Archive York St John College Lord Mayor's Walk York North Yorkshire YO31 7EX T: 01904 716550 F: 01904 716552 E: yfa@yorksj.ac.uk
Yorkshire - South
Archives & Local Studies Central Library Walker Place Rotherham South Yorkshire S65 1JH T: 01709-823616 F: 01709-823650 E: archives@rotherham.gov.uk W: www.rotherham.gov.uk 1901 census
Barnsley Archives and Local Studies Department Central Library, Shambles Street, Barnsley S70 2JF T: 01226-773950 T: 01226-773938 F: 01226-773955 E: Archives@barnsley.gov.uk librarian@barnsley.gov.uk W: www.barnsley.gov.uk 1901 census
Central Library Surrey Street Sheffield South Yorkshire S1 1XZ T: 0114 273 4711 F: 0114 273 5009 E: sheffield.libraries@dial.pipex.com
Doncaster Archives King Edward Road Balby Doncaster DN4 0NA T: 01302-859811 E: doncasterarchives@hotmail.com W: www.doncaster.gov.uk Diocesan Record Office for the Archdeaconry of Doncaster (Diocese of Sheffield) 1901 census
Sheffield Archives 52 Shoreham Street Sheffield South Yorkshire S1 4SP T: 0114-203-9395 F: 0114-203-9398 E: sheffield.archives@dial.pipex.com W: www.sheffield.gov.uk/in-your-area/libraries/archives W: www.familia.org.uk/services/england/sheffield.html Please include a postal address when contactinmg by Email 1901 census

Yorkshire - West
Bradford Archives West Yorkshire Archive Service 15 Canal Road Bradford West Yorkshire BD1 4AT T: 01274-731931 F: 01274-734013 E: bradford@wyjs.org.uk W: www.archives.wyjs.org.uk
John Goodchild Collection Local History Study Centre Below Central Library Drury Lane Wakefield West Yorkshire WF1 2DT T: 01924-298929 Primarily concerned with regional history; many tens of 000s of index cards, many tons of MSS, maps, illustrations. SAE essential for reply. No photocopying; use by prior appointment. All services free of charge, including lectures and guided walks and advice. 50 years experience in the field; no genealogical research undertaken
Local Studies Library Leeds Central Library Calverley Street Leeds West Yorkshire LS1 3AB T: 0113 247 8290 F: 0113 247 4882 E: local.studies@leeds.gov.uk W: www.leeds.gov.uk/library/services/loc_reso.html
National Museum of Photography, Film & Television see National
Wakefield Library Headquarters - Local Studies Department Balne Lane Wakefield West Yorkshire WF2 0DQ T: 01924-302224 F: 01924-302245 E: wakehist@hotmail.com W: www.wakefield.gov.uk 1901 census
West Yorkshire Archive Service
Wakefield & Headquarters Registry of Deeds Newstead Road Wakefield West Yorkshire WF1 2DE T: 01924-305980 F: 01924-305983 E: wakefield@wyjs.org.uk W: www.archives.wyjs.org.uk This Office hold county-wide records of the West Riding and West Yorkshire and records of Wakefield Metropolitan District. Appointment always required.
Kirklees Central Library Princess Alexandra Walk Huddersfield West Yorkshire HD1 2SU T: 01484-221966 F: 01484-518361 E: kirklees@wyjs.org.uk W: www.archives.wyjs.org.uk Appointment always required
Bradford 15 Canal Road Bradford West Yorkshire BDI 4AT T: 01274-731931 F: 01274-734013 E: bradford@wyjs.org.uk W: www.archives.wyjs.org.uk Appointment always required
Calderdale Central Library Northgate House Northgate Halifax West Yorkshire HX1 1UN T: 01422-392636 F: 01422-341083 E: calderdale@wyjs.org.uk W: www.archives.wyjs.org.uk Appointment always required
Leeds Chapeltown Road Sheepscar Leeds West Yorkshire LS7 3AP T: 0113-214-5814 F: 0113-214-5815 E: leeds@wyjs.org.uk W: www.archives.wyjs.org.uk Also at Yorkshire Archeaological Society, Claremont, 23 Clarendon Road, Leeds LS2 9NZ (0113-245-6362; fax 0113-244-1979)
Yorkshire Archaeological Society Claremont 23 Clarendon Rd Leeds West Yorkshire LS2 9NZ T: 0113-245-6342 T: 0113 245 7910 F: 0113-244-1979 E: j.heron@sheffield.ac.uk (Society business) yas@wyjs.org.uk (Library and Archives) W: www.yas.org.uk Opening Hours: Tues,Wed 2.00 to 8.30pm; Thurs, Fri 10.00 to 5.30; Sat 9.30 to 5.00 Appointment necessary for use of archival material.

Wales
National Library of Wales Penglais Aberystwyth Ceredigion SY23 3BU T: 01970 632800 T: 01970 632902 Marketing F: 01970 615709 E: holi@llgc.org.uk W: www.llgc.org.uk
Department of Manuscripts Main Library, University of Wales College Road Bangor Gwynedd LL57 2DG T: 01248-382966 F: 01248-382979 E: iss04@bangor.ac.uk
National Monuments Record of Wales Royal Commission - Ancient & Historical Monuments Wales Crown Building Plas Crug Aberystwyth SY23 1NJ T: 01970 621200 F: 01970 627701 E: nmr.wales@rchamw.org.uk W: www.rchamw.org.uk

Anglesey
Anglesey County Archives Service Shirehall Glanhwfa Road Llangefni Anglesey LL77 7TW T: 01248-752080 W: www.anglesey.gov.uk 1901 census
Carmarthenshire
Carmarthenshire Archive Service Parc Myrddin Richmond Terrace Carmarthen Carmarthenshire SA31 1DS T: 01267 228232 F: 01267 228237 E: archives@carmarthenshire.gov.uk W: www.carmarthenshire.gov.uk
Ceredigion
Archifdy Ceredigion, Ceredigion Archives Swyddfa'r Sir, County Offices Glan y Mor, Marine Terrace Aberystwyth Ceredigion SY23 2DE T: 01970-633697 E: archives@ceredigion.gov.uk W: www.ceredigion.gov.uk
National Screen and Sound Archive of Wales Unit 1 Science Park Aberystwyth Ceredigion SY23 3AH T: 01970 626007 E: http://screenandsound.llgc.org.uk
Conwy
Conwy Archive Service Old Board school Lloyd Street Llandudno Conwy LL30 2YG T: 01492 860882 F: 01492 860882 E: archifau.archives@conwy.gov.uk W: www.conwy.gov.uk/archives 1841-1901 census, parish records, non-parochial records, school records, rate books, maps, newspapers, photographs

Denbighshire

Denbighshire Record Office 46 Clwyd Street Ruthin Denbighshire LL15 1HP T: 01824-708250 F: 01824-708258 E: archives@denbighshire.go.uk W: www.denbighshire.gov.uk Extensive refurbishment until early Summer 2002 - telephone before visiting

Flintshire

Flintshire Record Office The Old Rectory Rectory Lane Hawarden Flintshire CH5 3NR T: 01244-532364 F: 01244-538344 E: archives@flintshire.gov.uk W: www.flintshire.gov.uk

Glamorgan

Glamorgan Record Office Glamorgan Building King Edward VII Avenue Cathays Park Cardiff CF10 3NE T: (029) 2078 0282 F: (029) 2078 0284 E: GlamRO@cardiff.ac.uk W: www.glamro.gov.uk 1901 census

Neath Central Library (Local Studies Department) 29 Victoria Gardens Neath Glamorgan SA11 3BA T: 01639-620139 W: www.neath-porttalbot.gov.uk

Swansea Reference Library Alexandra Road Swansea SA1 5DX T: 01792-516753 F: 01792 516759 E: central.library@swansea.gov.uk W: www.swansea.gov.uk

Gwent

Blaenavon Ironworks Blaenavon Tourist Information Office North Street Blaenavon Gwent NP4 9RQ T: 01495 792615 W: www.btinternet.com~blaenavon.ironworks/pages/genealogy.htm

Gwent Record Office County Hall Croesyceiliog Cwmbran Gwent NP44 2XH T: 01633-644886 F: 01633-648382 E: gwent.records@torfaen.gov.uk W: www.llgc.org.uk/cac

Gwynedd

Archifdy Meirion Archives Swyddfeydd y Cyngor Cae Penarlag Dolgellau Gwynedd LL40 2YB T: 01341-424444 F: 01341-424505 E: EinionWynThomas@gwynedd.gov.uk W: www.gwynedd.gov.uk/archives/

Caernarfon Area Record Office, Gwynedd Archives Caernarfon Area Record Office Victoria Dock Caernarfon Gwynedd LL55 1SH T: 01286-679095 F: 01286-679637 E: archifau@gwynedd.gov.uk W: www.gwynedd.gov.uk/adrannau/addysg/archifau 1901 census

Pembrokeshire

Pembrokeshire Libraries The County Library Dew Street Haverfordwest Pembrokeshire SA61 1SU T: 01437 775248 F: 01437 769218 E: sandra.matthews@pembrokeshire.gov.uk W: www.pembrokeshire.gov.uk The Local Studies Library covers people, places and events relating to the County of Pembrokeshire past and present. The Library also houses the Francis Green Genealogical Collection consisting of over 800 pedigree sheets and 35 volumes of information relating to the prominent families of Pembraokeshire, Cardiganshire and Carmarthenshire.

Pembrokeshire Record Office The Castle Haverfordwest Pembrokeshire SA61 2EF T: 01437-763707 F: 01437 768539 E: record.office@pembrokeshire.gov.uk W: www.pembrokeshire.gov.uk

Tenby Museum Tenby Museum & Art Gallery Castle Hill Tenby Pembrokeshire SA70 7BP T: 01834-842809 F: 01834-842809 E: tenbymuseum@hotmail.com W: www.tenbymuseum.free-online.co.uk Archives & Museum Mainly Tenby Town & immediate area. Search fee £5

Powys

Powys County Archives Office County Hall Llandrindod Wells Powys LD1 5LG T: 01597 826088 F: 01597 826087 E: archives@powys.gov.uk W: http://archives.powys.gov.uk 1901 census

Newport

Newport Library & Information Service Newport Central Library John Frost Square Newport South Wales NP20 1PA T: 01633-211376 F: 01633-222615 E: reference.library@newport.gov.uk W: www.earl.org.uk/partners/newport/index.html The Local Studies Collection contains information on all aspects of Monmouthshire and or Gwent. A fee paying postal research service is available, which uses the library's own resources.

West Glamorgan

West Glamorgan Archive Service County Hall Oystermouth Road Swansea West Glamorgan SA1 3SN T: 01792-636589 F: 01792-637130 E: archives@swansea.gov.uk W: www.swansea.gov.uk/archives 1901 census

West Glamorgan Archive Service - Neath Archives Access Point Neath Mechanics Institute Church Place Neath Glamorgan SA11 3BA T: 01639-620139 W: www.swansea.gov.uk/archives 1901 census

West Glamorgan Archive Service - Port Talbot Access Point Port Talbot Library 1st Floor, Aberavon Shopping Centre Port Talbot West Glamorgan SA13 1PB T: 01639 763430 W: www.swansea.gov.uk/archives 1901 Census - West Glamorgan area

Wrexham

Wrexham Local Studies and Archives Service A N Palmer Centre for Local Studies and archives Wrexham Museum, County Buildings Regent Street Wrexham LL11 1RB T: 01978-317976 F: 01978-317982 E: archives@wrexham.gov.uk W: www.wrexham.gov.uk/heritage 1901 census E: localstudies@wrexham.gov.uk

Isle of Man

Civil Registry Registries Building Deemster's Walk Bucks Road Douglas Isle of Man IM1 3AR T: 01624-687039 F: 01624-687004 E: civil@registry.gov.im

Isle of Man Public Record Office Unit 3 Spring Valley Industrial Estate Braddan Douglas Isle of Man IM2 2QR T: 01624 613383 F: 01624 613384

Manx National Heritage Library Douglas Isle of Man IM1 3LY T: 01624 648000 F: 01624 648001 E: enquiries@mnh.gov.im W: www.mnh.gov.im 1901 census

Guernsey

Guernsey Island Archives 29 Victoria Road St Peter Port Guernsey GY1 1HU T: 01481 724512 F: 01481 715814

Jersey

Jersey Archives Service - Jersey Heritage Trust Clarence Road St Helier Jersey JE2 4JY T: 01534 833303 F: 01534 833301 Do not hold genealogical sources but do have 30,000 registration cards for the population of the island 1940 - 1945 during the German occupation. 1901 census

Judicial Greffe Morier House Halkett Place St Helier Jersey JE1 1DD T: 01534-502300 F: 01534-502399/502390 E: jgreffe@super.net.uk W: www.jersey.gov.uk

SCOTLAND

National

General Register Office for Scotland New Register House Edinburgh EH1 3YT T: 0131-334-0380 T: Certificate Order 0131 314 4411 F: 0131-314-4400 E: records@gro-scotland.gov.uk W: www.gro-scotland.gov.uk A fully searchable index of Scottish birth and marriage records from 1553 to 1901 and death records from 1855 to 1926 can be accessed on the internet at W: www.origins.net

Scottish Genealogy Society & Library 15 Victoria Terrace Edinburgh EH1 2JL T: 0131-220-3677 F: 0131-220-3677 E: info@scotsgenealogy.com W: www.scotsgenealogy.com

National Archives of Scotland HM General Register House 2 Princes Street Edinburgh EH1 3YY T: 0131 535 1334 F: 0131 535 1328 E: enquiries@nas.gov.uk W: www.nas.gov.uk The Scottish Record Office holds the National Archives of Scotland

National Monuments Record of Scotland Royal Commission on the Ancient & Historical Monuments of Scotland John Sinclair House 16 Bernard Terrace Edinburgh EH8 9NX T: 0131 662 1456 F: 0131 662 1477 or 0131 662 1499 E: nmrs@rcahms.gov.uk W: www.rcahms.gov.uk Website gives access to the searchable database of NMRS Records - 'CANMORE'

National Library of Scotland - Department of Manuscripts National Library of Scotland George IV Bridge Edinburgh EH1 1EW T: 0131 466 2812 F: 0131 466 2811 E: mss@nls.uk W: www.nls.uk The division will answer general enquiries but cannot undertake detailed genealogical research

National Archives of Scotland - West Search Room West Register House Charlotte Square Edinburgh EH2 4DJ T: 0131-535-1413 F: 0131-535-1411 E: wsr@nas.gov.uk W: www.nas.gov.uk All correspondence to: National Archives of Scotland, HM General Register House, Edinburgh EH1 3YY

National Register of Archives (Scotland) H M General Register House 2 Princes Street Edinburgh EH1 3YY T: 0131 535 1405/1428 T: 0131 535 1430 E: nra@nas.gov.uk W: www.nas.gov.uk The papers mentioned on the Register are not held by the NRA(S) but are deposited elsewhere or remain in private hands. While the NRA staff are always happy to answer limited and specific POSTAL enquiries about the existence of papers relating to a particular individual or subject, they are unable to undertake research on behalf of enquirers. Once they have advised on possible sources it is then up to enquiriers either to carry out the research themselves or to engage a record agent to do so on their behalf. Where papers remain in private hands written applications for access should be made in the first instance to the NRA(S)

Glasgow University Library & Special Collections Department see Glasgow

Glasgow University Archive Services 13 Thurso Street Glasgow G11 6PE T: 0141 330 5515 F: 0141 330 4158 E: archives@archives.gla.ac.uk W: www.archives.gla.ac.uk

Scottish Brewing Archive 13 Thurso Street Glasgow G11 6PE T: 0141 330 2640 F: 0141 330 4158 E: sba@archives.gla.ac.uk W: www.archives.gla.ac.uk/sba/

Heriot-Watt University Archives see Edinburgh

St Andrews University Library - Special Collections Department see Fife

Strathclyde University Archives McCance Building 16 Richmond Street Glasgow G1 1XQ T: 0141 548 2397 F: 0141 552 0775

Aberdeen

Aberdeen City Archives Aberdeen City Council Town House Broad Street Aberdeen AB10 1AQ T: 01224-522513 F: 01224 638556 E: archives@legal.aberdeen.net.uk W: www.aberdeencity.gov.uk also covers Aberdeenshire

Aberdeen City Archives - Old Aberdeen House Branch Old Aberdeen House Dunbar Street Aberdeen AB24 1UE T: 01224-481775 F: 01224-495830 E: archives@legal.aberdeen.net.uk W:

www.aberdeencity.gov.uk

Angus

Angus Archives Montrose Library 214 High Street Montrose Angus DD10 8PH T: 01674-671415 F: 01674-671810 E: angus.archives@angus.govuk W: www.angus.gov.uk/history/history.htm Family history research service. Archive holdings for Angus County, Arbroath, Brechin, Carnoustie, Forfar, Montrose, Monifieth, Kittiemuir.

Argyll

Argyll & Bute District Archives Manse Brae Lochgilphead Argyll PA31 8QU T: 01546 604120

Ayrshire

Ayrshire Archives Centre Craigie Estate Ayr Ayrshire KA8 0SS T: 01292-287584 F: 01292-284918 E: archives@south-ayshire.gov.uk W: www.south-ayrshire.gov.uk/archives/index.htm includes North Ayrshire, East Ayrshire and South Ayrshire.

East Ayrshire Council District History Centre & Museum Baird Institute 3 Lugar Street Cumnock Ayrshire KA18 1AD T: 01290-421701 F: 01290-421701 E: Baird.institute@east-ayrshire.gov.uk W: www.east-ayrshire.gov.uk

North Ayrshire Libraries Library Headquarters 39 - 41 Princes Street Ardrossan Ayrshire KA22 8BT T: 01294-469137 F: 01924-604236 E: reference@naclibhq.prestel.co.uk W: www.north-ayrshire.gov.uk

Clackmannanshire

Clackmannanshire Archives Alloa Library 26/28 Drysdale Street Alloa Clackmannanshire FK10 1JL T: 01259-722262 F: 01259-219469 E: libraries@clacks.gov.uk W: www.clacksweb.org.uk/dyna/archives

Dumfries & Galloway

Dumfries & Galloway Library and Archives Archive Centre 33 Burns Street Dumfries DG1 1PS T: 01387 269254 F: 01387 264126 E: libsxi@dumgal.gov.uk W: www.dumgal.gov.uk Open : Tues, Wed, Fri, 11am to 1pm, 2pm to 5pm and on Thurs 6pm to 9pm. Please book. Postal and consultation genealogical service available. Details on application.

Ewart Library Ewart Library Catherine Street Dumfries DG1 1JB T: 01387 260285 T: 01387-252070 F: 01387-260294 E: ruth_airley@dumgal.gov.uk W: www.dumgal.gov.ukf Fee paid research service availble

Dundee

Dundee City Archives 21 City Square (callers use 1 Shore Terrace) Dundee DD1 3BY T: 01382-434494 F: 01382-434666 E: archives@dundeecity.gov.uk W: www.dundeecity.gov.uk/archives.html

Dundee City Council - Genealogy Unit 89 Commercial Street Dundee DD1 2AF T: 01382-435222 F: 01382-435224 E: grant.law@dundeecity.gov.uk W: www.dundeecity.gov.uk/registrars

East Dunbartonshire

East Dunbartonshire Local Record Offices and Reference Libraries William Patrick Library 2 West High Street Kirkintilloch East Dunbartonshire G66 1AD T: 0141-776-8090 F: 0141-776-0408 E: libraries@eastdunbarton.gov.uk W: www.eastdunbarton.gov.uk

East Renfrewshire

East Renfrewshire Record Offices East Renfrewshire District Council Rouken Glen Road Glasgow East Renfrewshire G46 6JF T: 0141-577-4976

Edinburgh

Edinburgh City Archives City Chambers High St Edinburgh EH1 1YJ T: 0131-529-4616 F: 0131-529-4957

Heriot-Watt University Archives Coporate Communications Heriot-Watt University Edinburgh EH14 4AS T: 0131 451 3218 T: 0131 451 3219 & 0131 451 4140 F: 0131 451 3164 E: a.e.jones@hw.ac.uk W: www.hw.ac.uk/archive

Scottish Archive Network Thomas Thomson House 99 Bankhead Crossway North Edinburgh EH11 4DX T: 0131 242 5800 F: 0131 242 5801 E: enquiries@scan.org.uk W: www.scan.org.uk

Falkirk

Falkirk Library Hope Street Falkirk FK1 5AU T: 01324 503605 F: 01324 503606 E: falkirk-library@falkirk-library.demon.co.uk W: www.falkirk.gov.uk Holds Local Studies Collection

Falkirk Museum History Research Centre Callendar House Callendar Park Falkirk FK1 1YR T: 01324 503778 F: 01324 503771 E: callandarhouse@falkirkmuseums.demon.co.uk W: www.falkirkmuseums.demon.co.uk Records held: Local Authority, business, personal and estate records, local organmisations, trade unions, over 28,000 photographs Falkirk District

Fife

Fife Council Archive Centre Carleton House, Haig Business Park Balgonie Road Markinch Glenrothes Fife KY6 6AQ T: 01592 416504 E: andrew.dowsey@fife.gov.uk W: www.fifedirect.org.uk Open Mon to fri 9.00.a.m. to 5.00.p.m. by appointment

St Andrews University Library - Special Collections Department North Street St Andrews Fife KY16 9TR T: 01334 462339 E: speccoll@st-and.ac.uk W: http://specialcollections.st-and.ac.uk

Glasgow

Scottish Screen Archive Scottish Screen 1 Bowmont Gardens Glasgow G12 9LR T: 0141 337 7400 W: www.scottishscreen.com

Glasgow City Archives Mitchell Library North Street Glasgow G3 7DN T: 0141-287-2913 E: archives@cls.glasgow.gov.uk W: http://users.colloquium.co.uk/~glw_archives/src001.htm

Glasgow University Archive Services 13 Thurso Street Glasgow G11 6PE T: 0141 330 5515 F: 0141 330 4158 E: archives@archives.gla.ac.uk W: www.archives.gla.ac.uk

Glasgow University Library & Special Collections Department Hillhead Street Glasgow G12 8QE T: 0141 330 6767 F: 0141 330 3793 E: library@lib.gla.ac.uk W: www.gla.ac.uk/library

Royal College of Physicians and Surgeons of Glasgow 232 - 242 St Vincent Street Glasgow G2 5RJ T: 0141 221 6072 F: 0141 221 1804 E: library@rcpsglasg.ac.uk W: www.rcpsglasg.ac.uk

Strathclyde University Archives McCance Building 16 Richmond Street Glasgow G1 1XQ T: 0141 548 2397 F: 0141 552 0775

Highland

North Highland Archive Wick Library Sinclair Terrace Wick KW1 5AB T: 01955 606432 F: 01955 603000

Invernesshire

Highland Council Genealogy Centre Inverness Public Library Farraline Park Inverness IV1 1NH T: 01463-236463 : T: 01463 220330 ext 9 F: 01463 711128 E: genealogy@highland.gov.uk W: www.highland.gov.uk/publicservices/genealogy.htm

Isle of Lewis

Stornoway Record Office Town Hall 2 CromwellStreet Stornoway Isle of Lewis HS1 2BD T: 01851-709438 F: 01851 709438 E: emacdonald@cne-siar.gov.uk

Lanarkshire

South Lanarkshire Council Archives 30 Hawbank Road College Milton East Kilbride South Lanarkshire G74 5EX T: 01355 239193 F: 01355 242365

Midlothian

Midlothian Archives and Local Studies Centre 2 Clerk Street Loanhead Midlothian EH20 9DR T: 0131 271 3976 F: 0131 440 4635 E: local.studies@midlothian.gov.uk W: www.midlothian.gov.uk

Moray

Moray Local Heritage Centre Grant Lodge Cooper Park Elgin Moray IV30 1HS T: 01343 562644 T: 01343 562645 F: 01343-549050 E: graeme.wilson@techleis.moray.gov.uk W: www.morray.org/heritage/roots.html

North Lanarkshire

North Lanarkshire - Lenziemill Archives 10 Kelvin Road Cumbernauld North Lanarkshire G67 2BA T: 01236 737114 F: 01236 781762 W: www.northlan.gov.uk

Orkney

Orkney Archives The Orkney Library Laing Street Kirkwall Orkney KWl5 1NW T: 01856-873166 F: 01856-875260 E: alison.fraser@orkney.gov.uk W: www.orkney.gov.uk Open Mon to Fri 9am to 1pm & 2pm to 4.45pm. Appointments preferred

Orkney Library The Orkney Library Laing Street Kirkwall Orkney KWl5 1NW T: 01856-873166 F: 01856-875260 E: karen.walker@orkney.gov.uk W: www.orkney.gov.uk

Perthshire

Dunkeld Cathedral Chapter House Museum Dunkeld PH8 0AW T: 01350 728732 T: 01350 728971 W: www.dunkeldcathedral.org.uk contains Scottish Horse Regimental Archives

Perth and Kinross Council Archives A K Bell Library 2 - 8 York Place Perth Perthshire PH2 8EP T: 01738-477012 T: 01738 477022 F: 01738-477010 E: archives@pkc.gov.uk W: www.pkc.gov.uk/library/archive.htm

Scottish Horse Regimental Archives - Dunkeld Cathedral Dunkeld PH8 0AW T: 01350 727614 F: 01350 727614 Scottish Horse Regimental Museum closed 1999 - archives now held in Dunkeld Cathedral Chapter House Museum. View by prior appointment

Regimental Museum and Archives of Black Watch Balhousie Castle Hay Street Perth Perthshire PH1 5HR T: 0131 310 8530 F: 01738-643245 E: archives@theblackwatch.co.uk W: www.theblackwatch.co.uk

Renfrewshire

Renfrewshire Archives Central Library & Museum Complex High Street Paisley Renfrewshire PA1 2BB T: 0141-889-2350 F: 0141-887-6468 E: local_studies.library@renfrewshire.gov.uk W: www.renfrewshire.gov.uk

Scottish Borders

Scottish Borders Archive & Local History Centre Library Headquarters St Mary's Mill Selkirk Scottish Borders TD7 5EW T: 01750 20842 T: 01750 724903 F: 01750 22875 E: archives@scotborders.gov.uk W: www.scotborders.gov.uk/libraries

Shetland

Shetland Archives 44 King Harald St Lerwick Shetland ZE1 0EQ T: 01595-696247 F: 01595-696533 E: shetland.archives@zetnet.co.uk

Unst Heritage Centre Haroldswick Unst Shetland ZE2 9ED T: 01957 711528 T: 01957 711387 (Home)

Stirlingshire

Stirling Council Archives Unit 6 Burghmuir Industrial Estate Stirling FK7 7PY T: 01786-450745 F: 01786 473713 E: archive@stirling.gov.uk W: www.stirling.gov.uk

Strathclyde
Registrar of Births, Deaths and Marriages - Glasgow The Register Office 22 Park Circus Glasgow G3 6BE T: 0141 287 8350 F: 0141 287 8357 E: bill.craig@pas.glasgow.gov.uk
Tayside
Dundee University Archives Tower Building University of Dundee Dundee DD1 4HN T: 01382-344095 F: 01382 345523 E: archives@dundee.ac.uk W: www.dundee.ac.uk/archives/
West Lothian
West Lothian Council Archives - Archives & Records Management 7 Rutherford Square Brucefield Industrial Estate Livingston West Lothian EH54 9BU T: 01506 460 020 F: 01506 416 167

NORTHERN IRELAND
Belfast Family History & Cultural Heritage Centre 64 Wellington Place Belfast BT1 6GE T: (028) 9023 5392 F: (028) 9023 9885
General Register Office of Northern Ireland Oxford House 49 - 55 Chichester Street Belfast BT1 4HL T: (028) 90 252000 F: (028) 90 252120 E: gro.nisra@dfpni.gov.uk W: www.groni.gov.uk
Belfast Central Library Irish & Local Studies Dept Royal Avenue Belfast BT1 1EA T: (028) 9024 3233 F: (028) 9033 2819 E: info@libraries.belfast-elb.gov.uk W: www.belb.org.uk
Derry City Council Heritage & Museum Service Harbour Museum Harbour Square Derry Co Londonderry BT48 6AF T: (028) 7137 7331 F: (028) 7137 7633
Banbridge Genealogy Services Gateway Tourist Information Centre 200 Newry Road Banbridge County Down BT32 3NB T: 028 4062 6369 F: 028 4062 3114 E: banbridge@nitic.net
Northern Ireland Film Commission 21 Ormeau Avenue Belfast BT2 8HD T: W: www.nifc.co.uk
Presbyterian Historical Society of Ireland Church House Fisherwick Place Belfast BT1 6DW T: (028) 9032 2284 Opening hours: Mon to Fri 10am to 12.30pm. Wed afternoons 1.30pm to 3.30pm
Public Record Office of Northern Ireland 66 Balmoral Avenue Belfast BT9 6NY T: (028) 9025 5905 F: (028) 9025 5999 E: proni@dcalni.gov.uk W: www.proni.nics.gov.uk Recent publications

IRELAND
Church of Ireland Archives see Church Records
Genealogical Office / Office of The Chief Herald Kildare Street Dublin 2 Co Dublin T: +353-1-6030 200 F: +353-1-6621 062 E: herald@nli.ie W: www.nli.ie
Grand Lodge of Ireland see Masonic
National Archives Bishop Street Dublin 8 T: 01-407-2300 F: 01-407-2333 E: mail@nationalarchives.ie W: www..nationalarchives.ie
Registrar General for Ireland Joyce House 8 - 11 Lombard Street East Dublin 2 T: Dublin-711000
Presbyterian Historical Society of Ireland see Church Records
County Donegal
Donegal Local Studies Centre Central Library & Arts Centre Oliver Plunkett Road Letterkenny County Donegal T: 00353 74 24950 F: 00353 74 24950 E: dgcolib@iol.ie W: www.donegal.ie/library
Donegal Ancestry Old Meeting House Back Lane Ramleton Letterkenny County Donegal T: 00353 74 51266 F: 00353 74 51702 E: donances@indigo.ie W: www.indigo.ie/~donances
Donegal County Council Archive Centre 3 Rivers Centre Lifford County Donegal T: + 00353 74 72490 F: + 00353 74 41367 E: nbrennan@donegalcoco.ie W: www.donegal.ie
Dublin
Dublin City Archives City Assembly House 58 South William Street Dublin 2 T: (01)-677-5877 F: (01)-677-5954
County Clare
Clare County Archives Clare County Council New Road Ennis Co Clare T: 065-28525 T: 065 21616 W: www.clare.ie
County Dublin
Dublin Heritage Group Ballyfermot Library Ballyfermot Road Ballyfermot Dublin 10 T: 6269324 F: E: dhgeneal@iol.ie
County Limerick Limerick City Library Local History Collection The Granary Michael Street Limerick T: +353 (0)61-314668 T: +353 (0)61-415799E: noneill@citylib.limerickcorp.ie W: www.limerickcorp.ie/librarymain.htm
Limerick Regional Archives Limerick Ancestry, The Granary Michael Street Limerick T: 061-415125W: www.mayo-ireland.ie
County Louth
Louth County Archive Service Old Gaol, Ardee Road, Dundalk T: 00 353 (0)42 933 9387 E: archive@louthcoco.ie W: www.louthcoco.ie/louthcoco/louth/html/archive.htm
County Mayo
Local Record Offices The Registration Office New Antrim Street Castlebar Co Mayo T: 094-23249 094 23249
County Waterford
Waterford Archives and Local Records St Joseph's Hospital Dungarvan Co Waterford T: 058-42199

AUSTRALIA
National Archives of Australia - Canberra PO Box 7425, Canberra Mail Centre, Canberra, ACT, 2610 T: 02-6212-3600 E: archives@naa.gov.au W: www.naa.gov.au
National Archives of Australia - Hobart 4 Rosny Hill Road, Rosny Park, Tasmania, 7018 T: 03-62-440101 F: 03-62-446834 E: reftas@naa.gov.au W: www.naa.gov.au
National Archives of Australia - Northern Territories Kelsey Crescent, Nightcliffe, NT, 810 T: 08-8948-4577
National Archives of Australia - Queensland 996 Wynnum Road, Cannon Hill, Queensland, 4170 T: 07-3249-4226 F: 07-3399-6589 W: www.naa.gov.au
National Archives of Australia - South Australia 11 Derlanger Avenue, Collingwood, South Australia, 5081 T: 08-269-0100
National Archives of Australia - Sydney 120 Miller Road, Chester Hill, Sydney, New South Wales, 2162 T: 02-96450-100 F: 02-96450-108 E: refnsw@naa.gov.au W: www.naa.gov.uk
National Archives of Australia - Victoria PO Box 8005, Burwood Heights, Victoria, 3151 T: 03-9285-7900
National Archives of Australia - Western Australia 384 Berwick Street East, Victoria Park, Western Australia, 6101 T: 09-470-7500 F: 09-470-2787,
New South Wales - State Archives Office 2 Globe Street, Sydney, New South Wales, 2000 T: 02-9237-0254
Queensland State Archives PO Box 1397, Sunnybanks Hills, Brisbane, Queensland, 4109 T: 61-7-3875-8755 F: 61-7-3875-8764 E: qsa@ipd.pwh.qld.gov.auWWW: www.archives.qld.gov.au
South Australia State Archives PO Box 1056, Blair Athol West, South Australia, 5084 T: 08-8226-8000 F: 08-8226-8002,
Tasmania State Archives Archives Office of Tasmania, 77 Murray Street, Hobart, Tasmania, 7000 T: (03)-6233-7488 E: archives.tasmania@central.tased.edu.au W: www.tased.edu.au/archives
Victoria State Archives - Ballerat State Offices, Corner of Mair & Doveton Streets, Ballarat, Victoria, 3350 T: 03-5333-6611 F: 03-5333-6609,
Victoria State Archives - Laverton North 57 Cherry Lane, Laverton North, Victoria, 3028 T: 03-9360-9665 F: 03-9360-9685,
Victoria State Archives - Melbourne Level 2 Casselden Place, 2 Lonsdale Street, Melbourne, Victoria, 3000 T: 03-9285-7999 F: 03-9285-7953,
Western Australia - State Archives & Public Records Office Alexander Library, Perth Cultural Centre, Perth, Western Australia, 6000 T: 09-427-3360 F: 09-427-3256,

NEW ZEALAND
National Archives of New Zealand PO Box 10-050, 10 Mulgrave Street, Thorndon, Wellington, New Zealand T: 04-499-5595 E: national.archives@dia.govt.nz W: www.archives.dia.govt.nz

AFRICA
South Africa
Cape Town Archives Repository Private Bag X9025, Cape Town, 8000, South Africa T: 021-462-4050 F: 021-465-2960,
Dutch Reformed Church Archive PO Box 398, Bloemfontein, 9301, South Africa T: 051-448-9546,
Dutch Reformed Church Archive of O.F.S P O Box 398, Bloemfontein, 9301, RSA T: 051 448 9546,
Dutch Reformed Church Records Office PO Box 649, Pietermaritzburg, 3200 T: 0331-452279 F: 0331-452279,
Dutch Reformed Church Synod Records Office of Kwa Zulu-Natal P O Box 649, Pietermaritzburg , 3200, RSA T: 0331 452279 F: 0331 452279 E: ngntlargrief@alpha.futurenet.co.za,
Free State Archives Private Bag X20504, Bloemfontein, Free State, 9300, South Africa T: 051-522-6762 F: 051-522-6765
Free State Archives Repository Private Bag X20504, Bloemfontein, 9300, South Africa T: 051 522 6762 F: 051 522 6765,
National Archives - Pretoria Private Bag X236, Pretoria, 1, South Africa T: 323 5300
South Africa National Archives Private Bag X236, Pretoria, 1
South African Library - National Reference & Preservation P O Box 496, Cape Town, 8000, South Africa T: 021 246320 F: 021 244848 E: postmaster@salib.ac.za

NAMIBIA
National Archives of Namibia Private Bag, Windhoek, 13250, Namibia T: 061 293 4386 E: Renate@natarch.mec.gov.na W: www.witbooi.natarch.mec.gov.na

ZIMBABWE
National Archives of Zimbabwe "Hiller Road, off Borrowdale Road", Gunhill, Harare, Zimbabwe T: 792741/3 F: 792398

EUROPE
BELGIUM
Archives de l'Etat a Liege 79 rue du Chera, Liege, B-4000, Belgium T: 04-252-0393 F: 04-229-3350 E: archives.liege@skynet.be
De Kerk van Jezus Christus van den Heiligen Der Laaste Dagen, Kortrijkse Steenweg 1060, Sint-Deniss-Westrem, B-9051, Belgium T: 09-220-4316

Provinciebestuur Limburg Universititslaan 1, Afdeling 623 Archief, Hasselt, B-3500, Belgium

Rijks Archief te Brugge Academiestraat 14, Brugge, 8000, Belgium T: 050-33-7288 F: 050-33-7288 E: rijksarchief.brugge@skynet.be

Rijksarchief Kruibekesteenweg 39/1, Beveren, B-9210, Belgium T: 03-775-3839

Service de Centralisation des Etudes Genealogique et Demographiques Belgique Chaussee de Haecht 147, Brussels, B-1030, Belgium T: 02-374-1492

Staatsarchiv in Eupen Kaperberg 2-4, Eupen, B-4700, Belgium T: 087-55-4377

Stadsarchief te Veurne Grote Markt 29, Veurne, B-8630, Belgium T: 058-31-4115 F: 058-31-4554

CYPRUS

Cyprus Center of Medievalism & Heraldry P O Box 80711, Piraeus, 185 10, Greece T: 42-26-356

DENMARK

Association of Local History Archives P O Box 235, Enghavevej 2, Vejle, DK-7100, Denmark F: 45-7583-1801 W: www.lokalarkiver.dk

Cadastral Archives Rentemestervej 8, Copenhagen NV, DK-2400, Denmark F: 45-3587-5064 W: www.kms.min.dk

Danish Data Archive Islandsgade 10, Odense C, DK-5000, Denmark Fax: 45-6611-3060, W: www.dda.dk

Danish Emigration Archives P O Box 1731, Arkivstraede 1, Aalborg, DK-9100, Denmark T: 045 9931 4221 F: 45 9810 2248 E: bfl-kultur@aalbkom.dk W: www.cybercity.dk/users/ccc13656

Danish National Archives Rigsdagsgaarden 9, Copenhagen, DK-1218 T: 45-3392-3310 F: 45-3315-3239 W: www.sa.dk/ra/uk/uk.htm

Det Kongelige Bibliotek POB 2149, Copenhagen K, DK-1016 T: 045-3393-0111 F: 045-3393-2218

Frederiksberg Municipal Libraries Solbjergvej 21-25, Frederiksberg, DK-2000, Denmark F: 45-3833-3677 W: www.fkb.dk

Kobenshavns Stadsarkiv Kobenhavns Radhus, Kobenhavn, DK01599, Denmark T: 3366-2374 F: 3366-7039

National Business Archives Vester Alle 12, Aarhus C, DK-8000, Denmark T: 45-8612-8533 E: mailbox@ea.sa.dk W: www.sa.dk/ea/engelsk.htm

Provincial Archives for Funen Jernbanegade 36, Odense C, DK-5000, Denmark T: 6612-5885 F: 45-6614-7071 W: www.sa.dk/lao/default.htm

Provincial Archives for Nth Jutland Lille Sct. Hansgade 5, Viborg, DK-8800, Denmar T: 45-8662-1788 W: www.sa.dk/lav/default.htm

Provincial Archives for Southern Jutland Haderslevvej 45, Aabenraa, DK-6200, Denmark Tel: 45-7462-5858 W: www.sa.dk/laa/default.htm

Provincial Archives for Zealand etc Jagtvej 10, Copenhagen, DK-2200, Denmark F: 45-3539-0535 W: www.sa.dk/lak.htm

Royal Library Christains Brygge 8, Copenhagen K, DK-1219, Denmark F: 45-3393-2219 W: www.kb.dk

State Library Universitetsparken, Aarhus C, DK-8000, Denmark Tel: 45-8946-2022 F: 45-8946-2130 W: www.sb.aau.dk/english

FINLAND

Institute of Migration Piispankatu 3, Turku, 20500Tel: 2-231-7536 Fax: 2-233-3460 E: jouni.kurkiasaaz@utu.fi W: www.utu.fi/erill/instmigr/

FRANCE

Centre d'Accueil et de Recherche des Archives Nationales 60 rue des Francs Bourgeois, Paris Cedex, 75141, France T: 1-40-27-6000 F: 1-40-27-6628

Centre des Archives d'Outre-Mer 29 Chemin du Moulin de Testas, Aix-en-Provence, 13090

Service Historique de la Marine Chateau de Vincennes, Vincennes Cedex, 94304, France

Service Historique de l'Armee de l'Air Chateau de Vincennes, Vincennes Cedex, 94304, France

Service Historique de l'Armee de Terre BP 107, Armees, 481, France

Military (Army), Service Historique De L'Armee De Terre, Fort de Vincennes, Boite Postale 107 T: 01 4193 34 44 F: 01 41 93 38 90

Military (Navy), Service Historique De La Marine, Chateau de Vincennes, Boite Postale 2 T: 01 43 28 81 50 F: 01 43 28 31 60 E: shistorique@cedocar.fr

GERMANY

German Emigration Museum Inselstrasse 6, Bremerhaven, D-2850 T: 0471-49096

Historic Emigration Office Steinstr. 7, Hamburg, (D) 20095, Germany T: 4940-30- 51-282 F: 4940-300-51-220 E: ESROKAHEA@aol.com W: users.cybercity.dk/gccc13652/addr/ger_heo.htm

Research Centre Lower Saxons in the USA Postfach 2503, Oldenburg, D-2900, Germany T: 0441 798 2614 E: holtmann@hrzl.uni-oldenburg.de W: www.uni-oldenburg.de/nausa

Zentralstelle fur Personen und Familiengeschichte Birkenweg 13, Friedrichsdorf, D-61381 T: 06172-78263 W: www.genealogy.com/gene/genealogy.html

GREECE

Cyprus Center of Medievalism & Heraldry P O Box 80711, Piraeus, 185 10, Greece T: 42-26-356

LIECHENSTEIN

Major Archives Record Offices & Libraries Liechtenstein W: www.genealogy.com/gene/reg/CH/lichts.html

NETHERLANDS

Amsterdam Municipal Archives P O 51140, Amsterdam, 1007 EC

Brabant-Collectie Tilburg University Library, P O Box 90153, Warandelaan, Tilburg, NL-5000 LE, Netherlands T: 0031-134-662127

Gemeentelijke Archiefdienst Amersfoort P O Box 4000, Amersfoort, 3800 EA T: 033-4695017 F: 033-4695451

Het Utrechts Archief Alexander Numankade 199/201, Utrecht, 3572 KW, T: 030-286-6611 F: 030-286-6600 E: Utrecht@acl.archivel.nl

Rijksarchief in Drenthe P O Box 595, Assen, 9400 AN, Netherlands T: 0031-592-313523 F: 0031-592-314697 E: RADR@noord.bart.nl W: obd-server.obd.nl/instel/enderarch/radz.htm

Rijksarchief in Overijssel Eikenstraat 20, Zwolle, 8021 WX, Netherlands T: 038-454-0722 F: 038-454-4506 E: RAO@euronet.nl W: www.obd.nl/instel/arch/rkarch.htm

Zealand Documentation CTR P O Box 8004, Middelburg, 4330 EA, Netherlands

NORWAY

Norwegian Emigration Centre Strandkaien 31, Stavanger, 4005, Norway T: 47-51-53-88-63 Email: detnu@telepost.no W: www.emigrationcenter.com

POLAND

Head Office Polish State Archives Ul Dluga6 Skr, Poczt, Warsaw, 1005-00-950 F: 0-22-831-9222

RUSSIA

Moscow
Russian State Military Historical Archive 2, Baumanskaya 3, 107864, Moscow T: 7 (095) 261-20-70

St Petersburg
Russian State Historical Archive (RGIA), Naberejnaya 4 (English Embankment), 1900000 St Petersburg T: 7 (812) 315-54-35 , T: 7 (812) 311-09-26 F: 7 (812) 311-22-52

SPAIN

Archivo Historico National Serrano 115, Madrid, 28006 T: 261-8003-2618004

Instituucion Fernando el Catolico Plaza de Espagna 2, Zaragoza, 50071, Espagn T: 09-7628-8878 E: ifc@isendanet.es.mail

SWEDEN

Harnosand Provincial Archive Box 161, Harnosand, S-871 24, Sweden T: 611-835-00 E: landsarkivet@landsarkivet-harnosand.ra.se W: www.ra.se/hla

Goteborg Provincial Archive Box 19035, Goteborg, S-400 12, Sweden T: 31-778-6800

House of Emigrants Box 201, Vaxjo, S-351 04, Sweden T: 470-201-20 E: info@svenskaemigrantinstitulet.g.se

Kinship Centre Box 331, Karlstad, S-651 08, Sweden T: 54-107720

Lund Provincial Archive Box 2016, Lund, S-220 02 T: 046-197000 F: 046-197070 E: landsarkivet@landsarkivet-lund.ra.se

Orebro Stadsarkiv Box 300, Orebro, S-701 35 T: 19-211075 F: 19-211050

Ostersund Provincial Archive Arkivvagen 1, Ostersund, S-831 31, Sweden T: 63-10-84-85 E: landsarkivet@landsarkivet-ostersund.ra.se W: www.ra.se/ola/

Stockholm City & Provincial Archives Box 22063, Stockholm, S-104 22 T: 8-508-283-00 F: 8-508-283-01

Swedish Military Archives Banergatan 64, Stockholm, S-115 88 T: 8-782-41-00

Swedish National Archives Box 12541, Stockholm, S-102 29, Sweden T: 8-737-63-50

Uppsala Provincial Archive Box 135, Uppsala, SE-751 04, Sweden T: 18-65-21-00

Vadstena Provincial Archive Box 126, Vadstena, S-592 23, Sweden T: 143-130-30

Visby Provincial Archive Visborgsgatan 1, Visby, 621 57, Sweden T: 498-2129-55

SWITZERLAND

Achives de la Ville de Geneve Palais Eynard, 4 rue de la Croix-Rouge, Geneve 3, 1211 T: 22-418-2990 E: didier.grange@seg.ville-ge.ch

Archives Canonales Vaudoises rue de la Moulne 32, Chavannes-pres-Renens, CH 1022, Switzerland T: 021-316-37-11 F: 021-316-37-55

Archives de l'Ancien Eveche de Bale 10 rue des Annonciades, Porrentruy, CH-2900, Suisse

Geneva
Archives d'Etat, 1 Rue de l'Hotel de Ville, Case Postale 164, Geneve 3 T: 41 21 319 33 95 F: 41 21 319 33 65

Lausanne
Archives De La Ville De Lausanne, Rue de Maupas 47, Case Postale CH-1000 Lausanne 9 T: 41 21 624 43 55 F: 41 21 624 06 01

Staatsarchiv Appenzell Ausserhoden Obstmarkt, Regierungsgebaede,

Herisau, CH-9100, T: 071-353-6111 E: Peter.Witschi@kk.ar.ch
Staatsarchiv des Kantons Basel-Landschaft Wiedenhubstrasse 35, Liestal, 4410 T: 061-921-44-40 E: baselland@lka.bl.ch W: www.baselland.ch
Staatsarchiv des Kantons Solothurn Bielstrasse 41, Solothurn, CH-4509, Switzerland T: 032-627-08-21 F: 032-622-34-87
Staatsarchiv Luzern Postfach 7853, Luzern, 6000 T: 41-41-2285365 E: archiv@staluzern.c W: www.staluzern.ch

UKRAINE
Odessa, Odessa State Archive, 18 Shukovskovo Street, Odessa 270001

NORTH AMERICA - CANADA
Archives & Special Collections
PO Box 7500, Fredericton, New Brunswick, E3B 5H5 T: 506-453-4748 F: 506-453-4595,
Archives Nationales PO Box 10450, Sainte Foy, Quebec, G1V 4N1 T: 418-643-8904 F: 418-646-0868
Glenbow Library & Archives 130-9th Avenue SE, Calgary, Alberta, T2G 0P3 T: 403-268-4197 F: 403-232-6569
Hudson's Bay Company Archives, 200 Vaughan Street, Winnipeg R3C 1T5 T: 204-945-4949 F: 204-948-3236 E: hbca@chc.gov.mb.ca W: http://www.gov.mb.ca/chc/archives/hbca/index.html
Loyalist Collection & Reference Department PO Box 7500, Fredericton, New Brunswick, E3B 5H5 T: 506-453-4749 F: 506-453-4596,
Manitoba Provincial Archives 200 Vaughan Street, Winnepeg, Manitoba, R3C 1T5 T: 204-945-4949 F: 204-948-3236,
National Archives of Canada 395 Wellington Street, Ottawa, Ontario, K1A 0N3 T: 613-996-7458 W: http://www.archives.ca,
New Brunswick Provincial Archives PO Box 6000, Fredericton, New Brunswick, E3B 5H1 T: 506-453-2122 E: provarch@gov.nb.ca W: www.gov.nb.ca/supply/archives
Newfoundland & Labrador Archives Colonial Building, Military Road, St Johns, Newfoundland, A1C 2C9 T: 709-729-0475 F: 709-729-0578,
Nova Scotia State Archives 6016 University Avenue, Halifax, Nova Scotia, B3H 1W4 T: 902-424-6060,
Ontario Archives Unit 300, 77 Grenville Street, Toronto, Ontario, M5S 1B3 T: 416-327-1582 E: reference@archives.gov.on.ca W: www.gov.on.ca/MCZCR/archives
Public Archives & Record Office PO Box 1000, Charlottetown, Prince Edward Island, C1A 7M4 T: 902-368-4290 F: 902-368-6327 E: archives@gov.pe.ca W: www.gov.pe.ca/educ/
Saskatchewan Archives Board - Regina 3303 Hillsdale Street, Regina, Saskatchewan, S4S 0A2 T: 306-787-4068 E: sabreg@sk.sympatico.ca W: www.gov.sk.ca/govt/archives
Saskatchewan Archives Board - Saskatchewa Room 91, Murray Building, University of Saskatchewan, 3 Campus Drive, Saskatoon, Saskatchewan, S7N 5A4 T: 306-933-5832 E: sabsktn@sk.sympatico.ca W: www.gov.sk.ca/govt/archives
Yarmouth County Museums & Archives 22 Collins Street, Yarmouth, Nova Scotia, B5A 3C8 T: (902)-742-5539 E: ycn0056@ycn.library.ns.ca W: www.ycn.library.ns.ca/museum/yarcomus.htm

UNITED STATES OF AMERICA
Alaska State Archives 141 Willoughby Avenue, Juneau, Alaska, 99801-1720, United States of America, T: 907-465-2270 E: sou@bham.lib.al.usarchives@educ.state.ak.us,
Arizona Department of Library Archives & Public Records State Capitol, 1700 West Washington, Phoenix, Arizona, 85007, United States of America, T: 602-542-3942
Arizona Historical Foundation Library Hayden Library, Arizona State Univeristy, Tempe, Arizona, 85287, United States of America, T: 602-966-8331
Arkansas History Commission OneCapitol Mall, Little Rock, Arkansas, 72201 T: 501-682-6900,
California State Archives Office of the Secretary of State, 1020 O Street, Sacramento, 95814 T: (916)-653-7715 E: archivesweb@ss.ca.gov W: www.ss.ca.gov/archives/archives.htm
Colorado State Archives Room 1b-20, 1313 Sherman Street, Denver, Colorado, 80203-2236, United States of America, T: 303-866-2390,
Connecticut State Archives 231 Capitol Ave, Hartford 6106, T: 0860 757 6580 E: isref@cslib.org W: www. cslib.org
Daughters of the American Revolution Library 1776 D Street N W, Washington, District of Columbia, 20006-5392, United States of America, T: 202-879-3229,
District of Columbia Archives 1300 Naylor Court North West, Washington, District of Columbia, 20001-4225 T: 203-566-3690,
Family History Library of the Church of Jesus Christ of LDS 35 N West Temple Street, Salt Lake City, Utah, 84150, USA,
Georgia State Archives 330 Capital Avenue SE, Atlanta 30334-9002 T: 404-656-2350 W: http://www.state.ga.us/SOS/Archives/,
Hawaii State Library 478 South King Street, Honolulu, Hawaii, 96813
Indiana Archives Room117, 140 N Senate Avenue, Indianapolis, Indiana, 46204-2296 T: 317-232-3660 F: 317-233-1085,
Kansas State Historical Society - Archives 6425 SW Sixth Street, Topeka, Kansas, 66615-1099 T: 913-272-8681 F: 913-272-8682 E: reference@hspo.wpo.state.ks.us W: www.kshs.org
Maryland State Archives Hall of Records Building, 350 Rowe Boulevard, Annapolis, Maryland, 21401 T: 410-974-3914,

Missouri State Archives PO Box 778, Jefferson City, Missouri, 65102 T: 314-751-3280,
National Archives - California 100 Commodore Drive, San Bruno, California, 94066-2350
National Archives - Colorado PO Box 25307, Denver, Colorado, 80225-0307 T: 303-866-2390,
National Archives - Georgia 1557 St Joseph Avenue, East Point, Georgia, 30344, T: 404-763-7477 F: 404-763-7059 W: www.nara.gov
National Archives - Illinois 7358 South Pulaski Road, Chicago, Illinois, 60629
National Archives - Massachusetts 380 Trapelo Road, Waltham, Massachusetts, 2154,
National Archives - Massachusetts 100 Dan Fox Drive, Pittsfield, Massachusetts, 01201-8230
National Archives - Missouri 2306 East Bannister Road, Kansas City, Missouri, 64131
National Archives - New York 201 Varick Street, New York, New York, 10014 - 4811
National Archives - Northwest Pacific Region 6125 Sand Point Way NE, Seattle, Washington, 98115 T: 206-524-6501 E: archives@seattle.nara.gov,
National Archives - Pennsylvania Rom 1350, 900 Market Street, Philadelphia, PA 19144,
National Archives - Texas Box 6216, 4900 Hemphill Road, Fort Worth, Texas, 76115
National Archives - Washington Pennsylvania Avenue, Washington, District of Colombia, 20408,
National Archives - Pacific Alaska Region 654 West 3rd Avenue, Anchorage, Alaska, 99501 - 2145 T: 011-1-907-271-2443 F: 011-1-907-271-2442 E: archives@alaska.nara.gov W: www.nara.gov/regional/anchorage.html
National Archives (Pacific Region) 1st Floor East, 24000 Avila Road, Orange County, Laguna Niguel, California, 92677 T: (949)-360-2641 F: (949)-360-2624 E: archives@laguna.nara.gov W: www.nara.gov/regional/laguna.html
Nevada State Archives Division of Archives & Records, 100 Stewart Street, Carson City, Nevada, 89710 T: 702-687-5210,
New Jersey State Archives PO Box 307, 185 West State Street, Trenton, New Jersey, 08625-0307 T: 609-292-6260,
New Mexico State Archives 1205 Camino carlos Rey, Sante Fe, New Mexico, 87501 T: (505)-827-7332 F: (505)-476-7909 E: cmartine@rain.state.nm.us W: www.state.nmus/cpr
Ohio State Archives 1982 Velma Avenue, Columbus, Ohio, 43211-2497 T: 614-297-2510,
Pennsylvania State Archives PO Box 1026, 3rd & Forster Streets, Harrisburg, Pennsylvania, 17108-1026 T: 717-783-3281,
South Carolina Department Archives & History 8301 Parklane Road, Columbia, South Carolina, 292223 T: 803-896-6100,
South Carolina State Archives PO Box 11669, 1430 Senate Street, Columbia, South Carolina, 29211-1669 T: 803-734-8577,
South Dakota Archives Cultural Heritage Center, 900 Governors Drive, Pierre, South Dakota, 57501-2217 T: 605-773-3804,
Tennessee State Library & Archives 403 7th Avenue North, Nashville, Tennessee, 37243-0312 T: 615-741-2764 E: reference@mail.state.tn.us W: www.state.tn.us/sos/statelib
Texas State Archives PO Box 12927, Austin, Texas, 78711-2927 T: 512-463-5463,
Vermont Public Records Division PO Drawer 33, U S Route 2, Middlesex, Montpelier, Vermont, 05633-7601 T: 802-828-3700 and 802-828-3286 F: 802-828-3710,
Vermont State Archives Redstone Building, 26 Terrace Street, Montpelier, Vermont, 05609-1103 T: 802-828-2308,
Virginia State Archives 11th Street at Capitol Square, Richmond, Virginia, 23219-3491 T: 804-786-8929,
West Virginia State Archives The Cultural Center, 1900 Kanawha Boulevard East, Charleston, West Virginia, 25305-0300 T: 304-558-0230,
Wisconsin State Archives 816 State Street, Madison 53706 T: 608-264-6460 F: 608-264-6742 E: archives.reference@ccmail.adp.wisc.edu W: www.wisc.edu/shs-archives
Wyoming State Archives Barrett State Office Building, 2301 Central Avenue, Cheyenne, Wyoming, 82002 T: 307-777-7826

Registrars of Births, Marriages & Deaths - England, Wales and Scotland

Following is a list of Superintendent Registrars of Births, Marriages and Deaths in alphabetical order by County. We have also included details of Registration Sub Districts. **Note:** Many of the Registration Officers listed here share Office accommodation with other parties. When using the addresses given they should be prefixed "Superintendent Registrar, Register Office ...." *We offer the following advice to help readers and Superintendent Registrars* The volume and page number references which are found on the microfiche and film indexes of the General Register Office must only be used when applying for certificates from the GRO. These reference numbers are not a reference to the filing system used at local register offices and do not assist Superintendent Registrars in any way to find the entry. The General Register Office hold the records for the whole of England and Wales and therefore have their own filing system, whereas the majority of register offices are still manually searching handwritten index books which is extremely time consuming. Most offices only became computerised in the early 1990s and do not hold records before this date on computer and will never have the staff time to backlog 150 years of records. Finally, many offices are only part time, some just open a few hours per week. Unlike the larger offices they do not have receptionists or staff employed specifically to assist people researching their family history, and have to devote the majority of their time to providing certificates urgently required for passport applications, marriage bookings and pension applications. Once the applicant has carried out their research fully using all the records and data widely available to them at no cost, they can apply to their local office with sufficient information for the Registrar to trace the entry within minutes instead of hours.

England,
The General Register Office, Trafalgar Road, Birkdale, Southport, PR8 2HH T: 0870 243 7788
Bath & North East Somerset, The Register Office, 12 Charlotte Street, Bath, BA1 2NF T: 01225 312032 F: 01225 334812
Bedfordshire
The Register Office, Pilgrim House, 20 Brickhill Drive, Bedford, MK41 7PZ T: 01234 290450 F: 01234 290454
Berkshire
Bracknell Forest, Easthampstead House, Town Square, Bracknell, RG12 1AQ T: 01344 352027 F: 01344 352010
West Berkshire, Peake House, 112 Newtown Road, Newbury, RG14 7EB T: 01635 48133 F: 01635 524694
Reading , The Register Office, Yeomanry House, 131 Castle Hill, Reading, RG1 7TA T: 0118 901 5120 F: 0118 951 0212
Slough, Slough Register Office, The Centre, Farnham Road, Slough, SL1 4UT T: 01753 787601 F: 01753 787605
Windsor & Maidenhead, Town Hall, St Ives Road, Maidenhead, SL6 1RF T: 01628 796422 F: 01628 796625
Wokingham, The Old School, Reading Road, Wokingham, RG41 1RJ T: 0118 978 2514 F: 0118 978 2813
Buckinghamshire
Aylesbury Vale, County Offices, Walton Street, Aylesbury, HP20 1XF T: 01296 382581 F: 01296 382675
Chiltern Hills, Wycombe Area Offices, Easton Street, High Wycombe, HP11 1NH T: 01494 475200 F: 01494 475040
Birmingham
Birmingham, The Register Office, 300 Broad Street, Birmingham, B1 2DE T: 0121 212 3421 F: 0121 303 1396
Bournemouth
Bournemouth, The Register Office, The Town Hall, Bourne Avenue, Bournemouth, BH2 6DY T: 01202 454945,
Brighton & Hove
Brighton & Hove, Brighton Town Hall, Bartholomews, Brighton, BN1 1JA T: 01273 292016 F: 01273 292019
Cambridgeshire
Cambridge, Castle Lodge, Shire Hall, Castle Hill, Cambridge, CB3 0AP T: 01223 717401 F: 01223 717888 All churches on computer index from 1837 to date. For general searches please arrange in advance.
Ely, Old School House, 74 Market Street, Ely, CB7 4LS T: 01353 663824
Fenland, The Old Vicarage, Church Terrace, Wisbech, PE13 1BW T: 01945 467950 F: 01945 467950
Huntingdon, Wykeham House, Market Hill, Huntingdon, PE29 3NN T: 01480 375821 F: 01480 375725
Oundle and Thrapston, The Old Courthouse, 17 Mill Road, Oundle, Peterborough, PE8 4BW T: 01832 273413
Peterborough, The Lawns, 33 Thorpe Road, Peterborough, PE3 6AB T: 01733 566323 F: 01733 566049
Cheshire
Chester West, Goldsmith House, Goss Street, Chester, CH1 2BG T: 01244 602668 F: 01244 602934
Halton, The Register Office, Heath Road, Runcorn, WA7 5TN T: 0151 471 7636 F: 01928 573616
Cheshire East, The Register Office, Park Green, Macclesfield, SK11 6TW T: 01625 423463 F: 01625 619225
Cheshire Central, The Register Office, Delamere House, Chester Street, CW1 2LL T: 01270 505106 F: 01270 505107
Warrington, The Register Office, Museum Street, Warrington, WA1 1JX T: 01925 442762 F: 01925 442739
Bristol
The Register Office, Quakers Friars, Bristol, BS1 3AR T: 0117 903 8888 F: 0117 903 8877
Cornwall
Bodmin, Lyndhurst, 66 St Nicholas Street, Bodmin, PL31 1AG T: 01208 73677 F: 01208 73677
Camborne-Redruth, The Register Office, Roskear, Camborne, TR14 8DN T: 01209 612924 F: 01209 719956
Falmouth, Berkeley House, 12-14 Berkeley Vale, Falmouth, TR11 3PH T: 01326 312606 F: 01326 312606

Kerrier, The Willows, Church Street, Helston, TR13 8NJ T: 01326 562848 F: 01326 562848
Launceston, 'Hendra', Dunheved Road, Launceston, PL15 9JG T: 01566 772464 F: 01566 775980
Liskeard, 'Graylands', Dean Street, Liskeard, PL14 4AH T: 01579 343442 F: 01872 327554
Penzance, The Register Office, Alphington House, Alverton Place, Penzance, TR18 4JJ T: 01736 330093 F: 01736 369666
Stratton, The Parkhouse Centre, Ergue Gaberic Way, Bude, EX23 8LF T: 01288 353209 F: 01288 359968
St. Austell, The Register Office, 12 Carlyon Road, St Austell, PL25 4LD T: 01726 68974 F: 01726 67048
St. Germans, The Register Office, Plougastel Drive, St Germans, Saltash, PL12 6DL T: 01752 842624 F: 01752 848556
Truro, Dalvenie House, New County Hall, Truro, TR1 3AY T: 01872 322241 F: 01872 323891
Coventry
Coventry, The Register Office, Cheylesmore Manor House, Manor House Drive, CV1 2ND T: (024) 7683 3137 F: (024) 7683 3110
Cumbria
Barrow-in-Furness, Nan Tait Centre, Abbey Road, Barrow-in-Furness, LA14 1LG T: 01229 894510 F: 01229 894513
Carlisle The Register Office, 23 Portland Square, Carlisle, CA1 1PE T: 01228 607432 F: 01228 607434
Cockermouth The Register Office, Fairfield, Station Road, Cockermouth, CA13 9PT T: 01900 325960 F: 01900 325962
Kendal The Register Office, County Offices, Kendal, LA9 4RQ T: 01539 773567 F: 01539 773565
Millom The Millom Council Centre, St Georges Road, Millom, LA18 4DD T: 01229 772357 F: 01229 773412
Penrith The Register Office, Friargate, Penrith, CA11 7XR T: 01768 242120 F: 01768 242122
Ulverston Town Hall, Queen Street, Ulverston, LA12 7AR T: 01229 894170 F: 01229 894172
Whitehaven College House, Flatt Walks, Whitehaven, CA28 7RW T: 01946 852690 F: 01946 852673
Wigton Wigton Registry Office, Station Road, Wigton, CA7 9AH T: 016973 66117 F: 016973 66118
Darlington
The Register Office, Central House, Gladstone Street, Darlington, DL3 6JX T: 01325 346600,
Derbyshire
Derby The Register Office, 9 Traffic Street, Derby, DE1 2NL T: 01332 716025 This office holds all the South Derbyshire (formerly Swadlingcote and Gresley District) records
Amber Valley, The Register Office, Market Place, Ripley, DE5 3BT T: 01773 841380 F: 01773 841382
Ashbourne, Town Hall, Market Place, Ashbourne, DE6 1ES T: 01335 300575 F: 01335 345252
Bakewell, The Register Office, Town Hall, Bakewell, DE45 1BW T: 01629 812261 F:
Chesterfield, The Register Office, New Beetwell Street, Chesterfield, S40 1QJ T: 01246 234754 F: 01246 274493
Erewash, The Register Office, 87 Lord Haddon Road, Ilkeston, DE7 8AX T: 0115 932 1014 F: 0115 932 6450
High Peak, Council Offices, Hayfield Road, Chapel-en-le-Frith, SK23 0QJ T: 01663 750473
High Peak (Buxton Sub-district), The Registrar's Office, Hardwick Square West, Buxton, SK17 6PX T: 01298 25075
High Peak (Chapel en le Frith Sub-district), The Town Hall, Chapel en le Frith, SK23 0HB T: 01298 813559
High Peak (Glossop Sub-district), 46-50 High Street West, Glossop, SK13 8BH T: 01457 852425
South Derbyshire, The Register Office, Traffic Street, Derby, DE1 2NL T: 01332 716020, 01332 716025 F: 01332 716021
Devon
North Devon, The Register Office, Civic Centre, Barnstaple, EX31 1ED T: 01271 388456
Torridge, Council Offices, Windmill Lane, Northam, Bideford, EX39 1BY T: 01237 474978 F: 01237 473385

Exeter, 1 Lower Summerlands, Heavitree Road, Exeter, EX1 2LL T: 01392 686260 F: 01392 686262

East Devon, The Register Office, Dowell Street, Honiton, EX14 1LX T: 01404 42531 F: 01404 41475

South Hams, Follaton House, Plymouth Road, Totnes, TQ9 5NE T: 01803 861234 F: 01803 868965

Mid Devon, The Great House, 1 St Peter Street, Tiverton, EX16 6NY T: 01884 255255 F: 01884 258852

Teignbridge, The Register Office, 15 Devon Square, Newton Abbot, TQ12 2HN T: 01626 206340 F: 01626 206346

Plymouth, The Register Office, Lockyer Street, Plymouth, PL1 2QD T: 01752 268331 F: 01752 256046

West Devon, Town Council Offices, Drake Road, Tavistock, PL19 0AU T: 01822 612137 F: 01822 618935

Torbay, The Register Office, Oldway Mansion, Paignton, TQ3 2TU T: 01803 207130 F: 01803 525388

Doncaster
The Register Office, Elmfield Park, Doncaster, DN1 2EB T: 01302 364922

Dorset
East Dorset, King George V Pavilion, Peter Grant Way, Ferndown, BH22 9EN T: 01202 892325 F:

North Dorset, The Register Office, Salisbury Road, Blandford Forum, DT11 7LN T: 01258 484096 F: 01258 484090, This is a part-time office with only 2 members of staff and no receptionist. All Blandford births and deaths from 1837 to 1974 are held at Poole Register Office

South and West Dorset, The Guildhall, St Edmund Street, Weymouth, DT4 8AS T: 01305 760899 F: 01305 771269

Dudley
Priory Hall, Priory Park, Dudley, DY1 4EU T: 01384 815373 F:

Durham
Durham Central, The Register Office, 40 Old Elvet, Durham, DH1 3HN T: 0191 386 4077 F:

Durham Eastern, Register Office, York Road, Acre Rigg, Peterlee, SR8 2DP T: 0191 586 6147 F: 0191 518 4607

Durham Western, Cockton House, 35 Cockton Hill Road, Bishop Auckland, DL14 6HS T: 01388 607277 F: 01388 664388

East Sussex
Hastings & Rother, The Register Office, Summerfields, Bohemia Road, Hastings, TN34 1EX T: 01424 721722 F: 01424 465296

Lewes, Southover Grange, Southover Road, Lewes, BN7 1TP T: 01273 475589 F: 01273 488073

Essex
Braintree, John Ray House, Bocking End, Braintree, CM7 9RW T: 01376 323463

Brentwood, The Register Office, 1 Seven Arches Road, Brentwood, CM14 4JG T: 01277 233565 F: 01277 262712

Chelmsford, The Register Office, 17 Market Road, Chelmsford, CM1 1GF T: 01245 430700 F: 01245 430707

Colchester, Stanwell House, Stanwell Street, Colchester, CO2 7DL T: 01206 572926 F: 01206 540626

Epping Forest, The Register Office, St Johns Road, Epping, CM16 5DN T: 01992 572789 F: 01992 571236

Harlow, Watergarden Offices, College Square, The High, Harlow, CM20 1AG T: 01279 427674 F: 01279 444594

Havering, 'Langtons', Billet Lane, Hornchurch, RM11 1XL T: 01708 433481 F: 01708 433413

Redbridge, Queen Victoria House, 794 Cranbrook Road, Barkingside, Ilford, IG6 1JS T: (020) 8708 7160 F: (020) 8708 7161

Southend-on-Sea, Civic Centre, Victoria Avenue, Southend-on-Sea, SS2 6ER T: 01702 534351 F: 01702 612610, This office now covers Southend-on-Sea, Castle Point and Rochford Registration District

Thurrock, The Register Office, 2 Quarry Hill, Grays, RM17 5BT T: 01375 375245 F: 01375 392649

Uttlesford, Council Offices, London Road, Saffron Walden, CB11 4ER T: 01799 510319 F: 01799 510332

Castle Point and Rochford, Civic Centre, Victoria Avenue, Southend-on-Sea, SS2 6ER T: 01702 534351,

Gateshead
Civic Centre, Regent Street, Gateshead, NE8 1HH T: 0191 433 3000, 0191 433 2200 F: 0191 477 9978

Gloucestershire
Cheltenham, The Register Office, St Georges Road, Cheltenham, GL50 3EW T: 01242 532455 F: 01242 254600

Cirencester, Old Memorial Hospital, Sheep Street, Cirencester, GL7 1QW T: 01285 650455 F: 01285 640253

Gloucester, Maitland House, Spa Road, Gloucester, GL1 1UY T: 01452 425275 F: 01452 385385

North Cotswold, North Cotswold Register Office, High Street, Moreton-in-Marsh, GL56 0AZ T: 01608 651230 F: 01608 651226

Stroud, The Register Office, Parliament Street, Stroud, GL5 1DY T: 01453 766049 F: 01453 752961

Forest of Dean, Belle Vue Centre, 6 Belle Vue Road, Cinderford, GL14 2AB T: 01594 822113 F: 01594 826352

Hampshire
Alton, The Register Office, 4 Queens Road, Alton, GU34 1HU T: 01420 85410

Andover, Wessex Chambers, South Street, Andover, SP10 2BN T: 01264 352943, 01264 352513 F: 01264 366849

Hampshire North, Hampshire North Register Office, Goldings, London Road, Basingstoke, RG21 4AN T: 01256 322188 F: 01256 350745

Droxford, Bank House, Bank Street, Bishop's Waltham, SO32 1GP T: 01489 894044

New Forest, Public Offices, 65 Christchurch Road, Ringwood, BH24 1DH T: 01425 470150 F: 01425 471732

North-East Hampshire, The Register Office, 30 Grosvenor Road, Aldershot, GU11 3EB T: 01252 322066 F: 01252 338004

Petersfield, The Old College, College Street, Petersfield, GU31 4AG T: 01730 265372 F: 01730 261050

Romsey, Hayter House, Hayter Gardens, Romsey, SO51 7QU T: 01794 513846 F: 01794 830491

South-East Hampshire, The Register Office, 4-8 Osborn Road South, Fareham, PO16 7DG T: 01329 280493 F: 01329 823184

Winchester, The Register Office, Station Hill, Winchester, SO23 8TJ T: 01962 869608, 01962 869594 F: 01962 851912

Hartlepool
The Register Office, Raby Road, Hartlepool, TS24 8AF T: 01429 236369 F: 01429 236373 E: registrar@hartlepool.gov.uk

Herefordshire
Bromyard, Council Offices, 1 Rowberry Street, Bromyard, Hereford, HR7 4DU T: 01432 260258 F: 01432 260259

Ledbury, Town Council Offices, Church Street, Ledbury, HR8 1DH T: 01531 632306

Hereford, County Offices, Bath Street, Hereford, HR1 2HQ T: 01432 260565 F: 01432 261720, Owing to the large number of sub-districts operational from 1837 to 1935 this office has a preference for genealogical enquiries by post rather than visits in person.

Kington, The Register Office, Old Court House, Market Hall Street, Kington, HR5 3DP T: 01544 230156 F: 01544 231385

Leominster, The Register Office, The Old Priory, Church Street, Leominster, HR6 8EQ T: 01568 610131 F: 01568 614954

Ross, The Old Chapel, Cantilupe Road, Ross on Wye, HR9 7AN T: 01989 562795 F: 01989 564869

Hertfordshire
Bishops Stortford, The Register Office, 2 Hockerill Street, Bishops Stortford, CM23 2DL T: 01279 652273 F: 01279 461492

Broxbourne, Borough Offices, Churchgate, Cheshunt, EN8 9XH T: 01992 623107 F: 01992 627605

Dacorum, The Bury, Queensway, Hemel Hemstead, HP1 1HR T: 01442 228600 F: 01442 243974

Hatfield, The Register Office, 19b St Albans Road East, Hatfield, AL10 0NG T: 01707 283920 F: 01707 283924

Hertford & Ware, County Hall, Pegs Lane, Hertford, SG13 8DE T: 01992 555590 F: 01992 555493

Hitchen & Stevenage, The Register Office, Danesgate, Stevenage, SG1 1WW T: 01438 316579 F: 01438 357197

St Albans, Hertfordshire House, Civic Close, St Albans, AL1 3JZ T: 01727 816806 F: 01727 816804

Watford, The Register Office, 36 Clarendon Road, Watford, WD17 1JQ T: 01923 231302 F: 01923 246852

Hull,
Municipal Offices, 181-191 George Street, Kingston Upon Hull, HU1 3BY T: 01482 615401 F: 01482 615411

Isle of Wight, The Register Office, County Hall, High Street, Newport, PO30 1UD T: 01983 823230 F: 01983 823227

Isles of Scilly, The Register Office, Town Hall, St Marys, TR21 0LW T: 01720 422537,

Kent
Bexley, Manor House, The Green, Sidcup, DA14 6BW T: (020) 8300 4537 F: (020) 8308 4967

Bromley, Room S101, Bromley Civic Centre, Stockwell Close, Bromley, BR1 3UH T: (020) 8313 4666 F: (020) 8313 4699

Kent, The Archbishop's Palace, Palace Gardens, Mill Street, Maidstone, ME15 6YE T: 0845 678 5000, 01622 701922 F: 01622 663690

Medway, Medway Register Office, Ingleside, 114 Maidstone Road, Chatham, ME4 6DJ T: 01634 844073 F: 01634 840165

LB of Camden Camden Register Office, Camden Town Hall, Judd Street, London, WC1H 9JE T: (020) 7974 1900 F: (020) 7974 5792

LB of Croydon, The Register Office, Mint Walk, Croydon, CR10 1EA T: (020) 8760 5617 F: (020) 8760 5633

LB of Barking & Dagenham, Arden House, 198 Longbridge Road, Barking, IG11 8SY T: (020) 8270 4743 F: (020) 8270 4745

LB of Barnet The Register Office, 182 Burnt Oak, Broadway, Edgware, HA8 0AU T: (020) 8731 1100 F: (020) 8731 1111

LB of Brent Brent Town Hall, Forty Lane, Wembley, HA9 9EZ T: (020) 8937 1010 F: (020) 8937 1021

LB of Ealing Ealing Town Hall, New Broadway, Ealing, W5 2BY T: (020) 8825 7272 F:

LB of Enfield Public Offices, Gentlemen's Row, Enfield, EN2 6PS T: (020) 8367 5757 F: (020) 8379 8562

LB of Greenwich The Register Office, Town Hall, Wellington Street, London, SE18 6PW T: (020) 8854 8888 F: (020) 8317 5754

LB of Hackney The Register Office, Town Hall, Mare Street, London, E8 1EA T: (020) 8356 3376 F: (020) 8356 3552

LB of Hammersmith & Fulham Register Office, Fulham Town Hall, Harwood Road, Fulham, London, SW6 1ET T: (020) 8753 2140 F: (020) 8753 2146

LB of Haringey The Register Office, Civic Centre, High Road, Wood Green, London, N22 4LE T: (020) 8489 2605, (020) 8489 2601 F: (020) 8489 2912

LB of Harrow The Civic Centre, Station Road, Harrow, HA1 2UX T: (020) 8424 1618 F: (020) 8424 1414

LB of Hillingdon The Register Office, Hillingdon Civic Centre, Uxbridge, UB8 1UW T: 01895 250418 F: 01895 250678

LB of Hounslow The Register Office, 88 Lampton Road, Hounslow, TW3 4DW T: (020) 8583 2090, (020) 8583 2086 F: (020) 8577 8798

LB of Islington The Register Office, Islington Town Hall, Upper Street, London, N2 2UD T: (020) 7527 6347 F: (020) 7527 6308

LB of Kensington & Chelsea Register Office, Chelsea Old Town Hall, Kings Road, London, SW3 5EE T: (020) 7361 4100 F: (020) 7361 4054

LB of Lambeth The Register Office, 357-361 Brixton Road, Lambeth, London, SW9 7DA T: (020) 7926 9420 F: (020) 7926 9426

LB of Lewisham The Register Office, 368 Lewisham High Street, London, SE13 6LQ T: (020) 8690 2128 F: (020) 8314 1078

LB of Merton Morden Park House, Morden Hall, London Road, Morden, SM4 5QU T: (020) 8648 0414 F: (020) 8648 0433

LB of Newham The Register Office, Passmore Edwards Building, 207 Plashet Grove, East Ham, London, E6 1BT T: (020) 8430 2000, (020) 8430 3616 F: (020) 8430 3127

LB of Richmond upon Thames The Register Office, 1 Spring Terrace, Richmond, TW9 1LW T: (020) 8940 2853 F: (020) 8940 8226

LB of Southwark, Southwark The Register Office, 34 Peckham Road, Southwark, London, SE5 8QA T: (020) 7525 7651 F: (020) 7525 7652

LB of Tower Hamlets The Register Office, Bromley Public Hall, Bow Road, E3 3AA T: (020) 7364 7883 F: (020) 7364 7885, This office holds the records of the former RDS of Stepney, Whitechapel, Bethnal Green, Poplar Mile end of Old Town and St George in the East. Please note records of the former East London RD are held by Islington Register Office.

LB of Waltham Forest The Register Office, 106 Grove Road, Walthamstow, E17 9BY T: (020) 8496 2716 F: (020) 8509 1388

LB of Wandsworth The Register Office, The Town Hall, Wandsworth High Street, London, SW18 2PU T: (020) 8871 6120 F: (020) 8871 8100

LB of Westminster The Register Office, Westminster Council House, Marylebone Road, London, NW1 5PT T: (020) 7641 1161 F: (020) 7641 1246

City of London The Register Office, Islington Town Hall, Upper Street, Islington, London, N1 2UD T: (020) 7527 6347, (020) 7527 6357 F: (020) 7527 6308

Kingston upon Thames The Register Office, 35 Coombe Road, Kingston upon Thames, KT2 7BA T: (020) 8547 4600 F: (020) 8547 6188

Merseyside
Knowsley, District Council Offices, High Street, Prescot, L34 3LH T: 0151 443 5210 F: 0151 443 5216

Lancashire
Blackburn with Darwen, The Register Office, Jubilee Street, Blackburn, BB1 1EP T: 01254 587524 F: 01254 587538

Blackpool , The Register Office, South King Street, Blackpool, FY1 4AX T: 01253 477177 F: 01253 477176

Bolton, The Register Office, Mere Hall, Merehall Street, Bolton, BL1 2QT T: 01204 331186

Burnley and Pendle, The Register Office, 12 Nicholas Street, Burnley, BB11 2AQ T: 01282 436116 F: 01282 412221

Bury, Town Hall, Manchester Road, Bury, BL9 0SW T: 0161 253 6027 F: 0161 253 6028

Chorley, The Register Office, 16 St George's Street, Chorley, PR7 2AA T: 01257 263143 F: 01257 263808

Hyndburn & Rossendale, The Mechanics Institute, Willow Street, Accrington, BB5 1LP T: 01254 871360 F: 01254 871877

Lancaster The Register Office, 4 Queen Street, Lancaster, LA1 1RS T: 01524 65673 F: 01524 842285

Preston and South Ribble, The Register Office, PO Box 24, Bow Lane, Preston, PR1 8SE T: 01772 533800 F: 01772 531012

Ribble Valley, The Register Office, Off Pimlico Road, Clitheroe, BB7 2BW T: 01200 420492 F: 01200 420491

West Lancashire, Greetby Buildings, Derby Street, Ormskirk, L39 2BS T: 01695 585779 F: 01695 585819

Fleetwood and Fylde, The Register Office, South King Street, Blackpool, FY1 4AX T: 01253 477177 F: 01253 477176

Leeds
Belgrave House, Belgrave Street, Leeds, LS2 8DQ T: 0113 224 3604, 0113 247 6707 F: 0113 247 6708

Leicestershire
Leicester, The Register Office, 5 Pocklington's Walk, Leicester, LE1 6BQ T: 0116 253 6326 F: 0116 253 3008

Leicestershire, Leicestershire Register Office, County Hall, Glenfield, Leicester, LE3 8RN T: 0116 265 6585 F: 0116 265 6580, Covering Coalville, Loughborough, Market Harborough, Melton Mowbray, Hinckley, South Wigston

Lincolnshire
The Register Office, 4 Lindum Road, Lincoln, LN2 1NN T: 0845 330 1400 F: 01522 589524

Liverpool
Liverpool Register Office, The Cotton Exchange, Old Hall Street, Liverpool, L3 9UF T: 0151 233 4972 F: 0151 233 4944

Luton
The Register Office, 6 George Street West, Luton, LU1 2BJ T: 01582 722603 F: 01582 429522

Manchester
Heron House, 47 Lloyd Street, Manchester, M2 5LE T: 0161 234 5502 F: 0161 234 7888, E: , register-office@manchester.gov.uk

Middlesbrough
The Register Office, Corporation Road, Middlesbrough, TS1 2DA T: 01642 262078 F: 01642 262091

Milton Keynes
Bracknell House, Aylesbury Street, Bletchley, MK2 2BE T: 01908 372101 F: 01908 645103

Newcastle-upon-Tyne
Civic Centre, Barras Bridge, Newcastle-upon-Tyne, NE1 8PS T: 0191 232 8520 F: 0191 211 4970

Norfolk
Depwade, Council Offices, 11-12 Market Hill, Diss, IP22 3JX T: 01379 643915

Downham, The Register Office, 15 Paradise Road, Downham Market, PE38 9HS T: 01366 387104

East Dereham, The Breckland Business Centre, St Withburga Lane, Dereham, NR19 1FD T: 01362 698021,

Fakenham, The Register Office, Fakenham Connect, Oak Street, Fakenham, NR21 9SR T: 01328 850122 F: 01328 850150

Great Yarmouth, 'Ferryside', High Road, Southtown, Great Yarmouth, NR31 0PH T: 01493 662313 F: 01493 602107

King's Lynn, St Margaret's House, St Margaret's Place, King's Lynn, PE30 5DW T: 01553 669251 F: 01553 769942

North Walsham, The Register Office, 18 Kings Arms Street, North Walsham, NR28 9JX T: 01692 406220 F: 01692 406220

Norwich, Churchman House, 71 Bethel Street, Norwich, NR2 1NR T: 01603 767600 F: 01603 632677

Wayland, Kings House, Kings Street, Thetford, IP24 2AP T: 01842 766848 F: 01842 765996

North-East Lincolnshire
The Register Office, Town Hall Square, Grimsby, DN31 1HX T: 01472 324860 F: 01472 324867

North Lincolnshire
Register Office, 92 Oswald Road, Scunthorpe, DN15 7PA T: 01724 843915 F: 01724 872668

North Somerset
The Register Office, 41 The Boulevard, Weston-super-Mare, BS23 1PG T: 01934 627552 F: 01934 412014

North Tyneside
Maritime Chambers, 1 Howard Street, North Shields, NE30 1LZ T: 0191 200 6164,

Nothamptonshire
Corby, The Old Stables, Cottingham Road, Corby, NN17 1TD T: 01536 203141,

Daventry, Council Offices, Lodge Road, Daventry, NN11 5AF T: 01327 302209 F: 01327 300011

Kettering, The Register Office, 10 London Road, Kettering, NN15 7QU T: 01536 514792 F: 01536 526948

Northampton, The Guildhall, St Giles Square, Northampton, NN1 1DE T: 01604 745390 F: 01604 745399

Towcester & Brackley, Sunnybanks, 55 Brackley Road, Towcester, NN12 6DH T: 01327 350774

Wellingborough, Council Offices, Swanspool House, Wellingborough, NN8 1BP T: 01933 231549,

Northumberland
Northumberland Central, The Register Office, 94 Newgate Street, Morpeth, NE61 1BU T: 01670 513232 F: 01670 519260

Northumberland North First, The Register Office, 5 Palace Street East, Berwick upon Tweed, TD15 1HT T: 01289 307373

Northumberland North Second, The Register Office, 6 Market Place, Alnwick, NE66 1HP T: 01665 602363 F: 01665 510079

Northumberland West, Abbey Gate House, Market Street, Hexham, NE46 3LX T: 01434 602355, 01434 602605 F: 01434 604957

Nottinghamshire
Basford, The Register Office, Highbury Road, Bulwell, NG6 9DA T: 0115 927 1294 F: 0115 977 1845

East Retford, Notts County Council Offices, Chancery Lane, Retford, DN22 6DG T: 01777 708631 F: 01777 860667

Mansfield, Registry Office, Dale Close, 100 Chesterfield Road South, Mansfield, NG19 7DN T: 01623 476564 F: 01623 636284

Newark, County Offices, Balderton Gate, Newark, NG24 1UW T: 01636 705455 F: 01636 679259

Nottingham, The Register Office, 50 Shakespeare Street, Nottingham, NG1 4FP T: 0115 947 5665 F: 0115 941 5773
Rushcliffe, The Hall, Bridgford Road, West Bridgford, NG2 6AQ T: 0115 981 5307 F: 0115 969 6189
Worksop, Queens Buildings, Potter Street, Worksop, S80 2AH T: 01909 535534 F: 01909 501067
Oldham
Metropolitan House, Hobson St, Oldham, OL1 1PY T: 0161 678 0137
Oxford
Register Office, Tidmarsh Lane, Oxford, OX1 1NS T: 01865 816246
Poole
The Register Office, Civic Centre Annexe, Park Road, Poole, BH15 2RN T: 01202 633744 F: 01202 633725
Portsmouth
The Register Office, Milldam House, Burnaby Road, Portsmouth, PO1 3AF T: (023) 9282 9041, (023) 9282 9042 F: (023) 9283 1996
Redcar and Cleveland
The Register Office, Westgate, Guisborough, TS14 6AP T: 01287 632564 F: 01287 630768
Rochdale
Town Hall, The Esplanade, Rochdale, OL16 1AB T: 01706 864779 F: 01706 864786
Rutland
Catmose, Oakham, LE15 6JU T: 01572 758370 F: 01572 758371
Salford
'Kingslea', Barton Road, Swinton, M27 5WH T: 0161 909 6501 F: 0161 794 4797
Sefton
Sefton North, Town Hall, Corporation Street, Southport, PR8 1DA T: 01704 533133 F: 0151 934 2014
Sefton South, Crosby Town Hall, Great Georges Road, Waterloo, Liverpool, L22 1RB T: 0151 934 3045 F: 0151 934 3056
Sheffield
The Register Office, Surrey Place, Sheffield, S1 1YA T: 0114 203 9423 F: 0114 203 9424
Shropshire
Bridgnorth, The Register Office, 12 West Castle Street, Bridgnorth, WV16 4AB T: 01746 762589 F: 01746 764270
Clun, The Pines, Colebatch Road, Bishop's Castle, SY9 5JY T: 01588 638588
Ludlow, The Register Office, Stone House, Corve Street, Ludlow, SY8 1DG T: 01584 813208 F: 01584 813122
North Shropshire, Edinburgh House, New Street, Wem, Shrewsbury, SY4 5DB T: 01939 238418
Oswestry, The Register Office, Holbache Road, Oswestry, SY11 1AH T: 01691 652086
Shrewsbury, The Register Office, Column Lodge, Preston Street, Shrewsbury, SY2 5NY T: 01743 252925 F: 01743 252939
Telford and Wrekin, The Beeches, 29 Vineyard Road, Wellinton, Telford, TF1 1HB T: 01952 248292 F: 01952 240976
Solihull
The Register Office, Homer Road, Solihull, B91 3QZ T: 0121 704 6100 F: 0121 704 6123
Somerset
Mendip The Register Office, 19b Commercial Road, Shepton Mallet, BA4 5BU T: 01749 343928 F: 01749 342324
Sedgemoor, Morgan House, Mount Street, Bridgewater, TA6 3ER T: 01278 422527 F: 01278 452670
Taunton, Flook House, Belvedere Road, Taunton, TA1 1BT T: 01823 282251 F: 01823 351173
West Somerset, 2 Long Street, Williton, Taunton, TA4 4QN T: 01984 633116
Yeovil, Maltravers House, Petters Way, Yeovil, BA20 1SP T: 01935 411230 F: 01935 413993
South Gloucestershire
Poole Court, Poole Court Drive, Yate, BS37 5PT T: 01454 863140 F: 01454 863145
South Tyneside
The Register Office, 18 Barrington Street, South Shields, NE33 1AH T: 0191 455 3915 F: 0191 427 7564, Records from Jarrow on abolition 2001 transferred here
Southampton
The Register Office, 6A Bugle Street, Southampton, SO14 2LX T: (023) 8063 1422 F: (023) 8063 3431, Visa, Switch, etc are accepted. Marriage indexes are computerised from 1837 - 1900 and some others. Births and deaths computerised from 1988.
St Helens
The Register Office, Central Street, St Helens, WA10 1UJ T: 01744 23524, 01744 732012 F: 01744 23524
Staffordshire
Cannock Chase, The Register Office, 5 Victoria Street, Cannock, WS11 1AG T: 01543 512345 F: 01543 512347
East Staffordshire, Rangemore House, 22 Rangemore Street, Burton-upon-Trent, DE14 2ED T: 01283 538701 F: 01283 547338
Lichfield, The Old Library Buildings, Bird Street, Lichfield, WS13 6PN T: 01543 510771 F: 01543 510773
Newcastle-under-Lyme, The Register Office, 20 Sidmouth Avenue, The Brampton, Newcastle-under-Lyme, ST5 0QN T: 01782 297581

F: 01782 297582 Wolstanton Registration District is split between Newcastle-under-Lyme and Stoke-on-Trent Register Offices.
South Staffordshire, Civic Centre, Gravel Hill, Wombourne, Wolverhampton, WV5 9HA T: 01902 895829 F: 01902 326779
Stafford, Eastgate House, 79 Eastgate Street, Stafford, ST16 2NG T: 01785 277880 F: 01785 277884
Staffordshire Moorlands, The Register Office, High Street, Leek, ST13 5EA T: 01538 373166 F: 01538 386985
Stockport
Town Hall - John Street Entrance, Stockport, SK1 3XE T: 0161 474 3399 F: 0161 474 3390
Stockton-on-Tees
Nightingale House, Balaclava Street, Stockton-on-Tees, TS18 2AL T: 01642 393156 F: 01642 393159
Tel no is a direct line for family history enquiries,
Stoke-on-Trent
Town Hall, Albion Street, Hanley, Stoke on Trent, ST1 1QQ T: 01782 235260 F: 01782 235258
Suffolk
Bury St. Edmunds, St Margarets, Shire Hall, Bury St Edmunds, IP33 1RX T: 01284 352373 F: 01284 352376
Deben, Council Offices, Melton Hill, Woodbridge, IP12 1AU T: 01394 444331
Gipping & Hartismere, Milton House, 3 Milton Road South, Stowmarket, IP14 1EZ T: 01449 612054
Ipswich, St Peter House, County Hall, 16 Grimwade Street, Ipswich, IP4 1LP T: 01473 583050 F: 01473 584331
Sudbury, The Register Office, 14 Cornard Road, Sudbury, CO10 2XA T: 01787 372904
Waveney, St Margarets House, Gordon Road, Lowestoft, NR32 1JQ T: 01502 405325 F: 01502 508170
Sunderland
Town Hall & Civic Centre, PO Box 108, Sunderland, SR2 7DN T: 0191 553 1768 F: 0191 553 1762
Surrey
East Surrey, East Surrey Register Office, The Mansion, 70 Church Street, Leatherhead, KT22 8DP T: 01372 832815, , This Office now deals with all enquiries for the Reigate Office which closed in 2000
North Surrey, 'Rylston', 81 Oatlands Drive, Weybridge, KT13 9LN T: 01932 794700 F: 01932 794701
West Surrey, Artington House, Portsmouth Road, Guildford, GU2 4DZ T: 01483 562841 F: 01483 573232
Sutton, Russettings, 25 Worcester Road, Sutton, SM2 6PR T: (020) 8770 6790 F: (020) 8770 6772
East Sussex
Eastbourne, Town Hall, Grove Road, Eastbourne, BN21 4UG T: 01323 415051 F: 01323 431386
Crowborough, Beaconwood, Beacon Road, Crowborough, TN6 1AR T: 01892 653803 F: 01892 669884
Swindon
1st Floor, Aspen House, Temple Street, Swindon, SN1 1SQ T: 01793 521734 F: 01793 433887
Tameside
Education & Development centre, Lakes Road, Dukinfield, SK16 4TR T: 0161 330 1177
Trafford
Sale Town Hall, School Road, Sale, M33 7ZF T: 0161 912 3025 F: 0161 912 3031
Warwickshire
Mid Warwickshire, Pageant House, 2 Jury Street, Warwick, CV34 4EW T: 01926 494269 F: 01926 496287
North Warwickshire, Warwick House, Ratcliffe Street, Atherstone, CV9 1JP T: 01827 713241 F: 01827 720467
Nuneaton and Bedworth, Riversley Park, Coton Road, Nuneaton, CV11 5HA T: (024) 7634 8944, (024) 7634 8948 F: (024) 7635 0988
Rugby, The Register Office, 5 Bloxam Place, Rugby, CV21 3DS T: 01788 571233 F: 01788 542024
South Warwickshire, The Register Office, 7 Rother Street, Stratford-on-Avon, CV37 6LU T: 01789 293711 F: 01789 261423
West Sussex
Crawley, Town Hall, The Boulevard, Crawley, RH10 1UZ T: 01293 438341 F: 01293 526454
Haywards Heath, West Sussex County Council Offices, Oaklands Road, Haywards Heath, RH16 1SU T: 01444 452157 F: 01444 410128
Horsham, Town Hall, Market Square, Horsham, RH12 1EU T: 01403 265368 F: 01403 217078
Worthing, Centenary House, Durrington Lane, Worthing, BN13 2QB T: 01903 839350 F: 01903 839356
Chichester, Greyfriars, 61 North Street, Chichester, PO19 1NB T: 01243 782307 F: 01243 773671
West Midlands
Sandwell, Highfields, High Street, Sandwell, B70 8RJ T: 0121 569 2480 F: 0121 569 2473
Walsall, The Register Office, Civic Centre, Hatherton Road, Walsall, WS1 1TN T: 01922 652260 F: 01922 652262
Wigan & Leigh
New Town Hall, Library Street, Wigan, WN1 1NN T: 01942 705000

Wiltshire
Chippenham, The Register Office, 4 Timber Street, Chippenham, SN15 3BZ T: 01249 654361 F: 01249 658850
Devizes & Marlborough, Browfort, Bath Road, Devizes, SN10 2AT T: 01380 722162
Salisbury, The Laburnums, 50 Bedwin Street, Salisbury, SP1 3UW T: 01722 335340 F: 01722 326806
Trowbridge, East Wing Block, County Hall, Trowbridge, BA14 8EZ T: 01225 713000 F: 01225 713096
Warminster, The Register Office, 3 The Avenue, Warminster, BA12 9AB T: 01985 213435 F: 01985 217688
Wirral
Town Hall, Mortimer Street, Birkenhead, L41 5EU T: 0151 666 4096 F: 0151 666 3685, This office now holds the records formerly held at the Wallasey office, which has been closed and amalgamated with Birkenhead. Registration District now named "Wirral"
Wolverhampton
Civic Centre, St Peters Square, Wolverhampton, WV1 1RU T: 01902 554989 F: 01902 554987
Worcestershire
Bromsgrove, The Register Office, School Drive, Bromsgrove, B60 1AY T: 01527 578759 F: 01527 578750
Droitwich, Council Offices, Ombersley Street East, Droitwich, WR9 8QX T: 01905 772280
Evesham, County Offices, Swan Lane, Evesham, WR11 4TZ T: 01386 443945 F: 01386 448745
Pershore, Civic Centre, Queen Elizabeth Drive, Station Road, Pershore, WR10 1PT T: 01386 565610 F: 01386 553656
Kidderminster, Council Offices, Bewdley Road, Kidderminster, DY11 6RL T: 01562 829100 F: 01562 60192
Malvern, Hatherton Lodge, Avenue Road, Malvern, WR14 3AG T: 01684 573000 F: 01684 892378
Redditch, The Register Office, 29 Easmore Road, Redditch, B98 8ER T: 01527 60647 F: 01527 584561
Tenbury, Council Buildings, Teme Street, Tenbury Wells, WR15 8BA T: 01584 810588 F: 01584 819733
Worcester, The Register Office, 29-30 Foregate Street, Worcester, WR1 1DS T: 01905 765350 F: 01905 765355
Yorkshire
York, The Register Office, 56 Bootham, York, YO30 7DA T: 01904 654477 F: 01904 638090
Yorkshire East
East Riding of Yorkshire, The Register Office, Walkergate House, Walkergate, Beverley, HU17 9EJ T: 01482 393600 F: 01482 873414
Yorkshire North
North Yorkshire Registration Service - North Yorkshire (Headquarters), Bilton House, 31 Park Parade, Harrogate, HG1 5AG T: 01423 506949 F: 01423 502105, Holds all historical records for the County of North Yorkshire (except the City of York)
Yorkshire South
Barnsley, Town Hall, Church Street, Barnsley, S70 2TA T: 01226 773085, 01226 773080,
Rotherham, Bailey House, Rawmarsh Road, Rotherham, S60 1TX T: 01709 382121 F: 01709 375530
Yorkshire West
Bradford, The Register Office, 22 Manor Row, Bradford, BD1 4QR T: 01274 432151
Calderdale, The Register Office, 4 Carlton Street, Halifax, HX1 2AH T: 01422 353993 F: 01422 253370
Dewsbury, The Register Office, Wellington Street, Dewsbury, WF13 1LY T: 01924 324880
Huddersfield, Civic Centre, 11 High Street, Huddersfield, HD1 2PL T: 01484 221030 F: 01484 221315
Keighley, Town Hall, Bow Street, Keighley, BD21 3PA T: 01535 618060 F: 01535 618208
Pontefract, The Register Office, Town Hall, Pontefract, WF8 1PG T: 01977 722670 F: 01977 722676
Wakefield, The Register Office, 71 Northgate, Wakefield, WF1 3BS T: 01924 302185 F: 01924 302186
Wales
Anglesey
Ynys Môn, Shire Hall, Glanhwfa Road, Llangefni, LL77 7TW T: 01248 752564
Caerphilly, The Council Offices, Ystrad Fawr, Caerphilly Road, Ystrad Mynach, Hengoed, CF82 7SF T: 01443 863478 F: 01443 863385
Cardiff, The Register Office, 48 Park Place, Cardiff, CF10 3LU T: (029) 2087 1690, (029) 2087 1680 F: (029) 2087 1691
Carmarthenshire
Carmarthen, Carmarthen Register Office, Parc Myrddin, Richmond Terrace, Carmarthen, SA31 1DS T: 01267 228210, 01267 228212 F: 01267 228215
Llanelli, Llanelli Register office, 2 Coleshill Terrace, Llanelli, SA15 3DB T: 01554 744202 F: 01554 749424
Ceredigion
Cardiganshire Central, The Register Office, 21 High Street, Lampeter, SA48 7BG T: 01570 422558 F: 01570 422558

Cardiganshire North, Swyddfar Sir, Marine Terrace, Aberystwyth, SY23 2DE T: 01970 633580
Cardiganshire South, Glyncoed Chambers, Priory Street, Cardigan, SA43 1BX T: 01239 612684 F: 01239 612684
Conwy
Colwyn, New Clinic and Offices, 67 Market Street, Abergele, LL22 7BP T: 01745 823976
Denbighshire
Denbighshire North, Morfa Hall, Church Street, Rhyl, LL18 3AA T: 01824 708368 F: 01745 361424
Denbighshire South, The Register Office, Station Road, Ruthin, LL15 1BS T: 01824 703782 F: 01824 704399
Flintshire
Flintshire East, The Old Rectory, Rectory Lane, Hawarden, CH5 3NN T: 01244 531512 F: 01244 534628
Flintshire West, The Register Office, Park Lane, Holywell, CH8 7UR T: 01352 711813 F: 01352 713292
Glamorgan
Bridgend, County Borough Offices, Sunnyside, Bridgend, CF31 4AR T: 01656 642391 F: 01656 667529
Merthyr Tydfil, The Register Office, Ground Floor, Castle House, Glebeland Street, Merthyr Tydfil, CF47 8AT T: 01685 723318 F: 01685 721849
Vale of Glamorgan, The Register Office, 2-6 Holton Road, Barry, CF63 4RU T: 01446 709490 F: 01446 709502
Gwent
Blaenau Gwent (Abertilley), Council Offices, Mitre Street, Abertilley, NP3 1AE T: 01495 216082
Blaenau Gwent (Ebbw Vale & Tredegar), The Grove, Church Street, Tredegar, NP2 3DS T: 01495 722769
Newport, The Register Office, 8 Gold Tops, Newport, NP20 4PH T: 01633 265547 F: 01633 220913
Gwynedd
Aberconwy, The Library, Mostyn Street, Llandudno, LL30 2RP T: 01492 574045
Ardudwy, Bryn Marian, Church Street, Blaenau Ffestiniog, LL41 3HD T: 01766 830217
Bangor, The Register Office, Town Hall, Bangor, LL57 2RE T: 01248 362418
Caernarfon, Swyddfa Arfon, Pennrallt, Caernarfon, LL55 1BN T: 01286 682661
De Meirionndd, Meirionnydd Area Office, Cae Penarlag, Dolgellau, LL40 2YB T: 01341 424341
Dwyfor, The Register Office, 35 High Street, Pwllheli, LL53 5RT T: 01758 612546 F: 01758 701373
Penllyn, Penllyn Register Office, Fron Faire, High Street, Bala, LL23 7AD T: 01678 521220, 01678 520893 F: 01678 521243
Monmouthshire
Monmouth, Coed Glas, Firs Road, Abergavenny, NP7 5LE T: 01873 735435 F: 01837 735429
Neath Port Talbot, The Register Office, 119 London Road, Neath, Port Talbot, SA11 1HL T: 01639 760020 F: 01639 760023
Pembrokeshire
Pembrokeshire, The Register Office, Tower Hill, Haverfordwest, SA61 1SS T: 01437 775176 F: 01437 779357
Powys
Brecknock Neuadd Brycheiniog, Cambrian Way, Brecon, LD3 7HR T: 01874 624334 F: 01874 625781
Hay The Borough Council Offices, Broad Street, Hay-on-Wye, HR3 5BX T: 01497 821371 F: 01497 821540
Machynlleth, The Register Office, 11 Penrallt Street, Machynlleth, SY20 8AG T: 01654 702335 F: 01654 703742
Mid Powys, Powys County Hall, Llandrindod Wells, LD1 5LG T: 01597 826020
Newtown, Council Offices, The Park, Newtown, SY16 2NZ T: 01686 627862
Radnorshire East, The Register Office, 2 Station Road, Knighton, LD7 1DU T: 01547 520758
Welshpool & Llanfyllllin, Neuadd Maldwyn, Severn Road, Welshpool, SY21 7AS T: 01938 552828 Ext 228 F: 01938 551233
Ystradgynlais
County Council Offices, Trawsffordd, Ystradgynlais, SA9 1BS T: 01639 843104
Rhondda Cynon Taf
The Register Office, Courthouse Street, Pontypridd, CF37 1LJ T: 01443 486869 F: 01443 406587
Swansea
The Swansea Register Office, County Hall, Swansea, SA1 3SN T: 01792 636188 F: 01792 636909
Torfaen
The Register Office, Hanbury Road, Pontypool, NP4 6YG T: 01495 762937 F: 01495 769049
Wrexham
Ty Dewi Sant, Rhosddu Road, Wrexham, LL11 1NF T: 01978 292670 F: 01978 292676

Isle of Man
Civil Registry Registries Building Deemster's Walk Bucks Road Douglas IM1 3AR T: 01624-687039 Fax: 01624-687004 E: civil@registry.gov.im
Channel Islands
Guernsey
Greffe Royal Court House St Peter Port GY1 2PB T: 01481 725277 Fax: 01481 715097
Jersey
Judicial Greffe Morier House Halkett Place St Helier JE1 1DD T: 01534-502300 Fax: 01534-502399/502390 E: jgreffe@super.net.uk W: www.jersey.gov.uk
Northern Ireland
General Register Office of Northern Ireland Oxford House 49 - 55 Chichester Street Belfast BT1 4HL Northern Ireland T: (028) 90 252000 Fax: (028) 90 252120 E: gro.nisra@dfpni.gov.uk W: www.groni.gov.uk

Scotland
Aberdeen, St Nicholas House, Upperkirkgate, Aberdeen, AB10 1EY T: 01224 522616 F: 01224 522616 E: registrars@legal.aberdeen.net.uk
Aberdeen City Council
Peterculter, Lilydale, 102 North Deeside Road, Peterculter, AB14 0QB T: 01224 732648 F: 01224 734637
Aberdeenshire
Braemar, The Braemar Royal Highland So, Hillside Road, Braemar, AB35 5YU T: 01339 741349
Inverurie, Oldmeldrum, Skere and Echt, Gordon House, Blackhall Road, Inverurie, AB51 3WA T: 01467 620981 F: 01467 628012 E: diane.minty@aberdeenshire.gov.uk incorporating Inverurie (319) Oldmeldrum(320) , Skere and Echt (323)
Maud, County Offices, Nethermuir Road, Maud, AB42 4ND T: 01771 613667 F: 01771 613204 E: maureen.stephen@aberdeenshire.gov.uk
Peterhead, Arbuthnot House, Broad Street, Peterhead, AB42 1DA T: 01779 483244 F: 01779 483246 E: shirley.dickie@aberdeenshire.gov.uk
Stonehaven, East Kinkardine & Inverbervie, Viewmount, Arduthie Road, Stonehaven, AB39 2DQ T: 01569 768360 F: 01569 765455 E: cressida.coates@aberdeenshire.gov.uk Incorporates Inverbervie (343)
Strathdon, Arca Office, School Road, Alford, AB33 8PY T: 01975 564811
Tarves, Area Office, Schoolhill Road, Ellon, AB41 7PQ T: 01358 720295 F: 01358 726410 E: kathleen.stopani@aberdeenshire.gov.uk
Turriff, Towie House, Manse Road, Turriff, AB53 4AY T: 01888 562427 F: 01888 568559 E: sheila.donald@aberdeenshire.gov.uk
Skere and Echt, Operating from Inverurie Inverurie, AB32 6XX T: 01467 628011 (Direct) E: diane.minty@aberdeenshire.gov.uk incorporating Inverurie (319) Oldmeldrum(320) , Skere and Echt (323)
Aberfoyle & Mentheith, Aberfoyle Local Office, Main Street, Aberfoyle, FK8 3UQ T: 01877 382986
Aboyne and Torphins, District Council Offices, Bellwood Road, Aboyne, AB34 5HQ T: 01339 886109 F: 01339 86798 E: esther.halkett@aberdeenshire.gov.uk
Alford, Sauchen and Strathdo, Council Office, School Road, Alford, AB33 8PY T: 01975 562421 F: 01975 563286 E: anne.shaw@aberdeenshire.gov.uk incorporating Sauchen (327)
Arbroath, The Register Office, 69/71 High Street, Arbroath, DD11 1AN T: 01241 873752 F: 01241 874805 E: macpherson@angus.gov.uk
Ardgour, The Register Office, 9 Clovullin, Ardgour, by Fort William, PH33 7AB T: 01855 841261
Argyle and Bute
Rosneath, Registration Office, Easter Garth, Rosneath, by Helensburgh, G84 0RF T: 01436 831679 E: elsa.rossetter@eastergarth.co.uk W: www.eastergarth.co.uk
Dunoon, Council Offices, Hill Street, Dunoon, PA23 7AP T: 01369 704374 F: 01369 705948 E: ann.saidler@argyll-bute.gov.uk
Lismore, Baleveolan Isle of Lismore, PA34 5UG T: 01631 760274
Campbeltown, Council Office, Dell Road, Campbeltown, PA28 6JG T: 01586 552366 F: 01586 552366 E: isabella.soudan@argyll-bute.gov.uk W: www.argyll-bute.gov.uk
Kilbrandon and Kilchattan, Dalanasaig, Clachan Seil, By Oban, PA34 4TJ T: 01852 300380
South Cowal, Copeswood, Auchenlochan High Road, Tighnabruaich, PA21 2BE T: 01700 811601
Strachur, Crosshaig Strachur, PA27 8BY T: 01369 860203
Strontian, Easgadail, Longrigg Road, Strontian Acharacle, PH36 4HY T: 01967 402037
Tobermory, County Buldings, Breadalbane Street, Tobermory, PA75 6PX T: 01688 302051 E: iainmackinnon03@argyll.bute.gov.uk
Arrochar, The Register Office, 1 Cobbler View, Arrochar, G83 7AD T: 01301 702289
Assynt, Post Office House, Lochinver, Lochinver by Lairg, IV27 4JY T: 01571 844201
Auchinleck, The Register Office, 28 Well Road, Auchlinleck,

Cummock, KA18 2LA T: 01290 420582
Auchterarder, The Ayton Hall, 91 High Street, Auchterarder, PH3 1BJ T: 01764 662155 F: 01764 662120 E: mmellis@pkc.gov.uk
Aviemore, Tremayne, Dalfaber Road, Aviemore, PH22 1PU T: 01479 810694
Ayr
Ayr, Sandgate House, 43 Sandgate, Ayr, KA7 1DA T: 01292 284988 E: ayr.registrars@south-ayrshire.gov.uk
Ballater, An Creagan, 5 Queens Road., Ballater, AB35 5NJ T: 01339 755535
Banchory, Aberdeenshire Council, The Square, High Street, Banchory, AB31 5RW T: 01330 822878 F: 01330 822243 E: christine.handsley@aberdeenshire.gov.uk
Banff, Seafield House, 37 Castle Street, Banff, AB45 1DQ T: 01261 813439 E: kate.samuel@aderdeenshire.gov.uk
Barra, Council Offices, Castlebay, Barra, HS9 5XD T: 01871 810431
Barrhead, Council Office, 13 Lowndes Street, Barrhead, G78 2QX T: 0141 577 35551 E: mcquadem@eastrenfrewshire.gov.uk
Beauly Operates from Inverness E: kathleen.chisholm@highland.gov.uk
Bellshill, The Register Office, 20/22 Motherwelt Road, Bellshill, ML4 1RB T: 01698 346780 F: 016989 346789 E: registrars-bellshill@nothlan.gov.uk
Benbecula, Council Offices, Balivanich, Benbecula, South Uist, HS7 5LA T: 01870 602425
Biggar, The Register Office, 4 Ross Square, Biggar, ML12 6DH T: 01899 220997
Bishopbriggs, Council Offices, The Triangle, Kirkintilloch Road, Bishopbriggs, G64 2TR T: 0141 578 8557 E: mary.neill@eastdunbarton.gov.uk
Black Isle, Black Isles Leisure Centre, Deans Road, Fortrose, IV10 8TJ T: 01381 620797 F: 01381 621085 E: marion.phimister@highland.gov.uk
Blairgowrie, Council Buildings, 46 Leslie Street, Blairgowrie, PH10 6AW T: 01250 872051 F: 01250 876029
Bo'ness and Carriden, Registration Office, 15a Seaview Place, Bo'ness, EH51 0AJ T: 01506 778992
Boisdale, Post Office House, Daliburgh, South Uist, HS8 5SS T: 01878 700300
Bonar and Kincardine, Post Office, Bonar Bridge, Ardgay, IV24 3EA T: 01863 766219
Bonnybridge, Operating from Denny T: 01324-504280
Brechin, Contact Arbroath
Bressay, The Register Office, No 2 Roadside Bressay, Lerwick, ZE2 9EL T: 01595 820356
Broadford, The Register Office, Fairwinds, Broadford, IV49 9AB T: 01471 822270
Buckie, Town House West, Cluny Place, Buckie, AB56 1HB T: 01542 832691 F: 01542 833384 E: Jill.addison@chief.moray.gov.uk
Bucksburn, Area Office, 23 Inverurie Road, Bucksburn, AB21 9LJ T: 01224 712866 F: 01224 716997
Carnoch, Operating from Dingwall, IV15 9QR T: 01349 863113
Carnoustie, Council Chambers, 26 High Street, Carnoustie, DD7 6AP T: 01241 853335/6 F: 01241 857554
Castle Douglas, District Council, 5 St Andrew Street, Castle Douglas, DG7 1DE T: 01557 330291 E: ruthpe@dumgal.gov.uk
Castleton, Castleton, 10 Douglas Square, Newcastleton, TD9 0QD T: 01387 375606 E: maaitchison@scotborders.gsx.gov.uk
Chryston, The Register Office, Lindsaybeg Road, Muirhead, Glasgow, G69 9DW T: 0141 779 1714
Clackmannanshire
Clackmannanshire, Marshill House, Marshill, Alloa, FK10 1AB T: 01259 723850 F: 01259 723850 E: registration@clacks.gov.uk,
Clyne, Brora Service Point, Gower Street, Brora, KW9 6PD T: 01408 622644 E: margaret.mackintosh@highland.gov.uk
Coalburn, Pretoria, 200 Coalburn Road, Coalburn, ML11 0LT T: 01555 820664
Coigach, 29 Market Street Ullapool, IV26 2XE T: 01854 612426
Coldstream, 73 High Street, Coldstream, TD12 4AE T: 01890 883156 E: sbrodie@scotborders.gsx.gov.uk
Coll, The Register Office, 9 Carnan Road, Isle of Coll, PA78 6TA T: 01879 230329
Colonsay & Oronsay, Colonsay Service Point, Village Hall, Colonsay, PA61 7YW T: 01951 200263
Comhaire Nan Eilean Siar
Stornoway and South Lochs, Town Hall, 2 Cromwell Street, Stornoway, HS1 2DB T: 01851 709438 F: 01851 709438 E: emacdonald@cne-siar.gov.uk W: www.cne-siar.gov.uk/w-isles/registrars
Coupar-Angus, Union Bank Buildings Coupar Angus, PH13 9AJ T: 01828 628395 F: 01828 627147 E: legalservices@wandlb.co.uk
Crawford, Raggengill, 45 Carlisle Road, Crawford, Biggar, ML12 6TP T: 01864 502633
Crieff, Crieff Area Office, 32 James Square, Crieff, PH7 3EY T: 01764 657550 F: 01764 657559
Cumbernauld, Council Offices, Bron Way, Cumbernauld, G67 1DZ T: 01236 616390 F: 01236 616386

Dalbeattie, Town Hall Buildings, Water Street, Dalbeattie, DG5 4JX T: 01557 330291 Ext 323

Dalmellington, Dalmellington Area Centre, 33 Main Street, Dalmellington, KA6 7QL T: 01292 552 880 F: 01292 552 884

Dalry, 42 Main Street, Dalry, Castle Douglas, DG7 3UW T: 01644 430310

Delting, Soibakkan Mossbank, ZE2 9RB T: 01806 242209

Denny, Carronbank House, Carronbank Crescent, Denny, FK4 6GA T: 01324 504280 E: fiona.mitchell@falkirk.gov.uk

Dornoch, Service Point Office, The Meadows, Dornoch, IV25 3SG T: 01862 812008 E: lesley.conner@highland.gov.uk

Douglas, Post Office, Ayr Road, Douglas, ML11 0PU T: 01555 851227

Dumbarton, 18 College Street Dumbarton, G82 1NR T: 01389 738350 F: 01389 738352 E: tony.gallagher@west-dunbarton.gov.uk

Dumfries
Municipal Chambers, Buccleuch Street, Dumfries, DG1 2AD T: 01387 245906 F: 01387 269605 E: isabeld@dumgal.gov.uk incorporating New Abbey (861)

Dumfries and Galloway
Annan, Council Offices, 15 Ednay Street, Annan, DG12 6EF T: 01461 204914 F: 01461 206896 E: shirleymo@dungal.gov.uk

Gretna, Registration Office, Central Avenue, Gretna, DG16 5AQ T: 01461 337648 F: 01461 338459 E: gretnaonline@dumgal.gov.uk W: www.gretnaonline.net, CC accepted

Kirkcudbright, District Council Offices, Daar Road, Kirkcudbrigbt, DG6 4JG T: 01557 332534 W: www.dumgal.gov.uk

Lockerbie, Town Hall, High Street, Lockerbie, DG11 2ES T: 01576 204267 E: janeta@dumgal.gov.uk

Moffat, Town Hall, High Street, Moffat, DG10 9HF T: 01683 220536 F: 01683 221489

Stranraer Area, The Register Office, Council Offices, Sun Street, Stranraer, DG9 7JJ T: 01776 888439 E: murielc@dumgal.gov.uk

Thornhill, One Stop Shop, Manse Road, Thornhill, DG3 5DR T: 01848 330303 E: margaretbr@dumgal.gov.uk

Wigtown Area, Council Sub-office, County Buildings, Wigtown, DG8 9JH T: 01988 402624 F: 01988 403201 E: marm@dumgal.gov.uk

Whithorn Area, The Register Office, 75 George Street, Whithorn, DG8 8NU T: 01988 500458 E: archietaylor@supanet.com

Dundee
Dundee City Council - Genealogy Unit, 89 Commercial Street, Dundee, DD1 2AF T: 01382-435222 F: 01382-435224 E: grant.law@dundeecity.gov.uk W: www.dundeecity.gov.uk/registrars

Dunrossness, Baptist Manse Dunrossness, ZE2 9JB T: 01950 460792

Duns, The Register Office, 8 Newtown Street, Duns, TD11 3DT T: 01361 882600

Durness, Service Point, Highlands of Scotland Tourist Board, Sangomore, Durness, IV27 4PZ T: 01971 511368 E: sheila.mather@highland.gov.uk

East Ayrshire
Catrine, The Register Office, 9 Co-operative Avenue, Catrine, KA5 6SG T: 01290 551638

Darvel, Galston, Newmilns, The Register Office, 11 Cross Street, Galston, KA4 8AA T: 01563 820218

Kilmarnock, Civic Centre, John Dickie Street, Kilmarnock, KA1 1HW T: 01563 576695/6 E: cathy.dunlop@east-ayrshire.gov.uk

East Kilbride
East Kilbride, Civic Centre, Cornwall Street, East Kilbride, Glasgow, G74 1AF T: 01355 806474 E: aileen.shiells@southlanarkshire.gov.uk CC accepted

East Lothian
Dunbar, Town House, 48 High Street, Dunbar, EH42 1JH T: 01368 863434 F: 01368 865728 E: fwhite@eastlothian.gov.uk

Haddington, The Register Office, John Muir House, Brewery Park, Haddington, EH41 3HA T: 01620 827308 F: 01620 827438 E: sforsyth@eastlothian.gov.uk

Eastwood and Mearns
Eastwood and Mearns, Council Offices, Eastwood Park, Roukenglen Road, Giffnock, G46 6UG T: 0141 577 3100 E: jim.clarke@eastrefrewshire.gov.uk

Eday and Pharay, Redbanks, Eday, Orkney, KW17 2AA T: 01857 622219

Edinburgh
Edinburgh (India Buildings) 2 India Buildings, Victoria Street, Edinburgh, EH1 2EX T: 0131 220 0349 F: 0131 220 0351 E: registrars.indiabuildings@edinburgh.gov.uk CC accepted

Edinburgh (Ratho) Operating from 2 India Buildings, Victoria Street, Edinburgh Ratho T: 0131 220 0349 F: 0131 220 0351 E: registrars.indiabuildings@edinburgh.gov.uk CC accepted

Edinburgh (Currie) The Register Office, 138 Lanark Road West, Currie, EH14 5NY T: 0131 449 5318

Edinburgh (Kirkliston) 19 Station Road Kirkliston, EH29 9BB T: 0131 333 3210

Edinburgh (Leith) The Register Office, 30 Ferry Road, Edinburgh, EH6 4AE T: 0131 554 8452 E: registrars.leith@edinburgh.gov.uk

Edinburgh (Queensferry) Council Office, 53 High Street, South Queensferry, EH30 9HP T: 0131 331 1590 E: margaret.kenny@edinburgh.gov.uk

Ellon, Area Office, Neil Ross Square, 29 Bridge Street, Ellon, AB41 9AA T: 01358 720295 F: 01358 726410 E: kathleen.stopani@aberdeenshire.gov.uk

Eyemouth, Community Centre, Albert Road, Eyemouth, TD14 5DE T: 01890 750690 E: pjohnston@scotborders.gsx.gov.uk

Falkirk (Falkirk) Old Burgh Buildings, Newmarket Street, Falkirk, FK1 lJE T: 01324 506580 F: 01324 506581 E: elinor.laing@falkirk.gov.uk

Fife
Fife (Auchterderran) The Register Office, 145 Station Road, Cardenden, KY5 0BN T: 01592 414800 F: 01592 414848

Fife (Auchtermuchty) Local Office, 15 High Street, Auchtermuchty, KY14 7AP T: 01337 828329 F: 01337 827166

Fife (Benarty) Benarty Local Office, 6 Benarty Square, Ballingry, KY5 8NR T: 01592 414343 F: 01592 414363 E: dorothy.thomson@fife.gov.uk

Fife (Buckhaven) Local Office, Municipal Buildings, College Street, Buckhaven, KY8 1AB T: 01592 414446 F: 01592 414490 E: martha.shields@fife.gov.uk

Fife (Cowdenbeath) The Register Office, 123 High Street, Cowdenbeath, KY4 9QB T: 01383 313190

Fife (Cupar) County Buildings, St Catherine Street, Cupar, KY15 4TA T: 01334 412885

Fife (Dunfermline) The Register Office, 34 Viewfield Terrace, Dunfermline, KY12 7HZ T: 01383 312121 F: 01383 312123 E: anne.williamson@fife.gov.uk

Fife (East Neuk) Anstruther Local Office, Ladywalk, Anstruther, KY10 3EX T: 01333 592110 F: 01333 592117 E: helen.moist@fife.gov.uk

Fife (Glenrothes) Albany House, Albany Gate Kingdom Centre, Glenrothes, KY7 5NX T: 01592 416570 F: 01592 416565 E: sophia.semple@fife.gov.uk

Fife (Inverkeithing) Civic Centre, Queen Street, Inverkeithing, KY11 1PA T: 01383 313570 F: 01383 313585 E: alexandra.birrell@fife.gov.uk

Fife (Kelty) Kelty Local Services, Sanjana Court, 51 Main Street, Kelty, KY4 0AA T: 01383 839999 E: karen.henderson@fife.gov.uk

Fife (Kennoway) 6/7 Bishops Court, Kennoway, Fife, KY8 5LA T: 01333 352635

Fife (Kirkcaldy) District Office, Town House, Kirkcaldy, KY1 1XW T: 01592 412121 F: 01592 412123 E: jennifer.brymer@fife.gov.uk

Fife (Leven) Carberry House, Scoonie Road, Leven, KY8 4JS T: 01333 592412 E: irene.ballantyne@fife.gov.uk

Fife (Lochgelly) Lochgelly Local Office, Town House, Hall Street, Lochgelly, KY5 9JN T: 01592 418180 F: 01592 418190 E: jacqueline.redpath@fife.gov.uk

Fife (Newburgh) Tayside Institute, 90-92 High Street, Newburgh, KY14 6DA T: 01337 883000 E: sophia.semple@fife.gov.uk

Fife (Newport on Tay) Blyth Hall, Scott Street, Newport On Tay, DD6 8DD T: 01382 543345 E: carol.traill@fife.gov.uk

Fife (St Andrews) Area Office, St Mary's Place, St Andrews, KY16 9UY T: 01334 412525 F: 01334 412650 E: jennifer.millar@fife.gov.uk

Fife (Tayport) Burgh Chambers Tayport, DD6 9JY T: 01382 552544

Fife (West Fife) The Health Centre , Chapel Street, High Valleyfield, Dunfermline, KY12 8SJ T: 01383 880682

Forfar, The Register Office, 9 West High Street, Forfar, DD8 1BD T: 01307 464973 E: regforfar@angus.gov.uk

Forres, 153 High Street, Forres, IV36 1DX T: 01309 694070 E: forres.registrar@chief.moray.gov.uk

Fort Augustus, Highland Council Service Point, Memorial Hall, Oich Road, Fort Augustus, PH32 4DJ T: 01320 366733 E: heather.smart@highland.gov.uk

Forth, The Register Office, 4 Cloglands, Forth, ML11 8ED T: 01555 811631

Fraserburgh, The Register Office, 14 Saltoun Square, Fraserburgh, AB43 9DA T: 01346 513281 E: eyoung.la@aberdeenshire.gov.uk

Gairloch, The Service Point, Achtercairn, Gairloch, IV22 2BP T: 01445 712572 E: trudy.mackenzie@highland.gov.uk

Gairloch (South) Gairloch, The Service Point, Achtercairn, Gairloch, IV21 2BP T: 01445 712572 F: 01445 712911 E: trudy.mackenzie@highland.gov.uk

Gigha, 10 Ardminish, Gigha, PA41 7AB T: 01583 505249

Girthon and Anwoth, 63 High Street, Gatehouse of Fleet, DG7 2HS T: 01557 814646 E: mhairiw@dumgal.gov.uk

Glasgow
Glasgow (Martha Street) The Register Office, 1 Martha Street, Glasgow, G1 1JJ T: 0141 287 7677 F: 0141 287 7666 E: robert.sneddon@pas.glasgow.gov.uk

Glasgow (Park Circus) The Register Office, 22 Park Circus, Glasgow, G3 6BE T: 0141 287 8350 F: 0141 287 8357 E: bill.craig@pas.glasgow.gov.uk

Golspie, Council Offices, Main Street, Golspie, KW10 6RB T: 01408 635200 F: 01408 633120 E: moira.macdonald@highland.gov.uk

Grangemouth, Municipal Chambers, Bo'ness Road, Grangemouth, FK3 8AY T: 01324 504499

Hamilton (Blantyre) Local Office, 45 John Street, Blantyre, G72 0JG T: 01698 527901 F: 01698 527923 E: carole.cartwright@southlanarkshire.gov.uk CC accepted

Harris, Council Offices Tarbert, HS3 3DJ T: 01859 502367 F: 01859 502283 E: marionmorrison@cne-siar.gov.uk

Hawick, Council Offices, Town Hall, Hawick, TD9 9EF T: 01450 364710 F: 01450 364720 E: mfhope@scotborders.gsx.gov.uk

Helensburgh, Scotcourt House, 45 West Princes Street, Helensburgh, G84 8BP T: 01436 658822 F: 01436 658821

Helmsdale, Operating from, Gower Street, Brora, KW8 6LD T: 01408 622644 F: 01408 622645

Applecross, Coire-ringeal, Applecross, Kyle, IV54 8LU T: 01520 744248

Area Repository Ross and Cromarty, Council Offices, Ferry Road, Dingwall, IV15 9QR T: 01349 863113 F: 01349 866164 E: alison.matheson@highland.gov.uk NOTE: All Statutory Registers (1855-1965) are held here for the following Districts: Alness, Applecross, Avoch, Carnoch, Coigach, Contin, Cromarty, Dingwall, Edderton, Fearn, Fodderty, Gairloch, North Gairloch, South Glensheil, Killearnan, Kilmuir Easter Kiltearn, Kincardine, Kinlochluichart, Kintail, Knockbain, Lochalsh, Lochbroom, Lochcarron, Logie Easter Nigg, Resolis, Rosemarkie, Rosskeen, Shieldaig, Strathoykel, Tain, Tarbat, Urquart and Logie Wester Urray. All Ancestry Enquiries should be addressed to this Office. Records from 1965 to present at local Offices

Dingwall and Carnoch, Council Offices, Ferry Road, Dingwall, IV15 9QR T: 01349 863113 F: 01349 866164 E: alison.matheson@highland.gov.uk anna.gallie@highland.gov.uk Area Repository for Ross and Cromarty

Dunvegan, Tigh-na-Bruaich Dunvegan, IV55 8WA T: 01470 521296 F: 01470 521519

Fort William and Ballachulish, Tweeddale Buildings, High Street, Fort William, PH33 6EU T: 01397 704583 F: 01397 702757 E: isobel.mackellaig@highland.gov.uk W: www.highland.gov.uk

Glenelg, Taobh na Mara, Na Mara, Glenelg Kyle, IV40 8JT T: 01599 522310 Only holds records from 1965

Grantown-on-Spey and Nethyridge, Council Offices, The Square, Grantown On Spey, PH26 3HF T: 01479 872539 F: 01479 872942 E: diane.brazier@highland.gov.uk

Inverness, Moray House, 16/18 Bank Street, Inverness, IV1 1QY T: 01463 239792 F: 01463 712412 E: margaret.straube@highland.gov.uk W: www.highland.gov.uk

Mallaig and Knoydart, Sandholm, Morar, Mallaig, PH40 4PA T: 01687 462592 F: 01687 462592

Rosskeen, Invergordon Service Point, 62 High St, Invergordon, IV18 0DH T: 01349 852472 F: 01349 853803 E: alison.mathieson@highland.gov.uk

Thurso, Strathy and Mey, Library Buildings, Davidsons Lane, Thurso, KW14 7AF T: 01847 892786 F: 01847 894611 E: pauline.edmunds@highland.gov.uk

Tain, 24 High Street, Tain, IV19 1AE T: 01862 892122

Tarradale, Service Point Office, Seaforth Road, Muir Of Ord, IV6 7TA T: 01463 870201 F: 01463 871047 E: lorraine.ross@highland.gov.uk

Kirkton and Tongue , The Service Point, Naver Teleservice Centre, Bettyhill, By Thurso, KW14 7SS T: 01641 521242 F: 01641 521242 E: mary.cook@highland.gov.uk

Wick, Town Hall, Bridge Street, Wick, KW1 4AN T: 01955 605713 E: margaret.wood@highland.gov.uk

Thurso, Strathy and Mey, District Office, Library Buildings, Davidson's Lane, Thurso, KW14 7AF T: 01847 892786 F: 01847 894611 E: pauline.edmunds@highland.gov.uk Caithness Area Repository - Genealogical Repository with on line access to GRO(S)

Huntly, The Register Office, 25 Gordon Street, Huntly, AB54 8AN T: 01466 794488

Insch, Marbert, George Street, Insch, AB52 6JL T: 01464 820964

Inveraray, Operating from Lochgilphead PA32 8UZ T: 01546 604511

Inverclyde, The Register Office, 40 West Stewart Street, Greenock, PA15 1YA T: 01475 714250 F: 01415 714253 E: maureen.bradley@inverclyde.gov.uk

Inveresk, Brunton Hall, Ladywell Way, Musselburgh, EH21 6AF T: 0131 653 4224 E: acurrie@eastlothian.gov.uk

Irvine, The Register Office, 106-108 Bridgegate House, Irvine, KA12 8BD T: 01294 324988 F: 01294 324984 E: jmcdowall@north-ayrshire.gov.uk

Islay, Council Office, Jamieson Street, Bowmore, Islay, PA43 7HL T: 01496 301301 E: sharon.mcharrie@argyll-bute.gov.uk

Isle of Bute, Council Office, Mount Pleasant Road, Rothesay, PA20 9HH T: 01700 503l-551

Isle of Eigg, Small Isles, Kildonan House Isle Of Eigg, PH42 4RL T: 01687 482446

Isle of Lewis, Carloway, The Registry, Knock, Carloway, HS2 9AU T: 01851 643264

Isle Of Tyree, Tyree, The Register Office Crossapol, PA77 6UP T: 01879 220349

Jedburgh, Library Building, Castlegate, Jedburgh, TD8 6AS T: 01835 863670 F: 01835 863670 E: aveitch@scotborders.gov.uk W: www.scotborders.gov.uk

Johnstone, The Register Office, 16-18 McDowall Street, Johnstone, PA5 8QL T: 01505 320012 F: 01505 382130, W: www.renfrewshire.gov.uk

Jura, Forestry Cottage, Craighouse, Jura, PA60 7XG T: 01496 820326

Kelso, Town House Kelso, TD5 7HF T: 01573 225659 E: dgittus@scotborders.gsx.gov.uk incorporates Gordon District

Kenmore, Operating from Aberfeldy Acharn by Aberfeldy, PH15 2HS T: 01887 829218

Kilbirnie, Beith & Dalry, 19 School Wynd Kilbirnie, KA25 7AY T: 01505 682416 F: 01505 684334 E: amcgurran@north-ayrshire.gov.uk

Kilfinichen & Kilvickeon, The Anchorage Fionnphort, PA66 6BL T: 01681 700241

Kilwinning, The Regsitrar's Office, 32 Howgate, Kilwinning, KA13 6EJ T: 01294 552261/2 F: 01294 557787 E: mmccorquindale@north-ayrshire.gov.uk

Kingussie, Council Offices, Ruthven Road, Kingussie, PH21 1EJ T: 01540 664529 F: 01540 661004 E: lorna.mcgregor@highland.gov.uk CC accepted

Kinlochbervie, Operating from Service Point Durness IV27 4RH T: 01971 511259 E: sheila.mather@highland.gov.uk

Kinlochluichart, The Old Manse Garve, IV23 2PX T: 01997 414201

Kirkconnell, Nith Buildings, Greystone Avenue, Kelloholm, Kirkconnel, DG4 6RX T: 01659 67206 F: 01659 66052

Kirkintilloch and Lennoxtown, Council Office, 21 Southbank Road, Kirkintilloch, G66 1NH T: 0141 776 2109 E: rab.macaulay@eastdunbarton.gov.uk

Kirkmabreck, The Bogue, Creetowm, Newton Stewart, DG8 7JW T: 01671 820266

Kirriemuir, Contact Arbroath

Lairg, The Service Point, Main Street, Lairg, IV27 4DB T: 01549 402588

Langholm, Town Hall Langholm, DG13 0JQ T: 01387 380255 F: 01387 81142

Larbert, The Register Office, 318 Main Street, Stenhousemuir, FK5 3BE T: 01324 503580 F: 01324 503581

Larkhall, Council Office, 55 Victoria Street, Larkhall, ML9 2BN T: 01698 882864

Latherton, Post Office Latheron, KW5 6DG T: 01593 741201

Laurencekirk, Royal Bank Buildings Laurencekirk, AB30 1AF T: 01561 377245 F: 01561 378020

Leadhills, Operating from Lanark Temporarily Leadhills T: 01555 673220

Lerwick, County Buildings Lerwick, ZE1 0HD T: 01595 744562 E: registrar@sic.shetland.gov.uk

Lesmahagow, The Register Office, 40/42 Abbeygreen, Lesmahagow, ML11 0EQ T: 01555 893812

Loch Duich, Operating from Hamilton House Kyle Of Lochalsh, IV40 8EZ T: 01599 534270

Lochalsh, Hamilton House, Plock Road, Kyle, IV40 8BL E: joyce.smith@highland.gov.uk

Lochbroom and Coigach, Locality Office, North Road, Ullapool, IV26 2XL T: 01854 613900 E: doreen.macleod@highland.gov.uk

Lochcarron and Shieldaig, Lochcarron Service Point, Main Street, Lochcarron, IV54 8YB T: 01520 722241 E: fiona.sproule@highland.gov.uk

Lochgilphead, Dairiada House, Lochnell Street, Lochgilphead, PA31 8ST T: 01546 604511 E: isabella.soudan@argyll-bute.gov.uk

Lochgoilhead, Dervaig, Lettermay, Lochgoilhead, PA24 8AE T: 01301 703306

Lonforgan, The Register Office, 8 Norval Place, Longforgan, Dundee, DD2 5ER T: 01382 360283

Mauchline, The Register Office, 2 The Cross, Mauchline, KA5 5DA T: 01290 550231 F: 01290 551991

Melrose, Ormiston Institute, Market Square, Melrose, TD6 9PN T: 01896 823114 E: jnorman@scotborders.gsx.gov.uk

Mid and South Yell, Schoolhouse, Ulsta, Yell, ZE2 9BD T: 01957 722260

Midlothian

Dalkeith, The Register Office, 2-4 Buccleuch Street, Dalkeith, EH22 1HA T: 0131 271 3281 F: 0131 663 6842 E: dkregistrars@midlothian.gov.uk

Milnathort, Rowallan, 21 Church Street, Milnathort, KY13 9XH T: 01577 862536

Mochrum, 13 South Street, 85 Main Street, Port William, Newton Stewart, DG8 9SH T: 01988 700741 E: francess@dumgal.gov.uk

Montrose, The Register Office, 51 John Street, Montrose, DD10 8LZ T: 01674 672351 E: regmontrose@angus.gov.uk

Moray Council

Elgin inc Tomintoul, The Register Office, 240 High Street, Elgin, IV30 1BA T: 01343 554600 F: 01343 554644 E: heather.grieg@moray.gov.uk

Morayshire

Keith and Upper Speyside, Area Office, Mid Street, Keith, AB55 5BJ T: 01542 885525 F: 01542 885522 E:

keith.registrar@chief.moray.gov.uk

Morvern, The Register Office, Dungrianach, Lochaline, Morvern, PA34 5XT T: 01961 421662

Motherwell and Wishaw, Civic Centre, Windmillhill Street, Motherwell, ML1 1TW T: 01698 302206 E: muiris@northlan.gov.uk

Muckhart and Glendevon, Operating from Alloa T: 01259 723850

Muirkirk, 44 Main Street, Muirkirk, KA18 3RD T: 01290 661227 E: muirkirk@east-ayrshire.gov.uk

Nairn, The Court House Nairn, IV12 4AU T: 01667 458500 E: anthea.lindsay@highland.gov.uk

New Cumnock, Town Hall, The Castle, New Cumnock, KA18 4AN T: 01290 338214

New Kilpatrick, Council Office, 38 Roman Road, Bearsden, G61 2SH T: 0141 942 2352/3

Newton Stewart Area, McMillan Hall, Dashwood Square, Newton Stewart, DG8 6EQ T: 01671 404187 E: marm@dumgal.gov.uk

North Ayrshire

Isle of Arran, District Council Office Lamlash, KA27 8LB T: 01770 600338 F: 01770 600028 E: ladamson@north-ayrshire.gov.uk incorporates Lochranza (552)

Largs , Moorburn, 24 Greenock Road, Largs, KA30 8NE T: 01475 676552 E: gmcginty@north-ayrshire.gov.uk W: www.north-ayrshire.gov.uk, CC accepted
Also covers Cumbrae (551)

Saltcoats, The Register Office, 45 Ardrossan Road, Saltcoats, KA21 5BS T: 01294 463312 F: 01294 604868 E: jkimmett@north-ayrshire.gov.uk W: www.north-ayrshire.gov.uk

West Kilbride, Kirktonhall, 1 Glen Road, West Kilbride, KA23 9BL T: 01294 823569 F: 01294 823569 E: jkimmett@north-ayrshire.gov.uk W: www.north-ayrshire.gov.uk

Cumbrae, Operating from Largs Largs T: 01475 674521 F: 01475 687304 E: gmcginty@north-ayrshire.gov.uk W: www.north-ayrshire.gov.uk, CC accepted
Also covers Largs (660)

North Berwick, The Register Office, 2 Quality Street, North Berwick, EH39 4HW T: 01620 893957 E: ddoman@eastlothian.gov.uk

North Lanarkshire

Airdrie, Area Registration Office, 37 Alexander Street, Airdrie, ML6 0BA T: 01236 758080 F: 01236 758088 E: registrars-airdrie@northlan.gov.uk

Coatbridge, The Register Office, 183 Main Street, Coatbridge, ML5 3HH T: 01236 812647 F: 01236 812643 E: registrars-coatbridge@northlan.gov.uk W: www.northlan.gov.uk

Kilsyth, Health Centre, Burngreen Park, Kilsyth, G65 0HU T: 01236 826813

Shotts, Council Offices, 106 Station Road, Shotts, ML7 4BH T: 01501 824740

North Ronaldsay, Hooking North Ronaldsay, KW17 2BE T: 01857 633257

North Uist, Fairview, Lochmaddy, North Uist, HS6 5AW T: 01876 500239

Oban, Lorn House, Albany Street, Oban, PA34 4AW T: 01631 567930 F: 01631 570379 E: gemma.cummins@argyll-bute.gov.uk

Old Cumnock, Council Office Millbank, 14 Lugar Street, Cummock, KA18 1AB T: 01290 420666 F: 01290 426164

Old Kilpatrick, Council Offices, Rosebery Place, Clydebank, G81 1TG T: 01389 738770 F: 01389 738775

Oldmeldrum, operating from Inverurie AB51 0EX T: 01467 628011 E: diane.minty@aberdeenshire.gov.uk incorporating Inverurie (319) Oldmeldrum(320) , Skere and Echt (323)

Orkney

Birsay, Sandveien, Dounby, Orkney, KW17 2HS T: 01856 771226

Orphir, The Bu, Orphir, Kirkwall, KW17 2RD T: 01856 811319

Sanday, The Register Office, Hyndhover, Sanday, KW17 2BA T: 01857 600441

Firth & Stenness, The Register Office, Langbigging, Stenness, KW16 3LB T: 01856 850320

Flotta, Post Office, Flotta , Stromness, KW16 3NP T: 01856 701252

Harray, New Breckan Harray, KW17 2JR T: 01856 771233

Holm and Paplay, The Register Office, Netherbreck , Holm, KW17 2RX T: 01856 781231

Hoy, Laundry House, Melsetter, Longhope, KW16 3NZ T: 01856 791337

Kirkwall, Council Offices, School Place, Kirkwall, KW15 1NY T: 01856 873535 F: 01856 873319 E: chief.registrar@orkney.gov.uk W: www.orkney.gov.uk

Shapinsay, The Register Office, Girnigoe, Shapinsay, KW17 2EB T: 01856 711256 E: jean@girnigoe.f9.co.uk W: www.visitorkney.com/accommodation/girnigoe

Stromness, The Register Office, Ferry Terminal Building, Ferry Road, Stromness, KW16 3AE T: 01856 850854

Westray, Myrtle Cottage, Pierowall, Westray, KW17 2DH T: 01857 677278

Papa Westray, Bewan Papa Westray, KW17 2BU T: 01857 644245

Penicuik & Glencorse, The Registry Office, 33 High Street, Penicuik, EH26 8HS T: 01968 672281 F: 01968 679547

Perth & Kinross - Aberfeldy, Duntaggart, Crieff Road, Aberfeldy, PH15 2BJ T: 01887 829218

Blair Athol, Operating from Pitlochry

Kinross, Kinross Area Office, 21/25 High Street, Kinross, KY13 8AP T: 01577 867602

Logierait, Operating from Pitlochry

Perth, The Register Office, 3 High Street, Perth, PH1 5JS T: 01738 475122 F: 01738 444133 E: ringham@pkc.gov.uk Incorporates Dunkeld (388)

Pitlochry, District Area Office, 26 Atholl Road, Pitlochry, PH16 5BX T: 01796 472323 F: 01796 474226

Dunkeld, Operating from Perth Perth, PH8 0AH T: 01738 475121 F: 01738 444133 E: ringham@pkc.gov.uk

Polmont and Muiravonside, Council Offices, Redding Road, Brightons, Falkirk, FK2 0HG T: 01324 503990

Portree and Raasay, Registrars Office, King's House, The Green, Portree, IV51 9BS T: 01478 613277 F: 01478 613277 E: meg.gillies@highland.gov.uk

Portsoy, The Register Office, 2 Main Street, Portsoy, AB45 2RT T: 01261 842510 F: 01261 842510

Prestonpans, Aldhammer House, High Street, Prestonpans, EH32 9SH T: 01875 810232 F: 01875 814921 E: sross@eastlothian.gov.uk

Prestwick, The Register Office, 2 The Cross, Prestwick, KA9 1AJ T: 01292 671666

Rannoch and Foss, Altdruidhe Cottage, Kinloch-rannoch, Pitlochry, PH17 2QJ T: 01882 632208

Renfrew, Town Hall Renfrew, PA4 8PF T: 0141 886 3589

Paisley, Registration Office, 1 Cotton Street, Paisley, PA1 1BU T: 0141 840 3388 F: 0141 840 3377 E: marion.mcglynn@refrewshire.gov.uk W: www.renfrewshire.gov.uk

Rousay, Egilsay and Wyre, Braehead , Rousay, Kirkwall, KW17 2PT T: 01856 821222

Sanquhar, Council Offices, 100 High Street, Sanquhar, DG4 6DZ T: 01659 50697

Scottish Borders

Chirnside, Operating from , 8 Newton Street, Duns, TD11 3XL T: 01361 882600 E: mdick@scotborders.gsx.gov.uk

Galashiels, Library Buildings, Lawyers Brae, Galashiels, TD1 3JQ T: 01896 752822 E: eczajka2@scotborders.gsx.gov.uk

Lauder, The Old Jail, Mid Row, Lauder, TD2 6SZ T: 01578 722795 E: bgoldie@scotborders.gsx.gov.uk

Peebles, Chambers Institute, High Street, Peebles, EH45 8AG T: 01721 723817 F: 01721 723817 E: showitt@scotborders.gsx.gov.uk

Selkirk, Municipal Buildings, High Street, Selkirk, TD7 4JX T: 01750 23104 E: jstock@scotborders.gsx.gov.uk

West Linton, Council Office West Linton, EH46 7ED T: 01968 660267 E: ptodd@scotborders.gsx.gov.uk

Scourie, Operating from, Assynt, Lochinver, IV27 4TD T: 01571 844201

Shetland

Burra Isles, Roadside, Hannavoe, Lerwick, ZE2 9LA T: 01595 859201

Sandness, The Register Office, 13 Melby, Sandness, ZE2 9PL T: 01595 870257

Tingwall, Vindas, Laxfirth, Tingwall, ZE2 9SG T: 01595 840450

Whiteness and Weisdale, Vista Whiteness, ZE2 9LJ T: 01595 830332

Fair Isle, Field Fair Isle, ZE2 9JU T: 01595 760224

Sandsting and Aithsting, The Register Office, Modesty, West Burrafirth, Aithsting, ZE2 9NT T: 01595 809428 F: 01595 809427

Fetlar, Lower Toft Funzie Fetlar, ZE2 9DJ T: 01957 733273

Foula, Magdala Foula, ZE2 9PN T: 01595 753236

Lunnasting, Vidlin Farm Vidlin, ZE2 9QB T: 01806 577204

Nesting, Laxfirth Brettabister North Nesting, ZE2 9PR T: 01595 890260

North Yell, Breckon, Cullivoe, Yell, ZE2 9DD T: 01957 744244 F: 01957 744352

Northmaven, Uradell Eshaness, ZE2 9RS T: 01806 503362

Papa Stour, North House Papa Stour, ZE2 9PW T: 01595 873238

Sandwick, The Register Office, Lee Cottage, Sandwick, Stromness, KW16 3JF T: 01856 841518

Sandwick and Cunningsbur, The Register Office, Pytaslee Leebitton, Sandwick, ZE2 9HP T: 01950 431367

Walls, Victoria Cottage, Walls, Lerwick, ZE2 9PD T: 01595 809478

Whalsay, Conamore, Brough, Whalsay, ZE2 9AL T: 01806 566544 CC accepted

Whalsay-Skerries, Fairview, East Isle, Skerries, ZE2 9AR T: 01806 515255

Slamannan, Operating from Falkirk T: 01324 506580

South Ayrshire

Girvan, Barrhill, Barr, Dailly, Colmonell, Ballantrae, Registration Office, 22 Dalrymple Street, Girvan, KA26 9AE T: 01465 712894 F: 01465 715576 E: girvan.registrars@south-ayrshire.gov.uk

Maybole, Crosshill, Dunure, Kirkmichael, Kirkoswald, Straiton, Council Office, 64 High Street, Maybole, KA19 7BZ T: 01655 882124 E: maybole.registrars@south-ayrshire.gov.uk CC accepted

South Lanarkshire
Cambuslang, Council Office, 6 Glasgow Road, Cambuslang, G72
7BW T: 0141 641 9605 F: 0141 641 8542 E:
registration@southlanarkshire.gov.uk W:
www.southlanarkshire.gov.uk, CC accepted
Carluke, The Register Office, 9 Kirkton Street, Carluke, ML8 4AB
T: 01555 777844 F: 01555 773721 E:
catherine.watson@southlanarkshire.gov.uk
Hamilton, The Register Office, 21 Beckford Street, Hamilton, ML3
0BT T: 01698 454213 F: 01698 455746 E:
jean.lavelle@southlanarkshire.gov.uk CC accepted
Lanark, The Register Office, South Vennel, Lanark, ML11 7JT T:
01555 673261 CC accepted
Rutherglen, 1st Floor, 169 Main Street, Rutherglen, G73 2HJ T:
0141 613 5332 F: 0141 613 5335 E:
wndy.cranston@southlanarkshire.gov.uk
South Ronaldsay, The Register Office, West Cara, Grimness, South
Ronaldsay, KW17 2TH T: 01856 831509
Stirling
Callander, The Register Office, 1 South Church Street, Callander,
FK17 8BN T: 01877 330166
Dunblane, Municipal Buildings Dunblane, FK15 0AG T: 01786
823300 E: muirm@stirling.gov.uk
Killin, 8 Lyon Villas, Killin, FK21 8TF T: 01567 820655
Stirling, Municipal Buildings, 8 - 10 Corn Exchange Road, Stirling,
FK8 2HU T: 01786 432343 F: 01786 432056 E:
registrar@stirling.gov.uk
Strathendrick, Balfron Local Office, 32 Buchanan Street, Balfron,
G63 0TR T: 01360 440315 CC accepted
Strathaven, Royal Bank of Scotland Buildings, 34 Common Green,
Strathaven, ML10 6AQ T: 01357 520316
Strathclyde
Glasgow, The Register Office, 22 Park Circus, Glasgow, G3 6BE T:
0141 287 8350 F: 0141 287 8357 E: bill.craig@pas.glasgow.gov.uk
Stronsay, The Register Office, Strynie, Stronsay, Kirkwall, KW17
2AR T: 01857 616239
Tarbat, The Bungalow, Chaplehill, Portmahomack, Portmahom Tain,
IV20 1XJ T: 01862 871328
Tarbert, Argyll House, School Road, Tarbert, PA29 6UJ T: 01880
820374
Tayinloan, Bridge House, Tayinloan, Tarbert, PA29 6XG T: 01583

441239
Tranent, The Register Office, 8 Civic Square, Tranent, EH33 1LH T:
01875 610278 F: 01875 615420 E: bmcnaught@eastlothian.gov.uk
Troon, Municipal Buildings, 8 South Beach, Troon, KA10 6EF T:
01292 313555 F: 01292 318009
Uig (Lewis) The Register Office, 10 Valtos, Uig, Lewis, HS2 9HR T:
01851 672213
Uig(Skye) (Inverness) The Register Office, 3 Ellishadder, Staffin,
Portree, IV51 9JE T: 01470 562303 Records held are from 1967 to
date. all previous records now held at Portree
Unst, New Hoose, Baltasound, Unst, ZE2 9DX T: 01957 711348
Wanlockhead, Operating from Sanquhar T: 01659 74287
West Dunbartonshire
Vale of Leven, The Register Office, 77 Bank Street, Alexandria, G83
0LE T: 01389 608980 F: 01389 608982 E: brenda.wilson@west-
dunbarton.gov.uk
West Lothian
West Lothian (Bathgate) The Register Office, 76 Mid Street,
Bathgate, EH48 1QD T: 01506 776192 F: 01506 776194 E:
agnesmcconnell@westlothian.gov.uk
West Lothian (Linlithgow) The Register Office, High Street,
Linlithgow, EH49 7EZ T: 01506 775373 F: 01506 775374 E:
joyce.duncan@westlothian.gov.uk
West Lothian (East Calder) East Calder Library, 200 Main Street,
East Calder, EH53 0EJ T: 01506 884680 F: 01506 883944 E:
gillian.downie@wled.org.uk
West Lothian (Livingston) Lammermuir House, Owen Square,
Avondale, Livingston, EH54 6PW T: 01506 773754 E:
frances.kane@westlothian.gov.uk
West Lothian (Uphall) Strathbrock Partnership, 189a West Main
Street, Broxburn, EH52 5LH T: 01506 775509 E:
laura.clarke@westlothian.gov.uk
West Lothian (West Calder) The Register Office, 24 - 26 Main
Street, West Calder, EH55 8DR T: 01506 874704 E:
gary.bandoo@westlothian.gov.uk
West Lothian (Whitburn) The Register Office, 5 East Main Street,
Whitburn, EH47 0RA T: 01501 678005 F: 01506 678085 E:
agnes.mcconnell@westlothian.gov.uk
Western Ardnamurchan, Operating from Strontian Acharacle, PH36
4HY T: 01967 402037

Registration Records in The Republic of Ireland
Oifig An Ard-Chlaraitheora (General Register Office) Joyce House, 8/11 Lombard Street East, Dublin, 2.

The General Register Office and Research Room are open
Monday to Friday, (excluding public holidays) from 9.30 a.m. to
12.30 p.m. and from 2.15 p.m. to 4.30 p.m. for the purpose of
searching the indexes to birth, death and marriage records

The following records are deposited in the General Register
Office:-
1. Registers of all Births registered in the whole of Ireland from
1st January, 1864, to 31 December, 1921, and in Ireland (excluding
the six north-eastern counties of Derry, Antrim, Down, Armagh,
Fermanagh and Tyrone know as Northern Ireland) from that date.
2. Registers of all Deaths registered in the whole of Ireland from
1st January, 1864, to 31st December 1921, and in Ireland
(excluding Northern Ireland) from that date.
3. Registers of all Marriages registered in the whole of Ireland
from 1st April 1845, to 31st December 1863, except those
celebrated by the Roman Catholic clergy.
4. Registers of all Marriages registered in the whole of Ireland
from 1st January, 1864, to 31st December, 1921, and in Ireland
(excluding Northern Ireland) from that date.
5. Registers of Births at Sea of children, one of whose parents was
Irish, registered from 1st January, 1864, to 31st December, 1921.
Register of Births at Sea of Children one of whose parents was
born in the Republic of Ireland, registered after 1921.
6. Register of Deaths at Sea of Irish-born persons, registered from
1st January, 1864, to 31st December, 1921, and after 1921 of Irish
born persons other than those born in Northern Ireland.
7. Registers of Births of children of Irish parents, certified by
British Consuls abroad, from 1st January, 1864 to 31st December,
1921.
8. Registers of Deaths of Irish-born persons, certified by British
Consuls abroad, from 1st January, 1864, to 31st December, 1921.
9. Register of Marriages celebrated in Dublin by the late Rev. J F
G Schulze, Minister of the German Protestant Church, Poolbeg
Street, Dublin, from 1806 to 1837, inclusive.
10. Registers under the Births, Deaths and Marriages (Army) Act,
1879.

11. Adopted Children Register – legal adoptions registered in the
Republic of Ireland on or after 10th July, 1953. Note: Cost of
certificates issued from the Adopted Children Register: £5.50 for
full certificate: £3.50 for short certificate: £0.70 for certificate for
Social Welfare purposes.
12. Birth and Death Registers under the Defence (Amendment)
(No. 2) Act, 1960.
13. Registers of certain births and deaths occurring
outside the State (The Births, Deaths and Marriages
Registration Act, 1972, Sec. 4).
14. Register of Certain Lourdes Marriages (Marriages Act, 1972,
Sec.2).
15. Registers of Stillbirths registered in Republic of Ireland from
1st January 1995 (certified copies available to parents only).

Reading Room Searches.
There are two types of searches available to the public.
A search for a maximum of 5 years or a general search for one day
covering all years. Fees apply Photocopies may be purchased

Records for births, deaths and Catholic marriages commenced in
1864. Records for non-Catholic marriages date from 1845.
Information prior to this (1864) may be available from parish
records which are kept in the Genealogical Office in the National
Library, Kildare Street, Dublin, 2. Records of births, deaths and
marriages for Northern Ireland are only available up to 1921.

The indexes are complied on a yearly/quarterly basis in
alphabetical order. Records for the years 1878 to 1903 and 1928 to
1965 are divided into four quarters ending March, June, September
and December. Marriages are indexed under both the maiden name
of the bride and the grooms surname, therefore, if you check under
each name you find a cross reference which will indicate it is the
correct entry relating to the marriage.

Museums

National
Battlefields Trust 33 High Green Brooke Norwich NR15 1HR T: 01508 558145 F: 01508 558145 E: BattlefieldTrust@aol.com W: www.battlefieldstrust.com
The Boat Museum & David Owen Waterways Archive see Cheshire
Black Cultural Archives 378 Coldharbour Lane London SW9 8LF T: (020) 7738 4591 F: (020) 7738 7168 E: info@99mbh.org.uk W: www.99mbh.org.uk
British Empire & Commonwealth Museum Clock Tower Yard Temple Meads Bristol BS1 6QH T: 0117 925 4980 0117 925 4983 E: staff@empiremuseum.co.uk W: www.empiremuseum.co.uk
British Museum The Secretariat Great Russell St London WC1B 3DG T: (020) 7323 8768 T: (020) 7323 8224 F: (020) 7323 8118 E: jwallace@thebritishmuseum.ac.uk W: www.thebritishmuseum.ac.uk
British Red Cross Museum and Archives 44 Moorfields, London EC2Y 9AL T: 0870 170 7000 F: (020) 7562 2000 E: enquiry@redcross.org.uk W: www.redcross.org.uk/museum&archives Open by appointment 10am to 4pm Monday to Friday.
Commonwealth War Graves Commission 2 Marlow Road Maidenhead SL6 7DX T: 01628 634221 F: 01628 771208 W: www.cwgc.org
The Galleries of Justice Shire Hall High Pavement Lace Market Nottingham NG1 1HN T: 0115 952 0555 F: 0115 993 9828 E: info@galleriesofjustice.org.uk W: www.galleriesofjustice.org.uk
Imperial War Museum - Duxford Imperial War Museum The Airfield Duxford Cambridge CB2 4QR T: 01223 835 000 F: 01223 837 237 E: duxford@iwm.org.uk
Imperial War Museum Film & Video Archive Lambeth Rd London SE1 6HZ T: 020 7416 5291 W:www.iwm.org.uk/collections/film.htm
Labour History Archive and Study Centre People's History Museum 103 Princess Street Manchester M1 6DD T: 0161 228 7212 F: 0161 237 5965 E: archives@nmlhweb.org_lhasc@fs1.li.man.ac.uk W: http://rylibweb.man.ac.uk
Ministry of Defence - Fleet Air Arm Records Service CS(R)2, Bourne Avenue, Hayes, Middlesex UB3 1RF F: 0181 573 9078 E: lhearn.defencerecords.hayes@gtnet.gov.uk
Ministry of Defence - Army Records Centre CS(R)2b, Bourne Avenue, Hayes, Middlesex UB3 1RF F: 0181 573 9078 E: lhearn.defencerecords.hayes@gtnet.gov.uk
Royal Marines Historical Records and Medals Centurion Building, Grange Road, Gosport, Hampshire PO13 9XA
Ministry of Defence - Royal Naval Personnel Records Centre CS(RM)2 Navy Search, Bourne Avenue, Hayes, Middlesex UB3 1RF F: 0181 573 9078
The National Coal Mining Museum for England Caphouse Colliery New Road Overton Wakefield WF4 4RH T: 01924 848806 F: 01924 840694 E: info@ncm.org.uk W: www.ncm.org.uk
National Museum of Photography, Film and Television Bradford BD1 1NQ T: 01274-202030 F: 01274 -723155 W: www.nmpft.org.uk
National Gallery St. Vincent House 30 Orange St London WC2H 7HH T: (020) 7747 5950
Natural History Museum Cromwell Rd London SW7 5BD T: (020) 7938 9238 F: 020 7938 9290 W: www.nhm.ac.uk
National Portrait Gallery 2 St. Martins Place London WC2H 0HE T: (020) 7306 0055 F: (020) 7206 0058 W: www.npg.org.uk
National Railway Museum Leeman Road York YO26 4XJ T: 01904 621261 F: 01904 611112 E: nrm@nmsi.ac.uk W: www.nrm.org.uk
National Tramway Museum Crich Tramway Village Crich Matlock DE4 5DP T: 01773 852565 F: 01773 852326 E: info@tramway.co.uk W: www.tramway.co.uk cc accepted
The National Waterways Museum Llanthony Warehouse Gloucester Docks Gloucester GL1 2EH T: 01452 318054 F: 01452 318066 E: curatorial1@nwm.demon.co.uk W: www.nwm.demon.co.uk
Royal Armouries Armouries Dr Leeds LS10 1LT T: 0990 106666
Royal Armouries H.M Tower Of London Tower Hill London EC3N 4AB T: (020) 7480 6358 ext 30 F: (020) 7481 2922 E: Bridgett.Clifford@armouries.org.uk W: www.armouries.org.uk
The Science Museum Exhibition Rd London SW7 2DD T: 0870 8704868 E: sciencemuseum@nmsp.ac.uk
Victoria & Albert Museum Cromwell Rd South Kensington London SW7 2RL T: (020) 7942 2164 T: (020) 7638 8500 F: (020) 7942 2162 W: www.nal.vam.ac.uk

Bedfordshire
Bedford Museum Castle Lane Bedford MK40 3XD T: 01234 353323 F: 01234 273401 E: bmuseum@bedford.gov.uk W: www.bedfordmuseum.org
Bedfordshire Yeomanry Castle Lane Bedford MK40 3XD T: 01234 353323 F: 01234 273401 E: bmuseum@bedford.gov.uk W: www.bedfordmuseum.org
Bedfordshire and Hertfordshire Regimental Museum Luton Museum Wardown Park Luton LU2 7HA T: 01582 546722 F: 01582 546763 W: www.luton.gov.uk/enjoying/museums

Cecil Higgins Art Gallery Castle Close Castle Lane Bedford MK40 3RP T: 01234 211222 F: 01234 327149
Elstow Moot Hall Elstow Bedford MK42 9XT T: 01234 266889 E: wilemans@deed.bedfordshire.gov.uk W: www.bedfordshire.gov.uk
John Dony Field Centre Hancock Drive Bushmead Luton LU2 7SF T: 01582 486983
Luton Museum Service & Art Gallery Wardown Park Luton LU2 7HA T: 01582 546725 F: 01582-546763 E: adeye@luton.gov.uk
Museum of Defence Intelligence Chicksands Shefford SG17 5PR T: 01462 752340 F: 01462 752341
Shuttleworth Collection Old Warden Aerodrome Old Warden Biggleswade SG18 9ER T: 01767 627288 F: 01767 626229 E: collection@shuttleworth.org W: www.shuttleworth.org
Shuttleworth Veteran Aeroplane Society PO Box 42 Old Warden Aerodrome Biggleswade SG18 9UZ T: 01767 627398 E: svas@oldwarden.fsnet.co.uk
Station X - Bletchley Park Bletchley Park Trust The Mansion Bletchley Milton Keynes MK3 6EB T: 01908 640404 W: www.bletchelypark.org.uk

Berkshire
Blake's Lock Museum Gasworks Rd Reading RG1 3DS T: 0118 939 0918
Friends of Royal Borough Collection, Windsor 14 Park Avenue Wraysbury TW19 5ET T: 01784 482771
Maidenhead Heritage Centre 41 Nicholsons Centre Maidenhead SL6 1LL T: 01628 780555
Museum of English Rural Life, Rural History Centre University of Reading Whiteknights PO Box 229 Reading RG6 6AG T: 0118 931 8664 F: 0118 975 1264 E: j.s.creasey@reading.ac.uk W: www.ruralhistory.org/index.html Appointments required
R.E.M.E. Museum of Technology Isaac Newton Road Arborfield Reading RG2 9NJ T: 0118 976 3375 F: 0118 976 3375 E: reme-museum@gtnet.gov.uk W: www.rememuseum.org.uk
Royal Berkshire Yeomanry Cavalry Museum T A Centre Bolton Road Windsor SL4 3JG T: 01753 860600 F: 01753 854946
Royal Borough Museum (Windsor & Maidenhead) Tinkers Lane Windsor SL4 4LR T: 01628 796829 E: olivia.gooden@rbwm.gov.uk
Slough Museum 278-286 High St Slough SL1 1NB T: 01753 526422
The Household Cavalry Museum Combermere Barracks Windsor SL4 3DN T: 01753 755112 F: 01753 755161 Admission Free
The Museum of Berkshire Aviation Trust Mohawk Way Woodley Reading RG5 4UE T: 0118 944 8089 E: museumofberkshireaviation@fly.to W: http://fly.to/museumofberkshireaviation
The Museum of Reading Town Hall Blagrave Street Reading RG1 1QH T: 0118 939 9800 W: www.readingmuseum.org.uk
Wantage Vale & Downland Museum Church Street Wantage OX12 8BL T: 01235 771447
Wellington Exhibition Stratfield Saye House Reading RG7 2BT T: 01256 882882 F: 01256 882882 W: www.stratfield-saye.co.uk
West Berkshire Heritage Service - Newbury The Wharf Newbury RG14 5AS T: 01635 30511 F: 01635 38535 E: heritage@westberks.gov.uk W: www.westberks.gov.uk/tourism
West Berkshire Museum The Wharf Newbury RG14 5AS T: 01635 30511 F: 01635 38535 E: heritage@westberks.gov.uk W: www.westberks.gov.uk

Bristol
Ashton Court Visitor Centre Ashton Court Long Ashton Bristol BS41 8JN T: 0117 963 9174
Blaise Castle House Museum Henbury Bristol BS10 7QS T: 0117 903 9818 F: 0117 903 9820 E: general_museum@bristol-city.gov.uk W: www.bristol-city.gov.uk/museums
Bristol Industrial Museum Princes Wharf Wapping Road Bristol BS1 4RN T: 0117 925 1470
British Empire & Commonwealth Museum see National
City Museum & Art Gallery Queens Road Bristol BS8 1RL T: 0117 921 3571 F: 0117 922 2047 E: general_museum@bristol-city.gov.uk W: www.bristol-city.gov.uk/museums
Clevedon Story Heritage Centre Waterloo House 4 The Beach Clevedon BS21 7QU T: 01275 341196
Clifton Suspension Bridge Visitor Centre Bridge House Sion Place Bristol BS8 4AP T: 0117 974 4664 F: 0117 974 5255 E: visitinfo@clifton-suspension-bridge.org.uk W: www.clifton-suspension-bridge.org.uk
Georgian House 7 Great George St Bristol BS1 5RR T: 0117 921 1362
Harveys Wine Museum 12 Denmark St Bristol BS1 5DQ T: 0117 927 5036 E: alun.cox@adwev.com W: www.j-harvey.co.uk
Red Lodge Park Row Bristol BS1 5LJ T: 0117 921 1360 W: www.bristol-city.gov.uk/museums
SS Great Britain and Maritime Heritage Centre Wapping Wharf Gasferry Road Bristol BS1 6TY T: 0117 926 0680

Buckinghamshire

Amersham Local History Museum 49 High Street Amersham HP7 0DP T: 01494 725754 F: 01494 725754

Bletchley Park Trust The Mansion Bletchley Park Bletchley Milton Keynes MK3 6EB T: 01908 640404 F: 01908 274381 E: info@bletchleypark.org.uk WWW: www.bletchleypark.org.uk

Blue Max Wycombe Air Park Booker Marlow SL7 3DP T: 01494 449810

Buckinghamshire County Museum Church Street Aylesbury HP20 2QP T: 01296 331441 F: 01296 334884 E: museum@buckscc.gov.uk

Buckinghamshire Military Museum Trust Collection Old Gaol Museum Market Hill Buckingham MK18 13X T: 01280 823020 F: E: ian.beckett@luton.ac.uk

Chesham Town Museum Project Chesham Library Elgiva Lane Chesham HP5 2JD T: 01494 783183

Chiltern Open Air Museum Ltd Newland Park Gorelands Lane Chalfont St. Giles HP8 4AB T: 01494 871117 F: 01494 872774

Milton Keynes Museum Stacey Hill Farm Southern Way Wolverton Milton Keynes MK12 5EJ T: 01908 316222

Pitstone and Ivinghoe Museum Society Vicarage Road Pitstone Leighton Buzzard LU7 9EY T: 01296 668123 W: http://website.lineone.net/~pitstonemus Pitstone Green Museum and Ford End Watermill

Wycombe Museum Priory Avenue High Wycombe HP13 6PX T: 01494 421895 E: enquiries@wycombemuseum.demon.co.uk W: www.wycombe.gov.uk/museum

Cambridgeshire

Cambridge Brass Rubbing The Round Church Bridge St Cambridge CB2 1UB T: 01223 871621

Cambridge Museum of Technology Old Pumping Station Cheddars Lane Cambridge CB5 8LD T: 01223 368650

Cromwell Museum The Cromwell Museum Huntingdon T: 01480 375830 E: cromwellmuseum@cambridgeshire.gov.uk http://edweb.camcnty.gov.uk/cromwell

Cromwell Museum Grammar School Walk Huntingdon PE18 6LF T: 01480 375830 F: 01480 459563

Duxford Aviation Society Duxford Airfield Duxford Cambridge CB2 4QR T: 01223 835594

Duxford Displays Ltd Duxford Airfield Duxford Cambridge CB2 4QR T: 01223 836593

Ely Museum The Old Goal Market Street Ely CB7 4LS T: 01353-666655 E: elymuseum@freeuk.com W: www.ely.org.uk includes Cambridge Regiment displays

Farmland Museum Denny Abbey Ely Rd Waterbeach Cambridge CB5 9PQ T: 01223 860988 F: 01223 860988 E: f.m.denny@tesco.net W: www.dennyfarmlandmuseum.org.uk

Fenland & West Norfolk Aviation Museum Lynn Rd West Walton Wisbech PE14 7 T: 01945 584440

Folk Museum 2 - 3 Castle St Cambridge CB3 0AQ T: 01223 355159 E: info@folkmuseum.org.uk W: www.folkmuseum.org.uk

March & District Museum Society Museum High St March PE15 9JJ T: 01354 655300

Museum of Classical Archaeology Sidgwick Avenue Cambridge CB3 9DA T: 01223 335153 W: www.classics.cam.ac.uk/ark.html/

Nene Valley Railway Wansford Station Peterborough PE8 6LR T: 01780 782833 T: 01782 782855

Norris Library and Museum The Broadway St Ives PE27 5BX T: 01480 497317 E: bob@norrismuseum.fsnet.co.uk

Octavia Hill Birthplace Museum Trust 1 South Brink Place Wisbech PE13 1JE T: 01945 476358

Peterborough Museum & Art Gallery Priestgate Peterborough PE1 1LF T: 01733 343329 F: 01733 341928 E: museum@peterborough.gov.uk

Prickwillow Drainage Engine Museum Main St Prickwillow Ely CB7 4UN T: 01353 688360

RAF Witchford Display of Memorabilia Grovemere Building Lancaster Way Business Park Ely T: 01353 666666 T: 01353 664934

Railworld Museum - Nene Valley Railway Oundle Road Peterborough PE2 9NR T: 01733 344240 W: www.railworld.net

Ramsey Rural Museum The Woodyard Wood Lane Ramsey Huntingdon PE17 1XD T: 01487 815715

Sedgwick Museum University of Cambridge Downing St Cambridge CB2 3EQ T: 01223 333456 T: 01223 333450 E: mgd2@esc.cam.ac.uk

Soham Community History Museum PO Box 21 The Pavilion Fountain Lane Soham CB7 5PL T:

Wisbech and Fenland Museum Museum Square Wisbech PE13 1ES T: 01945-583817 F: 01945-589050 E: wisbechmuseum@beeb.net

Cheshire

Catalyst Gossage Building Mersey Road Widnes WA8 0DF T: 0151 420 1121

Cheshire Military Museum The Castle Chester CH1 2DN T: 01244 327617 Cheshire Yeomanry elements of 3rd Carabiniers and 5th Royal Inniskilling Dragoon Guards

Cheshire Military Museum The Castle Chester CH1 2DN T: 01244 327617 W: www.chester.cc.uk/militarymuseum

Chester Heritage Centre - closed August 2000 St. Michaels Church Bridge St Chester CH1 1NQ T: 01244 317948

Deva Roman Experience Pierpoint Lane off Bridge Street Chester CH1 2BJ T: 01244 343407 F: 01244 343407

Griffin Trust The Hangars West Road Hutton Park airfield Ellesmere Port CH65 1BQ T: 0151 350 2598 F: 0151 350 2598

Grosvenor Museum 27 Grosvenor St Chester CH1 2DD T: 01244 402008 F: 01244 347587 E: s.rogers@chestercc.gov.uk W: www.chestercc.gov.uk/heritage/museums

Hack Green Secret Nuclear Bunker PO Box 127 Nantwich CW5 8AQ T: 01270 623353 F: 01270 629218 E: coldwar@dial.pipex.com W: www.hackgreen.co.uk

Lion Salt Works Trust Ollershaw Lane Marston Northwich CW9 6ES T: 01606 41823 F: 01606 41823 E: afielding@lionsalt.demon.co.uk W: www.lionsaltworkstrust.co.uk

Macclesfield Museums Heritage Centre Roe St Macclesfield SK11 6UT T: 01625 613210 F: 01625 617880 E: postmaster@silk-macc.u-net.com

Macclesfield Silk Museums Paradise Mill Park Lane Macclesfield SK11 6TJ T: 01625 612045 F: 01625 612048 E: silkmuseum@tiscali.co.uk W: www.silk-macclesfield.org

Miniature AFV Association (MAFVA) 45 Balmoral Drive Holmes Chapel CW4 7JQ T: 01477 535373 F: 01477 535892 E: MAFVAHQ@aol.com W: www.mafva.com

Nantwich Museum Pillory St Nantwich CW5 5BQ T: 01270 627104

Norton Priory Museum Trust Ltd Tudor Road Manor Park Runcorn WA7 1SX T: 01928 569895 F: 01928 589743 E: info@nortonpriory.org W: www.nortonpriory.org

Stockport Air Raid Shelters 61 Chestergate Stockport SK1 1NG T: 0161 474 1942 F: 0161 474 1942

The Boat Museum & Waterways Archive see National

Warrington Library, Museum & Archives Service 3 Museums Street Warrington WA1 1JB T: 01925 442733 T: 01925 442734 E: museum@warrington.gov.uk W: www.warrington.gov.uk/museum

West Park Museum Prestbury Rd Macclesfield SK10 3BJ T: 01625 619831

Cleveland

HMS Trincomalee Maritime Avenue Hartlepool Marina Hartlepool TS24 0XZ T: 01429 223193 F: 01429 864385 W: www.thisishartlepool.com

Captain Cook Birthplace Museum Stewart Park Marton Middlesbrough TS7 6AS T: 01642 311211 W: www.aboutbritain.com/CaptainCookBirthplaceMuseum

Captain Cook & Staithes Heritage Centre High St Staithes Saltburn-By-The-Sea TS13 5BQ T: 01947 841454

Dorman Musuem Linthorpe Rd Middlesbrough TS5 6LA T: 01642 813781 E: dormanmuseum@middlesbrough.gov.uk W: www.dormanmuseum.org.uk

Green Dragon Museum Theatre Yard High St Stockton-On-Tees TS18 1AT T: 01642 393938

Hartlepool Historic Quay Maritime Avenue Hartlepool Marina Hartlepool TS24 0XZ T: 01429 860077 F: 01429 860077 E: arts-museum@hartlepool.gov.uk W: www.thisishartlepool.com

Margrove Heritage Centre Margrove Park Boosbeck Saltburn-By-The-Sea TS12 3BZ T: 01287 610368 F: 01287 610368

Preston Hall Museum Yarm Road Stockton-On-Tees TS18 3RH T: 01642 781184

Stockton Museums Service Education, Leisure & Cultural Services, Po Box 228 Municipal Buildings Church Road Stockton on Tees TS18 1XE T: 01642 415382 F: 01642 393479 E: rachel.mason@stockton.gov.uk W: www.stockton.gov.uk

The Tom Leonard Mining Experience Deepdale Skinningrove Saltburn TS13 4AA T: 01287 642877

Cornwall

Automobilia The Old Mill Terras Rd St. Austell PL26 7RX T: 01726 823092

Bodmin Museum Mount Folly Bodmin PL31 2DB T: 01208 77067 F: 01208 79268

Cable & Wireless Archive & Museum of Submarine Telegraphy Eastern House, Porthcurno Penzance TR19 6JX T: 01736 810478 E: info@tunnels.demon.co.uk W: www.porthcurno.org.uk

Charlestown Shipwreck & Heritage Centre Quay Rd Charlestown St. Austell PL25 3NX T: 01726 69897 F: 01726 68025

Duke of Cornwall's Light Infantry Museum The Keep Bodmin PL31 1EG T: 01208 72810 F: 01208 72810 E: dclimis@talk21.com W: www.britrishlightinfantry.org.ca

Flambards Village and Cornwall Aircraft Park Flambards Village Theme Park Culdrose Manor Helston TR13 0GA T: 01326 573404F: 01326 573344 E: info@flambards.co.uk W: www.flambards.co.uk

Helston Folk Museum Market Place Helston TR13 8TH T: 01326 564027 F: 01326 569714 E: enquiries@helstonmuseum.org.uk W: www.helstonmuseum.org.uk

John Betjeman Centre Southern Way Wadebridge PL27 7BX T: 01208 812392

Lanreath Farm & Folk Museum Lanreath Farm Near Looe PL13 2NX T: 01503 220321

Lawrence House Museum 9 Castle St Launceston PL15 8BA T: 01566 773277

Maritime Museum 19 Chapel Street Penzance TR18 4AF T: 01736 68890

Merlin's Cave Crystal Mineral & Fossil Museum & Shop Molesworth St Tintagel PL34 0BZ T: 01840 770023

National Maritime Museum (Falmouth, Cornwall) 48 Arwenack St Falmouth TR11 3SA T: 01326 313388

National Maritime Museum (Saltash, Cornwall) Cotehele Quay Cotehele Saltash PL12 6TA T: 01579 350830

Penryn Museum Town Hall Higher Market St Penryn TR10 8LT T: 01326 372158 F: 01326 373004

Penzance Maritime Museum 19 Chapel St Penzance TR18 4AW T: 01736 368890

Potter's Museum of Curiosity Jamaica Inn Courtyard Bolventor Launceston PL15 7TS T: 01566 86838 F: 01566 86838

Royal Cornwall Museum River St Truro TR1 2SJ T: 01872 272205

Mevagissey Museum Society Frazier Ho The Quay Mevagissey Cornwall PL26 6QU T: 01726 843568 T: 01726 844692 F: E: haycas02@yahoo.co.uk W: www.geocities.com/mevamus All correspondence to: "An Cala", 55 Lavorrick Orchards, Mevagissey, St Austell, Cornwall PL26 6TL

Trinity House National Lighthouse Centre Wharf Road Penzance TR18 4BN T: 01736 60077 F: 01736 64292

Cumbria

Aspects of Motoring Western Lakes Motor Museum The Maltings The Maltings Brewery Lane Cockermouth CA13 9ND T: 01900 824448

Birdoswald Roman Fort Gilsland Brampton CA6 7DD T: 01697 747602 F: 01697 747605

Border Regiment & Kings Own Royal Border Regiment Museum Queen Mary's Tower The Castle Carlisle CA3 8UR T: 01228 532774 F: 01228 521275 E: rhq@kingsownborder.demon.co.uk W: www.armymuseums.org

Dove Cottage & The Wordsworth Museum Town End Grasmere Ambleside LA22 9SH T: 015394 35544

Friends of The Helena Thompson Museum 24 Calva Brow Workington CA14 1DD T: 01900 603312

Haig Colliery Mining Museum Solway Road Kells Whitehaven CA28 9BG T: 01946 599949 F: 01946 618796 W: www.haigpit.com

Keswick Museum & Art Gallery Station Rd Keswick CA12 4NF T: 017687 73263 F: 1768780390 E: hazel.davison@allerdale.gov.uk

Lakeland Motor Museum Holker Hall Cark In Cartmel Grange-Over-Sands LA11 7PL T: 015395 58509

Lakeside & Haverthwaite Railway Haverthwaite Station Ulverston LA12 8AL T: 01539 531594

Laurel & Hardy Museum 4c Upper Brook St Ulverston LA12 7BH T: 01229 582292

Maritime Museum 1 Senhouse Street Maryport CA15 6AB T: 01900 813738 F: 01900 819496

Maryport Steamship Museum Elizabeth Dock South Quay Maryport CA15 8AB T: 01900 815954

North Pennines Heritage Trust Nenthead Mines Heritage Centre Nenthead Alston CA9 3PD T: 01434 382037 F: 01434 382294 E: administration.office@virgin.net W: www.npht.com

Penrith Museum Middlegate Penrith CA11 7PT T: 01768 212228 F: 01768 867466 E: museum@eden.gov.uk

Roman Army Museum Carvoran House Greenhead Carlisle CA6 7JB T: 016977 47485 F:

Ruskin Museum Yewdale Rd Coniston LA21 8DU T: 015394 41164 F: 015394 41132 W: www.coniston.org.uk

Senhouse Roman Museum The Battery Sea Brows Maryport CA15 6JD T: 01900 816168 F: 01900 816168 E: romans@senhouse.freeserve.co.uk W: www.senhousemuseum.co.uk

Senhouse Roman Museum The Battery The Promenade Maryport CA15 6JD W: www.aboutbritain.com/SenhouseRomanMuseum.htm

Solway Aviation Museum Aviation House Carlisle Airport Carlisle CA6 4NW T: 01227 573823 F: 01228 573517 E: info@solway-aviation-museum.org.uk W: www.solway-aviation-museum.org.uk

The Dock Museum North Rd Barrow-In-Furness LA14 2PW T: 01229 894444 E: docmuseum@barrowbc.gov.uk W: www.barrowtourism.co.uk

The Guildhall Museum Green Market Carlisle CA3 8JE T: 01228 819925

Tullie House Museum and Art Gallery Castle Street Carlisle CA3 8TP T: 01228-534781 F: 01228-810249

Ulverston Heritage Centre Lower Brook St Ulverston LA12 7EE T: 01229 580820 F: 01229 580820 E: heritage@hitch.demon-house.demon.co.uk W: www.rootsweb.com/~ukuhc/

William Creighton Mineral Museum & Gallery 2 Crown St Cockermouth CA13 0EJ T: 01900 828301 F: 01900 828001

Windermere Steamboat Museum Rayrigg Rd Windermere LA23 1BN T: 015394 45565 F: 1539448769 W: www.steamboat.co.uk

Derbyshire

Chesterfield Museum & Art Gallery St Mary's Gate Chesterfield S41 7TY T: 01246 345727 F: 01246 345720

Derby Industrial Museum Silk Mill Lane Derby DE1 3AR T: 01332 255308

Derby Industrial Museum Silk Mill Lane Off Full Street Derby DE1 3AF T: 01332 255308 F: 01332 716670 W: www.derby.gov.uk/museums

Derby Museum & Art Gallery The Strand Derby DE1 1BS T: 01332-716659 F: 01332-716670 W: www.derby.gov.uk/museums

Derwent Valley Visitor Centre Belper North Mill Bridge Foot Belper DE56 1YD T: 01773 880474

Donington Grandprix Collection Donington Park Castle Donington Derby DE74 2RP T: 01332 811027

Donington Park Racing Ltd Donington Park Castle Donnington Derby DE74 2RP T: 01332 814697

Elvaston Castle Estate Museum Elvaston Castle Country Park Borrowash Road Elvaston Derby DE72 3EP T: 01332 573799

Erewash Museum The Museum High Street Ilkeston DE7 5JA T: 0115 907 1141 E: 0115 907 1121 E: museum@erewash.gov.uk W: www.erewash.gov.uk

Eyam Museum Eyam S32 5QP T: 01433 631371 F: 01433 631371 E: johnbeck@classicfm.net W: www.eyam.org.uk

Glossop Heritage Centre Bank House Henry St Glossop SK13 8BW T: 01457 869176

High Peak Junction Workshop High Peak Junction Cromford Matlock DE4 5HN T: 01629 822831

High Peak Trail Middleton Top Rise End Middleton Matlock DE4 4LS T: 01629 823204

Midland Railway Centre Butterley Station Ripley DE5 3QZ T: 01773 570140

National Stone Centre Porter Lane Wirksworth Matlock DE4 4LS T: 01629 824833

Peak District Mining Museum The Pavilion South Parade Matlock Bath DE4 3NR T: 01629 583834 F: 01629 583834 E: mail@peakmines.co.uk W: www.peakmines.co.uk

Pickford's House Museum 41 Friar Gate Derby DE1 1DA T: 01332 255363 F: 01332 255277 W: www.derby.gov.uk/museums

Regimental Museum of the 9th/12th Royal Lancers Derby City Museum and Art Gallery The Strand Derby DE1 1BS T: 01332 716656 F: 01332 716670 E: angela.tarnowski@derby.gov.uk W: www.derby.gov.uk/museums

Devon

Allhallows Museum of Lace & Antiquities High St Honiton EX14 1PG T: 01404 44966 F: 01404 46591 E: dyateshoniton@msn.com W: www.honitonlace.com

Bill Douglas Centre for the History of Cinema and Popular Culture University of Exeter Queen's Building Queen's Drive Exeter EX4 4QH T: 01392 264321 W: www.ex.ac.uk/bill.douglas

Brixham Museum Bolton Cross Brixham TQ5 8LZ T: 01803 856267 E: mail@brixhamheritage.org.uk W: www.brixhamheritage.org.uk

Century of Playtime 30 Winner St Paignton TQ3 3BJ T: 01803 553850

Crownhill Fort Crownhill Fort Road Plymouth PL6 5BX T: 01752 793754 F: 01752 770065

Devon & Cornwall Constabulary Museum Middlemoor Exeter EX2 7HQ T: 01392 203025

Dunkeswell Memorial Museum Dunkeswell Airfield Dunkeswell Ind Est Dunkeswell Honiton EX14 0RA T: 01404 891943

Fairlynch Art Centre & Museum 27 Fore St Budleigh Salterton EX9 6NP T: 01395 442666

Finch Foundary Museum of Rural Industry Sticklepath Okehampton EX20 2NW T: 01837 840046

Ilfracombe Museum Wilder Rd Ilfracombe EX34 8AF T: 01271 863541 E: ilfracombe@devonmuseums.net W: www.devonmuseums.net

Museum of Barnstaple & North Devon incorporating Royal Devon Yeomanry Museum Peter A Boyd The Square Barnstaple EX32 8LN T: 01271 346 747 F: 01271 346407 E: admin@sal.org.uk

Newhall Visitor & Equestrian Centre Newhall Budlake Exeter EX5 3LW T: 01392 462453

Newton Abbot Town & Great Western Railway Museum 2A St. Pauls Rd Newton Abbot TQ12 2HP T: 01626 201121

North Devon Maritime Museum Odun House Odun Rd Appledore Bideford EX39 1PT T: 01237 422064 F: 01237 422064 W: www.devonmuseums.net/appledore

North Devon Museum Service St.Anne's Chapel Paternoster Row Barnstaple EX32 8LN T: 01271 378709

Otterton Mill Otterton Budleigh Salterton EX9 7HG T: 01395 568521 E: escape@ottertonmill.com W: www.ottertonmill.com

Park Pharmacy Trust Thorn Park Lodge Thorn Park Mannamead Plymouth PL3 4TF T: 01752 263501

Plymouth City Museum Drake Circus Plymouth PL4 8AJ T: 01752 304774 F: 01752 304775 E: plymouth.museum@plymouth.gov.uk W: www.plymouthmuseum.gov.uk W: www.cottoniancollection.org.uk
Royal Albert Memorial Museum Queen Street Exeter EX4 3RX T: 01392 265858
Seaton Tramway Harbour Road Seaton EX12 2NQ T: 01297 20375 F: 01297 625626 E: info@tram.co.uk W: www.tram.co.uk
Sidmouth Museum Hope Cottage Church St Sidmouth EX10 8LY T: 01395 516139
Teignmouth Museum 29 French St Teignmouth TQ14 8ST T: 01626 777041
Tiverton Museum of Mid Devon Life Beck's Square, Tiverton, Devon EX16 6PJ T: 01884 256295 E: tiverton@eclipse.co.uk W: www.tivertonmuseum.org.uk**The Dartmouth Museum** The Butterwalk Dartmouth TQ6 9PZ T: 01803 832923
The Devonshire and Dorset Regiment (Archives) RHQ, Devonshire and Dorset Regiment, Wyvern Barracks Barrack Road Exeter EX2 6AR T: 01392 492436 F: 01392 492469
The Museum of Dartmoor Life West Street Okehampton EX20 1HQ T: 01837 52295 F: 01837 659330 E: dartmoormuseum@eclipse.co.uk W: www.museumofdartmoorlife.eclipse.co.uk

Dorset

Bournemouth Aviation Museum Hanger 600 Bournemouth International Airport Christchurch BH23 6SE T: 01202 580858 F: 01202 580858 E: admin@aviation-museum.co.uk_phil@philbc.freeserve.co.uk W: www.aviation-museum.co.uk
Bridport Harbour Museum West Bay Bridport DT6 4SA T: 01308 420997
Cavalcade of Costume Museum Lime Tree House The Plocks Blandford Forum DT11 7AA T: 01258 453006 W: www.cavalcadeofcostume.com
Christchurch Motor Museum Matchams Lane Hurn Christchurch BH23 6AW T: 01202 488100
Dinosaur Land Coombe St Lyme Regis DT7 3PY T: 01297 443541
Dorset County Museum High West Street Dorchester DT1 1XA T: 01305 262735 F: 01305 257180 E: dorsetcountymuseum@dor-mus.demon.co.uk W: www.dorsetcc.gov.uk
Dorset Volunteers, Dorset Yeomanry Museum Gillingham Museum Chantry Fields Gillingham SP8 4UA T: 01747 821119 W: www.brWebsites.com/gillingham.museum
Lyme Regis Philpot Museum Bridge St Lyme Regis DT7 3QA T: 01297 443370 E: info@lymeregismuseum.co.uk W: www.lymeregismuseum.co.uk
Nothe Fort Barrack Rd Weymouth DT4 8UF T: 01305 766626 F: 01305 766425 E: fortressweymouth@btconnect.com W: www.fortressweymouth.co.uk
Portland Museum Wakeham Portland DT5 1HS T: 01305 821804
Priest's House Museum 23-27 High St Wimborne BH21 1HR T: 01202 882533
Red House Museum & Gardens Quay Rd Christchurch BH23 1BU T: 01202 482860
Royal Signals Museum Blandford Camp Nr Blandford Forum DT11 8RH T: 01258-482247 F: 01258-482267 F: 01258-482084 W: www.royalsignalsarmy.org.uk/museum/
Russell-Cotes Art Gallery & Museum East Cliff Bournemouth BH1 3AA T: 01202 451858 F: 01202 451851 E: diane.edge@bournemouth.gov.uk W: www.russell-cotes.bournemouth.gov.uk
Shaftesbury Abbey Museum & Garden Park Walk Shaftesbury SP7 8JR T: 01747 852910
Shaftesbury Town Museum Gold Hill Shaftesbury SP7 8JW T: 01747 852157 Open Daily 10.30.a.m. to 4.30.p.m. Closed wednesdays. Admission charge Adults
Sherborne Museum Association Abbey Gate House Church Avenue Sherborne DT9 3BP T: 01935 812252
Tank Museum Bovington BH20 6JG T: 01929 405096 F: 01929 462410 E: librarian@tankmuseum.co.uk_davidw@tankmuseum.co.uk W: www.tankmuseum.co.uk
The Dinosaur Museum Icen Way Dorchester DT1 1EW T: 01305 269880 F: 01305 268885
The Keep Military Museum The Keep Bridport Road Dorchester DT1 1RN T: 01305 264066 F: 01305 250373 E: keep.museum@talk21.com W: www.keepmilitarymuseum.org CC accepted
Tolpuddle Museum TUC Memorial Cottages, Tolpuddle, Dorset DT2 7EH T: 01305 848237 W: www.tolpuddlemartyrs.org.uk
Wareham Town Museum 5 East St Wareham BH20 4NS T: 01929 553448
Waterfront Musuem and Local Studies Centre 4 High St Poole BH15 1BW T: 01202 683138 T: 01202 262600 F: 01202 660896 E: museums@poole.gov.uk_mldavidw@poole.gov.uk W: www.poole.gov.uk 1901 census
Weymouth & Portland Museum Service The Esplanade Weymouth DT4 8ED T: 01305 765206

Weymouth Museum Brewers Quay, Hope Square, Weymouth, Dorset DT4 8TR T: 01305 777622 F: 01305 761680E: admin@brewers-quay.co.uk W: www.brewers-quay.co.uk
West Bridport Museum Trust - Local History Centre The Coach House Grundy Lane Bridport DT6 3RJ T: 01308 458703 F: 01308 458704 E: sh-bridportmus@btconnect.com

Durham

The 68th (or Durham) Regiment of Light Infantry Display Team 40 The Rowans Orgill Egremont CA22 2HW T: 01946 820110 E: PhilMackie@aol.com W: www.68dli.com
The Bowes Museum Newgate Barnard Castle DL12 8NP T: 01833 690606 F: 01833 637163 E: info@bowesmuseum.org.uk W: www.bowesmuseum.org.uk
Darlington Railway Centre & Museum North Road Station Station Rd Darlington DL3 6ST T: 01325 460532
Darlington Railway Preservation Society Station Rd Hopetown Darlington DL3 6ST T: 01325 483606
Discovery Centre Grosvenor House 29 Market Place Bishop Auckland DL14 7NP T: 01388-662666 F: 01388-661941 E: west.durham@groundwork.org.uk
Durham Cultural Services Library and Museums Department County Hall Durham DH1 5TY T: 0191 384 3777 F: 0191 384 1336 E: culture@durham.gov.uk W: www.durham.gov.uk
Durham Heritage Centre St Mary le Bow North Bailey Durham DH1 5ET T: 0191-384-5589
Durham Light Infantry Museum Aykley Heads Durham DH1 5TU T: 0191-384-2214 F: 0191-386-1770 E: dli@durham.gov.uk W: www.durham.gov.uk/dli
Durham Mining Museum Easington Colliery Welfare Memorial Road Easington T: 07931 421709 W: www.dmm.org.uk
Fulling Mill Museum of Archaeology The Banks Durham T: 0191 374 3623
Durham University Library Archives and Special Collections Palace Green Section, Palace Green, Durham DH1 3RN T: 0191 334 2932 F: 0191 334 2942E: pg.library@durham.ac.uk W: www.dw.ac.uk/library/asc
Killhope Lead Mining Centre Cowshill Weardale DL13 1AR T: 01388-537505 F: 01388-537617 E: killhope@durham.gov.uk W: www.durham.gov.uk/killhope/index.htm
Timothy Hackworth Victorian & Railway Museum Shildon DL4 1PQ T: 01388-777999 F: 01388-777999
Weardale Museum South View 2 Front Street Ireshopeburn DL13 1EY T: 01388-537417

Essex

Barleylands Farm Museum & Visitors Centre Barleylands Farm Billericay CM11 2UD T: 01268 282090
Battlesbridge Motorcycle Museum Muggeridge Farm Maltings Road Battlesbridge Wickford SS11 7RF T: 01268 560866
Castle Point Transport Museum Society 105 Point Rd Canvey Island SS8 7TJ T: 01268 684272
Chelmsford Museum Oaklands Park Moulsham Street Chelmsford CM2 9AQ T: 01245 615100 F: 01245 262428 E: oaklands@chelmsfordbc.gov.uk
East England Tank Museum Oak Business Park Wix Rd Beaumont Clacton-On-Sea CO16 0AT T: 01255 871119
East Essex Aviation Society & Museum Martello Tower Point Clear Clacton on Sea T: 01255 428020 T: 01206 323728
Epping Forest District Museum 39-41 Sun St Waltham Abbey EN9 1EL T: 01992 716882
Essex Police Museum Police Headquarters PO Box 2 Springfield Chelmsford CM2 6DA T: 01245 491491-ext-50771 F: 01245 452456
Essex Regiment Museum Oaklands Park Moulsham Street Chelmsford CM2 9AQ T: 01245 615101 F: 01245 262428 E: pompadour@chelsfordbc.gov.uk W: www.essexregimentmuseum.co.uk
Essex Secret Bunker Crown Building Shrublands Road Mistley CO11 1HS T: 01206 392271 (24 hour information line)
Essex Volunteer Units Colchester Museums 14 Ryegate Road Colchester CO1 1YG T: 01206 282935 F: 1206282925 E: tomhodgson@colchester,gov,uk
Essex Yeomanry Collection Springfield Lyons TA Centre Colchester Road Chelmsford CM2 5TA T: 01245 462298
Great Dunmow Maltings Museum The Maltings Mill Lane Great Dunmow CM6 1BG T: 01371 878979
Harwich Maritime Museum Low Lightouse Harbour Crescent Harwich T: 01255 503429 F: 01255 503429 E: theharwichsociety@quista.net W: www.harwich-society.com
Harwich Redoubt Fort Behind 29 Main Road Harwich T: 01255 503429 E: theharwichsociety@quista.net W: www.harwich-society.com
Hollytrees Museum High St Colchester CO1 1DN T: 01206 282940
Kelvedon Hatch Secret Nuclear Bunker Kelvedon Hall Lane Kelvedon Common Kelvedon Hatch Brentwood CM15 0LB T: 01277 364883 F: 01277 372562 E: bunker@japar.demon.co.uk W: www.japar.demon.co.uk Visitor Access via A128

Leigh Heritage Centre & Museum 13a High St Leigh-On-Sea SS9 2EN T: 01702 470834 E: palmtree@nothdell.demon.co.uk
Maldon District Museum 47 Mill Rd Maldon CM9 5HX T: 01621 842688
National Motorboat Museum Wattyler Country Park Pitsea Hall Lane Pitsea Basildon SS16 4UH T: 01268 550077 F: 01268 581903
Royal Gunpowder Mills Beaulieu Drive Powdermill Lane Waltham Abbey EN9 1JY T: 01992 767022 F: 01992 710341 E: info@royalgunpowder.co.uk W: www.royalgunpowder.co.uk
Saffron Walden Museum Museum Street Saffron Walden CB10 1JL T: 01799 510333 E: museum@uttlesford.gov.uk
Southend Central Museum Museum Victoria Avenue Southend-On-Sea SS2 6EW T: 01702 434449 F: 01702 349806
The Cater Museum 74 High St Billericay CM12 9BS T: 01277 622023
The Museum of Harlow Muskham Rd Harlow CM20 2LF T: 01279 4549569 F: 01279 626094 W: www.tmoh.com
Thurrock Museum Ossett Road Grays RM17 5DX
Valence House Museum Valence House Museum Becontree Avenue Dagenham RM8 3HT T: 020 8270 6866 F: 020 82706868 W: www.barking-dagenham.gov.uk

Gloucestershire
Campden & District Historical & Archaeological Society (CADWAS) The Old Police station High Street Chipping Campden GL55 6HB T: 01386 848840 E: enquiries@chippingcampdenhistory.org.uk W: www.chippingcampdenhistory.org.uD
Dean Heritage Centre Soudley Cinderford Forest of Dean GL14 2UB T: 01594 822170 F: 01594 823711 E: deanmuse@btinternet.com
Frenchay Tuckett Society and Local History Museum 247 Frenchay Park Road Frenchay BS16 ILG T: 0117 956 9324 F: E: raybulmer@compuserve.com W: www.frenchay.org/museum.html
Gloucester City Museum & Art Gallery Brunswick Rd Gloucester GL1 1HP T: 01452 524131
Gloucester Folk Museum 99-103 Westgate St Gloucester GL1 2PG T: 01452 526467 F: 01452 330495 E: christopherm@glos-city.gov.uk
Holst Birthplace Museum 4 Clarence Rd Cheltenham GL52 2AY T: 01242 524846 F: 01242 580182
Jet Age Museum Hangar 7 Meteor Business Park Gloucestershire Airport Cheltenham Road East Gloucester GL2 9QY T: 01452 715100 W: www.aboutbritain.com/JetAgeMuseum.htm
John Moore Countryside Museum 42 Church St Tewkesbury GL20 5SN T: 01684 297174
Nature In Art Wallsworth Hall Tewkesbury Rd Twigworth Gloucester GL2 9PG T: 01452 731422 F: 01452 730937 E: rinart@globalnet.co.uk W: www.nature-in-art.org.uk
Regiments Of Gloucestershire Museum Gloucester Docks Gloucester GL1 2HE T: 01452 522682
Shambles Museum Church Street Newent GL18 1PP T: 01531 822144 Museum of Victorian Life
Soldiers of Gloucestershire Museum Custom House Gloucester Docks Gloucester GL1 2HE T: 01452 522682 F: 01452 31116 W: www.glosters.org.uk
The Great Western Railway Museum (Coleford) The Old Railway Station Railway Drive Coleford GL16 8RH T: 01594 833569 T: 01594 832032 F: 01594 832032
The Guild Of Handicraft Trust Silk Mill Sheep Street Chipping Campden GL55 6DS T: 01386 841417
The Jenner Museum Church Lane Berkeley GL13 9BH T: 01453 810631 F: 01453 811690 E: manager@jennermuseum.com W: www.jennermuseum.com
The National Waterways Museum see National
Wellington Aviation Museum Broadway Road Moreton in the Marsh GL56 0BG T: 01608 650323 W: www.wellingtonaviation.org Collection of Royal Air Force Treasures
Gloucestershire(TidenhamParish) Chepstow Museum Bridge St Chepstow NP16 5EZ T: 01291 625981 F: 01291 635005 E: chepstowmuseum@monmouthshire.gov.uk

Hampshire
Action Stations Boathouse No 6 HM Naval Base Portsmouth PO1 3LR T: 023 9286 1512
Airbourne Forces Museum Browning Barracks Aldershot GU11 2BU T: 01252 349619 E: airbourneforcesmuseum@army.mod.uk.net
Aldershot Military Historical Trust Evelyn Woods Rd Aldershot GU11 2LG T: 01252 314598 F: 01252 342942
Aldershot Military Museum Queens Avenue Aldershot GU11 2LG T: 01252-314598 F: 01252-342942 E: musmim@hants.gov.uk W: www.hants.gov.uk/museum/aldershot
Andover Museum & Iron Age Museum 6 Church Close Andover SP10 1DP T: 01264 366283 F: 01264 339152 E: andover.museum@virgin.nbet_musmda@hants.gov.uk_musmad@hants.gov.uk W: www.hants.gov.uk/andoverm

Army Medical Services Museum Keogh Barracks Ash Vale Aldershot GU12 5RQ T: 01252 868612 F: 01252 868832 E: museum@keogh72.freeserve.co.uk Records the history of the army Medical Services which includes medical, veterinary, dental and nursing services CC accepted
Army Physical Training Corps Museum ASPT Fox Line Queen's Avenue Aldershot GU11 2LB T: 01252 347168 F: 01252 340785 E: regtsec@aptc.org.uk W: www.aptc.org.uk
Balfour Museum of Hampshire Red Cross History Red Cross House Weeke Winchester SO22 5JD T: 01962 865174
Bishops Waltham Museum Trust 8 Folly Field Bishop's Waltham Southampton S032 1EB T: 01489 894970
Broadlands Romsey SO51 9ZD T: 01794 505056 F: 01794 505040 E: admin@broadlands.net W: www.broadlands.net
D-Day Museum and Overlord Museum Clarence Esplanade Southsea PO5 3NT T: 023 9282 7261 F: 023 9282 7527
Dockyard Apprentice Exhibition Portsmouth Royal Dockyard 19 College Road HM Naval Base Portsmouth PO1 3LJ T:
Eastleigh Museum 25 High St Eastleigh SO50 5LF T: (023) 8064 3026 E: musmst@hants.gov.uk W: www.hants.gov.uk/museum/eastlmus/index.html
Eling Tide Mill Trust Ltd The Tollbridge Eling Hill Totton Southampton SO40 9HF T: (023) 80869575
Explosion! The Museum of Naval Firepower Priddy's Hard Gosport PO12 4LE T: 023 9258 6505 F: 023 9258 6282 E: info@explosion.org.uk W: www.explosion.org.uk
Gosport Museum Walpole Rd Gosport PO12 1NS T: (023) 9258 8035 F: (023) 9250 81951 E: musmie@hunts.gov.uk
Hampshire County Museums Service Chilcomb House Chilcomb Lane Winchester SO23 8RD T: 01962 846304
Havant Museum Havant Museum 56 East Street Havant P09 1BS T: 023 9245 1155 F: 023 9249 8707 E: musmop@hants.gov.uk W: www.hants.gov.uk/museums
Historic Ships and The Naval Dockyard HM Naval Base Portsmouth PO1 3LR T: 023 9286 1512 T: 023 9286 1533 W: www.flagship.org.uk
HMS Victory Victory Gate HM Naval Base Portsmouth PO1 3LR T: (023) 9277 8600 F: (023) 9277 8601 E: info@hmswarrior.org W: www.hmswarrior.org
HMS Warrior (1860) Victory Gate HM Naval Base Portsmouth PO1 3LR T: (023) 9277 8600 F: (023) 9277 8601 E: info@hmswarrior.org W: www.hmswarrior.org
Hollycombe Steam Collection Iron Hill Midhurst Rd Liphook GU30 7LP T: 01428 724900
Museum of Army Chaplaincy Amport House Nr Andover Andover SP11 8BG T: 01264 773144 x 4248 T: 01264 771042 E: rachdcurator@tiscali.co.uk
Museum of Army Flying Middle Wallop Stockbridge SO20 8DY T: 01980 674421 F: 01264 781694 E: daa@flying-museum.org.uk W: www.flying-museum.org.uk
New Forest Museum & Visitor Centre High St Lyndhurst SO43 7NY T: (023) 8028 3914 F: (020) 8028 4236 E: nfmuseum@lineone.net
Portsmouth City Museum and Record Office Museum Road Portsmouth PO1 2LJ T: (023) 92827261 F: (023) 92875276 E: portmus@compuserve.com 1901 census
Priddy's Hard Armament Museum Priory Rd Gosport PO12 4LE T: (023) 92502490
Rockbourne Roman Villa Rockbourne Fordingbridge SP6 3PG T: 01725 518541
Royal Armouries - Fort Nelson Fort Nelson Down End Roadd Fareham PO17 6AN T: 01329 233734 F: 01329 822092 E: enquiries@armouries.org.uk W: www.armouries.org.uk
Royal Marines Museum Eastney Southsea PO4 9PX T: (023) 9281 9385-Exts-224 F: (023) 9283 8420 E: matthewlittle@royalmarinesmuseum.co.uk W: www.royalmarinesmuseum.co.uk
Royal Naval Museum H M Naval Base (PP66) Portsmouth PO1 3NH T: (023) 9272 3795 F: (023) 9272 3942 W: www.royalnavalmuseum.org
Royal Navy Submarine Museum Haslar Jetty Road Gosport PO12 2AS T: (023) 92510354 F: (023) 9251 1349 E: admin@rnsubmus.co.uk W: www.rnsubsmus.co.uk
Sammy Miller Motor Cycle Museum Bashley Manor Farm Bashley Cross Rd New Milton BH25 5SZ T: 01425 620777
Search 50 Clarence Rd Gosport PO12 1BU T: (023) 92501957
Southampton Hall of Aviation Albert Road South Southampton SO1 1FR T: 01703 635830
Southampton Maritime Museum Bugle St Southampton SO14 2AJ T: (023) 80223941
The Bear Museum 38 Dragon St Petersfield GU31 4JJ T: 01730 265108 E: judy@bearmuseum.freeserve.co.uk W: www.bearmuseum.co.uk
The Gurkha Museum Peninsula Barracks Romsey Road Winchester SO23 8TS T: 01962 842832 F: 01962 877597 E: curator@thegurkhamuseum.co.uk W: www.thegurkhamuseum.co.uk

The King's Royal Hussars Museum (10th Royal Hussars PWO 11th Hussars PAO and The Royal Hussars PWO) Peninsula Barracks Romsey Road Winchester SO23 8TS T: 01962 828540 F: 01962 828538 E: beresford@krhmuseum.freeserve.co.uk W: www.hants.gov.uk/leisure/museum/royalhus/index.html

The Light Infantry Museum Peninsula Barracks Romsey Road Winchester SO23 8TS T: 01962 868550

The Mary Rose Trust 1-10 College Road HM Naval Base Portsmouth PO1 3LX T: (023) 92750521

The Museum of The Adjutant General's Corps RHQ Adjutant General's Corps Worthy Down Winchester SO21 2RG T: 01962 887435 F: 01962 887690 E: agc.regtsec@virgin.net

The Royal Green Jackets Museum (Oxford and Bucks Light Infantry King's Royal Rifle Corps and The Rifle Brigade) Peninsula Barracks Romsey Road Winchester SO23 8TS T: 01962 828549 F: 01962 828500 E: museum@royalgreenjackets.co.uk W: www.royalgreenjackets.co.uk

The Willis Museum Of Basingstoke Town & Country Life Old Town Hall Market Place Basingstoke RG21 7QD T: 01256 465902 F: 01256 471455 E: willismuseum@hotmail.com W: www.hants.gov.uk/leisure/museums/willis/index.html

West End Local History Society 20 Orchards Way West End Southampton S030 3FB T: 023 8057 5244 E: westendlhs@aol.com W: www.telbin.demon.co.uk/westendlhs Museum at Old Fire Station, High Street, West End

Westbury Manor Museum West St Fareham PO16 0JJ T: 01329 824895 F: 01329 825917 W: www.hants.gov.uk/museum/westbury/

Whitchurch Silk Mill 28 Winchester St Whitchurch RG28 7AL T: 01256 892065

Winchester Museums Service 75 Hyde St Winchester SO23 7DW T: 01962 848269 F: 01962 848299 E: museums@winchester.gov.uk W: www.winchester.gov.uk/heritage/home.htm

Herefordshire

Churchill House Museum Venns Lane Hereford HR1 1DE T: 01432 260693 F: 01432 267409

Cider Museum & King Offa Distillery 21 Ryelands St Hereford HR4 0LW T: 01432 354207 F: 01432 341641 E: thompson@cidermuseum.co.uk W: www.cidermuseum.co.uk

Leominster Museum Etnam St Leominster HR6 8 T: 01568 615186 F:

The Judge's Lodging Broad St Presteigne LD8 2AD T: 01544 260650 F: 01544 260652 W: www.judgeslodging.org.uk

Teddy Bears of Bromyard 12 The Square Bromyard HR7 4BP T: 01885 488329

Waterworks Museum 86 Park Street Broomy Hill Hereford HR1 2RE T: 01432-356653

Weobley & District Local History Society & Museum Weobley Museum, Back Lane, Weobley, Herefordshire, HR4 8SG T:01544 340292

Hertfordshire

Bushey Museum, Art Gallery and Local Studies Centre Rudolph Road Bushey WD23 3HW T: 020 8420 4057 F: 020 8420 4923 E: busmt@bushey.org.uk W: www.busheymuseum.org 1901 census for Bushey and aldenham

De Havilland Heritage Centre inc The Mosquito Aircraft Museum PO Box 107 Salisbury Hall London Colney AL10 1EX T: 01727 822051 F: 01727 826400 W: www.hertsmuseums.org

First Garden City Heritage Museum 296 Norton Way South Letchworth Garden City SG6 1SU T: 01462 482710 F: 01462 486056 E: fgchm@letchworth.com

Hertford Museum (Hertfordshire Regiment) 18 Bull Plain Hertford SG14 1DT T: 01992 552100 F: 01992 534797 E: enquiries@hertfordmuseum.org W: www.hertfordmuseum.org

Hertford Regiment Museum Hertford Museum 18 Bull Plain Hertford SG14 1DT T: 01992 582686 F: 01992 534797

Hitchin British Schools 41-42 Queen St Hitchin SG4 9TS T: 01462 420144 F: 01462 420144 E: brsch@britishschools.freeserve.co.uk W: www.hitchinbritishschools.org.uk

Hitchin Museum Paynes Park Hitchin SG5 1EQ T: 01462 434476 F: 01462 431316 W: www.nndc.gov.uk

Kingsbury Water Mill Museum St. Michaels Street St. Albans AL3 4SJ T: 01727 853502

Letchworth Museum & Art Gallery Broadway Letchworth Garden City SG6 3PF T: 01462 685647 F: 01462 481879 E: l.museum@north-herts.gov.uk W: www.north-herts.gov.uk

Mill Green Museum & Mill Mill Green Hatfield AL9 5PD T: 01707 271362 F: 01707 272511

Rhodes Memorial Museum & Commonwealth Centre South Rd Bishop's Stortford CM23 3JG T: 01279 651746 F: 01279 467171 E: rhodesmuseum@freeuk.com W: www.hertsmuseums.org.uk

Royston & District Museum 5 Lower King St Royston SG8 5AL T: 01763 242587

Stondon Transport Museum Station Road Lower Stondon SG16 6JN T: 01462 850339 F: 01462 850824 E: info@transportmuseum.co.uk W: www.transportmuseum.co.uk

The De Havilland Aircraft Museum Trust P.O Box 107 Salisbury Hall London Colney St. Albans AL2 1EX T: 01727 822051

The Environmental Awareness Trust 23 High St Wheathampstead St. Albans AL4 8BB T: 01582 834580

The Forge Museum High St Much Hadham SG10 6BS T: 01279 843301

Verulamium Museum St. Michaels St St. Albans AL3 4SW T: 01727 751810 T: 01727 751824 F: 01727 836282 E: d.thorold.stalbans.gov.uk

Walter Rothschild Zoological Museum Akeman St Tring HP23 6AP T: (020) 7942 6156 F: (020) 7942 6150 E: ornlib@nhm.ac.uk W: www.nhm.ac.uk

Ware Museum Priory Lodge 89 High St Ware SG12 9AD T: 01920 487848

Watford Museum 194 High St Watford WD1 2DT T: 01923 232297

Welwyn Hatfield Museum Service Welwyn Roman Baths By-Pass-Road Welwyn AL6 0 T: 01438 716096

Hull

4th Battalion East Yorkshire Regiment Collection Kingston upon Hull City Museums Wilberforce House 23-25 High Street Kingston upon Hull HU1 T: 01482 613902 F: 01482 613710

Ferens Art Gallery Kingston upon Hull City Museums Queen Victoria Square Kingston upon Hull HU1 3RA T: 01482 613902 F: 01482 613710

Wilberforce House Kingston upon Hull City Museums 23-25 High Street Kingston upon Hull HU1 T: 01482 613902 F: 01482 613710

Isle Of Wight

Bembridge Maritime Museum & Shipwreck Centre Providence House Sherborne St Bembridge PO35 5SB T: 01983 872223

Calbourne Water Mill Calbourne Mill Newport PO30 4JN T: 01983 531227

Carisbroke Castle Newport PO30 1XL W: www.english-heritage.org.uk

Carisbrooke Castle Museum Carisbrooke Castle Newport PO30 1XY T: 01983 523112 F: 01983 532126 E: carismus@lineone.net

East Cowes Heritage Centre 8 Clarence Rd East Cowes PO32 6EP T: 01983 280310

Guildhall Museum Newport High St Newport PO30 1TY T: 01983 823366 F: 01983 823841 E: rachel.silverson@iow.gov.uk W: www.iwight.com

Natural History Centre High St Godshill Ventnor PO38 3HZ T: 01983 840333

Needles Old Battery West High Down Totland Bay PO39 0JH T: 01983 754772 F: 01983 7596978

The Classic Boat Museum Seaclose Wharf Town Quay Newport PO30 2EF T: 01983 533493 F: 01983 533505 E: ebmiow@fsmail.net

The Island Aeroplane Company Ltd Embassy Way Sandown Airport Sandown PO36 9PJ T: 01983 404448 F: 01983 404448

The Lilliput Museum of Antique Dolls & Toys High St Brading Sandown PO36 0DJ T: 01983 407231 E: lilliput.museum@btconnect.com W: www.lilliputmuseum.co.uk

Ventnor Heritage Museum 11 Spring Hill Ventnor PO38 1PE T: 01983 855407

Kent

Brenzett Aeronautical Museum Ivychurch Road Brenzett Romney Marsh TN29 0EE T: 01233 627911 W: www.aboutbritain.com/renzettAeronauticalMuseum

Buffs Regimental Museum The Royal Museum & Art Gallery 18 High Street Canterbury CT1 2RA T: 01227-452747 F: 01227-455047 E: museum@canterbury.gov.uk W: www.canterbury-museums.co.uk

Canterbury Roman Museum Butchery Lane Canterbury CT1 2JR T: 01227 785575

Chartwell House Chartwell Westerham TN16 1PS T: 01732 866368 F: 01732 868193 E: chartwell@nationaltrust.org.uk W: www.nationaltrust.org.uk Home of Sir Winston Churchill from 1924 until his death in 1965

Chatham Dockyard Historical Society Museum Cottage Row Barrack Rd Chatham Dockyard Chatham ME4 4TZ T: 01634 844897(museum)

Cobham Hall Cobham DA12 3BL T: 01474 823371 F: 01474 822995 and 01474 824171

Dickens House Museum 2 Victoria Parade Broadstairs CT10 1QS T: 01843 861232 T: 01843 862853

Dolphin Sailing Barge Museum Crown Quay Lane Sittingbourne ME10 3SN T: 01795 423215

Dover Castle Dover CT16 1HU T: 01304 211067

Dover Museum Market Square Dover CT16 1PB T: 01304 201066 F: 01304 241186 E: museum@dover.gov.uk W: www.dovermuseum.co.uk

Dover Transport Museum Old Park Barracks Whitfield Dover CT16 2HQ T: 01304 822409 F:

Fleur De Lis Heritage Centre 13 Preston St Faversham ME13 8NS T: 01795 534542 E: faversham@btinternet.com W: www.faversham.org

Fort Armherst Dock Road Chatham ME4 4UB T: 01634 847747 W: www.fortamhurst.org.uk

Fort Luton Museum Magpie Hall Road Chatham ME4 5XJ T: 01634 813969

Guildhall Museum Guildhall Museum High Street Rochester ME1 1PY T: 01634 848717 F: 01634 832919 E: guildhall@medway.gov.uk W: www.medway.gov.uk

Guildhall Museum Rochester High St Rochester ME1 1PY T: 01634 848717 From 22/7/00 museum only responsible for the museum and Brook Pumping Station

Gunpowder Chart Mills Off Stonebridge Way Faversham ME13 7SE T: 01795 534542 F: 01795 533261 E: faversham@btinternet.com W: www.faversham.org

Herne Bay Museum Centre 12 William St Herne Bay CT6 5EJ T: 01227 367368 F: 01227 742560 E: museum@canterbury.gov.uk W: www.hernebay-museum.co.uk

Kent and Sharpshooters Yeomanry Museum Hever Castle Edenbridge TN8 7DB T: 020 8688 2138

Kent Battle of Britain Museum Aerodrome Rd Hawkinge Folkestone CT18 7AG T: 01303 893140

Lashenden Air Warfare Museum Headcorn Aerodrome Headcorn Nr Ashford TN27 9HX T: 01622 890226 F: 01622 890876

Maidstone Museum & Art Gallery St. Faith St Maidstone ME14 1LH T: 01622 754497

Margate Old Town Hall Museum Old Town Hall Market Place Margate CT9 1ER T: 01843 231213

Masonic Library & Museum St. Peters Place Canterbury CT1 2DA T: 01227 785625

Minster Abbey Gatehouse Museum Union Rd Minster On Sea Sheerness ME12 2HW T: 01795 872303

Minster Museum Craft & Animal Centre Bedlam Court Lane Minster Ramsgate CT12 4HQ T: 01843 822312

Museum of Kent Life Cobtree Lock Lane Sandling Maidstone ME14 3AU T: 01622 763936 F: 01622 662024 E: enquiries@museum-kentlife.co.uk W: www.museum-kentlife.co.uk

The Patterson Heritage Museum 2 - 6 Station Approach, Birchington on Sea, Kent CT7 9RD T: 01843 841649 E: pattersonheritage@tesco.net W: www.pattersonheritage.co.uk Please address all mail to 4 Station Approach, Birchington on Sea Kent CT7 9RD. No fees Donations welcome

Penshurst Place & Gardens Penshurts Tonbridge TN11 8DG T: 01892 870307 F: 01892 870866 E: enuiries@penshurstplace.com W: www.penshurstplace.com

Powell-Cotton Museum, Quex House and Gardens Quex Park Birchington CT7 0 T: 01843 842168 F: 01843 846661 E: powell-cotton.museum@virgin.net W: www.powell-cottonmuseum.co.uk

Princess of Wales's Royal Regt & Queen's Regt Museum Howe Barracks Canterbury CT1 1JY T: 01227-818056 F: 01227-818057 Covers Infantry Regiements of Surrey, Kent, Sussex, Hampshire and Middlesex

Quebec House Quebec Square Westerham TN16 1TD T: 01892 890651 F: 01892 890110

RAF Manston History Museum The Airfield Manston Road Ramsgate CT11 5DF T: 01843 825224 E: museum@rafmanston.fsnet.co.uk W: www.rafmuseum.fsnet.co.uk

Ramsgate Maritime Museum Clock House Pier Yard Royal Harbour Ramsgate CT11 8LS T: 01843 587765 F: 01843 582359 E: museum@ekmt.fsnet.co.uk W: www.ekmt.fsnet.co.uk

Ramsgate Maritime Museum The Clock House Pier Yard Royal Harbour Ramsgate CT11 8LS T: 01843 570622 F: 01843 582359 E: museum@ekmt.fsnet.co.uk W: www.ekmt.fsnet.co.uk

Rochester Cathedral Militia Museum Guildhall Museum High Street Rochester ME1 1PY T: 01634 848717 F: 01634 832919 E: guildhall@medway.gov.uk

Roman Dover Tourist Centre Painted House New street Dover CT17 9AJ T: 01304 203279

Roman Museum Butchery Lane Canterbury CT1 2JR T: 01227 785575 W: www.aboutbritain.com/CanterburyRomanMuseum

Romney Toy & Model Museum New Romney Station Romney TN28 8PL T: 01797 362353

Royal Engineers Library Brompton Barracks Chatham ME4 4UX T: 01634 822416 F: 01634 822419

Royal Engineers museum of Military Engineering Prince Arthur Road Gillingham ME4 4UG T: 01634 822839 F: 01634 822371 E: remuseum.rhgre@gtnet.gov.uk W: www.army.mod.uk/armymuseums

Royal Museum & Art Gallery 18 High St Canterbury CT1 2RA T: 01227 452747

Sheerness Heritage Centre 10 Rose St Sheerness ME12 1AJ T: 01795 663317

Shoreham Aircraft Museum High Street Shoreham Sevenoaks TN14 7TB T: 01959 524416 W: www.s-a-m.freeserve.co.uk

Spitfire and Hurricane Memorial Building The Airfield Manston Road Ramsgate CT11 5DF T: 01843 821940 F: 01843 821940 W: www.spitfire-museum.com

St Margaret's Museum Beach Road St Margaret's Bay Dover CT15 6DZ T: 01304 852764

Tenterden Museum Station Rd Tenterden TN30 6HN T: 01580 764310 F: 01580 766648

The Buffs Regimental Museum The Royal Museum 18 High Street Canterbury CT1 2JE T: 01227 452747 F: 01227 455047

The C.M Booth Collection Of Historic Vehicles 63-67 High St Rolvenden Cranbrook TN17 4LP T: 01580 241234

The Charles Dickens Centre Eastgate House High St Rochester ME1 1EW T: 01634 844176

The Grand Shaft Snargate Street Dover CT16 T: 01304 201066

The Historic Dockyard Chatham ME4 4TZ T: 01634 823800 F: 01634 823801 E: info@chdt.org.uk W: www.chdt.org.uk

The Queen's Own Royal West Kent Regiment Museum Maidstone Museum and Art Gallery St. Faith's Street Maidstone ME14 1LH T: 01622 602842 F: 01622 685022 E: simonlace@maidstone.gov.uk

The Romney, Hythe & Dymchurch Railway New Romney Station Romney TN28 8PL T: 01797 362353

The West Gate St Peters Street Canterbury T: 01227 452747 F: 1227455047

Timeball Tower Victoria Parade Deal CT14 7BP T: 01304 360897

Victoriana Museum Deal Town Hall High St Deal CT14 6BB T: 01304 380546

Walmer Castle and Gardens Kingsdown Road Walmer Deal CT14 7LJ T: 01304 364288 W: www.english-heritage.org.uk

Watts Charity Poor Travellers House 97 High St Rochester ME1 1LX T: 01634 845609

Whitstable Museum & Gallery 5a Oxford St Whitstable CT5 1DB T: 01227 276998 W: www.whitstable-museum.co.uk

Lancashire

Blackburn Museum and Art Gallery Museum Street Blackburn BB1 7AJ T: 01254 667130 F: 01254 685541 E: paul.flintoff@blackburn.gov.uk W: www.blackburnworld.com

Bolton Museum & Art Gallery Le Mans Crescent Bolton BL1 1SE T: 01204 332190 F: 01204 332241 E: bolwg@gn.apc.org

British in India Museum Newton Street Colne BB8 0JJ T: 01282 870215 T: 01282 613129 F: 01282 870215

Duke of Lancaster's Own Yeomanry Stanley St Preston PR1 4AT T: 01722 264074

East Lancashire Railway Bolton Street Station Bolton Street Bury BL9 0EY T: 0161 764 7790 F: 0161 763 4408 E: admin@east-lancs-rly.co.uk W: www.east-lancs-rly.co.uk

East Lancashire Regiment Towneley Hall Burnley BB11 3RQ T: 1282424213 F: 01282 436138 E: towneleyhall@burnley.gov.uk W: www.towneleyhall.org.uk

Ellenroad Trust Ltd Ellenroad Engine House Elizabethan Way Milnrow Rochdale OL16 4LG T: 01706 881952 E: ellenroad@aol.com W: http:\\ellenroad.homepage.com

Fleetwood Museum Queens Terrace Fleetwood FY7 6BT T: 01253 876621 F: 01253 878088 E: fleetwood.museum@mus.lancscc.gov.uk W: www.nettingthebay.org.uk

Gawthorpe Hall Habergham Drive Padiham Burnley BB12 8UA T: 01282 771004 E: gawthorpehall@museumsoflancs.org.uk W: www.museumsoflancs.org.uk

Hall I'Th' Wood Museum Hall I Th' Wood Tonge Moor Bolton BL1 8UA T: 01204 301159

Heaton Park Tramway (Transport Museum) Tram Depot Heaton Park Prestwich Manchester M25 2SW T: 0161 740 1919

Helmshore Textile Museums Holcombe Road Helmshore Rossendale BB4 4NP T: 01706 226459 F: 01706 218554

Heritage Trust for the North West within Pendle Heritage Centre Colne Rd Barrowford Nelson BB9 6JQ T: 01282 661704

Judge's Lodgings Museum Church St Lancaster LA1 1LP T: 01524 32808

King's Own Royal Regimental Museum The City Museum Market Square Lancaster LA1 1HT T: 01524 64637 F: Fax: 01524 841692 E: kingsownmuseum@iname.com

Kippers Cats 51 Bridge St Ramsbottom Bury BL0 9AD T: 01706 822133

Lancaster City Museum Market Square Lancaster LA1 1HT T: 01524 64637 F: 01524 841692 E: awhite@lancaster.gov.uk

Lancaster Maritime Museum Custom House St George's Quay Lancaster LA1 1RB T: 01524 64637 F: 01524 841692

Lytham Heritage Group 2 Henry St Lytham St. Annes FY8 5LE T: 01253 730767

Manchester Museum University of Manchester Oxford Rd Manchester M13 9PL T: 0161 275 2634

Manchester Museum Education Service University of Manchester Oxford Rd Manchester M13 9PL T: 0161 275 2630 F: 0161 275 2676 E: education@man.ac.uk W: http://museum.man.ac.uk

Museum of Lancashire Stanley Street Preston Lancashire PR1 4YP T: 01772-264079 E: museum@lancs.co.uk

Museum of Lancashire (Queen's Lancashire Regiment Duke of Lancaster's Own Yeomanry Lancashire Hussars 14th/20th King's Hussars) Stanley Street Preston PR1 4YP T: 01772 534075 F: 01772 534079 Credit Cards accepted

Museum of the Manchester Regiment Ashton Town Hall Market Place Ashton-u-Lyne OL6 6DL T: 0161 342 3078 E: museum.manchester@nxcorp1.tameside.gov.uk W: www.tameside.gov.uk

Museum of the Queen's Lancashire Regiment (East South and Loyal (North Lancashire) Regiments, Lancashire Regiment (PWV) and The Queen's Lancashire Regiment Fulwood Barracks Preston PR2 8AA T: 01772 260362 F: 01772 260583 E: rhq.qlr@talk21.com Including associated Volunteer, TA and Militia Units

North West Sound Archive Old Steward's Office Clitheroe Castle Clitheroe BB7 1AZ T: 01200-427897 F: 01200-427897 E: nwsa@ed.lancscc.gov.uk W: www.lancashire.gov.uk/education/lifelong/recordindex

Oldham Museum Greaves St Oldham OL1 1 T: 0161 911 4657

Ordsall Hall Museum Taylorson St Salford M5 3HT T: 0161 872 0251

Pendle Heritage Centre Park Hill Colne Rd Barrowford Nelson BB9 6JQ T: 01282 661702 F: 01282 611718

Portland Basin Museum Portland Place Ashton-Under-Lyne OL7 0QA T: 0161 343 2878

Queen St Mill Harle Syke Queen St Briercliffe Burnley BB10 2HX T: 01282 459996

Rawtenstall Museum Whitaker Park Haslingden Road Rawtenstall T: 01706 244682 F: 01706 250037

Ribchester Museum of Roman Antiquities Riverside Ribchester Preston PR3 3XS T: 01254 878261 W: www.aboutbritain.com/Ribchester Roman Museum.htm

Ribchester Roman Museum Riverside Ribchester Preston PR3 3XS T: 01254 878261 F: 01772 264080

Rochdale Museum Service The Arts & Heritage Centre The Esplanade Rochdale OL16 1AQ T: 01706 641085

Rochdale Pioneers Museum Toad Lane Rochdale OL12 0NU T: 01706 524920

Saddleworth Museum & Art Gallery High St Uppermill Oldham OL3 6HS T: 01457 874093 F: 01457 870336

Salford Museum & Art Gallery Peel Park Salford M5 4WU T: 0161 736 2649 E: info@lifetimes.org.uk W: www.lifetimes.org.uk

Slaidburn Heritage Centre 25 Church St Slaidburn Clitheroe BB7 3ER T: 01200 446161 F: 01200 446161 E: slaidburn.heritage@htnw.co.uk W: www.htnw.co.uk_slaidburn.org.uk

Smithills Hall Museum Smithills Hall Dean Road Bolton BL1 7NP T: 01204 841265

South Lancashire Regiment Prince of Wales Volunteers Museum Peninsula Barracks Warrington

The British in India Museum Newtown Street Colne T: 01282 613129 0976 665320 F: 01282 870215 Open April to september Wednesday & Saturdays 2pm to 5pm

The Fusiliers Museum (Lancashire) Wellington Barracks Bolton Road Bury BL8 2PL T: 0161 764 2208

The Greater Manchester Police Museum 57 Newton St Manchester M1 1ES T: 0161 856 3287 0161 856 3288 F: 0161 856 3286

The Museum of Science and Industry In Manchester Liverpool Rd Castlefield Manchester M3 4JP T: 0161 832 2244 0161 832 1830 (24 hour info line) F: 0161 833 2184 E: marketing@msim.org.uk W: www.msim.org.uk

The Rochdale Pioneers' Museum 31 Toad Lane Rochdale T: 01706-524920

Weaver's Cottage Bacup Road Rawtenstall T: 01706 229937 01706 226459 E: rossendale_leisure@compuserve.com

Weavers Cottage Heritage Centre Weavers Cottage Bacup Rd Rawtenstall Rossendale BB4 7NW T: 01706 229828 F: 01706 210915

Whitworth Museum North Street Whitworth T: 01706 343231 01706 853655 E: rossendale_leisure@compuserve.com

Leicestershire

New Walk Museum New Walk Museum 53 New Walk Leicester LE1 7AE T: 0116 247 3220 E: hide001@leicester.gov.uk W: www.leicestermuseums.co.uk

Abbey Pumping Station Corporation Rd Abbey Lane Leicester LE4 5PX T: 0116 299 5111 F: 0116 299 5125 W: www.leicestermuseums.ac.uk

Ashby De La Zouch Museum North St Ashby-De-La-Zouch LE65 1HU T: 01530 560090

Belgrave Hall & Gardens Church Rd Belgrave Leicester LE4 5PE T: 0116 266 6590 F: 0116 261 3063 E: marte001@leicester.gov.uk W: www.leicestermuseums.org.uk

Bellfoundry Museum Freehold St Loughborough LE11 1AR T: 01509 233414

Bosworth Battlefield Visitor Centre Sutton Cheney Market Bosworth Nuneaton CV13 0AD T: 01455 290429 T: 0116 265 6961 (Rosemary Mills) F: 01455 292841 E: bosworth@leics.gov.uk W: www.leics.gov.uk

British Aviation Heritage Bruntingthorpe Aerodrome Bruntingthorpe Lutterworth LE17 5QH T: 0116 221 8426 E: Banmuseums@hotmail.com W: www.jetman.dircon.co.uk/brunty

Charnwood Museum Granby St Loughborough LE11 3DU T: 01509 233754 F: 01509 268140 W: www.leics.gov.uk/museums/musinliecs.htm#charnwood

Foxton Canal Museum Middle Lock Gumley Rd Foxton Market Harborough LE16 7RA T: 0116 279 2657

Harborough Museum Council Offices Adam and Eve Street Market Harborough LE16 7AG T: 01858 821085 F: 01509 268140 E: museums@leics.gov.uk W: www.leics.gov.uk/museums/musinliecs.htm#harborough

Hinckley & District Museum Ltd Framework Knitters Cottage Lower Bond St Hinckley LE10 1QU T: 01455 251218

Jewry Wall Museum St. Nicholas Circle Leicester LE1 4LB T: 0116 247 3021

Leicester City Museum & Art Gallery 53 New Walk Leicester LE1 7EA T: 0116 255 4100

Leicester Gas Museum - Closed Archive material transferred to The National Gas Archive.

Leicestershire Ecology Centre Holly Hayes Environmental Resources Centre 216 Birstall Rd Birstall Leicester LE4 4DG T: 0116 267 1950 F: 0116 267 7112 E: dlott@leics.gov.uk

Leicestershire Yeomanry, Leicestershire Tigers Museum Loughborough War Memorial Queen's Park Loughborough T: 01509 263370

Melton Carnegie Museum Thorpe End Melton Mowbray LE13 1RB T: 01664 569946 F: 01664 569946 E: museums@leics.gov.uk W: www.liecs.gov.uk/museums/#melton

Royal Leicestershire Regiment Museum Gallery New Walk Museum New Walk Leicester LE1 7FA T: 0116 2470403 closed for refurbishment to 2005 Postal enquiries: Newarke Houses Museum, The Newarke, Leicester LE2 7BY

Royal Leicestershire Regimental Gallery New Walk Museum 53 New Walk Leicester LE1 7AE T: 0116 247 3220 E: hide001@leicester.gov.uk W: www.leicestermuseums.co.uk

Snibston Discovery Park Ashby Rd Coalville LE67 3LN T: 01530 510851 F: 01530 813301 E: museums@leics.gov.uk W: www.leics.gov.uk/museums/musinliecs.htm#snibston

The Guildhall Guildhall Lane Leicester LE1 5FQ T: 0116 253 2569

The Manor House Manor Rd Donington Le Heath Coalville LE67 2FW T: 01530 831259 F: 01530 831259 E: museums@leics.gov.uk W: www.leics.gov.uk/museums/musinliecs.htm#manor

Lincolnshire

50 and 61 Suadrons' Museum The Lawn Union Road Lincoln

Alford Civic Trust Manor House Museum West Street Alford LN13 9DJ T: 01507 463073 Closed Sept 2003 to 2005 for refurbishment.

Ayscoughfee Hall Museum & Gardens Churchgate Spalding PE11 2RA T: 01775 725468 F: 01775 762715

Battle of Britain Memorial Flight Visitor Centre R.A.F Coningsby Coningsby Lincoln LN4 4SY T: 01526 344041 F: 01526 342330 E: bbmf@lincolnshire.gov.uk W: www.lincolnshire.gov.uk/bbmt

Bomber County Aviation Museum Ex RAF Hemswell Hemswell cliff Gainsborough T: 01724 855410 T: 01482 215859

Boston Guildhall Museum South Street Boston PE21 6HT T: 01205 365954 E: heritage@originalboston.freeserve.co.uk

Church Farm Museum Church Rd South Skegness PE25 2HF T: 01754 766658 F: 01754 898243 E: wifff@lincolnshire.gov.uk

Cranwell Avation Heritage Centre Heath Farm North Raunceby Near Cranwell Sleaford NG34 8QR T: 01529 488490 F: 01529 488490

Gainsborough Old Hall Parnell St Gainsborough DN21 2NB T: 01427 612669

Gordon Boswell Romany Museum Hawthorns Clay Lake Spalding PE12 6BL T: 01775 710599

Grantham Museum St. Peters Hill Grantham NG31 6PY T: 01476 568783 F: 01476 592457

Lincolnshire Aviation Heritage Centre East Kirkby Airfield East Kirkby Spilsby PE23 4DE T: 01790 763207 F: 01790 763207 E: enquiries@lincsaviation.co.uk W: www.lincsaviation.co.uk cc accepted

Lincs Vintage Vehicle Society Whisby Rd North Hykeham Lincoln LN6 3QT T: 01522 500566

Louth Naturalists Antiquarian & Literary Society 4 Broadbank Louth LN11 0EQ T: 01507 601211

Metheringham Airfield Visitor Centre Westmoor Farm Martin Moor Metheringham LN4 3BO T: 01526 378270E: foma-lincs@hotmail.com

Museum of Lincolnshire Life Old Barracks Burton Road Lincoln LN1 3LY T: 01522-528448 F: 01522-521264 E: lincolnshirelife_museum@lincolnshire.gov.uk W: www.lincolnshire.gov.uk/museumoflincolnshirelife

National Fishing Heritage Centre Alexander Dock Great Grimsby DN31 1UZ T: 01472-323345 W: www.nelincs.gov.uk

RAF Digby Ops Room Museum RAF Digby Scopwick Lincoln LN4 3LH T: 01526 327503 W: www.airops.freeserve.co.uk

Royal Lincolnshire Regiment Lincolnshire Yeomanry Museum Old Barracks Burton Road Lincoln LN1 3LY T: 01522-528448 F: 01522-521264 E: finchj@lincolnshire.gov.uk

The Incredibly Fantastic Old Toy Show 26 Westgate Lincoln LN1 3BD T: 01522 520534

The Queen's Royal Lancers Regimental Museum (16th/5th and 17th/21st Lancers) Belvoir Castle nr Grantham NG32 1PD T: 0115 957 3295 F: 0115 957 3195

Thorpe Camp Visitor Centre Tattersall Thorpe Lincoln LN T: 01205 361334 E: mjhodgson@lancfile.demon.co.uk W: www.thorpecamp.org.uk

Lincolnshire – North

Baysgarth House Museum Caistor Rd Barton-Upon-Humber DN18 6AH T: 01652 632318

Immingham Museum Immingham Resorce Centre Margaret St Immingham DN40 1LE T: 01469 577066

North Lincolnshire Museum Oswald Rd Scunthorpe DN15 7BD T: 01724 843533 E: David.Williams@northlincs.gov.uk W: www.northlincs.gov.uk\museums

Liverpool

King's Regiment Collection Museum of Liverpool Life Pier Head Liverpool L3 1PZ T: 0151-478-4062 Collection of 8th Kings Liverpool Regiment 1685 to 1958 & the Kings Regt 1958 to date.

Liverpool Maritime Museum William Brown Street Liverpool L3 8EN T: 0151-2070001

London

Alexander Fleming Laboratory Museum / St Mary's NHS Trust Archives St Mary's Hospital Praed Street Paddington London W2 1NY T: (020) 7886 6528 F: (020) 7886 6739 E: kevin.brown@st-marys.nhs.uk W: www.st-marys.nhs.uk

Bank of England Archive Archive Section HO-SV The Bank of England Threadneedle Street London EC2R 8AH T: (020) 7601-5096 F: (020) 7601-4356 E: archive@bankofengland.co.uk W: www.bankofengland.co.uk

Berkshire and Westminster Dragoons Museum Cavalry House, Duke of York's Headquarters Kings Road Chelsea London SW3 4SC T: 020 7414 5233

Bethlem Royal Hospital Archives and Museum Monks Orchard Road Beckenham BR3 3BX T: (020) 8776 4307 T: (020) 8776 4053 F: (020) 8776 4045 E: museum@bethlem.freeserve.co.uk

Bethnal Green Museum of Childhood Cambridge Heath Rd London E2 9PA T: (020) 8980 2415 F: (020) 8983 5225 E: k.bines@vam.ac.uk

Black Cultural Archives see National

Britain at War Experience Winston Churchill 64-66 Tooley Street London Bridge London SE1 2TF T: 020 7403 3171 F: 020 7403 5104 E: britainatwar@dial.pipex.com W: www.britainatwar.co.uk

British Dental Association Museum (MUSEUM CLOSED) 64 Wimpole Street London W1M 8AL T: (020) 7935-0875-ext-209

British Museum see National

British Red Cross Museum and Archives see National

Cabinet War Rooms Clive Steps King Charles Street SW1A 2AQ T: (020) 7930 6961 E: cwr@iwm.org.uk W: www.iwm.org.uk

Church Farmhouse Museum Greyhound Hill Hendon NW4 4JR T: (020) 8203 0130 F: (020) 8359 2666 W: www.earl.org.uk/partners/barnet/churchf.htm

Crystal Palace Museum Anerley Hill London SE19 T: 020 8676 0700

Cutty Sark King William Walk London SE10 9HT T: (020) 8858 2698 F: (020) 8858 6976 E: info@cuttysark.org.uk W: www.cuttysark.org.uk Postal address:2 Greenwich Church Street London SE10 9BG

Design Museum Butlers Wharf 28 Shad Thames London SE1 2YD T: (020) 7940 8791 T: (020) 7403 6933 F: (020) 7378 6540 E: enquiries@designmuseum.org.uk W: www.designmuseum.org

Dickens House Museum 48 Doughty St London WC1N 2LF T: (020) 7405 2127 E: DHmuseum@rmplc.co.uk W: www.dickensmuseum.com

Doctor Johnson's House 17 Gough Square London EC4A 3DE T: (020) 7353 3745

Firepower - The Royal Artillery Museum Royal Arsenal Woolwich London SE18 6ST T: (020) 8855 7755 E: info@firepower.org.uk W: www.firepower.org.uk

Florence Nightingale Museum 2 Lambeth Palace Road London SE1 7EW T: (020) 7620-0374 F: (020) 7928-1760 E: curator@florence-nightingale.co.uk W: www.florence-nightingale.co.uk

Freud Museum 20 Maresfield Gardens London NW3 5SX T: (020) 735-2002 T: (020) 735-5167 F: (020) 431 5452 E: freud@gn.apc.org W: www.freud.org.uk

Fusiliers' London Volunteer Museum 213 Balham High Road London SW17 7BQ T: 020 8672 1168

Geffrye Museum Kingsland Rd London E2 8EA T: (020) 7739 9893 F: (020) 7729 5647 E: info@geffrye-museum.org.uk W: www.geffrye-museum.org.uk CC Accepted

Golden Hinde Living History Museum St. Mary Overie Dock Cathedral St SE1 9DE T: 08700 118700 F: 020 7407 5908 E: info@goldenhinde.co.uk W: www.goldenhinde.co.uk

Grange Museum of Community History The Grange Neasden Lane Neasden London NW10 1QB T: (020) 8452 8311 T: (020) 8937 3600 F: (020) 8208 4233

Greenwich Heritage Centre Artillery Square, Royal Arsenal, Woolwich, London SE18 4DX T: 020 8854 2452 E: heritage.centre@greenwich.gov.uk W: www.greenwich.gov.uk

Grenadier Guards Record Office Wellington Barracks Birdcage Walk London SW1E 6HQ E: rhqgrengds@yahoo.co.uk Access is by appointment made in advance. Search fee of £25.00 per search

Guards Museum Wellington Barracks Birdcage Walk London SW1E 6HQ T: (020) 7414 3271/3428 F: (020) 7414 3429

Gunnersbury Park Museum Gunnersbury Park Popes Lane W3 8LQ T: (020) 8992 1612 E: gp-museum@cip.org.uk

H.M.S. Belfast Morgans Lane Tooley Street London SE1 2JH T: (020) 7940 6300 F: (020) 7403 0719 W: www.iwm.org.uk

Hackney Museum Service Parkside Library Victoria Park Rd London E9 7JL T: (020) 8986 6914 E: hmuseum@hackney.gov.uk W: www.hackney.gov.uk/hackneymuseum

Handel House Museum 25 Brook Street London W1K 4HB T: (020) 7495 1685 F: (020) 7495 1759 E: mail@handelhouse.org W: www.handelhouse.org

Hogarth's House Hogarth Lane Chiswick London W4 2QN T: (020) 8994 6757

Honourable Artillery Company Armoury House City Road London EC1Y 2BQ T: 020 7382 1537 F: 020 7382 1538 E: hac@hac.org.uk W: www.hac.org.uk

Horniman Museum 100 London Rd Forest Hill London SE23 3PQ T: (020) 8699 1872 F: (020) 8291 5506 E: enquiries@horniman.co.uk W: www.horniman.co.uk

House Mill River Lea Tidal Mill Trust , Three Mills Island Three Mill Lane Bromley by Bow London E3 3DU T: (020) 8980-4626

Imperial War Museum Lambeth Road London SE1 6HZ T: (020) 7416-5000 T: (020) 7416 5348 F: (020) 7416 5374 (020) 7416 5246 E: books@iwm.org.uk W: www.iwm.org.uk

Imperial War Museum Film and Video Archive see National

Inns of Court and City Yeomanry Museum 10 Stone buildings Lincoln's Inn London WC2A 3TG T: 020 7405 8112 Open Mon to Fri 1000 - 1600 by appointment only

Island History Trust St. Matthias Old Church Woodstock Terrace Poplar High St London E14 0AE T: (020) 7987 6041

Islington Museum Foyer Gallery Town Hall Upper St N1 2UD T: (020) 7354 9442

James Clavell Library Royal Arsenal (West) Warren Lane Woolwich London SE18 6ST T: 020 8312 7125 E: library@firepower.org.uk W: www.firepower.org.uk

Jewish Museum The Sternberg Centre for Judaism 80 East End Road Finchley London N3 2SY T: 020 8349 1143 F: 020 8343 2162 E: enquiries@jewishmuseum.org.uk W: www.jewishmuseum.org.uk

Keats House Museum Wentworth Place Keats Grove NW3 2RR T: (020) 7435 2062

Kensington Palace State Apartments Kensington Palace London W8 4PX T: (020) 7937 9561

Leighton House Museum 12 Holland Park Rd London W14 8LZ T: 020 7602 3316 F: 020 7371 2467 E: museums@rbkc.gov.uk W: www.rbkc.gov.uk/leightonhousemuseum

Library of the Royal College of Surgeons of England 35-43 Lincoln's Inn Fields London WC2A 3PN T: (020) 7869 6520 F: (020) 7405 4438 E: library@rseng.ac.uk W: www.rseng.ac.uk Research enquiries are not undertaken. Appointments required.

Livesey Museum for Children 682 Old Kent Rd London SE15 1JF T: (020) 7639 5604 F: (020) 7277 5384 E: livesley.museum@southwark.gov.uk

Lloyds Nelson Collection Lloyds of London Lime Street London EC3M 7HA T: 020 7327 6260 F: 020 7327 6400

London Borough of Greenwich Heritage Centre Museum and Library Building 41 Royal Arsenal Woolwich London SE18 6SP T: (020) 8858 4631 F: (020) 8293 4721 E: local.history@greenwich.gov.uk W: www.greenwich.gov.uk

London Canal Museum 12-13 New Wharf Rd London N1 9RT T: (020) 7713 0836 W: www.charitynet.org/~LCanalMus/

London Fire Brigade Museum 94a Southwark Bridge Rd London SE1 0EG T: (020) 7587 2894 F: (020) 7587 2878 E: esther.mann@london-fire.gov.uk

London Gas Museum Twelvetrees Crescent London E3 3JH T: (020) 7538 4982 Closed. Exhibits in storage John Doran Gas Museum 0116 250 3190 or National Gas Archive 0161 777 7193

London Irish Rifles Regimental Museum Duke of York's Headquarters Kings Road Chelsea London SW3 4SA

London Scottish Regimental Museum RHQ 95 Horseferry Road London SW1P 2DX T: 020 7233 7909 E: smallpipes@aol.com

London Toy & Model Museum 21-23 Craven Hill London W2 3EN T: (020) 7706 8000

London Transport Museum Covent Garden Piazza London WC2E 7BB T: (020) 7379 6344 F: (020) 7565 7250 E: contact@ltmuseum.co.uk W: www.ltmuseum.co.uk

Mander & Mitchenson Theatre Collection c/o Salvation Army Headquarters PO BOx 249 101 Queen Victoria Street London EC49 4EP T: (020) 7236 0182 F: (020) 7236 0184

Markfield Beam Engine & Museum Markfield Rd London N15 4RB T: (020) 8800 7061 T: 01763 287 331 E: alan@mbeam.org W: www.mbeam.org

Metropolitan Police Historical Museum c/o T.P.H.Q., Fin & res 4th Floor Victoria Embankment London SW1A 2JL T: (020) 8305-2824 T: (020) 8305-1676 F: (020) 8293-6692

Museum in Docklands Library & Archives Library & Archive No 1 Warehouse, West India Quay Hertsmere Road London E14 4AL T: (020) 7001 9825 (Librarian) F: (020) 7001 9801 E: bobaspinall@museumindocklands.org.uk W: www.museumindocklands.org.uk

Museum of London London Wall London EC2Y 5HN T: F: 0171-600-1058 E: info@museumoflondon.org.uk

Museum of the Order of St John St John's Gate St John's Lane, Clerkenwell, London EC1M 4DA T: (020) 7253-6644 F: (020) 7336 0587 W: www.sja.org.uk/history

Museum of the Royal Pharmaceutical Society Museum of the Royal Pharmaceutical Society 1 Lambeth High Street London SE1 7JN T: (020) 7572 2210E: museum@rpsgb.org.uk W: www.rpsgb.org.uk

Museums Association 42 Clerkenwell Close London EC1R 0PA T: (020) 7250 1789 F: (020) 7250 1929

National Army Museum Royal Hospital Road London SW3 4HT T: (020) 7730-0717 F: (020) 7823-6573 E: info@national-army-museum.ac.uk W: www.national-army-museum.ac.uk incorporating Middlesex Regiment Museum & Buffs regiment Museum

National Army Museum Department of Archives (Photographs, Film & Sound) Royal Hospital Road London SW3 4HT T: (020) 7730-0717 F: (020) 7823-6573 E: info@national-army-museum.ac.uk W: www.national-army-museum.ac.uk

National Gallery see National

National Portrait Gallery see National

Newham Museum Service The Old Town Hall 29 The Broadway Stratford E15 4BQ T: (020) 8534 2274

North Woolwich Old Station Musuem Pier Rd North Woolwich London E16 2JJ T: (020) 7474 7244

Percival David Foundation of Chinese Art 53 Gordon Square London WC1H 0PD T: (020) 7387 3909 F: (020) 7383 5163

Petrie Museum of Egyptian Archaeology University College London Gower St WC1E 6BT T: (020) 7504 2884 F: (020) 7679 2886 E: petrie.museum@ucl.ac.uk

Pitshanger Manor & Gallery Mattock Lane London W5 5EQ T: (020) 8567 1227 F: (020) 8567 0595 E: pitshanger@ealing.gov.uk

Polish Institute & Sikorski Museum 20 Princes Gate London SW7 1PT T: (020) 7589 9249

Pollock's Toy Museum 1 Scala St London W1P 1LT T: (020) 7636 3452

Princess Louise's Kensington Regiment Museum Duke of York's Headquarters Kings Road Chelsea London SW3 4RX T:

Pump House Educational Museum Lavender Pond & Nature Park Lavender Rd Rotherhithe SE16 1DZ T: (020) 7231 2976

Ragged School Museum Trust 46-50 Copperfield Rd London E3 4RR T: (020) 8980 6405 F: (020) 89833481 W: www.ics-london.co.uk/rsm

Royal Air Force Museum Grahame Park Way Hendon London NW9 5LL T: (020) 8205-2266 F: (020) 8200 1751 E: groupbusiness@rafmuseum.org.uk W: www.rafmuseum.org.uk

Royal Armouries see National

Royal London Hospital Archives and Museum Royal London Hospital Newark Whitechapel London E1 1BB T: (020) 7377-7608 F: (020) 7377 7413 E: r.j.evans@mds.qmw.ac.uk W: www.bartsandthelondon.org.uk

Royal Observatory Greenwich Romney Road Greenwich London SE10 9NF T: (020) 8858-4422 F: (020) 8312-6632 W: www.nmm.ac.uk

Sam Uriah Morris Society 136a Lower Clapton Rd London E5 0QJ T: (020) 8985 6449

Sir John Soane's Museum 13 Lincolns Inn Fields London WC2A 3BP T: (020) 7430 0175 F: (020) 7831 3957 W: www.soane.org

St Bartholomew's Hospital Archives & Museum Archives and Museum West Smithfield London EC1A 7BE T: (020) 7601-8152 F: (020) 7606 4790 E: marion.rea@bartsandthelondon.nhs.uk W: www.brlcf.org.uk

The Association of Jewish Ex-Service Men and Women Military Museum AJEX House East Bank Stamford London N16 5RT T: 020 8800 2844 020 8802 7610 F: 020 8880 1117 W: www.ajex.org.uk

The Clink Prison Museum 1 Clink St London SE1 9DG T: (020) 7403 6515 F:

The Fan Museum 12 Crooms Hill London SE10 8ER T: (020) 8858 7879 F: (020) 8293 1889 E: admin@fan-museum.org W: www.fan-museum.org

The Iveagh Bequest Kenwood House Hampstead Lane London NW3 7JR T: (020) 8348 1286

The Museum of Women's Art 3rd Floor 11 Northburgh St London EC1V 0AN T: (020) 7251 4881

The Natural History Museum Cromwell Road London SW7 5BD T: (020) 7942 5000 W: www.nhm.ac.uk

The Old Operating Theatre Museum & Herb Garret 9a St. Thomas's St London SE1 9RY T: (020) 7955 4791 F: (020) 7378 8383 E: curator@thegarret.org.uk W: www.the garret.org.uk

The Royal Regiment of Fusiliers H M Tower of London London EC3N 4AB T: (020) 7488 5610 F: (020) 7481 1093

The Science Museum see National

The Sherlock Holmes Museum 221b Baker St London NW1 6XE T: (020) 7935 8866 F: (020) 7738 1269 E: sherlock@easynet.co.uk W: www.sherlock-holmes.co.uk

The Wellcome Trust 183 Euston Rd London NW1 2BE T: (020) 7611 8888 F: (020) 7611 8545 E: infoserv@wellcome.ac.uk W: www.wellcome.ac.uk

Theatre Museum Russell Street Convent Garden London WC2 T: 020 7943 4700 E: info@theatremuseum.org W: www.theatremuseum.org

Valence House Museum see Essex

Vestry House Museum Vestry Road Walthamstow London E17 9NH T: (020) 8509-1917 E: vestry.house@al.lbwf.gov.uk W: W: www.lbwf.gov.uk/vestry/vestry.htm 1901 census

Veterinary Museum Royal Vetinerary College Royal College Street London NW1 0TU T: (020) 768-5165 T: (020) 768-5166 F: (020) 7468 5162 E: Email: fhouston@rvc.ac.uk W: W: www.rvc.ac.uk

Victoria & Albert Museum see National

Wallace Collection Hertford House Manchester Square London W1V 3BN T: 020 7563 9500 F: 020 7224 2155 E: enquiries@wallacecollection.org W: www.wallacecollection.org

Wellington Museum - Apsley House Apsley House 149 Piccadilly Hyde Park Corner London W1J 7NT T: 020 7499 5676 F: 020 7493 6576 W: www.apsleyhouse.org.uk

Westminster Abbey Museum Westminster Abbey Deans Yard SW1P 3PA T: (020) 7233 0019

Wimbledon Lawn Tennis Museum The All England Lawn Tennis & Croquet Club Church Road Wimbledon London SW19 5AE T: (020) 8946 6131 F: (020) 8944 6497 E: museum@aeltc.com W: www.wimbledon.org/museum CC accepted

Wimbledon Museum of Local History 22 Ridgeway London SW19 4QN T: (020) 8296 9914

Manchester

Manchester Jewish Museum 190 Cheetham Hill Road Manchester M8 8LW T: 0161 834 9879 F: 0161 834 9801 E: info@machesterjewishmuseum.com W: www.machesterjewishmuseum.com

Manchester Museum of Science and Industry Liverpool Road Castlefield Manchester M3 4FP T: 0161 832 2244 F: 0161 833 1471 E: n.forder@msim.org.uk W: www.msim.org.uk

Wigan Heritage Service Museum History Shop Library Street Wigan WN1 1NU T: 01942 828020 F: 01942 827645 E: heritage@wiganmbc.gov.uk W: www.wiganmbc.gov.uk 1901 census

Merseyside

Beatle Story Ltd Britannia Vaults Albert Dock Liverpool L3 4AA T: 0151 709 1963 F: 0151 708 0039

Botanic Gardens Museum Churchtown Southport PR9 7NB T: 01704 227547 F: 01704 224112

Liverpool Scottish Regimental Museum 15 Rydal Bank Lower Bebington Wirral L23 2SH T: 0151 645 5717 E: ilriley@liverpoolscottish.org.uk W: www.liverpoolscottish.org.uk

Merseyside Maritime Museum Maritime Archives and Library Albert Dock Liverpool L3 4AQ T: 0151-478-4418 T: 0151 478 4424 F: 0151-478-4590 E: archives@nmgmarchives.demon.co.uk W: www.nmgm.org.uk

National Museums & Galleries on Merseyside 127 Dale St Liverpool L2 2JH T: 0151 207 0001

Prescot Museum 34 Church St Prescot L34 3LA T: 0151 430 7787

Shore Road Pumping Station Shore Rd Birkenhead CH41 1AG T: 0151 650 1182

Western Approaches 1 Rumford St Liverpool L2 8SZ T: 0151 227 2008 F: 0151 236 6913

Middlesex

Forty Hall Museum Forty Hill Enfield EN2 9HA T: (020) 8363 8196

Harrow Museum & Heritage Centre Headstone Manor Pinner View Harrow HA2 6PX T: 020 8861 2626

HQ No 11 (Fighter) Group Battle of Britain Operations Room RAF Uxbridge Uxbridge UB10 0RZ T: 01895 815400 F: 01895 815666

Kew Bridge Steam Museum Green Dragon Lane Brentford TW8 0EN T: (020) 8568 4757 F: (020) 8569 9978 E: info@kbsm.org W: www.kbsm.org

Royal Military School of Music Museum Kneller Hall Twickenham TW2 7DU T: 020 8744 8652 F: 020 8898 7906 E: rmsm.kellerhall@btinternet.com

The Musical Museum 368 High St Brentford TW8 0BD T: (020) 8560 8108

Norfolk
Battlefields Trust see National
100th Bomb Group Memorial Museum Common Road
Dickleburgh Diss IP21 4PH T: 01379 740708 Correspondence
address: 41 Vancouver Avenue, Kings Lynn, Norfolk PE30 5RD
Air Defence Radar Museum RAF Neatishead Norwich NR12 8YB
T: 01692 633309 F: 01692 633214 E: curator@radarmuseum.co.uk
W: www.radarmuseum.co.uk
Bressingham Steam & Gardens Bressingham Diss IP22 2AB T:
01379 687386 T: 01379 687382 (24 hour info line) F: 01379 688085
Bure Valley Railway Norwich Road Aylsham NR11 6BW T: 01263
733858
Castle Museum Castle Hill Norwich NR1 3JU T: 01603 493624
Cholmondeley Collection of Model Soldiers Houghton Hall
Houghton Kings Lynn PE31 6UE T: 01485 528569 F: 01485 528167
E: administrator@houghtonhall.com W: www.houghtonhall.com
City of Norwich Aviation Museum Hosham St Faith Norwich NR10
3JF T: 01603 893080 F: 01692 633214
City of Norwich Aviation Museum Ltd Old Norwich Rd Horsham
St. Faith Norwich NR10 3JF T: 01603 893080
Diss Museum The Market Place Diss IP22 3JT T: 01379 650618
EcoTech Swaffham PE37 7HT T: 01760 726100 F: 01760 726109 E:
info@ecotech.rmplc.co.uk W: www.ecotech.org.uk
Elizabethan House Museum 4 South Quay Great Yarmouth NR30
2QH T: 01493 855746
Feltwell (Historical and Archaeological) Society 16 High Street
Feltwell Thetford IP26 4AF T: 01842 828448 E:
peterfeltwell@tinyworld.co.uk The Museum is at The Beck, Feltwell
Glandford Shell Museum Church House Glandford Holt NR25 7JR
T: 01263 740081
Iceni Village & Museums Cockley Cley Swaffham PE37 8AG T:
01760 721339
Inspire Hands On Science Centre Coslany St Norwich NR3 3DJ T:
01603 612612
Lynn Museum Old Market St King's Lynn PE30 1NL T: 01553
775001 F: 01553 775001 W: www.norfolk.gov.uk/tourism/museums
Maritime Museum for East Anglia 25 Marine Parade Great
Yarmouth NR30 2EN T: 01493 842267
Norfolk Motorcycle Museum Station Yard Norwich Rd North
Walsham NR28 0DS T: 01692 406266
Norfolk Rural Life Museum & Union Farm Beach House
Gressenhall East Dereham NR20 4DR T: 01362 860563 F: 01362
860563 E: frances.collinson.mus@norfolk.gov.uk W:
www.norfolk.gov.uk
Royal Norfolk Regimental Museum Shirehall Market Avenue
Norwich NR1 3JQ T: 01603 493649 F: 01603 765651 E:
regimental.museum@central.norfolk.gov.uk W: www.norfolk.gov.uk
Sheringham Museum Station Rd Sheringham NR26 8RE T: 01263
821871
Shirehall Museum Common Place Walsingham NR22 6BP T: 01328
820510 F: 01328 820098 E: walsinghammuseum@farmline.com
The Air Defence Battle Command & Control Museum Neatishead
Norwich NR12 8YB T: 01692 633309
The Muckleburgh Collection Weybourne Holt NR25 7EG T: 01263
588210 F: 01263 588425 E: info@muckleburgh.co.uk W:
www.muckleburgh.co.uk
The North Norfolk Railway The Station Sheringham NR26 8RA T:
01263 822045 F: 01263 823794 W: www.nnrailway.co.uk

Northamptonshire
**Abington Museum and Museum of The Northamptonshire
Regiment** Abington Park Museum Abington NN1 5LW T: 01604
635412 F: 01604 238720 E: museums@northampton.gov.uk W:
www.northampton.gov.uk/museums
Canal Museum Stoke Bruerne Towcester NN12 7SE T: 01604
862229
Naseby Battle Museum Purlieu Farm Naseby Northampton NN6
7DD T: 01604 740241
National Dragonfly Museum Ashton Mill Ashton Peterborough PE8
5LB T: 01832 272427 E: ndmashton@aol.com W:
natdragonflymuseum.org.uk
Northampton Iron Stone Railway Trust Hunsbury Hill Country
Park Hunsbury Hill Rd West Hunsbury Northampton NN4 9UW T:
01604 702031 T: 01604 757481 ; 01908 376821 E:
bnile98131@aol.com_raf968y@aol.com
Northampton & Lamport Railway Preservation Society Pitsford
& Brampton Station Pitsford Road Chapel Brampton Northampton
NN6 8BA T: 01604 820327
Rushden Historical Transport Society The Station Station
Approach Rushden NN10 0AW T: 01933 318988
Wellingborough Heritage Centre Croyland Hall Burystead Place
Wellingborough NN8 1AH T: 01933 276838

Northumberland
**A Soldier's Life 15th/19th The King's Royal Hussars
Northumberland Hussars and Light Dragoons** Discovery Museum
Blandford Square Newcastle-upon-Tyne NE1 4JA T: 0191 232 6789
F: 0191 230 2614 E: ralph.thompson@twmuseums.org.uk

Berwick Borough Museum The Barracks The Parade Berwick-
Upon-Tweed TD15 1DG T: 01289 330933
Bewick Studios Mickley Square Mickley Stocksfield NE43 7BL T:
01661 844055
Border History Museum and Library Moothall Hallgate Hexham
NE46 3NH T: 01434-652349 F: 01434-652425 E:
museum@tynedale.gov.uk W: www.tynedale.gov.uk
Chesterholm Museum Vindolanda Trust Bardon Mill Hexham NE47
7JN T: 01434 344 277 F: 01434 344060 E: info@vindolanda.com W:
www.vindolanda.com
Chesters Roman Fort and Clayton Collection Museum
Vindolanda Trust Chollerford Humshaugh Hexham NE46 4EP T:
01434 681 379 E: info@vindolanda.com W: www.vindolanda.com
Corbridge Roman Site Corbridge NE45 5NT T: 01434 632349 W:
www.english-heritage.org.uk
Fusiliers Museum of Northumberland The Abbot's Tower Alnwick
Castle Alnwick NE66 1NG T: 01665-602151 F: 01665-603320 E:
fusmusnorthld@btinternet.com
Housesteads Roman Fort Museum Haydon Bridge Hexham NE47
6NN T: 01434 344363
King's Own Scottish Borderers Museum The Barracks The Parade
Berwick upon Tweed TD15 1DG T: 01289 307426 W:
www.kosb.co.uk
Marine Life Centre & Fishing Museum 8 Main St Seahouses NE68
7RG T: 01665 721257
North East Mills Group Blackfriars Monk Street Newcastle upon
Tyne NE1 4XN T: 0191 232 9279 F: 0191 230 1474 E:
nect@lineone.net W: //welcome.to/North.East.Mill.Group
Roman Army Museum Carvoran Greenhead CA6 7JB T: 01697
747485 F: 01697 747487 E: info@vindolanda.com W:
www.vindolanda.com
The Heritage Centre Station Yard Woodburn Road Bellingham
Hexham NE48 2DF T: 01434 220050 E:
bell.heritage@btopenworld.com W: www.bellingham-heritage.org.uk
The Vindolanda Trust Chesterholm Museum Bardon Mill Hexham
NE47 7JN T: 01434 344277 F: 01434 344 060 E:
info@vindolanda.com W: www.vindolanda.com
Tynedale Council Museums Department of Leisure & Tourism,
Prospect House, Hexham, Northumberland NE46 3NH T: 01461
652351 E: museum@tynedale.gov.uk W: www.tynedale.gov.uk

Nottinghamshire
D.H Lawrence Heritage Durban House Heritage Centre Mansfield
Rd Eastwood Nottingham NG16 3DZ T: 01773 717353
Flintham Museum & Flintham Society Flintham Museum Inholms
Road Flintham NG23 5LF T: 0163.6 525111 E:
flintham.museum@lineone.net W: www.flintham-museum.org.uk
Greens Mill & Science Musuem Windmill Lane Sneinton
Nottingham NG2 4QB T: 0115 915 6878
Harley Gallery Welbeck Worksop S80 3LW T: 01909 501700
Mansfield Museum & Art Gallery Leeming Street Mansfield NG18
1NG T: 01623-463088 F: 01623-412922
Millgate Museum of Folk Life 48 Millgate Newark NG24 4TS T:
01636 655730 F: 01636 655735 E: museums@newark-
sherwood.gov.uk W: www.newark-sherwood.gov.uk
Natural History and Industrial Musuem Wollaton Hall Wollaton
Park Nottingham NG8 2AE T: 0115 915 3910 F: 0115 915 3941
Newark Museum Appletongate Newark NG24 1JY T: 01636
655740 F: 01636 655745 E: museums@nsdc.info W: www.newark-
sherwooddc.gov.uk
Newark (Notts & Lincs) Air Museum The Airfield Winthorpe
Newark NG24 2NY T: 01636 707170 E: mail@newarkair.lineone.net
W: www.newarkairmuseum.co.uk
Newark Town Treasures and Art Gallery The Town Hall Market
Place Newark NG24 1DU T: 01636 680333 F: 01636 680350 E:
post@newark.gov.uk W: www.newarktowntreasures.co.uk
Newstead Abbey Museum Newstead Abbey Park Ravenshead
Nottingham NG15 8NA T: 01623 455900 F: 01623 455904 E:
sally@newsteadabbey.org.uk W: www.newsteadabbey.org.uk
Nottingham Castle Museum & Art Gallery Castle Rd Nottingham
NG1 6EL T: 0115 915 3700 F: 0115 915653
Ruddington Framework Knitters' Museum Chapel St Ruddington
Nottingham NG11 6HE T: 0115 984 6914 F: 0115 984 1174 W:
www.rfkm.org
Ruddington Village Museum St. Peters RoomsChurch
StRuddingtonNottinghamNG11 6HD Tel: 0115 914 6645
Sherwood Foresters Museum & Archives RHQ WFR, Foresters
House Chetwynd Barracks Chilwell NottinghamNG9 5HA Tel: 0115
946 5415 F: 0115 946 9853 E: curator@wfrmuseum.org.uk W:
www.wfrmuseum.org.uk
Sherwood Foresters (Notts and DerbyRegiment) Museum The
Castle Nottingham NG1 6EL Tel: 0115 946 5415 F: 0115 946 9853
E: rhqwfr-nottm@lineone.net W: www.wfrmuseum.org.ukAddress for
enquiries: RHQ WFR, Foresters House, Chetwynd Barracks,
Chilwell, Nottingham NG9 5HA
The Museum of Nottingham Lace 3-5 High Pavement The Lace
Market Nottingham NG1 1HF Tel: 0115 989 7365 F: 0115 989
7301 E: info@nottinghamlace.org W: www.nottinghamlace.org

The Vina Cooke Museum Dolls & Bygone Childhood The Old Rectory, Cromwell, Newark, Nottinghamshire NG23 6JE T: 01636 821364

Whaley Thorn Heritage & Environment Centre Portland TerraceLangwithMansfieldNG20 9HA Tel: 01623 742525

Oxfordshire

Abingdon Museum County Hall Market Place Abingdon OX14 3HG Tel: 01235 523703 F: 01235 536814

Ashmolean Museum University of Oxford Beaumont StreetOxfordOX1 2PH Tel: 01865 278000

Chipping Norton Museum 4 High Street Chipping NortonOX7 5AD E: museum@cn2001.fsnet.co.uk

Edgehill Battle Museum The Estate Yard Farnborough Hall Farnborough Banbury OX17 1DU Tel: 01926 332213

Great Western Society Ltd Didcot Railway Centre Station Rd Didcot OX11 7NJ Tel: 01235 817200

Oxfordshire and Buckinghamshire Light Infantry Regimental Museum Slade Park Headington OxfordOX3 7JL Tel: 01865 780128

Pitt Rivers Museum University Of Oxford South Parks Rd Oxford OX1 3PP Tel: 01865 270927 F: 01865 270943 E: prm@prm.ox.ac.uk W: www.prm.ox.ac.uk

River & Rowing Museum Rowing & River MuseumMill MeadowsHenley on ThamesRG9 1BF Tel: 01491 415625 F: 01491 415601 E: museum@rrm.co.uk W: www..rrm.co.uk

The Oxfordshire Museum Fletchers House Park St Woodstock OX20 1SN Tel: 01993 811456 T: 01993 814104 F: 01933 813239 E: oxon.museum@oxfordshire.gov.uk

Vale & Downland Museum 19 Church St WantageOX12 8BL Tel: 01235 771447 E: museum@wantage.com

Wallingford Museum Flint House High StWallingfordOX10 0DB Tel: 01491 835065

Witney & District Museum Gloucester Court MewsHigh StWitneyOX8 6LX Tel: 01993 775915 E: janecavell@aol.com

Rutland

Rutland County Museum Catmose StreetOakhamLE15 6HW Tel: 01572-723654 F: 01572-757576 W: www.rutnet.co.uk

Rutland Railway Museum Iron Ore Mine SidingsAshwell RdCottesmoreOakhamLE15 7BX Tel: 01572 813203

Shropshire

Acton Scott Historic Working Farm Wenlock LodgeActon ScottChurch StrettonSY6 6QN Tel: 01694 781306

Blists Hill Open Air Museum Ironbridge Gorge Museum Trust Ltd Legges Way Madeley TelfordTF7 5DU Tel: 01952 586063Fax: 01952 588016

Coalport China Museum Ironbridge Gorge Museum Trust Ltd High St Coalport Telford TF8 7AW Tel: 01952 580650

Cosford Royal Air Force Museum Cosford ShifnalTF11 8UP Tel: 01902 376200 E: cosford@rafmuseum.org W: www.rafmuseum.org

Ironbridge Gorge Museum , Library & Archives The WharfageIronbridgeTelfordTF8 7AW Tel: 01952 432141 F: 01952 432237 E: library@ironbridge.org.uk W: www.ironbridge.org.uk

Museum Of The River Visitor Centre Ironbridge Gorge Museum Trust LtdThe WharfageIronbridgeTF8 7AW Tel: 01952 432405

Jackfield Tile Museum Ironbridge Gorge Museum Trust LtdJackfieldTelfordTF8 7AW Tel: 01952 882030

Ludlow Museum Castle StLudlowSY8 1AS Tel: 01584 875384

Midland Motor Museum Stanmore HallStourbridge RdStanmoreBridgnorthWV15 6DT Tel: 01746 762992

Museum Of Iron Ironbridge Gorge Museum Trust LtdCoach RdCoalbrookdaleTelfordTF8 7EZ Tel: 01952 433418

Oswestry Transport Museum Oswald RdOswestrySY11 1RE Tel: 01691 671749 Email:lignetts@enterprise.netWWW: www.cambrian-railways-soc.co.uk

Queen's Own Mercian Yeomanry Museum Bridgeman House Cavan Drive, Cemetery Road DawleyTelfordTF4 2BQ Tel: 01952 632930 F: 01952 632924

Rosehill House Ironbridge Gorge Museum Trust LtdTelfordTF8 7AW Tel: 01952 432141Fax: 01952 432237

Rowley's House Museum Barker StreetShrewsburySY1 1QH Tel: 01743 361196 F: 01743 358411

Shropshire Regimental Museum (King's Shropshire Light Infantry, Shropshire Yeomanry) Shropshire Militia, Volunteers and TA The Castle Shrewsbury SY1 2AT Tel: 01743 358516 T: 01743 262292 F: 01743 270023 E: shropshire@zoom.co.uk W: www.shropshireregimental.co.uk

Somerset

Abbey Barn - Somerset Rural Life Museum Abbey Barn Chilkwell St Glastonbury BA6 8DB Tel: 01458 831197Fax: 01458 834684 Email:county-museum@somerset.gov.ukWWW: www.somerset.gov.uk/museums

Admiral Blake Museum Bridgwater HouseKing SquareBridgwaterTA6 3AR Tel: 01278 435399 F: 01278 444076 E: Museum s@sedgemoor.gov.uk

American Museum Claverton ManorBathBA2 7BD Tel: 01225 460503 T: 01225 463538 F: 01225 480726

Bakelite Museum Orchard MillBridge St WillitonTauntonTA4 4NS Tel: 01984 632133

Bath Postal Museum 8 Broad StBathBA1 5LJ Tel: 01225 460333 F: 01225 460333 E: a.swindells@virgin.net W: www.bathpostalmuseum.org

Bath Royal Literary & Scientific Institution16-18 Queen SquareBathBA1 2HN Tel: 01225 312084

Blake Museum Blake StreetBridgwaterTA6 3NB Tel: 01278 456127 F: 01278 456127 E: Museum s@sedgemoor.gov.uk W: www.sedgemoor.gov.uk

Blazes Fire Museum Sandhill ParkBishops LydeardTauntonTA4 3DE Tel: 01823 433964

Bruton Museum Society The Dovecote Building High StreetBruton Tel: 01749 812851 W: www.southsomersetmuseum.org.uk

Chard & District Museum Godworthy HouseHigh StChardTA20 1QB Tel: 01460 65091Contact: 17 Cedric Close, Chard, Somerset TA20 1NR Tel: 01460 64017

Fleet Air Arm Museum R.N.A.S Yeovilton Yeovil BA22 8HT Tel: 01935 840565

Fleet Air Arm Museum Records Research Centre Box D61RNAS YeoviltonNr IlchesterBA22 8HT Tel: 01935-840565

Glastonbury Lake Village Museum The Tribunal 9 High St Glastonbury BA6 9DP Tel: 01458 832949

Holburne Museum of Art Great Pulteney St Bath BA2 4DB Tel: 01225 466669 W: www.bath.ac.uk/holbourne

Lambretta Scooter Museum 77 Alfred St Weston-Super-Mare BS23 1PP Tel: 01934 614614 F: 01934 620120 E: lambretta@wsparts.force.net

Museum of Bath at Work Camden Works Julian Road Bath BA1 2RH Tel: 01225 318348 F: 01225 318348 E: mobaw@hotmail.com W: www.bath-at-work.org.uk

Museum of South Somerset HenfordYeovil Tel: 01935 424774 F: 01935 424774 E:
heritage.services@southsomerset.gov.uksouthsomersetmuseums.org.uk

No.1 Royal Crescent 1 Royal Crescent Bath BA1 2LR Tel: 01225 428126 Fax:01225 481850 Email:no1@bptrust.demon.co.ukWWW: www.bath-preservation-trust.org.uk

North Somerset Museum Service Burlington St Weston-Super-MareBS23 1PR Tel: 01934 621028 F: 01934 612526 E: Museum .service@n-somerset.gov.uk W: www.n-somerset.gov.uk

Radstock, Midsomer Norton & District Museum Waterloo RoadRadstockBathBA3 3ER Tel: 01761 437722 E: radstockmuseum@ukonline.co.uk W: www.radstockmuseum.co.uk

Roman Baths Museum Abbey ChurchyardBathBA1 1LZ Tel: 01225 477773 F: 01225 477243

Somerset County Museum Service Taunton CastleTauntonTA1 4AA Tel: 01823 320200

Somerset & Dorset Railway Trust Washford StationWashfordWatchetTA23 0PP Tel: 01984 640869 T: 01308 424630 E: info@sdrt.org W: www.sdrt.org

Somerset Military Museum (Somerset Light Infantry, YeomanryMilitia and Volunteers) County Museum The County Museum Taunton CastleTauntonTA1 4AA Tel: 01823 333434 F: 01823 351639 E: info@sommilmuseum.org.uk W: www.sommilmuseum.org.uk

The Building of Bath Museum The Countess of Huntingdon's ChapelThe VineyardsBathBA1 5NA Tel: 01225 333 895 F: 01225 445 473 E: admin@bobm.freeserve.co.uk W: www.bath-preservation-trust.org.uk

The Haynes Motor Museum Castle Cary RdSparkfordYeovilBA22 7LH Tel: 01963 440804Fax: 01963 441004 Email:mike@gmpwin.demon.co.ukWWW: www.haynesmotormuseum.co.uk

The Helicopter Museum The HeliportLocking Moor RoadWeston-Super-MareBS24 8PP Tel: 01934 635227Fax: 01934 645230 E: office@helimuseum.fsnet.co.uk W: www.helicoptermuseum.co.uk

The Jane Austen Centre40 Gay StreetBathBA1 2NT Tel: 01225 443000 E: info@janeausten.co.uk

The John Judkyn Memorial Garden ThorpeFreshfordBathBA3 6BX Tel: 01225 723312

The Muscum Of East Asian Art12 Bennett StBathBA1 2QL Tel: 01225 464640Fax: 01225 461718 Email:museum@east-asian-art.freeserve.co.ukWWW: www.east-asian-art.co.uk

The South West Museum s Council Hestercombe HouseCheddon FitzpaineTauntonTA2 8LQ Tel: 01823 259696 F: 01823 413114 E: robinbourne@swmuseums.co.uk

Wells Museum 8 Cathedral GreenWellsBA5 2UE Tel: 01749 673477

West Somerset Museum The Old SchoolAllerfordMineheadTA24 8HN Tel: 01643 862529

William Herschel Museum 19 New King StBathBA1 2BL Tel: 01225 311342

Staffordshire

Bass Museum Horninglow Street Burton on TrentDE14 1YQ Tel: 0845 6000598 F: 01283 513509 W: www.bass-museum.com

Borough Museum & Art Gallery Brampton ParkNewcastleST5 0QP Tel: 01782 619705

Clay Mills Pumping Engines Trust Ltd Sewage Treatment WorksMeadow LaneStrettonBurton-On-TrentDE13 0DB Tel: 01283 509929

Etruria Industrial Museum Lower Bedford StEtruriaStoke-On-TrentST4 7AF Tel: 01782 233144Fax:01782 233144 E: etruria@swift.co.uk W: www.stoke.gov.uk/museums

Gladstone Pottery Museum Uttoxeter RdLongtonStoke-On-TrentST3 1PQ Tel: 01782 319232Fax: 01782 598640

Hanley Museum & Art Gallery Bethesda StHanleyStoke-On-TrentST1 3DW Tel: 01782 232323

Museum of The Staffordshire Regiment Whittington BarracksLichfieldWS14 9PY Tel: 0121 311 3240 T: 0121 311 3229 F: 0121 311 3205 E: Museum @rhqstaffords.fsnet.co.uk

Museum of the Staffordshire Yeomanry The Ancient High HouseGreengate StreetStaffordST16 2HS Tel: 01785 619130

Samuel Johnson Birthplace Museum Breadmarket StLichfieldWS13 6LG Tel: 01543 264972 W: www.lichfield.gov.uk

The Potteries Museum & Art Gallery Bethesda StreetHanleyStoke-On-TrentST1 3DE Tel: 01782 232323 E:museums@stoke.gov.uk WWW: www.stoke.gov.uk/museums

Uttoxeter Heritage Centre34-36 Carter StUttoxeter ST14 8EU T: 01889 567176Fax:01889 568426

Suffolk

390th Bomb Group Memorial Air Museum Parham AirfieldParhamFramlington Tel: 01743 711275 F: 01728 621373

British Resistance Organisation Museum Parham AirfieldParhamFramlingham Tel: 01743 711275 F: 01728 621373 E: bretwar@supanet W: www.auxunit.org.uk

Christchurch Mansion & Wolsey Art Gallery Christchurch ParkSoane StIpswichIP4 2BE Tel: 01473 253246

Dunwich Museum St. James's StreetDunwichSaxmundhamIP17 3DT Tel: 01728 648796

East Anglia Transport Museum Chapel RdCarlton ColvilleLowestoftNR33 8BL Tel: 01502 518459

Felixstowe Museum Landguards FortFelixstoweIP11 8TW Tel: 01394 674355

Gainsborough House Society Gainsborough St Sudbury CO10 2EU Tel: 01787 372958 E:mail@gainsborough.org W: www.gainsborough.org

HMS Ganges Museum Victory HouseShotley Point MarinaIpswichIP9 1QJ Tel: 01473 684749

International Sailing Craft Association Maritime Museum Caldecott RdOulton BroadLowestoftNR32 3PH Tel: 01502 585606 F: 01502 589014 E: admin@isca-maritimemuseum.org

Ipswich Museum & Exhibition Gallery High StIpswichIP1 3QH Tel: 01473 213761

Ipswich Transport Museum Ltd Old Trolley Bus DepotCobham RdIpswichIP3 9JD Tel: 01473 715666

Long Shop Steam Museum Main StLeistonIP16 4ES Tel: 01728 832189Fax: 01728 832189 W: www.suffolkcc.gov.uk/libraries_and_heritage/sro/garrett/index.html

Lowestoft Museum Broad HouseNicholas Everitt ParkOulton BroadLowestoftNR33 9JR Tel: 01502 511457 T: 01502 511795 F: 01502 513795

Maritime Museum Sparrows Nest The Museum Whapload RdLowestoftNR32 1XG Tel: 01502 561963

Mid Suffolk Light Railway Brockford StationWetheringsettStowmarketIP14 5PW Tel: 01449 766899

Mildenhall and District Museum 6 King Street Mildenhall Bury St Edmunds IP28 7EX Tel: 01638 716970 T: 01638 713835

Norfolk and Suffolk Aviation Museum Buckeroo Way The Street Flixton Bungay NR35 1NZ Tel: 01986 896644 E: nsam.flixton@virgin.net W: www.aviationmuseum.net

R.A.F. Regiment Museum Home of The RAF RegimentR A F HoningtonBury St EdmondsIP31 1EE Tel: 01359 269561 ext 7824 F: 01359 269561 ext 7440

Rougham Tower Association Rougham Estate OfficeRoughamBury St. EdmundsIP30 9LZ Tel: 01359 271471 F: 01359 271555 E: bplsto@aol.com

Royal Naval Patrol Association Museum Sparrows NestLowestoftNR32 1XG Tel: 01502 586250 F: 01502 586250

Suffolk Regiment Museum The Keep, Gibraltar BarracksOut Risbygate StreetBury St EdmondsIP33 3RN The Museum is closed pending relocation

Suffolk Regiment Museum -Museum closed to the public Suffolk Record Office77 Raingate StreetBury St EdmundsIP33 2AR Tel: 01284-352352 F: 01284-352355 E: bury.ro@libher.suffolkcc.gov.ukhttp:// W: www.suffolkcc.gov.uk/sro/

The National Horseracing Museum 99 High St NewmarketCB8 8JH Tel: 01638 667333

West Stow Country Park & Anglo-Saxon Village Icklingham Rd West Stow Bury St Edmunds IP28 6HG Tel: 01284 728718

Surrey

Bourne Hall Museum Bourne HallSpring StEwellEpsomKT17 1UF Tel: (020) 8394 1734 W: www.epsom.townpage.co.uk

Chertsey Museum The Cedars33 Windsor StChertseyKT16 8AT Tel: 01932 565764Fax: 01932 571118 E:enquiries@chertseymuseum.org.uk

Dorking & District Museum Dorking & District Museum The Old Foundry62a West StDorkingRH4 1BS T: 01306 876591

East Surrey Museum 1 Stafford RdCaterhamCR3 6JG Tel: 01883 340275

Elmbridge Museum Church StWeybridgeKT13 8DE Tel: 01932 843573 F: 01932 846552 E: info@elm-mus.datanet.co.uk W: www.surrey-online.co.uk/elm-mus

Godalming Museum 109a High StGodalmingGU7 1AQ Tel: 01483 426510Fax: 01483 869495 E:musaeum@goldaming.ndo.co.uk

Guildford Museum Castle ArchQuarry StGuildfordGU1 3SX Tel: 01483 444750 E: Museum @remote.guildford.gov.uk

Haslemere Educational Museum 78 High StHaslemereGU27 2LA Tel: 01428 642112Fax: 01428 645234 E: haslemere_museum@compuserve.com

Kingston Museum & Heritage Service North Kingston CentreRichmond RoadKingston upon ThamesKT2 5PE Tel: (020) 8547-6738 F: (020) 8547-6747 E: local.history@rbk.kingston.gov.uk W: www.kingston.gov.uk/museum/

Kingston Upon Thames Museum North Kingston CentreRichmond RoadNew MaldenKT3 3UQ Tel: 020 8547 67381901 census

Merton Heritage Centre The CannonsMadeira RdMitchamCR4 4HD Tel: (020) 8640 9387

Queen's Royal Surrey Regiment Museum (Queen's Royal, East Surrey & Queen's Royal Surrey Regiments) Clandon ParkWest ClandonGuildfordGU4 7RQ Tel: 01483 223419 E: queenssurreys@caree4free.net W: www.surrey-online.co.uk/queenssurreys_www,queensroyalsurreys.org.uk

Regimental Museum Royal Logistic Corps Princess Royal Barracks Deepcut Camberley GU16 6RW Tel: 01252 833371 E: query@rlcmuseum.freeserve.co.uk W: www.army-rlc.co.uk/museum

Reigate Priory Museum Reigate Priory Bell St ReigateRH2 7RL Tel: 01737 222550

Rural Life Centre Old Kiln Museum The Reeds Tilford FarnhamGU10 2DL Tel: 01252 795571Fax: 01252 795571 E: :rural.life@argonet.co.uk

Sandhurst Collection Royal Military Academy Sandhurst CamberleyGU15 4PQ Tel: 01276 412489 F: 1276421595

Staff College Museum Old Staff College BuildingCamberleyGU15 4NP Tel: 01276 41271901276 412602

Surrey Heath Museum Knoll Road, Camberley, Surrey GU15 3HD T: 01276 707284 E: museum@surreyheath.gov.uk W: www.surreyheath.gov.uk/leisure

Wandle Industrial Museum Vestry Hall AnnexLondon RdMitchamCR4 3UD Tel: (020) 8648 0127 W: www.wandle.org

Woking Museum & Arts & Craft Centre The GalleriesChobham RdWoking GU21 1JF Tel: 01483 725517 F: 01483 725501 E: the.galleries@dial.pipcx.com

Sussex

Brighton Fishing Museum 201 Kings RoadArchesBrightonBN1 1NB Tel: 01273-723064 F: 01273-723064

Museum of The Royal National Lifeboat Institution King Edward Parade Eastbourne BN Tel: 01323 730717

Royal Military Police Museum Roussillon Barracks Chichester PO19 6BL Tel: 01243 534225 F: 01243 534288 E: Museum @rhqrmp.freeserve.co.uk W: www.rhqrmp.freeserve.co.uk

Sussex Combined Services Museum (Royal Sussex Regiment and Queen's Royal Irish Hussars) Redoubt Fortress Royal Parade Eastbourne BN22 7AQ Tel: 01323 410300

Tangmere Military Aviation Museum Tangmere Chichester PO20 2ES Tel: 01243 775223 F: 01243 789490 E: admin@tangmere-museum.org.uk W: www.tangmere-museum.org.uk

Sussex – East

Sussex Yeomanry Museum 198 Dyke Road Brighton BN1 5AS

Anne of Cleves House Museum 52 SouthoverHigh StLewesBN7 1JA T: 01273 474610

Battle Museum Langton Memorial Hall High StBattleTN33 0AQ T: 01424 775955

Bexhill Museum Egerton Rd Bexhill-On-SeaTN39 3HL T: 01424 787950 E: Museum @rother.gov.uk W: www.1066country.com

Bexhill Museum of Costume & Social History Assoc Manor Gardens Upper Sea Rd Bexhill-On-Sea TN40 1RL T: 01424 210045

BN1 Visual Arts Project Brighton Media Centre 9-12 Middle St BrightonBN1 1AL T: 01273 384242

Booth Musuem 194 Dyke Rd BrightonBN1 5AA T: 01273 292777 F: 01273 292778 E: boothmus@pavilion.co.uk

Dave Clarke Prop Shop Long BarnCross In HandHeathfieldTN21 0TP T: 01435 863800

Ditchling Museum Church Lane DitchlingHassocksBN6 8TB T: 01273 844744 F: 01273 844744 E: info@ditchling-museum.com

Eastbourne Heritage Centre2 Carlisle RdEastbourneBN21 4BT T: 01323 411189 T: 01323 721825

Filching Manor Motor Museum Filching ManorJevington RdPolegateBN26 5QA T: 01323 487838
Fishermans Museum Rock A Nore RdHastingsTN34 3DW T: 01424 461446
Hastings Museum & Art Gallery Johns PlaceBohemia RdHastingsTN34 1ET T: 01424 781155Fax: 01424 781155 E: Museum @hastings.gov.uk W: www.hmag.org.uk
Hove Musuem & Art Gallery19 New Church RdHoveBN3 4AB T: 01273 290200Fax: 01273 292827 Email:abigail.thomas@brighton-hove.gov.ukWWW: www.brighton-hove.gov.uk
How We Lived Then Museum of Shops20 Cornfield Terrace EastbourneBN21 4NS T: 01323 737143
Michelham Priory Upper Dicker Hailsham BN27 3QS
Newhaven Fort Fort Rd Newhaven BN9 9DL T: 01273 517622 F: 01273 512059 E: ian.everest@newhavenfort.org.uk W: www.newhavenfort.org.uk
Newhaven Local & Maritime Museum Garden Paradise Avis WayNewhavenBN9 0DH T: 01273 612530
Preston Manor Musuem Preston DroveBrightonBN1 6SD T: 01273 292770 F: 01273 292771
Rye Castle Museum East StRyeTN31 7JY T: 01797 226728
Seaford Museum of Local History Martello Tower The Esplanade SeafordBN25 1NP T: 01323 898222 E: Museum seaford@tinyonline.co.uk W: www.seaforedmuseum.org

The Engineerium The Droveway Nevill Rd Hove BN3 7QA T: 01273 554070 Email:info@britishengineerium.com
Wish Tower Puppet Museum Tower 73 King Edwards Parade Eastbourne BN21 4BY T: 01323 411620 E: puppet.workshop@virgin.net W: www.puppets.co.uk
Sussex - West
Amberley Working Museum Station Rd Amberley ArundelBN18 9LT T: 01798 831370 F: 1798831831 E: office@amberleymuseum.co.uk W: www.amberleymuseum.co.uk3
Chichester District Museum 29 Little LondonChichesterPO19 1PB T: 01243 784683 F: 01243 776766 E: Email: chichmus@breathemail.net
Fishbourne Roman Palace Roman WaySalthill RdFishbourneChichesterPO19 3QR T: 01243 785859 F: 01243 539266 E: adminfish@sussexpast.co.uk W: www.sussexpast.co.uk
Horsham Museum 9 The Causeway Horsham RH12 1HE T: 01403-254959 F: 01403 217581 E: Museum @horsham.gov.uk
Marlipins Museum High StShoreham-By-Sea BN43 5DA T: 01273 46299401323 441279 F: 01323 844030 E: smermich@sussexpast.co.uk W: www.sussexpast.co.uk
Petworth Cottage Museum 346 High StPetworthGU28 0AU T: 01798 342100 W: www.sussexlive.co.uk
The Mechanical Music & Doll Collection Church RdPortfieldChichesterPO19 4HN T: 01243 372646
Weald & Downland Open Air Museum SingletonChichesterPO18 0EU T: 01243-811363 F: 01243-811475 E: wealddown@mistral.co.uk W: www.wealddown.co.uk

Tyne and Wear
101 (Northumbrian) Regiment Royal Artillery (Volunteers) Museum Napier ArmouryGatesheadNE8 4HX T: 0191 239 6130 F: 0191 239 6132
Military Vehicle Museum Exhibition Park PavilionNewcastle upon TyneNE2 4PZ T: 0191 281 7222
Arbeia Roman Fort Baring St South ShieldsNE33 2BB T: 0191 4561369 F: 0191 4276862 E: liz.elliott@tyne-wear-museums.org.uk
Arbeia Roman Fort and Museum Baring StreetSouth ShieldsNE33 2BB T: 0191 456 1369 F: 0191 427 6862 E: lis.elliott@rwmuseums.org.uk W: www.aboutbritain.com/ArbeiaRomanFort.htm
Bede's World Museum Church BankJarrowNE32 3DY T: 0191 4892106
Castle Keep Castle GarthSt. Nicholas StNewcastle Upon TyneNE1 1RE T: 0191 2327938
Fulwell Windmill Newcastle Road, Sunderland, Tyne and Wear SR5 1EX T: 0191 516 9790 M: 07989 409 296 E: fulwell.windmill@sunderland.gov.uk W: www.fulwell-windmill.com
Hancock Museum Barras BridgeNewcastle Upon TyneNE2 4PT T: 0191 2227418 F: 0191 2226753 E: hancock.museum@ncl.ac.uk
Military Vehicles Museum Exhibition Park PavilionNewcastle Upon TyneNE2 4PZ T: 0191 2817222 E: miltmuseum@aol.com W: www.military-museum.org.uk
Newburn Motor Museum Townfield Gardens Newburn Newcastle Upon Tyne NE15 8PY T: 0191 2642977
North East Aircraft Museum Old Washington Road Sunderland SR5 3HZ T: 0191 519 0662
Ryhope Engines Trust Pumping Station Stockton Rd Ryhope Sunderland SR2 0ND T: 0191 5210235 W: www.g3wte.demon.co.uk
Segedunum Roman Fort, Baths and Museum WallsendNE T: 0191 236 9347 F: 0191 295 5858 E: segesunum@twmuseums.org.uk W: www.twmuseums.org.ukI

South Shields Museum & Art Gallery Ocean RoadSouth ShieldsNE33 2JA T: 0191-456-8740 F: 0191 456 7850
Stephenson Railway Museum Middle Engine LaneNorth ShieldsNE29 8DX T: 0191 200 7146 F: 0191 200 7146
Sunderland Maritime Heritage1st Floor Office, North East SideSouth DockPort of SunderlandSunderlandSR1 2EE T: 0191 510 2055 E: info@sunderlandMH.fsnet.co.uk W: www.sunderlandmaritimeheritage.com
Sunderland Museum & Art Gallery and Monkwearmouth Station Museum Borough RoadSunderlandSR1 1PP T: 0191 565 0723 F: 0191 565 0713 E: martin.routledge@tyne-wear-museums.org.uk
The Bowes Railway Co Ltd Springwell RdSpringwell VillageGatesheadNE9 7QJ T: 0191 4161847 T: 0191 4193349 E: alison_gibson77@hotmail.com W: www.bowesrailway.co.uk

Warwickshire
Leamington Spa Art Gallery & Musuem Royal Pump Rooms The Parade Leamington Spa CV32 4AA T: 01926 742700 E:prooms@warcickdc.gov.ukW: www.royal-pump-rooms.co.uk
Lunt Roman Fort Coventry Road Baginton Coventry T: 024 7683 2381
Midland Air Museum Coventry Airport Baginton CV8 3AZ T: 01203 301033 W: www.discover.co.uk/~mam/
Nuneaton Museum & Art Gallery Riversley Park NuneatonCV11 5TU Tel: (024) 76376473
Regimental Museum of The Queen's Own Hussars (The 3rd King's Own Hussars and 7th Queen's Own Hussars) The Lord Leycester Hospita l High StreetWarwickCV34 4EW T: 01926 492035 F: 01926 492035 E: trooper@qohm.fsnet.co.uk
Shakespeare Birthplace Trust - Museum Henley Street Stratford upon AvonCV37 6QW T: 01789-204016 F: 01789 296083 E: Museum s@shakespeare.org.uk
The Royal Regiment of Fusiliers Museum (Royal Warwickshire) St. John's HouseWarwick CV34 4NF T: 01926 491653
Warwick Castle WarwickCV34 4QU T: 01926-406600 F: 01926 401692 W: www.warwick-castle.co.uk
Warwick Doll Museum Okens HouseCastle StWarwickCV34 4BP T: 01926 495546
Warwickshire Market Hall Museum Market PlaceWarwickCV34 4SA T: 01926 412500 F: 01926 419840 E: Museum @warwickshire.gov.uk W: www.warwickshire.gov.uk/museumcc accepted
Warwickshire Yeomanry Museum The Court HouseJury StreetWarwick CV34 4EW T: 01926 492212 F: 01926 494837 E: wtc.admin@btclick.com
Wellesborough Aviation Museum Control Tower EntranceWellesboroughWarwickCV34 4EW

West Midlands
Aston Manor-Road Transport Museum Ltd208-216 Witton LaneBirminghamB6 6QE T: 0121 322 2298
Bantock House & Park Bantock Park,Finchfield RdWolverhamptonWV3 9LQ T: 01902 552195 F: 01902 552196
Birmingham & Midland Museum Of Transport Chapel LaneWythallB47 6JX T: 01564 826471 E: enquiries@bammot.org.uk W: www.bammot.org.uk
Birmingham Museum & Art Gallery Chamberlain SquareBirminghamB3 3DH T: 0121 235 2834 F: 0121 303 1394 W: www.birmingham.gov.uk/bmag
Birmingham Railway Museum Ltd670 Warwick RdTyseleyBirminghamB11 2HL T: 0121 707 4696
Black Country Living Museum Canal StTipton RdDudleyDY1 4SQ T: 0121 522 9643 F: 0121 557 4242 E: info@bclm.co.uk W: www.bclm.co.uk
Blakesley Hall Blakesley Rd Yardley Birmingham B25 8RN T: 0121 783 2193
Dudley Museum & Art Gallerey St James's Road Dudley DY1 1HU
Haden Hall & Haden Hill House Haden Hill Park Barrs Road Cradley Heath B64 7JX T: 01384 569444
Herbert Art Gallery & Museum Jordan Well Coventry CV1 5QP T: 024 76832381
Midland Air Museum Coventry AirportCoventry RdBagintonCoventryCV8 3AZ Tel: (024) 76301033
Museum of theJewellery Quarter75-79 Vyse St Hockley BirminghamB18 6HA T: 0121 554 3598Fax: 0121 554 9700
Oak House Museum Oak Rd West Bromwich B70 8HJ T: 0121 553 0759
Selly Manor Museum Maple Rd Birmingham B30 2AE T: 0121 472 0199
The Lock Museum 55 New RdWillenhallWV13 2DA T: 01902 634542 F: 01902 634542http://members.tripod.co.uk/lock_museum/
Walsall Leather Museum Littleton St West WalsallWS2 8EN T: 01922 721153 E: leather.museum@walsall.gov.uk
West Midlands Police Museum Sparkhill Police Station Stratford Rd Sparkhill Birmingham B11 4EA T: 0121 626 7181
Whitlocks End Farm Bills Lane Shirley Solihull B90 2PL T: 0121 745 4891

Wiltshire

Alexander Keiller Museum High St Avebury Marlborough SN8
1RF T: 01672 539250 E: avebury@nationaltrust.org.uk
Atwell-Wilson Motor Museum Trust Stockley Lane Calne SN11 0
T: 01249 813119
Lydiard House Lydiard Park Lydiard Tregoze Swindon SN5 9PA T:
01793 770401
RGBW (Salisbury) Museum The Wardrobe 58 The Close Salisbury
SP1 2EX T: 01722 419419 W: www.thewardrobe.org.uk
Royal Wiltshire Yeomanry Museum A (RWY) Sqn Royal
Yeomanry Church Place Swindon SN1 5EH T: 01793 523865 F:
01793 529350 E: arwsqn@hotmail.com
Salisbury & South Wiltshire Museum The King's House 65 The
Close SalisburySP1 2EN T: 01722 332151 F: 01722 325611 E:
Museum @salisburymuseum.freeserve.co.uk
Sevington Victorian School Sevington Grittleton ChippenhamSN14
7LD T: 01249 783070
Steam: Museum of the Great Western Railway Kemble Drive
SwindonSN2 2TA T: 01793 466646 F: 01793 466614 E:
tbryan@swindon.gov.uk
The Infantry and Small Arms School Corps Weapons Collection
HQ SASCHQ Infantry Warminster Training CentreWarminsterBA12
0DJ T: 01985 222487
The Science Museum Wroughton Wroughton Swindon SN4 9NS T:
01793 814466 E: enquiries.wroughton@nmsi.ac.uk W:
www.sciencemuseum.org.uk/wroughton
Wiltshire Heritage Museum Library Wiltshire Archaeological &
Natural HS 41 Long Street DevizesSN10 1NS T: 01380 727369 E:
wanhs@wiltshireheritage.org.uk W: www.wiltshireheritage.org.uk
Yelde Hall Museum Market Place Chippenham SN15 3HL T: 01249
651488
Wirral Historic Warships at Birkenhead East Float Dock Dock
Road Birkenhead L41 1DJ T: 0151 6501573 E:
manager@warships.freeserve.co.uk W:
www.warships.freeserve.co.uk

Worcestershire

Almonry Museum Abbey Gate Evesham WR11 4BG T: 01386
446944 W www.almonry.ndo.co.uk
Avoncroft Museum of Historic Buildings Redditch RdStoke
HeathBromsgroveB60 4JR T: 01527 831363 T: 01527 831886 E:
Avoncroft1@compuserve.com W: www.avoncroft.org.uk
Bewdley Museum Research Library Load StreetBewdleyDY12 2AE
T: 01229-403573 E: Museum
@online.rednet.co.uk_angela@bewdleyhistory.evesham.net W:
www.bewdleymuseum.tripod.com
Kidderminster Railway Museum Station DriveKidderminsterDY10
1QX T: 01562 825316
Malvern Museum Priory GatehouseAbbey RoadMalvernWR14 3ES
T: 01684 567811
MLA West Midlands Regional Council for Museums Libraries &
Archive 2nd Floor Grosvenor House14 Bennetts HillB2 5RS T:
01527 872258 F: 01527 576960
Museum of Worcester Porcelain The Royal Porcelain Works Severn
Street WorcesterWR1 2NETel:Email: rwgeneral@royal-
worcester.co.uk
The Almonry Heritage Centre Abbey GateEveshamWR11 4BG T:
01385 446944 E: tic@almonry W: www.almonry.ndo.co.uk
The Commandery Civil War Museum SidburyWorcesterWR1
2HU T: 01905 361821 E: thecommandery@cityofworcester.gov.uk
W: www.worcestercitymuseums.org.uk
The Elgar Birthplace Museum Crown East LaneLower
BroadheathWorcesterWR2 6RH T: 01905 333224Fax: 01905
333224WWW: www.elgarfoundation.org
The Mueseum of Local Life Tudor HouseFriar StreetWorcesterWR1
2NA T: 01905 722349 W: www.worcestercitymuseums.org.uk
The Museum of the Worcestershire Yeomanry Cavalry Worcester
City Museum & Art GalleryForegate StWorcesterWR1 1DT T:
01905 25371Fax:01905 616979 E: tbridges@cityofworcester.gov.uk
W: www.worcestercitymuseums.org.uk
The Worcestershire Regiment Museum Worcester City Museum &
Art GalleryForegate StreetWorcesterWR1 1DT T: 01905-25371
Museum T: 01905 354359 Office F: 01905-616979 Museum 01905
353871 Office E: rhq_wfr@lineone.net Postal Address: The Curator,
The Worcestershire Regimental Museum Trust, RHQ WFR, Norton
Barracks, Worcester WR5 2PA
Worcestershire City Museum and Art Gallery Foregate
StreetWorcesterWR1 1DT T: 01905 25371 F: 01905 616979 E:
artgalleryandmuseum@cityofworcester.gov.uk W:
www.worcestercitymuseums.org.uk
Worcestershire County Museum Hartlebury CastleHartleburyDY11
7XZ T: 01229-250416 F: 01299-251890 E: Museum
@worcestershire.gov.ukhttp:// W:
www.worcestershire.gov.uk/museum
Worcestershire Regiment Archives (Worcestershireand Sherwood
Forester's Regiment)RHQ WFR Norton BarracksWorcesterWR5
2PA T: 01905 354359 F: 01905 353871 E: rhg_wfr@lineone.net

Yorkshire – East

Museum of Army Transport FlemingateBeverleyHU17 0NG T:
01482 860445 F: 01482 872767
East Riding Heritage Library & Museum Sewerby HallChurch
LaneSewerbyBridlingtonYO15 1EA T: 01262-677874 T: 01262-
674265 E: Museum @pop3.poptel.org.uk W:
www.bridlington.net/sew
The Hornsea Museum Burns Farm11 NewbeginHornseaHU18 1AB
T: 01964 533 443WWW: www.hornseamuseum.comVictorian
farmhouse Museum .
Withernsea Lighthouse Museum Hull RdWithernseaHU19 2DY T:
01964 614834

Yorkshire – North

Eden Camp Museum MaltonYO17 6RT T: 01653 697777 F: 01653
698243 E: admin@edencamp.co.uk W: www.edencamp.co.uk
Green Howards Regimental Museum Trinity Church
SquareRichmondDL10 4QN T: 01748-822133 F: 01748-826561
Story of the Green Howards (Alexandra, Princess of Wales's Own
Yorkshire Regiment from 1688 to date)
Royal Dragoon Guards Military Museum (4th/7th Royal
Dragoon Guards& 5th Royal Inniskilling Dragoon Guards)3A
Tower StreetYorkYO1 9SB T: 01904-662790 T: 01904 662310 F:
01904 662310 E: rdgmuseum@onetel.net W: www.rdg.co.uk Also
Prince of Wales' Own Regt of Yorkshire Military Museum (West &
East Yorkshire Regiments)
The Real Aeroplane Museum The Aerodrome Breighton Selby YO8
7DH T: 01757 289065 F: 01977 519340
Upper Wharfedale Museum Society & Folk Museum The
SquareGrassingtonBD23 5AU
War Room and Motor House Collection30 Park
ParadeHarrogateHG1 5AG T: 01423 500704
Yorkshire Air Museum Halifax WayElvingtonYorkYO41 4AU T:
01904 608595 E: Museum @yorkshireairmuseum.co.uk W:
www.yorkshireairmuseum.co.uk Canada Branch, (Doug Sample CD),
470 Petit Street, St Laurent, Quebec Canada. H4N 2H6
Aysgarth Falls Carriage Museum Yore Mill Asgarth
FallsLeyburnDL8 3SR T: 01969 663399
Beck Isle Museum of Rural Life PickeringYO18 8DU T: 01751
473653
Captain Cook Memorial Museum Grape Lane Whitby YO22 4BA
T: 01947 601900 E: captcookmuseumwhitby@ukgateway.net W:
www.cookmuseumwhitby.co.uk
Captain Cook Schoolroom Museum 10 High Street Great Ayton
TS9 7HB T: 01642 723358
Dales Countryside Museum Station Yard Burtersett Rd Hawes DL8
3NT T: 01969 667494 F: 01969 667165 E:
dcm@yorkshiredales.org.uk
Life In Miniature 8 Sandgate Whitby YO22 4DB T: 01947 601478
Malton Museum The Old Town Hall Market Place Malton YO17
7LP T: 01653 695136
Micklegate Bar Museum Micklegate York YO1 6JX T: 01904
634436
Nidderdale Museum Council Offices King Street Pateley Bridge
HG3 5LE T: 01423-711225
Old Courthouse Museum Castle Yard Knaresborough T: 01423
556188 F: 01423 556130 W: www.harrogate.gov.uk/museums
Richard III Museum Monk Bar York YO1 2LH T: 01904 634191
W: www.richardiiimuseum.co.uk
Richmondshire Museum Ryder's Wynd Richmond DL10 4JA T:
01748 825611 Contact by letter only - queries dealt with by
volunteer staff as soon as possible
Ripon Museum Trust Ripon Prison & Police Museum St Marygate
Ripon HG4 1LX T: 01765-690799 E: ralph.lindley@which.net
Rotunda Museum Vernon Rd Scarborough YO11 2NN T: 01723
374839
Royal Pump Room Museum Crown Place Harrogate T: 01423
556188 F: 01423 556130 E: lg12@harrogate.gov.uk W:
www.harrogate.gov.uk
Ryedale Folk Museum Hutton le Hole YO62 6UA T: 01751 417367
E: library@dbc-lib.demon.co.uk
The Forbidden Corner Tupgill Park Estate Coverham Middleham
Leyburn DL8 4TJ T: 01969 640638 T: 01969 640687
The North Yorkshire Moors Railway Pickering Station Pickering
YO18 7AJ T: 01751 472508 E:
info@northyorkshiremoorsrailway.com W:
www.northyorkshiremoorsrailway.com
The World of James Herriott 23 Kirkgate Thirsk YO7 1PL T:
01845 524234 F: 01845 525333 E: anne.keville@hambleton.gov.uk
W: www.hambleton.gov.uk
Whitby Lifeboat Museum Pier Rd Whitby YO21 3PU T: 01947
602001
Whitby Museum Pannett Park Whitby YO21 1RE T: 01947
602908 F: 01947 897638 (Telephone first) E:
graham@durain.demon.co.uk W: www.durain.demon.co.uk

Yorkshire – South
Abbeydale Industrial Hamlet Abbeydale Road South Sheffield S7 2 T: 0114 236 7731
Bishops' House Norton Lees Lane Sheffield S8 9BE T: 0114 278 2600 W: www.sheffieldgalleries.org.uk
Bishops House Museum Meersbrook Park Nortin Lees Lane Sheffield S8 9BE T: 0114 255 7701
Cannon Hall Museum Cannon Hall Cawthorne Barnsley S75 4AT T: 01226 790270
Clifton Park Museum Clifton Lane Rotherham S65 2AA T: 01709 823635 E: guy.kilminster@rotherham.gov.uk W: www.rotherham.gov.uk
Fire Museum (Sheffield) Peter House 101-109 West Bar Sheffield S3 8PT T: 0114 249 1999 F: 0114 249 1999 W: www.hedgepig.freeserve.co.uk
Kelham Island Museum Alma St Kelham Island Sheffield S3 8RY T: 0114 272 2106
Magna Sheffield Road Templeborough Rotherham S60 1DX T: 01709 720002 F: 01709 820092 E: info@magnatrust.co.uk W: www.magnatrust.co.uk
Sheffield Police and Fire Museum 101-109 West Bar Sheffield S3 8TP T: 0114 249 1999 W: www.hedgepig.freeserve.co.uk
Sandtoft Transport Centre Ltd Belton Rd Sandtoft Doncaster DN8 5SX T: 01724 711391
Sheffield City Museum Weston Park Sheffield S10 2TP T: 0114 278 2600 W: www.sheffieldgalleries.org.uk

Yorkshire – West
Manor House Art Gallery & Museum Castle Yard Castle Hill Ilkley LS29 9D T: 01943 600066
Middleton Railway The Station Moor Road Hunslet Leeds LS10 2JQ T: 0113 271 0320 E: howhill@globalnet.co.uk w W: www.personal.leeds.ac.uk/mph6mip/mrt/mrt.htm
National Museum of Photography, Film & Television see National
Royal Armouries see National
Shibden Hall Lister Rd Shibden Halifax HX3 6AG T: 01422 352246 E: shibden.hall@calderdale.gov.uk W: www.calderdale.gov.uk
Skopos Motor Museum Alexandra Mills Alexandra Rd Batley WF17 6JA T: 01924 444423
Temple Newsham House Temple Newsham Road off Selby Road Leeds LS15 0AE T: 0113 264 7321
Thackray Medical Museum Beckett Street Leeds LS9 7LN T: 0113-244-4343 F: 0113-247-0219 E: info@thackraymuseum.org W: www.thackraymuseum.org
The Colour Museum 1 Providence Street Bradford BD1 2PW T: 01274 390955 F: 01274 392888 E: Museum s@sdc.org.uk W: www.sdc.org.uk
Thwaite Mills Watermill Thwaite Lane Stourton Leeds LS10 1RP T: 0113 249 6453
Vintage Carriages Trust Station Yard Ingrow Keighley BD21 1DB T: 01535 680425 F: 01535 610796 E: admin@vintagecarriagestrust.org W: www.vintagecarriagestrust.org
Wakefield Museum Wood St Wakefield WF1 2EW T: 01924 305351 F: 01924 305353 E: cjohnstone@wakefield.gov.uk W: www.wakefield.gov.uk/culture
Yorkshire & Humberside Museum s Council Farnley Hall Hall Lane Leeds LS12 5HA T: 0113 263 8909

Yorkshire – York
Archaeoilogical Resource Centre St Saviourgate York YO1 8NN T: 01904 654324 F: 01904 627097 E: enquiries.ar.yat@yorkarch.demon.co.uk W: www.jorvik-viking-centre.co.uk
Bar Convent 17 Blossom Street York YO24 1AQ T: 01904 643238 F: 01904 631792 E: info@bar-convent.org.uk W: www.bar-convent.org.uk
York Castle Museum The Eye of York York YO1 9RY T: 01904 687687 F: 01904 671078 W: www.yorkcastlemuseum.org.uk/
Yorkshire Museum Museum Gardens York YO1 7FR T: 01904 629745 F: 01904 651221 W: www.york.gov.uk

WALES
Anglesey
Beaumaris Gaol Museum Bunkers Hill Beaumaris LL58 8EP T: 01248 810921 T: 01248 724444 01248 750282 E: beaumariscourtand gaol@anglesey.gov.uk
The Maritime Museum Beach Rd Newry Beach Holyhead LL65 1YD T: 01407 769745 E: cave@holyhead85.freeserve.co.uk
Caernarfon
Welsh Slate Museum Padarn Country Park Llanberis Gwynedd LL55 4TY T: 01286 870630 F: 01286 871906 E: wsmpost@btconnect.com W: W: www.nmgw.ac.uk
Cardiff
1st The Queen's Dragoon Guards Regimental Museum Cardiff Castle Cardiff CF10 2RB T: (029) 2022 2253 T: (029) 2078 1271 F: (029) 2078 1384 E: clivejmorris@lineone.net W: www.qdg.org.uk

Cardiff Castle Castle Street Cardiff CF1 2RB T: (029) 20822083 F: (029) 2023 1417 E: cardiffcastle@cardiff.gov.uk
Museum of Welsh Life St Fagans Cardiff CF5 6XB T: (029) 2057 3500 F: (029) 2057 3490 E: post@nmgw.ac.uk W: W: www.nmgw.ac.uk/mwl/
Techniquest Stuart St Cardiff CF10 5BW T: (029) 20475475
Carmarthenshire
Parc Howard Museum & Art Gallery Mansion House Parc Howard Llanelli SA15 3LJ T: 01554 772029
Ceredigion
Cardigan Heritage Centre Teifi Wharf Castle St Cardigan SA43 3AA T: 01239 614404
Ceredigion Museum Coliseum Terrace Rd Aberystwyth SY23 2AQ T: 01970 633088 F: 01970 633084 E: Museum @ceredigion.gov.uk W: W: www.ceridigion.gov.uk
Mid-Wales Mining Museum Ltd Llywernog Silver Mine Ponterwyd Aberystwyth SY23 3AB T: 01970 890620
Mid-Wales Mining Museum - Silver River Mines Ltd Llywernog Mine Ponterwyd Aberystwyth SY23 3AB T: 01970 890620 F: 01545 570823 E: silverrivermine@aol.com W: www.silverminetours.co.uk
Conwy
Great Orme Tramway Tramffordd Y Gogarth Goprsaf Victoria Church Walks Llandudno LL30 1AZ T: 01492 575350 E: enq@greatormetramway.com W: www.greatormetramway.com
Sir Henry Jones Museum Y Cwm Llangernyw Abergele LL22 8PR T: 01492 575371 T: 01754 860661 E: info@sirhenryjones-museums.org W: www.sirhenryjones-museums.org
Denbighshire
Cae Dai Trust Cae Dai Lawnt Denbigh LL16 4SU T: 01745 812107 T: 01745 817004
Llangollen Motor Museum Pentrefelin Llangollen LL20 8EE T: 01978 860324
Dyfed
Kidwelly Industrial Museum Broadford Kidwelly SA17 4UF T: 01554 891078
Pembrokeshire Motor Museum Keeston Hill Haverfordwest SA62 6EH T: 01437 710950
Wilson Museum of Narberth Market Square Narberth SA67 7AX T: 01834 861719
Glamorgan Brecon Mountain Railway Pant Station Merthyr Tydfil CF48 2UP T: 01685 722988 E: enquiries@breconmountainrailway.co.uk W: www.breconmountainrailway.co.uk
Gwent
Abergavenny Museum The Castle Castle St Abergavenny NP7 5EE T: 01873 854282
Big Pit Mining Museum Blaenavon Torfaen NP4 9XP T: 01495-790311
Castle & Regimental Museum Monmouth Castle Monmouth NP25 3BS T: 01600 772175 E: curator@monmouthshirecastlemuseum.org.uk W: www.monmouthshirecastlemuseum.org.uk
Drenewydd Museum 26-27 Lower Row Bute Town Tredegar NP22 5QH T: 01685 843039 E: morgac1@caerphilly.gov.uk
Newport Museum & Art Gallery John Frost Square Newport NP20 1PA T: 01633-840064 F: 01633 222615 E: Museum @newport.gov.uk
Pillgwenlly Heritage Community Project within Baptist Chapel Alexandra Rd Newport NP20 2JE T: 01633 244893
Roman Legionary Museum High Street Caerleon NP6 1AE T: 01633 423134 W: www.nmua.ac.uk
Valley Inheritance Park Buildings Pontypool Torfaen NP4 6JH T: 01495-752036 F: 01495-752043
Gwynedd
Bala Lake Railway Rheilfford Llyn Tegid The Station Yr Orsaf Llanuwchllyn LL23 7DD T: 01678 540666 F: 01678 540535 W: www.bala-lake-railway.co.uk
Betws-y-Coed Motor Museum Museum Cottage Betws-Y-Coed LL24 0AH T: 01690 710760
Caernarfon Air World Caernarfon Airport Dinas Dinlle Caernarfon LL54 5TP
Gwynedd Museum s Service Victoria Dock Caernarvon LL55 1SH T: 01286 679098 F: 01286 679637 E: amgueddtlydd-museums@gwynedd.gov.uk
Llanberis Lake Railway Rheilffordd Llyn Padarn LLanberis LL55 4TY T: 01286 870549 F: 01286 870549 E: info@lake-railway.co.uk W: www.lake-railway.co.uk
Llandudno & Conwy Valley Railway Society Welsh Slate Museum Llanberis T: 01492 874590
Llandudno Royal Artillery Llandudno Museum 17-19 Gloddaeth Street Llandudno LL30 2DD T: 01492 876517
Lloyd George Museum Llanstumdwy Criccieth LL52 0SH T: 01766 522071 W: www.gwynedd.gov.uk/adrannau/addysg/amgueddfeydd/english/lg_1.htm
Porthmadog Maritime Museum Oakley Wharf 1 The Harbour Porthmadog LL49 9LU T: 01766 513736
Segontium Roman Museum Beddgelert Rd Caernarfon LL55 2LN T: 01286 675625 F: 01286 678416 W: www.nmgw.ac.uk

Snowdon Mountain Railway Llanberis LL55 4TY T: 0870 4580033 F: 01286 872518 E: info@snowdonrailway.co.uk W: www.snowdonrailway.co.uk

Teapot Museum 25 Castle St Conwy LL32 8AY T: 01492 596533

The Royal Welch Fusiliers Regimental Museum The Queen's Tower The Castle Caernarfon LL55 2AY T: 01286 673362 F: 01286 677042 E: rwfusiliers@callnetuk.com W: www.rwfmuseum.org.uk

Welsh Highland Railway Tremadog Road Porthmadog LL49 9DY T: 01766 513402 W: www.whr.co.uk

Welsh Slate Museum Llanberis LL55 4TY T: 01286 870630 F: 01286 871906 E: slate@nmgw.ac.uk W: www.nmgw.ac.uk

Home Front Experience New Street Llandudno LL30 2YF T: 01492 871032 W: www.homefront-enterprises.co.uk

Mid Glamorgan

Cyfartha Castle Museum Cyfartha Park Brecon Road Merthyr Tydfil CF47 8RE T: 01685 723112 T: 01685 723112

Joseph Parrys Cottage 4 Chapel Row Merthyr Tydfil CF48 1BN T: 01685 383704

Pontypridd Historical & Cultural Centre Bridge St Pontypridd CF37 4PE T: 01443 409512 F: 01443 485565

Ynysfach Iron Heritage Centre Merthyr Tydfil Heritage Trust Ynysfach Rd Merthyr Tydfil CF48 1AG T: 01685 721858

Monmouth Nelson Museum & Local History Centre Priory St Monmouth NP5 3XA T: 01600 710630 E: nelsonmuseum@monmouthshire.gov.uk

Chepstow Museum Bridge St Chepstow NP16 5EZ T: 01291 625981 E: chepstowmuseum@monmouthshire.gov.uk

Monmouthshire Royal Engineers (Militia) Castle and Regimental Museum The Castle Monmouth NP25 3BS T: 01600-712935 E: curator@monmouthcastlemuseum.org.uk W: www.monmouthcastlemuseum.org.uk

Monmouthshire Usk Rural Life Museum The Malt Barn New Market Street Usk NP15 1AU T: 01291-673777 E: uskrurallife.museum@virgin.net W: www.uskmuseum.members.easyspace.com

Pembrokeshire

Haverfordwest Town Museum Castle St Haverfordwest SA61 2EF T: 01437 763087 W: www.haverfordwest-town-museum.org.uk

Milford Haven Museum Old Customs House The Docks Milford Haven SA73 3AF T: 01646 694496

Pembroke Yeomanry, Royal Pembroke Militia, Pembrokeshire Volunteers Museum Scolton Manor Museum Spittal Haverfordwest SA62 5QL T: 01437 731328 F: 01437 731743

Pembrokeshire Museum Service Castle Gallery Castle St Haverfordwest SA61 2EF T: 01437 775246 F: 01437 769218

Tenby Museum Tenby Museum & Art Gallery Castle Hill Tenby SA70 7BP T: 01834-842809 F: 01834-842809 E: tenbymuseum@hotmail.com W: www.tenbymuseum.free-online.co.uk Archives & Museum Mainly Tenby Town & immediate area. Search fee £5

Powys

Brecknock Militia Howell Harris Museum Coleg Trefeca Brecon LD3 0PP T: 01874 711423 F: 01874 711423 E: post@trefeca.org.uk W: www.trefeca.org.uk

Llanidloes Museum Town Hall Great Oak Street Llanidloes SY18 6BN T: 01686 413777 W: http://powysmuseums.powys.gov.uk

Powysland Museum The Canal Wharf Welshpool SY21 7AQ T: 01938 554656 W: http://powysmuseums.powys.gov.uk Local Museum with display on Montgomeryshire Yeomanry Cavalry

Powysland Museum & Montgomery Canal Centre Canal Yard Welshpool SY21 7AQ T: 01938 554656 F: 01938 554656

Radnorshire Museum Temple St Llandrindod Wells LD1 5DL T: 01597 824513 E: radnorshire.museum@powys.gov.uk

South Wales Borderers & Monmouthshire Regimental Museum of the Royal Regt of Wales (24th/41st Foot) The Barracks Brecon LD3 7EB T: 01874 613310 F: 01874 613275 E: swb@rrw.org.uk W: www.rrw.org.uk

The Judge's Lodging Broad St Presteigne LD8 2AD T: 01544 260650 F: 01544 260652 W: www.judgeslodging.org.uk

Water Folk Canal Centre Old Store House Llanfrynach Brecon LD3 7LJ T: 01874 665382

South Glamorgan

National Museum & Galleries of Wales Cathays Park Cardiff CF10 3NP T: (029) 20397951 F: (029) 2057 3389

Welch Regiment Museum of Royal Regiment of Wales The Black & Barbican Towers Cardiff Castle And Grounds Cardiff CF10 3RB T: 029 2022 9367 E: welch@rrw.org.uk_john.dart@rrw.org.uk W: www.rrw.org.uk

West Glamorgan

Cefn Coed Colliery Museum Blaenant Colliery Crynant Neath SA10 8SE T: 01639 750556

Glynn Vivian Art Gallery Alexandra Rd Swansea SA1 5DZ T: 01792 655006 F: 01792 651713 E: glynn.vivian.gallery@business.ntl.com W: www.sawnsea.gov.uk

Neath Museum The Gwyn Hall Orchard Street Neath SA11 1DT T: 01639 645726 F: 01639 645726 Open Tuesday to Saturday 10.00.a.m. to 4.00.p.m. Admission free

Wrexham

Wrexham County Borough Museum County Buildings Regent Street Wrexham LL11 1RB T: 01978-317970 F: 01978-317982 E: Museum @wrexham.gov.uk W: www.wrexham.gov.uk/heritage

SCOTLAND

Royal Museum & Museum of Scotland Chambers St Edinburgh EH1 1JF T: 0131 247 4115 T: 0131-225-7534 W: www.nms.ac.uk

National War Museum of Scotland The Castle Museum Square Edinburgh EH1 2NG T: 0131 225 7534 F: 0131 225 3848 E: library@nms.ac.uk W: www.nms.ac.uk/war

Aberdeenshire

Aberdeen Maritime Museum 52-56 Shiprow Aberdeen AB11 5BY T: 01224 337700 E: johne@arts-recreation.aberdeen.net.uk W: www.aagm.co.uk

Alford Heritage Centre Alford & Donside Heritage Association Mart Road Alford AB33 8BZ T: 019755 62906

Arbuthnot Museum St. Peter St Peterhead AB42 1DA T: 01779 477778 F: 01771 622884

Fraserburgh Heritage Society Heritage Centre Quarry Rd Fraserburgh AB43 9DT T: 01346 512888 W: www.fraserburghheritage.com Open 1st April to 31st October

Gordon Highlanders Museum St Lukes Viewfield Road Aberdeen AB15 7XH T: 01224 311200 F: 01224 319323 E: Museum @gordonhighlanders.com W: www.gordonhighlanders.com

Grampian Transport Museum Alford AB33 8AE T: 019755-62292

Hamilton T.B Northfield Farm New Pitsligo Fraserburgh AB43 6PX T: 01771 653504

Provost Skene's House Guestrow Aberdeen AB10 1AS T: 01224 641086

The Museum of Scottish Lighthouses Kinnaird Head Fraserburgh AB43 9DU T: 01346-511022 F: 01346-511033 E: enquiries@lighthousemuseum.demon.co.uk

Satrosphere The Tramsheds, 179 Constitution Street, Aberdeen, Aberdeenshire AB11 6LU T: 01224 640340 F: 01224 211 685 E: info@satrosphere.net W: www.satrosphere.net

Angus

Arbroath Museum Signal Tower Ladyloan Arbroath DD11 1PY T: 01241 875598 F: 01241 439263 E: signal.tower@angsu.gov.uk W: www.angus.gov.uk/history

Glenesk Folk Museum The Retreat Glenesk Brechin DD9 7YT T: 01356 670254 E: retreat@angusglens.co.uk W: www.angusglens.co.uk

Montrose Air Station Museum Waldron Road Montrose DD10 9BB T: 01674 673107 T: 01674 674210 F: 01674 674210 E: info@RAFmontrose.org.uk W: www.RAFmontrose.org.uk

The Meffan Institute 20 High St. West Forfar DD8 1BB T: 01307 464123 F: 01307 468451 E: the.meffan@angus.gov.uk

Argyll

Campbeltown Heritage Centre Big Kiln Witchburn Rd Campbeltown PA28 6JU T: 01586 551400

Campbeltown Library and Museum Hall St Campbeltown PA28 6BU T: 01586 552366 F: 01586 552938 E: mary.vanhelmond@argyll-bute.gov.uk W: www.argyle-bute.gov.uk/content/leisure/museums

Castle House Museum Castle Gardens Argyll St Dunoon PA23 7HH T: 01369 701422 E: info@castlehousemuseum.org.uk W: www.castlehousemuseum.org.uk

Kilmartin House Trust Kilmartin House Kilmartin Lochgilphead PA31 8RQ T: 01546 510278 F: 01546 510330 E: Museum @kilmartin.org W: www.kilmartin.org

Ayrshire

Ayrshire Yeomanry Museum Rozelle House Monument Road Alloway by Ayr KA7 4NQ T: 01292 445400 (Museum)

Dalgarven Mill Dalry Rd Dalgarven Kilwinning KA13 6PL T: 01294 552448

East Ayrshire Council District History Centre & Museum Baird Institute 3 Lugar Street Cumnock KA18 1AD T: 01290-421701 F: 01290-421701 E: Baird.institute@east-ayrshire.gov.uk W: www.east-ayrshire.gov.uk

Glasgow Vennel Museum 10 Glasgow Vennel Irvine KA12 0BD T: 01294 275059

Irvine Burns Club & Burgh Museum 28 Eglinton St Irvine KA12 8AS T: 01294 274511

McKechnie Institute Dalrymple St Girvan KA26 9AE T: 01465 713643 E: mkigir@ukgateway.net

North Ayrshire Museum Manse St Saltcoats KA21 5AA T: 01294 464174 F: 01294 464174 E: namuseum@globalnet.co.uk

Rozelle House Rozelle Park Ayr KA7 4NQ T: 01292 445447

The Largs Museum Kirkgate House Manse Court Largs KA30 8AW T: 01475 687081

The Scottish Maritime Museum Gottries Road Irvine KA12 3QE T: 01294 278283 F: 1294313211 E: jgrant5313@aol.com

West Lowland Fencibles Culzean Castle Maybole KA19 8LE T: 01655 884455 F: 01655 884503 E: culzean@nts.org.uk W: www.culzeancastle.net

Banffshire

The Buckie Drifter Maritime Heritage Centre Freuchny Rd Buckie AB56 1TT T: 01542 834646

Berwickshire Coldstream Guards Coldstream Museum 13 Market Square Coldstream TD12 4BD T: 01890 882630
The Jim Clark Room 44 Newtown St Duns TD11 3DT T: 01361 883960
Caithness
Clangunn Heritage Centre & Museum Old Parish Kirk Latheron KW5 6DL T: 01593 741700
Dunbeath Preservation Trust Old School Dunbeath KW6 6EG T: 01593 731233 F: 01593 731233 E: info@dunbeath-heritage.org.uk W: www.dunbeath-heritage.org.uk
The Last House John O'Groats Wick KW1 4YR T: 01955 611250
Dumfrieshire
Robert Burns House Burns Street Dumfries DG1 2PS T: 01387 255297
Dumfries Museum & Camera Obscura The Observatory Dumfries DG2 7SW T: 01387 253374 F: 01387 265081 E: info@dumgal.gov.uk W: www.dumfriesmuseum.demon.co.uk
Ellisland Trust Ellisland Farm Dumfries DG2 0RP T: 01387 740426
Gretna Museum & Tourist Services Headless Cross Gretna Green DG16 5EA T: 01461 338441 F: 01461 338442 E: info@gretnagreen.com W: www.gretnagreen.com
John Paul Jones Birthplace Museum Arbigland Kirkbean Dumfries DG2 8BQ T: 01387 880613 W: www.jpj.demon.co.uk
Old Bridge House Museum Old Bridge House Mill Rd Dumfries DG2 7BE T: 01387 256904 W: www.dumfriesmuseum.demon.co.uk
Robert Burns Centre Mill Road Dumfries DG2 7BE T: 01387 264808 F: 01387 264808 E: dumfreis.museum@dumgal.gov.uk W: www.dumgal.gov.uk/museums
Sanquhar Tolbooth Museum High St Sanquhar DG4 6BL T: 01659 50186
Savings Banks Museum Ruthwell Dumfries DG1 4NN T: 01387 870640 E: tsbmuseum@btinternet.com
Shambellie House Museum of Costume New Abbey Dumfries DG2 8HQ T: 01387 850375 F: 01387 850461 E: info@nms.ac.uk W: www.nms.ac.uk
Dundee
Dundee Heritage Trust Verdant Works West Henderson's Wynd Dundee DD1 5BT T: 01382-225282 F: 01382-221612 E: info@dundeeheritage.sol.co.uk W: www.verdant-works.co.uk
HM Frigate Unicorn Victoria Dock Dundee DD1 3JA T: 01382 200893 T: 01382 200900 F: 01382 200923 E: frigateunicorn@hotmail.com W: www.frigateunicorn.org
Royal Research Ship Discovery Discovery point Discovery Quay Dundee DD1 4XA T: 01382 201245 F: 01382 225891 E: info@dundeeheritage.sol.co.uk W: www.rrs-discovery.co.uk
East Lothian
Dunbar Museum High St Dunbar EH42 1ER T: 01368 863734
John Muir House Museum 126-128 High St Dunbar EH42 1JJ T: 01368 862585
Myreton Motor Museum Aberlady EH32 0PZ T: 01875 870288 T: 07947 066 666 F: 01368 860490
North Berwick Museum School Rd North Berwick EH39 4JU T: 01620 895457
Edinburgh
Heritage Projects (Edinburgh) Ltd Castlehill Royal Mile Midlothian EH1 2NE T: 0131 225 7575
Museum of Edinburgh Huntly House 142 Canongate Edinburgh EH8 8DD T: 0131 529 4143 F: 0131 557 3346 W: www.cac.org.uk
Royal Scots Regimental Museum The Castle Edinburgh EH1 2YT T: 0131-310-5014 F: 0131-310-5019 E: rhqroyalscots@edinburghcastle.fsnet.co.uk W: www.theroyalscots.co.uk
Scots Dragoon Guards Museum Shop The Castle, Edinburgh, Midlothian EH1 2YT T: 0131 220 4387
Royal Yatch Britannia & Visitor Centre Ocean Drive Leith Edinburgh EH6 6JJ T: 0131 555 5566 T: 0131 555 W: www.royalyatchbritannia.co.uk
Scottish Museum Council County House 20-22 Torphichen Street Edinburgh EH3 8JB T: 0131 229 7465 F: 0131 229 2728 E: inform@scottish.museums.org.uk W: www.scottish.museums.org.uk
The Real Mary King's Close 2 Warriston's Close Writers' Court Edinburgh EII1 1PG T: 08702 430160 W: www.realmarykingsclose.com
Falkirk
Falkirk Museum History Research Centre Callendar House Callendar Park Falkirk FK1 1YR T: 01324 503778 F: 01324 503771 E: ereid@falkirkmuseums.demon.co.uk W: www.falkirkmuseums.demon.co.uk
Fife
Andrew Carnegie Birthplace Museum Moodie St Dunfermline KY12 7PL T: 01383 724302
Dunfermline Museum Viewfield Dunfermline KY12 7HY T: 01383 313838 F: 01383 313837 Enquiries can be made at this address for: Inverkeithing Museum , Pittencrief House Museum & St Margaret's Cave
Fife and Forfar Yeomanry Museum Yeomanry House Castlebrook Road Cupar KY15 4BL T: 01334 656155 F: 01334 652354

Inverkeithing Museum The Friary Queen St Inverkeithing KY11 T: 01383 313595
John McDouall Stuart Museum Rectory Lane Dysart Kirkcaldy KY1 2TP T: 01592 653118
Kirkcaldy Museum and Art Gallery War Memorial Gardens Kirkcaldy KY1 1YG T: 01592 412860 F: 01592 412870
Methil Heritage Centre 272 High St Methil Leven KY8 3EQ T: 01333 422100
Pittencrieff House Museum Pittencrieff Park Dunfermline KY12 8QH T: 01383 722935
Scotland's Secret Bunker Underground Nuclear Command Centre Crown Buildings (Near St Andrews) KY16 8QH T: 01333-310301
Scottish Fisheries Museum St. Ayles Harbourhead Anstruther KY10 3AB T: 01333 310628 E: andrew@scottish-fisheries-museum.org W: www.scottish-fisheries-museum.org
The Fife Folk Museum High St Ceres Cupar KY15 5NF T: 01334 828180
Verdant Works - A Working Jute mill West Henderson's Wynd Dundee DD1 5BT T: 01382-225282 F: 01382-221612 E: info@dundeeheritage.sol.co.uk W: www.verdantworks.co.uk
Glasgow
Fossil Grove Victoria Park Glasgow G14 1BN T: 0141 287 2000 W: www.glasgowmuseums.com
Glasgow Museum of Transport 1 Burnhouse Road Glasgow G3 8DP T: 0141 287 2720 W: www.glasgowmuseums.com
Glasgow Police Museum 68 St Andrews Square Glasgow G2 4JS T: 07788 532691 E: curator@policemuseum.org.uk W: www.policemusaeum.org.uk
Heatherbank Museum Glasgow Caledonian University Cowcaddens Road Glasgow G4 0BA T: 0141 331 8637 F: 0141 331 3005 E: A.Ramage@gcla.ac.uk W: www.lib.gcal.ac.uk/heatherbank
Kelvingrove Art Gallery and Museum Kelvingrove Glasgow G3 8AG T: 0141 287 2699 F: 0141 287 2690 W: www.cis.glasgow.gov.uk The Gallery and Museum closed on 29 June 2003 for 3 years for refurbishment
Martyrs School Parson street Glasgow G4 0PX T: 0141 552 2356 F: 0141 552 2356 W: www.glasgowmuseums.com
McLellan Galleries 270 Sauchiehall Street Glasgow G2 3EH T: 0141 565 4100 F: 0141 565 4111 W: www.glasgowmuseums.com
Museum of Piping The Piping Centre 30-34 McPhater Street Cowcaddens Glasgow T: 0141-353-0220
Open Museum 161 Woodhead Road South Nitshill Industrial Estate Glasgow G53 7NN T: 0141 552 2356 F: 0141 552 2356 W: www.glasgowmuseums.com
Pollok House Pollok Country Park 2060 Pollokshaws Road Glasgow G43 1AT T: 0141 616 6410 F: 0141 616 6521 W: www.cis.glasgow.gov.uk
Provand's Lordship 3 Castle Street Glasgow G4 0RB T: 0141 552 8819 F: 0141 552 4744 W: www.glasgowmuseums.com
Scotland Street School Museum 225 Scotland St Glasgow G5 8QB T: 0141 287 0500 F: 0141 287 0515 W: www.glasgowmuseums.com Scotland Street School
St Mungo Museum of Religious Life and Art 2 Castle Street Glasgow G4 0RH T: 0141 553 2557 F: 0141 552 4744 W: www.glasgowmuseums.com
The Burrell Collection Pollok Country Park 2060 Pollokshaws Road Glasgow G43 1AT T: 0141 287 2550 F: 0141 287 2597 W: www.glasgowmuseums.com
The Hunterian Museum Glasgow University Glasgow G12 8QQ T: 0141 330 3711 F: 0141 330 3617 E: e.smith@admin.gla.ac.uk
The Lighthouse 11 Mitchell Lane Glasgow G1 3NU T: 0141 221 6362 F: 0141 221 6395 E: enquiries@thelighthouse.co.uk W: www.thelighthouse.co.uk
Inverness-shire – Highland
Regimental Museum of The Highlanders (The Queen's Own Highlanders Collection) Fort George IV2 7TD T: 01463 224380 E: rhqthehighlanders@btopenworld.com
Clan Cameron Museum Achnacarry Spean Bridge PH34 4EJ T: 01397 712090 E: Museum @achnarcarry.fsnet.co.uk W: www.clan-cameron.org
Culloden Visitor Centre Culloden Moor Inverness IV2 5EU T: 01463 790607 F: 01463 794294 E: dsmyth@nts.org.uk W: www.nts.org.uk
Highland Folk Museum Duke St Kingussie PH21 1JG T: 01540 661307 F: 01540 661631 E: rachel.chisholm@highland.gov.uk
Highland Folk Museum Aultlarie Croft Kingussie Rd Newtonmore PH20 1AY T: 01540 673551 E: highland.folk@highland.gov.uk W: www.highlandfolf.com
Highland Railway Museum 5 Druimlon Drumnadrochit Inverness IV63 6TY T: 01456 450527
Inverness Museum & Art Gallery Castle Wynd Inverness IV2 3ED T: 01463 237114
Mallaig Heritage Centre Station Rd Mallaig PH41 4PY T: 01687 462085 E: curator@mallaigheritage.org.uk W: www.mallaigheritage.org.uk
Queen's Own Cameron Highlanders Fort George Arderseir Inverness IV1 2TD T: 01667 462777 Fort George is owned by Historic Scotland

The Clansman Centre Canalside Fort Augustus PH32 4AU T: 01320 366444

West Highland Museum Cameron Square Fort William PH33 6AJ T: 01397 702169 F: 01397 701927 E: info@westhighlandmuseum.org.uk W: www.westhighlandmuseum.org.uk

Queen's Own Highlanders (Seaforth & Camerons) Regimental Museum Archives Fort George Ardersier Inverness IV1 7TD T: 01463-224380

Isle Of Arran

Arran Heritage Museum Rosaburn House Brodick KA27 8DP T: 01770 302636

Isle Of Islay

Finlaggan Trust The Cottage Ballygrant PA45 7QL T: 01496 840644 F: 01496 810856 E: lynmags@aol.com W: www.islay.com

Isle Of Mull

The Columba Centre Fionnphort Isle Of Mull PA66 6BN T: 01681 700660

Isle Of North Uist

Taigh Chearsabhagh Trust Taigh Chearsabhagh Lochmaddy HS6 5AE T: 01876 500293 E: taighchearsabhagh@zetnet.co.uk W: www.taighchearsabhagh.org.uk

Isle Of South Uist

Kildonan Museum Kildonan Lochboisdale HS8 5RZ T: 01878 710343

Kirkcudbrightshire

The Stewartry Museum St Mary Street Kirkcudbright DG6 4AQ T: 01557 331643 F: 01557 331643 E: david@dumgal.gov.uk W: www.dumgal.gov.uk/museums Information service for family and local history research for Kirkcudbrightshire

Lanarkshire

Auld Kirk Musuem The Cross Kirkintilloch Glasgow G66 1 T: 0141 578 014

Biggar Museum Trust Moat Park Kirkstyle Biggar ML12 6DT T: 01899 221050

Discover Carmichael Visitors Centre Warrenhill Farm Warrenhill Road Thankerton Biggar ML12 6PF T: 01899 308169

Greenhill Covenanters House Museum Kirkstyle Biggar ML12 6DT T: 01899 221572

Heritage Engineering 22 Carmyle Avenue Glasgow G32 8HJ T: 0141 763 0007

Hunter House Maxwellton Rd East Kilbride Glasgow G74 3LW T: 01355 261261

John Hastie Museum Threestanes Road Strathaven ML10 6EB T: 01357 521257

Lanark Museum 7West Port Lanark ML11 9HD T: 01555 666680 E: paularchibald@hotmail.com W: www.biggar-net.co.uk/lanarkmuseum

Low Parks Museum 129 Muir St Hamilton ML3 6BJ T: 01698 283981 T: 01698 328232 F: 01698 328232

New Lanark Conservation Trust Visitors Centre Mill No 3 New Lanark Mills Lanark ML11 9DB T: 01555 661345 F: 01555 665738 E: visit@newlanark.org W: www.newlanark.org

The Cameronians (Scottish Rifles) Museum & Low Parks Museum c/o Low Parks Museum 129 Muir Street Hamilton ML3 6BJ T: 01698 452163 T: 01698 328232 F: 01698 328412

The People's Palace Glasgow Green Glasgow G40 1AT T: 0141 554 0223 F: 0141 550 0897 W: www.glasgowmuseums.com

Weavers' Cottages Museum 23-25 Wellwynd Airdrie ML6 0BN T: 01236 747712

Midlothian

History of Education Centre East London St Edinburgh EH7 4BW T: 0131 556 4224

Lauriston Castle 2a Cramond Rd South Edinburgh EH4 5QD T: 0131 336 2060

Newhaven Heritage Museum 24 Pier Place Edinburgh EH6 4LP T: 0131 551 4165 F: 0131 557 3346 W: www.cac.org.uk

Scottish Mining Museum Trust Lady Victoria Colliery Newtongrange Dalkeith EH22 4QN T: 0131 663 7519 F: 0131 654 1618 E: enwuiries@scottishminingmuseum.com W: www.scottishminingmuseum.com

Scots Dragoon Guards Museum Shop The Castle Edinburgh EH1 2YT T: 0131 220 4387

Morayshire

Elgin Museum 1 High St Elgin IV30 1EQ T: 01343 543675 F: 01343 543675 E: curator@elginmuseum.demon.co.uk W: www.elginmuseum.demon.co.uk

Falconer Museum Tolbooth St Forres IV36 1PH T: 01309 673701 F: 01309 675863 E: alasdair.joyce@techleis.moray.gov.uk W: www.moray.gov.uk

Grantown Museum & Heritage Trust Burnfield House Burnfield Avee Grantown-On-Spey PH26 3HH T: 01479 872478 E: Molly.Duckett@btinternet.com W: www.grantown-on-spey.co.uk

Lossiemouth Fisheries Museum Pitgaveny St Lossiemouth IV31 6TW T: 01343 813772

Nairnshire

Nairn Museum Viewfield House King St Nairn IV12 4EE T: 01667 456791

Orkney

Orkney Farm & Folk Museum Corrigall Farm Museum Harray KW17 2LQ T: 01856 771411

Orkney Farm & Folk Museum Kirbister Farm Birsay KW17 2LR T: 01856 771268

Orkney Fossil & Vintage Centre Viewforth Burray KW17 2SY T: 01856 731255

Orkney Museum Tankerness House Broad Street Kirkwall KW15 1DH T: 01856-873191 F: 01856 871560

Orkney Wireless Museum Kiln Corner Kirkwall KW15 1LB T: 01856-871400

Scapa Flow Visitor Centre Lyness Stromness KW16 3NT T: 01856 791300 W: www.scapaflow.co.uk

Stromness Museum 52 Alfred Street Stromness T: 01856 850025 F: 01856 871560

Perthshire

Atholl Country Collection The Old School Blair Atholl PH18 5SP T: 01796-481232 E: r.cam@virgin.net

Atholl Highlanders Blair Castle Blair Atholl PH18 5TL T: 01796 481207 E: office@blair-castle.co.uk W: www.blair-castle.co.uk

Clan Donnachaidh (Robertson) Museum Clan Donnachaidh Centre Bruar Pitlochry PH18 5TW T: 01796-483338 E: clandonnachaidh@compuserve.com

Clan Menzies Museum Castle Menzies Weem by Aberfeldy PH15 2JD T: 01887-820982

Dunkeld Cathedral Chapter House Museum Dunkeld PH8 0AW T: 01350 728732 T: 01350 728971 W: www.dunkeldcathedral.org.uk contains Scottish Horse Regimental Archives

The Hamilton Toy Collection 111 Main St Callander FK17 8BQ T: 01877 330004

Meigle Museum Dundee Rd Meigle Blairgowrie PH12 8SB T: 01828 640612

Regimental Museum and Archives of Black Watch Balhousie Castle Hay Street Perth PH1 5HR T: 0131 310 8530 F: 01738-643245 E: archives@theblackwatch.co.uk W: www.theblackwatch.co.uk

Scottish Horse Regimental Archives - Dunkeld Cathedral Dunkeld PH8 0AW T: 01350 727614 F: 01350 727614 Scottish Horse Regimental Museum closed 1999 - archives now held in Dunkeld Cathedral Chapter House Museum View by prior appointment

Renfrewshire

Mclean Museum & Art Gallery 15 Kelly St Greenock PA16 8JX T: 01475 715624

Old Paisley Society George Place Paisley PA1 2HZ T: 0141 889 1708

Paisley Museum Paisley Museum & Art Galleries High Street Paisley PA1 2BA T: 0141-889-3151

Ross-Shire

Dingwall Museum Trust Town Hall High St Dingwall IV15 9RY T: 01349 865366

Highland Museum of Childhood The Old Station Strathpeffer IV14 9DH T: 01997 421031 E: info@hmoc.freeserve.co.uk W: www.hmoc.freeserve.co.uk

Tain & District Museum Tain Through Time Tower St Tain IV19 1DY T: 01862 894089 E: info@tainmuseum.edmon.co.uk

The Groam House Museum High St Rosemarkie Fortrose IV10 8UF T: 01381 620961

Ullapool Museum & Visitor Centre 7 & 8 West Argyle St Ullapool IV26 2TY T: 01854 612987 E: ulmuseum@waverider.co.uk

Roxburghshire

Borders Museum of Arms Henderson's Knowe Teviot Hawick TD9 0LF T: 01450 850237

Hawick Museum & Scott Gallery Wilton Lodge Park Hawick TD9 7JL T: 01450 373457 F: 01450 378506 E: hawickmuseum@hotmail.com

Jedburgh Castle Jail Museum Castlegate Jedburgh TD8 6BD T: 01835 863254 F: 01835 864750

Mary Queen of Scots House and Visitor Centre Queens St Jedburgh TD8 6EN T: 01835 863331 F: 01835 893331 E: hawickmuseum@hotmail.com fionacolton@hotmail.com

Selkirkshire

Halliwells House Museum Halliwells Close Market Place Selkirk TD7 4BL T: 01750 20096 F: 01750 23282 E: Museum s@scotborders.gov.uk

Shetland

Fetlar Interpretive Centre Beach Of Houbie Fetlar ZE2 9DJ T: 01957 733206 E: fic@zetnet.co.uk W: www.zetnet.co.uk/sigs/centre/

Old Haa Museum Burravoe Yell Shetland ZE2 9AY T: 01957 722339

Shetland Museum Lower Hillhead Lerwick ZE1 0EL T: 01595 695057 E: shetland.museum@zetnet.co.uk W: www.shetland-museum.org.uk

Tangwick Haa Museum Tangwick Eshaness Shetland ZE2 9RS T: 01806 503389

The Shetland Textile Working Museum Weisdale Mill Weisdale Shetland ZE2 9LW T: 01595 830419

Stirlingshire
Stirling Smith Art Gallery & Museum Dumbarton Road Stirling FK8 2RQ T: 01786 471917 F: 01786 449523 E: Museum @smithartgallery.demon.co.uk
Regimental Museum Argyll and Sutherland Highlanders Stirling Castle Stirling FK8 1EH T: 01786 475165 F: 01786 446038
Stranraer
Stranraer Museum 55 George Street Stranraer DG9 7JP T: 01776 705088 F: 01776 705835 E: JohnPic@dumgal.gov.uk W: www.dumgal.gov.uk
Strathclyde
Museum of The Royal Highland Fusiliers (Royal Scots Fusilers and Highland Light Infantry) 518 Sauchiehall Street Glasgow G2 3LW T: 0141 332 0961 F: 0141 353 1493 W: www.rhf.org.uk
Sutherland
Strathnaver Museum Bettyhill KW14 7SS T: 01641 521 418 E: strathnavermuseum@ukonline.co.uk W: www.aboutbritain.com/StrathnaverMuseum.htm W: www.strathnaver.org
Tayside
Perth Museum & Art Gallery Perth Museum & Art Gallery George Street Perth PH1 5LB T: 01738-632488 F: 01738 443505 E: Museum @pkc.gov.uk W: www.pkc.gov.uk/ah
West Lothian Almond Valley Heritage Trust Livingston Mill Farm Millfield Livingston EH54 7AR T: 01506 414957
West Lothian Bennie Museum Mansefield St Bathgate EH48 4HU T: 01506 634944 W: www.benniemuseum.homestead.co.uk
Kinneil Museum Kinneil Estate Bo'Ness EH51 0AY T: 01506 778530
Queensferry Museum 53 High St South Queensferry EH30 9HP T: 0131 331 5545 W: www.cac.org.uk
The Linlithgow Story Annet House 143 High St Linlithgow EH49 7EJ T: 01506 670677 F: 011506 670677 E: enquiries@linlithgowstory.fsnet.co.uk W: www.linlithgowstory.org.uk
Wigtownshire
Taylor's Farm Tradition, Barraer Newton Stewart DG8 6QQ T: 01671 404890 E: jtaylor@bosinternet.com

NORTHERN IRELAND
Armagh County Museum The Mall East Armagh BT61 9BE T: (028) 37523070 F: (028) 37522631 E: acm.um@nics.gov.uk W: www.magni.org.uk
Ballymoney Museum & Heritage Centre 33 Charlotte St Ballymoney BT53 6AY T: (028) 2762280
Fermanagh County Museum Enniskillen Castle Castle Barracks Enniskillen BT74 7HL T: 028 66 32 5000 F: 028 66 32 73 42 E: castle@fermanagh.gov.uk
Friends of the Ulster Museum 12 Malone Road Belfast BT9 5BN T: (028) 90681606
Garvagh Museum 142 Main St Garvagh Coleraine BT51 5AE T: (028) 295 58216 T: (028) 295 58188 F: (028) 295 58993 E: jclyde@garvaghhigh.garvagh.ni.sch.uk
Down County Museum The Mall Downpatrick BT30 6AH T: (028) 44615218
Downpatrick Railway Museum Railway Station Market St Downpatrick BT30 6LZ T: (028) 44615779
Foyle Valley Railway Museum Foyle Rd Londonderry BT48 6SQ T: (028) 71265234
NI Museum s Council 66 Donegall Pass Belfast BT7 1BU T: (028) 90550215 F: (028) 9055 0216 W: www.nimc.co.uk
Odyssey Science Centre Project Office Project Office NMGNI Botanic Gardens Belfast BT9 5AB T: (028) 90682100
Roslea Heritage Centre Church St Roslea Enniskillen BT74 7DW T: (028) 67751750
Royal Inniskilling Fusiliers Regimental Museum The Castle Enniskillen BT74 7BB T: (028) 66323142 F: (028) 66320359
Royal Irish Fusilers Museum Sovereign's House Mall East Armagh BT61 9DL T: (028) 3752 2911 F: (028) 3752 2911 E: rylirfusilier@aol.com W: www.rirfus-museum.freeserve.co.uk
The Museum Of The Royal Irish Regiment St. Patricks Barracks Demesne Avenue Ballymena BT43 7BH T: (028) 2566 1386 T: (028) 2566 1383 F: (028) 2566 1378
Royal Ulster Rifles Regimental Museum RHQ Royal Irish Regiment 5 Waring Street Belfast BT1 2EW T: (028) 90232086 E: rurmuseum@yahoo.co.uk W:www.rurmuseum.tripod.com
The Somme Heritage Centre 233 Bangor Rd Newtownards BT23 7PH T: (028) 9182 3202 F: (028) 9182 3214 E: sommeassociation@dnet.co.uk W: www.irishsoldier.org
Ulster American Folk Park Project Team Belfast 4 The Mount Albert Bridge Rd Belfast BT5 4NA T: (028) 90452250
Ulster Aviation Heritage Centre Langford Lodge Airfield Belfast T: 028 9267 7030 T: 028 9445 4444 E: emie@aimi.freeserve.co.uk W: www.d-n-a.net/users/dnetrAzQ
Ulster American Folk Park Centre for Migration Studies Mellon Rd Castletown Omagh BT78 5QY T: (028) 8225 6315 F: 028 8224 2241 E: uafp@iol.ie W: www.folkpark,com_ W: www.qub.ac.uk/cms/
The Ulster History Park Cullion Lislap BT79 7SU T: (028) 8164 8188 F: (028) 8164 8011 E: uhp@omagh.gov.uk W:

www.omagh.gov.uk/historypark.htm
Ulster Museum Botanic Gardens Botanic Gardens Stranmillis Road Belfast BT9 5AB T: (028) 90381251

IRELAND
Irish Jewish Museum 3 - 4 Walworth Road South Circular Road Dublin 8 Ireland T: 453-1797
Dublin Civic Museum 58 South William Street Dublin 2 Ireland T: 679-4260 677 5954

ISLES OF SCILLY
Isles of Scilly Museum Church Street St Mary's Isles of Scilly TR21 0JT T: 01720-422337
Valhalla Museum Tresco Abbey Tresco Isle of Scilly TR24 0QH T: 01720 422849 F: 01720 422106 W: www.tresco.co.uk/gard/f_gard.htm

CHANNEL ISLANDS
Alderney
The Alderney Society Museum Alderney GY9 3TG T: 01481 823222
Guernsey
18th Century Loopholed Tower PO Box 23 St Peter Port Guernsey GY1 3AN Located at Rousse headland, Vale, Guernsey
Clarence Battery Fort George St Peter Port Guernsey
Fort Grey Rocquaine Bay St Saviours Guernsey
German Direction Finding Tower PO Box 23 St Peter Port Guernsey GY1 3AN Tower at Plienmont Headland, Torteval, Guernsey
German Military Underground Hospital La Vassalerie Road St Andrew's Guernsey T: 01481 239100
German Naval Signals Headquarters St Jacques Guernsey
German Occupation Museum Les Houards Forest Guernsey GY8 0BG T: 01481 328205 W: www.aboutbritain.com/OccupationMuseum.htm
La Valette Underground Military Museum St Peter Port Guernsey T: 01481 722300
Royal Guernsey Militia and Royal Geurnsey Light Infantry Castle Comet St Peter Port Guernsey T: 01481 726518 T: 01481 721657 F: 01481 715177 W: www.museum.guernsey.net/castle.htm
Jersey
Elizabeth Castle - Jersey Militia St Aubin's Bay St Helier Jersey T: 01534 633300 F: 01534 633301
German Underground Hospital Meadowbank St Lawrence Jersey T: 01534 863442
Island Fortress Occupation Museum 9 Esplanade St Helier T: 01534 633300 F: 01534 633301
La Hougue Bie Grouville Jersey T: 01534 633300 F: 01534 633301
Maritime Museum and Occupation Tapestry Gallery New North Quay St Helier Jersey T: 01534 811043 F: 01534 874099 E: marketing@jerseyheritagetrust.org W: www.jerseyheritagetrust.org
Mont Orgueil Castle Gorey St Martin Jersey T: 01534 633300 F: 01534 633301
Noirmont Command Bunker Noirmont Point St Brelade Jersey T: 01534 482089
St Peter's Bunker Museum of Wartime German Equipment and Occupation Relics La Petite Rue De L'eglise St Peter Jersey JE3 7AF T: 01534 723136
The Channel Islands Military Museum The Five Mile Road St Ouen Jersey T: 01534 23136
Sark
German Occupation Museum Rue Lucas Sark Sark T: 01481 832564 F: 01481 832135

CANADA
Manitoba
Manitoba Museum of Man and Nature 190 Rupert Avenue Winnipeg Manitoba R3B 0N2 Canada W: www.manitobamuseum.mb.ca

SOUTH AFRICA
Kafframan Museum PO Box 1434 King William's Town 5600 T: 0430-24506 F: 0433-21569 E: stephani@hubertd.ry.ac.2a
Huguenot Memorial Museum PO Box 37 Franschoek Western Cape 7690 T: 021-876-2532

UNITED STATES OF AMERICA
Arizona
Arizona Historical Society Pioneer Museum , The PO Box 1968 2340 North Fort Valley Rd Flagstaff Arizona 86002 T: 602-774-6272
Phoenix Museum of History PO Box 926 1002 West Van Buren Street Phoenix Arizona 85001 T: 602-253-2734
Nevada
Museum Division of Museum s & History 700 Twin Lakes Drive Las Vegas Nevada 89107 T: 702-486-5205

Military Museums

Military Records
Ministry of Defence - Fleet Air Arm Records Service CS(R)2, Bourne Avenue, Hayes, Middlesex UB3 1RF F: 0181 573 9078 E:lhearn.defencerecords.hayes@gtnet.gov.uk
Ministry of Defence - Army Records Centre CS(R)2b, Bourne Avenue, Hayes Middlesex UB3 1RF F: 0181 573 9078 E: lhearn.defencerecords.hayes@gtnet.gov.uk
Ministry of Defence - Royal Naval Personnel Records Centre CS(RM)2, Navy Search, Bourne Avenue, Hayes, Middlesex UB3 1RF F: 0181 573 9078
Battlefields Trust see Museums - National
The Museum of The Adjutant General's Corps see Museums - Hampshire
Museum of Army Flying see Museums - Hampshire
Army Medical Services Museum see Museums - Hampshire
Army Physical Training Corps Museum see Museums - Hampshire
Commonwealth War Graves Commission see Museums - National
Coldstream Guards Record Office Wellington Barracks Birdcage Walk London SW1E 6HQ Access is by appointment made in advance. Search fee of £25.00 per search
Fleet Air Arm Museum Records Research Centre Box D61 RNAS Yeovilton Nr Ilchester BA22 8HT T: 01935-840565
Firepower - The Royal Artillery Museum see London
Grenadier Guards Record Office see Museums - National
Guards Museum see London
Imperial War Museum see Museums - National
IWM Film & Video Archive see Museums - National
Irish Guards Record Office Wellington Barracks Birdcage Walk London SW1E 6HQ E: bigbillaqq119@aol.com W: www.army.mod/ig~assoc
Museum of Defence Intelligence Chicksands Shefford SG17 5PR T: 01462 752340 F: 01462 752341
National Army Museum see London
National Army Museum Department of Archives (Photographs, Film & Sound) see Museums - National
Royal Air Force Museum see Museums - National
Royal Marines Museum see Museums - Hampshire
Royal Marines Historical Records and Medals Centurion Building, Grange Road, Gosport, Hampshire PO13 9XA
National Maritime Museum Romney Road Greenwich London SE10 9NF T: (020) 8858-4422 F: (020) 8312-6632 W: www.nmm.ac.uk
Royal Military School of Music Museum see Museums - Middlesex
Royal Naval Museum see Museums - Hampshire
Royal Navy Submarine Museum see Museums - Hampshire
RHQ Scots Guards Archives Wellington Barracks Birdcage Walk London SW1E 6HQ E: sgarchives@dial.pipex.com
Welsh Guards Record Office Wellington Barracks Birdcage Walk London SW1E 6HQ E: rhqwelshguards@milnet.uk.net Access is by appointment made in advance. Search fee of £25.00 per search
The Light Infantry Museum see Museums - Hampshire
Royal Military Police Museum see Museums - Sussex
England
Bedfordshire
Bedford Museum Bedfordshire Yeomanry
Bedfordshire and Hertfordshire Regimental Museum
Museum of Defence Intelligence
The Shuttleworth Collection see Museums - Bedfordshire
Buckinghamshire
Military Museum Trust Collection Old Gaol Museum Market Hill Buckingham MK18 13X T: 01280 823020 E: ian.beckett@luton.ac.uk
Berkshire
Commonwealth War Graves Commission see Museums - National
R.E.M.E. Museum of Technology
Royal Berkshire Yeomanry Cavalry Museum
The Household Cavalry Museum see Museums - Berkshire
Wellington Exhibition see Museums - Berkshire
Cambridgeshire
Ely Museum see Museums - Cambridgeshire
RAF Witchford Display of Memorabilia see Museums - Cambridgeshire
Cheshire
Cheshire Military Museum
Deva Roman Experience
Griffin Trust
Miniature AFV Association (MAFVA)
Stockport Air Raid Shelters see Museums - Cheshire
Cleveland
HMS Trincomalee see Museums - Cleveland
Cornwall
Duke of Cornwall's Light Infantry Museum
Flambards Village & Cornwall Aircraft Park see Museums - Cornwall

Cumbria
Border Regiment & Kings Own Royal Border Regiment Museum see Museums - Cumbria
Senhouse Roman Museum see Museums - Cumbria
Solway Aviation Museum see Museums - Cumbria
Derbyshire
Regimental Museum of the 9th/12th Royal Lancers see Museums - Derbyshire
Devon
Brixham Museum see Museums - Devon
Museum of Barnstaple & North Devon incorporating Royal Devon Yeomanry Museum see Museums - Devon
The Devonshire and Dorset Regiment (Archives) see Museums - Devon
Dorset
Bournemouth Aviation Museum see Museums - Dorset
Dorset Volunteers, Dorset Yeomanry Museum see Museums - Dorset
Royal Signals Museum see Museums - Dorset
Tank Museum see Museums - Dorset
The Keep Military Museum see Museums - Dorset
The Nothe Fort Museum of Coastal Defence see Museums - Dorset
Durham
The 68th (or Durham) Regiment of Light Infantry Display Team
Durham Light Infantry Museum see Museums - Durham
Essex
East Essex Aviation Society & Museum see Museums - Essex
Essex Regiment Museum see Museums - Essex
Essex Secret Bunker see Museums - Essex
Essex Volunteer Units see Museums - Essex
Essex Yeomanry Collection see Museums - Essex
Harwich Maritime Museum see Museums - Essex
Harwich Redoubt Fort see Museums - Essex
Kelvedon Hatch Secret Nuclear Bunker see Museums - Essex
Royal Gunpowder Mills see Museums - Essex
Gloucestershire
Jet Age Museum see Museums - Gloucestershire
Soldiers of Gloucestershire Museum see Museums - Gloucestershire
Wellington Aviation Museum see Museums - Gloucestershire
Hampshire
Action Stations see Museums - Hampshire
Airbourne Forces Museum see Museums - Hampshire
Aldershot Military Museum see Museums - Hampshire
Army Medical Services Museum see Museums - Hampshire
Army Physical Training Corps Museum see Museums - Hampshire
Broadlands see Museums - Hampshire
D-Day Museum and Overlord Museum see Museums - Hampshire
Explosion! The Museum of Naval Firepower see Museums - Hampshire
Historic Ships and The Naval Dockyard see Museums - Hampshire
HMS Victory see Museums - Hampshire
The Light Infantry Museum Peninsula Barracks Romsey Road Winchester SO23 8TS T: 01962 868550
Museum of Army Chaplaincy see Museums - Hampshire
Museum of Army Flying see Museums - Hampshire
Royal Hampshire Regimental Museum Serle's House Southgate Street Winchester SO23 9EG T: 01962 863658 F: 01962 888302
Royal Marines Museum see Museums - Hampshire
Royal Naval Museum see Museums - Hampshire
Royal Navy Submarine Museum see Museums - Hampshire
Southampton Hall of Aviation see Museums - Hampshire
The Gurkha Museum see Museums - Hampshire
The King's Royal Hussars Museum (10th Royal Hussars PWO 11th Hussars PAO and The Royal Hussars PWO) see Museums - Hampshire
The Museum of The Adjutant General's Corps see Museums - Hampshire
The Royal Green Jackets Museum (Oxford and Bucks Light Infantry King's Royal Rifle Corps and The Rifle Brigade) see Museums - Hampshire
Royal Military Police Museum Roussillon Barracks Chichester PO19 6BL T: 01243 534225 E: Museum @rhqrmp.freeserve.co.uk W: www.rhqrmp.freeserve.co.uk
Hertfordshire
De Havilland Heritage Centre inc The Mosquito Aircraft Museum see Museums - Hertfordshire
Hertford Museum (Hertfordshire Regiment) see Museums - Hertfordshire
Hertford Regiment Museum see Museums - Hertfordshire
Hull
4th Battalion East Yorkshire Regiment Collection see Museums - Hull
Isle of Wight
Needles Old Battery see Museums - Isle of Wight
Kent
Brenzett Aeronautical Museum see Museums - Kent

Buffs Regimental Museum see Museums - Kent
Dover Castle Dover CT16 1HU T: 01304 201628 W: www.english-heritage.org.uk
Fort Armherst see Museums - Kent
Fort Luton Museum see Museums - Kent
Gunpowder Chart Mills see Museums - Kent
Kent and Sharpshooters Yeomanry Museum see Museums - Kent
Kent Battle of Britain Museum see Museums - Kent
Lashenden Air Warfare Museum see Museums - Kent
Princess of Wales's Royal Regt & Queen's Regt Museum see Museums - Kent
Quebec House see Museums - Kent
RAF Manston History Museum see Museums - Kent
Rochester Cathedral Militia Museum see Museums - Kent
Roman Dover Tourist Centre see Museums - Kent
Roman Museum see Museums - Kent
Royal Engineers Library see Museums - Kent
Royal Engineers Museum of Military Engineering see Museums - Kent
Shoreham Aircraft Museum see Museums - Kent
Spitfire and Hurricane Memorial Building see Museums - Kent
St Margaret's Museum see Museums - Kent
The Buffs Regimental Museum see Museums - Kent
The Grand Shaft see Museums - Kent
The Historic Dockyard see Museums - Kent
The Queen's Own Royal West Kent Regiment Museum see Museums - Kent
The West Gate see Museums - Kent
Timeball Tower see Museums - Kent
Walmer Castle and Gardens see Museums - Kent
Lancashire
British in India Museum see Museums - Lancashire
East Lancashire Regiment see Museums - Lancashire
King's Own Royal Regimental Museum see Museums - Lancashire
Museum of Lancashire (Queen's Lancashire Regiment Duke of Lancaster's Own Yeomanry Lancashire Hussars 14th/20th King's Hussars) see Museums - Lancashire
Museum of the Manchester Regiment see Museums - Lancashire
Museum of the Queen's Lancashire Regiment (East South and Loyal (North Lancashire) Regiments, Lancashire Regiment (PWV) and The Queen's Lancashire Regiment see Museums - Lancashire
South Lancashire Regiment Prince of Wales Volunteers Museum see Museums - Lancashire
The Fusiliers Museum (Lancashire) see Museums - Lancashire
Leicestershire
Bosworth Battlefield Visitor Centre see Museums - Leicestershire
British Aviation Heritage see Museums - Leicestershire
Leicestershire Yeomanry, Leicestershire Tigers Museum see Museums - Leicestershire,
Royal Leicestershire Regiment Museum Gallery see Museums - Leicestershire
Royal Leicestershire Regimental Gallery see Museums - Leicestershire
Lincolnshire
50 and 61 Suadrons' Museum see Museums - Lincolnshire
Battle of Britain Memorial Flight see Museums - Lincolnshire
Bomber County Aviation Museum see Museums - Lincolnshire
Cranwell Avation Heritage Centre see Museums - Lincolnshire
Lincolnshire Aviation Heritage Centre see Museums - Lincolnshire
Metheringham Airfield Visitor Centre see Museums - Lincolnshire
RAF Digby Ops Room Museum see Museums - Lincolnshire
Royal Lincolnshire Regiment Lincolnshire Yeomanry Museum see Museums - Lincolnshire
The Queen's Royal Lancers Regimental Museum (16th/5th and 17th/21st Lancers) see Museums - Lincolnshire
Thorpe Camp Visitor Centre see Museums - Lincolnshire
Liverpool
King's Regiment Collection see Museums - Liverpool
London
Berkshire and Westminster Dragoons Museum see Museums - London
Britain at War Experience see Museums - London
Coldstream Guards Record Office Wellington Barracks Birdcage Walk London SW1E 6HQ Access is by appointment made in advance. Search fee of £25.00 per search
Firepower - The Royal Artillery Museum see Museums - London
Fusiliers' London Volunteer Museum see Museums - London
Grenadier Guards Record Office see Museums - London
Guards Museum see Museums - London
Honourable Artillery Company see Museums - London
Imperial War Museum see Museums - London
Inns of Court and City Yeomanry Museum see Museums - London
Irish Guards Record Office Wellington Barracks Birdcage Walk London SW1E 6HQ E: bigbillaqq119@aol.com W: www.army.mod/ig~assoc For archives information contact Achivist in first instance Search fee of £25.00 per search

Ministry of Defence - Army Records Centre see Museums - London
James Clavell Library see Museums - London
London Irish Rifles Regimental Museum see Museums - London
London Scottish Regimental Museum see Museums - London
National Army Museum see Museums - London
National Army Museum Department of Archives (Photographs, Film & Sound) see Museums - London
Princess Louise's Kensington Regiment Museum see Museums - London
Royal Air Force Museum see Museums - London
The Royal Regiment of Fusiliers see Museums - London
RHQ Scots Guards Archives Wellington Barracks Birdcage Walk London SW1E 6HQ E: sgarchives@dial.pipex.com Access is by appointment made in advance. Search fee of £25.00 per search
The Association of Jewish Ex-Service Men and Women Military Museum see Museums - London
The Polish Institute and Sikorski Museum see Museums - London
Wellington Museum - Apsley House see Museums - London
Welsh Guards Record Office Wellington Barracks Birdcage Walk London SW1E 6HQ T: 020 7414 3291 E: rhqwelshguards@milnet.uk.net Access is by appointment made in advance. Search fee of £25.00 per search
Merseyside
Liverpool Scottish Regimental Museum see Museums - Merseyside
Middlesex
HQ No 11 (Fighter) Group Battle of Britain Operations Room see Museums - Middlesex
Ministry of Defence - Army Records Centre Defence Records 2 Bourne Avenue Hayes UB3 1RF F: 0181 573 9078 E: lhearn.defencerecords.hayes@gtnet.gov.uk
Royal Military School of Music Museum see Museums - Middlesex
Norfolk
Battlefields Trust see Museums - National
100th Bomb Group Memorial Museum see Museums - Norfolk
Air Defence Radar Museum see Museums - Norfolk
Cholmondeley Collection of Model Soldiers see Museums - Norfolk
City of Norwich Aviation Museum see Museums - Norfolk
Royal Norfolk Regimental Museum see Museums - Norfolk
The Muckleburgh Collection see Museums - Norfolk
Northamptonshire
Abington Museum & Museum of The Northamptonshire Regt
Abington Park Museum Abington NN1 5LW T: 01604 635412 E: Museum s@northamton.gov.uk W: www.northampton.gov.uk/museums
Naseby Battle Museum Purlieu Farm Naseby Northampton NN6 7DD T: 01604 740241
Northumberland
A Soldier's Life 15th/19th The King's Royal Hussars Northumberland Hussars and Light Dragoons see Museums - Northumberland
Chesterholm Museum see Museums - Northumberland
Chesters Roman Fort and Clayton Collection Museum see Museums - Northumberland
Corbridge Roman Site see Museums - Northumberland
Fusiliers Museum of Northumberland see Museums - Northumberland
Housteads Roman Fort Museum see Museums - Northumberland
King's Own Scottish Borderers Museum see Museums - Northumberland
Roman Army Museum see Museums - Northumberland
Nottinghamshire
Newark (Notts & Lincs) Air Museum see Museums - Nottinghamshire
Sherwood Foresters Museum and Archives see Museums - Nottinghamshire
Sherwood Foresters (Notts and Derby Regiment) Museum see Museums - Nottinghamshire
Oxfordshire
Edgehill Battle Museum see Museums - Oxfordshire
Oxfordshire and Buckinghamshire Light Infantry Regimental Museum see Museums - Oxfordshire
Shropshire
Cosford Royal Air Force Museum see Museums - Shropshire
Queen's Own Mercian Yeomanry Museum see Museums - Shropshire
Shropshire Regimental Museum (King's Shropshire Light Infantry, Shropshire Yeomanry) Shropshire Militia, Volunteers and TA see Museums - Shropshire
Somerset
Blake Museum see Museums - Somerset
Fleet Air Arm Museum see Museums - Somerset
Somerset Military Museum (Somerset Light Infantry, YeomanryMilitia and Volunteers) County Museum see Museums - Somerset
Staffordshire
Museum of The Staffordshire Regiment see Museums -

Staffordshire
Museum of the Staffordshire Yeomanry see Museums - Staffordshire
The Potteries Museum & Art Gallery see Museums -Staffordshire
Suffolk
390th Bomb Group Memorial Air Museum see Museums - Suffolk
British Resistance Organisation Museum see Museums - Suffolk
Norfolk and Suffolk Aviation Museum - East Anglia's Aviation Heritage Centre see Museums - Suffolk
R.A.F. Regiment Museum see Museums - Suffolk
Royal Naval Patrol Association Museum see Museums - Suffolk
Suffolk Regiment Museum see Museums - Suffolk
Suffolk Regiment Museum -Museum closed to the public
Surrey
Queen's Royal Surrey Regiment Museum (Queen's Royal, East Surrey & Queen's Royal Surrey Regts) see Museums - Surrey
Regimental Museum Royal Logistic Corps see Museums - Surrey
Sandhurst Collection see Museums - Surrey
Staff College Museum see Museums - Surrey
Sussex
Sussex Combined Services Museum (Royal Sussex Regiment and Queen's Royal Irish Hussars) see Museums - Sussex
Tangmere Military Aviation Museum see Museums - Sussex
Sussex - East Newhaven Fort see Museums - Sussex East
Sussex Yeomanry Museum see Museums - Sussex
Tyne and Wear
101 (Northumbrian) Regiment Royal Artillery (Volunteers) Museum see Museums - Tyne & Wear
Military Vehicle Museum see Museums - Tyne & Wear
Arbeia Roman Fort and Museum see Museums - Tyne & Wear
North East Aircraft Museum see Museums - Tyne & Wear
Segedunum Roman Fort see Museums - Tyne & Wear
Warwickshire
Lunt Roman Fort see Museums - Warwickshire
Midland Air Museum see Museums - Warwickshire
Regimental Museum of The Queen's Own Hussars (The 3rd King's Own Hussars and 7th Queen's Own Hussars) see Museums - Warwickshire
The Royal Regiment of Fusiliers Museum (Royal Warwickshire) see Museums - Warwickshire
Warwickshire Yeomanry Museum see Museums - Warwickshire
Wellesborough Aviation Museum see Museums - Warwickshire
Wiltshire
RGBW (Salisbury) Museum see Museums - Wiltshire
Royal Wiltshire Yeomanry Museum see Museums - Wiltshire
The Infantry and Small Arms School Corps Weapons Collection see Museums - Wiltshire
Wirral
Historic Warships at Birkenhead see Museums - Wirral
Worcestershire
Commandery Civil War Museum see Museums - Worcestershire
The Museum of the Worcestershire Yeomanry Cavalry see Museums - Worcestershire
The Worcestershire Regiment Museum see Museums - Worcestershire
Worcestershire Regiment Archives (Worcestershire and Sherwood Forester's Regiment) see Museums - Worcestershire
Yorkshire – East
Museum of Army Transport see Museums - Yorkshire – East
Yorkshire – North
Eden Camp Museum see Museums - Yorkshire – North
Green Howards Regimental Museum see Museums - Yorkshire – North
Royal Dragoon Guards Military Museum (4th/7th Royal Dragoon Guards & 5th Royal Inniskilling Dragoon Guards) see Museums - Yorkshire – North
The Real Aeroplane Museum see Museums - Yorkshire – North
War Room & Motor House Collection see Museums - Yorkshire – North
Yorkshire Air Museum see Museums - Yorkshire – North
Yorkshire – South
Doncaster AeroVenture - The South Yorkshire Air Museum Aero Venture Lakeside Doncaster T: 01302 761616 F: 01302 316610
King's Own Yorkshire light infantry Regimental Gallery Doncaster Museum and Art Gallery Chequer Road Doncaster DN1 2AE T: 01302 734293 F: 01302 735409 E: Museum @doncaster.gov.uk W: www.doncaster.gov.uk/museums 51st (2nd Yorkshire, West Riding) the King's Own Light infantry regiment; 51st (2nd Yorkshire, West Riding) Regiment of Foot (Light Infantry); 51st (2nd Yorkshire, West Riding) Regiment of Foot; 51st Brudenell's Regiment of Foot; 53rd Napier's Regiment of Foot; 105th Madras (Light Infantry) regiment; 2nd Madras European Regiment (Light Infantry) (Honourable East India Company)
Regimental Museum 13th/18th Royal Hussars and The Light Dragoons Cannon Hall Cawthorne Barnsley S75 4AT T: 01226 790270
York and Lancaster Regimental Museum Library and Arts Centre

Walker Place Rotherham S65 1JH T: 01709 823635 F: 01709 823631 E: karl.noble@rotherham.gov.uk W: www.rotherham.gov.uk
Yorkshire – West
Bankfield Museum & Gallery Boothtown Rd Halifax HX3 6HG 01422 354823 F: 01422 349020 E: bankfield-museum@calderdale.gov.uk W: www.calderdale.gov.uk Also holds Duke of Wellington's Regimental Museum
Duke of Wellington's Regimental Museum Bankfield Museum Akroyd Park Boothtown Road Halifax HX3 6HG T: 01422 354823 F: 01422 249020
Leeds Rifles Museum c/o 7 Wentworth Court Raistrick Brighouse HD6 3XD
Yorkshire – City of York
Kohima Museum c/o Legal Branch, HQ 2 Div, Imphal Barracks Fulford Road York YO10 4AU T: 01904 662086 01904 635212 F: 01904 662377 E: thekohimamuseum@hotmail.com A small collection of memorabilia donated by veterans of 2nd division who served in India and Burman 1942-1946
Northern Ireland
The Museum Of The Royal Irish Regiment see Museums Morthern Ireland
Royal Irish Fusiliers Museum see Museums Morthern Ireland
County Down The Somme Heritage Centre 233 Bangor Road Newtownards BT23 7PH T: 028 9182 3202 F: 028 9182 3214 E: sommeassociation@dnet.co.uk W: www.irishsoldier.org
Royal Inniskilling Fusiliers Regimental Museum see Museums Morthern Ireland
Royal Ulster Rifles Regimental Museum see Museums Morthern Ireland
Ulster Aviation Heritage Centre see Museums Morthern Ireland
Scotland
Aberdeenshire
Gordon Highlanders Museum see Museums - Aberdeenshire
Angus
Montrose Air Station Museum see Museums - Angus
Ayrshire
Ayrshire Yeomanry Museum see Museums - Ayrshire
West Lowland Fencibles see Museums - Ayrshire
Berwickshire
Coldstream Guards see Museums - Berwickshire
Dundee
HM Frigate Unicorn see Museums - Dundee
Edinburgh
Royal Scots Regimental Museum see Museums - Edinburgh
Fife
Fife and Forfar Yeomanry Museum see Museums - Fife
Glasgow
Kelvingrove Art Gallery and Museum see Museums - Glasgow
The Burrell Collection see Museums - Glasgow
Highland
Regimental Museum of The Highlanders (The Queen's Own Highlanders Collection) see Museums - Highland
Inverness-shire
Culloden Visitor Centre see Museums - Inverness-shire
Queen's Own Cameron Highlanderssee Museums - Inverness-shire
Queen's Own Highlanders (Seaforth & Camerons) Regimental Museum Archivessee Museums - Inverness-shire
Lanarkshire
The Cameronians (Scottish Rifles) Museum & Low Parks Museum see Museums - Lanarkshire
Orkney
Stromness Museum see Museums - Orkney
Perthshire
Atholl Highlanders see Museums - Perthshire
Regimental Museum & Archives of Black Watch see Museums - Perthshire
Scottish Horse Regimental Archives - Dunkeld Cathedral see Museums - Perthshire
Roxburghshire
Borders Museum of Arms see Museums -Roxburghshire
Stirlingshire
Regimental Museum Argyll and Sutherland Highlanders Roxburghshire see Museums -Stirlingshire
Strathclyde
Museum of The Royal Highland Fusiliers (Royal Scots Fusiliers and Highland Light Infantry) see Museums -Strathclyde
Wales
Cardiff
1st The Queen's Dragoon Guards Regimental Museum see Museums - Cardiff
Gwent
Roman Legionary Museum see Museums - Gwent
Gwynedd
Caernarfon Air World see Museums - Gwynedd
Llandudno Royal Artillery see Museums - Gwynedd
Segontium Roman Museum see Museums - Gwynedd
The Royal Welch Fusiliers Regimental Museum see Museums -

Gwynedd
Monmouth
Nelson Museum see Museums - Monmouth
Monmouthshire Royal Engineers (Militia) see Museums -
Monmouth
Pembrokeshire
**Pembroke Yeomanry, Royal Pembroke Militia, Pembrokeshire
Volunteers Museum** see Museums - Pembrokeshire
Powys
Brecknock Militia see Museums - Powys
**South Wales Borderers & Monmouthshire Regimental Museum
of the Royal Regt of Wales (24th/41st Foot)** see Museums - Powys
Isle of Man
Regimental Museum of the Manx Regiment The MacClellan Hall
Tromode Road Douglas T: 01624 803146
Channel Islands
Guernsey
18th Century Loopholed Tower see Museums - Guernsey
Clarence Battery see Museums - Guernsey
Fort Grey Rocquaine Bay St Saviours
German Direction Finding Tower see Museums - Guernsey
German Underground Hospital see Museums - Guernsey
German Naval Signals Headquarters St Jacques

La Valette Underground Military Museum see Museums -
Guernsey
German Occupation Museum see Museums - Guernsey
Royal Guernsey Militia and Royal Geurnsey Light Infantry see
Museums - Guernsey
Jersey
Elizabeth Castle - Jersey Militia see Museums - Jersey
German Underground Hospital see Museums - Jersey
La Hougue Bie see Museums - Jersey
Maritme Museum and Occupation Tapestry Gallery see
Museums - Jersey
Noirmont Command Bunke see Museums - Jersey
**St Peter's Bunker Museum of Wartime German Equipment and
Occupation Relics** see Museums - Jersey
The Channel Islands Military Museum see Museums - Jersey
Island Fortress Occupation Museum see Museums - Jersey
Sark
German Occupation Museum see Museums - Sark
Belgium
In Flanders Fields Museum Lakenhallen Grote Markt 34 Ieper B-
8900 T: 00-32-(0)-57-22-85-84 F: 00-32-(0)-57-22-85-89 W:
www.inflandersfields.be

Police Records & Museums

**International Police Association - British Section - Genealogy
Group** Thornholm Church Lane South Muskham Newark
Nottinghamshire NG23 6EQ T: 01636 676997 E:
ipagenuk@thornholm.freeserve.co.uk
National Police Officers' Roll of Honour Roll of Honour project
Lancashire Contabulary Headquarters Hutton Preston Lancashire PR4
5SB
Police History Society 37 Greenhill Road Timperley Altrincham
Cheshire WA15 7BG T: 0161-980-2188 E:
alanhayhurst@greenhillroad.fsnet.co.uk W:
www.policehistorysociety.co.uk Whilst the society is not primarily
interested in family history and having no personal records of its own
is unable to answer enquiries re individual officers. Howcver
members may contact each other via the Newsletter or ask for
specific information which maybe available. shortly to have a 'notice
board' on the website which may assist researchers, as well as links
to many police-related sites
Berkshire
Thames Valley Police Museum Sulhamstead Nr Reading Berkshire
RG7 4DX T: 0118 932 5748 F: 0118 932 5751 E:
ken.wells@thamesvalley.police.uk W: www.thamesvalley.police.uk
Thames Valley Police formed April 1968 from Berkshire,
Oxfordshire, Oxford City and Reading Borough constabularies. Only
records of officers are those who served in Reading Borough and
Oxfordshire. Appointments only with Curator
Essex
Essex Police Museum Police Headquarters PO Box 2 Springfield
Chelmsford Essex CM2 6DA T: 01245 491491-ext-50771 F: 01245
452456 Open by appointment only.
Greater Manchester
The Greater Manchester Police Museum 57 Newton St
Manchester Lancashire M1 1ES T: 0161 856 3287 T: 0161 856
3288 F: 0161 856 3286
Lancashire
The Greater Manchester Police Museum see Greater Manchester
London
Metropolitan Police Archives Room 517, Wellington House 67-73
Buckingham Gate London SW1E 6BE T: 020 7230 7186 E:
margarter.bird@met.police.uk The Metropolitan Police do not hold
any records. All records that have survived are in the National
archives. Do not hold records for City of London Police or other
police forces or constabularies. The Archives have some finding aids.
SAE for information
Metropolitan Police Historical Museum c/o T.P.H.Q., Fin & res
4th Floor Victoria Embankment London SW1A 2JL T: (020) 8305-
2824 T: (020) 8305 1676 Visits by appointment only
Oxfordshire
Thames Valley Police Museum see Berkshire
Tyne and Wear
North Eastern Police History Society Brinkburn Cottage 28
Brinkburn St High Barnes Sunderland SR4 7RG T: 0191-565-7215
E: harry.wynne@virgin.net W: http://nepolicehistory.homestead.com
Research into Family and Police History 52 Symons Avenue
Eastwood Leigh on Sea Essex SS9 5QE T: 01702 522992 F: 01702
522992 E: fred@feather1.demon.co.uk
Surrey
Surrey Police Museum Mount browne Sandy Lane Guildford
Surrey GU3 1HG T: 001483 482155 W:
www.surreymuseums.org.uk/museums/Police.htm
Sussex

Royal Military Police Museum Roussillon Barracks Chichester
Sussex PO19 6BL T: 01243 534225 F: 01243 534288 E: Museum
@rhqrmp.freeserve.co.uk W: www.rhqrmp.freeserve.co.uk Depicts
Military Police history from Tudor times to present day
West Midlands
West Midlands Police Museum Sparkhill Police Station Stratford
Rd Sparkhill Birmingham West Midlands B11 4EA T: 0121 626
7181 W: stvincent.ac.uk/Resourcews/WMidPol
Yorkshire – North
Ripon Workhouse - Museum of Poor Law Allhallowgate Ripon
HG4 1LE T: 01765 690799
Yorkshire – South
Sheffield Police and Fire Museum 101-109 West Bar Sheffield
South Yorkshire S3 8TP T: 0114 249 1999 W:
www.hedgepig.freeserve.co.uk
Scotland
Glasgow Police Heritage Society & Glasgow Police Museum 68
St Andrews Square Glasgow G2 4JS T: 07788 532691 E:
curator@policemuseum.org.uk W: www.policemusaeum.org.uk
Ireland
Garda Síochána Museum & Archives The Records Tower Dublin
Castle Dublin 2 Ireland T: +353 1 6719 597 W:
www.geocities.com/CapitolHill/7900/museum.html

List of Current Police Forces
England and Wales - Avon and Somerset Constabulary,
Bedfordshire Police, Cambridgeshire Constabulary, Cheshire
Constabulary, City of London Police, Cleveland Constabulary,
Cumbria Constabulary, Derbyshire Constabulary, Devon and
Cornwall Constabulary, Dorset Police, Durham Constabulary, Dyfed-
Powys Police, Essex Police, Gloucestershire Constabulary, Greater
Manchester Police, Gwent Constabulary, Hampshire Constabulary,
Hertfordshire Constabulary, Humberside Police, Kent County
Constabulary, Lancashire Constabulary, Leicestershire Constabulary,
Lincolnshire Police, Merseyside Police, Metropolitan Police, Norfolk
Constabulary, North Wales Police - Heddlu Gogledd Cymru , North
Yorkshire Police, Northamptonshire Police, Northumbria Police,
Nottinghamshire Constabulary, South Wales Police - Heddlu de
Cymru, South Yorkshire Police, Staffordshire Police, Suffolk
Constabulary, Surrey Constabulary, Sussex Police, Thames Valley
Police, Warwickshire Constabulary, West Mercia Police, West
Midlands Police, West Yorkshire Police, Wiltshire Constabulary
Scotland - Central Scotland Police, Dumfries and Galloway
Constabulary, Fife Constabulary, Grampian Police, Lothian and
Borders Police, Northern Constabulary, Strathclyde Police, Tayside
Police
Non Geographic Police Forces
British Transport Police, Ministry of Defence Police, UK Atomic
Energy Constabulary, Port of Dover Police, The National Crime
Squad
Ireland
Northern Ireland - Police Service of Northern Ireland (Royal Ulster
Constabulary)
Southern Ireland - Garda Síochána
Channel Islands - Guernsey Police, States of Jersey Police
Isle of Man - Isle of Man Constabulary
Other Forces - Royal Military Police, Belfast Harbour Police,
Mersey Tunnels Police, Port of Bristol Police, Port of Tilbury London
Police, Royal Parks Constabulary, Port of Liverpool Police

The National Family History Fair

Saturday 10th September 2005
10.00a.m. - 4.30.p.m.

Gateshead International Stadium
Neilson Road Gateshead NE10 0EF

Admission £3.00
Accompanied Children under 15 Free

Meet the national experts!

A must for family historians in 2005

Full list of exhibitors at:
www.nationalfamilyhistoryfair.com

2006 - Saturday 9th September 2006

Index to Advertisers

1837online.com 4

ABM Publishing Ltd 29, 237 & 245
Accommodation
    Belmont Guest House - Sunderland 49
    London School of Economics Accommodation 129
    Yorkshireancestors.com 278

Achievements Ltd 24
Acorns2Oaks - Printed Family Trees and Charts 290
Adolph, Anthony 249
Ancestors Magazine 61
Anglo-Jewish Research - Judith Joseph 68
Ancestor Seeker 146
Archive CD Books Ltd 254, 255 & 256

British Association for Local History 38
Barnes, David J - Military Research 336
Barnett, Len - Research 101 & 326
Belmont Guest House - Sunderland 49
Bigwood, Rosemary - Scottish Research 236
Birmingham and Midland Society for
    Genealogy and Heraldry 52
Black Country Society 34
Blood's Thicker than Water 95
Boucher, Mrs Carolynn 23
Brown, Ian LRPS - Zebrafoto 273
Buxton, Audrey 68

CDI - Photographic Restoration 262
Chartists, The 166
Christopher Swan 17
City of York Family History Society 28 & 79
Cleaves, Sue 37
Cleveland Family History Society 62
Clwyd Family History Society 203
Cumbria Family History Society 108
Custodian - Computer Program 241

Derbyshire Family History Society 96
Devon Ancestry 12
Devon Family History Society 56
Dixon Smith, Rosemary 75
DNA Heritage 244
Doncaster Family History Society 120
Durham Records Online 257
Dyfed Family History Society 210

Evans, Jill 33

Family Chronicle Magazine 130
Family History Fairs 70
Family History Monthly 6, 7 & 18
Family & Local History Handbook 194
Family Tree Magazine 237 & 245
Faversham Society 42
Family History Online 269
Federation of Family History
    Societies Publications 165

Footsteps 23
Fred Feather 96
Future Publishing 51

Genealogy Printers 293
GenFair 269
Genfile 87
General Register Office for Scotland 220
Glasgow Police Museum 224
Gloucestershire Family History
    Research Service 33
Gould Genealogy - Australia 141
Gray, Sheila
    - The South African War 1899 - 1902 79
GW Research 87

Hamby, Jane - Lancashire & Cumbria 68
Hand Written & Illustrated Family Trees 27
Historical Maps of Ireland 290
Historical Research Associates - Ireland 213
Hodgson, Leslie FSA (Scot) 236
House of Lords Record Office 101
Huddersfield Family History Society 62

Imrie, Jennifer - Scottish Research 236
Institute of Local & Family History 108
Irish Family Research 262

Jewish Family History Society 65
JiGrah 241
Joan Dexter 95
Joseph, Judith - Anglo-Jewish Research 68

Keighley Family History Society 120
Kent County Archives 42
Kinship 50

Lancashire Ancestors 108
Lancashire Record Office 69
Leicester & Rutland Research - Pat Grundy 60
Leicestershire Research - Audrey Buxton 68
Lichfield Archives 37
Link Investigations 17
Lochin Publishing 23
London Ancestor 290
London Research - Timothy Saxon 120
London School of Economics Accommodation 129
Longhorn, Victor 96
Lynskey, Marie 27

Marathon Microfilm 262
McDonald CG^{SM}, David 33
MC Research Services - M P McConnon M.A 213
Microfilm Shop 52
MM Publications 48
My History 257
Murder Files 157, 159 & 198

National Archives Publications Inside Back Cover

Name Shop	56
National Family History Fair	13, 193 & 442
National Library of Wales	207
New Zealand Genealogy Ltd	69
Nicholson, Geoff - Northumberland and Durham	22
Northumberland Research - Neil Richardson	120
North Wales Family History Fair	70
Northern Writers Advisory Services	141
Parchment (Oxford) Ltd	33
Parish Chest	253
Parkinson, C W & S	24
Parkes, Elizabeth	69
Past Homes Ltd	290
Pinpoint Historical Research Services	60
Police - Glasgow Police Museum	224
Powys Family History Society	210
Pontefract FHS (1359)	123
Practical Family History Magazine	29
Raymond, S A & M J	141 & 148
Richardson, Neil - Northumberland & Durham	12
Rutland - Research Audrey Buxton	68
Saxton, Timothy	17
Scottish Family History Research Service	236
Scottish Genealogy Society	235
Scottish Roots	236
Sheffield Family History Society	163
Shropshire & Staffordshire Research	
- Sue Cleaves	37
Society of Genealogists	128
Society of Genealogists Family History Show	125
South African Research	75

South African War 1899 - 1902, The	
- Sheila Gray	79
Staffordshire Ancestry	
Research Services	37
Staffordshire Archives	37
Stepping Stones Inside Front Cover, , 344 & 448	
Suffolk Local & Family	
History Research	113 & 156
Suffolk Record Office	96
The Chartists	166
The Family & Local History Handbook	194
The Name Shop	56
The National Family History Fair	13, 193 & 442
Tyne Bridge Publications	104
Ulster Historical Foundation	213
U S of America - David McDonald CG^{SM}	
33	
Wakefield Family History Society	146
Western Front Association	320
West Sussex Record Office	41
Whitehand, Ray	113 & 156
Worcestershire Library & History Centre	69
www.durhamrecordsonline.com	257
www.irishfamilyresearch.co.uk	262
Yorkshireancestors.com	278
York Family History Society, City of	28 & 79
Yorkshire Family History Fair	164
Your Family Tree Magazine	51
Zebrafoto - Ian Brown LRPS	273

Email and Internet or Web Addresses

Email and Web addresses shown in this book have been notified to us by the Organisation or advertiser. Unlike a normal postal address these addresses are subject to frequent change. In the case of businesses Email forwarding and Website transfer are usually provided by links to the original address. This does not always happen and the only solution is to use the various search engines available on the internet.

Disclaimer

The Editors and Publishers of The Family & Local History Handbook make every effort to verify all information published. Nearly every organisation in this handbook has been contacted and asked to confirm that our information is correct. We provided reply paid envelopes and are grateful to those organisations who took the time to reply. We must express our disappointment that there were some organisations who did not reply. We cannot accept responsibilty for any errors or omissions or for any losses that may arise.

Advertisers are expected to provide a high standard of service to our readers. If there is a failure to provide such a service the Editor and Publishers reserve the right to refuse to accept advertising in future editions.

The Editors and Publishers cannot be held responsible for the errors, omissions or non performance by advertisers. Where an advertiser's performance falls below an acceptable level readers are asked to notify the Publisher in writing.

The views and opinions expressed in each of the articles are those of the author and do not necessarily reflect the opinions of the Editors.

Index

Adoption 49
America
   Tracing American Service Personnel 300

Beginners
   Starting Out A Beginners Guide 8
Brewing
   Haigh Brewery 109
Bygone Days in a Lancashire
      Mill Town 19

Cemeteries & Crematoria 386
Census
   Census Dates 14
   Census Enumerator's Instructions 221
   Irish Censuses & Census Substitutes 214
Certificates
   Family Records Centre 45
   General Register Office 46
The Clopton Oak 80
Conservation & Preservation
   of your family archives 15
Computers & Genealogy
   see Digital Genealogy & Internet
County & Country Codes 14
Crime
   An Irresitible Sense of duty 225
   Maria's Murderer 157
   Britain's Hangmen 195
   Crime and Punishment
      in the 18th Century 102
   www.oldbaileyonline.org 263

Death and the Victorians 57
Digital Genealogy
   A Basic Guide to Computers
      for Family History 238
   Caveat Internet! 246
   David Tippey's Top Research Websites 279
   Discovering family history with
      1837online.com 258
   DNA Heritage 270
   Easy Access to Records 242
   Electronic Indexes - Pain or Pleasure 252
   Family History in the Media 247
   Get Online! 295
   Heredis - a genealogy program 294
   If We Only Had Old Ireland Over Here 274
   Irish Genealogy with Eneclann 296
   Newsplan - Database of
      Local Newspaper Titles 292
   The Archive CD Books Story 255
   The Scotlands People Internet Service 291
   Trace Your British & Irish
      Family History using the Internet 265
   www.oldbaileyonline.org 263
Editorial 5
Education
   The Inspector calls 121

Family History Centres 370
Family History Societies
Family History Research
   A Hodge Podge of Duckenfields 160
   Blood's Thicker than Water 90
   Family History in the media 247
   I'm not tracing my Ancestors...really 43
   My Great Grand Aunt Maria 144
   The Little Drummer Boy 176
   No 2 Potash Cottages Pettistree 154
   Your ancestor's Family Planning 53
Family Records Centre 45
Family History Societies - listings 346
Ferries - History of 178
Ferries - Wawne Ferry 179
Food
   London Treacle, Syrup of Roses 134

Emigration
   Shovelling out the Poor 117

Gas Workers - National Gas Archive 186
General Register Office 46
   Adoption 49
   Overseas Records 50

Haigh Brewery 109

Index - Advertisers 443
Index 445
Indexes
   Caveat Internet 246
   Electronic Indexes- Pain of Pleasure 252
Ireland
   If only we had Ireland Overhere 274
   Irish Censuses & Census Substitutes 214
   Irish Genealogy with Eneclann 296
   Public Record Office of N Ireland 211
   Registration Records 417
Industry
   The Black Country Society 35
   Bygone Days in a Lancashire
      Mill Town 19
   Captain of Industry 152
   Civil Unrest in the Black Country 30
   Faversham Gunpowder Factories 39
   Haigh Brewery 109
   Understanding Old Trades
      and Occupations 131
   Showing their mettle ..
      Industries of the West Midlands 97

Internet
   Caveat Internet 246
   Get online! National Archives 295
   Irish Genealogy with Eneclann 296
   Newsplan - database of
      local newspaper titles 292
   www.oldbaileyonline.org 263

Jewish
A Wedding has been arranged 63

Leisure
The Georgians at the Seaside 114
Letter writing
Eavesdropping on the dead
- something to write home about 149
Libraries
The National Library of Wales 202
Libraries - listings 372
Local History Articles
A Hodge Podge of Duckenfields 160
The Black Country Society 35
Carmarthenshire Antiquarian Society 208
The Clopton Oak 80
Faversham Gunpowder Factories 39
No 2 Potash Cottages Pettistree 154

Local History Societies - Listings 357

Marine
Registry of Shipping & Seamen 170
Twentieth Century State Registers
of Merchant Mariners 167
Medical Reports
Your Ancestor's Family Planning 53
Military History
Belgium Refugees in Britain
during the First World War 317
Imperial War Museum 298
Waiting and Hoping 313
The Beckett Soldiers Index A-C 311
A Red Cross VAD in Wartime 321
Touring the Western Front 337
Air Force
The Inter War Years & Losses
1919 - 1939 303
Army
Tracing American Service Personnel 300
Tracing Army Ancestry 342
Imperial War Museum 298
Navy
Imperial War Museum 298
The Royal Navy -historical
background for genealogists 327
The Fleet Air arm & Casualties 331
Military Museums - Listings 438
Miscellaneous Information 447

Murder
An Irrestible Sense of duty 225
Maria's Murderer 157
Britain's Hangmen 195
Museums - Listings 418

Navy
The Royal Navy -historical
background for genealogists 327

Newspapers
Newsplan - database of
local newspaper titles 292

Overseas Records 50
Police
An Irrestible Sense of duty 225
Hobby Bobbies 182
Police Records & Museums 441
Poor
19th Century Plagues of the Poor 25
People of the Parish 105
Probate 199
How William Coleman Lived 147

Red Cross
A Red Cross VAD in Wartime 321
Record Offices and Archives
The National Archives 88
London's Genealogy Village 124
West Dorset History and
Genealogical Centre 83
Record Offices & Archives - Listings 393
Registrars
Registrars of Births, Marriages & Deaths
England, Wales and Scotland 408
Registration Records in Ireland 417
Rutlands Records - where to find them 66

Schools
The Inspector calls 121
Society of Genealogists
London's Genealogy Village 124
South Africa
Deceased Estates
in South African Genealogy 76
Finding South African Forebears 71

Scotland
General Register Office for Scotland 220
Census Enumerator's Instructions 221
The Search for Scottish Sources 217
Scotlands People Internet Service 291
Scottish Term Days 232
The Origin of Christianity in Scotland 228

United States of America
Tracing American Service Personnel 300

Wales
Carmarthenshire Antiquarian Society 208
J Llewellyn - Aberystwyth Brigantine 204
The National Library of Wales 202
West Dorset History and
Genealogical Centre 83
Windmills 84
Workhouse
Ipswich Workhouses 188
World War I
Touring the Western Front 337
Websites
David Tippey's Top Research Websites 279
Get Online! 295
Easy Access to Records 242
The Scotlands People Internet Service 291

About the Editor and Publisher

Robert Blatchford LL.B (Hons)
is a law graduate of The University of Hull,
England and has been involved in genealogy for
several years. He is a member of The Society of
Genealogists as well as Cleveland, The City of
York, Devon, Dyfed, Glamorgan, Somerset &
Dorset and Gwent Family History Societies. A
member of The British Association for Local
History and The Poppleton History Society. He is
a former Chairman of The City of York Family
History Society and former Vice Chairman of the
North East Group of Family History Societies. He
has undertaken research in the United Kingdom
& Australia. He has undertaken research in
England, Wales, Scotland, Belgium and France as
well as in Ireland, Australia and the United
States.

Published by
Robert Blatchford Publishing Ltd
33 Nursery Road, Nether Poppleton YORK, YO26 6NN England

E: sales@genealogical.co.uk   W: www.genealogical.co.uk

The Genealogical Services Directory
1st Edition Published March 1997   ISBN 0 9530297 0 0 ISSN 1368-9150
2nd Edition Published January 1998   ISBN 0 9530297 1 9 ISSN 1368-9150
3rd Edition Published January 1999   ISBN 0 9530297 2 7 ISSN 1368-9150
4th Edition Published January 2000   ISBN 0 9530297 3 5 ISSN 1368-9150

The Family & Local History Handbook
5th Edition Published January 2001   ISBN 0 9530297 4 3
6th Edition Published February 2002   ISBN 0 9530297 5 1
7th Edition Published February 2003   ISBN 0 9530297 6 X
8th Edition Published March 2004   ISBN 0 9530297 7 8

9th Edition Published March 2005 ....ISBN 0 9530297 8 6

ISSN 1745-3887   **ISBN 0 9530297 8 6**

Printed by
A1 Press Ltd
Dryson House, York Road, Wetherby, West Yorks, Tel 01937 588750